Contemporary
Literary Criticism

Guide to Gale Literary Criticism Series

For criticism on	Consult these Gale series
Authors now living or who died after December 31, 1959	*CONTEMPORARY LITERARY CRITICISM (CLC)*
Authors who died between 1900 and 1959	*TWENTIETH-CENTURY LITERARY CRITICISM (TCLC)*
Authors who died between 1800 and 1899	*NINETEENTH-CENTURY LITERATURE CRITICISM (NCLC)*
Authors who died between 1400 and 1799	*LITERATURE CRITICISM FROM 1400 TO 1800 (LC)* *SHAKESPEAREAN CRITICISM (SC)*
Authors who died before 1400	*CLASSICAL AND MEDIEVAL LITERATURE CRITICISM (CMLC)*
Black writers of the past two hundred years	*BLACK LITERATURE CRITICISM (BLC)*
Authors of books for children and young adults	*CHILDREN'S LITERATURE REVIEW (CLR)*
Dramatists	*DRAMA CRITICISM (DC)*
Hispanic writers of the late nineteenth and twentieth centuries	*HISPANIC LITERATURE CRITICISM (HLC)*
Native North American writers and orators of the eighteenth, nineteenth, and twentieth centuries	*NATIVE NORTH AMERICAN LITERATURE (NNAL)*
Poets	*POETRY CRITICISM (PC)*
Short story writers	*SHORT STORY CRITICISM (SSC)*
Major authors from the Renaissance to the present	*WORLD LITERATURE CRITICISM, 1500 TO THE PRESENT (WLC)*

Volume 87

Contemporary Literary Criticism

Excerpts from Criticism of the Works
of Today's Novelists, Poets, Playwrights,
Short Story Writers, Scriptwriters, and
Other Creative Writers

Christopher Giroux
EDITOR

Brigham Narins
ASSOCIATE EDITOR, *CLC*

Jennifer Brostrom
Jeff Chapman
Pamela S. Dear
John D. Jorgenson
Matt McDonough
Sean René Pollock
Deborah A. Stanley
Aarti D. Stephens
Polly A. Vedder
Thomas Wiloch
Kathleen Wilson
Janet Witalec
ASSOCIATE EDITORS

Gale Research Inc.

An International Thomson Publishing Company

I(T)P
Changing the Way the World Learns

NEW YORK • LONDON • BONN • BOSTON • DETROIT • MADRID
MELBOURNE • MEXICO CITY • PARIS • SINGAPORE • TOKYO
TORONTO • WASHINGTON • ALBANY NY • BELMONT CA • CINCINNATI OH

STAFF

Christopher Giroux, *Editor*

Jennifer Brostrom, Jeff Chapman, Pamela S. Dear, John D. Jorgenson, Matt McDonough,
Brigham Narins, Sean René Pollock, Deborah A. Stanley, Aarti D. Stephens,
Polly A. Vedder, Thomas Wiloch, Kathleen Wilson, Janet Witalec, *Associate Editors*

John Benci, George H. Blair, Jennifer Giroux, Kelly Hill,
Kristin Palm, Annette Petrusso, John Stanley, *Assistant Editors*

Marlene H. Lasky, *Permissions Manager*
Margaret A. Chamberlain, Linda M. Pugliese, *Permissions Specialists*

Susan Brohman, Diane Cooper, Maria Franklin, Arlene Johnson, Michele Lonoconus, Maureen Puhl, Shalice Shah,
Kimberly F. Smilay, Barbara A. Wallace, *Permissions Associates*
Edna Hedblad, Margaret McAvoy-Amato, Tyra Y. Phillips, Lori A. Schoenenberger, *Permissions Assistants*

Victoria B. Cariappa, *Research Manager*
Mary Beth McElmeel, Donna Melnychenko, Tamara C. Nott, Tracie A. Richardson, Norma Sawaya, *Research Associates*

Shirley Gates, Michele P. Pica, Amy Terese Steel, *Research Assistants*

Mary Beth Trimper, *Production Director*
Shanna Heilveil, *Production Assistant*

Barbara J. Yarrow, *Graphic Services Supervisor*
Sherrell Hobbs, *Macintosh Artist*
Willie F. Mathis, *Camera Operator*
Pamela A. Hayes, *Photography Coordinator*

Library of Congress Catalog Card Number 76-38938
ISBN 0-8103-4997-3
ISSN 0091-3421

Printed in the United States of America

10 9 8 7 6 5 4 3 2 1

I(T)P™ Gale Research Inc., an International Thomson Publishing Company.
ITP logo is a trademark under license.

Contents

Preface vii

Acknowledgments xi

Preface

A Comprehensive Information Source
on Contemporary Literature

Named "one of the twenty-five most distinguished reference titles published during the past twenty-five years" by *Reference Quarterly*, the *Contemporary Literary Criticism (CLC)* series provides readers with critical commentary and general information on more than 2,000 authors now living or who died after December 31, 1959. Previous to the publication of the first volume of *CLC* in 1973, there was no ongoing digest monitoring scholarly and popular sources of critical opinion and explication of modern literature. *CLC*, therefore, has fulfilled an essential need, particularly since the complexity and variety of contemporary literature makes the function of criticism especially important to today's reader.

Scope of the Series

CLC presents significant passages from published criticism of works by creative writers. Since many of the authors covered by *CLC* inspire continual critical commentary, writers are often represented in more than one volume. There is, of course, no duplication of reprinted criticism.

Authors are selected for inclusion for a variety of reasons, among them the publication or dramatic production of a critically acclaimed new work, the reception of a major literary award, revival of interest in past writings, or the adaptation of a literary work to film or television.

Attention is also given to several other groups of writers—authors of considerable public interest—about whose work criticism is often difficult to locate. These include mystery and science fiction writers, literary and social critics, foreign writers, and authors who represent particular ethnic groups within the United States.

Format of the Book

Each *CLC* volume contains about 500 individual excerpts taken from hundreds of book review periodicals, general magazines, scholarly journals, monographs, and books. Entries include critical evaluations spanning from the beginning of an author's career to the most current commentary. Interviews, feature articles, and other published writings that offer insight into the author's works are also presented. Students, teachers, librarians, and researchers will find that the generous excerpts and supplementary material in *CLC* provide them with vital information required to write a term paper, analyze a poem, or lead a book discussion group. In addition, complete bibliographical citations note the original source and all of the information necessary for a term paper footnote or bibliography.

Features

A *CLC* author entry consists of the following elements:

- The **Author Heading** cites the author's name in the form under which the author has most commonly published, followed by birth date, and death date when applicable. Uncertainty as to a birth or death date is indicated by a question mark.

- A **Portrait** of the author is included when available.

- A brief **Biographical and Critical Introduction** to the author and his or her work precedes the excerpted criticism. The first line of the introduction provides the author's full name, pseudonyms (if applicable), nationality, and a listing of genres in which the author has written. To provide users with easier access to information, the biographical and critical essay included in each author entry is divided into four categories: "Introduction," "Biographical Information," "Major Works," and "Critical Reception." The introductions to single-work entries—entries that focus on well-known and frequently studied books, short stories, and poems—are similarly organized to quickly provide readers with information on the plot and major characters of the work being discussed, its major themes, and its critical reception. Previous volumes of *CLC* in which the author has been featured are also listed in the introduction.

- A list of **Principal Works** notes the most important writings by the author. When foreign-language works have been translated into English, the English-language version of the title follows in brackets.

- The **Excerpted Criticism** represents various kinds of critical writing, ranging in form from the brief review to the scholarly exegesis. Essays are selected by the editors to reflect the spectrum of opinion about a specific work or about an author's literary career in general. The excerpts are presented chronologically, adding a useful perspective to the entry. All titles by the author featured in the entry are printed in boldface type, which enables the reader to easily identify the works being discussed. Publication information (such as publisher names and book prices) and parenthetical numerical references (such as footnotes or page and line references to specific editions of a work) have been deleted at the editor's discretion to provide smoother reading of the text.

- Critical essays are prefaced by **Explanatory Notes** as an additional aid to readers. These notes may provide several types of valuable information, including: the reputation of the critic, the importance of the work of criticism, the commentator's approach to the author's work, the purpose of the criticism, and changes in critical trends regarding the author.

- A complete **Bibliographical Citation** designed to help the user find the original essay or book precedes each excerpt.

- Whenever possible, a recent, previously unpublished **Author Interview** accompanies each entry.

- A concise **Further Reading** section appears at the end of entries on authors for whom a significant amount of criticism exists in addition to the pieces reprinted in *CLC*. Each citation in this section is accompanied by a descriptive annotation describing the content of that article. Materials included in this section are grouped under various headings (e.g., Biography, Bibliography, Criticism, and Interviews) to aid users in their search for additional information. Cross-references to other useful sources published by Gale Research in which the author has appeared are also included: *Authors in the News, Black Writers, Children's Literature Review, Contemporary Authors, Dictionary of Literary Biography, DISCovering Authors, Drama Criticism, Hispanic Literature Criticism, Hispanic Writers, Native North American Literature, Poetry Criticism, Something about the Author, Short Story Criticism, Contemporary Authors Autobiography Series,* and *Something about the Author Autobiography Series.*

Other Features

CLC also includes the following features:

- An **Acknowledgments** section lists the copyright holders who have granted permission to reprint material in this volume of *CLC*. It does not, however, list every book or periodical reprinted or consulted during the preparation of the volume.

- Each new volume of *CLC* includes a **Cumulative Topic Index,** which lists all literary topics treated in *CLC, NCLC, TCLC,* and *LC 1400-1800.*

- A **Cumulative Author Index** lists all the authors who have appeared in the various literary criticism series published by Gale Research, with cross-references to Gale's biographical and autobiographical series. A full listing of the series referenced there appears on the first page of the indexes of this volume. Readers will welcome this cumulated author index as a useful tool for locating an author within the various series. The index, which lists birth and death dates when available, will be particularly valuable for those authors who are identified with a certain period but whose death dates cause them to be placed in another, or for those authors whose careers span two periods. For example, Ernest Hemingway is found in *CLC,* yet a writer often associated with him, F. Scott Fitzgerald, is found in *Twentieth-Century Literary Criticism.*

- A **Cumulative Nationality Index** alphabetically lists all authors featured in *CLC* by nationality, followed by numbers corresponding to the volumes in which the authors appear.

- A **Title Index** alphabetically lists all titles reviewed in the current volume of *CLC.* Listings are followed by the author's name and the corresponding page numbers where the titles are discussed. English translations of foreign titles and variations of titles are cross-referenced to the title under which a work was originally published. Titles of novels, novellas, dramas, films, record albums, and poetry, short story, and essay collections are printed in italics, while all individual poems, short stories, essays, and songs are printed in roman type within quotation marks; when published separately (e.g., T. S. Eliot's poem *The Waste Land*), the titles of long poems are printed in italics.

- In response to numerous suggestions from librarians, Gale has also produced a **Special Paperbound Edition** of the *CLC* title index. This annual cumulation, which alphabetically lists all titles reviewed in the series, is available to all customers and is typically published with every fifth volume of *CLC.* Additional copies of the index are available upon request. Librarians and patrons will welcome this separate index: it saves shelf space, is easy to use, and is recyclable upon receipt of the next edition.

Citing *Contemporary Literary Criticism*

When writing papers, students who quote directly from any volume in the Literary Criticism Series may use the following general forms to footnote reprinted criticism. The first example pertains to material drawn from periodicals, the second to material reprinted in books:

[1]Alfred Cismaru, "Making the Best of It," *The New Republic,* 207, No. 24, (December 7, 1992), 30, 32; excerpted and reprinted in *Contemporary Literary Criticism,* Vol. 85, ed. Christopher Giroux (Detroit: Gale Research Inc., 1995), pp. 73-4.

[2]Yvor Winters, *The Post-Symbolist Methods* (Allan Swallow, 1967); excerpted and reprinted in *Contemporary Literary Criticism,* Vol. 85, ed. Christopher Giroux (Detroit: Gale Research Inc., 1995), pp. 223-26.

Suggestions Are Welcome

The editor hopes that readers will find *CLC* a useful reference tool and welcomes comments about the work. Send comments and suggestions to: Editor, *Contemporary Literary Criticism,* Gale Research Inc., Penobscot Building, Detroit, MI 48226-4094.

Acknowledgments

The editors wish to thank the copyright holders of the excerpted criticism included in this volume and the permissions managers of many book and magazine publishing companies for assisting us in securing reprint rights. We are also grateful to the staffs of the Detroit Public Library, the Library of Congress, the University of Detroit Mercy Library, Wayne State University Purdy/Kresge Library Complex, and the University of Michigan Libraries for making their resources available to us. Following is a list of the copyright holders who have granted us permission to reprint material in this volume of *CLC*. Every effort has been made to trace copyright, but if omissions have been made, please let us know.

COPYRIGHTED EXCERPTS IN *CLC*, VOLUME 87, WERE REPRINTED FROM THE FOLLOWING PERIODICALS:

The American Book Review, v. 7, March-April, 1985; v. 9, January-February, 1988. © 1985, 1988 by *The American Book Review.* Both reprinted by permission of the publisher.—*American Film,* v. XIV, January-February, 1989 for "Darkness at the Edge of Towne" by Michael Sragow. Copyright 1989 by *American Film.* Reprinted by permission of the author.—*American Indian Culture and Research Journal,* v. 4, 1980 for "The Uses of Oral Tradition in Six Contemporary Native American Poets" by James Ruppert. Copyright © 1980 The Regents of the University of California. Reprinted by permission of the author./ v. 18, 1994. © 1994 The Regents of the University of California. Reprinted by permission of the publisher.—*American Literature,* v. 46, March, 1974. Copyright © 1974 Duke University, Durham, NC. Reprinted with permission of the publisher.—*The American Scholar,* v. 62, Winter, 1993 for "Death and the Maiden" by Ann M. Begley. Copyright © 1993 by the author. Reprinted by permission of the publishers.—*Belles Lettres: A Review of Books by Women,* v. 4, Fall, 1988. Reprinted by permission of the publisher.—*Book World—The Washington Post,* October 26, 1986; January 6, 1991. © 1986, 1991, The Washington Post. Both reprinted with permission of the publisher.—*Books and Bookmen,* n. 369, July, 1986 for "Terrors of Civilization" by Michelene Wandor. © copyright the author 1986. Reprinted by permission of the author.—*The Boston Globe,* October 6, 1987. © 1987 Globe Newspaper Co. Reprinted courtesy of *The Boston Globe.*—*Boston Review,* v. IX, October, 1984 for "In the Company of M.F.K. Fisher" by Christopher Benfey. Copyright © by the Boston Critic, Inc. Reprinted by permission of the author.—*Callaloo,* v. 13, Summer, 1990. Copyright © 1990 by Charles H. Rowell. All rights reserved. Reprinted by permission of the publisher.—*Chicago Tribune—Books,* January 27, 1991. © copyrighted 1991, Chicago Tribune Company. All rights reserved. Used with permission.—*The Christian Science Monitor,* May 12, 1993. © 1993 The Christian Science Publishing Society. All rights reserved. Reprinted by permission from The Christian Science Monitor.—*Commonweal,* v. LXXXVIII, April 12, 1968. Copyright © 1968 Commonweal Publishing Co., Inc. Reprinted by permission of Commonweal Foundation.—*Comparative Literature,* v. 32, Summer, 1991. © 1991 by the Regents of the University of Wisconsin. Reprinted by permission of The University of Wisconsin Press.—*Comparative Literature Studies,* v. 24, September, 1987. Copyright © 1987 by The Pennsylvania State University. Reproduced by permission of The Pennsylvania State University Press.—*Critique: Studies in Contemporary Fiction,* v. XXXI, Winter, 1990. Copyright © 1990 Helen Dwight Reid Educational Foundation. Reprinted with permission of the Helen Dwight Reid Educational Foundation, published by Heldref Publications, 1319 18th Street, N.W., Washington, DC 20036-1802.—*Critique: Studies in Modern Fiction,* v. XXVIII, Summer, 1987. Copyright © 1987 Helen Dwight Reid Educational Foundation. Reprinted with permission of the Helen Dwight Reid Educational Foundation, published by Heldref Publications, 1319 18th Street, N.W., Washington, DC 20036-1802.—*Film Comment,* v. 26, November-December, 1990 for "Fault Lines" by Mark Horowitz. Copyright © 1990 by the author. Reprinted by permission of the author.—*History Today,* v. 31, October, 1981. © History Today Limited 1981. Reprinted by permission of the publisher.—*The Hudson Review,* v. XLVI, Spring, 1993. Copyright © 1993 by The Hudson Review, Inc. Reprinted by permission of the publisher.—*The Journal of Ethnic Studies,* v. 18, Spring, 1990. Copyright © 1990 by *The Journal of Ethnic Studies.* Reprinted by permission of the publisher.—*Journal of Modern Literature,* v. 11, March, 1984. © Temple University 1984. Reprinted by permission

Sukenick. Poznań, 1986. Reprinted by permission of the publisher.—Tarbox, Katherine. From *The Art of John Fowles.* University of Georgia Press, 1988. © 1988 by the University of Georgia Press. All rights reserved. Reprinted by permission of the publisher.—From "Right and Left: Che Guevara," in *T.L.S.: Essays and Reviews from "The Times Literary Supplement"—1968, Vol. 7.* Oxford University Press, London, 1969. © Times Newspapers Ltd., 1969. All rights reserved. Reprinted by permission of Times Newspapers Limited.—Towne, Robert with John Brady. From an interview in *The Craft of the Screenwriter: Interviews with Six Celebrated Screenwriters.* Edited by John Brady. Simon and Schuster, 1981. Copyright © 1981 John Brady. All rights reserved. Reprinted by permission of the authors.

PHOTOGRAPHS AND ILLUSTRATIONS APPEARING IN *CLC*, VOLUME 87, WERE RECEIVED FROM THE FOLLOWING SOURCES:

AP/Wide World Photos: **pp. 1, 117, 221, 261, 349, 380;** © Jerry Bauer: **pp. 22, 134;** Archive Photos/Horst Tappe: **p. 70;** Photograph by Osvaldo Salas: **pp. 210, 216;** Photograph courtesy of White Pine Press, Fredonia, NY: **p. 237;** Cover of *Between Two Rivers: Selected Poems 1956-1984,* by Maurice Kenny. Copyright © 1987 by Maurice Kenny. Reprinted by permission of White Pine Press, Fredonia, NY: **p. 246;** Cover of *The Mama Poems,* by Maurice Kenny. Copyright © 1984 by Maurice Kenny. Cover drawing by Rokwaho. Reprinted by permission of White Pine Press, Fredonia, NY: **p. 256;** Photograph courtesy of Jonathan Cape: **p. 312;** Photograph courtesy of New Directions Publishing: **p. 332;** Photograph by Stephen Vaughan/Sygma: **p. 367;** Photograph by Ron Galella: **p. 373.**

James Clavell

1925-1994

(Full name James duMaresq Clavell) Australian-born English-American novelist, screenwriter, and author of children's books.

The following entry presents criticism on Clavell's works from 1981 through 1994. For further information on his life and works, see *CLC*, Volumes 6 and 25.

INTRODUCTION

Clavell is known primarily for his best-selling novel *Shōgun* (1975) and his other fictional works that focus on East Asian customs, history, and economic and political power struggles. Although *Shōgun* was praised by Asian historian Henry Smith for "[conveying] more information about Japan to more people than all the combined writings of scholars, journalists and novelists since the Pacific War," other scholars and critics have questioned the authenticity of Clavell's portrayal of feudal Japan and accused him of willfully distorting reality and sensationalizing history. In response, Clavell stated that he "played with history—the where and how and who and why and when of it—to suit my own reality and, perhaps, to tell the real history of what came to pass."

Biographical Information

Born in Australia, Clavell was the son of a British Royal Navy captain and cultivated his ear for storytelling listening to the sea tales of his father and grandfather, who was also a seaman. Intent on a military career, he joined the Royal Artillery in 1940 and was stationed in the Far East in 1941. Wounded by machine-gun fire while fighting in Malaysia, he hid in a local village for several months before the Japanese discovered him and sent him to Changi, a prisoner-of-war camp near Singapore. There, he survived three and one half years of severe living conditions and brutal treatment. Years later Clavell said of his experience: "Changi was a school for survivors. It gave me a strength most people don't have. I have an awareness of life others lack." After his release he returned to military service and was subsequently discharged in 1946 when disabled in a motorcycle accident. He briefly attended Birmingham University, but found the film industry alluring when he began to visit movie sets with his future wife, an aspiring actress. Working first as a distributor and then in production, Clavell and his wife emigrated to the United States in 1953, becoming naturalized citizens ten years later. Eventually earning a screenwriting contract, he completed his first screenplay—the enormously successful science-fiction film *The Fly*—in 1958. Based on a short story by George Langelaan, *The Fly* concerns an atomic scientist whose life is drastically changed by his work: when a common house fly is inadvertently caught in one of his experiments, the protagonist and insect exchange

physical qualities. A screenwriters' guild strike in 1960 necessitated that Clavell search for alternate means of employment in the publishing industry. Haunted by his memories of the Changi prison, Clavell recorded these experiences in his first novel, *King Rat* (1962). He died of cancer in September 1994.

Major Works

Clavell's writings are characterized by convoluted plots and a focus on such themes as war, advanced technology, power, romance, espionage, and international commerce. Based on historical incidents and figures, his works dramatize the tensions resulting when divergent cultures meet. First in a six-novel series known as the *Asian Saga, King Rat* is set in Changi, a prisoner-of-war camp, and focuses on the relationship between a British and an American soldier as they struggle to survive the brutal conditions. *Tai-pan* (1966) begins in 1841 and traces the founding of Hong Kong and the establishment of Noble House, an English trading empire controlled by Dirk Struan, the *tai-pan*, or merchant overlord of the company. The third novel of the series, *Shōgun*, concerns William Blackthorne, a character loosely based on Will Adams, an Englishman who arrived in Japan in 1600 after serving as a pilot on a Dutch ship and who remained in Japan until his death in 1620. After arriving in Japan, Blackthorne becomes a trusted foreign advisor to the *shōgun*, or overlord, Toranaga, and eventually the lover of Toranaga's polyglot, Christian wife. For introducing his Japanese host to Western warfare and navigational technology, Blackthorne is transformed from a "barbarian" into an honorable *samurai*. *Noble House* (1981) continues where *Taipan* concluded, portraying the modern-day financial power struggles of foreign trade. *Whirlwind* (1986) takes place in Iran in 1979 during the weeks following the revolution. Centering on a group of pilots employed by S-G Helicopters, a company owned by Noble House, the novel delineates their attempt to transfer the company's equipment out of the country before the government of Ayatollah Khomeini can seize it. *Gai-jin* (1993) also concerns the continuing saga of the Noble House trading dynasty. The novel is set in 1862 Yokahama, Japan, where the protagonist, Malcolm Struan, grandson of Dirk Struan of *Taipan,* struggles for dominance in the realm of foreign trade. In addition to his novels, Clavell has written two children's books, *The Children's Story* (1963), a fable on the dangers of not questioning authority and the vulnerability of children to propaganda, and *Thrump-o-moto* (1986), a fantasy tale about a young Australian girl suffering from polio and her apprentice-wizard mentor who leads her on a journey in search of self-discovery and the magical cure for her disease.

Critical Reception

Despite Clavell's astonishing success with popular audiences, reviews have been largely mixed. Many critics have agreed that Clavell's novels hold readers' attention because of their rich historical detail, suspenseful plots, and abundant information about East Asian culture and customs. However, other commentators have viewed these same attributes negatively, arguing that the novels tend to be too detailed, the plots too convoluted to follow, and the characters too stereotyped. In praise of *Shōgun,* which sold a record-breaking 3.5 million copies and was on the *New York Times* best-seller list for thirty-two weeks, novelist Tom Clancy stated "my favorite sort of novel is one in which two cultures meet—or collide—for the first time. Probably the best-ever book in this genre is James Clavell's *Shōgun.* "

PRINCIPAL WORKS

The Fly (screenplay) 1958
*Five Gates to Hell (screenplay) 1959
Watusi (screenplay) 1959
Walk like a Dragon (screenplay) 1960
†King Rat (novel) 1962
The Children's Story (children's book) 1963; first appeared in *Ladies Home Journal*
The Great Escape (screenplay) 1963
†Tai-pan: A Novel of Hong Kong (novel) 1966

*The Last Valley (screenplay) 1969
*To Sir with Love (screenplay) 1969
†Shōgun: A Novel of Japan (novel) 1975
†Noble House: A Novel of Contemporary Hong Kong (novel) 1981
Thrump-o-moto (juvenilia) 1986
†Whirlwind (novel) 1986
†Gai-jin (novel) 1993

*Clavell was also the producer and director of these films.

†These works are collectively referred to as the *Asian Saga.*

CRITICISM

Eliot Fremont-Smith   (review date 2 September 1981)

SOURCE: "Capture the Flag," in *The Village Voice,* Vol. XXVI, No. 36, September 2, 1981, p. 37.

[*In the following review, Fremont-Smith traces the publication history of* The Children's Story *and offers a negative assessment of its literary, political, and social value.*]

Once upon a time—this was before "Finlandization" and "secular humanism" were coined, and before James Clavell (***King Rat, Tai-Pan, Shogun, Noble House***) became a U.S. citizen and got really rich and famous (though not to weep, he was doing okay in Hollywood)—a little girl dashed home to tell her father what she had just learned by heart in school. "Daddy, Daddy, listen!" she cried, her cheeks rosy with excitement. And then, in a proud rush, she recited: "I plege' illegience to the flag . . ."

Michaela Clavell's father was touched, of course, and gave his daughter a dime at her request. But he was also curious and concerned. Had she, he grilled the five year-old, been taught in school what the words stood for—"pledge" and "allegiance" and whatnot? Michaela frowned and was perplexed. "Plege' illegience is plege' illegience," she finally offered. "I know I said it right," she tried again. "I was better than Johnny . . ."

But James Clavell was no longer there. Instead, he was out in the streets asking "all kinds of people of every age" what *they* thought the Pledge was all about. Everyone he buttonholed could parrot the words, though "almost always equally blurred," but no one had ever been told what they meant, or seemed even now to have the foggiest. ***The Children's Story*** "came into being that day. It was then that I realized how completely vulnerable my child's mind was—any mind for that matter—under controlled circumstances." Unhappily for Clavell, the circumstances of the story's original publication in *Ladies Home Journal* in 1963 weren't controlled enough.

It's a wee fable, set in a future conquered and supine America, wherein a wily new teacher indoctrinates a first-grade class *away* from faith in and loyalty to flag, country, honor, family, and God in 23 minutes flat. The kids, you see, were never taught the precise meaning of the Pledge—

and are therefore just blobs of putty in the new teacher's clever and presumably Communist hands. A tiny tale but, alas, beyond the comprehension of many *Ladies Home Journal* readers, at least back then. Of the 2400 who wrote in, a majority denounced **The Children's Story** as godless, possibly un-American, and probably subversive—as if the author (and *LHJ*'s editors) *approved* what the new teacher did.

Well. You can imagine the consternation *chez* Clavell. What was the matter with the country, anyway, that people couldn't recognize simple patriotism—a warning call to steel the minds and hearts of our young against potential alien corruption—right in front of their noses? Certainly nothing could be wrong with the *telling* of the story (wasn't **King Rat** a best-seller, wasn't **Tai-Pan** about to be?), so maybe it was the times that were out of joint or, in this instance, the writer was too far ahead of. Perhaps in 18 years . . . Somehow Clavell endured the '60s and the '70s—and then, suddenly, Reagan was president, and Clavell *very* rich and famous, and, what the heck, why not repackage the thing, run it up the pole, and see if this time it would sell out?

Eleanor Friede, Clavell's editor at Delacorte, and famous in her own right for bringing *Jonathan Livingston Seagull* to commercial attention, thought this was a grand idea. Why—properly packaged and promoted, **The Children's Story** might even become the *Jonathan Livingston Seagull* of the '80s! The timing could hardly be more ripe. Individual aspiration of the free human spirit was yesterday's bonanza; today's now-people are into God and national security. Me first then, America first now. Funny how these things go in cycles, and if you look closely seem sort of the same, eternal-veritywise. But that's book biz!

Yet nothing is automatic, success is best arranged, and **The Children's Story** no criticism intended, would have to be done just right. Thus, to enhance the eternally verified cuteness, nostalgia, and sincerity factors, Clavell would append a hand-written account explaining how the fable burst all-unbidden into consciousness and manuscript, and its purpose. And Michaela Clavell (now Crisman) would be brought in as "an integral part of the book's production" (a small *coup,* yet redolent with fealty and forgiveness). The book itself would be modestly unpaginated—why should readers fret over publisher's profit per paragraph? —but dressed up smartly with a jacket of red, a cover of white and blue, and six *Seagull*-like illustrations by Joan Stoliar depicting the swirly, smudgy void, absent a parsing of the Pledge, between our youngster's ears.

But beautiful and moving packaging only begins the promotion and marketing process. The Betsy Nolan Group would be brought in for the public relations job—especially important with reviewers—to emphasize the pluses of the reprint and overcome the minuses. The one big minus, no criticism intended, was the track record—that the whole point of **The Children's Story** eluded so many readers back in '63. Of course, times *have* changed, and today the old misunderstanding could be a million-dollar newspeg. Yet the possibility that some influential reviewer (or his/her mom) once subscribed to *Ladies*

Home Journal and even now harbors a sense of insult about the story, should not be over-looked. Alternatively, reviewers tend generally to be liberal in their politics (a few almost willfully so), which, unless properly assuaged, could be another source of unconscious hostility to the product. Clearly, a press kit would be in order. And it would include the following items:

First, a Betsy Nolan letterhead letter stating that **The Children's Story** "is truly a book for our times" and "not a children's book, but a book for all ages," and that it's to be an alternate of the Literary Guild and 11 other Doubleday clubs, and that *LHJ* has purchased second serial rights (!), and that 1000 copies have been sent to educators, legislators, and civic and religious leaders whose responses are "incredible."

Second, a picture of the book and James Clavell.

Third, a career biography of James Clavell.

Fourth, a release of the story behind this "parable of freedom," including Mrs. Crisman's involvement.

Fifth, a favorable (if also rather crisp) preview of the book from *Publishers Weekly.*

Sixth, a "short quiz" on the book, together with the words and legislative history of the Pledge of Allegiance and the last three stanzas of *The Star-Spangled Banner.*

And seventh, a sidebar item on how Clavell, who likes the number 3, came to select September 3, 1981, which can also be written 9/3/81, as the book's publication date: "9 - 3 x 3.9 + 3 - 12 (and 1 + 2 - 3). 8 + 1 - 9 (which is divisible by 3). Thus the September 3 date is derived from the number 3 in three different ways."

So much for lingering liberalism. As for the ancient charges of godlessness and subversion, the following endorsements would be gotten out (I read them in *New York*): From the Boy Scouts of America: "The moral [is] that we must all be vigilant." From Ayn Rand: "Very skillful." From Senator Strom Thurmond: "An incident [that] could actually happen." And from the White House, where the Clavells have been to dinner, in the words of Betsy Nolan: "The president said it's a book he and Nancy will talk about."

Well.

So far, I've dealt with the objective facts. Now I must get personal. I have several problems with **The Children's Story**. These range from minor to major, from aesthetic to philosophic. A minor aesthetic problem, for instance, is the Stoliar illustrations, which look to me like outer space as seen by Voyager II while its camera was on the blink, or microcosmic activity in a garbage dump. But this could be a moral problem, like I could have done them myself with a little charcoal on my toe. (I know, I know—they said the same thing about Malevitch.) Are the insides of children's heads really this murky and bleak? I, for one, don't think so—and you see how the problems intermix and multiply. *I* think God programmed five-year-olds better, anyway more vividly, than Stoliar suggests. And I think Clavell thinks so, too.

Then there's the matter of beauty *within* the story. If there's one thing Clavell's kids appreciate, it's pulchritude. In the story, their old teacher was a middle-ager gone physically to pot. Their new teacher is a young vivacious knockout. She's also efficient, knows every name right away. Plus she's intelligent, actually engages the class in philosophic argument, and makes it exciting and fun. Plus she doesn't lie; she even lets the kids in on the game of rewards. In short, there's a kind of radiance about her that the old teacher, apparently a real ignorant and insensitive grump, entirely lacked. This raises all sorts of issues like are all Communist Finlandicizers the terrific, and is Shanker's union detrimental to quality education? Clavell writes that he likes his story because "it keeps asking questions." But so do Charlie's Angels.

I have a problem, too, with the Pledge. I mean, I'm all for it on the one hand, community spirit and sense of commitment and oath and honor, one for all and all for one and whatnot—it's *important*—but, on the other hand, I think the truth these days is that *all* nations are indivisible, and that local allegiance is therefore rather complicated. It's a secular humanist view, perhaps, but seems to me realistic as well as scary. And I bet the president thinks so, too—even though we plainly disagree on the 1954 (thank you, Betsy Nolan!) addition to the Pledge of the rubric "under God," which for me ruins the poetic rhythm I grew up with. (In my book, poetic rhythm is right up there with the First Amendment. Pitch, too. I wish our anthem were singable by normal folk, like "Deutschland, Deutschland Uber Alles," "Rule, Britannia," or "You Deserve a Break Today.")

And then there's the question of what five-year-olds, or any of us, can or should take in, and when and how. Unlike Clavell, I have this faith that some good things are appropriately accomplished by osmosis. I'm all for precise meanings of words. But that isn't all to experience, or to the war against sociopathological phenomena and other invading evils. In fact, I'm practically a Reaganite on rote. Some things must be learned by infants and toddlers and five-year-olds that cannot be fully understood until later, if ever. 9 - 3 x 3 is one example. Don't bite is another. Dimes are not in endless supply is still another (and one that Michaels and her father's accountant may recall.)

And freedom? Independence? Conscience? Loyalty? Morality and God? *The flag?* These things come by *all* means, intellectual and otherwise, and I think mostly otherwise in very young children, and perhaps throughout our lives. This isn't to denigrate; it expresses an optimism about the Almighty and His balanced plan. The trouble with the Pledge of Allegiance is not that it's learned by heart without detail comprehension, or even that it has no plot, but that it's so small, and worse, doesn't scan. You want *real* (though supposedly nonsensical) fidelity to duty, country, and family against the foreign foe, read *Jabberwocky.* Compared to which, I have to say, the Pledge seems strictly tumtum, and *The Children's Story* both overly momewrathy and outgrabe. But that's by the bye—except that the freedom of captiousness is one I trust Clavell holds dear.

Thus a multitude of problems, and in the end too much

one is asked to take on trust. That, for instance, Clavell knows *any* beans at all about how children learn, or what the dangers are, or how readers may react to a murky tale that can signify anything and seems, beneath the production hoopla and assuaging hype, to mean exactly zilch. In my handy desk dictionary, the third definition of "fable" is "falsehood." Here's why I bring this up.

According to Clavell's account, little Michaela not only didn't know the meaning of the Pledge, but, as she recited, spelled it wrong. Yet "plege' illegience" seems to me *his* mistake. Or commercial plan. I'm a stickler for words, but think on it: Being quite young, not yet fully in control of her motor coordination, and extremely eager to please her father and show off her most recent wonderful accomplishment, she might have burbled "eyeplejuleejense" or somesuch. But she wasn't *dictating,* and there's no record of a hiccup in the text, and I think the apostrophe, at least, is something Clavell *made up.*

And so, with deference to Friede, Nolan, et alia, I think *The Children's Story* stinks. The publication story is, of course, another matter, and no one said freedom, including of enterprise, doesn't sometimes smell, as well as keep things moving and people who need jobs employed.

Henry Smith   (essay date October 1981)

SOURCE: "Reading James Clavell's *Shogun,*" in *History Today,* Vol. 31, October, 1981, pp. 39-42.

[*An American educator and historian, Smith has written widely on Japanese history and was the editor of* Learning from "Shōgun": Japanese History and Western Fantasy *(1980). In the following essay, Smith relates Clavell's sources and manipulation of Japanese culture and history in* Shōgun.]

When confronted with an extremely popular modern novel which is based on historical themes the first instinct of the historian, naturally enough, is to ascertain the 'historicity' of the work. The models for the major characters in James Clavell's **Shōgun** are easy to recognise but Clavell has considerably rearranged and refashioned the events and personalities of the time about which he writes.

These changes can be summarised briefly. The model for Blackthorne, the protagonist of **Shōgun,** is Will Adams (1564-1620), the circumstances of whose arrival in Japan in April 1600 as pilot of a Dutch ship correspond closely to those of Blackthorne. Blackthorne's eventual rise to the position of adviser and retainer of Yoshi Toranaga roughly parallels the career of Adams; a key difference is that Clavell telescopes these events into a single summer, whereas in reality the intimacy of Adams and the historical Tokugawa Ieyasu grew over a matter of years. Clavell also inflates the heroic stature of the historical Adams by having Blackthorne actually save Toranaga's life, by having him introduce effective warfare with guns to Japan (something which had been accomplished several decades before), and above all by having him fall in love with the wife of one of the great feudal lords of Japan.

The depiction of the military struggle for national supremacy in **Shōgun** corresponds to historical fact in broad outline, although the intricate subplots of the novel are wholly of Clavell's invention. Toranaga's scheming rival 'Ishido' is vaguely modelled after the *daimyo* Ishida Mitsunari (1560-1600), who did in fact organise the coalition against Ieyasu that was defeated at the Battle of Sekigahara in October 1600. The historical Ishida however, was not nearly so powerful as his counterpart in **Shōgun,** nor was his execution in 1600 anything like the gruesome punishment meted out to Ishido at the very end of the novel. Similar and even greater liberties have been taken with the other *daimyo* who appear in **Shōgun,** for many of whom it is even difficult to locate a specific model.

The model of Blackthorne's lover, the Lady Toda Mariko, is Hosokawa Gracia (1563-1600), whose husband Tadaoki (1563-1645) was one of the most cultivated men of his time and is done somewhat of a historical disservice by being transformed by Clavell into the boorish 'Buntaro'. The historical Gracia was one of the most famous of all the Christian converts in Japan of her era, and is revered to this day as a saint by Japanese Roman Catholics. While she was indeed versed in both Portuguese and Latin, the historical Gracia never served as an interpreter for Ieyasu. Nor did she even meet Will Adams, and she certainly would never have had a love affair with him or any other European seaman.

It is this transformation of a chaste Catholic heroine of the sixteenth century into a modish Madame Butterfly that has tended to shock and sometimes offend the sticklers for historicity. Edwin Reischauer, the distinguished American historian of Japan, has written indignantly that Clavell 'freely distorts historical fact to fit his tale' when he stoops to having such an 'exemplary Christian wife' as Hosokawa Gracia 'pictured without a shread of plausiblity as Blackthorne's great love, Mariko'.

These charges raise some difficult questions. As a novelist, is Clavell not free to transform his characters as he pleases? The author himself has claimed that there were really no exact 'models' for the characters in **Shōgun,** simply 'sources of inspiration' drawn from the pages of history. He did, after all, change the names of virtually all the historical characters (one notable exception being Gracia's maiden name, Akechi). 'I thought, to be honest', Clavell has said, 'that I didn't want to be restricted by historical personality.'

The more serious charge against Clavell is that of historical plausibility. Granted that the historical Will Adams never laid eyes on the historical lady Gracia, was that sort of liaison conceivable in Japan of the year 1600? Here the answer would certainly be that it was not. The daimyo ladies of sixteenth-century Japan were strictly sequestered and rarely had the chance to meet any men other than immediate family. Nor can one imagine any Japanese woman of good breeding entering the bath so casually with another man—much less a 'barbarian'. The only sort of woman who would have behaved with the sexual candor of Mariko in that era would probably [have] been a prostitute (such as **Shōgun's** 'Kiku').

The issue of historical plausibility arises on other occasions in **Shōgun.** A number of these relate to details about Japanese customs. The careful historian might insist, for example, that such a rare imported luxury as soap would not have been used to bathe a captured barbarian, or that traditional Japanese never celebrated birthdays (as Lady Ochiba does late in the novel), or that the Japanese did in fact eat meat from time to time (contrary to Mariko's claim of total avoidance). In these and other small ways, **Shōgun** will strike the historian as a somewhat flawed depiction of Japanese customs in the year 1600.

Rather more of a problem is the question of Japanese psychology and behaviour as represented in **Shōgun.** Were samurai in fact given to beheading commoners on a whim and the hacking the corpse into small pieces? Were all Japanese of that era (or any other era, for that matter) so utterly nonchalant about sex and nudity? Would a peasant really have been summarily executed for taking down a rotting pheasant? Was *'karma'* in fact such an everyday word among the Japanese of the year 1600? Although precise answers to these questions are not always easy, it can certainly be said that in every case Clavell exaggerates and often distorts the historical reality.

But the real problem is to understand *why* James Clavell has depicted the Japanese in ways that occasionally strike the historian as implausible. Most of the errors of detail were surely unintentional, and probably reflect nothing more than the inadequacy of the English-language materials on which Clavell, who reads and speaks no Japanese, was obliged to depend for his information. As a practical matter it must be admitted that such authenticity is probably of little concern to the average Western reader of **Shōgun,** who knows almost nothing about Japan or its history.

But the exaggeration of Japanese behaviour, particularly with respect to attitudes about such matters as love, death, food and bathing, is clearly intentional on the part of Clavell, since in every case he strives to contrast the values of the Japanese with those of Blackthorne and his fellow Europeans. Even more importantly, the final message of the author is that, as the confused Blackthorne comes to realise, 'much of what they believe is so much better than our way that it's tempting to become one of them totally'. Whereas Western man, as symbolised by Blackthorne, is depicted as ridden with shame over sex, obsessed with a fear of death, raised on an unwholesome diet of animal flesh and alcohol, and terrified of bathing, the Japanese are represented as paragons in each particular. They view sex and nudity as wholly 'natural', are able to face death with composure and even eagerness, eat only fish (preferably raw), rice, and pickles, and of course are wholly addicted to the pleasures of the hot bath.

It is precisely this rather didactic contrast that gives **Shōgun** so much of its interest, both for the average reader and for the historian. Clavell is in effect delivering a sermon on the errant ways of the West. More specifically, he is delivering a polemic against the Christian Church for instilling in Western man his (in Clavell's view) distorted attitudes to sex, death, and cleanliness. This anti-christian tone runs throughout **Shōgun** and manifests itself most clearly in the depiction of the European Jesuits. Although no responsible historian would claim that the Jesuits were without their faults as missionaries in Japan, it is hard to find the priests of *Shōgun* as anything but caricatures. While the Jesuits did indeed for a time rely on the silk trade to finance their mission, they were scarcely the greedy villains of *Shōgun,* ever ready to stoop to crude assassination plots to thwart their rivals.

The preferable religious attitude, *Shōgun,* insistently implies, is the meditative and fatalistic posture of the Japanese samurai, as epitomised by the great warrior Toranaga. About halfway through the novel there appears a description of Toranaga in a state of religious reverie; it is an effective summary of the type of mysticism which Clavell seems to advocate:

> Now sleep, *Karma* is *karma*. Be thou of Zen. Remember, in tranquility, that the Absolute, the Tao, is within thee, that no priest or cult or dogma or book or saying or teaching or teacher stands between Thou and It. Know that Good and Evil are irrelevant, I and Thou irrelevant, Inside and Outside irrelevant as are Life and Death. Enter into the Sphere where there is no fear of death nor hope of afterlife, where thou art free of the impediments of life or the needs of salvation. . . .

While drawing freely on elements of Asian mysticism (*karma,* Zen, Tao), this sermon is a personal statement by James Clavell. A more authentically Japanese Zen Buddhist, for example, would certainly be far more respectful of 'teachers' and the idea of 'salvation'. Yet the Zen spirit is certainly there, and the message is that the West has much to learn from Asian meditational practice—an idea to which many of Clavell's devotees would seem to be hospitable.

In a sense, then, *Shōgun* is a story of a spiritual quest. It is of course skilfully woven in among other stories—that of a tragic love affair and that of a ruthless power struggle—so that the sermon never becomes obtrusive. But it is a very important element in the overall logic of *Shogun.* Even less apparent to the normal reader is the fact that this 'quest' is closely related to James Clavell's personal experiences with the Japanese. As a young soldier in the British army, Clavell was captured by the Japanese in Southeast Asia in 1942 and spent the remainder of the war in Changi prison on Singapore. While his experience understandably left him with many hostile feelings about the Japanese, he grew in time to respect his captors, for much the same reasons that Blackthorne does. In short, the story of Blackthorne's progress, from horror over his captors' 'barbarity' to respect for their 'civilized' values as even more 'civilized' than those of the West, is also the story of Clavell himself.

It is in order to dramatise this theme of spiritual quest in *Shōgun* that the author tends in various ways to idealise, over-simplify, and sometimes distort Japanese values and attitudes. And it is here that the historian can perhaps step in to right the balance a little.

One common form of exaggeration in *Shōgun,* is the depiction of values which were historically limited to a certain segment of Japanese society as though they were universally 'Japanese'. Take the simple example of eating

meat. Mariko tells Blackthorne that the Japanese never eat meat. This was in fact true at the time only of the Buddhist clergy and the Kyoto aristocracy; the samurai class of which Mariko was a member was in fact fond of meat and frequently consumed wild game. One hastens to add that in terms of contrast with the Europeans, Clavell's depiction is still basically valid. Even samurai ate only wild game, and never raised animals or even fowl for consumption; and never did their level of meat consumption even approach that of the highly carnivorous Europeans of all but the lowest classes.

Another type of simplification which the historian is anxious to pick out is anachronism. An appropriate example here might be that of sexual attitudes, a matter of fundamental East-West contrast as depicted in *Shōgun*. Here the problem lies primarily in the characterisation of European seamen as squeamish about sexual matters as Blackthorne is. The depiction of Western sexuality in *Shōgun* conforms instead to the stereotype known as 'Victorian'—although many people now question whether such prudishness was in fact typical of the nineteenth century.

In this process of trying to 'deidealize' the sharp Europe-Japan contrasts that appear in *Shōgun,* however, the historian soon learns two important lessons. The first is that we still do not really know the answers to many of these questions about the historical evolution of Japanese attitudes to sex, love, death and other such basic human preoccupations. Nor, for example, do we really know what the Japanese of different classes ate in the sixteenth century. Nor indeed can we give a satisfactory explanation of the historical development and psychological workings of the peculiar samurai practice of ritual disembowelment (*seppuku*). The lament of French historian Lucien Febvre in 1941, would certainly still apply to Japan: 'We have no history of Love. We have no history of Death. We have no history of Pity or Cruelty, we have no history of Joy.' We cannot, quite simply, answer the hard historical questions about the stuff of which a popular novel like *Shōgun* is made.

The second realisation provoked by *Shōgun* is that no matter how much the historian seeks to qualify the rather stark contrasts between Japan and the West that run through *Shōgun,* there remains little doubt that in many ways Japan had by the year 1600 evolved customs and attitudes that really do seem to have been at sharp variance with those in the West. One has only to peruse some of the fascinating reports of European visitors to Japan to realise this. As the Italian Jesuit Alessandro Valignano (the model for Father Carlo dell'Aqua in *Shōgun*) wrote in 1583, 'The things which they do are beyond imagining and it may truly be said that Japan is a world the reverse of Europe'. This metaphor of Japan as a 'topsy-turvy' land, where everything is done in precisely opposite manner, is one that has appeared again and again in Western descriptions of Japan ever since.

Western understanding of Japan has, we may hope, reached the point where we can dismiss the 'topsy-turvy' argument as Europocentric nonsense. This is not, however, to deny the reality of general differences between Japan and the West—provided of course that one remains alert to the wide diversity among different classes in Japan and

An excerpt from *Gai-Jin*

"God Almighty, look there! It's the French girl . . ."

"What's amiss? Christ, look at her clothes . . ."

"Cor, it's her, the smasher, Angel Tits, arrived couple of weeks ago . . ."

"That's right, Angelique . . . Angelique Beecho or Re-echo, some Frog name like that. . . ."

"My God, *look at the blood!*"

Everyone began converging on her, except the Chinese who, wise after millennia of sudden trouble, vanished. Faces began to appear in windows.

"Charlie, fetch Sir William on the double!"

"Christ Almighty, look at her pony, poor bugger will bleed to death, get the vet," a corpulent trader called out. "And you, soldier, quick, get the General, and the Frog, she's his ward—oh for God's sake the French Minister, hurry!" Impatiently he pointed at a single-story house flying the French flag. "Hurry!" he bellowed, the soldier rushed off, and he trundled for her as fast as he could. Like all traders he wore a top hat and woolen frock coat, tight pants, boots, and sweated in the sun. "What on earth happened, Miss Angelique?" he said, grabbing her bridle, aghast at the dirt and blood that speckled her face and clothes and hair. "Are you hurt?"

"*Moi, non* . . . no, I think not but we were attacked . . . Japanners attacked us." She was trying to catch her breath and stop shaking, still in terror, and pushed the hair out of her face. Urgently she pointed inland westwards, Mount Fuji vaguely on the horizon. "Back there, quick, they need, need help!"

Those nearby were appalled and noisily began relaying the half news to others and asking questions: Who? Who was attacked? Are they French or British? Attacked? Where? Two-sword bastards again! Where the hell did this happen . . .

Questions overlaid other questions and gave her no time to answer, nor could she yet, coherently, her chest heaving, everyone pressing closer, crowding her. More and more men poured into the street putting on coats and hats, many already armed with pistols and muskets, a few with the latest American breech-loading rifles. One of these men, a big-shouldered, bearded Scot, ran down the steps of an imposing two-story building. Over the portal was 'Struan and Company.' He shoved his way through to her in the uproar.

"Quiet for God's sake!" he shouted, and in the sudden lull, "Quick, tell us what happened. Where's young Mr. Struan?"

"Oh Jamie, *je* . . . I, I . . ." The girl made a desperate effort to collect herself, disoriented. "Oh *mon Dieu!*"

James Clavell in his Gai-Jin, *Delacorte Press, 1993.*

among the many cultures that make up 'the West'. It is precisely the general differences that make Japan such a fruitful and fascinating object of study for the West; by understanding Japan, we come to understand ourselves. It was the genius of James Clavell to mobilize this learning process as a central theme of ***Shōgun***. It remains the task of the historian to probe the roots and refine the limits of Blackthorne's lessons.

Terry Teachout   (essay date 12 November 1982)

SOURCE: "James Clavell, Storyteller," in *National Review,* New York, Vol, XXXIV, November 12, 1982, pp. 1420-22.

[*In the following essay, based on an interview with Clavell, Teachout discusses Clavell's ideas on writing, political views, and his novels, particularly* Noble House.]

At 18, Sub-Lieutenant James Clavell of the British army was thrown into Changi, a Japanese prison camp in Singapore, where he spent the last three and a half years of the Second World War. At 29 he emigrated to Hollywood and made a name for himself as one of the most successful writer-producer-directors in town; he eventually became a naturalized American citizen. At 35, idled by a screenwriters' strike, he wrote ***King Rat,*** a novel about his struggle for survival in Changi. Three years later, when he sold the film rights to ***King Rat*** for a cool $157,000, Clavell pulled up stakes, headed for Hong Kong in search of inspiration—and found it.

Today, at 57, James Clavell is the author of four novels about Asia that have collectively sold some 14 or 15 million copies. Even non-readers have gotten pleasure out of his lucrative knack for telling an appealing story; two years ago, more than 125 million Americans watched a 12-hour, five-night television adaptation of ***Shogun,*** Clavell's most popular novel to date. To call him a "popular novelist" is an understatement: incredibly, he is now among the most widely read authors of the century.

"I'm not a novelist, I'm a storyteller," says Clavell. "I'm not a literary figure at all. I work very hard and try to do the best I can; and I try and write for myself, thinking that what I like, other people may like. My attitude is perhaps more romantic than psychiatric. I've never been trained as a writer, either. I stumbled into it in a funny way; I do not know how it works; and I'm petrified that it will vanish as easily as it came!"

Clavell's modesty about his literary reputation is plainly genuine, though he has been publicly accused of false modesty. "I'd certainly like the Nobel Prize for Literature," he says with a smile, "but I'm sure they're not going to give it to me this year! Seriously, my concern is with the people who read my books for pleasure. Hopefully, I can give them pleasure; hopefully, I can entertain them; hopefully, I can pass on a little information which I find interesting. And hopefully—perhaps—I can be a bridge between East and West."

There is a dignity in James Clavell's utterances that makes one approach his books with a sense of promise: and that promise is largely fulfilled in the reading of them. For Clavell is very much a born "storyteller," and an exceedingly craftsmanlike one as well. Even his most hostile critics acknowledge his ability to spin a ripping tale of derring-do. (*The New Yorker,* while dismissing **Shogun** as "a slick, ambitious, 802-page popular novel . . . which disadvantageously combines the worst qualities of the fact-crammed historical novel with the sort of flashy Hollywood dialogue . . . that [hasn't] been around much since the heyday of the Errol Flynn movie," admitted in the very next sentence that "Mr. Clavell does have a decided gift for storytelling.") What is not so often acknowledged, at least by the upper-crust critics, is the fact that James Clavell, within the sphere of his limits and inclinations, is a first-rate novelist of the second rank—the kind of popular writer, like Marquand or Maugham, who provides genuinely stimulating literary entertainment without insulting the sensibilities.

Clavell's methods are displayed to fine effect in his most recent novel, **Noble House**. The fourth volume of Clavell's *Asian Saga,* **Noble House** brings the activities of the Struan clan, first heard from in his 1966 novel **Tai-Pan,** up to date. A novel of unusual length—1,370 pages in softcover—**Noble House** is also unusual in its recognition of the unities; once past the prologue, which introduces Ian Dunross, the current "tai-pan" (merchant overlord) of Struan and Company (the fictional Hong Kong trading company known as "Noble House"), the novel confines itself to the events, chronologically narrated, of a single week in November 1963. Although the plot does not lend itself to elegant précis, this is roughly what happens: Two Americans come to Hong Kong with the intention of triggering a sort of Oriental proxy fight between Struan's and its historical archrival, Rothwell-Gornt, and feeding on the wreckage. Between one Sunday and the next, Hong Kong experiences an earthquake; all of the principal personages in the novel are involved in a fire on a floating restaurant; there is a disastrous run on several major banks; the KGB and the Mafia do their best to take advantage of the general confusion; and a substantial amount of what one reviewer called "decorous sex" is engaged in by a variety of characters. The good guys win.

Obviously, this sounds preposterous; and it must be conceded that Clavell piles one cataclysm on top of another with a slightly excessive—and transparently improvisational—panache. ("In **Noble House,**" he confesses amiably, "I wanted to write a story about two Americans who go to Hong Kong to try and usurp the Noble House, and en route they have lots of adventures. That's all I knew I was going to do beforehand." He adds, with a touch of regret: "In the old days—say, in **Tai-Pan**—when I got myself into a hole I could always kill somebody. It wasn't that easy in **Noble House.**") But what sounds preposterous in the telling is surprisingly convincing in the reading, and one races through **Noble House** like a fire engine, torn between savoring each tasty bit of local color and wanting to find out as soon as possible what new outrage Ian Dunross will put down next. Even the (generally) happy ending is satisfactory; anything else would have been contrived. (It should be noted that all of Clavell's other novels

are like this, more or less; and all of them are every bit as rousing as **Noble House.**)

Another unusual aspect of **Noble House** is its political stance. It is refreshing to note that each and every one of the KGB agents in **Noble House** is a no-good bastard gleefully committed to the destruction of the West. And it is even more wonderful to find that all the good guys in **Noble House** are . . . well, *conservative.* One of the most engaging characters in the book, an intelligence specialist for Her Majesty's Government who slips Ian Dunross an occasional high-level evaluation on the side, likes to toss off informal speeches about such things as (this is 1963, remember) the future of the Panama Canal:

> "Very well, plan that the Panama Canal will be lost to America."
>
> "That's ridiculous!"
>
> "Oh, don't look so shocked, Mr. Dunross! It's too easy. Give it ten or 15 years of enemy spadework and lots of liberal talk in America, ably assisted by do-gooders who believe in the benevolence of human nature, add to all this a modest amount of calculated Panamanian agitation, students and so on—preferably, ah, always students—artfully and secretly assisted by a few highly trained, patient, professional agitators and oh so secret KGB expertise, finance, and a long-range plan—ergo, in due course the canal could be out of U.S. hands into the enemy's."
>
> "They'd never stand for it."
>
> "You're right, Mr. Dunross, but they will sit for it."

Ian Dunross, for that matter, sums up his own personal politics as follows: "I'm royalist, I'm for freedom, for freebooting and free trade. I'm a Scotsman, I'm for Struan's, I'm for laissez-faire in Hong Kong and freedom around the world." When one considers that **Noble House,** jammed full of pleasingly inflammatory statements like the ones quoted above, sold a whopping 488,905 hardbound copies in 1981 alone, one is sorely tempted to say that James Clavell has written, without the pretentiousness of the original, the *Atlas Shrugged* [Ayn Rand's 1957 novel] of the Eighties. (The *New York Times,* which in the past has carried generally friendly reviews, now seems to have Clavell's political number. A profile of him that ran last year in the *Times Magazine* turned out to be a freelance scalpel job full of discreet sniggerings at his rightwing tendencies.)

In private life, Clavell expresses himself far more mildly, steering clear of the outright conservative label. "I don't *have* any political views," he claims. "Very seriously. Please be kind enough to point that out to your readers. I'm not a politician; I'm not a rabble-rouser, not a fanatic, not anything. I'm a *storyteller.*" But then comes the measured declaration: "Now if you're going to tell a modern-day story, such as I did in **Noble House,** you've got to consider the things that bother people in a modern way. Obviously, my position would be that we are under siege, and obviously it's quite clear that there's something wrong in the world. I am not limp and socialistic. I'm certainly for 'free trade and freebooting.' And I'm for the American way of life, and the English way of life, and the French way of life, and the German way of life—which is one of freedom. I think that if *that* is a political attitude, then I would say that is my attitude."

One issue on which Clavell parts company with American conservatives, though, is the China problem. "If I were President of the United States—and I did, in fact, write him a letter about this at one time—I would propose that our State Department should say openly to Mainland China: 'We would like to have eternal friendship with you. Tell us what you need. The Taiwanese problem? Well, you settle that—in a Chinese fashion. But don't rock the boat, and don't beat your breast in public, and don't wash your dirty linen in the streets.' You must remember that we in America have a historic attitude toward China that only recently has been screwed up: our historic task was to try and help them. That's all they want: to know that we're going to be friends. They have a billion people to feed, and enormous problems of every kind; and it seems to me that they're trying to do it in the best way they can. I obviously don't approve of the Communist attitude; but *that is their present government,* and the Chinese have a thing that whenever they're threatened from the outside, it's just like the Fourth of July—they support the Emperor and repel the barbarians, under any circumstances whatsoever. I get bonkers, as they say in England, at the stupid and unnecessary mistakes our country has made with respect to China. For instance, at the time of the Geneva Conference, when Chou En-lai was there with Foster Dulles, he went up to him and said: 'Please excuse me, Mr. Dulles, let me introduce myself.' He put out his hand, and Dulles looked at him, turned his back on him, and walked away. What the Americans don't understand is that *that's going to be remembered for ten thousand years.*"

When in the proper frame of mind, James Clavell will gladly expand on his "nonpolitical" attitudes; but he greatly prefers to stick to the business he knows best—the craft of writing popular fiction. Although he is superstitious about discussing his novel-in-progress ("I'll tell you what: how about this? It's about this handsome chap who writes for this famous right-wing paper, and he's got himself this beautiful bird"), other than to admit that it is about Japan and is tentatively called *Nippon,* he will tell you about his methods of revision ("I write twenty pages for every one that sees print"), his favorite writers (Hemingway and Steinbeck), or his tendency to get "apoplectic" when he runs across "one fraction of one word that's hostile in a thousand-word review."

And, with a directness that rules out any possibility of affectation, James Clavell refers to himself time and time again as "just a storyteller." The implied distinction is a fair one; his work, for all its enormous appeal, makes no real attempt at the ambiguity and intellectual complexity of serious fiction—though **King Rat,** his first novel, suggests an untapped and underrated potential in this quarter. But Clavell rightly insists on the appropriate credit due him. "It used to be that the profession of storyteller was very honorable, you know, and I think that I would like to be one."

One inevitably thinks of those lines from another famous "storyteller" with an eye on the East whose reviews, like those of James Clavell, tended to be mixed.

> Since the beginning of history men have gathered around the campfire or in a group in the marketplace to listen to the telling of stories. The desire to listen to them appears to be as deeply rooted in the human animal as the sense of property. I have never pretended to be anything but a storyteller. It has amused me to tell stories and I have told a great many.

So, near the end of his career, spoke W. Somerset Maugham: no great writer, but still a superlative teller of tales whose best work has turned out to be of interest to a generation of readers far too young to know or care about the fussy demurrers of his fastidious contemporaries. It is not a bad summing-up for James Clavell, either; and if he lives to be as old and prolific as Maugham was, the world will unquestionably be the happier for it. Short of genius, who could reasonably ask for more?

Burton R. Pollin (essay date June 1983)

SOURCE: "Poe in Clavell's *Shōgun: A Novel of Japan,"* in *Poe Studies,* Vol. 16, No. 1, June, 1983, p. 13.

[In the essay below, Pollin cites thematic and stylistic similarities between Edgar Allan Poe's 1849 poem entitled "A Dream within a Dream" and Clavell's Shōgun.*]*

Poe did not originate the title phrase of his 1849 poem, "A Dream within a Dream"; as T. O. Mabbott indicates [in *Collected Works of Edgar Allan Poe,* 3 vols., 1969-1978], it had previously appeared in two works known to Poe, Margaret Fuller's *Summer on the Lakes* (1844) and C. A. Washburn's sentimental story in *Graham's Magazine* (October 1848). But surely, the currency of the phrase is entirely owed to Poe's poem. And we can be certain that James Clavell was borrowing from Poe in his threefold use of the phrase in **Shōgun: A Novel of Japan,** a best selling work that has become a major document in popular American awareness of Japan. The phrase figures most prominently in a key scene in Book II of the novel, a flashback which presents the death of the Taikō or ruler of Japan, an event releasing all of the rival forces determining the plot. The context makes it clear that the author had Poe's poem directly in mind, for he draws upon its title as well as upon its basic idea, particularly as expressed in the following lines: "Yet if hope has flown away / In a night, or in a day, / In a vision, or in none, / Is it therefore the less *gone? / All* that we see or seem / Is but a dream within a dream." The passage from Clavell follows:

> The dying had been easy. For months the Taikō had been sick and tonight the end was expected. A few hours ago he had opened his eyes and smiled at Ochiba and at Yodoko, and had whispered, his voice like a thread: "Listen, this is my death poem:
>
> 'Like dew I was born
> Like dew I vanish
> Osaka Castle and all that I have ever done
> Is but a dream

Within a dream.'

. . . And then the eyes opaqued forever. Father
Alvito remembered how moved he had been by
the last poem, so typical of the Taikō.

There then ensues a quarrel between the widow Ochiba
and Father Alvito, whose power over her late husband is
now departed. He warns her to take heed of God; she replies, "What will you do, priest, if when you're dead you
discover there is no God, that there's no hell and your
eternal Salvation just a dream within a dream?"

Clavell next uses Poe's poem three quarters of the way
through the novel in one of the crucial episodes occurring
in Osaka castle. We are being informed about a key mystery involving the line of dynastic succession of the heir
to whom the hero Blackthorn and his mentor Lord Toranaga owe fealty: it appears that the Taikō had long suspected that his son Yaemon was engendered elsewhere
than in his bed. Again the death of the Taikō is recalled:

. . . his eyes weren't smiling now, just probing,
wondering, pondering the never-dared-to-be-
asked question that she was sure was forever in
his mind: Is Yaemon really my son?

"*Karma*, O-chan, *Neh*?" It was gently said but
Ochiba's fear that he would ask her directly
racked her and tears glistened in her eyes. "No
need for tears, O-chan. Life's only a dream within a dream," the old man said.

The final reference to the poem occurs on the last page of
the narrative, thus fulfilling the germinal nature of the
phrase "a dream within a dream," which symbolizes so
many issues in this enormous, detail-filled, yet oddly remote and artificial novel. The Shōgun-to-be, Lord Toranaga, is musing over his long-maintained and always-hidden
ambition to rule Japan:

I will continue to wait patiently and one day
those two usurpers inside will make a mistake
and then they will be gone and somehow Osaka
Castle will be gone, just another dream within
a dream, and the real prize of the Great
Game . . . will be won: *the Shōgunate.*

Everett Groseclose   (review date 7 October 1986)

SOURCE: "Kids' Stuff from an Old Asia Hand," in *The
Wall Street Journal,* October 7, 1986, p. 30.

[*In the following review, Groseclose praises Clavell's*
Thrump-o-moto *for its appeal to adults as well as children.*]

Has success bored James Clavell?

How else can one explain the author's latest entry into the
world of books? Not another *Tai-Pan* or *Shogun*—but
rather a handsome, oversized children's story called
Thrump-O-Moto.

Since Mr. Clavell's only other children's story was published 23 years ago, this new one is a departure worthy of
note. His *Whirlwind,* the fifth in his series of Asian sagas
that also will reach book-sellers soon, fetched a reported

record $5 million for U.S. rights alone at a publisher's auc-
tion back in January.

Whatever the author's reasons for doing the book,
Thrump-O-Moto is a delightful yarn. This reader's 14-
year-old daughter, a discerning veteran of countless children's stories good and bad, swiped the book and read it
in a single sitting during a recent lakeside holiday. She
pronounced it "charming" and, "not quite like anything
I've ever read before—part *Alice-in-Wonderland* and part
Arabian Nights."

The book takes its title from the main character, an apprentice-wizard who's still learning the ropes. It's a tale
of good versus evil, of hope and aspiration and courage.
It presumes a willingness to suspend logic and believe in
magic.

Thrump-O-Moto, age 465, height about two feet and be-
decked in a kimono, meets Patricia, a cheerful seven-year-
old who lives on the edge of the Australian Outback, when
he muffs a travel trick at home in Japan and ends up in
Australia. Patricia, who can move about only with the aid
of crutches, is soon "woozed" through time and space to
Japan by her new-found friend.

Patricia gradually regains the use of her legs after much
wizardly earlobe pulling and magic word saying, meets the
evil spirit Nurk-u when she goes to a forest with Thrump-
O-Moto and his mom. He is part of the same cabal of baddies that put her on crutches in Australia. It's a memorable encounter: "Nurk-u stood as high as the heavens and
he was dressed all in fire with five eyes and blue hair and
10 fingers on each hand, his nails like long knives. Green
poison dropped from the tips."

Mr. Thrump-O lops off the ghoul's head, but another
grows back, uglier than the first and with 10 eyes instead
of five. Virtue eventually triumphs but we learn that some
fights can't be avoided and that no one else can do it for
you.

So it goes with Mr. Clavell, from one moral lesson to another. Nurk-u finally gets tossed off a cliff, but that still
leaves Patricia with her difficulty walking. On advice from
a grandfather wizard, she and Thrump-O "wooz" to an
imaginary land to find Charlie Rednosebeerdrinker. He
knows where to find the essence of sunset primrose, which
the old wizard has said will make Patricia able to walk
again.

Then comes yet another memorable battle, this time with
Muldoona, Hag Queen of the Forest. Because of Patricia's
courage and determination, plus a little magic, the girl
wins. Soon she is "woozed" back home to her father's loving arms. Primrose essence in hand, she regains the use of
her legs and all is wonderful forever.

Too sweet and too pat, perhaps, but nice nonetheless. In
fact, the whole book is nice. Its illustrations, by George
Sharp, a painter and designer, are at once pleasing and appropriately horrifying. The printing, of unusual quality, is
by an Italian firm. Even the book's dust jacket, the highest
grade bond, is folded back at the edges, not trimmed by
machine.

The result must be pleasing to Mr. Clavell. At $20 a copy it may even make him a bit richer, thanks to doting parents and adoring grandparents, who may be the audience he wanted to reach in the first place.

Susan Crosland   (essay date 2 November 1986)

SOURCE: "Maybe I'm James Clavell," in *The Sunday Times,* London, November 2, 1986, pp. 41, 43-4.

[*In the following essay based on an interview with Clavell, Crosland discusses Clavell's experiences as a prisoner of the Japanese during World War II and his writing career.*]

James Clavell was 18 when he was captured in Java in 1942. The next three years were spent in Changi. Even among Japanese prison camps, Changi was notorious. One in 15 men survived. Not until the early Sixties was Clavell able to write about it in his first novel, *King Rat.* Yet 10 years after that, he wrote *Shogun,* the colossal historical novel that seems to be *pro* Japanese.

When *Shogun* was televised, Clavell became a millionaire. His fortune spiralled with film rights and continuous reissue of his Asian saga books, each a blockbuster. *Whirlwind,* about a team of British-based professional helicopter pilots caught up in Iran's nightmare (or is it the path to paradise?), will be published tomorrow. Clavell has been paid $5 million for the American book rights alone.

Where does he live? What is he like? Not easy to discover. He gives and receives sparingly. In Changi all his friends died. Changi formed him. Intensely private, guarded, he allows insights into himself only obliquely (like the Japanese). Though English in dress and speech, he has a rootlessness about him. "Changi taught me always to present a moving target." When he and his wife are in Europe, they move between *pieds-a-terre*—Sussex, Gstaad, the Riviera. Outsiders are not welcome in his home. "It's just not on," he says in a polite voice, the underlying steel unmistakable.

So we meet first on my territory. Assured, well over six feet tall, wide-shouldered in his navy blazer, he has light blue eyes and sandy hair, eyelashes and brows gold, gold hairs gleaming on sun-browned hands. He is friendly in a deeply reserved way until I ask a direct question about himself. Then the gold lashes come down over his eyes; he looks at his watch. The message is clear: *I don't have to answer you. Drop dead.*

Our second meeting is on his territory, currently the Riviera. He rings to finalise logistics. "How am I to let you know I'm on course?" I ask. Pause at the other end. Then: "I'll be staying with friends. Hang on while I get their telephone number." I've no doubt it's his own number, but that's the way he plays it, so I follow suit.

The James Clavell who walks into the Negresco, Nice's *belle époque* hotel, wears a robin's-egg blue short-sleeved shirt open at the neck, arms of a casually slung, sweater draped either side. While still secretive, this Clavell is relaxed, gradually willing to acknowledge the traps he lays in conversation. He has the brigand's pleasure in ambush. It's not malicious: it's to keep you on your toes.

Half Irish, half English, he was born in Australia. His family was Royal Navy, and he went to a service preparatory school in Portsmouth. From this narrow society he joined the Royal Artillery when he was 18. Months later he was shot by the Japanese and captured.

"My generation went from 17 or 18 to being shot at, killed, mutilated. Of course it's a shocker—to be petrified for short periods, find you have guns but no ammunition, discover senior officers are a bunch of bloody idiots." All this is said good-naturedly. But the residue of bitter resentment of government reveals itself recurrently.

The round scar on his right cheek is from the Japanese bullet that broke his jaw. When he was put in Changi, the wound was still open. As there weren't any antibiotics, he stuffed the hole with cotton wool dipped in vinegar. He couldn't chew. "It didn't make much difference," he says equally. "There wasn't anything to eat."

In Changi the basic unit was four men. "One guarded. One foraged. One was sick. One was about to be sick. Like a family. All for one and one for all, whatever you feel for each other. Governments come and go, 'isms' come and go. What matters is the family unit."

In *King Rat* he describes terror but little atrocity. I ask about this.

"By 1943 the Japanese accepted the Geneva Convention. Sometimes. Prior to that, to surrender put you off limits: they didn't go for our live-and-fight-another-day. You'd given up your claim to dignity. And it was the first time that large numbers of the British—the bosses—were captured, Shanghai down to Singapore. Normally if one Briton was attacked, lo and behold over the horizon came the battleships. Suddenly the Japanese conquer thousands, who are then paraded to show they're not all-powerful: the mask has been pulled away. This was a kind of a heady experience."

He insists that historically the Japanese do not go in for torture. "Generally." When you think Clavell has completed a statement, he throws the whole thing into doubt by adding: "sometimes", "generally", "perhaps".

"They get peed off with people," he says. "In the 17th century they were anti-Christian because Christians were whipping up the Japanese to favour the Shogun in Rome. Difficult to stamp out. So they got hold of the Jesuit priests and hung them by their feet over a pit until the blood went into their heads. It was extremely uncomfortable and probably would kill them. But the Japanese didn't get a kick out of it. Usually. They killed one in order to terrorise 10,000."

And their treatment of prisoners in World War II?

"The earlier marches were brutal, primitive, but they were not torture. People were marched until they dropped and died. You hadn't food. You had to build a bridge, and if you didn't they bashed you on the head. But they didn't slit your nose, weren't like red Indian women who used to insert a thorn in the penis and then pull it out. The Japanese are a very, very gentle people. They cry a lot—privately or inside."

He thinks being English plus his naval background enabled him to survive Changi. "I was given the ability to dominate my own fear. You had to have a highly developed sense of humour, which the English have—probably because the weather's so dreadful. And my heritage makes it impolite to show emotion." Most of the time. After Changi he was the only POW on the flat-top taking him back across the Pacific.

"People looked at me out of the sides of their eyes. One survivor out of 15 is a substantial mortality rate." And there wasn't much flesh on him. "A commander handed me a proclamation welcoming the glorious warrior home. I was suddenly so angry I tore it up and threw it in his face: I wasn't a conquering bloody hero. He said, English style: 'Oh. Let's go have a drink.' If he'd reacted in a different way, I'd probably have gone bonkers."

In England, he saw a friend who'd had the bottom half of his leg cut off. "He said: 'Do you know something? My pension depends on the inches of stump I've got.' That kind of stayed in my mind. 'You boys go off and fight the war and we'll look after you.' You come back and it's not true."

In his view, governments lie, cheat, look after themselves. "Survival instinct. Governments are not concerned with me and my family."

He has a stable marriage and is extremely family-orientated and protective. "Just before I went overseas as a young officer, at my sister's school there was this scruffy little 12-year-old who said: 'I'm going to marry you. Oh yes I am.' When I came back, this broken heroic figure," he says drily, "I was going up the escalator. I saw April Stride billed in a play. I went to see the show. It was the same person. She said: 'I *never* said that.' 'You bloody did, you know.' So we got married. She decided."

In 1953 they went to Hollywood, he became a script writer on rock-bottom wages, then a director. Two daughters, now in their twenties, were born.

Then in the early Sixties he began writing **King Rat;** the turned-in-on-itself experience of Changi surfaced. Clearly the book was a purge. Even so, how was he able 10 years later to make the leap to **Shogun** which subtly presents the Japanese in a sympathetic light?

"I don't know. You tell me."

"You must speculate sometimes."

"I speculate at length," he concedes. By now we're getting used to each other. "You might have a theory. I might have a theory. There's no one single answer."

He has written of a tremendous affinity between the British and Japanese before 1939. I ask about their different forms of stoicism in bearing pain.

"The English don't want to embarrass others. The Japanese don't want to shame themselves; their prime duty is to themselves, keeping in balance—yang, yin. They don't go in for the western thing of being their brother's keeper." In his teasingly sang-froid manner, he gives an example of a Japanese who screwed up a coup and therefore decided to commit ritual suicide with his wife as witness. Then she kills herself. "From the western point of view, he was terribly selfish: blood, crap, entrails all over the place, and she has to look at this mess, smell the smell. Then she writes: 'I witness my husband's death.' Then she cuts her throat: that's the way women commit *hara-kiri.* In *hara-kiri* you cut open your centre. Maybe for a woman the centre is her vocal chords," he says, laughing. "In western terms, the husband would kill her first, then himself. It's a matter of manners."

When I speak sloppily of "Japs", he says curtly: "Japanese." Manners are an essential in Clavell's personal ethos. In **King Rat,** for instance, he merely alludes to the prisoners' limited sexuality. "Instead of writing 'jerk off' or 'masturbate', I write: 'And they did that which was necessary.' There has to be good manners in things. Perhaps also that's more intriguing to a reader."

In **Shogun,** eroticism is presented from the Japanese point of view. What westerners today may call "the big O", Clavell in oriental guise calls "the clouds and the rain". He smiles at the image. "Not only is the expression more pleasant: it makes you smile." He refers to a series of paintings of *samurai* and courtesans locked in improbable contortions. "In one picture, they are both looking off. Over there is a mirror directed at their parts. The maid is coming in on her knees with two cups of tea. If you're English, the maid-coming-in situation would spoil everything. And I'm sure it's not normal for the maid in Japan to come in while they're banging away. But the picture is trying to describe it in an interesting way—for humour as well as eroticism."

A voracious reader, he did a couple of years' research on his new book, **Whirlwind.** It covers three ghastly weeks in Iran just after the Ayatollah's return. Clavell builds up almost unbearable suspense without eschewing his sense of "good manners in things". Generally, I ask why the Rakoczy torture scene had to be so drawn out and explicit.

"It's all in your head," he replies. "It's not on the written page. People come in and see the way he was wired up. I do not describe the rest. I don't say anything about the smell. 'They did unmentionable things.'"

"But we *hear* his response to the unmentionable things being done to him."

"You like violence," says Clavell.

"Why do you say that?"

"You keep bringing it up." He goes on to say that he himself had to watch the entire scene in his mind before presenting any part of it to the reader. "Sometimes I frighten myself: the whole thing is so awful. Where does it come from? Personally I detest violence of any sort."

I switch to a less morbid subject and ask about one of the erotic, rather ambiguous, scenes in **Whirlwind** where two delectable Iranian wives are sharing a bath. "Does the pleasure you describe of touching each other's skin evolve into a completed lesbian act?"

"What do you think?"

"I don't know."

"Re-read one sentence. Then you'll know. You'll probably be wrong. Maybe. Perhaps." This time he mocks both of us.

He takes no sides in **Whirlwind.** "Every author tries to transmute into the characters he's writing about. I know how the Mullah feels about his wife, about the man whose head he's just blown off. He doesn't consider himself cruel: it's the will of God. He's going to paradise."

But the James Clavell who is sitting here on the Riviera—does *he* feel a little squeamish about the Muslims' eye for an eye?

"When I'm western I find it absolutely shocking. Of course. But there are a billion Muslims out there who believe in it. I'm not going to editorialise: that's cheating. What I find appalling is there's little chance of their attitudes and our attitudes coming together. The irresistible force has met the immovable object. I'm very, very bothered. I don't want to be a politician—those bloody idiots. I don't want to pontificate. I'm a writer. I know very well there's not much I can do except open people's eyes to how others think."

He has enthralled a mass audience. Intellectual critics admire the spellbinding historical narrative. But they withhold the accolade of "literature". I expect this annoys him without eating into his soul. He raises it obliquely. I ask if he cares about anyone except his family.

"The lack of justice?" he says. "Of course. But I don't shout from the ramparts. I do it more subtly."

"In your novels?"

"You must decide. I'm merely a storyteller. Take a *real* writer like Dickens," he says deadpan. "Is he getting rid of his anger in a subtle way? Is he saying the poor are being jumped on by the industrial revolution? Or is he just telling a story? It's for you to understand these things."

He certainly doesn't care about literary laurels in 100 years. "By that time I'm a little dead." He's enjoying his rewards here and now. His second job is selling the film rights of his books. He skis, plays tennis, flies helicopters. He doesn't like a Cadillac or Rolls waiting at the airport. He cannot bear anyone else being in control of his life. (Sooner or later everything circles back to Changi.) If people ask him to do something he doesn't want to do, his "drop dead money" means he can tell them to push off. But he's polite about it. He sacked his agent politely. "Because of my experienced nature, I'd always try to give somebody face. Why create enemies?" His elder daughter, a relative newcomer to the publishing world, now handles his foreign rights. "She's tripled my foreign income."

He avoids cameras that may catch him unguarded. "Every time I'm photographed, a part of my soul is stolen." He uses various names on credit cards and bank accounts.

Christened Charles Edmund Dumaresq Clavell, he has a nice choice. "Dumaresq was the first Australian admiral. James is a nickname." As well as a device for anonymity, it's fun. I say: "I was told you live near Cap Ferrat."

"No, Near Menton." He starts laughing. "Today I think I shall tell you a truth. Sort of."

Recently he found he wanted to write a children's book—***Thrump-O-moto***. A sensitive, moving story about a crippled girl, it has been exquisitely produced. (He oversaw the whole thing the way *he* wanted and then offered it to the publishers). "Unlike your novels," I say, "here you openly take sides: goodness is rewarded, badness punished."

"It's a fantasy. And it's not that evil is punished. He just happens to be overcome. Good gets there in the end, but only if you give yourself a hand."

Once he said: "After Changi, nothing can hurt you ever again." "Why not?" I ask.

"Oh. Well. Having experienced Changi and still been physically and mentally alive, what hurts normal people does not hurt me, what hurts me does not hurt them. The fear of most people is to be fired. So what? I know I can feed my family on a bag of rice." Plainly he is talking of the years before his bulging bank account.

I ask him what he fears that others do not. This time he bursts out laughing straight away. "I'm certainly not going to tell you. You must be joking. I may not know myself. Maybe."

Dick Davis   (review date 5 December 1986)

SOURCE: "How the Tough Get Going," in *The Times Literary Supplement,* No. 4366, December 5, 1986, p. 1368.

[*Below, Davis provides a negative assessment of* Whirlwind, *claiming that the "version of Iranian society offered is tripe."*]

Whirlwind, which its author calls an "adventure story", is set in Iran shortly after the Islamic revolution: the plot concerns a rich international company's attempt to evacuate its pilots and helicopters to a friendly Arab Emirate on the other side of the Gulf. The first scene shows us a helicopter flying low over a praying mullah who furiously and incompetently shoots at the departing foreign intruder: this scene more or less encapsulates what the novel has to say and is repeated with variations *ad nauseam* for the next thousand or so pages. It is very difficult to see why the novel is so long—there is certainly no need for it—and it is almost as if gargantuan length were being offered as a guarantee of, or perhaps substitute for, quality.

The characterization is minimal: the pilots are differenti-ated largely by nationality (Australian, Finnish, British, etc) and by their slightly different swearing vocabularies: they are all tough men who are good in a crisis and good in bed and have hearts of gold beneath their rough-diamond exteriors. Despite the lack of subtlety with which they are depicted, they are intermittently—particularly when airborne—believable. The Iranians are completely unbelievable: the men are devious and cruel, the women are devious and sexy; the men play with jewelled dag-gers—or automatic weapons—and smile, the women are of the "curve of her breasts proud under the sweater" kind. The women are also good in a crisis (though not as good as the pilots) and in bed (every bit as good as the pi-lots); whereas Iranian men are highly strung in a crisis and—we are given to understand—nasty in bed. Beneath the polite surface all nationalities hate all other nationali-ties and think of them as consisting of dogs, sons of whores etc.

The actual escape is an exciting read: helicopters have to be flown from three different sites simultaneously, there are last minute delays, bad weather, scrambled fighters to intercept them and so on. This is easily the best part of the book and seems the kind of thing James Clavell was born to write: unfortunately it does not get under way until around page 800, and the reader's mind is by then almost numb with clichés about Islam, mullahs, fate, death, karma, good men in a crisis and breasts proud under sweaters.

Much of the novel's attraction must depend on the vicari-ous insight it claims to give into three seemingly glamor-ous worlds—high finance, the expatriate pilots' life, Iran in revolution—of which most readers will have little knowledge. Linked with this is what E. M. Forster called "the consolations of history": "we cannot visit either the great or the rich when they are our contemporaries, but by a fortunate arrangement the palaces of Ujjain and the warehouses of Ormus are open for ever and we can even behave outrageously in them without being expelled". And outrageously—with arrogance, sadism and self-congratulation—is how the reader of this bestselling novel is invited to behave.

I cannot vouch for the authenticity or otherwise of the scenes of high financial chit-chat given here, or of those of life in the helicopter pilot's hot seat/bed, but I can say that the version of Iranian society offered is tripe. The book bristles with solecisms about Iran, the caricatures of Iranians are offensive (perhaps understandable in a novel of this kind, which has to have baddies, but offensive nev-ertheless); there is not much Persian in the book but al-most all of what there is has been so garbled as to be gib-berish. The author insists on referring to Persian as "Farsi" throughout; this is very irritating—"They were speaking Farsi" is as silly a sentence in a novel written in English as "They were speaking deutsch" would be. About the only thing to do with Iran which Clavell con-veys with any accuracy is the nature of the scenery; as soon as people begin to populate the scenery accuracy is abandoned for cliché, and usually erroneous cliché at that.

> Unlike *Shogun, Whirlwind* does not even make a pretense of trying to understand a foreign country or sympathize with its culture but instead re-runs tired, unsavory cliches. Most of the Iranian men in this novel come across as religious fanatics, programmed for murder or martyrdom; or as leering sex maniacs, undone by the sight of a woman who's not wearing a chador.
>
> —*Michiko Kakutani in "Iran After the Shah,"* The New York Times, *November, 1986.*

Thomas R. Edwards (review date 18 December 1986)

SOURCE: "Gulp!" in *The New York Review of Books,* Vol. XXXIII, No. 20, December 18, 1986, pp. 58-60.

[*Edwards is an American educator and critic. In the follow-ing excerpt, he faults* Whirlwind *for its lack of appeal and believability, lamenting that the novel "has nothing to do with any life I've ever heard of."*]

Whirlwind, a "now" book for which the publisher report-edly paid Clavell $5 million, the highest price ever paid for a novel, takes place in Iran between February 9 and March 4, 1979, just after the flight of the Shah and the ad-vent of Khomeini but well before the hostage crisis. Al-most 1150 densely printed pages are devoted to these twenty-four days; the evident aim is to let us know just what all of an enormous international cast of characters were doing moment by moment. But they often weren't doing much of anything, and the consequence is not fic-tion but chronicle run mad, a triumph of "data overload" over the faintest illusion of reality:

> Inside the Range Rover it was warm and com-fortable. Azadeh wore padded, modern ski gear and a cashmere sweater underneath, matching blue, and short boots. Now she took off her jack-et and her neat woolen ski cap, and her full-flowing, naturally wavy dark hair fell to her shoulders. Near noon they stopped for a picnic lunch beside a mountain stream. In the early af-ternoon they drove through orchards of apple, pear, and cherry trees, now bleak and leafless and naked in the landscape, then came to the outskirts of Qazvin, a town of perhaps 150,000 inhabitants and many mosques.
>
> "How many mosques are there in all Iran, Azadeh?" he asked.
>
> "Once I was told twenty thousand," she an-swered sleepily, opening her eyes and peering ahead. "Ah, Qazvin! You've made good time, Erikki." A yawn swamped her and she settled more comfortably and went back into half sleep. "There're twenty thousand mosques and fifty

thousand mullahs, so they say. At this rate we'll
be in Tehran in a couple of hours. . . ."

This would be a good passage for a reading comprehension test:

> 1. How many mullahs are said to be in Iran? a)
> 150,000? b) twenty thousand? c) fifty thousand?
> d) many?
>
> 2. At this rate, in a couple of hours we'll be: a)
> in Qazvin; b) in Tehran; c) only on the next page.

It would also do as an outline for a miniseries, with cues to the coiffeur and the wardrobe department. But it can hardly be called writing.

The events—there is no story—cluster loosely around an Anglo-Scottish helicopter company which has been serving the Iranian oil fields. We follow its pilots, managers, and support employees through these chaotic days; some of them have Iranian wives and in-laws, who lead the narrative outward into the local landscape, culture, and politics; assorted mullahs, bandits, revolutionaries, bourgeois profiteers, and spies prowl and prowl around (as P.G. Wodehouse would say) like the troops of Midian. The Europeans are hard to keep straight since so many of them have Scottish names (or cute ones—there's a "Nogger," an "Effer," and a "Scragger") and since they're all doing the same thing, saving their personal and organizational hides. The Islamic characters appear to have lost something in translation; within a page, for example, a Kurdish sheik says "So you dare to disobey me?" "You wish to beg for mercy?" "What trickery is this" and "Are you mad?"—sounding more like a heavy from an old Universal serial than a descendent of the great Saladin. And the factionalism of this revolution, as Clavell scrupulously reports it, may give the unschooled Western reader a headache—I learned to remember that the Tudeh are Communists, the Green Bands Khomeini's Shi'ites, and the SAVAK the Shah's secret police, but I never did figure out who the *mujhadin* and the *fedayeen* are.

Much violence and some sex occur, but the sex consists largely of fanatic male Muslims exposing themselves to unveiled women while grunting about their brutish intentions, and the violence, though detailed, usually observes the rule that when good Europeans are on the verge of destruction, a mysterious shot will ring out to save them, while when bad Iranians think they have it made, the puritanical Green Bands will burst in from nowhere to spoil their sport. Clavell keeps alluding to excitements one would be only too grateful to feel, but an indecision about what his words mean to do continually stifles titillation:

> . . . Bayazid pulled the pin out of a grenade and tossed it through the doorway. The explosion was huge. Smoke billowed out into the corridor. At once Bayazid leaped through the opening, gun leveled, Erikki beside him.
>
> The room was wrecked, windows blown out, curtains ripped, the carpet bed torn apart, the remains of the guard crumpled against a wall. In the alcove at the far end of the huge room . . . the table was upended, a serving maid moaning, and two inert bodies half buried under table

cloth and smashed dishes. Erikki's heart stopped as he recognized Azadeh. In panic he rushed over and shoved the debris off her[,] . . . lifted her into his arms, her hair flowing, and carried her into the light. His breathing did not start again until he was sure she was still alive—unconscious, only God knew how damaged, but alive. She wore a long blue cashmere peignoir that hid all of her, but promised everything. The tribesmen pouring into the room were swept by her beauty.

Some of my problems here are minor. I don't understand how the grenade's *pin* could make such a "huge" explosion. And it's impressive of Erikki to hold his breath (or heartbeat?) long enough to get to the far end of a "huge" room, remove all that debris, pick Azadeh up, carry her into the light (wherever that is), and thoroughly check her vital signs. But the last two sentences are the most puzzling. I thought I was supposed to be enjoying the mayhem, but it's Azadeh's body and the "everything" it promises the tribesmen and me that are the bait. Yet there's no body there, only its ghostly paradigm—long hair, blue cashmere—left over from the previous passage.

Why would anyone, of any age, occupation, or state of culture, want to read such a book? To some customers, I suppose, it may seem to offer instruction in recent history—what *was* that Iranian business all about? But **Whirlwind** never really says what it was about. Clavell is rather reticent about the imperfections of the Pahlavi regime, and though he shows some interest in the motives of the Shah's enemies and in "the Islamic mind" generally, his Iranians are mostly pictured as an excitable, devious, venal, self-destructive lot. And the Western character's contempt for the Carter administration and the Callaghan government in England, so sweeping as to suggest that the author's own politics are showing, doesn't clarify issues.

Spies and counterspies are endemic in **Whirlwind,** but the serious devotee of espionage fiction will want to look elsewhere. We learn that the SAVAK was ruthless, M16 plucky but understaffed, the KGB cunning and brutal, and the CIA dumb and obvious, just about as we'd expect. (But I doubt that even the CIA would choose "Wesson Oil Marketing" as the name of a petroleum company it uses for cover.) Clavell's suspense fails because all the spies keep quadruple-and quintuple-crossing everyone in sight, to the reader's bewilderment; when anything clear emerges, it is on the order of the megalomaniac SAVAK man who plots to bend the Iranian multitudes to his will by feeding them psychedelic drugs. "How exciting this is," someone says late in the book, but my sentiments are those of the British agent who says, "Christ! Where will it all end?" (And when?)

As someone who has misspent much of his life reading and somehow enjoying commercial fiction, good and awful, I must say that **Whirlwind** is by far the worst novel I've ever finished. I can't imagine anyone reading it with pleasure, but reading is probably the wrong thing to do with it. Better just to have it handy as the sign of the intention, at least, to know more about important things, like Asia. . . . James Clavell's novel has nothing to do with any life I've ever heard of.

F. G. Notehelfer   (review date 18 April 1993)

SOURCE: "The Wild West of the Far East," in *The New York Times Book Review,* April 18, 1993, p. 13.

[*Notehelfer is an American educator, historian, and critic who specializes in Japanese history. In the following review of* Gai-jin, *he asserts that despite Clavell's gifts as a story-teller, Clavell treats Japanese history in a stereotypical and sensationalistic manner.*]

Few eras of Japanese history were more violent, turbulent and politically exasperating than the 1860's. Caught between a dying old regime and the revolutionary forces that sought to create a new Japan, the country seethed in what appeared to be a chaotic series of intrigues, plots, coups and counter-coups. To make sense of all this was a formidable task. As *The New York Tribune*'s Japan correspondent, Francis Hall, lamented, "To foretell what will be is impossible; to be sure of what has happened is not always attainable." Better to be a "rainmaker" in South Africa, he added, than a "seer" in Japan. "Tycoons, Mikados, supreme councilors, regents, governors, nokamis, daimios friendly and daimios hostile," he wrote, "have flitted before our eyes with all the changefulness of the magic lantern's phantasmagorfs."

James Clavell's new novel, *Gai-Jin* (meaning "foreigner"), concentrates on this period. As in the case of *Shogun,* Mr. Clavell revels in the turbulence of political death and rebirth. Here are all the "phantasmagorfs" mentioned above, and a few more: a boy shogun in the clutches of an imperial princess; a conniving member of the Tokugawa house bent on becoming shogun himself; the lords of Satsuma and Choshu, committed to destroying the shogunate; hordes of samurai whose hatred for uncouth and greedy foreigners is combined with loyalty to the Emperor. As the narrative progresses, *ronin* assassins, conspiring *shishi* (men of action), gunrunners and gun buyers mix with beautiful and obliging women whose world of willows and pillows perpetuates the ever-alluring stereotype of the Asian woman. Not that there aren't modern touches. There's a female *shishi* who throws a knifelike *shuriken* at the future shogun—killing not the lord but his ever-protective mistress. What the 19th-century Japanese would have done with a female *shishi* boggles the mind! But then, what would the 16th-century Japanese have done with Mariko, the heroine of *Shogun?*

Gai-Jin is not without interest. Many of the period's colorful characters are here in thin disguise, and so are many episodes from the early days of Yokohama. Mr. Clavell's novel opens in 1862 with a fictionalized version of the assassination of a British citizen, Charles Richardson, by samurai traveling with the rebellious lord of Satsuma on the great national highway known as the Tokaido. It ends with the British bombardment of Kagoshima in 1863, a seminal event on the road to the Meiji Restoration, which brought feudal Japan into the modern era. What we have in between is something the Japanese might compare to a *manga*—a kind of comic-book portrait of Yokohama and its people.

Take the heroine of the novel, Angelique Richaud, a nubile 18-year-old French beauty who accompanies the fictionalized Richardson (called John Canterbury) on the Tokaido, only to see him murdered. Witness the following scenes: Angelique is raped (while under the influence of laudanum) by Canterbury's *shishi* assassin, who sneaks into her room while the good doctor, Babcott, operates in the room below on Malcolm Struan, her husband-to-be and heir to the trading company known as Noble House; some days later, the same man rapes Angelique, again at knifepoint; she becomes pregnant and, despite having aborted the child, looks on these two encounters as the most fulfilling sexual experiences of her life. If this isn't an *ero manga* (erotic comic) of the type popular in Japan today, what is it? I'm reminded of a feature published some years ago in *Mad* magazine projecting what the West might have been like if peopled by characters from the silver screen. The conclusion, I remember, was that the West would have been even wilder. In Mr. Clavell's novel, Yokohama, which some called "the Wild West of the Far East," presents the same gap between fiction and reality.

Such reservations do not detract from what is a well-told story, but I feel obliged to mention them because Mr. Clavell prefaces his book with the remark that his tale "is not history but fiction," adding that works of history "do not necessarily always relate what truly happened." Mr. Clavell also tells us that he has "played with *history*—the where and how and who and why and when of it—to suit my own reality and, perhaps, to tell the real history of what came to pass." As one who has played with Yokohama's past, I am intrigued that when scholars like Francis Fukuyama declare the end of history, novelists like James Clavell take up the mantle to tell us the "real" story of what happened. I wonder if Charles Richardson (John Canterbury), Ernest Satow (Jamie McFay), Sir Rutherford Alcock (Sir William Aylesbury), Dr. William Willis (Dr. George Babcott) and some of the other men of Yokohama are turning over in their graves. Certainly Mrs. Borrodaile (Angelique Richaud), who accompanied Richardson on that fateful ride on the Tokaido, must be jumping up and down.

Ron Scherer   (review date 12 May 1993)

SOURCE: "Drama and Intrigue in Emerging Japan," in *The Christian Science Monitor,* May 12, 1993, p. 13.

[*In the following review of* Gai-jin, *Scherer provides a mixed assessment of the novel, lamenting the often stereotyped characters but praising its suspense.*]

The Japanese love fine *jubako*—lacquered boxes that fit within boxes that are in boxes. In *Gai-Jin: A Novel of Japan,* James Clavell has written a *jubako* of a novel. Its 1,038 pages are filled with plots within plots within plots.

The scheming takes place at a critical moment in Japan's history—September 1862 to January 1863, only 10 years after American Commodore Matthew Perry opened Japan to Western trading. In that period foreigners, called *gai-jin* by the Japanese, were vying for influence. Yankee traders were in abundance, but any United States ambitions were deflected by the Civil War. Instead, the British dominated, with plenty of imperial jealousy from the French and Russians.

The Japanese feudal system was in turmoil. The powerful Toranaga family ran the country through their control of the Shogun, the ruler who governed temporal affairs. However, they were challenged by other feudal lords who were constantly scheming to control the "Land of the Gods." At the same time, there was a strong undercurrent of nationalism represented by rogue samurai, who wanted all power returned to the Emperor, who was in charge of spiritual affairs. These samurai wanted to get rid of the *gai-jin.*

That is where Clavell begins. Two samurai attack three Western men and a woman. One of the men is killed. A second is badly wounded. He is Malcolm Struan, the heir to Noble House (the subject of a 1981 Clavell novel), the Hong Kong trading institution that dominates Asia. The woman, Angelique Richaud, races back to Yokohama, the only area where Westerners are allowed to live.

After the attack, Sir William Aylesbury, the British minister in Japan, demands restitution for the man who was killed and the apprehension of the killers. Call it the beginning of diplomatic incomprehension—West not understanding East.

Struan tries to regain his health. He is fighting not only for his life, but also for his family's empire. His chief Asian rival, the Brocks, have plotted the downfall of Noble House, now run by Tess Struan, Malcolm's mother.

Woven into these events are the love affairs of the community. Miss Richaud is intent on becoming Mrs. Struan. Many of the men have girlfriends in the Yoshiwara, a brothel run by the Japanese who use the women to collect intelligence. The Japanese men have wives and courtesans as well, and Clavell also constructs *jubako* for them.

Gai-Jin is part of Clavell's *Asian Saga,* which so far consists of *Shogun,* dealing with the period around 1600, *Tai-Pan* (1841), *Gai-Jin* (1862), *King Rat* (1945), *Noble House* (1962), and *Whirlwind* (1979).

The novel will keep many beachgoers glued to their blankets this summer. The compelling plot helps you forget that the characters sometimes seem stereotyped: The British are pompous, the French connivers, the Japanese cunning and arrogant.

The first two chapters lack order, but Clavell gets it all sorted out by page 30. After the next 1,000 pages, readers will look forward to the next novel in his saga.

Christopher Lehmann-Haupt   (review date 24 May 1993)

SOURCE: "The Sixth Episode in James Clavell's Asian Saga," in *The New York Times,* May 24, 1993, p. C16.

[*Below, Lehmann-Haupt provides a negative assessment of* Gai-jin.]

At the opening of James Clavell's intermittently absorbing but over-long new novel. *Gai-Jin* two previous works in the author's so-called *Asian Saga* collide with each other, producing a thousand pages of complications that never do get completely straightened out, although by the end the reader is happy to take a rest from them, at least until the three-pound sequel is born.

At the start of *Gai-Jin* which means foreigner in Japanese, *Tai-Pan* crashes into *Shogun.* On Sept. 14, 1862, three Englishmen and a Frenchwoman are traveling by horseback not far from Yokohama on the Tokaido the coastal toll road that joins the Shogun's forbidden capital, Yedo (today Tokyo), to the rest of Japan.

Not long after setting out, the riders meet two columns of samurai traveling in the other direction. They step aside politely to let the columns pass but two of the samurai confront them in a rage and then attack with their swords. While only one of the riders is killed outright, severely wounded is Malcolm Struan the 20-year-old heir apparent to the powerful Far East English trading company known as Noble House that was featured in two of Mr. Clavell's previous cinder blocks, titled, logically enough, *Tai-Pan* and *Noble House.*

Galloping home covered with blood and crying, "*Au secours . . . à l'aide,* help!" goes the woman identified in the list of principal characters at the back of the book as "Angelique Richaud, 18, beloved of Malcolm, daughter of Guy Richaud, French China trader, ward of the French Minister." On about page 700, when the plot of *Gai-Jin.* has at last got off the ground, you discover somewhat to your surprise that this Angelique is the central character of the novel. Judging by how much has been left still to untangle at the end, she will likely be near the center of Mr. Clavell's next novel too.

This seemingly unprovoked attack by the two samurai produces consequences so enormous that it would take the space of this entire newspaper to summarize them adequately. But they can be divided into two broad streams. It turns out that the attacking samurai are shishi, or "persons of courage" who are "fanatically xenophobic and anti-gai-jin." They were enraged by the lack of complete respect the foreigners showed their cortege, but more calculatingly they hoped to provoke a counterattack by the foreigners that would lead to a civil war among the country's feudal lords, a shift in power from the ruling Shogunate back to the deposed Emperor and the eventual expulsion of the hated gai-jin.

This political stream of the novel involves incredibly complicated intrigue, endless diplomatic meetings in which the Japanese draw in their breaths in outrage and a certain amount of "pillowing" during which a network of spies exchanges secrets.

In the more domestic stream, Malcolm slowly recovers from his terrible wound and struggles with his growing dependence on laudanum, while Angelique grows more and more in love with him. Meanwhile, seething in Hong Kong and delivering irate letters by clipper ship, Malcolm's mother, Tess, grows increasingly convinced that Angelique is a fortune-seeking harlot. This half of the plot, easier to get into because it is domestic and romantic, keeps promising to burst into flame but somehow never does much more than smolder. But then perhaps I am being impatient.

At its best, *Gai-Jin* achieves a grand historical perspective that makes us feel we're understanding how today's Japan came into being with its ambivalence toward outsiders. Mr. Clavell's revolutionary samurai desire nothing more than to purify the country of foreigners. They are infinitely patient and guileful about achieving this end. And then one of them who has got to know the foreign community begins to have second thoughts. "Eeee, he told himself through the throbbing of his headache, there's so much I do not understand, the world is turning upside down, everything different, I am different, no longer samurai yet totally samurai. It is these filthy gai-jin with their tempting, sickening, awesome, greed-making ideas. They must be thrown out—*sonno-joi sonno-joi sonno-joi*—but not yet. First *massu produk'shun,* the first to make rifles."

Mr. Clavell is skilled at pumping up an apparent villain in a couple of paragraphs and then letting the air out of him when necessary to make him seem like not such a terrible guy after all. *Gai-Jin* sounds like a pastiche of those political columns in which the writer divines the inner thoughts of world leaders. "Ah Russia, beautiful extraordinary Russia, what a shame we're enemies," thinks Sir William Aylesbury, the British minister to the Japans, while conversing with the Czarist minister. "Best time I ever had was in St. Petersburg. Even so you're not going to expand into these waters, we stopped your invasion of the Japanese Tsushima islands last year, and this year we'll prevent you from stealing their Sakhalin too."

On the other hand, however accurate it may be, the Japanese dialogue often reads like that of a World War II comic book. "Have idea, Taira-san," a character says. "Bad for me go now, I sure die. Want he'rp Ing'erish friends, want to be *va'ru'ber a'rry,* very va'ru'ber friend." There is even a character named Ah Soh. Occasional though such speeches may be, in a thousand pages they being to grate.

It isn't really that Mr. Clavell writes comic-book fiction. There is an entertaining tribute to Charles Dickens in *Gai-Jin.* In which he dramatizes how excited people got when another installment of *Great Expectations* appeared in a magazine and the extremes to which they would go to read it. *Gai-Jin* is in the mainstream of a great and enduring storytelling tradition, full of rich characters and complicated action. It's just that modernism makes such fiction seem unreal. In any case, *Gai-Jin* feels vaporous even by Mr. Clavell's standards. There's one memorable scene in which, after a burial at sea, a storm blows up and the coffin "attacks" the ship that disposed of it. But other than that, for all the activity in these thousand pages, precious little sticks in the reader's mind.

The New York Times (obituary date 8 September 1994)

SOURCE: An obituary in *The New York Times,* September 8, 1994, p. D19.

[*In the obituary below, the critic provides an overview of Clavell's career.*]

James Clavell, the author of *Tai-Pan, Shogun, Noble House* and other richly detailed historical novels set in the Far East, died on Tuesday in Vevey, Switzerland. He was 69 and had homes in Vevey and Cap Ferrat, France.

The cause was cancer, said his wife, April.

Although historians sometimes disputed the historical accuracy of Mr. Clavell's novels, no one doubted his gifts as a storyteller, or his ability to draw the reader into a faraway time and place. "It's almost impossible not to continue to read *Shogun* once having opened it," wrote Webster Schott in *The New York Times Book Review.* "Yet it's not only something that you read—you live it."

His ability to deliver a gripping narrative and establish an exotic setting won Mr. Clavell millions of readers and great wealth. *Tai-Pan* and *Noble House* were stunning commercial successes, remaining on the best-seller list for nearly a year and selling millions of copies. For *Noble House,* Mr. Clavell received a $1 million advance, and in 1986, William Morrow & Company paid a record $5 million for his novel *Whirlwind.* Mr. Clavell described himself as "just doing my job, trying to entertain people and illuminate the world and perhaps bridge East and West." He was, he said, "just a storyteller."

Mr. Clavell was born in Sydney, Australia, but was taken back to England by his parents while still an infant. His father was an officer in the Royal Navy. After completing his public schooling, Mr. Clavell joined the Royal Artillery in 1940. He underwent training for desert warfare, but after Japan entered the war he was sent to Singapore. In 1942 he was captured on Java and sent by the Japanese to the infamous Changi prison near Singapore, where only 1 in 15 prisoners survived.

"Changi became my university instead of my prison," he later told an interviewer. "Among the inmates there were experts in all walks of life—the high and the low roads. I studied and absorbed everything I could from physics to counterfeiting, but most of all I learned the art of surviving."

On returning to England with the rank of captain, he suffered a motorcycle accident that left him lame in one leg, ending his military career. He spent a year studying at Birmingham University and worked at odd jobs. Through his future wife, April Stride, an aspiring ballerina and actress, he became interested in directing films. He worked in film distribution for several years and in 1953 headed to the United States, working briefly in television production in New York before moving to Los Angeles, where he bluffed his way into a screenwriting job.

He wrote *The Fly* (1958) and *Watusi* (1959) and helped write *The Great Escape* (1963), which won a Writers Guild award for best screenplay. He wrote, directed and produced several films, including *Five Gates to Hell* (1959), *Walk Like a Dragon* (1960) and, more memorably, *To Sir, With Love* (1967), which cost a little more than $500,000 to make and took in $15 million at the box office.

During a writers' strike in 1960, Mr. Clavell first tried his hand at fiction. The result, *King Rat* (1962), was the story of an upper-class Englishman and an amoral, wheeler-dealer American who meet in Changi prison and, against the odds, become friends. The novel was praised as a gripping narrative and a classic of the prison-camp genre. The novel was made into a 1965 film starring George Segal, Tom Courtenay and John Mills.

In writing *King Rat,* Mr. Clavell found his imagination returning once again to the Far East. He had become an American citizen in 1963 but temporarily moved his family to Hong Kong, where he plunged himself into researching a historical novel, *Tai-Pan,* about the founding of the crown colony. The novel's hero, Dirk Struan, is the first taipan, or merchant overlord, determined to establish an outpost of British power on the unpromising soil of Hong Kong. The fruit of his labor is the Noble House trading company, whose story Mr. Clavell continued in his next novel, *Noble House*.

Shogun, set in Japan in the year 1600, follows the adventures of the fictional John Blackthorne, whom the novel presents as the first Englishman to reach Japan. Five rival warlords are scheming to become shogun, or supreme military dictator. One of them takes Blackthorne under his protection, hoping to use his Western knowledge as a lever to displace his rivals. Like its two predecessors, the novel was long (1,207 pages), densely researched and bubbling with character, incident and historical pageantry.

In 1980 *Shogun* was made into a five-part television mini-series that starred Richard Chamberlain and Toshiro Mifune and was seen by 120 million viewers, the largest audience for a mini-series since *Roots*. A 1990 Broadway musical based on the novel was not successful. *Tai-Pan* was made into a television movie starring Bryan Brown in 1986, and *Noble House* was made into a four-part television mini-series in 1988.

In his 1986 novel *Whirlwind,* Mr. Clavell shifted location, turning out a historical novel on Iran in the tumultuous weeks after the fall of the Shah in 1979. Although most critics found the novel too long, at more than 1,100 pages, and far less enthralling than Mr. Clavell's previous works, *Whirlwind* immediately shot to the top of the best-seller lists and stayed there for more than 20 weeks. *Gai-Jin,* published in 1993, explored the clash of East and West in 1860's Japan.

Mr. Clavell also wrote *Thump-o-moto,* a children's book, and *The Children's Story,* a political fable. All of Mr. Clavell's novels for adults are published by Dell, except for *Whirlwind,* which is an Avon paperback.

In addition to his wife, he is survived by two daughters, Michaela and Holly.

William F. Buckley, Jr.   (essay date 10 October 1994)

SOURCE: "James Clavell, RIP," in *National Review,* New York, Vol. XLVI, October 10, 1994, pp. 23-4.

[*Buckley is an American political commentator, nonfiction writer, and novelist. In the following tribute, he reminisces about his friendship with Clavell.*]

A dozen years ago Chilton Williamson, at the time our book-review editor, called me to deliver a mildly compli-cated diplomatic message. It was this, that the young writer Terry Teachout (this was before he became famous) wished to have an interview with James Clavell, for publication in *National Review*. But Mr. Clavell, or perhaps someone on his staff, had passed along the word that Mr. Clavell would grant the interview only if I called him on the phone and requested it. I thought that protocol a little unusual, but not preposterous; and so I did call him. I have no memory of the conversation, in which I presumably gave the bona fides of Terry Teachout and assured Mr. Clavell that his name was not on *National Review*'s secret list of evil people who needed to be impaled. But I walked away with the impression that James Clavell was rather formal in his habits.

He gave the interview (it was published on November 12, 1982). Mr. Teachout began his story by adducing Noël Coward's answer to the question, "Isn't there *anyone* worth reading on the best-seller lists any more?" Yes, Coward had said—James Clavell. Teachout went on, "To call Clavell a 'popular novelist' is an understatement: incredibly, he is now among the most widely read authors of the century." In the interview, Clavell repeated several times that he thought himself, pure and simple, a "storyteller."

Six years later we met in Switzerland, at our place in Rougemont. He was striking in appearance, in the Bengal Lancer mode, with greying hair and rubicund cheeks, a prominent chin and light blue eyes. He limped on his right leg but maneuvered without difficulty. In a matter of minutes (sometimes these things happen) we were talking as though we had been to school together. At one point, chewing on a chicken leg, he eloquently and indignantly spoke of how his third publisher had cheated him out of royalties, and I was nodding my head sympathetically as he gave the predatory details. At this moment a Khan (I can't remember which one) breezed by: "What are you two talking about?"

Clavell looked up with his furtive smile and determined voice: "Something that concerns you not at all: money." All three of us enjoyed it.

We were in regular touch, he and his wife, April; my wife, Pat, and I. The day before leaving Switzerland in March I wrote him, "Well, finished novel. Don't much like the very end, but easy to change down the line. We should chat, though of course I'll see you very soon"—James had told us he'd be in Connecticut to visit his daughter "in a couple of weeks." I concluded my note as I had so many others, with reference to a computer program I was (am) so wildly enthusiastic about, the *American Heritage Dictionary*. " . . . I yearn to hear from you that the dictionary has brought such joy into your life as it has into mine!!!"

He didn't call—and didn't, during the summer, send along any of his two-line faxes. His silence was surprising, and then a week ago Roger Moore, his close friend and ours, called to say James had died of cancer, which he had fought all summer long.

Three years ago I had teased James in a brief passage in one of my books (*Windfall*) about a long lunch we had had together. I wrote, "A spirited session, as always with

James, about this and that, with heavy emphasis on his bad luck with his failed musical, ***Shogun***. That evening . . . I remarked to my wife, 'You know—James didn't ask what *I've* done since we last met. If he had, I could have said, "Waal, James, let's see: In the ten weeks since I last saw you, I've played two harpsichord concerts; I've retired as editor of *National Review,* after 35 years; I've crossed the Atlantic Ocean on a sailboat; I've published two books, one fiction, one non-fiction; and I have become a senior citizen." ' (I am running no danger whatever that James will see these words—he doesn't read my books, and I haven't read all of his. And what I am recording is by no means intended as critical: mere social piquancy, curious, scientific bemusement over solipsistic social manners.)"

I wasn't surprised after my book was published, in January 1992, not to hear from James about it. But in August I had one of his quick faxes. "Hi. Whatcha mean I don't read your books? J." And at one point this winter, when I said I was finishing my writing assignment, he gave me his look, one-half sternness, one-half the derisive smile: "Don't you go and put me into this book."

He would never let out the *mise en scène* of his own ongoing book until galley-proof time. He would simply report that he had put in his day's work, which was ten to twelve pages of manuscript and, later, fifty pages of copy editing. He came regularly to inspect my electronic equipment, and referred to himself once as our "electrician."

We very much enjoyed our fax camaraderie. Feb. 19, 1994: "To: the guru of gurus. M'aidez si vous plait. Could you press THE button and tell me did King Kong come out of Conan Doyle's Lost World? cir 1912? J." And I'd fax him an occasional column, especially if I thought he'd be amused by it, as by the bizarre suicide of the Tory MP Milligan last February, who was discovered with odd pieces of this and that tucked into odd parts of his body. "Another of the great joys of having the Buckleys en residence is the daily fax illuminating the world that I would otherwise miss. Quelle horreur to be so uneducated. Poor Tory Milligan. Why in the mouth? I could understand if it was in the other place, particularly if he had been a socialist, for there is ample room for a baker's dozen. Poor fellow. Did he just like oranges? He clearly wanted to tell us something—or his friend, assailant, or partner. Another of life's sweet tapestries. Would you and herself care to come to lunch one day—dinner I presume is out for you this way. Yours till hell etc. J."

I never told him how many of his books I had read, to which the answer is—only two. The reason is that I read slowly and have a terrible time taking on books of the length of James Clavell's. But the two I read confirm the reasons for his popularity. He was the supreme storyteller. Socially he was a retiring man, the sometime Australian

who at age 18 was taken by the Japanese into one of their legendarily terrible war camps, where he stayed five years. He was in his thirties before he began to score his heavy successes as the great fiction chronicler of Asia.

When we put down the telephone, after Roger described his final weeks, we both felt a void of loneliness which will gnaw at us for years to come. Our friendship wasn't that of one writer for another. It was as simple as that I delighted in his company.

FURTHER READING

Criticism

Allen, Louis. "Images of Undivided Souls." *The Times Literary Supplement,* No. 4100 (30 October 1981): 1261-62.
   Reviews three books inspired by the success of *Shōgun* and the ensuing interest in Japanese history: Richard Tames's *Servant of the Shōgun,* Henry Smith's *Learning from Shōgun,* and Michael Macintyre's *The Shōgun Inheritance.*

Andrews, Peter. "Abandoned in Iran." *New York Times Book Review* (7 December 1986): 28.
   Laments *Whirlwind*'s excessive length and confusing, overly-detailed plot.

Clancy, Tom. "Great Escapes: Writers Pick Their Favorites." *The Washington Post Book World* XVI, No. 49 (7 December 1986): 4.
   Considers *Shōgun* one of the best books ever written about two opposing cultures meeting for the first time and praises Clavell's ability to present characters who are sympathetic to a twentieth-century audience yet remain consistent with the period they represent.

Gates, David. " 'Whirlwind': The Eye of a Storm." *Newsweek* CVIII, No. 19 (10 November 1986): 84.
   Discusses the publication and marketing of *Whirlwind.*

King, Paul. "Epics from a Maelstrom." *Maclean's* 99, No. 47 (24 November 1986): 65.
   Reviews *Whirlwind,* praising Clavell's ability to create suspense.

Kirkpatrick, Melanie. "The Rising Sun Never Sets on His Empire." *People Weekly* 39, No. 10 (10 May 1993): 27, 29.
   Mixed review of *Gai-jin.*

LaGuire, Camille Allen. "Wozzing across the World." *Fantasy Review* 10, No. 5 (June 1987): 42.
   Deems *Thrump-o-moto* a "wonderful story, recommended to parents looking for something to read aloud to their children."

Additional coverage of Clavell's career is contained in the following sources published by Gale Research: *Contemporary Authors,* Vol. 25-28 (rev. ed.), 146; *Contemporary Authors New Revision Series,* Vol. 26; *Contemporary Literary Criticism,* Vols. 6, 25; and *Major 20th-Century Writers.*

Robert Coover

1932-

(Full name Robert Lowell Coover) American novelist, short story writer, playwright, poet, and critic.

The following entry presents criticism of Coover's novels. For further information on Coover's life and works, see *CLC*, Volumes 3, 7, 15, 32, and 46.

INTRODUCTION

A respected contemporary experimental writer, Coover intends his fiction to startle and fascinate the reader, believing, with fellow American author John Barth, that traditional literature has exhausted its narrative possibilities. In his search for new approaches to literature, Coover produces works in which the distinction between fantasy and reality becomes blurred. By placing standard elements from fairy tales, popular culture, biblical stories, or historical events in a distorted context, he attempts to deconstruct the myths and traditions which people create to give meaning to life.

Biographical Information

Coover was born in Charles City, Iowa, and, at the age of nine, moved with his family to Indiana, where his father worked as a newspaper editor. He began writing short stories and poems while a young boy and later wrote for school newspapers. Coover attended Southern Illinois University at Carbondale, but received his B.A. from Indiana University at Bloomington in 1953. After graduation, he joined the U.S. Navy, serving from 1953 to 1957, and published his first work, *One Summer in Spain,* in 1960. Since earning his M.A. in 1965 from the University of Chicago, he has taught in universities throughout the United States.

Major Works

Coover uses familiar mythic or popular cultural materials as well as various literary forms and techniques to illustrate his belief that history and truth are human inventions. By parodying popular and traditional forms of narrative and by subverting myths, Coover attempts to alert his audience to significant new literary patterns. His novels *The Origin of the Brunists* (1966), *The Universal Baseball Association, Inc., J. Henry Waugh, Prop.* (1968), *The Public Burning* (1977), and *Gerald's Party* (1986) particularly exemplify these characteristics. While *The Origin of the Brunists,* a chronicle of the rise and fall of a fictitious cult, follows a more conventional structure than later novels, it displays Coover's typical investigation of the human need to create myths, not only to order an individual's perception of the world, but also to imbue it with some sort of meaning. Coover moves further away from the traditional novel in *The Universal Baseball Association,* where

the protagonist devises an imaginary game in which he decides the futures of eight baseball teams by loaded rolls of the dice. In an obvious parallel to the Hebrew god Yahweh, J. Henry Waugh creates a world complete with histories, newspaper articles, and interviews with the players. Waugh becomes so involved that the reality of his life merges with the reality of the game, leading the reader to question which of the worlds is invented. Similarly, Coover's portrayal of the conviction and execution of Julius and Ethel Rosenberg in *The Public Burning* demonstrates, according to Chester E. Eisinger, Coover's "conviction that reality, history and truth are 'made' or invented, that appearances are everything, that forms are really substance, that poetry is the art of subordinating facts to the imagination, and that objectivity is an impossible illusion." In *Gerald's Party,* Coover creates a disorienting, kaleidoscopic effect through continual disruptions of dialogue and action, and extensive use of non-sequiturs intended to subvert the conventions of the English detective story. Amid murders and slapstick, Gerald and his friends urbanely ruminate on art, time, love, and memory. Although the book is intended to be outrageous, *Gerald's Party* raises serious issues, according to Robert Christgau, including "the intransigence of death, the persistence of regret, the inadequacy of memory, [and] the unfathoma-bility of causation." Updating the legend of the Italian puppet who longs to be real, Coover's 1991 *Pinocchio in Venice* focuses on such themes as physical existence and literary artifice, and has been cited for its humor, use of double-entendres, and references to popular culture.

Critical Reception

Coover continues to receive critical acclaim for his experimental approach to fictional forms and for his originality and versatility as a prose stylist. He is frequently compared to such authors of postmodern literature as John Barth, Donald Barthelme, and Thomas Pynchon. Paul Gray commented that "Coover has earned his reputation as an avant-gardist who can do with reality what a magician does with a pack of cards: shuffle the familiar into unexpected patterns."

PRINCIPAL WORKS

One Summer in Spain: Five Poems   (poetry)   1960
The Origin of the Brunists   (novel)   1966
The Universal Baseball Association, Inc., J. Henry Waugh, Prop.   (novel)   1968
Pricksongs and Descants   (short stories)   1969
A Theological Position   (plays)   1972
The Water Pourer   (novella)   1972
The Public Burning   (novel)   1977
Hair o' the Chine   (short stories)   1979
After Lazarus: A Filmscript   (novella)   1980
Charlie in the House of Rue   (novella)   1980
A Political Fable   (novella)   1980
Bridge Hound   (play)   1981
The Convention   (short stories)   1981
Spanking the Maid   (novella)   1981
In Bed One Night, and Other Brief Encounters   (short stories)   1983
Gerald's Party   (novel)   1986
A Night at the Movies; Or, You Must Remember This (short stories)   1987
Pinocchio in Venice   (novel)   1991

*This work includes *A Theological Position, The Kid, Love Scene*, and *Rip Awake*.

CRITICISM

Kathryn Hume   (essay date Winter 1979)

SOURCE: "Robert Coover's Fiction: The Naked and the Mythic," in *Novel: A Forum on Fiction*, Vol. 12, No. 2, Winter, 1979, pp. 127-48.

[*Hume is an American educator and critic. In the following excerpt, she defends Coover against charges of pitilessness* *and sadism, and argues that Coover's fiction demonstrates the interconnected nature of "the naked," symbolizing human inadequacy, and "the mythic," through which characters attempt to overcome this sense of impotence. Focusing on the novels* The Origin of the Brunists, The Universal Baseball Association, *and* The Public Burning, *Hume also traces parallels between Coover's fiction and the postmodern works of such authors as Jorge Luis Borges, John Barth, and Kurt Vonnegut.*]

Reviewers of Coover's novels respond—critically, in the main—to his flamboyant use of archetypes. "Patterns, myths, symbols, and folklore are Coover's stock-in-trade" (*Commonweal* [28 October 1977]). *Newsweek* [8 August 1977] complains of the "predilection for theology, which has been an identifying thumbprint since he published his first novel." Although his interest in ritual and faith is non-religious, Coover does lead us through the overgrown byways of "GOD literature," [Leo J. Hertzel, *Critique* 11, 1969] into realms of messiahs, sacrificial victims, apocalypses, and even a down-at-heels god. Other reviewers [such as Donald Hall in *National Review,* 30 September 1977, and Paul Gray in *Time,* 8 August 1977], bothered by an indefinable coldness in the novels, recoil from what they take to be Coover's attitude toward mankind.

> The book's structure is not intellectual; it is comic and passionate obsession—and satire as moral and as repulsive as Swift's. Outrage is the book's method and its message. . . . The burden is human weakness, everywhere, in marriage, in public life, in journalism, in private life. And Coover's response to weakness is more misanthropy than compassion.
>
> Manias stalked the land in the '50s; public and private life had the quality of a Manichaean morality play. Coover knows this, presents all the evidence, and then denies his book the ability to touch hearts or minds instead of nerves. What might have been a long, compassionate look becomes a protracted sneer.

Coover's fictions are "overdetermined." This dream characteristic makes it all too easy for the reader to seize on one concern and ignore others of at least equal significance. To give but one example, Bruno McAndrew, O.S.B., sees *The Origin of the Brunists* (1966) as a vile travesty on the origins of Christianity [*Best Sellers,* 1 November 1966]. To someone with a different set of mind-forged manacles, the same story seems rather to explore the nature of religion—any religion—and the human cravings it satisfies. But both are possible. Indeed, most of Coover's stories may be read from a mythic, or theological, or archetypal standpoint, and each approach yields a slightly different significance. Likewise, one can respond to Coover's bleak portrayal of human nature by drawing back from the contemptible weakness displayed by his characters, or one may wince with them at their acute and helpless vulnerability.

But these are only two facets of Coover's stories. Other characteristics have attracted attention both favorable and hostile. Coover creates and presents obsessed men with what can only be called obsessive care for detail. Many of his stories describe violence, some of it sadistic or sexual.

Coover is also a humanitarian. "The City of Man is all there is," and in Noah's brother, as Margaret Heckard observes [in *Twentieth Century Literature* 22, 1976], Coover shows us "the suffering of the everyday people who were left behind to drown. . . . It does not matter [as far as the Bible is concerned] that some of those left behind were pregnant, had selected names for their ill-fated unborn children, had built cradles with carved animal figures, or had even worked on the ark itself." "Behind the razzle-dazzle and the intentional bad jokes, Coover is deeply angry, heartsick about his country and pessimistic about its future" [Walter Clemons in *Newsweek,* 8 August 1977].

Beyond the humane, there is also the humor. Black, slapstick, or witty: all abound. The philosophical jokes of Damonsday in *The Universal Baseball Association,* Nixon's taxi ride in *The Public Burning,* or the outrage and discomfort of the priest in *A Theological Position,* whose hand is bitten by the vagina dentata of the talking cunt whose utterances he is trying to stifle: these hilarious scenes are not much commented upon by reviewers, but they and others like them mark Coover's work indelibly.

Some attention ought also to go to the explosive vividness of his fictive worlds. *The Universal Baseball Association* encompasses an imaginary eight-team league through 157 seasons of play. *The Origin of the Brunists* presents a mining town: its ethnic diversity, life above and below the surface of the earth, life in the high school and the town hall, in Church, in bedrooms and dining rooms, in the back seats of cars, in the hospital and news office. *The Public Burning* creates nothing less than the American public of the early '50s—the government, the entertainment world, the newsprinted word, the radio tunes, the "culture" that gave man his structures of meaning. I say "creates" deliberately, for Coover's procedure is poesis, not mimesis, and the harshest criticisms yet levelled at him concern his refusal to label episodes fact, fiction, or faction.

The nature of Coover's achievement to date is not rightly reflected in the fragments which reviewers have isolated for comment. It manifests itself in the integration of these pieces, in their necessary interrelationship. Coover's works are not archetypal *or* Swiftian. Rather, his stories flow from a balance of forces. One of these, a nexus of ideas I call "the naked," consists of Coover's representation of man's weaknesses (for which man is at least partly responsible) and his vulnerability (which is inherent). The other force, "the mythic" or archetypal, is both an authorial structural device, and a part of his characters' spiritual lives. It is their response to their nakedness. Coover analyzes the fashions in which man summons up mythic value systems. Sometimes man creates such systems deliberately; at others, the archetypal patterns loom up in man's path, and man embraces them for their mysterious otherness, unaware that his unconscious needs have called them into being. The tension between these two sets of values, the mythic and the naked, provides the basic dynamic for all three novels. Once their informing presence is recognized as a common denominator, we can better appreciate the rich diversity of Coover's secondary worlds, and can make better sense of his bitter, controversial spectacular, *The Public Burning.*

By calling attention to "the naked," I do not mean merely the visibility of unclad flesh, for that need not express any sense of weakness or vulnerability.

> The nude is the idealized human body, both erotic and heroic in the noble tradition begun by the Greeks: the nude is appropriate to the context of Eros (undressing for bed) or for the athletic-heroic (stripping for the games); it is the apotheosis of human anatomy. The naked, on the other hand, means undressing in a wholly inappropriate context: the naked man is caught with his trousers down, caught in the act of guilt or shame. . . . Nakedness thus reduces man from the godlike to the animal. [Mark Hodgart in his *Satire,* 1969]

Both spiritual and physical nakedness are common in Coover's world. Again and again, his characters are forced to feel their own humiliating shortcomings. Some of the miners in *The Origin of the Brunists* cannot find work when the mine closes: their helplessness is social. For others, the realization of their unprotected state is somehow related to the animal nature of their bodies. They must die, or they feel threatened by sexual relationships, or they remain ignorant of their vulnerability, yet we see and respond to it.

The cultists in *The Origin of the Brunists* are terribly vulnerable, although themselves largely unaware of this. Eleanor Norton's spirit guide gives her such assurance of righteousness that she is unmoved by adverse opinion. Nonetheless, she and those who cluster about her are drawn by their fear of death, more especially by a terror of the void. They crave signs, a pattern, a mystery that exalts them in their own minds in compensation for their dreary lives. When a mine disaster kills nearly 100 out of 300 men, there is no logical cause to get excited just because Giovanni Bruno lives while six men trapped near him do not. Yet this "miracle" catalyzes intense response from dissatisfied townsfolk. Despite evidence of brain damage from mine gas, his every cryptic utterance is received as flaming word from the Beyond. When a note from a dead miner-preacher comes to light, a painful scribble expressing their all standing before the Lord "the 8th of . . . [note unfinished]," the inchoate yearnings take a definite apocalyptic turn. The preacher's widow, a lawyer crazed by numerology, Mrs. Norton, Marcella (Bruno's sister), two school boys, and the local newspaperman form the core of the cult. Justin "Tiger" Miller does not believe. He wants copy. Yet he goes to great lengths to stay involved with the movement. He shares the dissatisfactions of the others, despite his sophistication, for he is a "prince become a frog, living grimly ever after, drowned in debt, sick to death of the disenchanted forest, and knowing no way out."

The psychic vulnerability of West Condon's inhabitants sometimes crystallizes into images of physical nakedness. The final apocalyptic happening turns into a sadistic and masochistic orgy, whose roots in their sexual repressions are patent. Miller is attacked by the Brunists, and nearly castrated and killed. We see him spread-eagled, helpless in his nakedness. Others not directly involved in the cult are also displayed in their nakedness. The miner Vince

Bonali destroys his chance of civic position by getting drunk and trying to take a former mistress by force. He is caught trying to get his pants up when the police arrive. Bonali's daughter loses her maidenhead, and we see her shy physical nakedness transformed to psychic vulnerability when she breaks up with the boy a few days later. A sadistic preacher forces his children to strip themselves bare before he beats them.

In *The Universal Baseball Association, Inc., J. Henry Waugh, Prop.,* Coover explores the ramifications of such vulnerability more subtly. Waugh has created a baseball game which increasingly rules his life. Eight teams play out seasons through the offices of three dice. Waugh compiles ledgers on the play by play of each game, tape-records interviews, writes obituaries, outlines the history of the league politics, develops names and personalities and families of great players. He composes satires, newspaper columns, and even the ballads the players sing. Why his unconscious has called forth this particular world becomes apparent when we notice the themes of the songs. All but two concern being forced to retire, death, and the uselessness that follows upon outliving one's physical prime. Henry shares his athletes' acute awareness of the impermanence of the flesh. In their company, he surrounds himself with the locker-room world and locker-room language, a taboo tongue which excludes women. He shares with the men the intensity of awareness which the game-ritual gives to their lives. Winning matters desperately to him and them, even though a man running over a white mat on the ground is meaningless *sub specie aeternitatis.*

He shares the paradox of their lives: aside from the game, sex is their main bulwark against awareness of death. (The whore Hettie Irden "made them all laugh and forget for a moment that they were dying men"). Yet these men ultimately equate the feminine with death. Their psychic defenses are therefore doubly vulnerable, first because of their reliance on the body, and second, because sex threatens them with Otherness and death. In the religion they develop, "the whore of whores, Dame Society," measures the players sexually, lusts for their bodies, and roars for their sacrificial destruction.

Henry cannot face death, yet it fascinates him. He rolls dice at the end of each season to produce the necessary deaths.

> He dreaded, in short, the death blow, yet it was just this rounding off in the Book of each career that gave beauty to all these lives. . . . As to how they died, he made his own decisions while composing the obituary; if he was uncertain, he had another chart that provided him general descriptors, but usually he just *knew,* a certain definite feeling about it that would come on him suddenly while considering the ballplayer's past—Abe Flint's heart failure, Verne Mackenzie's liver, Holly Tibbett's tumor, Rupert Allen's suicide.

The same *déjà vu* "knowing" makes him assign his own age to the veteran star Brock Rutherford on "Brock Rutherford's Day" for the game at which Brock's son, Henry's

favorite rookie, is killed by a bean ball. Damon Rutherford's death nearly destroys Henry. It cuts too near the bone. He works off his grief as the other players do: with solemn music, the wake, drink, and sex. The will to live overcomes the will to grieve when, at the book's center, those at the wake call for the ballad of Long Lew's rape of Fanny McCaffree. But death has so upset Henry's fragile sense of meaning that he can preserve it only by making a conscious, deliberate leap into ritual. He sets the dice down to the combination he wants, and kills the bean-balling pitcher, Jock Casey. With passing seasons, this life-for-a-life becomes the players' central religious myth, a Manichean duel, annually re-enacted. Physical nakedness plays a negligible role in this novel, yet everyone in it, creator and his creatures, are terrified of their unaccommodated state as poor, bare, forked animals. They do not need to be undressed to feel their own helplessness.

The Public Burning is notorious for its use of literal nakedness. Richard Nixon appears by magic on the Rosenbergs' execution scaffold in Times Square, his pants about his ankles. And after the execution, his helplessness is driven home when he cannot prevent Uncle Sam from buggering him. In a review of *The Public Burning,* Robert Towers observes: "The image of a bare-assed man humiliatingly exposed as he stumbles about with his pants or underpants tangled around his ankles recurs in several climactic scenes in Coover's fiction." He mentions *The Public Burning, The Origin of the Brunists,* and *Pricksongs and Descants.* One could add that there are slight variations on this situation in **"The Cat in the Hat for President,"** *A Theological Position,* and **"McDuff on the Mound."**

> Whatever its private significance for Coover, the figure of the bare-assed, encumbered man is expressive of the emotional bias of his fiction. This I would describe as highly aggressive, directed toward domination in all its forms. But this macho stance carries with it, inevitably, a fascinated horror of masochistic subjugation, passivity, and shame, a horror so intense as to suggest a covert attraction. . . . There is seldom room for tenderness or even for fun except at someone's expense. The atmosphere is perpetually heated, the emotional terrain either arid or scorched. Human flesh tends toward mechanization. Women, when they are not cast in the role of dominatrix, are largely presented as objects to be collected, used, and pushed around—or as receptacles for phallic thrusting. [Robert Towers, *New York Review of Books,* 29 September 1977]

Towers over-emphasizes the humiliating side of the image. Pants down for the miner Bonali are embarrassing, but far more lingering a shame are his buddies' taunts calling him mayor. On that same memorable night, he was drunk enough to reveal this pipe-dream, and cannot escape its mocking echo. Tiger Miller's nakedness has no humiliation, at least to his modesty or privateness. His situation embodies pure fear of castration and death. Nixon is humiliated, but only momentarily. He stumbles his way through a brilliant piece of chicanery, and ends by persuading the entire execution audience to drop its pants for America. We enjoy, with him, this lunatic triumph. . . .

Yes, Coover's characters bear "marks of weakness, marks of woe." And Yes, the image of dropped pants or some near equivalent recurs with unusual frequency. To see this as a sado-masochistic expression of Coover's psyche, as Towers does, may have some validity, but is not the whole truth. Coover uses the image to embody many forms of helplessness and weakness. To Coover, man is quintessentially vulnerable—through his fears, through his inability to feel comfortable with a meaningless cosmos, and through his dying flesh. For such nakedness, the image is appropriate, if repetitious.

> **The nature of Coover's achievement to date is not rightly reflected in the fragments which reviewers have isolated for comment. It manifests itself in the integration of these pieces, in their interrelationship. Coover's works are not archetypal *or* Swiftian. Rather, his stories flow from a balance of forces.**
>
> **—*Kathryn Hume***

Something which feels vulnerable cries out for protection. The naked craves the mythic. By "mythic" I mean a wide variety of patterns that refer implicitly or explicitly to an extrinsic meaning-giving system. These patterns operate within the plot, and also as part of the fictional work's structure. The characters in the stories seek such value systems in their myths, rituals, and games. The stories themselves rely on mythic exostructures. The human situation, as Coover portrays it, is too like the drifting, formless misery of the *Inferno's* first circle to have an intrinsic form. The fiction and fiction-making both are vulnerable to the formlessness of misery and meaninglessness. Therefore the stories need myth to give them visible form. Readers too have need for the mythic shapes. We want to find some sort of pattern, some explanation, of the unhappiness we face in the stories.

Within the plot, Coover's characters seek meaning in at least four basic patterns. Religion is one. Political or social myth another. Game is a third. Magic, a fourth. . . .

The seriousness with which Coover uses such extrinsic patterns varies markedly. A superficial mythic layer is very prominent in many stories, often functioning as an in-joke for the reader to enjoy. Pattern is indulged in for the pure fun of creating pattern. . . .

The gamut from joke to the resacralization of everyday life is run by the fleeting myths in the final chapter of *The Origin of the Brunists.* As Tiger Miller recovers in the hospital from near dismemberment, he undergoes a protean list of mythic metamorphoses. "He rises from the dead." The nurse, whom he nicknamed Happy Bottom,

> pierced his side with a needle, and the nerve coated over. He relaxed, and though he plunged once more toward darkness, he plunged now

without dread; the nails in his palms were basketballs and his legs were lean and could run again. "I'll be back!" he said, and, distantly, he thought he heard rewarding laughter.

> His own connection came by then to lower him, turning a noisy crank at his feet: mechanized Descent. Later, she would prepare spices and ointments. For now, she only wrapped his body in the sterile linens, stuck a thermometer in his mouth. . . .

In a shadowy part of his mind, one possibly connected with the haze of drugs, he realizes that he is Judas too. He had betrayed the Brunists, and with them, the prophet's sister Marcella, whom Tiger had loved. When Happy confirms her pregnancy, she speaks of the embryos as "Sons of Noah," to which Tiger responds "Aha! sign of the covenant." When the two of them hammer out what is to be the new framework for their common life, he is Peter:

> "Listen, Happy," said Miller, celebrating the bath hour, "let's set up a private little cult of our own." He saw doubt cross her eyes, as she looked up from his wet belly to study his face. "Trade rings, break a pot, whatever it is they do these days, build for perpetuity." Blushing, she turned back to the belly, rained suds on it from a sponge squeezed high. "Anyway," he said, "it'd be something different."

> She dipped an index finger into his navel. "And on this rock . . ." she said, and they both watched the church grow. . . .

[Miller and Happy] are also Adam and Eve, the ascended, the beginning and the end. And they are an ordinary couple enjoying a holyday/holiday. They have learned not to expect too much out of life. They narrow their sights and accept a very imperfect order, one they know can be destroyed all too easily.

> Born to be caught and killed. Frail cages. Containing what? Staring at X rays of his fractured clavicle, right thumb and left humerus, which Happy held out for him to see one morning while one of her buddies gave him an enema, both of them joking about his torn ear, rooted-out hair, broken nose, blackened eyes, and chipped and loosened teeth, he suddenly felt himself out there on the hill again, being danced on, bedded with corpses, splayed for a good Christian gelding, saw again the massed-up nameless bodies, the mad frenzy for life, the loins giving birth, and deep despair sprayed up his ass and inundated his body. "Why did you bother, Happy?" he asked.

> He expected her to make some crack, but instead she only smiled and said, "I don't know. I guess because I like the way you laugh."

> Yes, there was that. Not the void within and ahead, but the immediate living space between the two. The plug was pulled and the sheet lifted, and the despair, a lot of it anyway, flooded out of him with a soft gurgle. "My message to the world," he said, and if he hadn't been afraid of swallowing half his teeth in the process, he might have laughed along with them.

In Happy's *Last Judgment,* one of her parables about God and divine doings, Jesus' offer of his blood and body becomes her husband's "come and have breakfast"— mundane, yet as meaningful as the religious equivalent

A similar spectrum from joke to new myth exists in *The Universal Baseball Association.* J. Henry Waugh (JHWH, Jahweh) creates his baseball world. He mourns the loss of Damon, and half leads his friend Lou to believe the dead boy is an illegitimate son. An overturned can of beer nearly "floods" the game out of existence. Henry considers "burning" the whole lot, rather than go on. But instead, he interferes with the dice to kill off the pitcher whose ball had killed Damon, and with Jock Casey's death, Henry is once more caught up in the game as his primary reality, forever. As he sets the dice down in the fatal combination, "a sudden spasm convulsed him with the impact of a smashing line drive and he sprayed a red-and-gold rainbow arc of half-curded pizza over his Association, but he managed to get to the sink with most of it." God has interfered with his creation, and now makes his rainbow covenant and withdraws.

The insanity of Henry's commitment to the game world is not in doubt. Insane also is the devotion lavished by later generations of players on a misunderstood bit of history. Yet even if we can stand back and condemn their religion as delusion, we have to recognize that Henry and his players get from their lives something that they could not if deprived of the game and the religion: the sense of intense involvement, the focus for all conscious thought which gives the feeling that life has meaning. What Henry liked about Damon (aside from his phenomenal success) was his cool, intense commitment to the moment in a game.

> Ingram expected him to reach for the rosin bag or wipe his hands on his shirt or tug at his cap or something, but he didn't: he just stood there waiting. . . . he looked back out at Rutherford, he saw that the kid still hadn't moved, still poised there on the rise, coolly waiting, ball resting solidly in one hand, both hands at his sides, head tilted slightly to the right, face expressionless but eyes alert.

But the same quality also characterizes Jock Casey.

> He [Henry] kept seeing Jock Casey, waiting there on the mound. Why waiting? Who for? Patient. Yes, give him credit, he was. Enduring. And you had to admit: Casey played the game, heart and soul. Played it like nobody had ever played it before. . . . Lean, serious, melancholy, even. And alone. Yes, above all; alone. . . . Casey waiting there. . . . but still Casey waited, and his glance: come on, get it over, only way. . . .
>
> Henry got up. . . . He picked up the dice, shook them. "I'm sorry, boy," he whispered, and then, holding the dice in his left palm, he set them down carefully with his right. One by one. Six. Six. Six.

Many seasons later, two promising rookies re-enact the duel, not sure if participation in the ritual will lead to the death of one of them or not. The one impersonating the catcher Ingram walks the ball out to "Damon."

> He hands it to Damon, standing tall and lean, head tilted slightly to the right, face expressionless but eyes alert. Paul tries to speak, but he can find no words. . . . And then suddenly Damon sees, *must see,* because astonishingly he says:
>
> "Hey, wait, buddy! you *love* this game, don't you?"
>
> "Sure, but. . . ."
>
> Damon grins. Lights up the whole goddamn world. "Then don't be afraid, Royce," he says. . . .
>
> And he doesn't know any more whether he's a Damonite or a Caseyite or something else again. . . . doesn't even know if he's Paul Trench or Royce Ingram. . . . it's all irrelevant, it doesn't even matter that he's going to die, all that counts is that he is *here* and here's The Man and here's the boys and there's the crowd, the sun, the noise.
>
> "It's not a trial," says Damon. . . . "It's not even a lesson. It's just what it is." Damon holds the baseball up between them. It is hard and white and alive in the sun.
>
> He laughs. It's beautiful, that ball. He punches Damon lightly in the ribs with his mitt. "Hang loose," he says, and pulling down his mask, trots back behind home plate.

What matters is the moment, an awareness of what is happening which is so intense that one hardly notices oneself anymore. Commitment to the game—to the crowd, the sun, the noise—frees one from past, from the future (which may be death). And as he lives each moment with these men, Henry achieves much the same intensity. He may be a shabby god, an unhappy fifty-six year old bachelor, fired and going insane. But he has a revelation—a mystic vision, the blazing illumination of the moment—to cling to.

Coover jokes about theology and cosmology: "God exists, and he is a nut"; the sun says 100 watt; another player remarks "I don't know if there's really a record-keeper up there or not. . . . But even if there weren't, I think we'd have to play the game as though there were." Man is *homo ludens.* And that is perhaps a good way for him to define himself. A game involves accepted rules; one limits one's actions and expectations to fit the game situation. By taking part, one takes part in a system which has built-in rewards. "Games were what kept Miller going. Games, and the pacifying of mind and organs. Miller perceived existence as a loose concatenation of separate and ultimately inconsequential instants. . . . Life, then, was a series of adjustments to these actions and, if one kept his sense of humor and produced as many of these actions himself as possible, adjustment was easier." He models his marriage on this game interpretation of life. Likewise, Henry is a game player. So are his creations. Insofar as they stick to games, their enjoyment is harmless. When religion intrudes, the results are serious and sinister.

Aside from using the mythic to modulate from the entirely comic to the tentatively serious, Coover uses it also in ways that are serious from the start. A related triad of archetypes—victim, sacrifice, scapegoat—is fundamental to his vision. Society devours its own members. . . .

Lacking compensation or consolation for the meaningless suffering in life, Coover's characters seek it in the non-material. In *The Origin of the Brunists,* the scribbled message from the dead preacher, Bruno's mystic phrases, and Eleanor Norton's spirit guide provide the millenialist framework to contain the longings and give them form. The cult's religious hysteria is riddled with Christian symbols and vocabulary because Christianity is the only code most of them have for discussing the sacred and mysterious. But Christianity has not supplied them with the sense of meaning they crave.

Henry seeks meaning in the game. His job as an accountant with Dunkelmann, Zauber, and Zifferblatt offers no challenge, no friends, and no rewards. The game provides him with a sense of the fitness of things (his *déjà-vu* experiences) and of meaning. Real baseball could not supply this.

> There were things about the games I liked. The crowds, for example. I felt like I was part of something there, you know, like in church, except it was more real than any church, and I joined in in the score-keeping, the hollering, the eating of hot dogs and drinking of Cokes and beer, and for a while I even had the funny idea that ball stadiums and not European churches were the real American holy places. . . . But I would leave a game, elbowing out with all the others, and feel a kind of fear that I could so misuse my life. . . . Then, a couple of days later, at home, I would pick up my scoreboard. Suddenly, what was dead had life, what was wearisome became stirring, beautiful, unbelievably real. . . . I found out the scorecards were enough. I didn't need the games.

Communion with those crowds still left Henry alone. Real baseball gave him no creative role. Nor could it provide any barricade against death. In the company of his imagined players, he can suffer with them through the little-death of retirement, take comfort in numbers as they all grow old together. Each of the players, of course, reflects some part of Henry's mind. Fenn McCaffree can recognize that Sandy, the balladeer, "did [the men at the wake] a disservice, provided them with dreams and legends that blocked off their perception of the truth." In that instant, Henry is Fenn. But Henry is also Sandy, who provides the dreams and legends.

> . . . like the cloudburst outside, a whole new Sandy Shaw ballad for the UBA had poured suddenly out of him. Nothing to it. Everything came easy today. He'd explained to a curious Hettie that songwriting was a kind of hobby. No, no luck so far, he'd lied. In the UBA, after all, they all sang Sandy's songs.

All the responses to Damon's death are Henry's, from the solemn reverence at the *Dies irae* to the mad, hysterical giggling as he listens to Purcell.

Ruefully, the sackbuts poop-poop-dee-pooped, discreetly distant. . . . Trompetta! blaa-aa-att! and a mocking rumble of the tympanic gut! Man that is born of woman, woman that is laid by man! Blaa-aa-att! He cometh out! He goeth in! Raunchy giggle of trumpets. . . . Hee hee! Spare us, Lord! . . . "Oh no! he is much lamented!" Tee hee hee hee hee, hee, boo hoo hoo hoo, tee hee hee hee, boo hoo hoo hoo, ha ha ha ha—oops! . . . "Oh, Lou!" . . . "why do we go on?" . . . A tavern song, after all! The secrets of our hearts! "Tonight!" whispered Rooney, jigging along under the burden. "Jakes!" The Hole in the Wall. Tweet-tweet-tootle and a rattle of tin spoons on a hollow hilarious bouncing skull!

At the carousing wake, Sandy Shaw triggers release from sorrow and forgetfulness of death when he sings his ballad about Long Lew's rape of Fanny McCaffree. This assertion of power over failure, of life over death, and the symbolic form the assertion takes, tell us much about the failures and imperfections of the world Henry comes from.

In *The Public Burning,* the American public derives its sense of meaning from a political religion. Americans are the sons of light, communists the sons of darkness. The Phantom (Communism) is pledged to destroy Uncle Sam, motherhood, and apple pie. Onto this spectre, Americans project all their own weaknesses, fears, and sins. From hating the Phantom, they gain a sense of power, a sense of community, and a sense of purpose. They also relieve themselves of their anxieties by projecting these fears of being different, unliked, dowdy, and weak on the Rosenbergs. The scapegoats will bear this burden of sins to the electric chair. Not just the nation, but Richard Nixon too, is shown to need the Rosenbergs for his own personal relief. He needs so desperately to feel that he is winning, that despite his attraction toward Ethel, he too craves their death. That way, someone other than he bears the label of failure. . . .

People in Coover's fiction are haunted by their vulnerability. For the most part, their work gives them no sense of protection or of belonging, or even of usefulness. Sex and society are variously unsatisfactory as well. Nothing provides the characters with belief or compensation for the sensed inadequacy. Ultimately, they are up against death, and few of them show much confidence in their answers to that riddle. In their quest for mythic clothing to hide their nakedness, people try to infuse the myths with life so their faith will seem justified. Feeding the myth blood—the blood of a victim, sacrifice, or scapegoat—is the most emphatic action open to them, and one they turn to all too readily in Coover's worlds. One could say, as Towers did of the dropped pants, that this victim/scapegoat/sacrifice archetype is overused. But here too, it signals the urgency of man's desperation, at least as much as it embodies his actions. When we put on the mythic, we feel, however briefly, that we transcend our weaknesses. Like Jurgen's shimmering, unearthly shirt, or the armor borne by the Red Cross Knight, the myth gives the sense of transpersonal identity, of defined relationship to the cosmos. For Coover's heroes, however, the myth is not an absolute (as Christians claim theirs to be). Like the little child in "The Emperor's New Clothes," we see the nakedness, and so do the characters themselves in their more honest or more depressed moments. The only characters who escape this cycle at all are Tiger and Happy, and their victory is severely circumscribed.

The criticisms levelled at Coover's work have tended to divorce the naked and the mythic, and have not taken into account their necessary connectedness. Separate, the naked can indeed seem to indicate a Swiftian perspective—sneering and unsympathetic. And the mythic, taken alone, emerges as a superficial gimmick rather than as something intrinsic to the subject. Other criticisms of this fiction seem similarly askew. To object to the obsessive qualities of the works is to dislike them on personal grounds, for Coover's obsessions are his statements of meaning, and they are not so eccentric that they can be dismissed as the ravings from one in a padded cell. Obsessions characterize many of the writers of the last six or seven decades. Coover's works benefit from comparison with those of authors often deemed similar—Borges, Kafka, Joyce, Barth, and Vonnegut. The nature of Coover's achievement—both its weaknesses and strengths—is discernible when the novels are contrasted to those works with similar concerns.

That Coover's creations are obsessive at several levels is undeniable. The characters in *The Origin of the Brunists* are obsessed; the unhappy care with which Coover piles up detail can be called obsessive. Towers responded to this quality in *The Universal Baseball Association,* calling it "the most painfully claustrophobic novel I have ever experienced and I doubt that even the most single-minded baseball freak could find it endurable. . . . It lingers like a certain kind of nightmare. Undeniably, a power of sorts has been exerted." Donald Hall likens Coover's creations to the construction of a man who builds a model of the Eiffel Tower from three million toothpicks, and he points out that all three novels deal with obsessed individuals. What differentiates Coover from Borges, also an obsessed and obsessive writer, is partly Borges' lack of personal involvement in his fiction, and partly a matter of scale. Some of Borges' most famous *ficciones* exemplify a truly astonishing purity of obsession. The "Library of Babel," and "The Babylon Lottery" are classics in this line. In each, a single institution—the library, the lottery—gradually unfolds until it comes to represent the entire world. In "Tlön, Uqbar, Orbis Tertius," a peculiar volume of an encyclopedia calls into existence an entire other world. But what we respond most to in Borges' *ficciones* is this crystallizing image—library, lottery—rather than the scope of the implicit world which unfolds from it. Borges crams very diversified worlds into his little stories, but his stories are *little,* and character remains largely undeveloped. Waugh's baseball game is a similar seed crystal, but the personalities which Coover allows the players give these creations a size and substantiality which would burst the bonds of a refined, cameo world. The sophistication of Borges' lapidary productions seems to us now praiseworthy. Coover's works, like English sheep dogs, are boisterous and hard to control, and seem worlds apart from Borges' cool gems. Yet the English (and even more the American) literary tradition has specialized in Coover's approach rather than

Borges'. Elder Olson describes the two kinds of literature in his famous comparison of Shakespeare and Racine:

> Shakespeare is concerned with processes, Racine with situations. Shakespeare individualizes, particularizes, circumstantializes; Racine generalizes. Shakespeare correlates action with action, character with character; Racine selects. . . . The technique of Shakespeare is that of aggregation; the technique of Racine, like that of the ancients on whom he modelled, is that of isolation. [*Tragedy and the Theory of Drama,* 1961]

As Donald Hall points out, "If the novel [*The Public Burning*] survives, it will survive as a monster—but then, American literature is a collection of monsters." Monsters grow familiar with time, and lovable in their monstrosity. We come to cherish such additions to the aggregate as the porter in *Macbeth.* But they are not always lovable on first sight. . . .

This quality of being rooted in the twentieth-century American experience characterizes Coover's fictive worlds when they are compared to those of John Barth, Thomas Pynchon, or James Joyce.

—*Kathryn Hume*

The number of episodes portraying fatal or near fatal violence in Coover's fiction is very high. He has experimented extensively with physical brutality and disaster. But whereas the violence is raw in *The Origin of the Brunists,* and sexual in some of the short stories, it becomes symbolic and allusive by *The Public Burning,* thematically subordinated to the whole. Kafka's deaths are less often direct murders, but they serve much the same function of directing attention to the tormenters. Coover is hardly unique in displaying such torment.

Obsession, elephantine scale, and violence are also found in Barth's later fantasies. Moreover, Barth creates in *Giles Goat-Boy,* a secondary world as skewed, yet as rich, as that of *The Public Burning.* Where these two authors are perhaps most usefully compared, however, is in their humor. Coover flashes with verbal wit: *The Public Burning* reaches some of its most distressing depths on humorous notes. The brilliant parody of the Marx brothers on the execution scaffold, for instance, is funny in its own right, funny as parody, and gruesomely funny as contrast to the coming execution. In *The Universal Baseball Association,* the players' jokes, Coover's theological parody, the black comedy of the wake, are all painfully funny. But Coover's laughs rarely escape the realm of desperation. Almost always there is an edge of self-awareness and pain. Barth's humor in *Giles, The Sot-Weed Factor,* and *Chimera* sometimes escapes the pain by embracing the absurd. Tertullian embraced Christianity enthusiastically *quia impossible,* because it is absurd and impossible. Barth laughs because unself-conscious laughter is impossible, and this absurd assertion helps us win free from our self-awareness and awareness of pain. "The Dunyazadiad" ends on just such a *quia impossible* note.

> "Let's end the dark night! All that passion and hate between men and women; all that confusion of inequality and difference! Let's take the truly tragic view of love! Maybe it *is* a fiction, but it's the profoundest and best of all! Treasure me, Dunyazade, as I'll treasure you! . . ."
>
> "It won't work."
>
> "Nothing *works!* But the enterprise is noble; it's full of joy and life, and all other ways are deathy. Let's make love like passionate equals."
>
> "You mean *as if* we were equals," Dunyazade said. "You know we're not. What you want is impossible. . . ."
>
> "Let it be *as if!* . . ."
>
> "It's absurd. You're only trying to talk your way out of a bad spot."
>
> "Of course I am! And of course it's absurd! Treasure me!"

He wins the argument, and all four main characters emerge from the dark hour before dawn having learned that the key to the treasure is the treasure. Barth achieves a rollicking effect, partly made possible by his retreat to various distant and thoroughly fictional pasts (Colonial America, Ancient Greece). Coover mostly stays within what is recognizably twentieth-century America: all three novels start from a realistic setting. As a result, his plots do not convert pain to ornamentation as readily as do Barth's. Moreover, Barth concentrates on individuals almost exclusively, and sees some hope of salvation for them. Coover sees society as well as the individual, and sees the individual only in terms of his relationship to society, and therefore finds salvation far more tenuous, and the overall future of man more hopeless. Because he insists on affirming the human, however, he does not escape to the absurd as readily as Barth does, for Barth can make even the individual absurd. For Coover, laughter offers no easy or total escape.

This quality of being rooted in the twentieth-century American experience characterizes Coover's fictive worlds when they are compared to those of Barth, Pynchon, or Joyce. Pynchon works with America, but projects it as the paranoid, schizophrenic fantasy of his characters. Coover's America in *The Public Burning* may be as skewed, but the narrative stances he uses are ostensibly those of objective reporter, so his America gives the impression of existing outside of any one character's mind. Only Joyce works similarly grounded in a specific national and temporal location, and clearly *Ulysses* has heavily influenced *The Public Burning.* Joyce's one day is replaced by three. The Nixon sections play about the same role as Bloom's. Instead of Stephen and Molly, however, the other voices are those of the Rosenbergs, of divers politicians, of *vox populi,* and of Uncle Sam. Both Coover and Joyce develop characters' minds, wishes, and weaknesses. Pynchon, who created secondary worlds nearly as stupen-

dous in *Gravity's Rainbow* and *V,* rarely gives us coherent enough human portraits for us to accept the characters as people. They embody psychoses. They blunder through insane settings primarily to display those settings. Joyce and Coover create settings in order to display, echo, and magnify the problems of being human.

Critics who castigate Coover for his lack of pity seem to me to misunderstand the nature of his fiction. They are quite correct that we are not invited to feel pity. But then pity allows the pitier to feel superior to the pitied. Pity enforces a distance, because we who pity are aware that we do not suffer as the protagonist is suffering. Vonnegut is a master at inducing pity. It feels so *good* to join him in his low-keyed, sohisticated indignation. We feel flattered at our own moral wisdom. His objects are entirely worthy, his causes just, and his own response may be deeply felt. But his creations do invite facile sympathy, or even sardonic pity toward his fantastically exaggerated victims—such as the man who is deprived of livelihood, status, Ph.D., M.A., and B.A. when it is discovered that he never completed the physical education requirement necessary for college graduation. We enjoy ourselves all too readily when pitying some of Vonnegut's creations. We enjoy the lump in the throat which rises as we realize that prelobotomized Unc wrote a letter which his post-operation self reads (*Sirens of Titan*). We share Vonnegut's indignant pity toward tertiary stage syphilitics who have been turned into jerky, faulty machines by their diseased nervous systems; toward the poor—black and white—oppressed by the capitalist system (*God Bless You, Mr. Rosewater, Breakfast of Champions*), toward those firebombed in Dresden (*Slaughterhouse-Five*).

Coover does not allow us the luxury of such pity. The anesthetic quality of some of his violence may indeed be prompted by a desire to discourage pity. The Rosenbergs' electrocuted bodies are reduced to jerky, mechanical things. As bodies, their vulnerability is all too apparent. But the response evoked is partly miserable whimpers of laughter. Bergsonian reification makes the jerking marionettes funny as well as sickening, even while forcing us to acknowledge that we too are just as vulnerable to death through our bodies. The one character we are inclined to pity is Nixon. Pity may be Coover's ultimate weapon, for in a way, pity degrades the recipient.

Misunderstandings like that concerning Coover's lack of pity have dogged the reception of **The Public Burning.** Paul Gray of *Time,* after dismissing it as an "overwritten bore," expresses one version of this discomfort:

> Political figures, so the paranoia goes, are fair game. It is assumed in this genre that the most scabrous inventions can be brandished publicly and still fall short of the awful truth. Coover handles the rather limited demands of this artless form with ease. Those who are amused by gross fantasy will find much to admire in **The Public Burning:** Supreme Court Justices slipping and sliding in a pile of elephant dung; an aspirant to the presidency being sodomized by Uncle Sam.

Norman Podhoretz (in *Saturday Review* [17 September 1977]) attacks with more deadly precision:

> But the more important difference lies in the freedom Coover grants himself from respect for the evidence, respect for the known facts, by which any historian is bound, no matter how politically tendentious he may be. When it suits Coover's polemical purposes, he too relies on the record—which incidentally helps to establish the credibility of his thesis with the innocent reader: he certainly seems to know what he is talking about. But when the evidence for his position is either weak or nonexistent or goes against him altogether—which is, in truth, most of the time—he simply turns his back on it and (to use one of his own favorite tropes) "shazams" himself from a historian into a novelist. In the guise of a novelist, he is liberated from the limitations and restraints of the ordinary mortal historian. He can soar above the evidence or below it.

Podhoretz goes on to call the book

> . . . a lie. And because it hides behind the immunities of artistic freedom to protect itself from being held to the normal standards of truthful discourse, it should not only be called a lie, it should also be called a cowardly lie.

One answer to this kind of judgment is offered by Celia Betsky [in *Commonweal* (28 October 1977)]:

> The Rosenbergs' guilt or innocence is immaterial in *The Public Burning* and they are not really the center of attention. Coover is more interested in putting an entire generation, era, and system on trial. His book condemns the accusers and along with them an American tradition of persecution from the Salem witch-hunts to Sacco and Vanzetti.

For me, at least, the arguments for innocence were far less interesting than the indictment of our national outlook. Thomas LeClair offers another answer in his review in *The New Republic* [17 September 1977]:

> . . . his anthropological perspective suggests history is a fiction, perhaps finer-gauged than most yet without finality. But it is by stretching fact past "faction" to myth that Coover obviates history and makes *The Public Burning* a major achievement of conscience and imagination.

Clearly the American public did want scapegoats, and created them on a grand scale during the McCarthy era. Coover exposes this longing for a mythic pattern which will explain experience and protect one from knowledge of one's own weaknesses.

The third answer to Podhoretz's wrath lies in Coover's determination to break down readers' mental barriers. Insofar as we label and classify what we read, we are using our intellectual concerns as a defense against emotional response and commitment. We feel satisfaction when we can label an episode fact or fiction. In *The Public Burning,* Coover invites such frustration as to throw our mental equilibrium out of balance, and leaves us without some of our usual defenses. Clearly any strategy to violate the reader's sense of security can backfire: stories centering on rape will lose one segment of an audience; stories treating Christianity irreverently will lose another. That Podhoretz cannot tolerate someone playing fast and loose with history merely exposes the myth which he clings to for meaning in his cosmos. . . .

We may resent Coover's varyingly successful acts of violation. We certainly resent his calculated destruction of all the comforting myths we hide behind. Coover offers us little compensation for their destruction. We may find some comfort in a tenuous shared physicality; we may grow brave from facing our human limitations, especially if we face them together with a partner. We may find intensity of involvement in a game, which is less destructive than involvement in most religions, sacred or political. We may become involved with an inner struggle, and derive our sense of meaning by coming to terms with ourselves. We may find some release from the tension of awareness in humor.

Robert Coover on *The Public Burning:*

All I've written so far—the novels, stories, plays—have all emerged from a small kernel of an idea, something that in each case could be put in just a few words. But once examined more closely, they all hinted at a a lot more packed away inside, and my task then was to unpack them, unwrap them, make them reveal themselves. This is an artistic problem and it's what I'm always most interested in: this intransigent penetration of a metaphor. It's a little like chasing a vision. Most of the time, I might say, you end up in the dark. The germ idea behind the Rosenbergs project was a simple one, and partly set off by anger, I suppose, and an affinity with the times—this was the mid-sixties, Vietnam War days, a time of gathering protest in the United States, countered by a mounting right-wing reaction. I chanced to come across a book on the Rosenbergs and wondered with some embarrassment why we'd forgotten them. I was working with some theater ideas at the time and it occurred to me that we ought to restage the execution, some theater in Times Square maybe. I elaborated the idea a little—and then came that pregnant kernel: what if I wrote a *story* about doing this? That is, what if I wrote a kind of documentary history of the event, only instead of holding the executions at Sing Sing prison, transpose them to Times Square as a kind of circus event and bring the nation there to see it? That was all there was to it at the time and I thought of it as a short piece, thirty or forty pages long. Only when I started working seriously with it—*morally,* you might say—did it start to fatten out into this large complex communal metaphor we have now.

Robert Coover, in The Radical Imagination and the Liberal Tradition: Interviews with English and American Novelists, *1982.*

[In an interview in *Critique* 11 (1969), Coover says], "I tend to think of tragedy as a kind of adolescent response to the universe—the higher truth is a comic response . . . there *is* a kind of humor extremity which is even more mature than the tragic response." Walpole's apothegm that tragedy is for those who feel, comedy for those who think, may not tell the whole truth. One may find the stimuli of the world so painful that some protection is necessary. But laughter, ambivalent or absurd, is a possible, if only partial, protection. We sense Coover's contemptuous amusement at the earnest discomfort we feel when deprived of our myths, and of the luxury of feeling pity. Yet the laughter that echoes through his novels suggests that he feels—at some level—all too sharply the pain of existence. And he shows us an alternative defense to be used in place of myth. Laughter is no complete escape. We are still aware of the pain. But laughter can be shared, and even when solitary, it can induce an outlook which helps shield our naked nerve ends.

Larry McCaffery   (essay date 1982)

SOURCE: "Robert Coover and the Magic of Fiction Making," in his *The Metafictional Muse: The Works of Robert Coover, Donald Barthelme, and William H. Gass,* University of Pittsburgh Press, 1982, pp. 25-97.

[*McCaffery is an American educator and critic. In the following excerpt, originally published in slightly different form in 1979, he examines Coover's portrayal of the human tendency to manufacture myths in* The Origin of the Brunists *and* The Public Burning.]

Although flawed in certain respects, Robert Coover's first novel, *The Origin of the Brunists,* presents a clear, fairly comprehensive view of his metafictional impulses. Using the founding of the Christian religion as its primary analogue, *The Brunists* seeks to examine the hold which the fictions of religion and history maintain over men. Based in part on some actual experiences Coover had as a youngster in southern Illinois, the plot of the book is built around a mining disaster which kills ninety-seven men. One of the survivors is Giovanni Bruno, a quiet, enigmatic man disliked by most of his fellow workers. Due to a variety of circumstances, coincidences, and local needs, Bruno becomes the unlikely center of a small religious cult, "the Brunists." The story climaxes when most of the participants gather together on the Mount of Redemption (a small hill near the mine) in a wild, orgiastic finale. Here they wait (unsuccessfully, as it turns out) for the end of the world or the coming of the White Dove—no one is quite sure which. As the book concludes, we discover that despite the failure of the predicted cataclysm, the Brunists have struck a responsive chord in the world's religious needs; their cult has spread to all the major areas of the United States, prospects for overseas recruitment look excellent, and scriptural books and records are topping all the best-seller lists. Meanwhile the faithful are solemnly being prepared to meet their maker "on the eighth of January, possibly next year, but more likely 7 or 14 years from now."

Such a general plot summary gives little sense of what happens in the novel because apparent digressions and subplots dominate its development. More than any of Coover's other works, the strengths of this book are drawn from traditional fiction, especially the realistic novel. Thus *The Brunists* has more than twenty vividly drawn, realistic characters and provides most of the other elements of plot and setting familiar to conventional fiction. Indeed, it often seems as if Coover is using his first novel to polish up conventional narrative methods before he moves on to more ambitious, unusual approaches. . . .

Yet if Coover is "paying his dues" to traditional fiction in *The Brunists,* his payments often seem to be made with ambivalent feelings. For example, he constantly undercuts the realistic impulses of the book by borrowing elements from the surreal, the fantastic, and the absurd. Like Thomas Pynchon and Herman Melville—*V.* and *Moby Dick* are the two books which most obviously influenced *The Brunists*—Coover often halts his plot to present asides such as anecdotes, jokes, songs, and esoteric information. Such techniques make it obvious that Coover is more interested in exploring a complex idea through any fictional means than he is in following the conventions of realism.

The focus which holds the disparate parts of the novel together—and which ties this work firmly to Coover's other fictions—can be explained by some remarks he makes in the prologue to *Pricksongs and Descants.* The novelist, says Coover, should use "familiar or historical forms to combat the content of those forms and to conduct the reader . . . to the real, away from mystification to clarification, away from magic to maturity, away from mystery to revelation." Thus in *The Brunists,* as in most of Coover's other works, we are presented with a plot founded upon a prior "mythic or historical" source from which we will eventually be released by what Jackson Cope has termed an "anti-formal revelation." In other words, Coover hopes to use the familiar forms—be they the Christian analogues of *The Brunists,* the popular mythologies of sports (*The Universal Baseball Association*), fairy tales (*Pricksongs*), or the factual events of the Rosenberg case (*The Public Burning*)—to undercut the hold which the content of these forms still has on people. In *The Brunists* Coover uses the familiar, narrow Christian *contexts* but extends them so that the book becomes a metafictional commentary on the fictive process of history itself or, rather, on the ways in which human experience is conveniently translated and mythicized by chroniclers and historians.

By focusing *The Brunists* on religion and religious history, Coover provided himself with an obvious context in which to show the way that human intervention is imposed upon the world to give it meaning. In times of crisis or chaotic disruption, religious and historical perspectives have always provided men with the attractive notion that events actually contain a recognizable order and meaning despite their apparent absurdity. Coover makes it clear that the initial impetus for the Brunist development is the desire on the part of the survivors of the dead miners to attribute some purpose to the catastrophe, to justify it somehow. Faced with a destructive event of such major proportions, the townsfolk find in the Brunist religion a fictional system which endows the terrible events they have experienced with an illusion of order and purpose.

After Bruno is found unconscious but alive in an area of the mine where most of the men were killed, Coover sets several subplots in motion which gradually converge. Although nearly every conceivable potboiler element can be found in these subplots (adultery, incest, adolescent sex play, sadism, voyeurism—all the usual soap-opera materials), none is gratuitous or included merely for sensation's sake. All of them in fact serve Coover's central purpose of establishing the wide range of elements which eventually contribute to the rise of the Brunist cult. Coover is well aware that it takes more than small-town religious fanaticism to start a major religion. Helpful circumstances, unlikely coincidences, unwitting and unwilling support, and just plain luck are all also essential. Perhaps most important of all, a religion needs an effective prophet or PR man to get the word out and drum up interest. Christianity, of course, had all of these factors operating in its favor; and so do the Brunists.

The original Brunists are mainly satirized as answer-seeking fanatics who see in Bruno the fulfillment of their various needs. Their cause attracts such crackpots as Eleanor Norton and Ralph Himebaugh who develop their own fictional systems in ways that illuminate the approaches of later Coover characters such as J. Henry Waugh and Richard Nixon. What all of these characters share is the tendency to rely on mythic notions of causality—notions which operate differently from the more recently developed views of science and logic. Ernst Cassirer, who examines mythic thought in great detail in the second volume of his *Philosophy of Symbolic Forms,* remarks that for mythic thought "every simultaneity, every spatial coexistence and contact, proves a real causal 'sequence.' It has been called a principle of mythic causality and of the physics based on it that one takes every contact in time and space as an immediate relation of cause and effect." It is easy to see how religious explanations of events grow very naturally from such mythic conceptions of reality. A similar mythic basis of thought underlies the numerological orientation of Norton, Himebaugh, and many of Coover's other characters.

Numerology relies in an obvious fashion on a mythic notion of causality. Like astrology—which also influences Mrs. Norton—numerology assumes that some sort of causal relationship exists between two entities (in this case, number and event) which do not have any logical or scientific (i.e., empirical) connection. Ela Norton, for example, tries obsessively to decipher hidden meanings in everyday events. In her frantic desire to discover these veiled implications, she relies on "divine dispatches" sent to her from a spirit called "domiron." Not surprisingly, one system of hidden order which she has uncovered is based on numerological inferences, especially relating to the number seven.

Lawyer Ralph Himebaugh is also a firm believer in numerology and is, as well, a parody of the mathematically oriented post-Renaissance scientist. Himebaugh's metaphysical notions amusingly parallel what has been called the "mathematical metaphysics" which developed after Galileo. Like Descartes, Galileo, Newton, and other formulators of the metaphysical foundations of modern science, Himebaugh is confident that all events can be explained in terms of mathematically determined forces and formulas:

> Ralph's system was nevertheless for him a new science, and if he did not yet embrace the whole truth of the universe, it was only because he still lacked all the data, lacked some vital but surely existent connection—in short had not yet perfected his system.

Thus Himebaugh fills his spare time collecting and graphing statistical information, attempting to discover within the numbers before him a pattern, a basis for predictability. Ralph's theories, like those of the empirical scientist that Coover is satirizing, are "founded always in some concrete event in the world" and are "altered, revised with each discovery of new data." Yet, despite his carefully formulated statistics and graphs, Ralph is also clearly a crackpot: not only does he devote most of his time to deciphering very *un*-empirical numerological signs, but also he is convinced that all events are controlled by a demonic force called "the destroyer."

Mrs. Norton's confident overview of events (from above by divine dispatches) and Ralph's slow assimilation of facts and numbers into a general framework seem to represent comic analogues of the two basic methods of achieving all knowledge—the rationalistic, deductive approach and the empirical, inductive method. In this case, as in the case of science itself, the two systems help support each other. As the novel's main character, Tiger Miller, summarizes at one point, "They shared, that is, this hope for perfection, for final complete knowledge, and their different approach actually complemented each other, or at least seemed to." As we might expect of people who are seeking "final complete knowledge," their search for "final complete knowledge" ends in failure, just as all similar searches end in Coover's fiction. Thus Coover pokes a great deal of fun at both these methods and makes it obvious that Mrs. Norton and Ralph Himebaugh are simply projecting their own distorted personalities onto the world. Yet Coover also subtly undercuts this view by establishing a "real" numerological foundation in his own novel and thus indirectly creates an "objective basis" for the positions he mocks.

It isn't too difficult to uncover some sort of numerological pattern in the events of *The Brunists.* We probably laugh first at Ralph Himebaugh's analysis in the following passage, but further consideration may make us wonder if the pattern Ralph is describing isn't *really there* after all:

> The number ninety-seven, the number of the dead, was itself unbelievably relevant. Not only did it take its place almost perfectly in the concatenation of disaster figures he had been recording, but it contained internal mysteries as well: nine, after all, was the number of the mine itself, and seven, pregnant integer out of all divination, was the number of trapped miners. The number between nine and seven, eight, was the date of the explosion, and the day of the rescue was eleven, two one's or two, the difference between nine

and seven. Nine and seven added to sixteen, whose parts, one and six, again added to . . . seven!

Just as in a Nabokovian puzzle, certain patterns do mysteriously appear if we follow these numerological hints. If we take the number seven, for example, we find that Tiger Miller's high school basketball number was seven; the number of miners trapped was ninety-eight, which is itself composed of fourteen sevens (with fourteen itself being another multiple of seven); ninety-eight, if taken in a series leads first to seven (the number of miners trapped with Bruno) and then to six (the number who died); on the night of the mining disaster the basketball game is stopped with the score 14-11 (as noted above, fourteen is a multiple of seven, and is also the date Bruno is rescued); Vince Bonali just happens to have seven children. After just a little of this sort of number-chasing, we sense that Coover is playing a joke on us—inducing *us* to establish fictional patterns in much the same way that we laughed at Ralph and Ela for doing. But Coover also seems to be demonstrating a more subtle point which is often made by Nabokov (most notable in *Pale Fire*): that seemingly random appearances, under subjective human scrutiny, do often cohere into a pattern which can be applied to the world. And as we follow this game of creating a system from this series of elements, we are inevitably pointed back to the original fiction maker of the story—Coover himself. As he does in many of his stories, Coover begins by laughing at analytic machinery when used by his characters, turns his humor upon our own tendency to dig up hidden meanings, and all the while he mocks himself, the reader-critic within the writer, the creator who can't resist exposing himself in his formal strategies.

If the fiction-making impulses of the original small cult of the Brunists are fairly clear, it is even more evident that Giovanni Bruno himself is nothing more than a befuddled pawn who is manipulated by the religious needs of others. Certain that Bruno is "the One who is to come," Eleanor Norton becomes the unofficial spokesperson and high priestess of a small group of devoted believers. Most of these believers are people like Clara Collins who are desperately seeking some means of making sense of the recent tragedy at the mine. Bruno himself is brought home to sit in bed and mutter bizarre, often incoherent remarks ("The tomb is its message"; "Baptize . . . light"), each of which is reverently noted and carefully "decoded" by the message-hungry followers.

Coover's handling of the cult itself often seems one-dimensional and at times slips into pure farce; his treatment of the response of the West Condon folk to Brunism, however, is more complicated and ultimately less sympathetic. Without exception the townspeople of West Condon are shown to act solely in terms of their own selfish interests. Although these interests are not religiously motivated as are those of the Brunists, they nonetheless all unknowingly aid the Brunist cause—and this is what ties their sections to the novel's primary structure. Banker Ted Cavanaugh, for example, is never sympathetic to the Brunist cause and in fact recognizes them for the crackpots that they are. But because he is also concerned about the town's dismal economic situation and its inability to

attract outsiders, he is willing to use Bruno for a little free publicity. Thus when Bruno is ready to leave the hospital, he sees to it that Bruno is brought home in style:

> Bruno's big homecoming was Ted Cavanaugh's idea. There was a national—even international—focus on the man, why not put it to the whole town's service? Already Bruno had emerged as something of a town hero, a symbol of the community's own struggle to survive, so why not make the most of it? . . . For the moment—no matter how arbitrary it might seem—he stood for West Condon, and they all had to lift West Condon high!

Even less sympathetic to the Brunists is preacher Abner Baxter, who inherits his job when Ely Collins is killed in the blast. Uncertain of his congregation's loyalty, Baxter sees the Brunist movement as a threat to his own security. Hopeful of stabilizing his new position—and supported with historical parallels to religious situations in the past—Baxter declares a holy war on the Brunists and urges his parishioners to use any means to drive the new religion from their community. Thus begins the "Brunist Persecution" which, as was true with Christianity and many other religions, only serves to draw the Brunists together and publicize their cause. Baxter's children, after making off with the disembodied hand of a charred miner, play cruel and devilish tricks on the neighborhood (feeding ground glass to dogs, placing excrement in the rival preacher's pulpit) under the "Sign of the Black Hand"; the Brunists, who are willing to assimilate anything which will fit into their pattern of beliefs, quickly interpret these pranks as otherworldly messages or warnings. Like almost any organism which hopes to prosper, the Brunists deftly take advantage of whatever local conditions might aid in their development. Thus in the process of establishing their creed—a purely arbitrary, invented fiction—they provide an excellent example of why fiction-making is so useful to man.

By far the most important figure to aid the Brunists is the local newspaper editor, Justin "Tiger" Miller. Miller's name supplies the first clue about his role, for Justin was a second-century writer and apologist for Christianity. But Miller and his newspaper *The Chronicle* are peculiarly modern sorts of religious apologists; although Miller becomes the Brunists' public relations man, their historian, prophet, and gospel-maker, he also is aware that they are a hoax. He also introduces an important concept which is found in many of Coover's fictions: the concept of game.

Tiger Miller's background may remind us of Updike's Rabbit Angstrom (in *Rabbit Run*), for it too is dominated by his legendary feats as a high school basketball player. In a revealing passage, we are told that games help provide some semblance of order in Miller's life:

> Games were what kept Miller going. Games, and the pacifying of mind and organs. Miller perceived existence as a loose concatenation of separate and ultimately inconsequential instants, each colored by the action that preceded it, but each possessed of a small wanton freedom of its own. Life then, was a series of adjustments to these actions, and if one kept his sense of

humor and produced as many of these actions himself as possible, adjustments were easier.

This passage helps explain Miller's role in the book as a pseudo-historian or fiction-maker. It also offers a view of the world and man's position in it that seems to coincide with Coover's own view. The idea that life is a "loose concatenation of separate and ultimately inconsequential instants" directly opposes, of course, the historical view which attempts to explain and define meaningful relationships between events. Indeed, the notion that each moment possesses "a small wanton freedom of its own" opposes *any* concept of an *externally imposed* system of order. Once this view is accepted, the alternatives are evident: either man can adopt the despairing outlook that life is fundamentally and irrevocably absurd and chaotic; or he can consider the "freedom" of each moment as a sign that man can create his own system of order and meaning. If this latter alternative is accepted—and it is accepted by Miller, Waugh, and Nixon—the attraction of games, sports, and rituals of any kind becomes obvious—for here there is order, definite sets of rules to be followed, a series of signs that can be interpreted, noncapricious rewards and punishments, and a sense of stasis and repetition that seems somehow freed from the demands of process. The meaning and order of games are fictitious and arbitrary in the sense that they are invented subjectively and then applied to the transformational possibilities within the system. But unlike the equally fictitious sense of order provided by history, politics, or religion, games allow man to act with awareness of his position, without dogmatic claims to final truths and objectivity.

When the novel opens, Tiger Miller is presented as a game player without a "big game" to look forward to. Then when the Brunist controversy arises, Miller sees a chance to become involved in a new, potentially amusing game whose rules he is familiar with from his knowledge of the Bible and history—that is, the game of creating a religion. That Miller consciously conceives of his role in the Brunist affair as that of a player in a game is evident in the following passage:

> Their speculations amused Miller—who himself at age thirteen had read Revelations and never quite got over it—so he printed everything he thought might help them along, might seem relevant to them. . . . Once the emotions had settled down and the widows themselves had established new affairs or found mind-busying work, their eccentric interest of the moment would be forgotten, of course. Which, in a way, was too bad. *As games went, it was a good game, and there was some promise in it.* (emphasis added)

Late in the novel when Miller explains to a minister his own role in the Brunist affair, we discover that, for Miller, historians and theologians have always been engaged in the game of fiction making:

> "Exactly! It doesn't matter. Somebody with a little imagination, a new interpretation, a bit of eloquence, and—zap!—they're off for another hundred or thousand years." Miller passed his hand over the heap of manila folders on his desk. "Anyway, it makes a good story."

Edwards gazes down at the folders. "But Justin, doesn't it occur to you? These are human lives—one-time human lives—you're toying with!"

"Sure, what else?"

"But to make a game out of—"

Miller laughed. "You know, Edwards, *it's the one thing you and I have got in common."* (emphasis added)

The point established here is crucial: Edwards recognizes that to Miller the process of creating a religion and presenting a historical version of it is a game, an arbitrary fiction conjured up by an imaginative mind. Miller agrees and adds that Edwards is likewise engaged in game playing. But while Miller is very much aware of the fictional basis of *his* game, Edwards and the Brunists are unaware of what they are doing (or at least they are unwilling to acknowledge it). This directly anticipates the situation that J. Henry Waugh (in *The UBA*) and most of the American public (in *The Public Burning*) find themselves in.

Ironically it is precisely Miller's game playing which enables the Brunists to develop and maintain their tenuous foothold in the community. As Miller has told Edwards, history has always been presented by men willing to embellish some here and add a little there to "make a good story." The fact that historical perspectives result from human intervention and selection is usually ignored by an uncritical public hungry for order and truth. Such a public is an easy prey for an "entertainer" such as Miller:

> Once a day, six days a week and sometimes seven, year in, year out, the affairs of West Condon were compressed into a set of conventionally accepted signs and became, in the shape of the West Condon *Chronicle,* what most folks in town thought of as life, or history. . . . That its publisher and editor, Justin Miller, sometimes thought of himself as in the entertainment business and viewed his product, based as it was on the technicality of the recordable fact, as a kind of benevolent hoax, probably only helped to make the paper greater.

This view of the historical procedure being "a benevolent hoax" is dramatized even more clearly early in the book: when Miller discovers that a United Press representative has considerably embellished a wholly falsified report that Miller himself dreamed up about the mine rescue, he laughs and comments, "Such are history's documents."

A good fiction promoter, Miller meets with great success in furthering the Brunist cause. Near the end of the novel, however, when Miller tries to remind everyone that the whole Brunist uprising has only been an amusing game, he discovers too late the tenacity with which people cling to their fictions and is nearly killed by an angry mob of Brunists. Like some of Coover's later characters who do not fully understand the appeal of arbitrary systems (the sheriff in *The Kid,* Lou Engels in *The UBA,* Julius Rosenberg in *The Public Burning*), Miller is underestimating the fanatical desire of people to cling to their illusions of order and meaning. When he encounters a frenzied mob of

Brunists on the Mount of Redemption, an ironic reversal occurs as Miller-the-Tiger nearly becomes a sacrificial lamb.

The Brunists eventually go on to establish themselves as a major religion. They succeed in welding a creed and church hierarchy and set the foundations for precious and sacred traditions—all bearing considerable resemblance to the early stories, miracles, and wonders of Christianity. Naturally these parallels serve to parody the origins of Christianity; but as Leo Hertzel notes, Coover hopes to extend the range of the implications of this book into a "commentary on history, on the fantastic complexity and ignorance that lie at the root of all recorded and revered experience." Coover also includes a brief, puzzling epigraph to his novel entitled "Return" which—like the final chapter to *The UBA*—throws into doubt many of the mythic and historical parallels and associations developed earlier. For example, we probably have identified Marcella Bruno's death with that of Christ, for it unites the Brunists and is even presented to us in a chapter entitled "The Sacrifice." But the last chapter invites us to see Miller's near-death as being the Christ parallel. Thus the first thing that Miller's girlfriend, Happy Bottom, says to Miller when he revives is, "And how feels today the man who redeemed the world?" Later while Miller is delirious, he identifies himself on the cross: "He saw himself, crosshung, huge below, head soaring out of sight. . . . Something knocked against his cross: vibrations racked him and screaming, he fell." But before these new parallels are firmly established, we are reminded that Miller also betrayed the new religion and helped cause the death of the first sacrificial victim, Marcella Bruno. Not surprisingly, then, Miller is also identified at times in this last section with Judas—a confusion of mythic parallels that continues when Miller considers his own role in the rise of the Brunists and decides that "crucifixion was a proper end for insurgents: it dehumanizes them." The closest thing to a resolution of this mythic mixup comes in another ambiguous passage in which the Christ analogue vaguely seems to win out over that of the Judas:

> Jesus, dying, disconnected, was shocked to find Judas at his feet. "Which . . . one of us," Jesus gasped, "is really He: I . . . or thou?" Judas offered up a hallowing, omniscient smile, shrugged, and went away, never to be seen in these parts again.

All this may be a metaphorical way of demonstrating the struggle going on within Miller to assess his role in creating the rise of the Brunists. Or it may be a puzzling diversion, included by Coover for reasons that Miller would appreciate: it makes a good story. At any rate, it is obvious that although Coover invites us to establish parallels and note associations, he also does not want us to create too many easy one-to-one relationships. As he continually reminds us, life just isn't as straightforward and easily interpreted as most fictions—including those of history, religion, and realistic novels—would like to make it seem. This brief epilogue thus tears down, or at least calls into question, some of the mythic and archetypal machinery that Coover has earlier set in motion. In doing so, it reminds us that such pattern is useful in guiding our re-

sponses to both literary works and to life, but this utility is maintained only if we are aware that other perspectives are also possible. Only if we are able to develop an awareness of our own participation in the creation of fictions can we reject dogmatic attitudes and begin to take advantage of the fiction-making process. In short, we can be free only when we can distinguish our own creations from those which exist in the world. . . .

In certain fundamental ways, *The Public Burning* extends the vision of a chaotic, disruptive universe and the enormously complex operations of history that Coover presents in all his fiction. Likewise, the metafictional intent behind this work is again very evident as Coover examines the relationship between man's fictional systems and the reality they seek to explore. But although Coover continues to deal with man's need for order and the incredible variety of ways he has developed to cope with flux, *The Public Burning* is in almost every way a broader and more ambitious work than anything he had previously published. Beyond these major thematic concerns, *The Public Burning,* at its most accessible level, does a brilliant job of recreating the apocalyptic mood and paranoiac spirit of the early 1950s; even more remarkably, its portrait of Richard Nixon proves to be a subtle, credible, and strangely compassionate characterization.

The complexity and breadth of Coover's vision here results in part from his intricate interweaving of an enormous amount of factual data into his fictional narrative. Indeed, in a very important sense this book is a tribute to language's ability to create coherence, and it literally embodies Coover's central point about man's talent in manipulating the elements of his existence into new, exciting plots and patterns. As Coover commented, the role of the artist—the exemplary fiction-maker who represents us all—is to become "the mythologizer, to be the creative spark in this process of renewal: he's the one who tears apart the old story, speaks the unspeakable, makes the ground shake, then shuffles the bits back together into a new story." Much like Joyce in *Ulysses* (probably the best analogue of Coover's attempt), Coover meticulously builds his mythic framework out of a welter of facts, figures, dates, public testimony, and other real data. Everything that might possibly have a bearing on the Rosenberg case—from the cold war crisis (including the Korean War background) and political intrigues in Washington right up through a wide range of cultural and pop-culture events in America—is included here. As a result the book seems to operate on what we might term a deliberate strategy of excess, with the reader's difficulties in approaching the text mirroring Richard Nixon's own dilemma in unraveling the complexities of the Rosenberg case. Like Nixon, we are confronted with a bewildering assortment of facts, figures, lists, quotes, pseudo-quotes, song lyrics, trial testimony, movie plots, and dozens of other potential clues. It seems as if everything that was going on in America and around the world during this period had some sort of direct bearing on the Rosenberg case—even the significance of such films as *High Noon* and *House of Wax* which are repeatedly referred to and which provide meaningful cultural analogues to the larger dramas that are unfolding. All this material is transformed by Coover's hand to create a vivid sense of exactly what was occurring in the public consciousness on June 19, 1953 when the Rosenbergs were executed. The central magic of this work is therefore similar to Joyce's achievement in *Ulysses* or Pynchon's in *Gravity's Rainbow* and *V.* in that Coover succeeds in making his encyclopedic details seem aesthetically appropriate: all the details *seem* to be meaningful, seem to be forming themselves into the shapes and patterns that Coover wishes to establish. And it is precisely the nature of these shapes that is the focus of Coover's metafictional concern here, for these shapes represent the fictions that we all generate to create a bulwark against chaos: the shape of history, the shape of paranoia, the shape of simplistic oppositions (us versus them, communism versus democracy, God versus the devil, good versus evil), the shape of art, the shape of literary narratives.

The story of *The Public Burning* is told in twenty-eight sections which are narrated alternately by Richard Nixon and, in various voices, by Coover. Although a prologue and epilogue extend the action somewhat, the book focuses on the two days and nights that precede the execution of the Rosenbergs. Coover stages this execution at Times Square—the "luminous navel" of the United States, a "place of feasts, spectacle, and magic . . . the ritual center of the Western World." The actual execution itself, which is highly reminiscent of the climactic ending of *The Origin of the Brunists,* is presented as a powerful, circus-like finale that serves as a public exorcism and ceremonial return to what Coover has called "dreamtime." As he explains, "dreamtime" involves "the inner truths, legends, mythos of the race, the origins, the mysterious beginnings of the tribe. . . . The point of a ceremonial return to dreamtime is basically regenerative: to recover belief in the tribe and get things moving again." It is crucial to understanding Coover's intentions in *The Public Burning* to see that the Rosenbergs are supposed to represent something much more than mere pawns of the cold war strategy or cogs destroyed when our judicial machinery runs amuck. Instead, Coover presents the Rosenbergs as archetypal victims, the central participants in a celebratory ritual which Uncle Sam hopes will enable America to recapture a sense of community and momentum which it has lost in its battle with the Phantom. That their execution takes place in the spring at Times Square—"an American holy place long associated with festivals of rebirth"—helps underscore this fundamental association. At one point Uncle Sam bluntly explains to Nixon the specific purpose of the extravagantly staged execution: "Oh, I don't reckon we could live like this all year round . . . we'd only expunctify ourselves. But we do need an occasional peak of disorder and danger to keep things from just peterin' out, don't we." The execution is a blatantly theatrical spectacle designed to combine ritualistically elements of entertainment (Cecil B. DeMille chairs an entertainment committee and is assisted by Busby Berkeley, Betty Crocker, Walt Disney, Ed Sullivan, and the Mormon Tabernacle Choir—among others), religious archetypes celebrating rebirth and regeneration, and various anarchical and sexual impulses which will presumably free the populace for renewal once they have torn everything apart.

Although Coover fills nearly all the sections of the book

with a sense of bitterness, irony, and outrage, he also manages to suggest a sympathetic understanding of how communities are led to such destructive results. The chief danger to which all of the major participants in the novel succumb—except, curiously, Richard Nixon—is the familiar mistake made by so many Coover characters: the danger of dogmatizing beliefs, the danger of taking self-generated fictions too literally, the danger of relying too completely on fragile, oversimplified systems (such as historical or political perspectives) and of not seeing how utterly inadequate they are to deal with the enormously complex, constantly shifting nature of reality. Thus all the major characters—the Rosenbergs, Uncle Sam, Nixon, the Phantom—react to the prospect of randomness in the same way: they storify it, creating soothing possible fictions that they can feel comfortable with. Like *The Brunists* and *The UBA, The Public Burning* exhibits Coover's obvious fascination with the power of history to subjugate events to pattern—to create connections, causal relationships, and stories when most observers can find no meaning at all. As a result, one of the central preoccupations in the novel is with "the mosaic of history," how man is able, through language, to arrange and rearrange the random elements of existence into historically significant events. In trying to uncover all the relevant facts in the labyrinthine Rosenberg case, Richard Nixon is soon led to ponder the nature of man's efforts to organize his experience and to analyze the crucial role which language has in creating this system:

> What was fact, what intent, what was framework, what was essence? Strange, the impact of History, the grip it had on us, yet it was nothing but words. Accidental accretions for the most part, leaving most of the story out. We have not yet begun to explore the true power of the Word, I thought. What if we broke all the rules, played games with the evidence, manipulated language itself, made History a partisan ally? Of course, the Phantom was already onto this, wasn't he? Ahead of us again. What were his dialectical machinations if not the dissolution of the natural limits of language, the conscious invention of a space, a spooky artificial no-man's land, between logical alternatives?

Nixon here voices a view of history-as-artifice that we have seen being developed in much of Coover's earlier fiction, and he is also perceptive about the ability of the Phantom to organize the random elements of history into fictions useful to his cause. But what Nixon fails to realize at this stage is that Uncle Sam is also involved in such deceptive manipulations. While making a complete fool of himself in a hilarious game of golf with Uncle Sam, Nixon listens as his boss presents his own cynical view of history:

> Hell, *all* courtroom testimony about the past is ipso facto and teetotaciously a baldface lie, ain't that so? Moonshine! Chicanery! The old gum game! Like history itself—all more or less bunk . . . the fatal slantindicular futility of Fact! Appearances, my boy, appearances. Practical politics consists in ignorin' facts! *Opinion* ultimately governs the world. . . . And so a trial in the midst of all this flux and a slippery past is just one set of bolloxeratin' sophistries agin an-

other—or call'em mettyfours if you like, approx-imations, all the same desputt humbuggery.

Nixon at this point is still too desperate for Uncle Sam's favor to see the deeper relevance of this message ("I still hadn't figured out what Uncle Sam was up to," he admits). Uncle Sam, relying on the American public's bewilder-ment and rage over their loss of world power, has con-structed a simple fiction which conveniently reduces the complex political and historical realities of the world into a neatly organized black-and-white scenario: the Phantom (communism) is after us (the "Free World") and is willing to do anything to destroy us, including the adoption of any number of insidious disguises; anything connected with us is good and must be protected at all costs, while anything connected with the Phantom is evil and must be de-stroyed.

This simplistic good-versus-evil world view is subtly as-sisted by news media anxious to present their own picture of a tidy universe reducible to the "5 W's." Coover is care-ful to establish that the role of supposedly neutral news disseminators such as *Time* or even the more reputable *New York Times* is to grab onto details and organize them into coherent patterns. Like the role of historians, then, the function of journalists exactly parallels the role of Coover in this book, or the role of any artist. But journal-ists also falsify this experience for the public by pretending that the circuit is closed, that interpretation and ingenious organization is actual fact. Like the West Condonites in *The Brunists* and Dame Society in *The UBA,* the Ameri-can public in *The Public Burning* is shown to be desperate for assurances and frighteningly susceptible to effective manipulators who wish to establish their own rules. Cer-tainly it is not an accident that the actual deaths of the Ro-senbergs and the near-deaths of Tiger Miller and the Asso-ciation's ballplayers all derive from the public's inability to accept the arbitrary nature of fictional systems.

Although Coover is once again mocking our tendency to be uncritical in accepting the literal veracity of our inven-tions, he is also well aware of man's basic fear of paradox and transformation. Here, as in all of Coover's fiction, the desire for coherence is presented as intimately related to the artistic impulse itself which seeks to organize a selec-tive number of elements drawn from life's overabundance into an aesthetically pleasing and significant whole. As we read *The Public Burning,* we are constantly aware of Coover's efforts to transform the events of history into the system of language called the novel. Richard Nixon in-forms us that language is used "to transcend the confu-sions, restore the spirit, recreate the society!" In a crucial sense, then, Coover's efforts in this novel become an exem-plary achievement of the imagination to cope with confu-sion via language; Nixon's own struggles to solve the Ro-senberg puzzle become a metafictional representation of Coover's efforts to create a truthful presentation of an enormously complex set of elements. In one of the most important theoretical passages in all of his work, Coover summarizes his view of how man tries to deal with disor-der and randomness with the fiction-making process:

> Raw data is paralyzing, a nightmare, there's too much of it and man's mind is quickly engulfed

by it. Poetry is the art of subordinating facts to the imagination, of giving them shape and visi-bility, keeping them *personal.* It is, as Mother Luce has said, "fakery in allegiance to the truth," a kind of interpretive re-enactment of the overabundant flow of events, "an effective mosa-ic" assembled from "the fragmentary docu-ments" of life, quickened with audacious imag-ery and a distinct and original prosody: "noses for news lie betwixt ears for music." Some would say that such deep personal involvement, such metaphoric compressions and reliance on inner vision and imaginary "sources," must make ob-jectivity impossible, and TIME would agree with them, but he would find simply illiterate anyone who concluded from this that he was not serving Truth. More: he would argue that objec-tivity is an impossible illusion, a "fantastic claim" ("gnostic" is the word on his tongue these days), and as an ideal perhaps even immor-al, that *only* through the frankly biased and dis-torting lens of art is any real grasp of the facts—not to mention Ultimate Truth—even remotely possible.

This passage, with its acknowledgment of the "frankly bi-ased and distorting lens of art" and its insistence on "sub-ordinating facts to the imagination" could well stand as Coover's assessment of his own attempts in *The Public Burning* to present "an effective mosaic" of the age. It also demonstrates the combination of irony, sympathy, and honesty which typifies Coover's presentation of man's ef-forts to discover reliable and objective systems.

The Uncle Sam of *The Public Burning* embodies a pecu-liar mixture of wild energy, folksiness, meanness, and op-portunism—a mixture which has helped shape the United States. In the novel's shocking epilogue, however, all of his folksiness disappears and the ugly realities behind his cruel, power-seeking nature are unmasked. When Nixon accuses him of being "a butcher," "a beast," and "no bet-ter than the Phantom!", Uncle Sam defends himself by saying that death and destruction are part of what we must accept if the "game" is to be kept running smoothly: "It ain't easy holdin' a community together, order ain't what comes natural, you know that, boy, and a lotta peo-ple gotta get killt tryin' to pretend it is, that's how the game is played." Moments later as he prepares to sodo-mize Nixon—thereby investing him with the "Incarnation of Power" that will manifest itself publicly fifteen years later—Uncle Sam brutally announces that if he is to be loved, he should be loved for the powerful, lusty figure that he has always been:

> You wanta make it with me . . . you gotta love me like I really am: Sam Slick, the Yankee Ped-dler, gun-totin' hustler and tooth-n'-claw tamer of the heathen wilderness, lusty and in every-thing a screamin' meddler, novus ball-bustin' ordo seclorum, that's me, boy—and goodnight Mrs. Calabash to any damfool what gets in my way! . . . You said it yourself: they's a political axiom that wheresomever a vacuum exists, it will be filled by the nearest or strongest power! Well, you're lookin' at it, mister: an example and fit instrument, big as they come in this world and gittin' bigger by the minute! Towerin' genius dis-

dains a beaten path—it seeks regions hitherto unexplored—so clutch aholt on somethin' an say your prayers, cuz I propose to move immee-jitly upon your works!

This frightening revelation, which seems uncomfortably accurate even as a caricature, suggests that the real source of evil in America grows precisely out of its strength and power and its willingness to use these assets to dominate others.

Caught in the midst of these titanic struggles, the Rosenbergs are presented as tragic, largely sympathetic pawns who are perhaps too eager to accept their roles as exemplary victims. Part of their trouble, as Nixon sees it, is their "self-destructive suspicion that they were being watched by some superhuman presence," a suspicion which dehumanizes them by suggesting that they are acting out predetermined roles in a drama controlled by exterior forces. At one point Nixon wonders if the whole Rosenberg case might be simply a complete fabrication, a story which the main characters have duped themselves into believing: "And then what if, I wondered, there were no spy ring at all? What if all these characters *believed* there was and acted out their parts on this assumption, a whole courtroom full of fantasists . . . the Rosenbergs, thinking everybody was crazy, nevertheless fell for it, moving ineluctably into the martyr roles they'd been waiting for all along, eager to be admired and pitied." The Rosenbergs are destroyed, in part, because of their foolish trust in the operations of such arbitrary systems as history and justice. Even Nixon, who is at once both naive and cynical about the operations of history, is quick to realize that "they've been seduced by this. If they could say to hell with History, they'd be home free." Julius especially seems to have been too quick to place his trust in the judicial process, and thus he becomes an easy victim for men like J. Edgar Hoover who know the rules of the game and are able to manipulate all the angles to their own benefit. Unaware that the opposition has changed the rules and rigged the outcome with the umpire, Julius continues to believe until it is too late that justice will somehow prevail. Ethel, on the other hand, is a less passive and more passionate victim; because she is more cynical and self-conscious about the struggle she is engaged in, she is less gullible than Julius and ultimately her death is therefore more heroic. Certainly their willingness to accept their tragic roles is nurtured by their involvement with communism with its own dogmatic insistence that there exist objective systems (historical patterns, economic forces) which are inevitable but which man can decipher to his advantage. Consequently the Rosenbergs not only are victimized but even emphasize their "stage roles" as abstract pawns.

Remarkably, Richard Nixon emerges as the novel's most perceptive and sympathetic character as he lurches, clownlike, toward his destiny "at the center" of apocalypse in Times Square. Coover obviously did extensive research into Nixon's background, from his youth right up through his early political career. All the familiar Nixon qualities are here: the smug self-righteousness, the obvious malice and insecurity masked by a phony affability, the self-pity combined with an appetite for power and success. But Coover's portrayal is no mere caricature, for Nixon emerges as a resilient figure who manages to get up after every pratfall, whose intentions are often misunderstood and misrepresented, and whose paranoia and other peculiar personality traits are convincingly portrayed. We are probably expected to laugh at Nixon's constant comparisons between himself and various other American heroes like Lincoln, Teddy Roosevelt, Horatio Alger; but one of the most telling aspects of the way Coover uses Nixon is the fact that Nixon's career really does seem to embrace a lot of the American Dream. In his own bungling but energetic manner, Nixon's desire to be near the sacred "center" represents a fundamental faith in the American way. As he explains, "I have faith: I believe in the American dream, I believe in it because I have seen it come true in my own life. TIME has said that I've had 'a Horatio Alger-like career,' but not even Horatio Alger could have dreamed up a life so American—in the best sense—as mine." From our perspective today—a perspective that is crucial to the many oppositions and juxtapositions that Coover wishes to establish—our awareness of the many abuses and deceits that would follow Nixon's eventual "incarnation" allows us to realize that his career does indeed teach us a great deal about what has gone wrong with the American Dream.

Nixon's role in *The Public Burning* is really twofold: he is both clown and middleman. First of all, he plays the important role of clown who assists the ringmaster—Coover—by creating laughter which will release tension and allow the audience to refocus its attention on the main entertainment at hand. As Coover explains in an interview, this first role helps explain why Nixon was created as a basically sympathetic character: "My interest in Nixon—or my story about him—grew out of my concept of the book as a sequence of circus acts. That immediately brought to mind the notion of clown acts, bringing the show back down to the ground. You have to have a thrilling high-wire number, and then the clown comes on, shoots off a cannon, takes a pratfall, drops his pants, and exits. And then you can throw another high-wire act at them. So naturally I looked for the clownish aspects of my narrator, and you can't have an unsympathetic clown." Obviously the clownish aspect of Nixon's role is very evident: we watch him smear himself with dog excrement, make a fool of himself in front of his family, unwittingly hand Uncle Sam an exploding cigar, and—as a capper—become magically transported from a sexual encounter with Ethel Rosenberg onto the stage in Times Square with his pants down.

Nixon's second role is more complex and difficult to define, but it is equally significant: it is the role of middleman caught between his desire to be loyal to Uncle Sam (and perhaps move himself closer to the day he can be transformed into Sam's incarnation) and his sympathetic identification with the Rosenbergs. As Nixon himself explains his role, "Dwight Eisenhower and Julius Rosenberg would never understand each other, but I could understand—and contain—both." A bit earlier, Nixon had elaborated on his "middle" position by saying, "As the villain, I was also the hero, the bridging took place in me, and I had ever since been the healer of rifts, the party unifier, the fundamentalist who could perceive the Flux."

What Nixon wants desperately is what all of Coover's major characters want: some sort of balance, a center point which will provide relief from paradox and the freedom to operate within the extremes of chaos and rigidly fixed patterns. "Paradox was the one thing I hated more than psychiatrists and lady journalists," he admits, and much later in the novel he complains, "Ah, why did nothing in America keep its shape, I wondered? Everything was so fluid, nothing stayed the same, not even Uncle Sam." Nixon yearns for assurances and stability, but as he begins to involve himself in the incredible maze of clues and false scents of the Rosenberg case, he finds himself—like the Unwilling Participant in **"Panel Game"**—drowning in a sea of undecipherable signs and ambiguous messages. Ironically, Nixon's "drive to center," to which all the events in the book serve to propel him, can only serve to defeat his quest for final answers, for Times Square "is the most paradoxical place in all America." Nixon's role as a sort of super sleuth offers some interesting parallels (and contrasts) to the attempts of the American public at large to uncover meaning. Despite his vested interest in the case, Nixon actually shows more sensitivity and perceptiveness in the Rosenberg proceedings than does the general public. Realizing that the easy explanations of the prosecution and news media are false and oversimplified, Nixon is the only major character other than Justice Douglas who seriously doubts the Rosenbergs' guilt and is willing to do something about it. There is a lot of J. Henry Waugh in Coover's Richard Nixon: his numerological speculations, his mythic concept of names, his corny dramatic daydreams into which he is constantly projecting himself. Above all, Nixon shares with Waugh a terrifically active imagination which he uses to link up details into theories, to constantly invent false scents, and strained, improbable connections. For poor Nixon, everything seems to reverberate with a mysterious significance; thus finding a story he can believe in becomes an almost impossibly heroic effort. "I felt like I'd fallen into a river and was getting swept helplessly along," he whines during the middle of his investigations. In his humorous and occasionally poignant efforts to make sense of a shifting, ambiguous universe, Nixon represents us all.

One of the most fascinating results of Nixon's overactive imagination is his tendency to discover—or invent—identifications between himself and the Rosenbergs. As he gradually begins to sort through the details of the case, Nixon soon decides that he and the Rosenbergs are at once both psychic doubles and mirror opposites of one another. In thinking of Julius Rosenberg, for example, Nixon gets right to the heart of the matter when he suggests that their "mirror images" of each other also reflect an intimate bond: "We were more like mirror images of each other, familiar opposites. Left-right, believer-nonbeliever, city-country, accused-accuser, maker-unmaker. I built bridges, he bombed them. . . . He moved to the fringe as I moved to the center." Nixon's sympathetic identification with the Rosenbergs results in part from his finding in their shattered lives a distorted echo of his own Horatio Alger career. Like him, for example, the Rosenbergs were always anxious to uncover the secrets of political and historical events and to participate in the destiny of America. In considering their radical days as college students,

Nixon concludes that the Rosenbergs wanted to "get out of the overt activities of college days and withdraw to the very center of the heresy that excited them: why not? After all, I'd become Vice-President of the United States of America by a chain of circumstances not all that different, one thing drifting into the next, carried along by a desire, much like theirs, to reach the heart of things, to participate deeply in life." More fundamental to understanding his obsession with the Rosenbergs, however, is the fact that the Rosenbergs represent to Nixon a secret side of himself that he has always longed to explore but which he has never been allowed to acknowledge publicly. Extremely self-conscious about his own personal inadequacies, Nixon is especially drawn to Ethel Rosenberg, for he finds in her the warmth, idealism, and passion that have been absent in his own life. In his vivid daydreams of the courtship of Ethel and Julius, Nixon, like Henry Waugh, constantly projects himself into the scenes. Significantly, one of his most striking conjurings involves the moment when Ethel said to Julius concerning his political involvements, "I'll help you." To this, Nixon—who has felt rejected and victimized since childhood—comments with a sense of bitterness and longing, "No one had ever said anything like that to me."

Nixon's desire to be at the center of things, to be a part of Uncle Sam's vision, is clearly a yearning for power, but just as importantly, it is a yearning for love. Certainly these desires help illuminate the book's final scene in which Nixon is first of all raped by Uncle Sam and then responds to Sam's conciliatory remarks—"You're my everything, sunshine—*you're my boy!*"—by thinking, "Of course, he was an incorrigible huckster, a sweet-talking con artist, you couldn't trust him, I knew that—but what did it matter? Whatever else he was, he was beautiful (how had I ever thought him ugly?), the most beautiful thing in all the world." Nixon is now "ready at last to do what [he] had never done before," and confesses, "I . . . I *love you, Uncle Sam!*" These same impulses had led Nixon to various sexual fantasies about Ethel Rosenberg earlier in the novel and eventually to a dramatic confrontation with her at Sing Sing in which, for the first time, he is able to act out the role of impassioned lover that he always imagined he could play. Spouting all sorts of melodramatic corn—"Admit it, Ethel! You've dreamed of love all your life! You dream of it now! I know, because I dream of it too! . . . You're an artist, Ethel, a poet! You know what love is, what it might be! All the rest is just lies!"—Nixon finally grabs Ethel and urges her to reject all the "lies of purpose" that have led her to the gas chamber:

> "We've both been victims of the same lie, Ethel! There *is* no purpose, there *are* no causes, all that's just stuff we make up to hold the goddam world together—all we've really got is what we have right here and now: being alive! *Don't throw it away, Ethel!*"

This comic but occasionally moving love scene between Nixon and Ethel is Nixon's finest moment in the novel, for it is the one time that he is able to overcome his role as clown and victim and become his "own man at last!"

In his efforts to sort out meanings and create for himself

a freedom in which to maneuver, Nixon should remind us of the UBA's ballplayers. This analogy works on several levels. Like them, Nixon is trying to unravel myth and separate fact from invention; unknown to Nixon, just as it was unknown to the players, everything within his sphere of action has been laid out in advance, in part by Coover (the shaper of elements within the novel) and in part by history itself. Just as Paul Trench struggled in the last chapter of *The UBA* with his tragic role, Nixon is constantly bothered with the sensation that he is an actor in a play that has already been written: "Applause, director, actor, script: yes, it was like—and this thought hit me now like a revelation—it was like a little morality play for our generation!" What distresses Nixon about this realization is what lies behind the classic existentialist argument against the existence of God: to admit a higher order is to deny one's own freedom to operate. Yet to deny this higher authority and confront the "lie of purpose" is also difficult for Nixon, as is indicated by his desire to discover final answers and assign everything to predetermined categories. Thus part of his attraction to Uncle Sam is that he views Sam as "our Superchief in an age of Flux." In one of the book's most important scenes, Nixon takes a harrowing ride with the disguised Phantom, whose later designation as "The Creator of Ambiguities" helps crystallize the opposition, and is given a lecture which should sound familiar to readers acquainted with Coover's previous work:

> "Look," he said, his voice mellowing, losing its hard twang, "can't we get past all these worn-out rituals, these stupid fuckin' reflexes?" It wouldn't do any good to grab him, I knew. The ungraspable Phantom. He was made of nothing solid, your hand would just slip right through, probably turn leprous forever. "They got nothin' to do with life, you know that, life's always new and changing, so why fuck it up with all this shit about scapegoats, sacrifices, initiations, saturnalias—? . . . life's too big, you can't wrap it up like that!"

At this stage, Nixon is too frightened to grasp the importance of this message; later, however, he begins making discoveries of his own that confirm the Phantom's basic premise. Realizing that what has been bothering him all along was "that sense that everything was somehow inevitable, as though it had all been scripted out in advance," Nixon goes on to provide a neat summary of what much of Coover's work suggests:

> But bullshit! There were no scripts, no necessary patterns, no final scenes, there was just *action,* and then *more action!* Maybe in Russia History had a plot because one was being laid on, but not here—*that was what freedom was all about!* It was what Uncle Sam had been trying to tell me: *Act—act in the living present! . . .* This, then, was my crisis: to accept what I already knew. That there was no author, no director, and the audience had no memories—they got reinvented every day! . . . It served to confirm an old belief of mine: that all men contain all views, right and left, theistic and atheistic, legalistic and anarchical, monadic and pluralistic; and only an artificial—call it political—commitment to consis-

tency makes them hold steadfast to singular positions.

It is because of his recognition that "nothing is predictable, anything can happen" that Nixon decides to work out his own script: to go to the Rosenbergs and try to extract a confession, even though he rightly senses that "in a sense [he] was no more free than the Rosenbergs were, [they had] both been drawn into dramas above and beyond those of ordinary mortals." Nixon's few moments with Ethel Rosenberg represent the culmination of his efforts to extract a kind of freedom within the rigid confines of history; the portrayal of these struggles, which blend comedy, pathos, and tragedy in near equal proportions, is *The Public Burning*'s major triumph.

Robert Coover on the evolution of *The Universal Baseball Association*:

After the story (which is, essentially, the second chapter of the book) was written, I felt that I hadn't gotten everything out of the metaphor, that I hadn't yet fully understood it. So over the years that followed I set about playing with the images, working out the Association history, searching out the structure that seemed to be hidden in it.

Even though structure is not profoundly meaningful in itself, I love to use it. This has been the case ever since the earliest things I wrote when I made an arbitrary commitment to design. The reason is not that I have some notion of an underlying ideal order which fiction imitates, but a delight with the rich ironic possibilities that the use of structure affords. Any idea, even one which on the surface doesn't seem very interesting, fitted with a perfect structure, can blossom into something that even I did not suspect was there originally. Engaging in that process of discovery is the excitement of making fiction.

Robert Coover, in First Person: Conversations on Writers & Writings, *edited by Frank Gado, 1973.*

David Montrose   (review date 5 May 1986)

SOURCE: "A Hell of a Party," in *The Times Literary Supplement,* No. 4335, May 5, 1986, p. 486.

[*In the following review, Montrose faults* Gerald's Party *for being uninspired and for failing to attain Coover's "usual standard of excellence."*]

In form, if not in quality, Robert Coover's latest novel, *Gerald's Party*—his first full-length work since the savage Cold War burlesque, *The Public Burning,* eight years ago—is reminiscent of Flann O'Brien's *The Third Policeman.* Both feature a murder as the starting-point for a chain of comic bizarrerie recounted by a hero—on this occasion, Gerald himself—who, though regularly disconcerted, sees nothing fundamentally unnatural about each new turn of events.

Coover begins *in media res:* the eponymous shindig—densely populated by the affluent and arty—is advanced enough for widespread insobriety to have set in. Then a body is observed face-down on the carpet, stabbed to death: Ros, an untalented but beautiful actress who has been the lover of almost every man present, Gerald especially. The police are summoned. The ensuing investigation, commanded by the metaphysically-inclined Inspector Pardew, lampoons the conventions of the detective story. Pardew, like the best Golden Age sleuths, appears to be a man of superior intellect:

> Murder, like laughter, is a muscular solution of conflict, biologically substantial and inevitable, a psychologically imperative and, in the case of murder, death-dealing act that *must* be related to the *total ontological reality!*

His methods, however, prove unreliable: having, for example, confiscated everyone's watch in order to calculate (quite how is unclear) the time of the killing, he pinpoints it at half an hour after his arrival. What's more, "for all his fancy talk", as one of his two underlings remarks, Pardew "still seems to suspect foreigners, perverts, freaks and bums, just like the rest of us". He also presides over hard-boiled interrogations: early on, claiming self-defence, his men beat to death (with croquet mallets) the much-cuckolded husband of the deceased. The plot-twists are familiar to the genre. Possible clues and murder weapons come to light and puzzling incidents occur. And, of course, there are further corpses, including one supplied by Gerald, who puts a mortally wounded friend out of his misery. Coover, though, offers obscurity rather than fair and square mystification. Little is clarified.

While the investigation proceeds, the party—recharged by an influx of new arrivals—picks up and flourishes riotously. As in *The Public Burning,* Coover's humour relies heavily on ribald slapstick. Ros's corpse is its chief butt. Kept on the premises at Pardew's insistence, the dead girl suffers frequent indignities: assorted maulings and gropings; having her panties removed, cut into pieces, and distributed among the party-goers as souvenirs; being posed for sensationalist press photographs; and, finally "playing herself " in a play mounted on the spot by former theatrical colleagues.

Meanwhile, the characters tell each other weird stories and consume huge quantities of food and drink; sporadic outbreaks of violence cause damage to persons and property (Gerald's furnishing undergo extensive maltreatment); sexual couplings and triplings occur. Gerald's stream-of-consciousness enhances the prevailing air of strangeness and ambiguity: his perceptions are hazily incomplete, the line of his narrative regularly fractured by snatches of overheard speech, things glimpsed, reminiscences, meditations on love and drama. Unfortunately, this time, Coover's black comedy rarely shows inspiration.

Gerald's Party is intended as social satire, exposing the crude sensualism which underlies the guests' cultural pretensions, the moral insensibility which blinds them to all but pleasure: "You *know* what kind of world we live in", one tells his host in a rare moment of gravity, "so why are they letting you even *have* parties like this?" The signs are,

indeed, that the cartoon universe they inhabit does not merely represent modern America, satirically distorted, but (as in *The Third Policeman*) a circular hell they, or perhaps Gerald alone, have earned for such vices. O'Brien's nameless hero was condemned forever to repeat a series of terrible adventures, on each occasion experiencing them—together with the attendant surprise and fear—as for the first time. Gerald recurrently experiences vague feelings of *déjà vu* from the start of the novel, finally being reminded—when he laments, "It will never be the same again"—that the night's events are not unique: "You said that last time, Gerald. After Archie and Emma and . . . ." On the closing page, he remembers, without sharing the memory, "why it was we held these parties. And would, as though compelled, hold another."

Significantly, too, one of Pardew's orotund pronouncements concerns a theory of time similar to that advanced by the philosopher, J. W. Dunne, whose influence O'Brien acknowledged. In *The Third Policeman,* the nature of hell fits the sin. If the same applies here, Coover's damned have earned, through self-indulgence and callousness, an afterlife where those sins are unconfined. These parallels do not, alas, prevent the novel failing by some distance to reach Coover's usual standard of excellence.

Lois Gordon on Robert Coover's style:

Coover has developed a style unique among his contemporaries, mixing so-called fact and fiction with realism and surrealism, merging narrative line with adjacent and "descanting" poetic or fragmentary evocations of moral, mythic, historical, philosophical, and psychological dimensions. He writes in virtually every form, including short story, poetry, fairy tale, filmscript, drama, and novel. Within each, he demonstrates a remarkable diversity of styles and manipulates the trappings of every conventional literary form from old comedy to theater of the absurd; he also translates or transposes techniques associated with other art forms—e.g., film montage and operatic interludes. Any of these might then be transformed into the most extreme forms of parody. Coover has the uncanny ability to reproduce or mimic verbally the written, spoken, or even kinesthetic styles of literally hundreds of historical or popular figures. He can also arouse the emotions traditionally associated with tragedy. Regardless of length—and he has published noticeably long and short fiction—his work is always rich and difficult. Throughout, one would have a hard time finding an ill-chosen word or awkward phrase.

Lois Gordon, in her Robert Coover: The Universal Fictionmaking Process, *1983.*

Janusz Semrau   (essay date 1986)

SOURCE: "Robert Coover," in his *American Self-Conscious Fiction of the 1960s and 1970s: Donald Barthelme, Robert Coover, Ronald Sukenick,* Poznan, 1986, pp. 64-98.

[*In the following excerpt, Semrau cites* The Origin of the Brunists, The Public Burning, *and* The Universal Baseball Association *as examples of Coover's "musicalization of literature."*]

Robert Coover ranks unquestionably among the most versatile contemporary authors. A "literary polyglot," as one critic has called him, he has tried his hand at poetry and translation, has written a collection of plays, a book of short stories and many uncollected short fictions, six novellas (two of them in the form of film-scripts), and three novels ranging from the mere two-hundred-page *The Universal Baseball Association*—through the solid, four hundred pages long *The Origin of the Brunists*—to the truly encyclopedic *The Public Burning.*

While Barthelme foregrounds artifice in his writing basically through miniaturization, contraction and linguistic terseness, Coover secures it very often through flamboyant, almost extravagant elaboration. Though it is largely a function of the author's style, in his two longest works it is also very much a structural property. In general, however, Coover's fiction lacks overtly self-reflective or otherwise aggressive strategies aimed at instantaneous piercing of the reader's habitual universe of discourse by, as Barthelme would have it, "kicking him in the knee." "I don't like, on the whole, assaults on the audience. I don't like assaults on anybody really" [*Shanti,* Summer 1972]. Commenting on the innovative writing of his generation (both Barthelme and Sukenick are mentioned here), Coover said: "We were all working in a vacuum. It was only our books appeared in the . . . early sixties that we realized we were dealing with the same kinds of things" [*Antioch Review,* Summer 1982]. The "same kinds of things" had to do with the growing sense of dissatisfaction with conventional formulas of literature and the subsequent radical reaction against them. The main character of Coover's first novel voices a rather desperate reflection: "Should have never invented the written word. Kept folly hopelessly alive." It clearly partakes of Barthelme's observation that signs are only signs and some of them are "lies" or, even more closely, of his motion to retract "the whole written world."

The Origin of the Brunists (1966) is, both from a critical and biographical point of view, a rather uncomfortable book. As the author has repeatedly stressed, it is not his first work, most of *Pricksongs and Descants* and the core story of *The Universal Baseball Association* having been written before it. Although formally acknowledged as the best first novel by an American author of the year, its reception was from the beginning mixed, and in the overall perspective of Coover's writing it is not regarded as his outstanding work.

By saying that his intention was to present an exemplary realistic narrative, the author himself seems to be "responsible" for the misinterpretation of the book. Actually, on more than one occasion he has identified himself as a realistic writer. But then the same label could be easily applied to Barthelme who, having found the world to be absurd committed himself to affirm its absurdity by simply recording it. This is also the essence of Coover's understanding of literary realism: "All these topics . . . of the realis-

tic novel are not realistic topics. They are not out there in the world" [unpublished interview with Janusz Semrau]. Although with *The Origin of the Brunists* he thought of it as "paying dues"—"I didn't feel I had the right to move into more presumptuous fictions until I could prove I could handle the form as it was"—in the process he "turned it into [his] kind of book" [Frank Gado, *First Person,* 1973]. As Larry McCaffery notes: "From our perspective today, it is obvious that *The Origin of the Brunists* shares with other innovative books of the time (*V.,* Barth's *Giles Goat-Boy,* Barthelme's *Snow White,* Sukenick's *Up*) a sense of self-consciousness, outrageousness, and a flaunting of artifice" [*Dictionary of Literary Biography,* Vol. 2]. In formal terms the sense of artistic self-consciousness derives here basically from the use of certain organizing principles of musical composition. The paradox about *The Origin of the Brunists* is that as far as events are concerned there is really nothing unreal in it, but the novel's design is born of "something else," namely the nineteenth-century symphonic form: "I was looking for a way I could get the movement set up and the way the sections inside could work." In larger terms, Coover explains that he has a vision of narrative as "a certain kind of motion":

> Music is a particularly strong example of this because you're riding the time line in a very specific way. It's a time line that is so abstract, and yet carrying us from here to there in a very clear narrative way.

The earliest attempts at systematic musicalization of literature are usually attributed to the German Romantic poets and the French symbolists of half a century later. André Gide and Aldous Huxley were the first to theorize about the role of music in the novel, and to implement the idea on a large scale in their own work. As William Freedman says, the aim of the musical novel is "not to halt time in pattern of imagery, but somehow to reproduce its insistent flow in moving patterns of narrative, memory, and thought" [*Laurence Sterne and the Origins of the Musical Novel,* 1978]. The symphonic form, normally taken to signify an extended and thoroughly developed work for orchestra, seems to be very well suited for this kind of undertaking.

The Origin of the Brunists opens with a short prologue adumbrating the story and anticipating its resolution. The section can be compared to the first, fast allegro movement of a symphony which provides a point of departure and often also the title for the whole composition. Coover's prologue is very lively and quick:

> Hiram Clegg, together with his wife Emma and four friends of the faith from Randolph Junction, were summoned by the Spirit and Mrs. Clara Collins, widow of the beloved Nazarene preacher Ely Collins, to West Condon on the weekend of the eighteenth and nineteenth of April, there to await the End of the World. What did he really expect?

In the classical symphony the allegro is followed by a slow movement introducing some variation of form. Accordingly, the beginning of Part One in Coover's novel is marked by a perceptibly different tempo than the Prologue:

> Clouds have massed, dooming in the small world of West Condon. The patches of old snow, crusted black with soot in full daylight, now appear to whiten as the sky dulls toward evening. The temperature descends. Slag smoke sours in the air.

As the narrative sketches leisurely its setting, we are also introduced in the first ten pages of the chapter to most of the characters. Soon, the work reveals its full, orchestralike amplitude, with the impressive, diverse cast of over twenty vividly delineated major figures and a host of lesser ones. When the story gets properly under way the book begins vibrating with a dazzling variety of styles and voices, resembling the symphonic principles of transformation and flexibility. Combined with conventional third-person narration and occasional journalistic reportage are sermons, lyrics, monologues, unattributed dialogues, stream-of-consciousness passages and voices from the supernatural. Some sections are written in italics, some in boldface, some are typographically spaced out. There are also sequences endowed with rhythm and musicality of their own, and later in the novel the scale of its narrative technique is enriched with the epistolary form and elements of staged drama.

On the thematic plane the book achieves the symphonic effect of multiformity and kinetic movement through a number of apparently independent subplots, digressions, anecdotes, and jokes.

> Meditate on Beethoven. The changes of moods, the abrupt transitions. Majesty alternating with a joke, for example, in the first movement of the B flat major Quartet. Comedy suddenly hinting at prodigious and tragic solemnities. . . . All you need is a sufficiency of character and parallel, contrapuntal plots.

All these ideas of musical contrast, transition and modulation on which Philip Quarles speculates in *Point Counter Point* are very much present in *The Origin of the Brunists.* Exemplary in this respect is the theme of love and sex. Idealism and purity of feeling are juxtaposed with adultery and crude desire; adolescent initiation is set next to voyeurism and sadism. This is, incidentally, where Coover reveals at one point more conspicuously than anywhere else in the novel his playful, "manipulative" authorial disposition. Part Three closes with a routine, forced marital bedscene:

> She runs her hands inside his pajama pants. He is still irritated with her for having turned him on. . . . "Is he risen?" she asks in his ear then, astonishingly resurrecting this old premarital collegetime joke of theirs. . . . "Indeed," he whispers, rolling on his back to receive her: "he is risen!"

The opening of Part Four continues this play on words, but the context is totally different:

> West Condon, as though unable to gaze and longer look upon the deep black reach of night, rolls

over on its back to receive the Monday sun, now rising, as men say. . . .

In traditional literary terms, Coover's first novel follows, as Richard Andersen has noted, a variety of modes: novel of manners, psychological novel, social satire, fabulous story, religious parody, black humor novel, soap opera, and radical protest novel [*Robert Coover,* 1981].

Obviously, musical expansion is not endless and the classical symphony is probably more than any other form marked by unity of design and rigor of execution. It usually consists of four distinct major movements and is characteristically circular, being governed by the principles of exposition, development, and return or dramatic recapitulation of its motifs. *The Origin of the Brunists* is made up of four parts and all the subplots eventually converge to produce a quasi-apocalyptic ending. The musical idée fixe introduced into the symphony by Berlioz at the beginning of the nineteenth century is present in the book in the guise of an obsessive religious cult whose growth is its principle, immediate theme. The novel ends with an epilogue entitled appropriately "Return," which rounds off the main story lines. In this sense—with its tail in the mouth, so to speak, as well as its movements of repetition and return—the novel clearly departs from the linearity of structure inherited from Aristotle and basically observed in literature until the twentieth century. As we have suggested earlier and as Larry McCaffery stresses in *The Metafictional Muse,* "if Coover is 'paying dues' to traditional fiction in *The Brunists,* his payments often seem to be made with ambivalent feelings [since] he constantly undercuts the realistic impulses of the book."

An interesting, if familiar, element signalling (the need for) creative self-consciousness is the figure of Justin Miller, a newspaper editor who is the central character of the novel. "[His] name supplies the first clue about his role, for Justin was a second-century writer and apologist for Christianity" [Larry McCaffery, in *The Metafictional Muse,* 1982]. Miller becomes somewhat inadvertently the new cult's public relations man and its historian, and thus sets much of the story in motion. However, although he does not altogether lack a sense of order and is aware of the "fictionality" of the movement, he gets entangled in it like most of the others. As Coover explains elsewhere, "his confused vision of things spreads through the narrative like a mild high, comforting, sleep-inducing." The only one to preserve personal integrity and to maintain distance toward the maddening Brunists controversy is Miller's enigmatic assistant, Lou Jones. Though seemingly a marginal character, this is precisely where the author of the book, Robert Coover, otherwise practically absent from it, can be located.

> Jones had a knack . . . [for] a goddamn song-and-dance act that had had the whole klatch laughing and crying at the same time. . . . [He was] gifted with an uncommonly facile feedback system, making his way any way he could, keeping a perverse eye out and telling good stories about what he saw . . . though his humor sometimes had a way of biting too deep.

In this respect *The Origin of the Brunists* reminds of *King,*

Queen, Knave with its minor figure of perverse old Enricht as Nabokov's Machiavellian double. Enricht passes noiselessly through this apparently conventional narrative only to declare surprisingly at one point: "I do everything . . . I make everything. I alone." When he reveals later in the novel to be a "famed illusionist and conjuror," we need not even be told that "the whole world was but a trick of his, and all those people . . . owed their existence to the power of his imagination." Although Coover does not grant his own surrogate just as much power, Lou Jones likewise leaves an occasional imprint on the progress of the story:

> "Mount of Redemption," said Sal.
>
> "I never heard it called that," Vince said. "When did it—?"
>
> "Tiger Miller's old buddy Lou Jones made it up."
>
> "What's the point?"
>
> "What's the point of any cunt?" asked George, and they all laughed idiotically at that.

Significantly enough, the Mount of Redemption provides setting for the climatic scene of the novel, and Lou Jones is the sole person who remains unaffected by the general frenzy of the moment. This is only natural since he seems to be in fact orchestrating the whole event. The posture in which he is presented brings to mind none other than that of Velazquez in "Las Meninas":

> . . . now Miller saw him, moving impassively up the hill, photographing them as he went, kneeling for angles. . . . Jones, in drooping fedora and glistening raincoat, shaped like a big dark bag made an odd contrast to the frenetic worshipers who performed for his lens. There was something almost contemplative . . . almost statuesque about him as he crouched to peer into the instrument in his lap. . . . [Again] he . . . saw Jones, slyly amused, in modest retreat partway down the hill, photographing it all.

The book divorces itself from the earnestness of its proclaimed/supposed genre also through various, often quite elaborate patterns of numerological coincidences and recurrences. Most of them center on the number 7. Initially, with epigraphs like "Write what you see in the book and send it to the Seven Churches," "Of every clean beast thou shalt take to thee seven and seven, the male and his female . . . ," they might seem to add to the atmosphere surrounding the evolution of the new religious cult. However, after just a little of this sort of number-chasing, "we sense that Coover is playing a joke on us—inducing *us* to establish fictional patterns in much the same way" [McCaffery, in *The Metafictional Muse*]. Indeed, as a subjective choice, any given number can generate imaginative and perfectly autonomous games and fantasies. In this case seven and its multiples can be in fact regarded as the writer's peculiar self-conscious trademark or ironic signature. The frequency with which it appears in the world of *The Origin of the Brunists,* or rather the way it is forced upon it, clearly defies all standards of probability. When

we first meet Justin Miller, he is sitting in his office staring out the window—"unwashed in fourteen years." His high-school basketball number was 14, and so is the sum of the figures on the license plate of his car. One night he realizes within a dream that all this had happened to him when he was "in the seventh grade." Vince Bonali, the other major character of the novel, happens to have seven children; a shot of whiskey hits him one morning like "seven hundred blazing bicarbonates," and one of his sons is reported to have been AWOL "since the seventh of April." When the novel opens the Brunists history is in its fourteenth week, and at this point the community is "just seven short months" from city elections. The mining disaster which sparks off the movement "reduces itself to numbers," and so does the whole cult. In the fatal accident from which Giovanni Bruno emerges as a prophet he is the only survivor out of 98 trapped miners ("the infamous product of fourteen and seven"). There are six other men with him at the time, they entomb themselves up in a room around the fourteenth east and seventh south shaft of the mine, and on that particular night a local basketball game is stopped with the score 14-11. Furthermore: "The number between nine and seven, eight, was the date of the explosion, and the day of the rescue was eleven, two one's or two, the difference between nine and seven." Fourteen is the number of weeks separating the critical event and the expected end of the world; March 21 proves to be "the first day of the sign of rebirth and the night Mrs. Collins' house burned, marking mystically the commencement of their final trial," and the new creed itself is based on "the seven Words" Giovanni Bruno ever manages to utter following his rescue. Finally, all but one of the four Parts of the novel consist of seven chapters; the other one has twelve sections, but together with the Prologue and the Epilogue it makes another multiple of the notorious number. It is also in this context that we may say after Barthelme that "repetition is reality" since by recalling again and again the number 7 *The Origin of the Brunists* creates its arbitrary and independent, numerological, reality. What emphasizes the nature of the book are frequent, deliberately baffling time-checks. They may contribute to the growing intensity of action, but their ultimate inconsequentiality and obtrusive manner in which they are presented clearly punctuate the text with another bluntly artificial element.

Five years after the appearance of *The Origin of the Brunists* Coover published a quasi-novella *The Water Pourer* which was originally to be included as a chapter in the novel. In a two-page preface to it the author explains "the process of something coming in and going out of the text and what the text is like." This short essay can be seen in itself as an outline of his creative aesthetics. Since in general, Coover argues, art is "a polarizing lens" and the narrative—"like the universe"—is "explosive," at some point you have to "contain" it. Obviously, "weak vision is not suited for these explosions." The symphonic form and numerological games (the principles of design and modulation) is what informs the strength of Coover's vision in *The Origin of the Brunists.* They contain its narrative flow and draw the reader to see what the author himself sees, thus preventing "the loss of the reader to the explosion itself." The general idea is to "make an attractive and curious shape and drive the narrative through it, absorbing part of [the reader's] peripheral vision." In more personal terms, Coover has explained in an interview:

> Even though structure is not profoundly meaningful in itself, I love to use it. This has been the case ever since the earliest things I wrote when I made an arbitrary commitment to design. The reason is not that I have some notion of an underlying ideal of order which fiction imitates, but a delight with the rich ironic possibilities that the use of structure affords.

The Public Burning (1977), a real whale of a book which established Coover as a major voice in contemporary fiction, brings considerable extension and refinement of the stylistic technique and the narrative strategy employed in *The Origin of the Brunists.* With all parts divided into seven chapters each and some pertinent (if only marginal) numerological speculations, the author's playful trademark is unmistakably present in the novel. Its four major movements, clearly marked opening and finale, sophisticated musical vocabulary, song lyrics and breath-taking rhythmical sequences seem to suggest another symphonic composition. Still, for all its disruptiveness as a structural principle in literature, the classical symphony goes historically only too well with the nineteenth-century concept of the realistic novel.

> Apart from *The Brunists* everything else that I did does not belong to that time. People have heard me say about the influence of music on my writing and then have tried to find a parallel and have criticized me on the ground that they do not see what they expected. I tend to like best of all either pre-Monteverdian music or contemporary music. I like Penderecki, for example, or Ligeti. The idea of cramming tons and tons of little bits of sounds.

Donald Barthelme's appreciation of twentieth-century music [quoted in *The Radical Imagination and the Liberal Tradition,* 1982] comes in particularly useful here:

> . . . it has to do with bombardment . . . and that's a structural concept. . . . The aesthetic idea being what it would be like if we had all this noise pulled together and then turned up very high—increase the volume. . . . It's late twentieth-century music, which is, clearly, noise.

The subject matter of *The Public Burning* is even more "outrageous" than that of the previous book. It focuses on the famous and controversial Rosenberg spy case of the early 1950s and dramatizes a well-known political figure, Richard Nixon. Basically, the narrative deals with the two days and nights preceding the execution, but the novel includes absolutely everything that might have had any bearing on the trial—from the Korean War and contemporary government scandals and intrigues to cultural and pop cultural aspects of America. The author's vast and ironic vision makes him put in the pages of *The Public Burning* things that are normally considered to be outside the realm of belles-lettres. The mode of presentation deliberately confounds rather than expounds the action, which is thus immediately charged with literariness. We are bombarded with what appears to be an endless recitation of documentary facts, figures, dates, quotes, testimonies, speeches, interviews, autonomous essays, and various topical "debris" gathered from newspapers, magazines, movies, TV and radio programs, Broadway plays, advertisements, sports scores, etc.

> . . . like the 4998732500 foreign aid bill, little numbers like the 5 tons of gravel and dirt that Jimmy Willi is buried under in Lambertsville. The 6-2 record of Vinegar Bend Mizell. *The 500 Fingers of Dr. T.* by Dr. Seuss—You've got to see 480,000-key piano hit an atomic clinker! WITH STEREOPHONIC SOUND! Allison Choate of Apawamis cards a 77. 55 Chinese are ordered out of the country, Eleanor Hortense Almond dies at 103. Volume declines to 1010000 shares on the New York Stock Exchange. The President is visited by 100 schoolchildren, and the Vice President tells Senator Taft: "I broke 100 at Burning Tree Sunday, Bob!"

As Coover appears to be somewhat teasingly explaining at the outset of the novel, the "reasons" for this general strategy of diffusion (more specifically of informational excess and radical recontextualization) are "theatrical, political, whimsical." While the book aims at and succeeds in projecting the sense of dynamism and constant movement of American life and character ("I was striving for a text that would seem to have been written by the whole nation through all its history. . . . I wanted thousands of echos, all the sounds of the nation."), its primary goal is to expose the complex and ultimately stupifying operations of history and social myths. The writer's frankly biased treatment of history goes back to the roots of his creative philosophy, namely to his commitment to a relativistic vision of reality. In *The Public Burning* he calls objectivity "an impossible illusion," and has Nixon wonder: "What was fact, what intent, what was framework, what was essence?" At this point, with his famous pronouncement that all visible objects are but as pasteboard masks, Melville invites another interesting comparison. Many of Coover's chapter headlines seem to be taken out of *Moby Dick:* "All Aboard the 'Look Ahead, Neighbor Special'," "High Noon," "The Eye in the Sky," "Spreading the Table of Glory," "A Rash of Evil Doings," "The Phantom's Hour," "How to Handle a Bloodthirsty Mob," "Something Truly Dangerous," "Uncle Sam Strikes Back." Both works share many features, such as proliferation of characters, improbable coincidences, dramatic tension, density of references and allusions, elements of other genres.

Robert Coover ranks unquestionably among the most versatile contemporary authors.

—*Janusz Semrau*

Based on the belief that "the more elaborate the attempt to hide fiction, the creakier it becomes," *The Public Burning* features artifice as an essential element of its total reality and brings the reader's attention to the fiction-making process or, in the author's own words, "exposes its activity as it goes along."

> I've never had anyone come up and ask: "Were they really executed in Time Square?". . . . The main thing, I think, is that anyone reading the book is aware from the very first line that he's reading a book of fiction.

Not only in this respect, but in a more general artistic sense the power of the novel resides just as much in its style as in its content. On the level of language the narrative seems to delight in elaboration and sheer extravaganza. Much of it is self-apparent or, to use the writer's favorite phrase, "look-ma-no-hands" virtuosity fiction. The book includes in its stylistic repertoire rhetorical parody, deliberate agrammatical utterances, abstruse and protruded puns and anagrams, finally various paralinguistic gestures.

> "Who—Whoo—Whoop! Who'll come gouge with me? Who'll come bite with me? Rowff—Yough—Snort—YAHOO!"

> "Knock knock!" Eh? Who dere? "Grassy!" Grassy? Grassyquien? "Grassy-ass, amigos! Mooch-ass grassy-ass! Ha ha, de nada, jefe!"

> "Ah see no pahticulah point in sendin' may-un to Ko-REE-ya to dai, Mistah Cheymun," declaims Congressman Wheeler, "whahl ay-tomic spies are allowed to liy-uv heah at HOME! One Justice yieldin' to the voCIF'rous my-NOR-utty preshuh groups of this yere CUNT-tree is indee-FENsuble! Ah can-NOT sit ahdly by HEah in this yere layjus-LaY-tuv BAHDY without seekin' to DO somethin' abaout it!"

> The new President was packaged and sold by BBDandO as "Strictly a No-Deal Man Clean as a Hound's Tooth Who Will Go to Korea Restore Faith in God and Country On a Crusade to Clean Up Creeping Socialism Five-Percenters the Mess in Washington Crook Cronies Mink Coats Deep Freezers and Rising Inflation."

> "Too many have gawn CRAY-zy ovuh so-cawled SS-EVIL rahhts, a CUM-yunist propaganda FAY-vrit, and this heah class a PEE-pul is ri-SPWAN-subble fer this heah FOO-lishnuss!"

Earl Rovit's perceptive review of *The Public Burning* [*The American Book Review*, Vol. 15, December, 1977] concludes by asserting that it is not ultimately "about" the Rosenberg trial, the Cold War, or the early traumas of Richard Nixon—"Coover's central concern . . . is with words." In larger terms, the book is characterized by constant changes in point of view and narrative tempo, shifts from the present to the past tense, juxtaposition, montage and unexpected intercuttings. At one point Nixon comes up with an emotionally voiced reflection which proves to be an apt commentary on the novel's performance:

> There were no scripts, no necessary patterns, no final scenes, there was just action, and then more action! . . . that was what freedom was all about! . . . Act—act in the living present!

The Public Burning underscores its fictionality with various graphic elements: captions, italics, ellipse and typographical designs, e.g.,

> it
> was a
> sickening and
> to americans almost
> incredible history of men
> so fanatical that they would destroy
> their own countries and col
> leagues to serve a
> treacherous
> utopi
> a

Apart from song lyrics, similarly inserted in the text are Coover's own, rather peculiar, nursery rhymes:

> He's in here, boys, the hole's wore slick!
> Run here, Sam, with ye forked stick!
> Stand back, boys, an' le's be wise,
> Fer I think I see his beaded eyes!

There are also bigger, topological designs. The narrative assumes several times the guise of staged drama or musical/music hall, with scene descriptions (including costumes, props, etc.) and stage directions in self-contained "Intermezzo" pieces of some ten pages each. They might, as they do in music, connect the main parts of the composition, but their primary impact is only too obviously disruptive. Although the novel is so meticulously documented, it is unmistakably Coover himself who manages the stage and directs the drama. As Robert Alter observes [in *Partial Magic: The Novel as a Self-Conscious Genre*, 1975]: "the theater within the novel is a conspicuous vehicle of fictional self-consciousness, beginning with Master Pedro's puppet show in *Don Quixote;* and . . . we cannot escape . . . from the awareness that in abandoning the artifice of narration [the author] has adopted the artifice of the theater."

Five years before the publication of *The Public Burning* Coover said in a general context: "I love spectacle and virtuosity and risk-taking and the feeling of being surrounded by the setting." All these elements are certainly present in the book. In the final analysis the most intriguing of them is probably willed "risk-taking." One of the most ambitious and audacious contemporary works of fiction, the novel appears to be a precarious high-wire act. Initially, it may give the impression of disarray, uncontrollable narrative flow and ungraspable spatial realities. On closer scrutiny, however, it teems with symmetries and proves to be tightly contained. What gives the book an immediate sense of control and discipline of execution is its outer numerological organization. Inner balance is achieved by means of regularly alternating narrative voices of the author (text) and the main hero, Richard Nixon. The former offers chapters of straight impersonal presentation which, in general, are characterized by dynamism and linguistic as well as formal exuberance. The latter is by comparison more conventional, obtuse and meditative. The single most important structural (also thematic) entity is Uncle Sam. As the embodiment of the American spirit or, as is the case here, American hysteria and as such an apt extension of the atom bomb image, he/it is the centrifugal and centripetal pivot of the novel. As Sharon Spencer suggests in *Space, Time and Structure in the Modern Novel* [1971],

> . . . an ideal image for the visualization of how motion is suggested by "constructed" fiction is the circle; its center must be thought of as representing the subject of the book; the circumference, the point of view or the perspective from which it is seen.

Although in the physical sense the author's stance is that of positive self-effacement, his personal bitter irony and hilarious humor (Nixon as clown) are readily recognizable and are felt throughout the novel. Even if, as defined self-reflexively through Justin Miller, Coover's humor sometimes has "a way of biting too deep," this is precisely the realm in which the book vests—next to imagination ("THIS WORLD IS BUT CANVAS TO OUR IMAGINATIONS!")—its ultimate message: " 'always leave 'em laughin' as you say good-bye!' ".

As for the overall intent and final effect of **The Public Burning,** Coover "uses [it] to fight a pestilential fire with a fire that purifies. And even if his success is limited and evanescent—as it must necessarily be—it is a success that aggrandizes all of us" [Earl Rovit].

Talking with Thomas Bass about characteristic features of his literary generation Coover mentioned—next to "the reaction against the sclerosis of old forms," and "the adoption of self-conscious narrators"—an interest in pre-novel forms: "allegories, saints' lives, myths, epistolary romances, fairy tales, legends." **The Universal Baseball Association, Inc., J. Henry Waugh, Prop.** (1968) partakes of most of these conventions, with the concept of allegory as its most conspicuous lineament. The clue to it is the book's epigraph taken from Kant's *Critique of Judgement:* "It is not at all requisite to prove that such an intellectus archetypus is possible, but only that we are led to the Idea of it . . ." The novel leads us to origins of creativity and subsequently takes to grotesque limits the authorial dream and sacred privilege of long standing—the demiurgic, absolute control over the work of art.

The hero of the book, an aged and lonely bachelor, invents a complicated game played with dice and charts. The game has its own dialectics, a huge history behind it, and a potentially infinite horizon ahead of it. The title suggests, in fact, that it is a universe in its own right, with Henry not only its sole proprietor but also its fundamental "prop." As several critics have observed, his full name, J. Henry Waugh, makes an acronym translating itself as Yahweh—the Hebrew name for God.

All the while Henry brings to life new characters, controls their fortunes, and plays arbitrarily with time. He is most attentive to detail and concerned with effect. He thinks long, for instance, before deciding on a name for a new player:

> Bus stop. Whistlestop. Whistlestop Busby, second base . . . Thornton's. He'd been looking for a name to go with Shadwell, and maybe that was it. Thornton Shadwell. Tim's boy. Pitcher like the old man? Probably. But a lefty.

The immediate excitement is obviously in the play itself

but the part of it he "enjoys most" is "writing it up in the Book." Henry had always been drawn to games and experimented with a variety of them, but in the long run it was "the beauty of the records system which found a place to keep forever each least action—that had led Henry to baseball as his final project." Much as he hates his real job, this is actually where the game connects with his professional skill and career as an accountant. Henry's boss explains to him one day: "Accounting like baseball is an art . . . and a rough competitive business. Some make it and some don't." The same applies even more directly to creative writing which seems to be precisely Henry's art. Not only does he develop financial ledgers for each club, tabulate and file box scores, but provides each player with a comprehensive biography, invents dialogues, looks, mannerisms, and keeps a running and permanent record of the whole activity. "Now it consisted of some forty volumes. . . . He seemed to find more to write about, the more he played the game."

Henry's is indeed an artistic experience, and certain of its principles can be spelled out from his behavior. "The first phase in the creative process consists of frustration in reality. The creative person is faced with some dilemma . . . that cannot be resolved through ordinary problemsolving techniques" [Jay and Jean Harris, *The Roots of Artifice,* 1981]. Henry's game is not only a response to his humdrum personal existence but also to the devastating dreariness and absurdity of the world at large. To start with, "how could anyone take seriously" a sign like "Dunkelmann, Zauber and Zifferblat, Licensed Tax and General Accountants, Specializing in Small Firms, Bookkeeping Services and Systems, Payrolls and Payroll Taxes, Monthly, Quarterly and Annual Audits, Enter Without Knocking." Inside the drab office, "the clock on the wall . . . in its fat white roundness and hard black numbers always reminded Henry of Horace Zifferblat himself," and thus, befitting the boss' name and personal characteristics, of tyrannizing conventionality of time and dogmatic reverence for authority and hard work. As Waugh joins daily "the sour community on its morning pilgrimage," the streets appear to be "pregnant with the vague threat of confusion and emptiness," only to give him "a sober sense of fatality and closed circuits." The buses are often late and jammed, the drivers are heard "barking orders" and when a waitress sponges for him the table one morning, "the rag . . . smelled like something between an old goat and a dead fish." When he wants to buy flowers to commemorate a tragically "killed" player from his game, the florist offers him a prickly wreath which, to Henry's dismay and horror, turns out to be made of plastic.

> . . . a deep gloom was on him. He looked out, not to sink in. A dog barked at a window. Cars passed. A child smashed ants on the sidewalk with an egg-shaped stone. No, not a stone. Plastic again.

Newspapers invariably speak about "Gold and silver shortages. Orgy that the cops broke up. Rapes and murder. Making of another large war." Henry registers more experience than others and he certainly does so with greater intensity:

Oh, yes, he was sick of it! He saw those news
guys, writing it all down . . . a pack of goddamn
leeches, inventing time and space, scared shitless
by the way things really were.

Actually, Waugh is something of a philosopher. He finds
it pleasant "to muse about the origins" and is often inclined to talk "about time and people and history and how
everything seemed to flow confusedly together." As a larger version of the journalistic distortion of reality, history
in fact deeply disturbs and depresses him: "History my
god. An incurable diarrhea of dead immortals." Henry develops a similar attitude toward popular values and stereotypes symbolized in the novel by real baseball, "THE
GREAT AMERICAN GAME":

"You don't go to games, real ones?"

"Not for years now. The first game I saw . . .
I nearly fell asleep. . . . I would leave a game,
elbowing out with all the others, and feel a kind
of fear that I could so misuse my life."

In the essay "Poetic Creativity, Process and Personality"
[from *Creativity and the Individual,* 1960], R.N. Wilson
defines acquisition of technique as the second stage of the
creative process. "Experience must be translated into
form, and to do so, the poet must acquire technique. . . .
Technical mastery develops from exposure to models and
practice in skills." This stage of artistic development can
be found in Henry's trial-and-error experimentation with
other games. Also, before he finally plunges into the world
of the Association he spends a long time meticulously per-
fecting its rules and the basic technique of play. Every artist is believed to entertain faith in his vocation and the
unique significance of his own work. "Being refused a social recognition on the basis of his work is the professional
creator's trauma. He resolves this trauma syndromatically
through his pursuit of the fantasy of greatness" [Harris
and Harris]. Even though his sole friend, Lou, suggests
that maybe "it's not worth it," for Henry his enterprise is
obviously "more than just another ball game," it is an
"event of the first order." Actually, he is aware that some
people might view his game as (at best) "a kind of running
away," and he does not even try to achieve any social reputation along this line. Instead, he does indeed fantasize
about greatness as such:

. . . what a wonderful rare thing it is to do
something, no matter how small a thing, with
absolute unqualified unsurpassable perfection! . . . to do a thing so perfectly that, even if
the damn world lasted forever, nobody could
ever do it better. . . .

The simple statistics are ruled by the dice, but the logs are
governed by Henry's imagination. This is where his disposition and behavior respond to the next two stages of the
paradigmatically defined creative process: "the envision-
ing of combinations and distillations" and "elucidation of
the vision" [Wilson]:

This has been called insight, inspiration, or intuition, [but it] cannot be planned or ordered . . .
[it] may occur in a flash, at the end of deep consideration, or it may be set off by external stimu-

li. [Finally] conscious application of energy to
master the insight gained arises.

With phrases for the Book flashing through his head,

Henry paced the kitchen, his mind on several
things at once. He poured what was left of the
coffee, put another pot on.

. . . to the refrigerator, to the sink, back to the
table. He slapped the back of the chair with his
hand. Incredible!

He wrote out a few possible lead sentences on
scratch paper, but none appealed to him. He
stood, poured himself another cup of coffee, carried it back to the table and stood there, staring
down at the open Book.

Naturally enough, Waugh goes occasionally through
"dull-minded stretches," feeling "much like giving up,"

until one day that astonishing event would occur
that brought sudden life and immediacy . . . excitement, a certain dimension, color. The magic
of excellence. Under its charm . . . it could happen! Henry reeled around his chair a couple
times, laughing out loud. . . .

However overwrought and burlesque, the presented intellectus archetypus seems to contain a tacit autobiographical disclosure on Coover's part:

The way I can do work is . . . I get a kind of new
idea about something. Sometimes it just happens
itself . . . I see it and sit down and write it—not
very often though; I'm very lucky when that
happens.

"Attempting to accept the identity as an artist is a significant factor in the life of an artist. This is one reason the
adult artist seeks the company of other artists" [Harris
and Harris]. Appropriately enough, Lou is presented as an
artist in his own right. He is a comical food-artist who can
all the same be admired for his confrontation with the
"raw stuff" of his vocation:

It was amazing to watch Lou when he really attuned to his eating. All clumsiness vanished and
his fingers played over the food as upon a musical instrument, his face flushing with pleasure
and mild exertion.

Henry's friendship with Lou does well to display two diametrically different levels or modes of creativity. As B.
Chiselin would define it, Henry's art is of the higher, "ap-
plicative" sort, as it "alters the universe of meaning by introducing into it some new elements [and] some new order
of significance"—Lou's vocation is "reproductive" since
it merely "gives development to an established body of
meaning through initiating some advance in its use." It is
not surprising, therefore, that when Henry finally introduces Lou to the Universal Baseball Association, it does
not stir any imaginative response in his friend and the evening's game ends as a pitiful disaster.

With his mind constantly drifting back to his table, Henry
is able to feel himself perfectly and absolutely in tune with
his characters, setting, and action: "sweating with relief
and tension all at once, unable to sit, unable to think, in

there, with them! . . . licking his lips, dry from excitement." Given also the fact that his Book is, essentially, a conventional project—"functional details of the game were never mentioned [in it]"—Henry can be instructively linked with the nineteenth-century novel and its tradition. "It was in this period that many major novelists began to talk about a hallucinated sense of the presence of their imaginary characters, began to record a feeling of loss when they finished a book" [Alter].

For all its immediate features such as brute force, boisterousness or crude jokes, the world of the Association offers precisely that which Henry's own life and reality as he knows it lack: beauty, affection, excitement, justice, magnitude, order, and—above all—a sense of achievement and self-identity.

> The game was over.
>
> Giddily, Henry returned to the bathroom and washed his hands. He stared down at his wet hands, thinking: he did it! And then, at the top of his voice, "WA-HOO!" he bellowed, and went leaping back into the kitchen, feeling he could damn well take off. . . .

Waugh is not, at least initially, completely devoid of specifically authorial self-consciousness. Still, although he is also aware that it could be "a defining of the outer edges" and that "total one-sided participation in the league would soon grow even more oppressive than his job," Henry finally overestimates his capacities and underestimates the problems of his art. When in the 56th season of the game he plays nearly a quarter of it in just twenty-four hours instead of, as it usually required, two weeks, he loses the sense of his real self and of his situation. Consequently, his precarious equilibrium between neurotic and genuinely artistic disposition is destroyed. He can no longer discriminate among his experiences, begins to assume unconsciously the personalities of his players in public places, and mixes the world of the Association with the real one in general. As his personality keeps dissipating, Henry gives up his job, loses all control over the artifact, and in the end inexplicably disappears from the novel ("down there a couple blocks ahead: lead on, Barney! lead on!").

The Universal Baseball Association is not—formally—a work breaking new ground in literary self-consciousness. Also, it is self-conscious insofar that it is a self-reflexive (authorial) consideration of some larger problems involved in fiction-making. Still, it is certainly one of the most fascinating books about self-consciousness in art. Its message leaves no doubt about Robert Coover's own creative philosophy. A mature, truly self-aware artist will, as John Barth actually did, call the kind of histrionic disposition presented in the novel "a lot of baloney" [*Wisconsin Studies in Contemporary Literature,* Winter-Spring 1965]. Barth can be cited in this context as a spokesman for post-modern literature at large:

> You hear respectable writers, sensible people like Katherine Ann Porter, say the characters just take over. I'm not going to let those scoundrels take over. I am in charge. . . . When writers speak of . . . characters taking over and

space-time grids, it's usually because they don't know why they do the things they do.

Even if, as Margaret Heckard for instance argues, "taken as a whole Coover's works do not form a single coherent canon" [*Twentieth Century Literature,* May 1976], the present novel is not only a kind of compendium of ideas about writing, but can be treated as a guidebook to the author's own fiction as well. Many of Coover's central thematic concerns and even formal concepts are ingrained in *The Universal Baseball Association.* Though published nearly ten years after it, *The Public Burning* echoes almost ad verbum Waugh's interpretation of history. Also, with the detailed analysis of Henry's Book, the author seems to have had developed the idea for *The Public Burning* in his hero's mind, as it were:

> Into the Book went the whole UBA, everything from statistics to journalistic dispatches. . . . Style varied from the extreme economy of factual data to the overblown idiom of the sportswriter, from the scientific objectivity of the theoreticians to the literary speculations of essayists and anecdotalists. There were tape-recorded dialogues, satires, prophecies, scandals. . . . [Its] shifting mood oscillat[ing] between notions of grandeur and irony, exultation and despair, enthusiasm and indifference, amusement and weariness.

Given the fact that the core of the story (basically the second chapter) had been written before *The Origin of the Brunists,* that novel may also be linked along the same line with *The Universal Baseball Association.* The Brunists story seems to be indebted to it for one of its most interesting and complex characters—Ralph Himebaugh. Engaging the Nabokovian game of cryptograms and logographics we can detect here a fairly explicit reference to Henry Waugh. Capitalizing and turning upside down the middle "m" and translating "i" and "e" as id est, it reads: H(i)(m)(e)(b)augh, i.e., "b"rother of H. Waugh. The analogy is indeed amazing. Like Henry, Himebaugh is an oldish, lonely and eccentric bachelor. He is a brilliant file cabinet lawyer, and thus his professional skill is also to a certain extent an art of paper records and statistics. Dedicated to private ways of truth and obsessed by "the horror of existence qua existence," he devotes his life to the construction of a numerological system that would order the "universe of screaming particles" and thus reveal the "truth beyond phenomena." Like Henry, he develops the project in the seclusion of his home; his writing is "pedantic" and "precise," the "logs and papers" are always "spread on the kitchen table." Finally Himebaugh decides on the number 7 as his organizing principle, and goes on to give letters alphabet value in numbers. After a time he also finds himself totally imprisoned by his fantasy and experiences a similar fate: "they all noticed how his health had deteriorated," "he was really cracking up!"

With the bulk of it written later, *The Universal Baseball Association* in fact "takes up the concept of fiction-making where *The Origin of the Brunists* left off" [McCaffery]. What is to be noted about it first, however, is the background presence of some other element characteristic for Coover's writing: contentious attitude toward the

Christian dogma, numerological structure, musical references, linguistic exuberance. Henry's game as well as his life translate themselves quite comprehensively in terms of numerological patterns and coincidences. All of them center, inevitably, round the number 7. Henry is 56 years old (as is the father of the all-time star of the league), we are introduced to the Association in its 56th year, and the 49th game of the season proves to be a turning point in its history. Seven is the number of opponents each team has, and there are fifty-six ways to advance players in the charts. The real sport of baseball itself is in a sense governed by the number—with its three main activities (pitching, hitting, fielding) performed around four bases. Although Henry's imagination is the prime mover of the game and its universe, they both depend just as much on intelligence, strategy and choice as on pattern, luck and accident. This is what gives him a feeling of some "ultimate mystery" since he is not aware, [though] his creator—Robert Coover—certainly is, that the game of dice is only seemingly devoid of assignable cause and final effect. Mathematical probabilities applying to it are predictable owing to the fact that the sum of the spots on each two opposite faces of a cube is constant, always totalling seven. The observant reader will note that all this is too neat. Although it might appear, as it does for example to Frank Shelton [*Critique,* August 1975], that "Coover suggests the possibility that another order of existence may be working behind the dice" and thus behind the number informing it, Henry's game is obviously meant to be ironic:

> . . . the design, the structure of the book is so self-revealing—and it's not a gloss on the text from which it borrows its design [Genesis I.1 to II.3], in the sense of being a theologian's gloss; it's an outsiders gloss. . . .

Everybody knows about the seven days of creation, the seven wonders of the world, the seven mortal sins, and the seven-year cycle of famine and plenty. Wisdom and Freedom are proverbially said to rest on seven pillars, and Shakespeare has platitudinized the seven ages of man in the famous passage "All the world's a stage . . . ." Also, seven is believed to mark off the climacterics of human life, and there is the inexorable combination of three spiritual elements with the four basic corporeal ones which is said to account for all human existence. Numerology in Coover's fiction is not, however, an example of how man can "navigate" in the world, but rather a perfect illustration of how—in the writer's own words—we can "stumble through it." Coover's numerological games serve to underscore the "manmade" nature of his art. In larger terms this is to make us aware that it is "one of the ways that the mind gets locked in fixed distorting patterns."

The concept of game as such which is the immediate subject matter of *The Universal Baseball Association* is probably the single most important element in Coover's literary aesthetics. Games feature prominently as a thematic motif throughout his fiction, but they provide essentially a formal principle. Even though Henry is absent from the last chapter of the novel, his game (100 seasons later) still goes on, as if endowed with vitality and life of its own. The past is brought into the ongoing present, the game becomes self-reflective, and the chapter gives the whole book a puzzling, unaccountably open finale. In effect, it challenges the mainstays of so-called objective reality, such as causality, the possibility of isolating objects and events, the sense of purpose, absolute time and space. Reminiscent of Donald Barthelme's suggestion that "there are always openings, if you can find them," the author voices through Henry the fundamental belief: "the circuit wasn't closed, his or any other—there were patterns, but they were shifting and ambiguous and you had a lot of room inside them." Also, "the game on his table was not a message, but an event."

Jackson I. Cope　(essay date 1986)

SOURCE: "Demon Number: Damon and the Dice," in *Robert Coover's Fiction,* The Johns Hopkins University Press, 1986, pp. 35-58.

[*Cope is an American critic and educator. In the following excerpt, Cope examines the significance of names and numbers in* The Universal Baseball Association.]

[Coover] knows that baseball is America's religión, and that it is so because it is America's special reaction to its own wildness, dream (or nightmare) of a lack of limits: It is the play that can be reduced to number. Or almost so. *The Universal Baseball Association, Inc., J. Henry Waugh, Prop.* is a meditation upon this paradox.

J. Henry Waugh, a fifty-six-year-old bachelor and petty accountant has invented a baseball game played with dice and charts, a double metonymy, a game substituted for a game. He is a genius at games, a mathematical genius who once invented "Intermonop," "a variation on Monopoly, using twelve, sixteen, or twenty-four boards at once and an unlimited number of players, which opened up the possibility of wars run by industrial giants with investments on several boards at once . . . strikes and rebellions by the slumdwellers between 'Go' and 'Jail.' " But his gameplaying originated in and ultimately returned to baseball. For a short time in his life he had gone to the ball park: "The first game I saw . . . the league's best pitcher that year threw a three-hit shutout. His own team got only four hits, but three were in one inning, and they won, 2-0. Fantastic game, and I nearly fell asleep . . . at home I would pick up my scoreboard. Suddenly, what was dead had life, what was wearisome became stirring, . . . unbelievably real . . . I found out the scorecards were enough. I didn't need the games." This "reality" is "the records, the statistics, the peculiar balances between individual and team . . . no other activity in the world had so precise and comprehensive a history." And, as Henry remarks to his one friend, Lou Engel, "History. Amazing, how we love it. And . . . without numbers or measurements, there probably wouldn't be any history." "Reality" is defined, rationalized, indeed, created by a history that is number. And in its "game" aspect, that is, the superimposition of limit by rule, reality is controlled by number. An accountant is the precisely correct metaphor for a Platonic God who made the world by weight and measure.

But number has another side, mysterious, a pattern beyond the pattern, a will to its own symmetries for which there is no rational accounting. As one player in the Association says: "Numerology. Lot of revealing work in that field lately." And Henry marvels at length about the unconscious but compelling patterns that make it impossible to alter the structure of his league: "Seven—the number of opponents each team now had—was central to baseball. Of course, nine, as the square of three, was also important: nine innings, nine players, three strikes and four balls . . . four bases."

This doubleness of number is reflected in baseball's own doubleness. If it epitomizes statistical balance and comprehensive history, the ultimate rationality of codification, baseball paradoxically "at the same time" involves, as Henry says, "so much ultimate mystery." It was this something discernible yet inscrutable, which Henry felt when he was attending ball parks: "I felt like I was part of something there, you know, like in church, except it was more real than any church . . . for a while I even had the funny idea that ball stadiums and not European churches were the real American holy places. Formulas for energy configurations where city boys came to see their country origins dramatized, some old lost fabric of unity."

The double realization of baseball as game and as mystery rite lies behind a remark by Henry that lies behind the complicated allegories that begin with the forgivable puns in the novel's title, concluding that the "prop" of the university is JHW: "Everywhere he looked he saw names. His head was full of them. Bus stop. Whistlestop. Whistlestop Busby, second base . . . Henry was always careful about names, for they were what gave the league its sense of fulfilment . . . the dice and charts . . . were only the mechanics of the drama, not the drama itself." Like Adam, like his own prototype Jehovah, he knows that "the basic stuff is already there. In the name. Or rather: in the naming."

Let us look at the names, then, in the several "eras" of the novel, the "realities" that mediate, repeat, absorb one another. First, there is what can be labeled the "continuous era," in which J. Henry Waugh is an accountant. "Continuous," because in it Henry's employer is the German Zifferblatt ("clock dial"), the personification of "Ziffer" ("number") and its application to time. In this era Henry watches Zifferblatt and his clock, hastens out from work early, arrives late. He has lost all interest in his job, makes accounting blunders with ledger entries (which terrify him only because he might tragically miscalculate something in the annals of his baseball league), and plays a self-invented horse-race game surreptitiously at his desk. He talks to himself, drinks far into the night, rushes home to the baseball game on his kitchen table, and generally worries his fat, shy fellow-accountant Lou Engel, whom, in this Germanic context, one must presumably translate "Lucifer Angel." When he leaves the universe on his kitchen table, it is to abandon pastrami and beer and the labor of the game for brandy at Pete's Bar (where Pete has been renamed Jake because Henry recognized in him Jake Bradley, retired second baseman of the Pastimers). Here he has a hearty friendship with a saggily aging B-girl, Hettie Irden—presumably Gea-Tellus, the earth mother ("she's everybody's type"). Once Henry brings the celibate Lou to Pete's and offers to fix him up with Hettie, but in the end himself takes her home. Once also he makes the great decision to share his secret game with Lou, but the latter's misunderstanding of the spirit of probability and reality, plus his spastic clumsiness, almost wrecks the Association, and Henry drives him out of his life and restores order—but only at the point where he must institute ritual in place of game. In this era it seems clear that Jehovah offers participation to Lucifer, wrests from him the woman in the duel for the earth, repairs the ruins of his universe inflicted by Satan (by the sacrificial death of a player preposterously named to combine the baseball and fertility and Christian myths, Jock Casey).

But in this era, too, the allegory presses least upon our attention, its obviousness buried in the comic actions and reactions of J. Henry Waugh, picaresque accountant. Let us remember truisms for a moment to explain and place the function of the comic absurd in *The Universal Baseball Association, Inc.*

"What terrible game will you play with us?" asks the narrator at the close of **"The Leper's Helix."** But he has surely learned in the brief but total revisions of his role that game is the opposite of play. Game implies an "end," a victory sought as the result of obeyed formulae with all of the statistics that Henry leans upon, the prop's props. Play is endless because pointless, mimesis of or escape from the unpredictable openness of causality. Plays are defined formally as unexpectedness: The "peripeteia," the untangling of comic and tragic patterns is, however often repeated, a recipe for the incalculable. There are so statistics for drama or child's play. Play denies the otherness even of that which it may mimic: There are no body counts at cowboys and Indians, no sickness in playing doctor, no funeral or finality at the end of *Lear*. We are gamesters and game, hunters and hunted, and as such we are deprived of that make-believe trying on of selves, masks, new starts that constitute the freedom of play. Even our freedom to make up the rules of the game turns into another measure of containment. These are the polarities between which Coover's creatures struggle toward definition or—that favorite word—fulfilment.

When he goes to Pete's (Jake's—old "Pastimer" he) Bar to relax from his game or to celebrate its triumphs, Henry is playful. He has imposed not only upon Pete but also upon Hettie and himself the names and images of his game. But he goes there as a "player" in every sense. And the players, unlike the statistics, the games, are names. Adopting the name of his favorite, an improbably successful rookie pitcher, letting that projected personality reproject into his own, Henry the aging recluse has a lavishly successful night of sexual play with Hettie.

> "The greatest pitcher in the history of baseball," he whispered. "Call me . . . Damon."
>
> "Damon," she whispered, unbuckling his pants . . . unzipping his fly . . . "Play ball" cried the umpire. And the catcher, stripped of mask and guard, revealed as the pitcher Damon Rutherford, whipped the uniform off the first lady ballplayer in Association history . . . then . . . they . . . pounded into first, slid into

second heels high, somersaulted over third, shot home standing up, then into the box once more, . . . and "Damon!" she cried, and "Damon!"

Nothing could seem more mediated, and yet this is one of two unmediated moments in the novel. Coover here permits the Germanic allegory of the continuous (and comic) era, to accept and to absorb into its sex play the metonymic baseball metaphor of the game. "Irden," Gea-Tellus, "had invented her own magic version, stretching out as the field, left hand as first base." When Hettie and Henry play ball it is to accept the metaphor of baseball, that merely "mythic or historical form" that Coover's "prólogo" said literature must simultaneously build upon and transcend. Learning Henry's mythic game vocabulary, she absorbs its geometrical limits into the unlimited world of play, offers him the recognition that the magic in names, words, is their limitless possibilities (was he not, after all, the one who "everywhere he looked . . . saw names"?) for freedom from any source they may have had: "I got it, Henry, I got it! come on! come on! keep it up! Behind his butt she clapped her cold soles to cheer him on . . . And here he comes . . . he's bolting for home, spurting past, sliding in—POW! . . . Oh, that's a game, Henry! That's really a great old game!"

But the allegory turns upon its source. On the night before introducing Lou to his Association, Henry has his second bout with Hettie, this time in the role of another player, Damon's rival, the veteran pitcher Swanee Law. As they leave the bar to go home, he thinks, "Earthy . . . Won't be the same, he realized. No magic." And the following morning he is edging dangerously close to a fatal, Quijote-like awakening:

> Not once, in the Universal Baseball Association's fifty-six long seasons of play, had its proprietor plunged so close to self-disgust, felt so much like giving it up, . . . an old man playing with a child's toy; he felt somehow like an adolescent caught masturbating.

With this mood upon Henry, Hettie discovers the imaginary nature of his enterprise, and it is with total silence that he rejects her humane understanding as she tries to reassure him of her affection. "Suddenly, astonishingly, she burst into tears. 'Ah, go to hell, you loony bastard!' . . . He heard her heels smacking down the wooden stairs and . . . out into the world." That same night Lou Engel physically and psychically all but destroys the Association, and Henry sends him out of his haven into hell with the appropriate curse: "You clumsy goddamn idiot!" Lou's last communication is a call from the office to inform Henry of his dismissal by Zifferblatt, a call highlighted by the final anguished and outraged cry of Zifferblatt, which sums up his, ours, and Henry's own attitude toward the strange conduct of J. Henry Waugh: "(WHAT THE HELL DOES THIS MEAN—!!)" And, finally, on this same tragic day the dice decree the death of the veteran Jake Bradley, Pete's player counterpart, so that Pete's Bar, too, must be given up forever.

Without the spirit of unmediated play which was only once possible in that magic night game between Hettie and Henry-cum-Damon, the old Pastimer's paradisal bar has no further function. All is gone, all lost now.

In the original days of the Association there began a breakdown into two political parties interested in capturing the chancellorship in the Association elections held every four years. One was the Bogglers, individualists led by the original chancellor, Barnaby North. The other was the Legalists, the party of Swanee Law, the star pitcher whom Damon Rutherford was about to transcend at his tragic death. Play is over, as Henry looks upon play, upon playing with oneself, as disgusting. J. Henry Waugh has joined the Legalists, as his assumption of Law's persona for his love games told us. He is an angry God of the Old Testament whose Pyrrhic victory now reverses the apparent reading of the German allegory. Hettie goes, like Eve, exiled out into the world of time; the world in which Lou the clumsy angel works for old clock face, Zifferblatt. And with Lou's call, Jehovah is exiled from that world, our world, into the solipsism imaged by his masturbating simile. Hettie's parting words ring prophetic: "Ah, go to hell, you loony bastard!" He did, by staying home. This is the novel's first version of, to borrow a phrase, the disappearance of God.

But with the world in shambles it does not end. And here begins the second and more complicated era of allegories: the era in which J. Henry Waugh is Proprietor of, and in closest touch with, the Universal Baseball Association. It is the "new Rutherford era," exciting and yet somehow melancholy. "Maybe it was only because this was Year LVI: he and the Association were the same age, though, of course, their 'years' were reckoned differently. He saw two time lines crossing in space at a point marked '56.' Was it the vital moment?" Numbers are having their mystic way again, to remind us that there are within Henry's Association the double aspect of rationalized history and of "ultimate mystery," which Henry found in baseball itself, mysteries ultimately hidden even from the Proprietor.

Let us recall the history of the Association. Under Barnaby North's chancellorship, the first truly great crop of rookies came up in Year XIX, the greatest being the Pioneers' pitcher Brock Rutherford; indeed, the glorious XXs became known as "the Brock Rutherford era." Now Brock, also fifty-six-years-old in Year LVI, had sired a second son (an earlier one only partially successful), Damon, the magic pitcher who might transcend the father, who pitches a perfect game, who overshadows veteran ace Swanee Law. But as Damon is pitching on Henry's complex Extraordinary Occurrences Chart a three-dice throw shows 1-1-1: "Batter struck fatally by beanball." The pitcher, innocent of intent, was the Knickerbockers' Jock Casey. Brock's former teammate Barney Bancroft, now manager of the Pioneers, and so of the fated Damon, carries on the season; so does J. Henry Waugh.

When Lou Engel is permitted to become the only other ever to share in Henry's game, it is at a point in the season when Jock Casey is once again to pitch against the Pioneers. Lou plays to win, and he wins against all logic, all averages, wildly. Henry has been playing the season through since Damon's death without keeping records, throwing and throwing the dice. He has lost imaginative contact with his players (but this is the first instance in which the contact is lost not by Henry's disengagement, but by that of his creatures): "It was strangely as though they were running from him afraid of his plan, seeing it for what it was: the stupid mania of a sentimental old fool." The "plan" becomes clear when Lou's rolls of the dice suddenly bring Jock Casey the killer into jeopardy upon the Extraordinary Occurrences Chart. Henry tenses in anticipation of order, throws the retributional dice, and sees "2-6-6, a lot less than he'd hoped for." At this moment Lou spills beer over the Association records and is cast out. After Lou's departure, Henry stands in terror at his crossroads: "Damon Rutherford . . . it was just a little too much, and it wrecked the whole league . . . He smiled wryly, savoring the irony of it. Might save the game at that. How would they see it? Pretty peculiar. He trembles . . . Now, stop and think, he cautioned himself. Do you really want to save it? . . . Yes, if you killed that boy out there, then you couldn't quit, could you? No, that's a real commitment, you'd be hung up for good, they wouldn't let you go." Casey stands ready to pitch: "Why waiting? Patient . . . Enduring . . . Casey played the game, heart and soul. Played it like nobody had ever played it before." Waiting Casey stands "alone": "Sometimes Casey glanced up at him—only a glance, split-second pain, a pleading." St. Mark reminds us that "at the ninth hour Jesus cried . . . My God, my God, why hast thou forsaken me?" And then the agony is over. Henry picks up the dice: " 'I'm sorry, boy,' he whispered, and then . . . he set them down carefully . . . One by one. Six. Six . . . Six." The number of the beast: pitcher killed by line drive.

One allegory cries out for attention. UBA, USA. Rutherford for Ruth, certainly, but also for rue. The Rutherfords, leaders of the Pioneers (read New Frontier) are special: "Maybe it was just the name that had ennobled them, for in a way . . . they were . . . the association's first real aristocrats." The Kennedy myth of national renewal aborted is reflected in a series of killings following upon Henry's assassination of Jock after the death of Damon. Barney Bancroft—the latter-day echo of Barnaby North —eventually becomes chancellor and is assassinated, bringing on a revolt of the Universalists. The chancellor in Year LVI is, like Henry, a Legalist, and like LBJ, a paradox: "He looked old-fashioned, but he had an abiding passion for innovation. He was the most restless activist ever to take office . . . He was coldly calculating, yet supremely loyal to old comrades." And when the season continues in an unprecedentedly gloomy and unpopular course, like Henry he must say: "And there's not a goddamn thing I can do about it." His heir and alter ego is that grand southerner Swanee Law. Again, allegory by metonymy. We are directed to read through the layer of the accountant Jehovah to the history of the USA in the sixties, to see the sacrifice of Casey, the consequent helpless commitment of Henry and the chancellor as Vietnam, to hear the surge of revolution rolling in from the future. Politics and war are, after all, the great American games.

But if Swanee Law, in his symbiotic relationship with the current Legalist chancellor, focuses analogy upon LBJ, he can show us an even darker layer of the allegorical palimp-

sest. Nothing will come of nothing. The mystery of history is the regress of its sources, each carefully measured effect having its cause until we arrive at the Zenonian paradox inverted, infinity the ineffable first cause. "To be good," Henry once thought, "a chess player, too, had to convert his field to the entire universe, himself the ruler of that private enclosure—though from a pawn's-eye view, of course, it wasn't an enclosure at all, but, infinitely, all there was." Theologically, it is safest to assume that the first cause is the will of God; as the chess passage suggests, associationalogically it seems safe to assume that the first cause is the will of J. Henry Waugh. There it began, properly, precisely, in Year I. Or did it? Does that "beginning" only raise the question of inscrutability again, hint at another history, a mirrorcorridor in which JHW is only some middle term? The question worries him: "The abrupt beginning had its disadvantages. It was, in a sense, too arbitrary, too inexplicable. In spite of the . . . warmth he felt toward those first ballplayers, it always troubled him that their life histories were so unavailable to him: what had a great player already in his thirties been doing for the previous ten years?." Nothing can come of nothing. "It was, in fact, when the last Year I player had retired that Henry felt the Association had come of age, and when, a couple of years ago, the last veteran of Year I, old ex-chancellor Barnaby North, had died, he had felt an odd sense of relief: the touch with the deep past was now purely 'historic,' its ambiguity only natural."

"The basic stuff is already there. In the name." What then of the name, the, to Henry, always ambiguous nature, of Barnaby North, first chancellor and so first projection of the Proprietor himself within the Association; or, if JHW is only a middle term, perhaps the prototype of the prop himself? What this name tells us in conjunction with the rise of Swanee Law is that the Association's history has moved from North to South, a steady fall on any map.

The major portion of Coover's novel takes place in the critical Year LVI, the "new Rutherford era" in the Association. And the allegory is obviously written over the New Testament. It confuses because Damon Rutherford is so clearly the life-bringer; Jock Casey, his killer, is so clearly the Christ. But it is nonetheless obviously written over the new Testament, in which Matthew told of the Wise Men "saying . . . we have seen his star in the east, and are come to worship him" (Matt. 2:2). And it is in this sacred geography that one can place Henry's baserunner: "Out of the east, into the north, push out to the west, then march through the south back home again; like a baserunner on the paths, alone in a hostile cosmos, the stars out there in their places, . . . he interposed himself heroically to defy the holy condition . . . not knowing his defiance was merely a part of it."

The sun rises in the East; as runner he moves at once toward the North. Lucifer, too, who said in his heart, "I will exalt my throne above the stars of God [Swanee Law is a Star, Damon only a Rookie]: I will sit also upon the mount of the congregation, in the sides of the north . . . I will be like the Most High" (Isa. 14:13-14). Is *he*, Barnaby North, original or image of the creator of the Universal Baseball Association? Or neither? Is he the founder because (infinite inscrutability of beginnings, or, mystery that denies beginnings) he is not the father but the son (remembering that, should this be so, the paradox is enacted twice over. Barney Bancroft, the Pioneer manager and future chancellor, being his namesake, whose assassination set off the revolution). So he seems when we recall, from the Acts of the Apostles, "Barnabas (which is being interpreted, the son of consolation)" (4:36).

Scripture speaks parables against the South (Ezek. 20:45-49), as does American politics, but we must return to the basic metaphors. Like JHW, the southerner is Law—the law of average, the opposite of Damon Rutherford who breaks them. "Law knew what he had going for himself: whenever sportswriters interviewed him, they were shown large charts he kept tacked to his wall, indicating his own game-by-game progress . . . ['Pappy'] Rooney [his manager] had to laugh at Law's prostrating himself before the dirty feet of history." Swanee Law the Legalist set against Barney Bancroft and his prototype, Barnaby North, founder of the opposed free party. The rationalization of history, number, the averages are where Henry, Jehovah, and the Association seem to be going, and we remember that it was Swanee who replaced Damon so tragically in Hettie's favors. But there is a countercurrent within the Association as there is within J. Henry Waugh. Damon Rutherford the son is dead, but Barney Bancroft—manager, elder father figure to Damon but nominally son to Barnaby North, the child (and yet the mysterious elder) of J. Henry Waugh—knows the limits of Henry's and Swanee Law's history. "Bancroft, the rationalist, disbelieved in reason. It was the beast's son, after all, not the father, and if it had a way of sometimes getting out of hand, there was always limits . . . Re: back again, the primitive condition, the nonreflective operating thing: res. His son."

When Damon was struck down, "the Proprietor of the Universal Baseball Association . . . brought utterly to grief, buried his face in the heap of papers on his kitchen table and cried for long bad time." Well he might, victim of his own laws: "Even though he'd set his own rules, . . . and though he could change whenever he wished, nevertheless he and his players were committed to the turns of the mindless and unpredictable—one might even say, irresponsible—dice." When Damon's fate is rolled, the players press around him crying "Do something! But do what? The dice were rolled." And yet, after this time of weeping Henry goes out into the accountant's world, and he carries into it his sense of deity: "Feeling sour. Undiscoverable sun at four o'clock in the hazy sky. But a kind of glow in the streets, mocking him. Later, he'd have it rain." God has not disappeared. He is a loony bastard, who thinks he controls the universe. But he has become mad because he has become a Legalist, lost contact with Barney Bancroft's, Barnaby North's boggling world, forgotten the paradox that he once had been able to apply to chess: "Henry enjoyed chess, but found it finally too Euclidean, too militant, ultimately irrational." Chess is game without the magic, without play; he found it, "in spite of its precision, formless really—nameless motion."

Names not numbers are the drama, that which defies the

predestinarian, "irresponsible" dice to turn formulaic number into mythic formulae. That is what happened to the Universal Baseball Association when JHW did something about it and tipped the die that killed Casey. The consequences were cosmic: He ceased to have connection with Hettie, Lou, Zifferblatt, but with his commitment he paradoxically also ceased to have conjunction with his players.

Here we must notice a principal narrative technique: After Damon's death, while Henry is gradually withdrawing himself from his accountant's world, he inversely projects himself into the players to the extent that the interior monologue of Henry, which seems the chief device of the earlier sections as he imagines activities in his Association, becomes a series of interior monologues on the part of individual players through which Henry's direct persona emerges less and less often until the day with Lou and Hettie, when he surfaces to almost give up his universe.

Yet one important example of Henry's absorption into his players both bears out and immensely modifies this general truth. It demonstrates Coover's technique of creating unbroken chains of interillumination between Henry's life world and his created universe. And it does so at the crucial point of choice, the point at which Damon dead, he can go on by the rules, quit the game, or sacrifice Jock Casey.

Henry, sleepless and broken by the death, visits the puzzled Lou's apartment (unable to be alone) to "imagine" /attend Damon's funeral. He seeks out a recording of Mozart's *Archduke,* drinks; the alarmed friend listens to his jumbled talk, assuming, of course, that the death has been that of a close friend. His innocent question, "Did he leave any . . . family?" gives Henry the first suggestion for how he could continue: To himself he muses "A son? Yes, he could have, he could have at that, and his name . . . ?" There is nothing in the previous image, imagings of Damon, of this golden child athlete, young hero, to make such a history probable, and Henry realizes it implicitly in his next move; fleeing Lou's apartment for Jake's Bar, he creates a wake, a death-drunk of all the Old Timers reflecting his own manic grief. Before it begins, he accounts for all who are *not* in attendance, including Damon's older brother, a failed second-class player from a few seasons earlier. But he *had* been a ballplayer, had his moment of history with the league, and bore the magic name. So Henry imagines through him a more plausible, if indirect route to continuities:

> He'd bolted for home the minute the burial was over, dragging his missus behind him, and there, pressed by an inexplicable urgency, had heisted her black skirts, and without even taking time to drop his pants, had shot her full of seed: yes, caught it! she said, and even he felt that germ strike home.

They were right. Later, horny and half-drunk in a restaurant, Henry gazes on a waitress, a young frump, and thinks about her as the possible mother of this new potential: "Young Brock was handsome, elegant in his way, but it was easy to see that in a real ball game he just didn't have it. Something vital was missing. How would this son—Henry assumed it would be a boy—turn out? . . . Might be worth twenty more seasons just to find out." But clearly his heart was not in it, for Henry has already re-made an improbable history on the little cue offered by Lou's innocent query.

Probably the oldest and most cynical of Henry's avatars among the Old Timers who gather for the wake at Jake's is Rags Rooney, whose idea it had been. Sycamore Flynn, the manager of the pitcher who had killed Damon, attends but leaves very early, and Rooney laments that "Sick Flynn was gone, he'd had a few more things he'd like to jab him with. Like shotgunning poor Damon for jumping his virgin daughter." While the wake is in progress, but before this remark, Hettie, unaware of the imaginary crowd at Jake's, approaches Henry in hopes of another great old game pitched at her by Damon:

> He hadn't noticed her there before. She winked cheaply and asked: "How's Damon's pitching arm tonight?"
>
> "He's dead."
>
> "Hunh?"
>
> "Damon Rutherford is dead."
>
> It was as though he'd struck her in the face . . . When he looked up again, she was gone.

The incident merges with a reaction the others have to Sycamore Flynn, himself merging with Henry: "It was funny abou Sic'em: they all loved the bastard, pure gold the man's heart, yet this night they couldn't get close to him. Wasn't his fault. Yet something was happening." Then Flynn emerges *from* Henry, having left the bar. He is on a train, "his mind in trouble pitched here and there, rocked by the wheels' pa-clockety-knock, jogged loose from the continuum . . . the sons and the fathers, the sons and the fathers." There are three rationales for Flynn's pa-rental concern. One is his emergence from Henry. A sec-ond is his long rivalry through his stellar playing years with Damon's father, Brock Rutherford. The two greats of their era, now known as the Brock Rutherford Era: "Brock the Great. Oh yes, damn it, damn him, he was?". The last is his own paternity, the guilt and the loss when his daughter, too, accepts some version (before or after the act) of Rooney's barb about Flynn having killed Damon out of a father's jealousy. When he killed Damon as her Daemon lover before Hettie's face in Jake's, she had fled Henry. Now we learn the name of Flynn's daughter, fled like Hettie from the man who robbed her of Damon's young sexuality once, maybe twice:

> His daughter had disappeared. She'd left no note. Hadn't been necessary. He knew what she was telling him and there was nothing he could do about it, nothing he could do that would bring her back. Harriet was as dead to him now as her Damon was to Brock. Even more so, be-cause Damon died and left no hate behind. In a way, Flynn envied Brock. No, that wasn't true. You're just trying to smooth it over, ease the guilt.

It is an immense inner narrative developed in a few strokes by Henry's imagination. This is not surprising, in any of its aspects but one. He has been working fast with the idea of Damon having an heir; he has dismissed Henrietta by discarding his Damon avatar brutally, as Flynn has lost Harriet. But Flynn *is* Henry's alter ago, and so neither in-tentionally beaned Damon—that was the mindlessness of the dice. What then, and it is crucial at this juncture, is Flynn's "guilt"?

He descends from the train near the ball park, a short walk to his hotel, and enters us into one of the most successful and eerie of those deliriums, which are not quite dreams, that punctuate Coover's work, but especially in the psy-chic life of Richard Nixon in *The Public Burning.*

It begins on this problem of "guilt." Flynn is in Damon's hometown; he might be recognized and harassed, so he walks, choosing "the dark streets. What was hounding him? That he didn't feel guilty *enough*?" He passes the sta-dium, which "bulked, unlit in the dark night, like a mas-sive ruin, exuding a black odor of death and corruption" (one remembers that Henry thinks that these now bare quires, "ball stadiums and not European churches were the real American holy places"). But Flynn's experience goes beyond this: the Pioneers' Park has become unfamil-iar. "No, no gates. Not even the hinges for one. And in-side: it shouldn't be that black in there." He feels about the walls of the suddenly unfamiliar passageways to the dugout, to the field. He discerns ghosts, he retreats, he finds himself disoriented. On the darkened ball field he feels the presence of all his players around him in the dark, Jock Casey, most poignantly, on the mound behind him. It is a ghost field because Casey is there: " 'That you, Jock?' Turn around and look, you ass. Can't. Sorry, just can't . . . Flynn was near tears. Behind him, he realized, past Casey, past home plate, there was an exit. Maybe it was a way out, maybe it wasn't."

Flynn has absorbed Henry, Henry's grief, taken Henry home into the old ball park of his lonely spooky apartment full of the deaths of all these paper heroes. "Maybe it was a way out, maybe it wasn't. But he'd never make it. He couldn't even turn around. And besides, he wasn't even sure what he'd find at home plate on the way. 'I quit,' he said. But then the lights came on." In Henry's apartment. And when they did, he had given up the notion of quitting or continuing the Rutherford myth on the sheerness of chance of those dice, those numbers he had for so long thought of as order. Out of that dark dream, Henry had decided to intervene.

When young Damon is about to pitch in the fatal game succeeding his perfect performance, Henry's imagination works overtime: " 'Go out and win one for the old man, son.' Who said that? Why old Brock! Yes, there he was, sitting in a special box . . . In fact, Henry realized sudden-ly, 'it must be Brock Rutherford Day at Pioneer Park.' " That "it must be" takes on a redimensioning ambiguity analogous to the ambiguous status of Barnaby North, when, observing the wake for Damon, Henry's conscious-ness is expressed through that of successive participants in the festivities until it emerges as that of the chancellor: "Brock Rutherford Day had been Fenn's own idea. The whole UBA was suddenly bathed in light and excitement and enthusiasm. Fenn had foreseen an election sweep . . . The Guildsmen [at the time it was written read Goldwaterites] couldn't find a candidate. Total mandate. And then that pitch. He wasn't sure what he could do about it . . . The only conceivable forms of meaningful action at a time like this were all illegal." But "illegality," breaking of the rules and the substitution of sacrifice for chance, commitment for causality, predestination for percentages—these are phrases to describe Henry's deliberate killing of Jock Casey with the number of the beast from the Book of Revelation: And we might here remind ourselves that Coover's "prólogo" speaks of fiction as the use of "familiar forms to combat the content of those forms, . . . to conduct the reader . . . away from magic to maturity, away from mystery to revelation." The mediation is so intensified that we are led to search for answers to impossible questions, those that haunt Henry's sense of history: Is the chancellor Henry's "persona," or Henry the chancellor's? A familiar gambit, echo of the doubleness of Barnaby North, of Montaigne's puzzle about his playful cat. Until we arrive at the mythic era with which the novel concludes, "Damonsday CLVII."

Now JHW is gone; this the second, the defining disappearance of the god of the game. The world has become a ritual because he sacrificed Jock Casey to save his universe, not man's. The Christian myth is reenacted as a myth of the Beast who is anti-Christ. In this era, "some writers even argue that Rutherford and Casey never existed—nothing more than another of the ancient myths of the sun, symbolized as a victim slaughtered by the monster or force of darkness." The New Testament sources of Coover's allegories, like the Old Testament sources, are turned back upon themselves.

There is no narrative interaction now between Henry and his players—they have absorbed his consciousness both in narrative style and in literal fact: One player named Raspberry Schultz "has turned . . . to the folklore of game theory, and plays himself some device with dice." J. Henry Waugh reduced to a Bronx cheer. He exists only in the tangled confusions of skepticism and ignorance with which the players attempt to understand the meaning of the political parties that in a ritual world have become theological sects, attempts to wring some meaning out of the annual reenactment of the game in which Damon Rutherford was killed, the games of "Damonsday." The sun dominates the players and the imagery on this mythic day that closes the novel, and the old interaction between the two levels of phenomena mediated by Henry's consciousness is allowed to appear in reverse just once in a player's joke: " 'Pull the switch on that thing, man!' Gringo hollers up to the sun . . . 'Yeah,' 'What does it say?' '100 Watt.' " They are all gone as though they never existed: JHW, Rutherford, and Casey. Only Damon remains.

The cynical rookie chosen for the role resents and fears it, lives in a surrealistic shadowland where an apparitional boy demands an autograph, where women surround him and tear at his fly as he struggles through an Orphic threat. He reviews the theological debate upon the meaning of the Parable of the Duel, which is about to be reenacted and rejects it all, all but one thing: "Damon the man,

legend or no." "Just remember," he tells himself as he dresses for the Duel, "how you love the guy, that second son who pitched such great ball, and died so young" (read JFK).

Dressed, he stands on the mound as Damon feeling the mark of the Beast. He "flexes his fist, staring curiously at it, . . . thinking he's got something special there today," feeling that mark "in the right hand," as before and after "in the forehead" that is the Beast's (Rev. 13:6; 2:4). The doubter who must enact the catcher walks toward him. "He has read all he can find on the Association's history, and he knows he is nothing"; "His despair is too complex for plain speech . . . He is afraid. Not only of what he must do. But of everything." "He stares at the sky, beyond which there is more sky, overwhelming in its enormity. He, . . . is utterly absorbed in it, entirely disappears, is nothing at all." Perhaps Henry has heard Gringo's joking command and turned out the light over the table, for as the doubter contemplates his terror, he realizes that "it's coming, Yes, now, today, here in the blackening sun." And then he arrives at the mound. It is the second unmediated moment in the novel. He confronts Damon and sees that "it's all there is." And Damon sees, too, but inverts the sense of the vision. The joke of the 100-watt sun echoes an image from Henry's consciousness at the very beginning, when he realizes that sometimes his game is just dead statistics to him, no names: "just a distant echo . . . But then . . . someone like Damon Rutherford came along to flip the switch, turn things on." Damon sees, and gives light and life again: "He says: 'Hey, wait, buddy! You love this game, don't you?' . . . Damon grins. Lights up the whole goddamn world. 'Then don't be afraid' . . . he says. And the black clouds break up, . . . and his [Trench's, the battery mate's] own oppressed heart leaps alive to give it one last try." " 'It's not a trial,' says Damon, glove tucked in his armpit, hands working the new ball . . . 'It's not even a lesson. It's just what it is.' Damon holds the baseball up between them. It is hard and white and alive in the sun."

Two young friends together in a numerical, Platonic world that defies cynicism. Damon, the Pythagorean who offered himself for Pithias in the name of friendship to save them both by love. To save them from death imposed by a tyrant.

Paul Trench's unmediated moment of life, like Henry's, is given through Damon. Both are moments in which the tyranny of game is converted into the improbability of play: "You love this game," he affirms for Trench; "That's really a great old game," affirms Hettie. The relationship of J. Henry Waugh and Jock Casey, Coover's God and Jesus Christ, had inverted the Christian myth upon which it was founded. But the third person of Coover's trinity rights it again, or rather rewrites it, with the central holy pun. J. Henry Waugh is inspired, as is his Association, by the presence of Damon, that holy name whose Greek original meant not only the inevitable divine power mediating between gods and men but also those souls of the dead whom we honor, especially, explains the *OED*, "deified heroes." As Henry said, "The basic stuff is already there. In the name. Or rather: in the naming." By naming,

Coover converts the dark parable of our insane culture into an affirmation that salvation is still possible through that daemonic sense of play with which we are so richly endowed.

Let us now reconsider *The Universal Baseball Association, Inc.* (for that is what it is, Lou's flood of beer and Henry's rainbow wiping out the carefully penned box-scores and histories of a world gone wrong) under a different rubric; let us consider it as a sophisticated metafiction, a novel in the tradition of writings about writings. It has been examined in this context, and it is reasonable that it should be. It narrates a history perfectly separated from the ambiguities and impossibilities that separate the historical, even the least historical, novel—one mimetic only of a generalized place, time, space—from the text. Because here the history is of a text, a history that claims existence only in ink. A novel about a man, or a god, or a madman who substituted writing for life. And then, within that writing there were all those groups, the Bogglers and Legalists, conservatives and radicals, mythologists and rational demystifiers, who interpret the first seven chapters in the eighth. And we are left to play out our own critical fantasies in the missing ninth inning, chapter, life of the cat (is not Coover's story **"The Cat in the Hat for President,"** like this novel, about a book that comes into independent life?). And none of this is true to our reading. John Barth's *Chimera* is about the telling of stories, about the impossibility of it. *The Universal Baseball Association, Inc.* is not. Or rather, it uses the notion of authorship and its authority to tell a story, a history, a *historia* just as the Quijote does. As the author of the association is drawn into his game of chance measured against balance (*is* the book we read, after all, perhaps Barney Bancroft's history of the *UBA in the Balance*?), we are drawn with him into the names, not the numbers. The argument of "writing" becomes the vehicle of a larger argument. In this larger argument, characters may argue the ontology of their self-existence, as did Raspberry Schultz, Paul Trench, and others on "Damonsday CLVII," but we do not argue their existence, we embrace it as the function of narrative. The writer's vehicle is always the reader's tenor: This collusion makes a story seem a history. And that is what makes the novel novel: It always purveys news of a new life.

Christopher Ames   (essay date Winter 1990)

SOURCE: "Coover's Comedy of Conflicting Fictional Codes," in *Critique: Studies in Contemporary Fiction*, Vol. XXXI, No. 2, Winter, 1990, pp. 85-99.

[*In the following excerpt, Ames discusses the variety of narrative codes in* Gerald's Party, *including "the patterns of detective story, slapstick comedy, masquerade, dream tale, and ritual sacrifice."*]

Gerald's Party, Robert Coover's most recent novel, is a bruising book. Gerald, the host, ends up with numerous literal bruises, as do most of the surviving guests, who collide, trip, and fall throughout the novel and are beaten with nightsticks, croquet mallets, and fists. The reader also emerges somewhat battered, worn away by the assaults upon time, coherence, and verisimilitude. The bruising shocks of *Gerald's Party,* however, are in keeping with its essentially carnivalesque nature, which is exemplified in the festive setting of the party and the interplay of different fictional codes or conventions. The novel's excitement and tension arise from the collision of different narrative codes: the patterns of detective story, slapstick comedy, masquerade, dream tale, and ritual sacrifice. This clashing of different generic standards of verisimilitude displaces the reader's expectations. At the party, Gerald speaks of "all these violent displacements . . . it was as though we'd all been dislodged somehow, pushed out of the frame, dropped into some kind of empty dimensionless gap like that between film cuts, between acts." This sense of being between acts arises from an overdetermination of narrative cues—narrative codes are not lacking but are invoked in such fertile profusion as to subvert reader recognition. These displacements are often disorienting and frustrating, but, in the context of Coover's novel and Gerald's party, they become comic, parodic, and even liberating.

The subversive effect of a collision of narrative discourses highlights the intersection of festivity and the modern novel. In exploring how the novel, especially prior to the eighteenth century, combined actual folk carnival elements with a carnival-style multiplicity of viewpoints or dialogism, Mikhail Bakhtin has argued that "[carnivalization] determined not only the content but also the very generic foundations of a work." *Gerald's Party* vividly illustrates the way in which the modern private party can become a similarly dialogic locus, a fictional "town square" within the province of the modern novel. Although Bakhtin identified "carnivalization" with an earlier (and now displaced) folk tradition, his perception of the way in which form and content intersect in the multivoiced language of literary festivity remains illuminating in considering works of contemporary fiction such as *Gerald's Party.*

A fictional code or convention here means a subgenre of the novel characterized by a particular set of images, narrative patterns, motifs, and modes of discourse. To borrow M. H. Abrams's modification of [Roland] Barthes, a code consists of "artifices, arousing conventional expectations, which function entirely within the system of literary writing itself." When an author modifies a code and combines it with other fictional codes, however, those conventional expectations can be deliberately frustrated. *Gerald's Party* is not a detective novel, for example, but it invokes enough of the elements of the detective code to generate (and then frustrate) conventional reader expectations. "Every effort to speak of the world involves a kind of fiction-making process," Coover has commented. "There are always other plots, other settings, other interpretations. So if some stories start throwing their weight around, I like to undermine their authority a bit, work variations, call attention to their fictional natures." This notion of "undermining" aptly describes Coover's narrative technique in *Gerald's Party,* in which a hearty and remorseless dialogism plays with conventions and expectations, and structures the novel.

The most powerful convention a modern novelist manipulates is that of realism. Many of the innovations of contemporary fiction are modes of playing with the realist frame, a frame that has conditioned the modern reader to expect the events of a work of fiction to mirror standards of social and psychological probability commonly associated with real life. An author might dispense with the realist convention at the outset, either through an invocation of an alternate and exclusive convention, such as the fairy tale, or through the rapid violation of certain realist consistencies (or reader expectations). Coover does not choose either of these nonrealist paths. Instead, certain realist conventions exist throughout the novel so that the violations of realism continually have a disruptive or absurdist force. The setting recalls much realist fiction: a suburban house party of intellectuals and professionals with familiar food, drink, and furnishings. The narrative, although it frequently becomes improbable or bizarre, never broaches the impossible: the dead do not speak; people do not turn into butterflies or armadillos. Gerald's perspective is presented consistently, and his concern and unease—and finally his sorrow and inarticulate anger—suggest a realistic human response to the increasingly strange events.

Within these realistic parameters, however, Coover challenges the convention in several ways. He creates a sense of absurdity by presenting unusual or startling events without any reactions of shock or surprise from witnessing characters. The novel opens with the discovery of a corpse—someone has been stabbed to death at the party. The situation is contained within realist probabilities as people gather around the corpse, the police are summoned, and Ros's newly widowed husband goes wild with grief. When the police beat the husband to death with croquet mallets, and Gerald's wife (unnamed in the text) continues making hors d'oeuvres while the guests continue to eat and drink, the realist frame threatens to dissolve. As the party continues, three more guests die violently. The wife continues to cook, serve, and clean, and the guests continue to flirt, tell jokes, and drink. Eventually the juxtapositions become more startling: " 'Yum!' enthused Bunky, stepping over Ros's body and plucking a melon ball."

The novel has many such discordant absurdities: as Gerald's wife is being tortured by police (for no apparent reason), she begs Gerald to check the nachos in the oven. When Gerald reports that his best friend, Vic, has bled to death, his wife asks him to carry coffee cups into the living room. As the police intimidate and torture people, the plumber is drafted to be a video cameraman, and as the child's toy soldiers are beheaded and his stuffed bunny dismembered, we sense that this is not a typical party of realist fiction. The reader's sense of verisimilitude is strained and revised, but never so thoroughly that the novel sacrifices the power of comically unusual events to disturb. The novel depends upon supporting and subverting the familiar realist parameters. This pattern is structured through gradually increasing chaos and grotesqueness as if the reader is being innoculated in his or her tolerance for the bizarre.

At the same time, the novel mirrors the cacophony of a wild party through its narrative interruptions. Scenes, paragraphs, and sentences are constantly interrupted. Parentheses abound, usually in mid-sentence to maximize the disruption. Gerald muses that, as with multiple parentheses, "all conversations were encased in others, spoken and unspoken. . . . It was what gave them their true dimension, even as it made their referents recede." Accordingly, Coover interweaves many dialogues without attribution. The effect is confusing but provocative. The reader becomes a guest at the party, concentrating on one conversation and ignoring others as "noise," or interpreting the interspersed dialogues as commenting upon one another in montage fashion. The reader can also "play back" the interrupted dialogues by rereading a passage and disentangling the different conversational threads. Much of the book's power arises from Coover's masterful involvement of the reader in such ways.

If the reader of a party novel is analogous to a guest, the narrator likely resembles a host. Gerald's haze infects us and renders the party more immediate, yet more blurred. We see through his eyes with immediacy, but they are not always well-focused. Amid the confusion, the general outlines of the action remain ascertainable. Unity of time and place helps to fix those outlines: the entire novel takes place at the party, and the narrative strays no further than the back yard.

The novel is also structured by the homicide investigation that occurs at the party. The police alter the closed system of the party when they enter, and they are directly responsible for the deaths of Roger and Vic. In between those deaths, Tania, the painter, dies mysteriously in the bathtub, evidently a suicide. Amid much eating and drinking, a panoply of sexual activities ensues, particularly in the outside garden and the downstairs rec room. Gerald has sexual involvements of various kinds with Alison, Sally Ann, and his wife. A long-standing couple, Cyril and Peg, breaks up when Peg leaves the party with Dickie, a notorious playboy. Meanwhile, the guests discuss artistic theory and tell dirty jokes, and Zack Quagg's theatre troupe enacts a funereal drama built around Ros's corpse. Yvonne breaks a leg, and Charley "Choo-Choo" Trainer slips a disc. Sally Ann and young Anatole become engaged. The party seems to epitomize Dick Diver's decadent desire in *Tender Is the Night:* "I want to give a really *bad* party . . . where there's a brawl and seductions and people going home with their feelings hurt and women passed out in the cabinet de toilette."

These bizarre events coalesce into a compelling tour de force through the collision of fictional codes and the rich symbolic associations of the party, which connect and reconcile the competing generic patterns of the novel. The abundance of fictional codes disrupts coherence, but the party setting (which allows for the interplay of many voices) restores it by celebrating the dialogic possibilities of festive and novel form.

The fictional code of the detective story permeates *Gerald's Party* and provides the most marked example of the way in which different fictional codes undermine one another. Detective fiction's distinctive relationship to fictionality *per se* and to the party in particular grants that subgenre special force in shaping reader expectations. Detective fiction is a kind of metafiction because it contains a narrative within the narrative—the detective functions as reader as he interprets and follows clues, and as writer as he presents them at the denouement. Coover exploits both of these fertile relationships in parodying and re-presenting the detective story.

In general, detective fiction depicts an investigator creating a chronological and causal narrative retrospectively from its conclusion at the murder scene. To do so, he must assemble narrative elements that have become disorganized like pieces of a puzzle (a common metaphor in detective fiction). Reader and detective share this perspective as well as the desire to render the scene intelligible through assembling the narrative pieces. The beauty and appeal of the game of detective fiction are often enhanced by limiting or closing the number of possible narratives, particularly by limiting the number of suspects. Thus the closed house party or country weekend becomes a frequent setting for murder dramas because the boundaries of the house double as boundaries for the "game." In detective fiction in which a party is not the setting for the murder, it is often the setting for the resolution: all suspects gather at a dinner or party at which the detective reveals the murderer.

Gerald's Party uses both of these intersections between the closed system of the party and the finite world of the detective novel. The murder clearly occurs at the party, and Inspector Pardew predictably warns, *"[n]obody moves! . . . Nobody leaves this house without permission!"* Two hundred and fifty pages later, the Inspector initiates the classic detective denouement: "I have called you all here, here to the scene of the crime." In between these two events, Coover intensifies the dramatic unity by having the police conduct their entire investigation at the party: they set up a lab, interrogate witnesses, examine the body, develop and test theories, catalog evidence, and conduct similar activities. As in traditional detective fiction, the party becomes a social microcosm, allowing the plot of narrative reconstruction to be dramatized more readily.

Tzvetan Todorov cites detective fiction as an example of the way in which genres possess individual internal standards of verisimilitude. The detective plot must be believable and logical but must also conform to an apparent antiverisimilitude, such as the rejection of the most likely suspect. Thus the detective subgenre exists within a narrow margin between the need for surprise and the need for believability. Coover parodies this balance by skewing the investigation far from both poles: it is filled with crazy illogic and implausibility, yet the denouement (the revelation of the supposed killer) is absurdly anticlimactic. The humor emerges from the incongruity between the familiar detective form and the novel's farcical content.

Pardew initially (and predictably) tries to determine the time of Ros's death. He does this, however, by collecting all the guests' watches. Everyone cooperates as if this approach were reasonable; perhaps it comically exaggerates our tendency to look at a watch when asked how long ago something happened. The collection of the watches is also a comment on the temporal inversion of the detective act—working backward from the conclusion. Pardew is

fascinated with such metaphysical implications of his own investigations: "It's a little like sorting out the grammar of a sentence. . . . You have the object there before you and evidence of at least the verb. . . . But you have to reach back in time to locate the subject." Fascinated with such paradoxes, he sees no contradiction in concluding from the watches that the murder took place half an hour after he arrived and examined the body. The characters do not comment on the strangeness of all this absurdity, which effectively lampoons the surprise element of the classic detective denouement: Pardew's conclusion is so ingenious that it is ridiculous.

Other absurdities enrich the investigation motif. The investigation includes such things as dismembering Gerald's son's stuffed bunny, Peedie; conducting comparative penis exams; and videotaping and viewing various moments of the party. Police laboratory procedures are comically exaggerated in the description of a Rube Goldberg-style temporary crime lab set up at the party. The most elaborate mockeries, however, are reserved for the narrative theories of detection. The Inspector speaks at times like a hard-boiled cop, at others like an obsessed literary critic analyzing crime detection. He is a self-parodying figure.

> "Holistic criminalistics *rejects* these narrow localized cause-and-effect fictions popularized by the media! Do you think that poor child in there died because of some arbitrary indeterminate and random act? Oh no, *nothing* in the *world* happens that way! It just by such simple atavistic thinking that we fill our morgues and prisons, missing the point, solving nothing!" Pardew stormed about the room, waving his arms. . . . "Murder, like laughter, is a muscular solution of conflict, biologically substantial and inevitable, a psychologically imperative and, in the case of murder, death-dealing act that *must* be related to the total *ontological reality!*"

The detective as interpreter or reader is similarly parodied in Pardew's dramatic revelation to Gerald that he has found a blueprint of the murder. His lengthy and, at times, brilliant analysis is undermined by Gerald's identification of the drawing as his son's depiction of the "Holy Family." These excessive interpretations warn the reader against the potential solipsism of interpretive zeal. Caught between the fictional codes of detective story, parody, and realistic novel, Pardew is rendered absurd. In carnivalistic spirit, the most authoritarian figure is the most ridiculed.

When Pardew triumphantly announces that he has solved Ros's murder, his climactic moment is deflated by his own contradictions and absurdities. His conclusion that the murderer is Vachel, a dwarf who arrives well after the murder, is neither logical nor stunning: it simply does not make sense. Pardew violates the detective frame by not explaining his detective process; he offers no coherent narrative in which Vachel is the villain. His climactic moment is further weakened by interruptions and slapstick physical comedy. He has to begin his speech three times because of different interruptions, ranging from slightly suppressed yawns to ribald jokes. In an elaborately detailed description, Pardew gets his fedora stuck first on one shoe, then the other, then both, until he finally shoots it off with his revolver. When the hat tricks abate long enough for the perpetrator to be revealed, the Inspector's scene dissolves into a Keystone Kops melee as the vaseline-greased dwarf struggles with the police. The comical anticlimax reduces the power of the detective fiction code so that it becomes but one of many voices in the text.

Coover has made use of literary equivalents of film techniques in his earlier fiction, particularly the montage and cut techniques. Film's power to show motion as story—and the possibilities for imitating that power in language—seems the most significant cinematic legacy in *Gerald's Party.* In particular, Coover seems interested in the pantomime comedy of slapstick. The pratfall belongs to pre-cinematic forms, such as circus and vaudeville, but it attained its greatest power in film, particularly silent film in which gesture and body movement substitute for language. The physical comedy of falling, slipping, tripping, spilling, and bumping into things is even more appropriate in the festive setting because traditional decorum is suspended, intoxication encouraged, and the boundary lines between body and building blurred.

Gerald's Party is filled with instances of physical comedy, and the humor of the slips and falls intensifies as they accumulate throughout the novel and become increasingly violent or theatrical. In the first (rather tame) instance, Gerald pours drinks to overflowing as his attention strays to the alluring Alison across the room. Later, in the chaos of Roger's frenzy after Ros's death, there is much slipping and sliding on blood. Eyeglasses are shattered, drapes torn, and lamps smashed. Big Louise falls, and, as Patrick comments later, "[w]hen she hit the floor I *skidded three feet in her direction.*" Guacamole dip dribbles off dentures onto chins, ashtrays tumble, and beer froths and overflows. Naomi shits her pants in fright; Yvonne tumbles down a flight of stairs and breaks a leg; Charley Trainer falls down the same stairs and slips a disc. The party becomes an arena in which ordinary movement is difficult or impossible, relentlessly transformed into slapstick.

But there is a difference. The slapstick performer uses grace and skill to pretend to be clumsy and awkward. The pratfall is a planned replication of something that is spontaneous by nature—falling down. The physical comedy in *Gerald's Party* is largely unintentional. In substance, the falls and spills are real, not theatrical, slapstick. In the theatrical context of the party and the literary context of the book, however, they take on the patterned artificiality of slapstick. Detective fiction plays with the tension between surprise and believability; similarly, slapstick plays with the tension between the planned and the spontaneous. Both the detective code and the slapstick code are transformed in the context of this novel.

We have seen how Coover manipulates the usual detective code of verisimilitude. Slapstick is similarly transformed, almost inverted. The good slapstick artist falls hard enough so that the planned physical comedy appears spontaneous. The party guests' hard falls are patterned enough (by the author) that they appear theatrical and comic: life imitates art. More appropriately, the literary representation of life imitates a cinematic representation

called slapstick. One example demonstrates Coover's descriptive technique.

> *"Hole on, Yvonne! GodDAMN it! Ole Chooch is comin'!"* But his knees started to cave about halfway down the landing and there was no negotiating the right angle turn there—Woody and Cynthia ducked, clinging to each other, as he went hurtling past behind them, smacking the banister with his soft belly and somersaulting on over the railing to the floor below: *"Pp-FOOOFF!"* he wheezed mightily as he landed on his back (I'd managed to jerk Mark out of the way just in time), bathrobe gaping and big soft genitals bouncing between his fat legs as though hurling them to the floor had been his whole intent. "Ohh, shit!" he gasped (Mark was laughing and clapping, my wife's mother shushing him peevishly), lying there pale and, except for the aftershock vibrations still rippling through his flaccid abdomen, utterly prostrate: *"Now wha've I done . . . ?!"*

The slapstick feeling here is created not only by the attention to gesture and physical detail (which creates an almost slow-motion effect as the prose unfolds more slowly than the action described), but also by Charley's drunken bravado turned into sheepishness, the comic book-style sound effects, and little Mark's laughter and applause.

The point of the slapstick descriptions is, first of all, comic. The carnival spirit celebrates the body at play and the ability to laugh at the body's limitations. Pratfalls remind our minds of our bodies and make us laugh. The fall also illustrates loss of control. A wild freedom exists in the moment between slip and impact—a moment of flight. Loss of control—as parties often remind us—can be frightening. The intensifying physical comedy of this party manifests its increasing chaos. The slapstick fits perfectly and comically into the festive setting, but it hints at a darker loss of control and tests the boundary between pleasure and pain. The triple juxtaposition of realist comedy of manners, detective story, and slapstick comedy generates multiple incongruities and exemplifies the festive mixing of modes characteristic of the carnivalized novel.

Loss of bodily control also manifests itself in the attention to vomiting and excretion at Gerald's party. The novel is a self-proclaimed "vomedy," a dark comedy of festive excess. Parties accentuate what Bakhtin terms the "lower bodily strata," most obviously in their attention to physical appetite, eating, and drinking. Traditional carnivals also celebrated an earthy regard for the consequences of that physical excess, as Bakhtin notes in Rabelais. In contemporary Anglo-American parties, the taboos surrounding bodily waste are the least likely to give way. Intoxication may be acceptable and even encouraged in the festive setting, but vomiting and passing out remain serious breaches of decorum. Excremental taboos remain strong, as the comment that Gerald's parties have "too much shit and blood" reminds us. Blood inspires fear and horror when it crosses the boundary of the flesh, when it is "spilled." Excrement is similarly taboo when it passes the bodily boundary. Taboos stem, as Mary Douglas has argued, from such societal classifications or compartmentalizations, the very classifications that festivity traditionally suspends. By assaulting and exposing those taboos least willingly suspended, Coover dramatizes the transgressive force of the celebration and the increasingly futile attempts to control that transgression. At the same time, he extends physical comedy into a code that more explicitly invokes the carnival tradition.

Ros's murder initiates the flow of blood and shit. Her blood (and later Roger's) darkens drapes, carpets, and clothing; her murder causes Naomi to defecate in her pants. Throughout the evening, Gerald and his wife battle this rising tide with attempts to clean up. Gerald actually cleans Naomi and finds her new clothes. His wife does several loads of laundry and lends out her own clothes. Guests make various attempts (usually feeble) to clean up spilled ashtrays or to change their stained clothing, but their efforts never seem to catch up with the flood of waste and blood. The upstairs toilet clogs so badly that the plumber cannot fix it, and guests begin to relieve themselves in the garden until it is transformed into a morass of urine and feces. The breakdown of taboos becomes oppressive, not liberating, in its reminder of the body's physical essence. Roger's blood-spattered suit, the begrimed bedsheets of the master bedroom, Naomi's shit-stained clothes, the clogged toilet—all these images echo the ultimate corporeal reminder of Ros's body.

"The grotesque body of carnival" is, however, essential to the festive spirit. Some festive celebration of the body emerges in Gerald's party's relentless libidinal energy—another glorification of the lower body—but that aspect is also frustrated or dammed up. Gerald's intense longing for the seductive Alison epitomizes frustrated desire as his attempts to rendezvous with her are repeatedly blocked. By the end of the evening, Alison has been abandoned to unspecified humiliations, and her exit from the party is marked by her husband's pulling a long string of scarves from her behind in a grotesque parody of "theatre." The bodily elements of carnival tradition are surely present at this party, but the context renders them negative; they reinforce a bondage to physicality rather than a reveling in it. Such "bondage" is reified ludicrously in Gerald's sexual encounter with Sally Ann, in which his penis becomes partially caught in her and has to be extricated by the doctor, Jim. Like the slapstick code, the motif of the lower body fits the festive frame but does not necessarily celebrate it.

The futile attempts to clean or change clothes initiate a comic masquerade that highlights the body's monstrosity. Gerald's party is not officially a masquerade, but it becomes one as blood transforms dress clothes into costumes and the theatre troupe joins in with liberally applied stage makeup. In their desire to shed their stained clothing, many of the guests borrow clothes from the hosts, resulting in an informal masquerade in which few guests are wearing what they wore at the beginning of the party. Much of the individual distinctiveness of characters magically disappears in the confusion of costume. The primitive phenomenon in which costume erases individuality emerges in the confusion of identity caused by the clothing changes. Gerald mistakes Kitty for his wife because she is wearing borrowed clothing; Sally Ann pretends to be Alison with the aid of a dark room and Alison's knitted

"peckersweater." Regina, arriving late, mistakes Yvonne for Ros. The injured Yvonne is also confused: "Honest to God, Jim, I think you guys pulled a fast one on me! This isn't my *body*." Talbot appears wearing a pair of Gerald's pants, as does Daffie later. In an extended comic scene, Ginger dons more and more articles of Inspector Pardew's clothing (overcoat, scarf, pipe); later, Fats appears wearing the Inspector's fedora "like a party hat." Modern equivalents of motley emerge in a variety of "patched" guests: Steve, the plumber, wears a name patch; a nameless guest is identified only by his patched elbows; Sally Ann adds various sexually suggestive patches to her clothing during the party; by the end of the evening, Alison sports a lewd road-sign patch.

The comical costume changes reflect a profound festive metamorphosis: the blurring of individual distinctions in the ritual setting. Identity depends upon certain taxonomic categories, and, in the chaos of the celebration, those distinctions can disappear. The primitive qualities of festive chaos remind individuals of their primal and bodily nature. All clothing becomes a masking of the bodily nature, and "even bare skin is a kind of mask." Such confusions of identity are temporary—even momentary—but they reflect the frightening side of the exhilarating potential of the party. The party reveals, for better or for worse, a monstrous side to the human.

What is the point of Coover's insistent invocation of the language of masquerade and monstrosity to describe the less formal costume changes of Gerald's party? The costume allows for and signals a release of that which is repressed by the mask of the everyday. As Terry Castle says of eighteenth-century masquerade, the transformation of public self represents "an almost erotic commingling with the alien." The dialogic natures of party and novel are especially receptive to this collective chaos of masking. The fictional code of masquerade fits naturally into the festive setting, but its context is deepened by the other codes of transformation—slapstick, injury, and waste—all of which depend upon illusion and metamorphosis, and contribute to the party's dreamlike, or nightmarish, character.

Distortions of the human image, visions of monsters, and the metamorphosis of the human form all suggest the logic of dream or nightmare, as well as the primitive festival. Gerald's party is not framed as a dream as are the "Alice" books or, in a sense, *Finnegans Wake*, but the party does contain specific retold dreams, and it does operate throughout with a certain visually associative dream logic.

When we call a fictional narrative "dream-like," first, we are identifying a kind of departure from novelistic realism. Dreams freely violate the realist conventions of fiction; time, causality, and probability are commonly altered or distorted. Dreams seem organized primarily by vivid images and dramatic moments. Most important, the shape of dreams appears to be directed by repressed wishes and fears; dreams are weighted with a significance that we sense but do not understand. Dreams are always in the past, recalled through memory's double remove, and the vagueness of retold dreams is always at least partially attributable to the limitations of memory. Narratives remind us of dreams, then, when they suspend normal notions of time and causality, move from one vivid image to another, and are vaguely suggestive of deeper significance. When the images are colored with horror or grotesqueness, narratives remind us of nightmares.

Works of literature are not dreams, however. Even "Kubla Khan" reflects the deliberateness of authorship. Dreams do become narratives when we tell them, however, and thus they have a particular resonance with fiction. Jackson Cope sees the dreamlike quality of *Gerald's Party* (he calls it a "detective novel woven with dreams") in its obsessive searching for obscured origins. Dreamwork and fiction both struggle with memory, "the primal crime." Thus Gerald's frequent reveries of vaguely remembered sexual encounters and Pardew's struggle to triumph over the force of time, which pushes the murder act into an unrecoverable past, are akin to dreamwork in their probing through confused memories to originating acts.

The breaking of boundaries and the voicing of the repressed articulate the transgressive power, which dreams and festivities share. Both realms present alternatives to the everyday world of waking, work, decorum, and rationality. Dreams, however, are individual, while festivals are communal. The difference is crucial, and it reminds us that Gerald's party is not a dream but is dreamlike. Dreams do become communal when they are told, and several are retold at Gerald's party. Perhaps these narratives are authorial attempts at connecting nightly individual transgressions with the sporadic communal transgressions. The novel contains five dream narratives and at least two dreamlike stories or visions. The most elaborate are those of the Inspector and Michelle; theirs present opposite views of revelation and comment upon one another and upon the novel itself.

One scene playfully frames the entire party as a dream. At the end of the party, Knud emerges from the TV room, having "slept through the whole goldarn party." He has had a remarkably vivid dream, which he begins to recount.

> I was like in some kind of war zone, see, only everyone was all mixed up and you didn't know who was on your side. . . . Since you couldn't be sure who anybody was, see, just to be safe you naturally had to kill everyone—right? Ha ha! You wouldn't *believe* the blood and gore! And all in 3-D and full color, too, I kid you not! I kept running into people and asking them, Where *am* I? They'd say: "What a *loony*," or something like that—and then I'd chop their heads off, right?

Metaphorically, Knud's dream is an equivalent to the party—certainly the blood and gore suggest such a parallel. The images of a confused war zone in an unknown location are darker, but they do evoke the neutral zone of festivity—here a festivity in which the only response to the breakdown of categories (no clear "us" and "them") is murderous violence. Perhaps the dream's most profound resemblance to the party is its hazy vagueness, which is especially acute in the novel's concluding pages: "You know . . . sometimes, Gerald," his wife comments, "it's almost as if . . . you were at a different party." Certainly

Knud was—but while he missed the communal festivity, he carries some trace of it in his foggy dream memories. The nightmare resonances of *Gerald's Party* blend with the magic of metamorphosis that characterizes the codes of slapstick and masquerade; at the same time, the dream haziness blunts the play with verisimilitude, upon which the detective code usually depends. The hints of communal dream experience suggest, finally, the importance of primitive ritual—the shared experience of magical transformation.

Throughout the novel, the phantasmagoria returns us to the initial image—Ros's corpse. Ros's character is presented almost entirely as a projection of male libido: the apotheosis of male sexual fantasy lies dead at the heart of the novel, signifying a dead end to desire. Ros's mysterious murder transforms her into a sacrificial victim, albeit a perverted sacrifice. Many elements of the ritual pattern and its traditional literary representations are clearly present: the death at the celebration, the near-sacred or legendary status of the victim, the lack of an individual clearly responsible for the murder, the use of the body in ritual performances, and the sale of articles of clothing as relics. Like the traditional *pharmakos,* Ros has a status that is both sacred and vilified, and she is elevated and killed, in a sense, by the whole community. The insistence that one's feelings for Ros are never unique but always shared ("You loved her very much." "Yes. Along with a thousand other guys") suggests the shared emotions the community invests in the sacrificial victim. Traditionally, the victim was killed by being stoned to death or driven off a cliff so that no one individual bore the guilt (or honor) of the deed. Here Ros is murdered, but, with the perpetrator unidentified, the party seems to share a vague and guilty sense of responsibility. Ros also has no relatives, which further improves her candidacy for sacred status.

Ros's death is not a primitive ritual but a murder at a contemporary party, and there is much to suggest that if she is a sacrificial victim, it is of a confused and perverted sacrifice that is life-destroying rather than preserving. Little in the events following her death suggests communal revitalization, except—significantly—that the party continues.

Ros apotheosizes the body as independent sensual entity. At the party she becomes, literally, all body, all corpse. The police desecrate the corpse in their investigation—taking film exposures, revealing the gaping stab wound along with her breasts, making an incision to take the liver temperature, cutting up and selling pieces of her panties, and encasing her in plastic bags. The true horror of the ultimate reduction to the physical—the separation of body and spirit—is revealed. The body remains on the floor throughout the party and is even used in an impromptu play staged by Zack Quagg's troupe:

> We got Ros playing herself—we use the corpse, I mean—but the rest of the cast interacts with it like she's alive, you dig? The trick being to make the audience get the sense she really is alive!

That trick fails. Ros reminds us of death's finality and omnipotence. Once, perhaps, she was "the flame at which all chilled men might well warm themselves." Now she reifies a boundary between art and life and reminds Gerald that "[n]o, we were not going around in circles, Ros wasn't anyway."

The death of the projection of male fantasy suggests the morbid and destructive consequences of the sexual imagination. The nature of Ros's wound implies that murder is a kind of sexual violation as well. Ros is stabbed to death, cut in her famous chest by some vicious weapon. Pointing to the corpse, the policeman Bob asserts, "Only one instrument could make a perforation like that! If we find the weapon that did it we'll have . . . our perpetrator. . . ." In *Gerald's Party,* an insistent parallel links the penis with a weapon—knife or ice pick. The mysterious ice pick, which seems at first to be a reification of a verbal misunderstanding, pops up repeatedly throughout the book, always in a phallic and guilt-related context. The cold undercurrent of the comedy of the mysteriously returning ice pick is the horrible realization that sexual desire exceeds individual control. Eventually we learn that the ice pick was planted by the Inspector: "One of the Old Man's favorite tricks. . . . His probe, he calls it. Stick it in, see what surfaces." One thing that surfaces is the shared guilt of the party in the murder of Ros. As the Inspector hyperbolically asserts, "The motive here was not merely irrational, it was preparational, atavistic, shared by all, you might say, and thus criminal in the deepest sense of the word." The party highlights the corruption of desire in a decadent world; the myriad of desperate or ridiculous sexual liaisons (Dickie's girls, Sally Ann's crushes, Janny Trainer's flirtations, Gerald's pursuit of Alison, Vic's brutal relationship with Eileen, Malcolm's unassisted orgasms) finds ultimate expression in Ros's corpse, in which the dream of vitalizing sexuality lies slaughtered.

The penis is the murder weapon, at least metaphorically. This conclusion is suggested by the comic links between ice pick and phallus, and by aspects of the homicide investigation. The police discover a series of photographs of Ros engaged in sexual intercourse with a costumed man. We later learn that the man is Gerald and that the costume is a disguise used once in a theatrical sexual romp for a photographer's benefit. Inspector Pardew irrationally concludes that the costumed man must be both a rapist and Ros's murderer. The penis is the only exposed part of his anatomy, and the police begin systematic penis examinations. The scenes, which include taking ink "penis prints" and an exchange in which a policeman revenges a suspect's erection by clubbing it with his nightstick, broadly parody police methodology. The comedy concludes with the interrogation of Gerald, in which the police browbeat him and shout, "Awright . . . *out with it!*" As Gerald reluctantly undoes his pants, the police confess that the interrogation is a joke: "We know it's not you. We showed your wife the photos and she said definitely not." The scene underscores the link between the murder and male sexuality; it pictures detection as a sort of undressing or humiliation. The phallic motif of the novel, epitomized in the pseudo murder weapon of the ice pick, mocks the traditional festival celebration of sexuality. Here, sexuality has become morbid and distorted.

Coover's development of the theme of sexual guilt around the murder of Ros illustrates his technique whereby the phantasmagoric themes of the novel gain intelligibility through the festive setting. We understand Ros's centrality better when we connect the party to ancient rituals and festivals. At that point, the image of the guests dancing around the corpse loses some of its initial strangeness. Death at the party is no longer an aberration but is part of the festive pattern. This is not to diminish the horror or to argue that Gerald's party follows a ritual pattern because it represents a revitalizing communal encounter with mortality. Rather, the very superimposition of the modern celebration on the ritual pattern reveals the alienation and despair in the world of Gerald and his friends. Ros's death does not discharge communal violence; it incites more violence in its wake (the murders of Roger and Vic and the various police beatings). Ros's communal being exists at the expense of her individual integrity, and her death reveals the lifenegating aspects of the party's supposed sexual freedom. Ultimately, we do not see in the party-goers' reactions to Ros a triumphant encounter with mortality; rather, we witness frantic avoidance as the guests satiate their desires around the blood-soaked body. The traditional wake, in which the encounter with death intensifies the celebration of life, is transformed into a festivity rendered ghastly by its desperate need to ignore the accumulating corpses.

The narrative structure of *Gerald's Party* is composed from the patterns associated with the detective story, slapstick comedy, carnivalistic celebration of the body, masquerade, dream tale, and ritual sacrifice. None of these codes is allowed to dominate, to "throw its weight around," in Coover's terms. Instead the novel's vitality emerges from the very incongruity of competing codes, which lends it a multivoiced richness that is greater than the sum of its narrative parts.

Constance Markey   (review date 27 January 1991)

SOURCE: "Professor Pinocchio," in *Chicago Tribune—Books,* January 27, 1991, pp. 1, 5.

[*Markey is an educator. In the review below, she offers a favorable assessment of* Pinocchio in Venice.]

Hide your eyes Walt Disney fans. Here comes a scary sequel to *Pinocchio* designed to squash the life out of Jiminy Cricket and trample in the dust his goody-good philosophy. But then maybe it is about time. Carlo Collodi's original 19th Century fairy tale was never meant to be a simpering Technicolor homily but an alarm, a sinister allegory on life's meager blessings and plentiful pitfalls.

And in this sense Robert Coover's adult fable *Pinocchio in Venice* comes closer to the stern morality of the early Italian story than Disney's saccharine film ever did. In fact, going beyond the earlier tale, Coover adds some frightening thoughts on human nature, questions that Collodi probably never even considered in the last century.

Can anyone—hapless wooden puppet or fragile human woodhead—ever honestly mend his ways? In the random confusion of contemporary life are real choices for the better possible? Have blue fairies, hope, happiness or heaven ever existed outside of movies or stories?

But before going on in his darkly amusing way to look closely at his own contemporary doubts, Coover happily fills the reader in on what became of the legendary puppet after the earlier fairy tale ended. Where did Pinocchio go after he escaped from the land of donkeys, after he saved his father Geppetto from the whale, after he became a "real boy"? To our delight we learn that, like many other Italians early in this century, he immigrated to America.

There he not only mastered his ABC's (something Collodi's lazy puppet was loath to do), but he also ironically won fame and fortune as a renowned university professor and author. Blue Fairy magic and modest living have obviously reformed our erstwhile hero. The new Pinocchio emerges as an American success story. Like a character out of Horatio Alger, a stubborn mule is transformed into a brilliant savant. Or is he?

Now, nearly a century after his youthful misadventures, we meet Pinocchio again, this time returning to Italy, changed maybe—but how? The novel tells us that he is much older, "an aging emeritus professor . . . burdened with illness, jet lag . . . and an excess of luggage." We learn that he has long since traded in his ancient *Abbecedario,* or speller, for a smart new portable computer. But these and other changes are on the surface.

We soon see that, inside, Professor Pinenut (as Pinocchio is slyly called in the novel) is still the same petulant piece of wood once whittled on father Geppetto's knee. Despite his publications, his "ennobling labor," he is still his naive younger self, "drawn back" impulsively to bawdy Venice "by the sudden vivid conviction that only by returning here—to his roots—would he find . . . that synthesizing metaphor that might adequately encapsulate the unified whole his life has been, and so provide him his closing chapter."

These are prophetic and self-fulfilling sentiments. Clearly our hero has done no more than come full circle. Already he senses that his legs "are turning to wood again," and this can only spell trouble (or arthritis). Whatever the case may be, bound by his stubborn wooden (or is it human?) nature, he is soon propelled on a nonstop, nightmare re-enactment of all his youthful follies.

Even disembarking he already has unwittingly collided with his two arch foes, the fox and the cat, now dressed as a porter and a hotel desk clerk. In no time he finds himself, as in the original story, back at the inn called the Gambero Rosso, where, as in the good old days, he is bilked of his "five pieces of gold," today in the shape of traveler's checks and credit cards.

Robbed and then abandoned to the beautiful but treacherous snow-swept panorama of Venice at carnival time, Pinenut-Pinocchio is aided by many of his former friends from earlier days, including his old puppet comrades from the Gran Teatro Dei Buratini. But in this version the puppets are a hilariously lecherous lot whose ideas of a good "festa" include "swapped parts" and showing off their brightly varnished bottoms.

Equally lascivious is the novel's Blue Fairy, easily Coover's funniest invention. A well-endowed bimbo in a tight blue angora sweater, she meets Pinenut-Pinocchio, her former teacher, in a Venetian church. There she takes him on a gum-chewing tour of the art treasures, complete with ribald commentaries on saints and madonnas and a Rabelaisian glance at a nearby painting of "the cute little butt on John-boy the Baptist."

At the book's beginning, our senile Pinocchio is hard-pressed to make sense of all these new mishaps. But as events grow more familiar to him, he is overcome by deja vu. "Something is bothering him about all this," Coover writes, "but he cannot think what it might be."

The author is a postmodernist with a vengeance. In drawing his new fairy tale from the traditional one, he has already done his homework very well, and now he expects the reader to do his.

One balances a copy of Coover in one hand and a copy of Collodi in the other in order not to miss the double-entendres, the subtle innuendo sandwiched between the two stories. Indeed, Coover is a master of the Italian cuss word, reveling in low-life erudition, lacing the book with prurient Italian not to be found in prudish vocabularies.

Also at hand one has a map of Venice, a guide to its museums and a history of the city and its art, indispensable tools to a reader bent on following Pinenut (alias "pignola" or fuss-budget in Italian) in his pursuit of his madcap destiny through the canals of Venice.

Pinocchio in Venice does not have a sweet ending because it asks too many questions. Exposing the safe, narrow world of the original fairy tale to the broad, haphazard realm of postmodernism is dangerous and challenging. It requires that the reader take a new hard look at his own wooden-headed ways, mulish choices and false blue fantasies.

What is human existence? Coover asks. Is it growing up or growing old? Is it a holy crusade or apocalypse now? Or is it the raucous round-trip this novel describes—a funny, frightening carnival ride hastily squeezed between howling birth and the reluctant return to mother oblivion?

Richard Eder   (review date 27 January 1991)

SOURCE: "Wooden Nickels for Pinocchio," in *Los Angeles Times Book Review,* January 27, 1991, pp. 3, 11.

[*An American critic, Eder received the 1987 Pulitzer Prize for Criticism and a 1987 citation for excellence in reviewing from the National Book Critics Circle. In the following, he provides a mixed review of* Pinocchio in Venice.]

In *Pinocchio in Venice,* Collodi's boy/puppet has become an elderly art-critic/puppet, winner of two Nobel Prizes in literature. Arriving in Venice at Carnival, he undergoes a series of misadventures roughly equivalent to those of his early days, though far raunchier. They are told in a learnedly witty logorrhea that knocks them askew; like reciting "Ode to a Nightingale" in stage-German.

It is *Pinocchio* and it is utterly different: a post-structuralist, litcrit demonstration that the language of a narrative does not convey the narrative but the narrator. Robert Coover, in this case.

Coover is not a bad subject; he is fierce and funny, campy at times, and Rabelaisian at others. When you get through the bramble hedges of his wordplay and reality-play, you find a winning sympathy for his stick-figure pedant, along with a meditation on humanity vs. art. As old Pinocchio thrashes once again in his lifelong (puppet-long?) agony over whether to be human flesh or wooden artifice, Coover's book teeters uneasily between the same choices.

In the children's classic, Pinocchio finally overcame his flaming temper, his incurable greed and his helpless acquiescence to every temptation. After many slips, he shed his puppet condition and dedicated himself to study and hard work, under the aegis of the Blue Fairy or Fairy Godmother.

A happy ending? Yes, if you are a 19th-Century Italian fabulist. No, if you are a late-20th-Century avant-garde ironist. Coover's aged Pinocchio obeyed his godmother so thoroughly that he became a world-renowned scholar. And yet, stumbling through the Venice railroad station with luggage, a word processor and no hotel reservations, he is as irascible, unappeased, greedy and naive as ever.

A decrepit porter takes him in tow. He leads him on a tortuous route through the empty midnight city, crossing and recrossing the same bridge—this is normal in Venice, the porter explains—and ends up at a deserted palazzo that he swears is a hotel run by a friend.

Porter and a friend—blind and one-armed—take the old visitor to a tavern where, they assure him, everything is on the house. They eat and drink tremendously, stick him with the bill, and abandon him. When he eventually struggles back to the "hotel" through a heavy fog, he finds it is empty and his luggage is gone. The two swindlers, of course, are the Fox and the Cat, grown old and mangy.

Pinocchio collapses in despair and humiliation, increased by a loss of control of his sphincter. Picked up by the police, who abuse him, he is rescued and cleaned up by Alidoro and Melampetta, the two giant mastiffs he once befriended, now as old and decrepit as he is.

He falls into a canal, is rescued and bilked once more by the Fox, this time masquerading as a gondolier. He is thrown into a trash can and mocked by a troupe of performing puppets until they recognize him as their own comrade, and invite him to join their performance of "When You Wish Upon a Star." Coover shuffles his texts with deliberate glee.

Pinocchio is taken in hand by Eugenio, the schoolmate whose braining by a heavy mathematics book first launched Pinocchio on his sea of troubles. Eugenio had been another victim of the wicked coachman and master of Pleasure Island; but instead of being turned into a donkey, he became the coachman's sex partner and, eventual-

ly, his successor. He has turned Pleasure Island into a vast and noxious industrial park, and swindled his way into owning much of Venice. Now, after putting Pinocchio up in luxury, he swindles him as well.

The picaresque misadventures proliferate through all kinds of bawdy and phantasmagoric variations, and page after page of historical, philosophical and autobiographical self-searching. Pinocchio is in anguish. For one thing, he is turning back into wood, and unsound, splintery wood, at that. For another, he is trying to figure out the meaning of his life and troubles as man and as puppet.

He is obsessed above all with the mysterious, polymorphous figure who has ruled his life. In the original *Pinocchio,* she was, whether as the dead child who became a spectral playmate or as the loving but reproachful Fairy Godmother, an unqualified angel. But to Coover's Pinocchio, she is passion, salvation and corruption all in one.

He recalls her, as dead child and as godmother, mingling pure love with the most squalid eroticism; and making use of his wooden parts—his nose, particularly—for sexual gratification. She reappears in Venice, this time as a voluptuous, blue-haired college student, cuddly and aloof at the same time.

He had owed his Nobel-laureated success to her insistence that he become human, with a human's dedication to work and achievement. Why, then, is he turning back into a puppet? Why do his fellow-puppets entreat him to join them?

As a wooden puppet he was free, he realizes. Choosing to become a boy, he became the puppet of "she who, whipping him with guilt and the pain of loss, has broken his spirit and bound him lifelong to a crazy dream, this cruel enchantment of human flesh. In effect, liberated from wood, he was imprisoned in metaphor."

I admire *Pinocchio in Venice* and I like some of it a great deal. But it has two difficulties. It is overpriced, and I don't mean the $19.95 that Linden Press is charging.

There is the baroque subversion of its own story, jumping ahead and slowly catching up, like a mountaineer throwing up his rope and hoisting himself behind it. There are the punning, the wonderfully obscene Venetian argot, the emotional whirligig of feelings not felt but provisionally tried on, the encrustation of jokes and philosophical asides, the simultaneous specificity and vagueness of events; as a dream is both specific and vague. All this sets up a dense screen we get through at considerable cost.

At too much cost, I think, for what is there. A lot "happens" and yet it often seems—not always—that all that is happening is Coover. And whereas a story will move and change from page to page, here, despite the frenetic activity, each page seems curiously the same.

The second difficulty is only partly related to the book. It is related also to my reading the book. This is self-referential, if you like. Considering the nature of Coover's writing, perhaps that is appropriate.

In any case, the reading was done some two weeks before this review is being published. Inevitably, through the complex fabric of words that aim at being essentially about themselves, other words came, via radio. It was the Congressional debate, it was the countdown.

"Body-bags," "massive airstrikes," "Saddam Hussein," "The Constitution," "gas-masks," "the draft." Each of these words contained not only reality, but the likelihood of drastic shifts of reality. That made it hard to pay attention to words that struggled and dazzled so hard to be about themselves, and to tell us that essentially they could be about nothing else.

Lorna Sage   (review date 31 May 1991)

SOURCE: "A Puppet-Show in the Great Bitch," in *The Times Literary Supplement,* No. 4596, May 31, 1991, p. 19.

[*In the following favorable review of* Pinocchio in Venice, *Sage praises the novel's humor, brilliance, and intensity.*]

In 1985 Cardinal Biffi, the Archbishop of Bologna, wrote a theological commentary on *Pinocchio,* showing how the story of the puppet whose nose grows every time he tells a lie is a most satisfactory allegory of original sin. Pinocchio, created by a carpenter-father, painfully weaned away from Toyland at the last, via the mediation of the mysterious blue-haired fairy, and turned into a flesh-and-blood human, is a brand plucked from a burning, a toy-boy who proves to have a soul after all. Robert Coover, celebrating the centenary of the death of Pinocchio's author Carlo Lorenzini (who was, even the good Cardinal admitted, a bit of an agnostic), has produced [**Pinocchio in Venice**] a hilariously phallic riposte, a carnivalesque reprise all about the agonies and delights of turning back to wood. His Pinocchio, after a century of humanity, opts for the dry rot and the unstrung joints, follows his nose and looks to his roots.

But why to Venice? This is a piece of poetical licence. Pinocchio's native Tuscany, despite the tourism and the cosmopolitan trendiness, wouldn't have provided anything like such an appropriate setting for this *fin-de-siècle* fantasy. Venice, thanks not only to Thomas Mann, but also to Calvino, Spark and McEwan, has become fiction's Toyland. Coover explains why, with panache—"this fake city built on fake pilings with its fake fronts and fake trompes l'oeil"; "the revel of the earth, the Masque of Italy", set on "a kind of itchy boundary between everywhere and somewhere, between simultaneity and history, process and stasis, geometry and optics." In other words, Venice is always sinking, never sunk, an icon of decadence and meretricious beauty, hallucinatory and penetrated by suggestive stinks, "Una vera cuccagna", which I think translates as the Great Bitch. So it is the right place for a terminal Festa, and a celebration of people as puppets.

This Pinocchio ("Professor Pinenut") has had a long and distinguished career in the United States as an art historian and philosopher, "living proof of the power of redemption through education". But now all that "scholarship, writing and tenured self-denial" is stripped away. First, on arriving at the station, he is robbed of his luggage, computer discs and credit cards—an episode done with natural-ism enough, though if you know the original *Pinocchio* you'll recognize the old villains, the Cat and the Fox, in the pair of crooks who part him from his possessions. And soon, he finds himself caught up on a tide of alternating euphoria and despair, lost in dirty, empty night-time piazzas, taking refuge in a church, only to find the paintings coming to life, and his erstwhile preceptress, the blue-haired fairy, ludicrously reincarnated in a gum-chewing tourist co-ed ("Call me Bluebell") who once did her nails in his first-year lectures, and now leads him a merry dance through the city's scary labyrinth. Led by the famous nose, he forgets the lessons of soulfulness and self-discipline he used to teach, and rediscovers the fatal power of fun. Meanwhile, hideously, he's falling apart, bits dropping off, his flesh peeling into tatters, the wood within asserting its rights.

Coover's readers will possibly be prepared for the manic pace with which one ecstatic disaster follows on another. It is like being at a non-stop party, where the energies are endlessly recharged with newcomers just when you long for it all to be over. Fun, Coover-style, is perfectly nightmarish—murderous in its intensity, chilling in the thoroughness with which it scatters and splinters the remnants of "character". And here, the whole process is rendered yet more exhausting by a continuous barrage of cunning cross-references to the original Pinocchio tale. For instance, his old friend Eugenio (a goody-goody in the original) is here reintroduced as a prancing carnival Queen, with a finger in every one of the rackets and scams that keep Venice afloat. And the other puppets, Harlequin and Columbine and the cast of *commedia dell'arte* characters, come screaming back in the form of The Great Puppet Show Vegetal Punk Rock band. The trick (a good old picaresque trick) is to rescue your hero from the fire or the gallows, as it were, in every chapter, cranking up the impossible odds each time. It is what blurb writers call a *tour de force:* brilliant and all-but-unbearable.

Nor would you need to be a Cardinal to find it shocking. "The Wood was made Flesh and Dwelt among us"; but now the flesh is made wood, our "seasoned sage, laureled, laquered and lionised" finds his way back to his own version of home and womb, and is apotheosized as—a dildo, all nose at last, climaxing in a euphoric narrative sneeze. Professor Pinenut catches an everlasting cold, and all the innocently obscene connotations of the children's book ("The boy who had to wear on his face what other people hid in their pants") are detonated at once, like fireworks. The ribaldry and the "fun" are a lot more strenuous and obsessive than self-denial ever was. But then, that is Coover's specialism—the joke on the joker, that the world without soul, far from being easy, is absurdly hard. There's "no end to it", laments poor creaky old Pinocchio, it's "like jumping, over and over, through a ring at the circus". Desire pulls the strings, we fall about, and watch ourselves in the act. Among the comedians of this extremity, Coover is the most indefatigable and wily, Toyland's master of ceremonies.

Brooke Horvath   (review date Fall 1991)

SOURCE: A review of *Pinocchio in Venice,* in *The Review*

of Contemporary Fiction, Vol. 11, No. 3, Fall, 1991, pp. 267-68.

[*In the following, Horvath offers a favorable review of* Pinocchio in Venice.]

I'm afraid I know how we may soon hear **Pinocchio in Venice** described: as tour-de-force postmodern intertextuality and "superposition" amenable to Bakhtinian analysis, as an allegorical account of all of us puppets ravaged by childhood traumas in our yearning for selfhood, as . . . But let's leave all that for somebody else to say. What **Pinocchio in Venice** more simply is, amico mio, is a very adult (mature, that is, not pornographic, though often ribald and decidedly irreverent) appropriation of and sequel to *The Adventures of Pinocchio,* a book already rich in psychological and fabulistic (whoops!) implication (if you don't believe me, check out the Carlo Collodi entry in *Children's Literature Review*). As such, *Pinocchio* is perfect source material for Coover, and the thematizing reader, tooled for profundity, will find an ample supply of lumber here with which to construct any number of elaborately useful readings.

In **Pinocchio in Venice** Coover's signature themes are all present and particularly getatable, for his Pinocchio (a.k.a. Dr. Pinenut) is a highly articulate two-time Nobel laureate and "world-renowned art historian and critic, social anthropologist, moral philosopher, and theological gadfly," the "lionized author" of such modern classics as *The Wretch* and *The Transformation of the Beast.* As the novel opens, Pinocchio—reverting to wood in his old age and suffering myriad physical ailments from weevil infestation to warping—has just arrived in Venice, hoping to find the inspiration needed to complete his magnum opus *Mamma* (a tribute to the Blue-Haired Fairy) but encountering instead, mostly in wonderfully transmogrified form, all his former friends and enemies: Eugenio, the Cat and the Fox, the Little Man, and the rest. As the novel unfolds, he endures one pathetic-comic misadventure after another, each provoking reflections upon art and nature, life and death, essence and existence, wisdom and woodenheadedness, and so on and so forth—those standard Coover themes.

I don't mean to shortchange the novel's serious intentions; indeed, some of Coover's finest passages are to be found during the novel's more meditative moments, as when San Giorgio Maggiori is described as sitting "gravely at anchor like an ordered thought within a confused sensuous dream, this damp dream called Venice"—though such austere moments don't overstay their welcome: this description of Venice ends with the city characterized as "the original wet dream," thus making the sentence a fine example of Coover's penchant for shifting tones quickly and bringing unlikely materials into boisterous collision. Indeed, it is at the level of verbal performance—of wordplay, antic set piece, and the hammering together of diverse styles and moods—that I find myself arrested, almost every scene a small triumph of picaresque slapstick and Rabelaisian excess, every paragraph a "mad skein" of epithets ("you cuntless whore" is the one I'm saving for a special occasion), bad puns (for instance, Pinocchio's observation that only he and Jonah "fully understand what

a gut feeling really is"), and provocative, often reflexive observations (e.g., the "little fagot's" belief that art today is "nothing more than, like scrimshaw, a decorated fossil"). In short, **Pinocchio in Venice** is one very funny, solid book; moving, too, with not a wooden line or ill-mortised joint to be found. One recommendation: to appreciate fully Coover's cleverness and his book's charm, reread *The Adventures of Pinocchio* first. Besides, like me, you may find a preliminary run through Collodi an unexpected treat in itself.

FURTHER READING

Bibliography

Andersen, Richard. *Robert Coover.* Boston: Twayne Publishers, 1981, 156 p.
    Combines an essay discussing the role of the fictionmaker in Coover's fiction with an annotated bibliography.

Criticism

Caldwell, Roy C., Jr. "Of Hobby-Horses, Baseball, and Narrative: Coover's *Universal Baseball Association.*" *Modern Fiction Studies* 33, No. 1 (Spring 1987): 161-71.
    Discusses the intertwining elements of baseball and fiction-making in *The Universal Baseball Association.*

Durand, Régis. "The Exemplary Fictions of Robert Coover." In *Les américanistes,* edited by Ira D. Johnson and Christiane Johnson, pp. 130-37. Port Washington, N.Y.: Kennikat Press, 1978.
    Compares various critical perspectives on Coover's fiction and offers a sympathetic yet objective approach.

Gordon, Lois. *Robert Coover: The Universal Fictionmaking Process.* Carbondale: Southern Illinois University Press, 1983, 182 p.
    Focuses on innovative aspects of Coover's fiction.

Hite, Molly. "A Parody of Martyrdom: The Rosenbergs, Cold War Theology, and Robert Coover's *The Public Burning.*" *Novel* 27, No. 1 (Fall 1993): 85-101.
    Assesses Coover's treatment of the cultural context of the Rosenbergs' execution in *The Public Burning.*

Kennedy, Thomas E. *Robert Coover: A Study of Short Fiction.* New York: Twayne Publishers, 1992, 153 p.
    A study of Coover's short story collections that includes interviews and a compilation of criticism from additional sources.

Maltby, Paul. "Robert Coover." In his *Dissident Postmodernists: Barthelme, Coover, Pynchon,* pp. 82-130. Philadelphia: University of Pennsylvania Press, 1991.
    Comments on the subversion of literary-narrative conventions, the use of pattern, and the instrumentalization of meaning in Coover's fiction.

Mazurek, Raymond A. "Metafiction, the Historical Novel, and Coover's *The Public Burning.*" *Critique: Studies in Modern Fiction* XXIII, No. 3 (Spring 1982): 29-42.
    Argues that *The Public Burning* represents a "new kind of historical novel."

Orlov, Paul A. "A Fiction of Politically Fantastic 'Facts': Robert Coover's *The Public Burning.*" In *Politics and the Muse: Studies in the Politics of Recent American Literature,* edited by Adam J. Sorkin, pp. 111-23. Bowling Green, OH: Bowling Green State University Popular Press, 1989.

> Examines the relationship between politics and fiction in *The Public Burning.*

Pearce, Richard D. "Robert Coover's Kaleidoscopic Spectacle." In his *The Novel in Motion: An Approach to Modern Fiction,* pp. 102-17. Columbus: Ohio State University Press, 1983.

> Analyzes Coover's use of rapid motion and spectacle to simultaneously engage and upset his readers.

Siegle, Robert B. "Coover's 'The Magic Poker' and the Techniques of Fiction." *Essays in Literature* VIII, No. 2 (Fall 1981): 203-17.

> Assesses Coover's narrative technique in "The Magic Poker."

Interviews

Gado, Frank. "Robert Coover." In his *First Person: Conversations on Writers & Writing,* pp. 142-59. Schenectady, N.Y.: Union College Press, 1973.

> Interview with Coover in which he discusses his literary influences, the writing process, and formal and thematic aspects of his fiction.

McCaffery, Larry. "Robert Coover on His Own and Other Fictions: An Interview." *Genre* XIV, No. 1 (Spring 1981): 45-63.

> Interview in which Coover discusses the role of the contemporary writer in America as well as his short fiction, novels, poetry, and plays.

Additional coverage of Coover's life and career is contained in the following sources published by Gale Research: *Contemporary Authors,* Vols. 45-48; *Contemporary Authors New Revision Series,* Vols. 3, 37; *Contemporary Literary Criticism,* Vols. 3, 7, 15, 32, 46; *Dictionary of Literary Biography,* Vol. 2; *Dictionary of Literary Biography Yearbook: 1981; Major 20th-Century Writers;* and *Short Story Criticism,* Vol. 15.

Jacques Derrida

1930-

Algerian-born French philosopher, critic, and educator.

The following entry presents an overview of Derrida's career through 1994. For further information on his life and works, see *CLC*, Volume 24.

INTRODUCTION

Since 1967, when he simultaneously published three of his most important works, Derrida has been an extraordinarily influential and controversial voice in contemporary philosophy and critical theory. While his theories deal primarily with philosophical issues, his critique of traditional Western philosophy as a "metaphysics of presence" has had an equally profound impact on contemporary literary theory, where critics have appropriated his theories on language into the movement known as "deconstructionism."

Biographical Information

Derrida was born to middle-class Jewish parents in El Biar, Algeria. During his childhood, he was traumatized by the anti-Semitism of Algeria's Christian majority. In 1940, Jewish children were expelled from Algeria's schools, and violence against Jews became officially sanctioned. Derrida remarked later that these experiences left him feeling profoundly alienated and hinted that they were formative influences on the central themes of his philosophy. When he was eighteen years old, Derrida moved to France, having earned his baccalaureate degree in Algeria. After hearing a radio broadcast about the French novelist and philosopher Albert Camus, Derrida decided to enroll in philosophy classes at the École Normale Supérieure in Paris. While a university student, Derrida was influenced by the philosophy of Jean-Paul Sartre, although he later repudiated Sartrean existentialism. By 1957 Derrida was planning his doctoral dissertation, to be titled "The Ideality of the Literary Object." However, at this time he became immersed in the phenomenological writings of the German philosopher Edmund Husserl and shifted his attention to formulating a critique of metaphysics, the central branch of traditional philosophy, which consists of the search for the ultimate foundations of reality. Since 1960 Derrida has been a professor of philosophy at universities in Paris and the director of the École des Hautes Etudes en Sciences Sociales, also in Paris.

Major Works

Derrida first introduced his ideas about language and philosophy in his *Traduction et introduction à l'origine de la géométrie d'Edmund Husserl* (1962; *Edmund Husserl's*

"Origin of Geometry: An Introduction"), which contains a lengthy introduction and a translation of Husserl's 1939 essay "Die Frage nach dem Ursprung der Geometrie." However, Derrida did not attract widespread notice until 1967, when he published *La voix et le phénomène* (*Speech and Phenomena, and Other Essays on Husserl's Theory of Signs*), *De la grammatologie* (*Of Grammatology*), and *L'écriture et la différence* (*Writing and Difference*). *Of Grammatology* is Derrida's most extensive and conventionally argued presentation of his central theme, that Western philosophy systematically portrays writing as the debased "supplement" of the voice, which is assumed to have a more privileged access to philosophical truth because of its supposedly more intimate correspondence with thought itself. Utilizing the method known as "deconstruction," a form of close textual interpretation which analyzes the internal contradictions of philosophical discourse, Derrida demonstrates that Western philosophy's arguments against writing consist of metaphors and figures of speech—the very elements of rhetoric which philosophers since Plato have denigrated as unphilosophical. For Derrida, the metaphysical philosopher's inherently rhetorical argumentation betrays his desire for a transcendental truth beyond the imperfections of language—a per-

ception which Derrida expresses very succinctly in his famous statement, "There is nothing outside the text." Applying these insights in *Speech and Phenomena*, Derrida contends that Husserl's phenomenology—a branch of philosophy which seeks to establish the absolute foundations of human perception—relies on metaphors or allegories of the metaphysical belief that language (in particular, written language) is too contradictory and concrete a medium to embody absolute truth. *Writing and Difference* is a collection of essays on various seminal figures in the history of philosophy which further illustrates Derrida's method of deconstruction. In 1972, Derrida again published three books nearly simultaneously. The most important of these, *La dissémination* (*Dissemination*), signalled a new direction in Derrida's work. While a large section of the book presents a critique of Plato's doctrine of truth, it begins and ends with a practical demonstration of Derrida's ideas on writing. Focusing on the concept of "dissemination," which refers to the inherent indeterminacy of meaning in language (due to the arbitrary relationship between words and the objects they signify), Derrida invents unusual words and sentence structures to demonstrate the fundamental instability and contradictoriness of philosophical discourse. The complexity of this "playful" mode of deconstruction reached its zenith in Derrida's following work, *Glas* (1974; *Glas*), which presents his discussion of the German philosopher Georg Wilhelm Friedrich Hegel and the French dramatist, novelist, and poet, Jean Genet. The commentary is arranged in parallel columns—Hegel on the left, Genet on the right, with an occasional third in the middle—which modify and reflect upon one another. The typographical and etymological wordplay of *Glas* has led to comparisons with James Joyce's *Finnegans Wake* (1939), which was written in a blend of different languages. Critics generally have not regarded *Glas* as a work of philosophical significance, beyond the fact that its format puts into practice Derrida's thesis that literary and philosophical texts are distinguished only by the structure of their metaphors and rhetoric. Derrida's subsequent works, while not as extreme in their experimentation as *Glas*, continue to display his concern with conflating literary and philosophical modes of discourse. In *La carte postale* (1980; *The Post Card*) Derrida utilizes metaphors of postal communication to interpret psychoanalysis as a series of transmissions between a sender and a receiver in which meaning is mediated, detoured, and deferred by language. Moreover, Derrida composes the first section of *The Post Card* as a series of fictitious letters which parody epistolary literature and flout the conventions of "serious" philosophy. Two of Derrida's works, *Éperons* (1976; *Spurs*) and *De l'esprit* (1987; *Of Spirit*) are considered important because they present Derrida's commentary on the German philosophers Friedrich Nietzsche and Martin Heidegger, whom Derrida and many of his interpreters have cited as his primary philosophical influences. He derived the word and the concept of deconstruction from Heidegger's use of the German word *destruktion;* and Heidegger's definitive four-volume study of Nietzsche, in which he argues that his philosophy is both the culmination and "overturning" of traditional metaphysics, provided a model for Derrida's deconstructive readings of philosophers.

Critical Reception

Derrida's works have tended to incite passionately divergent reactions from critics. Philosophers oriented toward the analytical and logical positivist schools, such as John Searle, refute Derrida by arguing that his championing of "indeterminacy" and linguistic freeplay leads to extreme forms of skepticism and nihilism. However, critic Christopher Norris defends Derrida by pointing out that deconstruction is actually an exceedingly rigorous form of analysis, and that Derrida's understanding of philosophy as a rhetorically structured form of writing indistinguishable in its essence from literature has been espoused by numerous other philosophers, notably Nietzsche. Derrida's reception among literary critics has been no less contentious. Part of the controversy may be attributed to the casual linkage of Derrida's name to the literary deconstructionists. As Rodolphe Gasché has pointed out, Derrida's philosophy does not concern itself directly with literary texts, and literary deconstruction is actually an independent movement which has for the most part only loosely applied Derrida's theories. Given that ideological and intellectual differences of opinion have made Derrida an extremely controversial figure, there can be no critical consensus as to the value of his work. However, his prominence in the history of philosophy seems assured. Philosopher Richard Rorty argues that the lasting value of Derrida's work is in its critical analysis of traditional Western philosophy. Rorty concludes: "Having done to Heidegger what Heidegger did to Nietzsche is the negative achievement which, after all the chatter about 'deconstruction' is over, will give Derrida a place in the history of philosophy."

PRINCIPAL WORKS

Traduction et introduction à l'origine de la géométrie d'Edmund Husserl [translator] [*Edmund Husserl's "Origin of Geometry: An Introduction"*] (philosophy) 1962

De la grammatologie [*Of Grammatology*] (philosophy) 1967

L'écriture et la différence [*Writing and Difference*] (philosophy) 1967

Le voix et le phénomène: Introduction au problème du signe dans le phénoménologie de Husserl [*Speech and Phenomena, and Other Essays on Husserl's Theory of Signs*] (philosophy) 1967

La dissémination [*Dissemination*] (philosophy) 1972

Marges de la philosophie [*Margins of Philosophy*] (philosophy) 1972

Positions (interviews) 1972

Glas [*Glas*] (criticism) 1974

L'archéologie du frivole: Lire Condillac [*The Archeology of the Frivolous: Reading Condillac*] (criticism) 1976

Éperons: Les styles de Nietzsche [*Spurs: Nietzsche's Styles*] (philosophy) 1976

La vérité en peinture [*The Truth in Painting*] (criticism) 1978

La carte postale: De Socrate à Freud et au-delà [*The Post Card: From Socrates to Freud and Beyond*] (philosophy) 1980

Signéponge [*Signsponge*] (criticism) 1984

Parages (criticism) 1986

De l'esprit: Heidegger et la question [*Of Spirit: Heidegger and the Question*] (philosophy) 1987

Psyché: Inventions de l'autre [*Psyche: Inventions of the Other*] (philosophy) 1987

†*Limited Inc* (philosophy) 1988

Du droit à la philosophie (philosophy) 1990

Le problème de la genèse dans la philosophie de Husserl (philosophy) 1990

---

*Derrida translated this work from the original German to French and wrote a lengthy introduction. The English translation is by John P. Leavey, Jr.

†This volume contains three essays, including "Limited Inc abc . . ." which originally appeared in the journal *Glyph*, No. 2, 1977.

CRITICISM

Denis Donoghue (review date 16 April 1977)

SOURCE: A review of *Of Grammatology*, in *The New Republic*, Vol. 176, No. 16, April 16, 1977, pp. 32-4.

[*Donoghue is an Irish critic and educator. In the following review, he asserts that* Of Grammatology, *in spite of its "excruciating" difficulties, is a work of great importance for students of philosophy and literature.*]

In April 1970 a colloquium of French philosophers and critics was held at Cluny on certain major themes in contemporary thought. By all accounts the most voluble presence at the proceedings was a man who was not present at all: the Algerian-French philosopher Jacques Derrida. Most of the discussions turned, twisted and swirled upon his work, especially the three books he had published in 1967, *La voix et le phénomène,* a critique of Husserl's theory of signs, *L'écriture et la différence* and *De la grammatologie.* For all I know, there may have been some philosophers at Cluny who claimed to have felt the first tremor of recognition several years before Derrida became famous; perhaps when he published his first book, a translation of Husserl's *The Origin of Geometry* (1962) which included a long introductory analysis of the work. But I doubt it. Derrida's reputation in France in the years before 1967 was provoked mainly by the essays brought together in *L'écriture et la différence.* The books published in 1967 have now been extended in several directions by Derrida's *La dissémination* (1972), *Marges de la philosophie* (1972), *Positions* (1972) and the bizarre production, *Glas* (1974). It is clear that Derrida and Jacques Lacan largely define the spirit of the age, or at least the spirit of the present moment, in French philosophy and criticism.

The position in the United States is different. David B. Allison's translation of *La voix et la phénomène* was pub-

lished by Northwestern University Press in 1973 as *Speech and Phenomena,* but it did not cause a stir, so far as I recall. But gradually, over the last few years, some of Derrida's most important essays have been translated and published in such periodicals as *Diacritics* and *New Literary History.* The result is that where two or three avant-grade critics are gathered together at any university from Yale to Irvine, Derrida is in the midst of them, as present and absent as he was at Cluny. Students who are satisfied that they have taken the gist of Lévi-Strauss, Barthes and Foucault are now doing their homework on Derrida. I assume they are finding the experience extraordinarily difficult. So [Gayatri Chakrovorty] Spivak's translation of *De la grammatologie* has arrived at the precise moment of its necessity. Her long introductory essay is nearly as difficult as the text it precedes, but it is extremely perceptive and helpful.

Derrida has described his philosophic project as "a general strategy of deconstruction which would avoid both simply neutralizing the binary oppositions of metaphysics and simply residing, while upholding it, in the closed sphere of these oppositions." This description, if it could be embodied in anything but its desire, would put Derrida beyond metaphysics and Structuralism alike. The main force of his critique has always been directed against nostalgia; particularly against those cries of nostalgia which constitute, in his view, the metaphysics of presence and origin. Those lost paradises are places of yearning for origin and end. Derrida opposes in Husserl the metaphysics of self-consciousness which accords privileged status to speech and voice: nostalgia is logocentric, phonocentric, it speaks of being and experience, universal logic, alphabetic writing, and its only theme is loss. Derrida wants to turn us away from that predicament. He is concerned with everything that escapes or refutes the metaphysics of presence and refuses to return to a paternal source. Deconstruction is an effort to dismantle the axioms upon which a metaphysical argument is based: it requires a critical parsing of a terminology, so that even when the philosopher uses the given terms his use of them is heretical. Much of Derrida's work is a series of arguments with his predecessors, especially Nietzsche, Freud, Heidegger and Husserl; in recent work he is arguing with Hegel, Foucault, Lacan, Sollers. *Of Grammatology* is a meditation provoked by Derrida's reading of Rousseau's *Essay on the Origin of Languages,* supplemented by critical glosses upon Saussure and Lévi-Strauss. Grammatology itself arises from Derrida's dissatisfaction with these predecessors and especially with tinges of nostalgia which he finds in their writings. As for the word: it is available already to mean "a treatise upon letters, upon the alphabet, syllabation, reading, and writing," but in Derrida's use the word points only toward a possibility which he is the first to declare at the same time an impossibility. Grammatology, were it to exist, would be beyond semiology, it would dismantle logocentrism and use conventional signs only while erasing them, *"sous rature."* Spivak's introductory essay is splendid on this aspect of Derrida, and especially on the bearing of his technical vocabulary, such words as *l'écriture, différance, alterité, errance, jeu, trace,* and *déconstruction.* A philosopher, like a poet, is revealed in his diction: by his choice of words he is known. Just as Derrida discloses in Rousseau a writer who distrusts writing and longs for the prox-imity of the self to its voice, so Spivak approaches Derrida through the structure of his diction; no ideas but in the words themselves.

It would be misleading to say that Derrida is trying to bring metaphysics to an end. Either metaphysics has al-ready come to an end or the question of its end is beside the point. Besides, it would be lonelier without the loneli-ness. Like any honest heretic, he wants to retain religion if only to pervert it; retaining its terms while erasing them, deleting the words while keeping their trace still legible. He does not claim to have stepped beyond philosophy, but rather to have read the philosophers in a certain spirit. I do not think much would be lost or abused if we called that spirit Irony and referred to Derrida as an ironist. Irony smiles upon contradiction and speaks blithely of ca-tastrophe: it dislikes residence and offers itself, like Derri-da's work, as a philosophy for nomads. Derrida circum-vents residence by resorting to the concept of *jeu* as an act logically prior to the possibility of presence or absence. The final intention of ***De la grammatologie,*** according to Derrida, is "to make enigmatic what one thinks one un-derstands by the words 'proximity,' 'immediacy,' and 'presence.'" Could any stated aim express the spirit of Irony more precisely? Not to clarify, but to retain the enig-matic state; and to put every crucial noun within the scru-tiny of those inverted commas. No philosopher is more in-clined than Derrida to the inverted commas: every ab-stract noun is forced to reveal its speciousness. Derrida takes pleasure in showing that when we have ostensibly demonstrated the coherence of a structure we have merely revealed the force of a desire. He loves to ascribe to objects only a virtual status; their existence is less reliably sub-stantial than the shadow they cast. If someone points to a center, Derrida does not deny that there is or may be a center, but he asserts that the center is a function, not a being. It would be no pleasure to Derrida to have his mind praised for its creative force; it has no creative ambition. Criticism as he practices it is a contraceptive act, appropri-ate in his view to an age of mass populations and mass cli-ches. Indeed he is willing to use his mind only as a double agent: never what it seems or says, always an accomplice, its promises at best provisional, its language an honest lie; its vocality a form of equivocation. Such a mind could not have been a native Structuralist, because Structuralists be-lieve in the structures of opposed terms they employ. Der-rida employs such terms only on the understanding that belief is not required of him: his mind is willing to be stained, contaminated or provoked by nouns, but it admits no obligation to them. Derrida tends to explain things on the ground of their impossibility; and then to admit possi-bility by admitting desire. Faced with something that is thought to be an attribute, he rejects the appellation, drives it away from ontology, and locates it in a space of need, desire, or play. He loves to be able to say of some-thing that it may always not have taken place, "il peut tou-jours n'avoir pas lieu," or that its operation cannot be on-tologically sustained. The long meditation on Rousseau which accounts for most of ***De la grammatologie*** is mainly concerned with supplementarity *(supplémentarité),* a mode of replacement and substitution, and Derrida con-cedes that supplementarity "makes possible all that con-stitutes the property of man: speech, society, passion etc." But lest we think anything has been achieved or money lodged in the human bank, he asks: "But what is this prop-erty of man?" Answer:—

> On the one hand, it is that of which the possibili-ty must be thought before man, and outside of him. Man allows himself to be announced to himself after the fact of supplementarity, which is thus not an attribute—accidental or essen-tial—of man. For on the other hand, supplemen-tarity, which *is nothing,* neither a presence nor an absence, is neither a substance nor an essence of man. It is precisely the play of presence and absence, the opening of this play that no meta-physical or ontological concept can compre-hend.

Presence is already absence: what seems an origin is al-ready belated. Derrida endorses only that presence which goes out of itself and returns to itself in the forms of substi-tution. He is patient only with demonstrably fugitive forms of immediacy.

I have mentioned that Spivak seeks Derrida in his techni-cal vocabulary and that it is the right place to start look-ing. But there is a simple sentence in ***De la grammatologie*** which I offer as especially revealing: it does not contain any technical terms, but rather a gesture which is pure De-rrida. The sentence reads: "Penser, c'est ce que nous savons déjà n'avoir pas encore commencé à faire"; 'think-ing is what we already know that we have not yet begun.' Pure Derrida; because it enacts nothing but the gap be-tween belatedness and futurity, placing a void where tradi-tional metaphysics would place a presence. There are many philosophers who love to use both hands to achieve precision: on the one hand, and yet on the other. Derrida uses both hands to say the same thing: no, the situation is neither this nor that but the play between them.

How can we account, then, for Derrida's bearing upon contemporary thought in philosophy and criticism? There are a few obvious considerations. His work is clearly con-genial to a situation in which Europe has been displaced from the center of the metaphysical circle: metaphysics is no longer permitted to proceed along white Caucasian as-sumptions, history is no longer understood merely as the history of meaning. No orchids are currently offered to ethnocentrism, eschatology, teleology, or idealism: the no-tion of play is deemed to make up for the lack of a stable center. Structuralism is on the decline: only the most ar-dent believers would wish to have the decline arrested. De-rrida finds in the very notion of structure a longing for presence, origin, and center. It may be that ***De la gramma-tologie*** is one of those books which not only create the au-dience by which they are appreciated, but are willing to wait until an even more sluggish audience is in the mood to receive them: they wait for readers to catch up with them.

I have implied my own view of Derrida, that his work is important chiefly because it extends the possibilities of irony: it brings post-Nietzschean joy and gaiety to bear upon circumstances which, left to their own attributes, would make for demoralization and *ennui.* If you read

Derrida for the plot, you would shoot yourself. Paul de Man has described the main theme of Derrida's work as "the recurrent repression, in Western thought, of all written forms of language, their degradation to a mere adjunct or supplement to the live presence of the spoken word." Hence the reading and misreading of Rousseau in *De la grammatologie.* Students of philosophy are likely to find Derrida's meaning chiefly in the idea of *différance;* students of literature will probably come upon it more congenially through the idea of *jeu,* relating it to other and more readily available terminologies of literature as play. In either case there is cause for rejoicing in the translation of *De la grammatologie,* an excruciatingly difficult work in any language. Spivak's translation is deliberately literal, and she knows that there is bound to be a pedantic air in the English which the French accommodates more cheerfully. "Nous sommes donc d'entrée de jeu dans le devenir-immotivé du symbole" sounds more at home to itself than the English version, "From the very opening of the game, then, we are within the becoming-unmotivated of the symbol." I suppose it would be easier to say, ". . . we are taken up in the unmotivated play of the symbol," but that would make Derrida sound more agreeable and less 'Germanic' than his French. The same would apply if we tried to translate Derrida's "d'exhiber son être-inacceptable dans un miroir contre-ethnocentrique" as something more gracious than Ms. Spivak's version, "of exhibiting its being-unacceptable in an anti-ethnocentric mirror." Spivak's understanding of Derrida's work is extremely acute: she is determined that if we encounter him at all we will earn the right to do so by coping with his recalcitrance. An easy translation would be a bad translation.

Christopher Norris   (essay date 1982)

SOURCE: "Jacques Derrida: Language against Itself," in *Deconstruction: Theory and Practice,* 1982. Reprint by Routledge, 1988, pp. 18-41.

[*Norris is an English critic and educator who has authored numerous studies on Derrida and deconstruction. In the following excerpt, he offers a detailed summary of Derrida's theories on language, philosophy, and writing.*]

The texts of Jacques Derrida defy classification according to any of the clear-cut boundaries that define modern academic discourse. They belong to 'philosophy' in so far as they raise certain familiar questions about thought, language, identity and other longstanding themes of philosophical debate. Moreover, they raise those questions through a form of critical dialogue with previous texts, many of which (from Plato to Husserl and Heidegger) are normally assigned to the history of philosophic thought. Derrida's professional training was as a student of philosophy (at the École Normale Supérieure in Paris, where he now teaches), and his writings demand of the reader a considerable knowledge of the subject. Yet Derrida's texts are like nothing else in modern philosophy, and indeed represent a challenge to the whole tradition and self-understanding of that discipline.

One way of describing this challenge is to say that Derrida refuses to grant philosophy the kind of privileged status

it has always claimed as the sovereign dispenser of reason. Derrida confronts this claim to power on its own chosen ground. He argues that philosophers have been able to impose their various systems of thought only by ignoring, or suppressing, the disruptive effects of language. His aim is always to draw out these effects by a critical reading that fastens on, and skilfully unpicks, the elements of metaphor and other figurative devices at work in the texts of philosophy. Deconstruction in this, its most rigorous form acts as a constant reminder of the ways in which language deflects or complicates the philosopher's project. Above all, deconstruction works to undo the idea—according to Derrida, the ruling illusion of Western metaphysics—that reason can somehow dispense with language and arrive at a pure, self-authenticating truth or method. Though philosophy strives to efface its textual or 'written' character, the signs of that struggle are there to be read in its blindspots of metaphor and other rhetorical strategies.

In this sense Derrida's writings seem more akin to literary criticism than philosophy. They rest on the assumption that modes of rhetorical analysis, hitherto applied mainly to literary texts, are in fact indispensable for reading *any* kind of discourse, philosophy included. Literature is no longer seen as a kind of poor relation to philosophy contenting itself with mere 'imaginary' themes and forgoing any claim to philosophic dignity and truth. This attitude has, of course, a long prehistory in Western tradition. It was Plato who expelled the poets from his ideal republic, who set up reason as a guard against the false beguilements of rhetoric, and who called forth a series of critical 'defences' and 'apologies' which runs right through from Sir Philip Sidney to I. A. Richards and the American New Critics. The lines of defence have been variously drawn up, according to whether the critic sees himself as *contesting* philosophy on its own argumentative ground, or as operating outside its reach on a different—though equally privileged—ground.

In the latter camp it is F. R. Leavis who has most forcefully asserted the critic's right to dissociate his habits of thought from the logical checks and procedures demanded of philosophic discourse. Criticism on Leavis's term is a matter of communicating deep-laid intuitive responses, which analysis can point to and persuasively *enact,* but which it can by no means *explain* or *theorize* about. Philosophy is kept at arm's length by treating literary language as a medium of 'lived' or 'felt' experience, a region where the critic's 'mature' responses are his only reliable guide and where there is no support to be had from abstract methodology. Hence Leavis's insistence on the virtues of 'practical' criticism (or close reading), allied to such moral imperatives as 'relevance', 'maturity' and an 'open reverence before life'. The effect of this programme is to draw a firm line of demarcation between literary language and the problems of philosophy. Leavis rejects the idea that criticism need concern itself with epistemological problems, or rhetorical modes of working, implicit in literary texts. His ideal critic works within a discipline defined by qualities of responsiveness and intuitive tact, rather than subtlety of philosophic grasp.

Such was the tenor of Leavis's famous 'reply' to Rene Wellek [in 'Literary Criticism and Philosophy,' *Scrutiny* VI], who had asked (in an otherwise appreciative essay) why Leavis should not provide a more coherent or worked-out rationale for his critical judgements. To do so would amount to a betrayal, it seemed, of the different but equally disciplined activity required of the literary critic. That activity was justified in so far as it preserved the life-giving wholeness of critical response from the deadening weight of abstract theory.

Leavis represents the most rooted and uncompromising form of resistance to philosophy on the part of literary criticism. The American New Critics, with their penchant for rhetorical system and method, tended to strike a somewhat more ambiguous stance. . . . [Allen Tate has written] despairingly of criticism as a middle-ground activity torn between the warring poles of imagination and philosophic reason. Typically, the New Critics managed to contain these tensions by devising a rhetoric of figure and paradox which closed the poem off within its own formal limits. Poetry (and fiction, so far as they dealt with it) took on a kind of self-authenticating status, confirmed by the various dogmas of critical method. Conceptual problems—like that of relating poetic 'form' to communicable 'meaning'—were neatly side-stepped by being treated as if they were somehow constitutive of poetry's uniquely complex mode of existence. Paradox and irony, which Tate saw as bearing (to some extent at least) on the critic's own predicament, were generally regarded by the New Criticism as objectively 'there' in the poem's structure of meaning.

Hence the circularity and self-sufficient character of New Critical rhetoric. It kept philosophy at bay, not, like Leavis, by flatly denying its relevance, but by translating its questions into a language of irreducibly *aesthetic* paradox and tension. As critics came to interrogate this rhetoric of closure, so it became more evident that the problems had merely been repressed or displaced, and that criticism had yet to discover its relation to the modes and exigencies of 'philosophic' discourse. It was at this point in the history of American criticism and its discontents that Derrida's influence came as such a liberating force. His work provided a whole new set of powerful strategies which placed the literary critic, not simply on a footing with the philosopher, but in a complex relationship (or rivalry) with him, whereby philosophic claims were open to rhetorical questioning or *deconstruction.* Paul de Man has described this process of thought in which 'literature turns out to be the main topic of philosophy and the model of the kind of truth to which it aspires' [*Allegories of Reading: Figural Language in Rousseau, Nietzsche, Rilke, and Proust,* 1979]. Once alerted to the *rhetorical* nature of philosophic arguments, the critic is in a strong position to reverse the age-old prejudice against literature as a debased or merely deceptive form of language. It now becomes possible to argue—indeed, impossible to deny—that literary texts are less deluded than the discourse of philosophy, precisely because they implicitly acknowledge and exploit their own rhetorical status. Philosophy comes to seem, in de Man's work, 'an endless reflection on its own destruction at the hands of literature'.

> **Above all, deconstruction works to undo the idea—according to Derrida, the ruling illusion of Western metaphysics—that reason can somehow dispense with language and arrive at a pure, self-authenticating truth or method.**
>
> **—*Christopher Norris***

Derrida's attentions are therefore divided between 'literary' and 'philosophical' texts, a distinction which in practice he constantly breaks down and shows to be based on a deep but untenable prejudice. His readings of Mallarmé, Valéry, Genet and Sollers are every bit as rigorous as his essays on philosophers like Hegel and Husserl. Literary texts are not fenced off inside some specialized realm of figurative licence where rational commentary fears to tread. Unlike the New Critics, Derrida has no desire to establish a rigid demarcation of zones between literary language and critical discourse. On the contrary, he sets out to show that certain kinds of paradox are produced across all the varieties of discourse by a motivating impulse which runs so deep in Western thought that it respects none of the conventional boundaries. Criticism, philosophy, linguistics, anthropology, the whole modern gamut of 'human sciences'—all are at some point subjected to Derrida's relentless critique. This is the most important point to grasp about deconstruction. There is no language so vigilant or self-aware that it can effectively escape the conditions placed upon thought by its own prehistory and ruling metaphysic.

The passage 'beyond formalism' was broached in various ways. Some critics (like Geoffrey Hartman) have adopted a wayward and teasingly indirect style, while others—notably Paul de Man—have attempted to *think through* the paradoxes of New Critical method. De Man's essays in *Blindness and Insight* (1971) were a powerful application of Derridean ideas to the rhetoric of modern poetics. To read the New Critics with an eye to their founding metaphors is to discover, in de Man's terminology, a 'blindness' inseparable from their moments of greatest 'insight'. Their formalist notion of the poem as 'verbal icon'—a timeless, self-possessed structure of meaning—is shown to deconstruct its own claim through unrecognized twists of implication. Their obsession with 'organic' form was undermined by those very 'ambiguities' and 'tensions' which they sought out in order to praise, and so contain, them. 'This unitarian criticism', as de Man puts it, 'finally becomes a criticism of ambiguity, an ironic reflection on the absence of the unity it had postulated'. 'Form' itself turns out to be more an operative fiction, a product of the interpreter's rage for order, than anything vested in the literary work itself. The organicist metaphors of New Critical parlance result from what de Man calls the 'dialectical interplay' set up between text and interpreter. 'Because such patient and delicate attention was paid to the reading of forms, the critic pragmatically entered into the hermeneu-

tic circle of interpretation, mistaking it for the organic circularity of natural processes'.

Deconstruction draws no line between the kind of close
reading appropriate to a 'literary' text and the strategies
required to draw out the subtler implications of critical
language. Since *all* forms of writing run up against perplexities of meaning and intent, there is no longer any
question of a privileged status for literature and a secondary, self-effacing role for the language of criticism. De
Man fully accepts the Derridean principle that 'writing',
with its own dialectic of blindness and insight, precedes all
the categories that conventional wisdom has tried to impose on it.

This amounts to a downright refusal of the system of priorities which has traditionally governed the relation between 'critical' and 'creative' language. That distinction
rested on the idea that literary texts embodied an authentic or self-possessed plenitude of meaning which criticism
could only hint at by its roundabout strategies of reading.
For Derrida, this is yet another sign of the rooted Western
prejudice which tries to reduce writing—or the 'free play'
of language—to a stable meaning equated with the character of *speech*. In spoken language (so the implication runs),
meaning is 'present' to the speaker through an act of inward self-surveillance which ensures a perfect, intuitive
'fit' between intention and utterance. Literary texts have
been accorded the status of a self-authenticated meaning
and truth, a privilege deriving (in Derrida's view) from the
deep mistrust of textuality which pervades Western attitudes to language. This mystique of origins and presence
can best be challenged by annulling the imaginary boundaries of discourse, the various territorial imperatives
which mark off 'literature' from 'criticism', or 'philosophy' from everything that stands outside its traditional domain.

This redistribution of discourse implies some very drastic
shifts in our habits of reading. For one thing, it means that
critical texts must be read in a radically different way, not
so much for their interpretative 'insights' as for the symptoms of 'blindness' which mark their conceptual limits. De
Man puts the case most succinctly:

> Since they are not scientific, critical texts have
> to be read with the same awareness of ambiva-
> lence that is brought to the study of non-critical
> literary texts, and since the rhetoric of their dis-
> course depends on categorical statements, the
> discrepancy between meaning and assertion is a
> constitutive part of their logic.

This argument cuts both ways when it comes to defining
the critic's position *vis-à-vis* the literary text. Clearly it denies him the kind of methodical or disciplined approach
which has been the recurrent dream of a certain critical
tradition. On the other hand it offers a way beyond the
rigid separation of roles which would cast him as a mere
attendant upon the sovereign word of the text. What it
loses in methodical self-assurance, criticism stands to regain in rhetorical interest on its own account. A similar
reversal of priorities occurs in the deconstructive reading
of 'literary' texts. There is no longer the sense of a primal
authority attaching to the literary work and requiring that

criticism keep its respectful distance. The autonomy of the
text is actively invaded by a new and insubordinate style
of commentary which puts in question all the traditional
attributes of literary meaning. But at the same time this
questioning raises literature to a point of rhetorical complexity and interest where its moments of 'blindness' are
often more acutely revealing than anything in the discourse of philosophy.

Such has been the effect of Derrida's writing on a deeply
entrenched conservative tradition—that of American
New Criticism—which had already started to question its
own ideology. What might have carried on as a series of
skirmishing tactics (or virtuoso exercises in Hartman's
manner) was galvanized by Derrida into something far
more radical and deeply unsettling. We can now look
more closely at the major texts in which Derrida sets forth
the terms and implications of deconstructive reading.
Rather than take his books one by one, I shall fasten upon
certain crucial themes and argumentative strategies, acting as far as possible on Derrida's reiterated warning that
his texts are not a store of ready-made 'concepts' but an
activity resistant to any such reductive ploy.

If there is a single theme which draws together the otherwise disparate field of 'structuralist' thought, it is the principle—first enounced by Saussure—that language is a *differential* network of meaning. There is no self-evident or
one-to-one link between 'signifier' and 'signified', the word
as (spoken or written) vehicle and the concept it serves to
evoke. Both are caught up in a play of distinctive features
where differences of sound and sense are the only markers
of meaning. Thus, at the simplest phonetic level, *bat* and
cat are distinguished (and meaning is generated) by the
switching of initial consonants. The same is true of *bag*
and *big,* with their inter-substitution of vowels. Language
is in this sense *diacritical,* or dependent on a structured
economy of differences which allows a relatively small
range of linguistic elements to signify a vast repertoire of
negotiable meanings.

Saussure went on from this cardinal insight to construct
what has become a dominant working programme for
modern linguistics. His proposals broke with traditional
thinking in two main respects. He argued, first, that linguistics could be placed on a scientific basis only by adopting a 'synchronic' approach, one that treated language as
a network of structural relations existing at a given point
in time. Such a discipline would have to renounce—or
provisionally suspend—the 'diachronic' methods of historical research and speculation which had dominated
nineteenth-century linguistics. Second, Saussure found it
necessary to make a firm distinction between the isolated
speech-act or utterance (*parole*) and the general system of
articulate relationships from which it derived (*la langue*).
This system, he reasoned, had to underlie and pre-exist
any possible sequence of speech, since meaning could be
produced only in accordance with the organizing ground-
rules of language.

Structuralism, in all its manifold forms and applications,
developed in the wake of Saussure's founding programme
for modern linguistics. This is not the place for a detailed
account of that development, which the reader will find

expounded in Terence Hawkes's *Structuralism and Semiotics* (1977). Briefly, structuralism took over from Saussure the idea that *all* cultural systems—not only language—could be studied from a 'synchronic' viewpoint which would bring out their various related levels of signifying activity.

The precise status of linguistics in regard to this new-found enterprise was a topic of considerable debate. Saussure had argued that language was but one of many codes, and that linguistics should therefore not expect to retain its methodological pre-eminence. With the advent of a fully fledged *semiotics,* or science of signs, language would assume its proper, participant place in the social life of signs in general. Paradoxically, it was Roland Barthes—the most versatile of structuralist thinkers—who originally wanted to reverse this perspective and reinstate linguistics as the master-science of semiology. Barthes was quick to exploit the possibilities of structuralist method across a diverse field of cultural codes, from literary texts to cookery, fashion and photography. Yet in his *Elements of Semiology* (1967) Barthes is to be found expressing the conviction that 'the moment we go on to systems where the sociological significance is more than superficial, we are once more confronted with language'. And this, he explains, because 'we are, much more than in former times . . . a civilization of the written word'.

Of course, this text belongs to an early stage of Barthes's development, a phase he was later to criticize precisely for its overdependence on concepts of metalinguistic or 'scientific' knowledge. . . . [He] eventually travelled toward deconstructing such concepts through a textual activity aware of its own shifting and provisional status. But the kind of linguistic analogy that Barthes once deployed is representative of structuralism at a certain definite point in its development. It was at this point that Derrida intervened, with the object of wrenching structuralism away from what he saw as its residual attachment to a Western metaphysics of meaning and presence. In particular, he questioned the role of linguistics in dictating the methodological priorities of structuralist thought. Derrida's critique of Saussure, in his essay '**Linguistics and Grammatology**' [in *Of Grammatology*], is therefore a crucial point of encounter for the deconstructive enterprise.

The argument turns on Saussure's attitude to the relative priority of *spoken* as opposed to *written* language, a dualism Derrida locates at the heart of Western philosophic tradition. He cites a number of passages from Saussure in which writing is treated as a merely derivative or secondary form of linguistic notation, always dependent on the primary reality of speech and the sense of a speaker's 'presence' behind his words. Derrida finds a dislocating tension here, a problem that other structuralists (Barthes included) had been content to regard as a puzzling but unavoidable paradox. What are we to make of this privileged status for speech (*parole*) in a theory which is otherwise so heavily committed to the prior significance of language-as-system (*langue*)? Barthes presents the question most succinctly:

> A language does not exist properly except in 'the speaking mass'; one cannot handle speech except

by drawing on the language. But conversely, a language is possible only starting from speech; historically, speech phenomena always precede language phenomena (it is speech which makes language evolve), and genetically, a language is constituted in the individual through his learning from the environmental speech. [*Elements of Semiology*]

The relation of language and speech is thus 'dialectical'; it sets in train a process of thought which shuttles productively from one standpoint to the other.

Where Derrida differs with Barthes is in his refusal simply to accept this paradox as part of a larger, encompassing project (that of semiology) which would overcome such apparent contradictions. For Derrida, there is a fundamental *blindness* involved in the Saussurian text, a failure to think through the problems engendered by its own mode of discourse. What is repressed there, along with 'writing' in its common or restricted sense, is the idea of language as a signifying system which exceeds all the bounds of individual 'presence' and speech. Looking back over the passage from Barthes quoted above, one can see how 'speech' terminology prevails, even where the argument is ostensibly stating the rival claims of language-as-system. Thus Barthes (drawing on Saussure) refers metaphorically to 'the speaking mass' in a context which purportedly invokes the totality of language, but which appeals even so to actual speakers and their speech as the source of that totality. Barthes may state, as a matter of principle, that language is at once the 'product and the instrument' of speech, that their relationship is always 'dialectical' and not to be reduced to any clear-cut priority. In practice, however, his theorizing leans upon metaphors which implicitly privilege individual speech above the system of meaning that sustains it.

Derrida's line of attack is to pick out such loaded metaphors and show how they work to support a whole powerful structure of presuppositions. If Saussure was impelled, like others before him, to relegate writing to a suspect or secondary status, then the mechanisms of that repression are there in his text and open to a deconstructive reading. Thus Derrida sets out to demonstrate

> 1 that writing is systematically degraded in Saussurian linguistics;
>
> 2 that this strategy runs up against suppressed but visible contradictions;
>
> 3 that by following these contradictions through one is led *beyond* linguistics to a 'grammatology', or science of writing and textuality in general.

Derrida sees a whole metaphysics at work behind the privilege granted to speech in Saussure's methodology. *Voice* becomes a metaphor of truth and authenticity, a source of self-present 'living' speech as opposed to the secondary lifeless emanations of writing. In speaking one is able to experience (supposedly) an intimate link between sound and sense, an inward and immediate realization of meaning which yields itself up without reserve to perfect, transparent understanding. Writing, on the contrary, destroys this ideal of pure self-presence. It obtrudes an alien, depersonalized medium, a deceiving shadow which falls between intent and meaning, between utterance and understanding. It occupies a promiscuous public realm where authority is sacrificed to the vagaries and whims of textual 'dissemination'. Writing, in short, is a threat to the deeply traditional view that associates truth with self-presence and the 'natural' language wherein it finds expression.

Against this tradition Derrida argues what at first must seem an extraordinary case: that writing is in fact the *pre-condition* of language and must be conceived as prior to speech. This involves showing, to begin with, that the concept of writing cannot be reduced to its normal (i.e. graphic or inscriptional) sense. As Derrida deploys it, the term is closely related to that element of signifying *difference* which Saussure thought essential to the workings of language. Writing, for Derrida, is the 'free play' or element of undecidability within every system of communication. Its operations are precisely those which escape the self-consciousness of speech and its deluded sense of the mastery of concept over language. Writing is the endless displacement of meaning which both governs language and places it for ever beyond the reach of a stable, self-authenticating knowledge. In this sense, oral language already belongs to a 'generalized writing', the effects of which are everywhere disguised by the illusory 'metaphysics of presence'. Language is always inscribed in a network of relays and differential 'traces' which can never be grasped by the individual speaker. What Saussure calls the 'natural bond' between sound and sense—the guaranteed self-knowledge of speech—is in fact a delusion engendered by the age-old repression of a 'feared and subversive' writing. To question that bond is to venture into regions as yet uncharted, and requires a rigorous effort of conceptual de-sublimation or 'waking up'. Writing is that which exceeds—and has the power to dismantle—the whole traditional edifice of Western attitudes to thought and language.

The repression of writing lies deep in Saussure's proposed methodology. It shows in his refusal to consider any form of linguistic notation outside the phonetic-alphabetical script of Western culture. As opposed, that is, to the non-phonetic varieties which Derrida often discusses: hieroglyphs, algebraic notions, formalized languages of different kinds. This 'phonocentric' bias is closely allied, in Derrida's view, to the underlying structure of assumptions which links Saussure's project to Western metaphysics. So long as writing is treated as a more or less faithful transcription of the elements of speech, its effects can be safely contained within that massive tradition. As Derrida puts it:

> The system of language associated with phonetic-alphabetic writing is that within which logo-centric metaphysics, determining the sense of being as presence, has been produced. This logocentrism, this *epoch* of the full speech, has always placed in parenthesis, *suspended,* and suppressed for essential reasons, all free reflection on the origin and status of writing. [*Of Grammatology*]

There is a deep connection between the craving for self-presence, as it affects the philosophy of language, and the

'phonocentrism' which prevents linguistic method from effectively broaching the question of writing. Both are components of a powerful metaphysic which works to confirm the 'natural' priority of speech.

Derrida shows that these assumptions, though consistent and mutually reinforcing at a certain level, lie open to disruption as soon as one substitutes 'writing' for 'speech' in the conceptual order that governs them. The effect is unsettling not only for linguistics but for every field of enquiry based on the idea of an immediate, intuitive access to meaning. Derrida traces the exclusion or degradation of writing as a gesture perpetually re-enacted in the texts of Western philosophy. It occurs wherever reason looks for a ground or authenticating method immune to the snares of textuality. If meaning could only attain to a state of self-sufficient intelligibility, language would no longer present any problem but serve as an obedient vehicle of thought. To pose the question of writing in its radical, Derridean form is thus to transgress—or 'violently' oppose—the conventional relation of language and thought.

Such is the deconstructive violence to which Derrida subjects the texts of Saussure and his structuralist successors. It is not a question, he repeats, of rejecting the entire Saussurian project or denying its historical significance. Rather it is a matter of driving that project to its ultimate conclusions and seeing where those conclusions work to challenge the project's conventional premises. In Derrida's words,

> It is when he is not expressly dealing with writing, when he feels he has closed the parentheses on that subject, that Saussure opens the field of a general grammatology . . . then one realizes that what was chased off limits, the wandering outcast of linguistics, has indeed never ceased to haunt language as its primary and most intimate possibility. Then something which was never spoken and which is nothing other than writing itself as the origin of language writes itself in Saussure's discourse. [*Of Grammatology*]

Saussure is thus not merely held up as one more exemplar of a blind and self-deceiving tradition. Derrida makes it clear that structuralism, whatever its conceptual limits, was a necessary stage on the way to deconstruction. Saussure set the terms for a development which passed beyond the grasp of his explicit programme but which could hardly have been formulated otherwise. By repressing the problem which his own theory of language all but brought into view, Saussure transcended the express limitations of that theory. The very concept of 'writing' was enlarged through this encounter into something primordial and far removed from its place in traditional usage.

The point will bear repeating: deconstruction is not simply a strategic reversal of categories which otherwise remain distinct and unaffected. It seeks to undo both a given order of priorities *and* the very system of conceptual opposition that makes that order possible. Thus Derrida is emphatically *not* trying to prove that 'writing' in its normal, restricted sense is somehow more basic than speech. On the contrary, he agrees with Saussure that linguistics had better not yield uncritically to the 'prestige' that written texts have traditionally enjoyed in Western culture. If the opposition speech/writing is not subjected to a full critique, it remains 'a blind prejudice', one which (in Derrida's phrase) 'is no doubt common to the accused and the prosecutor'. Deconstruction is better provided with texts, like Saussure's, which foreground the problematic status of writing precisely by adopting a traditional perspective. A repressed writing then reasserts itself most forcibly through the detours and twists of implication discovered in Saussure. It is the 'tension between gesture and statement' in such critical texts which 'liberates the future of a general grammatology'.

Deconstruction is therefore an activity of reading which remains closely tied to the texts it interrogates, and which can never set up independently as a self-enclosed system of operative concepts. Derrida maintains an extreme and exemplary scepticism when it comes to defining his own methodology. The deconstructive leverage supplied by a term like *writing* depends on its resistance to any kind of settled or definitive meaning. To call it a 'concept' is to fall straight away into the trap of imagining some worked-out scheme of hierarchical ideas in which 'writing' would occupy its own, privileged place. We have seen how structuralism proved itself amenable to such uses. The *concept* of structure is easily kidnapped by a tame methodology which treats it as a handy organizing theme and ignores its unsettling implications. Derrida perceives the same process at work in the structured economy of differential features which Saussure described as the precondition of language. Once the term is fixed within a given explanatory system, it becomes (like 'structure') usable in ways that deny or suppress its radical insights.

Hence Derrida's tactical recourse to a shifting battery of terms which cannot be reduced to any single, self-identical meaning. *Differance* is perhaps the most effective of these, since it sets up a disturbance at the level of the signifier (created by the anomalous spelling) which graphically resists such reduction. Its sense remains suspended between the two French verbs 'to differ' and 'to defer', both of which contribute to its textual force but neither of which can fully capture its meaning. Language depends on 'difference' since, as Saussure showed once and for all, it consists in the structure of distinctive oppositions which make up its basic economy. Where Derrida breaks new ground, and where the science of grammatology takes its cue, is in the extent to which 'differ' shades into 'defer'. This involves the idea that meaning is always *deferred,* perhaps to the point of an endless supplementarity, by the play of signification. *Differance* not only designates this theme but offers in its own unstable meaning a graphic example of the process at work.

Derrida deploys a whole rhetoric of similar terms as a means of preventing the conceptual closure—or reduction to an ultimate meaning—which might otherwise threaten his texts. Among them is the notion of 'supplement', itself bound up in a supplementary play of meaning which defies semantic reduction. To see how it is put to work we can turn to Derrida's essays on Rousseau and Lévi-Strauss [in *Of Grammatology*], where the theme is that of writing

in the context of anthropology and the cultural 'sciences of man'.

For Derrida, writing (in its extended sense) is at once the source of all cultural activity and the dangerous knowledge of its own constitution which culture must always repress. Writing takes on the subversive character of a 'debased, lateralized, displaced theme', yet one that exercises 'a permanent and obsessive pressure . . . a feared writing must be cancelled because it erases the presence of the self-same (*propre*) within speech'. This passage occurs in the course of a chapter on Rousseau, whose *Essay on the Origin of Languages* is the starting point for one of Derrida's most brilliant meditations.

Rousseau thought of speech as the originary form and the healthiest, most 'natural' condition of language. Writing he regarded with curious distrust as a merely derivative and somehow debilitating mode of expression. This attitude of course falls square with Rousseau's philosophy of human nature, his conviction that mankind had degenerated from a state of natural grace into the bondage of politics and civilized existence. Language becomes an index of the degree to which nature is corrupted and divided against itself by the false sophistications of culture. What Derrida does, in a remarkable tour of argument, is to show that Rousseau contradicts himself at various points in his text, so that far from proving speech to be the origin of language, and writing a merely parasitic growth, his essay confirms the priority of writing and the illusory character of all such myths of origin.

Rousseau, for instance, treats of writing as the 'supplement' of spoken language, existing in a secondary relation to speech just as speech itself—by the same token—is at one remove from whatever it depicts. Such arguments have a long prehistory in Western thought. Like Plato's mystical doctrine of forms, the effect is to devalue the activities of art and writing by constant appeal to a pure metaphysics of presence, their distance from which condemns them to an endless play of deceitful imitation. For Derrida, the 'supplementarity' of writing is indeed the root of the matter, but not in the derogatory sense that Rousseau intended. Writing is the example *par excellence* of a supplement which enters into the heart of all intelligible discourse and comes to define its very nature and condition. Derrida shows that Rousseau's essay submits to this reversal even in the process of condemning the subversive influence he attributes to writing and its 'supplementary' character. A whole strange thematics of the supplement runs through the detail of Rousseau's argument like a guilty obsession and twists his implications against their avowed intent. That Rousseau cannot possibly *mean what he says* (or say what he means) at certain crucial junctures is the outcome of Derrida's perverse but utterly literal reading. Rousseau's text, like Saussure's, is subject to a violent wrenching from within, which prevents it from carrying through the logic of its own professed intention.

Music was one of the manifold interests which went toward the Rousseauist philosophy of culture, and Derrida has some fascinating pages relating Rousseau's ideas on the subject to the general theme of speech *versus* writing. The argument turns on Rousseau's preference for the vocal or melodic style, which he identified with the Italian music of his time, as against the harmonic or contrapuntal, which typified the supposed weakness and decadence of French tradition. As a matter of musical history this view is open to all kinds of scholarly question. Derrida, however, is not concerned so much with musicological fact as with the *textual* symptoms of doubt and duplicity which mark Rousseau's argument. The primacy of melody in music is held to follow from its closeness to song, which in turn represents the nearest approach to the passionate origins of speech itself. Harmony enters music by the same 'degenerate' process of supplementarity which marks off writing from speech. As music developed, melody (as Rousseau explains it) 'imperceptibly lost its former energy, and the calculus of intervals was substituted for nicety of inflection'.

Derrida fastens upon this and similar passages in Rousseau's text, and shows that what Rousseau is really describing is the condition, not of music in a phase of historical decline, but of *any* music which aspires beyond the stage of a primitive, inarticulate cry. Forgetfulness of origin may be the ruse by which harmony and writing manage to efface the primordial 'warmth' of a pure communion with nature. Yet Rousseau is forced obliquely to acknowledge (through the blind-spots and contradictions of his text) that music is strictly *unthinkable* without the supplement of harmony, or swerve from origin, which marks the possibility of its progress. Rousseau's 'embarrassment' is plainest when he attempts to define the originary nature of melody and song. If song is already, as Rousseau suggests in his *Dictionary of Music,* 'a kind of modification of the human voice', then how can he assign to it (Derrida asks) 'an absolutely characteristic (*propre*) modality'? The text unconsciously confesses what Rousseau is at such pains to deny: that thought is incapable of positing a pure, unadulterated origin for speech or song. Rousseau's argument, as Derrida describes it,

> twists about in a sort of oblique effort to act *as if* degeneration were not prescribed in the genesis and as if evil *supervened upon* a good origin. As if song and speech, which have the same act and the same birth pangs, had not always already begun to separate themselves.

Rousseau's text cannot mean what it says, or *literally* say what it means. His intentions are skewed and distorted by the 'dangerous supplement' of writing as it approaches the theme of origin.

Derrida perceives such discrepancies at every turn of Rousseau's argument. Wherever the primacy of 'nature' (or speech) is opposed to the debasements of 'culture' (or writing), there comes into play an aberrant logic which inverts the opposition and cuts away the ground of its very meaning. Thus Rousseau's quest for the 'origin' of language turns out to *presuppose* an already articulate movement of production which must be cut off at source from any such originating presence. The supplement has to be inserted, Derrida writes, 'at the point where language begins to be articulated, is born, that is, from falling short of itself, when its accent or intonation, marking origin and

passion within it, is effaced under that *other* mark of origin which is articulation'.

'Accent', 'intonation' and 'passion' are bound up together as positive terms in Rousseau's philosophy of man and nature. They all belong to that ruling ideology of voice-as-presence which equates the primacy of speech with the virtues of an innocent, unclouded self-knowledge. Rousseau constructs an elaborate mythology based on the contrast between 'natural' languages which remain close to their sources in passionate utterance, and 'artificial' language where passion is overlaid by the rules and devices of convention. The former he associates with 'the South', with a culture largely indifferent to progress and reflecting in its language the gracefulness and innocence of origins. The latter is identified with those 'Northern' characteristics which, for Rousseau, signalize the decadence of progress in culture. Passion is overcome by reason, community life invaded by the forces of large-scale economic order. In language the polarity (according to Rousseau) is equally marked. In the passionate, mellifluous, vowel-based language of the South one encounters speech near the wellspring of its origin. The tongues of the North, by contrast, are marked by a harsh and heavily *consonantal* structure which makes them more efficient as communicative instruments but widens the rift between feeling and meaning, between instinct and expression.

For Derrida, this Rousseauist mythology is a classic instance of the reasoning that always comes up against its limits in trying to locate any origin (or 'natural' condition) for language. He shows how Rousseau associates the threat of writing with that process of 'articulation' by which language extends its communicative grasp and power. 'Progress' involves a displacement from origin and a virtual supersession of all those elements in speech—accent, melody, the marks of passion—which bound language to the speaking individual and community at large. To deconstruct this mythology of presence, Derrida has only to pursue that 'strange graphic of supplementarity' which weaves its way through Rousseau's text. What emerges is the fact that language, once it passes beyond the stage of a primitive cry, is 'always already' inhabited by writing, or by all those signs of an 'articulate' structure which Rousseau considered decadent. As with Saussure's linguistic methodology, so with Rousseau's historical speculation: speech in its imaginary plenitude of meaning is disrupted at source by the supplement of writing.

This is why Rousseau occupies such a central place in *Of Grammatology* and Derrida's writing generally. He represents a whole constellation of themes which, in one form or another, have dominated subsequent discourse on language and the 'sciences of man'. His texts are a constant, obsessive repetition of gestures which miss their rhetorical mark and display the insufficiency of language when it strives for an origin beyond all reach. The deadlocked prolixity of Rousseau's text is also a lesson to the modern philosopher or linguist:

> Our language, even if we are pleased to speak it, has already substituted too many articulations for too many accents, it has lost life and warmth, it is already eaten by writing. Its accentuated

features have been gnawed through by the consonants.

Speech itself is always shot through with the differences and traces of non-present meaning which constitute articulate language. To attempt to 'think the origin' in Rousseau's fashion is therefore to arrive at a paradox which cannot be resolved or surpassed: 'The question is of an originary supplement, if this absurd expression may be risked, totally unacceptable as it is within classical logic.' The supplement is that which both signifies the lack of a 'presence', or state of plenitude for ever beyond recall, and *compensates* for that lack by setting in motion its own economy of difference. It is nowhere present in language but everywhere presupposed by the existence of language as a pre-articulated system. Philosophies that take no account of its activity are thereby condemned (Derrida argues) to a ceaseless repetition of the paradoxes brought to light in his reading of Rousseau.

This critique is extended to the structuralist anthropology of Claude Lévi-Strauss, where Derrida finds the same issues raised in terms of nature versus culture. Lévi-Strauss was among the first to perceive that the insights of structural linguistics could be applied to other 'languages' or signifying systems in the effort to elucidate their underlying codes. This gave rise to what is perhaps the most impressive single achievement of structuralism in its broadbased interpretative mode. Lévi-Strauss rests his analyses of myth and ritual on the conviction that, behind all the surface varieties thrown up by the world's different cultures, there exist certain deep regularities and patterns which reveal themselves to structural investigation. It is a matter of looking beyond their manifest content to the structures of symbolic opposition and sequence that organize these various narratives. At a certain level of abstraction, he argues, it is possible to make out patterns of development and formal relations which cut right across all distinctions of culture and nationality. Myths can then be seen as a problem-solving exercise, adapted to context in various ways but always leading back to the great abiding issues of human existence—mainly the structures of law and taboo surrounding such institutions as marriage, the family, tribal identity, and so forth. The end point of such analysis may well be to discover, as Lévi-Strauss frequently does, a formula of algebraic power and simplicity to express the logic underlying a dispersed corpus of myths.

Derrida reads Lévi-Strauss as an heir to both Saussure's 'phonocentric' bias and Rousseau's nostalgic craving for origins and presence. The two lines of thought converge in what Derrida shows to be a subtle but weighted dialectic between 'nature' and 'culture'. The phonocentric basis of Lévi-Strauss's method derives, quite explicitly, from the structural linguistics of Saussure and Roman Jakobson. But along with this methodological commitment there is also, according to Derrida, a '*linguistic* and *metaphysical* phonologism which raises speech above writing'. In effect, Lévi-Strauss is seen as performing for modern (structuralist) anthropology the same ambiguous service that Rousseau performed for the speculative science of his day. The nature/culture opposition can be shown to deconstruct itself even as Lévi-Strauss yields to the Rousseauistic dream of an innocent language and a tribal community untouched by the evils of civilization.

Derrida's arguments are largely based on a single brief excerpt—'The Writing Lesson'—from Lévi-Strauss's book *Tristes Tropiques* (1961). Here the anthropologist sets out to analyse the emergence of writing and its consequences among a tribe (the Nambikwara) whose transition to 'civilization' he describes with undisguised feelings of sadness and guilt. He records how the motives of political power ('hierarchization, the economic function . . . participation in a quasi-religious secret') manifested themselves in the earliest responses to written language. Lévi-Strauss gives expression, like Rousseau, to an eloquent longing for the lost primordial unity of speech-before-writing. He takes upon himself the burden of guilt produced by this encounter between civilization and the 'innocent' culture it ceaselessly exploits. For Lévi-Strauss, the themes of exploitation and writing go naturally together, as do those of writing and violence.

Derrida's answer is not to deny the inherent 'violence' of writing, nor yet to argue that it marks a stage of irreversible advance beyond the 'primitive' mentality. On the one hand he points out that the Nambikwara, on Lévi-Strauss's own evidence, were already subject to a tribal order marked 'with a spectacular violence'. Their social intrigues and rituals of power are in manifest contrast to the retrospective feelings of the anthropologist, who elsewhere presents an idealized picture of their playful and uncorrupted nature. Moreover, as Derrida argues, this suggests that writing is always already a part of social existence, and cannot be dated from the moment when the anthropologist, that guilty spectator, introduced its merely graphic conventions. In truth, there is no such pure 'authenticity' as Lévi-Strauss (like Rousseau) imagines to have been destroyed by the advent of writing in this narrow sense. 'Self-presence, transparent proximity in the face-to-face of countenances . . . this determination of authenticity is therefore classic . . . Rousseauistic but already the inheritor of Platonism'. From this point it is possible for Derrida to argue that the violence of writing is there at the outset of all social discourse; that in fact it marks 'the origin of morality as of immorality', the 'non-ethical opening of ethics'.

> **For Derrida, writing (in its extended sense) is at once the source of all cultural activity and the dangerous knowledge of its own constitution which culture must always repress. Writing takes on the subversive character of a "debased, lateralized, displaced theme," yet one that exercises "a permanent and obsessive pressure."**
>
> —*Christopher Norris*

Thus Derrida's critique of Lévi-Strauss follows much the same path as his deconstructive readings of Rousseau and Saussure. Once again it is a matter of taking a repressed or subjugated theme (that of writing), pursuing its various textual ramifications and showing how these subvert the very order that strives to hold them in check. Writing, for Lévi-Strauss, is an instrument of oppression, a means of *colonizing* the primitive mind by allowing it to exercise (within due limits) the powers of the oppressor. In Derrida's reading this theme of lost innocence is seen as a romantic illusion and a last, belated showing of the Rousseauist mystique of origins. 'Writing' in Lévi-Strauss's sense is a merely derivative activity which always supervenes upon a culture already 'written' through the forms of social existence. These include the codes of naming, rank, kinship and other such systematized constraints. Thus the violence described by Lévi-Strauss presupposes, 'as the space of its possibility, the violence of the arche-writing, the violence of difference, of classification, and of the system of appellations'.

This latter has to do with the function of *names* in Nambikwara society, their significance and mode of designation. Lévi-Strauss offers a casual anecdote about some children who took out their private animosities by each revealing the other's name in a round of mutual revenge. Since the Nambikwara, according to Lévi-Strauss, place strict prohibitions on the use of proper names, this episode becomes symbolic of the violence that intrudes upon preliterate cultures when their language gives way to promiscuous exchange (or writing). Derrida counters with evidence—again from Lévi-Strauss's own text—that these were *not*, in fact, 'proper names' in the sense the anecdote requires, but were already part of a 'system of appellation'—a social arrangement—which precludes the idea of personal possession. The term 'proper name' is itself improper, so the argument runs, because it carries an appeal to authentic, individuated selfhood. What is really involved is a system of classification, a *designated* name which belongs to the economy of socialized 'difference' and not to the private individual. In this instance, what is prohibited by the Nambikwara is not the breach of any personal rights but rather the utterance of 'what *functions* as the proper name':

> The lifting of the interdict, the great game of the denunciation . . . does not consist in revealing proper names, but in tearing the veil hiding a classification . . . the inscription within a system of linguistico-social differences.

Derrida's strategies are most clearly on view in these pages devoted to Lévi-Strauss. The 'nature' which Rousseau identifies with a pure, unmediated speech, and Lévi-Strauss with the dawn of tribal awareness, betrays a nostalgic mystique of presence which ignores the self-alienating character of *all* social existence. Writing again becomes the pivotal term in an argument that extends its implications to the whole prehistory and founding institutions of society.

Moreover, the evidence pointing to this conclusion is *there* in the texts of Lévi-Strauss, as it was in the writings of Rousseau and Saussure. It is not some novel and ultra-sophisticated 'method' of reading devised to keep criticism one jump ahead. Nor does it impinge from outside and above, like certain forms of Marxist criticism which treat 'the text' as a handy support for their own superior knowledge of its meaning or mode of production. . . . Indeed, one of the myths or metaphysical ruses Derrida often attacks is the notion that writing is somehow *external* to language, a threat from outside which must always be countered by the stabilizing presence of speech. Carried down through a long tradition, from Plato to Saussure, this idea is most visibly (and paradoxically) inscribed in the Rousseauistic leanings of Lévi-Strauss. Writing becomes an exteriorized agency of violence and corruption, constantly menacing the communal values so closely identified with speech. Derrida's aim to is to show that, on the contrary, writing emerges both within the very *theme* of speech and within the *text* which strives to realize and authenticate that theme. Deconstruction is in this sense the active accomplice of a repressed but already articulate writing. In Derrida's much-quoted phrase, 'Il n'y a pas de hors-texte' ('There is nothing outside the text').

Richard Rorty   (review date 16 February 1984)

SOURCE: "Signposts along the Way That Reason Went," in *London Review of Books,* Vol. 6, No. 3, February 16, 1984, pp. 5-6.

[*An American philosopher, critic, and educator, Rorty is the most prominent contemporary advocate for the discipline known as pragmatism. In the following review of* Margins of Philosophy, *he examines the philosophical contexts relevant to Derrida's theories on language. While he argues that Derrida's position vis-à-vis the Western philosophical tendency to privilege reason over rhetoric is not original, he predicts that Derrida will be considered an important philosopher by future generations of scholars.*]

If you want to know what the common sense of the bookish will be like fifty years from now, read the philosophers currently being attacked as 'irrationalist'. Then discount the constructive part of what they are saying. Concentrate on the negative things, the criticisms they make of the tradition. That dismissal of the common sense of the past will be the enduring achievement of the long-dead 'irrationalist'. His or her suggestions about what to do next will look merely quaint, but the criticisms of his or her predecessors will seem obvious.

For example, everybody has doubts about the superman and the Oedipus complex, but nobody wants to revive the moral psychology which Nietzsche and Freud found in place. Everybody has doubts that truth is just 'what works', but nobody (well, almost nobody) wants to revive the 'copy theory of ideas' which James and Dewey criticised. Fifty years from now, nobody will want to listen to the Voice of Being, or to deconstruct texts, but nobody will take seriously the ways of distinguishing between science, philosophy and art which Heidegger and Derrida criticise. Nowadays both men look like eccentrics, an impression they do their best to encourage. Their writings are filled with explanations of how very marginal, how very different and unlike all other philosophers they are.

But in time they will be seen as central to the philosophical tradition, as having overcome certain ways of thinking which were 'mythic' or 'self-deceptive' or 'culture-bound' (or whatever near-synonym of 'irrational' is then in fashion). 'Reason' is always being redefined in order to accommodate the irrationalists of the preceding generation.

Heidegger and Derrida get called 'irrationalist' because they want us to stop looking for a final resting-place for thought—the sort of thing which Being or Mind or Reason were once thought to be. Capitalised words of this sort were thought to name things such that, if one knew enough about them, one would be in a better (perhaps the best possible) position to know about everything else. If one knew about Being as such, maybe everything else would seem merely a special case. If one knew what Mind or Reason was, maybe one could tell when one's mind had done its job, or gauge one's own rationality better. If one knew the nature of Language, perhaps one would have a standpoint from which to choose among all those competing languages—the Christian, the liberal, the Marxist, the Freudian, the sociobiological etc—which claim to 'place' all other jargons, to supply the meta-instruments which will test out every new-fangled conceptual instrument.

The suggestion that Language might be the Archimedean point sought by the philosophical tradition was explored by analytic philosophy—a movement which was fascinated by the idea that 'logic' or 'conceptual analysis' named instruments by which all the rest of culture could be held at arm's length, seen in a clear cold light. From Heidegger's and Derrida's point of view, that movement was just one more effort at 'metaphysics' or 'totalisation'—one more attempt to give the perturbed spirit rest. It was also bound to be short-lived, for Language is simply not as plausible a candidate for a resting-place as its predecessors. What Heidegger called 'the onto-theological tradition' made it possible to think of 'Being' or 'Mind' as names for a causal force, a power with which it would be desirable to stand well, something big and strong enough to put everything else in its place. But 'Language' doesn't sound like the name of a thing, a locus of causal power. It is not a suitable sobriquet for Omniscience. 'Language' suggests something sprawling, something which dissipates its forces by rambling on. That is why, in the philosophical tradition, language has usually been something to be avoided—sometimes by replacing lots of little words with one big Word, sometimes by concentrating on 'logic', envisaged as a sort of concentrated essence of language, all the language the philosopher really needs to know.

Derrida's principal theme in these essays [collected in **Margins of Philosophy**] is the attempt of the tradition to make language look less sprawling by trimming off unwanted growth. This is done by making invidious distinctions between true (e.g. 'literal' or 'cognitively meaningful') language and false (e.g. 'metaphorical' or 'meaningless') language. He is arguing that this attempt cannot succeed, because it is just the latest version of the onto-theological attempt to contrast the Great Good Resting-Place with the sprawling world of time and chance. He wants to convince us that there is no natural hierarchy of discourses or jargons, no structure topped off by the super-language which gives us a grip on all the others, the words which classify all the other words. There is no privileged language in which to state invidious distinctions between true and false language. There is no linguistic material out of which we can forge clippers with which to snip off unfruitful linguistic suckers. He thinks Heidegger betrayed his own project by trying to separate 'real' language (the Call of Being, the kind of language which 'is what it says') from 'inauthentic' language (words used as means to technocratic ends, chatter, the jargon of this or that disciplinary matrix).

Derrida is one of the very few philosophers, perhaps the only one so far, to go along enthusiastically and wholeheartedly with Heidegger's criticism of 'onto-theology' while still resisting the old wizard's spell. After learning all that Heidegger had to teach, he still manages to look Heidegger in the eye and stare him down. Heidegger's own writing combined enormous respect for such predecessors as Plato and Nietzsche with a fierce will to be free of them. Derrida has the same filial relation to Heidegger himself. Having done to Heidegger what Heidegger did to Nietzsche is the negative achievement which, after all the chatter about 'deconstruction' is over, will give Derrida a place in the history of philosophy. By the year 2034, after a new generation of 'irrationalists' has made Heidegger and Derrida look like pussycats, the genealogical charts for the philosophers of our century are likely to show Derrida as standing to Heidegger as Wittgenstein stands to Russell. What Russell did to Mill, Wittgenstein did to Russell by finding something right in Mill after all—the empirical character of the *a priori*. What Heidegger did to Nietzsche, Derrida has done to Heidegger by recovering Nietzsche's slaphappy *je-m'en-foutisme,* his refusal to be 'serious' and concentrated and Thoughtful.

Nobody on our side of the Channel has as yet managed to face down the later Wittgenstein. Wittgenstein has as yet had no brave, strong, parricidal sons. But even though we have not struggled with him properly, we Anglo-Saxon philosophers know Wittgenstein better than Heidegger: so, because much of what Derrida says about language sounds pretty much like what the *Philosophical Investigations* said, we may conclude that in France they are just now catching up with what we learned as students. We were raised to sneer at Hegelian absolute knowledge, Marxist certainty about the direction of history, Husserlian apodicticity, Russellian logical form, positivist 'meaning-analysis', and the rest of the bag of onto-theological tricks. We learned while still young that logic was not something sublime, that philosophy consisted in 'assembling reminders for a particular purpose' rather than constructing 'theories of meaning', and that our aim was to show ourselves the way out of the fly-bottle. We were taught to be suspicious of the kinds of cuts between good and bad language suggested by Russell and Ayer, and to be equally suspicious of the *Tractatus*'s concluding injunction to sacred silence. To a philosophical generation raised on Wittgenstein's advice to think of language as a tool rather than a medium, and urged by Quine to be as holistic and behaviouristic as possible in our account of how language works, a climb to the top of a hierarchy of language-games has little appeal. Such philosophers find Derrida more fervid than necessary. His advice not to capitalise Language, to *let* it sprawl, seems unneeded.

This is one reason for resistance to Derrida. There are at least two others. One is that he has become a fad among students of literature, who have mastered a gimmick called 'deconstructive reading', one which rivals 'psycho-analytic reading' as a formula for producing lots of seemingly original articles very quickly. This gimmick should not be confused with anything Derrida himself does (nor with 'Yale'—the diverse things which a remarkable constellation of original critics, Harold Bloom, Geoffrey Hartman, J. Hillis Miller and the late Paul de Man, were already doing before Derrida came along to join them). Derrida did write some things which encouraged the belief that he had discovered a brand-new whiz-bang method of finding out what texts 'were really about'. But, mercifully, he did not write many of them. He should not get more blame for his blithe and brutal young followers than Freud gets for his.

Another, less accidental reason Derrida is distrusted is that he occasionally assumes an analytic, argumentative stance which is entirely inappropriate to what he is doing. There are passages (especially in his earlier, more 'academic' work, some of which is translated in the volume under review) in which he seems to be saying that other philosophers' views of Language can be shown to be wrong by appealing to some commonly recognised criteria. But, in the first place, it betrays Derrida's own project to suggest that there is something out there—Language—to get right or wrong. In the second place, there are no criteria of the sort which he seems to invoke.

Consider, as a sample of Derridean argument, the last essay in this volume—**'Signature Event Context'**. This begins with the question: 'Is it certain that there corresponds to the word *communication* a unique, univocal concept, a concept that can be rigorously grasped and transmitted, a communicable concept?' It proceeds to show that this is not certain, for there is no 'rigorous and scientific conception of *context*' which one can invoke to 'reduce the field of equivocity covered by the word *communication*'. Derrida writes as if we could all tell a 'rigorous scientific conception' or a 'univocal concept' when we see one, and as if he were going to show us that our criteria for univocity or rigour have, alas, not been fulfilled.

We have to have swallowed this suggestion that we want, and thought we had, a 'univocal concept' of communication if we are going to be impressed by Derrida's (perfectly correct) claim that 'every sign . . . can be *cited,* put between quotation-marks; thereby it can break with every given context, and engender infinitely new contexts in an absolutely non-saturatable fashion.' That fact does indeed show that 'there are only contexts, without any centre of absolute anchoring,' but few readers would have thought that communication required absolute anchors if Derrida hadn't been so skilful at insinuating that this was a presup-

position of 'the entire history of philosophy', that throughout this history it had been believed that 'meaning, the content of the semantic message, is . . . *communicated . . .* within an homogenous element across which the unity and integrity of meaning is not affected in an essential way.' The reader is supposed to say to himself or herself: 'Gee, I guess I *had* believed that; how credulous I have been.' He or she then becomes a prospective customer for the 'new logic, a graphematics of iterability' which Derrida suggests we are going to have to develop. Why would anybody think that the fact that you can always create a new context (and thus a new meaning) for any given sign entails that you can't communicate univocally, that you can't get your message across without 'the unity and integrity of meaning being affected in an essential way'? Does anyone really think of the meaning of a sign as being like the shape of a coin, rather than like its value (something which is different from year to year, and different for currency exchanges, scrap-metal dealers, numismatists etc)? There are certainly people who have to pretend to think in this way. 'Would a reasonable man have taken the meaning of this letter to be . . . ?' is a proper question to pose to a jury. But even people who invoke such professional pretences are quite aware that you can give any sign a new meaning by putting it in quotation-marks. They don't think that they need 'a rigorous scientific notion of context', a way of drawing a neat line between sign and context, in order to say that quoting something provides a new context for it. They would regard this demand for rigorous demarcation as being like the demand for a distinction between a thing and its properties, or an artichoke and its leaves. Only a *philosopher* would want such a thing.

But maybe this is enough for Derrida? His essay was, after all, 'a communication to the Congrès International des Sociétés de Philosophie de Langue Française' (which was staging a colloquium on 'Communication'). Maybe it is only 'the entire history of philosophy' which has believed all these silly things, while the laity have always been too sensible to do so? Actually, this *is* pretty close to what Derrida thinks. He does not think that all those French-speaking philosophers in his original audience were that dumb, but he does think that there is a useful definition of 'philosophy' according to which it names just that sort of belief—beliefs in clear and distinct ideas, in concepts so shiny that contexts roll right off them, in signs so sharp-edged that they cut right through attempts to use them equivocally, in thinking and writing whose clarity is intrinsic, not just a matter of familiarity to a readership.

Philosophy, so defined, is the subject—the only subject—of *Margins of Philosophy*. If read as essays on that subject, rather than on communication or meaning or metaphor or Language, this book makes admirable sense. But if one gets stuck on questions like 'Has Derrida really *demonstrated* that our concept of communication is equivocal, our conception of metaphor internally inconsistent, our notion of sign in need of revision through the development of a graphematics of iterability?' one will soon get disgusted with the book. Not only does he not demonstrate anything like this, he is not really trying to. He is continually pretending to play the professional game of searching for clear and distinct ideas, eliminating equivocity, being rigorous in some absolute way (not simply a way which is relative to a given readership). He is also continually giving you sly hints that he would not be caught dead doing anything of the sort. He plays this game of mirrors brilliantly, but it palls quickly. The way to avoid getting caught up in it is to not take questions like 'What is Language?' seriously enough to think that Derrida is going to give you some nice new answers to them. Do not read this book in search of contributions to an understanding of the nature of signs, or metaphors, or anything else. Avoid letting Derrida use you as a straight person. Do not let the weak and question-begging character of his arguments lead you to think that he has not made his case. When you hit something that looks like an argument, remember that an argument requires speaker and hearer to share a vocabulary and a set of beliefs, and that Derrida has no intention of sharing *yours*. If he seems to do so, he only does it to annoy, because he knows it teases. Distrust of Derridean argumentation is perfectly justified, but it is distrust of an unfortunate mannerism, one which Derrida dropped in his later work.

Do not, on the other hand, think that, since you have never (or at least not since reading Wittgenstein) taken clear and distinct ideas seriously, you need not read one more book debunking them. The onto-theological tradition is not shrugged off so easily. Anybody who thinks of himself as having some non-philosophical arguments with which to expose the silliness of the philosophers, or some position outside philosophy from which to view it, is already a philosopher within the meaning of Derrida's redefinition. Derrida is aiming at the very idea of argument which is more than invocation of the implicit assumptions of a current vocabulary, of a position which is more than a bit of logical space carved out by such a vocabulary. He wants to make trouble for the very ideas of an 'intellectual position', of 'a clear view of a subject', or 'a clear non-metaphorical presentation of the substantive issues'. Let him who can keep thinking without falling back on such ideas, without hoping for a resting-place which will bring his thinking to an end, cast the first blackball.

But what, since he does not argue, *does* Derrida do to make (or help) us give up our hopes of eternal rest? Roughly, he writes about the self-destructive character of the philosophical tradition and about the difficulty of finding a way out of that tradition: the difficulty of avoiding the self-referential absurdity of adopting a philosophical position which is opposed to the idea of philosophical positions. This could be a very boring subject, and in many philosophers' hands it is. Derrida is saved by being a magnificent writer (and saved for us Anglo Saxons by having found translators—notably Alan Bass—who are able to carry off a nearly impossible task). To see Derrida at his best, try the essay **'White Mythology'**. This is the most convincing piece in this volume (except perhaps for a remarkable essay on Heidegger, **'Ousia and Grammé'**, which is, however, impenetrable for those unfamiliar with Heidegger).

> **Having done to Heidegger what Heidegger did to Nietzsche is the negative achievement which, after all the chatter about "deconstruction" is over, will give Derrida a place in the history of philosophy.**
>
> —*Richard Rorty*

Derrida starts off this essay by quoting Anatole France: 'the very metaphysicians who think to escape the world of appearances are constrained to live perpetually in allegory. A sorry lot of poets, they dim the colours of the ancient fables, and are themselves but gatherers of fables. They produce white mythology.' He comments: 'Metaphysics—the white mythology which reassembles and reflects the culture of the West: the white man takes his own mythology, Indo-European mythology, his own *logos,* that is to say the *mythos* of his idiom, for the universal form of that he must still wish to call Reason.' In the Heideggerean sense in which Derrida is using 'metaphysics', it includes physical science—not physical science as an instrument for prediction and control, as a set of devices for synthesising antibiotics and bombs, but physical science as Archimedean point for thought, as the way the world really and truly is, as offering a language which gives us 'matter of fact' rather than one more jargon. Metaphysics, in this sense, is the belief that one has found a vocabulary that is not merely a metaphorics, a kind of language which is really and truly Language because somehow isomorphic with what it represents, *literal* language as opposed to one more 'way of speaking'.

One could say that Derrida's point in this essay is that we are never going to have a standpoint outside of language from which to judge that a given language is literal, from which to draw the metaphorical-literal distinction. Any language which pats itself on the back by declaring itself to be literal is just developing one more metaphor (that of 'matter of fact'). Such a summary would be accurate enough, but would be like saying that Nabokov's point in *Lolita* is that life never quite lives up to art. What counts is the detail in which the point is made. Derrida makes his by an unparaphrasable series of exhibitions of the fact that 'philosophy is incapable of dominating its general tropology and metaphorics. It could perceive its metaphorics only around a blind spot or central deafness.' The central image of the essay is that of the heliotrope—the mind as plant which follows the motion of the sun (Plato's supersensible sun, that quasi-deity whose rays cut through all confusion, all obscurity, all metaphor). Derrida concludes the essay by saying that the heliotropic vision, the 'dream at the heart of philosophy', is to 'reduce the play of metaphors to one "central" metaphor'. Then 'there would be no more true metaphor, but only, through the one true metaphor, the assured legibility of the proper.' As he says:

> Metaphor, then, always carries its death within itself. And this death, surely, is also the death *of*

philosophy. But the genitive is double. It is sometimes the death of philosophy, death of a genre belonging to philosophy, which is thought and summarised within it, recognising and fulfilling itself as philosophy; and sometimes the death of a philosophy which does not see itself die and is no longer to be found within philosophy.

The dream at the heart of Derrida's writing is to achieve the second sort of death, to escape the self-referential predicament that anything you say against metaphysics is going to look like more metaphysics, that any metaphor you use for writing about metaphor will look like one more attempt to give the plain, literal facts about what metaphor is. In a sort of foreword to the volume called **Tympan,** he asks: 'Can one violently penetrate philosophy's field of listening without its immediately . . . making the penetration resonate within itself, appropriating the emission for itself, familiarly communicating it to itself between the inner and middle ear . . . ? In other words, can one puncture the tympanum of a philosopher and still be heard and understood by him?'

The answer, so far, has been 'no'. Only the first sort of death, the death of a particular genre of metaphysics (e.g. theological, idealistic) which is immediately succeeded by another (e.g. scientist, positivistic, phenomenological), has been achieved. Derrida would like to find a kind of writing which is not one more such genre. The presence of such writing in the world would serve as a black hole, into which all future metaphysics which pretends to be scientific would disappear. Such a writing would be a new sort of philosopher's stone, not one which locks within itself the whole light of the sun, but a sort of anti-heliotrope. Derrida ends **'White Mythology'** by saying: 'Heliotrope also names a stone, a precious stone, greenish and streaked with red veins, a kind of oriental jasper.'

Such a concluding gesture towards the East, away from the white man's effort to characterise the dissemination of 'the Greek miracle' as the march of Reason through the world, is common to Derrida and Heidegger. I suggested at the outset that the gesture would fail, that when the bearers of the white man's philosophical burden tire of denouncing these two as slackers they will proceed to marmorealise them, gestures and all—to set them up as signposts along the way that Reason went. But the more writers of this sort we have had (and Heidegger and Derrida are by no means the first), the less Greek, perhaps even the less white, we have become. Perhaps we are already closer than Derrida thinks to a point at which we can afford to fudge the distinctions between rationality and irrationality, and between philosophy, art and science—a point where all thinking and writing will become grist for a single mill. If this is so, then Derrida may be writing about metaphors which few people take seriously. Maybe it is only the philosophers *ex professo* who still dream of a nonmetaphorical statement of the substantive issues, of 'rigorous and scientific concepts', unequivocal meanings. If so, the philosophers of the future may no longer be charting the march of Reason. They may find some other medium in which to freeze Derrida's gesture. A cameo of curiously streaked bloodstone, suitable for wear as a protective amu-

let, would be more appropriate than the usual colossus of white marble.

An excerpt from *Writing and Difference*

It would be easy enough to show that the concept of structure and even the word "structure" itself are as old as the *epistēmē*—that is to say, as old as Western science and Western philosophy—and that their roots thrust deep into the soil of ordinary language, into whose deepest recesses the *epistēmē* plunges in order to gather them up and to make them part of itself in a metaphorical displacement. Nevertheless, up to the event which I wish to mark out and define, structure—or rather the structurality of structure—although it has always been at work, has always been neutralized or reduced, and this by a process of giving it a center or of referring it to a point of presence, a fixed origin. The function of this center was not only to orient, balance, and organize the structure—one cannot in fact conceive of an unorganized structure—but above all to make sure that the organizing principle of the structure would limit what we might call the *play* of the structure. By orienting and organizing the coherence of the system, the center of a structure permits the play of its elements inside the total form. And even today the notion of a structure lacking any center represents the unthinkable itself.

Nevertheless, the center also closes off the play which it opens up and makes possible. As center, it is the point at which the substitution of contents, elements, or terms is no longer possible. At the center, the permutation or the transformation of elements (which may of course be structures enclosed within a structure) is forbidden. At least this permutation has always remained *interdicted* (and I am using this word deliberately). Thus it has always been thought that the center, which is by definition unique, constituted that very thing within a structure which while governing the structure, escapes structurality. This is why classical thought concerning structure could say that the center is, paradoxically, *within* the structure and *outside it*. The center is at the center of the totality, and yet, since the center does not belong to the totality (is not part of the totality), the totality *has its center elsewhere*. The center is not the center. The concept of centered structure—although it represents coherence itself, the condition of the *epistēmē* as philosophy or science—is contradictorily coherent. And as always, coherence in contradiction expresses the force of a desire.

Jacques Derrida, in his Writing and Difference, *University of Chicago Press, 1978.*

Rodolphe Gasché   (essay date 1986)

SOURCE: "Deconstructive Methodology," in *The Tain of the Mirror: Derrida and the Philosophy of Reflection,* Harvard University Press, 1986, pp. 121-76.

[Gasché is a Luxembourgian-born American critic and educator. In the following excerpt, he defines the methodology

of deconstruction, examining it implications for the analy-
sis of philosophical discourse in relation to Hegel's specula-
tive metaphysics.]

If deconstruction reaches out for "ultimate foundations," it may be said to represent a methodical principle of philosophical foundation and grounding. Such a statement, however, must be rendered more precise and secured against a number of misunderstandings. All the concepts implied in this statement will have to be put in quotation marks.

Methods are generally understood as roads (from *hodos:* "way," "road") to knowledge. In the sciences, as well as in the philosophies that scientific thinking patronizes, method is an instrument for representing a given field, and it is applied to that field from the outside. That is, it is on the side of the subject and is an external reflection of the object. It is an instrumental approach to knowledge from an entirely subjective position. Yet such a relation of scientific representation as a form exterior to a given content is in principle extraneous to any thinking philosophy. This, however, is not to say that methodical thought should be replaced "by the non-method of presentiment and inspiration, or by the arbitrariness of prophetic utterance, both of which despise not only scientific pomposity, but scientific procedure of all kinds," as Hegel puts it [in his *Phenomenology of Spirit*]. For genuine philosophical thought, methods are always *determined* methods, which have their source in the region to which they apply and which are dependent on the nature and specificity of that region. For this reason the ultimate method—that is, the method that represents the philosophical itinerary to truth—must be one that describes the intrinsic and spontaneous movement of truth itself. The philosophical method, as the road toward truth in a domain that is itself determined in terms of truth, implies philosophy's self-implication, and the necessity to reflect itself into self-consciousness. Since Plato such a method has been called *dialektike,* the science of dividing (*diairesis*) and reunification (*synagoge*). Such a method is nothing other than the patient pursuit of the conceptual activity of truth as it develops its own coherence. It is thus not a formal procedure or rule separate from the content of truth. Method, then, is no longer simply the way to truth; it is truth itself. This is what Hegel means when, in the last chapter of the greater *Logic,* entitled "The Absolute Idea," he finally thematizes the concept of method: "From this course the method has emerged as the *self-knowing Notion that has itself,* as the absolute, both subjective and objective, *for its subject matter,* consequently as the pure correspondence of the Notion and its reality, as a concrete existence that is the Notion itself" [Hegel, *The Science of Logic*]. What is called "method" in Hegel is thus the totalizing dynamic description of the intellectual activity that, as "the soul of being," attains its most complex and complete fulfillment in the Notion or Concept wherein that activity achieves full self-determination. In other words, method for Hegel is identical to the structure of thought, insofar as thought is also the systematic and genetic exposition of the successive moments that constitute it as a whole. In Hegel it coincides with the self-experience of thought.

To the extent that Derrida's work is a genuinely philosophical inquiry that takes the standard rules of philosophy very seriously, its "method" is certainly not characterized by any exteriority to its object. But is this to say that, in the last resort, it would tend to coincide with the movement of the self-exposition of truth as Concept? Undoubtedly not, since deconstruction also manifestly includes the deconstruction of dialectics, in both a Platonic and a Hegelian sense. As a method, deconstruction is very much determined by the region and the regions of philosophy to which it applies. Yet Derrida has argued that deconstruction is exorbitant to the totality of philosophical knowledge, in particular as that knowledge culminates in the Hegelian Concept. It proceeds from a certain point of exteriority to the whole of the region of all regions of philosophy so as to reinscribe or reground that totality in or with regard to what is exorbitant to it. Obviously, such a procedure not only makes it impossible to give the usual methodological or logical intraorbitary assurances for an operation such as deconstruction, but it also raises the question whether deconstruction can be thought of in terms of method.

Taking off from a certain point outside the totality of the age of logocentrism,—that is, the totality constitutive of philosophy, and in particular speculative philosophy, which claims to have achieved that totality— deconstruction seems to flirt with the scientific idea of method that is characterized precisely by its exteriority to its object. But as we shall see, this point of exteriority to the totality is not that of the subject. Deconstruction is never the effect of a subjective act of desire or will or wishing. What provokes a deconstruction is rather of an "objective" nature. It is a "must," so to speak. "The *incision* [*l'entame;* also 'opening,' 'beginning,' 'broaching'] of deconstruction, which is not a voluntary decision or an absolute beginning, does not take place just anywhere, or in an absolute elsewhere. An incision, precisely, it can be made only according to lines of force and forces of rupture that are localizable in the discourse to be deconstructed" [Derrida, ***Positions***].

Deconstruction, as a methodical principle, cannot be mistaken for anything resembling scientific procedural rules, in spite of its departure from a certain point outside philosophy, nor does it yield to philosophy's classical definition of method, according to which the method must not be irreducibly alien to the field through which it leads. Although deconstruction is an eminently philosophical operation, an operation of extreme sensibility toward the immanence or inherence of the ways of thought to that which is thought—the subject matter (the identity of method and concept, as Hegel would say)—it is not *strictu sensu* methodical, since it does take place from a certain point outside such an identity. Therefore, deconstruction is also the deconstruction of the concept of method (both scientific and philosophical) and has to be determined accordingly.

As in Heidegger, the scientific and philosophical concepts of method are reductive concepts for Derrida. According to Heidegger, the concept of method, by inaugurating the technologization of thought, has radically disfigured the essence of the road (*hodos*) as the proper mode of philosophical thought. In his debate with method, however, Derrida does not attempt to oppose a more fundamental notion of method to scientific or philosophical method. If method for Derrida is a reductive concept, it is so in a different sense than for Heidegger. For Derrida, method is by nature reductive, whether it is fundamental or only derived. Yet it would be a great mistake to conclude that because deconstruction is critical of the discourse of metaphysics and its concept of method (scientific or philosophical), it would, in total disrespect of all levels, indulge in uncontrollable free play. Although a deconstruction of method, deconstruction is not a nonmethod, an invitation to wild and private lucubrations. The rigor of deconstruction is exemplified, for example, by the discrete steps it takes to deconstruct method. Like those of dissemination, the steps of deconstruction, says Derrida, "allow for (no) *method* [*pas de méthode*]: no path leads around in a circle toward a first step, nor proceeds from the simple to the complex, nor leads from a beginning to an end . . . We here note a point/lack of method [*point de méthode*]: this [however] does not rule out a certain marching order" [*Dissemination*].

It is therefore important to emphasize the systematism of deconstruction. It represents a procedure all of whose movements intertwine to form a coherent theoretical configuration. Thus deconstructive "methodology" as a whole cannot be characterized by any impressionistic or empiricist appropriation of one or two of its "moments." A mere evocation of some of these moments, or of some of the themes with which deconstruction is concerned, will never lead to any true insight into what deconstruction purports to achieve.

Derrida makes varied use of the term *deconstruction*. In the early writings especially, *deconstruction* sometimes merely translates *Abbau* or *Destruktion;* at other times it metonymically names its own different movements or steps as well; and finally by appositional qualifications it now and again appears to differentiate between a multiplicity of operations. Yet for the most part, the term has a very definite meaning. Even if the operation of deconstruction also affects the concept of method, nothing prevents our formalizing to some extent the different theoretical movements that make up one rigorous notion of deconstruction. Before we can discuss the methodical aspect of deconstruction, however, we must clarify its theoretical presuppositions, determining the specific point at which it becomes compelling and operational, the different steps that lead up to that point, and finally the aims of deconstruction. Only against such a background can the formal characteristics of deconstruction be fully understood.

Let us recall Gadamer's contention that absolute reflection as it is articulated by Hegel anticipates all logically possible reflective stands on the speculative totality of philosophy by turning them into particular moments of that totality. More generally speaking, Hegel's discourse is thought to have taken account of all possible Otherness to that totality, including the concept of Otherness and exteriority, of a remainder or a beyond to the system, by making them simple elements in the process of the self-elaboration of truth. With this, of course, philosophy

reaches its completion and its end. Derrida recognizes this completion of philosophy in speculative thought as well when he writes that "in completing itself, [philosophy] could both include within itself and anticipate all the figures of its beyond, all the forms and resources of its exterior; and could do so in order to keep these forms and resources close to itself by simply taking hold of their enunciation" [*Writing and Difference*]. The compelling problem at that moment is how to break the silence without falling back behind the logical achievements of Hegel's position when in the end there is nothing left to be said. Like all other philosophies, starting with the Hegelian left, which in the wake of Hegel's completion of the metaphysical project of philosophy became aware of the dilemma posed by Hegel's thought, Derrida acknowledges that Hegel's superior solution of the traditional problems of philosophy is a terrible challenge to philosophical thought. Obviously that challenge cannot be met either through a deliberate decision to overcome Hegel's completion of metaphysics or by simple indifference. That brief segment of the history of the tradition of contesting metaphysics in the aftermath of Hegel, which, . . . began with Nietzsche, clearly shows what is at stake. Instead of ignoring the task, such a tradition, on the contrary, testifies to the increasing urgency of meeting that challenge, as well as to an equally increasing vigilance concerning all the methodological tools and themes that purport to unhinge the discourse of absolute knowing. After Heidegger's destruction, Derrida's deconstruction is the latest and most complex development of that tradition.

How, then, are we to characterize, in as succinct a manner as possible, Derrida's approach to the problem? Hegel's philosophy must be described as an attempt to overcome the aporias of traditional philosophical positions, which arise from a naive adoption of a set of inherited conceptual oppositions, by constructively destroying them in a purely conceptual genesis. Derrida's concern is with a naivety unthought by philosophy in general, a blindness constitutive of philosophical thought, Hegel's speculative system included. This naivety is an *essential* one and is a function of the logical (dialectical or not) consistency sought and achieved by the philosophical discourse. It is not a naivety that would hamper the solution of traditional philosophical problems; on the contrary, it is a blindness without which there may be no hope of ever solving them. This naivety is that of the philosophical *discourse,* of its practice of arguing toward and exposing its concepts. Derrida, who is particularly concerned with the discursive strategies constitutive of the speculative solution (in all its forms) of the aporias to which the traditional formation of concepts leads, has described the approach of singling out this discursive naivety as follows:

> A task is then prescribed: to study the philosophical text in its formal structure, in its rhetorical organization, in the specificity and diversity of its textual types, in its models of exposition and production—beyond what previously were called genres—and also in the space of its *mises en scène,* in a syntax which would be not only the articulation of its signifieds, its references to Being or to truth, but also the handling of its

proceedings, and of everything invested in them.
[*Margins of Philosophy*]

The naiveties brought to light by such a study—a study that is *not yet* the deconstruction of the philosophical text but only its negative and *prior* moment—are not, properly speaking, logical deficiencies. Thus, after pointing out in **"The Double Session"** [in ***Dissemination***] that, for organizational reasons concerning the text of *Philebos,* Plato's contention of a priority of the imitated over imitation is problematic in the text itself, Derrida warns us "not to be too quick to call [it] contradictory." Contradictions are in principle susceptible to a (dialectical) solution. What Derrida is pointing out here is an inconsistency on the level of philosophical argumentation that cannot be mended, but that nevertheless makes it possible to obtain the desired authoritative results. The very success of Plato's dialogue hinges on such inconsistencies.

These naiveties are contradictions owing neither to an inconsistency in logical argumentation nor to the rhetorical force of the discourse of philosophy. To call these naiveties logical deficiencies or to make them dependent on the inevitable rhetorical use of language in philosophy is to describe only very approximately the sorts of problems exhibited in what may be called the propaedeutics of deconstruction. It is even misleading, because the logical and the rhetorical are, precisely, corresponding intraphilosophical norms of the coherence and cohesion of the philosophical discourse, whose unthought is being focused upon here. In its apparent contradiction to the logical exigencies of philosophical discourse, the rhetorical, figural, and improper use of language combines with the logical use of language to achieve the desired conceptual transparency.

In order to understand the full impact of the shift from one sort of criticism of naivety to another—from the philosophical criticism of the unscientific and unphilosophical consciousness and its "natural attitude" (from Parmenides to Husserl) to the critique of the naiveties implied by the discursive pragmatics of the first type of criticism (speculative or not)—it is necessary to recall that at least since Plato, all major philosophical concepts have represented desiderata, values not of what is but of what *ought* to be. As Derrida has shown, since its inception philosophy has been conceived of as an antidote to the Other of philosophy, either in the form of the masters of illusion, the charlatans and thaumaturges (in the *Republic* for instance), or in the form of the unrepresentable and unnameable, which in Kant's Third Critique is thematized under the name of the disgusting, against which it is said that we strive with all our might. Moreover, all of philosophy's concepts and values are *dreams* of plenitude. It would be simplistic to retort that such would be true only of idealist philosophy, since even the most empirical description in philosophy of what is is normative, even were it only for the inevitably axiological dimension of the concepts used in description. As desiderata, all philosophical concepts are in a way utopian and atopic; they represent what Derrida calls ethico-teleological or ethico-ontological values. Hence the history of philosophy is the expression of the need to think these concepts, again and again, in a satisfactory and desirable manner—satisfactory, that is, according to the principle of noncon-

tradiction. All these desiderata of philosophy are thus concepts of unity, totality, identity, cohesion, plenitude, states of noncontradiction, in which the negative has been absorbed by the positive, states that lack, and by all rights precede, all dissension, difference, and separation, states of peace and reconciliation. Yet Derrida's contention is not simply that it would be impossible to think noncontradiction in a noncontradictory way. By focusing on the formal, organizational, and textual production of noncontradiction in the philosophical discourse, he shows that, on the contrary, what makes noncontradiction possible and successful within the limits of philosophy's expectations is precisely the evasion of insight that results from the failure to question the discrepancies and inconsistencies of philosophy's *mise en scène.* This is the naivety that is thematized in Derrida's writings.

This inquiry into the process of philosophical conceptualization, as well as into the practice of discursive exposition and the structures of philosophical argumentation, brings to light a whole new field of "contradictions" and "aporias," which, instead of simply belying the philosophical enterprise, are rather constitutive of its successful completion. If one could venture to say that Heidegger reveals a *theme* unthought by metaphysics—the question of the ontico-ontological difference—one could certainly say that Derrida discloses the unthought *syntax* (a word that I shall have to render more precise) of philosophical conceptualization and argumentation. Since the "contradictions" and "aporias" that spring from this unthought dimension of philosophical practice have never been thematized by philosophy itself and are thus in a certain way exterior to the traditional and coded problems of philosophy, they cannot be construed as contradictions or aporias proper. Therefore, rigorously speaking, it is misleading to define deconstruction as an operation that, as [Paul] Ricoeur puts it [in *The Rule of Metaphor,* 1977], "always consists in destroying metaphysical discourse by reduction to aporias," without further clarification. Derrida's own occasional use of the words *aporia* and *contradiction* does not render such an effort toward clarification dispensable, since understanding deconstruction depends on it. As we shall see, Derrida does not limit the notions of aporia and contradiction to fallacies of philosophical description and predication. Neither are these concepts borrowed from the conceptual arsenal of the skeptical tradition in philosophy, a tradition that throws doubt upon philosophical knowledge only from the perspective of a higher mode of truth. *Aporia* and *contradiction* must be understood in Derrida as referring to the general dissimilarity between the various ingredients, elements, or constituents of the discourse of philosophy as such. Indeed, Derrida's parallel inquiry into the formation of philosophical concepts and the argumentative, discursive, and textual structures of philosophy leads to the recognition of an essential nonhomogeneity between the concepts and philosophical texts or works themselves. All major philosophical concepts, he contends, are ethico-teleological values of unbroached plenitude and presence. But, as respectable as they may be, they "live on a delusion and nonrespect for . . . [their] own condition of origin" [*Of Grammatology*]. They exist precisely on a disregard for their own bipolar opposite, to which they deny a value similar to their own. Philosophical concepts would be entirely homogeneous if they possessed a nucleus of meaning that they owed exclusively to themselves—if they were, in other words, conceptual atoms. Yet since concepts are produced within a discursive network of differences, they not only are what they are by virtue of other concepts, but they also, in a fundamental way, inscribe that Otherness within themselves.

Let us outline several ways in which the teleological value of the homogeneity of concepts is disproved by the very process of the formation of concepts. First, since a concept is not a simple point but a structure of predicates clustered around one central predicate, the determining predicate is itself conditioned by the backdrop of the others. Second, each concept is part of a conceptual binary opposition in which each term is believed to be simply exterior to the other. Yet the interval that separates each from its opposite and from what it is not also makes each concept what it is. A concept is thus constituted by an interval, by its difference from another concept. But this interval brings the concept into its own by simultaneously dividing it. The property of a concept depends entirely on its difference from the excluded concept. No concept, including the concept of ethics ("There is no ethics without the presence *of the other* but also, and consequently, without absence, dissimulation, detour, differance, writing," [*Of Grammatology*]), can be thought rigorously without including the trace of its difference from its Other within itself. Yet that is as much as to say that the concept—of ethics, for example, but all other concepts as well—includes within itself the trace of that to which it strives (teleologically) to oppose itself in simple and pure exteriority. As a result of this law constitutive of concepts, all concepts are in a sense paradoxical. Take, for instance, the concept of the center:

> It has always been thought that the center, which is by definition unique, constituted that very thing within a structure which while governing the structure, escapes structurality. This is why classical thought concerning structure could say that the center is, paradoxically, *within* the structure and *outside* it. The center is at the center of the totality, and yet, since the center does not belong to the totality (is not part of the totality), the totality *has its center elsewhere.* The center is not the center. The concept of centered structure—although it represents coherence itself, the condition of the *episteme* as philosophy or science—is contradictorily coherent. And as always, coherence in contradiction expresses the force of a desire. [*Writing and Difference*]

Third, concepts are always (by right and in fact) inscribed within systems or conceptual chains in which they constantly relate to a plurality of other concepts and conceptual oppositions from which they receive their meaning by virtue of the differential play of sense constitution, and which thus affect them in their very core. And fourth, one single concept may be subject to different functions within a text or a corpus of texts. It may function as a citation of itself as well as of another meaning that this same concept may have in a different place or stratum or on another occasion. This citational play, far from being innocent,

also affects the ideal closure of the concepts. True, the different meanings to which any one concept may be subjected within the same context are not a problem for philosophy. If philosophy does not simply ignore the question, it solves it hermeneutically, as an index of a more profound and hidden meaning, or it solves the question of relating the two kinds of meaning of one concept by elevating one of these meanings into the more true, complete meaning, of which the other is but a derivation. As an example, let us refer to Kant's distinction between *pulchritudo vaga* and *pulchritudo adhaerens*. Although these two determinations of beauty are of a predicating nature, the question of beauty in general—that is, of the common root that would precomprehend the two concepts and make them communicate—is denied consideration. The essence of beauty is understood in terms of one of the determinations only. For Kant there is no single common source of the two forms of beauty: "We do not pre-understand the essence of beauty in the commonality of the two types, but rather from the perspective of the free beauty that gives rise to a pure aesthetic judgement. It is the pure that gives us the meaning of beauty in general, the pure *telos* of beauty (as a *non-telos*). It is the most beautiful that allows us to think essential beauty and not the less beautiful, which remains a groping approximation *en vue de l'errance*" [Derrida, *The Truth in Painting*].

In short, then, philosophical concepts are not homogeneous. Their nonhomogeneity is manifold, caused by the very process of concept formation and concept use. Yet the variety of dissimilarities that turn concepts into paradoxical structures must not concern us further, since at this point I am interested only in accentuating the generality of their contradictory and aporetic nature. We must note, however, that these different incoherences constituting concepts, which are either absolutely fundamental insofar as concepts are formed within a differential play, or seemingly contingent if they stem from a varied, if not contradictory, usage within a single context, are overshadowed by philosophy's desire for coherence. What Derrida calls the "regulated incoherence within conceptuality" cannot, therefore, be thematized in philosophy. But the motive of homogeneity—a teleological motive par excellence—not only blurs the incoherence within concepts but also organizes the philosophical conception of texts. Let us first consider how philosophy regulates differences in homogeneity relative to philosophical description and the construction of an argument. Derrida's investigation of philosophical works (and of literary texts as well) brings into view a variety of discrepancies between the various strata that make up a work's argumentation and description, and that make it thoroughly illusionary simply to maintain the metaphysical desire for the pure coherence of their volume.

Let us dwell for a moment on the specific nature of what, in the light of Althusser's concept of uneven development, I have chosen to call discursive inequalities or dissimilarities, which are due to these conflicting strata within the coherence of texts or works. Their nature is manifold too. One example of such a disparity between levels of argumentation is Derrida's demonstration of a contradiction

> **Derrida's concern is with a naivety unthought by philosophy in general, a blindness constitutive of philosophical thought, Hegel's speculative system included.**
>
> —*Rodolphe Gasché*

within Saussure's scientific project. This contradiction stems from the fact that Saussure, in determining the object of structural linguistics according to the principle of differentiality as a system of marks comparable to writing, belies his strong condemnation in *Cours* of writing as harmful to speech. Both a logo and a phonocentric valorization of speech cohabit in this discourse, as well as another scientific stratum that is a radical questioning of the former orientation. Another example is the tension between gesture and statement in Rousseau's discussion of the origin of language. In *Of Grammatology,* Derrida distinguishes between Rousseau's explicit declarations as to how he *wishes* to think the origin of language and his matter-of-fact *description* of it. Rousseau's declared intention is to think the origin as a simple one unbroached by any difference. "But in spite of that declared intention, Rousseau's discourse lets itself be constrained by a complexity which always has the form of the supplement of or from the origin." Yet instead of concluding, based on what follows from his own description of the origin, that from the outset difference has corrupted the origin, Rousseau prefers to believe that the supplement *"must (should) have"* been enclosed in, in the sense of being confused with, the origin. "There *must (should) have* been plenitude and not lack, presence without difference." As a result of this ethico-theoretical decision, which valorizes originarity as a desideratum, everything that had emerged in the description of the origin as already broaching it—that is, as being more originary than the origin—is turned into secondariness, into something that *"adds itself from the outside as evil and lack* to happy and innocent plenitude." The dangerous supplement, then, "would come from an outside which would be simply the outside." Consequently, the tension between gesture and statement, description and declaration, far from resulting in mutual annihilation contributes to the coherence of the text by means of the grid of the "ought to be," or the conditional mood. "*Should [devrait]*: it is the mode and tense of a teleological and eschatological anticipation that superintends Rousseau's entire discourse," writes Derrida. Through this mood the contradiction is made to be no more than apparent, and Rousseau can think the two incompatible possibilities, the origin and the supplement, simultaneously. As the conditional mood reveals, it is itself the unity of a desire. Derrida writes, "As in the dream, as Freud analyzes it, incompatibles are simultaneously admitted as soon as it is a matter of satisfying a desire, in spite of the principle of identity, or of the excluded third party—the logical time of consciousness" [*Of Grammatology*]. These discursive contradictions are united by desire into a contradictory coher-

ence regulated by what Freud calls the sophistry of the borrowed kettle. Derrida sums up this kind of reasoning, which according to Freud is supposed to illustrate dream logic, in the following passage: "In his attempt to arrange everything in his favor, the defendant piles up contradictory arguments: (1) The kettle I am returning to you is brand new; (2) The holes were already in it when you lent it to me; (3) You never lent me a kettle, anyway" [*Dissemination*].

The various arguments concerning the origin and the supplement, speech and writing, are organized by Saussure and Rousseau in a similar manner: (1) The supplement and writing are totally exterior and inferior to the origin and to speech, which are thus not affected by them and remain intact; (2) they are harmful because they are separate from the origin and thereby corrupt living speech, which otherwise would be intact; and (3) if one needs to fall back on the supplement or on writing, it is not because of their intrinsic value but because the origin was already deficient, and because living speech was already finite before it became supplemented by writing. Hence, supplement and writing do not harm origin or speech at all. On the contrary, they mend the deficiencies of origin and speech.

Because of this logic within discursive contradiction, or contradictory arguments held together by the desire for unity, it is insufficient simply to say "that Rousseau thinks the supplement without thinking it, that he does not match his saying and his meaning, his descriptions and his declarations." Rather, the contradiction is regulated, which gives these texts their very coherence and totality. Instead of permitting these contradictions to cancel each other out, Rousseau, like Saussure "accumulates contradictory arguments to bring about a satisfactory decision: the exclusion of writing," difference, or the supplement. But this organization of incompatibles into a unity dominated by ethico-teleological values, which maintains and contains the adverse arguments and strata in the very act of decision by which philosophy institutes itself, is possible only through the evasion of a number of questions and implications that follow from the fact that "Rousseau, caught, like the logic of identity, *within* the graphic of supplementarity, says what he does not wish to say, describes what he does not wish to conclude" [*Of Grammatology*].

A last example of such contradictions concerning the gap between declaration and, this time, factual practice concerns the often perceived contradiction in the Platonic condemnation of writing in writing. How could Plato, Rousseau, and others subordinate writing to speech while writing themselves? Derrida asks:

> What law governs this "contradiction," this opposition to itself of what is said against writing, of a dictum that pronounces itself against itself as soon as it finds its way into writing, as soon as it writes down its self-identity and carries away what is proper to it *against* this ground of writing? This "contradiction," which is nothing other than the relation-to-self of diction as it opposes itself to scription, as it *chases* itself (away) in hunting down what is properly its *trap*—this contradiction is not contingent. [*Dissemination*]

The sort of discursive inequalities that I have pointed out concern contradictory strata of description within the argumentation of a single work, discrepancies between explicit statements and the desiderata of thought, between declaration and factual practice. But the analysis preceding deconstruction—the propaedeutics of deconstruction—is not limited to bringing into prominence conceptual aporias on the one hand and, on the other, discursive inequalities of all sorts. There is a third type of discursive heterogeneity which in fact defies categorization properly speaking. In each instance it comprises a multiplicity of very different and radically incommensurable layers, agencies, or sediments that invariably make up discursive wholes. Through thematizing this kind of contradiction or aporia in the philosophical text, it becomes evident that the philosophical concept of contradiction or aporia is incapable of covering and comprehending these types of inconsistencies, not only in isolation but especially when taken together. Indeed, these discrepancies stem from differences in the importance, scope, and status of parts or elements of philosophical discourses, as well as from the irreducibly disproportionate and dissimilar nature of various constituents of these parts or elements. Let us, then, look at some paradigmatic types of this sort of discursive inequality, which, contrary to appearances, have not been problematized in the perspective outlined above.

The analysis of philosophical discourses reveals that they are composed not only of pure concepts and philosophemes but also of metaphors and mythemes. As discursive elements, the last two are of an entirely different status from that of concepts, yet they necessarily combine with concepts, whose purity as to mythical and figural residues should be beyond all question. Certainly the relation between myth and logos is a philosophical problem of long standing; the same must be said of the relation between concept and figure. But what Derrida is concerned with—in **"Plato's Pharmacy"** [in *Dissemination*], for instance—is not so much the way in which philosophy tries to master its relation to myth or to figures as the manner in which this intimate combination, within a whole of such dissimilar elements as concepts and nonconcepts, philosophemes and mythemes, instead of simply resisting absorption into the homogeneity of the concept contributes to the creation of an effect of such purity. In other words, Derrida's concern is with the irreducibility and inevitability of the combination of opposite genres in the philosophical discourse.

Such an analysis may also accentuate a lexicological inconsistency arising from the different and repeated use of one particular so-called key word or key signification in a text. The emphasis of such an analysis is on the singularity and inextricability of the juxtaposition of these significations in one ensemble. The different citations of one and the same word within one text or context can be *opposed* to one another, but they can also be simply dissimilar and irreducible to one another, in which case they resist all hermeneutical solution. "There cannot be any such thing as key words," writes Derrida [in *Dissemination*]. These multiple different usages of the same term in one work or textual unity must thus be analyzed as the background against which the hermeneutical search for an ultimate signified takes place.

The analysis may also focus on a chain of words similar to one another, which may have the same etymological root but are nonetheless not supposed to communicate within the text. *Pharmakeia-pharmakon-pharmakeus* in Plato's *Phaedros,* which Derrida analyzes in **"Plato's Pharmacy,"** is an instance of such a chain.

This sort of analysis may also throw into relief unsublated and unmediated statements or propositions about one particular theme within a text or a corpus of texts, for instance the theme of the "woman" in Nietzsche, analyzed by Derrida in *Spurs.* It may also point out the cohabitation in one text or corpus of two or more irreducible types of one general thing (such as *pulchritudo adhaerens* and *pulchritudo vaga* in the Third Critique, analyzed by Derrida in **"Parergon"** [in *The Truth in Painting*]); of a variety of information in a text and a context; or simply of the repeated and dissimilar functions within one text or context of mere signifiers, such as the letters *i* and *r* in Mallarmé. [Gasché is referring to the repetition of letters in Mallarmé's poetry, not his actual name; Derrida's discussion of this appears in *Dissemination*.]

Other such discursive inequalities can be found between parts of a text, for example a preface and the main body of a text, as discussed by Derrida in **"Outwork, Prefacing"** [in *Dissemination*]; between the title and the main part of the text, as thematized in **"Titre à préciser"** [in *Parages*]; or between two segments of a text divided by an intermediary space which is marked either by a blank, as in Blanchot's *L'Arrêt de mort,* analyzed in **"Living On: Border Lines"** [*Parages*], or marked by an interpolated text as in Nietzsche's *Ecce Homo,* treated in **"L'Otobiographie de Nietzsche"** [in *The Ear of the Other*]. For present purposes, it is not necessary to accumulate further evidence of such discursive discrepancies arising from a grafting of thoroughly heterogeneous elements upon one another. Let us recall for the moment that they are multiple, different in status, and different in essence. The analysis presupposed by all deconstruction, properly speaking, consists of such an assessment of the various heterogeneous levels of philosophical discourse, as well as of the heterogeneous elements or agencies that combine on these levels. It is not a question of reducing these variegated discursive and conceptual disparities to one model of divergency, especially not to that of contradiction as the major criterion of the necessary falsehood of statements. Nor is the question one of how to reduce these disparities, inconsistencies, and dissimilarities through any of the traditional procedures. What is at stake is the assessment of the generality and irreducibility of these various inequalities. Under this condition only can the second step of deconstruction take place. Deconstruction is thus the attempt to account for the heterogeneity constitutive of the philosophical discourse, not by trying to overcome its inner differences but by maintaining them.

To sum up: deconstruction starts with a systematic elucidation of contradictions, paradoxes, inconsistencies, and aporias constitutive of conceptuality, argumentation, and the discursiveness of philosophy. Yet these discrepancies are not logical contradictions, the only discrepancies for which the philosophical discourse can account. Eluded by the logic of identity, they are consequently not contradictions properly speaking. Nor are these necessary inconsistencies the result of inequality between form and content. Their exclusion from the canon of philosophical themes is precisely what makes it possible to distinguish between form and content, a distinction that takes place solely against the horizon of the possibility of their homogeneous reunification.

As its first step, deconstruction thus presupposes a concretely developed demonstration of the fact that concepts and discursive totalities are already cracked and fissured by necessary contradictions and heterogeneities that the discourse of philosophy fails to take into account, either because they are not, rigorously speaking, logical contradictions, or because a regulated (conceptual) economy must avoid them in order to safeguard the ethico-theoretical decisions that orient its discourse. These fissures become apparent when we follow to its logical end that which in the process of conceptualization or argumentation is only in a certain manner said. Deconstruction thus begins by taking up broached but discontinued implications—discontinued because they would have contradicted the intentions of philosophy. In the case of Rousseau's text, Derrida formulates this procedure as follows:

> Rousseau's text must constantly be considered as a complex and many-leveled structure; in it, certain propositions may be read as interpretations of other propositions that we are, up to a certain point and with certain precautions, free to read otherwise. Rousseau says A, then for reasons that we must determine, he interprets A into B. A, which was already an interpretation, is reinterpreted into B. After taking cognizance of it, we may, without leaving Rousseau's text, isolate A from its interpretation into B, and discover possibilities and resources there that indeed belong to Rousseau's text, but were not produced or exploited by him, which, for equally legible motives, he *preferred to cut short* by a gesture neither witting nor unwitting. [*Of Grammatology*]

The demonstration of these unexploited possibilities and resources, which contradict the ethico-theoretical decisions characteristic of conceptualization and philosophical argumentation and haunt the concepts and the texts of philosophy, corresponds to the thematization of a naivety unthought by discursive philosophical practice. Such naivety complies with and is a function of the ethical orientation of theorizing and is in no way a naivety or deficiency owing to the finitude of the philosophizing subject, Rousseau or Saussure, for instance. On the contrary, such naivety is the very possibility of theory.

Alexander Nehamas   (essay date 5 October 1987)

SOURCE: "Truth and Consequences," in *The New Republic,* Vol. 197, No. 14, October 5, 1987, pp. 31-6.

[*Nehamas is a Greek-born American educator and critic whose philosophical study,* Nietzsche: Life as Literature *(1986), was widely praised as one of the most important book-length interpretations of Nietzsche. In the following essay, he outlines and critiques the main themes of Derrida's philosophy.*]

Jacques Derrida has been the focus of furious controversy ever since he startled his audience, at a conference in 1966 intended to mark the coming of age of structuralism in America, by arguing that it was already too late, that structuralism was already effectively dead. In the years that followed, Derrida became an institution in his own right. His lectures attract huge crowds. At least 13 of his books have been published in English, including these newly translated, though not so recently written, works [*Glas, The Post Card: From Socrates to Freud and Beyond,* and *The Truth in Painting*]; and books about him are appearing wherever you look. Many of Derrida's terms—"grammatology," "logocentrism," "margin," "*différance*," and, of course, "deconstruction," after which a whole approach to literary criticism has been named—are now commonplace in many academic disciplines, and they are entering wider, even journalistic, usage as well.

The passions surrounding Derrida have been extraordinary, uniting in their intensity his partisans and his detractors. Some consider him to be one of the truly great writers of the second half of the century. Others dismiss him as a charlatan. Many see his work as a profound, innovative, and perhaps constructive critique of many of our most basic ideas and institutions. Others suspect it of fostering relativism, irrationalism, and nihilism, all alluringly clothed in the haute couture of French irony, polymathy, and sophistication.

Both camps agree that Derrida is radically subversive. They are united in finding in the content of his work, as well as in its form, a general attack on the notions of truth, clarity, reason, definiteness, and understanding. The two camps disagree only over the value of these notions, not over Derrida's attitude toward them. Those who want to defend the values of truth and reason, and the institutions that serve them, despise him; those who think that Derrida's writings are the unmaking of these values, and the institutions connected with them, adore him. In fact, a careful reading of Derrida's work shows that he is less relativist and nihilist than his opponents fear, and less innovative and original than his proponents wish.

Many literary critics, and a few philosophers, have hailed Derrida for having liberated us from "the logocentric tradition of Western metaphysics"—a sweeping generalization that, not without some justification, goes against every instinct and value of analytical philosophers. "Logocentrism" is derived from the Greek *logos,* which means "word" or "definition," the true account that states correctly what each thing really is. In the Gospel of St. John, *logos* is identified with God, who is taken as the ultimate source of all truth. And since the *logos,* as John writes, was "in the beginning," error arises from the Fall from God. The *logos* has ceased being "present" to us; the truth, which was there first, has now been hidden.

Logocentrism, accordingly, is the view, held to be dominant in philosophy and in most "serious" activities, that there is such a thing as the objective truth about the world.

Moreover, whether or not this truth can ever actually be recaptured, logocentrism is supposed to include the desire to return to it, and to confront it directly, without distortion, once and for all. Derrida's advocates claim that he has shown conclusively that such a conception represents an impossible, self-undermining dream.

This is where deconstruction enters the picture. Consider, for example, "phonocentrism," one of logocentrism's specific manifestations. (Derrida is an inveterate purveyor of technical terms, which always seem to provide his supporters with something to say and his opponents with something to be suspicious of.) Phonocentrism begins from the fact that thought cannot be communicated directly. Among the indirect expression of thought, phonocentrism considers speech or voice (*phoné* in Greek) the best, because it seems that spoken sounds, which coincide temporally with our thoughts, do not obscure them and do not therefore mask the meaning we want to express. Thought is "present," or as "present" as it can possibly be, when it is being expressed in speech. Moreover, we can always avoid unclarity by answering questions, until our meaning is finally clear to our listeners.

But writing, according to phonocentrism, is different. In contrast to speech, writing is essentially opaque. It interposes an additional layer of signs between us and the meaning we need to understand. Written marks have a solidity of their own, masking the meaning that originally animated them. Thus writing functions, and is intended to function, in the "absence" of the person with whom it originated. It necessarily requires interpretation; and, especially in the author's absence, it can always be misinterpreted and misappropriated.

A "deconstruction" of the dichotomy between speech and writing aims to undermine the primacy of the preferred, or "valorized," term. The strategy is to show that the very features that have been supposed to make writing unreliable are in fact present in speech as well, and that this fact is always suppressed by logocentrism.

According to deconstruction, speech too consists of signs with their own material nature, signs that can be iterated in isolation from the context of their original use. Derrida argues that many authors who have devalued writing as a mere "supplement" to speech, like Rousseau or Saussure, have also demonstrated a fear that writing somehow is able to pervert the living voice. Their fear is justified, Derrida continues, only on the supposition that writing can affect speech because the two share the same nature.

Does this, then, make writing better than speech? Many have taken Derrida to make just this claim; but his answer is that it does not. Deconstruction refuses to reverse the hierarchy implicit in logocentrism. This, after all, would be to perpetuate logocentrism in a new guise, since logocentrism is essentially the view that *some* method for reaching the truth is better than others. Instead, deconstruction reveals that, despite their superficial differences, speech and writing are both special cases of a general set of conditions for communication, rather pompously called "archi-writing," to which the possibility of misunderstanding is endemic.

In sum, there simply is no such thing as communication or knowledge that is guaranteed to be successful, there is no undistorted perception of the truth, there is no identification, as Hegel would have put it, between subject and object. Truth is not prior to error, capable of being grasped by itself; the two go hand in hand. Neither can exist without the other. On its own terms, therefore, the privileging of speech over writing, since it ultimately attributes to both the same features, shows that the opposition it sets up is untenable or, as Derrida often puts it, "undecidable."

Derrida has been concerned to display the undecidability of a whole host of distinctions, notably the pairs presence/absence, concept/sign, intelligible/sensible, center/margin, and others. In close and detailed readings of philosophers like Plato, Aristotle, Kant, and Husserl, he has argued that in each case the first member of each pair is considered more valuable, and a better guide to the truth, only because the features it shares with the second, which make both equally fallible, have been ignored or repressed.

Husserl, for example, privileges what is present to consciousness, and considers it as the basis from which all our knowledge and our understanding proceed. But he is able to do this, according to Derrida, only because he suppresses the fact that what is present is thought of as such by being implicitly contrasted with something that is no longer present (the past) as well as with something that is not yet present (the future). Both past and future are cases of "absence." And the only way the present can be at all conceived is by contrast to what is absent; what is present, Derrida would characteristically say, is a special case of what is absent. It has no special claim to priority of any sort. Moreover, Derrida argues, these philosophical works deconstruct themselves: read closely, they themselves provide the evidence that undermines the hierarchical distinctions that it is their official purpose to set up.

Since the two terms of each pair are always implicated in this way, Derrida claims that it is not possible to say definitely what the works that employ them ultimately mean. Saussure, for example, finally equated speech with writing. Does his text "really" mean that speech is better than writing? That writing is better than speech? Both? Neither? The answer is not clear; such works cannot be univocally interpreted. The very effort to use some definite standard—for example, the author's explicit intention—in order to determine their real meaning is itself a special case of logocentrism, since it is an attempt to state definitely the truth about them.

This controversial cluster of ideas is to be found mainly in the works Derrida composed in the '60s and '70s (they include the books under review). These writings established deconstruction as the vanguard approach to literary criticism, which now saw philosophy, supposedly still trapped in the snares of logocentrism, at its mercy. But many philosophers remained either ignorant or disdainful of this new act of aggression. Nor did many literary critics join the new group, which they accused of being simply a mechanical application of a few tired principles. They saw deconstruction as an empty celebration of "the interminable play of *différance*," an obscure if ubiquitous principle that allegedly prevents any literary work from communicating a clear and single meaning. Taking interpretation as the effort to determine precisely such a clear and single meaning, and deconstruction as the desire to show that precisely such an interpretation is impossible, the opponents of deconstruction saw it as nothing short of an attempt to undermine the very idea of literary criticism.

Against certain Derrideans, if not against Derrida himself, this objection is often justified. But a look at the reception of the New Criticism in American universities in the '40s and '50s shows that such objections, such fears, are inevitable in criticism, as they are in many of the disciplines of the human sciences, where the difference between fact and fashion is not always easy to tell. More serious and more disturbing, however, is the charge that Derrida's views are relativist and nihilist. If written texts (or any acts of communication) cannot be definitively interpreted, if meaning is undecidable, is it not the case (as some deconstructive critics, in moments of intoxication, have claimed) that any text can be made to mean anything at all? How can even the view that meaning is undecidable itself be definitively communicated? The very statement of this view, if it can be understood at all, seems to undermine itself: to succeed in communicating the view that meaning cannot be communicated is to show that the thesis is wrong.

Equally important, Derrida's suspicion of the idea of objective truth that can be captured without distortion raises a further question: If truth does not exist, isn't every view as valid as every other? If truth is no longer available as a standard, we simply cannot any longer distinguish between better and worse ideas. Reason, and reasons, are discarded: this leads to irrationalism. Truth is abandoned: nihilism follows. Standards are lacking: relativism remains the only alternative. How can anyone, especially a professor who is sustained by the institutions these very views call into question, hold these views? The moral charge of bad faith is added to the philosophical objection.

In fact, however, in the light of much of what he has written, Derrida is not an advocate of irrationalism, relativism, or nihilism. The undecidability of meaning does not make of every text a blank slate on which any interpretation can be imposed. Undecidability is specific. Derrida does not, as many fear, "make the author nothing and the reader everything." It is not meaning in general that is undecidable: Derrida does not hold that nothing means anything in particular, that every text is at its readers' mercy. What is undecidable is only whether a text "really" means that speech communicates the truth better than writing—or, for that matter, the opposite, since the distinction between the two is being questioned.

The second issue, the matter of Derrida's rejection of truth, is very complicated. As Rodolphe Gasché definitively (if turgidly) shows in his study, Derrida attacks Hegel's idea that absolute, total, and non-distorting knowledge is achieved through Reason's reflecting on itself, through the identification of subject and object. Hegel's view is as obscure as anything ever written by a philosopher. The question whether it even makes sense has never been answered, Gasché's equanimity notwithstanding. But the main point, in Gasché's lovely meta-

phor, is that even the most perfect mirror requires a tain, the lusterless and invisible backing without which reflection would not be possible, and which is left out of the picture in Hegelian speculation on reflection. Once again, a purely positive result—perfect and transparent reflection—is made possible only by suppressing the opposing term—non-reflecting and invisible—that allows it to occur in the first place.

Derrida's position on truth is not in fact very shocking at all. It belongs within a distinguished family of views that, deriving directly or indirectly from the writings of Nietzsche and William James, constitute the modern attack on essentialism. Essentialism is the idea that some features of the world are absolutely indispensable to it, that they are possessed by the world in itself, independently of any point of view. Further, essentialism is the idea that some methods of acquiring knowledge are better guides to the truth than others, because they are better suited to mirror these essential features of the world in a faithful manner.

Varieties of anti-essentialist arguments can be found in the writings of a number of recent American philosophers (notably W. V. Quine, Wilfrid Sellars, Nelson Goodman, Richard Rorty, and Hilary Putnam). In one way or another, these philosophers have claimed that knowledge has no "foundations," that there are no indubitable experiences of basic undistorted truths or facts on which the rest of our knowledge can securely be based. They deny that knowledge can ever be certain, that there are any absolute facts that everyone must always acknowledge.

What counts as a fact, according to the anti-essentialists, is always relative to a theory, to a particular system of representation. The facts of one theory may always appear, from another point of view, as a theory concerned with some further facts, themselves capable, in further contexts, of playing a theoretical role. We are very close to Derrida here. In his idiom, the notion is that the reality represented or described by any text can itself be, on analysis (or deconstruction), a text representing a further reality, itself subject to the same predicament. Hence his notorious slogan, "There is nothing outside the text."

It is important to realize that this view, in Derrida's case or more generally in the case of anti-essentialism, is not relativism or nihilism. Anti-essentialism does not deny that there are standards by which two competing approaches to the same subject matter can be evaluated. It only denies that there is a single standard by which all approaches, whatever their subject matter, can be judged. It is like denying that there is a single God for all people, and leaving people to order their lives according to their faiths in various deities. It is not like claiming that there are no gods at all.

These views are sometimes unclear, and often controversial. But they are neither absolutely new nor absolutely wild. Derrida is not subverting the values of truth and objectivity, at least any more than many respectable philosophers do. By the standards of modern philosophy, his views on truth and objectivity can even be called traditional. What, then, is all the fuss about? What is it about Derrida that stirs such passions?

> Derrida is not an advocate of irrationalism, relativism, or nihilism. The undecidability of meaning does not make of every text a blank slate on which any interpretation can be imposed. What is undecidable is only whether a text "really" means that speech communicates the truth better than writing.
>
> —*Alexander Nehamas*

Part of the problem is that Derrida has been ill-served by many of his literary followers. He has read carefully many of the texts that he has "deconstructed." But generalizations similar to his own are constantly being made by people with no understanding of philosophy, who, having read a few of Derrida's essays, declare on the basis of the deconstruction of some minor text that "logic is a self-enclosed system" whose time has come and gone, or that "Western metaphysics" has finally been overcome—at which point what was merely suspicious becomes positively ludicrous.

Then there is the problem of Derrida's form. I have in mind not his difficulty, his dense, allusive, and indirect style, or his strange, idiosyncratic vocabulary. There is a certain philistine criticism of Derrida, a kind of anti-intellectualism really, that harps upon these features of his work; but these are features that characterize the writings of many respectable philosophers, indeed of some great ones. I am concerned, rather, with the fact that Derrida's works are often designed not to look like books or essays at all. And the obscurity of Derrida's form is designed to make a philosophical point.

Recall Derrida's view that logocentrism, the search for truth and for determinate meaning, undermines itself. This is not to say that logocentrism is something we can simply abandon. Of course we cannot turn our back on the search for truth. There is a profound paradox here, first articulated by Nietzsche. To try to show that the search for truth is, for whatever reason, misguided is to try to show, whether we like it or not, that it is true that the search for truth is, for whatever reason, misguided. In other words, an attack on truth is here being waged, inevitably, in the name of truth. And if the attack is successful, and the search for truth is somehow discredited, then the truth has won out again.

This is the point Derrida makes in a well-known passage:

> There is no sense in doing without the concepts of metaphysics in order to attack metaphysics. We have no language—no syntax and no lexicon—which is alien to this history; we cannot utter a single destructive proposition which has not already slipped into the form, the logic, and the implicit postulations of precisely what it seeks to contest.

Derrida's effort to come to terms with this predicament accounts for some of the most characteristic, most brilliant, and most objectionable features of his work. For it is this problem that led him to conclude that straightforward discursive prose, argument, proof, all the traditional forms of scholarly communication—essays, monographs, books—are suspect. They are the very tools of logocentrism. Any effort to attack logocentrism directly, by these means and in these forms, will inevitably perpetuate it, and become itself the object of a deconstruction.

Thus Derrida has been experimenting with alternative forms of writing and composition. In addition, he has consistently maintained an ironic stance toward his own writings, inevitably prompting his readers to ask whether he can really mean what he says. But, as with all questions regarding "real" meaning, his reply, too, is undecidable: a shrug of the shoulders, in person or in prose. This question, he responds, is itself logocentric. But how can a scholar, one still wants to know, and a professor of philosophy at that, *not* be serious about his own ideas? And if he isn't, why should we be? But Derrida's response has a point. Though not self-consciously, we frequently take ideas seriously without any notion of their authors' attitude toward them; sometimes we don't even know whose ideas they were in the first place. Derrida's ironic attitude toward his views aims to bring this fact explicitly to our attention.

Readers of *Glas* (originally published in 1974), *The Truth in Painting* (1978), or *The Post Card* (1980) are bound to be disturbed both by the form of these works and by Derrida's ambiguous attitude toward his own views. Since Derrida constantly employs multilingual puns, wordplay, and intentional ambiguity (all in order not to produce univocal meaning), his works are also a translator's nightmare. This explains why these remarkably successful English versions took so long to appear. Only very determined readers will master these forbidding works. Yet it is likely that much of what they find there will strike them as a set of esoteric jokes.

It's almost as if these texts were composed by a professor gone mad in Borges's Library of Babel. In the Library, every possible bit of writing means something; it is not even possible accidentally "to combine some characters, *dhcmrlchtdj*, which the divine Library has not foreseen . . . and which in one of its secret tongues do not contain a terrible meaning." But the principle governing *The Post Card* in particular seems to be the exact contrary of Borges's fantasy. Not only does the work contain a non-sensical character-sequence, EGEK HUM XSR STR, but its central claim is that error and nonsense, the impossibility of determinate meaning, are built into the essence of every code of communication.

The Post Card is an immense meditation on this idea, particularly in connection with psychoanalysis. (*The Truth in Painting* pursues similar themes in art, its criticism, and its philosophy.) It includes brilliant readings of Freud and Lacan. But Derrida's method is perhaps best illustrated by *Envois,* the first and by far the longest part of the work, and a parody of the epistolary novel in which Derrida aims to expose what he calls "the Postal Principle." The Postal Principle is Derrida's metaphor for what he considers to be one of the founding ideas of our culture. This is the idea that acts of communication proceed from an undisputed sender to an equally undisputed recipient. Therefore they always occur in a definite context which fixes their meaning, and which it is the task of interpretation to determine and express without remainder. The Postal Principle is the assumption that every message hits its mark, that every letter is delivered to its addressee.

But there always is a remainder, Derrida believes, that is forever beyond our grasp. The message does not always hit its mark. The postcards of which *Envois* consists are sent by someone named "Derrida" (whose name is woven throughout the book's prose) to someone who could be his wife, his reader, or himself. The postcards all carry a reproduction of the cover of a book of prophecy depicting, contrary to everything we know, Socrates writing at Plato's dictation. This prompts Derrida to engage in a long questioning of our usual understanding of priority, order, and communication. Open to inspection, postcards often carry elliptical, indeterminate messages, especially when both their source and destination remain unclear. And right in the center of "the Postal System," showing that its failure is as inherent as its success, is the dead-letter office, containing those messages that have completely missed their mark.

Yet a careful reading of *Envois* shows that Derrida holds two views. The first is that any statement can function in many contexts, none of which is indisputably the proper one, and that in each context the statement in question will have a different meaning. The question of what the statement "really" means, therefore, cannot receive an answer, though the statement can still communicate something definite in each specific context. It is not, Derrida reasonably writes, "that the letter never arrives at its destination, but it belongs to the structure of the letter to be capable, always, of not arriving."

Derrida's second view is more radical, and much less defensible. The possibility of different contexts sometimes seems to suggest to Derrida that no statement ever has a determinate meaning: "a letter can always not arrive at its destination, and . . . therefore it never arrives. . . . The condition for it to arrive is that it ends up and even that it begins by not arriving." This position assumes that a statement would have a determinate meaning only if it communicated that very meaning in all possible contexts; or, to put it another way, only if that statement were meaningful in one and only one context.

But this is a remarkably strong criterion of what it is to have a determinate meaning. In fact, it is nothing other than the old "logocentric" ideal, according to which communication can be successful only through a perfect coincidence between a sign and its meaning. Amazingly, Derrida seems to confess to just this dream in *Envois*:

> I would like to write to you so simply, so simply, so simply. Without having anything ever catch the eye, excepting yours alone, and what is more while erasing all the traits, even the most inapparent ones, the ones that mark the tone, or the belonging to a genre (the letter, for example, or the post card), so that above all the language re-

mains self-evidently secret, as if it were being invented at every step, and as if it were burning immediately, as soon as any third party would set eyes on it.

The contradiction in Derrida's thinking here is striking: the deconstructionist appears as a logocentrist. It is in this surprising, second, immoderate view of Derrida's that he parts company with the tradition of Nietzsche and James, and at which his critics should properly take aim.

Glas, whose every page contains two columns, is surely the most remarkable-looking of Derrida's works. The left column discusses Hegel, particularly his notion of Absolute Knowledge. This logocentric ideal, *savoir absolu* in French, is abbreviated as SA, a homonym of *ça,* the French neuter pronoun, and is thereby connected with Freud's *id,* which is the Latinization of the corresponding German pronoun *es.* There is also a discussion of Hegel's views on the family (connected with the Immaculate Conception, or IC), of his own family situation, of the relations between the two, and of his name, which in France is pronounced like *aigle,* the word for eagle. The right column is concerned with Genet, whose name is a homonym of *genêt,* broomflower, and traces floral motifs in his works, including his *Notre-Dame-Des-Fleurs,* which, naturally, is connected with IC. Each column contains numerous inserts. The space between the columns also sometimes contains writing. There are innumerable puns, variations on the sound "gl," meditations on Derrida's own name, and an examination of the connections between authors' names ("signatures") and the themes and words in their works—this last having become one of Derrida's central preoccupations in recent years.

A number of people have written about this book. Nobody knows what it is about. Is *Glas,* after all, a "book"? Is it "about" anything? As Gregory Ulmer writes in *Glassary* (which traces every term and every reference in *Glas*—a most scholarly enterprise), *Glas* "is not composed in the conventional manner of the academic book because it is explicitly an anti-book. . . . The Book as such reflects a certain model of thought based on the platonic, and ultimately on the logocentric paradigm of thought." So then how are we to read this text? First one column all the way through and then the other? First one column on each page and then the other? Should we interrupt our reading of the columns to read the inserts? Should *Glas* and *Glassary* (large, square volumes) be displayed on coffee tables, to be read a little at a time over long periods?

Certainly Derrida's experiments with the printed form have produced some remarkable works. But his assumption that words, sentences, paragraphs, and books can, by themselves, reflect a commitment to logocentrism, that to write a book is already to accept "the logocentric paradigm of thought," is a grave mistake. All logocentric works have been composed in traditional forms, but not all works composed in traditional forms have been logocentric. A commitment to a philosophical theory is not reflected simply in the form in which ideas are presented, in words and books taken in themselves, independently of what they are used to say. It is, rather, reflected by the combination of form and content, by what we *do* with our words and our books, by what we say and what we believe.

Derrida writes seductively, playfully, hauntingly. He offers philosophical readings of literary authors and literary analyses of the heroes of philosophy. He seems to have convinced many people that he believes that philosophy is simply a species of literature, fiction mistaking itself for the pursuit of truth. Many (but not all) literary critics have been delighted, and many (but not all) philosophers have been infuriated, by this idea. But it is a wrong interpretation of his work. Derrida's writing resists such obvious classifications. It poses, once again, the question of the relation between philosophy and literature; but it gives no consistent answer.

In recent years Derrida has been writing about the place of philosophy within the university and within the general culture, about the function of universities, about political issues such as nuclear war and racism. Though always written in his characteristic style, these essays betray a new seriousness, as readers of the collection *For Nelson Mandela,* which Derrida edited and to which he contributed a long essay, are bound to notice. Could it be, then, that 21 years after his scandalous entry into the American academy, the enfant terrible may be growing up after all?

Undoubtedly deconstructive criticism has greatly profited from Derrida's thought, both thematically and methodologically. But to quarry from Derrida's writings is not automatically to become deconstructive in the eminent sense. Indeed, many deconstructionist critics have chosen simply to ignore the profoundly philosophical thrust of Derridean thought, and have consequently misconstrued what deconstruction consists of and what it seeks to achieve.

—*Rodolphe Gasché, in his* The Tain of the Mirror: Derrida and the Philosophy of Reflection, *1986.*

Richard Rorty   (essay date Spring 1989)

SOURCE: "Is Derrida a Transcendental Philosopher?" in *Yale Journal of Criticism,* Vol. 2, No. 2, Spring, 1989, pp. 207-17.

[*In the following essay, Rorty disputes the interpretations of Derrida's work put forth by such critics as Christopher Norris and Rodolphe Gasché, who argue that Derrida is a rigorous logician and a transcendental philosopher in the tradition of Hegel and Kant.*]

For years a quarrel has been simmering among Derrida's American admirers. On the one side there are the people who admire Derrida for having invented a new, splendidly ironic way of writing about the philosophical tradition. On the other side are those who admire him for having given us rigorous arguments for surprising philosophical conclusions. The former emphasizes the playful, distancing, oblique way in which Derrida handles traditional philosophical figures and topics. The second emphasize what they take to be his results, his philosophical discoveries. Roughly speaking, the first are content to admire his manner, whereas the second want to say that the important thing is his matter—the truths that he has set forth.

Geoffrey Hartman's *Saving the Text* set the tone for the first way of appropriating Derrida. At the same time that I was picking up this tone from Hartman, and imitating it, Jonathan Culler was criticizing Hartman for light-mindedness. The term "Derridadaism," Culler said [in *On Deconstruction*], was "a witty gesture by which Geoffrey Hartman blots out Derridean argument." I weighed in on Hartman's side, claiming that Culler was too heavy-handed in his treatment of Derrida, too anxious to treat him as having demonstrated theorems which literary critics might now proceed to apply. I thought it too much to ask of "deconstruction" that it be, in Culler's words, *both* "rigorous argument within philosophy and displacement of philosophical categories and philosophical attempts at mastery." Something, I claimed, had to go. I suggested we jettison the "rigorous argument" part.

This suggestion was contested by Christopher Norris. [In a footnote, Rorty cites articles in which he and Norris debated this question. These include: Norris's "Philosophy as *not* just a 'kind of writing': Derrida and the claim of reason" and Rorty's "Two senses of 'logocentrism': a reply to Norris," both in *Redrawing the Lines: Analytic Philosophy, Deconstruction and Literary Theory,* edited by Reed Way Dasenbrock.] Norris was concerned to show that Derrida has arguments, good solid arguments, and is not just playing around. Like Culler, he was also concerned to block my attempt to analogize deconstruction to pragmatism. Whereas a pragmatist view of truth, Culler said, treats conventionally accepted norms as foundations, deconstruction goes on to point out that "norms are produced by acts of exclusion." "Objectivity," Culler quite justly pointed out, "is constituted by excluding the views of those who do not count as sane and rational men: women, children, poets, prophets, madmen." Culler was the first to make the suggestion, later taken up and developed in considerable detail by others, that pragmatism (or at least my version of it) and deconstruction differ in that the one tends toward political conservatism and the other toward political radicalism.

In his recent book on Derrida [*Derrida,* 1987], Norris repeats this suggestion, and reaffirms that to read Derrida in Hartman's and my way is

> to ignore the awkward fact that Derrida has devoted the bulk of his writings to a patient working-through (albeit on his own, very different terms) of precisely those problems that have occupied philosophers in the "mainstream" tradition, from Kant to Husserl and Frege. And this because those problems are indubitably *there,* installed within philosophy and reaching beyond

it into every department of modern institutional-ized knowledge.

The quarrel about whether Derrida has arguments thus gets linked to a quarrel about whether he is a private writ-er—writing for the delight of us insiders who share his background, who find the same rather esoteric things as funny or beautiful or moving as he does—or rather a writ-er with a public mission, someone who gives us weapons with which to subvert "institutionalized knowledge" and thus social institutions. I have urged [in "From Ironist Theory to Private Allusions: Derrida," in his *Contingency, Irony and Solidarity*] that Derrida be treated as the first sort of writer, whereas most of his American admirers have treated him as, at least in part, the second. Lumping both quarrels together, one can say that there is a quarrel between those of us who read Derrida on Plato, Hegel and Heidegger in the same way as we read Bloom or Cavell on Emerson or Freud—in order to see these authors transfig-ured, beaten into fascinating new shapes—and those who read Derrida to get ammunition, and a strategy, for the struggle to bring about social change.

Norris thinks that Derrida should be read as a transcen-dental philosopher in the Kantian tradition—somebody who digs out hitherto unsuspected presuppositions. "Der-rida," he says, "is broaching something like a Kantian transcendental deduction, an argument to demonstrate ('perversely' enough) that *a priori* notions of logical truth are *a priori* ruled out of court by rigorous reflection on the powers and limits of textual critique" [*Derrida*]. By con-trast, my view of Derrida is that he nudges us into a world in which "rigorous reflection on the powers and limits . . ." has as little place as do "*a priori* notions of logical truth." This world has as little room for transcen-dental deductions, or for rigor, as for self-authenticating moments of immediate presence to consciousness.

On my view, the only thing that can displace an intellectu-al world is another intellectual world—a new alternative, rather than an argument against an old alternative. The idea that there is some neutral ground on which to mount an argument against something as big as "logocentrism" strikes me as one more logocentric hallucination. I do not think that demonstrations of "internal incoherence" or of "presuppositional relationships" ever do much to disabuse us of bad old ideas or institutions. Disabusing gets done, instead, by offering us sparkling new ideas, or utopian vi-sions of glorious new institutions. The result of genuinely original thought, on my view, is not so much to refute or subvert our previous beliefs as to help us forget them by giving us a substitute for them. I take refutation to be a mark of unoriginality, and I value Derrida's originality too much to praise him in those terms. So I find little use, in reading or discussing him, for the notion of "rigorous argumentation."

Culler and Norris have now been joined, on their side of the quarrel I have been describing, by Rodolphe Gasché. Gasché's *The Tain of the Mirror* is by far the most ambi-tious and detailed attempt to treat Derrida as a rigorous transcendental philosopher. Gasché says that

> [i]n this book I hope that I have found a middle ground between the structural plurality of Der-

rida's philosophy—a plurality that makes it im-possible to elevate any final essence of his book into its true meaning—and the strict criteria to which any interpretation of his work must yield, if it is to be about that work and not merely a private fantasy. These criteria, at center stage in this book, are, as I shall show, philosophical and not literary in nature.

Just as in the case of Culler I doubted that one could dis-place philosophical concepts while still having rigorous philosophical arguments, so in Gasché's case I doubt that one can eschew the project of stating Derrida's "true meaning" while still judging him by "strict criteria." I do not think that one should try to pay good old logocentric compliments to enemies of logocentrism.

In what follows, I shall try to spell out why the compli-ments Gasché offers Derrida seem to me misapplied. To my mind, "private fantasy" is, if not entirely adequate, at least a somewhat better compliment. Many responsibili-ties begin in dreams, and many transfigurations of the tra-dition begin in private fantasies. Think, for example, of Plato's or St. Paul's private fantasies—fantasies so original and utopian that they became the common sense of later times. Someday, for all I know, there may be some social changes (perhaps even changes for the better) which retro-spection will see as having originated in Derrida's fanta-sies. But the *arguments* which Derrida can be read as of-fering on behalf of his fantasies seem to me no better than the ones Plato offered for his. Anybody who reads through Plato in search of rigorous arguments is in for a disap-pointment. I think that the same goes for Derrida.

I can begin quarreling with Gasché by taking up his dis-tinction between philosophy and literature. On my view, "philosophy" is either a term defined by choosing a list of writers (e.g., Parmenides, Plato, Aristotle, Kant, Hegel, Heidegger) and then specifying what they all have in com-mon, or else just the name of an academic department. The first sense of the term is hard to apply to a writer who, like Derrida, is trying to extricate himself from the tradi-tion defined by such a list. But the second sense of the term is not much help either, for in this sense "philosophy" is just an omnium gatherum of disparate activities united by nothing more than a complicated tangle of genealogical connections—connections so tenuous that one can no lon-ger detect even a family resemblance between the activi-ties. [In a footnote Rorty adds: "There is no interesting least common denominator of, for example, Rawls, Croce, Frege, Nietzsche and Gödel—no feature which makes them all representative of the same natural kind. One can only explain why all six are studied within a single aca-demic department by developing a complicated historico-sociological story."] Only if one buys in on the logocentric idea that there just *must* be an autonomous discipline which adjudicates ultimate questions would "philosophy" have a third sense, one appropriate for Gasché's purposes. It is only by reference to some such idea that it makes sense to worry, as he does, about the lines between philos-ophy and literature.

For my purposes, the important place to draw a line is not between philosophy and non-philosophy but rather be-tween topics which we know how to argue about and those we do not. It is the line between the attempt to be objective—to get a consensus on what we should believe—and a willingness to abandon consensus in the hope of transfiguration. Gasché, by contrast, thinks that we can separate the philosophical books (or, at least, the important philosophical books of recent centuries) from other books by a fairly straightforward test. The former are the books in which we find a specifically *transcendental* project—a project of answering some question of the form "what are the conditions of the possibility of . . . ?"—of, for example, experience, self-consciousness, language or philosophy itself.

I have to admit that asking and answering that question is, indeed, the mark of a distinct genre. But unlike Gasché I think that it is a thoroughly self-deceptive question. The habit of posing it—asking for non-causal, nonempirical, nonhistorical conditions—is the distinctive feature of a tradition which stretches from the *Critique of Pure Reason* through Hegel's *Science of Logic* to *Being and Time* (and, if Gasché is right about the early Derrida's intentions, through *Of Grammatology*). The trouble with the question is that it looks like a "scientific" one, as if we knew how to debate the relative merits of alternative answers, just as we know how to debate alternative answers to questions about the conditions for the *actuality* of various things (e.g., political changes, quasars, psychoses). But it is not. Since that for which the conditions of possibility are sought is always *everything* that any previous philosopher has envisaged—the whole range of what has been discussed up to now—anybody is at liberty to identify any ingenious gimmick that he dreams up as a "condition of possibility."

The sort of gimmick in question is exemplified by Kantian "transcendental synthesis," Hegelian "self-direction of the concept," Heideggerian *Sorge,* and (on Gasché's interpretation) Derridean *différance.* These suggestions about transcendental conditions are so many leaps into the darkness which surrounds the totality of everything previously illuminated. In the nature of the case, there can be no preexistent logical space, no "strict criteria" for choosing among these alternatives. If there were, the question about "conditions of possibility" would automatically become merely "positive" and not properly "transcendental" or "reflective." [In a footnote Rorty remarks: "Another way of putting this point is to note that each successive figure in the tradition in question has had to invent his own 'central problem of philosophy' rather than work on some issue previously agreed to be problematic. Consider, in this light, Gasché's claim that 'Arche-writing is a construct aimed at resolving the philosophical problem of the very possibility (not primarily the empirical fact, which always suffers exceptions) of the usurpation, parasitism and contamination of an ideality, a generality, a universal by what is considered its other, its exterior, its incarnation, its appearance, and so on.' Nobody knew *that* was a 'philosophical problem' before Derrida came along, any more than we knew that 'the conditions of the possibility of synthetic a priori judgments' was a problem before Kant came along."] Once again, I would want to insist that you cannot have it both ways. You cannot see these leaps in the dark as the magnificent poetic acts they are and still

talk about "philosophical rigor." Rigor just does not come into it.

This insusceptibility to argument is what makes "the philosophy of reflection"—the tradition of transcendental inquiry within which Gasché wishes to embed Derrida—the *bête noir* of philosophers who take public discussability as the essence of rationality. Habermas's polemic against the late Heidegger and against Derrida has the same motives as Carnap's attack on the early Heidegger. Like Carnap, Habermas thinks that philosophy ought to be argumentative. He thinks that Heidegger and Derrida are merely oracular. My own view is that we should avoid slogans like "philosophy ought to be argumentative" (or any other slogan that begins "philosophy ought to be . . .") and recognize that the writers usually identified as "philosophers" include both argumentative problem-solvers like Aristotle and Russell and oracular world-disclosers like Plato and Hegel—both people good at rendering public accounts and people good at leaping in the dark.

But this conciliatory ecumenicism still leaves me hostile to those who, like Gasché, think that one can synthesize world-disclosing and problem-solving into a single activity called "reflection." In particular, I object to the idea that one can be "rigorous" if one's procedure consists in inventing new words for what one is pleased to call "conditions of possibility" rather than playing sentences using old words off against each other. The latter activity is what I take to constitute argumentation. Poetic world-disclosers like Hegel, Heidegger and Derrida have to pay a price, and part of that price is the inappropriateness to their work of notions like "argumentation" and "rigor." [In a footnote Rorty continues: "Consider Gasché's claim that Derrida has 'demonstrated' that 'the source of all being beyond being is *generalized,* or rather *general,* writing.' This is just the sort of claim which inspired the logical positivists to say that metaphysics lacked 'cognitive status.' Their point was that such a claim cannot be 'demonstrated,' unless 'demonstration' means something very different from 'can be argued for on the basis of generally shared beliefs.' "]

Habermas differs with me and agrees with Gasché in thinking that philosophy ought to be argumentative, but he agrees with me and differs from Gasché in refusing to see the transitions in Hegel's *Logic,* or the successive "discoveries" of new "conditions of possibility" which fill the pages of [Heidegger's] *Being and Time,* as *arguments.* Habermas and I are both in sympathy with Ernst Tugendhat's nominalist, Wittgensteinian rejection of the idea that one can be nonpropositional and still be argumentative. Tugendhat sees the attempt of a German tradition stemming from Hegel to work at a subpropositional level, while nevertheless claiming the "cognitive status" which people like Carnap want to deny them, as doomed to failure. By contrast, Gasché explicitly rejects Tugendhat's "theoretical ascetism," his self-confinement to "linguistic and propositional truth." [In a footnote, Rorty elaborates, quoting Gasché in *The Tain:* " 'For Tugendhat, and the analytic tradition he represents, knowledge and truth can only be propositional. . . . [But] by eliminating altogether the ontological dimension of self-identity in self-consciousness (and, for that matter, in absolute reflection), one deprives oneself of the possibility of thinking the very foundations of propositional knowledge and truth, as well as of the very idea of epistemic self-consciousness. . . . Without the presupposition of ontological or formal-ontological identity of being and thought, of subject and object, of the knower and what is known, there is no ground for any propositional attribution whatsoever.' On the 'analytic' view I share with Tugendhat and Habermas, the very idea of a 'ground' for 'propositional attribution' is a mistake. The practice of playing sentences off against one another in order to decide what to believe—the practice of argumentation—no more requires a 'ground' than the practice of using one stone to chip pieces off another stone in order to make a spear-point."] Gasché thinks that such confinement will forbid one to do something which needs to be done, and which Derrida may in fact have accomplished.

Whereas Gasché thinks that words like "différance" and "iterability" signify "infrastructures"—structures which it is Derrida's great achievement to have unearthed—I see these notions as merely abbreviations for the familiar Peircean-Wittgensteinian anti-Cartesian thesis that meaning is a function of context, and that there is no theoretical barrier to an endless sequence of recontextualizations. I think the problems with taking this Derridean jargon as seriously as Gasché does are the same as those which arise if one takes the jargon of *Being and Time* as a serious answer to questions of the form "How is the ontic possible? What are its *ontological* conditions?" If one thinks of writers like Hegel, Heidegger, and Derrida as digging down to successively deeper levels of noncausal conditions—as scientists dig down to ever deeper levels of causal conditions (molecules behind tables, atoms behind molecules, quarks behind atoms . . .)—then the hapless and tedious metaphilosophical question "How can we tell when we have hit bottom?" is bound to arise. More important, so will the question "Within what language are we to lay out arguments demonstrating (or even just making plausible) that we have *correctly* identified these conditions?"

Anybody who reads through Plato in search of rigorous arguments is in for a disappointment. I think that the same goes for Derrida.

—Richard Rorty

The latter question causes no great embarrassment for physicists, since they can say in advance what they want to get out of their theorizing. But it *should* embarrass people concerned with the question of what *philosophical* vocabulary to use, rather than with the question of what vocabulary will help us accomplish some specific purpose (e.g., splitting the atom, curing cancer, persuading the populace). For either the language in which the arguments are given is itself an antecedently given one or it is a dis-

posable ladder-language, one which can be forgotten once it has been *aufgehoben*. The former alternative is impossible if one's aim is to cast doubt on *all* final vocabularies previously available—an ambition common to Hegel, Heidegger and Derrida. Seizing the latter horn of the dilemma, however, requires admitting that the arguments which one uses must themselves be thrown away once they have achieved their purpose. But that would mean, on the normal understanding of the term, that these were not *arguments,* but rather suggestions about how to speak differently. Argumentation requires that the same vocabulary be used in premises and conclusions—that both be part of the same language-game. Hegelian *Aufhebung* is something quite different. [According to the *Encyclopedia of Philosophy,* a "concept or view that is *aufgehoben* (is one that has been) transcended without being wholly discarded."] It is what happens when we play elements of an old vocabulary off against each other in order to make us impatient for a new vocabulary. But that activity is quite different from playing old beliefs against other old beliefs in an attempt to see which survives. An existing language-game will provide "standard rules" for the latter activity, but *nothing* could provide such rules for the former. Yet Gasché tells us that "Derrida's work is a genuinely philosophical inquiry that takes the standard rules of philosophy very seriously."

On my view, it is precisely *Aufhebung* that Derrida is so good at. But one could only think of this practice as *argumentative* if one had a conception of argument as subpropositional—one which allowed the unit of argumentation to be the word rather than the sentence. That is, indeed, a conception of argumentation which, notoriously, we find in Hegel's *Logic*—the text to which Gasché traces back "the philosophy of reflection." Hegel tried to give a sense to the idea that there are inferential relations among individual concepts which are not reducible to inferential relations among sentences which use the words signifying those concepts—that there is a "movement of the concept" for the philosopher to follow, not reducible to the reweaving of a web of belief by playing beliefs off against each other. Hegel thought that he followed this movement as he went from "Being" at the beginning of the *Logic* to "the Absolute Idea" at its end.

Nominalists like myself—those for whom language is a tool rather than a medium, and for whom a concept is just the regular use of a mark or noise—cannot make sense of Hegel's claim that a concept like "Being" breaks apart, sunders itself, turns into its opposite, etc., nor of Gasché's Derridean claim that "concepts and discursive totalities are already cracked and fissured by necessary contradictions and heterogeneities." The best we nominalists can do with such claims is to construe them as saying that one can always make an old language-game look bad by thinking up a better one—replace an old tool with a new one by using an old word in a new way (e.g., as the "privileged" rather than the "derivative" term of a contrast), or by replacing it with a new word. But this need for replacement is *ours,* not the concept's. *It* does not go to pieces; rather, we set it aside and replace it with something else.

Gasché is quite right in saying that to follow Wittgenstein

and Tugendhat in this nominalism will reduce what he wants to call "philosophical reflection" to "a fluidization or liquefaction (*Verflüssigung*) of all oppositions and particularities by means of objective irony." Such liquefaction is what I am calling *Aufhebung* and praising Derrida for having done spectacularly well. We nominalists think that all that philosophers of the world-disclosing (as opposed to the problem-solving) sort can do is to fluidize old vocabularies. We cannot make sense of the notion of discovering a "condition of the possibility of language"—nor, indeed, of the notion of "language" as something homogeneous enough to have "conditions." If, with Wittgenstein, Tugendhat, Quine and Davidson, one ceases to see language as a medium, one will reject *a fortiori* Gasché's claim that "[language] must, in philosophical terms, be thought of as a totalizing medium." That is only how a certain anti-nominalistic philosophical tradition—"the philosophy of reflection"—must think of it.

If one does think of it that way, to be sure, then one will have to worry about whether one has got hold of a true or a false totality. One will worry about whether one has burrowed deeply enough (whether, for example, Derridean infrastructures, though doubtless deeper than mere Heideggerian *Existentiale,* may not conceal still deeper and more mysterious entities which underlie *them.*) But if, with Wittgenstein, one starts to think of vocabularies as tools, then totality is no longer a problem. One will be content to use lots of different vocabularies for one's different purposes, without worrying much about their relation to one another. (In particular, one will be more willing to accept a private-public split: using one set of words in one's dealings with others, and another when engaged in self-creation.) The idea of an overview of the entire realm of possibility (one made possible by having penetrated to the conditionless conditions of that realm) seems, from this Wittgensteinian angle, crazy. For we nominalists think that the realm of possibility expands whenever somebody thinks up a new vocabulary, and thereby discloses (or invents—the difference is beside any relevant point) a new set of possible worlds.

Nominalists see language as just human beings using marks and noises to get what they want. One of the things we want to do with language is to get food, another is to get sex, another is to understand the origin of the universe. Another is to enhance our sense of human solidarity, and still another may be to create oneself by developing one's own private, autonomous, philosophical language. It is possible that a single vocabulary might serve two or more of these aims, but there is no reason to think that there is any great big meta-vocabulary which will somehow get at the least common denominator of all the various uses of all the various marks and noises which we use for all these various purposes. So there is no reason to lump these uses together into something big called "Language," and then to look for its "condition of possibility," any more than to lump all our beliefs about the spatio-temporal world together into something called "experience" and then look, as Kant did, for *its* "condition of possibility." Nor is there any reason to lump all attempts to formulate great big new vocabularies, made by people with many different purposes (e.g., Plato, St. Paul, Newton, Marx, Freud, Heideg-

ger), into something called "the discourse of philosophy" and then to look for conditions of the possibility of that discourse.

How does one go about deciding whether to read Derrida my way or Gasché's way? How does one decide whether he is really a much-misunderstood transcendental "philosopher of reflection," a latter-day Hegel, or really a much-misunderstood nominalist, a sort of French Wittgenstein? Not easily. Derrida makes noises of both sorts. Sometimes he warns us against the attempt to hypostatize something called "language." Thus early in *Of Grammatology* he says "This inflation of the sign 'language' is the inflation of the sign itself, absolute inflation, inflation itself." But, alas, he immediately goes on to talk in a grandiloquent, Hegel-Heidegger, "destiny of Europe" tone about how "a historico-metaphysical epoch *must* finally determine as language the totality of its problematic horizon." [In a footnote, Rorty continues: "I have criticized Derrida's tendency to adopt this tone in 'Deconstruction and Circumvention.' For a more general criticism of the Heideggerian, un-'playful' side of Derrida, see Barbara Herrnstein Smith, 'Changing Places: Truth, Error and Deconstruction' in her *Contingencies of Value.* Smith argues that ' "the metaphysics of Western thought" *is* thought, all of it, root and branch, everywhere and always' and that 'as figure and ground change places, the unravelling of Western metaphysics weaves another Western metaphysics.' I agree, and take the point to be that each generation's irony is likely to become the next generation's metaphysics. Metaphysics is, so to speak, irony gone public and flat—liquefaction congealed, providing a new ground on which to inscribe new figures. From my angle, the attempt to make Derrida into somebody who has discovered some 'philosophical truths' is a premature flattening-out of Derrida's irony. I think that he ought to be kept fluid a while longer before being congealed (as eventually he must be) into one more set of philosophical views, suitable for doxographic summary."]

Derrida himself, I have to admit, used to use words like "rigorous" a lot. There is a lot in his early work which chimes with Gasché's interpretation. But as he moves along from the early criticisms of Husserl through *Glas* to texts like the "Envois" section of *The Post Card,* the tone has changed. I should like to think of Derrida as moving away from the academic, "standard rules of philosophy" manner of his early work to a manner more like the later Wittgenstein's. Indeed, I should like to see his early work as something of a false start, in the same way that *Being and Time* seems to me, in the light of Heidegger's later work, to have been a false start, and as Wittgenstein thought his *Tractatus* had been a false start.

But perhaps it is just too soon for a judgment to be rendered on whether Gasché or I am looking at Derrida from the right angle, or whether we both may not be somewhat squinty-eyed. For Derrida is, to put it mildly, still going strong. Still, it may be a service to those coming to Derrida for the first time to have a choice between opposed readings at their disposal.

James Arnt Aune   (review date August 1989)

SOURCE: A review of *Glas* and *Glassary,* in *The Quarterly Journal of Speech,* Vol. LXXV, No. 3, August, 1989, pp. 355-57.

[*In the following review of* Glas, *Aune remarks that its barriers to comprehension are even greater than in Derrida's earlier books, yet he praises it for its erudition and scholarly rigor.*]

My first reaction upon receiving *Glas* in the mail was that it may have inaugurated a new literary genre: the coffee-table book for academics. Elegantly printed (in several different typefaces, which correspond to the multiple "voices" of the text) and 10¼ inches *square,* *Glas* looks like the sort of book one would display or read in, but never read.

And, alas, *Glas* probably will remain unread by most readers. . . . Conversation between American-style rhetoricians and deconstructionists seems impossible, and the recent de Man case may well serve as a convenient excuse for evading such a conversation indefinitely. Thus far, David Cratis Williams, Dilip Gaonkar, and Martha Solomon are the only rhetoricians who have expressed sympathy with deconstruction, and I suspect *Glas* will send even them screaming into the night.

Derrida, of course, never was terribly accessible—with the possible exception of his early work on Husserl, *Speech and Phenomena,* and the essay, **"Structure, Sign, and Play in the Discourse of the Human Sciences,"** in *Writing and Difference. Dissemination* began what most might perceive as a descent into a Babel of parody, word-plays, and typographical tomfoolery. *Glas* is even more difficult than the later sections of *Dissemination.*

"Glas" means "knell" in French, and the title remains untranslated because throughout the book Derrida will search for the uncanny recurrence of the phoneme "gl" in the works of his two chief subjects: Hegel and Jean Genet, the French homosexual playwright/novelist and thief. The book consists of two seemingly unrelated columns of text, with an occasional third column, the first of which is excerpts from and commentary on Hegel's writings on primitive religion, Judaism, Christianity, and the family, and the second of which does the same for Genet. It is possible that the two columns also represent the two sides of a bell, with the third representing the bell's "clapper," which makes "communication" between the two sides of the bell possible. The book enacts stylistically Derrida's familiar preoccupations with the relationships among philosophy, rhetoric, and literature; the impossibility of absolute knowledge; the priority of writing over speech; and the semantic status of proper names. There is a relatively new focus on deconstructing sexuality, which should make the book of interest to American followers of the new French feminism. There is also a brief stab at a deconstructive reading of Marx. Any attempt, however, at isolating Derrida's "argument" is pointless, because *Glas* is finally "about" the experience of reading and about the peculiarities of academic prose, which Derrida continues ruthlessly to parody.

Gregory L. Ulmer, in an essay included in the companion volume, *Glassary,* makes an elegant defense of Derrida's style. *Glas* is "an essay in postcriticism in which style is assigned an epistemic or cognitive function." Derrida himself puts it this way: "Let us space. The art of this text is the air it causes to circulate between its screens. The chainings are invisible, everything seems improvised or juxtaposed. This text induces by agglutinating rather than demonstrating, by coupling or decoupling, gluing and ungluing rather than by exhibiting the continuous, and analogical, instructive, suffocating necessity of a discursive rhetoric."

Perhaps a better way of illustrating Derrida's point is to cite a quotation from Genet in *Glas:* "When one is cunning . . . one can pretend to believe that words do not budge, that their sense is fixed or has budged thanks to us who become, voluntarily, one feigns to believe, if our appearance is modified just a bit, gods. As for me, when confronted with the enraged, engaged herd in the dictionary, I know that I have said nothing and will ever say nothing. And the words don't give a fuck." *Glas* enacts the difference between these two views of language, the first characteristic of Hegel (or philosophy in general) and the second characteristic of Genet. It is not a question of *choosing* between the two (Derrida, it seems to me, is continually misread on this point), but of miming that moment in history and conceptual space where the seeming necessity of such a choice becomes possible. *Glas* provides, to the patient reader, an insight into the vexing problem of the ontology of rhetoric. Rhetorical theory, since the 1960s, has tried to cope with the Western binary opposition between philosophy and rhetoric by collapsing philosophy into rhetoric or, at least, by exalting rhetoric into the Great White Hope of Western ethics and politics. *Glas* projects the reader into a state in which even the hitherto most grandiose conception of rhetoric's epistemic status seems too tame. For traditional notions of rhetoric, like philosophy, are premised on the assumption that language is somehow controllable by human beings. Derrida, like Genet, helps us posit (a more realistic?) conception of language as "not giving a fuck."

An attentive reading of *Glas* will pay off for contemporary scholars of rhetoric. In a way, *Glas* is the most joyous and interesting of Derrida's writings. His painstaking and loving attention to his sources should once and for all acquit him of charges of nihilism. Such charges are also persuasively refuted by the companion volume, *Glassary,* which includes a preface by Derrida, an essay by the chief translator, and an essay by Gregory L. Ulmer on the relationship between Derrida and Lacanian psychoanalysis. It also includes a useful index and an explanation of choices made by Leavey in translating a work whose untranslatability must compare only to *Finnegans Wake.* Ulmer's essay is the most lucid introduction to Derrida's theory of communication I have read.

Glassary, however, is probably not the best introduction to *Glas.* Geoffrey Hartman's *Saving the Text* is a better overview of *Glas,* and pays special attention to the continuity between deconstruction and rabbinical biblical interpretation. Although it is possible to overestimate Derrida's Jewishness (Leavey's essay points out that Derrida, somewhat surprisingly, does not know Hebrew), *Glas* is the most explicitly theological of his writings. His most intriguing observation on Hegel is that Hegel's arguments about the history of Christian theology are really "about" rhetoric. By that, I think Derrida means that the status of the relationship between Jesus and the Father is similar to that of a rhetorical figure and "reality."

Glas will probably make few new disciples of Derrida. My own experience of reading the book refuted my earlier perception that he is a destructive nihilist. For what *Glas* reveals—despite its narcissism, preciosity, and irritatingly French naughtiness—is a thoroughgoing commitment by Derrida and his friends to (dare I say it?) the central virtues of scholarship in the humanities: close reading, mastery of languages, loving attention to the central texts of Western culture, and—above all—a commitment to what Ezra Pound described as the main function of art: "MAKE IT NEW," the renewal of perception.

Charles E. Winquist   (review date January 1990)

SOURCE: "Derrida and the Study of Religion," in *Religious Studies Review,* Vol. 16, No. 1, January, 1990, pp. 19-21.

[*In the following review of* Glas, The Truth in Painting, *and* The Post Card, *Winquist summarizes Derrida's philosophy and considers its relation to theology.*]

> Deconstruction is always deeply concerned with the "other" of language. I never cease to be surprised by critics who see my work as a declaration that there is nothing beyond language, that we are imprisoned in language; it is, in fact, saying the exact opposite. The critique of logocentrism is above all else the search for the "other" and the "other of language." [Derrida, in an interview with Richard Kearney in Kearney's *Dialogues with Contemporary Continental Thinkers,* 1984]

Western theology and the study of religion are both deeply implicated in the logocentric framework of the Western philosophical tradition that has become the object of a radical deconstructionist critique. In particular, it has been the work of Jacques Derrida that has most recently "problematized" any easy alliance of theology and the study of religion with unquestioned logocentric assumptions and trajectories in their discursive practices. Derrida has made conscious the often unthought syntax of philosophical thinking that is itself the often unthought context for the study of religion. Whether we agree or disagree with Derrida's analyses and readings of the tradition, studies in religion are subject to the interrogative force of his inquiry and can choose to be naive only by casting a shadow on their credibility.

Derrida's impact on English language studies in religion follows three waves of publication and subsequent English translations. *Speech and Phenomena, Of Grammatology,* and *Writing and Difference* were published in 1967; *Disseminations, Positions,* and *Margins in Philosophy* were published in 1972; and, *Glas, The Truth in Painting,* and

The Post Card were published in 1974, 1978 and 1980. All of these works are difficult and require philosophically sophisticated readings; and it is the lack of philosophical knowledge that has led to so many misreadings and clichéd understandings that are at best a caricature of Derrida's thought and more often a falsification of his positions in the growing secondary literature on deconstruction. The publications that are under the explicit focus of this review [the last three just mentioned], sometimes thought of as his more "playful" or "literary" works, are particularly subject to misreading because of their nonconventional organization. I, however, do agree with Rodolphe Gasché in his excellent book, *The Tain of the Mirror: Derrida and the Philosophy of Reflection,* that "all the motifs of the earlier texts continue to inform and direct Derrida's more 'playful' texts." There are philosophical arguments in these texts even when they manifest themselves in nonsystematic differential play.

What we must first account for in our reading of any of Derrida's major texts is that Derrida is a careful reader and that reading Derrida is also reading Plato, Rousseau, Kant, Hegel, Nietzsche, Freud, Husserl, and Heidegger and sometimes reading them in juxtaposition with Bataille, Mallarmé, Blanchot, Genet, Sollers, or other literary and visual artists. Derrida teaches us to read *in extremis* and to read carefully. It is in this reading that we discover the "other" and the "other of language." That is, Derrida reads philosophy and literature without denying their internal tensions, inconsistencies, and constitutive complexities. He is thereby able to locate and follow lines of force within the differential play of signifiers of the text to ruptures and gaps that witness to the originary trauma and undecidability of bringing force to textual experience. His readings resemble a transcendental interrogation of the conditions for the possibilities of discursive practices and textual productions. This is why Gasché properly refers to Derrida's undecidables, *archetrace, différance, supplementarity, iterability,* and *re-mark,* as quasitranscendental and as infrastructures of discourse. These undecidables are conditions, infrastructural syntheses, that constitute philosophy's *mise en scène.* They are themselves not concepts but mark the inscription of concepts within differential chains of signifiers that constitute their sense. Identity is in difference and it is the conditions that make possible this coming into difference that are interrogated in a deconstructive reading.

What Derrida fundamentally disturbs is the philosophy of reflection with its notion of the self-grounded thinking subject. The *signature* of the self is decentered in the heterogeneity of conditions that constitute its possibility. Inscription is more than and other than intention. "The alterity that splits reflection from itself and thus makes it able to fold itself into itself—to reflect itself—is also what makes it, for structural reasons, incapable of closing upon itself. The very possibility of reflexivity is the subversion of its own source" (Gasché). There will be traces of the "other" than the text even when they are repressed or under erasure that makes possible the "double gesture" of deconstruction, a phase of reversal and appropriation of formative concepts and a phase of reinscription and displacement into the context of their infrastructural possibilities.

Contrary to some criticisms of Derrida, the indeterminacy of undecidable traces in the text does not justify irresponsible interpretive play or gratuitous readings; nor is deconstruction a reconstructed "new criticism." The locus of deconstruction is the given text; and its reading maintains a fidelity with the text since "the interpretive efficiency of the infrastructures or signifying structures depends on their *insistence within* a given text or discourse" (Gasché). In *Positions,* Derrida very clearly states that: "The *incision* of deconstruction, which is not a voluntary decision or an absolute beginning, does not take place just anywhere, or in an absolute elsewhere. An incision, precisely, it can be made only according to lines of force and forces of rupture that are localizable in the discourse to be deconstructed." However, the articulation of this *incision* is not predetermined by the formal constraints of the text under examination. Derrida's "more playful" texts carefully read the tradition but acknowledge the heterogeneity of context and text production by experimenting with syntax and organization. Fidelity to the text is also fidelity to its supplementarity.

Glas, the first of the major experimental works to be published, confronts the reader with a strategic decision as to how it is to be read. Composed of two columns with parenthetical and grafted subtexts, one might suspect (for which there is some evidence), a complex orchestration that needs to be deciphered. There, however, is a warning inserted into the text to caution the reader against organizational unity: "one column here [*ici*]—let one think [to compensate] then the other one over there. The one shows when the other descends, but isn't the level almost constant, almost only because you count for nothing in the time [*mesure*] of the two heterogeneous columns. No common measure at the very moment you think you are clutching/declutching, manipulating, orchestrating, making the liquid music rise or fall by playing the pedals, by making use of fags [*en jouant des pédales*]. The columns deceive and play with you, threaten to beat on each other without leaving you any issue."

The reader reads within a tension of readings of Hegel and Genet chiasmatically crossing between the *Sa,* an acronym for the *savoir absolu* of Hegel, and the *ça,* it, this and that, of Genet's incorrigible heterogeneity of immediate experience. *Glas,* a death knell, is a study of Hegel's *Aufhebung.* It is explicitly theological and christological by holding one of its columns close to the Hegelian achievement and profoundly secular by holding the other column close to Genet's dark witness to the body of particularity. The reading of Hegel is uncompromising with revisionist accommodations that make the Hegelian project more easily assimilable in contemporary theology. "The deconstructive undoing of the *greatest totality,* the totality of ontotheology, faithfully repeats this totality in *its* totality while simultaneously making it tremble, making it *insecure* in its most assured evidences" (Gasché).

Sublation and subversion are the warp and woof of Derrida's textual fabric in *Glas,* making it difficult to determine when to read the text ironically and parodically and when

to read it straightforwardly. The one hand of his writing has as its object the *morsel* and the other hand writes the implications of the Hegelian *Aufhebung* in the ascent toward absolute knowledge, *Sa.* He follows the Hegelian trajectory into the heart of Christianity while in the adjacent column he works in and under Genet's gluey textual veil of drool, spit, and milk. *Glas* is not a text of moderation. To read Hegel seriously is to think "God's infinite revelation revealing itself in its infinity." "To claim to think absolute, true and revealed religion, and maintain, as Kant does, the limits of a finite subjectivity is to *prohibit* oneself from thinking what thinking is said to be, is not to think what one already thinks, is to chitchat—in the infidelity, idolatry, formalist abstraction of the understanding." Derrida does not claim that Hegelianism is true Christianity or that Hegel can think "infinity" without fissuring his text, but he does claim that ". . . one must be certain that, for Hegel at least, no ontology is possible before the Gospel or outside it."

What we must first account for in our reading of any of Derrida's major texts is that Derrida is a careful reader and that reading Derrida is also reading Plato, Rousseau, Kant, Hegel, Nietzsche, Freud, Husserl, and Heidegger and sometimes reading them in juxtaposition with Bataille, Mallarmé, Blanchot, Genet, Sollers, or other literary and visual artists.

—Charles E. Winquist

The preaching of love and its subjective interiorization is the paradigmatic expression of the *Aufhebung.* "If *Sein* cannot be what it is, cannot posit itself, become and unfold itself without traversing Christianity's destiny, that is first because *Sein* must first determine itself as subjectivity. Being perhaps lets itself be re-covered and dissembled, bound or determined by subjectivity (Heidegger), but that is, for Hegel, in order to think itself. First in Christ." Absolute religion precedes the *Sa.* "The immortality of the one who is God's anointed, who is a being [*Wesen*] only as the son of God, this immortality, the glorious resurrection of his body, consists in letting itself be thought."

Hegel's analysis of the family, particularly the holy family, is the conceptual matrix for absolute knowledge. "[T]he Christian holy mother is named *Aufhebung* . . . *Aufhebung* is the productive imagination." The textual juxtaposition of this analysis with Genet's *Our Lady of the Flowers* does not mean that we can dismiss the overtly theological entailments of the reading of Hegel and attend only to the nonconventional format of Derrida's text. The text has a context and a content. Language is "filled, fulfilled, filled in, accomplished, inflated, curved (*galber*), *rounded* by the sense that penetrates it."

Derrida's readings of Hegel and Genet in *Glas* are lessons

in the specificity of reading. These, however, are not lessons in constraint. Derrida's readings are errant readings. They stray within texts and between texts and in this way reveal texts in their richness and complexity, incompleteness and otherness, including their religious and theological sensibilities.

The Truth in Painting and *The Post Card* are not unlike *Glas* in their being serious readings of the philosophical tradition in a nonconventional style. The recurrent theme of *The Truth in Painting* is framing; and Derrida's stated strategy is to make a disturbance in the philosophy that dominates discourse on painting, to decrypt the linkage between the phonic and graphic traits, to analyze systems of *duction* (production, reproduction, reduction, etc.) and the desire for restitution of the *truth* in painting. An important question for this discourse on art and also an important question for the study of religion is: "What happens when a surplus value places itself *en abyme*?" This question will insist upon itself in the interrogation of *parergon,* all that is neither in the work [*ergon*] nor outside of it.

Derrida's disturbance to philosophy is primarily through a reading of Kant's third *Critique* and secondarily through the construction of a polylogue discussing a debate between Heidegger and Meyer Schapiro of a Van Gogh painting of unlaced shoes. The questions of the *trait,* the *idiom of the trait* [signature] and systems of *duction* are woven into discussions of Adami's *The Journey of the Drawing* and Titus-Carmel's *The Pocket Size Tlingit Coffin.* All of the essays investigate the parerga of the discourse on art. They are discourses on art and also discourses on thinking.

Derrida's reading of the third *Critique* [in *The Truth in Painting*] is a radical exercise in the purity of thinking that follows and seduces the text and the problematics of the whole of the Kantian project to lines of fissure and expressions of absurdity. It is in an interlacing of the first two *Critiques* that "an abyss is established between the domain of the concept of nature, that is, the sensible, and the domain of the concept of freedom, that is the supersensible, such that no passage is possible from one to the other" (Kant quoted in *The Truth in Painting*). The identification of art as a middle term to resolve the separation between mind and nature becomes in Derrida's reading the deconstruction of a system of pure philosophy. The parergonal function of the analytic of concepts in the analytic of the beautiful mixes discourses; and its framing effect of subjectivity can be effaced only by naturalizing the frame to infinity, placing it in the hands of God. Only then could we have "the pureness which gives us the sense of beauty in general, the pure telos of beauty (non-*telos*)."

This and other paradigmatic but parabolic formulations of pure beauty and the refusal of the pure sublime to adequate presentation confound resolution of the opposition of mind and nature. We have frames without works; and it is the frames that are determined in their undecidability. It would appear that the truth *in* painting eludes the philosophical gesture that reduplicates itself.

This comment applies to Derrida's reading of Heidegger as well as Kant. Heidegger has paired "Van Gogh's" unlaced shoes, "he has loaded these shoes, invested them, arraigned them, compulsively laced them around peasant ankles, when nothing in the picture expressly authorized this." Then, it is this pair of shoes "in this painting which opens to the truth of the being-product. But which opens to it in its unveiled-unveiling presence, letting itself be traversed—toward truth." In this parodic reading of Heidegger the movement toward truth does not bring us to the truth in painting. The desire for restitution is an onto-theological desire. Perhaps there is something "other" in the truth in painting.

The Post Card is constructed of "*envois,*" essays and an interview. It is, among other movements, a reading of Freud and the psychoanalytic tradition. "You might read these *envois* as the preface to a book I have not written. It would have treated that which proceeds from the *postes* of every genre, to psychoanalysis." This "unwritten book" is about delivery systems and the delivery of truth. "To post is to send by 'counting' with a halt, a relay, or a suspensive delay, the place of a mailman, the possibility of going astray and of forgetting." It is the "post" that brings us to an awareness of the materiality of the text to be delivered and the possibility of its loss without return.

Derrida, however, does not write a history of the post, he writes of a postcard inverting the historical images of Socrates and Plato, or mixing up the names, while he, Derrida, mixes a personal correspondence with philosophical speculation. "A correspondence: this is still to say too much, or too little. Perhaps it was not one (but more or less) nor very correspondent. This still remains to be decided." The question of too much or too little, undecidable excess, is a focus of interrogation throughout this text.

In a reading of Freud's *Beyond the Pleasure Principle,* "How to gain access to the *resistance* of *Beyond* . . . ?" is the dominant motif. The difficulty and necessity of *translating* an observation into a description, ". . . these trajectories—transitional, transcriptive, transpositional and transgressive, transferential trajectories—open the very field of speculation." In the prefixes of speculation, the *trans* or the *Über,* we confront the return of the problematic of the *Aufhebung* and the displacement of subjectivity in the accession into the symbolic, the logic of the signifier.

The Post Card, The Truth in Painting, and *Glas* keep bringing us back to the "other" and the "beyond" of the multiple manifestations of the desire for the *savior absolu.* Derrida writes that "what makes me write . . . would represent in this respect only one offer. An offer on the scene in which attempts to occupy the place of the *Sa* . . . are multiplying, that is, simultaneously all the places, those of the seller, the buyer, and the auctioneer."

"Who is writing? To whom? And to send, to destine, to dispatch what? To what address?" Is this a scene of writing that demands and allows for a theological response? Even if Derrida's writings have been misdirected into the study of religion, their arrival and presence poses questions of the delivery of the truth that is religious and theological.

John D. Caputo   (review date January 1990)

SOURCE: "Derrida and the Study of Religion," in *Religious Studies Review*, Vol. 16, No. 1, January, 1990, pp. 21-5.

[*In the following review of* The Post Card, The Truth in Painting, *and* Glas, *Caputo discusses Derrida's use of psychoanalytic and theological ideas in his critique of traditional philosophy.*]

On the cover of **The Post Card: From Socrates to Freud and Beyond** there is a reproduction of a drawing taken from a thirteenth-century fortune telling book by Matthew of Paris that portrays Socrates seated at a writing desk, diligently at work on a manuscript, while behind him stands a rather more diminutive Plato who appears to be dictating to him. Upon this "catastrophic" reversal of roles Derrida comments:

> Be aware that everything in our bildopedic culture, . . . in our telecommunications of all genres, in our telematicometaphysical archives, . . . everything is constructed on the protocolary charter of an axiom, that could be demonstrated, displayed on a large *carte*, . . . [that] Socrates comes *before* Plato, there is between them—and in general—an order of generations, an irreversible sequence of inheritance.

Our tradition has always assumed that Socrates did not write and that Plato, who did, regarded his writings as a written copy, a mimesis, of the living dialogue of Socrates; in other words we have always imagined Plato seated and Socrates whispering in his ear. And just as Socrates breathed on Plato, Plato got Aristotle going (and Aristotle Aquinas, etc.), thus setting up the irreversible line(age) called the Western tradition.

Derrida is clearly charmed by the outrageous reversal perpetrated by the drawing, as if Matthew of Paris were a thirteenth-century deconstructionist. But as always there is a point to the joke, a fine tip on the Derridean stylus. The point is *not* to announce the "end of the tradition," even if that is what Allan Bloom and former Education Secretary Bennett think he is up to. For careful readers of Derrida know that he regards declamations about the "end" of the tradition, or of metaphysics, or of literature (or of whatever you want) as just more metaphysics, more tele-communication, more apocalyptic pronouncements from on high. Derrida's idea is that the telecomunicatory life of the tradition, the "postal" process of sending out messages over the lines of Western philosophy, theology, and literature is a lot more complicated than defenders of the tradition have been wont to allow. It is not, by a long shot, a process whereby original messages, *ipsissima verba*, are passed on to a legacy of faithful followers whose job is then to return them faithfully to their author, which is the classical hermeneutic circuit(ry). On the contrary, messages have been scrambled, garbled, even lost; and filial lines have come out backwards. So many voices, so many writers: who is saying what to whom? Who is the sender and who is the receiver? This is not just bad luck but a structural necessity inscribed in the very nature of the postal process. Communication necessarily depends upon writing, not just in the narrow sense of written documents, but in the general sense of *écriture,* of the tangled chain of signifiers which is the condition of possibility—and of impossibility—of any attempt to communicate in any kind of medium at all.

Consider a theological analogy. Instead of an image of an evangelist with pen in hand and ear cocked heavenwards waiting for his next line—a theological "postal principle"—imagine the Derridean counterpart: a large Jesus seated at a writing desk, while diminutive evangelists whisper in his ear; and not just the evangelists, but whole communities, churches, clusters of even more diminutive figures whose names and faces we cannot make out, feeding Jesus lines that grew out of oral traditions and liturgical practices, passed on and altered, altered and passed on, and put into his mouth. The sayings of Jesus are dictated by those who followed him; the Teacher is the effect produced by those who are supposed to be receiving the teaching. You see the Derridean, deconstructionist reversal here: Jesus as effect, i.e., not an original content which is preserved and communicated—according to the classical postal principle—but a content which is produced by the followers; the founder is founded.

Derrida tries to get all this across—i.e., tries to make the idea of getting things across problematic—by writing a book or, better, patching together a text, about transmissions, correspondences, communications called **The Post Card** that has been very ably translated by Alan Bass. Indeed Derrida has been very fortunate with his English translators; and they have made available in the cluster of books here under discussion [**The Post Card, The Truth in Painting,** and **Glas**] an exceedingly important dimension of his work. The (a)thesis (like Kierkegaard, Derrida has to write a book in such a way as not to write a book) of **The Post Card** is that a letter is always *able not* to arrive at its destination. The tip of that point is directed at Lacan, who in the concluding line of his 1956 seminar on Edgar Allan Poe's "The Purloined Letter" claims that a letter *always* arrives at its destination. . . . Freud had said in *Beyond the Pleasure Principle* that the unconscious desire for forbidden pleasure is constantly being rerouted, directed along alternate paths, postponed and deferred, or "purloined" (which is why Freud is one of Derrida's sources for his notion of *différance.*) Lacan's innovation was to treat this process of rerouting as a linguistic operation, according to which the "transactions" between the unconscious and experience are governed by linguistic laws. The life of the subject is a function of "the symbolic order," a metonomic and metaphoric transformation of unconscious desire. The subject passes along a fated path marked out by the symbolic chain and is entirely traversed by the symbolic order. Lacan sees in Poe's story a literary illustration of this theoretical point (which for Derrida betokens a whole metaphysics of "literature"): the fate of each of the characters in the story is governed by the place of the stolen letter. They do not have the letter but the letter has them. Eventually the detective Dupin, who recovers the stolen letter, is himself drawn into the cycle, sent skidding down the route to which the letter destines everyone and so misses his chance to occupy the place of the doctor/detective/psychoanalyst, the place of Poe and Lacan themselves. The duped Dupin is a bad psychoanalyst (and the dissident Lacan, excommunicated by official Freudianism, is the good one).

The Post Card is very much an attempt to upset Lacan's cart(e). Derrida objects that Lacan harbors a theory of a master hermeneut, a master of the truth who, by listening to the inverted letters sent out by the unconscious, claims to return them to their sender in decoded form. The doctor/hermeneut knows the "truth" of the unconscious, the law of its letter, which he has gained in virtue of his transcendental, doctoral advantage. Derrida in turn is defending a poststructuralist Freudianism, one that must proceed without the help of a master key. Derrida does not reject the very idea of the unconscious—for it is central to his attempt to disrupt the Husserlian, Cartesian, Platonic notion of intentional consciousness—but only that the unconscious operates according to laws that can be deciphered. Derrida thinks the unconscious is constantly "disseminating" its effects all over conscious life in such a way that the letter may always not reach its destination. The letter does not mean anything determinate, but it is constantly lost and going astray. Indeed it does not "mean" at all, but it is a much more "grammatological" operation than Lacan allows. We ought not to say that Derrida's "point" is "illustrated"—for that is to subordinate literature (fiction) to philosophy (truth)—but that this athesis is enacted in *The Post Card* by the exchange of lost and torn love letters which constitute the opening "*Envois*" ("Sendings," "Epistles"?), which includes not incidentally an important critique of Heidegger's postal principle, his letters from Being (*Seinsschickungen*).

Readers of *The Purloined Poe* will discover that Derrida and Lacan may not be as far apart as Derrida contends, that Derrida like Dupin is too tough on Lacan, that Derrida is being drawn into the cycle! (Cf. Barbara Johnson's study *A World of Difference*, 1987.) For one thing, Derrida's whole idea of Freudianism as a transcription system, a system of writing, which he defended in *Writing and Difference*, is originally Lacan's. Furthermore, it may be that the contested sentence, that a letter always arrives at its destination, means only that the rule of the symbolic order is unbroken, that no one escapes the symbolic order. What the analyst sees is not a master plan, as Derrida contends, but the necessity of the symbolic order, the inescapability of the chain of signifiers—that there is nothing outside the text (= the symbolic order), which is precisely Derrida's own view. The position of the analyst is not a transcendental one but one of Socratic vigilance, alertness to what Derrida calls the play of signifiers and to what Lacan calls the insistence of the letter. On that reading, "the letter always arrives at its destination" means about the same as "there is nothing outside the text." It is obvious—it hanging from the fireplace for everyone to see—that Derrida and Lacan are saying the same thing, but Derrida/Dupin does not see it.

In *The Truth in Painting* Derrida is again out to deflate the pretensions of the masters of truth, not this time the master of the truth of the unconscious, but the *Kunstwissenschaftler,* the learned art historian, master of the work of art. This whole discussion applies as well to the art historian in *The Post Card* who intends to straighten

Derrida out about the true meaning of the illustration in Matthew of Paris's book. This time detective Meyer Schapiro, the Columbia University art historian, is stalking a stolen work of art that he intends to restore to its proper owner. A painting of Van Gogh has been lifted by Heidegger, who has pilfered it right from under the nose of Van Gogh experts by cloaking it with his sentimental, unscientific, Schwarzwaldian mythology of the "peasant woman" that makes it speak of "earth and world." Schapiro (Dupin) sets Heidegger up, asking him, innocent as a lamb—did I say Columbia or Columbo?—just what painting Heidegger was describing. Then Schapiro moves in for the kill, explaining with scientific deftness that in the painting that Heidegger must have had in mind the shoes were not peasant shoes, but city shoes, indeed the shoes of Van Gogh himself, at that time a man of the town.

Derrida is not out to defend Heidegger—he is also worried by the peasant ideology, a point that is directly related to Heidegger's involvement with National Socialism (see Derrida's *De L'esprit,* 1987)—but to deflate Schapiro. He casts a series of doubts over Schapiro's arguments: Couldn't a city dweller paint peasant shoes? Are we sure these are men's shoes? Are we sure they even make a pair? Isn't Schapiro's urbane Jewishness just an opposite ideology? In short, Derrida rejects not only Heidegger's onto-hermeneutics of the Being of the work of art that is supposed to open up a Greco-Germanic world of earth and sky, mortals and gods, but also Schapiro's scientific hermeneutics which brings the work under scientific control. He wants to unlace the shoes, to free them up, to extricate them from the art-historical police as well as from those who fantasize about standing in peasant fields receiving messages from the gods (Heidegger's Hölderlinian hermeneutics). In the end, Derrida thinks, "there is" only the painting:

> Nobody's being accused, or above all condemned, or even suspected. *There is* painting, writing, restitutions, that's all. . . . The shoes are *there for* (figure, representing, remarking, depicting) painting at work. Not in order to be reattached to the feet of somebody or other, in the painting or outside it, but there *for-painting* (and vice versa).

The painting cannot be reduced one way or the other, restored definitively to any proprietor. It is marked with an irreducible residuum or remnance. It cannot be assimilated, appropriated, thematically determined. The painting is stuck to its canvass, imbedded in its textuality, pasted down in and by the rough strokes of Van Gogh's brush. The painting is glued down to the canvas. And with that remark we come to the glue of *Glas,* to Derrida's most outrageous moment, his academic *skandalon* which has rent more than one academic robe.

Glas not only resists thematic summary; it is like many of Derrida's writings a disruption of the very idea of thematic summary. The book is printed in two columns, each of which is cut into by numerous insert paragraphs called Judas peep holes and which look like little windows on a computer display terminal peering into other texts. On the left is a commentary on Hegel, on the right a commentary on Jean Genet, the well known French novelist and dramatist, convicted thief, and homosexual who was celebrated in Sartre's *Saint Genet*, a study of Genet which Derrida very much dislikes. *Glas* deals with Hegel and Genet. With Hegel, which in French sounds like *aigle*, eagle, which embodies the cold, soaring conceptuality of absolute knowledge, *savoir absolue* (*Sa*). With Genet, that is, with *genêt*, a mountain flower, with the flowers that fill the pages of *The Miracle of the Rose, Our Lady of the Flowers*, and *The Thief's Journal*. *Glas:* on Hegel and Genet, that is, on *aigle* and *genêt*.

One can imagine the difficulty of translating a book like this but Leavey and Rand have done a remarkable job. And Leavey and Ulmer have added to their contribution with a completely indispensable companion book—called, what else? *Glassary* (1986)—which supplies an exhaustive index to *Glas*, tracks down all of its references, and adds two excellent introductory essays.

Now we who have long ago succumbed to onto-theologic, who are Greek down to our toes (shoes?), want to dismiss this *aigle/genêt* with a wave of our academic gowns and cut through to Derrida's *idea;* we want to know what the logos is here and to cut the wordplay. But it is Derrida's claim that whatever logos is to be found here sticks like glue to the glossa and the glotta—and that is its glas. In short, we have run up against Derrida's quasi-psychoanalytic theory of the signature, that an author is constantly signing his name both *in* the text as well as on the title page outside the text. The signature is both inside and outside, unable to be contained by the "classical" (*glas* is derived etymologically from *classicus*) distinction between author and text, unable to be circumscribed by the frame which literary theory puts around the text. Such signing is not a conscious, intentional act, of course. On the contrary, an author's signature seems to act for Derrida like an opaque medium or even a scrambling machine through which the exchanges between the unconscious and conscious life are transacted. Like a classical trope called antonomasia, which treats a proper name as a common name, Genet keeps turning his name into flowers, into a thing, making it a kind of rebus; Genet's antonomasia is an anthonomasia. In the same way, Derrida himself is fascinated with his own name: the *-da* reminds him of Heidegger's *Da-sein* and also of Freud's famous *fort-da* game, both frequent subjects of Derrida's writing. And then there is the Reb Derissa; the derisoriness of "rida" (*ridere*); and finally *derriere*, e.g., Plato behind Socrates, which among others things is a homosexual behind.

"Thematically" (a bell should go off at this word, for *Glas* tolls the death knell of thematics) *Glas* is about religion. The Hegel column is interested in the transition from religion to absolute knowledge, to a conception which has purified itself of contamination by *Vorstellung*, to a pure *Begriff*, an immaculate conception. *Glas* is specifically interested in jamming the gears of this transition, putting a glitch in its works (and so can be read as rejection of the claim that religion and art can be transcended). Derrida knows that you can not "oppose" *Sa* with anything because *Sa* will just eat it, that is, *Sa* assimilates any opposition as its "negative moment." So you have to jam *Sa*

with writing, gum up its works, show how writing sticks to its operations like glue. The result will be to have shown that there is always something left out by *Sa*, always a remnant that the absolute system failed to digest, an excess that exceeded the grasp of the system, a transcendental excess or ex-position, i.e., a transcendental that is out-of-place.

For Derrida, that transcendental is Hegel's sister—both with and without citation marks. Without the scare quotes, because Derrida inserts numerous "cuts" from Hegel's letters about his real life sister whom, on Derrida's quasi-psychoanalytic theory of the signature, Hegel is always writing. With the scare quotes, because Derrida treats the "theme" of the "sister" in Hegel's works as just this transcendental excess. The reasoning behind this is as follows. For Derrida Hegel's "system" is a kind of "holy family," and the transition from religion to philosophy is a transition from a "holy family" to the "speculative family." A family is a process of division and reappropriation, a life process by which the separate (husband/wife) unite to bring forth the individual that is their own, that itself separates and unites, and so on. It is a circular system by which the proper ap-propriates, keeps returning to home and hearth, until the process culminates in absolute homecoming, *Sa*.

So the family is *in* the system but it also *is* the system; the family is inside/outside the system. Now within the family the sister occupies a unique role because her relationship with her brother is according to Hegel the most "spiritual" of all relations. That is because, while she and her brother are a couple made up of members of the opposite sex, their relationship is without sexual desire and hence without the battle of recognition. Yet the system would seem to exclude the possibility that a relationship could ever be formed without that battle. Hence the most perfectly spiritual and beautiful relationship that *Sa* knows is excluded by *Sa*. *Sa* turns on the possibility of what it excludes, depends upon what it renders impossible. The sister is in a position of transcendental excess. You see what Derrida's idea of the transcendental is: that which is excluded from a certain place in order to open up that place; that which makes something possible and in making it possible, breaches it.

Derrida develops all of this by means of an insightful account of: (1) Hegel's early *Life of Jesus*—which accentuates Hegel's invidious distinction between the alienated, divided, ugly, soulless, slavishishness of Judaism and the living, breathing unity of the spiritual life of love that Jesus initiated; (2) the conflict between the divine and the human law in Sophocles' *Antigone;* (3) the culminating analysis of the next to last chapter of the *Phenomenology of Spirit* in which Hegel includes the "religion of flowers." Enter Genet (*genêt*).

In column (b) we meet the most bizarre counterparts to the holy family and the immaculate conception: Genet's underworld of convicts and "fags" (*pédale, tante*). "Convicts garb is striped rose and white," *The Thief's Journal* opens; "there is a close relationship between flowers and convicts." Cut off from bourgeois society, Genet's figures occupy a space parallel to that of the family in Hegel's, a sphere of love prior to that of law. Still, they are not a moment in the growth of society that contributes its sons to the public sphere, but outlaws whose illicit love is mocked by bourgeois society. Genet signifies their other-worldly status by an act of nomination, giving them names like First Communion, Divine, and Our Lady of the Roses—like members of religious communities who have also "left the world." There is a smell of incense and burning candles and of altars decked with beautiful flowers throughout these novels that deal with the most sordid characters. When the Judge calls Divine by her(his) civil name at his trial for murder, Divine is already lost. You can betray persons just by giving the authorities their name. Genet does not hesitate to compare his homosexual convict lovers who face the guillotine to Jesus (mocked, spat upon, betrayed). Or to compare himself: abandoned by his father at birth, taking his mother's name, lacking what Hegel called a *wirklich* father, his is a kind of virgin birth.

There is an explosion of Derridean motifs in Genet, the likes of which are to be found perhaps only in Joyce and Mallarmé. For one thing, so much turns on naming and nomination: Genet has written his name all over these books, has signed his Jean (the Gospel of John) and his *genêt* wherever he could. Furthermore, Derrida reads Genet in strongly anti-Lacanian terms. (See Ulmer's essay in *Glossary.*) For Genet's virgin birth means the displacement of the father and of the rule of phallocentrism. Genet (his mother's name) takes the feminine side (*Sa* has become *sa,* her), makes himself into a flower, adorns his fags like the lillies of the field and compares them to the Blessed Mother. Thus Genet refuses Lacan's identification of logos with the name of the father and accentuates the cultural element in gender over natural sexual difference. (Derrida is always testing the limits of the *physis/nomos* distinction.)

But, as I have repeatedly insisted here, it is not the thematic issues that interest Derrida. He is not opposed to Sartre's *Saint Genet,* which distills from Genet an ontology of freedom, because Sartre got the thematics wrong. He is contesting thematic interpretation (hermeneutics) itself. What interests Derrida above all about Genet is the operation of writing, the grammatological play, the glas. He finds in Genet's writings an omnipresent discussion of cutting: of whores with roses embroidered strategically to their dresses, of cut flowers, of guillotined convicts, of the photos of notorious criminals cut from the newspapers and pasted on cell walls ("head cuts"!), of multiple castrations of the "antherection" (the flower/convict). Now it is not Derrida's intention to submit all this *"coupture"* to psychoanalytic hermeneutics, to reduce it to the fear of castration, which would just be to oppose Sartrean hermeneutics with Lacanian. He wants not to op-pose one position with another, but to jam the pos-tional-thetic-phallic mode altogether. He writes in double columns and not linearly, but not because *Glas* constitutes a phallic war, a battle for recognition between opposing columns. We have already seen that Derrida favors Hegel's sister from whom this battle is missing. Derrida writes this way so that we cannot castrate him, not because he has gained an unconquerable phallic advantage, but because we are always already castrated, i.e., divided by writing, subject to the inci-

sions of the law. We have always already lacked the phallus. Our veil has always already been ripped down the middle; our columns are always already circumscribed (-cised) with writing.

Now once again this is not a *third* thematic, an anti-Oedipal one, to be opposed to the Sartrean and Lacanian, but a description of writing, of *écriture* itself, which is the condition of the (im)possibility of thematics. In other words, when Genet writes *genêt* he/it is writing about writing, about cutting and pasting together, about the spider's web of textuality. And the wild vines that grow this way and that on the right side of *Glas* cross the line cut down the middle of the page and wrap around the Hegel column on the left, eating at its surface, hollowing out and invaginating its doric, let us say its Greco-Germanic eminence. This cut and paste job, this gluing together of fragments and torn pieces, this agglutination is the *glas* that gums up the glide of the Hegelian transitions, the glitch in its machine, the glottal stop in its logos. It pushes *Sa*'s head back into the text, causing its fragments and globules to stick in its throat, leaving it sticky with glue and glucose. I could go on (and Derrida does).

If I am asked what significance Derrida holds for theology I would say that he represents in part at least the latest installment in the debate between Athens and Jerusalem, the latest and most subtle version of de-Hellenization. Deconstruction in my view is *not* the latest version of death of God theology, a more ruthlessly atheistic theology, an atheism with a Saussurean twist, as Mark Taylor holds. It is more feasibly put to work, I suggest, in a low christology, to take but one example, a very low christology which is ruthless about the limiting, textualizing conditions from which the logos of christology tries to ascend. Derrida stalks the claims of logo-centrism with a maddening patience. He does not let anything get by; he picks up everything, every slip, every chance, every loose thread. Every time we think we are breathing the air of the living logos and are filled with the spirit, Derrida clogs our throat with the thick mucous of textuality, chokes us with the glue of glas. Now theo-logy is no more immune from logo-centrism than any of the other -ologies, no more free from the illusion that it deals with gifts which have dropped from the sky than the rest of us. Indeed its critics would say that it is particularly vulnerable to such illusions, that anyone who speaks of divine revelation has made his whole enterprise turn on such an illusion.

I do not think that Derrida undoes the very idea of religious revelation but that he undoes a lot of the ideas of revelation that religious writers have proffered for some time now. He thinks that all immaculate conceptions are always already contaminated with writing. He would insist—patiently, ruthlessly, indefatigably—that textuality sticks like glue to what religious traditions hold dear, that textuality insinuates itself into religious "positions." (Are religious beliefs in the positional-thetic mode? Are confessions of faith "claims"? Are *doxa* in the phallic-thetic mode? Or is doxa just praise?) Deconstruction wants to cut off the illusion of immediacy—of immediate experience, immediate revelation. Derrida thinks that immediacy is both philosophically unjustifiable and politically dangerous.

I do not think that Derrida is an antagonist of religion but rather a powerful and novel critic of the illusions and tom foolery to which mortals are prone; and that includes religious mortals. But why end on such a critical note? After all, cutting is to be followed by gluing. *Glas* glues. So maybe Derrida does not just stick it to theology; maybe he can teach theologians a thing or two about how to make things gel.

Charles E. Scott (essay date Fall-Winter 1991)

SOURCE: "Beginning with Belonging and Nonbelonging in Derrida's Thought: A Therapeutic Reflection," in *Soundings,* Vol. LXXIV, Nos. 3-4, Fall-Winter, 1991, pp. 399-409.

[*In the following essay, Scott links Derrida's notion of* différance *with Freud's theories of the unconscious, and speculates on the possible therapeutic uses of deconstruction.*]

I do not know how to speak of Derrida's writing. That much, at least, I can say about his writing. My difficulty is two fold: to speak properly about his writing I need to put in question the words and concepts that I use as I use them so that a sense of simple, continuing presence and meaning is not communicated. Otherwise I mislead by the seeming clarity with which I place and define his thought. And second, if I speak that way I will not be understood by those who are not careful readers of Derrida.

Why do I face such a difficulty when I speak about Derrida's writing? Primarily because of the way in which he responds to the following descriptive claims about language. First, vocalized speech dominates the western experience of communication and provides a deep illusion of unbroken meaning. Second, vocalized speech is quite different to writing which belongs to something unspeakable. And third, language in all of its parts is constructed by strife among multiple lineages of expression and meaning, and by both meaning and no meaning at all. I can state initially and oversimply the problem before us by saying that our patterns of certainty and truth, our manners of being clear and unambiguous with each other, and our communal proprieties are constructed by many different and often contradictory elements. These constitutive differences are often forced or blurred into simplified habitual structures of value and thought that seem to be clear in their consistency with each other. When I *speak* about Derrida's writing, I am of course, implicated in the very questions that he addresses, and if I make his writing manageable and usable in conventional terms I mislead you. If, on the other hand, I put in question our conventional ways of understanding others and texts as I give you an account of Derrida's writing, and if you hear the presentation conventionally, you will find what I am doing perverse because your way of understanding will be resisted by what you want to understand.

To what, indeed, do we belong if not to our language, institutions, values, and customs? Are we not together in our broad communal traditions and above all in our common

language? The thought I want to pursue is that in belonging together as we do are also in a situation that I shall call nonbelonging. I mean that there is something about language and tradition to which we cannot belong and that whatever this "something" might be (or not be), Derrida's writing provides us with a remarkable entrée into its question. This is not entirely unlike encountering unconsciousness which obliterates consciousness and makes us look again and again until the limits of consciousness give us pause and drive us to reconsider the seeming totality of consciousness and the completeness of our belonging to it.

So my difficulty in speaking about Derrida's writing is like the difficulty in speaking about what escapes consciousness and cannot belong to consciousness. Derrida's writing writes something that is not articulable. His writing attempts to follow "something" that is like a thoroughly repressed dimension in our language and thought, the trace of something erased, he says. And the danger that I face is like the danger of speaking as though I have mastered unconsciousness. You would know in that case that my confidence reveals an anxious ignorance about something that is misconstrued when it is addressed directly and held by concepts. Although we can address Derrida directly and diagram his sentences and follow the lineage of his thought, we confront in his writing "something" that does not belong to our heritage of direct address and meaningfulness, "something" that is heard, as he says, beyond all reckoning. [All quotes in this essay come from *Derrida and Différance,* edited by David Wood and Robert Bernasconi, 1988.] Hence, as I address you directly and reckon with Derrida's writing within this circumscription of meaning, I face the question of how to speak appropriately before an unspeakable dimension of language that is traced indirectly in Derrida's writing.

First, a note on Derrida's experience of nonbelonging as we approach the question of how to speak before "something" to which we cannot belong and which we cannot appropriate, "something," he says, that "somehow marks you without belonging to you." "As a child" Derrida said in an interview, "I had the instinctive feeling that the end of the world is at hand, a feeling which at the same time was most natural, and, in any case, the only one I ever knew. Even for a child incapable of analyzing things, it was clear that all this would end in fire and blood. No one could escape that violence and fear. . . ." This feeling accompanying his life as a Jew in Algeria who "knew from experience that knives could be drawn at any moment, on leaving school, in the stadium, in the middle of those racist screams which spared no one, Arabs, Jews, Spanish, Maltese, Italians, Corsicans." In 1940 he with all other Jews was expelled from school. He found that friends no longer knew him, public insults to Jews became socially proper for the majority, and social order appeared to depend on such persecution. "It's an experience that leaves nothing intact," he said, "something you can never again cease to feel."

He felt "displaced" both in the Jewish community, which closed in on itself, and in the Christian culture in which he had been assimilated. The antisemitism that characterized France, where he moved when he was eighteen, was not directed toward him, but he found that it was there for many others. His acceptance in the non-Jewish culture and his acceptance of that culture further displaced him. He felt a desire to be integrated into the non-Jewish community, but he distrusted the desire, found it painful, and felt a "nervous vigilance, a painstaking attitude to discern signs of racism." "From all of this comes a feeling of nonbelonging that I have doubtless transposed . . . everywhere."

This feeling of nonbelonging includes, I believe, a sense of difference that pervades each instance of identity. This is not a question of conflict between more than one identity or of conflicting values. Rather the limits of identity as such are before us in this sense of nonbelonging: "something" that identity and belonging do not encompass seems to resonate in the margins and spaces of identity, "something" that we might over-hear as though it were a barely audible, retreating sound or like silence in the woods that falls after a gun fires. Derrida's sense of nonbelonging means that things in their continuities stand out in a resonance of no continuity, it means that not anything breaks the seeming promise of unbroken time and life. He found himself neither properly Jew nor properly non-Jew, neither a proper Algerian nor a proper Frenchman, neither secure in his family nor insecured by his family. He was and was not his name. Before the frequently drawn knives he was alive and threatened at once. Everything was in question and undecidable, and normally so in his experience. In his world the limited Algerian persecution fell against the backdrop of the fires of Holocaust, and Derrida felt his own blood in the ashes of incinerators.

> **Derrida found himself neither properly Jew nor properly non-Jew, neither a proper Algerian nor a proper Frenchman. Everything was in question and undecidable, and normally so in his experience. In his world the limited Algerian persecution fell against the backdrop of the fires of Holocaust, and Derrida felt his own blood in the ashes of incinerators.**
>
> —*Charles E. Scott*

"The final word," he said, "is never fully master. . . . the vibrant desire to write binds you to a terror that you try to control, to handle, all the while trying to keep it intact, audible, in 'this' place where you must find yourself, hear yourself out, yourself and your reader, beyond all reckoning, thus at once saved and lost." In this combination of vibrant desire to write, terror, sense of determinate place, and incalculable danger and pleasure, I hear the inscription of nonbelonging, of undecidability, investing being and nonbeing, of a strangeness in our lives that threatens destruction precisely where our satisfactions are strongest. Two distinct directions arise for Derrida in this absence

of a final word. On the one hand he asks, what kind of culture do we have in which our culture's own radical violence seems to stand at such a distance from it? With this question he faces institutions and practices whose exchanges of power are structured by values and words that have lost touch with their own depression, scapegoating, and anxiety over primal differences. By this question concerning the seeming distance of our violence everything that is normal and the processes of normalization appear not only optional, but fragmented by the disorder and lack of identity that they cover over with a veneer of stability that is raised to the order of fundamental truth and right. Efforts in his thought to destabilize our cultural orders constitute one form of response that Derrida makes to those forms of stabilization that are diffused by the fragmentation and nonbelonging that seems to belong to them.

He finds this type of subversion in the lineage of psychoanalysis: "psychoanalysis," he says,

> should make us rethink a great many convictions, for example to reconstruct the whole axiomatics of law, morality, "human rights," the entire discourse constructed upon the demands of the "me," the concept of torture, the whole system of legal psychiatry, etc. Not to renounce ethical affirmations or politics, but on the contrary, to insure their very future. This would not be done within the psychoanalytic community nor within society as such, in any case, not extensively enough, nor soon enough. Such, perhaps, is a task for thought.

". . . Not to renounce ethical affirmations or politics, but on the contrary to insure their very future." Just as in consequence to psychoanalysis complications, mixed desires, and cross purposes emerge to unsettle the pathogenic normalcies of ordinary life, and just as this analysis allows for noninnocent affirmation of what seems valuable in the midst of uncertainty—affirmation even to the point of endangering one's self in struggling for communal benefits—so Derrida wants to uncover the destinies of violence that are invested in our normal structures of thought and life for the sake of ethical affirmation and politics, both of which—ethical affirmation and politics—he will also put in question. And this process for him is found in thought, in taking apart the concepts and values that provide the grid of meaning for knowledge and truth. Thought can allow a movement in advance of institutional and communal change: his work belongs securely neither to relevance nor irrelevance, but to continuous questioning of the shared structures of our lives.

One direction that comes out of Derrida's experience of nonbelonging is thus that of unsettling in his own thought the cultural structures that suppress their own fragility and thereby produce violently a dream-like reality that promises unbroken identity and certainty. When we lose our perception of violence within our normal systems, do we have any way of avoiding that very violence?

The second direction that comes out of the absence of a final word, and one closely related to the first, addresses "the unconscious conspiracy" in our heritage to establish unity, continuing presence, and univocity of meaning as the structure of true discourse. The first direction puts emphasis on violence, institutions, and responsibility. The second is directed to the texts and language that have formed our capacities for thought, judgment, and communication. Each direction involves the other, but there is a difference of shading and tone. We should bear in mind that Derrida was first a teacher of the history of philosophy at the Ecole Normal Superieur and that a major part of his work has addressed the canonical texts of western thought. Regarding traditional thought, he said,

> . . . I feel that I am also a beneficiary: faithful as much as possible, a lover, avid for the re-readings and for the philosophical delights which are not merely ascetic games. I like repetition: it is as if the future trusted in us, as if it waited for us, encoded in an ancient work—which hasn't yet been given voice. All of this makes for a strange mixture, I realize, of responsibility and disrespect. The attention given all this on the present scene is at once intense, hopeless, and a bit vacant—rather anachronistic, that. But without this bizarreness, nothing seems desirable to me. We have received more than we think we know from the "tradition," but the gift scenario also necessitates a kind of filial impiety, both serious and not, with regard to those thoughts to which we owe most.

"But without this bizarreness, nothing seems desirable to me." Desire: a movement out of need, energy toward the missing, a movement from absence, a seeking movement in distance, energy that dies in its fulfillment, energy that continues in its dissatisfaction. Derrida feels in debt to our tradition, indebted like a lover is indebted to the beloved, like one who receives more than he can give, desiring to return again and again to the texts—the bodies—that inspire and that seem to offer something that is missing. But he is also in the tradition like an impious son, one who owes much to father and mother heritage, not the least of the gifts being impiety. Is he a lover or a son? Both and neither in the metaphors' ambiguity, which holds him at a distance from the tradition to which the metaphors connect him. The bizarreness of being traditional now—and Derrida is in many ways a traditionalist—the bizarreness of expecting within the tradition something unspeakable and unthinkable that is encoded in proper language, expecting something not proper, and something to which the future belongs, something that has been sealed off or erased but has left the trace of its disappearance in the dominating language, the bizarreness of waiting for a voice to emerge as though from the grave of what is lost to sound and sense and expecting this voice—doubtless a hollow, unintelligible voice in the context of present sounds and values—to give a future that has been lost in the structures and forces of our best efforts: this bizarreness that produces intensity, hopelessness, and scholarship on foreign and old texts makes things desirable for Derrida. I believe he means that everything becomes desirable because of the senselessness that our good sense embodies, and I believe that the metaphor behind his words is the beloved's body that inspires love not in mute materiality, but in an animation that stands outside of reason and common sense, an animation that speaks of lack and unfulfillment as well as of an ambivalent promise, not of the loss of desire, but of desire's continued life in its hunger for the missing. The missing and not a full and sufficient presence animates Derrida, who finds his animation in a heritage of undecidable valences, a heritage that is like the beloved who, in his or her closeness, is all the more beyond reckoning, is all the more unpossessible than he or she is in the distance of first attraction.

In this context we are prepared to see that the term *deconstruction* does not suggest destructiveness, nihilism, or skepticism. The word, which he took from Heidegger, comes early in Derrida's work and, true to his statements about reading and speaking, has been disseminated in many other texts with meanings quite other to his sense. It is a careful, highly specific word in Derrida's thought. By it he names a process of taking apart the signifying structures in a text, finding what signs substitute and replace other signs, finding the ambiguities invested in relations of meaning, following chains of references in which signs differ from each other, space out each other, and defer their sense to other references. What is always in question is the systematic totality of our conceptuality and the rule-governed polarities that control our sense of difference and identity. By undoing these connections, unraveling them, if you will, out of the patterns that they weave, Derrida finds not only economies of exchange in a text whereby much that constitutes them is elided or suppressed. He also finds that our language in its systematic use establishes senses of identity which elide the continuous processes of substitution, dissemination, annulment, fictionalizing, supplementation, and displacement of absence that characterize language.

We can see Derrida's kinship to Freud in this thought of deconstruction. The question concerns the manner in which something unpresentable—in Freud's case, the unconscious—is carried over into signs and images. Freud's deconstruction of the authority of consciousness is carried out in part by showing that the unconscious is always deferred by the conscious processes that refer to it. In Derrida's language the unconscious is *traced* in its total alterity vis-a-vis consciousness. Consciousness and unconsciousness are in a relation of continuous differing, and consciousness in its difference postpones unconsciousness—puts it off—by giving expression to unconsciousness and by making reference to it. Unconscious traces are produced and detoured in the difference of conscious activity. And an indirect access to unconsciousness is also opened as consciousness is breached by unconscious traces that both relay the unconscious and defer conscious appropriation in their difference. Consciousness has no authority over the traces that fracture its identity and limit the range of its mastery. Consciousness cannot even think the simultaneity of its occurrence with unconsciousness; it cannot grasp the reserve of energy that moves it and withdraws from it anymore than it can think the expenditure of energy that accompanies its retention of energy. In the Freudian context we can say that the presence of the unconscious never happens, that the unconscious is not like a past *present* that is now recalled in its absence. Rather, the unconscious has no conscious presence except as a disappearing trace that opens consciousness through a radical alterity.

In the trace of unconsciousness consciousness belongs neither to unconsciousness nor to itself. This thought contradicts our intuitive good sense: surely consciousness belongs together with whatever occurs with it. Surely the trace of unconsciousness is present in consciousness and consciousness is present with it. But that good sense is what Freud's account of unconsciousness puts in question. Like Derrida's boyhood world, consciousness is always before its own loss in unconscious traces that have neither ownership nor belonging. Freudian thought is deconstructive as it follows the traces of what it cannot think and struggles for words and concepts that hold in question the authority that it would give to itself.

In a similar way Derrida deconstructs the language whereby our culture has privileged singular identity, wholeness, and continuing presence. He finds unspeakable and unthinkable traces that seam our good sense, and he develops a language, a manner of writing and thinking, that maintains the fragility of meaning in its element of no meaning at all. In the space remaining I shall note a therapeutic implication of deconstruction. I make this move on the assumption that our ability to recognize pathological and therapeutic processes can be produced by a language in which we expect ourselves to belong to something that has the promise of full presence such as human dignity and identity.

The question that I wish to raise regarding therapy is one that I cannot answer: how do we work therapeutically with people when we do not make belonging an organizing value in our perceptions regarding psychological help? If Derrida is accurate in his descriptive claim that the language and thought of our culture, by giving overwhelming privilege to presence, identity, and wholeness, have thoroughly repressed primordial and "originary" difference, alterity, non-meaning, and non-presence, repressed them to such a degree that like the unconscious they are without the possibility for communicative speech, then our values regarding health will be structured by an anxiety that systematically directs us away from the conditions of our lives. One of the implications of his work is that the language by which we care for ourselves and understand ourselves is itself under the impact of anxiety over non-presence, an anxiety that silently traverses our individual and communal lives. The deconstructive strategy is to reread the major documents of our tradition in order to show the repression that occurs within them. Although that is a kind of therapeutic project—one that unsettles us and gives no satisfaction to the values that bond us and establish our destinies—it is not a psychotherapeutic venture oriented toward individuals seeking release from emotional pain. We do wish to deconstruct the pathogenic patterns. But we do not engage in deconstructing the normalizing values regarding identity and presence to self in order to establish a new normalcy. The direction of Derrida's work includes a dismantling of our normative thought that intends to tell us how we are to be when we are at our best.

How would a therapist relate to patients and clients if he or she were thoroughly aware of the repressive aspect of the ideal of wholeness of identity? If the therapist suspected, as I believe that Derrida suspects, that the holocaust was made possible by the dominance of presence and meaning over non-presence and non-meaning in our history? If the therapist were in touch with the traces of non-belonging that give fissure to our presumed selves? If the therapist, without pessimism or depression, knew the darkness that makes possible the light of our minds?

A final word in this first step into Derrida's thought. I have made belonging and nonbelonging the organizing words for my remarks, and I have linked them to Derrida's personal experiences as a strategy for approaching a conception of connection in the midst of no connection at all. This conception suggests the possibility that the ideal language of wholeness and unity regarding both identity and community is misleading and may well put us at odds with the occurrences of knowledge and of our lives. Were we able to let opposites be together as opposites, if we were able to understand the therapeutic in a language in which difference, and not identity, gave us our perceptions—if, that is, we experienced ourselves and our world as belonging only to their own occurrences—then, not expecting our belonging together to override all that cannot belong at all, we might experience a freedom for the affirmation of the opposites, differences, and nonbelonging without a drive to normalize and appropriate the radically other. Would this constitute a therapy that addresses a traditional desire to make unity and to produce wholeness in a broken world of difference, a world in which identity can expand itself only by ignoring its not belonging to anything but the differences that resist it? Would this be a freedom from that peculiar brutality that comes from making the other one's own? Would we learn to speak differently enough so that we did not expect to overcome everything that puts in question our highest values and most spiritual experiences? Would we learn to affirm ourselves without belonging to anything final or whole, to affirm our difference from everything that shows us to be incomplete and arbitrary in our finest moments?

FURTHER READING

Bibliography

Schultz, William R., and Fried, Lewis L. B. *Jacques Derrida: An Annotated Primary and Secondary Bibliography.* New York: Garland Publishing, 1992, 882 p.

    Comprehensive primary and secondary bibliography, including sources in English, French, German, Italian, Japanese, and other languages.

Criticism

Behler, Ernst. *Confrontations: Derrida/Heidegger/Nietzsche.* Stanford: Stanford University Press, 1991, 180 p.

    Analyzes the complex interrelations between the works of Derrida, Martin Heidegger, and Friedrich Nietzsche.

Brunette, Peter, and Wills, David. *Screen/Play: Derrida and Film Theory.* Princeton: Princeton University Press, 1989, 210 p.

Applies Derridean concepts to such aspects of film theory as frame-analysis and genre classifications.

Coward, Harold. *Derrida and Indian Philosophy.* Albany: State University of New York Press, 1990, 200 p.

Comparative study of Derrida and various classical Indian philosophers which asserts that Derrida's work "provides a challenging and creative bridge between traditional Indian and modern Western philosophy."

————, and Foshay, Toby, eds. *Derrida and Negative Theology.* Albany: State University of New York Press, 1992, 337 p.

Considers Derrida's relation to "negative theology," a discipline in which traditional theological conceptions are deconstructed. The collection includes three essays by Derrida.

Evans, Claude J. *Strategies of Deconstruction: Derrida and the Myth of the Voice.* Minneapolis: University of Minnesota Press, 1991, 205 p.

Assesses the validity of Derrida's critique of "phonocentric" and "logocentric" assumptions in Western philosophy, focusing on two of his earliest publications, *Speech and Phenomena* and *Of Grammatology.*

Gasché, Rodolphe. *The Tain of the Mirror: Derrida and the Philosophy of Reflection.* Cambridge: Harvard University Press, 1986, 348 p.

Highly acclaimed study of Derrida's philosophy that situates him in the tradition of transcendental speculation which began with René Descartes and includes Immanuel Kant and Georg Wilhelm Friedrich Hegel.

Hirsch, E. D., Jr. "Derrida's Axioms." *London Review of Books* 5, No. 13 (21 July-3 August 1983): 17-18.

Sharply critical essay in which Hirsch argues that many of Derrida's basic ideas unwittingly contradict themselves.

Hoy, David. "Deciding Derrida: David Hoy on the Work (and Play) of the French Philosopher." *London Review of Books* 4, No. 3 (18 February 1982): 3-5.

Review of *Dissemination* which argues against some of Derrida's major themes, such as the concept of semantic "undecidability."

Leavey, John P. *Glassary.* Lincoln: University of Nebraska Press, 1986, 320 p.

A companion guide to *Glas* by one of the translators of the work into English. It includes a glossary of Derrida's puns and neologisms, a preface by Derrida, and an essay by Gregory L. Ulmer which reviewer James Arnt Aune calls "the most lucid introduction to Derrida's theory of communication I have read."

Madison, Gary B., ed. *Working Through Derrida.* Evanston, Ill.: Northwestern University Press, 1993, 284 p.

Collection of essays which explore the ethical dimensions of Derrida's thought and its contrasts with the ideas of such philosophers as Richard Rorty, John R. Searle, and Jurgen Habermas.

Megill, Allan. *Prophets of Extremity: Nietzsche, Heidegger, Foucault, Derrida.* Berkeley: University of California Press, 1985, 399 p.

Highly theoretical study which views Derrida's work as the culmination of a trend in philosophy toward a radical critique of traditional metaphysical values.

Michelfelder, Diane P., and Palmer, Richard E., eds. *Dialogue and Deconstruction: The Gadamer-Derrida Encounter.* Albany: State University of New York Press, 1989, 352 p.

Collection that includes the transcript of a 1981 debate between Derrida and Hans-Georg Gadamer, a leading interpreter of Martin Heidegger and the main exponent of philosophical hermeneutics, a philosophy of interpretation which contrasts sharply with deconstruction. The other essays examine various aspects of deconstruction and hermeneutics.

Neel, Jasper. *Plato, Derrida, and Writing.* Carbondale: Southern Illinois University Press, 1988, 252 p.

Examines the radically diverse functions and theories of writing in Derrida and Plato's works. Neel, a theoretician of rhetoric and composition, attempts to "deconstruct" both Plato and Derrida, and thereby "argue for a new sort of writing, a rhetorical writing that quite self-consciously admits its own rhetoricity and carefully delineates the ethical ramifications of its operation at all times."

Norris, Christopher. *Derrida.* Cambridge: Harvard University Press, 1987, 271 p.

Study of Derrida's philosophy that examines his relations with various seminal thinkers including Plato, Kant, Hegel, Ferdinand de Saussure, Jean-Jacques Rousseau, and Nietzsche.

————. "Limited Think: How Not to Read Derrida." *Diacritics* No. 1 (Spring 1990): 17-36.

Critiques John Searle's rejection of deconstruction, and reviews John M. Ellis's book *Against Deconstruction* (1989).

Rorty, Richard. "Philosophy as a Kind of Writing: An Essay on Derrida." *New Literary History* X (1978-79): 141-60.

Interprets Derrida in the context of Rorty's own pragmatist philosophy, contending that, for Derrida, philosophy is merely another "genre" of writing indistinguishable in its essence from literature and other rhetorical modes of discourse.

Ryan, Michael. *Marxism and Deconstruction: A Critical Articulation.* Baltimore: The Johns Hopkins University Press, 1982, 232 p.

Examines the theoretical interrelations between Marxism and deconstruction, arguing that "deconstructive philosophy has positive implications for Marxism and that these implications are not only philosophical, but political."

Sallis, John, ed. *Deconstruction and Philosophy: The Texts of Jacques Derrida.* Chicago: The University of Chicago Press, 1987, 207 p.

Collection of essays which examine the transcendental and metaphysical aspects of Derrida's thought. The volume closes with an essay by Derrida entitled "*Geschlecht* II: Heidegger's Hand."

Smith, Joseph H., and Kerrigan, William, eds. *Taking Chances: Derrida, Psychoanalysis, and Literature.* Baltimore: The Johns Hopkins University Press, 1984, 185 p.

Essay collection which discusses the impact of Derrida's philosophy on psychoanalysis and literary criticism. The book begins with an essay by Derrida entitled "My Chances/*Mes Chances*: A Rendezvous with Some Epicurean Stereophonies."

Wood, Michael. "Deconstructing Derrida." *New York Review of Books* XXIV, No. 3 (3 March 1977): 27-30.
    Reviews *Of Grammatology* and *Glas,* and critiques the main themes of Derrida's philosophy.

Additional coverage of Derrida's life and career is contained in the following sources published by Gale Research: *Contemporary Authors,* Vols. 124 and 127; and *Contemporary Literary Criticism,* Vol. 24.

M. F. K. Fisher

1908-1992

(Full name Mary Frances Kennedy Fisher; born Mary Frances Kennedy; also wrote under the pseudonyms Victoria Bern and Mary Frances Parrish) American essayist, short story writer, memoirist, novelist, translator, journalist, and author of children's books.

The following entry presents an overview of Fisher's career. For further information on her life and works, see *CLC*, Volume 76.

INTRODUCTION

Fisher is best known for essays and reminiscences in which she combines sensual descriptions of food with observations about life and culture. In addition to gastronomical essays, Fisher wrote autobiographical short stories, two novels, travel sketches, and memoirs. Although she was primarily known as a food writer during the early years of her career, Fisher is now considered one of America's finest essayists. She was elected to the American Academy of Arts and Letters in 1991.

Biographical Information

Fisher was born in Albion, Michigan, in 1908, the daughter of Rex Brenton Kennedy, an editor, and Edith Oliver Holbrook Kennedy, a real estate broker. Two years later her family moved to Whittier, a small Quaker community in southern California. In 1929 Fisher married her first husband and began attending the University of California in Los Angeles and then the University of Dijon in France, where she developed her lifelong passion for French cuisine and culture. She divorced in 1938 and remarried twice, in 1942 and 1945. Residing alternately in California and Europe, Fisher traveled extensively, particularly throughout France, and her experiences there inform the setting and subject matter of many of her books. In her later years she suffered from Parkinson's disease but continued writing, examining both the indignities and consolations of aging. She died in Glen Ellen, California, in 1992.

Major Works

Fisher's first book, *Serve It Forth* (1937), is recognized as an unusually stylized and artful collection of gastronomic essays with its mélange of personal reminiscence, anecdote, and erudite observations on the cuisine of ancient cultures. *Consider the Oyster* (1941) and *How to Cook a Wolf* (1942) are similarly eclectic, combining practical advice on food preparation with insightful commentary on the historical and philosophical significance of cuisine. *The Gastronomical Me* (1943) has been described as an autobiography using food as the unifying motif for diverse memories. The first of Fisher's two novels, *Not Now but*

Now (1947), presents four interrelated stories about an adventurous girl named Jennie. The work received mixed reviews by critics who considered it contrived in comparison with the engaging directness of her essays. A later novel, *The Boss Dog* (1991), is based on Fisher's experiences in Aix-en-Provence and is considered suitable for children as well as adults. Fisher's memoirs and travel sketches include *Maps of Another Town* (1964) and *Long Ago in France* (1991). Also highly regarded for her work as a translator, Fisher is known for the 1949 English-language version of *The Physiology of Taste,* a work by Jean Anthelme Brillat-Savarin.

Critical Reception

While early reviewers of Fisher's works recognized the originality and excellence of her prose, they tended to focus on her merits as a "food writer." As critics began to view her work in a broader context, she acquired a reputation as a neglected writer of immense sophistication and formal skill. Among her more famous admirers was W. H. Auden, who once said, "I do not know of anyone in the United States today who writes better prose." Although she remains relatively obscure among the mass public, Fisher has acquired the status of a major writer among critics who cherish her idiosyncratic and highly cultured prose style.

PRINCIPAL WORKS

*Serve It Forth [as Mary Frances Parrish] (essays) 1937
*Consider the Oyster [as Mary Frances Parrish] (essays) 1941
*How to Cook a Wolf (essays) 1942
*The Gastronomical Me (essays) 1943
Here Let Us Feast: A Book of Banquets (nonfiction) 1946
Not Now but Now (novel) 1947
*An Alphabet for Gourmets (essays) 1949
The Physiology of Taste [translator and editor] (nonfiction) 1949
A Cordiall Water: A Garland of Odd & Old Recipes to Assuage the Ills of Man or Beast (nonfiction) 1961
The Story of Wine in California (nonfiction) 1962
Maps of Another Town: A Memoir of Provence (memoir) 1964
The Cooking of Provincial France (nonfiction) 1968
With Bold Knife and Fork (nonfiction) 1969
Among Friends (memoir) 1970
A Considerable Town (travel sketch) 1978
Sister Age (memoir) 1983
The Boss Dog (novel) 1991
Long Ago in France: The Years in Dijon (memoir) 1991
To Begin Again: Stories and Memoirs, 1908-1929 (anthology) 1992

*These works were published as The Art of Eating: The Collected Gastronomical Works of M. F. K. Fisher in 1954 and reprinted as The Art of Eating: Five Gastronomical Works in 1976.

CRITICISM

Katherine Woods (review date 20 June 1937)

SOURCE: "About the Various Pleasures of Eating," The New York Times Book Review, June 20, 1937, p. 3.

[In the following review, Woods offers enthusiastic praise for Serve It Forth.]

This is a book about food; but though food is universal, this book is unique. The first adjective for Serve It Forth must certainly be "different." And as one reads on the mind takes note again and again of that different quality, and is charmed and shocked and entertained by it, in what the author has to say and in the way she says it, and even, too, in the quaint illustrations scattered through the text. This is a delightful book. It is erudite and witty and experienced and young. The truth is that it is stamped on every page with a highly individualized personality. Sophisticated but not standardized, brilliant but never "swift-

moving" or "streamlined," perfumed and a little mocking, direct and yet almost précieuse, the style of Serve It Forth is as unusual as its material is unfamiliar and odd.

And it really is a book about food. Mrs. Fisher even goes so far, in spite of preliminary assurances to the contrary, as to include two recipes—rare ones, both. But this is no book of practical counsel. These pages are filled with odd fact and obscure fantasy, illuminating comment, personal reflection and remembrance. The young author goes back to the simple and democratic food of the Egyptians and their simple lives; she dwells a bit on the Greeks. Then, with some horrible particularity of detail, she tells how "in their furious delicacy of palate and heavy-handed subtlety of selection the wealthy Romans left Greeks far behind." She explains how good cooking, like learning, was kept alive in the monasteries in the Dark Ages. She has surprising notes from Elizabethan England and Catherine de' Medici's France.

Of all the present nations France, says Mrs. Fisher, "has the simplest school of cooking." But when she explains the proper preparation of snails at their best (they ought to be starved to death, to be most appetizing), one realizes that there are different kinds of simplicity! Mrs. Fisher has lived in provincial France, and much of her oddest research and most pungent comment comes from that land of culinary supremacies; she brings some responsive human anecdotes from France, too. But most Americans, she declares, don't know how to eat: they are "taste blind."

The New York Times Book Review (review date 28 June 1942)

SOURCE: "A Guide for Cooks When Wolves Prowl," The New York Times Book Review, June 28, 1942, p. 3.

[In the following review of How to Cook a Wolf, the critic praises Fisher's highly informative and vivacious writing style.]

If the wolf is snuffling at the keyhole—well, it's possible to make a dish that will keep you going for several days, says M. F. K. Fisher, if you can succeed in borrowing 50 cents. Here, she continues [in How to Cook a Wolf], is exactly how to prepare it.

This suggestion—which is admittedly a counsel of desperation and should be appreciatively received as such—is the farthest point of the wolf-hunt beguilingly organized by the author of Consider the Oyster and Serve It Forth. And even if practical value may be sought first in the recipes and hints offered by this original young writer, her book's enjoyment is no less conspicuously high. Whether these recipes are as irresistibly seductive as they sound, a mere review can't say. But there is no possible question about the book's good reading, or, for that matter, about its basic good sense.

The good sense is most obviously employed in carrying out the theme that the quality of informed choice is important in keeping the wolf from the kitchen door as well as in setting really excellent meals on the dining-room table. Far from being ashamed of discussing food, Mrs. Fisher insists, we should make a point of it. And to that end she writes of luscious soups, of the difficulties and delights of egg cookery, of the most civilized ways of serving potatoes; she provides a long course in meats, from the simple rare beefsteak to kidneys and calves' brains and on to pigeon and rabbit; and general hints on vegetables are followed by notes on very particular economies, from other days as well as our own.

This highly individualistic adviser is never afraid to puncture a convention of which she disapproves or to protect a tradition she believes worth honoring. Nor is she afraid to individualize her dishes themselves by her individual phrasing: do we, for instance, prefer the "bland, unctuous broth" known as Vichysoisse to that "thick unsophisticated soup," the "heart-warming and soul-staying" minestrone? Her book is lively and amusing and intelligent; and a real cook book, too.

John W. Chase   (review date 31 August 1947)

SOURCE: "Jennie's Clever Trick of Vanishing," *The New York Times Book Review,* August 31, 1947, p. 7.

[*In the following review, Chase offers a mixed assessment of* Not Now but Now.]

At first careless glance one might wonder why the author of **How to Cook a Wolf** and other books of culinary exoticism should try her hand at fiction. Strictly speaking, Mrs. Fisher has not produced a unified narrative [in **Not Now But Now**]. Upon a not too cumbersome framework, she has created four stories involving the girl Jennie, at different periods of time and in quite separate settings. But no matter what the circumstances, Jennie is always an extraordinary gal, possessing a quality that raises havoc wherever she appears. In the early pages the author gives this frank appraisal of Jennie:

> She attended to herself as if she were a trainer with a fine show-bitch: baths and feedings and exercise, all fit and proper. Then she enjoyed herself too, like the employer of the trainer of the show-bitch, and she felt proud ownership in all her own points, standing off to judge, coming close to caress.

It is the pattern of Jennie's various lives to capitalize on her exterior assets and then, when the moment of horrible reckoning is at hand, to disappear into the mists like the village of Brigadoon—thus escaping the hateful people who insist on misunderstanding her motives. This literary device might easily have slipped into the commonplace, but it is a tribute to Mrs. Fisher's skill that she generally holds our interest and credulity in this world of fact and fantasy.

What, for instance, could have seemed duller to a blasé Jennie than the Swiss family of Jeannetôt—bourgeois father, conceited young son, convent-ridden daughter? Let the reader discover the bittersweet result. Or does life as chambermaid in a London town house of the mid-nineteenth century appear drab for our Jennie? Alas, ask poor Mr. Spackle, that most devoted and upright of butlers. And how fares Jennie in the giddy life of San Francis-

co in the Eighties, where the worldy-wise Sir Harry acts as her "sponsor"? A memorable cut of cards furnishes the answer.

It is not easy to convey the ironic charm with which Mrs. Fisher presents her stories. She has the sophistication to write simply, with a minimum of affectation. Her mockery is not jaundiced; she laughs with you at Jennie but is careful to make you keep your distance. The dialogue has a natural sparkle rarely found in a first novel. Mrs. Fisher loves the flow of dresses, the intimacies of food.

In the midst of such praise, it is perhaps boorish to add that this novel is not without a serious blemish. The third tale, set in an Ohio college town, seems definitely out of place. Here Mrs. Fisher loses her sureness of touch, and her characters bog down in a mire of unconvincing detail. It is difficult to account for this relapse; perhaps the author somehow felt compelled to add a touch of "significance" to her book. A lesser criticism involves her occasional overuse of fanciful images—Jennie's bones "yawn" too often; people are forever "sucking" at her, and so on. However, the best of cooks at times scorches a soufflé and these are essentially minor defects in a diverting book.

Rex Stout   (review date 9 October 1949)

SOURCE: "Suggestions for the Sensitive Palate," *The New York Times Book Review,* October 9, 1949, p. 25.

[*An American novelist, journalist, and critic, Stout was best known as the author of the popular "Nero Wolfe" detective mysteries. In the following review of* An Alphabet for Gourmets, *he lauds Fisher's culinary expertise and writing skills.*]

It would be fun to argue the question: which is the greater treasure, a gifted cook or a gifted writer on cooking? But M. F. K. Fisher—to stick to the lady's pseudonym—could not be cited in evidence on either side, because she is both. For the first I can offer only hearsay, from people who have had the good fortune to eat at her table; for the second, here is this book I have just read [**An Alphabet For Gourmets**], the sixth that this authority on cooking and eating has written about food since 1937.

With most books it is the highest praise to say you simply couldn't lay it down, but not with books on cookery. Their excellence as manuals depends, of course, on how they meet the tests and trials in the seasons and years to come, but their excellence as books can be judged by the number of times, while reading, you have to fight the impulse to make for the kitchen, lay the book down propped open, and go to it. That happened to me a dozen times with **An Alphabet for Gourmets,** which gives it this year's pennant with none other even in sight. Once, indeed, the impulse was irresistible, and I did lay it down, to go to the garden for four eggplants and get the preliminaries started for Peasant Caviar Recipe Number Two.

But though I expect it to go through the tests with a high mark as a manual, as a book there is no question about it. Since Mrs. Fisher wrote it, naturally it is witty, pungent and highly civilized, but also it has a special charm. It tells of the bad as well as the good. It tells how to scramble eggs with love and wisdom, and it also tells how to scramble them with ignorance and rancor. It describes the finest meal the author ever ate, and it also describes the most ghastly one. It not only guides and titillates; it warns.

A couple of times Mrs. Fisher disappointed me. I have long felt that nothing is good on raw oysters except salt or caviar, and that serving horseradish, tabasco, or that unspeakable red mixture with them is gastronomical felony. Mrs. Fisher does mention the wedding of an oyster with a bit of caviar, but she does not denounce the felony, and I wish she had, for she has a great reputation and influence. On bread she is sound but not outspoken enough for me. The tasteless stuff that passes for bread on ninety-nine American tables out of a hundred is an insult and an outrage, and I wish Mrs. Fisher had fired a hotter blast at it.

She does make her general position plain, as for instance in her remarks on the fruit cup. She doesn't say so, but I feel sure she chose the fruit cup as the symbol of the canned and cellophaned insipidity that threatens to dominate the American menu, both at home and "out." She may have thought it impolite to launch a direct attack and preferred to come at it on a flank. Was that why she slyly made a place for the recipe for Garum (400 B.C.)? And did that inspire the grotesque chapter entitled *Y for Yak?* I would guess so.

If you are yourself getting fed up with fruit cups and inane bread and soup canned to startle no palate, by all means read that recipe for Garum (400 B.C.) It will make your taste buds do a jig. If you are man enough not only to read it but also to make it and eat it, not even fruit cups can ever get you down.

I like this book. It is filled with anecdotes, provocations, and stimulating suggestions and facts. But in one paragraph Mrs. Fisher was worse than impolitic; she was foolhardy. She might have known reviews of her book would be entrusted to writers, and surely she likes favorable reviews. Yet she tells about a writer who lived for five months on hen mash, with no expression of sympathy or regret. Why did it have to be a writer? Why couldn't she have made it a banker or a bus conductor? I can tell her one thing: if I had been living on hen mash for five months when her book reached me, this review would have given her something to think about.

Rex Stout   (review date 19 September 1954)

SOURCE: "Cooking for Sauce," *The New York Times Book Review,* September 19, 1954, p. 12.

[*Below, Stout praises* The Art of Eating, *commenting on the skill and occasional eccentricity of Fisher's writing.*]

Someone has said of Casanova's Memoirs that it is a wonderful book about life with the accent on love and sex. M. F. K. Fisher's **The Art of Eating** is a wonderful book about life with the accent on food and cooking. Casanova could certainly love, but his book is wonderful because he could write; and Mrs. Fisher can certainly cook, but her book is wonderful because she too can write. It is an omnibus volume containing her **Serve It Forth, Consider the**

Oyster, How to Cook a Wolf, The Gastronomical Me and **Alphabet for Gourmets.**

It has scores of recipes, from gentle and creamy scrambled eggs to *Riz à l'Impératrice* and pheasant with sauerkraut. It has hundreds of hints and comments on cuisine and gastronomy—historical, practical, wayward, sound, imaginative, provocative, mad. Anyone who reads it will forever after be a better cook and a better host (or hostess)—and a more dangerous guest.

There is your money's worth, but there is much more. A recipe to cure bruised withers for ladies who ride straddle. How to wash dishes and get them clean, without an electric dish washer and without getting your hands wet. How to keep the fumes from permeating your hair when you fry onions. How a woman can eat alone and like it, in public, and get away with it.

Mrs. Fisher can be utterly cuckoo, as when she says beer is better from a bottle than from a tap. She can be irresponsible, as when she says you should save the caps of beer bottles and adds in parentheses that she has forgotten why. She can be too cryptic to live, as when she suggests, "If you want to feel like a character from one of the James brothers' looser romantic moments you can float a few drops of oil of lavender in a silver bowl filled with hot water." Jesse and Frank? Or William and Henry? In either case, what on earth! If I am being thick and she is merely taking a playful sideswipe at the stories of the last-named, I apologize, for he gives me a pain, too.

Even when Mrs. Fisher is writing specifically of food her remarks may often be more widely applied with no strain. She closes a chapter on feeding a family in wartime with the admonition, "Use as many fresh things as you can, always, and then trust to luck . . . and what you have decided, inside yourself, about the dignity of man."

Certainly good advice, even for those who have never coddled an egg and never will.

Jan Morris   (review date 4 June 1978)

SOURCE: "Marseille Ramble," *The New York Times Book Review,* June 4, 1978, p. 10.

[*Morris is an English journalist, travel writer, and autobiographer. In the following review, she extols* A Considerable Town *as an exceptionally perceptive portrait of the French city of Marseille.*]

Most city essays are awful—I have written some really ghastly ones—and most city books are worse still. Is there any literary product more depressing than your archetypal urban travelogue, with its statutory folios of lush photography interspersed among the obligatory historical gobbets and hashed-up anecdotes?

It is a delight, then, to welcome another distinctly *un*-city book from dear M. F. K. Fisher—"dear" because Mrs. Fisher stands to so many of us, wherever we live, in the office of an endlessly entertaining and slightly mysterious aunt. She has written one such book before, about Aix-la-Chapelle, but in **A Considerable Town** she develops the genre much further, and weaves a meditative, discursive and sometimes enigmatic spell about that Chicago of European seaports, Marseille.

I use the Chicago analogy not because of Marseille's old reputation for vice and violence, but because it has always seemed to me, with the possible exception of Barcelona, the most elemental city of the Mediterranean seaboard, as Chicago is of the North American continent. Mrs. Fisher indeed is at pains to balance the black legend of Marseille with its vivacity, age, strength and even occasional compassion, and she succeeds wonderfully: Nobody who reads this book, I swear, will ever think of the place in quite the same way again.

Not that it is, as I say, really a city book. Mrs. Fisher could have written a book not unlike it if her subject had been lawn tennis, say, or dandelions. Marseille is only obliquely the subject of her reportage. The star of the piece is always Mrs. Fisher, and it is only by way of her quirks of temperament and sentiment that we get a veiled but intensely suggestive view of the Vieux Port, the Quai des Belges, Notre Dame de la Garde and all that.

E. M. Forster said that the best way to see Alexandria was to "wander aimlessly about." Mrs. Fisher herself believes that strolling is a lost art these days, but in fact she is the perfect rambler. *A Considerable Town* is one long ramble. It rambles through the city, its monuments, its quays, its shops and its cafes, but more important, it rambles through the author's mind and memory—she has known Marseille since 1932, and seems to have forgotten nothing.

> I keep an eye on things, like what wars do to little shops. Some are empty now that once looked smart and thriving: a place that sold elegant leather gloves and belts and purses is a snack bar, as I remember . . . something fleeting like that. There used to be an English pub, but War and the Exchange and perhaps the Common Market closed it, as happened to a lot of British pharmacies and bars all along the Côte d'Azur, and now it is bleak and boarded up. Some noble old buildings are "modernized" into one-room studio apartments, and a once-stylish café is now an airline agency.
>
> And one time when the Place was hastily being transformed into a little park for a Christmas present to Marseille, I watched the tall plane trees that ring three sides of it being pruned in what seemed a crazily brutal way. . . . Then, magically, for Christmas Eve and the formal opening with its speeches and music, the tall trees turned into *arbres de Noël,* twinkling with thousands of little lights the color of champagne. By now they are still Christmas trees every winter, but lend cool green beauty to everything around them in the summertime, like fashion models, artificially tall and graceful.
>
> After World War II, there seemed to be an extra lot of thin tumblers and jugglers doing shaky handstands on old carpets rolled out on the pavement of what was still the Place de la Bourse, but since about 1971 when the Old Girl got her face lifted again and wore a new if somewhat unwelcome name, she has become a charming if comparatively colorless little square, and it is rather difficult to think of it screaming with furious citizens, running with blood, blazing with firebrands.

Sometimes, I have to say, I found it a little *too* rambling, a little too dependent, like many letters from aunts, upon rows of dots and exclamation marks. Civilized editors do not, I know, fiddle unnecessarily with the prose of beloved and distinguished authors, but even so I think somebody at Knopf ought gently to have pointed out, if not simple repetitions in Mrs. Fisher's typescript, at least the same thing told us three or four times.

But of course one forgives her everything, even occasional passages of actual incomprehensibility, for her absolute originality and her always winning ways. I forgive her as easily as anyone, if it is not an impertinence to say so, because I agree with every word she ever says, and share almost all her many and diverse enthusiasms.

Mrs. Fisher loves ships, docks and harbors. She likes fresh fish with dry white local wine at lunchtime. She has a susceptible fondness for rogues and vagabonds, and a Dickensian taste for the scramble, the rasp, the blarney and even the petty pretensions of city life. Nobody can describe the sound of bells or the feel of churches better than Mrs. Fisher, and surely nobody in the history of gastronomy has more exactly defined the pleasures of eating. "[Tomatoes] make understandable at once, without words, why the men of the South of France know that the reason their women ('strong, wild, fertile,' they have been called) are more lastingly seductive than others is that they are fed from the cradle on the local love apples."

Food has been her literary specialty for 40 years, and it is above all through the chapter on food in this book that she projects the sensations of Marseille. A simple aside from the stuffed mussels—a passing reference to restaurant décor—some fleeting memory of a courteous waiter, an empty room, a window-dressing, a curious fellow diner—and miraculously not just the occasion, or the taste or the company comes to life, but the very presence of the city.

From time to time I am almost persuaded by the literary intelligentsia that places are better described by fiction than by fact—that the novel is a more effective instrument of evocation than the travel book. Mrs. Fisher bolsters me in my contrary conviction. Undistracted by reservations of plot or plausibility, she often expresses in a single flick of reminiscence more than most novelists could communicate in pages of descriptive allusion, however artfully inserted between segments of what is so often called *truly* creative writing.

For really no writer could be much more creative than Mrs. Fisher. A gallery of characters looks back at us from the chapters of this not very long book, and they are all vivid and in the round—if not unwaveringly true in the detail, unmistakably authentic in the whole. A plethora of emotions is exposed, too, emotions public and private, past and present, emotions in the author, emotions in us.

In short, *A Considerable Town* is a considerable book, perhaps a kind of classic. I only wish (if a reviewer may pay the ultimate compliment to an author), I only wish I had written it myself.

Raymond Sokolov   (review date 6 June 1982)

SOURCE: "On Food and Life and Herself," *The New York Times Book Review,* June 6, 1982, pp. 9, 44-6.

[*Sokolov is an American critic, cookbook author, novelist, and translator. In the following review of* As They Were, *he presents an overview of Fisher's career and considers her to be a major American writer.*]

In a properly run culture, Mary Frances Kennedy Fisher would be recognized as one of the great writers this country has produced in this century. A few acute readers have understood this. Nearly 20 years ago, W. H. Auden said: "I do not know of anyone in the United States today who writes better prose." Perhaps *As They Were,* her new anthology, consisting of well-chosen work spanning the past five decades, will take the gastronomic curse off Mrs. Fisher and convince a world quite ready to acclaim her as the *doyenne* of food writers that she deserves much higher literary status. *As They Were* certainly provides the proper occasion to look again at all her books and to think about M. F. K. Fisher's peculiar eminence.

Almost housebound now among the grapes of the Sonoma Valley in California and nudging 75, she has had plenty of time to think about the way she's misconstrued. "People ask me," she wrote in the foreword to *The Gastronomic Me* in 1943, "Why do you write about food and eating and drinking? Why don't you write about the struggle for power and security, and about love, the way others do?"

Her reply to this inquisition can stand as her credo: "The easiest answer is to say that, like most other humans, I am hungry. But there is more than that. It seems to me that our three basic needs, for food and security and love, are so mixed and mingled and entwined that we cannot straightly think of one without the other. So it happens that when I write about hunger, I am really writing about love and the hunger for it, and warmth and the love of it and the hunger for it . . . and then the warmth and richness and fine reality of hunger satisfied . . . and it is all one."

Food is the prism that refracts all of life for this highly sensitive sensualist. Oh, she has the basic cooking skills too; she gets the recipes right and cares deeply about cooking. You could, in fact, mount a strong and detailed argument proving that M. F. K. Fisher led the way to our current culinary sophistication. From her expatriate years between the wars in Dijon and Vevey, she brought Americans their earliest honest chance to master the art of French (and Swiss) cooking. As self-conscious and esthetically preoccupied a writer in her way as Flaubert, she also insisted on the bluff Californian note. She promoted gumbos and casseroles and other provincial Americanisms with as much zeal as she ever devoted to the higher thoughts of her idol, Jean Anthelme Brillat-Savarin, whose *Physiology of Taste* she translated and provided with amusing and learned notes in 1949.

In the nostalgic essay **"Three Swiss Inns"** included in *As They Were,* she captures the aura and delight that so many of us have felt as tenderfeet abroad, stumbling upon supernal cooking in an out-of-the way European restaurant. The menu in this case was trout; the earthy joy of such discovery lies at the heart of the American expatriate experience. Hemingway had the same kind of epiphany chasing bulls in Pamplona. M. F. K. Fisher had her ecstatic European spiritual awakening at table.

She was and is, before all else, a food writer. And when she abandoned the table in her contrived novel, *Not Now But Now,* she misfired—with elegance, but misfired nonetheless. On the other hand, when Mrs. Fisher tries to squeeze herself as demurely as she can into the tight brown oxfords of the meat-and-potatoes recipe expounder, life sweeps into the kitchen like a Santa Ana through the Central Valley.

Winding up for an essay on coming to terms with frozen fish, she wrote: "I knew a man who gave up what could be called an enviable life in Central Nevada because he refused to eat any sea fish more than a day old and got tired of the fresh trout which often leaped in mountains all around him. He was rich, powerful, famous, sadly limited, and now he is dead. He reminds me of one of Brillat-Savarin's anecdotes about a devout gastronomer. . . ." The vigor here is typical, as is the incredible gastronomic memory in service of a wider purpose than gastronomy. "The first thing I remember tasting and then wanting to taste again," she has written, "is the grayish-pink fuzz my grandmother skimmed from a spitting kettle of strawberry jam."

The close reader will notice the strategic cantilevering of this sentence, the repetition in "tasting" and "wanting to taste" and how it dramatizes the child's tentative progress toward enthusiasm for the initially off-putting grayish-pink fuzz (the perfect description, as anyone knows who has ever looked at boiling strawberry jam), expressed in language that is implicitly childlike ("spitting") to suggest the child's point of view; and the whole structure built to mimic the final discovery: This stove top Scylla is only an apparent monster metamorphosing into a delicious and comforting sweet that a girl called Mary Frances can put in her mouth with magical pleasure.

Now *that* is the joy of cooking. And there are hundreds of similarly intense moments in other kitchens and at other tables tucked into piece after piece in the two justly famous collections of cookery articles, *The Art of Eating* and *With Bold Knife and Fork.* This is neither the place nor the moment to catalogue the quirky brilliance of such practical triumphs as *How to Cook a Wolf,* Mrs. Fisher's wartime book on coping with scarcity in the larder. Nor is it necessary anymore to point out the good sense of her perky catalogue of vegetables and how to deal with them in **"Having Fallen Into Place"** other than to quote the entry on rutabaga: "Down with it."

All these worthy achievements have been well and wisely praised before. Every serious cook will find much to treasure in those pages, but the juiciest meat is elsewhere, in two complementary volumes of autobiography.

The new anthology begins appropriately with long extracts from one of them. *Among Friends* is a memoir of an Episcopal girlhood in the overwhelmingly Quaker town of Whittier outside Los Angeles in the era of World War I and just after. Mary Frances's father, Rex Kennedy, ran the newspaper. The Quaker establishment shunned the Kennedys, who prospered anyway and had a fine time making the best of summers at a then undeveloped place called Laguna Beach, driving there through canyons where a rifle was standard equipment in the car as insurance against big cats.

This was Southern California before freeways, before the heyday of Hollywood. By ironic coincidence, the same Whittier produced another crucial Californian, Richard Nixon. Both he and Mary Frances Kennedy went to the local college. She does not mention him in *Among Friends.* No doubt the two never crossed paths, but the omission of the man's name in a book about Whittier published while he was President is a sort of statement. Some might call it a subtle return for the cold shoulder the Kennedys got from the local Quaker majority. "I was never asked inside a Friend's house, in the more than forty years I lived in Whittier," she wrote, recalling with suppressed, queenly, magnificent fury her Quaker schoolmates' "composed remote mothers, always seen from a polite distance, and their quiet fathers, the men who looked over my own sire for several years and then almost smiled at him, as they met in passing on the corner of Greenleaf and Philadelphia."

The Kennedys came to Whittier from Albion, Mich., and brought with them both an Iowan farmhouse heritage and, through Mary Frances's mother, who was a finishing-school alum and Anglomaniac, a touch of class. *Among Friends* is the story of how they made a rich life for themselves among the Whittier people who did not snub them: batty relatives, an eccentric neighbor called Aunt Gwen, servants and assorted "lame ducks" who fitted into Whittier even less well than the Kennedys themselves.

Out of this youthful complexity, this strained mix of exuberant yet genteel family warmth and social ostracism, sprang the restless, pants-wearing, sweet-liqueur-disdaining, big, warmhearted M. F. K. Fisher we meet in her very best book, *The Gastronomical Me.* Nominally, this is an autobiography told in a series of culinary vignettes. No question that the food matters for itself, but it also functions as a structural organizing principle for holding together swatches of Mrs. Fisher's life from 1912 to 1941.

Even though I once met the author of this book, I have trouble, as I read it, not imagining Katharine Hepburn in the leading role of the film that should be made of it. Starting as a good Californian child, our heroine becomes her own woman, in the brave style of the liberated (but not too liberated) woman of the 20's and 30's. She crosses oceans with impunity, changes husbands in midstream, launches herself in a career and in motherhood, tends her tragically ailing and enigmatic second husband, encounters Nazism and decadent sexuality in a Burgundian boarding house and a transvestite mariachi singer in Guadalajara. What this philistine summary leaves out is the depth and the mastery of M. F. K. Fisher's treatment of these potentially

melodramatic episodes. By the time she came to write *The Gastronomic Me,* she had learned everything Hemingway and Colette had to teach her about literary control and about the importance of what is left out.

She omits, for instance, any account, any explanation of the collapse of her marriage to Al, the young professor whom she seems, even after the divorce, never to have stopped loving. Yet, as we learn abruptly at the start of an episode, great passion has impelled her into a new marriage with Chexbres, who dies horribly and on camera, as it were. Mostly, however, the essential events happen in the gaps between episodes. The action we see centers around eating; the main "plot," when there is any, takes place as if it were a side dish.

The virtue of this technique is that it pushes unwieldy plot machinery into the wings and cuts out the heavy load of sentimentality that dramatic turns of fortune tend to bring in train.

What is left? Vivid freeze frames: the way it was when Mary Frances and Chexbres lived idyllically in a Swiss house on a "sloping green meadow, held high in the air above the Lac Leman by stone walls." Dinner was a form of white magic, a chthonic rite, and M. F. K. Fisher was the good witch stirring the pot: "As fast as Father and Chexbres could pick the peas, Mother and I would shell them, and then on a little fire of shavings I'd cook them perhaps four or five minutes in a heavy casserole, swirling them in butter and their own steam. We'd eat them with little cold pullets cooked for us in Vevey, and good bread and the thin white wine of the coast that lay about us."

On other occasions, other pots brew darker potions. During a dismal, endless sailing home from Europe in 1932 on an Italian ship, with Al and her younger sister Norah, there is a hint that the marriage is on the rocks ("I had found out several things about my relationship to my family, and to other men than Al . . .", but the real give-away comes when she and Al aren't able to eat compatibly. Al shuns the ship's wines. Al stays aboard and doesn't go with Mary Frances and Norah to shore restaurants at Central American landfalls (he hates insects). She temporizes: "Probably he was sickened to think of my coming back from those dreamy trips ashore, covered with invisible pests." Or perhaps it was stomach trouble.

M. F. K. Fisher not only uses food as a way into character, she also believes, like some westernized tribal shaman who still practices magic despite his education, that food changes people's bodies and their natures. She has written with high seriousness about folk medicine. *A Cordiall Water* (reissued by San Francisco's North Point Press last year) is no joke, despite its quaint nostrums, its purgatives, even its whole chapter on the efficacy of eating excreta. Mrs. Fisher thinks *A Cordiall Water* contains her best writing. It is certainly the key to her thaumaturgical approach to food as literature and literature as food.

The little treatise ends with two recipes which no other writer (and certainly no food writer but her) would have thought to print together. One is for a potion of snails and earthworms, eryngo root and milk, prescribed for a "consumpsion" in Shakespeare's time. The other is the text of a handbill advertising a faith healer's laying on of hands. "The handbill," she concludes, "was no stranger to me than the other recipe, for both spoke of incantation, and mystery, and ageless faith: the essentials of healing." And they are also the ingredients of M. F. K. Fisher's cuisine of the soul, giving body and flavor to what she has called, in a modest self-appraisal that is neither false nor truly modest, her "pleasant honesty of style."

Frances Taliaferro   (review date 29 May 1983)

SOURCE: "The Art of Aging," *The New York Times Book Review,* May 29, 1983, pp. 10-11.

[*In the following review, Taliaferro assesses* Sister Age *as an artful though uneven collection of meditations on aging.*]

To describe M. F. K. Fisher as the *doyenne* of food writers would be an absurd reduction, as if one were to call Mozart the greatest Freemason composer or Cézanne the leading painter of apples. Food, it is true, often happens to be Fisher's subject, but the narrow certainties of the home economist and the restaurant critic have no place in her gastronomic or her emotional vocabulary. She is, after all, the philosopher who wrote years ago (in **How to Cook a Wolf,** 1942), "No recipe in the world is independent of the tides, the moon, the physical and emotional temperatures surrounding its performance." It is for her dauntless appreciation of those physical and emotional temperatures that we most value her.

M. F. K. Fisher is 75 this year. In the present collection of mostly autobiographical short stories, *Sister Age,* she turns her clear gaze to the art of aging and finds inspiration for her title in the "family" of St. Francis. We know his gentle reverence for Brother Sun and Sister Moon, but "it is not always easy," she writes, "for us lesser people to accept gracefully some such presence as that of Brother Pain and his cousins, or even the inevitable visits of a possibly nagging harpy like Sister Age." If we can heed these visits, however, they have mysterious and valuable lessons to teach.

Sister Age instructs us subtly, firmly and usually by example or quiet implication. All of the stories consider people who are no longer young. The most admirable pieces do not lend themselves to summary; they are marvels of context in which simple objects and small gestures are inseparable from the larger harmony. At her best, Fisher relies for her effect on silence and slow time, on the accumulation of ordinary detail and the power of one slight displacement to reveal the underlying order.

"Moment of Wisdom," for example, is Fisher's recollection of herself as a child alone one hot, dry day long ago at an orange ranch in California where her family lives surrounded by flowers—poppy and lupine, wild roses and "weeds of beauty." A tiny man makes his way to the door, dressed in black and carrying a valise—clearly he is a Bible salesman. The child, polite in spite of herself, offers him some cool water but does not buy a Bible. The old man, "dry as a ditch weed," picks up his dusty satchel and walks back down the long driveway to the county road,

stopping on the way to pick up one of the dusty roses by the gate. The child, watching as she leans against the porch screen, is "astounded and mystified to find slow fat quiet tears roll from my unblinking eyes and down my cheeks."

> To describe M. F. K. Fisher as the *doyenne* of food writers would be an absurd reduction, as if one were to call Mozart the greatest Freemason composer or Cézanne the leading painter of apples.
>
> —*Frances Taliaferro*

These tears of mysterious sympathy, "the tears of new wisdom," "the slow, large tears that spill from the eye, flowing like unblown rain according to the laws of gravity and desolation—these are the real tears, I think. They are the ones that have been simmered, boiled, sieved, filtered past all anger and into the realm of acceptive serenity." To call this "moment of wisdom" an epiphany seems moony and unduly literary, but such moments quicken many of these stories.

In **"The Second Time Around"** we are in familiar M. F. K. Fisher territory, as the author celebrates the formidable Mme. Duval, her landlady 30 years ago in Aix-en-Provence. With ineluctable graciousness and "unaffrontable detachment," the old woman presides over her houseful of boarders like Mme. de Maintenon defending the barricades of civilization, regardless of poverty, postwar shoddiness and social change. The household swirls madly about her; Mme. Duval's unswerving dignity is both a rebuff and an illumination to the callow, middle-aged American visitor still in her "racial adolescence."

Another homage, somewhat less emotionally complex, is Fisher's **"The Oldest Man,"** an account of several days spent in the wild country of the Aveyron with her two young daughters and their French hosts, Georges and his ancient, spirited father, Pépé, a man in his hundredth year. There is great clarity and sweetness in the portrait of Pépé doing the dishes according to his own sloshy system, Pépé singing, Pépé reciting all of La Fontaine's fables "in a spate of magnificent rhythmic rhyme."

In a very different vein, **"Answer in the Affirmative"** recalls "Mr. Ardamanian and the time I let him make love to me." The narrator, now in her 40's, remembers the day in her young womanhood when old Mr. Ardamanian, the rug man, lightly caressed her body as a sculptor might touch his statue. "He had the most fastidiously intelligent hands I had ever met with. . . . I stood, silent and entranced, for I do not know how long, while Mr. Ardamanian seemed to mold my outlines into classical loveliness." Lust is irrelevant to this lovely story of tacit ecstasy.

M. F. K. Fisher's prose, never less than lucid, is sometimes startlingly astute. On a passenger freighter bound for Antwerp, the waiter "poured out my coffee the way a murder-er might fill a cup with poison—attentively, hopefully." An elderly passenger "had the patient, sweet, sickening half-smirk so often found on the face of a person who is afraid and at the same time voluptuously involved with her fear." Blanchette, Mme. Duval's maid, "strode with a kind of cosmic disgust from market place to meatshop and wine merchant, a fierce frown on her dark-browed face, and her firm breasts high." At home, "she was deft, silent, attentive, almost invisible in her correct black-and-white uniform—which was something like seeing the Victory of Samothrace in livery."

Sister Age is a somewhat uneven collection. A few of the stories depend on a supernatural element; they seem artificial and dated. One or two others are, to my mind, long and insufficiently shapely. But the best of the pieces, those that read like memoirs, are vigorous and perhaps less cranky than some of Fisher's earlier work. ("I notice," she writes, "that as I get rid of the protective covering of the middle years, I am more openly amused and incautious and less careful socially, and that all this makes for increasingly pleasant contacts with the world.") These forthright stories remind us that the writer's wisdom is as exemplary as her vitality.

Christopher Benfey   (essay date October 1984)

SOURCE: "In the Company of M.F.K. Fisher," in *Boston Review*, Vol. IX, No. 5, October, 1984, pp. 9-11.

[*In the following essay, Benfey offers an appreciation of Fisher's career, focusing on the autobiographical and "American" qualities of her writing.*]

If you go to a library to look for M.F.K. Fisher's books, you will find them scattered all through the stacks. If the library is big—big enough to hold a history of California wine-making, say, or a book about Aix-en-Provence (Fisher has written both)—you will have to climb up and downstairs searching through different categories. You will probably find more of her works among the cookbooks than elsewhere (in a university library these will be under some such heading as "Technology," next to books on building dams), but you will also find her works among books of fiction, travel, and autobiography. In its sheer diversity, in its consistently high quality and occasional perversity, Fisher's work resembles (although it resembles in little else) the work of Robert Graves. She too could have filled in her passport, "Occupation: Writer."

Although Fisher's range is enormous, she pretends to have a narrow appeal. The pretense has little to do with the actual size of her readership—which seems to be growing steadily—and everything to do with the sense of shared intimacy she offers her readers. In an early book she acknowledges the pleasure of knowing that "I, I with my brain and my hands, have nourished my beloved few, that I concocted a stew or a story, a rarity or a plain dish, to sustain them truly against the hungers of the world." Hidden in the hyperbole is Fisher's artistic credo. She writes, as she cooks, for a small audience—Stendhal's "happy few." Her books often resemble collections of good letters—informative, bristling with anecdote and detail,

bravely digressive. She assumes an audience that shares her taste for the exotic, but whose staple diet is the plain and the true. And she has a hardy faith in the nourishment art provides.

The letter is a first-person genre, even when it is a letter to the world, and Fisher's genius is resolutely first person: "*I, I* with *my* brain and *my* hands." The words come from a book called, significantly, *The Gastronomical Me* (reprinted in *The Art of Eating*). Yet Fisher manages to take an interest in herself and her life without becoming preoccupied with them. She confirms John Updike's insight that "literature can do with any amount of egoism, but the merest pinch of narcissism spoils the flavor." And to those who cannot grasp that distinction, Fisher replies: "People ask me: Why do you write about food, and eating and drinking? Why don't you write about the struggle for power and security, and about love, the way others do?" Fisher's answer, too long to quote entirely—and in a sense her answer consists of all her books—rests on her discovery that "There is a communion of more than our bodies when bread is broken and wine drunk."

> I tell about myself, and how I ate bread on a lasting hillside, or drank red wine in a room now blown to bits [she is writing in 1943], and it happens without my willing it that I am telling too about the people with me then, and their other deeper needs for love and happiness.

And with that august faith (Montaigne's rather than Pascal's) she can confidently begin a book with the sentence: "The first thing I remember tasting and then wanting to taste again is the grayish-pink fuzz my grandmother skimmed from a spitting kettle of strawberry jam" (*The Gastronomical Me*). She has the courage of her own sensuality.

The buzz of words on lip and palate—fuzz, skim, spit, jam—probably gives Fisher as much pleasure as the remembered taste of strawberries. "Most minds," as she observes at the outset of *Among Friends,* "have someplace in them a scrappy collection of phrases that are *there,* caught like gnats in the honey of memory . . . flies in the amber." Fisher has had to dip into the honey of verbal memory more than many writers for she has spent much of her life away from the English language. This distance has purified her idiom, just as certain isolated communities in Appalachia are said to preserve the Elizabethan dialect. In the preface to *A Cordiall Water,* a meditation on folk medicine which is her best book, Fisher remarks on the "purity" she discerns in the prose of writers, such as Conrad and Nabokov, "who are thinking in two languages." "I never tried to attain this," she remarks. "But for a few hours, while I was writing about horny cats and aching bones and nosebleeds, and all that clutter of life, I was stripped of banality, and I wrote simply in my native tongue, because I was temporarily detached from it." In voluntary exile from America and the English language, she learned to experience both more clearly. "I read even the banalities of an American newsweekly with cleared eyes and ears," she remarks.

Gertrude Stein made this discovery while living in Paris, Fisher while in Aix-en-Provence. But while Stein's language is highlighted, or foregrounded, in its opaque materiality, Fisher aims for a transparent idiom, where her almost conversational language is as unobtrusive as possible. She attains this purity more often than she claims. She is better at short forms than at long, best of all at the shortest prose form: the sentence. A well-packed but representative sentence from *A Cordiall Water* runs: "When I was little, my grandmother lived with us, or vice versa, and she prescribed a few remedies which I see now were from her years of life on the prairies that later became the state of Iowa." It is a snake of a sentence, not quite elegant, perhaps, but muscular and flexible; it reaches forward and back in time, back and forth in perspective, and curls back on itself. And of course it is in the first person—in the casual, trusting manner of one person writing to other people.

Fiction is not her forte. There is something pinched and uncomfortable about her novel and some of her stories: one senses the labor of making up characters' names and disguising autobiographical events. Fisher herself seems to be aware of this not entirely fruitful exertion. Looking back at an account of overcoming panic during a blizzard on Long Island, she remarks: "It seems odd, by now, that I wrote in the third person, because it is one of the most directly personal accounts I have ever given of something that has happened to me . . . Unless I look at the story I do not even remember what name I gave myself." The impersonal complexities of the novel are entirely foreign to Fisher's temperament.

Her novel *Not Now but Now,* bravely reprinted by North Point Press (it was first published in 1947), does not seem a labor of love. The whole book might well have been written in a pout:

> The nearest Jennie ever came to being untrue to Jennie was the night all four of them were staying with her. It was not just one of the people who adored her, not even two: they were all there, wary and jealous and demanding.

The narrative derives from a dinner party, as though the natural way to assemble a group of characters and have them take part in a story were to invite them to a meal. (Fisher calls herself, elsewhere, a "self-styled culinary *raconteuse,*" and she seems peculiarly sensitive to the ways in which remarkable meals, as subject and setting, engender stories.) A somewhat mechanical manipulation of time, on the novelist's part, allows Jennie to examine her four guests in different times and places: Lausanne in 1939, London in 1847, a midwestern college town in 1927, and San Francisco in 1882. The shifting time scheme may remind readers of another Jennie: the central character in the Robert Nathan novel and its better-known film version, *Portrait of Jennie.* Despite an appealing sensuality in Fisher's novel—Colette seems the presiding spirit—the awkward machinery of plot and mask keeps intruding. *Not Now but Now* (the title comes from parachute-jumping) finally left me bewildered, with the insecure feeling one may have after listening attentively to a long joke and not "getting it." I didn't get *Not Now but Now.*

Fisher's best stories are fragments of undisguised autobiography. They are, to borrow her own term, "reports"

rather than short stories—brief, honest, news-gathering forays into her own life. The term "report" may have entered Fisher's vocabulary through her father's trade. He edited the local newspaper in Whittier, California (the Quaker community where Richard Nixon received his college education), and it was at his work place that she was "impregnated forever with the tantalizing itching excitement of any place in the world where newsprint is . . . the cold smell of ink, with its indescribable bite . . . the mystery of paper. . . ." (Her ellipses.) She may also have picked up from the Whittier Quakers some of her trust in what she calls "straight plain telling." Whatever the source of the term, as a *reporter* Fisher has a good nose for a scoop, and what she is scooping is the shape and texture of her own life.

Among the finest of these reports is an account of a brief sojourn in Reno, where Fisher went for a peculiar kind of quick divorce.

> I went up to Reno from San Francisco after a long illness, to break a pattern of convalescence. Most people go there for amorous or marital or financial reasons, but I went to get a divorce from myself, the sick or malingering self. It was early spring, and I felt like a refugee from clinics and the test tubes.
>
> On the train . . . I looked with deliberate interest from my window. . . .

That is the opening of **"The Changeover,"** one of several reports and stories dealing with the theme of convalescence. (The curious historical link between remedies and recipes—*A Cordiall Water* collects "odd and old *receipts* to cure the ills of people and animals"—gives a satisfying coherence to Fisher's twin concerns of cuisine and convalescence.) **"The Changeover"** strangely resembles another narrative about the moods of convalescence, Poe's classic "The Man of the Crowd."

> Not long ago, about the closing in of an evening in autumn, I sat at the large bow-window of the D—Coffee-House in London. For some months I had been ill in health, but was now convalescent, and, with returning strength, found myself in one of those happy moods. . . .

If there is a debt here, it is insignificant. A period of convalescence after a long illness, the healing seasons of spring and autumn, the seat at the window with a view outside—these assembled elements constitute a perfect moment for a story: the passage from sickness to health. "I felt that my vision was ready, cleared by illness," Fisher reports in **"The Changeover."** The Reno hotel is wonderfully observed—the bellboy dressed as a cowboy who tells her that not only is it safe to go downstairs alone to the gambling area and the bar, but "Y'all's safer here than in your own home"; the three meals available at any hour; the tension between an Indian band and the rednecks at the bar. And **"The Changeover"** ends superbly: "The sun would be along soon, and meanwhile I knew that I was not ill anymore. The divorce had been granted. I had complete custody of myself."

The passage from sickness to health is the guiding narrative thread of *A Cordiall Water,* and Fisher's most poignant account of convalescence occurs toward the beginning of that book. The theme is in part the onset of age, though not in this case of human aging. It is the tale of "the cat Blackberry" who, after nine years of abstinence—"I was convinced," Fisher comments, "that he had been born a feline eunuch"—enters the realm of the senses. He disappears for a week and returns, "a shadow but quiet, and that year almost every kitten born in the Valley was Blackberry's, for when the moon was right he would leave again." But the other tomcats take their revenge on the feline Don Juan, and Fisher has to go look for the victim.

> I heard a small cheeping sound now and then, so like a bird's that I did not heed it at first. It came from the canyon, a narrow rocky place with a few straggly, ancient eucalyptus trees shading the muddy bottom, and for the knowing there were paintings on hidden and protected stones, done in the mysterious and ineradicable reddish stuff of ancient times, by Indians who came here to pray and be healed.

A day's search ends here, for "down in the muddy slit in the hills lay the cat Blackberry."

> He lay so flat into the mud that I almost stepped on him, and he was stretched out so long and far that he looked more like the shape of a dead reptile than a living animal. The mud was so coated on his fur that it was cracked in the dry air. I could not tell which end was the head of the horrid dead-alive thing, until he made another faint cry and I saw the feeble opening of his caked lips.

This is Blackberry's trip to Reno, his own way of divorcing himself from his sick self. As in the Reno report, Fisher is acutely aware of the placing of the story, with its arrival in "a narrow rocky place with a few straggly, ancient eucalyptus trees shading the muddy bottom." All her books testify to a homing pigeon's sense of place.

Fisher often seems to have been everywhere, seen everything, but only a few places have been home to her. She quotes Jean Giono: " 'It is very probable that if I had to draw the portrait of Paris, I would, one more time, draw it of myself.' " Fisher's own self-portrait, drawn across several books—and all her books are, in a sense, self-portraits—would first include Whittier, California, where she grew up "Among Friends," an experience she recorded, often bitterly, in her memoir of that ambiguous title. The Quakers of Whittier were often less than friendly to the Episcopalian family in their midst. "I was never asked inside a Friend's house," Fisher complains, "in the more than forty years I lived in Whittier." More friendly were the great French towns on the ancient Roman road—Dijon and Aix. Living in Burgundy and Provence taught Fisher much about culture, culinary and otherwise. It also gave her a complex understanding of what it means to be an American.

The American traveler runs the risk of becoming what Henry James called a "European"—cultured and countryless. The more M. F. K. Fisher travels, however, the more consciously American she seems to become. She

writes movingly of her role as stranger, ghost, invisible woman; and this seems to her a peculiarly American role.

> There are myriad facets to invisibility, and not all of them reflect comfort or security. Often I have been in pain, in my chosen role of The Stranger. Just as often I have counted on being so, and was not. Learning to be invisible has, of course, some moments worse than others.

Fisher's Americanness is brought home to her (so to speak) in her dealings with the older societies of Europe. "In Aix," she notes, "I came in for a certain amount of the old patronizing surprise that I did not have an 'American accent,' which I do; that I did not talk through my nose, which I don't; that I knew how to bone a trout on my plate and drink a good wine (or even how to drink at all), which I do." The innocent abroad is easily lulled by such compliments; but Fisher lived in Aix long enough to suffer from her own lucidity.

> What was harder to take calmly, especially on the days when my spiritual skin was abnormally thin, was the hopeless admission that the people that I really liked would never accept me as a person of perception and sensitivity perhaps equal to their own. I was forever in their eyes the product of a naive, undeveloped, and indeed infantile civilization, and therefore I was incapable of appreciating all the things that had shaped them into the complicated and deeply aware supermen of European culture that they firmly felt themselves to be.

Fisher's irony in those lines is difficult to read: did she indeed "really like" such arrogant "supermen of European culture"?

Her best defense, in any case, is to acknowledge her own Americanness. The first time she and her two daughters left Aix, Fisher wasn't sure why she had to leave, "except," she notes, "that I wanted the girls to stay American." In her own writing the determination to "stay American" is evident. She isn't chauvinistic about this patriotism; rather, she seems refreshingly willing to admit whatever innocence and youthfulness and cultural poverty might accompany her nationality.

If Fisher is the most interesting character in her reports and stories, she is hardly the only one. The family—mother, grandmother, daughters, often-absent father—is ever present; but there are other significant people in Fisher's world. These seem to fit into two main categories. There are, first, the not entirely unexpected, yet not quite invited, visitors to the house. Three of the best stories in *Sister Age* unfold from such visit—by a Bible salesman, an Armenian rugmaker, a wax-man. Such figures share, in peculiar ways, our privacy. They are admitted to our circle even though they are strangers. Or because they are strangers. The surprise, and the pivot, of these stories is that such people may suddenly cease to be strangers and become, unexpectedly, party to our intimacy. There is, for example, the moment when the wax-man, extraordinarily named Mr. Bee, becomes a man who simply happens to sell wax, and has mysterious, unaccountable feelings, pricked by the presence of a mountain in the distance. "Funny what these old mountains do to you, all right!"

> Matey saw in amazement, in a kind of horror, that his pale grey eyes were thick with tears, and that his mouth, which she had never really looked at, was trembling and bluish over his even white false teeth. She saw that his neat clothes were very loose upon his frame. He was old. He was much more than five years older than he had been five years ago, she saw. . . . Oh, Mr. Bee, she thought, weak with compassion.

If these itinerant salesmen occasionally share our domestic intimacy, another group of characters in Fisher's narratives shares our lives when *we* become itinerant. Waiters and porters and bartenders are ubiquitous in Fisher's writing. After a loving homage to Ange, a favorite waiter, Fisher notes that "because of our strangely permanent impermanence and our dependence upon restaurants and cafés, we got to know many other waiters in Aix." These figures are continually and palpably present, too, in Fisher's remarkable tribute to that monument of *La Belle Époque,* the Gare de Lyon in Paris. "As far as I can know or learn," she comments, "no other railroad station in the world manages so mysteriously to cloak with compassion the anguish of departure and the dubious ecstasies of return and arrival" (*As they Were*). And in her book about Aix, Fisher makes such a graceful transition from churches to cafés that the shift seems inevitable: these are both sites of communion, where one partakes of bread and wine.

> For more than three years, on and off, this place nurtured various phases of our varied souls. It was a solace and refuge from everything: wind and blasting heat and rain, disasters, anxieties, too much noise or silence. It was protective of us, always aloof, able to do without us.

This particular clean, well-lighted place is the Deux Garcons in Aix, the Café—and the name is significant—of the Two Waiters.

Perhaps because Fisher knows so much about traveling, she has a special appreciation for what it means to belong somewhere, to live intensely in one place. She is, of course, a connoisseur of kitchens. **"Two Kitchens in Provence"** are lovingly described in *As They Were,* and among the stories in *Sister Age* is **"A Kitchen Allegory."** Fisher also knows something about houses; and at the close of *As They Were,* in a piece called **"Nowhere But Here,"** she offers a loving description of her own house, a two-room *palazzina* built for her, in Glen Ellen, California, by her friend the architect David Bouverie. "I said I wanted two rooms and a big bath, with an arch at each end to repeat the curved doors of his [she lives on Bouverie's ranch] two big barns. I wanted tile floors. He did not blink . . . and I went back to Aix for several months to grow used to a new future." Bouverie built the house, the first new house Fisher had ever lived in. "It took a couple of years, once here, for me to feel that this was and would be . . . my 'home,'" she remarks. "Slowly and willingly I grew into the place, so that I was *here.*"

Fisher shares with many of our finest writers an American fascination with the meaning of the words "here" and "place." Her preoccupation with finding proper housing for her thoughts recalls Emerson and Thoreau and Dickinson. But it is characteristic of her (as it is of Thoreau) that these preoccupations find their place in her own experience. She teaches us, if we can receive the lesson, to take an interest in our own lives, to match her interest in hers. Even now there are important things to report, here in this place. A hungry circle of friends is waiting in the next room, eager for the next stew or story.

> **While no one talks about Proust as a food writer because of his memorable madeleine, M. F. K. Fisher has been so identified because she has chosen gastronomy as her central subject, her all-purpose metaphor. But Fisher's gastronomical self exists within a larger life, food acting as a transport to memory and the élan vital.**
>
> **—David Lazar, in "The Usable Past of M. F. K. Fisher: An Essay on Projects," in Southwest Review, *1992.***

Mary Hawthorne   (essay date 11 January 1993)

SOURCE: "A Hunger Artist," in *The New Yorker,* Vol. LXVIII, No. 47, January 11, 1993, pp. 107-10.

[*In the following essay, Hawthorne reflects upon Fisher's life and career, emphasizing the importance of sensual experience and memory in her writing.*]

Mary Frances Kennedy Fisher's just issued book, ***To Begin Again: Stories and Memoirs, 1908-1929,*** is mostly about the years of her youth in California, before her first marriage and her now celebrated sojourns in France and Switzerland. Some of these pieces were written as recently as a couple of years ago, when she was fully in the grip of the indignities of old age and Parkinson's, and could be found propped in bed on pillows, drinking strange pink cocktails through a straw and feeding on—what else? —oysters. She died last June, on the verge of her eighty-fourth birthday.

Since the publication, in 1937, of ***Serve It Forth,*** her first book, M. F. K. Fisher has hovered, continuously and vaguely, in the public imagination as a kind of Katharine Hepburn of culinary arts and letters. She was well bred and well loved as a child, beautiful (Man Ray photographed her), gifted, shrewd, and—therefore, perhaps—possessed of an occasionally noteworthy arrogance. ("I was a haughty child," she has said with some pride.) People have tended to embrace her as "the grande dame of gastronomy" or "the doyenne of food writers," or else to avoid her, skeptical of arguments that her work is really about something beyond mere *food,* and suspecting a chilly élitism and superficiality in the very lustre of her style, to say nothing of her ostensible subject.

What *was* Fisher writing about all those years? **Serve It Forth** was followed by eighteen other books, not including her famous 1949 translation of Brillat-Savarin's **The Physiology of Taste.** Even she seemed to feel the need to defend herself. In the foreword to her book **The Gastronomical Me** (1943) she wrote, "People ask me: Why do you write about food, and eating and drinking? Why don't you write about the struggle for power and security, and about love, the way others do? They ask it accusingly, as if I were somehow gross, unfaithful to the honor of my craft. The easiest answer is to say that, like most other humans, I am hungry. But there is more than that. It seems to me that our three basic needs, for food and security and love, are so mixed and mingled and entwined that we cannot straightly think of one without the others." The explanation—repeatedly quoted, as if in proof—is, in fact, a mostly good and accurate one. Hunger is a messy, tangled business, and Fisher does indeed acknowledge, in both subtle and overt ways, the reach of appetite into the realm of power—something she was keenly aware of from a young age, when she began cooking for her own family: "The stove, the bins, the cupboards, I had learned forever, make an inviolable throne room. From them I ruled; temporarily I controlled. I felt powerful, and I loved that feeling." Later, she added, "I . . . was basically what Beerbohm calls, somewhat scornfully, 'a host' and not 'a guest': I loved to entertain people and dominate them with my generosity."

As for love, there is ample, if often oblique or ambiguous, reference to it in her work; again, longing is much in evidence. And sometimes Fisher wanders into the sexual in surprising and delightful ways. Her own infatuation with food commenced in childhood with the simple discovery of the pleasures of the forbidden. Again and again in her books Fisher describes the influence of her puritanical Grandmother Holbrook, who lived with the family, in Whittier, California, until her death, when Fisher was eleven. The tale is a classic of its day. Because Grandmother held the purse strings (Fisher's father was a struggling Episcopalian newspaper editor in an alien, sometimes hostile Quaker community, her mother a "prairie princess" from Iowa), she also held the grocery list, and dictated the family diet, adjusting it to accommodate her own "despotic bowels" and her singular revulsion at pleasure or sensuality in any form:

Grandmother's Boiled Dressing

1 cup cider vinegar
Enough flour to make thin paste
Salt to taste

Mix well, boil slowly fifteen minutes or until done, and serve with wet shredded lettuce.

Periodically, Grandmother would travel to the sanatorium in Battle Creek for a cure, or to a religious convention in Asbury, New Jersey, and the entire family—closet bacchanalians all—would indulge in a riotous dining-room hedonism. And a few years later Fisher, ensconced in an all-girls boarding school and surrounded by admiring ad-

hoc lesbians at the annual Christmas dinner-dance, experiences the heady sway of more wicked sin: "With the unreasoning and terrible persnicketiness of a sixteen-year-old I knew that I would be sick if I had to swallow anything in the world alive, but especially a live oyster," she writes. "I remembered hearing Mother say that it was vulgar as well as extremely unpleasant to do anything with an oyster but swallow it as quickly as possible, without *thinking,* but that the after-taste was rather nice."

Then there is the profound solace of food—security like no other. Fisher, especially in her stories of Provence, where she lived with her two daughters in the late fifties and early sixties, describes a world that, in her rendering of the particulars of time and place and *soil,* is immensely satisfying and at the same time makes us nearly ill with nostalgia. Nostalgia, furthermore, for something that was never part of the experience of most of us to begin with. What *is* part of our experience is the horrible recognition of that era's passing, and today, jostling one's way through any farmers' market, one cannot help remarking the profound sense of gratitude and astonishment everywhere as dazed customers shyly feast their senses on shimmering rows of Biblical fruits, perfect in their imperfection: apples, pears, figs, quinces, pomegranates—tiny orchards in a box. Fisher has been instrumental in bringing an appreciation of these timeless creations to our conscious attention, and the adoration of food nowadays constitutes a virtual pagan splinter religion, its icons the paintings of Bartolomeo Bimbi, Giovanna Garzoni, Cézanne, Chardin, and countless others. It seems miraculous, given the general decrepitude and gloom of the urban world, that not only do certifiable vestiges of paradise remain but it is still actually possible to partake of them. The dearly purchased truffle whose perfume wafts from one's pocket is thus no mere truffle but something much larger—something that extends to the little sow, the *chercheuse,* who found it buried at the foot of an oak tree in the historic dirt of Périgord. There are also the pleasures of more idiosyncratic indulgences, as Fisher points out—like tangerine sections roasted on a radiator in winter in Strasbourg, or a bowl of potatoes mashed with ketchup—which have a poignancy all their own. (And what, I wonder, would Fisher have made of the last meals commonly requested by death-row inmates: T-bone steak, French fries, iced tea?)

But what Fisher doesn't mention about her subject is what seems to me to be at the core of her work: her rather touching desire—perhaps compulsion—simply to honor her own intensely sensual experience of the world. Fisher possessed the instinctive fierce hauteur of an animal that knows its own worth and place in a hierarchy, and thrills at the superiority of its keenness and its cunning; you can almost feel the metronomic twitching of a tail as she surveys her surroundings with both rapt attention and a certain detachment. Metaphors of the natural world abound in her work ("I was surprised at how beautiful her body was . . . with high firm breasts and a clear triangle of golden hair, like an autumn leaf "; "Anita-Patita would move like an imperturbable cricket about the kitchen"; "I fled family and friends and security like a suddenly freed pigeon, or mole, or wildcat"; "Her hair was like mud"). Her coup was in finding a niche in which to display the fruits of her desire. A. J. Liebling, for example, writes of his gastronomic exploits with gleeful and hilarious abandon ("I had chosen *côtes d'agneau* as the safest item in the mediocre catalogue that the Prospéria's prospectus of bliss had turned into overnight. They had been cut from a tired Alpine billy goat and seared in machine oil, and the *haricots verts* with which they were served resembled decomposed whiskers from a theatrical-costume beard"); Fisher instead offers exquisite and precisely remembered collages of sensation ("In my mouth the chocolate broke at first like gravel into many separate, disagreeable bits. I began to wonder if I could swallow them. Then they grew soft, and melted voluptuously into a warm stream down my throat"). These memories then blossom into delicate essays and stories and reminiscences—larger but equally artful arrangements of her closely observed experience. The beauty of the best of them lies in their insularity and incompleteness. Her pieces frequently suggest the qualified plot of a dream; they tend not so much to end as to evanesce, like a Satie "Gymnopedie," into uncomplaining melancholy or query.

At the start of *Among Friends* (1970), her book of memoirs about growing up among the Quakers, Fisher writes (in a chapter entitled, incidentally, "Then Begin Again"), "Most minds have someplace in them a scrappy collection of phrases that are *there,* caught like gnats in the honey of memory. . . . Why do I still chant now and then, even aloud . . . 'Begin, and cease, and then begin again.' " The question not only highlights the title of her new collection—what was the spell of Arnold's "Dover Beach" for Fisher? —but also suggests the repetitive, homing nature of her memory, hence of her writing. Much of what Fisher wrote was some form of memoir, so it's surprising that her work isn't particularly confiding or revelatory. And, even for those who don't subscribe to the idea that the contents of medicine cabinets or diaries marked for burning necessarily reveal the secrets of the soul, Fisher seems oddly, though no doubt calculatedly, closemouthed. Perhaps, like many women of her generation, she found the idea of revelation not only foreign but unseemly, indulgent—worst of all, foolish. (Fisher did not, of course, suffer fools gladly.) Her revelations are incompletely articulated apercus of isolated moments and events. In fact, she is most compelling—and seems most natural and at home—when her subject *is* surface and immediate sensation. There is a magic in her description of, say, a scorching Provencal summer:

> I could almost feel the food in the baskets swelling with juice, growing soft, splitting open in an explosive rush toward ripeness and disintegration. The fruits and vegetables of Provence are dying as they grow—literally leaping from the ancient soil, so filled with natural richnesses and bacilli and fungi that they seem a kind of summing up of whatever they *are.*

Or an Alsatian winter:

> I used to go across into the Orangerie when I felt too cold to sit still, and watch what animals had thick enough fur to wander outside their cages. I'd stand and stand, waiting for some sign of life from the rumpled creatures on the other side of

the bars, but even the guinea pigs were too stiff to carry out their usual haphazard copulations. The storks, symbol of Alsace, would stare bleakly at me and occasionally drop a languid feather into the frozen filth, and I would turn back to my home, stumbling a little in my haste to get there before the fire went out again.

And it is Fisher's own complete absorption that accounts for her magic. That, and perhaps the fact that her absorption is not interrupted by profound considerations of a great deal else. The questions we might have about her life reside in the realm of the intimate and, often, the painful; it seems unfair to criticize her for not having written about anything beyond what she chose to. Still, we are haunted by ghostly remembrances of husbands, for example, who figure prominently in her work and then vanish, almost without comment. (There is a peculiar addendum at the end of **"Tree Change,"** a story in the current collection which concerns a lovely Christmas memory from childhood: "I got married in September of 1929, but Christmas was always the same while Rex and Edith [her parents] were alive.") Of her three marriages she said not long ago, with laconic ambivalence and frost, "They were fine marriages as marriages go. I don't like marriage myself."

In 1983, Fisher published a book of stories, *Sister Age,* that took as its subject the pain of growing older. It is as personal and sad and stoic a volume as she ever wrote, and perhaps offers the best chance of understanding the complexity of her aloofness. In **"A Kitchen Allegory,"** Mrs. Quayle, "an agreeable and reasonable woman—in her private estimation, at least," in preparation for a visit from her daughter and grandson, compulsively stocks the house with food that she knows does not interest her daughter. The daughter arrives with her son on a bus and hastily announces her forthcoming marriage to a man unknown to Mrs. Quayle. Having barely tasted a morsel of the lonely woman's offerings, the two leave, six hours later.

> She heard again the bus whining off into the dark, and saw through its blue window glass the tiny hand, like a sea anemone, of her grandson. Behind him, a more earthly flower, was her dear child, the purposeful shadow of a fine relationship. "Until soon," she called into the glass. They made mouths back at her, compassionately. And then she returned to the confrontation with her stores of unwanted, uneaten, unneeded nourishment.

At last, food fails. Along with so much else.

In *To Begin Again* Fisher has, for the most part, moved on from those unhappy tales, which were principally the anticipations of old age, into the real thing—the freer and, to a certain extent, dottier realm of someone who has actually passed into it. The book is foremost a curiosity, innocently redundant. It feels as if it were written by someone whose powers have peaked, even though not all the pieces in it are actually the work of an enfeebled Fisher. But its focus, youth, is the traditional subject of the old, who so often can recall the most obscure moments of childhood with extraordinary clarity as they approach full circle ("Inside the Orpheum, all was pulsating excitement and the throb of drums to such young ears as ours, so uncalloused by the artful assaults of radio and TV. Outside, there was the still-timid tinny sound of what was beginning to be called traffic"). The draw of this collection is the evidence it provides of what Fisher, as an old person, thought worth bringing to light. Her home in Glen Ellen, California, where she spent the last twenty years of her life, housed a myriad of boxes, which, in turn, housed innumerable notes, clippings, and drafts of things she thought she might one day like to write about. Why these stories? There is a piece on the place of her birth (Albion, Michigan) and why it has always rankled her not to have been born in California. There is one on a superstitious attachment she had to a particular coral pendant in childhood. There is a story about an invisible childhood playmate of her brother's, and about an invisible little old man she held her hand out to for protection and comfort every night for many years after she first married, and who has now simply left her: "Speaking dispassionately, I would say that I need his warm strong hand in mine more now than ever, but he is not there. My hand, left out, would grow cold and awkward." There are pretty childhood reminiscences, like **"Tree Change"** and **"A Few Notes About Aunt Gwen,"** and a rather uncharitable one, **"Mother and 'Miss E.,' "** about the "dried-up" hometown librarian to whom Fisher's mother gave an annual Christmas gift of "a flamboyantly sexy and extravagant nightgown." There are the journals of adolescence. And then there is **"Gracie,"** a story, written in 1957, about childhood cruelty and its roots—in this case, racism and classism—which is one of the best. "I watched her straight blue-black hair hanging down, and I knew that I would never see her again. I knew that I was damned forever to be pink and white, as my mother had told me several years before, and I felt like crying. . . . I hope that if she is alive she does not remember me." In **"The Jackstraws,"** another tale of remorse, written thirty years later, Fisher muses, with uncharacteristic introspection, "Every thinking man is prone, particularly as he grows older, to feel waves large or small of a kind of cosmic regret for what he let go past him. He wonders helplessly—knowing how futile it would be to feel any active passion—how he could have behaved as he did or let something or other happen without acknowledging it." The elliptical evidence suggests that Fisher did suffer, in her sensitivity and in her superciliousness, and that her retreat into the circumscribed world of food provided her not only with a source of sensuous pleasure without risk of pain but with a sanctuary in which she could practice her own particular brand of alchemy. From the shelter of this world, she could add, hopefully, rightly, "The only salve to this occasional wound, basically open until death, no matter how small and hidden—is to admit that there is potential strength in it: not only in recognizing it as such but in accepting the long far ripples of understanding and love that most probably spread out from its beginning."

Brenda Wineapple (review date March 1993)

SOURCE: "Feasting on Life," in *The Women's Review of Books,* Vol. X, No. 6, March, 1993, pp. 14-15.

[*Wineapple is an American educator, critic, and biographer. In the following review of* To Begin Again, *she provides an account of her personal acquaintance with Fisher and an overview of the author's life.*]

M.F.K. Fisher changed my life. Not in direct, obvious ways: her ways, like her prose, are subtle, graceful and not a little mischievous.

I first spoke with her almost eight years ago when researching a biography of Janet Flanner, the *New Yorker's* longtime Paris correspondent. I had known that the two women were first acquainted in the summer of 1966, when Fisher was in Paris writing on the foods of the world for Time-Life. She was then 58, author of some eight books on the art of eating and translator of Brillat-Savarin's ***The Physiology of Taste.*** But though W.H. Auden had just called her "America's greatest writer," she was, in her own words, a comparative unknown. And she was nervous: although she'd been in Paris many times before 1966, never before had she been completely on her own.

Seventy-four-year-old Janet Flanner, Fisher's neighbor in an attic room at the Hotel Continental, took care of that. "Janet was much spryer than I," Mary Frances recalled in her introduction to *The Alice B. Toklas Cookbook,* "but was used to deputizing her many disciples, so that I spent most of that summer happily puffing around Paris on errands for her, fending off her fans at concerts, sampling a new batch of Sancerre in a cool cellar under the Luxembourg, with an ancient vintner she had known for countless years." "Janet exhausted me," Mary Frances Fisher told me by telephone, "but I loved her."

Several phone calls and a few months later, I set off from the San Francisco airport in my small rented car, maps and directions strewn over the front seat. (Remember every morsel you eat, begged a friend of mine.) I drove through California's lush Sonoma Valley looking for the Smokey the Bear sign she used as a landmark for the many visitors to her home. Mary Frances would not hear of my staying in a motel or an inn. I was to be her guest for several days while interviewing her reclusive friend, Hildegarde Flanner, Janet Flanner's sister, who lived across the mountains in the Napa Valley. I was to tell Mary Frances *everything.*

Flattered, nervous, even a bit suspicious, I hardly knew what to expect. Neither, I learned, did she. Minutes after my arrival, she happily confided she'd expected a dried-up, elderly, Eastern academic and was delighted to find me younger and jazzier than she'd imagined. Tall, almost lanky, robed in a bright, flowing caftan, Mary Frances for her part bore slight resemblance to the pictures on the dust-jackets of her books. She was much more regal, her lipstick was redder, her gray-green eyes bluer, and the hint of blond could still be seen in her long white hair, wound to a bun near the top of her head. Her hands were long and graceful, although she said she could no longer control them as much as she liked. Arthritis and Parkinson's disease were taxing all of her physical movements, a fact she mentioned and then dismissed, as if such tiresome infirmities should be lightly tolerated, not indulged.

She gently steered me toward the kitchen table where she'd set out milk and cookies for the elderly academic.

The kitchen occupied the entire wall in a large, airy room that also served as living room, reading room, dining room and no doubt writing room. Situated on the rolling grounds of the Bouverie ranch, hidden from the main road and surrounded by yellow wildflowers, her house had been built to her specifications: only two rooms, she'd insisted, a public one and a bedroom joined by a large foyer and the enormous bathroom she'd always coveted. Each room was spacious, the white walls flushed with the color of brightly woven rugs over the tiles, painted Mexican pottery, and desks and tables laden with papers, pens, a small kaleidoscope, photographs, books and galley proofs; she said it seemed as if hundreds of them came every day, begging for her comment.

We drank the crisp white wine produced in the valley and talked long and late over a simple, delicious plate of cold pink shrimp. It was one of those nights, rarer as we grow old, of stories, speculations, confidences. We talked about Janet Flanner and Flanner's sister, about writing, about living alone and about living with others, about two of her three husbands, and about her life in California, Switzerland and France. She mentioned her two daughters, whom she raised more or less on her own, and her first collection of essays, *Serve It Forth* (1937), which had been encouraged by her second husband Dillwyn Parrish. She was still amused when readers assumed the genderless "M.F.K." to be a man and admits the initials were chosen, in part, because she preferred ambiguity—especially because she wrote about food. (I have written a novel, but it's terrible; I am *not* a novelist, she insisted.)

Before I went to sleep, I asked why she had extended so much hospitality to me, a stranger, offering bed and board and even her literary agent before she'd even met me face to face. She smiled broadly. I had nothing to lose, she said.

A Californian by choice and disposition, Mary Frances Kennedy was born on July 3, 1908 in Albion, Michigan. "I still feel embarrassed that I was not born a native Californian because I truly think I am one," Fisher admits in *To Begin Again,* a posthumous collection of stories and memoirs, some written or revised in the last few years and some going back as early as 1927. For those familiar with Fisher's twenty or so other books, *To Begin Again* is a refreshing reminder of her tonic, unpretentious prose as well as the autobiographical details that often appear in her work.

Mary Frances didn't arrive in the Golden State until she was past two. Her father Rex Kennedy had sold his share in Albion's local newspaper, packed up his well-bred Episcopalian wife Ethel and their two small daughters, and bolted. "[T]he four of us," writes Fisher, "were undoubtedly among the first beatniks of the Far West— unwittingly, of course." Like all good Midwesterners, they aimed for the Pacific. But after speculating on a half-dead orange grove, Rex and Ethel Kennedy decided they'd all fare much better on a steady income in a sturdy house. (One of Fisher's earliest memories is of her small sister sleeping peacefully in the top drawer of a hotel bureau.) Rex bought the *Whittier News,* the local paper of the small Quaker community in southern California destined for modest renown as the birthplace of Richard Nixon.

Nixon, however, meant as little to the young Mary Frances as the words "smog" or "pollution," all of which had not yet been born. During her childhood the air smelled of dusty eucalyptus, wild mustard and orange; the poppies grew as tall as little girls. Only the stern, self-righteous asceticism of the Whittier Quakers dimmed the otherwise lovely vista of half-wild roses, lupine and sage. "I was never asked inside a Friend's house, in the more than forty years I lived in Whittier," Fisher recollected.

Yet her family never lacked for warmth, companionship, or their own prejudices and arrogance, which Fisher recalls unflinchingly in *To Begin Again.* She remembers how she taunted her schoolmate Gracie with the casual and unforgettable cruelty of childhood. With her navy-blue hair and a dark complexion the color of a polished hardwood floor, Gracie was an outcast among the pink and white girls of grammar school. And though the young Mary Frances loved Gracie almost as much she loved being pink and white, she blithely ignored Gracie's poverty, she made fun of Gracie's name, she made Gracie cry. "I wonder what ever happened to her," Fisher mused more than a half a century later. "I hope that if she is alive she does not remember me."

Laced with reminiscences, M.F.K. Fisher's books never submit to nostalgia or sentimentality—no matter how green and aromatic was the southern California of yesteryear. In this, *To Begin Again* is no exception. Fisher is a tart writer who, for all her autobiographical urges, does not confess. She keeps a tidy, brisk distance between herself and the objects of her contemplation, whether these be her beloved, democratic father, her sensitive, traditional mother, or her maternal grandmother, a Victorian *grande dame* who took refuge from the duties of her gender and class in the privileges of a nervous stomach:

> The pattern was one they followed like the resolute ladies they were: a period of dogged reproduction, eight or twelve and occasionally sixteen offspring, so that at least half would survive the nineteenth-century hazards of colics and congestions; a period of complete instead of partial devotion to the church, usually represented in the Indian Territory where my grandmother lived by a series of gawky earnest missionaries who plainly needed fattening; and at last the blissful flight from all these domestic and extracurricular demands into the sterile muted corridors of a spa. It did not matter if the place reeked discreetly of sulphur from the baths and singed bran from the diet trays: it was a haven and a reward.

Fisher claims that her grandmother's nervous stomach indirectly accounts for the pleasure she herself began to take in sauces that weren't white, in marshmallows floating in hot chocolate, and in grilled sweetbreads with a dash of sherry on them. When Grandmother retreated to one of her spas, the family rioted in the pleasures of the pantry from which Mary Frances "formed my own firm opinions of where gastronomy should and indeed must operate in any happy person's pattern." Food nourishes the body and the soul. "Increasingly I saw, felt, understood the importance, especially between people who love and trust one another, of a full sharing of one of our three main hungers, which are for food, for love, and for shelter." So why not, Fisher asked herself, enjoy it all?

But it wasn't just Grandmother's Nervous Stomach that inspired Fisher to write about one of our basic hungers and the skills that go into satisfying it. She tells us in *To Begin Again* that as the oldest child of four, she discovered early the best way to get attention was to cook something, something a little different, something good. She would stand on a little stool so she could stir the double boiler and on Saturday mornings she helped the family cook mix ingredients for Sunday's cake. She entertained the family with new inventions, prepared with care and hope. And though she insisted that she always told the truth, she also captivated them with stories that sounded preposterous, so loaded were they with lurid details. Her father told her she'd make a good reporter.

Propped on one of Mary Frances' bookshelves was an old piece of painted leather she'd found in a junk shop in Zurich in 1936, a portrait of a wrinkled old woman, Ursula von Ott, born in 1767. Intrigued and recognizing something familiar in Ursula's gaze, Mary Frances bought the picture. It would teach her about aging, she thought; she planned to learn as much as possible and then write a book about the art of growing old.

Over the years, Mary Frances carried the picture wherever she went, hanging it above desk or bed. Silverfish ate much of the pigment surrounding the old woman, but the face itself remained ugly, vivid and oddly unperturbed. Mary Frances didn't write the book she planned, but she never stopped watching Sister Age, as she called Ursula von Ott, who calmly looked past her. "I am glad that I have been able to live as long as I have, so that I can understand why Ursula von Ott did not weep as she stood by the funeral urn of her son, surrounded by all the vivid sights of his short silly life. . . the fat cupids, the fatter Venuses whose satiny knees he lolled against," wrote Mary Frances in the afterword to the collection of short stories, *Sister Age,* published two years before we met. "She did not smile, but behind her deep monkey-eyes she surely felt a reassuring warmth of amusement, along with her pity that he never had tried to feel it too."

The last time I saw Mary Frances was in the spring of 1989. Her voice had sunk to a whisper. She could no longer guide her elegant hands, now knotted in her lap, but had managed to keep working by breathing notes and stories into a tape-recorder each night for her secretary to transcribe the following day. Even this method, never totally satisfactory, was now exhausting. Not impossible, however, not for Mary Frances. Curled in her wheelchair, wraithlike and twisted, she greeted guests with unwavering courtesy and charm. Her lips were still bright red, her

eyes still glittered, her courage (though she would hate such a pretentious word) was steady.

She had written me that she was working on a Secret Project. I don't know if that project became *To Begin Again,* but I like to think it did. And I like to think it was she who chose the book's title. Mary Frances was a person who began again, every day. And what she gave me, Ursula von Ott had shown her: that in spite of our wrinkling limbs and fading voices and despite the inevitable slowing down of physical things, we can go on—with forbearance and understanding and no small measure of wit.

"Parts of the Aging Process are scary, of course," she wrote in *Sister Age,*

> but the more we know about them, the less they need be. That is why I wish we were more deliberately taught, in early years, to prepare for this condition. It would leave a lot of us freed to enjoy the obvious rewards of being old, when the sound of a child's laugh or the catch of sunlight on a flower petal is as poignant as ever was a girl's voice to an adolescent ear, or the tap of a golf-ball into its cup to a balding banker's.

Composed under the shadow of *Sister Age, To Begin Again* records Mary Frances Kennedy Fisher's abiding appetite for life.

FURTHER READING

Criticism

Fisher, M. F. K. "Swiss Journal." *Antaeus,* No. 61 (Autumn 1988): 129-46.
> Relates Fisher's visit to Switzerland in 1938.

Gillespie, Elgy. "The Art of Living." *The Washington Post Book World* XXIII, No. 4 (24 January 1993): 2.
> Adulatory review of *To Begin Again,* which Gillespie calls "a revelation as well as a bit of a mystery."

Glendinning, Victoria. "The Gastronomical Her." *The New York Times Book Review* (9 June 1991): 15.
> Review of *The Boss Dog, Long Ago in France: The Years in Dijon,* and Jeannette Ferrary's *Between Friends,* in which the latter is described as a "collection of appreciations" of Fisher's life and career.

Lazar, David. "The Usable Past of M. F. K. Fisher: An Essay on Projects." *Southwest Review* 77, No. 4 (Autumn 1992): 515-31.
> Relates how the author befriended Fisher, whom he had long idolized, and speculates on the psychological basis for her artistry.

John Fowles

1926-

(Full name John Robert Fowles) English novelist, short story writer, novella writer, poet, nonfiction writer, and screenwriter.

The following entry provides an overview of Fowles's career through 1994. For further information on his life and works, see *CLC*, Volumes 1, 2, 3, 4, 6, 9, 10, 15, and 33.

INTRODUCTION

Fowles's reputation as an important contemporary author rests on novels that incorporate elements of mystery, realism, and existential thought. An allusive writer, Fowles has experimented with such traditional prose forms as the mystery novel, the Victorian novel, and the medieval tale, and his writings are characterized by strong narration; vital, resourceful characters confronted with complicated situations; and lavish settings permeated with references to historical events, legends, and art. Other distinguishing features of Fowles's works include his rejection of the omniscient narrator and his use of ambiguous, open endings lacking resolution. Readers have often been annoyed at this refusal to offer satisfactory conclusions, but Fowles believes his responsibility as an artist demands that his characters have the freedom to choose and to act within their limitations. This practice parallels his conception of "authentic" human beings, or people who resist conformity by exercising free will and independent thought.

Biographical Information

Born in Essex, England—on the outskirts of London—Fowles attended a suburban prepatory school until his family moved to Devonshire to escape the German air raids of World War II. There, in England's southwestern countryside, he first experienced the "mystery and beauty" of the natural world, the importance of which is evident in his fiction, philosophical writings, and his avocation as an amateur naturalist. He served two years as a lieutenant in the Royal Marines, but never saw combat since the end of his training coincided with the end of the war. After receiving a B.A. with honors in French from Oxford University in 1950, Fowles taught English at numerous schools in England and Europe, including the University of Poitiers in France, Anargyrios College on the Greek island of Spetsai, and St. Godric's College in Hampstead, England, where he was head of the English department. The two years he spent in Greece during the early 1950s were particularly important to his artistic development. It was there that he first began to write, and the fictive island of Phraxos from *The Magus* (1965) is modeled on Spetsai. In 1963 Fowles published *The Collector,* and the novel's success allowed him to retire from teaching. Though not his first attempt at a novel—Fowles had produced several manuscripts since 1952—it was the

first he deemed worthy of publication. Since 1966, Fowles has lived in Lyme Regis, a coastal town in southern England and the setting for *The French Lieutenant's Woman* (1969).

Major Works

The Collector concerns the interaction between a kidnapper, a lower-middle-class clerk named Frederick Clegg, and his victim, an upper-class art student called Miranda Grey. Narrated by Clegg and Grey, the novel highlights the struggle between the elite and the masses, criticizing contemporary society's obsession with control and possession. One common interpretation of *The Collector* is that the authentic individual, who represents a code of behavioral excellence, is endangered by the pressures exerted by conventional society. Fowles discussed this idea in *The Aristos* (1964), a nonfiction work outlining his thoughts on art, religion, politics, and society. The concepts outlined in *The Aristos*—specifically the need "to accept limited freedom . . . [and] one's isolation . . . , to learn one's particular powers, and then with them to humanize the whole"—are integral to *The Magus* and *The French Lieutenant's Woman*. Set primarily on the fictitious Greek island of Phraxos, *The Magus* centers on Nicholas Urfe and his experiences as a participant in Maurice Conchis's illusive and seemingly amoral "godgame," a type of living drama or metatheater which, in the case of Urfe, includes many scenes of humiliation and perverse, malicious cruelty. Designed to provoke participants into reevaluating their identities through confronting their weaknesses and the mystery of existence, the godgame is a central device in many of Fowles's works. In *The French Lieutenant's Woman,* for instance, Charles Smithson undergoes a godgame at the hands of Sarah Woodruff, who guides him to an understanding of his desire to free himself from Victorian restraints. Considered Fowles's most ambitious and innovative work, *The French Lieutenant's Woman* examines Victorian manners and morals from a present-day perspective. While Fowles's manipulation of time and space in the novel allows his characters to discover certain truths, they also lead to further ambiguities for the reader, as Fowles includes a number of possible resolutions to the novel, all of which are consistent with earlier events in the narrative. The novella and short stories contained in *The Ebony Tower* (1974) are variations on Fowles's previous themes and narrative methods, and focus on failed attempts at self-discovery. They also imitate and expand on elements contained in Marie de France's twelfth-century romance *Eliduc,* a translation of which is included in the book. *Daniel Martin* (1977), which Fowles has described as "emotionally autobiographical," is a long, discursive work about a man's search for himself. In this novel, in which the protagonist appears to be its author and reader, events from different time periods intertwine as Daniel relates them from multiple perspectives in order to see himself objectively. Although some critics have regarded *Daniel Martin* as an attempt by Fowles to achieve a more realistic style, others have viewed the characters in the novel as symbols of the relationship between individuals and generations. Described as an allegory of the creative process, *Mantissa* (1982) combines such diverse topics as sex and literary theory in an examination of the writer's role in modern literature. A sexual scenario between an author named Miles Green and his psychiatrist becomes a literary debate between a writer and Erato, the Greek muse of poetry. Set in eighteenth-century England, *A Maggot* (1985) consists of court transcripts of an inquiry into the disappearance of an unnamed nobleman and facsimile excerpts from the "Historical Chronicle," a column appearing in the eighteenth-century journal *Gentleman's Magazine.* Rebecca Hocknell, an unreliable narrator who has presented at least two contradictory accounts of the lord's disappearance, is the key witness at the proceedings and the future mother of Ann Lee, the founder of the Shaker movement. In her responses to barrister Henry Ayscough, Rebecca tells a fantastic tale about an otherworldly spaceship or "maggot." While the science-fiction aspects of the novel are a departure from Fowles's previous works, *A Maggot* embodies one of his characteristic themes: a concern with freedom from social conventions.

Critical Reception

Critical reaction to Fowles's work has centered on his treatment of historical and existential themes and his narrative methods. Scholars have noted, for instance, that in both *The French Lieutenant's Woman* and *A Maggot,* Fowles assumes a modern authorial consciousness, presenting history as incomplete and thoroughly connected with the present. Commentators have looked to such devices as the godgame and recurring traits ascribed to his characters to thematically link Fowles's works. They note that his characters frequently live outside the conventional moral boundaries of society and typically reach crucial turning points requiring a reevaluation of self. The women are intelligent and independent, while the men are usually uncertain and isolated, in search of answers to the enigmatic situations in which they are enmeshed. In most cases, however, they do not find simple solutions; rather, their quests for answers result in additional mystification. Critics argue that Fowles's concern with mystery and ambiguity, which is particularly evident in his reluctance to provide authoritative resolutions to many of his works, prompts active audience participation in the quest for answers and emphasizes that reality is illusory and alterable. Describing Fowles as a literary explorer, Ellen Pifer has commented: "Fowles has investigated a wide range of styles, techniques, and approaches to writing. . . . He has affirmed the resources of language and at the same time delineated the strictures inherent in representing reality within literature and art. By acknowledging these limitations, yet continuing to struggle against them, Fowles has indeed proved himself a dynamic rather than a static artist."

PRINCIPAL WORKS

The Collector (novel) 1963
The Aristos: A Self-Portrait in Ideas (nonfiction) 1964; revised edition, 1968
The Collector [with Stanley Mann and John Kohn] (screenplay) 1965
The Magus (novel) 1965; revised edition, 1977
The Magus (screenplay) 1968
The French Lieutenant's Woman (novel) 1969
Poems (poetry) 1973
The Ebony Tower (novella and short stories) 1974
Shipwreck (nonfiction) 1974
Daniel Martin (novel) 1977
Islands (nonfiction) 1978
The Tree (nonfiction) 1979
The Enigma of Stonehenge (nonfiction) 1980
Mantissa (novel) 1982
A Short History of Lyme Regis (history) 1982
A Maggot (novel) 1985
Lyme Regis Camera (nonfiction) 1990

CRITICISM

Frank G. Novak, Jr. (essay date Spring 1985)

SOURCE: "The Dialectics of Debasement in *The*

Magus," in *Modern Fiction Studies,* Vol. 31, No. 1, Spring, 1985, pp. 71-82.

[*In the following essay, Novak analyzes the "disturbing" aspects of* The Magus *and the novel's cultural significance.*]

Commentators and readers alike have praised *The Magus* as a fascinating and powerful novel of great audacity, richness, and intellectual depth. I am sure that many, like myself, have also found it to be an eminently teachable work that rarely fails to intrigue and to challenge those who study it. Yet *The Magus* profoundly disturbs many college students; it often affects these young readers in unexpected and unsettling ways. Although praising the novel as a compelling and absorbing work, students frequently express an uneasy concern about various problems: the meaning of Nicholas Urfe's bizarre experience, the extent to which he learns and changes, the unresolved ending, the motives and morality of those who conduct the godgame. One detects a sense of desperate urgency as these readers struggle to address such problems and to solve the book's mysteries. At the same time, surprisingly, students resist Fowles's assertion that the individual reader has the right as well as the obligation to decipher the events narrated. They typically view his advice on interpreting *The Magus* as an evasion, a "cop-out": "Its meaning is whatever reaction it provokes in the reader, and so far as I am concerned there is no given 'right' reaction." Although readily accepting this sort of interpretative principle when studying other literary works, many students, perhaps unaccustomed to experiencing agitation and anxiety as a consequence of reading a literary work, insistently demand an explanation of the book's meaning, a denunciation of the ethics of the godgame, or a scenario of what will transpire after Nicholas and Alison are reunited at the end of the novel.

Rather than advancing what Fowles terms a "right" interpretation, the purpose of this essay is to account for the confusion, uneasiness, and—not infrequently—genuine terror *The Magus* is likely to evoke in the reader, especially the college student. Although the book is a complex, multilayered work possessing many themes and capable of sustaining numerous interpretations, the elements responsible for this troubling effect compose a particularly important dimension of the novel—an import perhaps not immediately apparent or specifically intended by Fowles. This dimension endows *The Magus* with relevance and significance as a work of cultural criticism, for the novel serves as a troubling and, I think, profound commentary on contemporary man and civilization.

Several aspects of the novel contribute to the work's unsettling effect; these include the episodes of perverse and wanton cruelty, the apparent amorality of those who conduct the godgame, the unresolved ambiguities and unexplained mysteries. Yet the distressing, haunting impact of *The Magus* resides in a pervasive logic more fundamental and insidious than these individual scenes and problematic elements: the novel develops a dialectic of debasement whose final synthesis asserts a view of life that is both empty and terrifying. The view the book propounds is a compound of nihilism and narcissism; it is the response of impotent, insignificant man attempting to cope with immense, threatening, and often mysterious forces he can neither understand nor control. As a microcosm of a world beset by these vast forces of negation, the godgame advances the nihilistic doctrine that there is no meaning. Conchis' premise that "an answer is always a form of death" and the assumption of Wimmel and his fellow Nazis that "nothing is true, everything is permitted" are versions of this "meaningless meaning" that resonates throughout the book. In an attempt to protect his ego against this dehumanizing and terrifying nihilism, Nicholas responds to the godgame in a defensive if not logical way: he adopts a self-absorbed and self-directed narcissism. These nihilistic and narcissistic themes are major elements of a pervasive logic of despair that is part of the work's general cultural significance.

This pervasive logic, the dimension of the novel responsible for its unsettling impact, is composed of three major elements. First of all, Conchis' protean guises, especially his function as a god figure, contribute to the confusion and perturbation both Nicholas and the reader experience. In whatever role Conchis assumes—physician, teacher, or divinity—his manipulative, deceptive actions travesty the usual function, for he confuses and demeans Nicholas rather than helping or educating him. A second component of the novel's pervasive logic consists of the selfish, even malign motives of Conchis and the others who stage the godgame. Their willful disregard for traditional moral standards or conventional notions of propriety contributes significantly to the book's disquieting character. Lacking constructive educational value or moral purpose, the godgame promotes a nihilistic "antitheology" of degradation, terror, and chaos. Finally, Nicholas Urfe's personality and his response to the godgame comprise the most significant component of the book's general dialectical pattern. As described in the devastating psychological analysis presented at the trial, Nicholas is selfish, alienated, socially and spiritually "sterile." His failure to respond creatively to the godgame—his inability to learn, to change, to wrest any meaning from the experience—is a fundamental aspect of the novel's overall logic of despair. He becomes the prototypical "antihero" who experiences a desperate masochistic pleasure in his role as "victim." Much of the work's power and relevance lies in the extent to which Nicholas embodies a cultural type, a personality representative of contemporary man. These three aspects combine to produce a dialectic of debasement that accounts for both the novel's disturbing, haunting impact on many readers and its general cultural significance.

Assuming a variety of roles and personae throughout the novel, Conchis never discloses his true identity. Nor does he reveal the intent of the godgame. In fact, one of the best clues to the purpose of the godgame appears not in the novel itself but in Fowles's Foreword to the revised version of the text. Here Fowles states that he occasionally regrets rejecting *The Godgame* as the book's title because he intends Conchis "to exhibit a series of masks representing human notions of God . . . that is, a series of human illusions." There is a sense in which each of the various roles Conchis plays, each of the several guises he assumes, embodies a different conception or facet of God—or, at least, a general notion of divine power and purpose. He often functions as the omnipotent divinity whose mysterious ways and supernatural powers control and enthrall Nicholas. Like Prospero in *The Tempest,* to which the novel several times alludes, Conchis seems to control the spirits of the air as well as the demons of the underworld on his enchanted island. He also plays the artist-producer who employs and directs the strange masque enacted on Phraxos. Other times, he assumes the role of a psychiatrist-god who patronizingly endures the whims of the "deranged" Julie and encourages Nicholas to confess his own neuroses. Although Nicholas soon discounts his initial impression that Conchis is merely a voyeur seeking gratification by clandestinely observing him and Julie (and sometimes June) together, he is never free of the suspicion that Conchis is always near, constantly observing. Although he never discloses his identity or purpose, Conchis most consistently functions as a sadistic god who enjoys watching his victim struggle in the bizarre, often degrading situations he creates for him. Baffled by Conchis' protean and often capricious roles, Nicholas speculates that "perhaps he saw himself as a professor in an impossible faculty of ambiguity, a sort of Empson of the event." In spite of his confusion, Nicholas finds himself enchanted by Conchis and the godgame, but neither Nicholas nor the reader ever discovers Conchis' identity or purpose.

Compounding the confusion created by Conchis' various guises and his refusal to explain his purposes are the arrogance and willfulness with which he and the others conduct the game. There is little evidence that their motives and values are higher than those of unprincipled sadists who wantonly torture and humiliate Nicholas. Although the novel may imply from time to time that Conchis' motive consists of a disinterested concern for Nicholas' therapeutic reeducation, an irresponsible compulsion to debase and to destroy appears to be the dominant impulse shaping the events of the godgame. Attempting to place Nicholas in the same sort of dilemma he faced during the German occupation of Phraxos, Conchis assumes the role and character of Wimmel so completely that he undermines whatever beneficial purposes the godgame might otherwise possess. Although the stakes of the godgame are obviously not so high as those in occupied Phraxos, the experience of deception and torment that Nicholas endures at Conchis' hands exceeds the limits of basic decency; it becomes disturbingly similar to the excruciating ordeal of psychological terror to which Wimmel had subjected Conchis ten years earlier. Moreover, Wimmel and Conchis use essentially the same rationale to justify the methods of both situations. Wimmel had excused the hideous torture and wanton murder perpetrated during his reign of terror on the basis of "one supreme purpose . . . the German historical purpose." Madame de Seitas uses an identical self-exonerating logic of inevitability to justify the extremes of the godgame: "All that we did was to us a necessity." Conchis argues that the Nazis were successful because "they imposed chaos on order"; the effect of the godgame is similar in that it obliterates what little order had existed in Nicholas' life and substitutes chaos—the confusion of unanswered questions and ambiguous purposes. As he is forced to watch Lily and Joe make love during the final phase of his "disintoxication," Nicholas realizes that the axiom underlying the actions of Wimmel

and his fellow Nazis also serves as the only "principle" behind the godgame: "Nothing is true, everything is permitted." The references to de Sade and Nazism throughout the novel echo and reinforce the motiveless malignity of the "meta-theatre."

Perhaps the most insidious aspect of their motives and rationale is the fact that Conchis and the others do not consider themselves obligated to justify or to explain the meaning of what they do to Nicholas. The only justification they offer is that they act according to a different and higher moral standard than that assumed by "ordinary" humans. Madame de Seitas tells Nicholas that "we" are "more moral" and excuses their actions by saying "we are rich and we are intelligent and we mean to live rich, intelligent lives." When Nicholas asks her to explain what they have been attempting to accomplish in the godgame, he receives the same sort of evasive response Conchis had given him some time earlier: "An answer is always a form of death." This reply not only absolves Conchis of any moral responsibility but also compounds the confusion in Nicholas' life. The cruelties of the godgame make one skeptical of Conchis' "higher" moral standards, which, apparently, can be twisted to permit almost any extreme providing selfish or sadistic amusement. Whatever benefits and meaning Nicholas may derive from the godgame, therefore, the motives of Conchis and the others are fundamentally selfish; and they acknowledge few if any strictures on the extent of deception or the type of abuse to which they subject him. This philosophy of negation coupled with a totally egocentric view can vindicate any number of aberrant responses to life: from the "historically mandated" promulgation of terror, sadism, and murder endorsed by Wimmel and his fellow Nazis, on the one hand, to the impotent though no less nihilistic alienation and narcissism of Nicholas, on the other.

Therefore, although in various roles and guises Conchis may embody different versions of divine power and purpose, he is ultimately a figure who represents the opposite, even the absence of God. He does not advance any meaningful, transcendent truths or values; rather, "hazard" (chance) and chaos lie at the heart of his "theology." During the early stages of the godgame, Conchis states a principle that quite accurately describes all that he does to Nicholas: "There is no plan. All is hazard. And the only thing that will preserve us is ourselves." And he later tells Nicholas that man "needs the existence of mysteries. Not their solution." Assuming that religion exists to give life purpose, meaning, and value—to provide what Paul Tillich calls the "dimension of depth"—Conchis' function as a god-figure is a curious one indeed. Conchis' notion of what it means to become "elect" is also unconventional; his definition seems identical to that of Henrik Nygaard for whom "elect" means "especially chosen to be punished and tormented." Upon being informed at the end of the "disintoxication" that he is "now elect," Nicholas is baffled; he is "elect" only insofar as he recognizes Conchis' irony and ruthlessness. In the Christian scheme, the mysterious ways of God, even though they may require the individual to suffer, eventually result in understanding, faith, and ultimately salvation. Yet the godgame fulfills no discernible purpose beyond debasing and confusing Nicholas and providing a perverse sort of gratification for Conchis and his associates. Conchis' role and motives, therefore, advance an "antitheology" consisting of humiliation, ambivalence, and chaos. As the only "god" Nicholas ever knows, Conchis assumes many guises but provides no answers; he is a god as "magus" who creates an illusory world but who deceives and ultimately absconds, leaving his victims in the abyss of chaos.

The view *The Magus* propounds is a compound of nihilism and narcissism; it is the response of impotent, insignificant man attempting to cope with immense, threatening, and often mysterious forces he can neither understand nor control.

—*Frank G. Novak, Jr.*

Whatever misshapen purposes and twisted values motivate Conchis, Nicholas clearly has the opportunity to forge some meaning from his baffling and often degrading experience—just as the previous English master of the Lord Byron School, John Leverrier, apparently acquired something of value as a result of his involvement in an earlier godgame. Unlike Leverrier, however, Nicholas does not possess the intelligence, creativity, or character to derive any enduring lessons from the experience. He never recognizes that life can be more than a mysterious and ambiguous theatrical game. The godgame itself is a patently staged illusion; after perceiving the emptiness of this illusion, the "victims" must create for themselves whatever meaning the strange masque may possess without "divine" assistance. But for Nicholas, order, purpose, and meaning are illusions; selfhood and freedom are mere dreams. Beyond his own dark purposes, Conchis may have been attempting to teach him a lesson in self-awareness, the importance of maintaining larger perspectives beyond the self, or the difference between reality and illusion. Yet Nicholas learns none of this; he is fundamentally the same person at the end of the experience that he was at the beginning: isolated, selfish, indecisive, lacking moral or spiritual commitment. Unlike Charles Smithson, the protagonist of *The French Lieutenant's Woman,* who acquires something of meaning and value from a similar ordeal of fabulation and mystery, Nicholas' essential nature remains unchanged during the course of the novel. Whereas Fowles may assert that the destruction of such illusions as those contained in the godgame is "an eminently humanist aim," Nicholas clearly fails to perceive, much less to accept, such a challenge. He maintains and even extends his illusions about himself, and Conchis' antitheology becomes his as well.

This response and, more significantly, the personality lying behind it comprise an aspect of the novel even more disturbing than the irresponsibility and cruelty of those who stage the godgame. Not only is Nicholas incapable of forming any enduring values, but he is also superficial, aimless, and thoroughly narcissistic. Although these personal inadequacies are apparent throughout the novel, the devastating psychoanalytic portrait presented during the trial depicts his essential self more vividly and acutely than any other scene. In spite of the contrived situation and the Freudian jargon, this analysis provides the key to understanding Nicholas' personality as well as the novel's unsettling effect on many readers. The analysis describes Nicholas' life as one lacking "social content"; he allegedly exhibits "fear and resentment . . . revenge and counter-betrayal" in his relationships with others; he is said to exploit women with a "semi-incestuous ruthlessness." He is the failed artist who assumes an alienated and cynical demeanor in order to arouse the interest and sympathy of women; he is the existential poseur who fabricates a mask of ennui and isolation to conceal his personal inadequacies and failure to establish meaningful human relationships. Nicholas is described as being sterile and impotent insofar as his life lacks purpose and commitment. Particularly devastating is "Doctor Maxwell's" deterministic analysis of Nicholas' personality deficiencies, which, she says, deserve pity rather than condemnation; as a person who lacks purpose and vision, his "self-pity is projected so strongly on his environment that one becomes contaminated by it."

Given Nicholas' responses throughout the novel, one can only conclude that this analysis is an accurate one. [In a footnote, Novak adds: "Nicholas' personality is, of course, indicated in many other ways and places beyond the trial analysis. The images of imprisonment, entombment, and estrangement, for example, emphasize his alienation, helplessness, and paranoia. His 'favourite metaphor' for his life is 'the cage of glass' he imagines as existing between him and the rest of the world—yet Alison, with her instinctive perspicuity, observes that he likes such isolation because it gives him the illusion that he is different. Nicholas similarly describes the symbolic *'gabbia'* he had constructed 'out of light, solitude, and self-delusions' during his first months on Phraxos. There are also several individual scenes that convey the image and idea of isolation and helpless entrapment; these include the scene in which he regains consciousness immediately before the trial."] Nicholas is an apt "victim," indeed almost a clone specifically engineered to be the subject of Conchis' machinations. He is easily deceived, manipulated, and tyrannized; thoroughly egocentric, he lacks the moral standards and meaningful commitments that would give his life strength and purpose. He is the pseudo-intellectual, the failed poet whose studied pose of alienation and cynicism can neither hide nor mitigate the emptiness, purposelessness, and spiritual sterility that compose his true self. Nicholas fails to respond constructively to the godgame: he does not change significantly, nor does he acquire any enduring values. He can neither understand nor extricate himself from the complex predicament that threatens him. The godgame is meaningful to Nicholas only because he becomes the center of the artificial world it creates. He participates in it and becomes obsessed by it because the experience promotes the illusion that he is significant, that events occur and other people exist merely for his amusement and benefit. Nicholas, in short, not only assumes but also embodies Conchis' nihilistic antitheology.

Much of the novel's relevance and power lies in the extent to which this psychological portrait of Nicholas is also an accurate description of contemporary man; moreover, the symbolic relevance of Nicholas Urfe as cultural type, as a representative character, accounts for the disquieting impact of *The Magus* on many readers. According to the analysis presented at the trial, Nicholas is not a unique personality; his is "the characteristic personality type" of modern man. The analysts compare Nicholas with the representative personality described in Conchis' purported work *The Mid-century Predicament:* "the rebel with no specific gift for rebellion" who in society becomes a "sterile drone." Alienated and ineffectual in a world whose complexities and dangers are beyond his understanding or control, he is typical of the many who "adopt a mask of cynicism that cannot hide their more or less paranoic sense of having been betrayed by life." Thus the novel presents Nicholas as a representative modern man who fails to respond meaningfully to the challenges, the complexities, and the opportunities life holds.

During the trial, a "Professor Ciardi" argues that Nicholas represents the sort of personality that will become the norm in a world in which men must live under the constant "threat of a nuclear catastrophe." This is, I think, an important and suggestive identification. Like modern man grappling with the menace of nuclear extermination, Nicholas is confused and impotent. His response consists of a self-consuming narcissism and a morbid nihilism. The godgame projects, in miniature, the same sort of predicament that, on a much larger scale, confronts contemporary man; it reflects the ambiguity, chaos, and insensate violence pervading modern life. Nicholas is, in this regard, the "modern Everyman," the impotent clone, the "antihero" of the age. As the Everyman of the nuclear era, Nicholas evinces the pathological symptoms of the psychological and spiritual malaise that infects mankind. His solipsistic nihilism, the analysts argue, is the typical response of the middle-class person possessing an average intellect and living under the constant threat of nuclear obliteration. The anxiety that the book produces in so many readers, particularly college students, attests to the devastating accuracy of the description of Nicholas Urfe as the prototypical nuclear age personality.

The nihilistic and sadistic themes of the novel and the depiction of Nicholas as a nuclear age Everyman concur with the analysis developed by various eminent critics of contemporary culture. Erich Fromm's description [in his *The Heart of Man: Its Genius for Good and Evil,* 1971] of the narcissism that infects contemporary man, for example, closely parallels the character of Nicholas Urfe— particularly as he exploits others while assuming a self-protective mask of existential alienation. Fromm describes the fundamental narcissism of modern man as an "incestuous . . . craving to be freed from the risks of responsibility, of freedom, of awareness" and a "longing for unconditional love, which is offered without any expectation of loving response." Nicholas possesses a personality like that of those, as described by Fromm, "whose whole sense of self-worth is bound up with the relationship to the women who admire them unconditionally and without limits" and who become the type of " 'traitor' who cannot

be loyal to anybody." Throughout the novel, Nicholas exhibits both the "malignant narcissism" and the "symbiotic-incestuous fixation" Fromm sees as two basic components of the "syndrome of decay" pervading modern life. Nicholas describes how he uses his alienation as a "deadly weapon," making a show of unpredictability, cynicism, and indifference in order to seduce women; he even admits a "narcissistic belief in the importance of the life-style." The novel reveals the pathetic dimensions of such narcissism, as when Nicholas masturbates while lying on the beach, and also indicates its insidious elements, as embodied in the figure of de Deukans, who symbolizes the evil of solitary pleasure. In one of the novel's most intense scenes, Alison accurately identifies Nicholas' empty narcissism: "you're a filthy selfish bastard who can't, can't like being impotent, can't *ever* think of anything except number one. . . . You've built your life so nothing can ever reach you." This indictment, of course, adumbrates the later analysis that describes him as the sterile "drone" who assumes a mask of cynicism to conceal and to protect his self-obsessed ego.

Lewis Mumford is another cultural critic whose concerns and warnings are echoed in *The Magus.* Mumford has written extensively about the fate of man and the deterioration of culture in a world of complex, autonomous forces that dehumanize and threaten to annihilate the individual. The godgame and Nicholas' response to it are generally similar to what Mumford has described [in his *The Pentagon of Power,* 1970] as "the cult of anti-life." Mumford argues that "disillusion, cynicism, and existential nihilism" comprise the prevailing philosophy of contemporary life and art. Finding himself "at the mercy of forces over which he exercises no effective control, moving to a destination he has not chosen," modern man has adopted a negative philosophy of despair in response to the dangers posed by "his favored technological and institutional automatisms." Beginning as a reaction against the insidious and vastly powerful "pentagons of power" that threaten to destroy humanity, the cult of antilife has evolved into "an attack against civilization itself," against "all organized structures, all objective criteria, all rational direction." Beyond these general parallels, Mumford's description of the "symptoms of regression" bear an uncanny similarity to certain aspects of *The Magus.* Compare Conchis' antitheology with Mumford's evaluation of contemporary (lack of) faith: "Chance has become the ruling deity and chaos the new Heaven." As indicated earlier, Conchis and the others recognize no humane or moral constraint as they prosecute the godgame; similarly, citing the heroes of this cult of human degradation whose number includes the Marquis de Sade, Mumford says that "there is no limit to the forces of anti-life."

Throughout the novel Nicholas remains what his analysts term *"homo solitarius";* he leads a lonely existence suffused with ennui and impotent aimlessness. As the personality "norm" of the nuclear age, he finds identity and purpose only in narcissistic self-indulgence and self-delusion. Although he is tortured and confused by the machinations of the godgame, the experience does provide the opportunity for Nicholas to extend the fundamental fantasy that sustains him: he plays the leading role in a drama staged for his personal benefit, and he perversely enjoys the sadistic torment to which he is subjected. The ordeal verifies his identity and significance; it also confirms his egocentric, thoroughly selfish way of life. Even after the godgame has officially ended, Nicholas refuses to relinquish the patently contrived illusion. When given the opportunity to make a meaningful human commitment—to love Alison unconditionally and, thereby, to transcend himself—he is more concerned to know whether or not he is still the "victim." He remains enmeshed in his narcissistic solipsism. Is Conchis watching when Nicholas is reunited with Alison? Nicholas wants to believe he is; he wants to maintain the illusion that his selfish, purposeless life possesses the aura of mystery.

Herein lie the sources of the novel's troubling significance and haunting effect. The anxiety and terror *The Magus* may provoke reside in this subtle yet powerful thematic dialectic involving the role of Conchis, the way in which the godgame is conducted, and the personality and response of Nicholas. The godgame represents in microcosm a terrifying world man can neither control nor understand; the amoral, nihilistic qualities of the godgame are an expression of what Mumford has called the cult of antilife so pervasive in contemporary thought and art. The novel's unsettling effect also resides in the extent to which one recognizes, perhaps unconsciously, Nicholas Urfe as a contemporary Everyman. These aspects of the book strike a nerve of reality: the godgame symbolizes the contemporary predicament, and Nicholas Urfe typifies the personality of nuclear age man. Not incidentally do some of the novel's most vivid and memorable scenes contain graphic depictions of the worst sort of horrors the twentieth century has witnessed: the nightmare madness and bestiality of World War One trench warfare; the sadistic torture, barbaric mutilation, and wholesale human extermination perpetrated by the Nazis. Although the book does not describe the ultimate horror of nuclear holocaust, that lurking threat is indicated by the screaming jet fighter that shatters the idyllic placidity of Phraxos and the ominous fleet of warships that pass nearby—"cloud-grey shapes on the world's blue rim. Death machines holding thousands of gum-chewing, contraceptive-carrying men." The sight causes Nicholas to recognize "the fragility . . . of time itself."

The godgame and Nicholas' reaction to it, therefore, mirror contemporary man's response to the immense and inimical forces that threaten to obliterate him. The novel presents several options by means of which one may desperately attempt to assert the self in the face of such terrors: to assume a mask of alienation and cynicism that both conceals and protects the ego; to participate in insensate rituals of sexual gratification or sadistic amusement; to withdraw into narcissistic fantasies of self-importance and self-indulgence. Living in a world haunted by the specter of nuclear annihilation, contemporary man may feel as if he is caught in a complex web of forces he can neither control nor comprehend; he may find himself attempting to cope with what seems an inexorable dialectic of debasement, a sort of cosmic "godgame"—with, perhaps, a vicious Conchis "at web-center." Consequently, he may seek identity through a self-indulgent narcissism, and

he may choose nihilism as the only "logical" doctrine of last resort. Incapable of taking action against the vast forces that threaten him and finding his life empty and impotent, modern man may in desperation accept the axiom of Wimmel that underlies the godgame: "nothing is true, everything is permitted." Like Nicholas and Alison at the end of the novel, mankind precariously stands "trembling, searching, between all our past and all our future." Today's college students must feel intimidated and thwarted by the terrifying question, as posed by William Faulkner [in *Essays, Speeches, and Public Letters by William Faulkner,* 1965], "When will I be blown up?" Consequently, they may have lost or ignored something of their essential humanity—"the old verities and truths of the heart." Nicholas, of course, lacks and fails to discover such truths and values; and reading *The Magus,* I believe, makes students acutely and often painfully aware of this loss. For the novel is, to cite Faulkner again, "not of love but of lust, of defeats in which nobody loses anything of value, of victories without hope and, worst of all, without pity or compassion."

However, as indicated above, Nicholas does have the opportunity to change for the better, to derive something meaningful and beneficial from the godgame. The novel suggests another option by means of which one may assert the self and conduct one's life. Aside from the objectivity with which Nicholas retrospectively describes himself and his experience, the reader has no evidence that Nicholas ever discovers this option; the novel presents it by implication rather than description. This option involves a self-transcendence and the establishment of a meaningful social identity—both of which Nicholas lacks. It also involves discovering effective means of combating the vast forces of antilife that threaten to destroy the individual, culture, civilization itself. Recognizing something of the challenge and urgency of the problem, one approaches it with courage and resourcefulness rather than with terror, dread, or cynical despair; one seeks enduring values and creative activity rather than retreating into nihilism and narcissism. In this spirit, the reader may choose to view the godgame as the commencement of an "emancipation": "a restoration of the human world and of human relation-

---

Anthony Burgess on Fowles's view of history:

Fowles's view of our view of the past—and he states it unequivocally [in *A Maggot*]—is that we get things wrong because we get them from literary geniuses, who are untypical of their age. If we want the eighteenth century, we'd better not go to Pope, Addison and Johnson, who transcend the period that produced them. We'll taste its bitter otherness best by entering the narrow legal mind of Henry Ayscough, whose enquiry into certain strange events of the year 1736 makes up the bulk of the book.

Anthony Burgess, in his "Re-opening a Can of Worms," in The Observer, *22 September 1985.*

ships to man himself." Only through such an emancipation and restoration can man vanquish those terrors that the contemporary world poses and the novel reflects.

Bruce Bawer   (essay date April 1987)

SOURCE: "John Fowles and His Big Ideas," in *The New Criterion*, Vol. V, No. 8, April, 1987, pp. 21-36.

[*In the following excerpt, Bawer comments on the philosophical ideas presented in* The Aristos.]

The Aristos, originally subtitled "A Self-Portrait in Ideas," consists of several hundred related axioms which are organized into eleven chapters with titles like "The Universal Situation," "The Tensional Nature of Human Reality," and "The Importance of Art." The axioms, some of which consist of a single sentence and only one of which occupies so much as an entire page, are numbered chapter by chapter, like verses of the Bible. The book is nothing less than Fowles's answer to Plato's *Republic*—it represents his notion of what ideas on life, death, art, religion, politics, science, economics, education, and sex should govern a world run by superior men and women. And indeed his primary concern is with the superior individual, the *aristos.* The word is borrowed from Heraclitus, who, Fowles reminds us, "saw mankind divided into a moral and intellectual *élite* (the *aristoi,* the good ones, *not*—this is a later sense—the ones of noble birth) and an unthinking conforming mass—*hoi polloi,* the many." Fowles notes that Heraclitus has been condemned as "the grandfather of modern totalitarianism," but insists that

> in every field of human endeavour it is obvious that most of the achievements, most of the great steps forward, have come from individuals— whether they be scientific or artistic geniuses, saints, revolutionaries, what you will. And we do not need the evidence of intelligence testing to know conversely that the vast mass of mankind are not highly intelligent—or highly moral, or highly gifted artistically, or indeed highly qualified to carry out any of the nobler human activities.

Fowles thus divides mankind into two groups, the Few and the Many. Nonetheless he declares himself to be a socialist: "All my adult life I have believed that the only rational political doctrine one can hold is democratic socialism." His way of reconciling these two disparate views is to say that "*the dividing line between the Few and the Many must run through each individual, not between individuals.* In short, none of us are wholly perfect; and none wholly imperfect." Or, as he puts it at the end of the book, "We are all sometimes of the Many." If this is true, however, then why posit a "Few" and a "Many" in the first place?

Fowles sees life in terms of process: to him, everything is ultimately unknowable, indefinite, mysterious. But, though we will never reach perfection of any kind, we can nonetheless strive for it ("We build towards nothing; we build"—1.33). And it is this endless striving that makes life worth living. "Our universe is the best possible because it can contain no Promised Land; no point where we could

have all we imagine. We are designed to want: with nothing to want, we are like windmills in a world without wind" (1.34). What human beings need most of all in such a universe—and what David Williams so tragically lacks in *The Ebony Tower*—is freedom of will. It is "the highest human good" (1.64); to be true *aristoi,* men and women must overcome the "asphyxiating smog of opinions foisted on them by society," which forces ordinary people to "lose all independence of judgement, and all freedom of action" and to "see themselves increasingly . . . as parts of a machine" (3.29). We must, in short, commit existential acts—existentialism signifying, by his definition, "the revolt of the individual against all those systems of thought, theories of psychology, and social and political pressures that attempt to rob him of his individuality" (7.74). Fowles is not inciting mass revolution, though, for "existentialism is conspicuously unsuited to political or social subversion, since it is incapable of organized dogmatic resistance or formulations of resistance. It is capable only of one man's resistance; one personal expression of view; such as this book" (7.79). Fowles insists, moreover, on the importance of moral judgment, proclaiming that "[o]ur function is to judge, to choose between good and evil. If we refuse to do so, we cease to be human beings and revert to our basic state, of being matter" (5.45). As for risks, we need to take them in order to improve our lives and ourselves. "The purpose of hazard is to force us, and the rest of matter, to evolve" (2.61). . . .

[The] sort of freedom that usually figures most prominently in Fowles's fiction is sexual freedom. Fowles has a good deal to say about this subject in *The Aristos.* He speaks of the twentieth-century emergence of sex "from behind the curtains and crinolines of Victorian modesty and propriety" (9.97) and finds it necessary to say that "[s]exual attraction and the sexual act are in themselves innocent, neither intrinsically moral nor immoral. Sex is like all great forces: simply a force" (9.105). One has the feeling, after reading through Fowles's oeuvre, that his obsession with freedom has a great deal to do with his complicated feelings about sex; he often seems to be taking on an enemy—namely, the stifling sexual morality of the Victorian period—that no longer exists. Indeed, he has made reference, in several of his novels, to the Victorian notions of morality with which people of his generation were raised. "My contemporaries," notes the Fowles-like narrator of *Daniel Martin,* "were all brought up in some degree of the nineteenth century, since the twentieth did not begin till 1945."

A concept that is of central importance to Fowles is that of the "nemo," which Fowles defines as "a man's sense of his own futility and ephemerality; of his relativity, his comparativeness; of his virtual nothingness" (3.7). Fowles says that it is art, above all else, that "best conquers time, and therefore the nemo"; an art object is "as nearly immortal as an object in a cosmos without immortality can be." Fowles devotes much of his chapter on art to a description of the situation of the modern artist—a situation that, for all his criticism of Victorian vis-à-vis modern culture, he is not at all happy with. He deplores, for instance, "the tyranny of self-expression" (10.35); the narrowing of the artist's audience to "a literate few" (10.51); and the pressure on the artist to present "a mirror to the world around him" (10.36). He is disturbed by the rise of a type of intellectual that is interested mainly in "colour, shape, texture, pattern, setting, movement," rather than in "the properly intellectual (moral and socio-political) significance of events and objects"—more interested, in short, in style than in content, which to him is the single most woeful symptom of the modern temperament.

What *The Aristos* essentially amounts to, then, is a collection of opinions, some of which one agrees with, some of which one doesn't; there is much in it that is intelligent and thought-provoking, and much that is silly and wrongheaded. Fowles is often guilty of sentimental overgeneralization; in distinguishing between the craftsman and the genius, he says that the former "is very concerned with his contemporary success, his market value," while the latter "is indifferent to contemporary success." And Fowles can be unintentionally amusing when he is pretending to be objective about things that are close to him. For example, having decided that mankind should have a universal language, he arrives, by way of an elaborate and (he thinks) purely logical argument, at the conclusion that the language of choice should be—guess what?—English. Likewise, this man who chooses to identify himself at the beginning of the book as "a poet first; and then a scientist," determines—by means of an equally sophisticated and objective bit of dialectic—that "the great arts" are not equal, and that "[l]iterature, in particular poetry," is of all the arts "the most essential and the most valuable."

Despite such weaknesses, however, one cannot help but admire Fowles for his intellectual seriousness, his acute sense of the artist's dignity as well as of his moral and social responsibility, and his attempt to express and to codify his way of seeing the world. It is rare and admirable for a contemporary British or American novelist to be as intensely and seriously concerned as John Fowles is with the relations between art and ideas, art and morality. But *The Aristos* is chiefly of interest not as a work of philosophy but as a *catalogue raisonné*, as it were, of many of the thematic preoccupations of Fowles's fiction.

I have often said I have only written about one woman in my life. I mean, I feel that. I do not put it in the novels but I feel when writing that the heroine of one novel is the same woman as the heroine of another novel. They may be different enough in outward characteristic but they are for me a family—just one woman, basically.

—John Fowles, in an interview with Susana Onega, in her Form and Meaning in the Novels of John Fowles, *UMI Research Press, 1989.*

Magali Cornier Michael   (essay date Summer 1987)

SOURCE: " 'Who is Sarah?': A Critique of *The French Lieutenant's Woman*'s Feminism," in *Critique: Studies in Modern Fiction*, Vol. XXVIII, No. 4, Summer, 1987, pp. 225-36.

[*In the essay below, Michael discusses Fowles's portrayal of Sarah Woodruff and the theme of feminism in* The French Lieutenant's Woman, *concluding that the work "falls short of being a feminist novel."*]

The figure of Sarah Woodruff in John Fowles' *The French Lieutenant's Woman* has elicited a multiplicity of interpretations: Sarah has been described as feminist, symbol (especially of woman and of freedom), mythic figure, *femme fatale,* and various combinations of these. The most overt conflict among these interpretations is due to the difference in perspective between the critics who view the book as a feminist novel and those who make no such claims. The issue is more complex than this simple opposition suggests, however; and I see the critics of both camps as being partially correct. I attribute the many interpretations of Sarah and the partial validity of all of them to the fact that, although she has a speaking role and is thus a participant within the plot, she remains ambiguous. Sarah is the central figure rather than its protagonist. I see this ambiguity as stemming from the absence of Sarah's point of view, which is symptomatic of what I take to be the novel's internal contradiction: it wants to assert the theme of feminism and yet fails as a feminist novel.

Sarah is represented through a triple layering of voices which includes Charles', the male narrator', and Fowles' voices. Not only do Sarah's thoughts remain outside of the realm of the novel, but the perspective offered of Sarah is purely masculine. The novel's failure to realize Sarah as a character and human being in her own right, whether done intentionally or not, is due in part to its exclusive use of male views. The ideological nature of any perspective is undeniable and in this case the male perspective, which has been and still is dominant in western culture, brings to the novel all sorts of preconceptions and myths about women. Fowles seems to be aware of the limitations of male views about women since he brings these issues to the foreground, and yet his choice of narrative technique counters that impulse of masculine critique.

It could be argued that, by describing Sarah purely from an external position, the novel is presenting an honest view of male perspectives of women and not falling into the trap of projecting male thinking into Sarah's mind. My objection, however, is that Fowles is not explicit enough and thus relies too heavily upon the reader. He seems to assume that the reader will be able to see that the novel is depicting the imposition of male perspectives onto the portrait of Sarah. I have no great illusions, however, as to the capacity of most readers to step outside of their own masculine perspectives; and this includes female as well as male readers, since both are socialized within a patriarchal world. Fowles is not totally to blame, however, since he is himself a product of that same male-dominated culture. Because Sarah remains an ambiguous figure to the end of the novel and because Fowles does not make evident his critique of male ideology inherent in the representation of Sarah, many readers miss the irony and view Sarah precisely in the way the narrative presents her (proof of this can be found in much of the criticism and discussion of the novel). Fowles' failure to prevent this "straight" reading or misreading of Sarah and thus of the novel may suggest, however, that Fowles himself remains caught to a certain extent within the very ideological system he challenges.

It may be useful to begin by delineating what I find to be the undeniable presence of the issue of feminism or emancipation of women in *The French Lieutenant's Woman.* One way in which the issue of feminism is pushed to the forefront of the novel is by overt references to historical figures and events having a prominent place in the emancipatory progress of women: "Mrs. Caroline Norton" as "an ardent feminist" writer, "Florence Nightingale," "John Stuart Mill" and his argument that "now was the time to give women equal rights at the ballot box," the date of "March 30th, 1867" as marking "the beginning of feminine emancipation in England," the publication of "Mill's *Subjection of Women,*" and the founding of "Girton College." This kind of emphasis cannot be ignored and in fact fully supports the notion that the novel wants to claim feminism as one of its central concerns.

There is also evidence that it is more specifically "Sarah's emancipation" that is "central to the novel" and that Fowles is working to depict Sarah as a woman who "gradually develops a feminist consciousness" [Deborah Byrd, "The Evolution and Emancipation of Sarah Woodruff: *The French Lieutenant's Woman* as a Feminist Novel," *International Journal of Women's Studies* (September-October 1984)]. The feminism, which Fowles wants to attribute to Sarah, is apparent in the words she is made to speak. Sarah proudly asserts her developing independence when she states that she has "married shame" because there was "no other way to break out of what I was" and that as a result she now has "freedom" and "No insult, no blame, can touch" her. Fowles has Sarah create her own fictions in order to emphasize Sarah's attempt to step outside of conventional patriarchal society and to define herself outside of male fictions about women. Charles not only sees in her "an independence of spirit" and "a determination to be what she was" but also observes that she transcends the conventional portrait of Victorian woman by being both "completely feminine" and full of overt "sensuality." By the end of the novel, Sarah's words—"I wish to be what I am"—and Charles' perception that she has gained a "new self-knowledge and self-possession" indicate the Fowles wishes to portray Sarah as having realized a feminist consciousness. It is evident that, although Fowles to a certain degree romanticizes Sarah's quest for a feminist consciousness by depicting her as an enigmatic and tragic figure, the novel does assert this theme of emancipation and of Sarah's development into "the New Woman." Even Charles is enlisted in support of the feminism theme when he denounces "masculine prejudice" and the "bias in society": "They are to sit, are they not, like so many articles in a shop and to let us men walk in and turn them over and point at this one or that one." Although these words and thoughts are attributed to

Charles, they seem to contain a certain "double-voicedness": I distinctly hear an authorial voice, Fowles' voice, within these pro-feminist discourses.

This notion of double-voiced discourse is delineated within [Mikhail] Bakhtin's theory of the novel and involves the notion that the author cannot remain completely outside the text. Charles' language supporting women's emancipation contains an intermingling of both Charles' and Fowles' voices and thus serves in part to express the author's intentions, although in a refracted way. Although this layering of voices occurs throughout, it is particularly evident here because throughout most of the novel Charles is portrayed as chauvinistic and unable to step outside of his masculine perspective, so that his assuming a feminist stance is immediately suspicious. Fowles also uses the narrator's assertion that Charles "began to understand" the basis of the emancipation movement to create the illusion that the language supporting feminism is Charles' own, although it seems clear that Charles remains caught within masculine ideology to the very end—Charles, for example, tells Sarah in the first of the final endings that she could remain everything that she was if she became "Mrs. Charles Smithson" without realizing that this name change is symptomatic of masculine dominance. All of this suggests that Fowles' orchestration of the text includes his attempt to give the issue of feminism a primary position and that as a result his own voice has been inserted into the narrative.

Fowles' authorial voice thus asserts itself within the text, and its importance cannot be overlooked. As orchestrator of the text, Fowles holds a degree of power and is an essential voice within the novel. When the narrator steps into the novel as a character in Chapter 13, a sharper distinction is created between author and narrator that emphasizes the layering of voices making up the text. The narrator's claim that "This story I am telling is all imagination" draws attention to the fact that ultimately the novel is a work of fiction created by Fowles, which subsumes the narrator's as well as the characters' fictions. There is thus a layering of fictions as well as of voices. The narrator's statement that, even if the notion that fictional characters possess autonomy is granted, ultimately "The novelist is still a god" foregrounds Fowles' role as orchestrator and its implications for the novel. Fowles as author is a god in the sense that, since he creates from within a certain worldview (Western, masculine, late twentieth-century), his characters can never be totally free. The reference to the "patriarchal beard" of the author figure described near the end of the novel is an appropriate description of both the narrator as posited author and of Fowles as actual author: both are caught within a male perspective. If the novel is created within a masculine ideology and only masculine perspectives are allowed inside the text, then it necessarily follows that its characters cannot transcend that male ideology.

Although, as I have asserted, the issue of feminism is central to *The French Lieutenant's Woman,* it does not follow that the novel is "an almost ideal feminist fictional work". The way in which the novel ultimately projects Sarah runs counter to the theme of feminism. Because Sarah's point of view remains absent from the text, Sarah remains objectified and never becomes a subject in her own right. Everything known about Sarah is mediated through the male perspectives of Charles, the narrator, and ultimately Fowles himself as orchestrator. That the arena of Sarah's mind is left outside of the novel is a strategic move on Fowles' part. It is clear that this absence is intentional, both because Fowles is too good of a craftsman not to have consciously planned out the use of point of view, and because the novel abounds with narrative statements which emphasize this very absence of any knowledge of Sarah's thoughts from the text. The claim that "Fowles provides sufficient information about Sarah's personality traits, values, and experiences for one to understand her character and history by the time one has finished reading the novel" (Byrd) is symptomatic of a naive reading which fails to question the author's motives and to identify the means by which the author is manipulating the narrative. The problem with Byrd's assertion may be due to her strong wish to read *The French Lieutenant's Woman* as a feminist novel. As a result of this desire, she in effect is reading her own version of the novel, which is very different from the one I read. It is apparent to me that an inherent contradiction in the novel is its need both to retain Sarah as an enigma and to give her the status of a character; and I would assert that it is the first impulse, to keep Sarah as an object of mystery, which ultimately takes precedence.

Everything points to and supports the view of Sarah as an object of mystery. The information about Sarah that the novel slowly unveils consists solely of first-hand accounts mingled with assumptions, which are delivered by the narrator and various characters, as well as of Sarah's actual speech to the extent that it is included in the text. Many critics fall into the trap of treating Sarah as if she were a whole character, discussing her feelings, motivations, and beliefs; but I find this highly problematic since Sarah's point of view is not present. Since Sarah is seen exclusively through the perspective of others, male others to be more specific, any attempt to attribute thoughts to her mind is pure interpolation. Sarah's independence as a subject or character is an illusion that must be questioned and broken.

The novel itself seems to challenge that illusion since both Charles and the narrator overtly discuss their lack of knowledge about Sarah aside from what they actually observe of her. The narrator stresses that his presentation of Sarah is based upon an external and thus limited view: "I report, then, only the outward facts." Throughout the novel, the narrator uses expressions such as "perhaps," "as if," and "it was hard to say" when he refers to Sarah, which underlines the notion that even as he describes or discusses Sarah, the narrator never knows "what was going on in her mind." The narrator in fact sharply displays his ignorance about Sarah when he asks, "Who is Sarah?" Charles likewise admits that Sarah remains unknown to him and that it is in fact "the enigma she presented" which "obsessed him": when he writes to Sarah he addresses her as "mysterious Sarah" and "my sweet enigma." This supports Woodcock's assertion [in his *Male Mythologies: John Fowles and Masculinity,* 1984] that "the preservation of her [Sarah's] mystery is essential to her

function in the book." The plot seems to depend on Sarah's remaining an enigma, and the novel would have been a very different one if Sarah's perspective had been included. What is problematic and needs to be questioned is the relationship between Sarah as figure of mystery and Sarah as emerging feminist as well as its effect on the novel as a whole.

Not only do the narrator and Charles assert that they know nothing about Sarah's mind, but they (like many critics) interpolate her state of mind from her actions, expressions, and words. The illusion of Sarah as a full character is thus partially created through these interpretations of Sarah's mind, which often pretend or at least appear to be more legitimate than they really are. Because the novel sustains a continuous commentary on Sarah, the distinction between what is in actuality merely a distanced perspective of Sarah and Sarah herself becomes hazy. I would in fact assert that within the novel there is no representation of Sarah as an independent being. Charles' interpretations of Sarah are so varied and so inconsistent, ranging from Sarah as manipulator ("I have been led by the nose") to Sarah as an ideal and a symbol of "freedom," that it is clear that an objective portrait of Sarah is not to be found in his perspective of her. The trustworthiness of Charles' perception is also challenged by the text, which casts doubts on his interpretation of Sarah. When Charles goes to Sarah at the hotel in Exeter, for example, he distinctly says that "he felt her flinch with pain as the bandaged foot fell from the stool" and yet later is bewildered to and out that "there was no strained ankle." Because Charles is obviously taken in completely by Sarah's contrivance, the overall credibility of his view of Sarah is questioned. Charles' inability to understand what lies behind Sarah's actions and words, coupled with his admitted obsession with her as a symbol rather than as a specific human being, suggests that Charles' perspective of Sarah is biased, limited, and thus suspect.

The narrator's perspective of Sarah, which is more all-encompassing than Charles', is also thrown into question. The fact that the narrator is quickly revealed to be a twentieth-century male may serve as a warning (especially to feminist or pro-feminist readers) that the narrative will be biased accordingly. The narrator's perspective of Sarah is thus distanced in two ways, by time and by gender-specific ideology. He asserts a certain control over the information provided in the text, and at one point he even admits to having "cheated" by controlling how much or how little he revealed. The narrator's ironic statement in Chapter 13 that he "intended at this stage (*Chap. Thirteen—unfolding of Sarah's true state of mind*) to tell all" reveals the intentional absence of an accounting of Sarah's point of view and thus the narrator's manipulative powers. Within the narrator's discussion of the "autonomy" of characters in fiction, his particular emphasis on the fact that he must give the female characters "their freedom as well" is suspicious. The question that arises is whether a female character can be free within a work of fiction that denies her a point of view: I would answer in the negative, particularly since most readers come to the work with a perspective grounded in patriarchal society and thus male ideology and would therefore not necessarily interpret Sarah's lack of a point of view as a statement against male ideology.

The narrator's many intrusions into the narrative with his own commentary on the various situations and characters provide an internal bias toward what is presented. This happens, for example, when the narrator follows one of Sarah's speeches with a hint to the effect that Sarah is not telling the truth, thus introducing a suspicion against Sarah into the text: "That might have been a warning to Charles." The narrator in this way judges Sarah and makes that judgment a part of the perspective that the novel offers of Sarah. In the only extended scene that presents Sarah alone (the depiction of her arrival and settling at the hotel in Exeter), the narrator's presence is strongly felt as he presents all of her actions from an external and distanced position and never gets into her mind. His manipulation of the view of Sarah that he presents in this episode is made clear when he speaks of the gestures he has "permitted her" to make. Sarah's lack of independent existence outside of the perspectives of her offered by the novel is thus emphasized by Charles and the narrator's words; and this in turn implies that the orchestrator of the text, Fowles, chose to retain her as an enigmatic figure.

It is Charles then who is the novel's protagonist, despite the narrator's reference to Sarah as "the protagonist," in the sense that the plot follows his actions and reactions; and Sarah functions as the object of mystery around which the plot revolves. Sarah is in fact not present in many scenes, even though her image is central. In contradiction to [Thomas] Docherty's generalized assertion [in "A Constant Reality: The Presentation of Character in the Fiction of John Fowles," *Novel* (Winter 1981)] that Fowles does not subsume "character into function or pattern," I think that Sarah is a functional object. She functions, for example, as "the mystery woman who is both a male fantasy and the catalyst for male redemption" (Woodcock)—in both cases, woman is an object functioning for man—and as such Sarah's portrait deviates from a feminist one. Because Sarah is depicted exclusively through male perspectives (this includes women such as Mrs. Poulteney and Ernestina whose perspectives adhere to the dominant male ideology inherent in their society), her portrait remains a construct of masculine ideology and Sarah retains the status of object, figure, or symbol rather than of a whole female character.

The novel begins by presenting Sarah as a figure—she is both "the other figure" and "a figure from myth"—to which is then attached the symbolic names of "Tragedy" and "the French Lieutenant's Woman." This initial description of Sarah is overdetermined to the extent that she can never discard these associations with symbol, mythic figure, and Other. She is in fact not given an identity within society, "Sarah Woodruff," until the end of the fourth chapter. These symbolic and mythic representations of Sarah offered by the "fundamentally elitist and male" narrative voice(s) are inextricably caught within the dominant masculine ideology. Sarah is thus a male representation of a woman rather than an unbiased representation of a woman in her own right. As a male construct within a culture filled with male mythologies, Sarah also "stands for 'woman'—timeless, unchanging, mysterious" [Terry Lovell, "Feminism and Form in the Literary Adaptation: *The French Lieutenant's Woman,*" in *Criticism and Critical Theory,* edited by Jeremy Hawthorn, 1984]. Male mythologies are powerful in that they are "myths of ideology at work within history for the perpetuation" of male dominance (Woodcock). If Sarah is constructed of male fictions, then the status of the theme of feminism in the novel becomes problematic and even questionable.

Fowles' use of male myths about women is blatant and pervasive throughout, and what needs to be questioned is the impact that the use of these myths has on the novel. Because of his emphasis on the theme of women's emancipation, the assumption can be made that Fowles intends to use the myths in order to break them open—whether he succeeds, however, is questionable. The development of the relationship between Sarah and Charles initially takes place within the setting of the "Undercliff," which is overtly and significantly described as "an English Garden of Eden." Fowles thus appropriates the Eden myth complete with its Adam and Eve figures, Charles and Sarah, and the valorization of the male; and this serves to predetermine both the outcome and the way in which the two characters will be regarded and judged. Sarah is in this way determined as Eve the temptress, and she is depicted as manipulating and finally seducing Charles. She thus comes off as a type of *femme fatale,* which is yet another male symbol: Charles sees her as "a woman most patently dangerous" and at one point describes "Her expression" as "calm, almost fatalistic." The emphasis on her sensuality further accentuates Sarah's definition as seductress: when Charles comes upon her asleep, he describes her as lying in "complete abandonment" in a way that was "intensely tender and yet sexual." Even Sarah's sexuality is described in terms that transcend the concrete and seem to be connected to male fantasy, as is exemplified by Charles' perception of Sarah as "a figure in a dream." The image of Sarah as sensual is thus a symbol of sexuality and of potential sexual fulfillment for Charles as well as an indication of her proclivity as seductress.

The mythic figure of Eve is just as much a helpmate as a temptress, however, and likewise Sarah illustrates both roles. In opposition to her negative role as seductress, Sarah also embodies a potential redemption for Charles. Charles sees in Sarah "some possibility she symbolized," "a glimpse of an ideal world" or "a mythical world," and "the symbol around which had accreted all his lost possibilities, his extinct freedoms." Sarah thus functions as a symbol of the freedom for which Charles is questing; and Charles' obsession is directed toward the ideal that Sarah represents rather than toward the concrete woman, except maybe for his sexual attraction to her (but even that is idealized). Toward the end of the novel, Charles himself seems to have perceived the dichotomy between Sarah and his idealization of her, although the masculine perspective inherent within that idealization is left undiscussed: Charles "became increasingly unsure of the frontier between the real Sarah and the Sarah he had created in so many dreams: the one Eve personified, all mystery." There is thus no mistaking the parallel between the mythical Eve and the figure of Sarah.

The use of male myths in the portrayal of Sarah does not stop with the Eden myth but rather includes, among others, references which link Sarah to Greek myths, "a siren" and "a Calypso," to Christian myths, "the Virgin Mary," and to scientific myths. The last of these is particularly striking and is epitomized by Dr. Grogan's use of clinical cases to categorize Sarah. Dr. Grogan lives within "that masculine, more serious world," and his chauvinism is all too apparent. Women are objects to observe and diagnose. His joking admission to Charles that he likes to watch "his feminine patients" bathing in the sea through his "brass Gregorian telescope" suggests that both his personal and scientific perspectives are grounded in masculine ideology and thus heavily biased. This view in fact reflects the general perspective of women depicted in the novel, in which men look at women and believe that they can adequately interpret their actions and thoughts. Dr. Grogan objectifies Sarah by labeling her with the clinical term of "obscure melancholia," which limits his view of her. Charles' own chauvinistic idealization of women surfaces in his horrified reaction to the case studies on melancholia that Dr. Grogan gives him to read: "that such perversion existed—and in the pure and sacred sex." It is evident from these case studies that there is a whole stockpile of male scientific myths about women, all of which attempt to explain women's non-conformist behavior in terms of illness.

The major question is whether Fowles' use of these male myths does break them open and divulge them as masculine constructions aimed at creating images of women that work to keep women subjected to men. I think that ultimately Fowles fails to invalidate these male myths. In his book *Male Mythologies: John Fowles and Masculinity,* Woodcock formulates this failure very well in his central argument that Fowles "promotes a realigned version of the very myth of masculinity he lays bare" because he "is caught within the limits of masculine ideology." It is too bad, however, that Woodcock undercuts himself and falls prey to the same problem he attributes to Fowles. After a perceptive analysis of Fowles' use of male myths in his fiction, Woodcock makes the peculiar statement that Fowles' "revision" rather than destruction of "male mythologies" ultimately does not "undermine the credibility of seeing in Fowles' work a potential critique of masculinity and male power" since Fowles does "expose a critical self-awareness" and a "desire to reveal male ideologies at work." I think that Woodcock's weak attempt to retain Fowles as a critic of male ideology must be a result of Woodcock's own inability to transcend masculine ideology. It is contradictory to assert that a novel that remains caught up in male perspectives and myths to its very end can still be regarded as a credible critique of male ideology. I believe that male myths and ideology must be made more explicit, maybe even rejected, and not just exposed in order to constitute a critique of masculine ideology in a world whose values and beliefs are steeped in that same male ideology.

Fowles' failure to discard the male myths he exposes is intrinsically connected to his choosing to use only male perspectives. One way in which a male myth about woman can be broken is through its invalidation by a concrete and independent being (most likely a woman) standing outside of male ideology, although the possibility is questionable since western writers are products of that very ideology. Fowles wants to represent the development of such a feminist consciousness and yet he does not give Sarah a voice. The actions of Sarah that are reported do suggest that she is a woman who rebels against patriarchal society by casting herself outside that society and thus outside masculine ideology. The problem, however, is that the Sarah who performs these revolutionary acts has no existence outside of the male perspectives that depict her.

An alternative means of breaking male myths, for which Fowles seems to have opted, is through irony. His use of male perspectives, which render Sarah as an object, can in this way be viewed as an exposure of male ideology. I do not think, however, that irony works very well in this case. Irony depends on a clear and stable set of commonly held values, standards, or beliefs so that a difference can be seen between what is asserted in the text and what is known to be "true" or "real." In Fowles' novel, the ironic presentation of the way in which women are viewed is not different enough from most readers' commonly held assumptions and views about women. I think that many readers living within modern western patriarchal society fail to see Fowles' text as a critique of male ideology simply because readers are as often as not caught within male ideology themselves.

The two endings that culminate the novel support the claim that the novel perpetuates rather than breaks open male myths. All of the critics whom I read valorize the second ending, except for Woodcock, and I find this problematic. I do not think that one ending is more probable or plausible than the other or that Fowles wishes his reader to choose between them. It seems naive to disregard the narrator's emphasis on the fictional character of any ending and on the author's manipulative powers: fiction only "pretends to conform to the reality," whereas the writer "in fact fixes the fight." Although the narrator explains that he will solve the problem by showing "two versions" of "the fight," it is clear that any version will be biased and that in this case both endings are suspect since they are created from and remain caught within a masculine perspective. The narrator's further claim that "the second [ending] will seem, so strong is the tyranny of the last chapter, the final, the 'real' version" cannot be ignored but rather should render the whole idea of the double ending suspicious.

I think that both endings are possibilities but that neither can be valorized, because both are products of a totally male view and as such are limited: in both cases, the scene is described from Charles' side by the male narrator. Woodcock makes the noteworthy claim that in the first ending, Charles "is both apparently open to learn and the continuing victim-perpetrator of his sex's mythologies," and that in the second ending, "Charles's misogynistical misconceptions about Sarah win the day." This suggests that Charles remains caught within male ideologies in both endings, which in turn implies that the portrait of Sarah remains to the end a male product. The second ending, which is so often declared the "true" ending, in fact appears almost more chauvinistic than the first. In the first ending, Charles at least feels Sarah's "intellectual equality" and feels "admiration" for her even if he still does not understand her. In the second ending, however, Charles feels "his own true superiority to her" and finds "himself reborn" after having left Sarah for good. Sarah, in this second version, functions only as the catalyst for his rebirth and accordingly drops out of the story after Charles leaves her. The very last image of Sarah is symptomatically one of Sarah as "Sphinx." Both versions of the novel's conclusion thus show signs of remaining bound within male ideology, which explains why Sarah never achieves the independent existence as a character that Fowles tries to delineate for her.

If Sarah's point of view had been allowed into the novel and yet not subsumed within male ideology, she might have become a full character with the potential to reveal the bias against women inherent in the dominant and male ideology. With no voice with which to express her thoughts, however, Sarah remains an image and never becomes a woman or a female character in her own right. Rather than breaking open male myths, Fowles ultimately reinforces them by giving Sarah no being outside of those very myths or fictions with which she is presented—she is nothing more than a symbol, an ideal, a mythic figure, an Other—and giving readers no overt indications that Sarah's portrait may be a critique of male perspectives of women. Fowles does not make his use of male myths explicit and seems to assume that readers will discover for themselves the critique of masculine ideology within the text, which neglects to take into account that many readers are themselves caught within male ideology (although I acknowledge that readers of literature are also to blame for this shortcoming). This failure to account for the potential difficulties and even impossibility of many readers to transcend their own male-dominated ideologies suggests that Fowles to a certain extent remains caught within male ideology himself. The novel ultimately fails either to allow a place for woman's voice, which could open up the potential for woman's self-portrayal outside of male ideology as well as initiate a critique of male ideology, or to make its inherent exposure of male myths and ideology explicit. Regardless of the central position that the issue of feminism as theme takes in the novel and of Fowles' exposure of male myths and ideology, if only feminist or profeminist readers can see the novel's feminism, then I think that Fowles' *The French Lieutenant's Woman* falls short of being a feminist novel.

Katherine Tarbox   (essay date 1988)

SOURCE: An introduction to *The Art of John Fowles,* The University of Georgia Press, 1988, pp. 1-10.

[*In the following excerpt, Tarbox examines the underlying theme of Fowles's novels, analyzing the trials that his protagonists undergo in order to achieve self-realization and authenticity.*]

In my analyses of [Fowles's] novels I have been guided by one light alone: Fowles's implicit demand that the reader of his works "see whole." Seeing whole means diving bravely into the teeming substance of each Fowles text, into the glut of detail, the language play, the eccentric modes of narration, the bizarre events, the dislocations of time, the distinctive use of history, the structural architecture of patterning and counterpoint, the deviations from genre, the flagrant use of cinematic, novel-defeating conventions, the metafictional concerns, and so on. But seeing whole is a skill each reader must learn, and Fowles teaches his reader *how* to see whole by using the education of his protagonist as an example. Thus, each Fowles novel is about learning to see, but also about its own relation to that learning. . . .

[*The Ebony Tower*] is, in intent, theme, and technique, . . . similar to *The Magus.* In both novels an unsettled man invades the private domain of a much older man, a mentor or hierophantic figure. In each case the young man becomes involved in an elaborate game with two women—one wanton, one demure—in which sex plays a major part. Even the motifs of the novels—art, music, swimming, drinking—are the same. At the end of the game they disgorge their victim back into his ordinary life a changed man, not immediately understanding what has happened to him.

All the novels are the same story at bottom, and we shall soon see why. They begin with a protagonist who suffers some degree of narcissism. He (or in the case of *The Collector* and *A Maggot,* she) has been living an inauthentic life and playing roles that substitute for true identity. He lives, as Nicholas might say, as though someone were looking over his shoulder. Nicholas Urfe sees himself as the *homme revolté,* while Miranda sees herself as the *femme revoltée.* Charles Smithson tries to be a proper Vic-

---

Fowles on the double ending in *The French Lieutenant's Woman:*

Why did I put a double ending in *The French Lieutenant's Woman?* That was purely personal because I knew the novel required the hero and the heroine to part, to separate, yet I was slightly in love with both of them and I wanted them to come together and be happy. This is very familiar when you are writing a novel. You like two characters and you want them to come together and you want a happy ending; but some twentieth-century part of you, who is really the victim of black, absurdist art in a way, says they must split, they must separate. All that happened to me was that I thought, "Why don't I put both endings?" In a way it is so like life. Life also has forks. Very small matters sometimes do bring people together or separate them. We cannot control the present, let alone the future. It was simply that I had the idea that it would be interesting to use both possible ends and leave it to the reader to decide.

John Fowles, in an interview with Susana Onega, in her Form and Meaning in the Novels of John Fowles, *UMI Research Press, 1989.*

torian gentleman, Rebecca Hocknell tries to be the most depraved of whores, and Daniel Martin has simply forgotten who he really is. The protagonists are, however, always in a state of disequilibrium. They feel nebulously ill at ease in their inauthentic lives, but do not know why; in fact, they are not even aware that they are playing roles. They are, to use one of Fowles's favorite metaphors, schizophrenic—torn between what they perceive is expected of them and what they dimly intuit they need to be. Nicholas confesses, "I was not the person I wanted to be"; and Rebecca echoes his dilemma: "I would not be what I am, sir."

This statement of desire to escape a false identity, to shed one's self-imposed mask, seals the protagonist's election; and to be elect in Fowles's terms means to be poised on a fulcrum, prepared to change one's wayward course even though the personal risks involved are significant. Charles showed great courage in setting off on an irreversible course that would expose him to ridicule and loss. Victorian society was safe and predictable, while the freedom Sarah offered was decidedly dangerous. Dan needed a similar courage to divest himself of his easy, glib, but superficial life. He took a path that led him to the terrors of self-confrontation.

The elect individual is swept up by a benevolent magus who has already attained selfhood through some personal trial. This mentor draws the protagonist into what Fowles calls the godgame, a complex production designed to upset, disorient, and in all ways distress the "initiate." In the first phase of the godgame the magus takes the protagonist away from his familiar surroundings and thereby disturbs his tired habits of perception. Nick goes to Bourani, Miranda goes to her cell, Charles goes to the infamous Ware Cliffs, Dan goes up the Nile, and Rebecca journeys to Cleave Wood. Once the game is under way the protagonist becomes bereft of ordinary frames of reference. He will have to see with new eyes and use new standards of judgment.

The main strategy of the godgame is metatheater (though the metatheater is less overt in *The Collector* and *Daniel Martin*), a kind of living drama performed for and with the protagonist, without his knowledge of the artifice. The magus involves the protagonist in many layers of illusion by playing out, in metaphorical form, aspects of the protagonist's inauthenticity. Conchis dramatizes many of Nicholas's failings, such as his compulsive abstraction of women and his failure to understand his own nature. Sarah dramatizes, in her bizarre charade involving the French Lieutenant, Charles's struggling will to be free of Victorian restraints. Bartholomew shows Rebecca, in the extraordinary maggot vision, her own longing for peace, sanity, and "more love." The masque is meant to be a mirror in which one sees the reflection of one's self. The various anima figures throughout the novels also act as mirrors for the male initiates. June and Julie, for example, exist in their masque only to receive the projections of Nicholas; they will be whatever he wants them to be. Similarly, Sarah acts as the embodiment of everything Charles secretly wishes he were, just as Jane becomes the eyes through which Dan eventually sees himself.

> In his writings Fowles teaches his reader *how* to see whole by using the education of his protagonist as an example. Thus, each Fowles novel is about learning to see, but also about its own relation to that learning.
>
> —*Katherine Tarbox*

Sex is always a significant part of the masque because the erotic element functions as a symbol for the ways in which human relationships are deformed by the protagonist's habit of games playing. Sex within the masque is virtually always masturbatory, voyeuristic, or pornographic, suggesting physical analogues to existential conditions. Nicholas is narcissistic and Fowles reveals him masturbating often. Charles is afraid to leap into selfhood, but he enjoys being on the fringe of Sarah's rich life; hence, she makes him the voyeur to her affair with Varguennes. Rebecca debases herself in prostitution, so Bartholomew contrives to involve her in a degrading threesome.

As the protagonist becomes enmeshed in story upon story and endeavors to make sense of the chameleon players he is involved with, he has increasing difficulty in discerning what is real and what is not. The protagonist's habitual approaches to life are unworkable, and slowly the cyclone of appearances works to deconstruct him. This is the ultimate point of the game—to make of the elect what Nicholas calls "a litter of parts." The game works to stress and ultimately break down the protagonist's false identity. The last act of the magus and his players is to abscond; they leave the protagonist alone, in exile, thereby forcing him to put himself back together again in a new way. Each godgame illustrates the lines from "Little Gidding" that Conchis leaves for Nicholas to find:

> The end of all our exploring
> Will be to arrive where we started
> And know the place for the first time.

The major lesson of the godgame is that individual existential freedom, the insistence upon one's right to an authentic personal destiny, is the highest human good. Each protagonist learns that he must see through the roles we all play in ordinary life. The one who is elect must make a conscious choice to live his real life in the world, but choosing once is not enough. Charles, for example, has to suffer anew each day for the freedom he stole and therefore must be willing to be perpetually crucified. Rebecca Lee must suffer poverty, ridicule, and persecution to be true to her vision. Thus, the protagonist who sets himself against the conforming, role-playing masses must be willing to suffer exile for his dissent.

In the journey toward self-awareness Fowles asserts the primacy of intuition, what Dan calls "right feeling," as the vehicle for knowledge. The very point of the godgame is that it cannot be understood by science or logic. It resists rational scrutiny. Appearances are always deceptive, as the numerous spy-narrators prove. The narrators of both *A Maggot* and *The French Lieutenant's Woman* are consistently deceived by the evidence of their senses. Nicholas is deceived by the glut of "proof " that Conchis offers him: the photos, letters, newspaper clippings, and so on. The use of language to deceive is a major theme in all the novels. Fowles shows that in ordinary life we interpret our surroundings according to established codes. We tend to put experience in categories, interpret new material by received ideas, to see with others' eyes, and this epistemological habit is what Fowles calls collector-consciousness. The magus thwarts the protagonist's collector tendencies by giving him an experience that goes far beyond his ability to categorize it. There is, for example, no code that will help Rebecca understand her flying maggot, as there is no easy way for Nicholas to interpret his fantastic trial. The protagonist finds himself by looking inside rather than outside for explanations. Each must "turn in," as Anthony warns Dan, to find the "right feeling" that both reason and language are inadequate to convey.

Fowles uses characteristic metaphors and motifs throughout his novels to express his themes. He uses cinematic techniques (most notably the narrator, who rolls the story before us like a kind of living movie camera) to parallel the way in which we ordinarily perceive life. That is, we are all victims of the tyranny of a present tense that drags us on, treadmill style. We tend to see life as a progress from a beginning to an end, and as a result exclude the sense of "whole sight." Certainly Dan's problem is that he literally perceives his life as a film because films can only work in one tense at a time—the present. Fowles believes that linear time is an artificial measuring device imposed upon experience, that real time is nebulous, and that all time lies parallel. He believes in what he calls a "spinning top" model of history and holds as ideal vision the perception of all three tenses at once. This ideal is fully expressed in *A Maggot* when the silver woman first splinters into her three ages, then merges again.

The typical Fowles protagonist is temporarily blinded by the customs and fashions of his own time, and thus looks upon life with tunnel vision. A major characteristic of each godgame is that it takes the protagonist not only out of his physical space but out of his own time as well. All the elect become time travelers. Conchis throws Nicholas into a whirlwind of myth and archetype, and in his masque he meets Diana, Ashtaroth, Desdemona, a dead Edwardian girl, and so on. Dan's journey represents a going back in time, as he visits first the ancient ruins of Egypt, then, finally, the very roots of human civilization in Mesopotamia. Rebecca journeys into the future of the human race, and when she returns she finds she can also communicate with dead spirits. Of all Fowles's protagonists, she achieves what is perhaps the most nearly complete whole sight. Because Fowles believes in quantum time rather than linear time, he eschews the notion of endings. The godgame always leaves its subject in a quandary because the magus denies him a neat conclusion to his or-

deal. The protagonist is a "litter of parts" adrift in a sea of mysteries. But it is the existence of mystery, the denial of an artificial ending, that gives the protagonist the energy to quest on, to reconstruct himself and his perception of the world. His new life feeds on mystery.

The themes of time and perception are conveyed through different narratorial strategies in each novel, but Fowles always uses the motif of doors, rooms, and windows to express the difference between tunnel vision and whole sight. In these novels crucial discoveries take place outdoors. Nicholas has penetrating insights into his predicament when he awakes on a hillside after his trial. Charles finds himself on the Ware Cliffs, as Rebecca finds what she is looking for in Cleave Wood. Dan understands most about himself as he surveys the dismal waste of desert at Palmyra. Indoors, characters are confined and confused, and rooms, as well as closed doors, become a metaphor for lack of personal freedom. In his "stage-settings," in which he plays much with the physical structure of buildings, Fowles examines the ways in which humans enclose, confine, and limit space. The brain in *Mantissa* has a door but no apparent means of egress for Miles. The drawing rooms of *The French Lieutenant's Woman* are an appropriate counterpoint to the open spaces Sarah inhabits. Nicholas moves through the warren-like hallways and bedrooms of Bourani and ends in the trial cell before he earns his meeting with Alison, out of doors, in London. Ayscough's quarters are much like a prison, and in fact he often keeps his deponents under arrest. Miranda's prison is, of course, the ultimate metaphor for lack of freedom. Inside rooms people are confused and unreal. In each of the novels Fowles is looking for the door that leads out of the prison.

If the protagonist learns that all time is one, he also learns that he has a "linked destiny" with the rest of his human fellows. The protagonist who begins as *Homo solitarus* ends, as a result of his trial, with a sense of empathy. The godgame breaks down the walls he builds, the arbitrary categories he puts between himself and others. Nicholas, Charles, and Miranda all experience the deflation of their pretensions, the sense that they are somehow better, smarter, more astute than their fellows. Dan and Rebecca, both of whom had been exiled from friends and family, find their way back into the human fold and "the warm web of kin."

Thus the characters undergo complete metamorphosis. They begin with false, provisional identities and end as freer, more authentic beings. The metamorphosis encompasses the journey from narcissism to humanism, from games playing and artifice to a respect for decency, moderation, sanity, feeling, and caring. The Fowles protagonist comes to honor "the elementary decencies of existence—method, habit, routine . . . continuity." The orderly life is reflected in our last glimpse of Dan, who is standing beside Jane in her kitchen. It is also expressed in Rebecca's vision of the Shaker community.

Of course the most obvious question about any Fowles text is, why does there have to be a godgame at all? Through his various unusual technical strategies Fowles shows in each novel how limited our seeing is in everyday life, how time bound and tradition bound we are, how accustomed we are to looking at the world with collector-consciousness, and how sullied are our true natures. In our everyday lives we train ourselves to ignore and to conform. As Fowles said to me in conversation, "Life does condition us so frightfully, that it's terribly difficult to sense . . . the underlying nature of existence. You know, we are caged more and more by present society in roles, and I think being able to see through the roles is most important. . . . Most people like to be conditioned, unfortunately, it's a fallacy that everybody wants to be freer in the sense we're talking about. They're much happier I think, having fixed routines and a limited way of life." We need to be awakened from this existential torpor and, in his extravagant metaphor of the godgame, Fowles proposes that fiction itself is the great awakener, the great teacher. The maguses involve their subjects in fictions to teach them how to see. Thus the godgame is heuristic. The logic of the godgame is identical to Hamlet's logic when he says, "The play's the thing wherein I'll catch the conscience of the king." Fiction teaches by the method of metaphor because to interpret the difficult material of the story, material that always suggests and never assigns meaning, one must "turn in" to process the information. In this way fiction is a reflection of the protagonist. It illuminates what everything else in ordinary life conspires to hide: what is already there inside him. Because stories lead to self-understanding, fiction is the great existential adventure.

But Fowles always takes the godgame one step further. Through narrative technique he deconstructs the reader as well as the protagonist, and each reader is in turn the elect. Each novel is a parallel godgame in which both the protagonist and the reader grope through the multiple deceptions and illusions of the text. The same operations the protagonist performs, the reader must perform as well. Each novel itself is a dense tapestry of allusiveness, studied confusion, moral quandary, myth, archetype, symbol, and motif. The reader struggles with this polysemy as well as with the substance and mechanics of the protagonist's masque. This density mirrors the complexity of life and if the reader would see the text whole, he must undergo the same sort of reconstruction as the protagonist.

Like the protagonist, the reader must cast off his collector-consciousness and, in terms of the novel, that means he must give up certain generic expectations. He must not expect endings because endings, as Fowles shows us, are arbitrary and artificial. He must also, like the protagonist, not expect to have the mysteries solved for him. The traditional model of the novel's author is the fight fixer as Fowles describes him in *The French Lieutenant's Woman*: "Fiction usually pretends to conform to reality: the writer puts the conflicting wants in the ring and then describes the fight—but in fact fixes the fight, letting that want he himself favors win." Fowles consistently repudiates the notion of an author-god, and he assiduously avoids fight fixing. He refuses, in effect, to collect his readers. He desires in his fiction to allow the reader the same psychoanalytic, reconstructive experience as the protagonist, with its attendant, sometimes uneasy freedoms.

> The real art of John Fowles lies in his showing us the different ways by which we can come to know and be ourselves, despite formidable handicaps and pressures to conform.
>
> —*Katherine Tarbox*

Each novel ultimately tells the same story, and the story of the survival of individual freedom is the *only* story. Upon it are contingent all other human stories, such as history and evolution, because, as both Fowles and Jung affirm, the survival of the race depends upon the salvation of each individual soul. In *The Magus* Fowles uses Hitler to illustrate this idea. Conchis asserts that the real tragedy of Nazi Germany was not that one man had the courage to be evil, but that the millions who followed him, and who were basically sensible, decent people, had not the courage to be good.

In telling his urgent story again and again, Fowles is really conveying his sense that the process of understanding is what he considers important. The real art of John Fowles lies in his showing us the different ways by which we can come to know and be ourselves, despite formidable handicaps and pressures to conform. Always in his novels he compares the art of reading well with the art of living well. Both require considerable perceptual acuity, indeed whole sight. We transfer the methods by which we come to understand his texts onto the plots of our everyday lives. To study the art of Fowles is to study how fiction humanizes us.

Carol M. Barnum   (essay date 1988)

SOURCE: "*The Ebony Tower:* Variations on the Mythic Theme," in *The Fiction of John Fowles: A Myth for Our Time,* The Penkevill Publishing Company, 1988, pp. 77-99.

[*In the following excerpt, Barnum analyzes the predominant themes and imagery of the works collected in* The Ebony Tower.]

John Fowles's fourth work of fiction, *The Ebony Tower,* continues the theme of the novels in the more precise format of the short story. The working title for the collection was *Variations,* Fowles's intent being to show variations on the theme of his previous fiction. But since early readers found the title (and its connections) obscure, it was abandoned in favor of the present title. If, however, we consider Fowles's stated intent, we see a pattern emerging of the protagonist's struggles to take the journey toward self-discovery or individuation, the emphasis of the stories in this collection being on the bleaker aspects of failed attempts.

Also included in the collection is Fowles's translation of the medieval romance *Eliduc,* which, as he explains in "A

Personal Note" preceding it, is connected to [the novella] *The Ebony Tower* in the same way that medieval romance is connected to modern fiction—as a natural outgrowth. Thus, the stories of *The Ebony Tower* not only demonstrate variations on the ancient theme of the quest, but also variations on the theme of Fowles's fiction.

The title story describes a quester who inadvertently stumbles into the realm of myth, only to find that he cannot rise to the challenge of the quest and is therefore ejected from the mythic landscape. The other three stories in the collection are all centered on enigmas (one of the stories is titled **"The Enigma"**) or mysteries of modern life. These mysteries arise because "mystery" in the sacred sense no longer appears valid in modern man's existence. The movement of the stories is generally downward toward darkness, modern man depicted as being less and less able to take the mythic journey of self-discovery because he is trapped in a wasteland world that bewilders him.

David Williams of *The Ebony Tower* is the typical Fowlesian protagonist: well-born and bred, self-assured, and representative of his age and class. Driving through the forests of Brittany, the landscape of the Celtic romance, he is unsuspecting of the mythic encounter that awaits him. Since David's approach to life is one of "intelligent deduction," as opposed to "direct experience," he is ill prepared for the journey he is about to undertake. As a source of information, his journey will not be wasted; as a source of psychic growth, not the expressed purpose but the implied opportunity, his journey will be wasted because his rational response will prove insufficient to the challenge.

Turning off the main road into the forest lane, David comes to the "promised sign" announcing *Manoir de Coëtminais: coët* meaning "wood" or "forest" and *minais* meaning "of the monks," the sacred wood of the mythic quest. Fowles's description of David's experience within this mythic domain has similarities linking it to Robert Browning's poem " 'Childe Roland to the Dark Tower Came,' " not the least of which is the association between the dark tower and the ebony tower. The differences are also interesting. While Roland fears his journey because he knows its dangers, David relishes his journey, being unsuspecting of danger. Roland is directed to the path off the main road by a "hoary cripple" who is "posted there" to point the way; David is directed by the posted "promised sign." The day is bleak on Roland's arrival, sunny on David's; but when David leaves Coëtminais, the day becomes as bleak as it is in Browning's poem. For David's departure the sky is "clouded over" and the landscape is of "dull, stubbled plains," a setting which corresponds with "the gray plain all round" and "stubbed ground" of Roland's landscape. In Roland's view "all hope of greenness" is gone, and when David leaves Coëtminais the same holds true: "an end now to all green growth." The essential difference, however, between the two journeys is that Roland has spent his life preparing for his journey and will rise to the challenge, while David has spent his life avoiding the challenge, living comfortably but superficially. When he finds himself faced with the dark tower of his existence, he cannot rise to meet it; therefore, his departure

from the mythic landscape is as bleak as Roland's approach, or bleaker because Roland has at least the hope of success in the face of adversity, while David must live the rest of his life with the surety of his failure.

David comes to Breasley as an admirer of his art for its "mysterious" and "archetypal" qualities, which some critics called " 'Celtic' " "with the recurrence of the forest motif, the enigmatic figures and confrontations." Breasley pretends to downplay the Celtic influence but tells David at the same time:

> 'Just here and there, don't you know, David. What one needs. Suggestive. Stimulating, that's the word.' Then he went off on Marie de France and *Eliduc.* 'Damn' good tale. Read it several times. What's the old Swiss bamboozler's name. Jung, yes? His sort of stuff. Archetypal and all that.'

In discussing the significant influences on his art, Breasley links the medieval quest with the Jungian archetypes, seeing the two as united in his work, just as Fowles unites the two strains in this story and in his fiction as a whole.

David knows that his art, as well as his lifestyle, is different from Breasley's; therefore he is not entirely surprised to meet the two girls who live with Breasley: Anne, dubbed "the Freak," and Diana, dubbed "the Mouse." Like the twins in *The Magus,* these two girls serve as mirror images, two halves that complement one another as two aspects of womankind. Diana, the Mouse, is described as ethereal, distant, feminine, and almost always dressed in white. Her counterpart, Anne, the Freak, is described as "aboriginal," sexual, coarse, and almost always dressed in black. Taken together, Diana and Anne, Anne's name contained within Diana's, form the archetype of the anima for David. David is attracted to the Mouse, finding the Freak somewhat offensive. His later failure to meet the challenge of the quest stems partly from the fact that he cannot accept the "freak," her sexuality, in the Mouse and respond positively to it. Breasley understands the dual nature of both girls, but his secret about the significance of the Mouse's name—"muse" with the feminine "o" drawn in the shape of a vulva—strengthens her role as an anima figure in the story, not only for David but for Breasley. Fowles ascribes to the power of the muses as well, telling an interviewer, " 'I *do* believe in inspiration. I almost believe in muses. In fact, I wrote a short story last year that did bring the muses into modern life' " [John Fowles with Daniel Halpern, "A Sort of Exile in Lyme Regis," *London Magazine* (March 1971)].

Somewhat confused by his initial encounter, David feels like an outsider within the mythic domain, and he wishes his wife were with him to support his persona and protect him from the dangers of "so many ripening apples," an obvious reference to the temptation of the forbidden fruit in the Garden of Eden. At the same time, David thinks of his wife as "poor old Beth" and "predictable old Beth," revealing the nature of their relationship in its unfruitfulness. Thus to handle the confusing situation he faces, he provides himself with rational explanations for the things he sees in much the same way that Charles and Nicholas try to understand their own as well as others' behavior by ascribing rational explanations to them.

Related to David's need for a rational approach to life is his need to express everything verbally, to compartmentalize all experience within the boundaries of language. Language is certainly important, as any novelist will admit, but language cannot be a substitute for feeling. In an interview after the publication of **The Ebony Tower,** Fowles discusses David's use of language, calling it "a kind of smooth language . . . which is losing meaning" [Interview on *The Today Show,* NBC (11 November 1974)]. Breasley, on the other hand, is barely verbal, speaking for the most part in a kind of abbreviated language of fragments and phrases and communicating his important thoughts and feelings through his canvasses. Breasley can, however, use language effectively when necessary, as he demonstrates by means of a verbal attack upon David after dinner, drawing from him a symbolic "drop of blood." David mistakes the verbal wound for his initiation, thinking prematurely that he has passed the test. Unlike Gawain, the medieval quester who is similarly wounded by the Green Knight but who learns from the wound an important lesson, David has not learned anything yet except the art of carefully sidestepping an argument. In this case, however, he does not know how to respond to "the violently personal nature of the assault" Breasley mounts with such barbs as, " 'You really a painter, Williams? Or just a gutless bloody word-twister?'," to which David replies, " 'Hatred and anger are not luxuries we can afford anymore.' " This elicits further insults from Breasley who, by now quite drunk, explains to David that he is trying to tell him something important, although he confesses to his inadequacy with words (David's presumed strength). In his abbreviated style he summarizes: " 'Don't hate, can't love. Can't love, can't paint. . . . Bloody geometry. No good. Won't work. All tried it. Down the hole.' " He concludes "with a strange lucidity": " 'Ebony Tower. That's what I call it.' " The meaning of the term is not explained until later by the Mouse, who tells David that it signifies anything Breasley does not like about modern art, in particular the obscurity of artists who are afraid to be clear. Fowles elaborates on the meaning of the term:

> I see the ebony tower as not so much an 'opposite' of the ivory one, as an inevitable consequence of it . . . if one stays too long in retreat in the sacred combe. Thus, a great deal of unnecessary 20th century 'obscurity' is a direct cultural result of 19th century ivory-towerism—art for art's sake, and so on. The trouble for me is not, so to speak, at the top—let us say, in the genius with which Mallarmé uses ambiguity and obscurity (and with undoubted sincerity in his greatest stuff); but the only-too-easy loophole it provides for the less gifted. Deliberately making your work incomprehensible is uncomfortably close to making it impossible to judge. [Letter from Fowles to Barnum, 5 August 1981]

David recognizes the creative powers in the old man, as evidenced in his canvasses, but fails to see their absence in his own art or life; he merely sees his existence as different from Breasley's, thinking the old man's self-imposed

exile is based on the knowledge that "his persona would never wash in the Britain of the 1970s." He does, however, envy Breasley's lifestyle and success: "To someone like David, always inclined to see his own life (like his painting) in terms of logical process, its future advances dependent on intelligent present choices, it seemed not quite fair."

Logical process begins to break down within the mythic landscape as David realizes that much of what he is learning about Breasley cannot be put in his introduction because "like the forest itself, the old man had his antique mysteries." In the same vein, at a picnic in the woods with Breasley and the girls, he likens Coët to the Garden of Eden, seeing the place and its lifestyle as "faintly mythic and timeless." The Mouse concurs, telling David how she came to Coët: " 'Bump. You're in a different world.' " He also is beginning to recognize more in the Freak's character than he previously realized, seeing in her look, which is "both questing and quizzing," a directness and gentleness that he previously missed, and thus recognizing an identity and a complimentarity between the two girls (as aspects of the anima archetype). Quickly, he feels drawn toward the three as a part of a living quaternity, which he completes, the result of which brings him an experience of the mandala archetype.

At the same time, David is feeling the influence of the Mouse in her role as the projection of the anima archetype:

> He knew it and concealed it . . . not only to her, partly also to himself: that is, he analyzed what he had so rapidly begun to find attractive about her—why that precise blend of the physical and the psychological, the reserved and the open . . . called so strongly to something in his own nature. Strange, how these things hit you out of the blue, were somehow inside you almost before you could see them approaching. He felt a little bewitched, possessed; and decided it must be mainly the effect of being without Beth.

Several interesting points are revealed in this passage. One is that David recognizes the power of the Mouse as the anima archetype, even her power to bewitch or possess him, but he wants to *analyze* the situation so as to control it and to control the "something" it calls to in his nature: the anima within. In the midst of this analysis, a sentence intrudes in the second person where the sentences before and after are in the third person. Is this sentence, through the sudden use of "you," reflecting the voice of David's inner self, that which he seeks without knowing it? It speaks of the way "things hit you out of the blue" coming from "somewhere inside you," and it foreshadows the experience he will have with the Mouse in the garden. But the next sentence is safely back in the more distant third person as David attributes the strange things he is feeling to the absence of Beth, the projection of his persona.

Breasley, continuing in the archetypal role as David's guide, tells him that he does not provide answers to questions about his sources: " 'Let it happen. That's all. Couldn't even tell you how it starts. What half it means. Don't want to know.' " Like Conchis in **The Magus** who tells Nicholas that "every answer is a form of death," Breasley is interested in life, not answers. Speaking of *"trop de racine,"* he calls it " 'too much root. Origin. Past. Not the flower. The now. Thing on the wall. *Faut couper la racine.* Cut the root off.' " His message for David is that too much reliance on the past, the root, stifles growth in the present, the flower. Although the present is connected to the root of the past, it cannot be chained to it; if this happens, one must cut the root off to save the flower.

The more David learns from Breasley in his capacity as teacher and guide and the Mouse in her capacity as anima, the more he feels drawn into the quest. There is, however, the danger of becoming too attached to the mythic realm, thus fearing to leave it. Such a fate has befallen the Mouse who sees Coët as the " 'little forest womb. . . [where] everything remains possible.' " On the contrary, her possibilities for full growth cannot be realized as long as she stays within the protection of the domain. Part of David's task as mythic quester is to rescue her from her "forest womb" and provide her with safe passage back to the real world. David senses the challenge he faces:

> He felt he had traveled much farther than expected, into the haunted and unpredicted; and yet in some strange way it seemed always imminent. It had had to come, it had had causes, too small, too manifold to have been detected in the past or to be analyzed now.

For once he does not analyze, accepting that he has come to the central task of his journey. As he is awakened to the anima within, seen as Diana, she is awakened to the animus, which she projects on David, and the moment in which they must act in acknowledgment of each other is fast approaching.

The moment is "here, now, the unsaid" as they move to the Edenic garden with its "ghostly apple trees." And still, although it is "his move," David cannot make it, withdrawing instead, under the influence of the shadow archetype, "into speech." Knowing his inadequacy, he wishes for "two existences," finding himself unable to be united into one whole existence and yet not wanting to forsake this moment. Thoughts of Beth and the world he has left behind freeze him in inaction while one half of him nevertheless yearns to incorporate Breasley's teachings through his actions, as he thinks:

> Why deny experience, his artistic soul's sake, why ignore the burden of the old man's entire life? Take what you can. And so little: a warmth, a clinging, a brief entry into another body. One small releasing act. And the terror of it, the enormity of destroying what one had so carefully built.

Again his inner self speaks to him through the voice of the second person. Momentarily, the inner voice wins out and he takes Diana in his arms, but she, sensing his hesitation, pulls away, and he does not take her to him again, resorting instead to a fatherly kiss on the top of her head and ineffectual back-patting. From this point on, the struggle to regain a sense of the moment when all was potential is futile.

David has failed not only himself, by refusing to accept the anima within even after acknowledging its presence, but also Diana, by falling short of what she has needed to break the spell of Coët and facilitate her return to the real world. Thinking of his impending expulsion from the mythic landscape, he contemplates the ramifications of his failure, knowing that he cannot return, being "banned for life now." And worse than Adam, also banned for life from the Garden of Eden, he has left his Eve behind, the manifestation of the anima archetype in the person of Diana.

Leaving Coët, he runs over an object in the road. At first he thinks he has hit a mouse (an oblique reference to Diana, the Mouse) or a snake (a reference to the serpent in the Garden of Eden); but, on turning back, he discovers that he has hit a weasel, the same animal wounded in the tale of *Eliduc,* whose forest he now rides through. Fowles uses the weasel as a symbol that links the motif of his story with that of *Eliduc.* Unlike Eliduc, however, who successfully loved two women and whose tale demonstrates love as a connecting force, David cannot truly love either woman in his life. Thus, his tale demonstrates love as a dividing force since David is a divided man, caught between two worlds. Instead of being able to save the weasel that in *Eliduc* bears the life-restoring red flower, he kills it, and the blood that trickles from its mouth in the shape of the red flower now signifies his present psychic state of death without rebirth. The weasel's body is crushed but the head escapes, indicating the death of magic or creative powers with only the intellect or rational powers surviving.

The remainder of the story comprises David's analysis of his dilemma, not necessary for understanding the story's thesis, but in keeping with David's analytical character. He recognizes that fear, a manifestation of the shadow archetype, has prevented him from accepting the challenge of the quest, and he sees his art as reflecting his failure towards life: "You did not want how you lived to be reflected in your painting; or because it was compromised, so settled-for-the-safe, you could only try to camouflage its hollow reality under craftsmanship and good taste." Broadening the scope of his failure, David sees it as representative of his age. While Breasley is still connected to the past through a life-giving "umbilical cord," David and his contemporaries are "encapsulated in book knowledge." The authorial voice intones:

> David and his generation, and all those to come, could only look back, through bars, like caged animals, born in captivity, at the old green freedom. That described exactly the experience of those last two days: the laboratory monkey allowed a glimpse of his lost true self.

As the mythic quester who quests for all, David is correct in seeing his failure as the failure of his age.

Yet, knowing that he has failed, he also knows that he will eventually forget his failure. The "wound" he has suffered will be covered by a scar, which in time will fade, leaving no trace; but until that moment comes, he will have to live with the realization that "he had refused (and even if he had never seen her again) a chance of a new existence, and the ultimate quality and enduringness of his work had rested on acceptance." Now in Paris he thinks of Coët as "in another universe" and he feels the loss of his paradise as "the most intense pang of the most terrible of all human deprivations; which is not of possession, but of knowledge." Fowles elaborates on David's predicament in an [unpublished] interview: "I meant simply that David knows after Coëtminais that his life will never be the same, but restricted by his new knowledge of himself. His dreams of himself are shipwrecked; but because he is decent he must learn to live with what he knows, with his newly revealed lacks and faults." A last urge in him toward salvation through knowledge is kept in check by "the tall shadow of him," his inability to break through the complacency and confinements, perhaps even decency, of his persona. David is not shadow-possessed, like Clegg in *The Collector,* but neither has he conquered the shadow.

In the last passage, which describes Beth's approach from the plane, Fowles switches from past to present tense in the same way he does in the last page of the revised version of *The Magus.* The major difference, however, is that in *The Magus* the present tense expresses the limitless possibility of the future awaiting Nicholas. For David, the present is an entrapping tense, keeping him frozen in failure because of his denial of the future. The passage reads: "She comes with the relentless face of the present tense. . . . He composes his face into an equal certainty"; it continues: "He has a sense of retarded waking, as if in a postoperational state of consciousness some hours returned but not till now fully credited; a numbed sense of something beginning to slip inexorably away."

In Fowles's use of the "postoperational state" to describe David's condition, we hear an echo of T. S. Eliot's "The Love Song of J. Alfred Prufrock" in which the night is "spread out against the sky / Like a patient etherised upon a table." Other images reinforce the connection with Prufrock, another quester who dares not meet the challenge of life because, like David, he is a divided man, suffering from what Eliot calls "dissociation of sensibility." Like Prufrock who "prepare[s] a face to meet the faces that you meet," David wears a persona that allows him to meet the faces he meets, particularly the face of his wife who now approaches. Also like Prufrock, who has "heard the mermaids singing, each to each," David has caught a liberating glimpse of life's potential at Coët, only to suffer Prufrock's fate when "human voices wake us, and we drown." In similar terms, Fowles describes David as one who "knows one dreamed, yet cannot remember. The drowning cry, jackbooted day." He wakes to reality, the human voices of the present drowning out the dream of the anima (which for Prufrock is symbolized by the mermaids' cry); and "he surrenders to what is left: to abstraction." Eliot's "dissociated" man, Prufrock, becomes Fowles's abstract man, David Williams. In response to his wife's implied question about the weekend, David says, " 'I survived,' " a statement of hollow victory which concludes the novella and leaves us with the sinking sense of David's lost possibilities, his death-in-life in the eternal present, synonymous with Prufock's waking to drown. Had David succeeded in his quest, he would have done far more than survive: he would have lived.

The remaining stories in the collection are connected to the title story by the theme of lost opportunities. The sense of gloom that the ebony tower signifies becomes more pervasive, ending with the image of the dark cloud which overtakes the sun in the last story. In the first of these, **"Poor Koko,"** the narrator's "ordeal," as he calls his encounter with the young thief who burns his writing, brings him the closest of the protagonists of the remaining stories to an understanding of his personal failure, but it leaves him helpless to do anything more than explain it. His quest for self-knowledge is not voluntarily sought but forced upon him by the unusual circumstance of the robbery and his desire to understand it.

The details of the experience that begin the writer's journey are these: having gone to the country to work on his manuscript, he is awakened by a young thief. They engage in an encounter that crosses generational as well as attitudinal lines and that culminates in the thief's burning the writer's manuscript, a seemingly incomprehensible act. Following the act comes an equally incomprehensible gesture: the thief's cocked thumb in the writer's face. His departure leaves the writer the task of understanding the incomprehensible while subjected to "the acrid smell, surely the most distressing of all after burnt human flesh, of cremated human knowledge." What, in effect, has happened is that the heart of the writer, his life's work, has been put to death, and he must now construct a new one grounded in an understanding of his relationship and responsibility towards other people.

The writer begins by analyzing the robber's last "cocked thumb" gesture. At the time of its occurrence, he saw it puzzlingly as a sign of mercy when there was no mercy shown. Later he establishes other meanings for the gesture—all inappropriate to the situation. Finally, after seeing the gesture used by a football player to signal courage to the crowd before the game begins, the writer interprets the thief's gesture as a warning to him: "a grim match was about to start and the opposing team he represented was determined to win." Hidden also in the gesture, as the writer analyzes it, is the thief's feeling that the odds are stacked in the writer's favor. Burning the papers begins the match.

> **Through the stories in *The Ebony Tower*, Fowles sounds a warning by showing us the despair inherent in contemporary life if we cannot take the journey out of the darkness toward wholeness and undividuation.**
>
> **—*Carol M. Barnum***

The writer continues his analysis of the evening based on the linguistic implications of the thief's use of two words: "man" and "right." In the thief's frequent use of "man," the writer sees an attempt to bring them together within the family of man, while at the same time showing the vast differences that separate them. Through his use of "right" (with a question implied) he expresses his "underlying mistrust . . . of language itself." The writer, in his analysis, is, of course, expressing Fowles's view of the deterioration of language, a view he reiterates in discussing the story: "The point I was trying to make is that though I should like to see life become more simple in many (social) ways, language was not one of them" [Letter from Fowles to Barnum, 9 April 1980]. Thus, in the story, the young thief 's frustration at the old man comes from his inability to use language to express himself and his anger at the old man's refusal to share the power of language with him. Understanding this, the old man writes, "I must very soon have appeared to the boy as one who deprived him of a secret—and one he secretly wanted to possess."

On a larger scale, the clash between the boy and the writer is seen as the clash between generations, between a world in which language is meaningful and one in which it is empty, stripped of its "magic" and "mystery" in the profound sense. The writer, again probably speaking as Fowles's mouthpiece, raises the conflict to a universal plane, seeing the problem as extending beyond this particular encounter to include television, the arts, social and political institutions, and the educational system. To strengthen the universal nature of the conflict, Fowles refrains from assigning names to the two main characters; they maintain their generalized roles as the old man and the boy, the writer and the thief. Even while their clash takes on universal proportions, it does not absolve the writer of his responsibility in the matter, which he sees as stemming from his "deafness." The deafness, while not specifically elucidated, is linked to the title of the story, which the writer explains is deliberately obscure. In illuminating its various meanings, he sheds light on the problem existing between himself and the boy, between his view of life and the boy's, between a world in which language and symbol have meaning and the present state of the world in which they do not. For example, when he asked friends to analyze the meaning of the title of his story, the consensus was that it derived from an unusual spelling for Coco the clown. On one level, as the writer explains, this is an accurate interpretation if the title refers to both participants and if "poor" carries its several meanings. However, as the writer continues, he had in mind *koko*, the Japanese word meaning "correct filial behavior, the proper attitude of son to father"; thus, the title means inadequate or inferior filial behavior, indicating the failure of the relationship between the "father" and "son" of the story. Further, the writer illuminates the meaning of the "incomprehensible epigraph" following the title, saying that it "shall have the last word, and serve as judgment on both father and son":

> *Too long a tongue, too short a hand;*
> *But tongueless man has lost his land.*

Inherent in the epigraph, now brought to light through the still viable powers of the old man, is the idea that language must serve to reach out from father to son but must at the same time be accompanied by human love, the "hand." For if man loses his language, the power of the word to communicate, he loses his heritage, his roots. The epigraph "comes with a sad prescience" from old Cornish, an extinct language without a land, since it may foreshadow the fate of English and other contemporary languages if the writer, as the representative "father," keeps his "tongue" to himself, refusing to communicate through his "hand" the love and spirit of the language as a reflection of heritage, "the land." The title of the story and its epigraph are obscure, as is the meaning of the boy's action toward the old man—each requires translation. But the question remains as to whether the writer's new-found understanding, forced on him through such unusual circumstances, can save his age from the fate of extinction. It certainly comes too late to save the boy or provide him with the foundation for a correct filial relationship based on love, understanding, and the old man's transference of the creative power of language.

In the succeeding story, **"The Enigma,"** a mystery of a different kind is presented: the disappearance of John Marcus Fielding, prominent businessman, family man, Member of Parliament. Since the disappearance has no apparent criminal motivation, the question is raised as to why a man who seemed to have everything would want to abscond from life. The answer, as it is pieced together by hypothesis and conjecture, is that a life that seemed to offer a man everything in actuality provided him with an incurable feeling of emptiness; therefore, he set out to create his own mystery through his disappearance.

Since Fielding has disappeared before the story begins, the focus is on Sergeant Michael Jennings, whose life is connected to Fielding's by more than just the investigation. One of their connections involves their concern with keeping up appearances. Peter Fielding, the M.P.'s son, tells Jennings, "Maybe you don't know the kind of world I was brought up in. But its leading principle is never, never, never show what you really feel." Jennings is not much different, being described as one who took very good care indeed not to show his feelings when dealing with his peers and superiors on the force. He can just as easily "put on his public school manner" when addressing Mrs. Fielding. This ability to change face, that is, to assume the persona appropriate to the situation without revealing his true feelings, has served him well (as it has Fielding).

Another connection between Fielding and Jennings involves his attraction toward Isobel Dodgson, Peter's girl friend. At first sight of her, Jennings has "an immediate impression of someone alive, where everyone else has been dead, or playing dead; of someone who lived in the present, not the past." In her vitality, she serves as a potential anima figure for Jennings; and their meeting shifts the story's focus away from Fielding's disappearance to the developing relationship between Jennings and Isobel, such that the enigma now includes the young couple and the question of their future relationship. The conflict that caused Fielding to disappear soon manifests itself, however, in Jenning's relationship toward Isobel, whom he sees at first as fresh, independent, and not taken in by "the Sunday color-supplement view of values" which Fielding and his world represent, until she brings him abruptly down to earth with her crude statement about police brutality. His expectations dashed, Jennings feels "shocked more than he showed, like someone angling for a pawn who finds himself placed in check by one simple move." Disappointed unconsciously by her failure to live up to her potential as an anima figure for him, Jennings nevertheless feels himself consciously relieved to be returned to more familiar ground, now seeing Isobel as a sex object who appeals to him through the more familiar world of the senses.

Isobel is not easily categorized, however. When she tells Jennings her intuitions about Fielding, her ability to see " 'someone else, behind it all,' " she demonstrates again her potential as anima, her ability to see a man whole (Sarah's and Alison's gift), but her potential remains undeveloped since she is as much a product of the contemporary wasteland as is Fielding or Jennings, and, like Jennings, is not on the mythic journey.

From a small detail that she has not divulged to previous investigators, Isobel weaves a story for Jennings that "explains" Fielding's disappearance. Jennings listens while at the same time trying to "calculate how far he could go with personal curiosity under the cover of official duty." As they talk, they discover, despite their different backgrounds, "a certain kind of unspoken identity of situation." In the pragmatic world in which they exist, "identity of situation" rather than identity of feeling forms the basis for a relationship. Still, he sees in her something different that speaks to something inside him, but he does not know how to attain it because he has lost the means of communication; he therefore falls back on sexual communication as the only avenue he knows, despite the fact that

> something about her possessed something that he lacked: a potential that lay like unsown ground, waiting for just this unlikely corn-goddess; a direction he could follow, if she would only show it. An honesty, in one word. He had not wanted a girl so fast and so intensely for a long time. Nevertheless, he made a wise decision.

The allusion to Isobel as a corn-goddess relates her to the vegetative myths and the regeneration cycle. What Jennings seeks without knowing it is rebirth through the experience of the archetypes, here expressed as union with the anima, but he does not know how to journey toward such an experience and seeks direction from her. If she were serving in her potential capacity as anima, she might provide the direction he seeks, leading him to experience the archetypes and to approach wholeness. But she is not the anima; she only possesses the unrealized potential, as deeply locked inside her as it is in Jennings. His "wise decision" in its very nature reveals his inherent problem: decision does not produce archetypal encounter.

Isobel's "fiction" concludes open-endedly with Fielding's walking out. When prompted for a better ending, she says that the real author of the story is not she or anyone else, but the system: " 'Something that had written him. Had really made him just a character in a book.' " Using an analogy that figures prominently in *The French Lieutenant's Woman,* Isobel describes Fielding as being " 'like a fossil—while he's still alive.' " Trapped by the system that "limited" and "prevented" him from changing or evolv-

ing, he left it behind, thereby creating a sense of mystery his own life lacked. Of course, as Isobel tells her story about Fielding, she and Jennings, one cannot forget, are also characters in the story, just as much written by the system that defines them as is Fielding. Equally, they are products of Fowles's fiction, with Fowles using them and the various stories within the story to make a point about the condition of modern existence that "writes us" and denies us the freedom we need to take the mythic journey.

While Isobel tells her story, she is unconsciously tracing "invisible patterns" on the table top with her finger: "a square, a circle with a dot in it." What she traces is the archetype of the mandala, the circle-in-the-square pattern that indicates wholeness. [In an endnote, Barnum adds: "In a letter of 9 April, 1980, Fowles says that the circle with the dot 'was meant to be the universal printer's symbol for full stop, or period. The square, a space or paragraph symbol. But I will now claim your interpretation as conscious!' "] Significantly, Isobel's patterns are invisible, unrecognized by the pair as they discuss a man who, lacking wholeness and the creative powers of archetypal encounter, has killed himself. Jennings, now only referred to as "the sergeant," takes no notice of Isobel's patterns, wondering instead if she is naked beneath her dress. Meanwhile, Isobel raises "the pattern-making finger" and concludes, " 'Nothing lasts like a mystery.' " The finger which draws the pattern of the mandala but does not contain its power is the finger that points to the crux of Fielding's dilemma: life without mystery cannot be endured. Since Fielding, along with Isobel and the sergeant, lacks mystery in his life in the sacred sense, provided through an attachment to meaningful rituals and symbols, he can only attain mystery in the profane sense, created by his own disappearance and described in Isobel's story.

In similar fashion, Isobel and the sergeant create their own mystery in their budding relationship. What they are now faced with is not the solution to Fielding's mystery but the solution to the mystery between them, which the sergeant sees as still another "test," both "test" and "mystery" being used in the limited, non-mythic sense. Fowles writes, "The point was a living face with brown eyes, half challenging and half teasing; not committing a crime against that." The "crime" is not committed in that they plan to continue the relationship, but the language Fowles employs to describe their "first tomorrow" has a distinctly criminal cast when the sergeant "deprive[s]" her of her clothes, finding her "*defenseless* underneath, though hardly an innocent *victim* in what followed" italics mine). Since they are both consenting adults desirous of the anticipated sexual encounter, the criminal language Fowles employs is humorously ironic. Isobel and the sergeant create their own mystery on the sensual level, and while it does not lead to archetypal encounter since they are not on the mythic journey, it is not unpleasurable and provides some respite from the sterility of the wasteland. As the concluding sentence of the story attests: "The tender pragmatisms of flesh have poetries no enigma, human or divine, can diminish or demean—indeed it can only cause them, and then walk out." Although the two characters that remain do not take the mythic journey, whose potential has been hinted at but never realized, they do achieve a union of sorts which is "tender" even while being pragmatic. The flesh provides a poetry of its own, and it will have to suffice since it appears to be all that remains. Instead of clearing up the enigma of Fielding's disappearance, Fowles provides us with a new enigma, inherent in the last sentence with its deliberately ambiguous pronouns. Fowles, himself, may shed meaning on the story if we consider his words in *The Magus:* "To view life as a detective story, as something that could be deduced, hunted and arrested, was no more realistic (let alone poetic) than to view the detective story as the most important literary genre, instead of what it really was, one of the least." Perhaps Fowles is telling us that the detective story part of **"The Enigma"** is of less importance than the more "poetic" story between Jennings and Isobel. If that is the case, the conclusion to the story, which is no conclusion but a new beginning, will have to suffice since in the age of antimyth—the setting for this story and others in the volume—mystery in the sense of enigma is all that remains. Or, as John B. Humma writes [in "John Fowles' *The Ebony Tower:* In the Celtic Mood," *Southern Humanities Review* (1983)], "The Spillanesque winding-up (detective beds heroine) may seem to trivialize a serious story otherwise, but it is in keeping with the genre. Moreover, 'the tender pragmatisms of flesh' which Jennings achieves with Isobel counterpoint all that is lost by David Williams, who had hung back at his portal."

"The Cloud," the last story in the collection, continues the motif of the collection in its descent toward darkness. It begins by painting a picture of a summer day, "vivid with promise," but the participants are divided into sun and shadow, hinting from the start the breakdown in communication that is part of the story's thesis. Further, the two women described in the opening paragraph are lying "stretched as if biered," a description which introduces the image of death that dominates by the end of the story. The two men, Peter and Paul, have no connection to the wisdom of the apostles (although Peter is called "Apostle Peter"); their actions are futile and pointless for the most part. The scene even includes a snake which frightens the children, but of which Peter says philosophically, " 'Proves it's paradise, I suppose.' " All is not Edenic, however much the aura of a "different world" is suggested; the participants are divided from each other and themselves and find themselves strangers in paradise. The crux of the problem is stated by one of the voices (possibly Catherine's):

> What one lost, afterward, was what one had never had strongly at the best of times: a sense of continuity. . . . So now everything became little islands, without communication, without farther islands to which this that one was on was a stepping-stone, a point with point, a necessary stage. Little islands set in their own limitless sea, one crossed them in a minute, in five at most, then it was a different island but the same: the same voices, the same masks, the same emptiness behind the words. Only the moods and settings changed a little; but nothing else. And the fear was both of being left behind and of going on: of the islands past and the islands ahead.

We are again in the land where no one ever goes beneath

the level of the persona, where people meet only in masks. In this existence, actions have no meaning because man is going nowhere, having lost his sense of a past and finding himself without hope for the future. It is the age of anti-myth, the world of the wasteland. Yet the voice continues, asking to be proven wrong, to be surprised, to be provided with something or someone to "string the islands together again." But the narrative structure, islands of thought breaking from present into past tense and back again, moving from person to person without continuity, echoes the thesis of the story. Fowles strengthens thesis through his inclusion of a section from *The Waste Land:* "Hurry up please it's time. Goonight Bill. Goonight Lou. Goonight. Goonight," by means of which he connects Eliot's theme of the breakdown of communication in the wasteland world to his own.

Within this wasteland world, Catherine, the tragic figure of the piece, can relate least well to the others in the group and is incapable of maintaining the persona of happiness they wear, having succumbed to the archetype of the shadow in its manifestation as despair. Her view of life is contrasted with the others. Paul, for instance, exemplifies "decency, mediocrity, muddling through"; he copes with the future by continually "trying." Annabel, his wife, is the "presiding mother-goddess," although "slightly blowsy," indicating her connection with an ancient tradition but one that is greatly reduced in the contemporary world. While there is talk among them, the failure of language is as evident here as it is in Eliot's poem. Life in this wasteland full of the "tired rush of evening people, work drained automata" is life after "the harvest is in. All that's left are the gleanings and leasings: fragments, allusions, fantasies, egos. Only the husks of talk, the meaningless aftermath." The image of the harvest, traditionally associated with the vegetative myth of regeneration, now offers no hope for a new harvest to follow: only the "husks of talk" remain, language without the living symbol.

There remains, however, the power of the story, the repository of myth. Catherine is coaxed by her niece Emma into telling her a story about a princess. As Catherine creates her story of the lonely, sad princess, she also creates her own future (in much the same way that Fielding does in **"The Enigma"**), finding a myth she can become a part of. The story ends with the princess waiting for the return of the prince who has abandoned her, but with whom she will be reunited soon. As Emma returns to the picnickers, Catherine contemplates death, the future she had created for herself in the fairy tale. Like the princess in the tale, she fears men and can find no one to trust and love, since the man she loved committed suicide. Thus, like Prince Florio, he has gone away, but he returns as Smiling Death, "alive, almost fleshed; just as intelligent, beckoning." In a last, meaningless act and under the influence of the shadow archetype, she dryly seduces Peter who has come upon her on his walk away from the others. [In an endnote, Barnum adds: "Fowles gives his view of the act as 'not necessarily a final act of despair—at least possibly one of exorcizing self-disgust. It came to me first as that.' Letter from Fowles, 5 August, 1981."]

Afterwards, Peter descends from the hills and, like the

apostle for whom he is named, denies Catherine, claiming not to have seen her, as the Apostle Peter descended from the Mount of Olives and claimed not to have known Christ. Because he does not tell the others that he has been with Catherine, they leave her to her fate, assuming she has gone ahead. As they emerge into the clearing, they see "a mysterious cloud," which seems "feral and ominous, a great white-edged gray billow beginning to tower over the rocky wall, unmistakable bearer of heavy storm." The picnickers depart, "the princess calls [through the cry of the bird of Catherine's story], but there is no one, now, to hear her," as Catherine has apparently given in to her despair and committed suicide. [In an endnote, Barnum adds: "Curiously, Fowles says that he did not necessarily mean that Catherine commits suicide, remarking, 'If she dies, who tells the story?' Letter from Fowles, 5 August, 1981."] Only the black cloud remains to roll over the deserted meadow.

The dark mood introduced in the first story by the symbol of the ebony tower is now transformed into the symbol of the dark cloud. The characters in this collection of stories have failed, for the most part, in their lives because they have not reached out and communicated to their fellow man the love that is needed to turn the wasteland into the garden. David Williams sees what life lacks but is incapable of changing it; the old writer in **"Poor Koko"** learns through his failure to communicate with the young thief what the failure of language means for the future; the M.P. of **"The Enigma"** disappears in an attempt to create a mystery that is lacking in his meaningless existence, and we are left with "the tender pragmatisms of flesh" that form the basis for the relationship between the sergeant and the girl; and Catherine in **"The Cloud,"** having lost love and despairing of ever finding it again, commits suicide.

Although the general tone of these stories is dark, Fowles's view of life is not one of despair, as his novels *The Magus, The French Lieutenant's Woman,* and *Daniel Martin* attest, each treating protagonists who break out of wasteland existences into self-awareness and understanding because of their ability to take the mythic journey. As Robert K. Morris writes [in "A Forest of Fictions," *The Nation* (13 September 1975)]:

> Fowles's intent as a novelist, and as a writer of these fictions, is to strike the sane balance between art and life at a time when both seem vulnerable to excess, and neither seems susceptible to control. Perhaps only when art descends from the ebony tower will it be able to light up Fowles's cheerless 'bottomless night' and once more tell us, as it has in the past, something about life.

Through the stories in *The Ebony Tower,* Fowles sounds a warning by showing us the despair inherent in contemporary life if we cannot take the journey out of the darkness toward wholeness and individuation.

Susana Onega   (essay date 1989)

SOURCE: "Conclusion," in *Form and Meaning in the Novels of John Fowles,* UMI Research Press, 1989, pp. 165-74.

[*In the excerpt below, Onega examines the major themes and structural devices of Fowles's novels.*]

[The different trends at work in the contemporary English novel from the fifties onwards involve] the steady evolution from the "angry" reaction against experimentalism in the 1950s to a new form of experimentation best described as an overriding concern with the nature of fiction and reality. This concern has led in recent decades to a new kind of experimental writing, characterized by its self-conscious and systematic concern with its own status as an artifact and with the relationships between fiction and reality.

This general scheme is perfectly applicable to the literary evolution of John Fowles, who, with his double training in English realism and French experimentalism, seems as concerned with writing about the real as he is determined to test and undermine the received conventions of literary realism.

The tension created by this double, paradoxical endeavor finds complex but consistent expression in his novels. John Fowles's stylistic versatility, his remarkable capacity to create different styles according to the different requirements of the subject matter of each novel, combined with his thorough knowledge of history, work to produce an overriding effect of realism; while his repeated parodying of well-worn literary traditions and his breaking all rules of literary decorum work to produce the contrary effect of highlighting the literary nature of the world created.

Kerry McSweeney's description of John Fowles [in "Withering into the Truth: John Fowles and *Daniel Martin,*" in *Critical Quarterly* (Winter 1987)] as "more an unfolding than a growing artist" points to a most important characteristic of the writer, for it underlines Fowles's unflinching tendency to take up the same topics in every

---

Fowles on the presence of the anima in his works:

Anima . . . it's very difficult for me to say where it came from originally. I'd have to be analyzed to do that. But it's the idea of the female ghost inside one that's always been very attractive to me. Perhaps it's bound up with my general liking for mystery—the idea that there is a ghost like that inside one. In historical or social terms I've always had great sympathy for, I won't quite say feminism in the modern sense, but for a female principle in life. It doesn't always tie in with modern feminism. My wife would deny point blank that I'm a proper feminist. But I do, more for obscure personal reasons, hate the macho viewpoint. This is the one thing I can't swallow in America, both North and South. I find it detestable.

John Fowles, in an interview with Katherine Tarbox, in her The Art of John Fowles, *University of Georgia Press, 1988.*

novel, testing the thematic, the stylistic, and also the structural implications a bit further each time.

From the thematic point of view, every novel deals in one way or another with Fowles's major concern: human freedom, focused from two major perspectives. From the point of view of man in isolation, freedom is presented as a process of individuation of the self; from the point of view of man in relation to society, as a power-bondage relationship.

Following Heraclitus's theory of the Many (*hoi polloi*), the masses, the untaught, and the Few (*hoi aristoi*), the elect, the chosen and civilized, Fowles explains in **The Aristos** his belief that the status of the Few is a privileged one they have got through mere good luck, both socially and genetically. Consequently, for him, being an *aristos* means not so much that you are entitled to exert power on the less privileged, but rather that you are in "a state of responsibility" with respect to the masses.

In **The Collector,** Frederick Clegg, the representative of the Many, is a collector; Miranda, the prototypical *aristos,* an art student. In every novel by John Fowles, collecting and creating turn into activities symbolic of two basic attitudes to life to be found simultaneously in every balanced man: the collector is *l'homme moyen sensuel,* the intrinsic materialist, a man who only lives to satisfy his senses, watching, touching, possessing. So the collector is the least imaginative of men, for in order to exist he must tangibly possess the objects that obsess him, while the creator rejects this material reality and uses his imagination to create his own subjective alternatives to it.

From **The Magus** onwards, the immature *aristos* is invariably described as a collector: Nicholas Urfe collects "girlfriends" and the young Conchis bird-sounds; Charles Smithson, ammonites; Daniel Martin and his friend Anthony, orchids. Consequently, "learning" for them always implies the rejection of their collecting activities. Those who are unable to overcome this tendency, like Frederick Clegg in **The Collector** or Alphonse de Deukans in **The Magus,** are unbalanced or even mentally deranged—as unbalanced as, at the other extreme of the spectrum, Miles Green, the hero of **Mantissa,** a writer reduced to his mental activity of creating literary worlds, and suffering from total amnesia with regard to the material universe.

The struggle between collectors and creators; the teaching of the young by the mature *aristos;* and the use and abuse of power, are all subjects John Fowles touches on and develops along different lines in his novels. Whether the hero is confronted with a Prospero-like figure, a magus who either exerts power over him (or her) in order to teach him, as is the case with Nicholas Urfe with Conchis, or with Miranda with G. P.; or who confirms the route taken, as does Herr Professor Otto Kirnberger with Daniel Martin; whether he has to face, like Charles Smithson, or like Miles Green, a mysterious woman, pursuing her own, unimaginable ends; or whether he has to revolt against his father, as does Mr. Bartholomew, the result of the confrontation always takes the form of *anagnorisis,* a cathartic discovery of the utter isolation of man and of the remoteness of God. At this stage, the hero suffers an agonizing

phase of deterministic despair, as he apprehends the existentialist void or its equivalent. But as soon as he masters his angst, and accepts the void, he is seized by *une joie de vivre,* a *delirium vivens,* the passion to exist that comes together with the realization that man is radically free to choose even death, as Conchis or Dick Thurlow do. This realization of personal freedom, which is presented in psychological terms, brings about the hero's "individuation" and often follows the discovery of the polymorphous nature of reality.

The assumption that man must seek his freedom in order to mature and that reality is complex and many-sided, made up not only of the ontologically real but also of the imagined, not only of the actual, but also of the potentially possible, not only of what is or was, but also of what might have been, are perhaps the two basic messages John Fowles wants us to distill from his novels. These messages are to be found not only at the thematic level, but are also echoed and reflected structurally.

> From the thematic point of view, each of Fowles's novels deals in one way or another with Fowles's major concern: human freedom, focused from two major perspectives. From the point of view of man in isolation, freedom is presented as a process of individuation of the self; from the point of view of man in relation to society, as a power-bondage relationship.
>
> —*Susana Onega*

From the structural point of view, each novel works to affirm the polymorphous nature of reality by different means: by presenting two or more opposed, utterly divergent but also complementary worlds enjoying the same status; by the alternation of narrative voices; the shifts of time and space; the multiplication of realistic, mythical, psychological, and literary versions of the same events; and through the parodic use of well-known literary conventions. Indeed, from **The Collector** onwards, each novel consciously assumes and parodies one—or more—traditional novel-writing conventions, but as we move from **The Collector** to **A Maggot** we also move from a fiction that is predominantly realistic to a much more boldly experimental and specifically metafictional kind of fiction, for, even though in **Daniel Martin** Fowles seemed determined to adhere to the canons of realism, the novel naturally moves to the metafictional pole, affirming, along with the other novels, the importance of the psychological and of the literary aspects of reality.

In **The Collector,** John Fowles offers us two complementary versions of the events—Frederick Clegg's "objective" first-person account counterbalanced and undermined by Miranda's much more literary version recorded in her diary—and forces us to accept them as part of a unique whole by interrupting Clegg's narrative midway in order to have us read Miranda's diary, a diary Miranda has hidden under the mattress of her bed in the prison-cellar where it is likely to remain for ages after her death, unless Clegg himself finds it, and allows us access to it through his mind and eyes.

In the last entry of her diary, Miranda lapses from the preterite into the present tense. Being a metadiscourse within the main one, Miranda's present is included within Clegg's story time, so that the time of her narrative and the time of her story coincide in her present, though with reference to Clegg's narration they have taken place in the past. When Clegg's diegesis and narration overlap in the present, however, his present can only be measured with reference to our own present. Thus, when narrative and story time coincide at the end of the novel we realize with a pang that we are not dealing with the confession of a remote crime, but with the account of some horribly near experience that shows signs of intending to stretch into the future, threatening not only Marian, the next victim, but also the reader. The compression of narrative and story time in a pregnant present is a device John Fowles uses again in the following novels. With it he structurally expresses his existentialist conception of time as a succession of "nows," which precludes knowledge of the future.

In *The Collector,* Miranda intuits that it is possible to destroy her awful reality by striving to create a fictional alternative to it with her diary. In *The Magus* this alternative world is a reality so tangible that the hero, Nicholas Urfe, is able to bodily cross its boundaries and physically enter its realm. Again, the structure of the novel neatly echoes its message.

Structurally, *The Magus* may be said to follow a circular development involving three major stages: from London to Phraxos and back to London again. At the narrative level, the overall structure of *The Magus,* like that of *The Collector,* can be seen as linear, by virtue of the discourse narrated by Nicholas Urfe. Within this linear development, the central episodes corresponding to his visits to Bourani disrupt the linear development by the introduction of a second narrator: at Bourani Nicholas sometimes hands over the narrative role to Maurice Conchis, who in his turn narrates his own life-story to Nicholas Urfe.

Conchis's narration, like Miranda's, is to be considered as a metadiscourse engulfed by the primary narration, although the stories Conchis narrates refer to episodes of his own life and so must be viewed as retrospective heterodiegetic digressions, that is, as digressive anachronies related only analogically to the diegesis. At the end of the novel, a third narrator identifiable with the implied author omnisciently comments in two metalepses on the moral of the whole novel, thus adding to the discourse and the metadiscourse a third, ontological level.

Unlike the mythical hero, Nicholas Urfe undergoes at Bourani a series of trials exclusively intended to test and improve his perception of reality. If Nicholas is to mature, he must learn to distrust his senses and to foster his imagination. So the quality of the hero's quest is wholly fictional and psychological, and is carried out by means of three major literary tests: first, he has to participate in the metatheater, an allegorical masque consisting of two devices—portrait-like staging of iconic scenes by secondary actors, and performance of the *Three Hearts* story by Urfe himself and the twin sisters. Secondly, he hears the narration of Conchis's life-story; and thirdly he is made to listen to a series of tales with a moral, such as "The Tale of the Swiss and the Goats" or "The Tale of the Prince and the Magician."

From a thematic point of view, the situation Urfe has lived with Alison in England, the situation he is living with Lily at Bourani, and the situation Conchis describes when he narrates his life-story bear clear-cut analogies, so much so that both the metadiscourse and the metatheater may be considered as inverted *mises en abyme* of the primary discourse. Indeed, the function of the masque at Bourani is to enact materially the morals encapsulated in the iconic tales and in Conchis's life-story, in order to provide a concrete realization of the theoretical lessons imparted by them. Thus, for example, after Conchis has spoken of his long-deceased fiancée, Lily appears at the villa. Quite accurately, Nicholas himself interprets the incidents as devices "designated to deceive all his senses." As we learn later, Lily's role in the masque is meant to convince Urfe of the fact that it is possible to touch a woman who only exists in his imagination.

Structurally, then, if we take the main story (Alison and Nicholas) to represent the material, and the masque (Lily and Nicholas), the psychological aspects of reality, and Conchis's story (Lily and Conchis), the inverted mirror image of the first, we may understand *The Magus* as one tale containing three variations of the same story told from complementary perspectives which, when mixed, offer a polymorphous unique whole of a literary character. The fact that it is so difficult to separate these three theoretically different "variations" in practice points to one important structural characteristic of the novel: namely that the *mises en abyme* it contains are not "concentrating" but, on the contrary, are *mises en abyme éclatées,* that is, *mises en abyme* whose elements appear scattered and interwined with the elements of the main story and with the elements of each other, forming an inextricable unity.

At the very end of the novel, the narrator-author, breaking the rules of narrative decorum, takes over the narration to comment in a gnomic present on the insecure future of the hero. As he had already done in *The Collector,* John Fowles suddenly removes the gap between narrative and story time, to leave his hero and heroine in a *frozen present.* Alison and Nicholas frozen in an eternal present is John Fowles's verbal icon for the final truth he has tried to develop through the whole novel, namely that, for the contemporary existentialist hero, the aim of the quest is the quest itself.

Thus, in *The Magus,* the changes of intro-homodiegetic narrators and the metaleptic intrusions of the extra-heterodiegetic narrator-author work to confirm the thematic assertion that reality is polymorphous and that the boundaries between fiction and nonfiction are easily crossed and so, by implication, wholly artificial.

In *The French Lieutenant's Woman* John Fowles carries the game a step further, denying even the existence of these fragile barriers. In this novel, the contemporary "real" world of the twentieth-century heterodiegetic narrator is meant to set a contrast to the "fictional" Victorian world of the diegesis. In order to accommodate his narration to the Victorian convention, the narrator assumes the role of omniscience and sustains it with minor frame-breaks up to the beginning of chapter 13, where his answer to the rhetorical question which closes chapter 12, "Where is Sarah. Out of what shadows does she come?," acts as a major frame-break, shattering to its foundations the illusion of realism created so far: "I do not know. The story I'm telling is all imagination."

After this first major frame-break, the narrator toys with the convention: he corrects himself, confesses his ignorance about certain matters, admits that he is inventing them, and blurs the boundaries between fiction and reality by including historical figures like Hitler or Dante Gabriel Rossetti within the diegesis. Finally, he even allows himself to appear in the story in the flesh, first facing Charles Smithson in a train, and later on tossing a coin to help himself decide which of the two endings he has selected for his novel he will narrate first.

In this example, as in many others to be found throughout the novel, the narrator uses the Victorian convention of the omniscient narrator parodically. [In "The Novel Interrogates Itself: Parody and Self-Consciousness in Contemporary English Fiction," in *The Contemporary English Novel,* 1979] Robert Burden has defined parody as "a mode of imitation in subversive form," while pastiche is defined as "a nonsubversive form of imitation." These definitions of parody and pastiche may explain the major frame-breaks in the novels of John Fowles as well as the overriding use of traditional conventions: the "confession" and "diary" conventions in *The Collector;* the pattern of the mythical hero's quest in *The Magus,* in *Daniel Martin,* and in *A Maggot;* the Victorian convention of omniscience, and the thematic indebtedness to Victorian romance in *The French Lieutenant's Woman.* They also may explain the use of seemingly eighteenth- or nineteenth-century styles; the telling of tales; the literal quotations; the wealth of literary allusions, both to past and to contemporary literature: the echoes of Shakespeare, of Richardson and Defoe, of Jane Austen and Hardy, of T. S. Eliot and, in a word, every possible sort of imitation, enhancing the fictionality of the worlds created and expressing conscious indebtedness to the bulk of the Western literary tradition as a whole.

The inclusion of the author and of historical figures and events in the diegesis of *The French Lieutenant's Woman* are meant to blur the boundaries between fictional and ontological reality. The narration of three different endings (one imagined by Charles Smithson, and two others selected by the narrator) function to enhance the existentialist conviction that the future of man is not predetermined, but depends on successive acts of the will.

As in *The French Lieutenant's Woman,* in *Daniel Martin* a basic contrast is drawn between two worlds. In the later novel, the English world of Daniel's childhood and university years in the 1940s and 1950s is set in contrast with the American, movie-star world of his mature age in the 1970s. But, again, the English world endlessly transforms itself, as the adult narrator recalls particular episodes of it. To match the ever-changing nature of his past, the voice of the narrator simultaneously changes: he tells the story of his childhood and youth at Thorncombe and Oxford in the third person and in the preterite, but lapses into the first person and the present tense whenever he digresses about his recent past or present, and even sometimes in the middle of his reported memories. At the same time, he pretends to be writing an autobiographical novel about a fictional character called Simon Wolfe, while his girlfriend, Jenny McNeil, writes her own divergent and complementary version of the same story.

Following the pattern of *The Magus,* Daniel Martin undertakes a climactic journey at two different levels. On the one hand, the journey is an ontologically real trip from California through New York to England, and then Egypt and Palmyra, ending up in England again. On the other, it is a psychological quest for individuation, made up of Daniel Martin's flashbacks to his childhood and early adulthood in England. When, at the end of the novel, Daniel Martin and Jane are left at Oxford, exactly at the point where they had taken the wrong fork of the road twenty-six years before, the psychological and the ontological journeys fuse into each other in an all-enveloping "now," similar to the pregnant "nows" reached at the end of *The Collector,* of *The Magus,* and of *The French Lieutenant's Woman.*

In *A Maggot* the contrast of opposed and complementary worlds is set between the twentieth-century world of the heterodiegetic narrator-cum-chronicler and the eighteenth-century world of the fictional mother of Ann Lee, the historical founder of the Shakers. If the Gothic historical romance and the Victorian multiplot novel provide the patterns for parody in *The French Lieutenant's Woman,* *A Maggot* combines echoes of eighteenth-century edifying prose; of the sentimental and of the gothic novel, as of the genuine judicial reports made by Defoe and other early journalists on the confessions of convicts at Newgate. In the novel, the confessions are interspersed with diverse eighteenth-century genuinely historical chronicles from *The Gentleman's Magazine,* which further show John Fowles's relish in the use not only of parody but also of deliberate pastiche, and which again warns us against the temptation to separate the ontological from the fictional.

Although in *A Maggot* the eighteenth-century world is described with remarkable wealth and accuracy of detail, the novel simultaneously affirms its radical twentieth-century character. Matching the ontological, the psychological, and the literary layers described for *The Magus,* which find their counterpart in the simultaneous movement backwards and forwards of the ontological and of the psychological hero's quest in *Daniel Martin, A Maggot* offers the reader a rationalist, a metaphysical, and a psychological version of the events narrated which, although apparently existing in order to cancel each other out, actually work to affirm the possibility of their co-existence on a fourth, all-enveloping literary level.

The polymorphous nature of reality thus stated, it is easy to see that it not only affects the material and the psychological universe of the protagonists, but the protagonists themselves: in Fowles's novels, every man or woman contains within him or herself a number of divergent and complementary potentialities which must be discovered, comprehended, and fostered. Daniel Martin's infinite mirrored faces express his condition of creator, like Conchis's and Mr. B.'s ever-changing identities; and, from *The Magus* onwards, every heroine of John Fowles has in herself a duality of character that continuously baffles the hero: Alison's oxymoronic quality is expressed as the splitting into twin characters (Lily and Rose) in the metatheater; as their names indicate in the Victorian convention, Lily is spiritual and virginal, Rose down-to-earth and sexually aggressive.

This archetypal dichotomy of woman will reappear in *The Ebony Tower,* where the Mouse stands for the ideal and the Freak for the real; in *The French Lieutenant's Woman,* where Sarah is alternatively seen as an innocent, virginal maiden, and as a succuba; in *Daniel Martin,* in the parodically Victorian "Heavenly Twins" Nell and Jane; in the "Fairy Sisters" Marjory and Miriam; and in Nancy Reed's twin sisters Mary and Louise; in *Mantissa,* in the splitting of the muse into Dr. Delfie a Nurse Cory; and in *A Maggot,* where Rebecca Hocknell, also known as Fanny and Louise, a barren prostitute, mysteriously transforms herself into a pious visionary and the mother of a religious reformer.

The assumption that man must seek his freedom in order to mature and that reality is complex and many-sided are perhaps the two basic messages John Fowles wants us to distill from his novels.

—*Susana Onega*

Summing up the ideas discussed so far, we can say that if for Miranda the material reality had to be obliterated by a conscious effort of the imagination; if for Nicholas Urfe it was possible to walk in and out of the fictional world at will; and if for the narrator of *The French Lieutenant's Woman* these barriers did not seem to exist, for Daniel Martin the Cartesian proposition has become "I create, I am: all the rest is dream, though concrete and executed."

It is no wonder, then, that in the following novel, *Mantissa,* John Fowles should write a novel about the writing of a novel by a writer whose notion of reality is restricted to the workings of his mind. Doing away with ontological reality as a whole, *Mantissa* offers the reader a psychological reality in which space is restricted to the inside of Martin Green's skull, and time to a present devoid of past or future, exclusively filled by the obsessive skirmishes of muse and writer about the only possible topic: how to write still

one more variation of a unique, all-enveloping and life-generating text.

With the publication of *Mantissa* the contest inaugurated with *The Collector* between fact and fiction, between the tangible and the imaginary or, in Fowles's terms, between the English realistic pull and the French experimental temptation, is finally resolved in favor of metafiction. The publication of *A Maggot,* one year later, with its display of historical data and its wealth of realistic detail, apparently a pendular swing backwards from experimentalism into realism, similar to the one attempted in *Daniel Martin,* constitutes nevertheless—like *Daniel Martin* itself—a most radical study in the difficulty of separating the mental from the actual, "what might have been" from "what has been," the real from the unreal, and so thoroughly confirms Fowles's steady course in the direction of metafiction.

Although published after *The Collector, The Magus* is, as is well known, the first novel written by John Fowles. For years the writer had trouble with this novel, rewriting it once and again. One reason for Fowles's dissatisfaction with it might be attributed to the enormous scope and range of this novel, which may be said to sum up his whole vision of the world. So many and so important are the ideas Fowles compressed in this novel that he has spent twenty more years developing aspects of them in his subsequent fiction. When, for example, Daniel Martin exultantly cries "I create, I am" and decides to accommodate his life to this dictum, he is only discovering something Nicholas Urfe had already intuited when he affirmed, "Not *cogito,* but *scribo, pingo, ergo sum.*" And when in *A Maggot* Mr. B. burns his books in order to direct the actors he himself has hired, he is only putting into practice, of his own accord, the lesson Maurice Conchis wanted Urfe to take in; namely, that in order to mature, man has to become his own *magus.* The fact that Nicholas needed somebody to open his eyes, whereas Mr. B. did not, proves that after a long, painful process of refinement John Fowles's unique hero has reached the kind of superior understanding about the human condition that is sought for by all religions and which implies, in Buddhist terms, the rejection of "*lilas,* the pursuit of triviality" (*The Magus*).

At a surface level, the word "maggot," like the word "mantissa," may be said to evoke precisely the kind of triviality expressed by the Buddhist concept of *lilas.* At a deeper level, however, "the maggot" symbolizes, as we have seen, the cyclical movement of life and death which, visualized in the *mandala,* sums up, in archetypal terms, the basic pattern of the self's struggle into being.

Explaining the meaning of "maggot" in the preface of the novel, John Fowles said that he had written it "out of obsession with a theme." We might take the author's statement literally for . . . not only *A Maggot* but every one of the six full-length novels so far written by John Fowles depicts, beneath the profusion of contradictory data, alternative versions, and literary references, a major concern with one single theme, iconically expressed in the archetypal meaning of the word "maggot"—namely, the essence and purpose of human existence.

Being a twentieth-century agnostic, John Fowles time and again has expressed his need for human transcendence in the only terms available: through the kind of archetypal symbolism that Jung presented as the contemporary alternative to pre-rationalist myth and religion. The archetypal quality of Mr. B.'s journey is what confers on him his representative character.

His struggle for individuation synthesizes the never-ending striving not only of every John Fowles's hero, but of every man. The fact that this striving is presented as cyclical and progressive (that is, as endlessly yielding Christ-figures like Ann Lee, ready to take up the amelioration of mankind at the point where it was left in the preceding cycle), may be taken as evidence that John Fowles has finally reached beyond the hopelessness of existentialism in order to affirm a certain faith in a capacity for progressive improvement, not only of the individual, but of the human species at large.

However, undermining this hope, the doubt still remains as to whether Mr. B. stands for every man or whether John Fowles still holds the existentialist belief that general truths are mere illusions, that each individual has to work out his own salvation for himself, for, encapsulated in his own particularity, he is utterly alone. Or again, expressed in John Fowles's own terms, whether man is really free to aspire to and eventually to achieve the divine status of the Father, or whether his freedom is only an illusion made to appear temporarily real within a wholly unreal, literary world, ironically created by the power of John Fowles's magic wand.

Raymond J. Wilson III   (essay date Spring 1990)

SOURCE: "Fowles's Allegory of Literary Invention: *Mantissa* and Contemporary Theory," in *Twentieth Century Literature*, Vol. 36, No. 1, Spring, 1990, pp. 61-72.

[*In the following essay, Wilson interprets Fowles's novel* Mantissa *as an allegorical attack on poststructuralist theory.*]

> [*Interviewer*]: (*with reference to post-structuralists*): "*You seem to make fun of them in* Mantissa."
>
> [Fowles]: "Well, I did in *Mantissa* because I think they've been granted altogether too powerful a position on the intellectual side." [John Fowles with Carol M. Barnum, "An Interview with John Fowles," in *Modern Fiction Studies* (Spring 1985)]

An allegory of the creative process structures John Fowles's *Mantissa,* an allegory that proceeds by means of, and within, a parody of contemporary theoretical ideas on that same creative process. Within his parody, Fowles takes hold of the post-structuralist sexual metaphor of texts and transforms it into a unique image of the creative process—the remerging of the public/logical self with the secret/intuitive self in literary creation. Drawing primarily from Roland Barthes but also from Jacques Derrida and Jacques Lacan, Fowles ridicules the sexual theory of the text while simultaneously transforming it into an inter-

esting and plausible allegorical expression of the creative process. In the allegory, Miles and Erato, the traditional Muse of love poetry (who, in Fowles's novel, has been "stuck" with the whole of fiction as well), are parts of one person. Miles, in his amnesia, has remembered only his social "presentation" self, his logic, and his masculine vanity; all of his forgotten "frivolous," feminine, creative aspects, he sees as another person, Erato. As long as the two remain characters, the closest they can come to union is the sexual act; the impossible full recovery from amnesia would mean the remerging of the characters into one person. That this person is John Fowles emerges slowly because the reader does not at first recognize that this novel is transpiring within a skull. The delay leads to refutation; together the two principles of delay and refutation form a paradigm for the mechanism of Fowles's sexual allegory, of literary invention in *Mantissa.*

In providing the parodic vehicle for the allegory, *Mantissa*'s existence proclaims that John Fowles has decided to take the post-structuralist theorists at their word and produce a text that conforms to their explanations. Such parodic writing may take place in each age. For example, [in his *Inventions,* 1982] Gerald Bruns, interpreting Hugh Kenner, notes that "Joyce shares with Swift and the Swift-like Pope of *The Dunciad* a common point of departure: What would happen if things actually were as our Modern Philosophers represent them to be?" What, for example, would happen "if things were as naturalism represents them to be? Answer: they would be as they are in *Dubliners,*" says Bruns, and he continues: "Swift was no Lockean, but he understood how by parodying Locke one could produce Gulliver, whose mental failures are so many descriptions of how the Lockean mind is supposed to work." Bruns makes the same point about Locke in reference to Pope. Similarly, we may ask: What would a novel look like if the post-structuralists are right? John Fowles's answer: If they are right a novel will look like *Mantissa.* However, without recognition of the allegorical dimension, Fowles's novel will likely strike the reader as an absurd "mantissa," an unimportant, trivial addition to Fowles's discourse. The allegory exists within a context of this parody of contemporary theory.

Fowles's familiarity with contemporary academic schools of theory is undeniable. In an interview with Carlin Romano ["A Conversation with John Fowles," in *Boulevard: Journal of Contemporary Writing* (Spring 1987)], Fowles discusses his unsympathetic responses in his reading of Jacques Derrida and Jacques Lacan. More generally, Fowles's work radiates an overall feel that could lead Philip Thody, for example, in his introduction to the English translation of Roland Barthes' *Criticism and Truth,* to say that "contemporary novelists such as John Fowles . . . clearly owe a debt to the style of thinking about prose fiction which Barthes was one of the first to develop." And the books are sprinkled with specific references. Catherine, in Fowles's story **"The Cloud,"** which ends *The Ebony Tower,* decides that she hates a man named Peter when he responds unintelligently to her explanation of a book by Roland Barthes (possibly *Mythologies*), the translation of which she has been editing. Daniel Martin, in the novel of that name, develops his relationship with Jane, the main female character of the book, through their discussion of the writings of the Marxist theorists Georg Lukacs and Antonio Gramsci; Gramsci's words even provide Fowles with the opening epigraph for *Daniel Martin.* The primary transformation of character in the novel comes from Daniel's writing a novel, and his writing develops in response to Lukacs' and Gramsci's ideas, as Daniel interprets them during his conversations with Jane.

Within *Mantissa* itself, Fowles's character, Miles Green, tells Erato that "I feel sure we have one thing in common": resentment of the neglect she has suffered from "the campus faculty factories." In case anyone should wonder what, specifically, he attacks in *Mantissa,* Fowles has his character list the targets: "the structuralists and deconstructivists . . . the semiologists" and "the marxists." Miles adds "academic Uncle Tom Cobbleigh" to these, referring to an old Devon ballad; and since, according to a standard reference work, Old Tom was the "last named of the seven village worthies who borrowed Tom Pearce's grey mare on which to ride to 'Widecombe Fair,'" Fowles probably means to depict practitioners of all the schools as crowding comically on the back of the single overloaded mare of fiction.

Fowles, is, thus, almost certainly ridiculing contemporary theory in *Mantissa,* and yet he transforms a poststructuralist sexual theory of texts into his own allegory of the creative process. While limiting its action to the inside of a skull, the allegory performs a gamboling, comic commentary on the creative process and a hilarious debate—with structuralist and post-structuralist theorists—over the artist's position in the process of artistic creation. In an admitted pun, Fowles plays with words by naming one of Erato's avatars Dr. A. Delphie [The critic adds in a footnote: "*Adelphi* is a comedy by the Latin writer Terence, based on a lost Greek model, in which the son of a wealthy man falls in love with a slave dancing girl, possibly a model for Fowles's Erato. . . . Delphi, of course, is the city on the slopes of Mount Parnassus, home of Apollo and the Muses: the cave-shrine there was called 'the novel of the world.'"] Clinically and scientifically, she says "we can offer most" of the sexual positions "in the Kama Sutra," words which might be a direct parody of Roland Barthes' definition of writing [in *The Pleasure of the Text,* 1978] as a treatise of "the science of various blisses of language, its Kama Sutra." *Mantissa* may be an individual text of bliss that provides a critical entrance into the text of bliss as a category. Such an interpretation sees *Mantissa* as a novel that also functions as criticism, providing an insight into what Roland Barthes called the "text of bliss," which is "outside of criticism, *unless it is reached through another text of bliss.*"

Fowles transforms this into allegory when Erato and Miles identify storytelling with sexual intercourse, and she attaches a different sexual position to each letter of the alphabet which may be Fowles's deft analogy to the alphabetical arrangement of *The Pleasure of the Text.* The huge number of sexual positions they have tried, and that they plan to try, represents the infinite variety of narrative courses open to the author as he or she faces the terror of the blank page: "You know, it can be constant, even rather frightening, because you write every word, you have a hundred—or at least three—choices, anyway," says Fowles in the Romano interview. At the height of their union, the walls of the hospital room become transparent and people outside, in the position of readers looking into the author's head, can see the moment when the author's "presentation self" is grappling with his "inspiration"—as private and, in the post-structuralist parlance, as sexual a moment as Miles and Erato's mutual orgasm.

Most importantly, the creative self dominates. When Miles discovers that Erato is the author of *The Odyssey,* a work he can never hope to equal, he concedes her complete artistic ascendancy. And despite Miles's claim to be cured, she simply knocks him into a syncope with a blow to the jaw, or eludes his lunge so that he knocks himself out; she resumes her shape as Dr. A. Delphie, and continues her sexual "treatment" of his amnesia. Within the sexual rhythm between Miles and Erato, each time Miles relapses into unconsciousness, Fowles says that Miles drops into a "syncope," a word which has a medical and a grammatical meaning. Medically, the word indicates a break in consciousness caused by the failure of the heart's action; grammatically it means a break, a cutting short, an abbreviation, contraction, or sudden cessation or interruption. Fowles may again be absurdly fitting *Mantissa* to Barthes who [in *The Pleasure of the Text*] connects the "physics of bliss" to "the groove, the inscription, the syncope." In the syncopes, Miles does not cede his autonomy to an entity outside himself called language, but to Erato, who is, ultimately, a forgotten part of himself—and this is the point of Fowles's allegory, the workings of which we can understand through the paradigm that has two parts: delay and refutation.

The allegorical impact of *Mantissa* has a delayed effect in the book because Fowles has established the apparent setting as a hospital room, but the room's domed shaped and bumpy padding reveal its allegorical location as the inside of a writer's skull. This is an appropriate place for an allegory of the process of invention, as its analogy with Samuel Beckett's *Endgame* suggests. In Beckett's play, two high windows suggest the interior of a skull and the action revolves around a story that is always nearing its end but never does reach a conclusion. The room in *Mantissa* is lined with gray corrugations that Miles eventually identifies as standing for the gray matter of the human brain. Present from the beginning as the reader sees in retrospect, the skull/brain context is a fecund cavity for an allegory on the creative process.

The allegorical implications of the skull setting emerge in an aesthetic context when Miles tries, unsuccessfully, to walk out on Erato, whom he considers "essentially a mere call girl." In the episode Erato says, "You can't walk out of your own brain." First she makes the door and his clothes disappear, and when the door reappears, "All stands as in a mirror, or a Magritte." He can only respond, "Ridiculous." "Magritte's strategy," says yet another post-structuralist theorist, Michel Foucault, in *This Is Not a Pipe,* is to deploy "largely familiar images, but images whose recognizability is immediately subverted and rendered moot by 'impossible,' 'irrational,' or 'senseless' conjunctions." The scene in *Mantissa* reverses this process; the reader's shock comes from realizing that the items so gradually introduced by Fowles—a man in "a borrowed woman's purple bathrobe that is too small for him," a naked woman who is supposed to be a minor Greek deity, and a cuckoo clock with a pseudo-Grecian garment hanging ludicrously from it—are actually in improbable juxtaposition, "like in a Magritte." As with the painter, Fowles's shock induces a laugh, followed by an independent seeing. The laugh is partly on post-structuralist theory, a laugh that is the essence of the allegory's comic contradiction of contemporary theory; and by delaying recognition, Fowles makes it a laugh of insight.

The delay allows Fowles to establish a dialogue with contemporary criticism before the refutational implications of the allegory become clear. To be like Roland Barthes' writer, Miles Green would have to be "the blind spot of systems, adrift"; for Barthes, the writer "is the joker in the pack, the mana, a degree zero, the dummy in the bridge game." Just such a writer is Miles Green. In Part One of *Mantissa,* Miles Green—who is being treated for amnesia—stares uncomprehendingly at a nurse's cradling arms; she shows him a manuscript the way a maternity ward nurse shows a newborn infant to its mother who has been unconscious at its birth. When the nurse reads a few words, the "baby" turns out to be *Mantissa,* the writing of which, in line with contemporary theories that assign the author little or no importance, Miles has forgotten. Miles Green's total lack of memory of anything before this "birth" connects to a passage in Roland Barthes' "The Death of the Author" [in his *Image—Music—Text,* 1977] in which Barthes claims that "the modern scriptor is born simultaneously with the text," and is "in no way equipped with a being preceding or exceeding the writing," and the author "is not the subject with the book as predicate." The birth scene works better if the reader is still ignorant of the skull location; Fowles creates an enigma that the reader solves with dawning recognition of the allegorical location.

A similar delayed reaction also characterizes the dialectic structure of Fowles's argument with theory; *Mantissa's* characters first state a position about the source of literary creativity equivalent to the contemporary critic's; this statement is then refuted by an aspect of the novel's structure or by a second statement that carries the logic to the next step, reveals its absurdity, and so discredits it. For example, "At a certain level," says Miles Green, in what Harold Fawkner calls [in his *The Timescapes of John Fowles,* 1984] a "crypto-Derridean" comment, "there is in any case no connection between author and text. . . . The deconstructivists have proved that beyond a shadow of a doubt." While a wide variety of quotes from Jacques Derrida could be brought forward as examples to illustrate Miles's statement, the following from *Writing and Difference* might be accepted as typical:

> Furtiveness—in Latin—is the manner of the thief, who must act very quickly in order to steal from me the words which I have found . . . must purloin them before I have even found them, I am certain that I have always already been divested of them. . . . As soon as I speak, the words I have found (as soon as they are words) no longer belong to me.

Miles continues that the author "has no more significant status than the bookshop assistant or the librarian who hands the text *qua* object to the reader."

The delayed reaction works like an actor's double take; in his second statement, Miles goes beyond what Derrida says, but Miles's statement expresses the next logical stage of Derrida's argument. And in fact Derrida does quote Antonin Artaud on the necessity to renounce "the theatrical superstition of the text and the dictatorship of the writer" in a context that implies Derrida's approval. Embedding the conversation literally within a skull and figuratively within the allegorical structure, Fowles demonstrates the absurdity of his character's words in the novel's concrete context. When he makes this concept concrete, Fowles not only demonstrates its absurdity but also its inconsequentiality, which may account for his title, and for his waiting until near the end of the book to define it.

In delaying the definition of his title, Fowles hints that *Mantissa* is a novelist's reductio ad absurdum reply to contemporary critics who reduce the author's role in creating the text to an inconsequentiality. Fowles overtly defines "mantissa" as "an addition of comparatively small importance, especially to a literary effort or discourse," but the reader receives this information only after forming a similar opinion of *Mantissa.* The allegorical insight opens a second possibility. While Fowles quotes the obsolete sense of the word "mantissa" from the *Oxford English Dictionary* in a footnote, he omits that same source's entry for the word's operative meaning: the decimal point in a mathematical logarithm.

The first definition expresses the insignificant role in which contemporary critical theory casts the author. Miles says that contemporary theorists have proved that the author's role is purely "fortuitous and agential," in possible parody of the way Barthes entertains the possibility that the author is the "full subject" of the act of writing, but then, citing Jacques Lacan, concludes that "structural analysis is unwilling to accept such an assumption: *who speaks* (in the narrative) is not *who writes* (in real life) and *who writes* is not *who is*" [Barthes, *Image—Music—Text*]. "Who speaks?" In *Écrits,* Jacques Lacan says that "truth" alone answers "I speak," and Lacan says that there is "no speech that is not language." Like Fowles and his character, Jane Gallop interprets Lacan here [in her *Reading Lacan,* 1985] to mean that "only language speaks." In developing Lacan's idea, Barthes is more radical even than Tzvetan Todorov, who says, "The *I* in the novel is not the *I* of discourse, that is, the subject of the speech act" [*The Poetics of Prose,* 1971].

The result is a conditional proposition that only gradually assumes importance to the reader: if the author does not exist, then it would make no sense to say that one book by this author is more (or less) significant than any other. Thus Fowles cleverly makes the reader's own initial sense of *Mantissa* as a mantissa into an argument against the post-structuralist dissolving of the author. This theory of the author, in making a human being completely disappear, has created an absurdity. For Barthes, in the conscious mind, the writer is "a creature of language . . . never anything but a plaything" of "the language that constitutes him" [*The Pleasure of the Text*]. The "unconscious," says Lacan [in his 1988 *Seminars*], "is the discourse of the other. . . . It is the discourse of the circuit in which I am integrated. I am one of its links." If the writer is made up of consciousness and the unconscious, then the entire creature, the writer, *is* language. Significantly, Barthes accepts Jacques Lacan's notion that the unconscious is a system of writing, and thus has the structure of human language. Barthes says [in *The Pleasure of the Text*], "As institution, the author is dead: his civil status, his biographical person have disappeared." Todorov expresses the idea only a bit less radically: "Man has constituted himself out of language, as the philosophers of our century have so often observed, and we are likely to discover its schema in all our social activity."

The discourse-oriented definition of mantissa implies a light, comic addition to the continuing discourse that is Fowles's work, of little importance compared to his major novels. In its mathematical sense, the title suggests Fowles's regret at the increasing transfer of creative energy from art to rational theorizing about art; the work of fiction looks unimportant, just as the decimal looks small compared to the numerals in a logarithm, but its position gives it complete leverage over the meaning of the expression, which is exactly what happens with allegory in this novel. These lines of thought from Barthes, Lacan, and Todorov fit, but fit absurdly, with Miles Green's sneers to Erato.

Mr. Green's contemptuous, condescending tone becomes part of the second half of the allegorical paradigm: refutation. When Erato asks why, then, "writers still put their names on the title page," the author-character written by John Fowles replies, "because most of them are like you. Quite incredibly behind the times. And hair-raisingly vain. Most of them are still under the positively medieval illusion that they write their own books." Miles's openly unfair tone fits with Barthes' ridicule of the author who thinks he must "delay and indefinitely 'polish' his form": "Having buried the Author," the modern "scriptor" can thus no longer believe "the pathetic view of their predecessors," that the hand that writes "is too slow for his thought or passion." And later in "The Death of the Author," Barthes insists that what occurs is "a pure gesture of inscription (and not of expression)," which "traces a field without origin," or which at least, "has no other origin than language itself, language which ceaselessly calls into question all origins." And incidentally, for Barthes [in his 1970 *S/Z*], the same is true of the reader, and hence of the critic: "This 'I' which approaches the text is already itself a plurality of other texts, of codes which are infinite or, more precisely, lost (whose origin is lost)." In parallel, Fowles's Erato raises the issue of the origin of Miles Green, putative author of *Mantissa,* bringing us to the discrepancies.

The allegorical dimension of his characters' dialogue continues the refutation aspect of the allegorical paradigm; by this dialogue, Fowles demonstrates that an element is missing in the interpretation of Miles Green as an author,

an omission that further parodically demonstrates the absurdity of post-structuralist theory in Fowles's allegory. After complaining of her helplessness as a character in Miles's book, the Muse Erato challenges Miles: "To say nothing of *your* character. I notice there is not a word about his exceedingly dubious status. I wonder who's pulling *his* strings?" Rather than saying language is, Miles, the writer born simultaneously with the text, replies, "I am. I'm me. Don't be ridiculous." But he cannot answer Erato's smiling questions: "Then why's he being referred to as 'he' throughout? What are you trying to hide?" The answer, "John Fowles," necessarily supplied by the reader, is the punch line of Fowles's allegorical joke.

A similar discrepancy reveals how Fowles's allegorical action contradicts contemporary theory when the characters speak directly about it. Lording his intelligence over Erato, Miles says, "You'll be telling me next you've never heard of Todorov," and he asks in rhetorical exasperation, "how can one possibly discuss theory with you when you haven't even read the basic texts?" Offering to explain "in simple laymen's terms," he continues with a statement that includes "hypostatic and epiphanic *facies,* of the diegetic process" and especially, he says, "in terms of the anagnorosis." Knowing the post-structuralist vocabularies gives Miles an apparent advantage over Erato, who supposedly relies on enthusiasm—for both sexuality and fiction; but Miles's advantage is only an apparent one.

That the theoretician has only an illusory advantage over the artist is further confirmed by the refutation side of the paradigm of the allegorical strategy of *Mantissa:* allegorical action refutes the words of Miles, the spokesman of contemporary theory. Miles looks foolish when Erato applies the term "anagnorosis" correctly to the reversal point in the plot in *Mantissa,* supporting her earlier claim that the role-playing is all over now, "the pretending I haven't even heard of Tzvetan Todorov and hermeneutics and diegesis and deconstructivism." Miles had not mentioned Todorov's first name, so we can conclude that the Muse does know theory, but chooses intuitive inspiration.

By comic discrepancy, *Mantissa* also contradicts Barthes, who said that the text of bliss "could not be written." On page 183, Miles calls *Mantissa* "what would have been, if this wasn't an unwritable non-text, one hundred and eighty-three pages at least." The reader's reaction to Miles's "would-have-been" epitomizes the second half of the allegorical paradigm—Fowles's strategy of contradicting theory by narrative allegory—for the reader holds the supposedly unwritable, non-text book in her or his hands, demonstrating the absurdity of any such concept. Instead, a written text actually exists: the product of a process that Fowles depicts allegorically as the sexual union of Miles and Erato, the union of the creative artist's public and secret selves.

In total effect, the narrative depiction of an Erato as a lively, animated, but essentially brainless young woman is contradicted by the allegory in which she is not only an essential element of literary creation but the dominant partner. To Erato's mother Mnemosyne (memory) "is ascribed the art of reasoning and giving suitable names to everything, so we can describe them, and converse about them without seeing them," as Fowles reminds us by his epigram from Lemprière. While accepting Mnemosyne's traits as valuable, Fowles's allegorical structure in *Mantissa* allows him to demonstrate two points—that these traits are neither the only valuable human attributes, nor are they sufficient in themselves to generate literary invention. Thus, when Fowles parodies our modern philosophers in *Mantissa,* he transcends parody by re-crafting the post-structuralist sexual theory of the text into his own demonstrated sexual allegory of the creative process; by so doing, John Fowles has fashioned a text that is more than a mantissa.

Freedom for me is inalienably bound up with self-knowledge. I would say the two words are almost synonymous in this context. And so it's really *that,* you know, the ability to withstand the appalling brainwashing that we all get now through the media, to think of yourself and know yourself.

—*John Fowles, in an interview with Katherine Tarbox, in her* The Art of John Fowles, *The University of Georgia Press, 1988.*

Jaqueline Costello   (essay date 1990)

SOURCE: "When Worlds Collide: Freedom, Freud, and Jung in John Fowles's *Daniel Martin*," in *University of Hartford Studies in Literature,* Vol. 22, No. 1, 1990, pp. 31-44.

[*In the essay below, Costello examines the interplay of Freudian and Jungian concepts in* Daniel Martin.]

Like Proust's *Remembrance of Things Past,* Gide's *The Counterfeiters,* Nabokov's *Pale Fire,* or Borges's *Labyrinths,* John Fowles's *Daniel Martin* presents a protagonist who is also its author and implied reader, thus reminding us of the fictions that order our worlds by overtly linking fiction and life through the novel itself. Fowles analyzes the ways in which fiction can restrict or expand our ideas, our relationships, and our beings as he explores the extent to which one can write and revise one's life. His juxtaposition of the then and now, the real and reported, the narrator's first and third persons, discovers a realm in which fiction and reality, author and character, past, present, and future are no longer limited by clear distinctions. The title character is a middle-aged British playwright involved in Hollywood movie scripts and an affair with a young actress, Jenny McNeill. Called back to England at the behest of Anthony Mallory, an estranged Oxford friend who is dying of cancer, Dan finds himself scrutinizing past and present, thereby altering his future. Most important, Dan discovers commitments he has long resisted as his buried love for Anthony's widow, Jane, reemerges.

Within this floating world of introspection is a deeply rooted preoccupation with philosophical concerns, and Fowles has remarked that he would rather be "a sound philosopher" than "a good novelist." Indeed, a variety of ideologies coexist—and sometimes collide—in the Fowlesian universe, none more discordantly than the inherently incompatible systems of Freud and Jung. On the one hand, the novel frequently invokes Freud and derives both meaning and structure from a predominantly psychoanalytic foundation. Yet even as *Daniel Martin* rehearses the Freudian concept that art is a surrogate for an unsatisfactory reality (an idea flatly rejected by Jung), certain pivotal insights credited to Dan spring directly from Jungian constructs. For example, Dan contends that writers are traditionally poor at relationships "because we can always imagine better ones" and, echoing Freud, because "you create out of what you lack. Not what you have." Moreover, "a perfect world would have no room for writers."

In fact, the view of psychical temporality and causality that informs *Daniel Martin* is best understood through Freud's theory of *nachträglichkeit,* variously translated as belatedness, deferred action, or secondary revision. Belatedness describes the manner in which experiences, impressions, and memory traces are revised at later dates to accommodate subsequent experience of new stages of development, and "it is this revision which invests them with significance and even with efficacity or pathogenic force" [J. Laplanche and J. B. Pontalis, *The Language of Psychoanalysis,* 1973]. A clear privileging of belatedness is evident from the start as we witness Dan's reconstruction of characters and events. The novel opens with an overview of a field from Dan's boyhood and quickly focuses more closely, signalled by a switch from past to present tense: "There are four figures in the field." We see them working before the narrator centers on "the boy," who remains nameless for several pages. With the boy, we hear "the crackle of the stubble, the shock of the stood sheaves"; taste the "illicit scalded cream, its deep yellow crust folded into the voluptuous white"; smell the sweat; see a rabbit caught in the reaper's blades.

Here and elsewhere, images from the past recur in the future to become invested with new meaning in Dan's present. The boy, finally individualized when he is called "Danny," is "nursing his solitude, his terrible Oedipal secret; already at the crossroads every son must pass." The "quick and tortuous ancestral voices" of the boy's Devon become "All the ghosts," which "get you in the end" for the man. The Oedipal implications of his relationship with Jenny reverberate when he says "parentally" that she should be asleep, and "an unskilled adolescent in him still prizes the thousand-times-seen view" of her naked skin. The final paragraph of "The Harvest" introduces a new narrative voice, that of the first person, which will continue to interrupt the third ("Point of view of the hidden bird"):

> I feel in his pocket and bring out a clasp-knife; plunge the blade in the red earth to clean it of the filth of the two rabbits he has gutted; slit; liver; intestines; stench. He stands and turns and begins to carve his initials on the beech-tree.

Deep incisions in the bark, peeling the gray skin
away to the sappy green of the living stem.
Adieu, my boyhood and my dream.

D.H.M.

And underneath: 21 *Aug.* 42.

Through this representation, we see how the self is narrated by multiple voices. The first person in the foregoing passage is Dan as author; the character called "Dan" is clearly distinct. Throughout the novel, a hierarchy of narrative voices bridges past, present, and future: the authorial voice of the older Dan recreates the characters of his past selves, while an author in another guise comments on the Dan of the present, who is—*de facto*—in the past as well. Whether cast as character, author, or super author, Dan is interpreting—and thereby altering—personality and experience, self-consciously developing a persona, writing and being written. As both Freud and an epigraph taken from George Seferis's "Man" point out, memory is inherently subjective; like the novel, it selects, re-orders, and interprets those events that enable it to signify: "What can a flame remember? If it remembers a little less than is necessary, it goes out; if it remembers a little more than is necessary, it goes out. If only it could teach us, while it burns, to remember correctly."

Dan's attempt "to remember correctly," to appropriate his own history by rendering it in language much as the psychoanalytic patient does, takes the form of the novel we are reading. Along the way, he uncovers myths he has betrayed and been betrayed by and comes to see the authorial roles of history, background, and culture in the shaping of a self. This connection between fiction and reality—for "All writing, private and mental, or public and literal, is an attempt to escape from the conditioned past and future"—is foregrounded as Dan realizes that his "true Oedipus complex" is among the authors of his life, manifested not only in the incestuous subtext of his affair with Jenny but also in his brief romance with Jane many years ago. Indeed, the very notion of the Oedipus complex (so vigorously renounced by Jung) writes Fowles's own imagery here. Jane was engaged to Anthony and Dan would eventually marry her sister Nell, but it was Jane he loved, and his marriage "was broken long before that day" he and Jane made love. Dan "felt an inherent poison in the situation (. . .) an almost Jacobean claustrophobia, incest," and although "his sense of guilt ought to have been attached to Nell (. . .) it was much more oriented toward Anthony." Like Dan's father, a Church of England minister, Anthony is rigid and deeply religious. In retrospect, "he was a kind of father-substitute (. . .) The idea would have outraged me at the time, and killed the friendship, as I believed I had consciously 'killed' the spirit of my father and his antiquated world." Just as Dan had rebelled against his father, so he rebelled against Anthony, first by sleeping with Jane and later by attacking him in the play that caused their estrangement. Years later, as Dan reflects on his relationship with his daughter Caro, he comments: "I half sensed what could drive fathers and daughters to incest (. . .) that need to purge the spoken of the unspoken," while Caro's affair with her father's Oxford schoolmate is surely sexual transference. And of her cur-

rent lover, formerly Anthony's student, Jane says "there's always been that Oedipal undertone. The Jocasta thing."

Appealing directly to another Freudian motif, Fowles goes out of his way to show that narcissism, a phenomenon largely ignored by Jung yet crucial to the evolution of psychoanalytic thought, is a powerful agent in Dan's various poses and relationships. In fact, one of Freud's purposes in "On Narcissism: An Introduction" was to establish the concept of narcissism as a corrective to Jung's notion of libido as generalized psychic energy rather than specifically sexual energy. Freud observes that narcissism is the initial human condition; the infant seeks and believes all pleasure to be obtainable. This primary state is a pure narcissism because the child has no comprehension of boundaries between self and other, and any source of pleasure is presumed to belong to the self solely to produce pleasure. In normal development, narcissistic tendencies diminish as the child learns to invest in love objects outside of the self. Arrested maturation or regression results in secondary narcissism, in which the libido is directed toward aspects of the self and others are valued solely for what they give to the self.

Dan's narcissism is most patently manifest in the various postures he assumes to maintain emotional distance between self and other. Even conversation is one-sided: "He divides conversation into two categories: when you speak and when you listen to yourself speak. Of late, his has been too much the second. Narcissism: when one grows too old to believe in one's uniqueness, one falls in love with one's complexity." Jenny describes him as "something in transit, hardly ever altogether with you," like "a good suitcase in an airport lounge, neatly locked, waiting to be taken somewhere else, with a destination label you can't read." He is "deeply divorced (. . .) homeless, permanently mid-Atlantic," yet clings to "his Visit-Britain self." Her account of their first meeting discloses how derivative his poses are: "I think I thought he was rather pathetic, really. Like some character out of Hemingway. Or the man in *Under the Volcano.* You can see I'm tough and wise and virile and literary and lost and totally above all this because I'm drunk." Dan describes love as a sickness of his generation and attributes the barricade between Jenny and him to "a great chasm in twentieth-century history" in which time jumped forward three decades in one, leaving his generation "permanently out of gear," encumbered with "ridiculous decors of the heart." But scenes from Dan's past indicate that the "decors" of his heart have long been contrived. A description of his undergraduate lodgings points to a characteristic reliance on appearances in his pursuit of a self: "The most striking effect was of a highly evolved (if not painfully out-of-hand) narcissism, since the room had at least fifteen mirrors on its walls." Predictably, Dan's persona is the logical outgrowth of his milieu, a "callow attempt at a personal decor [that] existed against—or because of—a background of austerity, rationing, and universal conformity."

At various junctures, the Dan of the implied future tense—the "author" of ***Daniel Martin***—steps in to comment on the Dan of the novel's present. In one such instance he speculates on the homosexual implications of

Dan's relationships with women: Dan "liked looking for women who would interest him, for new specimens," much as he enjoys searching for new botanical finds. Along with the explicit egocentricity of this pattern (for "he was arguably not even looking for women in all this, but collecting mirrors still; surfaces before which he could make himself naked (. . .) and see himself reflected"), there is the self-serving prophecy that "his mistress was not loss so much as that he expected the loss of all his mistresses," which precludes both intimacy and rejection. While renewing his acquaintance with Jane, Dan realizes that he is looking for her "old self " as if it were a reality deliberately withheld, exposing a "retardation (. . .) a quasi-Freudian searching for the eternally lost, his vanished mother." Another pattern emerges: his relationships with women have all been variations on this theme and "broke down precisely because they could not support what his unconscious demanded of them," a "repetition compulsion" that accounts for his difficulties with Jane.

Here we see Dan rehearsing the myth of Freud "as the discoverer, the overcomer of his own resistances, the hero of an autobiographical as well as an analytic odyssey" [Perry Meisel, "Introduction. Freud as Literature," in *Freud: A Collection of Critical Essays,* edited by Perry Meisel, 1981]. Recalling Stanley Edgar Hyman's reading of the analytic quest, **Daniel Martin** assumes the moral shape of the epic romance as it replays the protagonist's return to domesticity, community, and culture after travel and trial, after quelling id and confronting neurosis. As Steven Marcus observes [in "Freud and Dora: Story, History, Case History," in Meisel's *Freud*] coherent narrative is not simply Freud's trope for mental health, it *is* mental health, and his exegesis of Freud's "Fragment of an Analysis of a Case of Hysteria" (1905), the case of Dora, applies equally well to **Daniel Martin:** "Everything," Marcus writes, "is transformed into literature, into reading and writing." Like Dora, Dan "does not merely provide the text, he also *is* the text, the writing to be read, the language to be interpreted." Returning to England at Anthony's request, Dan is "an I in the hands of fate, Isherwood's camera, not unhappily reduced to watching himself, as if he were indeed a fiction, a paper person in someone else's script." The possibility that a love of mirrors "can also be symbolic of an attempt to see oneself as others see one—to escape the first person, and become one's own third" not only suggests that we are all characters in novels, our own and those of others, but exactly describes Fowles's narrative technique here.

Indeed, Dan's assorted personae seem crafted by the psychic determinism of Freudian theory, calling into question the very notion of human freedom. Even his incompatibility with Nell "was at least as much a matter of history as of personal psychologies":

> If I had been born into an earlier world, where society punished the heretic, I should probably never have betrayed Nell—or at any rate I should have concealed the betrayal much better. But I was what the Victorians banned from their arts: a dramatist (. . .) The novel, print, is very English; the theater (despite Shakespeare) is not. I was always conscious of this paradox, of my

> all-hiding private self and my lying public one; my unwritten *Sonnets* and my all too written *plays.*

But can there be another way? A free way? Fowles is of two minds here and finally lets us see it. Dan appears to be entirely the product of forces acting on him—family, history, culture. Even his choice of medium is ascribed to his age, intimating that every text emerges from those that precede it, social, historical, and artistic. At the same time, it is Dan's belated recognition of these determinations that leads to the redefining idea of writing a novel. Initially he fears the last chapter has somehow been written, "What I've become," again yoking fiction and reality through the novel itself. Jenny insists this is the *first* chapter, that something will happen, "like a window opening (. . .) Like a door in a wall." Scanning the phone book for a suitable name for Dan's protagonist, she lights on "S. Wolfe," an anagram for Fowles and another link between author and character, novel and life.

As Dan wrestles with his incipient novel, he considers giving "Simon Wolfe" disadvantages he does not have, cancer perhaps, and then considers a character less self-conscious than himself. A third solution suddenly emerges: "To hell with cultural fashion; to hell with elitist guilt; to hell with existentialist nausea; and above all, to hell with the imagined that does not say, not only in, but behind the images, the real." Although this seems to dismiss existentialism, it also reiterates a central confusion in Fowles's work: some images equal "the real," and some do not. Because language, like all genres of signification, is by definition symbolic, description of "the real" is a contradiction of Fowles's own contention [in "Notes on an Unfinished Novel," in *Afterwords: Novelists on Their Novels,* edited by Thomas McCormack, 1969] that *"All human modes of description (. . .) are metaphorical."* Yet Dan speculates that the Victorians banned theater "because they knew the stage is a long step nearer an indecent reality than the novel." At different junctures, reality is "the immense forest constituted by the imagined" and "that ultimate ambiguous fiction of the enacted past." But at another moment, "the mode of recollection usurps the reality of the recalled," which implies that one's sense of reality exists somewhere *outside* of recollection—an assumption antithetical to the belatedness on which the novel is structured. Here and elsewhere, an existential rhetoric clashes with what is actually an inquiry into the systems that structure art and life. This dissonant insistence on an undefined real reality, presumably a realm unsullied by the network of signs, codes, and relationships that produce self and culture, unwittingly pits existentialism and the concept of authenticity against their opposites.

Dan's quest for "the real history of what I am," based as it is on language and memory, is similarly misguided, and his comparison of cinematic and prose images uncovers a kindred conflict of philosophies:

> Images are inherently fascistic because they *overstamp the truth,* however dim and blurred, of the *real* past experience; as if, faced with ruins, we must turn architects, not archaeologists. *The word is the most imprecise of signs.*

Only a science-obsessed age could fail to comprehend that this is its great virtue, not its defect. What I was trying to tell Jenny in Hollywood was that I would murder my past if I tried to evoke it on camera; and it is precisely because I can't really evoke it in words, can only hope to awaken some analogous experience in other memories and sensitivities, that it must be written [my italics].

Here we confront the novel's—and Fowles's general—bifurcated notion of fiction and reality. The novel strives for verisimilitude, poses as a paradigm for reality, pretends to create—and reflect—a "real world" that is itself a network of representations to which we all come belatedly. Furthermore, this third-hand reality is contingent upon the devices of fiction-making, a blatant contradiction. Thus, while purporting to convey some sort of truth about the human condition, the novel remains subjective, at best a portrait of its author's deferred perceptions of reality, themselves tardy fictions. Although Fowles frequently addresses the problematic of "reality" inside and outside of fiction proper, he manifests its symptoms as well: sometimes he believes in "truth," sometimes not.

Similarly, we find a certain chaos in the vocabularies employed to describe Jane. On the one hand, she is *sui generis,* "unique in not mirroring him [Dan] clearly"; her "spirit remained not quite like that of any other woman he had ever known (. . .) there are some people one can't dismiss, place, reify (. . .) who set riddles one ignores at one's cost." But crossing these descriptions of Jane as unique in an existential sense, distinct from any system or structure, is the assertion that she, like the novel, cannot be approached in the terms of Dan's métier, "terms of visual symbolisms, of sets, locations, movements, gestures; of the seen actor and actress." She (and the novel) belongs to "another art, another system, the one he was trying to enter." Yet both existentialism and the unique find their meaning *apart* from any system, which, by definition, would compromise their "authenticity."

Concurrent with such ambiguities is what may be called the heightening of the Freud/Jung conflict, unavoidable in the novel's final section, which takes Dan and Jane to Egypt, Syria, and home again. Dan's analysis of past and present points to the power of the unconscious, and he gradually experiences what Freud calls "the return of the repressed." He feels "not master of his own destiny at all" and wonders if he has "been formed in his father's image," recalling "the old man's flight into stasis, unchangingness, immemorial ritual and safe tradition." Dan has sought safety in movement, replacing his father's religious loyalties with non-attachment. So he decides nothing can be done about his relationship with Jane, for "the scenario was already written, by their past, by their present, by Anthony's ghost, by their family relationships and responsibilities; and Dan was a great believer in keeping to agreed lines in scripts." His admission that he is "profoundly English" is fundamental to "this peculiarly structured imagination, so dependent on undisclosed memories, undisclosed real feelings" for "we are above all the race that lives in flashback." This recognition is one impetus for *Daniel Martin* itself, a quest for "something dense, inter-

weaving, treating time as horizontal, like a skyline, not cramped, linear and progressive (. . .) thereby creating a kind of equivalency of memories and feelings."

But counter to these fundamentally Freudian discoveries is the baffling refuge in mysticism that the novel sometimes seeks. A number of Dan's epiphanies appear clearly indebted to Jung, and that these revelations supposedly liberate him from "the false freedoms of the past" indicates a common misreading of Jungian mythology. In fact, the conditions deemed necessary for the elusive Jungian goal of individuation, "the realization of self-hood," negate any notion of personal freedom. Jung explains [in *The Essential Jung,* edited by Anthony Storr, 1983] that "many are called, but few are chosen (. . .) for the development of personality is at once a charisma and a curse." Moreover, one who is chosen has no choice in the matter:

> What is it (. . .) that induces a man to rise out of unconscious identity? (. . .) Not necessity, for necessity comes to many, and they all take refuge in convention. Not moral decision, for nine times out of ten we decide for convention likewise. What is it, then, that inexorably tips the scales in favor of the *extra-ordinary?*
>
> It is what is commonly called *vocation:* an irrational factor that destines a man to emancipate himself (. . .) Vocation acts as a law of God from which there is no escape (. . .) One who has a vocation (. . .) must obey his own law, as if it were a daemon.

Edward Glover observes [in *Freud or Jung,* 1950] that "while objecting to Freudian concepts of *psychic determination*" Jung "is evidently prepared to preach *predestination,*" and points out that *bestimmung,* translated above as *vocation,* has also been translated as *destiny.* "The meaning Jung gives to 'vocation' is closer to 'destiny' in the sense of fate *(Geschick)* than to 'calling' in the sense of *beruf.*" Jung himself explains that "the original meaning of 'to have a vocation' is 'to be addressed by a voice,'" which is most clearly exemplified in the "avowals of the Old Testament prophets," thus underwriting Glover's contentions.

The contradictions in Fowles's work point to dualities inherent in the genre of the novel, to the fictions of realism and the impossibility of an uncontaminated text.

—*Jacqueline Costello*

Replaying Jung's complementary archetypes in the "soul images" of male and female, Dan identifies his sense of incompleteness with the ancient Egyptian concept of *ka* and *ba,* regarding himself as *ka,* "a would-be ambition," and Jane as *ba,* "a would-be selflessness," "both equally insufficient." Together these concepts "are ways of seeing man first as an individual (. . .) and then as one." Indeed, Jung cites these very concepts to explain a "synchronistic" event in the life of a patient's wife. Along similar lines, an Egyptologist excuses the pharaohs for the formality and rigid control of their art because time, "the source of all human illusion," is to blame. He recounts a transcendental experience in which he became part of a universal system beyond the confines of time, body, and ego, and once again we collide head-on with Jung:

> For a little interval time does not seem to exist. One is neither the original painter nor one's own self, a modern archaeologist. If one is anything (. . .) one is the painting. One exists, but it is somehow not in time. In a greater reality, behind the illusion we call time. One was always there. There is no past or future (. . .) This is not to do with mysticism. It is almost physical, something hidden in the nature of things. I once had a similar experience, also after many hours of work, with a difficult papyrus. I became the papyrus, I was beyond time. Yet it did not help me decipher it at all. So. It was not in that sense that I was the papyrus. Perhaps I was the river. For a few moments whatever in the river does not pass. That river between.

Jung tells us that our concepts of space and time become "fixed only in the course of [human] mental development, thanks largely to the introduction of measurement. In themselves space and time consist of *nothing*. They are hypostatized concepts born of the discriminating activity of the conscious mind" [*The Collected Works of Carl Jung*, 1959].

Thus, the psychoanalytic narrative that informs **Daniel Martin,** based as it is on psychic causality, temporality, and belatedness, is tainted by a concurrent Jungian yearning for the eternal, first hinted at when Dan experiences "an unchangingness, behind all the outward shifts of circumstance. Time lay quiescent, if not defeated." He is deeply affected by Tsankawi in New Mexico, which "transcended all place and frontier (. . .) defeated time, all deaths." Time as "the mother of metaphors" is reinforced by the cruise down the Nile, whose "waters seemed to reach not merely back into the heart of Africa, but into that of time itself." Its effect is only partly a result of the ancient sites that frame it, for "its origin lay in something deeper, to do with transience and agelessness, which in turn reflected their own heightened sense of personal past and personal present." The river "was the Heraclitean same and not the same. It was the river of existence."

Along the same contrary lines is the "WHOLE SIGHT; OR ALL THE REST IS DESOLATION" to which the novel is addressed (its opening statement and implied conclusion), a variant of Anthony's claim that the devil is "Not seeing whole" and a borrowing of E.M. Forster's "wittingly Arnoldian refrain" [Meisel] of seeing things "steadily" and seeing them "whole" (*Howards End*). "Whole sight" presumes the possibility of total consciousness posited by Jung, which is, of course, categorically opposed to Freudian theory. Moreover, Dan credits the natives of Tsankawi in New Mexico with "a totality of consciousness that fragmented modern man has completely lost." Such eclecticism attempts an impossible marriage,

yet Dan's "integration" at novel's end appears to be just that—a banishment of the unconscious itself. And all of this despite the psychoanalytic premises on which the novel and its principals are structured.

Further contaminating the Freudian foundation of the novel are certain coincidences. Too often, thinking about something precipitates miraculous materialization, calling up Jung's theory of synchronicity. Shortly after Jenny tells Dan that something will happen, like a door opening into his past, he receives the phone call from Jane that summons him back to England. Even more dramatic is the sudden appearance of Barney Dillon, a former schoolmate, on Dan's flight to London, which directly follows Dan's reverie about the day he and Jane had made love in his Oxford room. Barney's footsteps outside the door alarmed them, but shortly afterwards Dan "found (. . .) the chutzpah to go up and see Barney Dillon." In fact, Barney now echoes Dan's word of a few hours before, "Ghosts." Synchronicity, insofar as it can be understood, denies the scientific sense of causality in certain "chance" situations. Instead, it invests the coincidence of a psychic state in the observer and the occurrence of a simultaneous external event with mystical meaning. According to Jung, synchronicity confirms that "the psyche cannot be localized in space, or that space is relative to the psyche."

Still another instance of Jungian synchronicity not only enables Dan to understand the enigmatic "right feeling" to which Jane is privileged (reminiscent of the essentially emotional nature of Jung's anima archetype) but also to overcome "her obsession with solitary independence." Jung observes that synchronistic events "almost invariably accompany the crucial phases of individuation." After Dan and Jane finally sleep together, Dan finds roles reversed, "he Eve, she recalcitrant Adam." A fortuitous walk across a barren Syrian plain produces two young puppies, and the couple notices a mangy bitch some distance away. When Jane is suddenly overcome, Dan divines that "gods take strange shapes; find strange times and stranger climates for their truths":

> Beneath all her faults, her wrong dogmas, her self-obsessions, her evasions, there lay, as there had always lain—in some analogue of that vague entity the Marxists call totality, full consciousness of both essence and phenomenon—a profound, and profoundly unintellectual, sense of natural orientation . . . that mysterious sense he had always thought of as right feeling. But he had always thought of it as something static and unchanging—and conscious, even if hidden; when of course it had always really been living, mobile, shifting and quivering, even veering wildly, like a magnetic needle . . . so easily distorted, shaken out of true by mind, emotion, circumstance, environment. It had never meant that she could see deeper . . . It was simply that she *felt* deeper.

Jane projects her despair onto the seemingly deserted puppies and tells Dan that their night together was "a sort of madness. A blindness to all the realities." But the dog is simply exhibiting distraction behavior, offering herself as a trade and luring the interlopers away from her young.

In contrast, Jane's instincts have been thwarted by a narcissistic withdrawal into self, which she intellectualizes as a quest for autonomy. In "the oldest male gesture in the world," Dan wipes Jane's tears away, as the novel pursues the oldest pattern of all, separation and reunion, courtship and marriage.

In another discordant intrusion, one of the novel's culminant images seems predicated on Jung's "humanist psychology" as well. Standing before the late Rembrandt self-portrait, Dan sees "a presentness beyond all time, fashion, language; a puffed face, a pair of rheumy eyes, and a profound and unassuageable vision," which, like his lament for Tsankawi, exposes a Jungian yearning for the eternal as well as a "crucial myth of the modern (. . .) that thought and feeling are now disjoined compared to their former oneness in a happier age whose primacy we have lost" [Meisel]:

> He could see only one consolation in those remorseless and aloof Dutch eyes. It is not finally a matter of skill, of knowledge, of intellect; of good luck or bad; but of choosing and learning to feel. Dan began at last to detect it behind the surface of the painting; behind the sternness lay the declaration of the one true marriage in the mind mankind is allowed, the ultimate citadel of humanism. No true compassion without will, no true will without compassion.

Despite the distractions created by Jungian suppositions imposed on a Freudian edifice, Fowles does attain some resolution of the primary problems *Daniel Martin* addresses as he refines the relationship between fiction and reality, self and culture. Here even the concept of self, the idea of characters isolated in their own bodies and minds, like actions confined to a single place and time, is fundamentally fictive. Here individuals are inseparable from society, art, and language: in fiction and in life we achieve what freedom is possible within the contexts of these systems, through the recognition—and celebration—of communality. Like language, we acquire meaning through oppositions, interactions, varied frames of reference.

Dan's inquiry into the self he has become discovers an inertia that has dominated his life and craft, belying his insistence that "he needed freedom" and pointing to his immersion in the mythologies of his milieu. He feels "both artistically and really, in the age-old humanist trap: of being allowed (as by some unearned privilege) to enjoy life too much to make a convincing case for any real despair of dissatisfaction" and "dense with forebodings of a rich and happy year ahead . . . as if he were condemned to comedy in an age without it." This contemporary conviction—that the happy ending is inauthentic and only tragedy real—has informed each of Dan's scripts: "all through his writing life (. . .) he had avoided the happy ending, as if it were somehow in bad taste," a convention that both Dan's life and Fowles's earlier novels have largely observed. But Dan "was not wholly to blame" because no one "had ever suggested anything different for the close." They were "all equally brainwashed, victims of the dominant and historically understandable heresy (. . .) It had become offensive, in an intellectually privileged caste, to

suggest publicly that anything might turn out well in this world."

Most important, Dan's facade of freedom betrays a profound anxiety about the freedom to which artists are privileged: although not "genetically, environmentally, or technically free; imprisoned inside whatever gifts they have, whatever past and present experience," even their limited freedom is considerable "because of the immense forest constituted by the imagined, because of the permission Western society grants them to roam in it (. . .) That is the one reality." If the one reality is imagination and freedom springs from exploring its potential, both freedom and reality are equally grounded in fiction. Indeed, it is imagination that produces and interprets self, society, and art all alike, mediates between world and psyche. Dan, however, has chosen imitation over invention, craft over art. Most damaging has been his retreat from imagination, and "that was the horror of landing that drove the bird endlessly on: the risk of the real ground."

Like the Egyptians who "had used art, instead of letting art use them," Dan has allowed neither art nor life to happen. His past, his Englishness, and his defenses have indeed made him a character in someone else's script. Perceiving that Jane's "real lack of freedom" lies "in the inability to compromise" and the belief that "all was determined, predestined," Dan concludes that "the only true and real field in which one could test personal freedom was present possibility (. . .) One could so clearly only move and act from today, *this* present and flawed world." He begins revising when he realizes that "Love might be a prison" but "also a profound freedom" and proposes to Jane that they extend their holiday with a visit to Lebanon and Syria, a preliminary to a far more important proposal. Here we see that Jane, like other Fowlesian heroines, is redemptive, the agent of the male protagonist's return to domesticity, community, and culture:

> It was not a wanting to possess, even uxoriously, but a wanting to know one could always reach out a hand and (. . .) that shadow of the other shared voyage, into the night. She was also some kind of emblem of redemption from a life devoted to heterogamy and adultery, the modern errant ploughman's final reward; and Dan saw, or felt, abruptly for the first time in his life, the true difference between Eros and Agape.

The contradictions uncovered in Fowles's work point to dualities inherent in the genre of the novel, to the fictions of realism and the impossibility of an uncontaminated text. Fowles yearns for a comprehensive myth that somehow transcends self while also assuring its primacy, at once acknowledging the self as a social construct and affirming its autonomy. Despite the imposition of existential and Jungian rhetoric, *Daniel Martin* takes its inspiration from Freud, showing that we have been shaped by culture even as we are set against it, equally immersed in civilization and its discontents.

Frederick M. Holmes   (essay date Summer 1991)

SOURCE: "History, Fiction, and the Dialogic Imagination: John Fowles's *A Maggot*," in *Contemporary Literature*, Vol. 32, No. 2, Summer, 1991, pp. 229-43.

[In the following essay, Holmes examines Fowles's treatment of history, mystery, and rationalism in A Maggot, *as well as the novel's narrative structure.]*

Although all of John Fowles's works of fiction grapple with common themes, each new volume has seemed to be the fresh creation of an experimental writer determined not to repeat himself. To a degree, however, his latest novel, *A Maggot* (1985), seems to revert to the narrative method of what is widely regarded as his finest work, *The French Lieutenant's Woman* (1969). Both are unconventional historical novels which bring an explicitly modern authorial consciousness to bear on the past rather than pretending to be of the historical period during which the action takes place. This strategy makes it possible for both novels to examine history critically as a humanly constructed discourse rather than simply to present history dramatically as though it had an objective, unproblematic ontological status. Both novels are examples of what Linda Hutcheon calls [in "Beginning to Theorize Postmodernism," *Textual Practice* (1987)] "historiographic metafiction": "novels which are both intensely self-reflexive and yet lay claim to historical events and personages." Such works are inherently paradoxical in creating the illusion of bringing the reader into contact with independently existing historical events only to expose that experience as a fabrication. The implication of this procedure is one that most modern historians would accept: not that history is unreal but that it consists of fallible, provisional, relative sets of interpretations of a past to which we have no unmediated, complete access.

A Maggot foregrounds the textual nature of history by presenting itself as a heterogeneous mixture of various kinds of documents. It flaunts the media through which the story is transmitted rather than effacing them. Like *The French Lieutenant's Woman, A Maggot* features both segments of narrative in the manner of a realistic novel (this time set in the eighteenth rather than the nineteenth century) and the discursive reflections of a self-consciously literary narrator. Unlike the earlier novel, though, it also incorporates other kinds of documents, some of which Fowles has taken from authentic, eighteenth-century sources and some of which he has composed to masquerade as eighteenth-century texts. In the former category are excerpts from the "Historical Chronicle" for 1736 of the *Gentleman's Magazine* and a satire, culled from the same periodical, titled "Pretty Miss's Catechism." In the latter group are a newspaper report of the death of one of the novel's characters; personal letters; and transcripts in question and answer form of the sworn testimony which the barrister Henry Ayscough elicits from several characters in the process of investigating the disappearance of his employer's son, an unnamed young lord who has adopted the pseudonym Mr. Bartholomew. The sum total of this medley of texts is a novel which is itself a mixture of genres well described by the dust jacket blurb: "Part detective story, part science fiction, part gothic horror tale, part history of dissent, *A Maggot* is a contemporary novel, yet also in its way a true tale of Defoe's time."

In this essay I want to examine in more detail the relationship between this hybrid narrative structure and the wide-ranging implications of the novel's treatment of history. In Mikhail Bakhtin's well-known terms, the book is dialogic or polyphonic, an agglomeration of different discourses, voices, dialects, and points of view. As such, it relativizes history by offering a variety of perspectives on how the past should be interpreted. Of the many perspectives, two conflicting ones are particularly important: those embodied by Henry Ayscough and Rebecca Lee. Ayscough's scientific quest for certitude is at variance with the view of history that Fowles wishes to endorse and that Lee's mystical orientation gives rise to. Fowles associates each of these characters' approaches to truth, somewhat arbitrarily, it must be confessed, with a broad range of attitudes about politics, religion, and life in general. Ayscough is rational, empirical, legalistic, authoritarian, conservative, and misogynistic, whereas Lee is intuitive, imaginative, artistic, visionary, democratic, feminist, and revolutionary. Ayscough is obviously meant to be seen as a representative early-eighteenth-century man of reason and neoclassical tradition, whereas Lee, as the novel's epilogue makes clear, anticipates romantic individualism and reliance on feeling and intuition.

Fowles's far-from-neutral treatment of the conflict between what Ayscough and Lee represent easily expands to encompass a reworking of some of the novelist's favorite themes. As do his earlier novels and stories, *A Maggot* reveals his preoccupation with individual freedom and self-transformation. Lee and her aristocratic mentor Bartholomew prove equal to what Ayscough fears and avoids—vitalizing psychological change brought on by imaginative encounters with the mystery and hazard of existence. Whereas Lee and Bartholomew resist the received historical patterns, prefabricated identities, and iniquitous class distinctions which their society imposes on individuals, Ayscough is an agent of its tyranny. As Fowles has often done in the past, in *A Maggot* he stresses the relationship between freedom and creative imagination, and, by casting his protagonists in the role of surrogate novelists, he celebrates the novel as a vehicle for the imagination's transforming power. His remarks in the prologue on one of the meanings of the book's title leave no doubt that *A Maggot* itself is meant to serve as a paradigm of such metamorphosis: "A maggot is the larval stage of a winged creature; as is the written text, at least in the writer's hope."

The novel focuses attention on history not only because it is set in the eighteenth century but also because one strand of the plot involves Ayscough's attempt to reconstruct the past. The bulk of the novel consists of an inquiry into the disappearance of Bartholomew following a strange journey to a cavern in Devonshire, where an enigmatic series of events takes place. This setting recalls E. M. Forster's famous Marabar cave, but the ambiguity about what happens there to Adela Quested is mild compared to the radical uncertainty about what causes Bartholomew to vanish and his servant, Thurlow, to kill himself. Fowles declines to dramatize directly the events which take place in the cave. The only available report of the extraordinary affair is the unreliable testimony of Rebecca Lee, the lone eyewitness. What breeds doubt about the veracity of her account is not only the fantastic nature of her tale of visiting a heavenly city in a flying saucer or "maggot" but also the fact that she had earlier told David Jones an entirely different, contradictory version of the story in which she unwillingly participated in a Satanic orgy. Rather than supplying definitive answers about the real nature of Lee's experience in the cave and Bartholomew's fate, Ayscough's inquiry only raises questions. The reader is free to interpret Lee's testimony as evidence of an intent to deceive, a hallucination, a mystical vision, or an encounter with beings from another planet. None of these interpretations receives sufficient corroboration to become authoritative, however. Even the archempiricist Ayscough is ultimately forced to admit that the cloud of obscurity surrounding the events in the cave cannot be cleared away.

Fowles's decision not to dramatize the climactic episode in the cave objectively and unambiguously renders the novel's structure ironic since, as some of the reviewers noticed, much of the book is written as a kind of detective story, the whole point of which is to unearth a truth which stays obstinately buried. In the terms of Russian formalism, the effect of Fowles's refusal to introduce a solution is to thwart the reader's ability to deduce the whole of *A Maggot*'s *fabula* or story from its *sjuzet* or plot. The *fabula*, according to Seymour Chatman [in his *Story and Discourse: Narrative Structure in Fiction and Film,* 1978], is the "basic story stuff, the sum total of events to be related in the narrative," whereas the *sjuzet* is "the story as actually told by linking the events together." Or, in Tzvetan Todorov's simpler formulation [in his *The Poetics of Prose,* 1977], "the story is what has happened in life, the plot is the way the author presents it to us." In *A Maggot,* however, the stories "as actually told" by the narrator and by the characters who testify before Ayscough do not add up to one uniform "sum total of events" or reflect clearly "what has happened in life." The problem is not just insufficient information, for even if one is willing to accept on faith the truth of what Lee says as the inspired utterance of a visionary, one still cannot easily choose between her two versions of what took place in the cave. Although she repudiates the tale which she had told Jones, her sworn testimony does not cancel or replace that first account in the reader's consciousness but stands in addition to it. The effect of this duality is to place *A Maggot* in the category of texts which Chatman calls "antinarratives" because "what they call into question is, precisely, narrative logic, that one thing leads to one and only one other, the second to a third and so on to the finale."

Because Fowles's narrative is unconventional in the way that Chatman describes, it actually subverts the concept of *fabula* and corroborates Peter Brooks's assertion [in his *Reading for the Plot: Design and Intention in Narrative,* 1984] that "the apparent priority of *fabula* to *sjuzet* is in the nature of a mimetic illusion, in that the *fabula*—'what really happened'—is in fact a mental construction that the reader derives from the *sjuzet,* which is all that he ever directly knows." What Brooks appears to mean is that, since the events of narrative fictions are at least in part the authors' fabrications, there is no anterior reality to which the

sjuzet at every point corresponds. But, as Todorov has shown, detective fiction has traditionally created a powerful illusion of the independent reality of the *fabula,* the crime which has already occurred and which must be reconstructed in the *sjuzet* by the detective in order to be solved. Todorov argues that the second order of story, the detective's inquest, "has no importance in itself" but "serves only as mediator between the reader and the story of the crime." Fowles destroys this hierarchy, however. Because his detective fails, because the details of the "crime" cannot be determined with empirical accuracy, only the *sjuzet,* the second order of story, can have intrinsic importance. What I mean is that, despite Fowles's care to set the novel in a specific and detailed historical context, his strategy focuses attention on the fictional properties of the narrative as imaginative creation. His method forces us finally to assess the novel according to criteria other than mimetic adequacy or correspondence to historical fact. What must be judged is not the literal truth of Lee's stories but their imaginative richness as metaphors for psychological conditions.

The reader cannot contemplate those metaphors in isolation, though, but is forced to encounter them in the adversarial judicial context set up by Ayscough, whose only interest is in the literal truth of testimony. This conflict is a central aspect of what I have already referred to as the book's dialogic nature. Fowles's novel is polyphonic in mixing different kinds of discourses and in establishing "a special relationship with extraliterary genres of everyday life" [M. M. Bakhtin, *The Dialogic Imagination,* 1981] such as letters and transcripts of legal proceedings. Bakhtin thought that the raw materials out of which novels were formed endowed them with "an indeterminacy, a certain semantic openendedness, a living contact with unfinished, still evolving contemporary reality." We have already seen that *A Maggot* resists unambiguous interpretation and closure. Like the majority of Fowles's fictions, it suggests that to impose finality on narratives is to falsify the existential uncertainty which is an inescapable part of being alive. Though *A Maggot* is set in the eighteenth century, it is intent on demonstrating the presentness as well as the pastness of that era. As in *The French Lieutenant's Woman,* Fowles attempts to show that history is not safely complete and that it has a vital connection with the contemporary world of the reader.

A Maggot's open-ended, dialogic nature supports its obvious thematic bias in favor of the egalitarian political subtext of religious dissent. "You would talk in religious terms in the 1700's and 1600's," Fowles has said, "but you were really talking politics." The clash of voices and points of view in *A Maggot* serves explicitly what Bakhtin perceived to be the implicitly pluralistic and democratic tendencies of all novels. As David Lodge says [in "The Novel Now: Theories and Practices," *Novel: A Forum on Fiction* (1988)], there "is an indissoluble link between the linguistic variety of prose fiction, which [Bakhtin] called heteroglossia, and its cultural function as the continuous critique of all repressive, authoritarian, one-eyed ideologies." In the case of *A Maggot,* the despotic ideology in question is the vestige of feudalism, with its tenet that all social change is evil, fiercely defended by Ayscough. But it is not merely the overt opposition of Lee and her sect which prevents the monologic discourse of aristocracy from holding uncontested sway. A challenge to its dominance is mounted by the mere existence within the novel of heteroglossia. *A Maggot* presents us with the regional dialects of Devon and Wales, the writing and speaking styles of the aristocracy, the deferential speech patterns of those who serve them, the languages of the legal system and the stage, the specialized, tendentious vocabulary of Protestant dissent, and even the modern argot of a twentieth-century narrator who is trying to understand and explain the eighteenth-century world which his characters take for granted.

Rebecca Lee is herself aware that her religious and political conflict with established authority is in part a clash of "languages" and of the different mental worlds which they body forth. She more than once correlates her disagreements with Ayscough with what she terms their separate and opposed "alphabets." For example, after she has testified that Bartholomew was transported from the cavern to heaven in the "maggot," the following exchange takes place between her and Ayscough:

> Q. Can you deny that he may have left some otherwise than in your engine?
>
> A. I cannot, in thy alphabet; in mine I can, and do.
>
> Q. You say, he was brought to your June Eternal?
>
> A. Not brought, he is returned.

What Lee means is that their different vocabularies and ways of speaking reflect conflicting mind-sets and methods of apprehending truth.

Although as an artist Fowles clearly values the visionary/imaginative mode of Lee more than the rational/scientific one of Ayscough, his handling of the conflict is truly dialogic in that the narrator of *A Maggot* refuses to silence the very formidable opposition or to resolve the debate in favor of Lee. While the narrator does at times editorialize against Ayscough's bullying tactics and reactionary nature, he declines to usurp the barrister's dominant position in the text, the bulk of which is structured in the question and answer format which he imposes and to a large extent controls. The narrator speaks only in those briefer sections which are composed in the manner of a conventional novel, and even there his is just one of several limited perspectives. Fowles does not grant his narrator psychological and spatial omniscience but restricts his proximity to the characters. For example, the narrator is as much in the dark as the reader concerning the enigmatic motives and character of Bartholomew, and, as I have already said, the narrator is also ignorant of the crucially important happenings in the cave.

The point to be stressed is that Fowles is as wary of imposing in monologic fashion his own world view on the reader as he is vigilant to incorporate into the novel alternatives to Ayscough's repressive ideology. Moreover, as Fowles shows in *The Aristos,* he is not so naive as to believe that any idea or belief can exist without its opposite or counter-

pole, on which that idea or belief paradoxically depends for definition and energetic support. *A Maggot* endorses Fowles's view that "we exist mentally in a world of opposites, converses, negatives" (*Aristos*). Man is counterbalanced by woman, reason by imagination, the desire to preserve the status quo by the urge to transform society, and so on. Fowles also juxtaposes sections written in the present and past tenses because he believes that visionaries and artists such as himself "tend to live and wander in a hugely extended now, treating both past and future as present, instead of keeping them in control and order, firmly separated" (*Maggot*), whereas realists such as Ayscough reify the present by treating it as though it were completed in order to control experience intellectually and practically.

What *A Maggot* implies about Ayscough's rational empiricism is not that it has no place in life but that there are areas of experience which it is powerless to illuminate, and that an overreliance on this faculty is psychologically destructive. It is not merely the failure of Ayscough's method to get to the bottom of Bartholomew's disappearance that discredits it in the particular context that Fowles has set up. Readers are used to approving the motives behind the investigations of detective fiction, but Ayscough's deeds are sparked by nothing nobler than a reactionary fear of behavior not sanctioned by the existing social order and a toadying regard for one of the aristocrats on whom his practice depends. The barrister does have a passionate need to uncover the truth, but that need is itself the object of Fowles's disapproval. The novel shows that Ayscough is so intent to discover the objective facts of the case that he is blind to other dimensions of experience which are ethically and existentially important.

Ayscough is, in fact, the most recent example of a recognizable type in Fowles's fiction, characters who are afflicted with what William Palmer has dubbed [in his *The Fiction of John Fowles: Tradition, Art, and the Loneliness of Selfhood,* 1974] "collector-consciousness," the need to possess, to control, to understand totally. The counterpole of the vital incompleteness which Bakhtin exalted as the particular glory of the novel, a deadening preference for what is already finished, for the product over the process, is the hallmark of "collector-consciousness." Such a desire is evident in Ayscough's attempts to impose an investigative order on his witnesses and thereby cut short the natural, organic growth of their narratives in order to arrive more quickly at the only thing he values—the end result, the solution to the mystery. In her testimony, Lee consistently resists this sort of coercion and refuses to let the barrister dictate the structure and compromise the integrity and power of her story.

Ayscough's relentless application of the scientific method bespeaks an inability to accept uncertainty, the flux and hazard of existence which Fowles believes to be necessary for biological evolution and psychological growth (*Aristos*). This lack of what Keats called "negative capability" is therefore life-denying, as Fowles demonstrates most graphically in *The Collector,* in which Frederick Clegg literally kills Miranda Grey in a demented attempt to possess her with complete certainty. Ayscough's impatience with the unknown and the ungovernable is a product of his arrogant assumption that no approach other than the scientific can lead to genuine knowledge. Of course, as a respectable man of his time he assents notionally to the authority of the Church of England, but his true allegiance is to the monologic ideology of science. In *The Enigma of Stonehenge* Fowles identifies science as the most powerful of "all of the reifying and self-imprisoning systems" condemned by Keats's romantic predecessor William Blake for cutting humans off from the divinity of immediate experience. Fowles celebrates Stonehenge precisely because "there are not yet enough facts about it to bury it in certainty, in a scientific final solution to all its questions. Its great *present* virtue is . . . that something so concrete, so *sui generis,* so individualized, should still evoke so much imprecision of feeling and thought." It is no accident that Stonehenge figures prominently as one of the settings for the rituals enacted by Bartholomew and his minions, the rituals which culminate in the hidden occurrence at the heart of the novel. For the events in the cave are analogous in their effect to that with which Fowles credits Stonehenge—the "power to challenge the imagination of its beholders" (*Stonehenge*). What ultimately poses the challenge and stimulates the imagination is mystery. "Mystery, or unknowing, is energy," Fowles states in *The Aristos.* "As soon as a mystery is explained, it ceases to be a source of energy."

There seems little doubt that Lee's two conflicting accounts of what happened at Stonehenge and in the cave are meant to be embodiments of the vital energy which Fowles speaks of, not definitive explanations which drain it. In other words, however she conceives of them, Lee's narratives are intended by Fowles to be metaphoric expressions of the potent effect on her psyche of a mystery not to be understood rationally, not literally accurate descriptions of the sort which Ayscough craves. The ineradicable ambiguities of Lee's testimony in relation to an external standard of truth do not so much undermine as fuel the imaginative power of her stories. Fowles's point is not that scientific criteria are without validity but that there are aspects of life which are richer for being impervious to scientific investigation. He holds that what is not scientifically verifiable is not necessarily untrue. In *The Aristos* he glorifies art, for example, as "the expression of truths too complex for science to express."

It is as art, finally, as literature, that Lee's narratives, for all their religious content, are to be judged. If they seem less plausible than Ayscough's own narrative account of what happened—his flat, debunking speculation that Bartholomew duped Lee, committed suicide after failing in his dark experiments, and thus precipitated the suicide of his devoted servant—Lee's stories are more richly textured, suspenseful, and thematically suggestive. In short, they are aesthetically superior as narrative literature. They certainly perform the function which Northrop Frye thinks characteristic of literature: as evocations of damnation and salvation, they map the limits of our deepest fears and desires. For this reason, the primary significance of her stories as literature might well be psychological. It is possible to interpret them symbolically as the record of a psychological battle for growth and freedom in a social and political context hostile to these aspirations. Such an interpretation need not violate the text's dialogic open-endedness, the inexhaustible qualities for which good literature has traditionally been valued. A symbolic reading is merely one way to account for the power of the narratives, not the critical equivalent of a "scientific final solution" which saps their mystery and closes off other possibilities.

One advantage of a psychological perspective is that it allows us to see that the two versions of what happened do not so much contradict as complement one another as opposite but integral stages of one unified process. This is the belief of Walter Miller, Jr., who [in his review in *The New York Times Book Review* (September 8, 1985)] adopts a Jungian vantage point. Miller notices that each account features a "numinous female triad linked to a mysterious fourth—three witches and Satan (the lord transformed), or a female Holy Trinity joined by a harlot." Miller concludes that the "equivalence of the infernal and celestial versions of the scene in the cave conforms to Jung's psychology, and both versions of the cave scene are true."

Because Lee's narratives, as evocations of a struggle for freedom, serve what Fowles believes to be the basic function of art, which is "essentially a liberating activity" (*Aristos*), they constitute a paradigm of Fowles's goals for the novel which contains them. As I mentioned earlier, like most of Fowles's novels and stories, *A Maggot* is a metafiction which lays bare the problematics and exalts the possibilities of its own medium. Like *The Magus's* Maurice Conchis and *The French Lieutenant's Woman's* Sarah Woodruff, Lee is a storytelling substitute for Fowles within the fictional world of the book. By explicitly performing a facsimile of the novelist's task, by unfolding stories which tantalize us even as they trouble us with their indeterminate ontological status, Lee makes us more conscious of what is at stake in our engagement with the book and with the other narratives that inform and shape our lives. That Fowles intends Lee to act as his surrogate is made clear in the epilogue in his comments on the Shakers, the religious movement foreshadowed in Lee's visionary experience and founded by the real historical figure Ann Lee, whom Fowles imagines to be the daughter of his entirely fictional character Rebecca: "Something in Shaker thought and theology . . . has always seemed to me to adumbrate the relation of fiction to reality. We novelists also demand a far-fetched faith, quite often seemingly absurd in relation to normal reality; we too need a bewildering degree of metaphorical understanding from our readers before the truths behind our tropes can be conveyed."

The activities of the shadowy figure Bartholomew may also be seen as a self-reflexive image of those of Fowles himself as a novelist. Like *The Magus's* Conchis, Bartholomew is a surrogate author who does within the world of the novel what a postmodernist writer such as Fowles does with words: he creates various fictional scenarios to be acted out and in the process proliferates artifice and uncertainty about what is real. He is like Conchis in being a morally ambiguous character with Satanic associations who deceives and manipulates others but whose ultimate intention seems to be the benign one of bestowing freedom. And, again like Conchis, in absconding without warning or explanation, he performs the equivalent of what Fowles does in leaving his plot without a denouement and thus inviting readers to become more creatively involved with the text. In this regard, Bartholomew is also reminiscent of **"The Enigma"**'s John Fielding, the character whose unexplained disappearance activates the imaginations of the story's protagonists and, Fowles hopes, of its readers. Like the Fielding of Isobel Dodgson's speculation (**Ebony Tower**), Bartholomew is a member of the ruling elite who views the mores and behavior patterns of his class as a confining script which denies him the freedom to forge a meaningful identity. Those scripts are analogous to the conventional plots of narrative fiction which Fowles believes to be equally constraining and which he violates in not accounting for the disappearances of his characters. In vanishing, both become what Dwight Eddins calls [in "John Fowles: Existence as Authorship," *Contemporary Literature* (1976)] "existentialist authors of their own lives."

However opaque some of Bartholomew's motives might be, then, Fowles seems to expect us to associate the actions leading to his disappearance with his desire for liberating, radical change. Once again, a character's ambition mirrors that of the self-conscious novel which incarnates him. His recipe for transformation contains some of the ingredients which Kerry McSweeney has identified as recurring features of Fowles's previous works of fiction. The cave constitutes the by-now-familiar secret world into which his male protagonists penetrate by means of the vitalizing powers of sex and imagination. What is new in **A Maggot** is that Bartholomew is impotent and that, in one version of the story, transcendence follows not from the awakening of his sexual powers but from practicing an abstinence which conforms to the tenets of Lee's severe faith. Bartholomew's own "far-fetched faith," equally a metaphor for that of the novelist who has created him, is a peculiar, only vaguely presented blend of pagan and Christian elements. It seems to be derived in part from the religious life of the Celtic druids, who, according to the now-discredited eighteenth-century theory of William Stukely endorsed enthusiastically by Bartholomew, built Stonehenge and practiced "the purest form of primitive Christianity" (**Stonehenge**). While Bartholomew assumes the form of Satan in the first version of Lee's story, in the second she certainly presents him as a veritable emanation of the spirit of Christ, and she glosses the strangely close relationship between the aristocrat and his servant in the following allegorical fashion: "And now do I see they were as one in truth, Dick of the carnal and imperfect body, his Lordship of the spirit. . . . And as Jesus Christ's body must die upon the Cross, so must this latter-day earthly self, poor unregenerate Dick, die so the other half be saved."

Thurlow's death, and his earlier sexual couplings with Lee, can also be given a pagan interpretation, in relation to a widespread fertility rite which featured, in the words of Fowles, "the real or symbolic mating of a potent young man and a female representative of the earth-goddess, sometimes associated with the subsequent ritual sacrifice of one or both" (**Stonehenge**). Viewing Thurlow as a dying god figure in the tradition of pre-Christian vegetation cults makes even more sense when we remember that violets were found in his mouth by those who discovered his corpse.

The mythic and religious particulars of the novel, however, do not form a coherent whole which serves as a key to unlock the novel's mysteries. As I have already intimated, these details seem less important in their own right than the metaphoric resonances which they generate. However dialogic his method, it is difficult to forget that Fowles is himself an atheist who has rejected Christianity (**Maggot**) and consigned to the "lunatic fringe" the modern-day Bartholomews who would review pagan rites at Stonehenge (**Stonehenge**). What Fowles will not repudiate, though, is an urge which underlies most religions and motivates artists such as himself: the desire to overcome time. Fowles has said quite directly that "art best conquers time" (**Aristos**), and the attempts of his proxies within the fictional world to achieve states of timelessness can be seen to reflect his own preoccupations as creator of **A Maggot**. Lee's "June Eternal," as the very name suggests, is a condition of arrested time. And Bartholomew's absorption in the problem of defeating time is shown in his fascination with Stonehenge, whose builders, he holds, "had pierced some part of the mystery of time." Stonehenge itself, according to Fowles, overwhelms visitors with "the presentness of its past" (**Stonehenge**) and manifests "an obsession with defying time and death" (**Stonehenge**).

Considerations of the novel's treatment of time lead back to the topic with which I began, the peculiar status of **A Maggot** as an unorthodox historical novel, and suggest some conclusions about the nature of Fowles's intentions and achievements. What he would like to do, in a sense, is to abolish history, to remove the two-hundred-and-fifty-year gap between his characters and his readers and to institute an eternal world, that "hugely extended now" which he claims artists and mystics have the capacity to inhabit (**Maggot**). Ideally, the best art "constitutes that timeless world of the full intellect . . . where each artefact is contemporary, and as nearly immortal as an object in a cosmos without immortality can be" (**Aristos**). But this accomplishment requires the full imaginative involvement of both author and readers, which in turn depends upon what Fowles calls "the inmost characteristic of art—mystery. For what good science tries to eliminate, good art seeks to provoke—mystery, which is lethal to the one and vital to the other" (**Aristos**). Accordingly, Fowles envelops his eighteenth-century subject matter in a haze of uncertainty. The cost is a loss of scientific clarity and objective understanding. What Fowles hopes to gain is the freshness and immediacy of "that weird tense grammar does not allow, the imaginary present" (**Maggot**).

The novel implies that eliminating the pastness of the past has another salutary effect, that of destroying its deterministic power over the present and of thereby freeing the individual to fashion his or her own identity, as Bartholomew hopes to do by refusing the fixed part written for him by his own past, by his aristocratic origins. This existentialist goal, however, is incompatible with a knowledge of historical forces. "Choosing not to know," says Fowles, "in an increasingly 'known,' structured, ordained, predictable world, becomes almost a freedom, a last refuge of the self " (**Stonehenge**). One might object that such a sense of freedom is delusive since it is possible to be shaped by factors of which one is ignorant. It is worth asking, too, how one can choose not to know if one in fact already does know. This is a difficulty recognized by Bartholomew, who, as the actor Lacy testifies, contrasted the wise unknowing of the builders of Stonehenge with the constraining awareness of people of his own era:

> They knew they knew nothing. . . . We moderns are corrupted by our past, our learning, our historians; and the more we know of what happened, the less we know of what will happen; for as I say, we are like the personages of a tale, fixed it must seem by another intention, to be good or evil, happy or unhappy, as it falls. Yet they who set and dressed these stones lived before the tale began, Lacy, in a present that had no past.

What follows from Bartholomew's train of thought is the realization that it is not wholly possible to obliterate the past or to avoid being conditioned by it. History might well be the imperfect construction of human beings, and not the objective truth, but it has an undeniable reality which Fowles acknowledges. As Lacy reports, Bartholomew finally concluded that one's freedom is relative and limited: "he answered that we may choose in many small things as I may choose how I play a part . . . but yet must at the end, in greater matters, obey that part and portray its greater fate, as its author creates." Changing the vehicle of the metaphor from authorship to imprisonment, the narrator of **A Maggot** expresses the matter succinctly when he states that most of us are "equal victims in the debtors' prison of History, and equally unable to leave it."

The foregoing admission accounts for qualities of **A Maggot** which are not consistent with an intention to blur historical differences between the eighteenth and twentieth centuries and in the process to make a bygone age come to life for the contemporary reader. Fowles's narrator is often concerned to keep the past neatly separated and very remote from the present. As Pat Rogers correctly observes [in "Left Lobe and Right," *Times Literary Supplement* (September 20, 1985)], "Fowles leaves no room for sentimental identification with the past: he snaps down the alienation effect with a brisk, no-nonsense finality." Compared to **The French Lieutenant's Woman, A Maggot** is an austere, uncompromising book which is not easy of access for the casual reader. Despite **The French Lieutenant's Woman's** postmodernist pyrotechnics, its Victorian milieu has a coziness and charm that the more distant and foreign eighteenth century lacks. Fowles's learned explanations of various facets of eighteenth-century life are designed to measure the distance between then and now, not to eliminate it. It is to his credit that he will not dishonestly deny the otherness of history in order to give his maggot wings.

Lance St John Butler (essay date 1991)

SOURCE: "John Fowles and the Fiction of Freedom," in *The British and Irish Novel since 1960,* edited by James Acheson, Macmillan Academic and Professional Ltd, 1991, pp. 62-77.

[*Butler is an educator, editor, and critic. In the essay below, he discusses Fowles's focus on freedom, Existentialism, Poststructuralism, and intertextuality in his novels.*]

Fowles is an enigma in broad daylight. He is exceptionally open about his feelings and opinions, yet it is hard to be absolutely certain that one has understood his work or his position in post-1960s fiction. He is an erudite novelist who is at the same time immensely popular. He is obsessional about freedom and at the same time critical of the uses to which it has been put. Much of his work seems to have a left wing or feminist bias, yet he can also be seen as crypto-fascist and sexist. He is a self-proclaimed atheist whose most recent novel, **A Maggot,** presents a bigoted fanaticism of the eighteenth century as a necessary step towards freedom. He says that he has 'little interest' in the historical novel, yet he is an expert at the evocation of the past and at convincing period dialogue. The catalogue of enigmas could be continued almost indefinitely, but the daylight, the accessibility and the 'readerly' character of his work remains.

Some ways of approaching Fowles the novelist seem to hold more promise than others. [In *The Romances of John Fowles,* 1985] Simon Loveday, for instance, proposes the chivalric romance, a genre studied by Fowles at university and explicitly present in **The Ebony Tower,** as a clue. Like Chrétien de Troyes and the other authors of the late medieval romance, Fowles is interested in the traditional quest in which the hero will prove himself in ambiguous competition with some *belle dame,* often *sans merci,* and he toys with the quasi-magical environment of the enchanted castle (the 'domaine') with its wizard-wiseman. Loveday's book is convincing when it deals with some of the fiction (**The Collector, The Magus,** most of the stories in **The Ebony Tower**), but it begins to break down when its thesis is applied to **The French Lieutenant's Woman, Daniel Martin** and **A Maggot.**

Fowles himself has taken a psychoanalytic approach to his novels in a fascinating essay, **'Hardy and the Hag'** [published in *Thomas Hardy After Fifty Years,* edited by Lance St John Butler, 1977], in which he explores the source of fictional creativity in (male) novelists with the help of an analysis of **The French Lieutenant's Woman** undertaken by Gilbert Rose, an American psychiatrist. Here we feel close to the intimate springs of Fowles's work, but we are not, in the end, led to any very clear interpretations. While it seems probable that we would learn more about how writing occurs if we were to familiarise ourselves with, say, Melanie Klein's *Love, Guilt and Reparation,* this will not lead us to anything like a complete account of a ludic piece such as **The French Lieutenant's Woman** or a work as baffling as **A Maggot.**

For the purpose of this essay I would like to attempt a less partial account (not that I would deny the Romance element or the probability of Fowles's version of the psychic generation of fiction) and offer a picture of a novelist coming to terms with freedom, both in the Existentialist sense, which would require that freedom be an indispensable absolute (which I think Fowles believes, at least as far as the indispensability is concerned), and in the more recent Poststructuralist sense, which would require freedom to be a chimera, an endlessly deferred goal (which I think is what Fowles now also believes).

In this way Fowles is the novelist *par excellence* of the period since 1960, in Britain at least. He belongs to the generation most profoundly influenced by Existentialism, and his development has followed the same course as developments that have in part sprung from Existentialism. This may help to explain some of the enigma—the early interest in the freedom of the individual consciousness thrown into the world later becomes the more limited Barthesian freedom of the author playing with the text. The 'pleasure of the text', Barthes' explicit connection of the play of fiction with the play of sexual encounter, becomes in Fowles an elaborate erotics of fiction that takes us well beyond the search for authenticity. The author's self, always closely bound up with that of his hero-surrogates in Fowles, seems to be exploring Existentialist choices in an early work such as **The Magus,** but by the time we reach **Daniel Martin,** that self has itself come to seem part of the problem of fictional creation. We are not dealing with self-obsession but rather with the position of the Postmodern/Poststructuralist author for whom the problem of writing is that he is at once all-powerful (the ludic God, the magus) and indeterminable (the blank space, the 'Urfe'—private code, as Fowles has indicated, for 'earth').

Fowles's first novel, **The Magus,** drafted in the 1950s, is in some essential ways an alternative *L'Etranger,* the work of an English Camus. The themes of personal choice, freedom and responsibility, are at the heart of this novel, and the debts to the Romance tradition and to the 'domaine' of Alain-Fournier are, as it were, only scenery, the mechanism needed to put Nicholas Urfe through his Existentialist paces. Urfe is an outsider in the attitudes he demonstrates in London, just as he is the suicidal Camusian on his Greek island who, deeply in love with nature, nonetheless cannot escape the absurd.

In the later novels, however, the elusive goddess Eleutheria is pursued in ways that have become familiar to us in the 1970s and 1980s, rather than in the parabolic manner of Camus and Sartre. Instead of offering himself as the Authority or Origin that announces the Era of Freedom *ex cathedra,* Fowles *enacts* freedom in his later fiction at the same time as discussing it directly. The most obvious example of this lies in the famous 'double' (actually triple) ending of **The French Lieutenant's Woman** in which the novelist tries to put the reader into the same position as (a) the hero, Charles Smithson, and (b) the novelist, John Fowles. By the late 1960s, in other words, Fowles is no longer in the relatively innocent world of Camus, a world where heroic young men whose authenticity is guaranteed by their relationship with nature can defy Necessity and assert the freedom offered to them by Absurdity. We have instead been taken into the world of Barthes, Foucault and Derrida, where all assertion is textual, provisional and rhetorical. For Sartre and early Fowles man is condemned to freedom; for Barthes and later Fowles man is condemned to free play. Authenticity proves to be unavailable, so the later freedom settles for inauthentic 'play' (acting).

Fowles himself is quite open about the centrality of free-

dom to his work. He told Daniel Halpern in 1971: 'Freedom . . . That obsesses me. All my books are about that. The question is, is there really free will? Can we choose freely? Can we act freely? Can we *choose?* How do we do it?' ['A Sort of Exile in Lyme Regis,' *London Magazine* (March 1971)]. In his study of Fowles [*John Fowles,* 1978], Barry Olshen comments that 'The novels are predicated on the supposition of individual free will and the ideal of self-realisation'. Similarly, Peter Conradi [in his *John Fowles,* 1982] sees the novels as 'quests for personal authenticity'. But Conradi, writing with the advantage of four more years of Fowles's output to consider, is able to add what seems to me to be the necessary gloss: 'Each of his novels can best be read as in pursuit of the peculiar integrity of its own incompleteness, which is to say as braving a new kind of fictional logic by which to foreground, however inconclusively, its necessary inauthenticities'. This captures more exactly the move from Existentialism to Poststructuralism than a simple insistence on freedom *per se* as the dominant motif in Fowles. It is no longer a frustrated search for possible authenticity, as in **The Magus;** rather, it is a matter of Fowles playing with the inauthenticity to which we are all (and none more clearly than the novelist) condemned.

Fowles would, I think, have stopped writing or would in any case have faded from view if it were only true that, as Olshen says, his fiction is 'adolescent' in its 'exclusive fixation on the vision of the individual ego asserting itself in the world'. Fowles uses adolescent Absurdism as a springboard from which he is well able to launch himself into the unfathomable waves of Derridean arbitrariness. Who else, after all, is better able to *defer* the resolutions of his novels? Who is better able to postpone the closure that brings meaning? Fowles may have set out to write the fiction that celebrated or explored freedom, but he has stayed to demonstrate the other sense of the expression 'the fiction of freedom'.

Fowles's short novel **Mantissa** (1982) should be compulsory reading for those who wish to undertake a study of Fowles. It is an unusually neat parable about artistic creation, and it involves the reader to just the necessary degree. In it Fowles achieves the level of realism of which he is so easy a master, yet he throws it away—it wasn't reality at all that those opening paragraphs were related to—no, of course, they were just lines in an author's head, and, lo and behold, **Mantissa** is set in just that—a head. What does one find in an author's head, then, when creation is taking place? A Muse, of course, specifically Erato, the teasing Muse of lyric poetry, and for some reason that she is inclined to regret, of fiction, too.

The personification of the Muse is ready-made and to hand: she is female, Greek, attractive, musical. But Fowles has to demonstrate allegorically how she operates. In **'Hardy and the Hag'** he has indicated his preferences in this matter: the novelist, he says, 'longs to be possessed by the continuous underlying myth he entertains of himself'. (We notice that the yearning for the lost mother-stage is cast in literary terms: the longing is for a *myth*). This 'possession' would be the modern equivalent of the divine inspiration of the poet, and so is itself that which the Muse brings. It has to operate over *time,* and here is the Postmodern rub: the Muse is, in her original Greek form, relatively static—she *stands* for what she stands for. But what is it like for a writer to be possessed for the duration of a long novel? Fowles comments that the possession is 'a state that withdraws . . . as the text nears consummation'. Given the final noun here it is evident that something very like sexual teasing is involved, and Fowles makes this explicit a few pages later in **'Hardy and the Hag'** when, having written of Hardy's 'violent distaste for resolution, or consummation', he says that 'the endlessly repeated luring-denying nature of [Hardy's] heroines is not too far removed from what our more vulgar age calls the cock-tease'.

So in *Mantissa* the Muse takes on a complete sexual-allegorical persona. In her first incarnation as Dr Delfie, whose job it is to bring the amnesiac Miles Green back to reality by means of sex therapy, she points out, bearing in mind that Mnemosyne was the mother of the Muses, that 'the memory nerve-centre in the brain is closely associated with the one controlling gonadic activity'. When Dr Delfie persuades Miles to make love as part of his cure, her orgasm coincides with the words 'last syllable', and the result of their love-passage is a child of sorts, in fact a work of literature, *Mantissa.* Delfie/Erato explains to Miles/Fowles that when he is writing he does not know what he is doing; it is unplanned. Like Nicholas Urfe, perhaps, she would like to be in a position of 'eternally awaiting climax', and she looks forward to a Beckettian moment where she would be able to communicate entirely by sensation in a 'text without words' in which, she tells Miles, 'we could both be our real selves at last'. This Lacanian hopeless yearning for the lost paradise is at once, and most appropriately, verbal and sexual, the fusion is as complete as metaphor and allegory can make it. Erato, suggesting sexual variations, says 'there are all sorts of . . . narrative alternatives we haven't fully explored'; towards the end of the novel she refers to 'a tactile centimetre (or syllable)'.

Even in the revised version, *The Magus* is incomplete in Fowles's view, and this incompleteness stems from the same inability to close—to offer us anything other than possible narrative alternatives—that we see more violently exposed at the end of *The French Lieutenant's Woman* and *A Maggot.* It is emphatically not a matter of Fowles's not being able to bring off an ending. His skill as a fictional craftsman is beyond dispute, and he could have pursued a career as a writer of thrillers, erotica, historical novels or almost any of the other sub-genres of fiction. There is no satisfying ending because Fowles does not believe such a thing to be possible. Urfe does finally rediscover Alison, but she is utterly changed and may no longer want a relationship with him. No reconciliation is made, and the novelist steps in, playing his own godgame: 'She is silent, she will never speak, never forgive, never reach a hand, never leave this frozen present tense'. A resolution is whisked away from under the reader's nose. Fowles's interest in sexual teasing and postponement may be read as a symbol of this inability to make the final statement that will bring closure. However, in the first version of *The Magus* Fowles did partially yield to the temptation to close (the sentence quoted, with its reference to the present tense, be-

longs only to the revised version), and this shows why *The Magus* and *Daniel Martin* are problematic for the Fowles critic. The problem so stunningly solved in *The French Lieutenant's Woman* and satisfactorily kept at arm's length in *The Ebony Tower* and *A Maggot* is balked at in these two novels. In the revised *Magus* the balking is alleviated by the arrival of the novelist as *deus ex machina,* telling us that we will never know what happens to Urfe and Alison because he is going to stop writing now. The move from Existentialism to Poststructuralist play is rather obvious here.

In the Foreword to the revised edition of *The Magus* we learn that 'loss is essential for the novelist'. In **'Hardy and the Hag'** we find Fowles concurring with the psychoanalytic thesis that novelists are marked more deeply than other people by the traumatic separation from the mother and from the omnipotence that characterises the earliest phase of human development. The novelist, on this account, is always trying to staunch the psychic wound created by this separation by inventing surrogate worlds in which omnipotence is once again available, and in which author-surrogates can be rewarded by full possession of the mother-surrogate. This is the 'loss' that is so vital to fictional creativity, and in the case of Fowles it seems to explain why he so consistently tantalises his heroes: he needs to exercise his power as creator. Were he to stop, in this case to allow Urfe an explanation or a 'happy ending', the game (very much the 'godgame'—Fowles's original title for *The Magus,* as he tells us in the Foreword) would come to an end. The process must at all costs be *kept going;* closure, although it seems to bring the reward of the mother, necessarily also brings about the end of the game that was providing the satisfactions of omnipotence and freedom. Hence the great length of the two novels in which Fowles has failed to square this circle: it is as if he has to keep talking to postpone the moment when his lack of an exit-line will become apparent. Once again, this is not a matter of a lack of technical skill.

Fowles is an enigma in broad daylight. He is exceptionally open and honest about his feelings and opinions, yet it is hard to be absolutely certain that one has understood his work or his position in post-1960s fiction.

—Lance St John Butler

The giveaway in *The Magus* and *Daniel Martin* can be found in what might be called their pseudo-*Bildungsroman* status. In both novels there is a suggestion that the hero has developed, has learnt a moral truth, has moved to a better view of his own life and, in particular, of the responsibilities of personal relationships. The hero in Thomas Mann or Lawrence (one thinks of Paul Morel in *Sons and Lovers,* for example) has in some crucial way *grown up,* and this is the template that we unconsciously lay down beneath our reading of the two Fowles novels in question. But this reading of them is untenable. Nicholas Urfe does not grow up at all, or at least the thrust of the novel has little interest in this possibility. To the very end he remains committed to himself (rather than learning, say, that he should no longer be a cad). His long ordeal on Phraxos leaves him bitter and baffled rather than wiser and purer. The 'lesson', if there is one, is the non-lesson that 'the maze has no centre', and that *all* action is a form of theatre. Even Alison, who on the *Bildungsroman* reading would have to be a touchstone, a signal of the lesson having been learnt, a reward for having grown up, is explicitly described in theatrical terms. She is merely *'cast' as Reality'* (my italics), and the circumstances of her final ambiguous meeting with Urfe are stagey in the extreme. The only lesson is that there is nobody watching the performance any more. This is usually taken to mean that Conchis and his helpers are no longer operating their 'metatheatre', but it clearly has death-of-God overtones too. And yet Urfe knew at the very beginning that there was no God, and that he was alone; his suicide attempt (or pantomime) makes his nihilism quite clear.

All through *The Magus* we could echo Nicholas's question to Mrs De Seitas at the end: 'But why the colossal performance just to tell one miserable moral bankrupt what he is?'. Why indeed? Fowles toys with trying to convince us that Nicholas has changed. There are hints, for instance, that were he now to resume his affair with Alison, he would do so with greater understanding of some kind; but this is mere froth compared with what is happening underneath. 'In reality all is fiction', says Mrs De Seitas, and Fowles concurs. *This* lesson (that all is fiction) may rub off on Nicholas, but it is not, as it were, a lesson *internal* to the story which we might choose to apply to our own lives. Rather, it is a lesson that is entirely public, already something that belongs to the nature of writing novels, an open secret between Fowles and the reader. For if all is fiction, then fiction is all, including the 'real lives' to which we might more traditionally try to apply the lesson of 'fiction'. We are all in this fiction together, including the reader: the meaning of the novel, says Fowles in the Foreword, is 'whatever reaction it provokes in the reader'.

The Magus is a deeply anti-Romantic novel. Fowles is not as clear about this as he will be in later works: there is a ghost of a desire for God in the apparently omnipotent 'magus' Conchis, and a yearning for romanticised nature and a romantic view of the self that will be far less evident in *The French Lieutenant's Woman.* Conchis tries a little romanticism in his story of his visit to Norway; Henrik, the mad brother of his host in the remote north, teaches Conchis something by way of his extraordinary eremitic existence and his rare but overwhelming meetings with the 'pillar of fire' that is God. Conchis summarises: ' . . . in a flash all our explanations, all our classifications and derivations, our aetiologies, suddenly appeared to me like a thin net. That great passive monster, reality, was no longer dead, easy to handle . . . The net was nothing, reality burst through it'. The romantic notion that reality is a powerful beast, a Frankenstein's monster to be trammelled only with the greatest humility, cannot, however, stand up to the force of the godgame. Fowles may yearn

for the primal unity and seem to glimpse it in nature (here and in several memorable scenes, not surprisingly, of *Daniel Martin*), but the nets are in fact a good deal stronger than 'reality'. Henrik, after all, has to be insane and completely alone in a cabin in a remote part of Norway where the only access is by river, and even that for only part of the year; he is blind and has spoken to no one for twelve years. Very occasionally, after absolute concentration of the will upon this one end, he is vouchsafed the insight or vision of the pillar of fire. Clearly the price paid for a glimpse of reality is immensely high and, far from 'bursting through', 'reality' is practically a closed book. What we find in nature, then, is not the personification of the god or the contact with the elemental that Romanticism sought. For Fowles, nature too is part of the game: the mountain is Parnassus or it is no mountain; the Muses are the inhabitants of the natural; Alison is recruited into the godgame without explanation and without objection in a way that utterly subverts her status as 'reality'.

The Magus was Fowles's first novel, and *The Collector* (1963) his first *published* novel. *The Collector's* theme is the relationship between inarticulate power and articulate intelligence, between body and mind, between imprisonment and freedom, between Caliban and Ariel, and more literally, between Ferdinand and Miranda. Clegg/Caliban is imprisoned in inarticulacy and the commonplace; in revenge he imprisons Miranda in a converted cellar. The twist is that Clegg is unable successfully to fulfil his role: where Shakespeare's Caliban has at least a healthy lust, Clegg is effectively impotent, a supplementary theme of Fowles's being the inadequacy of certain sorts of Englishness. [In an endnote, the critic adds: 'Fowles has always been interested in this two-sided, articulate and inarticulate, Caliban-and-Ariel bifurcation of human nature. We think of Julie and June in *The Magus,* or of Henrik and his brother. But it is most fully confirmed in *A Maggot.* There "Mr Bartholomew" and his rather too-obviously-named servant, Dick, form two sides of a single personality. Dick is a deaf mute of great strength who, though gentle, is highly sexed. His master and alter ego is highly intellectual and apparently frigid. Faced with the revelations of the end of the novel Dick hangs himself while "Mr Bartholomew" vanishes into the future. Their relationship to the heroine Rebecca is simple: Dick loves her dumbly and physically while his master leads her to a view of an intellectual reality that will liberate her from the prison of the brothel in which she works.']

The Collector would be a very different sort of novel were it not for the Shakespearean intertext with which Fowles explicitly provides it. The thinker who dominated the French literary scene during the 1950s and 1960s when it was having such a profound impact on John Fowles was, after all, Roland Barthes, the father of intertextuality. Without this element *The Collector* would be a psychological novel, a brilliant study of a warped mind—brilliant because of Fowles's ability to write an English that catches so exactly the limitations and banalities of Clegg's mind; or it would be an allegory, perhaps, about the fear of the 'nasty' (the libido) deeply ingrained in a certain kind of English mind. Additionally it would be a study of Miranda's slightly contrived Existentialist tenets: she 'loves being to the full' and is in 'despair', and so must 'act' to obtain her 'freedom' and so on. Fowles signals his interest in the author's enactment of freedom by contriving 'play' between *The Tempest* and his own novel rather than merely endorsing 'realistically' these propositions about freedom. It is therefore not surprising that he has not remained merely 1950s or merely Existentialist. Like modern thought itself he has come on into the Postmodern and Poststructuralist world where intertextuality reigns.

In *The French Lieutenant's Woman* (1969) the intertextual is signalled in the first paragraph. It is not *all* Jane Austen, but without Jane Austen it would not read as it does:

> An easterly is the most disagreeable wind in Lyme Bay—Lyme Bay being that largest bite from the underside of England's outstretched south-western leg—and a person of curiosity could at once have deduced several strong probabilities about the pair who began to walk down the quay at Lyme Regis, the small but ancient eponym of the inbite, one incisively sharp and blustery morning in the late March of 1867.

The narrator presents us with two voices here, one slightly humorous and knowing, a voice interested in bitten legs, and the other the voice of that other author who set a crucial part of *Persuasion* in Lyme Regis on the Cobb. But then *The French Lieutenant's Woman* is in one sense nothing but intertext.

Not only is the novel thick with epigraphs and quotations of all sorts, but it keeps up a running fire of literary references, both explicit and concealed. Ernestina has an 'imperceptible hint of a Becky Sharp', Sam Farrow's name 'evokes immediately the immortal Weller'—these two are unmissable, but other details take some unearthing. Sarah Woodruff's father goes to the dogs partly on account of his obsession with his gentlemanly ancestry; Sarah herself becomes *déclassée* by being sent away to be educated above her station in life. The first of these cannot be unconnected with the fatal snobbery implanted in Tess Durbeyfield's father in Hardy's *Tess,* and the second echoes the return of Grace Melbury to Little Hintock in *The Woodlanders.* The Fallen Woman Sarah Woodruff is first approached at the end of the Cobb in the memorable opening scene in a way curiously reminiscent of a scene in *The Moonstone* where the Fallen Woman Rosanna is approached as she looks out to sea near the village of Cobb's Hole.

The list could be extended almost indefinitely. Fowles has made his novel out of Tennyson, Arnold, Hardy, Darwin, Marx, in a way that emphasises the paradox of the writer: playing around among texts, he can do precisely as he chooses; yet it really does seem as if it is not Fowles who is writing language, but language (more broadly, culture) that is writing Fowles. We have here moved beyond the Existentialist fear of the inauthenticity that might result from the domination of the 'They' (Heidegger's *Das Man,* Sartre's *On,* what in *The Aristos* Fowles calls the Many), and into the Lacanian resignation to our absolute inability to achieve any authentic voice or selfhood. Fowles has abandoned the quest for authenticity in *The French Lieutenant's Woman* and is enjoying his new-found freedom

to play. [In an endnote, the critic adds: 'In **"Notes on an Unfinished Novel"**, Fowles says that while writing *The French Lieutenant's Woman* he was "trying to show an [E]xistentialist awareness before it was chronologically possible". But the novel as written shows a greater gap between author and hero than was evident in *The Magus.* Nicholas Urfe is a Fowles-surrogate working out Existentialist themes, Charles Smithson is a plaything of the author's; we are never allowed to forget that the real freedom is not his but his creator's. It is as if the whole of *The French Lieutenant's Woman* is written in the spirit that inspired the authorially self-conscious changes made to the ending of *The Magus* when it was revised. Significantly, fifteen years after noting his attempt to show Existentialist awareness in *The French Lieutenant's Woman,* Fowles said in an interview: "I now think of Existentialism as a kind of literary metaphor, a wish fulfilment. I long ago began to doubt whether it had any true philosophical value in many of its assertions about freedom" (Quoted in *The Radical Imagination and the Liberal Tradition,* ed. Heide Ziegler and Christopher Bigsby, 1982).']

Daniel Martin, we have seen, is less ludic in appearance, more committed to the impossible old *Magus* project of bringing its hero through to some sort of authenticity or wisdom; but even here Fowles has not forgotten the Poststructuralist lessons he has learnt. The novel is, for one thing, far less an example of conventional realism and full of far more tricks than might at first appear. It is, for instance, a novel about Dan learning to write a novel; in the early pages he answers the suggestion that he write a novel with 'I wouldn't know where to begin', just as he (or rather, John Fowles) is beginning *Daniel Martin.* The hero of Dan's novel is to be one 'S. Wolfe', an anagram of 'Fowles'; Fowles's own life looms inescapably, too: Devon, the time spent at Oxford, the involvement with film, the similar age of the protagonist. His deliberate shifting from first- to third-person narration and back again means that, every time it happens, the reader is obliged to rethink his suspension of disbelief. And again the point at which this partially-concealed playfulness becomes apparent is when we realise how deeply intertextual *Daniel Martin* is.

> Fowles is perhaps a great realist born out of his time, but he has accepted his fate and now, having tried to write the fiction that proclaims freedom, he contents himself with the freedom that *is* the fictional play with texts.
>
> —*Lance St John Butler*

We feel the ghostly presence, behind *Daniel Martin,* of, for instance, *Jude the Obscure.* In Chapters 7 and 8 of the first part of that novel the scholarly Jude becomes attracted to the pig-breeder's daughter Arabella, who is a 'complete and substantial female animal'. She lures him into making love to her (something that he is strongly drawn towards in spite of his educational ambitions), but turns out to be hopelessly unsuited to him and eventually becomes a pub landlady. Similarly, in *Daniel Martin*, young Dan, working on a Devon farm, becomes attracted to a sexually-arousing girl of about Arabella's age, and in spite of class and educational differences, they begin a somewhat immature but extremely passionate liaison. Exactly as in Hardy Dan feels 'irresistibly drawn' to this casual encounter with Nancy. The affair is brought to an abrupt halt by parental intervention, and many years later, Nancy reappears at Dan's house, a middle-aged woman who has become very like the Arabella of later years: 'I hardly recognised her, she'd got so heavy-limbed and stout, her tinted hair done back and up in a kind of bouffant style, *like a pub landlady* in a last pathetic attempt at attractiveness' (my italics). This could be fleshed out in much greater detail, but the important thing is the structural intertextuality at work; it is clinched by the next phase of Dan's adolescent life. Just as Jude transfers his affections from the earthy Arabella to his intellectual and spiritually-minded cousin Sue Bridehead, so Dan transfers his from Nancy to his cousin Barbara. Sue is too fastidious about sexual relations to be a satisfactory mate for Jude, and is deeply affected by high church Anglicanism. Here is Fowles on Barbara:

> Her shyness and niceness in the flesh proved far stronger than a certain veiled emotion that had flavoured . . . some of her letters. Five years later she was to cause a great family to-do by 'turning' Catholic . . . and soon after becoming a nun. Her distaste for the flesh was already apparent.

The similarities between these two West Country novelists (both profoundly interested in the flesh and its opposites) are too great to be coincidental.

Besides *Jude the Obscure, Tess of the d'Urbervilles* is an intertext for *Daniel Martin.* The early scene in Fowles's novel, for instance, where the Devonshire harvesters massacre the rabbits trapped in the ever-shrinking area of wheat cannot possibly exist independently of the almost identical scene in *Tess* where Dorsetshire harvesters perform the same grisly ritual. Equally, the attentive reader will pick up all sorts of details from Dylan Thomas ('the scene had a deep humanity, a green fuse'), Conrad (of the Nile: 'Its waters seemed to reach not merely back into the heart of Africa, but into that of time itself') or Keats ('Some hidden warbler bubbled an out-of-season song. It was delicious . . . a profound and liquid, green and eternal peace'.) This is all quite apart from the echoes of Alain-Fournier, George Eliot, T. S. Eliot, Langland and D. H. Lawrence.

In *A Maggot* intertextuality is given a new and extraordinary form. The novel is studded with facsimile reproductions of pages from *The Gentleman's Magazine* and *The Historical Chronicle* for 1736 (the date in which the novel is set). These have almost no direct bearing on the text of the novel, and are hard to read, appearing in very small print. But nearly all of the facsimile pages contain some reference to the Porteous riots of 1736. Now the Porteous affair forms the core of Scott's *Heart of Midlothian,* so we

are offered a sort of palimpsest involving 1985 (*A Maggot*), 1818 (*Heart of Midlothian*) and 1736 (twice: the Porteous narrative written in the magazines of that year and the narrative concerning the characters in *A Maggot.*)

A Maggot involves time-travellers from the future bringing an indication of what history holds for mankind to the mid-eighteenth century. Its hero is taken away in a spaceship while its heroine is confirmed in her extreme form of Protestant Dissent and becomes the mother of a (historical) prophetess. This alarming plot appears quite alien to everything that Fowles has done hitherto (*Daniel Martin* was also greeted with surprise), but in truth we are in the same world as before. The freedom of the fiction writer is absolute, and his greatest interest is in exploring the implications of freedom for the human species, though in the end that becomes an exploration of his own freedom as a writer. Thus Rebecca in *A Maggot* becomes the most completely free thing she can, granted her sex, date and status; she frees herself from money, men and convention (as well as from the brothel), while her creator takes the liberty of the text as he sees fit. In *The French Lieutenant's Woman,* after all, he travelled in time, too. But the relativity of freedom is made clear here: in the political conditions of the early eighteenth century, the best way for Rebecca to assert herself may very well have been to join a tiny sect of religious extremists among whom she is able to be not her *herself* but at least *different* from the norms enforced by the dominant social ideology. Freedom in *A Maggot* (a deliberate echo of 'Magus', if that word is pronounced cor-

---

Fowles on the difficulties of writing:

I should think the revising part [is the hardest part of writing]. I write lots of drafts, but so does almost every writer I've ever heard of. I don't know anyone who can sit down and write a perfect text. I've quoted quite often the hypnotism chapter in *The Magus,* which I left out because I couldn't cope with it. All it was in the typescript was just a page with a note "Conchis hypnotizes Nicholas," or something like that. I couldn't actually see how to do it. I did it right at the very end; I wrote it in one morning, in fact. The accursed Erato was on my side on that occasion. This does happen in narrative: you'll get a chapter down very fast and then the most ridiculous little thing in some other one causes you hours and hours of problems. On the whole, dialogue is the most difficult thing, without any doubt. It's very difficult, unfortunately. You have to detach yourself from the notion of a lifelike quality. You see, actually lifelike, tape-recorded dialogue like this has very little to do with good novel dialogue. It's a matter of getting that awful tyranny of mimesis out of your mind, which is difficult. Evelyn Waugh is the man I admire. I don't like him on social or philosophical grounds, but I think he was an admirable handler of dialogue.

John Fowles, in an interview with Katherine Tarbox, in her The Art of John Fowles, *The University of Georgia Press, 1988.*

rectly) has been reduced to the freedom to assert one inauthenticity rather than another. The 'authentic' is no longer available.

At the beginning and end of *Daniel Martin* Fowles tries to proclaim the wisdom of something he calls 'whole sight', but this is not a piece of goods that he is able to deliver. He has tried very hard to find it, but this is no longer the century (it was the nineteenth) in which it can be found. Matthew Arnold of course felt that it had only been possible in Sophocles' day to see life steadily and 'whole', but from our perspective the great nineteenth-century novelists were much less fragmented in their view than we are. Fowles is perhaps a great realist born out of his time, but he has accepted his fate and now, having tried to write the fiction that proclaims freedom, he contents himself with the freedom that *is* the fictional play with texts.

Dominique Costa   (essay date 1991)

SOURCE: "Narrative Voice and Focalization: The Presentation of the Different Selves in John Fowles' *The Collector*," in *Subjectivity and Literature from the Romantics to the Present Day,* edited by Philip Shaw and Peter Stockwell, Pinter Publishers, 1991, pp. 113-20.

[*In the essay below, Costa analyzes Fowles's narrative technique and delineation of character in* The Collector.]

In 1963 the publication of *The Collector* initiated John Fowles' career as a full-time writer. In [this] first novel the story of Frederick Clegg, an emotionally disturbed young man from an unhappy lower middle-class family, and of Miranda Grey, an attractive art student from an upper-class family, is recounted to us in a most distinctive manner.

The aim of this paper is to examine Fowles' use of two specific narrative devices—voice and focalization—in order to present in a realistic way two fundamentally different selves, Clegg's and Miranda's; one static and destructive, the other striving for self-knowledge and improvement, each representative of two distinct social groups: 'the Few' and 'the Many'. For this analysis I shall use the concepts and terminology introduced by the French theorist Gérard Genette in his major work *Narrative Discourse: An Essay in Method* (1980).

The main plot of the novel may be conveyed in a few words. Having unexpectedly won a football pool, Clegg prepares to fulfil his secret aspiration of possessing Miranda with whom he is deeply obsessed. Letting his fantasies dominate his life, he kidnaps the young girl using chloroform as he does for his butterflies. Being a collector he keeps her for a long period in the cellar, especially prepared for her imprisonment in the old cottage he has recently bought, until she dies. Throughout the novel it is the strange relationship that develops between these characters—Clegg, the imprisoner and Miranda, the imprisoned—which unfolds dramatically in front of the reader's eyes.

The Collector opens with Clegg's account of the events which precede Miranda's kidnapping, followed by those during her captivity in the cellar, halting abruptly at a cru-

cial moment during her illness, within a few days of the girl's death. In fact, having arrived almost at the middle of the novel, Part Two suddenly starts not with Clegg's continuation of the events but, instead, with Miranda's account of the events her captor has already described. The main difference is that events are now seen by her and recounted from her own perspective, and I quite agree with Perry Nodelman who [in 'John Fowles' Variations in *The Collector*', *Contemporary Literature* (1987)] considers that 'it is this surprising switch of perspective *in medias res* that forms readers' attitudes to both Clegg and Miranda'. Fowles' selection of two distinct, traditionally called, 'first-person' voices and sharply contrastive focalizations on the same events—a selection that allows Clegg and Miranda to narrate the story of their relationship in their own manner with their own words—is, as will be seen, crucial to the presentation of these characters. By inserting in Part Two Miranda's narrative voice within, rather than before or after, Clegg's narrative sections, together with the juxtaposition of their contrastive voices, the author shows the narrators' differing, clashing viewpoints on the situation enhancing their different selves, and simultaneously causes the form of the novel to mirror the content. Miranda's story becomes entrapped in Clegg's, paralleling in this way her personal entrapment by him. These two sections of *The Collector,* in which Clegg's and Miranda's voices show their personal views on the situation, form the bulk of the novel and are followed by two shorter ones in which Clegg, taking up the narrative once more, unfolds in Part Three a chilling account of Miranda's last moments, finally ending in Part Four with the disclosure of his plans for his next victim.

By permitting direct access to his protagonists' narratives, Fowles removes himself from his novel leaving the reader to pass judgement alone. With the absence of the authorial voice the illusion that the characters themselves shape their own text is effective. While authenticity and credibility are thus achieved by having two 'surrogate authors'—Clegg and Miranda—provide their own narratives, their different selves become apparent to the reader.

I now want to look in more detail at the narrative voice which provides the frame of the novel, Clegg's. In the opening sentence of the novel we are at once confronted with the occurrence of two personal pronouns lacking any antecedent:

> When *she* was home from her boarding-school *I* used to see her almost every day sometimes, because their house was right opposite the Town Hall Annexe (my emphasis).

The 'I' of this 'etic opening'—ie one characterized by the absence of narrative preliminaries with predominance of personal pronouns without references—can here only indicate the narrator, a narrator whom the traditional theoretical studies on perspective generally and confusingly name a 'first-person narrator' failing, as Genette points out, to distinguish between *mode* (Who sees?) and *voice* (Who speaks?). As the opening sentence shows, this narrator is present as a character within the world of fictional events. He is what Genette calls a 'homodiegetic narrator' and, because he functions as the protagonist in the story he is narrating, he is also 'autodiegetic'—ie what is traditionally called a 'protagonist-narrator'.

Genette's crucial separation of mode and voice—distinguishing between the question 'Who sees?' (focalization) and the question 'Who talks? (narration)—is of great value here since a differentiation between Clegg the protagonist, whose perception orients the narrative perspective (the focus), and Clegg the narrator, who presents the events (the voice), is essential for the way in which Clegg's narrative is recounted and for the way the reader perceives his self. Basing their argument on Genette's concept of focalization, two later theorists, Mieke Bal [in *Narratology: Introduction to the Theory of Narrative,* 1985] and Shlomith Rimmon-Kenan [in *Narrative Fiction: Contemporary Poetics,* 1983], call such an agent the 'focalizer'; he is the vehicle of focalization 'through whose spatial, temporal and/or psychological position the textual events are perceived' [S. S. Lanser, *The Narrative Act: Point of View in Prose Fiction,* 1987]. What the focalizer perceives—all that is related to himself, Miranda and her captivity—is named the 'focalized object'. The relationship between focalizer (Clegg) and focalized object (Miranda) is offered from an 'internal focalization' since it is, as the following example reveals, through Clegg's thoughts, feelings and perceptions that the story is presented:

> *Seeing* her always made me *feel* like I was catching a rarity, going up to it very careful, heart-in-mouth as they say. A Pale Clouded Yellow, for instance. I always *thought* of her like that (my emphasis).

In his narrative then, Clegg plays a double role. He is at the same time a character within the story he is telling—the protagonist who underwent the experience in the past, the focus through which all is seen—and also the one who narrates it in the present, the narrating voice. Genette posits that these two identities—the narrating focus and the narrating voice—though found within the same character, are quite different in function as well as in the degree of their knowledge. He considers the following:

> The narrator almost always 'knows' more than the hero, even if he himself is the hero, and therefore for the narrator focalization through the hero is a restriction of field just as artificial in the first person as in the third. (Genette)

Because of the 'restriction of field' and especially because of the duality of focus-narration, the reader rapidly senses Clegg's unreliability as a narrator. Knowing, in fact, before the beginning of his narration what the end of Miranda's captivity will be, Clegg colours his treatment of the events from the very beginning and distorts reality to his advantage.

The reader also rapidly becomes aware that in Clegg's presentation of Miranda's captivity, certain terms and expressions are used to conceal his faults and to make him feel less guilty about her condition. For instance, he never directly refers to her as his prisoner but calls her his 'guest'. Furthermore, a similar process, a process of self-deceit by which Clegg distorts reality in his own favour in order to justify his actions and eliminate any responsibility, is frequently used, as the following example illustrates:

> About what I did, undressing her, when I thought after, I *saw it wasn't so bad; not many would have kept control of themselves . . . it was almost a point in my favour* (my emphasis).

Other negative aspects of Clegg's self, such as his obsession with collecting, quickly become noticeable in the novel. First, Miranda's name is revealingly marked in his entomological observations diary and throughout his narrative she is frequently compared to butterflies, as in 'It was like catching the Mazarine Blue again or a Queen of Spain Fritillary'. On one occasion Fowles explicitly draws our attention to his protagonist's obsession by making him refer to Miranda as 'it' instead of 'she': 'For a moment I thought her, *it* looked so different (my emphasis). This obsession is characterized in him by a need of possession. 'Having her', declares Clegg, 'was Nothing needed doing: I just wanted to have her'. As with his butterflies, he is interested in her image not in her self, as Miranda rightly observes:

> The sheer joy of having me under his power, of being able to spend all and every day staring at me. He doesn't care what I say or how I feel—my feelings are meaningless to him—it's the fact that he's got me . . . It's me he wants, my look, my outside; not my emotions or my mind or my soul or even my body. Not anything *human.* He's a collector. That's the great dead thing in him.

The writer's choice of the girl's name—Miranda, the Latin gerundive of *miror,* referring to 'she who ought to be wondered at'—clearly enhances this.

From the beginning of his narrative Clegg's language shows certain distinctive features. His personal way of narrating the events in a matter-of-fact, colloquial style, using banal expressions, emphasizes his low social background and poor level of education. The type of language and tone used by the narrator is frequently inappropriate to, and clashes with, the events that are being narrated. In his analysis of one of the most dramatic passages of the novel, when Clegg coldly describes Miranda lying dead in her bed, [G. Ronberg notes in 'Literature and the Teaching of English as a Foreign Language at University Level', *Triangle* (1985)] that 'the language does not accord with the field of discourse', a conflict arising from 'form not matching function'. This observation can be applied to other passages of the novel and it is also through such a device that Clegg's emotional, psychological, sexual and social inadequacies are revealed. Language is thus primarily used by the author as a means of revealing the deficiencies of his narrator's intellect and education, and exposing his emotional stuntedness and moral blindness. At the end of his narrative, Fowles shows how little Clegg has learned by letting us witness how, without any sense of guilt, he is prepared to repeat what he has done. The only difference is that this time he will catch an 'ordinary common shop-girl'—his previous mistake, he tells us, having been that of 'aiming too high'.

By means of such narrative Fowles lets his reader see how Clegg's disturbed mind works, how his obsession rules his and Miranda's lives. According to Clegg, his failure with Miranda has been caused by class difference: 'There was always class between us' he says. His resentment and sense of inferiority are quite evident when, in an outburst, he tells his prisoner:

> If you ask me, London's all arranged for the people who can act like public schoolboys, and you don't get anywhere if you don't have the manner born and the right la-di-da voice—I mean rich people's London, the West End, of course.

Miranda's views of her captor indicate that she sees him as, to some extent, a victim himself, as when, for example, she writes: 'I know he's a victim of a miserable nonconformist suburban world and a miserable social class, the horrid timid copycatting genteel in-between class'. Clegg is what he is as a result of social conditions, unequal opportunities, childhood deprivation and poor education, and Fowles asserts [in *The Aristos,* 1989] that in this novel he has tried 'to establish the virtual *innocence* of the Many'. The recurrence of expressions like 'I don't know why' or 'I don't know how' indicate that most of the time Clegg is at a loss, unable to understand what is happening. He has, as Fowles stresses in his preface to *The Aristos,* no control over what he is. Miranda clearly sees this when she tells him 'You're the one imprisoned in a cellar'.

Considering now Miranda's narrative voice, the beginning of her narration in Part Two of *The Collector,* with the date 'October 14th?', indicates at once that she is writing a diary in which her thoughts, feelings, perceptions and experiences about her present situation are going to be confided. In her diary she records all the events concerning her imprisonment and the painful experiences which accompany it, and at the same time she is able to recall memories of the past in which she can take refuge.

Miranda is, thus, in this part of the novel, as Clegg was in the others, an autodiegetic narrator since she is a narrator who tells a story in which she simultaneously plays a part as one of the fictional characters. It is she who acts as the focalizer—the agent of the narrative who concentrates her attention on the focalized object; ie all which concerns her present and Clegg, and also her past and G. P., George Paston, her artistic mentor. Her presentation of the fictional world, like Clegg's, is self-centred in that it is offered through her thoughts, memories and feelings—from an internal focalization. With such a process the reader is able to follow Miranda closely, observing her struggle and the transformations which her captivity effects in her inner self.

Fowles claims that Miranda 'is an existentialist heroine groping for her own authenticity', but he adds that 'her tragedy is that she will never live to achieve it. Her triumph is that one day she would have done so' [R. Newquist, 'John Fowles', *Counterpoint* (1964)]. Elsewhere he comments:

> I'm interested in the side of existentialism which deals with freedom: the business of whether we do have freedom, whether we do have free will, to what extent you can change your life, choose yourself, and all the rest of it. Most of my major characters have been involved in this 'Sartrian concept of authenticity and inauthenticity'.

[Kerry McSweeney, *Four Contemporary Novelists,* 1983]

While Clegg makes use of his memoir primarily as a means of self-justification, Miranda on the other hand uses her diary in order to discover her self. Writing is for her a creative activity. Through introspection and self-criticism she is able to expose her old self and her narrative allows us to follow the transformations she is undergoing:

> I want to use my feelings about life. I think and think down here. I understand things I haven't really thought about before.
>
> I am beginning to understand life much better than most people of my age.
>
> I'm growing up so quickly down here. Like a mushroom.

For Fowles, 'we must evolve to exist'. Contrasting with Clegg's spiritual inertia, deadness—subtly pointed out by his last name 'Clegg' which can be phonetically associated to the French 'clef', indicating his role as gaoler, but mainly in its meaning in dialect: a vampirish horsefly, and in its consonance with 'clog', suggesting heaviness and woodenness—Miranda is on the other hand to be seen as a symbol of moral growth, struggling to understand and become better. In *The Aristos* Fowles considers the following distinction: 'Adam is hatred of change', he 'is stasis or conservatism . . . Eve is the assumption of human responsibility, of the need for progress and the need to control progress . . . She is kinesis or progress'. Such distinction is clearly embodied in these two protagonists: Clegg (stasis or conservatism); Miranda (kinesis or progress).

Since she lives in the present of her captive world and she most desperately wants to escape from it, one sees Miranda making use of her memories, of her recollections of her past outside world, in order to escape, at least mentally if not physically, from her confined situation. She discloses this when she writes:

> I felt I was going mad last night; so I wrote and wrote and wrote myself into the other world. To escape in spirit, if not in fact. To prove it still exists.

Remembering the past, and especially her relationship with G. P., helps her in her present confinement. It is through the introduction of a certain type of 'analepsis' or 'flashback'—designated by Genette as 'external', whose 'only function is to fill out the first narrative by enlightening the reader on one or another "antecedent" '—that Fowles permits his reader to know his protagonist better. Through such analepses one is in fact able to follow Miranda's progress from her 'old Ladymont self' into a new and better self, her growth through suffering and her striving for self-knowledge. On one occasion she even goes so far as to admit:

> A strange thought: I would not want this not to have happened. Because if I escape I shall be a completely different and I think better person. Because if I don't escape; if something dreadful happened, I shall still know that the person I was and would have stayed if this hadn't happened was not the person I now want to be.

Being an artist with a creative temperament, Miranda's narrative voice is presented in her diary in various ways. She decides to use a variety of forms in her fiction including dialogue with stage directions, lists of thoughts and feelings and fictive letters. Her creativity can also be noticed in her use of language, offering a sharp contrast with her captor's. About her style Peter Wolfe rightly states [in *John Fowles, Magus and Moralist,* 1979] that 'Miranda's literary style gauges her personality, her values, and her ability to adapt to change'.

Throughout her diary Clegg has been referred to as one of 'the Many' or, as she derisively names him, one of the 'New People'—'the new-class people with their cars and their money and their tellies and their stupid vulgarities and their stupid crawling imitation of the bourgeoisie'—while she sees herself as one of 'the Few': 'a sort of band of people who have to stand against all the rest'. 'In this situation', Miranda claims, 'I'm a representative', but being a representative of 'the Few' does not mean that she is to be regarded as perfect and that the author's viewpoint is to be identified with his heroine's. Fowles himself draws our attention to this when he clearly asserts [in *The Aristos*]; 'That does not mean that she was perfect. Far from it she was arrogant in her ideas, a prig, a liberal-humanist snob, like so many university students'.

Miranda's flaws are apparent in her narrative. Like Clegg she makes use of clichés 'I love life so passionately, I never knew how much I wanted to live before', prefers avoiding verbal 'impropriety', and refers, for instance, to people by initials. What Fowles wants us to understand is that contrary to Clegg, who learns nothing, who cannot change or mature, 'if she had not died', he says about his heroine, 'she might have become something better, the kind of being humanity so desperately needs'. The author further explains his views on *The Collector* when he remarks:

> The actual evil in Clegg overcame the potential good in Miranda. I did not mean by this that I view the future with a black pessimism, nor that a precious *élite* is threatened by the barbarian hordes. I meant simply that unless we face up to this unnecessary brutal conflict (based largely on an unnecessary envy on the one hand and an unnecessary contempt on the other) between the biological Few and the biological Many; unless we admit that we are not, and never will be, born equal, though we are all born with equal human rights; unless the Many can be educated out of their false assumption of inferiority and the Few out of their equally false assumption that biological superiority is a state of existence instead of what it really is, *a state of responsibility*—then we shall never arrive at a more just and happier world. [*The Aristos*]

With Miranda's second 'autodiegetic narration' Fowles enhances the unbridgeable gap that exists between her and her captor. Through her narrative, Clegg's version of the events is complemented and often corrected, striking contrasts and ironies becoming thus apparent. Events which have been previously narrated by Clegg are treated differently in Miranda's narrative, disclosing to us his distorted self. Throughout the novel Clegg and Miranda appear to misread each other constantly. When he expects some understanding from her, none is shown, and when she sympathizes with him, he is not able to see it. Their mutual incomprehension is illustrated by Miranda when she writes 'We'll never understand each other. We don't have the same sort of heart', and also by Clegg when at a certain point he declares: 'We could never come together, she could never understand me, I suppose she would say I never could have understood her, or would have anyhow'. Apart from the different treatment of the events, the intersection of the autodiegetic narrations primarily reveals the fundamental differences between these two antagonistic selves.

This narrative process through which the writer presents his two autodiegetic narrators is fundamental for an effective treatment of the subject and points primarily to the two different selves of the protagonists. In *The Collector* Fowles appears thus as an author in full control of his material offering, through an effective handling of two specific narrative devices—voice and focalization—an existential parable which delineates Clegg's destructive *being* and Miranda's creative *becoming*.

FURTHER READING

Bibliography

Aubrey, James R. *John Fowles: A Reference Companion.* New York: Greenwood Press, 1991, 333 p.
> Contains a brief biography, an introduction to each of Fowles's fictional works, and a bibliography of works by and about Fowles.

Criticism

Balsamo, Gian. "The Narrative Text as Historical Artifact: The Case of John Fowles." In *Image and Ideology in Modern/Postmodern Discourse,* edited by David B. Downing and Susan Bazargan, pp. 127-52.
> Analyzes Fowles's two historical novels—*The French Lieutenant's Woman* and *A Maggot*—focusing on their themes, structure, and historical sources.

Boccia, Michael. " 'Visions and Revisions': John Fowles's New Version of *The Magus.*" *Journal of Modern Literature* 8, No. 2 (1980-1981): 235-46.
> Remarks on Fowles's revisions to *The Magus,* noting that most of the changes "make Fowles's themes more explicit or help to create sharper characterization."

Broich, Ulrich. "John Fowles, 'The Enigma' and the Contemporary British Short Story." In *Modes of Narrative: Approaches to American, Canadian and British Fiction,* edited by Reingard M. Mischik and Barbara Korte, pp. 179-89. Würzburg: Königshausen & Neumann, 1990.
> Contends that "The Enigma" is an amalgamation of experimentalism and realism, and is representative of contemporary British short fiction.

De Vitis, A. A., and Schwerdt, Lisa M. "*The French Lieutenant's Woman* and 'Las Meninas': Correspondences of Art." *The International Fiction Review* 12, No. 2 (Summer 1985): 102-04.

Brief essay focusing on the thematic parallels between Diego de Silva Velazquez's painting and Fowles's novel.

Doherty, Gerald. "The Secret Plot of Metaphor: Rhetorical Designs in John Fowles's *The French Lieutenant's Woman*." *Paragraph* 9 (March 1987): 49-68.

Argues that the three major plot designs in *The French Lieutenant's Woman* are "narrativized allegories" of the plots of metaphor that Paul Ricoeur presents in his study *The Rule of Metaphor*.

Dopp, Jamie, and Olshen, Barry N. "Fathers and Sons: Fowles's *The Tree* and Autobiographical Theory." *Mosaic* 22, No. 4 (Fall 1989): 31-44.

Relates *The Tree*'s contribution to autobiographical theory and an understanding of Fowles's theories on fiction writing and humankind's relationship with nature.

Fossa, John A. "Through Seeding to Mystery: A Reappraisal of John Fowles' *The Magus*." *Orbis Litterarum* 44, No. 2 (1989): 161-80.

Suggests an alternative reading of *The Magus* that "view[s] Nicholas not as a magus in the making, but as always having been a magus, though he himself only becomes aware of this through his experiences on the island of Phraxos."

Gaggi, Silvio. "Pirandellian and Brechtian Aspects of the Fiction of John Fowles." *Comparative Literature Studies* 23, No. 4 (Winter 1986): 324-34.

Argues that "the fiction of John Fowles has clear narrative correspondences to themes and techniques that occur in modern theatre."

Gallop, David. "Can Fiction Be Stranger than Truth? An Aristotelian Answer." *Philosophy and Literature* 15, No. 1 (April 1991): 1-18.

Contends that the double ending Fowles employed in *The French Lieutenant's Woman* "defeats the aim of fiction, constructed along Aristotelian lines, as moving and enlightening the reader."

Garard, Charles. *Point of View in Fiction and Film: Focus on John Fowles*. New York: Peter Lang, 1991, 142 p.

Analyzes the film adaptations of *The Collector, The Magus*, and *The French Lieutenant's Woman*.

Haegert, John. "Memoirs of a Deconstructive Angel: The Heroine as Mantissa in the Fiction of John Fowles." *Contemporary Literature* 27, No. 2 (Summer 1986): 160-81.

Examines the thematic and symbolic role of women in Fowles's fiction with the focus of the essay being *Mantissa*.

Holmes, Frederick M. "John Fowles's Variation on Angus Wilson's Variation on E. M. Forster: 'The Cloud,' 'Et Dona Ferentes,' and 'The Story of a Panic.'" *Ariel* 20, No. 3 (July 1989): 39-52.

Concludes that "Wilson's apparent influence on Fowles no more resulted in mere imitation than did Forster's apparent influence on Wilson. Rather Fowles turned his countryman's methods and concerns to his own distinct purposes in order to create a subtler and more compelling story."

Ireland, K. R. "Towards a Grammar of Narrative Sequence:

The Model of *The French Lieutenant's Woman*." *Poetics Today* 7, No. 3 (1986): 397-420.

Analyzes the novel's narrative progression by focusing on the relationships and transitions between chapters.

Lorsch, Susan E. "Pinter Fails Fowles: Narration in *The French Lieutenant's Woman*." *Film Literature Quarterly* 16, No. 3 (July 1988): 144-54.

Faults Harold Pinter's screenplay for failing to fully translate the spirit of Fowles's narrative through the film-within-a-film metaphor.

Mansfield, Elizabeth. "A Sequence of Endings: The Manuscripts of *The French Lieutenant's Woman*." *Journal of Modern Literature* 8, No. 2 (1980-1981): 275-86.

Analysis of Fowles's novel focusing on the creative process surrounding the multiple endings.

Miller, Walter, Jr. "Chariots of the Goddesses, or What?" *The New York Times Book Review* (8 September 1985): 11.

Favorably reviews *A Maggot*.

Modern Fiction Studies, Special Issue: John Fowles 31, No. 1 (Spring 1985): 3-210.

Contains essays on Fowles's major novels, an interview, and a bibliography of secondary sources.

Moynahan, Julian. "Fly Casting." *The New Republic* 193, No. 15 (7 October 1985): 47-9.

Comments on the literary and historical influences that inform *A Maggot*.

Smith, Frederick N. "The Endings of *The French Lieutenant's Woman*: Another Speculation on the Manuscript." *Journal of Modern Literature* 14, No. 4 (Spring 1988): 579-84.

Refutes Elizabeth Mansfield's claim (see article cited above) that Fowles originally intended the novel to have a single, happy ending and only later, on the advice of his wife, added the unhappy ending.

Vieth, Lynne S. "The Re-humanization of Art: Pictorial Aesthetics in John Fowles's *The Ebony Tower* and *Daniel Martin*." *Modern Fiction Studies* 37, No. 2 (Summer 1991): 217-33.

Discusses Fowles's concern with the relationship between imagistic and narrative insight as displayed in *The Ebony Tower*, "The Cloud," and *Daniel Martin*.

Ward, Carol. "Movie as Metaphor: Focus on *Daniel Martin*." *Literature Film Quarterly* 15, No. 1 (January 1987): 8-14.

Argues that a major thematic and structural component of *Daniel Martin* is "Fowles's comparison of the aesthetic properties of film and literature (represented by both fiction and drama)."

Interview

Foulke, Robert. "A Conversation with John Fowles." *Salmagundi*, Nos. 68-69 (Fall 1985-Winter 1986): 367-84.

Discussion relating Fowles's views on history and novel writing.

Additional coverage of Fowles's life and career is contained in the following sources published by Gale Research: *Concise Dictionary of British Literary Biography, 1960 to Present; Contemporary Authors,* Vols. 5-8, rev. ed.; *Contemporary Authors New Revision Series,* Vol. 25; *Contemporary Literary Criticism,* Vols. 1, 2, 3, 4, 6, 9, 10, 15, 33; *Dictionary of Literary Biography,* Vols. 14, 139; *Major 20th-Century Writers;* and *Something about the Author,* Vol. 22.

Che Guevara

1928-1967

(Full name Ernesto Guevara de la Serna) Argentine-Cuban nonfiction writer, essayist, diarist, and political theorist.

The following entry provides an overview of Guevara's career.

INTRODUCTION

The Marxist revolutionary who was chief military and ideological adviser to Fidel Castro during the Cuban Revolution of 1956-1959, Guevara is still recognized by leftists all over the world as a martyr to the cause of third-world revolution. Guevara's near-mythic reputation rests largely on his military exploits and his personal example of courage, self-sacrifice, and idealism, rather than any major original contributions to Marxist theory or revolutionary practice. As a writer of nonfiction, Guevara is best known for the training manual entitled *La guerra de guerrillas* (1960; *Guerrilla Warfare*) and his posthumously published *El diario de Che en Bolivia* (1968; *The Diary of Che Guevara*). He is also the author of numerous collections of speeches and articles on such wide-ranging topics as socialist morality and economic planning.

Biographical Information

Guevara was born in Argentina into an upper middle-class family with leftist sympathies. As a boy, he developed a severe asthma condition that would plague him throughout his life and contributed to his decision to pursue a career as a doctor. Guevara received his medical degree from the University of Buenos Aires in 1953 and then traveled around South and Central America, eventually settling in Guatemala, where he worked as an inspector for the agrarian land redistribution program launched by reformist President Jacobo Arbenz Guzman. Soon thereafter, a military coup organized and financed by the U.S. Central Intelligence Agency overthrew the Arbenz government. After fruitless attempts to organize local popular resistance to the military takeover, Guevara took asylum in the Argentine embassy, where he remained for two months before fleeing to Mexico. Guevara's first-hand experience of the coup deepened his anti-American sentiments and helped convince him that armed revolution was necessary for social reforms to occur in Latin America. In Mexico Guevara met the exiled Cuban brothers Fidel and Paul Castro, who were organizing a revolutionary movement against Cuban dictator Fulgencio Batista. Guevara agreed to join the Castros' "26 of July Movement" as their physician and thereby became the sole non-Cuban among eighty-three guerrilla fighters who landed in Cuba in December of 1956. The Cuban army crushed the force immediately, but Guevara and the Castros were among the twelve survivors who managed to reach the rugged Sierra

Maestra mountain range, where they began organizing the infrastructure for a prolonged guerilla insurgency. Guevara, nicknamed "Che" by his Cuban comrades, took up arms with the rest of the insurgents and displayed such leadership ability that he was named commander of a second guerrilla column composed of local peasant recruits. He also served as a trusted political advisor to commander-in-chief Fidel Castro, headed the insurgent medical corps, and organized military training camps, a radio station, a weapons plant, and a network of schools in the guerrilla zone of control. In late 1958 Guevara's soldiers routed a much larger and better equipped Cuban army contingent at the decisive battle of Santa Clara, which convinced Batista to resign from office and flee the country. Not long afterward, Guevara led the first rebel force into Havana and sealed the revolutionary victory. Guevara held a series of important positions in the early years of the new Cuban government, serving first as military commander of Havana's La Cabaña fortress and successively as a top official of the National Institute of Agrarian Reform, president of the National Bank of Cuba, and Minister of Industries. In the last two posts, Guevara (who was awarded full citizenship rights by the Castro government) was largely involved in the immensely complex and difficult task of converting a sugar-based, capitalist economy heavily dependent on the United States into a state-run system with a more diversified production and trading base. In 1960 Guevara helped negotiate an historic trading pact with the Soviet Union, exchanging sugar for capital goods; after the United States imposed an economic boycott of the island later in the year, he traveled to other Eastern bloc countries to develop new commercial relations. Better versed in Marxist economic theory than Castro, Guevara envisioned a socialist outcome for the Cuban Revolution and encouraged the Cuban leader to take the definitive step toward a state-run system by nationalizing virtually all of the country's industry in late 1960. Determined to break Cuba from its over-reliance on sugar exports, Guevara sought to industrialize the island with support from the Eastern Bloc, which provided generous aid and advantageous sugar prices. He believed, however, that the emergence of a new "socialist morality" among the Cuban people was the most expedient means of developing the island's economy. Consequently, he favored moral rather than material incentives to raise production and advocated voluntary work programs to strengthen revolutionary consciousness and solidarity. In early 1965 Guevara mysteriously disappeared from public view, with many speculating that he had disagreed with Castro over economic policy and had subsequently been "removed." Castro's official explanation that Guevara had freely departed Cuba to advance the cause of socialist revolution abroad was substantiated when Guevara later appeared in Africa with two hundred Cuban troops to assist Congolese rebels. In 1966 he returned to Havana, where he made plans to apply his military theories on guerrilla insurgency in South America. Guevara's ultimate goal was to create "two, three, many Vietnams" to challenge the hegemony of the United States—his greatest "imperialist" enemy. With Castro's support, he assembled a force of Cuban and Peruvian revolutionaries who secretly entered Bolivia in late 1966. Joined by Bolivian rebels, the group began its guerrilla campaign in southeastern Bolivia in March 1967 after its presence was revealed to local peasants. Guevara's far-reaching plans, however, proceeded disastrously since neither the local peasantry nor the Bolivian Communist Party provided the expected support. The Bolivian army, actively assisted by the C.I.A., finally annihilated the guerrillas. Guevara was captured on 8 October 1967 and, after being identified by Cuban agents of the C.I.A., was executed.

Major Works

Guevara's major political works reflect his attempt to adapt established Marxist revolutionary principles to Latin America's unique historical and social conditions. He drew on his combat experience in Cuba to write *Guerrilla Warfare,* a manual of guerrilla strategy, tactics, and logistics that was published in Cuba in 1960. In this work the author openly stated his hope that the Cuban example would trigger similar revolutions elsewhere in Latin America and argued that a dedicated guerrilla force of only a few dozen combatants could successfully initiate an insurgency virtually anywhere in the continent. Guevara's guerrilla manual found a readership not only among revolutionaries but within the ranks of the U.S. Army, where strategists were actively seeking solutions to the growing counter-insurgency war in South Vietnam. Guevara later wrote a series of articles describing his personal experiences in the Cuban insurgency that were published in book form as *Pasajes de la guerra revolucionaria* (1963; *Reminiscences of the Cuban Revolutionary War*). *The Nation* reviewer Jose Yglesias found this collection "simple, beautiful, and politically prophetic." Guevara's *Diary,* however, is considered by many critics his most significant work. Seized by the Bolivian army after the destruction of Guevara's guerrilla force, the manuscript created a media sensation, and publishers in Europe and the United States offered over one hundred thousand dollars in a bidding war for publishing rights. The matter was settled, however, when Fidel Castro acquired the manuscripts and international publishing rights from Bolivia's Minister of the Interior. Written in a German calendar notebook in a direct, unadorned style, *The Diary* is an intensely personal document recording Guevara's successes, failures, and frustrations as he attempted to establish the Bolivian guerrilla movement. Guevara summarized the group's activities at the end of each month, analyzing what had gone right as well as what had gone wrong. Scholars agree that the work provides invaluable insights into Marxist revolutionary theory in the field of guerrilla warfare. Guevara also addressed his conception of the socialist "new man" and other political and social issues confronting postcapitalist society in numerous speeches and articles published in Cuban journals. In these pieces, he wrote on such important international economic issues as the problem of third-world foreign debt, trade relations between industrialized and less-developed countries, and the controversy over "market socialism" versus centralized planning in the noncapitalist world. Frequently used in studying the philosophical and economic policies of China and the former Soviet Union, many of these articles and speeches have been translated into English and appear in the collections *Che Guevara Speaks* (1967) and *Venceremos!* (1968).

Critical Reception

Critical reaction to Guevara's works generally focuses on his ideas and not on his literary style and expertise. For example, while commentators point out that Guevara's *Diary* presents a uniquely personal picture of his life and political idealism during his days as a Bolivian rebel leader, it is his speeches and writings that continue to attract a wide popular and critical readership. Guevara's works are additionally considered key elements in any analysis of the growth and popularity of Marxist-Socialist ideology in Hispanic-American countries.

PRINCIPAL WORKS

La guerra de guerrillas [*Guerrilla Warfare*] (essays) 1960

Pasajes de la guerra revolucionaria [*Reminiscences of the*

Cuban Revolutionary War; also published as *Episodes of the Revolutionary War*] (reminiscences) 1963

Che Guevara Speaks: Selected Speeches and Writings (essays and speeches) 1967

Obra revolucionaria (essays) 1967

El diario de Che en Bolivia: noviembre 7, 1966, a octubre 7, 1967 [*The Diary of Che Guevara; Bolivia: November 7, 1966-October 7, 1967;* also published as *The Complete Bolivian Diaries of Che Guevara, and Other Captured Documents*] (diaries) 1968

Venceremos! The Speeches and Writings of Ernesto Che Guevara (essays and speeches) 1968

Che Guevara on Revolution: A Documentary Overview (diaries, essays, letters, and speeches) 1969

Obras, 1957-1967 (diaries, essays, and speeches) 1970

El hombre y el socialismo en Cuba (essays) 1973

Che Guevara and the Cuban Revolution: Writings and Speeches (essays and speeches) 1987

CRITICISM

Che Guevara with Laura Berguist (interview date 9 April 1963)

SOURCE: An interview in *Look,* Vol. 27, No. 7, April 9, 1963, pp. 26-7.

[*In the following excerpt, Berguist probes Guevara's views on Marxism, world politics, and social reform in Cuba.*]

[*Berguist*]: *Many early Castro supporters certainly didn't have today's Marxist-oriented revolution in mind. When you were fighting in the Sierra Maestra mountains, was this the future Cuba you envisioned?*

[*Guevara*]: Yes, though I could not have predicted certain details of development.

Could you personally have worked with a government that was leftist but less "radical"—government that nationalized certain industries, but left areas open for private enterprise and permitted opposition parties?

Certainly not.

Historically, the extreme Right and Left in Latin America (and Europe) have combined for different purposes, in an effort to topple "centrist" governments like Rómulo Betancourt's in Venezuela. Why does Cuba levy more violent attacks at Betancourt than at a dictator like Paraguay's Alfredo Stroessner?

Paraguay's dictatorship is obvious. Betancourt is a traitor; he has sold out to the imperialists, and his government is as brutal as any dictatorship.

But Nasser of Egypt takes help from the "imperialist" West, as well as from the East. Has he "sold out"?

No, he is a big anti-imperialist. We are friends.

You once said Cuba would resist becoming a Soviet satellite to the "last drop of blood." But how "sovereign" were you

when Khrushchev arranged with Kennedy for the missile withdrawal without consulting you?

As you know from Fidel's speech, we had differences with the Soviet Union.

You've traveled widely since our last talk—from the Punta del Este Conference in Uruguay to Moscow. Since you call yourself a "pragmatic Marxist" who learns from the "university of experience," what have you learned?

At Punta del Este, I learned in a shocking, first-hand way about the *servilismo* [servility] of most Latin-American governments to the United States. Your Mr. Dillon was a revelation to me.

I've heard many Cubans refer to the period when Anibal Escalante was a director of ORI as "our Stalin" period. But Anibalistas are still in the government. What can keep them from regaining power?

Escalante was shipped out of the country. He had to go. That period is finished. We are completely reorganizing ORI along different lines.

Bureaucracy seems a plague of most "Socialist" countries. I noticed it in Moscow. Hasn't it also invaded Cuba?

Bureaucracy isn't unique to socialism: General Motors has a big bureaucracy. It existed in Cuba's previous bourgeois regime, whose "original sins" we inherited. After the Revolution, because we were taking over a complex social apparatus, a "guerrilla" form of administration did develop. For lack of "revolutionary conscience," individuals tended to take refuge in vegetating, filling out papers, establishing written defenses, to avoid responsibility. After a year of friction, it was necessary to organize a state apparatus, using planning techniques created by brother Socialist countries.

Because of the flight of the few technicians we had, there was a dearth of the knowledge necessary to make sensible decisions. We had to work hard to fill the gaps left by the traitors. To counteract this, everyone in Cuba is now in school.

During the last mobilization, we had many discussions about one phenomenon: When the country was in tension, everyone organized to resist the enemy. Production didn't lessen, absenteeism disappeared, problems were resolved with incredible velocity. We concluded that various forces can combat bureaucracy. One is a great patriotic impulse to resist imperialism, which makes each worker into a soldier of the economy, prepared to resolve whatever problem arises.

What about Cuba's new school system, which separates many children from their parents? Isn't it completely disrupting family life?

The revolutionary government has never had a definite policy, or dealt with the philosophical question of what the family should be. When the process of industrial development takes place, as in Cuba, women are increasingly at work and less at home caring for children. Nurseries must be established to leave the child somewhere. In places like the Sierra Maestra, where there can be no central schools after a certain age, because pupils are too widely scattered in the countryside, we think it better for the children to receive schooling in a specialized center like Camilo Cienfuegos School City. There they can also train for their later work in life. The child spends his vacations with his family—certainly this is no worse than the "boarding schools" of the wealthy people we knew, who did not see their children for eight to ten months a year. There are the problems of families divided, where half the members are revolutionary, the other half not with the Revolution—even pathetic cases of parents who left for Miami, but whose children of 12 or 14 did not want to go. If we hurt the family, it is because we haven't thought about it, not because we are against the family.

Recently, at a trade-union banquet, you noted that "youth" was conspicuously lacking among "exemplary workers" honored that night. Since this is such a "young" Revolution—why?

Perhaps an artificial division has arisen in the thinking of our people. In the armed defense of the Revolution, young people have always been disposed to heroic adventure. Ask them to make long marches, to take to the trenches or mountains, to sacrifice their lives if need be, and they respond. But when the word "sacrifice" refers to an obscure, perhaps even boring job that has to be done daily with efficiency and enthusiasm, older people of experience still excel them. Socialism cannot be achieved by either armed fight or work alone. We must now create a new authentic national hero—a work hero whose example is contagious, as potent as any military hero's.

Finally, what of claims by Cubans that "socialism" here is "different"?

Perhaps it was more spontaneous, but we are part of the Socialist world. Our problems will be solved by our friends.

Fidel Castro   (speech date 18 October 1967)

SOURCE: "Introduction: Che's Enduring Contributions to Revolutionary Thought," in *Che Guevara and the Cuban Revolution: Writings and Speeches of Ernesto Che Guevara,* edited by David Deutschmann, Pathfinder/Pacific and Asia, 1987, pp. 19-32.

[*A leader of the Cuban Revolution and the current prime minister of Cuba, Castro considered Guevara an outstanding revolutionary leader and intellectual mentor. In the following essay, originally delivered as a speech at a memorial rally for Guevara in Havana's Plaza of the Revolution on October 18, 1967, Castro eulogizes Guevara's literary, military, and political achievements, noting "Che possessed the double characteristic of the man of ideas—of profound ideas—and the man of action."*]

Revolutionary compañeras and compañeros:

I first met Che one day in July or August 1955. And in one night—as he recalls in his accounts—he became one of the future *Granma* expeditionaries, although at that time the expedition possessed neither ship, nor arms, nor

troops. That was how, together with Raúl, Che became one of the first two on the *Granma* list.

Twelve years have passed since then; they have been twelve years filled with struggle and historical significance. During this time death has cut down many brave and invaluable lives. But at the same time, throughout those years of our revolution, extraordinary persons have arisen, forged from among the men of the revolution, and between those men and the people, bonds of affection and friendship have emerged that surpass all possible description.

Tonight we are meeting to try to express, in some degree, our feelings toward one who was among the closest, among the most admired, among the most beloved, and, without a doubt, the most extraordinary of our revolutionary compañeros. We are here to express our feelings for him and for the heroes who have fought with him and fallen with him, his internationalist army that has been writing a glorious and indelible page of history.

Che was one of those people who was liked immediately, for his simplicity, his character, his naturalness, his comradely attitude, his personality, his originality, even when one had not yet learned of his other characteristics and unique virtues.

In those first days he was our troop doctor. And so the bonds of friendship and warm feelings for him were ever increasing. He was filled with a profound spirit of hatred and loathing for imperialism, not only because his political education was already considerably developed, but also because, shortly before, he had had the opportunity of witnessing the criminal imperialist intervention in Guatemala through the mercenaries who aborted the revolution in that country.

A man like Che did not require elaborate arguments. It was sufficient for him to know that there were men determined to struggle against that situation, arms in hand. It was sufficient for him to know that those men were inspired by genuinely revolutionary and patriotic ideals. That was more than enough.

One day, at the end of November 1956, he set out on the expedition toward Cuba with us. I recall that the trip was very hard for him, since, because of the circumstances under which it was necessary to organize the departure, he could not even provide himself with the medicine he needed. Throughout the trip, he suffered from a severe attack of asthma, with nothing to alleviate it, but also without ever complaining.

We arrived, set out on our first march, suffered our first setback, and at the end of some weeks, as you all know, a group of those *Granma* expeditionaries who had survived was able to reunite. Che continued to be the doctor of our group.

We came through the first battle victorious, and Che was already a soldier of our troop; at the same time he was still our doctor. We came through the second victorious battle and Che was not only a soldier, but the most outstanding soldier in that battle, carrying out for the first time one of those singular feats that characterized him in all military

Che addresses the United Nations General Assembly, December 11, 1964.

action. Our forces continued to develop and we soon faced another battle of extraordinary importance.

The situation was difficult. The information we had was erroneous in many respects. We were going to attack in full daylight—at dawn—a strongly defended, well-armed position at the edge of the sea. Enemy troops were at our rear, not very far, and in that confused situation it was necessary to ask the men to make a supreme effort.

Compañero Juan Almeida had taken on one of the most difficult missions, but one of the flanks remained completely without forces—one of the flanks was left without an attacking force, placing the operation in danger. At that moment, Che, who was still functioning as our doctor, asked for two or three men, among them one with a machine gun, and in a matter of seconds set off rapidly to assume the mission of attack from that direction.

On that occasion he was not only an outstanding combatant but also an outstanding doctor, attending the wounded compañeros and, at the same time, attending the wounded enemy soldiers.

After all the weapons had been captured and it became necessary to abandon that position, undertaking a long return march under the harassment of various enemy forces, it was necessary for someone to stay behind with the wounded, and Che stayed with the wounded. Aided by a

small group of our soldiers, he took care of them, saved their lives, and later rejoined the column with them.

From that time onward, he stood out as a capable and valiant leader, one of those who, when a difficult mission is pending, do not wait to be asked to carry it out.

Thus it was at the battle of El Uvero. But he acted in a similar way on a previously unmentioned occasion during the first days when, following a betrayal, our little troop was attacked by surprise by a number of airplanes and we were forced to retreat under the bombardment. We had already walked a distance when we remembered some rifles of some peasant soldiers who had been with us in the first actions and had then asked permission to visit their families, at a time when there was still not much discipline in our embryonic army. Back then we had thought that possibly the rifles were lost. I recall that the problem was not brought up again and, during the bombardment, Che volunteered, and having done so, quickly went to recover those rifles.

This was one of his principal characteristics: his willingness to instantly volunteer for the most dangerous mission. And naturally this aroused admiration—and twice the usual admiration, for a fellow combatant fighting alongside us who had not been born here, a man of profound ideas, a man in whose mind stirred the dream of struggle in other parts of the continent and who nonetheless was so altruistic, so disinterested, so willing to always do the most difficult things, to constantly risk his life.

That was how he won the rank of commander and leader of the second column, organized in the Sierra Maestra. Thus his standing began to increase. He began to develop as a magnificent combatant who was to reach the highest ranks in the course of the war.

Che was an incomparable soldier. Che was an incomparable leader. Che was, from a military point of view, an extraordinarily capable man, extraordinarily courageous, extraordinarily aggressive. If, as a guerrilla, he had his Achilles' heel, it was this excessively aggressive quality, his absolute contempt for danger.

The enemy believes it can draw certain conclusions from his death. Che was a master of warfare! He was an artist of guerrilla struggle! And he showed that an infinite number of times. But he showed it especially in two extraordinary deeds. One of these was the invasion, in which he led a column, a column pursued by thousands of enemy soldiers over flat and absolutely unknown terrain, carrying out—together with Camilo [Cienfuegos]—an extraordinary military accomplishment. He also showed it in his lightning campaign in Las Villas Province, especially in the audacious attack on the city of Santa Clara, entering—with a column of barely 300 men—a city defended by tanks, artillery, and several thousand infantry soldiers. Those two heroic deeds stamped him as an extraordinarily capable leader, as a master, as an artist of revolutionary war.

However, now after his heroic and glorious death, some people attempt to deny the truth or value of his concepts, his guerrilla theories. The artist may die—especially when he is an artist in a field as dangerous as revolutionary struggle—but what will surely never die is the art to which he dedicated his life, the art to which he dedicated his intelligence.

What is so strange about the fact that this artist died in combat? What is stranger is that he did not die in combat on one of the innumerable occasions when he risked his life during our revolutionary struggle. Many times it was necessary to take steps to keep him from losing his life in actions of minor significance.

And so it was in combat—in one of the many battles he fought—that he lost his life. We do not have sufficient evidence to enable us to deduce what circumstances preceded that combat, or how far he may have acted in an excessively aggressive way. But, we repeat, if as a guerrilla he had an Achilles' heel, it was his excessive aggressiveness, his absolute contempt for danger.

And this is where we can hardly agree with him, since we consider that his life, his experience, his capacity as a seasoned leader, his authority, and everything his life signified, were more valuable, incomparably more valuable than he himself, perhaps, believed.

His conduct may have been profoundly influenced by the idea that men have a relative value in history, the idea that causes are not defeated when men fall, that the powerful march of history cannot and will not be halted when leaders fall.

That is true, there is no doubt about it. It shows his faith in men, his faith in ideas, his faith in examples. However—as I said a few days ago—with all our heart we would have liked to see him as a forger of victories, to see victories forged under his leadership, since men of his experience, of his caliber, of his really unique capacity, are not common.

We fully appreciate the value of his example. We are absolutely convinced that many men will strive to live up to his example, that men like him will emerge from the peoples.

It is not easy to find a person with all the virtues that were combined in Che. It is not easy for a person, spontaneously, to develop a character like his. I would say that he is one of those men who are difficult to match and virtually impossible to surpass. But I would say that the example of men like him contributes to the appearance of men of the same caliber.

In Che, we admire not only the fighter, the man capable of performing great feats. What he did, what he was doing, the very fact of his rising with a handful of men against the army of the ruling class, trained by Yankee advisers sent in by Yankee imperialism, backed by the oligarchies of all neighboring countries—that in itself constitutes an extraordinary feat.

If we search the pages of history, it is likely that we will find no other case in which a leader with such a limited number of men has set about a task of such importance; a case in which a leader with such a limited number of men has set out to fight against such large forces. Such proof of confidence in himself, such proof of confidence in the peoples, such proof of faith in man's capacity to fight, can be looked for in the pages of history—but the likes of it will never be found.

And he fell.

The enemy believes it has defeated his ideas, his guerrilla concepts, his point of view on revolutionary armed struggle. What they accomplished, by a stroke of luck, was to eliminate him physically. What they accomplished was to gain an accidental advantage that an enemy may gain in war. We do not know to what degree that stroke of luck, that stroke of fortune, was helped along, in a battle like many others, by that characteristic of which we spoke before: his excessive aggressiveness, his absolute disdain for danger.

This also happened in our war of independence. In a battle at Dos Ríos they killed the apostle of our independence; in a battle at Punta Brava, they killed Antonio Maceo, a veteran of hundreds of battles. Countless leaders, countless patriots of our war of independence were killed in similar battles. Nevertheless, that did not spell defeat for the Cuban cause.

The death of Che—as we said a few days ago—is a hard blow, a tremendous blow for the revolutionary movement because it deprives it, without a doubt, of its most experienced and able leader.

But those who boast of victory are mistaken. They are mistaken when they think that his death is the end of his ideas, the end of his tactics, the end of his guerrilla concepts, the end of his theory. For the man who fell, as a mortal man, as a man who faced bullets time and again, as a soldier, as a leader, was a thousand times more able than those who killed him by a stroke of luck.

Che brought the ideas of Marxism-Leninism to their freshest, purest, most revolutionary expression. No other man of our time has carried the spirit of proletarian internationalism to its highest possible level as Che did.

—Fidel Castro

However, how should revolutionaries face this serious setback? How should they face this loss? If Che had to express an opinion on this point, what would it be? He gave this opinion, he expressed this opinion quite clearly when he wrote in his message to the Latin American Solidarity Conference that if death surprised him anywhere, it would be welcome as long as his battle cry had reached a receptive ear and another hand reached out to take up his rifle.

His battle cry will reach not just one receptive ear, but millions of receptive ears. And not one hand but millions of hands will reach out to take up arms. New leaders will emerge. The men of the receptive ears and the outstretched hands will need leaders who emerge from the ranks of the people, just as leaders have emerged in all revolutions.

Those hands will not have available a leader of Che's extraordinary experience and enormous ability. Those leaders will be formed in the process of struggle. Those leaders will emerge from among the millions of receptive ears, from the millions of hands that will sooner or later reach out to take up arms.

It is not that we feel that his death will necessarily have immediate repercussions in the practical sphere of revolutionary struggle, that his death will necessarily have immediate repercussions in the practical sphere of development of this struggle. The fact is that when Che took up arms again he was not thinking of an immediate victory; he was not thinking of a speedy victory against the forces of the oligarchies and imperialism. As an experienced fighter, he was prepared for a prolonged struggle of five, ten, fifteen, or twenty years, if necessary. He was ready to fight five, ten, fifteen, or twenty years, or all his life if need be! And within that perspective, his death—or rather his example—will have tremendous repercussions. The force of that example will be invincible.

Those who cling to the idea of luck try in vain to deny his experience and his capacity as a leader. Che was an extraordinarily able military leader. But when we remember Che, when we think of Che, we do not think fundamentally of his military virtues. No! Warfare is a means and not an end. Warfare is a tool of revolutionaries. The important thing is the revolution. The important thing is the revolutionary cause, revolutionary ideas, revolutionary objectives, revolutionary sentiments, revolutionary virtues!

And it is in that field, in the field of ideas, in the field of sentiments, in the field of revolutionary virtues, in the field of intelligence, that—apart from his military virtues—we feel the tremendous loss that his death means to the revolutionary movement.

Because Che's extraordinary character was made up of virtues that are rarely found together. He stood out as an unsurpassed man of action, but Che was not only an unsurpassed man of action—he was a man of visionary intelligence and broad culture, a profound thinker. That is, in his person the man of ideas and the man of action were combined.

But it is not only that Che possessed the double characteristic of the man of ideas—of profound ideas—and the man of action, but that Che as a revolutionary united in himself the virtues that can be defined as the fullest expression of the virtues of a revolutionary: a man of total integrity, a man of supreme sense of honor, of absolute sincerity, a man of stoic and Spartan living habits, a man in whose conduct not one stain can be found. He constituted, through his virtues, what can be called a truly model revolutionary.

When men die it is usual to make speeches, to emphasize their virtues. But rarely as on this occasion can one say of a man with greater justice, with greater accuracy, what we say of Che: that he was a pure example of revolutionary virtues!

But he possessed another quality, not a quality of the intellect nor of the will, not a quality derived from experience, from struggle, but a quality of the heart: He was an extraordinarily human man, extraordinarily sensitive!

That is why we say, when we think of his life, that he constituted the singular case of a most extraordinary man, able to unite in his personality not only the characteristics of the man of action, but also of the man of thought, of the man of immaculate revolutionary virtues and of extraordinary human sensibility, joined with an iron character, a will of steel, indomitable tenacity.

Because of this, he has left to the future generations not only his experience, his knowledge as an outstanding soldier, but also, at the same time, the fruits of his intelligence. He wrote with the virtuosity of a master of our language. His narratives of the war are incomparable. The depth of his thinking is impressive. He never wrote about anything with less than extraordinary seriousness, with less than extraordinary profundity—and we have no doubt that some of his writings will pass on to posterity as classic documents of revolutionary thought.

Thus, as fruits of that vigorous and profound intelligence,

he left us countless memories, countless narratives that, without his work, without his efforts, might have been lost forever.

An indefatigable worker, during the years that he served our country he did not know a single day of rest. Many were the responsibilities assigned to him: as president of the National Bank, as director of the Central Planning Board, as minister of industry, as commander of military regions, as the head of political or economic or fraternal delegations.

His versatile intelligence was able to undertake with maximum assurance any task of any kind. Thus he brilliantly represented our country in numerous international conferences, just as he brilliantly led soldiers in combat, just as he was a model worker in charge of any of the institutions that he was assigned to. And for him there were no days of rest; for him there were no hours of rest!

If we looked through the windows of his offices, he had the lights on until all hours of the night, studying, or rather, working or studying. For he was a student of all problems; he was a tireless reader. His thirst for learning was practically insatiable, and the hours he stole from sleep he devoted to study.

He devoted his scheduled days off to voluntary work. He was the inspiration and provided the greatest incentive for the work that is today carried out by hundreds of thousands of people throughout the country. He stimulated that activity in which our people are making greater and greater efforts.

As a revolutionary, as a communist revolutionary, a true communist, he had a boundless faith in moral values. He had a boundless faith in the consciousness of man. And we should say that he saw, with absolute clarity, the moral impulse as the fundamental lever in the construction of communism in human society.

He thought, developed, and wrote many things. And on a day like today it should be stated that Che's writings, Che's political and revolutionary thought, will be of permanent value to the Cuban revolutionary process and to the Latin American revolutionary process. And we do not doubt that his ideas—as a man of action, as a man of thought, as a man of untarnished moral virtues, as a man of unexcelled human sensitivity, as a man of spotless conduct—have and will continue to have universal value.

The imperialists boast of their triumph at having killed this guerrilla fighter in action. The imperialists boast of a triumphant stroke of luck that led to the elimination of such a formidable man of action. But perhaps the imperialists do not know or pretend not to know that the man of action was only one of the many facets of the personality of that combatant. And if we speak of sorrow, we are saddened not only at having lost a man of action. We are saddened at having lost a man of virtue. We are saddened at having lost a morally superior man. We are saddened at having lost a man of unsurpassed human sensitivity. We are saddened at having lost such a mind. We are saddened to think that he was only thirty-nine years old at the time of his death. We are saddened at missing the additional

fruits that we would have received from that intelligence and that ever richer experience.

We have an idea of the dimension of the loss for the revolutionary movement. However, here is the weak side of the imperialist enemy: They think that by eliminating a man physically they have eliminated his thinking—that by eliminating him physically they have eliminated his ideas, eliminated his virtues, eliminated his example.

So shameless are they in this belief that they have no hesitation in publishing, as the most natural thing in the world, the by now almost universally accepted circumstances in which they murdered him after he had been seriously wounded in action. They do not even seem aware of the repugnance of the admission. They have published it as if thugs, oligarchs, and mercenaries had the right to shoot a seriously wounded revolutionary combatant.

Even worse, they explain why they did it. They assert that Che's trial would have been quite an earthshaker, that it would have been impossible to place this revolutionary in the dock.

And not only that, they have not hesitated to spirit away his remains. Be it true or false, they certainly announced they had cremated his body, thus beginning to show their fear, beginning to show that they are not so sure that by physically eliminating the combatant, they can eliminate his ideas, eliminate his example.

Che died defending the interests, defending the cause of the exploited and the oppressed of this continent. Che died defending the cause of the poor and the humble of this earth. And the exemplary manner and the selflessness with which he defended that cause cannot be disputed even by his most bitter enemies.

Before history, men who act as he did, men who do and give everything for the cause of the poor, grow in stature with each passing day and find a deeper place in the heart of the peoples with each passing day. The imperialist enemies are beginning to see this, and it will not be long before it will be proved that his death will, in the long run, be like a seed that will give rise to many men determined to imitate him, many men determined to follow his example.

We are absolutely convinced that the revolutionary cause on this continent will recover from the blow, that the revolutionary movement on this continent will not be crushed by this blow.

From the revolutionary point of view, from the point of view of our people, how should we view Che's example? Do we feel we have lost him? It is true that we will not see new writing of his. It is true that we will never again hear his voice. But Che has left a heritage to the world, a great heritage, and we who knew him so well can become in large measure his beneficiaries.

He left us his revolutionary thinking, his revolutionary virtues. He left us his character, his will, his tenacity, his spirit of work. In a word, he left us his example! And Che's example will be a model for our people. Che's example will be the ideal model for our people!

If we wish to express what we expect our revolutionary

combatants, our militants, our men to be, we must say, without hesitation: Let them be like Che! If we wish to express what we want the men of future generations to be, we must say: Let them be like Che! If we wish to say how we want our children to be educated, we must say without hesitation: We want them to be educated in Che's spirit! If we want the model of a man, the model of a man who does not belong to our time but to the future, I say from the depths of my heart that such a model, without a single stain on his conduct, without a single stain on his action, is Che! If we wish to express what we want our children to be, we must say from our very hearts as ardent revolutionaries: We want them to be like Che!

Che has become a model of what men should be, not only for our people but also for people everywhere in Latin America. Che carried to its highest expression revolutionary stoicism, the revolutionary spirit of sacrifice, revolutionary combativeness, the revolutionary's spirit of work. Che brought the ideas of Marxism-Leninism to their freshest, purest, most revolutionary expression. No other man of our time has carried the spirit of proletarian internationalism to its highest possible level as Che did.

And when one speaks of a proletarian internationalist, and

Che with his wife Aleida March and their children—Aleidita, Hildita, and Camilito.

when an example of a proletarian internationalist is sought, that example, high above any other, will be the example of Che. National flags, prejudices, chauvinism, and egoism had disappeared from his mind and heart. He was ready to shed his generous blood spontaneously and immediately, on behalf of any people, for the cause of any people!

Thus, his blood fell on our soil when he was wounded in several battles, and his blood was shed in Bolivia, for the liberation of the exploited and the oppressed, of the humble and the poor. That blood was shed for the sake of all the exploited and all the oppressed. That blood was shed for all the peoples of the Americas and for the people of Vietnam—because while fighting there in Bolivia, fighting against the oligarchies and imperialism, he knew that he was offering Vietnam the highest possible expression of his solidarity!

It is for this reason, compañeros and compañeras of the revolution, that we must face the future with optimism. And in Che's example, we will always look for inspiration—inspiration in struggle, inspiration in tenacity, inspiration in intransigence toward the enemy, inspiration in internationalist feeling!

Therefore, after tonight's impressive ceremony, after this incredible demonstration of vast popular recognition—incredible for its magnitude, discipline, and spirit of devotion—which demonstrates that our people are a sensitive, grateful people who know how to honor the memory of the brave who die in combat, that our people recognize those who serve them, which demonstrates the people's solidarity with the revolutionary struggle and how this people will raise aloft and maintain ever higher aloft revolutionary banners and revolutionary principles—today, in these moments of remembrance, let us lift our spirits, with optimism in the future, with absolute optimism in the final victory of the peoples, and say to Che and to the heroes who fought and died with him:

> Hasta la victoria siempre! [Ever onward to victory]
> Patria o muerte! [Homeland or death]
> Venceremos! [We will win]

Emile Capouya   (review date 12 April 1968)

SOURCE: "Che Guevara—the Loss Looms Larger," in *Commonweal*, Vol. LXXXVIII, No. 4, April 12, 1968, pp. 110-11.

[*Capouya is an American educator, editor, critic, and translator. In the following excerpt, he reviews Guevara's personal account of the Cuban revolution, focusing on* Reminiscences of the Cuban Revolutionary War *and* Guerrilla Warfare.]

In order to arrive at a true estimate of men like Ernesto Guevara and his fellow-revolutionary, Fidel Castro, we should first of all have to wake up to the world in which we are living. In that world, there are two hundred million Latin Americans, most of whom are very hungry, and their hunger is a necessary feature of the political and economic arrangements that make us North Americans rich.

They are ruled for the most part by armed degenerates whose brutality bears an exact proportion to the misery over which they preside, and the degenerates in question are subsidized out of the American treasury. In that waking world of hunger and hopelessness, Guevara and Castro took up the cause of the dispossessed. Most unfortunately—by our own standards of social decency, by our own ideals of freedom and personal dignity, by our own humane professions—they are in the right and we are in the wrong. That is what all the shooting is about.

Ernesto Guevara was, next to Fidel Castro, the most influential spirit and the best mind of the Cuban Revolution—both in its military phase and, after the overthrow of Batista, in the phase of intensive social reconstruction that still goes on. . . . Guevara's classic work is *Guerrilla Warfare.* Two translations have been published in this country, both of them technically and stylistically faulty. Guevara was, among other things, a first-rate writer, and no available translation of any of his works does him justice. Readers must be warned, accordingly, that the spirit of the man and sometimes the point and bearing of his ideas are misrepresented in English.

Guerrilla Warfare is more than a treatise of irregular military operations. It is a manual of political struggle in regions ruled as Latin America is ruled. For Guevara, guerrilla warfare is important because it is the most appropriate political instrument—and also the most effective instrument of political education—in countries like pre-revolutionary Cuba, where three general conditions exist: poverty, a predominantly rural economy, and no legal means of reform and redress. For understandable reasons, neither the conservatives nor the adherents of the traditional leftist sects and parties in North and South America are willing to accept the thesis.

Reminiscences of the Cuban Revolutionary War is Guevara's unadorned memoirs of his own service in that struggle. They suffer somewhat from having been set down as occasion offered, and because the author confined himself strictly to what he himself had done or observed. Guevara hoped that other participants in the revolution would write their own accounts in the same sober spirit, and produce collectively an accurate report of that turning-point in the history of the Western Hemisphere. The most interesting sections of the present book are concerned with the hand-to-mouth stage of the revolution, when, after the rout of the *Granma* expedition, the 12 survivors, including Guevara, Fidel Castro, and Camilo Cienfuegos, were fugitives rather than soldiers. Semi-starved, often bivouacking without shelter, for a long time, their object was mere survival and their immediate enemies were the climate and the terrain. Whether we are concerned with political and military history or with the history of particular souls, the transition from the stage of survivors in flight to the phase of effectual rebellion is of the highest interest. Despite the circumstantial character of Guevara's narrative, unfortunately, that transition accomplishes itself offstage, for there is a hiatus in the account precisely at the point where the material and moral current must have shifted to permit the first forays upon Batista's troops.

What does emerge clearly enough is Guevara's personal development in the course of the fighting. When it began, he was an enthusiast for revolution and the next thing to an invalid (he suffered all his life from incapacitating attacks of asthma), and, for all his spirit, hardly a likely soldier, one would think. But he fought along on sheer nerve, bearing severe physical hardship with his comrades, and showing reserves of will that marked him as a natural leader in difficult undertakings. Fidel Castro says of him that his failing as a soldier was excessive disregard of danger, and coming from that authority the judgment is one we had better accept. Yet there is no doubt that Guevara was one of the master tacticians of recent military history.

In that respect, *Guerrilla Warfare* is his witness; it is the only significant work on the subject written in the West—for the good reason that no other writers have had clear strategic notions in the light of which their tactics might be developed. The strategic aims of Western commentators tend to be, as it were, subconscious, and in any case unavowable. But in Guevara's writings, strategy is always conceived in terms of political evolution, and is necessarily more ample, more adequate in terms of reality, than the abstract geo-politics plus games theory that passes for military thought in other places.

For an example of his astuteness as a political analyst, the reader is referred to the epilogue to *Guerrilla Warfare,* in which, writing in 1959, he predicts the manner and means of the invasion of Cuba that was to take place in 1961. Another classic of analysis and polemic is his speech at the Punta del Este conference (reproduced in *Che Guevara Speaks*), called for the purpose of quarantining Cuba and containing the Latin-American revolution by means of the Alliance for Progress. Guevara's exposition of the program's defects, had they been heeded, might have saved Mr. Moscoso from resigning his directorship in despair

---

Martin Ebon on the origins and relevance of Guevara's nickname:

He liked to be called "Che." When Guevara was made a "native-born" Cuban by law, his nickname legally became part of his name. As director of the National Bank of Cuba, he brought his personal and informal touch to the face of all bank notes: they bore his signature, "Che Guevara." "Che" is a hail-fellow expression of camaraderie. He used to call those around him "Che" so often and consistently that they began to use the word back at him. And as "Che Guevara" he has become a symbol in contemporary history. Since his dramatic death in Bolivia, which ended an attempt at guerrilla warfare that was to spread to all of Latin America, the Guevara legend has achieved worldwide proportions. The myth of Che Guevara has set off a responsive vibration among thousands who see him as the gallant revolutionary—a symbol of rebellion—against hypocrisy, injustice, human suffering, and a society without soul.

Martin Ebon, in his Che: The Making of a Legend, *Universe Books, 1969.*

when time had made clear to everyone what was clear only to the Cuban delegation at Punta del Este.

The present volume ends with 26 remarkable letters written by Guevara, for the most part while he was serving as a bureaucrat of the revolution after the seizure of power. I think it impossible to read those letters—direct, unassuming, austere—and not know that one is in the presence of a rare being, a man of principle, deserving of Castro's eulogy: "Immensely humane, immensely sensitive."

Ernesto Guevara was wounded in the Bolivian mountains, captured, and apparently shot after capture. Then his body was exhibited to photographers by relieved officials. From his point of view, fair enough—he had sought out just such a fate. But our perspective must be different. He was a very great man. He died at 39. In terms of the political evolution of Latin America in this century, the loss cannot be made up.

Norman Gall (review date 5 May 1968)

SOURCE: "Guerrilla Saint," in *The New York Times Book Review,* May 5, 1968, pp. 3, 34-5.

[*In the following review, Gall analyzes several works by Guevara, tracing the development of his ideological position as revealed in his political essays.*]

The capture and murder last October in Bolivia of Ernesto "Che" Guevara was the most significant consequence of his own botched guerrilla insurgency. The story of his death—still subject to final refinement of detail—adds new mythic material to the reverence most Latin Americans feel for martyred guerrilla saints like Mexico's Emiliano Zapata. Nicaragua's Augusto Sandino and Colombia's rebel priest, Father Camilo Torres. Moreover, in Guevara's case, the flame of publicity has lighted candles in the literary salons of New York and Paris, as well as in the official eulogies of the Cuban Revolution and in the imagination of revolutionary youth throughout the world. The shadow, of course, has dwarfed the man; it has been enlarged by canonization and official tribute of the kind easily turned into a lean and flashy song.

The lacquered image of Che Guevara will not be beautified by the anemic spurt of quickie books issuing from his death [*Venceremos!, Reminiscences of the Cuban Revolutionary War, Episodes of the Revolutionary War* and *Che Guevara Speaks*]. Nor, as a result of their publication, will we understand more clearly the mystery of his restless romanticism, which has become an ideal for some of the more dynamic and concerned youth of both Americas. Offered here are diverse collections of the hero's wooden words, yielding little of Che's affecting presence and charm, and even less food for the nourishment of romantic illusion. Instead, human warmth gives way to the stilted, humorless prose of his official pronouncements, articles and speeches published by the Castro regime since 1959.

There are no unguarded moments here, only occasional signs of a momentous intellectual pilgrimage by a wanderer with the noble obsession of forming a pure and just human society, at whatever cost. Unfortunately, no independent editor or scholar has bothered to tell us of the origins and course of the pilgrimage, or of the intellectual milestones along the way. John Gerassi's introduction to *Venceremos!* is not what is needed. It merely provides a thin biographical sketch of the author, without any critical evaluation of his development or his political role.

The spirit shining through these hastily produced volumes is the fervent orthodoxy of the newly converted. They are full of exhortations for Cuban workers to work, to get organized, to produce, to correct the chaotic "errors" of the state-spawned bureaucracy that Che himself helped build to monster proportions. There is urgency throughout, as well as a healthy sense of vindication through the cyclonic social progress of the revolution.

Since Che was one of the key symbols and spokesmen of Cuba's revolutionary government, virtually every word in these books was uttered for its propaganda effect. His public personality shone strongest outside Cuba—and beyond the shadow of Fidel Castro—in cavalier appearances with beard and olive-green fatigues at international conferences such as the Punta del Este meeting of 1961 (when Cuba was expelled from the Organization of American States) and in Geneva at the 1964 United Nations Conference on Trade and Development. On that occasion he offered a modest proposal that, given the declining terms of trade for the Third World, the underdeveloped nations suspend payments of dividends, interest and amortization "until such time as the prices for [their] exports reach a level which will reimburse them for the losses sustained over the past decade."

Until he landed in Cuba in late 1956 in Fidel Castro's confused but momentous guerrilla expedition, Ernesto Guevara was part of Latin America's permanent floating population of young political bohemians; he had shown scant interest in "Marxist-Leninist" teachings. Relatives report that since his early adolescence he was prodigious in both his sympathy for the unfortunate and in his fondness for the open road.

As a teen-ager, he took marathon bike trips to read poetry to the inmates of a leper colony. His absorbing interest in leprosy and its victims led him, both as a medical student and a young doctor, into extravagant wandering (from the time of his first motor-bike trip across the Andes in 1952) into remote parts of South America to visit leprosariums and participate in anti-leprosy campaigns. By the time he met the Castro brothers in 1955 in Mexico City, where he earned his living as sidewalk photographer, Che already had obtained a much broader knowledge of Latin America than any of Cuba's top revolutionary leaders were ever to achieve. He had traveled through Bolivia just after the profound and convulsive 1952 revolution, when the tin miners had crushed the Bolivian Army and, in effect, seized the mines, when Indian serfdom was abolished and land and the vote given the hacienda peons. He had wandered about Colombia in the years of the *violencia,* the savage civil war that claimed 200,000 lives, then drifted to Guatemala just in time to witness the C.I.A.-organized invasion of right-wing exiles (conniving with key Guatemala Army officers) that ended the agrarian revolution of President Jacobo Arbenz, whose Communist and other leftist supporters did not rise to his defense. The lessons of these wanderings were hardened in Che's exemplary career as a guerrilla column leader in Cuba's Sierra Maestra, and only after he descended from the hills did the attitudes formed by these experiences begin to take doctrinal shape.

The formal crystallization of his revolutionary belief began when he became a kind of alter ego and lightning rod in Fidel Castro's maneuvers to consolidate his power. The formalization of his ideal was dramatized best in his last published essay, the utopian **"Man and Socialism in Cuba"** (reprinted in *Venceremos* and *Che Guevara Speaks*), which appeared in Uruguay shortly after his widely publicized disappearance in March, 1965, and proposes a new moral motor for socialist society. It underscored a common feeling in the young Cuban leadership that a new kind of Communist is being formed by the revolution, far better in breeding and behavior than the Stalinist party hacks implicated in sordid bargains with the old Batista dictatorship.

Che's last visionary essay foresees the day when

> man will begin to see himself mirrored in his work and to realize his full stature as a human being through the object created, the work accomplished. Work will no longer entail surrendering a part of his being in the form of labor-power sold, which no longer belongs to him, but will represent an emanation of himself reflecting his contribution to the common life, the fulfillment of his social duty. We are doing everything possible to give labor this new status of social duty and to link it on the one side with the development of a technology which will create the conditions for greater freedom, and on the other side with voluntary work based on a Marxist appreciation of the fact that man truly reaches a full human condition when he produces without being driven by the physical need to sell his labor as a commodity.

This is the glorification of the "moral incentives" to production—as opposed to material incentives of pay hikes pegged to economic performance advocated by Soviet-oriented Marxists—which under Che's influence have come to dominate the Cuban production ethos. Indeed, this moral formula bears a striking resemblance to that of China's communes and the disastrous "Great Leap Forward," and the analogies between Cuban and Chinese Marxism do not end there.

Just as Mao Tse-tung has been responsible for the adaptation of Marx and Lenin to Chinese cultural traditions, Castro and Guevara have been attempting another major mutation—under Chinese influence—by designing a program of revolutionary armed struggle for Latin America. Curiously, neither Che nor Castro nor Mao made any systematic study of Marxism-Leninism until they had come to power or—in Mao's case—retreated to a secure guerrilla base area.

Mao's peasant origins always have inclined him to a profoundly popular and violent form of revolutionary struggle, which was fed and inflamed by peasant self-defense against the scourge of Japanese invasion in the 1930's. On the other hand, the guerrilla theories of Che and Fidel are more narrowly rooted in the radical student politics of Latin-American universities, and contain the "élitist" flaw of imposing the guerrilla movement—as Che did, fatally, in Bolivia—from outside the peasant area, often with little preparation and less regard for local conditions.

Unfortunately, the anthologies published since Che's death fail to include—and barely mention—his little handbook, *Guerrilla Warfare,* which is probably the most influential book published in Latin America since World War II, even though its strategic precepts may be wrong and the guerrilla movements it guided may have failed. While Che's strategic formulation has failed so far to change the outcome of Latin America's revolutionary struggle, it has profoundly altered its focus and tone.

Of the four volumes under consideration here, two are separate editions of Che's recollections of the Cuban guerrilla insurrection in the Sierra Maestra mountains of Oriente Province, while John Gerassi's *Venceremos* anthology contains most of this text. These "reminiscences" were first published as separate articles in the Cuban armed forces magazine, *Verde Olivo,* for the political orientation of the military establishment. It is a skeletal official history told in the first person, strangely shy of personal reflection or any departure from normative political requirements.

In contrast, for example, to George Orwell's graphic and introspective memoir, in *Homage to Catalonia* of boredom and filth and starvation in the trenches of Spain, Ernesto Guevara steers clear of the "subjective" literary material that would seem to be of greatest interest: the inner life of the guerrilla band, the doubts, the sufferings, the quarrels, the factions, the diverse strains of human character tied together in a struggle to survive, the give and take of winning the loyalty of frightened peasants and of outwitting Batista's brutal, stupid, pot-bellied army.

As a result, the skirmishes are all here but the war is missing. The soldier-author affects a kind of Hemingwayesque curtness and stoicism, with little interest in personality save for a monotonous and perhaps abnormal adulation of Fidel Castro. Of the spear-carriers we learn little, save that Juan was a peasant who joined the guerrillas and became a good fighter, while José sneaked away one night to betray his comrades to the army, and that Che always knew that Pedro, the quiet one, was also a traitor, since after Castro came to power he went into exile in Miami.

Of the two anthologies reviewed here, the slimmer one, *Che Guevara Speaks,* has by far the more incisive and luminous selection of Che's writings, and costs much less than the bulky, repetitious and carelessly assembled Gerassi collection. Che in print is important because of his influence on the Cuban Revolution (his public utterances consistently anticipated Fidel's future moves) and his symbolic meaning to much of Latin America. But the warmth and weight of his personality are muffled in his official words, and the evolution of his intellectual character still needs to be described.

Raymond A. Sokolov   (review date 13 May 1968)

SOURCE: "Che Speaks," in *Newsweek,* Vol. LXXI, No. 20, May 13, 1968, p. 102.

Che playing golf with Fidel Castro.

[*Sokolov is a critic, novelist, and author of recipe and cooking books. In the following review, Sokolov offers a mixed assessment of* Venceremos!]

Even before his mysterious death last October, the Argentine revolutionary Ernesto Che Guevara had become the patron saint of the Third World and the guerrilla guru of the U.S. New Left. Raised in comfort, trained as a physician, he gave himself up totally to the revolutionary ideal. From early adolescence Guevara was an impassioned wanderer among his people; the underclass of feudal Latin America. He knew his continent and carried its sorrows with him from country to country. With each bloated baby and exploited peasant he saw, Guevara's hatred of the Latin overlords and their Yankee senior partners deepened. It was inevitable that Che would link up with a rebel government.

In 1956, at the age of 28, he sailed from Mexico to Cuba with Fidel Castro and 80 others on an old yacht called *Granma.* Two years later, Che emerged from the hills, a seasoned commander and a key figure in the new revolutionary government. Doctor, soldier, diplomat, economist—the careers multiplied and the prestige grew as his embattled new Cuba stabilized herself in spite of a U.S.-led trade embargo and, of course, the eventual and bumbled invasion of the Bay of Pigs. By 1965, Cuba was still far from self-sufficient, but for Guevara it was time to move on to new adventures. For months on end he fell from view, only to turn up murdered in Bolivia, where he had been fighting with local guerrillas.

He left behind him a legend of activist bravery, an unpublished diary tangled in copyright haggling and a great mass of speeches and writing. Shortly after Che's death, John Gerassi and a number of translators went to work making his currently printable literary legacy available to Yanqui readers. For the gringo Guevarista it would be a chance to commune with his hero, and for the outsider such a book should explain the bearded leader's charisma.

It [*Venceremos—The Speeches and Writings of Che Guevara*] doesn't. Charismatic he must have been, but on the printed page. Che's words don't even have the ring of Robert Taft's. "Let us go on now to Topic II of the Agenda," he says vibrantly to the leaders of the OAS at Punta del Este in 1961. Here he is wowing the cane cutters of Camagüey in 1963: "Under our agricultural conditions with 40,000 *arrobas* of cane to the *caballería,* six rows are needed to fill a cart. And a heavy cart that keeps getting heavier

> **Like most pep talks, the harangues and pseudo-essays collected in *Venceremos!* probably worked with the original audience but don't have much significance afterward except as historical documents in the archives of propaganda.**
>
> **—*Raymond A. Sokolov***

cannot be dragged along. A motor would be needed to move it."

Even at his most inspiring, Guevara does not really make the heart beat faster: "And you, comrades, you who are the vanguard of the vanguard, who have demonstrated your spirit of sacrifice toward work, your Communist spirit, your new attitude toward life, ought always to be worthy of Fidel's words, which you inserted in one of the boxes in this precinct: 'What we were at a time of mortal danger, may we also learn to be in production; may we learn to be workers of Liberty or Death!' "

Somehow the rhetoric comes unstrung; the over-all effect is turgid and flatfooted; and the message is repetitive. Like most pep talks, these harangues and pseudo-essays probably worked with the original audience but don't have much significance afterward except as historical documents in the archives of propaganda.

There are marginal exceptions to the general sweep of ennui. Che's personal account of the Cuban revolution is an engaging scenario; however, a fuller version was published three months ago by Monthly Review Press, as *Reminiscences of the Cuban Revolution.*

Che's knotty economics is hard for the non-Marxist to follow, but it led to Cuba's unorthodox but apparently workable substitution of moral for cash incentives. The Guevara myth is no fairy tale, but his talents were not on the printed page but as an activist exhorting peasants in the fields, leading irregulars in the mountains or improvising the structure of a new kind of state.

The Times Literary Supplement　　(review date 20 June 1968)

SOURCE: "The Cuban Revolution," in *The Times Literary Supplement,* No. 3460, June 20, 1968, p. 638.

[*In the following mixed review of* Reminiscences of the Cuban Revolutionary War, *the critic praises the volume's candor and humor but questions its value as an historical document.*]

When the history of the Cuban Revolution comes to be written—and perhaps the time is not yet ripe—Ernesto "Che" Guevara's *Reminiscences of the Cuban Revolutionary War* will probably be regarded as the outstanding contemporary account of the revolutionary war in the Sierra Maestra. There exist a number of excellent first-hand

reports by journalists (mostly foreign), but of the revolution's leaders only Guevara systematically recorded, from memory and "a few hasty notes", the most significant episodes of the war—experiences from which he derived the theories expounded in his now classic and, it seems, internationally (if sometimes inappropriately) influential *Guerilla Warfare.*

First published in installments in various Cuban periodicals during the early 1960s, Guevara's "fragmentary history" of the war ("a series of personal reminiscences") opens with a strikingly unheroic account of the voyage from Mexico to Cuba that Fidel Castro, his brother Raúl, the author (none of whom was over thirty years old) and some eighty other would-be revolutionaries made in the yacht *Granma:*

> With our lights extinguished we left the port of Tuxpan amid an infernal mess of men and all sorts of material. The weather was very bad. . . . We began a frenzied search for the anti-seasickness pills, which we did not find. We sang the Cuban national anthem and the "Hymn of the 26th of July" for perhaps five minutes and then the entire boat took on an aspect both ridiculous and tragic: men with anguished faces holding their stomachs, some with their heads in buckets, others lying in the strangest positions, immobile, their clothing soiled with vomit.
>
> Apart from two or three sailors and four or five other people the rest of the eighty-three crew members were seasick.

Three days after landing in Oriente province on December 2, 1956, and totally unprepared for immediate battle, they experienced at Algeria de Pìo a bloody baptism of fire at the hands of Batista's troops. Guevara himself, who was already suffering from an acute attack of asthma, was severely wounded:

> I immediately began to wonder what would be the best way to die, now that all seemed lost. I remembered an old story of Jack London's in which the hero, knowing that he is condemned to freeze to death in the icy reaches of Alaska, leans against a tree and decides to end his life with dignity.

Only twelve rebels survived the massacre to form the nucleus of the Rebel Army which two years later marched into Havana.

Guevara's narrative (complete with diagrams) of the rebels' skirmishes with government troops, the establishment of contacts with the local peasant population, the creation of a "liberated zone", and the way in which the *guerrilleros* (200 of them by June, 1957) coped with their everyday problems—the provision of food, water and clothing, the supply of arms and ammunition, the maintenance of discipline and morale (particularly during the early difficult months)—is one of unusual interest. Moreover, it is related with considerable frankness, modesty and, surprisingly, with a good deal of humour. Doctor, dentist (albeit a reluctant one), military commander of the Rebel Army's fourth column and responsible for the "political orientation" of new recruits. Guevara emerges from this book as a most attractive adventurer. "A virtuoso in the art of revolutionary war" (to use Castro's description of him), he became addicted to life in the *sierra* and came to believe in revolution as a kind of personal therapy: "revolution", he wrote, "purifies men, improves and develops them". The letters he wrote in the period after 1959, a number of which are printed as an appendix to the book, give some idea of the frustration he felt with his post-revolutionary life as a bureaucrat. It can have surprised no one who knew him when in 1965, having played his part in consolidating the Cuban Revolution "in its territory", he left in search of "new battlefronts" in the struggle against American imperialism—to meet his death two years later in a Bolivian jungle.

From the historian's point of view, Guevara's **Reminiscences** are of strictly limited value. Many of the questions crucial to any understanding of the origins, nature and development of the Cuban Revolution remain unanswered. There is little to be learned, for example, about the way in which the political aspirations of the rebels evolved beyond the desire to overthrow the Batista dictatorship. Guevara simply states that as they came into closer contact with the peasants of the Sierra Maestra (who were, of course, far from typical of the Cuban population as a whole)—"prematurely aged and toothless women, children with distended bellies, parasitism, rickets, general avitaminosis"—they began to see the need for "a definite change in the life of the people. The idea of agrarian reform became clear . . . ". His own ideological influence on the revolution—always said to be paramount—is still not clear. The relationship between the 26th of July Movement and the Partido Socialista Popular (the Communists) is scarcely discussed: "The P.S.P. joined with us in certain concrete activities", Guevara writes, "but mutual distrust hampered joint action and, fundamentally, the party of the workers did not understand with sufficient clarity the role of the guerrilla force, nor Fidel's personal role in our revolutionary struggle". The reasons for the ultimate rebel victory over Batista remain obscure. Guevara merely refers in vague terms to the oppressive nature of the existing regime, the privileged position of the *latifundistas* businessmen and foreign monopolists, and the demoralization and technical ineptitude of the military. In the last analysis, he says, in a statement which explains very little, "the war was won by the people, through the action of its armed fighting vanguard, the Rebel Army, whose basic weapons were their *morale* and their *discipline*". The narrative effectively ends with the second battle of Pino del Agua (February, 1958) and only a few pages are devoted to the events leading up to the seizure of power in January, 1959.

No one could reasonably accuse Guevara of exaggerating his own role in the Cuban revolutionary war: however brilliant, he was throughout Fidel Castro's second-in-command. At the same time one of the most curious features of his narrative is the infrequency with which Fidel himself figures in it. The explanation, of course, lies in the fact that the fourth column operated independently for much of the time and Guevara is describing *his* war. Yet no account of the war as a whole would be complete without an understanding of Castro's complex personality and his military and political skills.

Newsweek (essay date 15 July 1968)

SOURCE: "Che on Che," in *Newsweek,* Vol. LXXII, No. 3, July 15, 1968, pp. 41-2.

[*In the following essay, the critic examines Guevara's writing habits as well as the focus and publication history of his diaries.*]

Since his death in a squalid hamlet in the jungled mountains of Bolivia eight months ago, Ernesto (Che) Guevara has assumed a revered place in the romantic imagination of thousands of revolutionaries around the world. To many young people in particular, his bold attempt to carry the torch of Fidel Castro's Cuban revolution to the very heart of the South American continent was an act of high adventure and noble purpose. Last week, however, with the publication of his secret personal diary, Che himself revealed for the first time all the mundane details of his Bolivian sojourn—the constant battle he waged against jungle sickness, the bone-wearying effort to elude pursuing Bolivian troops, the internecine conflicts among his own Communist comrades. And for all the unquestioned drama contained in its 345 pages, the diary turned out to be the story of a blundering failure.

The diary, long thought to be tucked away in a heavily guarded safe in the Bolivian capital of La Paz, was released last week by the Cuban Government to a half dozen sympathetic foreign publishers, including *Ramparts* magazine in the U.S. Although Castro insisted that a Cuban "sympathizer" had provided Havana with the copy, there were a number of conflicting versions of just how the diary was spirited out of Bolivia.

For the occasion, Castro wrote a glowing introductory tribute to his old comrade-in-arms. "It was Che's habit during his days as a guerrilla," Fidel reminisced,

> to write down his daily observations in a personal diary. During the long marches over abrupt and difficult terrain, in the middle of the damp woods, when the lines of men, always hunched over from the weight of their *mochilas* [knapsacks], munitions and arms, would stop for a moment to rest, or when the column would receive orders to halt and pitch camp at the end of a long day's journey, one could see Che . . . take out his notebook and, with the small and almost illegible letters of a doctor, write his notes.

That, of course, was almost a decade ago, in Cuba's Sierra Maestra. But Che remained a faithful diarist in the Bolivian Andes, Castro explains, despite the fact that the struggle there "unfolded under incredibly hard material conditions." While the Cuban Premier carefully refrains from taking credit for sending Che to Bolivia to launch the insurrection, he leaves little doubt that he hoped, by presenting the diary to the world, to strengthen the cause of his militant philosophy of world revolution.

Indeed, a large portion of Castros' introduction is devoted to a bitter commentary on Che's conflicts with the conservative wing of the Bolivian Communist Party. Castro levels a searing blast at Communists, like those in Bolivia, who follow Moscow's line of peaceful coexistence rather than Fidels' own doctrine on the necessity for waging guerrilla wars. According to the Cuban Premier, Bolivian Communist Party Boss Mario Monje Molino did "nothing more than enter into shameful, ridiculous and unmerited claims for power" with Che and later actually "began to sabotage the movement, intercepting well-trained Communist militants in La Paz who were going to join the guerrillas."

In fact, as Che's diary makes clear, Monje and other Bolivian Communist leaders failed to share his vision of a "liberation" movement extending from a secure base in the Bolivian mountains to Argentina, Peru and other South American countries. Determined nonetheless to launch a "second Vietnam" in Latin America, Che left Cuba more than two years ago and flew to Europe (where he purchased his German diary in Frankfurt). Disguised as a balding Uruguayan businessman, he arrived in the Bolivian city of Santa Cruz sometime in the fall of 1966. From there, he journeyed to La Paz to confer with local Communists and then proceeded to a farm which had been purchased for him by his Bolivian sympathizers in the isolated area of Ñanchuhuasú, where he first began writing his diary.

Sometimes dramatic, sometimes tedious, the diary makes heavy reading due to its constant use of *noms de guerre*. The tangled geography of the region remains as confused to the reader as it was to the guerrilla chief himself. But what emerges is still a fascinating document of the painstaking mechanics of trying to start a revolution in an inhospitable land with groups of men (never more than 53) who frequently suffered not only from hunger, thirst and disease, but also from petty conflicts of personality and nationality. Che reveals himself as touchingly human by faithfully recording the birthdays of his comrades and his family. And as for Jules Régis Debray, the French Communist writer who, upon being captured and subsequently tortured by Bolivian Army troops, revealed the whereabouts of the Cuban's guerrilla hide-out, Che seems surprisingly uncritical. (Some experts, however, suspect that Che was not entirely happy with Debray's performance in the jungle—and let Castro know about this by radio.)

Castro gives his version of what happened to Che after he wrote the last entry in his diary on Oct. 7. The next day, he was caught by Bolivian soldiers and taken to the town of Higueras. There, on Oct. 9 in a small school house, writes Castro, "Maj. Miguel Ayoroa and Col. Andrés Selnich, rangers trained by the Yankees, instructed Officer Mario Terán to proceed with the killing. When the latter, completely drunk, went into the place, Che . . . saw that the assassin vacillated [and] said firmly, 'Shoot, don't be afraid!' "

Lee Lockwood   (review date 25 August 1968)

SOURCE: "The End of a Guerrillero," in *The New York Times Book Review,* August 25, 1968, pp. 1-2, 26, 28, 30.

[*Lockwood is a photojournalist, editor, and author of a*

book about Fidel Castro and Cuba. In the following review, in which he offers a highly favorable assessment of Guevara's Bolivia diary, Lockwood praises Guevara's writing style and comments on several events in the Bolivian campaign.]

> Dear Folks—Once again I feel the ribs of Rocinante between my heels; once again I take the road with my shield upon my arm. . . . Many will call me an adventurer, and that I am—only, one of a different sort, one who risks his neck to prove his platitudes. . . . Now a will which I have polished with delight will sustain some shaky legs and weary lungs. I will do it. Give a thought once in a while to this little twentieth century soldier-of-fortune. . . .
>
> —Che Guevara: farewell letter to his parents.

Last October, when the Bolivian Government gloatingly announced that it had not only captured and killed the great revolutionary *guerrillero,* Ernesto "Che" Guevara, but that among the contents of his rucksack had been found a complete war diary in Che's handwriting, minutely detailing his daily adventures and observations, publishers' agents from around the world flocked to La Paz to bid for the right to its publication.

Bolivian President René Barrientos, hoping to recoup some of the $3-million of Bolivia's meager funds which had been spent in bringing Guevara's tiny band to rout, hinted openly that he would like to get a million dollars for the package. At first, the publishers vied briskly with one another and intrigued secretly with members of the Government for the inside track. As months went by, however, most of the competitors dropped out, some because they feared a lawsuit from the Guevara heirs in Cuba (who presumably have some legal right to the diary), others out of dismay at the international scandal that had been stirred up by the crassness of the Bolivians, and still others out of unwillingness to accept the editorial conditions demanded by the Bolivian Government, i.e., that the full story "from the Bolivian side" must be included in any publication.

More than a simple war journal, Guevara's dairy is a rare self-portrait of the compleat revolutionary. Out of this diary of defeat emerges a triumphant legacy of courage, selflessness and devotion to principle of heroic dimensions.

—*Lee Lockwood*

Then, in July, Fidel Castro shocked La Paz by announcing that he had acquired a copy of Guevara's war diary "free of charge" from a mysterious source and would publish it immediately in Havana and other capitals. Within a week, an English translation of this Cuban edition, together with an introduction written by Castro, appeared in this country in *Ramparts Magazine,* and now reappears in a Bantam paperback [as *The Diary of Che Guevara; Bolivia: November 7, 1966—October 7, 1967*].

Almost simultaneously, Stein & Day publishers have come forth with what they call *The Complete Bolivian Diaries of Ché Guevara,* published under official license of the Bolivian Government. It is called "complete" because it contains Che's entries for 13 days that are missing from the Castro version (out of nearly 400 days). More interesting, it also includes the diaries of three other Cuban *guerrilleros* ("Pombo," "Rolando" and "Braulio," all officers of Cuba's Army), which shed further light on Che's fascinating narrative, and a 60-page introduction by Daniel James which, among other things, amply fulfills the obligation to present the Bolivian side of the story by devoting three effusive pages to a political biography of President Barrientos and an equal number to Gen. Alfredo Ovando, the army's Commander in Chief.

These two English versions of Che's diary have been compared, and they unquestionably derive from the same original. Both, however, suffer needlessly from inept and inaccurate translations. The Cuban translation, prepared in Havana (in obvious haste), is an especially messy job; the Stein & Day version is somewhat better, but far from perfect.

Che Guevara quietly dropped out of sight in April, 1965. "Other nations of the world call for my modest efforts," he had written at that time to his friend, chief and mentor, Fidel Castro, pledging "to carry to new battlefields the faith which you have taught me, the revolutionary spirit of my people, the feeling of fulfilling the most sacred of duties: to fight against imperialism." He was not seen again publicly until two and a half years later, when his grimy and stiffened cadaver, strangely saint-like in death, was brought to the Bolivian town of Vallegrande in the foothills of the Andes Mountains strapped to the runner of an army helicopter. Captured alive, he had been executed the next day on orders from La Paz.

Where had Guevara been all that time? The diaries provide a clue. He had gone first to the Congo. There, together with several other veterans of the Cuban Revolution, he had tried unsuccessfully to reorganize the remnants of Patrice Lumumba's forces. When they would not fight, Che returned secretly to Cuba in 1966. With Castro, he laid the plans for a guerrilla action in Bolivia that would serve as the base and training ground for a continental South American revolutionary movement, thus fulfilling Guevara's dream (expressed as early as 1959) of "transforming the Andes Mountains into the Sierra Maestra of Latin America."

As Fidel Castro has related, it was Che Guevara's custom during the guerrilla days in the Sierra Maestra to jot down his notes and observations each day in a notebook, "in the small and nearly illegible handwriting of a doctor." From this raw material Che later produced a series of accounts entitled *Passages From the Revolutionary War,* a book which ranks among the best war writing of modern times.

In this respect, the Bolivian diary of Che Guevara is no disappointment. In few writers does the style so transparently reflect the personality of the man. The writing is economical and matter-of-fact in tone, free of all hyberbole yet vivid, and leavened with a fine, dry sense of humor, the butt of which is often the author himself. The narrative begins slowly and gradually gains momentum. As it tersely unfolds one experiences a rising tension, a growing sense of tragic fate inexorably working itself out. As in all good adventure stories, though you know how it ends, you cannot put the book down.

The daily accounts begin with Che's arrival in Nancahuazú in November, 1966, and end the day before his capture the following October. The journal begins on a note of optimism and humor. Having traveled from Cuba via Prague, Frankfurt and São Paulo, bald and beardless and on a false passport, Che enters Bolivia and arrives at the farm which is intended to be his base of operations. The diary begins (reviewer's translation):

> (November 7, 1966) A new stage begins today. We arrived at the farm by night. The trip was quite good. After entering by way of Cochabamba, adequately disguised, Pachungo and I made the necessary contacts and traveled in two jeeps for two days. . . . On approaching the farm during the second trip, Bigotes, who had just learned my identity, nearly ran off a cliff, leaving the jeep stranded on the edge of a precipice. We walked about 20 km., arriving after midnight at the farm, where there are three Party workers.

Other Cuban guerrilla veterans arrive in the weeks that follow, in pairs, by various routes. In the end, Guevara's guerrilla *foco* will contain 20 Cubans (including at least 4 members of Cuba's Central Committee), 29 Bolivians and 3 Peruvians. Of the Bolivians, 4 will desert and several others will prove unfit for combat.

Things seem to go wrong almost from the beginning. Three days after Che's arrival, two Cubans carelessly let themselves be seen by a local peasant. For security purposes, the group is forced to leave the more comfortable farm and set up a new base camp in the jungle. At the end of December, Mario Monje, head of the pro-Moscow Bolivian Communist party, visits this camp and meets with Che. In return for support, he demands to be given military and political leadership of the revolution. Che refuses, and Monje departs in anger, withdrawing the party aid upon which Che had been counting as a source of men and supplies from the cities.

In the meantime, personality clashes have already broken out between some of the Cuban veterans, and there is friction between the Cubans and the Bolivians. Che is forced to discipline two Cuban *comandantes* and delivers a lecture to the entire group on the need to form "an exemplary nucleus made of steel."

It is clear from almost the initial entries in Che's journal that the Bolivian operation is intended to be only the first stage in a continental revolution. The strategy was to gain a foothold in Bolivia first, then to branch out north and south, thus creating "two, three, many Vietnams" (in Che's words). Peru and Argentina apparently were to be the next theaters of operations.

Guevara correctly saw that his real enemy was the United States; his theory was that the more brush fires that could be created, the more extended the United States would become in trying to put them out, and thus the greater the chances of any single revolutionary movement succeeding. That the United States understood and feared this strategy is evidenced by the alacrity with which it moved to send materiel and "advisers" to Bolivia once it was convinced that Che Guevara was there.

By the end of January the initial guerrilla group is complete. Che prepares to take his troop on a 25-day march through the jungle for training and toughening. In his monthly analysis for January he writes: "Now begins the real guerrilla phase, and we will test the troops. Time will tell what will happen and what the prospects are for the Bolivian revolution." To which he adds a comment that is an ominous portent of things to come: ". . . the incorporation of Bolivian fighters has taken the longest to accomplish."

Things continue to go poorly. The guerrilla force, lacking knowledge of the terrain, continually loses its way. Two men are accidentally drowned. Others contract malaria, and Che himself begins to suffer from recurrent bouts of asthma. All are hungry. The local peasantry, from whom Che hopes to enlist new recruits, exhibit stolid indifference to revolutionary ideals. Many villages speak an Indian dialect unknown even to the Bolivians in Che's force, making communication practically impossible. The march lasts 48 days instead of the planned 25.

As hardships and privations in crease, so does the friction between some of the veteran Cuban officers. One of the *comandantes* "Marcos," whom Che had intended to place in charge of the vanguard, is demoted for temperament and derelection of duty and ordered either to join the rear ranks as a common soldier or go back to Cuba. (He joins the rearguard and, much later, dies bravely in battle.)

The worst blow is reserved for Che's troop when it finally returns "home" to Nancahuazú; two of the Bolivian *guerrilleros* have deserted and have led army soldiers to the base camp, resulting in the capture of photographs, diaries and other documentary proof of Che Guevara's presence in Bolivia. Che records these events and their circumstances in his usual matter-of-fact way and then adds, gloomily, "An atmosphere of defeat prevailed."

Although a temporary period of military success will follow, this is actually the turning-point in Che Guevara's fortunes, for he is now compelled to abandon his training camp and go on the military offensive before he is ready and long before he had planned.

Beginning in Nancahuazú and moving southward, he fights a series of skirmishes with the poorly trained Bolivian Army troops and sustains a string of victories, most of them from carefully planned ambushes laid according to the classic model described by Guevara in his handbook, **On Guerrilla Warfare**. However, April proves one of the cruelest months for Che. On the 17th, he is accidentally separated from his rear guard, reducing his forces by more than 20 per cent, including five Cubans. (Though he will spend months searching for them, he will never see them

again.) On the 20th, the revolutionary ideologue Régis Debray, who had departed against Che's wishes after spending a month with him, is captured near Camiri and immediately becomes an international *cause célèbre.*

Guevara is now obliged to move northward again, taking to the inhospitable mountains and fighting as he goes. Victories continue, but now they are paid for with mortalities and casualties in his already meager forces which he is unable to replenish with even one Bolivian peasant recruit. He is cut off from support from the cities, and he has lost radio contact with Havana. Ascending into the mountains, Che is again visited with a series of horrendous asthma attacks. His medicine exhausted, he can no longer march and must alternately ride a mule (Rocinante?) or, when he loses consciousness, be carried on a litter. His sickness has begun to demoralize his men.

> The *Diary* is economical and matter-of-fact in tone, free of all hyberbole yet vivid, and leavened with a fine, dry sense of humor, the butt of which is often the author himself. The narrative begins slowly and gradually gains momentum. As it tersely unfolds a growing sense of tragic fate inexorably working itself out.
>
> *—Lee Lockwood*

The diary entries of this time, faithfully recording each detail of mounting adversity in an unbroken tone of incandescent courage and optimism, invoke a growing melancholy in the reader. Upon hearing on the radio that 16 American anti-guerrilla experts have arrived in La Paz to train the Bolivian rangers, Che notes with satisfaction: "We may be taking part in the first episode of a new Vietnam."

By August, Che records that his band is now down to 22 men, three of whom are disabled, and subsisting on horsemeat. Guevara's asthma is now so advanced that he has begun to lose control of his temper, berating his men and abusing his horse. For the man who had once written, "Now a will which I have polished with delight will sustain some weary lungs and shaky legs," this breach of self-discipline is a severe blow. He calls a meeting of his men:

> We are in a difficult situation . . . there are moments when I lose control of myself. This will change, but we must all share equally the burden of the situation, and whoever feels he cannot stand it should say so. This is one of those moments in which great decisions must be made, because a struggle of this type gives us the opportunity to become revolutionaries, the highest rung on the human ladder, and also allows us to graduate as men. Those who cannot reach either

of these stages should say so and leave the struggle.

By September, Che is bottled up in the mountains, desperately searching for an escape route from the tightening encirclement of the Rangers. Practically every new entry begins with the notation, "A black day." Though now aware that he is probably reaching his end, he still possesses enough spirit for a moment of humor: "I almost forgot to emphasize the fact that today, after something like six months, I bathed. This constitutes a record which several others are already approaching."

Why did Che Guevara fail? Unquestionably, the most significant cause of his defeat was his inability to attract the support of the Bolivian peasants. During 11 months of operations over an extensive rural area, not a single native joined the guerrilla band. Instead, as Che himself admits, the peasants responded to his urgings with indifference and duplicity, and many served as paid informers to Barrientos's troops.

One reason for this was lack of sufficient preparation. It seems incredible that neither Che nor any of the Cubans had taken the trouble to learn Quechua, the most common dialect spoken by the Bolivian Indians, before arriving in Bolivia; it is equally incredible that there was not at least one Bolivian in the group who spoke Guarani, the other prominent Indian tongue of the region.

More significant may have been a miscalculation by Castro and Guevara in attempting to duplicate the success of the Cuban revolution by transposing its tactics wholesale to a Bolivian setting. The two situations are not identical.

When Fidel Castro landed in the Sierra Maestra in 1956, he was a well-known Cuban patriot who was returning to his own country at the head of a revolutionary force who were 99 per cent Cubans. Castro had no avowed political program or ideology except that of ridding Cuba of a dictatorship and restoring a democratic government. He operated in a territory (Oriente Province) which he knew personally; he had, in fact, grown up among its peasants and spoke their dialect. Hence, Castro was able to obtain the overwhelming support of the peasantry, a factor which proved decisive to the success of his revolution.

By contrast, in Bolivia Che Guevara was a famous Cuban leader on foreign soil. He was the chief of a revolutionary band that was also largely made up of foreigners. He was an acknowledged Communist doctrinaire whose revolutionary program involved the communization not only of Bolivia but of all Latin America. In effect, he was the agent of a foreign power operating on Bolivian soil—at least, in the eyes of the Bolivians. He did not speak their language. Given these circumstances, it does not seem surprising that the Indian peasants offered a cool reception to the bearded foreign warriors, or that the Government was able to capitalize on their natural xenophobia and turn them into informers.

One wonders, also, at the inadequate planning that seems to have characterized the preparations for the Bolivian adventure. Were Castro and Guevara simply overconfident or overoptimistic? Why, for example, were not more Bolivians involved in the operation from the beginning, perhaps receiving their preliminary training in Cuba? Why did not the Cuban veterans (whom Che accuses of having grown soft and lazy in desk jobs during the nine years since the revolution) undergo a rigorous reconditioning before they left? (Some had no training.)

Once in Bolivia, why didn't the Cubans, instead of doing most of the fighting, function as "advisers" to the Bolivian *guerrilleros* (as did the United States experts to the Bolivian Rangers who ultimately defeated Che)? Why didn't Che, who knew beforehand that there would be trouble with the Bolivian Communist party, arrange other lines of support in advance to ensure that his *guerrilla* would not be cut off from the cities?

With more planning, better luck, and a guerrilla cadre mainly staffed and led by Bolivians, could the revolutionary effort have succeeded? There is no sure answer. "Pombo's" diary tells us that Che expected victory in Bolivia to take at least 10 years. Certainly many of the conditions that spawn revolutions do exist in Bolivia, among them extreme rural poverty, a feudal system of land ownership, exploitation and suppression of the tin miners, corruption at all levels of government, and a revolutionary tradition.

Daniel James, in his introduction to the Bolivian edition of Che's diaries, ascribes Che's defeat in part to his failure to appreciate the tremendous political popularity of President Barrientos, whom James characterizes as "a typical Latin-American revolutionary"—an assertion likely to cause guffaws even among Barrientos's cronies. Barrientos's regime, which began with a coup d'etat, is so shaky that it almost fell during Guevara's short-lived period of victories and is now tottering again because one of his ministers stole a copy of Che's diary and sent it to Fidel Castro, enabling him to publish it first.

Were there sufficient space, it would be interesting to compare the two introductions by Fidel Castro and Daniel James, which represent points of view that could not be more opposite. However, one matter in James's essay must be mentioned. At the beginning, and again at the end of his introduction, he devotes several pages to a discussion of what he calls the "rivalry" between Guevara and Castro.

According to James's somewhat muddled exposition, the two had never gotten along since their days together in the Sierra Maestra (though both had carefully hidden their feelings). When Che returned to Cuba in 1965 from Algeria, Castro, out of pique at Guevara's supposed efforts to assume the ideological leadership of the Cuban revolution, banished him first to the Congo and then to Bolivia (after which Fidel, "copied Che's ideological program"). When Guevara began to encounter adversity, James goes on, Fidel purposely withheld the aid and support that could have saved his life, and abandoned Che "to fight and die alone in the wilds of the Bolivian southeast," thus eliminating his chief rival to the leadership of the Latin-American armed struggle.

Suffice it to say that there exists not one shred of documentary evidence, either in Che's diaries of anywhere else, to support this fantastic story. In Cuba, since his departure in 1965, Guevara's name and image have been promoted incessantly by Castro's propaganda organs. If anything, Fidel's support of his comrade has been overenthusiastic, as witness the O.L.A.S. conference of 1967, where Che was clearly identified as the new Bolivar of South America's Socialist revolution—which no doubt helped stimulate United States action in Bolivia. As for Guevara's feelings for Castro, they are nowhere expressed more movingly than in his farewell letter to Fidel:

> If my final hour finds me under other skies, my last thought will be of this people [the Cubans] and especially of you. I am thankful for your teaching, your example, and I will try to be faithful to the final consequences of my acts. . . . I embrace you with all my revolutionary fervor!

It must be left to the reader to speculate why James (who has published a violently anti-Castro book about Cuba) sees fit to devote so much of his Introduction to this gratuitously vicious slur on Fidel Castro.

Yet no amount of scandal or intrigue will tarnish Che Guevara's Bolivian diary or prevent it from being read as one of the most transcendent documents of our time. More than a simple war journal, it is a rare self-portrait of the compleat revolutionary. Out of this diary of defeat emerges a triumphant legacy of courage, selflessness and devotion to principle of heroic dimensions. The revolutionary movement to which he so willingly sacrificed himself, though temporarily weakened by his death, must ultimately be fortified by the exemplary testament which he has left it.

The Times Literary Supplement (essay date 14 November 1968)

SOURCE: "Right and Left: Che Guevara," in *T.L.S.: Essays and Reviews from "The Times Literary Supplement"—1968, Vol. 7,* Oxford University Press, London, 1969, pp. 19-24.

[*In the following excerpt from a collection of essays written for* The Times Literary Supplement *during 1968, the critic discusses the insights that Guevara's diaries provide into his life and revolutionary activities in Bolivia. The critic also compares the Cuban and English editions of the diaries.*]

Early in the afternoon of October 8, 1967, at Quebrada del Yuro, in the remote south-east corner of Bolivia, a small guerrilla force, led by Ernesto 'Che' Guevara, found itself surrounded by units of the Bolivian Army's 2nd Ranger Battalion and suffered a decisive defeat. Six guerrillas were killed and Che himself was wounded and captured. Twenty-four hours later, on October 9, he was executed. Two diaries were found among his papers: the first, a spiral notebook, covered the period from November 7, 1966 (the day he arrived—heavily disguised—from Havana, via Prague, São Paulo and La Paz, at the guerrilla base of Nancahuazú), to the the end of the year; the second, an appointments book bearing the name of a German pharmaceutical company, ran from January 1, 1967, to October 7, the day before the final battle.

Clearly the Guevara diaries were documents of the great-

est political and historical interest and importance. However, neither the Bolivians nor the Americans—American counter-insurgency specialists had been training the Bolivian anti-guerrilla forces and the C.I.A. agents were apparently in at the kill—were at first prepared to authorize their publication. Photocopies of the diaries did nevertheless reach Havana, where, in June of this year, after their authenticity had been satisfactorily established, they were published, together with a 'Necessary Introduction' by Dr. Fidel Castro, in which he honoured the memory of Che, declared his solidarity with the Latin-American revolutionary movement, and argued strongly that although recent events in Bolivia constituted a setback for the Revolution they were not a defeat. The Cuban Government has consistently refused to reveal the source of the photocopies, but it is now known that they were handed over by Sr. Antonio Arguedas, the Bolivian Minister of the Interior, no less, whose defection in July triggered off a major political crisis in Bolivia. The Cape/Lorrimer edition of Che Guevara's Bolivian diaries is a translation of the Cuban edition complete with Dr. Castro's introduction and a translation of the July Proclamation by the Bolivian guerrilla, Inti Peredo, which begins with the stirring declaration, 'Guerrilla warfare in Bolivia is not dead! It has just begun.'

It has been widely assumed that besides being incomplete—in his introduction Dr. Castro admitted that a few pages were not yet in his possession—the Cuban edition of the Guevara diaries had been heavily edited in order to suppress or 'soften' passages damaging to the Castro regime. However, the publication in this country by Allen and Unwin of the American edition of the diaries, which their American publishers, Stein and Day, claim to be the 'only authentic, uncensored and complete version', makes it quite clear that this is not the case. Certainly the American edition is *complete*: it includes entries for January 4, 5, 8 and 9, February 8 and 9, March 14, April 4 and 5, June 9 and 10, July 4 and 5, which do not appear in the Cuban edition. Interesting as they are, however, Dr. Castro was quite correct when he wrote, 'they are entries for dates when nothing important happened and they in no way alter the diary's overall contents'. So far as the remaining 300 or so entries are concerned, there are minor variations in translation but no significant differences between the two editions. The very fact that both sides had the diaries (or photocopies of them)—and that each knew this to be the case—ensured that neither could tamper with the text and hope to get away with it.

> Without literary pretensions, the *Diaries* make compelling reading. Like the *Reminiscences* they include a great deal of information about the everyday problems of food supply, sickness, discipline and morale.
>
> —The Times Literary Supplement

Besides the thirteen entries missing from the Cuban version of the Guevara diaries, the American edition offers as an additional bonus, the captured diaries of three of Che's closest lieutenants, all, like himself, veterans of the Sierra Maestra and officers of the Cuban Revolutionary Army: first, *Pombo* (Captain Harry Villegas Tamayo), a 27-year-old Negro and one of the few survivors of the campaign, whose diary begins on July 14, 1966, and ends on May 29, 1967, and is therefore particularly valuable for the information it gives about the establishment of the guerrilla base before Che's arrival; secondly, *Rolando* (Captain Eliseo Reyes Rodríguez), a member of the central committee of the Cuban Communist Party, killed in action at the age of twenty-four, whose diary runs from August 11, 1966, to April 20, 1967: and, thirdly, *Braulio* (Lieutenant Israel Reyes Zayas), whose diary, the least interesting of the three, covers the period October 25, 1966, to August 9, 1967. The book also includes some fascinating photographs of Che himself, and the guerrilla camp, a useful chronology of the eleven-month campaign, and a complete list of the guerrillas, all of whom have been identified. (As is now well known from sensational newspaper stories, Tania [Laura], the only girl among the guerrillas, killed in August, 1967, was Haydee Tamara Bunke Bider, an East German double-agent keeping an eye on Che for the Soviet K.G.B.)

There is, moreover, a valuable, if poorly organized and at times inconsistent, introduction by the American editor of the diaries, Mr. Daniel James, a journalist and historian, who has had access to all the captured documents and who has for some time taken a close interest in the career of Che Guevara (a biography is expected to appear soon). In his introduction, Mr. James recounts Che's movements from the time of his 'disappearance' in March, 1965, to his arrival at Nancahuazú eighteen months later; he traces the idea of a Bolivian campaign back to the meeting between Dr. Castro and Sr. Mario Monje Molina, the First Secretary of the Bolivian Communist Party, during the Tricontinental Conference held in Havana in January, 1966; and he explains the purpose of the campaign which was to make Bolivia the catalyst for revolution against 'Yankee imperialism' throughout Latin America. Che is on record as saying: 'Bolivia will sacrifice itself so that conditions [for revolution] can be created in neighbouring countries. We have to make [Latin] America another Vietnam, with its centre in Bolivia.'

The *Diaries* themselves consist of daily jottings and monthly analyses relating to the guerrillas themselves— Che never had a fighting force of more than forty or so (almost half of whom were Cuban)—and guerrilla operations along a corridor approximately 200 miles long and seventy miles wide, within the triangle formed by the towns of Santa Cruz in the north, Sucre in the west, and Camiri in the south. No doubt they were very like the 'hasty notes' from which Che eventually compiled his *Reminiscences of the Cuban Revolutionary War,* which was also recently published in English. Without literary pretensions, the *Diaries* make compelling reading. Like the *Reminiscences* they include a great deal of information about the everyday problems of food supply, sickness, discipline and morale, as well as comments on Bolivian and Voice of America news broadcasts relating to the guerrilla war, and descriptions of patrols and skirmishes with Bolivian government troops. Again, as in the *Reminiscences,* Che writes with considerable self-awareness, frankness, modesty and not a little coarse humour (May 13: 'Day of belching, farting, vomiting and diarrhoea; a real organ concert'). As late as June-July Che was still optimistic (on July 7 the guerrillas had one of their greatest successes when they took Samaipata on the main Cochabamba-Santa Cruz highway), but it was from that time that things began to go wrong: the guerrilla force was gradually reduced in number and Che himself suffered a serious physical deterioration. The end came at Quebrada del Yuro early in October.

The most important question to be asked about Che Guevara's Bolivian campaign is why did it fail? The diaries themselves provide a number of clues. In the first place, and perhaps the most important, the peasants of southeast Bolivia failed to support the guerrillas. On the contrary, they seemed more disposed to assist the Bolivian army in tracking them down. Secondly, the guerrillas maintained little contact with the Bolivian miners, students and other urban revolutionary groups. One important reason for this was the deep rift which opened up between Che and the leaders of the Bolivian Communist Party. *Pombo's* diary reveals Che's bitterness over what became in effect communist sabotage of the guerrilla cam-

Che Guevara with Fidel Castro in Plaza of the Revolution, Havana, 1961.

paign, and in his introduction to the Guevara diaries Fidel Castro goes out of his way to denounce the Bolivian Communists for 'narrow and vulgar chauvinism'. And thirdly, the Bolivian army, hopelessly ineffective at first, improved its counter-insurgency methods as a result of intensive United States training and, in the end, had little difficulty in mopping up what remained of the guerrilla force.

Mose L. Harvey   (essay date January 1969)

SOURCE: A foreword to *"Che" Guevara on Revolution: A Documentary Overview,* edited by Jay Mallin, University of Miami Press, 1969, pp. 11-14.

[*A diplomat, educator, editor, and author, Harvey was known as an authority on Soviet affairs and East European trade. In the following excerpt from an essay written in early 1969, he briefly discusses the popularity and influence of Guevara's writings, noting his contributions to Marxist thought.*]

For any study of the Cuban revolution, the writings of Ernesto Guevara are of exceptional importance. Guevara played a number of roles in that revolution, and he alone of the top leaders was a prolific writer. Guevara's interests and official responsibilities were varied, and he wrote on diverse topics—plans for industrialization, processes of high finance, the evils of bureaucracy. Historical perspective will probably show, however, that his most significant work related to his continuing discussion and interpretation of Communist revolutionary theory, particularly in the field of guerrilla warfare.

Guevara viewed the Cuban revolution as but a part of a larger revolution that he was convinced would soon engulf all of Latin America. Much of his writings aimed at both stimulating and guiding struggle in other Latin American countries.

Guevara did not attempt to strike out on new theoretical paths. His evident objective was to adapt established Communist precepts to the Latin American scene—first in terms of demonstrating the Marxist-Leninist nature of the Castro revolution and second in terms of providing strategic, tactical, and operational guidelines for revolutionary drives elsewhere in Latin America. Nevertheless—and probably because he did not himself fully understand the tenets of the Communist theoreticians he sought to interpret—Guevara turned out to be an innovator in two very important particulars.

One, he viewed guerrilla war as a means to total victory in a revolutionary struggle. China's Mao Tse-tung and Viet Nam's Vo Nguyen Giap, the two master theorists on revolutionary war in Communist ranks, had emphasized the limitations of guerrilla war and had seen it as the prime form of struggle in only one of the three stages that would necessarily mark any successful "armed revolution." Guevara echoed the three stages concept, but in his mind the stages differed in a quantitative sense, that is, in consequence of increases in the size and strength of guerrilla forces. Mao and Giap saw the difference as qualitative, with guerrilla forces evolving into regular armies and with guerrilla-type methods and operations giving way to—or at least becoming subordinate to—regular, or conventional, warfare. Mao and Giap, in contrast to Guevara, ruled out success of an armed revolution through guerrilla war alone, no matter how large guerrilla forces might become.

Two, Guevara broke with the basic dictum of other Communist theorists that a generally favorable situation had to exist before an armed revolution could be successfully initiated. He argued that it was not "always necessary to await the existence of all the conditions for revolution: the insurrectional focus can create them." This was in direct contrast to:

> —Lenin: "If a revolutionary party has not the majority among the vanguard classes and in the country generally, there can be no question of insurrection. . . . To throw the vanguard alone into the decisive battle, before the whole class, before the broad masses have taken up a position either of direct support of the vanguard or at least one of benevolent neutrality towards it, and one in which they cannot possibly support the enemy, would be not merely folly but a crime."

> —Stalin: ". . . it must be born in mind that the overthrow of the bourgeoisie can be successfully accomplished only when certain absolutely necessary conditions exist, in the absence of which there can be even no question of the proletariat taking power."

> —Mao: ". . . strategically, we should despise all our enemies, but tactically we should take them all seriously . . . in dealing with concrete problems and particular enemies we shall be committing the error of adventurism unless we take them seriously . . . it is impossible to win victory in a people's war without taking full account of the enemy tactically and without regard to concrete conditions. . . . In seeking victory, those who direct a war cannot overstep the limitations imposed by objective conditions. . . ."

> —Lin Piao: ". . . every revolution in a country stems from the demands of its own people. Only when the people in a country are awakened, mobilized, organized, and armed can they overthrow the reactionary rule of imperialism and its lackeys through struggle; their role cannot be replaced or taken over by any people from outside."

Guevara's departure from the standard in these two regards had the effect of magnifying the potential of guerrilla warfare as an instrument of revolution. Guerrillas could not only get a revolutionary war under way; they could, if they applied "correct" strategy and tactics, carry it through to total victory. Even more important, a small guerrilla band, or nucleus, could, even if injected into an area from the outside, generate itself the conditions and dynamics necessary for a successful revolutionary struggle against an entrenched regime.

This thinking evidently lies at the root of the adventurism of the Castro government with respect to the training of Latin Americans in guerrilla warfare and the dispatch and support of guerrilla forces in a succession of Latin American countries. And . . . it well explains how Guevara could have brought himself to the abortive guerrilla effort in Bolivia that ended in his death.

Had Guevara lived out his days as a highly placed bureaucrat in Castro's Cuban government, what he wrote of revolutionary warfare would probably have been of interest and importance only to those specialists who seek to penetrate and explain the mysteries that surround the Castro takeover and the evolution of Cuba's domestic and foreign policies. It is true that for a brief period after the Castro triumph Guevara shone brightly from his Cuban setting and gave promise of a significant role in the shaping of worldwide radical thought. But as he settled into his post of *alto funcionario,* and proved somewhat bungling and over-voluble in the capacity, he lost his allure. Such romanticism as still attached to the Cuban revolution centered increasingly on Castro himself.

For any study of the Cuban revolution, the writings of Ernesto Guevara are of exceptional importance. Guevara's interests and official responsibilities were varied, and he wrote on diverse topics—plans for industrialization, processes of high finance, the evils of bureaucracy and interpretation of Communist revolutionary theory.

—Mose L. Harvey

Guevara, like a number of others through history, found a new and larger life in a bizarre death. His summary execution following the collapse of the tragicomic guerrilla campaign he and elements of the Cuban military imposed on an unwilling Bolivian peasantry projected the Guevara figure into a new dimension. Guevara the man gave way to Guevara the myth—and a myth that the dissidents of the world quickly seized upon for both symbol and example.

As part of Guevara's transformation from Cuban conspirator to hero of the New Left, widespread and avid interest has developed with regard to his writings and teachings. In less than a month after his death some 15,000 copies of his *Guerrilla Warfare* were sold in Italy alone. Guevara's thought on war and revolution has consequently become something far more than a guide to the formation of Cuban foreign policy. It has become a force to be reckoned with wherever men have become dissatisfied with their lot and with the societies in which they live. And here it can be of great importance that Guevara did not share the concern of other Communists over a premature or indiscriminate use of violence, but instead greatly exaggerated the ease and surety with which it could bring revolutionary changes in existing power structures. It can be of great importance that his counsel ran the exact opposite

of Lenin's "never play with insurrection" and Mao's "engage in no battle you are not sure of winning."

Given the unrest and searchings for new ways that mark the contemporary world as it passes through an era of great change, Guevara's theories can have widespread and traumatic impact. Guevara's own experiences, both as a manager and manipulator of insurrections from within the Cuban government and as a commander of guerrillas in Bolivia, demonstrated how small the chances are that application of his theories will lead in fact to the revolutionary overturns that he so ardently desired. But that appears of little moment to the angry and the impatient. For these, Guevara's concept that a handful of uninhibited men with guns, torches, and grenades can make a revolution where and as they choose obviously has great appeal. Would-be revolutionaries in a hurry to tear down existing orders have evidently long since wearied of the cautions of the older generation of Communists. Much more to their mood is a call to action such as Guevara sounds, no matter how rash and reckless the call might appear to others.

Jay Mallin   (essay date January 1969)

SOURCE: An introduction to *"Che" Guevara on Revolution: A Documentary Overview,* edited by Jay Mallin, University of Miami Press, 1969, pp. 19-44.

[*Mallin is the author of several books on Cuba and the Revolution, as well as works on Latin American and Caribbean politics. In the following excerpt, originally written in January 1969, he discusses Guevara's theories of guerrilla warfare as outlined in his various essays and in his* Guerrilla Warfare, *noting that "Guevara's ideas became the practical, as well as the theoretical guide for the Castro-Communist drive for power in Latin America."*]

Guevara's first book, *Guerrilla Warfare,* was less a theoretical work than a basic guidebook for guerrilla warfare. It contains detailed comments and instructions on tactics, techniques, weapons, training, propaganda, indoctrination, morale, and even "the role of the woman." The book was specifically written for use by future guerrillas in actual operations. As such, the Cuban government printed at least one small-sized edition which would fit handily into any guerrilla's pockets. A note at the end stated,

> *Compañero:* This book seeks to be a synthesis of the experiences of a people; if you believe anything should be added or changed, communicate it to the Department of Instruction of the MINFAR [Ministry of the Revolutionary Armed Forces].

Guerrilla Warfare was nevertheless a foretaste of the views Guevara would later project. There was a warning of things to come in his statement that the guerrilla goes to battle "with the intention of destroying an unjust order, and, therefore, more or less surreptitiously with the intention of putting something in place of the old," i.e., establishing a Communist regime.

Two years later Guevara brought his ideas to full fruition. He published an article entitled **"Guerrilla Warfare: A Method"** in *Cuba Socialista,* at that time the leading doctrinal publication of the Castro regime. In compact form, Guevara described how a guerrilla campaign can be started and carried out:

> Relatively small nuclei of people choose favorable places for guerrilla warfare, either to begin a counterattack, or to weather the storm, and thus they begin to act. The following must be clearly established: at first, the relative weakness of the guerrilla movement is such that it must work only to settle in the terrain, establishing connections with the populace and reinforcing the places that will possibly become its base of support.

Guevara agreed with Mao and Giap on basic tactics. But whereas they referred to the "three stages" as qualitatively different phases of a revolutionary war—the envolvement of guerrilla forces into regular armies and a changeover from guerrilla methods to more sophisticated methods of conventional warfare—Guevara thought in terms of a continuing guerrilla effort with the "stages" differing only in the sense of size and strength of guerrilla forces. Guevara used "guerrilla war" and "liberation war" and "revolutionary war" interchangeably. Mao and Giap viewed a "guerrilla war" as but one of the three stages of a "revolutionary war," or "war of liberation," although they allowed for the use of guerrilla methods and tactics in support of the conventional type of operations of the later stages.

Guevara echoed Mao in his listing of the conditions necessary for guerrilla survival: "Constant mobility, constant vigilance, constant distrust." He advocated the utilization of terror on the model of Giap. He saw terror not only as a means of intimidating civilians to support and help the guerrilla forces but also as a means of forcing increasingly harsh and indiscriminate countermeasures on the part of government forces. He explained this tactic on grounds that in Latin America there exists "a state of unstable balance between the oligarchic dictatorship and the popular pressure," and this balance "must be upset." Guevara said:

> The dictatorship constantly tries to operate without the showy use of force; forcing the dictatorship to appear undisguised—that is, in its true aspect of violent dictatorship of the reactionary classes, will contribute to its unmasking, which will intensify the struggle to such extremes that then there is no turning back. The manner in which the people's forces, dedicated to the task of making the dictatorship define itself—to hold back or to unleash the battle— carry out their function depends on the staunch beginning of a long-range armed action.

Guevara believed that a small nucleus of well-trained men could be formed in, or introduced into, any country, and that this nucleus, with the use of proper tactics, would with surety grow into a revolutionary movement and would step by step weaken and ultimately destroy opposing government forces. Guevara argued that it was "not always necessary to await the existence of all the conditions for revolution; the insurrectional focus can create them." An insurrection in the form of a guerrilla move-

ment can lead to a general revolution—so thought Guevara. In this, he differed importantly with both Mao and Giap and indeed with Communist thinking generally. He here reflected a naive faith in a sort of magic or mystique about guerrilla warfare that Fidel Castro and he had built up over the years, and which indeed became the foundation for much of Cuba's foreign policies. The mystique may be expressed as faith that any guerrilla operation, no matter how small or weak at its inception, can generate the means to its own success, that is, to a Castro-like takeover of power.

Castro and his followers, in speeches and writings, carefully nurtured the legend of the guerrilla "victory" in Cuba. Quite evidently the Castroites came to believe this legend, as evidenced by the fact that since 1959 efforts have been made to launch similar guerrilla campaigns in more than a dozen Latin American countries. Every one of these attempts has failed. In concentrating on rural guerrilla activities (with the partial exception of Venezuela, where "urban guerrillas" were also highly active for a period), the Castroites chose to overlook the fact that in Cuba the guerrilla campaign was but a phase of a general popular movement against Batista. Popular resentment against the Batista regime found expression in steadily widening clandestine activities: terrorism, sabotage, strikes, propaganda, passive resistance. It also found expression in the supply of the guerrillas with men, funds, and weapons. If it was true that the guerrillas were a major element in the wearing-away of the Batista army, it was also true that Castro rode—but did not generate or direct—a groundswell of national unrest.

Guevara's ideas became the practical, as well as theoretical, guide for the Castro-Communist drive for power in Latin America. His article was a blueprint for revolution. Tactics might vary somewhat from country to country, but basic emphasis was on fostering guerrilla warfare: "guerrilla warfare is . . . the central axis of the study," he declared.

> . . . The war [said Guevara] would be continental. This means also that it will be prolonged; there will be many fronts, it will cost much blood, innumerable lives for a long time. . . . In fact, the birth of the American struggle has begun. Will its vortex be in Venezuela, Guatemala, Colombia, Peru, or Ecuador . . . ? Will these present skirmishes be only manifestations of an unrest that does not bear fruit? It does not matter, for the final result, that one movement or another may be momentarily defeated. What counts is the decision to struggle that ripens day by day; the awareness of the need for revolutionary change, the certainty of its possibility.

Kenneth Minogue (essay date 1970)

SOURCE: "Che Guevara," in *The New Left: Six Critical Essays,* edited by Maurice Cranston, The Bodley Head, 1970, pp. 17-48.

[*Born in New Zealand, Minogue is an educator and critic who writes and lectures on issues related to political science.*

In the following excerpt, he articulates the principal tenets of Guevara's "concrete and practical" Marxism.]

Che was a Marxist in both his actions and his theories. His fame in his respect is such as to place him alongside Bernstein, Kautsky, Lenin, Rosa Luxemburg, Tito, Ho Chi Minh and Mao Tse-tung. Most of these leaders combined action with theory, but the theory is mostly subordinate to the action. Such was the case with Che.

What did his Marxism amount to? Here we need to observe the way in which Marxism itself has developed in the first century of its existence. Marxism in the nineteenth century claimed its following because it stood at the opposite pole from the attitudes of a professional revolutionary like Louis Blanqui, or a romantic anarchist like Mikhail Bakunin. Marxism recognised the fact that a man cannot simply 'make a revolution'. It recognised this fact by asserting that a great deal of preparatory work must go into building up the proletarian organisation that will make the revolution. But it developed these 'practicalities' of the activity of making revolutions vastly further, till they had become elaborated into the celebrated philosophy of history known as historical materialism. Every society was seen as a ferment of 'contradictions' working themselves out by a steady process of which the human participants were often quite unaware.

Marx developed this line of thought so far that he reached the conclusion that no society would be transformed by revolution until its potentialities had all been developed. Capitalism, for example, would have to go through a number of stages until everything inherent in it had been worked out. And when that point had been reached, then revolution would come about as part of the natural process. The Protestant reformers and the merchants of northern Europe, for example, had overthrown feudal society quite effectively, in spite of the fact that they had no theory of revolutionary social transformation and their conscious thoughts had been focused on quite different preoccupations. Now this version of Marxism evidently leaves very little room for the conscious making of revolutions. Up to the point at which potentialities had been exhausted, revolution could only fail or generate a monstrosity; and beyond that point, the resistance to revolution was so feeble that it would in all probability be a quick and relatively painless affair.

Now this is the version of Marxism which made it the most important brand of socialism of its time. On the basis of it, nineteenth-century Marxists expected the revolution to come first in the most advanced industrial countries. It took a man as strong minded as Lenin to overthrow this theory. He had already significantly revised Marxism by developing a theory of imperialism to explain why capitalism was lasting longer than had been expected, and a theory of the party as the vanguard of the proletariat in order to build up the revolutionary organisation he thought was needed in Czarist Russia. In 1917 at the Finland Station, he instructed his followers to work directly for an immediate proletarian revolution, in spite of the fact that capitalism was very little developed in the Russia of the early twentieth century.

Lenin was the first really talented revisionist of Marxism, and after his time the history of Marxism is the history of men who showed the theory who was boss. Mao Tse-tung defied Stalin's orthodox advice and built a successful revolution amongst the peasants. And Fidel Castro, along with Che, made a revolution in Cuba which was so much based upon a practical sense of local conditions that it was only some years later, and under the pressure of economic need, that the revolution came to be approximately squared with Marxist theory.

By the 1960s, even Marxists themselves, long immured as they were in Stalinist scholasticism about 'correct' lines of thought, had come to recognise this. Marxism, they began to proclaim, was not a dogma but a method, and for its elucidation they turned to the romantic strain which is prominent in the very early writings and which also appears in some of the very late pieces. Here we find a Marx who is the moral critic of contemporary capitalist society, and who develops the notion of alienation to explain why it is that human life as we moderns know it is so impoverished. The new Marxism of the mid-twentieth century has thrown off the fashionable positivism that Marx had absorbed a century before; it no longer advances Marxism as superior because it is 'scientific' socialism. On the contrary, it throws to the fore the elements of Marxism which appeal to hope, and which inflame the will to make revolutions and bring the long awaited terminus to the horrors of capitalism. What remains of the old Marx is the idea that all the evils of the world compose a single system and that each man must fight for the revolution in whatever circumstances he may find himself. The Marxism of Che belongs to this latter kind.

Yet Che does seek to restore the original unity between the romantic and the 'scientific' elements of Marxism, and he does so with a simplicity that can only be regarded as savage, and impatient:

> There are truths so evident, so much a part of people's knowledge, that it is now useless to discuss them. One ought to be "marxist" with the same naturalness with which one is "newtonian" in physics or "pasteurian" in biology, considering that if facts determine new concepts, these new concepts will never divest themselves of that portion of truth possessed by the older concepts they have outdated. . . . The merit of Marx is that he suddenly produces a qualitative change in the history of social thought. He interprets history, understands its dynamics, predicts the future, but *in addition* [my italics] to predicting it (which would satisfy his scientific obligation), he expresses a revolutionary concept: the world must not only be interpreted, it must be transformed. Man ceases to be the slave and tool of his environment and converts himself into the architect of his own destiny. . . . We, practical revolutionaries, initiating our own struggle, simply fulfil laws foreseen by Marx the scientist.

Marxism is, then, taken entirely for granted. A fully conscious revolutionary, as Che understands him, has the same sort of awareness that he lives in a world full of exploitation as the average man has that stones fall down, not up. Revolutionary struggle is as natural to him as walking and speaking; and as he walks and speaks he makes discoveries about the world which happen to correspond to the 'laws' of Marxian ideology. It is here—in the area where theory is related to practice—that the Cuban revolution has made its major contribution to Marxism; it is here that a kind of individualist renaissance has followed the frozen middle ages of Stalinism. This is the contribution of Che, of Fidel, and it was brought to its fullest maturity in the writings of Regis Debray. It amounts to a new version of the supremacy of practice over theory. Latin America had long been equipped with orthodox Marxists, but they had not succeeded in making revolutions. On the other hand, people who *did* succeed in making revolutions did in the end turn into orthodox Marxists. Such, at least, was the official view of the Cuban movement, a view which (it has been plausibly suggested) has allowed Castro to support guerrilla movements in Latin America and to by-pass the existing communist parties whilst yet claiming, for the benefit of his patron the Soviet Union, to be unimpeachably correct in his line.

Che's Marxism, like everything else about him, is concrete and practical. We hear little about historical epochs, and very little analysis of class relations. We do hear a great deal about the guerrilla. Developed into a theory, the guerrilla generates the idea of the *foco* the process of revolutionary detonation by which a small band of guerrillas set up a centre of attraction in the sierras and bring the capitalist or neo-colonialist regime to its knees. It is essential to this theory, certainly as developed by Debray, that the *foco* be regarded as simultaneously military and political. No longer does the commissar fight beside the soldier and guard the purity of his doctrine; for the two figures are fused together by practice, and the guerrilla will learn in the fires of experience what the urban communist has abstractly acquired from his books.

This development of Marxism runs very quickly into a problem which cannot but have struck anyone who has considered the history of Marxism. Marxism, we have seen, has largely been developed by its heretics—the men who knew when to throw aside the book and act on their own political judgment. Further, this has now happened so often that (as we have seen) it has received official recognition in the way in which Marxism is now conceived. The whole notion of orthodoxy, with its apparatus of 'correct' lines, has weakened in the poly-centric communist world of the mid-twentieth century. For those many, however, who wish to repair the fractured unity of theory and practice every break induces a desire to restore the unity. Consequently each change has been followed by a development of theory which purports to learn the lessons of the new experience.

The Russians, the Chinese, the Yugoslavs and the Cubans have all indulged in this exercise. Its logic is of course, inductive. It consists in transposing the most striking facts of the successful experience into abstract terms and generating theory from them. In this way, the successful landing of Castro and his guerrillas in Eastern Cuba, their difficult but successful struggle to survive, and their final overthrow of the Batista regime, turn into the theory of the *foco;* the fact that these men were revolutionaries

whose acquaintance with Marxist theory was slim, and that they became increasingly sweeping in their ambition to remodel the social order, turns into the thesis that under guerrilla conditions the military and political struggles fuse together.

This kind of argument is, we have noted, inductive, and inductive argument has been subject to devastating criticism. Why, the critics ask, does the inductive reasoner select *this* set of facts, and out of this set of facts generate *this* set of general principles? For since logically all experiences are very complex, and capable of generating very large numbers of facts and principles, the inductive reasoner must have left out of his account of what he was doing the crucial principle which led him to select (rather than to discover) what he has found. The attempt to learn lessons from practice very frequently gets shipwrecked on this difficulty, and political and military history, no less than that of ideologies, is full of people learning the wrong lessons and being surprised by the reality they encounter.

The Cuban experience, then, began by rejecting a good deal of Marxism as being inappropriate to the special conditions of Latin America. There was good warrant in Marxism itself—indeed in Marx himself—for such cavalier treatment of established principles. But the ideological passion to realign theory with practice led to the production of a revised ideology which *would* be appropriate to Latin American conditions. Such a production is immediately subject to the same criticism as that on which it is itself based: Need we assume that Latin America is homogeneous enough to be covered by such a general theory? Might it not be true that each region of Latin America, or even perhaps each separate country, might have its own particular conditions; might, in other words, require its own special theory? It would seem that Che, who worked hard to develop a Marxism appropriate to Latin America, did not carry his reasoning this far. But his fate has certainly provoked other Marxists to do so.

Here, to understand Che's Marxism, we need to consider the conditions of his Bolivian enterprise. Bolivia is a small and relatively underdeveloped country in the geographical heart of South America; and it seems that it was primarily this geo-political fact which made it attractive to Che as the detonator of the revolutionary liberation of the whole continent. It had a government which (like many in South America) called itself 'revolutionary', but was not so in any respect that Che would recognise; and it had an army which was small, ill-equipped, and had been savagely mauled back in the 1930s in a war with Paraguay, an even smaller and more primitive state. It had lots of jungle and plenty of peasants, and its economy depended upon tin, the miners of which commodity were frequently in a turbulent condition.

Anyone looking at these conditions with a fresh eye would light upon the tin miners as the evident beginning of a revolutionary movement in Bolivia. But it would seem that Che looked at Bolivia and saw only Cuba; looked at its wild and inhospitable countryside and saw the Sierra Maestra; looked at President Barrientos, and saw only the figure of Batista. What Che established in Bolivia was a carbon copy of what Fidel had done in Cuba. And since Che

Che in 1963.

was, far more than Fidel, a theoretical animal, the conclusion is tempting that Che was the victim of his own theory. He seems to have believed that Cuba was *nothing else but* the first instance of a pattern that could be repeated in other parts of Latin America. He had, like so many figures in history, learned the lessons of experience—the wrong lessons. For what was missing in Bolivia was a thousand particular characteristics—the radical organisation in the cities, the feebleness of the Batista government, and perhaps above all the fact of leadership by the able, articulate, intuitive and entirely native Fidel.

Thinking in international terms, Che clearly thought that a revolution could be induced in Bolivia without a prominent Bolivian leader. No doubt he had to think this, since no serious candidate was available; but even beyond this inevitable deficiency, Che (and Fidel) exhibited an astonishing indifference to local Bolivian sensibilities. They failed to win over the peasants, they alienated the local communist party and they never managed to have more than a few effective Bolivians fighting amongst their picked Cuban veterans.

In this respect, then, Che has run the whole gamut of experience available to a Marxist theoretician. He bucked the theory to make a revolution, reconstructed the theory to fit the revolution he had made, and then proceeded to demonstrate by his actions the inadequacy of his own the-

ory. It is not an enviable odyssey and it is unlikely to be frequently repeated.

Yet the adventures of a man are not the same as the premises of an ideology. The accidents which often lead to fatal consequences in the world of action are a standing *ceteris paribus* clause for an ideology; and an adroit use of this clause will prevent any theory from being refuted. We must therefore qualify our conclusion in two ways: firstly, that Che's failure in Bolivia does not necessarily indicate that the theory of the *foco* must be discarded, for it may simply be the case that ill-luck and poor preparation led to that particular disaster. More importantly, the very failure itself has abundantly the heroic quality which Che often spoke about in his writings and speeches. Whilst the Bolivian episode did—to some extent—refute one part of Che's Marxism, it also illustrated another part, and one which, although of less interest to practical revolutionaries, is far more important in generating the legend. This part of Guevara's Marxism is his preoccupation with 'the new man'.

The most suitable text for illustrating this preoccupation is **"Man and Socialism in Cuba,"** perhaps the most famous pamphlet he ever wrote. It is here that Che states what may be vulgarly called the ideals of the movement: and the central ideal is the creation of the new man. This figure of the inevitable future is sketched out against the familiar Marxist account of twentieth-century life. Man suffers a kind of death, we learn, during the eight hours of his daily work, and even the artistic creations by which he might express the (presumed) anguish of his environmentally determined situation have been restricted by an ideological conditioning through which the monopoly capitalists prevent art from becoming (what Che thinks it must become if it is to be authentic) a 'weapon of denunciation and accusation'.

Man is exploited, and consequently his moral stature is diminished; but this happens very largely without his awareness. His attention is focused (by the agents of the monopoly capitalists) upon the success of a Rockefeller, and diverted away from the unsavory facts which made such a gigantic accumulation of wealth in the hands of one man possible. Since this is a rhetorical document, it would be unfair to press too hard upon its logical inadequacies. We need merely to note that Che has in full measure the belief common among men of his time that human beings are 'conditioned' by the environment in which they live, and that the adoption of revolutionary Marxism, although not inexplicable in terms of social conditions, is the one form of human behavior in which man throws off his 'conditioning' and embraces freedom. Clearly this is an equivocation upon the notion of 'conditioning', for the conditioning that a man can throw off is no conditioning at all. What is evidently being used here is the commonsense distinction between proceeding thoughtlessly along the paths of habit on the one hand, and becoming more self-conscious and deliberate on the other. This latter is a casual distinction we commonly make; but as transposed into Marxist ideology, it is dressed in a different vocabulary and becomes a pseudo-science of social determination. What Che has to say about it is very little distinguished from the writings of any other exponent of Marxist beliefs; what does distinguish him is his intense interest in the other term of the contrast—the new man who will replace the spiritual cripple of today's capitalist world.

Often, the specification is extremely crude, since it derives from the easy device of inserting the word 'revolutionary' before moral words which are universally regarded as virtues. There are times when Che indulges in what is virtually self-parody, and exhorts us to engage in revolutionary struggle with revolutionary dedication towards revolutionary aims. In the end, the new man does not turn out to be very much more than a revolutionary paragon:

> We are seeking something new that will allow a perfect identification between the government and the community as a whole, adapted to the special conditions of the building of socialism and avoiding to the utmost the common-place of bourgeois democracy transplanted to the society in formation . . . the ultimate and most important revolutionary aspiration (is) to see man freed from alienation.

This freedom is specified in two main ways. The first is that the new man will be the possessor of a highly developed social consciousness. This means, presumably, that the category of the private will disappear from his thinking. It certainly means that the new man will hold the same beliefs about social reality which are already held by Che himself, along with the revolutionary vanguard. In

other words, the distinction between agreeing with Che's Marxist interpretation of the world, and disagreeing with it, has been transposed into the distinction between being socially conscious and remaining 'conditioned' and unaware. The doctrine of social consciousness, in other words, is a vehicle of dogmatism by which the promotion of one particular interpretation of social life is being passed off as the only possible thought on the subject.

The new man, then, will be a dedicated communist. His second general characteristic is that he will be a dedicated worker towards the communal goal of building up the community. Since Che speaks for an 'underdeveloped' country, the actual content of the work of building up the community is, quite simply, economic self-sufficiency. What it would be beyond that is very little specified. But there is one part of the revolutionary work which is so powerful that it has infused the entire picture:

> Let me say, with the risk of appearing ridiculous, that the true revolutionary is guided by strong feelings of love. It is impossible to think of an authentic revolutionary without this quality. This is perhaps one of the great dramas of a leader; he must combine an impassioned spirit with a bold mind and make painful decisions without flinching. Our vanguard revolutionaries must idealize their love for the people, for the most hallowed causes, and make it one and indivisible. . . . They must struggle every day so that their love of living humanity is transformed into concrete deeds, into acts that will serve as an example, as a mobilizing factor.

Love is the master passion of the new man. It involves 'doing away with human pettiness' and it will be both higher and more persistent than love found under contemporary conditions: 'There ought to be a spirit of sacrifice not reserved for heroic days only, but for every moment.' Again: 'One ought always to be attentive to the human mass that surrounds one.'

In praising the speech which has supplied these last quotations, Che's editor, Professor Gerassi, writes:

> '. . . the author gently criticizes Cuba's communist youth for its dogmatism, dependence on official directives, lack of inventiveness, lack of individuality—yes, Che was always fostering individualism—and continues with a beautiful, moving definition of what a communist youth ought to be.'

Che's emphasis on the new man may, then, be taken initially as evidence of his attachment to individuality, but to an individuality of a new and more complete kind than exists now. If there is any part of Che's Marxism (by contrast with other features of his career) which is responsible for the legend, it is to be found here. Communism has often been associated with a soulless collectivity, a kind of endless *corvée* directed towards some remote and abstract goal. But here is a major exponent of communism outflanking the appeal of capitalism on its own individualist ground.

Significantly enough, perhaps, it is in passages like this that Che sounds most like an old-fashioned Christian preacher; and he may easily be presented as a man trying to fuse the best of the old moral ideals with the most complete attention to the social realities which religious exhortation in the past has often ignored. Nor can this theme in Che be dismissed as merely the attractive rhetoric of a man who was, after all, something of a poet. For in his enjoyment of power, Che showed a powerful and continuous hostility to the capitalist device of material incentives, because he believed that such incentives split people off from one another; he believed that they stood in the way of developing the only truly socialist motive for working harder—socialist emulation.

Yet before we take Che's devotion to individuality entirely at its face value, we must consider two important qualifications. The first arises immediately if we ask: What exactly does Che mean by 'individuality'? A man like John Stuart Mill, who in his essay *On Liberty* supplied the classic account of individuality, believed that each person has his own unique thoughts to think and lines of action to pursue; and in what Che would call a capitalist society, which Mill would call a liberal one, the laws and governing institutions should be so framed as to permit the greatest possible development of such resources of individuality. But we can hardly believe that Che is thinking anything remotely like this when we read:

> Thus we go forward. Fidel is at the head of the immense column—we are neither ashamed nor afraid to say so—followed by the best party cadres, and right after them, so close that their great strength is felt, come the people as a whole, a solid bulk of individualities moving toward a common aim; individuals who have achieved the awareness of what must be done; men who struggle to leave the domain of necessity and enter that of freedom.

These are individualities only in the sense that a tray of buns straight from the baker's oven contains a collection of individualities. Each is separate, but in all essential respects they are made up of the same materials, they have the same awarness of the same 'what must be done'. And if we pursue this line of thought further we shall find many occasions on which Che speaks exactly like an old-fashioned Stalinist agitator—or 'orientator' as Fidel guilefully renamed the function: he harangues the workers to produce more and to rise above their personal preoccupations in order to join in the common struggle. Indeed, this theme becomes at times so obtrusive that the inspiring notion of the 'new man' looks like nothing so much as a carrot to induce people to drive tractors more carefully, or to ease pining for luxuries like chewing gum and lipstick which are no longer imported from the United States. And although it is perilous to extract a doctrine from writings which are fundamentally rhetorical, we must conclude that although Che makes use of the appeal of individualism, his view of the matter is consistently the one he expressed when he discussed revolutionary medicine:

> Individualism, in the form of the individual action of a person alone in a social milieu, must disappear in Cuba. In the future, individualism ought to be the efficient utilization of the whole individual for the absolute benefit of a collectivity.

There could be no better illustration than this of the way in which an ideological thinker appropriates an attractive term for propaganda purposes, and changes the meaning so that it means precisely the opposite of what once made it attractive.

The second qualification we must make to Che's individualism is closely related to the first. One of the most important differences between current capitalist society and the revolutionary society of the future is that the first has a government which must repress the people whilst the second has only leaders, or a vanguard, who are one in love and feeling with the people. The desire to eliminate politics from life, to create a community in which no one shall be rendered alien by his exercise of power, is as old as Rousseau and (in this century) as wide as the seven seas. It is by no means confined to Marxism, but it is a very powerful motor of that doctrine. To anyone who stands outside this current of thought, the aspiration can only seem delusory, the more so because it is precisely the leaders speaking most about love who have perpetrated some of the worst excesses of our time. The love which is supposed to unite Fidel and his people, for example, has had to emerge out of the early apparatus of televised executions and the constant hostility of some hundreds of thousands of Cubans who have preferred exile to the benefits of such a love.

We may go further: virtually all modern politics is an exercise of ventriloquism, in which the rulers speak *on behalf of* a populace which is most of the time necessarily mute. In the countries conventionally recognised as democratic—countries like Britain and America—this muteness is qualified by periodic elections, and by a fairly constant ferment of discussion and criticism. Nevertheless, it is of the nature of authority that whoever holds it must in the end make a pronouncement which shall be accepted as the political decision of the populace involved. Now most ideologies are devices by which this ventriloquial act may be carried on with virtually no interference from the puppet whatever. A democratic government, having to face elections, must come to some terms with the political opinions of its working class. But a Marxist government does not have a working class: it has a proletariat, whose consciousness may (by the rules of the ideology) be objectively determined, and instead of a political problem the government is faced by a pseudo-educational one: how to make the people conscious of what it *must* be thinking (but actually may not be). A great deal of what Che has to say is part of this kind of ventriloquial performance. The justification of it—as given to a group of communist youth—goes as follows:

> If we—disoriented by the phenomenon of sectarianism—were unable to interpret the voice of the people, which is the wisest and most orienting voice of all; if we did not succeed in receiving the vibrations of the people and transforming them into concrete ideas, exact directives, then we were ill-equipped to issue those directives to the Union of Young Communists.

In politics at least, a posture of humility often disguises arrogance; and those whom men wish to control they first drown in flattery. The 'concrete ideas' which the Cuban government articulates from the 'vibrations' of the people are indistinguishable from the practices of all the other countries in which Marxism has become the official creed. Here is Che discussing the central problem that arises from the pretence that there is no gap between a government and its people:

> And today . . . the workers consider the state as just one more boss, and they treat it as a boss. And since this [Che is referring to the new Cuba] is a state completely opposed to the State as Boss, we must establish long, fatiguing dialogues between the state and the workers, who although they certainly will be convinced in the end, during this period, during this dialogue, have braked progress.

This is one more version of the Stalinist argument that no safeguards (such as an opposition) are needed in a communist society, because the only oppression is class oppression, and classes have been abolished. It is a Quixotic argument in the most literal sense, for no intelligent worker is going to be taken in by propaganda pictures of Che or Fidel out in the fields humping bags of sugar. And it is particularly Latins who will, once the excitement of the moment is past, treat with amusement such exhortations as that of Che to 'raise our voices and make Fidel's radio vibrate. From every Cuban mouth a single shout: "Cuba si, Yankees no! Cuba si, Yankees no!' " The political problem is that when the puppet does get restless, and the 'dialogue' fails, the ventriloquist generally resorts to clouting him.

Our conclusion must be that although Che had a journalistic flair for the concrete detail, and although he was supremely sensitive to the intellectual and emotional atmosphere of his time, his Marxism is really very little distinguished from that of other Marxists. In the field of revolutionary guerrilla tactics, he will no doubt be remembered for a variety of devices and observations; he is the inventor, for example, of the 'beehive effect' whereby one of the leaders, 'an outstanding guerrilla fighter, jumps off to another region and repeats the chain of development of guerrilla warfare—subject, of course, to a central command.' But in the field of theory he has contributed very little, which is not surprising, since he was man who wrote gestures, postures, promises and exhortations, rather than arguments of any depth.

FURTHER READING

Biography

Berger, John. "Che Guevara." In *The Look of Things: Essays by John Berger,* edited by Nikos Stangos, pp. 42-53. New York: The Viking Press, 1974.
>   Focuses on events surrounding Guevara's death. Berger considers, in particular, the meaning of the recorded images of Guevara following his execution by the Bolivian army in 1967.

Ebon, Martin. *Che: The Making of a Legend.* New York: Universe Books, 1969, 216 p.
>   Biographical study focusing on Guevara's career as a revolutionary activist.

Gerassi, John. Introduction to *Venceremos! The Speeches and Writings of Ernesto Che Guevara,* edited by John Gerassi, pp. 1-22. New York: The Macmillan Co., 1968.
>   Surveys Guevara's political career, noting that Che "was primarily a doer, a revolutionary activist."

James, Daniel. Introduction to *The Complete Bolivian Diaries of Che Guevara and Other Captured Documents,* edited by Daniel James, pp. 11-69. New York: Stein and Day, 1968.
>   Analyzes "the background and course of the Bolivian campaign so that the reader will be able to grasp the import of the diaries and documents which make up the rest of the book."

———. *Che Guevara: A Biography.* New York: Stein and Day, 1969, 380 p.
>   Biographical study that concludes with an assessment of Guevara's political influence.

Criticism

"Already a Legend." *The Economist* 228, No. 6522 (24 August 1968): 36.
>   Favorable reviews of Guevara's *Reminiscences of the Cuban Revolutionary War,* translated by Victoria Ortiz, and *Venceremos! The Speeches and Writings of Ernesto Che Guevara,* edited by John Gerassi.

Lowy, Michael. *The Marxism of Che Guevara; Philosophy, Economics, and Revolutionary Warfare.* Translated by Brian Pearce. New York: Monthly Review Press, 1973, 127 p.
>   Provides an overview of Guevara's life and career. Lowy attempts "to show that Guevara's ideas constitute a coherent whole, and are built on the basic premises of Marxism-Leninism, their philosophical, humanistic, ethical, economic, sociological, political, and military themes, all closely linked together." The critic also discusses Guevara's contributions to Marxism and those points on which he differs from other contemporary communist leaders.

MacIntyre, Alasdair C. "Marxism of the Will." In his *Against the Self-Images of the Age: Essays on Ideology and Philosophy,* pp. 70-5. New York: Schocken Books, 1971.
>   Investigates Guevara's unique perspective on Marxist-Leninist theory, arguing that "in Guevara, although questions of organisation are treated with intellectual respect, it is the voluntarist component of Leninism which is appealed to as never before." This essay first appeared in *Partisan Review* in 1969.

Yglesias, Jose. "Book Marks." *The Nation* 207, No. 10 (30 September 1968): 316-18.
>   Reviews several collections of the works of Guevara, including *Venceremos!, Che Guevara Speaks,* and *The Diary of Che Guevara.*

Additional coverage of Guevara's life and career is contained in the following sources published by Gale Research: *Contemporary Authors,* Vols. 111, 127; *Hispanic Literature Criticism;* and *Hispanic Writers.*

"The Lottery"

Shirley Jackson

The following entry presents criticism on Jackson's short story "The Lottery" (1948). For further information on her life and works, see *CLC,* Volumes 11 and 60.

INTRODUCTION

Jackson's fiction is noted for exploring incongruities in everyday life, and "The Lottery," perhaps her most exemplary work in this respect, examines humanity's capacity for evil within a contemporary, familiar, American setting. Noting that the story's characters, physical environment, and even its climactic action lack significant individuating detail, most critics view "The Lottery" as a modern-day parable or fable which obliquely addresses a variety of themes, including the dark side of human nature, the danger of ritualized behavior, and the potential for cruelty when the individual submits to the mass will.

Plot and Major Characters

"The Lottery" concerns an annual summer drawing held in a small unnamed American town. As the townspeople gather and wait for the ceremony to begin, some calmly piling stones together, they discuss everyday matters of work and family, behaving in ways that suggest the ordinariness of their lives and of the impending event. Tessie Hutchinson, arriving late, talks with her friend, Mrs. Delacroix, about the household chores that almost made her miss the lottery. Although everyone appears to agree that the annual lottery is important, no one seems to know when it began or what its original purpose was. As Mr. Summers reads off an alphabetical list of names, the heads of each household come forward to select a folded slip of paper from an old black wooden box. Bill Hutchinson draws the paper with the black mark on it, and people immediately begin speculating about which Hutchinson will actually "win" the drawing. Each member of Bill's family then draws a slip from the box. Tessie selects the paper with the black mark on it, and she vigorously protests the unfairness of the drawing. The townspeople refuse to listen to her, and as the story ends they begin to pelt her with the stones they have gathered.

Major Themes

The principal themes of "The Lottery" rely on the incongruous union of decency and evil in human nature. Citing James G. Frazer's anthropological study of primitive societies, *The Golden Bough* (1890), many critics observe that the story reflects humankind's ancient need for a scapegoat, a figure upon which it can project its most undesirable qualities, and which can be destroyed in a ritually absolving sacrifice. Unlike primitive peoples, however, the townspeople in "The Lottery"—insofar as they repre-

sent contemporary Western society—should possess social, religious, and moral prohibitions against annual lethal stonings. Commentators variously argue that it is the very ritualization that makes the murder palatable to otherwise decent people; the ritual, and fulfilling its tradition, justifies and masks the brutality. As a modern parable on the dualism of human nature, "The Lottery" has been read as addressing such issues as the public's fascination with salacious and scandalizing journalism, McCarthyism, and the complicity of the general public in the victimization of minority groups, epitomized by the Holocaust of World War II.

Critical Reception

"The Lottery" was first published in *The New Yorker* magazine on 26 June 1948, and it generated hundreds of letters from readers, the vast majority of whom were confused as to the story's meaning. According to Lenemaja Friedman, three "main characteristics dominated the letters: bewilderment, speculation, and old-fashioned abuse." Since then, critical reception has generally been very favorable, and "The Lottery" has been anthologized many times. Those critics who read the story as a traditional narrative tend to fault its surprise ending and lack of character development as unrealistic, unbelievable, and making reader identification difficult. Other commentators, however, view "The Lottery" as a modern-day parable; they argue that the elements of the story often disparaged by its critics are actually consistent with the style and structure of New Testament parables and to stories from the Old Testament. Generally, critics agree only that the story's meaning cannot be determined with exactitude. While most critics concede that it was Jackson's intention to avoid specific meaning, some cite flatly drawn characters, unrevealing dialogue, and the shocking ending as evidence of literary infertility. The majority of commentators, though, argue that the story's art lies in its provocativeness and that with its parable-like structure Jackson is able to address a variety of timeless issues with contemporary resonance, and thereby stir her readers to reflective thought and debate.

PRINCIPAL WORKS

*The Road through the Wall (novel) 1948
The Lottery; or The Adventures of James Harris (short stories) 1949
Hangsaman (novel) 1951
Life among the Savages (nonfiction) 1953
†The Bird's Nest (novel) 1954
Witchcraft of Salem Village (juvenile fiction) 1956
Raising Demons (nonfiction) 1957
The Sundial (novel) 1958
The Bad Children: A Play in One Act for Bad Children (drama) 1959
‡The Haunting of Hill House (novel) 1959
We Have Always Lived in the Castle (novel) 1962
§The Magic of Jackson (short stories and novels) 1966
§Come along with Me: Part of a Novel, Sixteen Stories, and Three Lectures (short stories, novel, and lectures) 1968

*This work was published as *The Other Side of the Street* in 1956.

†This work was published as *Lizzie* in 1957.

‡This novel served as the basis for the film *The Haunting* (1963), written by Nelson Gidding and directed by Robert Wise.

§These works were edited by Stanley Edgar Hyman.

CRITICISM

Robert B. Heilman (essay date 1950)

SOURCE: "Shirley Jackson, 'The Lottery': Comment," in *Modern Short Stories: A Critical Anthology,* edited by Robert B. Heilman, Harcourt, Brace Jovanovich, 1950, pp. 384-85.

[*Heilman is an English professor and the author of several works on drama, comedy, and the humanities. In the following essay on "The Lottery," Heilman discusses how Jackson's shift "from a realistic to a symbolic technique" intensifies the shock value of the story's ending.*]

Miss Jackson's story ["The Lottery"] is remarkable for the tremendous shock produced by the ending. Let us ignore the problem of meaning for the moment and see how the shock is created. In general, the method is quite easily recognized. Up to the last six paragraphs the story is written in the manner of a realistic transcript of small-town experience: the day is a special one, true, but the occasion is familiar, and for the most part the people are presented as going through a well-known routine. We see them as decent, friendly, neighborly people; in fact, most of the details could be used just as they are in a conventional picture of idyllic small-town life. Things are easily, simply told, as if in a factual chronicle (note the use of date and hour). Suddenly, in the midst of this ordinary, matter-of-fact environment, there occurs a terrifyingly cruel action, official, accepted, yet for the reader mysterious and unexplained. It is entirely out of line with all the terms of actual experience in which the story has otherwise dealt. It is as if ordinary life had suddenly ceased and were replaced, without warning, without break, and without change of scene, by some horrifying nightmare. Hence the shock, which the author has very carefully worked up to. Note how the shock is enhanced by the deadpan narrative style, which in no way suggests that anything unusual is going on.

In one sense the author has prepared for the ending. A few slight notes of nervousness, the talk about giving up the tradition, and the emotional outburst by Mrs. Hutchinson all suggest some not entirely happy outcome. Still more important in building up an unusually strong sense of expectation is the entire absence of explanation of the public ceremony. (At the end, the reader recalls the gathering of stones earlier in the story. This unobtrusive introduction of stage properties for later use exemplifies the well-made kind of construction.) But all these preparations still look forward to an outcome which will fall within the realistic framework that the author has chosen to use. Yet the ending is not realistic: it is symbolic. We may summarize the method of the story by saying that it suddenly, without notice, shifts from a realistic to a symbolic technique. This is another way of describing the shock.

Here we come to the problem of meaning. The experienced reader will recognize immediately what Miss Jackson has done: she has taken the ancient ritual of the scapegoat—the sacrificing of an individual on whom the evils of the community are ceremonially laid (by looking up "scapegoat" in Frazer's *Golden Bough* the student can find accounts of many such practices)—and plunged it into an otherwise realistic account of contemporary American life. What the story appears to be saying, then, is that though ancient rituals die out, the habits of mind which brought them into being persist; that we still find scapegoats and "innocent victims."

The critical question is: Does the effect of shock really serve the symbolic intention of the story? Ideally, shock should have the effect of shaking up the accustomed habits of mind and, therefore, of compelling a more incisive observation of familiar ways of life. But shock may disturb as well as stimulate the mind and may leave the reader only feeling shaken up. The question here is whether the shock "seizes stage," so to speak, and so crowds out the revelation to which it should be secondary. It is difficult to shift from genial chatter—even with some overtones of fear—to ritual murder without leaving a sense of an unclosed gap. The risk would have been greatly lessened if atmosphere, instead of being used intentionally to emphasize the sense of the ordinary, had been used earlier in the story to introduce an element of the sinister. It would clearly have been most difficult to suggest the coexistence of the sinister and the innocuous from the start. But this would have been an ideal method, since that coexistence is really the human fact with which the story is concerned. But the story gives us the sinister after the innocuous, instead of the two simultaneously. To put it in other terms, the symbolic intention of the story could have been made clear earlier so that throughout the story we would have been seeking the symbolic level instead of being driven to look for it only retrospectively, after it has suddenly become apparent that a realistic reading will not work. (In [Kafka's] "The Hunger Artist," for instance, we have the symbolic figure—the hunger artist—as the center of attention from the start; we know immediately that the story goes beyond realism, and so we always read with an eye on the underlying meaning.) To set us immediately on the track of the symbolism would probably reduce the shock, but it might result in a more durable story.

Seymour Lainhoff (review date March 1954)

SOURCE: "Jackson's 'The Lottery,' " in *The Explicator*, Vol. XII, No. 5, March, 1954, p. 34.

[In the following essay, Lainhoff comments on the scapegoat theme in "The Lottery."]

Shirley Jackson's provocative **"The Lottery"** is a story in which anthropology provides the chief symbol. Frazer's *The Scapegoat* (*The Golden Bough,* Part VI, 3rd ed., 1913) makes it clear that the lottery is Miss Jackson's modern representation of the primitive annual scapegoat rite. The story imagines that, in some typical American community, the rite still flourishes.

The story begins on the morning of June 27. (Frazer: the rite often occurred at the time of the summer solstice.) The first to gather at the square where the lottery is to be held are the children. School recently over, they take to their new liberty uneasily, gathering together quietly at first before breaking into boisterous play, their talk "still of the classroom and the teacher, of books and reprimands." (Frazer: the rite was commonly preceded or followed by a period of general license, during which ordinary restraints were thrown aside and offenses went unpunished.)

The scapegoat rite had a double purpose: to exorcise the evils of the old year by transferring them to some inanimate or animate objects, and with that "solemn and public banishment of evil spirits" [*The Golden Bough*] to appease the forces of the new year, to insure fertility. Primitive man, it seems, could not distinguish natural from moral

phenomena: the forces of the seasons had to be placated. Similarly, the men of **"The Lottery"** (suburbanite and rural) cannot distinguish natural from social phenomena: anybody criticizing the social order works against the natural rightness of things. The evidence: on the public square, after the children have assembled, the men come—"Soon the men began to gather, surveying their own children, speaking of planting and rain, tractors and taxes." Old Man Warner says: "Listening to the young folks, nothing's good enough for *them*. Next thing you know, they'll be wanting to go back to living in caves, nobody work, live *that* way for a while. Used to be a saying about 'Lottery in June, corn be heavy soon.' "

The lottery is conducted by Mr. Summers, "who had time and energy to devote to civic activities. He was a round-faced jovial man and he ran the coal business, and people were sorry for him because he had no children and his wife was a scold." Summers is the appropriate leader of the rite, as his name would indicate, as his job would too, the providing of fuel, but who is more barren, more unhappy, more willing "to shift the burden of his pains and sorrows to another, who will suffer them in his stead" [*The Golden Bough*]?

The other characters are typical: Old Man Warner, the reactionary advocate of the lottery; Mr. Hutchinson, the typical citizen, disliking the lottery, but accepting it as inevitable; Mrs. Delacroix, the uneasy outsider, the most friendly to the destined victim before the lottery and the most ferocious in her attack afterwards.

The theme of the story: beneath our civilized surface, patterns of savage behavior are at work. The theme is mirrored in the gruesome unfolding of the lottery rite. However, Miss Jackson is optimistic: some villages have abandoned the lottery; and the children, unlike their elders, preserve an uncontaminated affection for one another.

Cleanth Brooks and Robert Penn Warren (essay date 1959)

SOURCE: "Shirley Jackson: 'The Lottery,' " in *Understanding Fiction,* edited by Cleanth Brooks and Robert Penn Warren, second edition, Appleton-Century-Crofts, 1959, pp. 72-6.

[Brooks was one of the most influential of the "New Critics"; he espoused a critical method characterized by a close reading of texts in which an individual work is evaluated solely on the basis of its internal components. Warren was the Pulitzer Prize-winning author of All the King's Men *(1947),* Promises: Poems, 1954-1956 *(1957), and* Now and Then: Poems, 1976-1978 *(1979). In the following essay, they examine Jackson's intentions in "The Lottery," contending that it is meant to be a parable whose "fictional form actually gives point and definition to social commentary."]*

The plot [of Shirley Jackson's **"The Lottery"**] is so simple that to some readers it may seem to lack sufficient complication to be interesting. The story seems to do no more than recount the drawing of lots to determine which citizen of the village shall be stoned to death. There is no conflict—at least of the kind that occurs between tangible forces—no decision to be arrived at, no choice between two goods or two evils. There is no development of plot through human struggle and effort: the issue of life and death turns upon pure chance. The suspense secured is the simplest kind possible: which unlucky person will chance determine to be the victim?

Even this suspense is largely undercut by the fact that character interest in the story is also at a minimum. We are not brought close up to any of the characters. We learn little about their inner natures. There is nothing to distinguish them from ten thousand other people and indeed it becomes clear that they represent no more than the typical inhabitants of a New England village. The author seems deliberately to have played down any distinguishing traits. The victim herself, it is made very clear, is simply the typical small-town housewife.

Yet the story makes a very powerful impact, and the handling of plot and character must finally be judged, in terms of the story's development, to be very skillful. Obviously this story, unlike "The Man Who Would Be King," and "The Secret Life of Walter Mitty," has been sharply titled toward theme. The reaction of most readers, as a matter of fact, tends to center on this problem: what does the story—granted its power—mean? It is not really a story about the victim, Mrs. Hutchinson. It is not literally about life in an American village, since the events portrayed are fantastic events. What then is the story "about"?

Before trying to answer the question specifically, one ought to say that this story is a kind of *fable*. The general flatness of characterization—the fact that the characters are all simply variants of the ordinary human being, and the fantastic nature of the plot make this rather clear. The most famous early fables, Aesop's fables, for example, give us fantastic situations in which animals are actuated by human motivations, speak like human beings, and reveal themselves as rather transparent instances of certain human types. But Aesop's fables usually express a fairly explicit comment on life which can be expressed as a moral. For example, a popular translation of the fable of the fox and the grapes concludes with the moral tag: "It is easy to despise what you cannot get."

The family resemblance of **"The Lottery"** to the fable is concealed in part by the fact that **"The Lottery"** does not end with a neat moral tag and indeed avoids focusing upon a particular meaning. This latter point, however, we shall consider a little later.

The general pattern of this story may also be said to resemble that of the *parable*. In a parable the idea or truth is presented by a simple narrative in which the events, persons, and the like, of the narrative are understood as being directly equivalent to terms involved in the statement of the truth. For example, let us look at the parable of the sower, in the Gospel according to Saint Mark:

> Hearken; Behold, there went out a sower to sow:
>
> And it came to pass, as he sowed, some fell by the way side, and the fowls of the air came and devoured it up.

> And some fell on stony ground, where it had not much earth; and immediately it sprang up, because it had no depth of earth:
>
> But when the sun was up, it was scorched; and because it had no root, it withered away.
>
> And some fell among thorns, and the thorns grew up, and choked it, and it yielded no fruit.
>
> And other fell on good ground, and did yield fruit that sprang up and increased; and brought forth, some thirty, and some sixty, and some an hundred.

Later, Jesus explains and interprets the parable to his disciples:

> The sower soweth the word.
>
> And these are they by the way side, where the word is sown; but when they have heard, Satan cometh immediately, and taketh away the word that was sown in their hearts.
>
> And these are they likewise which are sown on stony ground; who, when they have heard the word, immediately receive it with gladness;
>
> And have no root in themselves, and so endure but for a time: afterward, when affliction or persecution ariseth for the word's sake, immediately they are offended.
>
> And these are they which are sown among thorns: such as heat the word.
>
> And the cares of this world, and the deceitfulness of riches, and the lusts of other things entering in, choke the word, and it becometh unfruitful.
>
> And these are they which are sown on good ground; such as hear the word, and receive it, and bring forth fruit, some thirtyfold, some sixty, and some an hundred.

In a parable, it is plain, characterization is reduced to a minimum: the *sower* is any sower. And the action is reduced to a minimum too. We need only so much of narrative as will make the point that the speaker wishes to make. But if **"The Lottery"** in its relative thinness of characterization and its relative simplicity of narration resembles the parable, it is obviously not a naked parable. The author has taken pains to supply a great deal of concrete detail to make us "believe" in her village, in its goings on this morning of June 27th. It is also obvious that she has preferred to give no key to her parable but to leave its meaning to our inference. One may summarize by saying that **"The Lottery"** is a normal piece of fiction, even if tilted over toward the fable and the parable form. Yet the comparison with these two forms may be useful in indicating the nature of the story.

What of its meaning? We had best not try to restrict the meaning to some simple dogmatic statement. The author herself has been rather careful to allow a good deal of flexibility in our interpretation of the meaning. Yet surely a general meaning does emerge. This story comments upon the all-too-human tendency to seize upon a scapegoat and to visit upon the scapegoat the cruelties that most of us seem to have dammed up within us. An example out of our own time might be the case in which some sensational happening occurs in a family—a child is kidnapped, or a youthful member of the family is implicated in a weird crime. The newspapers sometimes hound the family past all decency, and we good citizens, who support those newspapers, batten upon their misery with a cruelty that would shock us if we ever could realize what we were doing. Or to take another case, a man's patriotism is impugned quite falsely; or, whether the charge against him is false or true, let us say that his wife is completely guiltless. Yet she is "stoned" by her self-righteous neighbors who are acting, of course, out of pure virtue and fervent patriotism. These two instances are merely suggestive. Neither would answer fully to the terms of the story, but they may indicate that the issues with which the story is concerned are thoroughly live issues in our time.

But the author has been wise not to confine the meaning to any precise happening of the sort we have suggested. For evidently she is concerned with the more general psychological basis for such cruelty as a community tends to manifest. **"The Lottery"** makes such points as these: the cruel stoning is carried out by "decent" citizens who in many other respects show themselves kind and thoughtful. The cruel act is kept from seeming the cruel thing it is by the fact that it has been sanctioned by custom and long tradition. When Mrs. Adams remarks that "Some places have already quit lotteries," Old Man Warner says, "Nothing but trouble in *that*. Pack of young fools." A further point is this: human beings find it difficult to become exercised over ills not their own. Once a family group sees that the victim is not to be selected from among themselves, they proceed to observe matters with a certain callous disinterest. Moreover, even the individual members of the Hutchinson family are themselves relatively unconcerned once each discovers that he is not the victim chosen. Thus, "Nancy and Bill, Jr., opened theirs at the same time, and both beamed and laughed, turning round to the crowd and holding their slips of paper above their heads." The French moralist Rochefoucald ruefully observed that we obtain a certain pleasure from news of misfortune to friends. There is truth in this, and our story savagely makes a related point. Only the victim protests "It isn't fair," and she makes her protest only after she has chosen a slip of paper marked with the black spot. We remember that earlier Mrs. Hutchinson had said to Mrs. Delacroix in neighborly good humor, "Clean forgot what day it was," and both had "laughed softly" together.

"The Lottery," then, deals indeed with live issues and issues relevant to our time. If we hesitate to specify a particular "point" that the story makes, it is not because the story is vague and fuzzy, but rather because its web of observations about human nature is too subtle and too complex to be stated in one or two brief maxims.

What requires a little further attention is a problem of a quite different sort: how does this story differ from a tract or a treatise on human nature? Are we actually justified in calling it a piece of fiction?

An answer to these questions might run like this: This is obviously not a tract or merely an essay. The village is

made to exist for us; the characters of Old Man Warner and Mr. Summers and Mrs. Hutchinson do come alive. They are not fully developed, to be sure, and there is a sense in which even the personality of the victim is finally subservient to the "point" to be made and is not developed in its own right and for its own sake. But, as we have said, this is not a "naked parable"—and the fact that we get an impression of a real village and real people gives the sense of grim terror.

The fictional form thus justifies itself by making vivid and forceful what would otherwise have to be given prosaically and undramatically. But it does something else that is very important: it provides a special shaping of the reader's attitude toward the climactic event and toward that from which the climactic event stems. The reader's attitude has been moulded very carefully from the very beginning. Everything in the story has been devised to let us know how we are to "take" the final events in the story. . . .

The very fact that an innocent woman is going to be stoned to death by her friends and neighbors and that this is to happen in an American small town during our own present day of enlightenment requires a special preparation. The apparently fantastic nature of the happening means that everything else in the story must be made plausible, down-to-earth, sensible, commonplace, everyday. We must be made to feel that what is happening on this June morning is perfectly credible. Making it seem credible will do two things: it will increase the sense of shock when we suddenly discover what is really going on, but it will ultimately help us to believe that what the story asserts does come to pass. In general, then, the horror of the ending is counter-balanced by the dry, even cheery, atmosphere of the scene. This contrast between the matter-of-factness and the cheery atmosphere, on one side, and the grim terror, on the other, gives us a dramatic shock. But it also indicates that the author's point in general has to do with the awful doubleness of the human spirit—a doubleness that expresses itself in the blended good neighborliness and cruelty of the community's action. The fictional form, therefore, does not simply "dress up" a specific comment on human nature. The fictional form actually gives point and definition to the social commentary.

Shirley Jackson   (essay date 1968)

SOURCE: "On the Morning of June 28, 1948, and 'The Lottery,' " in *The Story and Its Writer: An Introduction to Short Story Fiction*, edited by Ann Charters, St. Martin's Press, 1983, pp. 1192-95.

[*In the following edited version of a lecture on "The Lottery" that Jackson originally delivered in 1960 and published in* Come Along with Me *in 1968, she discusses public reaction to the story.*]

On the morning of June 28, 1948, I walked down to the post office in our little Vermont town to pick up the mail. I was quite casual about it, as I recall—I opened the box, took out a couple of bills and a letter or two, talked to the postmaster for a few minutes, and left, never supposing that it was the last time for months that I was to pick up the mail without an active feeling of panic. By the next week I had had to change my mailbox to the largest one in the post office, and casual conversation with the postmaster was out of the question, because he wasn't speaking to me. June 28, 1948, was the day *The New Yorker* came out with a story of mine in it. It was not my first published story, nor my last, but I have been assured over and over that if it had been the only story I ever wrote or published, there would be people who would not forget my name.

I had written the story three weeks before, on a bright June morning when summer seemed to have come at last, with blue skies and warm sun and no heavenly signs to warn me that my morning's work was anything but just another story. The idea had come to me while I was pushing my daughter up the hill in her stroller—it was, as I say, a warm morning, and the hill was steep, and beside my daughter the stroller held the day's groceries—and perhaps the effort of that last fifty yards up the hill put an edge to the story; at any rate, I had the idea fairly clearly in my mind when I put my daughter in her playpen and the frozen vegetables in the refrigerator, and, writing the story, I found that it went quickly and easily, moving from beginning to end without pause. As a matter of fact, when I read it over later I decided that except for one or two minor corrections, it needed no changes, and the story I finally typed up and sent off to my agent the next day was almost word for word the original draft. This, as any writer of stories can tell you, is not a usual thing. All I know is that when I came to read the story over I felt strongly that I didn't want to fuss with it. I didn't think it was perfect, but I didn't want to fuss with it. It was, I thought, a serious, straightforward story, and I was pleased and a little surprised at the ease with which it had been written; I was reasonably proud of it, and hoped that my agent would sell it to some magazine and I would have the gratification of seeing it in print.

My agent did not care for the story, but—as she said in her note at the time—her job was to sell it, not to like it. She sent it at once to *The New Yorker,* and about a week after the story had been written I received a telephone call from the fiction editor of *The New Yorker;* it was quite clear that he did not really care for the story, either, but *The New Yorker* was going to buy it. He asked for one change—that date mentioned in the story be changed to coincide with the date of the issue of the magazine in which the story would appear, and I said of course. He then asked, hesitantly, if I had any particular interpretation of my own for the story; Mr. Harold Ross, then the editor of *The New Yorker,* was not altogether sure that he understood the story, and wondered if I cared to enlarge upon its meaning. I said no. Mr. Ross, he said, thought that the story might be puzzling to some people, and in case anyone telephoned the magazine, as sometimes happened, or wrote in asking about the story, was there anything in particular I wanted them to say? No, I said, nothing in particular; it was just a story I wrote.

I had no more preparation than that. I went on picking up the mail every morning, pushing my daughter up and down the hill in her stroller, anticipating pleasurably the check from *The New Yorker,* and shopping for groceries.

The weather stayed nice and it looked as though it was going to be a good summer. Then, on June 28, *The New Yorker* came out with my story.

Things began mildly enough with a note from a friend at *The New Yorker:* "Your story has kicked up quite a fuss around the office," he wrote. I was flattered; it's nice to think that your friends notice what you write. Later that day there was a call from one of the magazine's editors; they had had a couple of people phone in about my story, he said, and was there anything I particularly wanted him to say if there were any more calls? No, I said, nothing particular; anything he chose to say was perfectly all right with me; it was just a story.

I was further puzzled by a cryptic note from another friend: "Heard a man talking about a story of yours on the bus this morning," she wrote. "Very exciting. I wanted to tell him I knew the author, but after I heard what he was saying I decided I'd better not."

One of the most terrifying aspects of publishing stories and books is the realization that they are going to be read, and read by strangers. I had never fully realized this before, although I had of course in my imagination dwelt lovingly upon the thought of the millions and millions of people who were going to be uplifted and enriched and delighted by the stories I wrote. It had simply never occurred to me that these millions and millions of people might be so far from being uplifted that they would sit down and write me letters I was downright scared to open; of the three-hundred-odd letters that I received that summer I can count only thirteen that spoke kindly to me, and they were mostly from friends. Even my mother scolded me: "Dad and I did not care at all for your story in *The New Yorker,*" she wrote sternly; "it does seem, dear, that this gloomy kind of story is what all you young people think about these days. Why don't you write something to cheer people up?"

By mid-July I had begun to perceive that I was very lucky indeed to be safely in Vermont, where no one in our small town had ever heard of *The New Yorker,* much less read my story. Millions of people, and my mother, had taken a pronounced dislike to me.

The magazine kept no track of telephone calls, but all letters addressed to me care of the magazine were forwarded directly to me for answering, and all letter addressed to the magazine—some of them addressed to Harold Ross personally; these were the most vehement—were answered at the magazine and then the letters were sent me in great batches, along with carbons of the answers written at the magazine. I have all the letters still, and if they could be considered to give any accurate cross section of the reading public, or the reading public of *The New Yorker,* or even the reading public of one issue of *The New Yorker,* I would stop writing now.

Judging from these letters, people who read stories are gullible, rude, frequently illiterate, and horribly afraid of being laughed at. Many of the writers were positive that *The New Yorker* was going to ridicule them in print, and the most cautious letters were headed, in capital letters: NOT FOR PUBLICATION or PLEASE DO NOT

PRINT THIS LETTER, or, at best THIS LETTER MAY BE PUBLISHED AT YOUR USUAL RATES OF PAYMENT. Anonymous letters, of which there were a few, were destroyed. *The New Yorker* never published any comment of any kind about the story in the magazine, but did issue one publicity release saying that the story had received more mail than any piece of fiction they had ever published; this was after the newspapers had gotten into the act, in midsummer, with a front-page story in the San Francisco *Chronicle* begging to know what the story meant, and a series of columns in New York and Chicago papers pointing out that *New Yorker* subscriptions were being canceled right and left.

Curiously, there are three main themes which dominate the letters of that first summer—three themes which might be identified as bewilderment, speculation, and plain old-fashioned abuse. In the years since then, during which the story has been anthologized, dramatized, televised, and even—in one completely mystifying transformation—made into a ballet, the tenor of letters I receive has changed. I am addressed more politely, as a rule, and the letters largely confine themselves to questions like what does this story mean? The general tone of the early letters, however, was a kind of wide-eyed, shocked innocence. People at first were not so much concerned with what the story meant; what they wanted to know was where these lotteries were held, and whether they could go there and watch.

Helen E. Nebeker　(essay date March 1974)

SOURCE: " 'The Lottery': Symbolic Tour de Force," in *American Literature,* Vol. 46, No. 1, March, 1974, pp. 100-07.

[*In the following essay, Nebeker discusses the underlying themes in "The Lottery," focusing on the religious symbolism and anthropological elements of the story.*]

Numerous critics have carefully discussed Shirley Jackson's **"The Lottery"** in terms of the scapegoat traditions of anthropology and literature, pointing out its obvious comment on the innate savagery of man lurking beneath his civilized trappings. Most acknowledge the power of the story, admitting that the psychological shock of the ritual murder in an atmosphere of modern, small-town normality cannot be easily forgotten. Nevertheless, beneath the praise of these critics frequently runs a current of uneasiness, a sense of having been defrauded in some way by the development of the story as a whole.

Virgil Scott [in *Studies in Short Story,* 1968], for example, writes that " . . . the story leaves one uneasy because of the author's use of incidental symbolism. . . . the black box, the forgotten tuneless chant, the ritual salute— indeed the entire reconstruction of the mechanics of the lottery—fail to serve the story as they might have." Robert Heilman [in *Modern Short Stories: A Critical Anthology,* 1959] discovers similar technical difficulties. While approving the "deadpan narrative style" which screens us from the "horrifying nightmare" to come, he nevertheless believes that the unexpected shock of the ending "crowds out" the impact of Jackson's thematic revelation. He sug-

gests that the "symbolic intention" should be evidenced earlier in the story because, while "to set us immediately on the track of the symbolism" might reduce the shock, it might, on the other hand, "result in a more durable story." [Cleanth] Brooks and [Robert Penn] Warren praise the story for its "web of observations about human nature" and the "all-too-human tendency to seize upon a scapegoat," visiting upon it "cruelties that most of us seem to have dammed up within us." But then they indicate structural weakness by asserting that Jackson has "preferred to give no key to her parable but to leave its meaning to our inference," allowing "a good deal of flexibility in our interpretation," while yet insisting that "everything in the story has been devised to let us know how we are to 'take' the final events in the story" [*Understanding Fiction,* 1959].

Perhaps the critical ambivalence illustrated above stems from failure to perceive that **"The Lottery"** really fuses two stories and themes into one fictional vehicle. The overt, easily discovered story appears in the literal facts, wherein members of a small rural town meet to determine by lot who will be the victim of the yearly savagery. At this level one feels the horror, senses clearly the "dichotomy in all human nature," the "doubleness of the human spirit" [*Understanding Fiction*], and recoils in horror. This narrative level produces immediate emotional impact. Only after that initial shock do disturbing questions and nuances begin to assert themselves.

It is at this secondary point that the reader begins to suspect that a second story lies beneath the first and that Miss Jackson's "symbolic intentions" are not "incidental" but, indeed, paramount. Then one discovers that the author's careful structure and consistent symbolism work to present not only a symbolic summary of man's past but a prognosis for his future which is far more devastating than the mere reminder that man has savage potential. Ultimately one finds that the ritual of the lottery, beyond providing a channel to release repressed cruelties, actually serves to *generate* a cruelty not rooted in man's inherent emotional needs at all. Man is not at the mercy of a murky, savage id; he is the victim of unexamined and unchanging traditions which he could easily change if he only realized their implications. Herein is horror.

The symbolic overtones which develop in this second, sub rosa story become evident as early as the fourth word of the story when the date of June 27th alerts us to the season of the summer solstice with all its overtones of ancient ritual. Carefully the scene is set—the date, the air of festivity, release, even license. The children newly freed from school play boisterously, rolling in the dust. But, ominously, Bobby Martin has already stuffed his pockets with stones and Harry Jones and Dickie Delacroix follow his example, eventually making a great pile of stones in the corner which they guard from the raids of other boys. By the end of just two paragraphs, Jackson has carefully indicated the season, time of ancient excess and sacrifice, and the stones, most ancient of sacrificial weapons. She has also hinted at larger meanings through name symbology. "Martin," Bobby's surname, derives from a Middle English word signifying ape or monkey. This, juxtaposed with "Harry

Jones" (in all its commonness) and "Dickie Delacroix" (of-the-Cross) urges us to an awareness of the Hairy Ape within us all, veneered by a Christianity as perverted as "Delacroix," vulgarized to "Dellacroy" by the villagers. Horribly, at the end of the story, it will be Mrs. Delacroix, warm and friendly in her natural state, who will select a stone "so large she had to pick it up with both hands" and will encourage her friends to follow suit. Should this name symbology seem strained, superimposed, a little later we shall return to it and discover that every major name in the story has its special significance.

Returning to the chronology of the story, the reader sees the men gather, talking of the planting and rain (the central issues of the ancient propitiatory rites), tractors and taxes (those modern additions to the concerns of man). The men are quieter, more aware, and the patriarchal order (the oldest social group of man) is quickly evidenced as the women join their husbands and call their children to them. When Bobby Martin tries to leave the group and runs laughing to the stones, he is sharply rebuked by his serious father, who knows that this is no game. Clearly this is more than the surface "idyllic" small-town life noted by Heilman [in *Modern Short Stories*], the symbolic undercurrents prepare us to be drawn step by step toward the ultimate horror, where everything will fuse.

In the fourth paragraph, Mr. Summers, who ironically runs the "coal" business, arrives with the postmaster, Mr. Graves, who carries the three-legged stool and the black box. Although critics have tended to see the box as the major symbol, careful reading discloses that, while the box is referred to three times in this paragraph, the stool is emphasized four times and in such strained repetition as to be particularly obvious. Further, in the next two paragraphs it will be stressed that the box rests upon, is supported by, the *three-legged stool*. It would thus seem that the stool is at least as important as the box: in my opinion, it is the symbol which holds the key to Jackson's conclusive theme. In the interest of structure and coherence, this point must be developed later in the article.

Returning to the symbol of the box, its prehistoric origin is revealed in the mention of the "original wood color" showing along one side as well as in the belief that it has been constructed by the first people who settled down to make villages here (man in his original social group). The chips of wood, now discarded for slips of paper, suggest a preliterate origin. The present box has been made from pieces of the original (as though it were salvaged somehow) and is now blackened, faded, and stained (with blood perhaps). In this box symbol, Jackson certainly suggests the body of tradition—once oral but now written—which the dead hand of the past codified in religion, mores, government, and the rest of culture, and passed from generation to generation, letting it grow ever more cumbersome, meaningless, and indefensible.

Jackson does not, however, attack ritual in and of itself. She implies that, as any anthropologist knows, ritual in its origin is integral to man's concept of his universe, that it is rooted in his need to explain, even to control the forces around him. Thus, at one time the ritual, the chant, the dance were executed precisely, with deep symbolic mean-

ing. Those chosen for sacrifice were not victims but saviors who would propitiate the gods, enticing them to bring rebirth, renewal, and thanking them with their blood. This idea explains the significance of Mrs. Delacroix's comment to Mrs. Graves that " 'there's no time at all between lotteries any more' " and her reply that " 'Time sure goes fast.' " To the ancients, the ritual was a highly significant time marker: summer solstice and winter solstice, light versus dark, life versus death. These modern women only verify the meaninglessness of the present rite. Later, in a similar vein, when one of the girls whispers, " 'I hope it's not Nancy,' " Mr. Warner replies, " 'People ain't the way they used to be,' " implying that, anciently, honor and envy were accorded those chosen to die for the common welfare. Another neat symbolic touch tied to the meaningful ritualistic slaughter of the past is suggested by the character Clyde Dunbar. He lies at home, unable to participate in this year's lottery because of his broken leg. This reminds us that in every tradition of propitiation the purity and wholeness of the sacrifice was imperative. This "unblemished lamb" concept is epitomized in the sacrifice of Christ. In view of the interweaving of these ideas, it is difficult to see only "incidental symbolism" or to overlook the immediate and consistent "symbolic intention" of the narrative.

From the symbolic development of the box, the story moves swiftly to climax. Tessie Hutchinson hurries in, having almost forgotten the lottery in her round of normal, housewifely duties. She greets Mrs. Delacroix and moves good-humoredly into the crowd. Summers consults his list, discovers that Clyde Dunbar is missing and asks who will draw for him. When Janey Dunbar replies, " 'Me, I guess,' " Summers asks, " 'Don't you have a grown boy to do it for you Janey?' *although Mr. Summers and everyone else in the village knew the answer perfectly well*" (italics added). In this seemingly innocent exchange the reader is jarred into a suspicion that the mentioned "grown boy" has been a previous victim and that his father cannot face the strain of being present, raising the question whether the breaking of his leg has been accidental or deliberate. At any rate, this loss of a son will explain the unusual encouragement given Janey by the women as she goes to draw her slip of paper, her great anxiety as she awaits results with her remaining two sons—" 'I wish they'd hurry. . . . I wish they'd hurry' "—and her sending her older son with the news to her husband who, we may surmise, waits in agony for the outcome.

Significantly, the name Dunbar may in itself suggest that thin gray line which separates those who have been personally marked by the horror of the lottery from those who have not. If this seems to be flagrant symbol hunting, we might remember that it is Mrs. Dunbar who, at the time of the stoning, holds back as Mrs. Delacroix urges her to action. Mrs. Dunbar, with only small stones in her hands, gasping for breath, says, " 'I can't run at all. You'll have to go ahead and I'll catch up.' " But we may believe that she will not. Marked by the loss of her son, she may still be a victim but she will not be a perpetrator. Herein lies the only humane hope raised in the story.

Next, because of the sequence of details, we are brought

to consider that Jack Watson is another villager touched personally by the lottery. Immediately after querying Mrs. Dunbar and making a note on his list, Mr. Summers asks, " 'Watson boy drawing this year?' " Note that the name Watson does not immediately succeed Dunbar; there seems to be a special quality about those whose names are checked previous to the actual lottery when the names will be called from A to Z. When Jack replies, " 'Here . . . I'm drawing for m'mother and me,' " blinking nervously and ducking his head, the crowd responds with " 'Good fellow, Jack,' " and " 'Glad to see your mother's got a man to do it,' " encouraging him excessively as they do Mrs. Dunbar. Later, after the drawing, they will specifically ask, " 'Is it the Dunbars?' " " 'Is it the Watsons?' " Surely, at least the elder Watson—and maybe others in the family—has been a previous victim of the rite.

Now the symbolic names crowd upon us: "Old Man Warner," prototype of the prophet of doom, voice of the past, foe of change, existing from everlasting to everlasting; Old Man Warner, seventy-seven (ancient magic number of indefiniteness) years old, the oldest of them all, juxtaposed with Jack Watson, the youngest patriarch, both part of the same unchanging horror. "Steve Adams"—Adam the father of the race and Stephen the first Christian martyr. "Baxter" [Richard Baxter, 17th-century English Puritan minister, who postulated the doctrine of free grace] Martin, the eldest brother of Bobby, again suggesting primitive origins changed only superficially by even the best thought of the centuries. Tessie Hutchinson, more subtle in reference but "Hutchinson" reminiscent of early American Puritan heritage, while "Tessie," diminutive for "Theresa," derives from the Greek *theizein* meaning "to reap," or, if the nickname is for "Anastasia" it will translate literally "of the resurrection." What deliberate symbolic irony that Tessie should be the victim, not of hatred or malice, or primitive fear, but of the primitive ritual itself.

Now, as Tessie stands at bay and the crowd is upon her, the symbols coalesce into full revelation. "Tessie Hutchinson," end product of two thousand years of Christian thought and ritual Catholic and Puritan merged, faces her fellow citizens, all equally victims and persecutors. Mrs. "Of-the-Cross" lifts her heavy stone in response to ritual long forgotten and perverted. "Old Man Warner" fans the coals (not fires) of emotions long sublimated ritualistically revived once a year. "Mr. Adams," at once progenitor and martyr in the Judeo-Christian myth of man, stands with "Mrs. Graves"—the ultimate refuge or escape of all mankind—in the forefront of the crowd.

Now we understand the significance of the three-legged stool—as old as the tripod of the Delphic oracle, as new as the Christian trinity. For that which supports the present day box of meaningless and perverted superstition is the body of unexamined tradition or at least six thousand years of man's history. Some of these traditions (one leg of the stool if you like), are as old as the memory of man and are symbolized by the season, the ritual, the original box, the wood chips, the names of Summers, Graves, Martin, Warner (all cultures have their priesthoods!). These original, even justifiable traditions gave way to or were absorbed by later Hebraic perversions; and the narrative pursues its "scapegoat" theme in terms of the stones, the wooden box, blackened and stained, Warner the Prophet, even the Judaic name of Tessie's son, David. Thus Hebraic tradition becomes a second leg or brace for the box.

Superimposed upon this remote body of tradition is one two thousand years old in its own right. But it may be supposed the most perverted and therefore least defensible of all as a tradition of supposedly enlightened man who has freed himself from the barbarities and superstitions of the past. This Christian tradition becomes the third support for the blood-stained box and all it represents. Most of the symbols of the other periods pertain here with the addition of Delacroix, Hutchinson, Baxter and Steve.

With this last symbolic intention clearly revealed, one may understand the deeper significance of Jackson's second, below-the-surface story. More than developing a theme which "deals with 'scapegoating', the human tendency to punish 'innocent' and often accidentally chosen victims for our sins" [Scott, *Studies in Short Story*] or one which points out "the awful doubleness of the human spirit—a doubleness that expresses itself in blended good neighborliness and cruelty . . ." [Brooks and Warren, *Understanding Fiction*], Shirley Jackson has raised these lesser themes to one encompassing a comprehensive, compassionate, and fearful understanding of man trapped in the web spun from his own need to explain and control the incomprehensible universe around him, a need no longer answered by the web of old traditions.

Man, she says, is a victim of his unexamined and hence unchanged traditions which engender in him flames otherwise banked, subdued. Until enough men are touched strongly enough by the horror of their ritualistic, irrational actions to reject the long-perverted ritual, to destroy the box completely—or to make, if necessary, a new one reflective of their own conditions and needs of life—man will never free himself from his primitive nature and is ultimately doomed. Miss Jackson does not offer us much hope—they only talk of giving up the lottery in the north village, the Dunbars and Watsons do not actually resist, and even little Davy Hutchinson holds a few pebbles in his hands.

Lenemaja Friedman (essay date 1975)

SOURCE: "The Short Stories," in *Shirley Jackson,* Twayne Publishers, 1975, pp. 44-77.

[*Friedman is an English professor and critic. In the following excerpt, she briefly discusses the publication history of "The Lottery" and examines the story's theme of social evil.*]

One of the ancient practices that modern man deplores as inhumanly evil is the annual sacrifice of a scapegoat or a god-figure for the benefit of the community. Throughout the ages, from ancient Rome and Greece to the more recent occurrences in African countries, sacrifices in the name of a god of vegetation were usual and necessary, the natives felt, for a fertile crop. Somewhere along the way, the sacrifice of a human for the sins of the people—to drive evil from themselves—became linked with the ritual of the vegetation god. In Mexico, among the Aztecs, the victims impersonated the particular gods for a one-year period before being put to death; death came then by the thrust of a knife into the breast and the immediate extraction of the heart. In Athens, each year in May, at the festival of the Thargelia, two victims, a man and a woman, were led out of the city and stoned to death. Death by stoning was one of the accepted and more popular methods of dispatching ceremonial victims.

But modern man considers such practices barbaric and, therefore, alien to his civilized behavior. For this reason, many persons were puzzled and shocked by **"The Lottery."** After its appearance in the June 28, 1948, issue of *The New Yorker,* a flood of mail—hundreds of letters—deluged both the editorial offices in New York and the post office in Bennington. No *New Yorker* story had ever received such a response. Of the many letters received, as Miss Jackson recalled, only thirteen spoke kindly to her; and those were from friends. Three main characteristics dominated the letters: bewilderment, speculation, and old-fashioned abuse. "The general tone of the early letters was a kind of wide-eyed shocked innocence. People at first were not so much concerned with what the story meant: what they wanted to know was where these lotteries were held, and whether they could go there and watch" [undated letter of Shirley Jackson to her mother]. Later, after the story had been anthologized, televised, and dramatized, the tone of the letters became more polite; but people still wondered what the story meant.

She had conceived the story idea, she said, on a fine June morning as she was returning from a trip to the grocery store and was pushing uphill the stroller containing her daughter and the day's groceries. Having the idea well in mind, she wrote the story so easily that the finished copy was almost the same word for word as the rough draft. Her agent, she recalls, did not care for the story; nor was the fiction editor of *The New Yorker* particularly impressed; however, the magazine was going to buy it. When Mr. Harold Ross, then editor of the magazine, indicated that the story might be puzzling to some people and asked if she would care to enlarge upon its meaning, she refused. But later, in response to numerous requests, she made the following statement, which appeared in the July 22 issue of the *San Francisco Chronicle:* "Explaining just what I had hoped the story to say is very difficult. I suppose, I hoped, by setting a particularly brutal ancient rite in the present and in my own village to shock the story's readers with a graphic dramatization of the pointless violence and general inhumanity in their own lives."

Several of Miss Jackson's friends had intimated that the village characters were modeled after actual persons in Bennington; but, if so, she took pains to disguise the fact. The names are plain, solid-sounding: Adams, Warner, Dunbar, Martin, Hutchinson, etc. The name Mr. Summers is particularly suitable for sunny, jovial Joe Summers; it emphasizes the surface tone of the piece and underscores the ultimate irony. Mr. Graves—the postmaster and the assistant to Mr. Summers in the administration of the lottery—has a name that might well signify the tragic undercurrent, which does not become meaningful until the end of the story. As in the other stories designating the presence of evil even in the least likely persons, such as in sweet old ladies, the reader discovers the blight in this deceptively pleasant community. In fact, much of the horror stems from the discrepancy between the normal outward appearance of the village life and its people and the heinous act these people commit in the guise of tradition.

The story begins with a fine sunny morning, June 27 (the fiction editor had asked for a change in date, to coincide with this particular edition of *The New Yorker*). At first, the village appears to have a holiday atmosphere; and the reader's expectations are that the lottery is a joyous occasion, ending with a happy surprise for some lucky individual. The whole lottery, one is told, takes less than two hours, so that, if it begins at ten o'clock, the villagers will be home in time for noon dinner. Not until the truth of the lottery is revealed can the reader appreciate the chilling callousness of this business-as-usual attitude on the part of the community and the willingness of the people to accept and dismiss torture-death as a common occurrence. The gathering of the stones in one corner of the square is the part of the ceremony performed by the schoolchildren during their "boisterous play." The children, too, are guilty; they show no sensitivity or emotion about the coming event. Miss Jackson's matter-of-fact description is allied to the attitude of the townspeople, and this objectivity sustains the suspense and heightens the shock of the ending.

As the men congregate, they talk of "planting and rain, tractors and taxes." The women exchange bits of gossip. One notices the first bit of tension when the families gather together; the women, standing by their husbands, call to their children. Mr. Martin speaks sharply to Bobby when the boy runs back to the pile of stones, and Bobby comes quickly. As the black box is set down, the villagers keep their distance, leaving a space between themselves and the stool; and there is hesitation at Mr. Summers's call for assistance. But Miss Jackson so skillfully weaves the tension of the present with description of the past and with the history of the black box that the reader is kept carefully unaware of anything more than what, he supposes, is the normal excitement of the occasion.

Jovial Mr. Summers who, it would seem, is the epitome of civic duty, conducts the lotteries, as he also conducts the square dances, the teen-age club, and the Halloween program. The incongruity of the purpose and the seriousness of these four activities is ironic and testifies to the guilt in Mr. Summers's soul, for he is a willing leader and thus a perpetrator of the evil. His conscience is as blank as the—all but one—little slips in the little black box. He does not recognize evil or, perhaps, know right from wrong. He does not question the tradition of the lottery; instead, his token civic improvements call not for elimination of the lottery but for the substitution of slips of paper for chips of wood—for convenience and expediency.

Mr. Summers's cheerful mien belies the seriousness of the occasion. When Tessie has been chosen, and the fatal moment has come, it is Mr. Summers who says, "All right, folks. . . . Let's finish quickly." He shows no hesitation and no compassion. Because of his position in the community, he is the one who might successfully repudiate tradition; but he is representative of conservative elements who, though outwardly progressive, are content to retain existing though harmful customs. He is aware of the changing conditions in other villages; for, as Mr. and Mrs. Adams point out, some villages have already "quit lotteries." The Adamses are among the few progressive people who question the tradition and who implicitly suggest action, but their convictions are not strong; worse, they go along with the majority. Indeed, when the mob is upon Tessie, the hypocritical Steve Adams, ready to kill, is at the front of the group.

Old Man Warner, who miraculously has survived seventy-seven lotteries, is a frightening individual because, still completely superstitious, he wholeheartedly believes in the lottery and is convinced that the ritual is necessary for the welfare of the corn crop. He resents the amiable spirit and the jokes of Mr. Summers ("Bad enough to see young Joe Summers up there joking with everybody"), for he senses the seriousness of the occasion and the necessity of preserving the religiosity of the ceremony. It is not the death of the victim that disturbs him but the possible consequences of an irreligious attitude on the part of the participants. To Mr. Adams, he repeats the old saw: "Lottery in June, corn be heavy soon." Then he adds, after the comment on stopping the lottery, "First thing you know, we'd all be eating stewed chickweed and acorns"—if the lottery were to be abandoned, the crops would be destroyed and man would soon be foraging for food as he did in his cave-dwelling days. He does not want to go back to living in a cave, although in terms of civilization and humanity, he has never emerged from one, "There's *always* been a lottery," he says, and that alone, he supposes, is reason enough to continue the practice.

Tessie Hutchinson shows both the evils and the weaknesses of mankind faced with immediate death. Her hypocrisy indicates that she would willingly take part in the stoning; but, when she is the chosen sacrifice, she protests the unfairness of the method; she is not willing to be a good sport about giving up her life. "Be a good sport, Tessie," Mrs. Delacroix calls; and Mrs. Graves says, "All of us took the same chance." Instead, Tessie reacts like a frightened animal; but, unlike the animal-mother, the human mother does not always seek protection for her offspring. In fact, instead of giving her life for her children, Tessie prefers that they take their chances also—and she tries to have her daughter Eva and her husband [Bill] included in the fatal drawing to increase her own chances for survival. The most pathetic figure of all is little Davy Hutchinson who survives the drawing but who is then forced, unknowing, to take part in the ordeal. Someone gives him a few pebbles so that he, too, may share in the collective murder of his mother; and his silence in this terrible moment is much more chilling than any other response Miss Jackson could have chosen for him.

If anything is illogical about the total ritual, it may be the stoicism of the participants and their complete willingness to sacrifice themselves or members of their families. As not all individuals are equally willing and able to endure pain, much less death, it would seem likely that during lottery time whole families might take to the woods or migrate to other villages. Even the Aztec god-figures, celebrated and worshipped until the sacrifice day, had to be guarded against escape. If the victim escaped, the captain of the guards became the substitute. But, since such practices are not literally a part of our culture, one may say that the story proceeds by way of realism to grimly realistic fantasy. As such, the lottery may be symbolic of any of a number of social ills that mankind blindly perpetrates.

Barbara Allen   (essay date December 1980)

SOURCE: "A Folkloristic Look at Shirley Jackson's 'The Lottery,'" in *Tennessee Folklore Society Bulletin,* Vol. XLVI, No. 4, December, 1980, pp. 119-24.

[*In the following essay, Allen analyzes the elements of folklore and ritual in "The Lottery," contending that Jackson successfully uses them to reveal various kinds of social behavior.*]

Most studies of folklore in literature fall into one of two categories. Either they are concerned with identifying specific items of folklore in works of literature, or they attempt to interpret the use of folklore as integral to the meaning of particular literary creations. Historically, folklore-in-literature research has been oriented more toward identification than interpretation; as a result, the preponderance of studies of folklore in specific literary works has focused on the stylistic uses of folklore to set a mood, to delineate a character, or to provide "local color." In spite of repeated pleas for scholars to go beyond the identification of folklore in literature to the interpretation of its use and meaning, relatively little research has been undertaken on the structural or functional use of folklore as thematic content or integral plot elements. . . . Furthermore, folklorists offering interpretive analyses of folklore in literature have, by and large, followed standard models of literary exegesis. That is, they have not brought their specialized training to bear on problems of interpretation. Their failure to do so seems to stem from the lack of a theoretical base for the folkloristic interpretation of folklore in literature.

In ["The Study of Folklore in Literature: An Expanded View"] published in *Southern Folklore Quarterly* in 1976, Mary Ellen B. Lewis attempts to fill this void, by urging scholars to consider folklore in processual terms rather than as discrete items. Specifically, Lewis argued that folklore can be analyzed on the three levels of text, context, and texture, and, therefore, that folklore can be represented in literature not just on the textual level (that is, as an item), but on the levels of situation (context) and medium (texture) as well. While the scheme which Lewis presents is intended primarily to expand the bases for the identification of folklore in literary works, it also offers a key for putting the interpretation of folklore in literature on a solid theoretical basis. If, as Lewis and others before her have contended, folklore should be viewed as behavior, as dynamic process rather than static item, then the use of folklore in literature can be examined not as the incorporation of specific items into a novel or poem, but as the literary representation or characterization of certain kinds of behavior. Taking this approach eliminates the logical inconsistency of identifying as true "items of folklore" what are actually representations or characterizations of folklore—or, more accurately, of folkloric performance or behavior.

The premise that folklore in literature is a representation of behavior is implicit in most folklore-in-literature studies, but making the notion explicit can provide objective grounds for what have previously been intuitively-based observations. Recognizing folklore in literature as a characterization of behavior rather than the behavior (or its product) itself makes it easy to account for the appearance in literature of certain items which look or sound like "folklore" but which have no analogues in published folklore collections. A character citing a proverb or telling a tall tale in a novel or short story, for example, is being represented by the author as engaging in expressive (folkloric) behavior, whether or not the particular proverb or tale being quoted in the narrative has parallels in oral tradition or is the product of the author's creative imagination. Taking this stance means that, instead of going through the sterile exercise of identifying and annotating specific folkloric items, such as traditional proverbs or tale types, in literature, we can concentrate instead on the representation of storytelling, proverb use, and other folkloric activities in literary works. This shift from an orientation toward folklore as item to a consideration of folklore as behavior frees us from the limitations of simple identification and allows us to see how an author uses folklore to create literary meaning.

In their preoccupation with the identification of folklore items in literature, scholars have failed to see that the point of using folklore in a literary work depends on the reader recognizing it as folkloric behavior. In other words, it is types of (folkloric) behavior that are being exploited in literature, not specific items of folklore. If an author considers the use of proverbs to be a traditional means of conveying social wisdom and inculcating desirable attitudes, then characters can be represented as respected authorities by having them use proverbs in interaction with others. If, on the other hand, the use of proverbs is considered to be a substitute for original thinking, then a character can be depicted as unthinking or unimaginative by representing him or her as citing them constantly. The simple identification of folklore items does not provide any clue to the nature of the behavior being characterized; it is only by looking at an author's conception of what kind of behavior is being represented in various forms of folklore that we can begin to interpret how folklore is used in literature to create meaning.

To illustrate my argument with a specific example, I offer Shirley Jackson's short story **"The Lottery"** as a case in point. The discussion in the following pages shows how standard techniques for identifying folklore in this particular story yield only minimum interpretive results, and then demonstrates how an examination of Jackson's conception of the nature of the ritual she describes accounts more fully for her choice of that particular kind of behavior to carry the message of her story.

. . . . .

"The Lottery" is a fictional account of an annual midsummer ceremony in a contemporary community. The story opens with the residents of a village gathering for the yearly lottery, the nature of which is not disclosed. The procedures of the ceremony are performed matter-of-factly: the head of each family draws a slip of paper from an old black wooden box; then lots are drawn among the members of the family, the Hutchinsons, to whom the first lot has fallen. When the wife and mother, Tessie, draws the paper with a black spot on it, the villagers begin to pelt her with stones.

The lottery which Jackson describes in her story sounds like an atrophied form of a scapegoat ritual. Evidence to support this argument can be found by comparing details in the story with descriptions of such rituals in the Bible, Frazer's *Golden Bough,* and Theodor Gaster's *Thespis.* The term scapegoat derives from the ritual described in Leviticus 16:21-22:

> . . . and Aaron shall lay both hands upon the head of a live goat, and confess over him all the iniquities of the people of Israel, and all their transgressions, all their sins; and he shall put them on the head of the goat, and send him away into the wilderness . . . . The goat shall bear all their iniquities upon him to a solitary land.

A scapegoat is more broadly defined by Frazer as:

> . . . an animal or human being used in public ceremonies to remove the taint or impairment consequent upon sin which, for one reason or other, cannot be saddled upon a particular individual. Such a scapegoat is a means of "cleansing" a community of a collective stain which cannot be wiped out by the normal procedure of individual penitence, restitution, and reform. The execution or despatch of it is always and necessarily accompanied by a blanket public confession. [*Golden Bough*]

Frazer discusses four aspects of scapegoats and scapegoat rituals which are reflected in Jackson's story. First, the scapegoat provides a "visible and tangible vehicle for bearing away a community's invisible and intangible evils." Tessie Hutchinson, the victim in the lottery, fills this role for her village. Secondly, according to Frazer, "When a general clearance of evils is resorted to periodically, the interval between the celebrations of the ceremony is commonly a year, and the time of year when the ceremony takes place usually coincides with some well-marked change of season." In **"The Lottery,"** the ritual falls on June 27, a date which closely follows the summer solstice, traditionally a significant occasion for agrarian communities such as Jackson's village. Old Man Warner's proverb, "Lottery in June, corn be heavy soon," makes it clear that the ceremony is associated with the success of the year's crop and, by implication, with the community's continued existence. Thirdly, Frazer continues, "This public and periodic expulsion of devils is commonly preceded or followed by a period of general license, during which the ordinary restraints of society are thrown aside." [In *Thespis: Ritual, Myth, and Drama in the Ancient Near East,* 1950] Gaster adds that the Hebrew scapegoat ritual, associated with the harvest, was marked by a suspension of normal activities. In Jackson's story, the ceremonial license is represented both in the children's sense of their recently gained freedom from school for the summer and in the suspension of work both at home and in the fields during the period in which the lottery takes place. Finally, Frazer notes that the scapegoat victim is often believed to be divine. Scapegoat Tessie Hutchinson's divinity seems to lie in her having been chosen, through the agency of the lottery, by some supernatural force such as fate or providence.

The process of identifying folkloric elements in this particular short story is comparatively simple, for they can be traced fairly easily to the descriptions of scapegoat rituals in published sources. But this identification does not account for the *fictional* aspect of the ritual—the lottery which Jackson describes has never taken place in real time and space. But, by thinking of the lottery as the representation of a kind of behavior, rather than as the replication of an actual occurrence, it is easier to understand how Jackson and other writers "create" folklore in the speech or actions of their characters by drawing upon traditional models.

The ritual of the lottery, as Jackson depicts it, is clearly characterized as a survival, that is, as a model of behavior which has devolved or degenerated through time until it is virtually meaningless. Jackson consistently describes the event in devolutionary, survivalistic terms.

—*Barbara Allen*

A second, and perhaps more important, limitation of simply identifying folkloric elements in the story is that doing so does not explain *why* Jackson chose the material she did to carry the meaning of the story. By looking at the ritual she describes as a fictionalized characterization of behavior, however, we can see how her conception of the *nature* of that behavior and the attitude she takes toward it explain how the ritual of the lottery is an apt vehicle for the story's message.

The annual lottery, Jackson intimates, has lost all meaning for the villagers. What keeps its performance going year after year is the momentum of tradition, embodied in the character of Old Man Warner who denounces neighboring villages that have abandoned the lottery as a "pack of crazy fools." It is clear from Jackson's description that the ritual has degenerated over time, for people only vaguely remember that:

> . . . there had been a recital of some sort . . . , a perfunctory, tuneless chant that had been rattled off duly each year; some believed that the official of the lottery used to stand just so when he said or sang it, others believed that he was sup-

posed to walk among the people, but years and years ago this part of the ritual had been allowed to lapse. There had been also a ritual salute, which the official of the lottery had had to use in addressing each person who came up to draw from the box, but this also had changed with time, until now it was felt necessary only for the official to speak to each person approaching.

Even the original paraphernalia of the ritual have been lost and substitutions made:

> Because so much of the ritual had been forgotten or discarded, Mr. Summers [the lottery official] had been successful in having slips of paper substituted for the chips of wood that had been used for generations. . . . Mr. Summers spoke frequently to the villagers about making a new box, but no one liked to upset even as much tradition as was represented by the black box. There was a story that the present box had been made with some pieces of the box that had preceded it, the one that had been constructed when the first people settled down to make a village here. Every year, after the lottery, Mr. Summers began talking again about a new box, but every year the subject was allowed to fade off without anything's being done.

The ritual of the lottery, as Jackson depicts it in her story, is clearly characterized as a survival, that is, as a model of behavior which has devolved or degenerated through time until it is virtually meaningless. Jackson consistently describes the event in devolutionary, survivalistic terms. Some parts of the ritual have been forgotten, such as the public confession of sin, presumably the predecessor of the "tuneless chant" which the official of the lottery used to perform before the ceremony began. Other aspects of the ritual, particularly physical objects, have changed in form. Frazer describes the lots used in the Purim festival as small stones; it is not difficult to imagine the replacement of the original stones with chips of wood and finally with the slips of paper used by Jackson's villagers. Still other components of the ceremony have become trivialized: the general feeling of license formerly enjoyed by the entire community is now relegated to the children; the suspension of normal activities has been abrogated to the two hours which it takes to accomplish the drawing of the lots.

In spite of the reduction of the lottery to empty ritual, the villagers cling tenaciously to it; thus, the lottery's continued existence, as presented in the story, is predicated on the idea that forms of behavior can persist through time even when their original meanings have been forgotten. Not only does our identification of the ceremony as a scapegoat ritual depend on this premise, but our recognition that the ritual is represented as a survival is crucial to an understanding of the story. The point of **"The Lottery"** is that blind adherence to traditional forms of behavior that have lost their original meanings and acquired no new, positive ones, can be destructive. This interpretation is not new, but in the past it seems to have been derived from implicit recognition of Jackson's conception of the behavior she describes as a survival and of the negative attitude she takes toward that behavior in this story. By making the recognition of Jackson's use of folkloric materials explicit, however, we can articulate how she uses those materials to create meaning in the story. By characterizing folklore as behavior and realizing that the use of folklore in literature is the representation of kinds of behavior, scholars can base their interpretations of folklore in literature on solid theoretical grounds rather than on intuitive feelings.

James M. Gibson   (essay date March 1984)

SOURCE: "An Old Testament Analogue for 'The Lottery,'" in *Journal of Modern Literature,* Vol. 11, No. 1, March, 1984, pp. 193-95.

[*In the following essay, Gibson identifies the similarities between the biblical story of Joshua 7:10-26 and "The Lottery," contending that while the biblical story emphasizes the supernatural triumph of good over evil, Jackson's story reveals a "chillingly impersonal world of gray amorality."*]

More than any other short story by Shirley Jackson, **"The Lottery"** has intrigued critics and provoked puzzled guesses about its enigmatic meaning. Seymour Lainoff early on invoked the "primitive annual scapegoat rite" discussed in Frazer's *The Golden Bough,* and Lenemaja Friedman [in her *Shirley Jackson,* 1975] more recently has compared the stoning of Tessie Hutchinson to the festival of the Thargelia in ancient Athens and to similar scapegoat rituals of the Aztecs in Mexico. Shyamal Bagchee [in his "Design of Darkness in Shirley Jackson's 'The Lottery,'" in *Notes on Contemporary Literature, IX,* December, 1979] has discovered the symbolism of "black magic and primitive pagan rituals" that expose the "hideous primitive faces" lurking under our "civilized modern masks," and Helen Nebeker [in "'The Lottery': Symbolic Tour de Force," *American Literature,* XLVI, 1974] has uncovered the triple symbolism of pagan ritual, Mosaic legalism, and Christian theology in the characters' names, the sacrifice, and the three-legged stool. Richard Williams [in "A Critique of the Sampling Plan Used in Shirley Jackson's 'The Lottery,'" *Journal of Modern Literature,* VII, 1979] has even produced a statistical analysis complete with equations and charts to determine the mathematical fairness of the lottery and ostensibly to support Tessie's objection that "It isn't fair, it isn't right." Shirley Jackson herself steadfastly refused to explain the story either to the editors of *The New Yorker* or to the writers of the 450 letters that overwhelmed her own post office and the editorial offices of *The New Yorker*—all demanding to know what the story meant. Maintaining that "it was just a story," Jackson commented only that the story came to her in an inspirational flash.

> The idea had come to me while I was pushing my daughter up the hill in her stroller—it was, as I say, a warm morning, and the hill was steep, and beside my daughter the stroller held the day's groceries—and perhaps the effort of that last fifty yards up the hill put an edge to the story; at any rate, I had the idea fairly clearly in my mind when I put my daughter in her playpen and the frozen vegetables in the refrigerator, and, writing the story, I found that it went quickly and easily, moving from beginning to

end without pause. [Shirley Jackson, **"Biography of a Story,"** in *Come Along With Me,* 1968]

Following Shirley Jackson's discreet silence, the search for pagan parallels and symbols both demonic and Christian has overlooked perhaps the closest analogue, if not the source, of **"The Lottery"**: an Old Testament story found in Joshua 7. Whether or not Jackson knew the story, she did not tell, but the parallels are there, and the contrasts point up nicely the sharp antithesis between the ironic mode of the modern story and the romance mode of its earlier counterpart. The story from the Book of Joshua recounts the abortive attack on Ai immediately following the spectacular and supernatural conquest of Jericho where Joshua had given the Israelites strict instructions to set fire to everything in the city except the silver and gold and vessels of copper and iron which were to be deposited in the tabernacle treasury. When some two or three thousand Israelites later attacked Ai, they were badly beaten, and Joshua threw dust on his head, lay on the ground before the Ark of the Lord, and lamented God's desertion of his people. The story then proceeds as follows:

> 10 And the Lord said unto Joshua, Get thee up; wherefore art thou thus fallen
>
> 11 upon thy face? Israel hath sinned; yea, they have even transgressed my covenant which I commanded them: yea, they have even taken of the devoted thing; and have also stolen, and dissembled also, and they have even put it
>
> 12 among their own stuff. Therefore the children of Israel cannot stand before their enemies, they turn their backs before their enemies, because they are become accursed: I will not be with you any more, except ye destroy the
>
> 13 devoted thing from among you. Up, sanctify the people, and say, Sanctify yourselves against to-morrow: for thus saith the Lord, the God of Israel, There is a devoted thing in the midst of thee, O Israel: thou canst not stand before
>
> 14 thine enemies, until ye take away the devoted thing from among you. In the morning therefore ye shall be brought near by your tribes: and it shall be, that the tribe which the Lord taketh shall come near by families; and the family which the Lord shall take shall come near by household; and the household
>
> 15 which the Lord shall take shall come near man by man. And it shall be, that he that is taken with the devoted thing shall be burnt with fire, he and all that he hath: because he hath transgressed the covenant of the Lord, and because he hath wrought folly in Israel.
>
> 16 So Joshua rose up early in the morning, and brought Israel near by their
>
> 17 tribes; and the tribe of Judah was taken: and he brought near the family of Judah; and he took the family of the Zerahites: and he brought near the family
>
> 18 of the Zerahites man by man; and Zabdi was taken: and he brought near his household man

by man; and Achan, the son of Carmi, the son of Zabdi, the

19 son of Zerah, of the tribe of Judah, was taken. And Joshua said unto Achan, My son, give, I pray thee, glory to the Lord, the God of Israel, and make confession unto him; and tell me now what thou hast done; hide it not from

20 me. And Achan answered Joshua, and said, Of a truth I have sinned against

21 the Lord, the God of Israel, and thus and thus have I done: when I saw among the spoil a goodly Babylonish mantle, and two hundred shekels of silver, and a wedge of gold of fifty shekels weight, then I coveted them, and took them; and, behold, they are hid in the earth in the midst of my tent, and the silver

22 under it. So Joshua sent messengers, and they ran unto the tent; and, behold, it

23 was hid in his tent, and the silver under it. And they took them from the midst of the tent, and brought them unto Joshua, and unto all the children of Israel;

24 and they laid them down before the Lord. And Joshua, and all Israel with him, took Achan the son of Zerah, and the silver, and the mantle, and wedge of gold, and his sons, and his daughters, and his oxen, and his asses, and his sheep, and his tent, and all that he had: and they brought them up unto the

25 valley of Achor [trouble]. And Joshua said, Why hast thou troubled us? the Lord shall trouble thee this day. And all Israel stoned him with stones; and

26 they burned them with fire, and stoned them with stones. And they raised over him a great heap of stones, unto this day; and the Lord turned from the fierceness of his anger. Wherefore the name of that place was called, The valley of Achor, unto this day. [Joshua 7: 10-26, *Holy Bible,* English Revised Version, 1885]

Although the lottery follows the same procedure in each story and the winner claims the same prize of death by stoning, the two stories do not affect the reader in the same way. Cruel as the punishment might be, the death of Achan does not grip one with the same nameless horror and dread provoked by the death of Tessie. The story world of the Book of Joshua is carefully ordered, and its moral laws are carefully defined. The reader, like the characters, knows the rules and the consequences of breaking them. The characters are sharply delineated in black and white to reinforce the clear demarcation between good and evil. The supernatural intervenes on the side of right and good in the conquest of Jericho immediately preceding the story and in the eventual destruction of Ai following this incident. More importantly, the beneficent supernatural

guides the lottery, giving instructions beforehand to Joshua and singling out the wrongdoer for his just punishment.

By contrast, the ironic story world of **"The Lottery"** is ruled by chance and caprice. The highest authority of the story world here is the lottery itself in which one's fate is sealed by chance irrespective of merit or demerit. Although Tessie vainly appeals to a higher law of fairness and right, the story world has no moral rules, for the lottery has rendered them meaningless. Instead of lining up clearly on the side of good or evil, the characters exist in a chillingly impersonal world of gray amorality. Mr. Summers performs equally well in organizing square dances and the teenage club or in presiding over the lottery. With equal enthusiasm Mrs. Delacroix exchanges neighborly chitchat with Tessie before the lottery and urges her neighbors to hurry with their stones after the lottery. Unlike the romance hero Joshua, who overcomes with the help of the supernatural, the ironic heroine Tessie is inferior to the laws of the story world and to the other characters. She is trapped in a predicament which she did not seek and from which she cannot escape. No beneficent supernatural exists in the ironic story world to rescue Tessie, and she suffers a punishment undeserved which can only be labeled senseless, meaningless, and capricious. With due allowance for archetypal displacement, then, the two stories follow the same plot, use the same plan for the lottery, and end with the same stoning for the winner; the major difference is that Jackson has shifted her story from the romance narrative mode of the Book of Joshua to the ironic mode of **"The Lottery."**

FURTHER READING

Criticism

Kosenko, Peter. "A Marxist/Feminist Reading of Shirley Jackson's 'The Lottery.' " *New Orleans Review* 12, No. 1 (Spring 1985): 27-32.

Investigates "The Lottery" from Marxist and feminist perspectives. This essay is included in *CLC*-60.

Oehlschlaeger, Fritz. "The Stoning of Mistress Hutchinson: Meaning and Context in 'The Lottery.' " *Essays in Literature* XV, No. 2 (Fall 1988): 259-65.

Examines the process of the lottery and argues that its "primary social consequence involves women turning over the control of their fertility to men." This excerpt is reprinted in *CLC*-60.

Williams, Richard H. "A Critique of the Sampling Plan Used in Shirley Jackson's 'The Lottery.' " *Journal of Modern Literature* 7, No. 3 (September 1979): 543-44.

Contends that there is "a flaw in the sampling plan used to select the victim" in "The Lottery." Williams also suggests "a more defensible plan."

Additional coverage of Jackson's life and career is contained in the following sources published by Gale Research: *Authors and Artists for Young Adults,* Vol. 9; *Concise Dictionary of American Literary Biography, 1941-1968; Contemporary Authors,* Vols. 1-4 (rev. ed.), 25-28 (rev. ed.); *Contemporary Authors New Revision Series,* Vol. 4; *Contemporary Literary Criticism,* Vols. 11, 60; *Dictionary of Literary Biography,* Vol. 6; *DISCovering Authors; Short Story Criticism,* Vol. 9; *Something about the Author,* Vol. 2; and *World Literature Criticism.*

Maurice Kenny

1929-

(Full name Maurice Francis Kenny) American poet, short story writer, editor, and playwright.

The following entry provides an overview of Kenny's career through 1994.

INTRODUCTION

Kenny has been a leading figure in the renaissance of Native American poetry since the 1970s. His works typically focus on the links between humanity and nature, the spiritual forces of renewal and creation, and prominent figures in the history of the Mohawk people. Although his works derive their subject matter primarily from Iroquois culture and traditions, he has also written knowledgeably and sympathetically about other Native American peoples; as Robert L. Berner has stated, "Maurice Kenny is perhaps the dean of American Indian poets."

Biographical Information

Kenny was born in Watertown, New York. When he was thirteen, his parents divorced, and he moved to New York City to live with his mother. Later, he returned to upstate New York to live with his father, who was of Mohawk descent. It was during this time that Kenny developed his ties to Iroquois culture. He attended Butler University, St. Lawrence University, and New York University, where he studied under Louise Bogan, whom Kenny has identified as a principal influence on his development as a poet. With her guidance, he published *Dead Letters Sent, and Other Poems* (1958), his first major collection of poetry. His epic poem *Blackrobe* (1982) was nominated for a Pulitzer Prize in 1982, as was *Between Two Rivers* (1987) in 1987. His collection *The Mama Poems* (1984) received the American Book Award of the Before Columbus Foundation in 1984. Kenny is the editor and publisher of the Strawberry Press and frequently travels to colleges and universities across the United States and Canada to give poetry readings.

Major Works

Kenny's works often draw on Iroquois traditions, and a recurring motif in his works is the strawberry, which possesses spiritual power in Mohawk culture. The poem "Wild Strawberry" and the short story "Yaikini," for instance, both depict the picking and eating of strawberries as sacred acts associated with growth and renewal. Many of the poems in *Dancing Back Strong the Nation* (1979) draw on the social dances and songs performed in the longhouse, the communal dwelling and center of social interaction for the Mohawk and other Native American peoples. Such poems as "Dance," "Drums," and "Mocca-

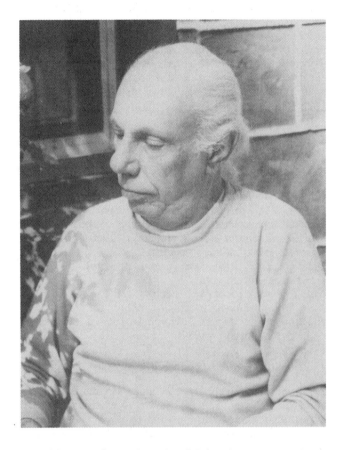

sin," for example, are based on Mohawk dance and drum rhythms and, like the songs, emphasize the ceremonial naming of objects as a means of locating the essence of their sacredness. Kenny has also written about historical confrontations between the Mohawk people and European missionaries and settlers. The epic poem *Blackrobe,* for example, centers on the brief career of Isaac Jogues, a Jesuit missionary whom the Mohawks killed in 1646, while the narrative poems in *Tekonwatonti/Molly Brant (1735-1795)* (1992) focus on the life of Molly Brant, a Mohawk woman who convinced the Mohawks to support the British during the French and Indian War and led the Mohawks in support of the British during the American Revolution. Kenny's works, however, are not limited to Mohawk history, culture, and concerns. The well-known poem "I Am the Sun," for instance, is based on a Lakota Ghost Dance song and was inspired by the armed confrontation between members of the American Indian Movement, U.S. federal marshals, and Federal Bureau of Investigation officers at Wounded Knee, South Dakota, in 1973. The short story "Rain," which concerns a Mohawk who travels with a Pueblo family to witness a rain dance in Santa Ana, New Mexico, similarly comments on questions of tribal identity and pan-Indianism.

Critical Reception

Praising Kenny's ability to depict a world in which humankind and nature are united, critics have noted his adept use of oral traditions, dance rhythms, and symbolic images from the longhouse to create a sense of community in his poetry. Commentators on his historical poems have additionally lauded his balanced treatment of European and Native American characters and articulate presentation of the Mohawk people's myth-oriented worldview. As Robert L. Berner has observed: "Kenny's most successful efforts derive from his greatest strength as a poet, his ability to let his themes emerge out of his Mohawk context."

PRINCIPAL WORKS

The Hopeless Kill   (poetry) 1956
Dead Letters Sent, and Other Poems (poetry) 1958
With Love to Lesbia: A Sheaf of Poems (poetry) 1958
And Grieve, Lesbia: Poems (poetry) 1960
North: Poems of Home (poetry) 1977
Dancing Back Strong the Nation (poetry) 1979; enlarged edition, 1981
Only as Far as Brooklyn (poetry) 1979
Kneading the Blood (poetry) 1981
Blackrobe: Isaac Jogues, b. March 11, 1607, d. October 18, 1646 (poetry) 1982
Boston Tea Party (poetry) 1982
The Smell of Slaughter (poetry) 1982
The Mama Poems (poetry) 1984
Is Summer This Bear (poetry and short stories) 1985
Rain, and Other Fictions (short stories and drama) 1985; enlarged edition, 1990
Between Two Rivers: Selected Poems 1956-1984 (poetry) 1987
Last Mornings in Brooklyn (poetry) 1991
Roman Nose, and Other Essays (essays) 1991
Tekonwatonti/Molly Brant *(1735-1795): Poems of War* (poetry) 1992

CRITICISM

Paula Gunn Allen (essay date 1978)

SOURCE: An introduction to *Dancing Back Strong the Nation: Poems* by Maurice Kenny, Blue Cloud Quarterly Press, 1979.

[*A Laguna Pueblo novelist, poet, nonfiction writer, educator, and critic, Allen edited* Studies in American Indian Literature: Critical Essays and Course Designs *(1983). In the essay below, which was originally written in 1978, she comments on the overall themes of* Dancing Back Strong the Nation, *noting that as a Native American poet, Kenny allows Native and non-Native readers to "discover what our*

common journey is about and to understand each step as within a totality."]

Poets are a unique breed of people, and Native American poets are, perhaps, even more so because of the nature of the modern Native American experience. Poets must say things that others might not allow themselves to think; they must transmute the ordinary into the extraordinary, and the extraordinary into the mundane. Poetry, that peculiar quirk of mind, requires that the hidden become clear while the evident sinks into obscurity. It is the poet's task to articulate the significance of human life by weaving discordant bits of life into meaningful patterns. The Native American poet, whose life is discordant at every level, faces the necessity of creating wholeness from a life that is biculturated—broken into pieces of the past and lumps of the fragmented present, and fuse them into coherence— make a meaningful rubric of beads and chrome, cities and wilderness, plants and machine, time immemorial and no-time-at-all. For the modern Native American lives a life in many worlds, and the Native American poet must make images and significances from these unfitting splinters— the Mohawk condemned to walk city streets, "Riding the sky on steel girders" reclaim tradition among the three or four who gather to enact ancient rites beneath the glare of electric bulb, feet moving in the ancient manner upon a linoleum floor, while the wild reservation fills with electrified HUD complexes and sixty-foot trailers.

Much is discordant; much jars the senses, refusing to make sense. But this is what the poet does—makes sense out of nonsense by fitting together bits of this and that experience into a form that articulates coherence in discordance, and discovers beauty and significance in apparent senselessness. By this process of making, we are allowed to discover what our common journey is about and to understand each step as within a totality.

Mr. Kenny's poetry allows us this discovery as he himself makes it: we understand that ache for what is lost, and that strength that comes when it is restored; alongside him, we walk each step back home, and we discover how it is that the past in its beauty of wilderness and warmth is part of this present, that it is quite possible for each of us to join in *Dancing Back Strong the Nation*. We are enabled to do this because he is compelled to, a half-breed has little choice, and a half-breed poet ultimately has no choice at all.

The volume moves with the consciousness of the poet recovering what has been lost, first articulating what that is, then how it came to be lost, then exploring the exact dimensions of the grief, pain and anger that must accompany loss. In the end a resolution occurs—one that has none of the phoniness of a sentimental love of the past, one that is beyond nostalgia, one that does not ask us to pretend that the modern will magically disappear, one that acknowledges grief and rage, and that can simultaneously celebrate the past by finding it in a meaningless present:

> I sit here in Brooklyn eating Mexican
> berries which I did not pick, nor do
> I know the hands which did, nor their
> stories . . .
> January snow falls, listen . . .

In this fusion, the poet discovers for himself and for us the real meaning of past and present, for the snow falls in Brooklyn as on the reservation, and there are stories everywhere, if we will hear.

James Ruppert (essay date 1980)

SOURCE: "The Uses of Oral Tradition in Six Contemporary Native American Poets," in *American Indian Culture and Research Journal*, Vol. 4, No. 4, 1980, pp. 87-110.

[*An American educator and critic, Ruppert specializes in Native American literature. In the excerpt below, he identifies the stylistic and thematic elements in Kenny's poetry that have been drawn from the Native oral tradition.*]

Maurice Kenny, publisher of Strawberry Press and Co-editor of *Contact/II*, among his many talents has developed a finely-tuned lyric voice. Kenny's background includes a seeking out of the works of Whitman, Williams and Louise Bogan after which he "returned with their teachings to my proper place . . . home / north." But to their world of things, men and especially nature, Kenny brings an atavistic self. He sees his role not so much as a storyteller, but as a singer of spirit. His song/poems express him as a medium for the voices he hears, the voices of the spirits of creation: plant spirit, animal spirit and human spirit. His poetry does not directly assume a *persona*, rather he sings the songs of everything and every thing. In assuming a *persona* we explain and explore character, whether personal, social, or mythical. Kenny wants to sing the songs, to praise and celebrate individual things, while a poet like Peter Blue Cloud may desire to pierce the web of spirit in nature or pick up the false-face to mask his own. Kenny at times becomes the nature he expresses. He has said "I am one of those pieces of sage" to indicate the extent of his unity with natural things.

"Wild Strawberry"

vines crawl across the grassy floor
of the north, scatter to the world
seeking the light of the sun and innocent
tap of the rain to feed the roots
and bud small white flowers that in June
will burst fruit and announce spring
when wolf will drop winter fur
and wrens will break the egg

my blood, blood berries that brought laughter
and the ache in the stooped back that vied
with dandelions for the plucking,
and the wines nourished our youth and heralded
iris, corn and summer melon

Here Kenny's fusion with the natural is so complete that it is almost unnoticed, a fusion and communion not achieved by Whitman's excellent, though "I" studded verse. His life and the life of the strawberry are irrevocably fused. The renewal of one is the renewal of spring which is the renewal of both, of all. Memory renews in recreating the past and the present. In creating an image, Kenny is exact in the memory of names—the names of animals, plants and minerals, for in naming those things he is in a sense calling on them, giving them a chance to speak. Here he reveals a commitment to Williams' "No ideas but in

things" because his use of natural imagery communicates elegantly its intellectual wisdom to mankind. Kenny's approach "through image, symbolically" lets him sing of natural objects such as the strawberry—a plant with a snow white flower which bursts into blood red nourishment in spring—and still tie those objects into the web of nature which incorporates us. His natural images may help us see the plant as plant, its place and voice in nature, its social use and symbolic significance and perhaps for the perceptive reader, its cultural significance. A complex web of meaning is created. In creating this web, he loans his voice to nature to carry back to the village so that nature, the song and the village will remain tied together and endure.

> For Kenny, song/poetry is always religious since its origin and strength lie in the ceremonies of the Longhouse, where the lyric, narrative and dramatic are woven together to praise and infuse spirit.
>
> —*James Ruppert*

Primary among the concerns in his song/poems is the need for endurance and survival, which the songs help make possible by being a medium for wisdom and knowledge. One feels little sense of separation between man, animal and plant. There is no dichotomy of nature in a human world or humans in a natural world. He wants to let his words carry that unified spirit so vital in oral tradition, instead of structuring the composition of a poem to force the capture of spirit. As a medium for song, the universal pushes through the personal, words "ride blood into song" and all Kenny asks is that we listen closely and think.

"Sweetgrass"

Seeded in the mud on turtle's back
Greened in the breath of the west wind
Fingered by the children of dawn
Arrowed in the morning sun
Blessed by the hawk and sparrow
Plucked by the many hands in the laughter
    of young girls and the art of old women
You hold the moments of the frost and the thaw
You hold the light of the star and the moon
You hold the darkness of the moist night and
    the music of the river and drum

Kenny's poetry is rich with the use of cultural and oral material pertaining to the old stories, to the clan animals—Turtle, Bear & Wolf, to the traditions of the Longhouse and to individuals still alive in oral history. Often these emerge through childhood remembrances, for in touching those important moments the singer and the listener participate in a personal renewal. This moment of renewal, which figures so significantly in his work, is best expressed in *Dancing Back Strong the Nation,* where the personal journey becomes a collective one for the Mohawk nation and by extension, all Indian nations. Through his song and poetry, Spirit—the motivating force behind Native American oral tradition—is expressed and confirmed; it re-animates the world. For Kenny, song/poetry is always religious since its origin and strength lie in the ceremonies of the Longhouse, where the lyric, narrative and dramatic are woven together to praise and infuse spirit. Song/poetry of today must be seen in that light.

> For thousands of years, verse-prayer has not been far from the Great Spirit. It has gathered together in ceremony not only its thanks to the Great Spirit, but composed the chronicle of time itself, the calendar of events of an historical culture, and includes love songs, victory songs, healing songs, the joy of creation, the surety of death and reunion with one's ancestors. [Maurice Kenny, **"Adowe: We Return Thanks,"** in *The Remembered Earth*, edited by Geary Hobson, 1979]

Kenny's work returns continually to this heart of oral tradition: "I believe that dramatic event, where poetry sprang from, was in the Longhouse or the altar."

Interestingly, the poems in [***Dancing Back Strong the Nation***] are the most purely oral in form of Kenny's work. Kenny's chant, **"I Am the Sun,"** based on a Lakota-Sioux Ghost Dance Song, however, may be in performance a more powerful example of oral form and oral material. The songs that followed the spread of the Ghost Dance consciousness were designed to help the singer/dancer achieve a trance-like state through a whirling song and a whirling motion. In this state the singer saw visions of the future and gathered power to aid the driving out of the Whites. In performance the chant builds through the disasters of the past to visions of strength for the future. On the page, the poems in ***Dancing Back Strong the Nation*** show a conscious expansion of the oral song form into contemporary poetry. He seems concerned with introducing on an extended basis the repetition and two-step beat of the dance in the Longhouse into his work. **"Drums"** is an example:

> **"Drums"**
>
> listen . . .
> drums drum
>   dance dance
> rattles rattle
>   sing sing
>
> drums dance
> rattles sing
> pause and
>   dance and
>
> drums drum
> to the song
>   of the young
>   warriors
>
> listen . . .
> thunder thunders
>   shakes
> thunder shakes the floor

Here the consistent way in which the two-step beat is worked into the poetic line may herald a break-through

in oral form in writing. His claim to be a singer of the spirit of things is confirmed by his commitment to oral form as well as cultural material. In much of his work, he becomes a traditional medium for the voices he hears around him.

An excerpt from "Prayer for Aroniateka/Hendrick"

> We are here
> We are here to listen
> We are here to listen to his voice
>   who has left us in sorrow
> We have brought flowers of remembrance
>   corn for his journey
>   songs for his pleasure
>   night for his peace
>   tears for his passing
>   this death
>   this father
>   we mourn

Maurice Kenny, in his Tekonwatonti/Molly Brant (1735-1795): Poems of War, *White Pine Press, 1992.*

Carolyn D. Scott   (essay date Winter 1983)

SOURCE: "Baskets of Sweetgrass: Maurice Kenny's *Dancing Back Strong the Nation* and 'I Am the Sun'," in *Studies in American Indian Literature*, Vol. 7, No. 1, Winter, 1983, pp. 8-13.

[*In the following essay, Scott examines Kenny's focus on nature and concern with community and tradition in* Dancing Back Strong the Nation *and* "I Am the Sun."]

Maurice Kenny's slim volume of only 23 poems, ***Dancing Back Strong the Nation,*** now out of print, has its origins, fittingly, in the sacred Longhouse of the Mohawk Nation, oldest in the country, resting on the borders of Canada and the U.S. A second printing adds six more poems, but preserves essentially the same mood and tone of the first. Both volumes move with the mystery of poetry especially found in Mohawk dance and drum rhythms which Kenny believes to be quintessential to his work.

Central to each volume is a series of poems inspired by the Longhouse dances, social dances that are not taboo, performed by the Wolf, Bear, and Turtle clans. When **"Drums," "Dance," "Moccasin,"** and **"The Women"** are heard as a simple rhythmic piece—though printed on alternate pages—the poems become music for the listener far away from "mice in the grass / chicory in the field." "Drums drum / . . . rattles rattle" from the lodge as the people "come to greet and thank / the strawberry plants / growing." The beginning soft whisper of "moccasin moccasin," like leather against an earthen floor, rises in pitch as the "wind howls like a wolf on the hill," then falls again to the sound of a single "moccasin." It creates that cosy tribal closeness of the people circling together inside to the beat of the water drum while wildness of thunder and wind provide a companion sound outside. Unlike most contemporary Western poetry, nature here is not alien; all is greeted and thanked alike, "hands gnarled in sweetgrass / . . . hands wet with babies." Kenny's own testimony to this effect declares his purpose in writing poetry: "I write about the Nation with the idea of keeping the campfires, village fires alive."

These dance poems, as well as many others in the volume, attest to Kenny's firm commitment to "our own natural speech in poetry." The first word of the untitled epigraph is "Listen . . ." Faces of listeners who have read the poems previously light up as Kenny's voice makes the words that have lain flat on the page dance with the chants of his childhood. Kenny, who once sang to himself in the fields where weeping willows were his sanctuary, thinks "every poem should be able to be sung, or it is not a poem." His song is the ceremonial naming of things—a listing so often heard in tribal song—discovering each thing's sacred center as in **"Yaikini,"** "when elms were sweet / squash tasted of sun / corn grew in circles." Each song is sensual with simple tastes, smells, and touches: "cedar scented afternoon / . . . sweetgrass is for weaving / and summer berries / for a child's tongue . . ."

Talk about orality in poetry is cheap these days, but with Kenny's poems it is not an attempt to "get with it" in the poetry circuit. He sees himself rather as "the medium for the voice of nature to come through . . . in the rebirthing of things." But he disavows all claims to being a "nature poet" like Frost or Dickinson who merely observe. "I use natural imagery because that's the imagery I know best. I am really not a nature poet. I try to become the nature itself. I am the birch tree . . . I am nature; you are nature." In **"Legacy"** such a binding of man and nature, incarnation if you will, is created. "[M]y face is grass / color of April rain; / arms, legs are the limbs of birch, cedar; / my thoughts are winds / which blow . . ."

From **Dancing Back** is forged the recurring symbolic language for much of his poetry. Strawberries, pollen, the sacred animals, sweetgrass, each spoken with reverence of ritual and litany from the sacred lore of his people. The recurrence of these images produces not the tiresome pretentiousness of private feeling, but rather intimations one can recognize as the belonging to home—the village fires.

Not all of Kenny's images are filled with the optimism of summer—"To go home / is always hard" (**"North in Winter"**). He avoids white Americans' need for Hiawatha dreams. Whether it is beating up a jeering white face outside the bowling alley (**"Saturday Night"**), "a little blood / wouldn't spoil our feathers much," or striking back against the pillagers of the reservation (**"Reynolds & Chevrolet"**), "aluminum hills strike against morning," Kenny is not forgetful that the "jails bulge with people / torn to booze to crime" (**"Warrior"**) or the St. Lawrence is dying with her brothers "in the summer mud of her shores" (**"St. Lawrence River"**). Rather than curse the darkness, Kenny believes "children should know hills / under their naked feet." He sets the tone for the dark / light visions of later poems in **Only As Far As Brooklyn, Kneading the Blood,** and **Blackrobe** exploring delusion, pain and death. As Paula Gunn Allen observes in her excellent foreword to the volume: "The Native American poet, whose life is discordant at every level, faces the ne-

cessity of creating wholeness from a life that is biculturated . . ."

Thus **"Wild Strawberry"**—symbol of Mohawk renewal—angrily laments the present loss of contact with even our own food. "I sit here in Brooklyn eating Mexican / berries which I did not pick, nor do / I know the hands which did, nor their stories . . ." A renewal of a simpler, holy age, like Thomas' "Fern Hill," equates the sacred act of picking and eating berries with firmness and growth, "we ate / wild berries with their juices running / down the roots of our mouths and our joy."

In the poem **"Legacy"** yet another aspect binds itself solidly to Kenny's work, the "legacy" of his Mohawk/Seneca heritage to loan his "word" as a poet to the communal cause. "The obligation I hand / to the blood of my flesh . . . / that carries my song / and the beat of the drum to the fires of the village / which endures." With these lines a deeper purpose to his sensual orality emerges. "If we keep in touch with our senses, our own tribalisms will merge . . . a collective spirit, community, can tap into it. It's still in our blood!" He means the latent tribalism of us all, "not just Indian people." Tribal takes on a new meaning. His poems embrace audiences with the words "we" and "you." Not only are the people of the Longhouse dancing back strong the Wolf, Bear, and Turtle, but listeners and readers return to the land with him.

Dancing Back leads us to an earlier, highly praised poem, **"I am the Sun,"** first published in 1973 in *Akwesasne Notes*. The present version by the White Pine Press (1979) appears as a chapbook. It serves as the end piece for most of his readings and reflects Kenny's most fervent feelings. Based on a Lakota Ghost Dance and inspired by the 1973 Wounded Knee confrontations, the poem's subtitle reveals its manifold purposes: "A Song of Praise, Defiance, and Determination." Like the Ghost Dances, the song is a plea for renewal through the return of the sacred arrows embodying the values of the Old Ones. Father (the Almighty), Mother (the earth), and Brother (all of us) are invoked to return the sun, the night, the earth, the spirit of the people. The sorry state of Mother Earth ("Mother, your breast is bare"), the loss of universal brotherhood of man for man and man for beast ("Brother, we cried for you"), and the loss of contact with things spiritual ("Our father has turned his face") motivate this cry for a vision, the *Hanblecheyapi*.

The chant is structured in incantorial fours and sixes, the sacred numbers of Native American religions, with invocative repetitions of the names of the sacred objects. This repetition is more formalized than in his other poems. The names, recall that terrible historical time of Wounded Knee—Sitting Bull, Black Coyote, Bigfoot—and the spirit of the chant, like **Dancing Back,** refers to the hypnotic attempts of the first Ghost Dancers to return the land to its primeval state. "We still plant the seed of the sacred tree in your country." (The Mohawk also have a legend that huge silver and gold snakes—Canada and the U.S.—will be driven back into the sea.) But there is more than a reproduction of Lakota dances here. Kenny's plea to the Father to make "a country into a home / a home into the sun" and the final supplication for renewal of spirituality,

"Father, give us back our arrows! / We have learned to hold them sacred!" could very well be the chant of any people's movement for a nuclear freeze, for release from oppression, for human dignity. Kenny rightly recognizes that the original Ghost Dance was not as destructive as its enemies supposed and emphasizes the aspects of renewal in its spirit. "We will fill the river with water / . . . We will build the walls of the dream." Kenny's performances of this chant at readings everywhere, sometimes with tears streaming on his cheeks, have at least electrified the jaded and drawn almost magically the unitiate [into] what poetry was always about but seldom is heard, the fusion of sound and object.

In retrospect, I realize I've not yet cast the standard critical aspersions for conventions not fulfilled. But with Kenny's poetry that is rarely a problem. These poems attest that he is a careful craftsman, not a self-indulgent scribbler. Rather, the expressive toughness and living sacredness of image in Kenny's poetry weave themselves tight like the sweetgrass of his people. It gnarls the hands with gathering, but the resulting odor is a lasting sweetness. Thus the natural objects cling to the sturdy form of his song—"Pinch of pollen / for your eyes"—so that there is no need for aesthetic alibis. His poetry is. "I learn rivers / by sitting still."

Joseph Bruchac   (review date September 1984)

SOURCE: A review of *The Mama Poems,* in *The Small Press Review,* Vol. 16, No. 9, September, 1984, p. 12.

[*Bruchac is a Native American educator, poet, and editor who has edited numerous works on Native American authors and literatures. Below, he offers a highly favorable assessment of* The Mama Poems.]

With the release of [*The Mama Poems*], Maurice Kenny moves closer towards achieving recognition as a major figure among American writers. Already seen by some critics as one of the 4 or 5 most significant Native American poets, Kenny speaks in *The Mama Poems* with a distinctive voice, one shaped by the rhythms of Mohawk life and speech, yet one which both defines and moves beyond cultural boundaries.

The Mama Poems is, somewhat like his earlier volume of poems centering around the figure of the Jesuit missionary Father Isaac Jogues, *Black Robe,* a flow of voices. The voices in this new book, though, are not those of historical figures. They are the voices of the poet himself—in childhood and at crucial points in the painful, powerful relationship with his family—and the voice of his mother, sometimes as an echo, sometimes (in the flatly powerful **"Telephone Call"**) as a direct monologue.

The world which Kenny opens for us is personal, yet never sentimental. The two prose poems for his mother which open and close the book, **"1911"** and **"1982"** are like the covers of a family album, presenting and enclosing this private universe. It is a world in which long-dead relatives can appear when they are needed, in which the drum sounds in rituals of curing; a world vibrant with the natural landscape of blackberry bushes, pine trees, animals and birds.

> birds weren't caged
> when I was a kid
> growing with mountains
>
> an old man might keep a crow
> on his shoulder
> but it could fly
> into alders when its mate called . . .

>   from **"Birds"**

As the book progresses, moving more or less chronologically through the poet's life and concluding with his mother's death and his attempts at an elegy, Kenny presents us with an experience which all of us share—the unpreventable loss of loved ones.

> I used to believe in the powers of
>   death.
> Until you died.
> It was the last belief.
> I believe in echoes now,
> in earth that holds you. I believe in a
>   bird,
> its flight, though I am not sure
>   which one, hawk
> or seagull . . .

>   from **"May 15, 1982"**

The transcendence which he finds is not simplistic or facile, nor does it reek of the easy and painless mysticism which certain recent imitators of Native American culture have foisted upon the public. But when one concludes the book, one feels that the dedication on the first page—juxtaposed with a section from the Iroquois story of Creation—has been justified. Speaking to his relatives, those living and dead, Kenny says: " . . . we are together again."

Kenny on oral tradition and "I Am the Sun":

I try to write in the oral tradition which is Indian, which is Iroquois. At the time I wrote "I Am the Sun," which was the time of the Wounded Knee confrontation in 1973, I personally was so angry and I physically couldn't do anything about it because I was suffering a heart attack. . . . [So] I had to sing it out of me. I sang it out in "I Am the Sun." I couldn't use an Iroquois traditional form because I was writing about Lakota people. So I chose a Ghost Dance song to pattern "I Am the Sun" after.

Maurice Kenny, in Survival This Way: Interviews with American Indian Poets, *by Joseph Bruchac, 1987.*

Edward Butscher   (review date March-April 1985)

SOURCE: "The Historic Present," in *The American Book Review,* Vol. 7, No. 3, March-April, 1985, p. 18.

[*Butscher is an American educator, poet, and critic. In the following excerpt, he reviews* Blackrobe, *noting Kenny's balanced treatment of French and Native American figures.*]

In **Blackrobe,** based upon the brief career of Isaac Jogues, a French Jesuit killed by the Mohawks in 1646, Indians and French are given voices, using letters and journal entries to alternate with the imagined or researched speeches of Iroquois witnesses and participants: "The third time he came / (with his book) / he brought raisins and brandy / but refused to throw them down to us. / We did not show him out of the woods."

It is clear that Father Jogues, initially treated with kindness by the contemptuous Mohawks, possessed a martyr's characteristic hysteria and tunnel rigidity, denigrating the mores and legends of a host people he deemed inferior. Kenny also suggests that he was more concerned about delivering rich fur country over to Cardinal Richelieu than about saving souls and had a closet attraction to pre-pubic boys. Courting persecution, he soon found it, was clubbed to death, his head impaled on "the highest pole of the village stockade," as was the head of a young companion, Jean de la Lande. But the white invasion could not be stemmed so easily, liquor and unknown diseases mounting a relentless assault no stone age civilization, however organizationally sophisticated, could hope to withstand.

Perhaps inescapably, **Blackrobe** is an uneven performance, unequal, at times, to the awesome task of recreating the ambiguous mesh of motives and psychologies at the cauldron heart of any culture clash. The best moments in the sequence, as when articulating myth-oriented Iroquois sensibilities, past and present—"My people have many war songs, / but we let them float / in the air as though canoes"—project a metaphoric vitality and lyric directness difficult to resist, and the sympathetic author is rarely less than fair to the views of Jogues' followers, native and European, such as Kateri Tekekwitha, a saintly convert dubbed "Lily of the Mohawks" for her sweet courage:

> Friend, be kind, accept this whip.
> Like winter wind let its leather thongs
> scream through the air and strike my flesh.
> Like juice of the raspberry blood shall
> trickle from my shoulder-blades, my arms.
> Each Sunday of the week I shall embrace purity.

If nothing else, apart from satisfying narrative expectations, **Blackrobe** reconfirms how madness manifests universal symptoms regardless of social nurture.

Maurice Kenny   (essay date February 1986)

SOURCE: A prelude to *Between Two Rivers: Selected Poems 1956-1984,* White Pine Press, 1987, pp. 1-5.

[*In the following excerpt from an essay originally written in 1986, Kenny reminisces about his education and development as a poet.*]

An excerpt from "Yaikini"

A soft breeze brought a bug into her bucket, a lady-bug fell into her fruit.

"Lady-bug, Lady-bug, fly away home. Your house is on fire and your children are alone. Lady-bug. Lady-bug, fly away home. Lady-bug, Lady-bug, your house is on fire, your children alone. Lady, Lady. Lady, Lady-bug . . ." She couldn't remember the entire rhyme. She chanted over and over, "Lady-bug, Lady-bug," hoping the rest of the words would follow. She worked herself into an anger so vicious she began pounding the air with her fists. Clenched hammers, the rolled hands struck the air, and the vines, the ground, her own chest.

"Ma! Ma, you alright?"

The women picking further away now in the wide meadow looked up from work.

"Ma, answer me. You alright?"

Her eyes looked up from the vines. They were seared with anger. She glanced toward the knoll. There he was again lurking in the woods. Mr. Peters. He stood in silence like a tree framed in windless mirage.

"Ma, answer me! You alright?"

Lulu's voice grew, concerned, louder as it came closer.

"Lady-bug, Lady-bug. Fly, fly, damn you, fly away home. Or I'll burn down your house. I'll cut off your children's heads. Damn you."

She picked up the bucket and flung out the berries.

Lulu stood by her mother and motioned to the other women to hurry. She looked at the old woman among the berries, her faded blue house dress soiled with scarlet juice, her hands and face running red, her bunned white hair framing the startled face was flecked with berry stain. She pulled out the comb that kept her hair in place and it cascaded down like the rapids of a swift river.

"She's a witch!" Annie screamed.

"Get out, get out," the old woman cried.

"Gramma, she's a witch, a witch!" little Annie screamed and screamed again as she stomped her feet.

"Get out of my bucket and go care for your children! Out of my woods. Out of my way. My house is burning and my children are alone."

Annie began to dance in a circle around her great-grandmother crying, and terrified, tearing at her own dark hair. She screamed and pushed her hands against her face and eyes to hide. She thrashed about, breaking from Lulu's inept grasp, and ran off to the women hurrying toward Lulu.

Maurice Kenny, in his Rain, and Other Fictions, *White Pine Press, 1990.*

To my creative spirit, it indeed seemed odd that a new book of my poems [*Between Two Rivers: Selected Poems 1956-1984*] was about to enter the jaws of a press, and I did not have any new words in it. This predicated the mulling of a 'prelude' to express an abiding and deeply-felt appreciation to those who have aided and abetted my years and successes as a writer.

My first poems were composed between two rivers—the St. Lawrence and the Black—somewhere between the ages of eight and fourteen. They were the songs of a shy, young boy, and I sang them to winds and clouds, the horse I rode, the creeks I fished, or the willow I sat beneath. Later, I learned to write them down and sent a few off to newspapers in the area. I went off to New York City and lived in the shadows of writers whose work I then admired, especially those who had survived in Greenwich Village: Edna St. Vincent Millay, e. e. cummings, Eugene O'Neill, and Edmund Wilson, who had a home in upstate New York not far from mine and who sent me a postcard in response to my query stating he "did not see young writers." No longer a boy, but still young, I traveled by sheer accident into the mid-west where I forgot my early pleasures in the poems of Robert Frost almost immediately and delighted in the poetry of William Carlos Williams, Louise Bogan, Dylan Thomas, Edwin Arlington Robinson, A. E. Housman, Gerard Manley Hopkins, and Denise Levertov—all of whom were galaxies away from my world.

I became acquainted with Blake, Wordsworth, and Keats. Wordsworth held a firm grip on me for years: I've always contended that my worst poetry was that influenced by him. Entering Butler University as a special student, I was soon indoctrinated by the Keats scholar Werner Beyer—who found me a rough thorn—and by Roy Marz, the religious poet. Roy felt I should turn my craft to prose fiction and away from poetry, and I privately turned, in letters, to John Crowe Ransom. He confirmed Marz' contention and added that I had no "sense of rhythm," meaning, naturally, his rhythms. I worked to complete a novel and was immediately discontented with it. I left Butler with Werner Beyer's blessing, and though without a cap and gown, I felt I led Pegasus by the reins. To this moment I feed on his advice.

Shortly after, I entered St. Lawrence University, where I took a course with the fine novelist Douglas Angus. He almost instantly pursuaded me back to poetry, and I will always be thankful to him. I returned to New York City to enter Columbia University on the strength of my father's urging. I passed a rigorous entrance examination in April of 1957 and took a job with the Marboro Book Store chain as a clerk. I was made a shop manager a month or two after employment, and that postponed my entering Columbia. In fact, I never did enter Columbia.

In autumn, 1958, I entered New York University to study with Louise Bogan. There was a sparkle in the air at that time, and a few of those sparks ignited me. Poetry was being born: Allen Ginsberg had published "Howl"; LeRoi Jones (Amiri Baraka) was writing poems and publishing his magazine *Yugen*. All sorts of little magazines were being printed, such as Tuli Kupferberg's *YEAH!*, in which I published a poem. Bob Wilson opened his Phoenix Book Shop, which was soon to be the first bookstore to place my work for sale. Sam Loveman also operated a second-hand book store in the Village. Oscar Williams walked up and down 8th Street with copies of his published anthologies in his armpits. Ezra Pound was released from St. Elizabeth's and one afternoon wandered into the Marboro Shop, stood before the poetry shelf, smiled to see his books in place, and briskly left. Muriel Rukeyser was attaining her peak and was a frequent visitor to the store, as was Paddy Chayefsky, who later became a friend. There was more than a sparkle in the heavens; there was a fire.

Poetry readings were being held all over this magical city, especially in Village coffeehouses and numerous churches. I applied to the Cafe Bizarre and Cafe Borgia to read my poems and was refused because the coordinators said I didn't look like a poet. (In those days I was forced to wear a white shirt and tie because of my job.) I was then living in a loft on Bleeker and Lafayette Streets, and in the building I had a young, French friend, Yves Bolomet, who was a rather sensual, handsome youth and looked the way a poet was expected to look. I wrote anti-flag poems and Yves read them at the readings; we split the passed-hat. There was fire, and sparkle and combustion.

No longer a boy—in fact, by then I was certainly losing that blush of youth altogether—I remained, however, shy and somewhat terrified of the literary scene. I remember meeting Jack Micheline (we shared a publisher) and being intimidated by his firm assurance, and I was totally awed by Asa Renveniste, who was not only a published poet, but published in Europe. I met Sam Loveman at this time, again at the Marboro shop, who took me under his wing, and, by coincidence, Willard Motley, the then-famous novelist. I was corresponding with Marianne Moore in Brooklyn and William Carlos Williams in New Jersey. I had become acquainted with the great, but I remained a shadowy figure looking in—a hungry man staring through the window at the diners.

Through Sam's auspices, I met Venable Herdon, who was co-editing *Chelsea Magazine*. I was tongue-tied. Herdon fervently wished to publish some "fragments" of Hart Crane's work never before published. They were in Sam's safekeeping, and he offered them to the magazine on the proviso that *Chelsea* also print my poems. Poor, good Sam. He lost. I don't know if Venable ever did acquire Crane's "fragments."

I did manage to place a few pieces in sporadic journals; I wrote drama reviews for Ed Corley's *Off-Broadway Magazine,* and taught a course in the history of drama at Mary Tarcai's School of Drama. Mary introduced me to many theatre people, but again the country bumpkin was totally tongue-cuffed and missed some terrific opportunities. Mary could not come to terms with my reluctance to hustle her theatrical friends—who were perfectly willing to be hustled. I'm sure with the hay still clinging to my hair and my north country accent, I was a respite from the fraudulent poses of their sophisticated salons.

I was comfortable with Paddy—I allowed him to do all the shouting—and with Sam Loveman, who wasn't as shy as I was but was certainly discreet. I spent many evenings with Sam in either his large apartment over the famous fish shop on upper Second Avenue or in the East 86th Cafeteria. With Sam I held my own; he actually listened to what I had to say and approved of my poetry. He believed I was another Hart Crane. I was not. Nor did I wish to be. It was a thrill to know this kind, informative man and to have him write the introduction for my first book, *Dead Letters Sent.*

But to fill in the gaps and set the tenor of my times, I have been rambling through a past and neglecting what I had set out to remember: Louise Bogan. Nearly thirty years later, it seems that her class on that first night was outrageously large—somewhere near fifty students, and we had been screened! I remember a few stood against the wall. Looking back, it seems to me that Louise was always dressed in black with lace at the collar. This reflection may simply be due to the fact that I remember her as being a very sad, pained woman, and I mistakenly shroud her in black cloth. She entered the classroom quietly with a few books clutched to her breast and holding a handkerchief to her mouth. She was never without that handkerchief—at least in class. She coughed into it a good deal of the time. I recognized instantly that she was my kind of woman: she was not merely shy, but was actually intimidated by her students. She did not enjoy teaching, and I soon gathered that she taught because of finances, even though she was in demand on the speaking circuit and often missed class to give a reading or a speech. Her substitute was always Donald Allen, who was then editing his classic anthology, *New American Poetry.*

The first evening, Louise announced that she could not teach us poetry, that no one could, it was not teachable, and that about all she could offer was how to punctuate and capitalize. She proceeded to do exactly that for the entire semester. We read our poems in class and the students made critical comments. She took them home, presumably read them, returned the poems to class, and occasionally made pronouncements—if that is not too harsh a word—on poems which exemplified particular ideas. She spoke of numerous contemporary poets; Allen Ginsberg's "Howl," she had decided, would get, if fortunate, a footnote in the literary history of the time. She often referred to literary politics and how one editor or anthologist could make or break a writer's career and reputation. She was faithful to her beliefs, and her beliefs were strong and deep. Early in the semester I approached her desk after class one night with the book *Poetry and Its Forms* by Mason Long clutched in hand. The handbook aroused her interest, and we marched to the subway together. The next day we met for lunch, and I gave her a copy of the Long book. After that, we met and talked frequently.

It was in these out-of-class sessions that I learned what she had to offer me. It was not so much her praise of my work nor the constructive criticism—and there was a large amount of both—but the suggestions she offered and my careful reading of her own magnificent poems. To her, a tree was not a tree but an elm, a white pine, a birch; a bird was not a bird but a hawk, a titmouse; a river was not a river but the St. Lawrence or the Mohawk. You establish communication by identification. This also aids the reflec-

tive juices. The first thought or the first image may be the best, but explore, define and refine, cut away what is not connotative. Fear nothing—not the personal nor the symbolic. Endure with the past, and your own past. Fear nothing knowing the worst shall happen.

Tragic experience was always near Louise Bogan; pain rarely took a holiday. When a youth, I was told that to create a great work of art one needed to suffer, and I always looked for suffering. Louise Bogan never had to look far: it appeared frequently at dawn, the breakfast table, the bedtime pillow. One of her greatest disappointments, a broken dream, was that she was never awarded a Pulitzer, which she adamantly prized and deserved. Louise Bogan was a fine teacher and a masterful poet—truly one of the great 20th century voices.

Upon leaving Louise Bogan's class, I was finished with formal, institutional learning. I was on my own and swimming in white water. Under her influence I had published *Dead Letters Sent* with Brayton Harris at Troubador Press, and shortly after, Aardvark printed *With Love to Lesbia* and *And Grieve, Lesbia,* both highly imitative of Catullus. I did not publish a collection again until after *Akwesasne Notes,* Alex Jacobs then poetry editor, first printed "I Am The Sun." "Sun" was printed in a pamphlet by dodeca and later again by White Pine Press. In those years I wrote little and published rarely. Much of my time was spent traveling to Mexico, California, the Southwest, Puerto Rico, and the Virgin Islands. I lived for exactly one year in Chicago where I wrote obituaries and advertisements for the Chicago *Sun-Times.* I returned to New York City in 1967, found an apartment in Brooklyn Heights, and took a job as waiter in a posh discoteque on Park Avenue where I was known as Maurice, the French waiter. I worked there on and off until a heart attack stopped work in 1974.

Since 1976 I have published nearly one book a year.

Daniela Gioseffi   (review date April 1987)

SOURCE: "Wild Berries," in *The Small Press Review,* Vol. 19, No. 4, April, 1987, pp. 4-5.

[*Gioseffi is an American poet, short story writer, novelist, nonfiction writer, and critic. In the review below, she remarks on Kenny's poems and stories in* Is Summer This Bear *and* Rain, and Other Fictions.]

Maurice Kenny, accomplished poet, winner of the 1984 American Book Award of The Before Columbus Foundation for his *Mama Poems,* in his new collection, *Is Summer This Bear,* continues in the fine nature tradition of Native-American poetry which he has helped to foster as one of its four or five most mature and significant voices. Kenny, whose *Blackrobe: Isaac Jogues,* was nominated for The Pulitzer Prize in 1982, is the author of several books of poetry.

Though Kenny's *Mama Poems*—because of their deep digging into the poet's family roots and his emotional connection to the upstate lands of his forefathers—still contain his most emotionally powerful works, there are many good pieces in this current collection of poems from The

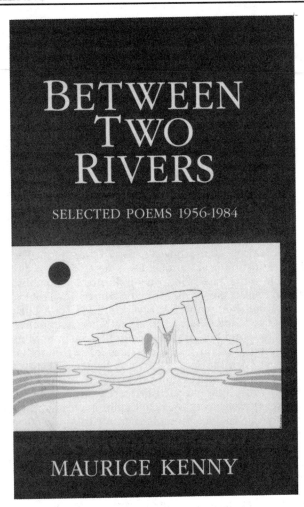

Cover for Between Two Rivers: Selected Poems 1956-1984.

Chauncy Press. *Is Summer This Bear* begins with a sensitive, poetically written preface which states: "I have never recognized humankind's supremacy. I have never granted humankind that boastful ego. Humans forget there was a time before them." Mr. Kenny goes on to talk about the fear of nuclear end which threatens all life and then he warns us to listen to the elders.

"Should they listen to the elders, humankind will be guided to the right path: should humankind respect hornet or fisher or willow, they will come to understand the nature of things and the design the Creator wove into the tapestry of life, all life." *Is Summer This Bear* is a collection of poems to remind us of the beauty of the natural world around us and to suggest our obligation to it.

Personified wolf, eagle, red tail, raccoon, bear, coyote, bobcat or turtle, anemone, loose-strife or wild strawberry exemplify her beauty and wisdom with their special gift or vital role in Kenny's lyrical chant, offering their indomitable wisdom of the earthly ages to the less wise, now often effete humankind who have stolen the American lands and who ignore the intelligence of earth and her native peoples. Nature's pristine powers and beauty are juxtaposed with the decadence the power of nature to which

it is attuned when a rain dance, despite the Coca-cola and carnival, *tourista* atmosphere in which it occurs, brings its longed for results from the skies. As the refraining drums drum and rattles rattle, the dry hot dusty traveler's thirst is quenched by the power of his Native-American people to dance down the rain—to respect nature and her sensual offerings better than the over-civilized white man can. **"Rain"** becomes the true power of this watery, blue clouded planet, marbled with nearly all swirling ocean.

Kenny is good as a visual imagist evoking scenes with short descriptive lines and sensual similes, as he creates the carnival atmosphere of the Pueblo rain dance festival, in New Mexico, for example:

> At the pueblo edge a Ferris wheel whirled. Music of a merry-go-round tinkled the afternoon. Sonny's face brightened with surprise, but his grandmother grasped his hand tightly. A smell of burning charcoal seamed the air. Young boys weaved in and out of the strolling crowd selling containers of Coca-cola from large wooden crates. Children, including Sonny, stared hungrily at the various booths selling cotton candy on plastic sticks. A tongue slid along the rim of a lip. Hundreds of people milled between craft stands and beverage counters, charcoal pits where great cauldrons of bubbling grease singed brown tortilla-like bread. Flies swarmed about the honey pots. A leather-skinned man wavered through the crowds hawking balloons: purple, the color of his lips; yellow as the sun; blue as the clear sky; red as the heat of the afternoon.

Despite all this, the rain does pour down, and the weary traveler who has witnessed the miracle, then quenches his thirst on slices of juicy melon from the lap of mother nature as he feels the power of his people to be in tune with her still. This is the very power of Native-American poetry—on a symbolic level, perhaps. Native-American poetry and writing is often better attuned to the actualities of our perilous time than is more academic prosody, or the dead metrics of English verse, in that it is vitally aware of the need to listen to the lessons that nature offers.

Kenny's work is full of the glories of the natural world with which he has a learned intimacy, the names of tree, bush, bird, flower or beast.

In the second story ["**Yaikini**"] of his collection, Kenny portrays three generations of Native-American women picking wild strawberries—central to the folklore and survival of their once Mohawk nation amid the foothills of the Adirondacks. The middle-aged woman—weighed down by the responsibility of her aging mother and her child—finds solace and comfort, or the ability to go on, in the wild strawberry juice brought to her by an aging medicine man of the region. The old medicine man's elliptical message is inherent in the cycle of the seasons. The grandmother, Lena, longs for winter—having barely survived her life away in the city—as she rebels against the heat of summer, symbolic of lost youth. Summer and its ripe fruit drives her momentarily mad in its heat and bloody juices as a lady-bug reminds her that she deserted her children and did not, herself, fly home to rescue them. "Lady-bug, lady-bug, fly away home, your house is on fire, your children will burn," she chants as the bug lands in her berry bucket, causing her to go berserk in the heat of summer. The medicine man reminds her that winter will come soon enough in his few American-Indian words, and then he leaves a jar of wild strawberry juice with Lena's daughter to give her the strength to go on past forgiving her mother for her desertion. Kenny tells this story in a mystical and elliptical fashion, with plenty of sensual imagery of the meadow and the wild strawberry patch, making the reader long to join his characters among the bright berries for a first-hand taste of their magical juice.

A central theme in Kenny's work is the theme of the wanderer between two worlds, who knows the value of one and doubts the real civilization of the other, yet must go back and forth to write and to read the meaning of his vision.

—Daniela Gioseffi

In his final story of the collection, he returns again to the theme of the wanderer as he recreates with the images and rhythms of his language the feeling of a long bus trip across country to San Jose, California, by Greyhound bus. We watch the scenic route through the bus windows with him, as a sixteen-year-old American-Indian youth travels in search of the father he's never seen, and a car salesman feels empathy with the Indian youth—longing for some kind of family connection of his own.

Again, Kenny is skilled at creating the scene:

> The Greyhound growled up street and down, at last pulling into the station dock. . . . Passengers trekked off. Some, naturally disgruntled about the long stop;

of a materialistic civilization, as in **"Am-traking to the Adirondacks"** where all sorts of wanderers, engrossed in, or deluded by, their separate civilizations or mysticism or religions, board the bus.

Kenny's Native-American voice carries the spirit of his symbolic folklore:

> Coyote
> Over the rain I hear your
> howl
> toothed into night. . . .
>
> Scrawny you run with
> hounds and poodles
> distract the gun's
> sight
> wearing grape leaves
> like a fox
> When that fails you whine
> into legend
> creep into the
> house to place
> your docile paw in

> the lap
> your joke, story on
> the table. . . .
> You are taken very
> seriously . . . for all
> the ridicule. . . .

Born and raised in northern New York near the St. Lawrence River and the foothills of the Adirondacks, Kenny lives in Brooklyn, often traveling back to his native land to teach or around the country to give readings. This living between two worlds, the culture of his Mohawk country realm and the urban blight of Brooklyn, has given rise to a central theme in Kenny's work—the theme of the wanderer between two worlds, who knows the value of one and doubts the real civilization of the other, yet must go back and forth to write and to read the meaning of his vision. **"Am-traking"** or **"Greyhounding"** appear in both his new verse and prose collections, in which the poet often appears as the wanderer or the visitor between worlds.

His short stories, *Rain, and Other Fictions,* carry the theme further. Issued as a volume in The Blue Cloud Quarterly Press series, with a charming drawing by Native-American poet/artist, Wendy Rose, on its pale blue cover, the book begins and ends with stories of traveling—the homebound wanderer in search of solace.

"Rain" begins with a small group of Native-Americans riding in a beat-up Pontiac to a rain dance festival which has become a tourist attraction. The fact that the car taking the American Indians to their festival is named for a great Indian chief offers an added irony. In this story, American-Indian mysticism is given

> others took an opportunistic outlook. The boy disappeared immediately into the crowded terminal; the man headed for the plastic cafeteria. . . . Time waddled like an old duck with chicks. Despite its surroundings, cool mountain tops checkered with snow, Salt Lake City was blistering hot. The sun's glare caught unpolarized eyes casting a blinding, sickening dizziness to the pit of the stomach. The polished sidewalks were poker hot. Few travelers ventured from the air-conditioned depot.

Kenny's *Rain, and Other Fictions,* continue to support the essence of the commentaries on his work as one of the most important voices of Native-American literature—one achieving a full-bodied maturity in the wisdom of the wanderer, between the nature of his homeland amidst the foothills of the Adirondacks and the urban blight and ironic civilization of Brooklyn's teaming cityscape.

It is easy to see where the poet's soul really lives in this short lyric titled **"Brooklyn Pigeon,"** (from *Is Summer This Bear*).

> Wings flash black on the
> sun,
> trick my thinking for a
> quick second:
> home, winter, snow
> crow on white fields
> sun thaws iced elms
> near blue waters

trout snagged in ice

may sun and pigeon fool my
                         eyes
again tomorrow . . .
and sight the mountains.

Robert L. Berner   **(review date Autumn 1988)**

SOURCE: A review of *Between Two Rivers: Selected Poems 1956-1984*, in *World Literature Today*, Vol. 62, No. 4, Autumn, 1988, p. 709.

[*In the following review, Berner surveys the strengths and themes of Kenny's poetry.*]

For three decades the work of the Mohawk poet Maurice Kenny has been largely ignored by the literary establishment but has been widely admired by the present generation of young Indian poets for its service to the old idea that poetry, before it is anything else, is an oral art. We can only hope that the handsome retrospective *Between Two Rivers* will bring his work to a larger audience.

Though Kenny is deeply committed to Iroquois traditions, he has at various stages of his career produced work which reveals a wide knowledge of other Indian cultures and a great sympathy for the condition of Indian people everywhere. "I Am the Sun," for example, is a sequence of chants which employ Lakota motifs to commemorate the 1890 "ghost dance" episode at Wounded Knee and the tragedy to which it led. Perhaps more significant are those poems which employ traditional Iroquois elements and Kenny's thorough understanding of Iroquois history. The sequence "Blackrobe: Isaac Jogues" deals with the early encounter of the Iroquois with the Jesuits who sought to convert them to Christianity but whose efforts were foiled finally by the intrusion of politics. These poems reveal a full knowledge of the historical factors, seen from the point of view of all the participants, Iroquois and European, and this broad perception is evidence of Kenny's profound historical imagination as well as his recognition of the universality of his story.

In my view, however, Kenny's best poems are those that address moments in his own experience which are often painful and which go beyond any narrowly defined ethnic definition while depending for their very existence upon his awareness of himself as a Mohawk. *Between Two Rivers* includes many such poems, but three of the most moving are **"Going Home,"** about the anguish inherent in the return to the reservation of one who best understands his origins because he has been away from them; **"Black River,"** a poem about a boy's drowning which reads like a scream of pain; and **"Wild Strawberry,"** which is both a profound personal statement and a reaffirmation of the traditional Mohawk symbolism of the strawberry. Maurice Kenny's is an original voice. It is time to take account of it.

> The authentic poetic voice is for Kenny not merely a lyrical inner voice, but an oracular public one. He consequently stresses his affinity with the traditional storyteller or public singer of tribal days, and his poetry bears the rhythmic influence of song and chant.
>
> —*"ASAIL Bibliography, No. 4: Maurice Kenny," in* Studies in American Indian Literature, *Winter, 1983.*

Maurice Kenny   **(essay date Winter 1989)**

SOURCE: A preface to *Rain, and Other Fictions*, White Pine Press, 1990, pp. 9-10.

[*In the excerpt below from an essay first written in 1989, Kenny comments on fiction and poetry writing.*]

Never have I seriously considered myself a storyteller. This is not to say that I do not take the writing of fiction seriously. I take all my writing seriously—poetry, plays, essays, book reviews, letters, and fiction. Writing is my life, and life is a most serious matter indeed. Not writing is almost like ceasing to breathe; it is breath itself, as important as the morning stroll down my Saranac Lake hill or the Oklahoma University campus walk through flowering ovals, the listening to bird song, wind rustle, water rapids, flutes and guitars, the human voice. All writing holds equal importance, although one form may prove to be of a better quality than another. My regret is that I could never present these stories to James Purdy, Faulkner, Checkov or Maugham for either their pleasure or their critique.

I have always proclaimed that I am a singer of poetic song, and that my betters in fiction—Simon J. Ortiz, Peter Blue Cloud, Leslie Silko, Elizabeth Cook-Lynn—can out-spin me for tales. I have, however, occasionally pursued narrative in both story and one-act plays, not necessarily to spin a tale but more to delineate character. Narrative is a challenge. For me, it is a morning exercise as well, an exercise in ridding poetry of the statement of prose. (James Purdy once confided that his morning exercise was composing poems to rid his prose of lyric overture.)

The stories and one-act play in [*Rain, and Other Fictions*] make a small bundle, and my clutch of narrative poems would make a smaller bundle, still. I will not deny my surprise at seeing these stories in print nor the pleasure I've experienced in putting these stories down.

Publishers Weekly **(review date 11 May 1990)**

SOURCE: A review of *Rain, and Other Fictions*, in *Publishers Weekly*, Vol. 237, No. 19, May 11, 1990, p. 254.

[In the following review, the critic offers a negative assessment of Rain, and Other Fictions.*]*

Introducing his five stories and a one-act play [in *Rain and Other Fictions*], Kenny says that writing these kinds of narrative is "an exercise in ridding poetry of the statement of prose." Regrettably, this disappointing collection suggests that the exercise also strips his tales of poetry, the element that may have lifted them above the mediocre. In **"And Leave The Driving to Us,"** a teenager rides a bus from Denver to San Jose, Calif., in search of the father he has never encountered. **"Wet Moccasins"** describes a man who refuses to take his wife hunting, returns empty-handed that evening, yet still has fresh rabbit—the one his wife shot in the backyard—for dinner; he eats it, one assumes, with a side dish of crow. A group of Pueblo Indians dances to bring an end to the dry spell, but the cultural and religious event yields tourists and vendors as well as "Rain." In the one-act play set in a shabby hotel room, two men who met in the El Paso bus station decide to become *Buddies,* but the hotel clerk breaks up their friendship when he sics the police on them.

Robert L. Berner   (review date Winter 1991)

SOURCE: A review of *Rain, and Other Fictions,* in *World Literature Today,* Vol. 65, No. 1, Winter, 1991, p. 169.

[In the following excerpt, Berner comments favorably on the play and stories in Rain, and Other Fictions, *noting their relationship to Kenny's poetry.]*

Maurice Kenny may be the most distinguished figure in the renaissance that has occurred in American Indian poetry over the last three decades. *Rain and Other Fictions* is his first collection of fiction. In its preface he tells us that he has never considered himself a storyteller and that his interest in his fiction, as in his narrative poems, has been "not necessarily to spin a tale but to delineate character." In fact, he suggests that he has used prose as a device to purify his poems, a kind of "morning exercise" in which he has sought to get "the statement of prose" out of his system before getting down to the more important task of making poems.

All this suggests that Kenny is, and considers himself, less a prose writer than a poet who happens to write fiction. He thus brings to his secondary form a poet's concern for precision and exactness in diction, but the tendency of poetry to suggest and connote, to make implicit, may conflict with the more explicit methods of prose. These strengths and these weaknesses are evident in the stories and the one-act play which make up *Rain.*

James Purdy, an unfortunately neglected novelist, is mentioned twice by Kenny in his preface, and his influence is apparent in the play *Buddies.* Here two young vagrants, who have encountered each other in El Paso and have made an excursion to the Mexican side of the river, take a cheap hotel room, antagonize each other until they begin to identify with Pat Garrett and Billy the Kid preparing for their final shoot-out, and at the end of the play are about to be arrested for an unspecified crime.

Kenny's most successful efforts derive from his greatest strength as a poet, his ability to let his theme emerge out of his Mohawk context. An example is **"Yaikini"** (the word means "strawberries"), in which an old woman's collapse while picking strawberries is defined in relation not only to her disreputable past as a Brooklyn barfly but also to the spiritual power of strawberries, a theme that Kenny has developed in several poems.

The title story [**"Rain"**] is perhaps the most significant. Certainly it is a basic text in the study of the significance of tribal identity within the context of pan-Indianism. The Mohawk narrator, accompanying a Pueblo family to a rain dance at Santa Ana, realizes that he is far from his cooler, more verdant origins and that, in spite of the obvious spiritual power of the rain dance, it has nothing to do with him: "I am a stranger in this country."

Robert L. Berner   (review date Spring 1992)

SOURCE: A review of *Last Mornings in Brooklyn,* in *World Literature Today,* Vol. 66, No. 2, Spring, 1922, p. 387.

[Below, Berner remarks favorably on Last Mornings in Brooklyn.*]*

Maurice Kenny is perhaps the dean of American Indian poets, and his *Between Two Rivers: Selected Poems 1956-1984* revealed a wide range of skills and approaches to verse. *Last Mornings in Brooklyn* is a sequence of forty-six very brief poems (or a single poem in forty-six brief parts), composed of everything perceived in a particular street from an apartment window in Brooklyn Heights on a particular Saturday morning. Though the poet may not consider it a major addition to his work, a careful reading suggests that there is more to it than meets the superficial eye.

Kenny's minimalist intentions—not to capture all the time and space of a city but only a small moment in a specific setting—are stated in the first poem: "I put down Williams' *Paterson* / and pick up the street." The last poem in the sequence provides an angle of vision for understanding his intentions in his reply to a friend's question as to how a Mohawk can live in Oklahoma: "I burn / Cedar and Sage / and keep / an eye / on the bridge." We must assume that the bridge here is the Brooklyn Bridge and that for Kenny, as for Hart Crane, it is a metaphor for metaphor itself. By keeping his eye on it in his memory, he bridges the space between Mohawk country and Oklahoma—and the rest of America.

Maurice Kenny   (essay date March 1992)

SOURCE: A preface to *Tekonwatonti/Molly Brant (1735-1795): Poems of War,* White Pine Press, 1992, pp. 9-14.

[In the following excerpt, written while Kenny was visiting the En'owkin Centre in Okanagan, Canada, he comments on Molly Brant and his reasons for writing a volume of poetry about her.]

This moment finds me far from Iroquois country. This March morning I sit before the t.v. watching the Syracuse and Seton Hall basketball teams battling for a berth in the Final Four Tournament. This is about as close as I can get now to Molly Brant and home country, the Mohawk Valley and the high peaks of the Adirondacks where I live in the village of Saranac Lake . . . currently covered in deep snow and bitter cold. This morning the Canadian sun shines on the balcony, nurturing my African violet, which has not been doing well this season. Across the city, Penticton, I can see from the veranda the Okanagan range of the Cascades. The sun is strong on the mountain shoulders. I can discern no snow, yet there must be some beds in the shadows beneath the conifers. Below me bloom crocus, daffodils, a few striped tulips and yesterday, walking to campus, I spotted a single wild violet of this early spring poking its tiny head through a clump of dry autumn leaves. Out beyond in the higher peaks of the range, I know the animals are contemplating the warmth of this new season: squirrels are bounding around, raccoon are scenting fish in the stream, rabbits are scratching behind the ears, and I cannot but believe that grizzlies are yawning and staring at the blockaded entrances to the dens while on the edged slopes—the precipices—the goats and sheep, stirred by the freshness of air and light of the skies, are trotting from rock to rock in hope of finding fresh grass. At home, the pines and maple bend in the wind under heavy snows, white tails stand shivering, chipmunks huddle in the nest, perhaps a single black crow caws in the white morning.

Molly, Tekonwatonti, sometimes called Lady Mary Brown, is not in her traditional lands, either. Her bones sleep in a grave in Kingston, Ontario, Canada, where she passed away at the age of 60 in 1795, more or less under the protection of the English Crown, subservient to the Crown's largess, to her embarrassment and chagrin. She was a most independent woman of her own council, indifferent to the world's censure. Molly has been, as many women in history, particularly Native American women, shockingly ignored by the historians. In most books she remains a footnote, at best; an accessory to her husband, Sir William Johnson, whom she married only through tribal ceremony, an accessory to her famed blood brother, Joseph Brant. In research, one book was found devoted to Molly, a novel published in 1951 based, perhaps, on hearsay or legend with few facts. As her star seemed to fade, the glow of other Native women brightened: Sacajawea, guide to Lewis and Clark, and, of course, the apocryphal legend surrounding the mysterious Pocohantas. Molly was flesh and bones, blood and guts, truth and physical beauty, wry intellect. Her importance to American history surpasses that of these other two women, though they, too, played a role in the early scenes.

This collection [*Tekonwatonti/Molly Brant (1735-1795): Poems of War*], mainly of personae poems, was composed to shed light on Molly Brant, assure her prominence in the starry firmament, and to right some historical inaccuracies or lies into a semblance of at least poetic truth, if not recorded fact. There has been an attempt at drama, character, and beauty, as well as truth and candor. Many historical and biographical volumes were consulted; a few are mentioned in the glossary. . . .

Shortly I will leave Penticton, British Columbia, the lands of the Okanagan people, Skaha Lake, and the eastern slope of the Cascades. I'll exchange this land for that of the Adirondacks, of home, exchange one mountain panorama for another. It will be good to sleep once more in the aura of the Iroquois though the spirit of the Okanagan has been gentle yet embracing. The only regret I take with me is that I never saw a grizzly bear tramping through canyons or woods. There is still a chance that the fruit trees will blossom in the Okanagan Valley before the car is loaded and departs from the riches of the orchards. Packed with books, clothes and memories is a glass jar of arrowroot and wild cherries, some wild rice, syrups of the blackberries and raspberries, and remembrance of warm handshakes.

Two Mohawks, Molly and her poet, return to home country having left, I hope, some mark in this more western country.

An excerpt from "Molly: Passions"

I loathe war and blood; I think constantly
of spring, wind rustling in green corn,
violets ripening at the wood's edge,
young possums sucking life into their jaws.

Maurice Kenny, in his Tekonwatonti/Molly Brant (1735-1795): Poems of War, *White Pine Press, 1992.*

Lisa A. Mitten   (review date 1 February 1993)

SOURCE: A review of *Tekonwatonti: Molly Brant (1735-1795); Poems of War*, in *Library Journal*, Vol. 118, No. 2, February 1, 1993, p. 84.

[*Below, Mitten comments favorably on* Tekonwatonti.]

Written mostly by white males, the history of Native Americans is peopled by warriors and chiefs. Though women have been ignored and trivialized, they have played an important role in the culture and government of their people. Among the Iroquois, for instance, women have always chosen the leaders, guided them, and removed them when they failed to carry out their duties. Tekonwatonti (also known as Molly Brant) was a Mohawk woman who played a very powerful role during the French and Indian War. Sister of the renowned leader Joseph Brant and widow of the influential Sir William Johnson, she led the Mohawk fighters in support of the British because she believed that cooperation would secure Mohawk land. These narrative poems [in *Tekonwatonti: Molly Brant (1735-1795); Poems of War*] speak in the voices of Molly, of her family, and of male historical figures and occasionally introduce other noted Native American women. Mohawk poet Kenny has gone far toward restoring these patriots to their rightful places in American history.

Robert L. Berner   (review date Summer 1993)

SOURCE: A review of *Tekonwatonti/Molly Brant (1735-1795): Poems of War*, in *World Literature Today*, Vol. 67, No. 3, Summer, 1993, pp. 649-50.

[*In the following review, Berner offers praise for* Tekonwatonti, *but questions Kenny's claims of historical accuracy.*]

Molly Brant was the sister of the great Mohawk chief Joseph Brant and the wife of Sir William Johnson, who during the French and Indian War convinced the Mohawks that their best hope for political survival was to side with the English. Molly herself led the Mohawks on behalf of the English during the American Revolution and after the defeat lived out the rest of her life in Canada.

Tekonwatonti is an account of the life of this extraordinary woman, told in a series of monologues by Molly, Sir William, and others. Maurice Kenny intends it as an act of homage to American Indian women, who generally have been neglected by historians, and he particularly intends, he tells us in his preface, "to shed light on Molly Brant . . . and to right some historical inaccuracies or lies into a semblance of at least poetic truth." The work is, in other words, a conscious exercise in myth-making, the legitimate act of every poet who deals with the past, whether public or personal. To put it another way, Aristotle was right in his distinction between history and poetry—that is, between what happened and what, given the poem's premises, must happen.

We ought not to object, for example, to Kenny's reinforcement, in one of the poems, of a myth believed by many American Indians, namely that the inspiration for the United States Constitution was the organization of the Iroquois League: "If you would listen . . . / you would remember always / where your freedoms and liberties / first captured your attention." The historical fact, of course, is that the matriarchal organization of Iroquois clans and the intricate bloc-voting system of the League council, remarkable as they were, bear no resemblance whatever to the political structure prescribed by the Constitution. And the fact that an Iroquois orator told the Albany Congress (and Benjamin Franklin agreed) that the colonies ought to unite is hardly evidence of Iroquois influence on the Bill of Rights.

It is unfortunate, therefore, that Kenny chose in his prose glossary and chronology to claim historical accuracy for the mythic elements of the poems. For example, the woman chief Aliquippa, about whom very little is known—the historical record cannot even agree on her tribal affiliation—is described by Kenny as "an important Seneca woman [whose] character seems fogged, as many historians refuse to mention or clarify her importance." The fact is that historians have not mentioned her much because they must depend on documents, and the documents say very little about her. Kenny implies that she had something to do with Washington's defense of Fort Necessity, but the records of that episode indicate only that her group of what Kenny says were "warriors" was largely made up of women and children, and that after eating up a substantial amount of Washington's provisions they moved on before the French arrived.

As for the poems themselves, the most interesting and most effective are the monologues of Johnson and Molly. Both were Homeric in their accomplishments, passions, and appetites, and their interplay in the drama of their story is an accomplishment in characterization.

Kenny on Native American themes in his poetry:

I think they're always there. Okay, there's that old bromide that if you're Indian you're going to write Indian. Not necessarily true. That's hogwash, quite frankly. The themes were there because that's what I grew up with. I didn't know there was anything different from that. It was already in my work when I was thirteen, when I was seventeen and heavily influenced by [Walt] Whitman. He was one of the poets I read a great deal. It didn't come out of Whitman, but his being a singer naturally appealed to me. The poems I was writing at that time which were in natural speech, natural rhythm, reflected my Indian background.

Maurice Kenny, in Survival This Way: Interviews with American Indian Poets, *by Joseph Bruchac, 1987.*

Craig S. Womack   (essay date 1994)

SOURCE: "The Spirit of Independence: Maurice Kenny's *Tekonwatonti/Molly Brant: Poems of War*," in *American Indian Culture and Research Journal*, Vol. 18, No. 1, 1994, pp. 95-118.

[*Womack is a critic of Creek-Cherokee descent. In the essay below, he examines* Tekonwatonti/Molly Brant, *focusing on Kenny's characterization, narrative voice, depiction of male-female tensions, and contribution to Native American history.*]

Citizens of the Six Nations have long been known as keepers of tribal histories. The Tuscaroran Reverend David Cusick probably wrote the first native tribal history, his *Sketches of Ancient History of the Six Nations*, published in 1848. Cusick "turned back to the blanket" after becoming disillusioned with Christianity, as did the Huron convert Peter Dooyentate Clarke, a missionary who later disappeared after writing *The Origins and Traditional History of the Wyandots* in 1870. Other examples include Tuscaroran chief Elias Johnson's 1881 *Legends, Traditions, and Laws of the Iroquois* and Arthur Parker's many works. The famous wampum belts, which served as mnemonic devices to help pass on cultural, historical, and ritual information by word of mouth, predated these written accounts.

Contemporary poet Maurice Kenny's unique combination of historic and poetic faculties is an excellent addition to this body of tribal histories as well as to American poetry in general. The author's work [*Tekonwatonti/Molly Brant: Poems of War*], a twelve-year effort, is an example of incarnation: Kenny gives historical data a voice, a personality, a spirit. He demonstrates that what one can imagine is as real, as vital, as important as written history.

The poet, through his creative vision, speaks to the silence of American history, which has reduced powerful women like Molly Brant, wife of Sir William Johnson and leader of forces against the Americans in the Revolution, to mere footnotes.

Kenny's poetry employs themes that are used also by other contemporary Native American writers. These themes include survival in a culture that has already declared native people vanished; the role of the past in creating the present; cultural decay and the shallowness of contemporary values; a universe infused with spirit that can guide and instruct those willing to listen; the ongoing presence of ancestors; and the reverence of language. As the narrator E. Pauline Johnson says in Kenny's poem **"Generations,"** "My poems drum as a partridge drums on the earth; / they do not sing in falsetto." The same can be said of Maurice Kenny, whose poems do not name the literati or contain pretentious literary allusions. Instead, he draws on the earth as text; the landscape and the natural world are the poetic tradition out of which he writes. In addition, he draws upon Iroquoian culture and history as well as both European written poetic forms and the oral tradition. In this he is consistent with many other contemporary Native American poets.

Kenny has written poems inspired by traditional chant and dances, influenced by what one critic [Michael Castro, in his foreword to Kenny's *Humorous And/Or Not So Humorous,* 1988] calls "moments of intersection" with nature and the past; his travels have inspired poems in which he recreates the spirit of place. As Andrew Wiget has observed [in *Native American Literature,* 1985], "Kenny sings of connections with the land and history, delighting in the smallest moments of being, which disclose in their sudden beauty and grace the oneness of all living things." His poems also deal with displacement and the difficulties incurred in returning home and creating home when separated from one's familiar landscape. Against such discomforting problems, however, Kenny invokes a continuous ceremonial naming of sacred elements of landscape. This naming demonstrates the possibility of living in relationship to the soil even when away from home, the potential for bringing home into exile through participation with nature. These feelings for the environment are not a mere romantic subjectivity. Carolyn D. Scott says [in "Baskets of Sweetgrass," *Studies in American Indian Literatures* (Winter 1983)], "The recurrence of these images produces not the tiresome pretentiousness of private feeling, but rather intimations one can recognize as those belonging to home—the village fires." In other words, the response to nature has specific ceremonial precedents among Kenny's people, the Iroquois.

What makes *Molly Brant: Poems of War* different from other historical accounts is that the author writes the poems from an insider's, rather than an outsider's, viewpoint. The poems provide an immersion in the past as complete as what James Welch accomplishes in *Fools Crow.* This recovery of traditional life differs somewhat from the aforementioned novel, however, in that Kenny keeps the past continually linked to the present and draws attention to Molly Brant's ongoing influence. Native authors have shown in their writing a sacred respect for ancestral voices; they have provided many portrayals of these formative influences and have discussed means in which they still speak; Kenny, however, has created a full cultural context for a historical figure. This work surpasses Kenny's earlier book *Blackrobe: Isaac Jogues* because of the depth he has achieved in presenting Molly's consciousness, personality, and philosophy. In addition to the portrayal of Molly Brant, the author gives voice to a number of other complex characters.

Maurice Kenny begins his history in a traditional manner, with an evocation of the sacred. Rather than beginning with Molly's birth, Kenny reaches back to legendary time, to earlier beginnings, as a traditional storyteller would. I use the terms *legendary* and *legend* because the author has expressed, in writing and in conversations, his preference for those words over *mythical* and *myth.* Kenny argues that stories have ongoing relevance and feels that the former terms express that sense better than the latter.

The poem **"Te-Non-An-At-Che"** names the elements of creation in order to show that all things begin with stories:

Water was first

    Morning rolled
fog steamed
from mud
where pollywogs
wiggled.

And legends began

            drop

                drop

Kenny links legends, dripping down through time, with water, the first element. Stories and creation occur simultaneously. A traditional oral historical sequence occurs in the poem. This progression begins with naming primordial elements, naming plants and animals, naming persons, naming the people's migration as they journey forth from the place of origin.

Maurice Kenny is a poet of concrete images, of vivid characterization, of realistic voices. When he employs symbols—blood and strawberries, for example—these work as recurring motifs that resonate with meaning because they have a place in the stories of his people, and they have a cumulative effect as they pile on meaning throughout the corpus of his work. Kenny is not an obscure symbolist. He believes in poetry as an oracular performance as much as a written form. Those who have heard him read know that, for him, poetry means movement, physicality, sound; the release of adrenaline and the pounding of the bloodstream. Kenny's poetry has a performative quality. For instance, one succinct poem, written in the French Jesuit Abbé Picquet's voice, simply reads, "Ah! / Behold / my dream." Picquet makes this proclamation as he gazes at the military fort he coerced Mohawk men into building. During an oral performance of this line, the listener witnesses Kenny becoming Abbé Picquet.

Kenny's presentation of poetry is consistent with oral cultures in which the storyteller becomes the story. Spoken words are, by definition, actions, not arbitrary symbols; thus, word and deed are closely related. This is the way stories can be passed on and remembered in the absence of written backups—by total emotional involvement of both teller and listener. Stories, then, are a re-experiencing of events. They come to pass in their tellings. The story-teller uses gesture, movement, voice modulation, sophisticated imitations of characters, and other techniques that all reduce the objective distance between listener, teller, and story. A complete identification between word and audience occurs. Maurice Kenny's use of repetition and parallelism gives his poems the rhythm of chant; and the purpose of chant, in oral cultures, is to aid listeners in remembering information passed down by word of mouth. Chant also has the larger spiritual purpose of creating being through language so that whatever is spoken of comes to pass. Kenny's poems convey an oral quality in another way—through the author's re-creation of the voices of Chief Hendrick, Aliquippa, Chief Cornplanter, and others. Through these Iroquoian voices, Kenny captures the superlative oratory for which his people are known.

The genius of *Tekonwatonti/Molly Brant* is that Kenny creates voices that are lyrical and, at the same time, convincing as speech.

—Craig S. Womack

Maurice Kenny makes the historical treatment of Molly Brant and other characters particularly interesting by creating an imaginative dialogue between historical accounts and poetic voices. For example, in an excerpt from a historical text, Kenny records James Thomas Flexner, an American historian and biographer of Sir William Johnson and George Washington. Flexner comments on Molly Brant's capacity for violence. On the following page, Molly specifically addresses the accusation herself and denies it, stating that she loathes war and will accept it only as the last alternative for survival. She says, "I hate war, but love this earth and my kin more / than I hate battles and bravery. This / is my passion . . . to survive with all around me."

For a poet who makes repeated claims not to be a story-teller, Kenny has demonstrated a strong narrative voice. Recently, he has experimented with short stories in *Rain and Other Fictions;* in the preface to that book, he says,

> Never have I seriously considered myself a sto-ryteller . . . . I have always proclaimed that I am a singer of poetic song, and that my betters in fiction—Simon J. Ortiz, Peter Blue Cloud, Leslie Silko, Elizabeth Cook-Lynn—can out-spin me for tales. I have, however, occasionally pursued narrative in both story and one-act plays, not necessarily to spin a tale but more to delineate character. Narrative is a challenge. For me, it is a morning exercise as well, an exercise in ridding

> poetry of the statement of prose. . . . The sto-ries and one-act play in this book make a small bundle, and my clutch of narrative poems would make a smaller bundle, still.

Yet Kenny's strongest previous works are *Blackrobe: Isaac Jogues* (1982) and *The Mama Poems* (1984). The former was nominated for a Pulitzer, the latter received the American Book Award. Both books focus on single persons—an ambitious and lascivious Jesuit missionary in the first case and the author's mother in the second. Both are books of narrative poems. In *Molly Brant: Poems of War,* the storytelling voice that the poet has been insecure about has risen to new heights of power.

The genius of the book is that Kenny creates voices that are lyrical and, at the same time, convincing as speech. A good example is the character George Croghan, an Irish immigrant, an important influence in the Mohawk Valley. The poet captures the feeling of Croghan's concerns as settler, trader, and farmer, and represents them with a voice at once colloquial and poetic:

> Unsung and I don't give a damn. Not medaled, and I don't give a fart. No recompense, no spoils, no vast acreage for valor, and I don't give a damn fart for that either. I'm a woodsman. A father. A friend. I till the soil, I arrow a bird, I shoot a deer.

In this book, Maurice Kenny demonstrates more than ever that he has an ear for American speech and can create a wide range of voices. Examples of this diversity appear in the poems about Jennie, a Black slave held by William Johnson, and her daughter Juba. When the reader encounters Juba for the first time, she is repeating something that sounds like a ceremonial incantation concerning fire, and one wonders if Juba is practicing some kind of voodoo:

> jumm jumm jumm jumm fire jump fire jump sprinkle beads onto these flames jumm jumm jumm jumm.

Juba continues by chanting a spell-like incantation, and a lively scene is created of a girl ritualistically feeding a fire. In a later poem spoken in Jennie's voice, Kenny reveals that Juba is mentally unstable and that her father is William Johnson:

> Some say Juba is his chile. Now. She ain't right in the head. She jumm-jumms most of the time. Now. He don't come back anymore. I ain't no chile no more.

Kenny captures a broad linguistic diversity in these poetic voices—Iroquoian orators, slaves, immigrants, French Jesuit missionaries, Mohawk women, as well as more contemporary figures such as Mohawk poet E. Pauline Johnson. He structures the book in such a way—as he did *Blackrobe: Isaac Jogues*—that multiple voices comment on the same person, and the characters are examined from many different angles. As with Juba, he reveals characters cumulatively, and their personalities fall together for the reader as the book progresses.

The center of attention, and an omnipresence in all the poems, is Molly herself. Through his creative act, the author has established a strong relationship between himself and Molly Brant, evident because the poems are so convincingly and lovingly rendered. This makes the book an interesting addition to the poet's corpus, since the Jogues poems reflect a certain enmity toward the central character, whom Kenny depicts as the culture slayer.

An important consideration in evaluating Molly's personality and actions is the fact that she frames her identity within the context of an oral and communal culture rather than as a lone individual. In the poem **"I, Tekonwatonti,"** Molly's actions, especially with regard to warfare, are predicated on the effect they will have on her community rather than on political loyalties to the British, French, or Americans:

> I,
> I,
> Tekonwatonti, I
> no, we.

In switching from *I* to *we*, Molly subjugates her individual needs to the needs of the community.

Another poem that reflects this communal identity is **"Prayer for Aroniateka/Hendrick,"** an expression of mourning as well as thanksgiving, based on the Mohawk Condolence Prayer. Those who are grieving at the death of a longhouse chief offer this prayer to ease their sorrow. Kenny's poem, a prayer for Hendrick after his death in the battle of Lake George in 1755, shows that an individual death is a group concern. The narrator of the poem is the communal *we*, the voice of the community, which calls upon a powerful assemblage of ancestral voices to honor and aid Hendrick:

> We come with his father and his father and his
>   father
>   father and his father and his father
>   father and his father and his father
>   father and his father and his father
>   father and his father and his father
>
>   until the memory no longer contains
>   his father
>   father and his father and his fa-
>   ther
>   to the morning sky woman fell
>   with birds from the highest sky
>   to the turtle's back
>   and brought his father and his cousin
>   the twins of the sky

Molly recognizes that her very survival depends on sticking to her blood, adhering to communal ties. After William's death, when she and their eight children are turned out of Johnson Hall, she says,

> We'll contend. Take less, perhaps.
> We won't starve. A roof
> remains over our heads.
> We stand in a circle.

Molly's tendency to see herself as *we* rather than *I* provides an important context for her becoming a woman warrior after she learns of George Washington's vow to wipe the Mohawk off the face of the earth. As a clan mother responsible for the safety of the community, Molly regards the danger to her people as a personal threat.

"I, Tekonwatonti" is the first of seven consecutive poems that give voice to Molly's memorable personality. The sequence of seven poems is significant, of course, because of the sacredness of the number seven in relation to the cardinal directions and the realms of earth, sky, and water.

The poem **"Picking Gooseberries"** places Molly in a legendary context of multiple voices in dialogue, arranged on the page like the text for a play. Molly converses with Blue Bird, Black Bird, and Red Bird about women's concerns and, more specifically, about William's demands. It is the talk of women at ease among themselves, out of the earshot of men. In his poems and in conversations, Maurice Kenny often has depicted berry-picking as an important time for socialization, gossip, jokes, and storytelling, and **"Picking Gooseberries"** is a wonderful addition to that association. Berries, especially strawberries, are central images for the poet: In Iroquois storytelling, the Little People, who lived in a quarry without meat, took in Ragged Boy, who shared game with them. They, in turn, gave him the gift of strawberries and stories to take back to the people. When he returned to his community, he found that his people had moved and were starving, and the strawberries and stories restored them to health.

Throughout the body of his work, Kenny associates berry-picking with blood—from the pricked fingers of the pickers. In **"What the Chroniclers Did Not Record,"** the narrator says of Molly, "[S]he gathered summer berries, stained cheeks / with their blood. . . ." Of Doris in *The Mama Poems,* the speaker recalls,

>   Girls were raised /
> to work, to carry water for the laundry, wash
>   dishes, scrub
> floors, /
> shake the tick in the morning wind, scythe the
>   grasses, and
> bend, bend, /
> forever bend in the berry fields where you bled
>   profusely on
> the fruit. /
> Your face and gingham spotted with your first
>   knowledge,
> your first /
> lesson. You were never able to wash the blood
>   away. It stuck,
> hard /
> and dark to your cheek, your hands. . . .

By associating Molly with berry-picking, Kenny links her to the contemporary women of power who recur throughout his poetry. The omnipresent blood imagery creates a simultaneity of past, present, and future. Blood, in the sense of bloodline, connects ancestors with those in the present, as well as those to come. A major theme in the book, which comes to the foreground in the last two sections, "Women/Memory" and "Epilogue," is Molly's continuing existence, in the landscape and in her contemporary progeny. In the poem **"Generations,"** E. Pauline Johnson contrasts William's diminishment and Molly's continuance. She proclaims Molly to have the stronger life, which lasts and continues to speak to people. She associates both Molly and William with blood: Molly in a positive way, because her blood is connected to the earth; William negatively, because his blood is associated with growing smaller:

> If I open a vein, I shall fill this hanky with valley
>   earth
> Molly brought to Canada, dragging
> her children along by the hairs on their heads,
> not with his bones and blood that she left
>   (against her will)
> in that shallow grave near the river.
> He's only a dab of blood on this hanky.

The claim that Johnson's blood has minimal influence is a damning statement, coming from a traditional culture that reckons kinship back many generations. The very last poem in the book, **"Old Coyote in the Adirondacks,"** contrasts William's waning power with Molly's continuing influence today, even on nonhumans. The poem describes a coyote singing "on the curve / of his hill." It does not say what song the coyote sings as it "enter[s] / the night," but the poem's silence is suggestive. Its placement at the end of the volume strongly implies that it is Molly's song the coyote sings. The penultimate poem in the collection backs up this assertion. In the midst of the cultural loss, destructive technologies, and waste depicted in **"Sitting in the Waters of Grasse River,"** the creative elements that survive, such as Coyote, such as E. Pauline Johnson, such as Maurice Kenny, continue to sing Molly's song. This perpetual song in the natural world counterbalances the obliteration of native women's voices from written American history. The poem entitled **"Beth Brant, 1981: Letter & Post Card"** establishes a relationship between women warriors from the past and contemporary women warriors, who use words. The poems move back and forth between past and present, and Molly's life dramatizes the fact that responsibility for language precedes action; thus contemporary native writers utilizing language for survival have an affinity with warriors from the past, who spoke and fought. Beth Brant, the contemporary Mohawk poet and fiction writer mentioned in the title of the poem, is a blood descendant of Molly.

Kenny depicts Molly as a woman in a community of women with strong voices; in Iroquoian culture, women have powerful positions in the longhouse and a strong influence on the political and social life of the nation. In her book *The Iroquois in the American Revolution,* Barbara Graymont states,

> The practice of matrilineal descent gave women a unique position. Each clan was entitled to a certain number of chiefs, and the matrons of the clans could appoint and depose these chiefs. The white wampum belts which indicated the hereditary names of the chiefs were kept by the women. When a chief died, he did not pass his title on to his son, for titles were hereditary only in the clan; the son belonged to his mother's, not his father's clan. The chief's title would be inherited by one of his brothers or one of his sister's sons, or another male member of his clan matron's lineage.

The mothers also had much influence with the warriors. During the American Revolution, Mary Brant [another name for Molly], Mohawk widow of Sir William Johnson and herself a clan mother, was able to sway the wavering warriors and keep them loyal to the British. The women, usually through a warrior chosen as their speaker, could always make their wishes known in council. Even an esteemed white woman living in Indian country could exercise unusual prerogatives, as did the Tory Sarah McGinnis when she prevented a wampum belt bearing news of an American victory over the British from going farther than her village. When the council could not agree on a certain issue, they referred the problem to the council of clan mothers. Among the Iroquois, the women thus had greater status and more control over the affairs of their nation than did the women of the European countries and their colonial settlements.

In Maurice Kenny's poems, Molly's boldness, her flouting of English tradition in her marriage to William, and her prodigious ability to learn white culture while remaining quintessentially Mohawk make her a singular personality. George Croghan, an Irish immigrant who became influential among the Iroquois, says of Molly in one poem,

> She knew how to hoe and how to sew.
> She could command servants and an army.
> She could birth a child and scalp a Frenchman.
> She could dine the governor and hunt mud frogs
> or snap a turtle's neck before presenting his
>   soup.
> Nothing was beyond her accomplishment, her
>   reach.

Molly's gentility and beauty are offset by a savvy and a refusal to be possessed like the white women of William's class. In spite of her access to white culture, she maintains a strong relationship with the earth and a spirit-based view of the universe. She combines the two cultures in creative and powerful ways. In **"Flight,"** a poem about her exile after the American Revolution, Molly says, "I left my son's placenta in leaves / tied with wild grapevines." This description of the return of life-giving tissue from Molly's own body to the soil strongly dramatizes her relationship with the earth. In the same poem, Molly goes on to say,

> I carried a small packet of soil,
> earth rich and dark in claim,
> moist from women's sweat working fields of
>   squash,
> still firm from feet dancing in celebration,
> warm with William's footprint,
> vibrant with Hendrick's oratory.
> I fled.

The passage shows Molly's recognition of the power of the earth to absorb human activity and to carry spirit voices. She carries a packet of earth to a new place, in a poignant attempt to bring home into her place of exile, to carry with her that which forms her, the most fundamental part of her identity. Molly's pain results from leaving behind part of herself in the landscape, the place where her kin and her ancestors lie buried. Kenny closely ties the soil to memory and culture: "A people who do not remember: / *rain which falls upon a rock.*" Rain that falls on a rock does not penetrate the soil; forgetting one's culture involves forgetting the place from which one comes, the soil beneath one's feet. The clan mother Aliquippa says,

> Memory
> does not die under autumn leaves, crisp and
>   brown;
> memory is on the wind, the shine of stars,
> the echo of song and story told winter nights.

Kenny brings out Molly's natural acceptance of inexplicable phenomena and mystery in the poem **"The Lights Are Always Near."** Here Molly lovingly explains that no one needs to fear the supernatural. The English mistake Molly's traditionalism for witchcraft, and they blame her for all the problems in the colonies: barrenness, drought, and war. Her husband William, however, recognizes that natural elements, not witchcraft, define Molly:

> Yes, I laugh.
> True, you are a witch, alchemist
> of September apples, red and savory
> in the bin of the springhouse;
> you are the bite of cider,
> the bitter of bush cranberries,
> the smart of fire rising under
> your kitchen kettles. . . .

This continues Kenny's custom of fusing characters so closely with the natural environment that there is no separation between their physical bodies and the elements of nature. Previous poems such as **"Mulleins Are My Arms"** and **"Legacy"** have emphasized the internalization of nature within the body of the speaker. This breaks down the division under which Western thought has labored for so long—the difference between an internal view and an external view of the physical world, the opposition of flesh and spirit. The fluidity of Maurice Kenny's work makes it seem natural for a human to speak for rocks and trees and water, because humans are composed of such elements themselves.

The poems can also be viewed as war literature, since they show the effects of war, not only on warriors but on a culture, on the landscape, on creation, on all one's relations. Molly fights against the extermination promised by George Washington. Barbara Graymont says,

> The expedition against the Six Nations would be one of the most carefully planned campaigns of the entire war. General Washington, fully aware of the significance of the Indian-Tory devastations on the frontier, wanted to remove the menace once and for all. . . . A strike against the Indians would humble them and perhaps cause them to ask for peace. Total destruction of their villages and crops, even if it did not pacify them, would make them a greater burden to the British and divert foodstuffs required by the British army to the support of the Indians.

Graymont points out that the Iroquois did not have the luxury of remaining neutral during the war. She writes that "for over a century [prior to the Revolution] the Iroquois had been accustomed to thinking of the English as one people—the children of the Great King beyond the sea." No matter who they sided with, the Iroquois would

face repercussions, and "because of both historic economic dependence and geographic contiguity, they could not withdraw completely, ignoring the whites and their quarrel." Graymont has documented that the colonists often employed barbarous methods of warfare. She reports that American troops led by Colonel Goose Van Schaick lay waste an entire Onondaga village, killing twelve and taking thirty-three prisoners, most of them women surprised in a cornfield. The Onondaga reported that the soldiers raped the women in spite of General James Clinton's earlier written warning: "Bad as the savages are, they never violate the chastity of any women, their prisoners. Although I have very little apprehension that any of the soldiers will so far forget their character as to attempt such a crime on the Indian women who may fall into their hands, yet it will be well to take measures to prevent such a stain upon our army."

Molly understands the unavoidable connection between war and loss, no matter what the justification:

> wolf
> clan
>   paints red
>   for war
>   paints black
>   for mourning

1984 AMERICAN BOOK AWARD WINNER

THE MAMA POEMS
by
MAURICE KENNY

Cover for Kenny's prizewinning collection The Mama Poems.

A loss is incurred the moment the decision is made to go to war, requiring ceremonial recognition of grief even before the first bodies fall. Even though Molly aligns her warriors with the British, she feels no great loyalty to their cause. She recognizes that the political power brokers do the talking, while young men and their families do the bleeding: "The rebels will win, and we lose, / not the red-coats; we, we the people, / the 'real people' will lose." The phrase *we the people* is ironic in that, in the United States Constitution, these same words exclude the native peoples who predated the loyalists and colonists. During the Revolution, these "real people" are the true losers, and their fight, against biological and cultural extinction, has much higher stakes.

As a leader, Molly accepts responsibility for the death of her warriors: "In death their blood / will scar my hands forever," and "the loss will be too great / to bear." She must avoid unnecessary waste of life, while at the same time protecting and insuring the survival of her people and culture. Thus, she prays,

> Give me good sense
> so I may not waste
> a single drop of the blood
> of these young and brave
> who fight for England now
> but truly for the survival
> and strength of the Longhouse.

In a poem entitled **"Molly: Passions,"** Molly summarizes her philosophy of war. She particularizes her viewpoint by first naming those elements of creation that make life worth living: "Yes, oh yes, passions for blackberry / blossoms, the clank of deer bones winning games, / river water sluicing against canoes. . . ." Molly will accept war only if it is the sole alternative to seeing her relatives wiped off the face of the earth: "I hate war, but love this earth and my kin more / than I hate battles and bravery. This / is my passion . . . to survive with all around me." She fights for the very thing that has created the Mohawk people: the land, which contains their stories and their dreaming of themselves, "for a long march to defend our priceless birthright / to new dawns and darknesses, our old stories / and old songs." Finally, Molly fights not only for humans but for the spirit and substance of the land and the creatures that occupy the land, against their potential destroyers:

> Who would not
> " . . . defend her mother's womb."
> All around me is my mother's womb.
> I lay claim to it.
> This is my passion: life. And the right
> to all it holds: blackberry blossoms,
> marsh iris, the growl of bear at night,
> light rising and falling upon our lodges,
> the rivers that bathe us and slack our thirst,
> and that old plum tree flowering winter with
>   snow.

Sir William Johnson, an Irish immigrant to the colonies who was appointed superintendent of Iroquois affairs in 1746 and who enlisted Mohawk warriors on the British side against the French, married Molly in a tribal ceremony but not according to British law. In the poem entitled

"Sir William Johnson: His Daily Journal," William explains that he falls philosophically between George Croghan, who believed in land acquisition through forceful moderation, and George Washington, who supported total extermination of those who occupied the land. William feels sympathy for the Mohawk, since he has Mohawk sons and thus a vested interest in the people's survival. However, he does not become a member of their community, and he posits value in his individual ownership of parts of the Mohawk Valley. William acts like a traditional only in order to gain advantages in trade. He displays genuine affection for Molly, but he does not love her enough to allow her to get in the way of land acquisition. In keeping with the incipient agrarian tradition of his time, William sees no value in the wilderness until it is turned under by the plow:

> Truly, do I thirst, tremble at the sight
> of unclaimed woods, woods which do not echo
> the sounds of an ax striking bark;
> earth unplowed, seedless, a womb virgin
> having borne neither phallic plow nor fruit.

This avowal of the virtues of a tamed landscape extends to his view of women. Just as William advocates penetration of the soil, he also values women in direct relationship to their fruitfulness:

> Ahhhhh! Woman, I'll round thy belly to a hun-
>   dred sons.
> Woman and land: the earth is a fallow woman,
> its portals dark and mysterious, yielding the ze-
>   nith
> in stratospheric music which men only hear
> when eyes are closed, chest and thighs sticky
> in lustful sweat, mucilaged to the fat of her
> scented flesh, writhing in groans, tendering
> her to orgasm. . . .

William comes across as a buffoon in this poem, and Kenny's hilarious performance of the piece with a macho Falstaffian bravado is highly memorable. Women and earth, according to William, do not have a fundamental integrity of their own apart from their usefulness to man. William seems both excited and threatened by Molly's power, a power not atypical for an Iroquoian woman but anathema from a British standpoint. He misinterprets Molly's abilities as an overbearing masculinity:

> Molly, I nearly said,
> man like man: Cut my tongue, couple my hands
> to be the step for your boot to mount the black
>   gelding,
> to ride off, possibly to die as I would die
> for these acres of woods and field, for this flag,
> the crown.

The strong castration image, suggested by the black gelding and by William as bootstep for Molly's mounting, implies that William fears this woman who can entertain aristocracy *and* lead warriors, yet he seems titillated by her manly qualities as well.

Although Molly plays a warrior's role, Kenny gives no indication that she has a warrior's spirit or a masculine sexual identity. In many cases in traditional cultures, a man or woman who had a homosexual orientation would have a matching social role that the tribe nurtured, accepted, and considered a part of the person's spiritual identity. The community saw such persons as powerful individuals who should be treated respectfully. Although Kenny was the first native author to publish an essay on the role of the berdache—he was concerned that much of this information had been purposely hidden by white anthropologists—he gives no indication that Molly is one of these two-spirited women (a person who can see from both the male and female worlds). Molly's warrior role seems to be borne strictly out of necessity. She states that she loathes war, and, if not for the threat of imminent extermination, she would have nothing to do with it. In addition, in Iroquoian culture, it was a norm for women to be closely involved in warrior activities. Graymont cites several instances of other Iroquoian women in battle; of the influence of women on warriors, she says,

> The women had significant influence with the warriors and could frequently make or break a war party by their support or disapproval of the warriors' enterprise. It was the women who provided the warriors with moccasins and charred corn pounded into meal and sweetened with maple sugar for their journey. The women also had the power to veto a war declaration by withholding these supplies.

Further, Molly's natural proclivities do not seem inclined toward a masculine role. In fact, Molly's natural femininity makes her male role as a warrior all the more striking. The Seneca clan mother Aliquippa explains women's reasons for involvement in the French and Indian War:

> Women warriors. We assumed we fought
> for freedom, our land, earth, for the joy
> of dawn and the rest of dark night.
> We were told the French would burn
> our villages, decimate our children,
> mutilate the prowess of our men.

Aliquippa goes on to say that women, as clan leaders, maintain serious responsibilities for leading men and instructing them in communal maintenance:

> Were we
> not the leaders of our clans, obliged to prod
> the men to hunt or war to feed and protect
> the village our hands constructed, our wombs
> populated, our minds furbished?

Thus, powerful women like Molly and Aliquippa, responsible for the welfare of the community, must defend it, if necessary.

In many interesting ways, both William and Molly resemble characters in earlier works like *Blackrobe* and *The Mama Poems*. Kenny depicts the two male figures, William Brant and Isaac Jogues, as being out of balance in terms of their sexual appetites. Jogues is attracted to the boys in the Mohawk village where he proselytizes. The poems show him casting furtive glances at the young men. This, in and of itself, would not create a problem in traditional Mohawk culture, which, generally speaking, accepted sexual variance with much more tolerance than

contemporary society does. However, Jogues, an outsider in every sense of the word, loathes the traditional ways of the people and spouts words of Christian damnation in response to Mohawk sexual practices. The poem **"Hoantteniate"** implicitly suggests that Jogues is involved sexually with his adopted Mohawk brother (at least, this reader interprets the poem that way). The poem shows a softer, more loving side of Jogues, but when he sees the same expression of sexuality among the people, he finds it abominable.

In the *Molly Brant* poems, Kenny depicts William's relationships with women as equally unbalanced. George Croghan says of him,

> He was profligate, Will was, and she courted his
> desires salaciously. She was young and ripe, ripe
> as the yellow pear hanging on his front yard tree.
> She was young, she was full of ginger, mustard;
> Will was lecherous, a woman masher, taken too
> early from his own mother's teat. . . .

William's lust takes the form of relationships with his slaves and myriad other women and includes bigamy. William purchased Catherine Weisenberg as an indentured servant from a Mohawk Valley farmer. The author states in the prologue that William, in blatant denial of his tribal marriage to Molly, "married Catherine the night she died and legitimized their union and children." Kenny indicates that "certain historians have hinted that Johnson may have fathered some two-hundred children, including Juba [a slave], by various women."

Further, a similarity exists in the tension between Sir William and Molly in this book and between Doris and Andrew in *The Mama Poems*. In both cases, adoring women devote themselves to men who behave sometimes lovingly and sometimes scandalously and rapaciously. Just as William is profligate and views women as valuable only in their usefulness to men, Andrew also can be cruel:

> No doubt he gave you a rough time,
> probably whacked you once or twice.
>
> .
>
> .
>
> .
> and I've heard it said he'd pinch
> a waitress' buttocks, never refused a bed.
> He taught you how to drive his car
> and promptly took the Ford away.
> He'd buy you a new dress and grumbled
> if you wore it. He even upbraided you
> for buying a pound of butter
> at fifteen cents a pound.

Andrew, like Jogues and William, seems to take advantage of the women in his life. (Jogues unfeelingly used Wolf Mother, the Mohawk woman who adopted him.) However, Andrew has qualities the speaker admires. In the context of the poems and in interviews, the author has described how his father provided a link to Mohawk culture and, in fact, rescued him in his teenage years when he got into trouble and risked being sent to a reformatory. It is difficult not to apply these autobiographical statements to *The Mama Poems,* since the author himself has chosen to begin the collection with a biographical statement about his mother. In the poems, Kenny states that the last word from Andrew's mouth is "Doris" and that he carries a snapshot of her until his death. So the male-female relationships in *Molly* and *The Mama Poems* involve a kind of love that stings yet endures, that remains healthy in some ways and disturbing in others.

Kenny presents the tension between William and Molly in a scene that is both taut and playful. William is seated before her. Knife in hand, she plucks his hair for battle:

> No, no,
> I won't take too much,
> my knife is sharp.
> You don't trust my knife?
> I wouldn't yank it from your scalp.

These relationships that grind against one another seem to have a kind of passion and vitality caused by the very elements that make them disturbing. If nothing else, each partner is so memorable to the other that they carry each other's spirit with them to the grave.

Kenny brings vitality to his presentation of characters by drawing on relationships that are familiar to him and infusing this personal background into his poetry.

—*Craig S. Womack*

In *The Mama Poems,* Doris, like Molly, has prodigious talents and can transcend male/female roles:

> Your qualities were never baking,
> but when you rolled up the sleeves
> and baited your own hook,
> or cleaned a mess of trout
> or string of November rabbits
> even when we demanded you darn
> socks or heal blisters, fight
> a cold. . . .

The Mama Poems end, as do the *Molly Brant* poems, with the speaker's realization that the lives of powerful women transcend death through their ongoing presence in the land:

> I believe in echoes now,
> in earth that holds you. I believe in a bird,
> its flight, though I'm not sure which one, hawk
> or seagull; the cedar near your grave, and the
>   lake
> not far away that you feared from childhood.

It seems, then, that Maurice Kenny brings vitality to his presentation of characters by drawing on relationships that are familiar to him and infusing this personal background into his poetry. The overall effect is compelling; what is particularly interesting is that it fits a larger cultural tension. The author begins *The Mama Poems* with the Mohawk version of the Iroquois creation story, which reports a strong male-female tension:

> Right-handed Twin came naturally from his

mother, the daughter impregnated by the West Wind, of Sky-woman. But his brother, Left-handed Twin, impatiently sprang early from his mother's armpit and killed her from his unnatural escape from her body.

The matricide in the legendary story comes up in an interesting way in **"On the Staten Island Ferry,"** from *The Mama Poems:*

> You brought me here when I was ten
> . . .
> A friend suggested I write
> a novel of how I wanted to push
> you off the ferry into the wake . . .
> fall like Sky-woman fell from the old world.
> My friend said impatience cured
> curiosity, but I don't think novels
> cure pain nor intention of guilt.
>
> This morning the sun hangs
> in the eastern sky and the moon
> sits in the west. They eye each other,
> jealous siblings never
> willing to share a dandelion
> nor rib of venison. As I could not do
> without a mother we cannot do
> without their argument.
> They'll continue contesting
> on such mornings as this, and I
> will continue pleased that you
> had not been swallowed in the ferry's wake.
> . . .
> My father took me home again.

The poem begins with the line about the boy's mother bringing him to the ferry and ends with his father taking him home. In the midst of all this ambivalence, the poem alludes to the legend about Left-handed Twin accidentally killing his mother, and it seems to suggest that the story that informs the poem actually keeps things in balance: "As I could not do / without a mother we cannot do / without their argument." In fact, the legend seems to help the speaker deal with his feelings and provides a cathartic release for his hostilities. The analysis here is not an attempt to be psychoanalytical, but, since the author himself raises these issues in the poems, it makes for an interesting comparison. In the whole body of work, one sees this kind of tension often: Wolf Mother protecting Jogues against the leaders of the Bear Moiety, who want to kill him; sibling, parental, and masculine and feminine tension in the poem "Sometimes . . . Injustice" in *The Mama Poems;* Molly with the knife to Sir William's scalp in *Molly Brant*. If anything, because of their consistency in all three books and the way they hearken back to legendary stories, these themes strengthen the poetry and broaden the author's vision, depicting vital, passionate, sometimes disturbing relationships between men and women.

In addition to these interesting personal relationships, *Molly Brant* reminds us of those persons who suffered under both banners—the Union Jack and the star-spangled one. The poems suggest that, in addition to honoring George Washington as father of our country, we must acknowledge other names for the first president if we wish to invoke the liberating power of truth. The Mohawk called him "town exterminator" because of his policy of total annihilation. Cornplanter, in 1790, had this to say to George Washington: "When your army entered the country of the Six Nations, we called you Town Destroyer: and to this day when that name is heard our women look behind them and turn pale, and our children cling close to the necks of their mothers."

Maurice Kenny's poetry demonstrates that, in order to understand historical figures like Washington, we need to know all their names. Contemporary people can heal the wrongs of the past only by creative empathy, not by "putting the past behind us." Cultural memory—accessible through the imagination and brought to life in this body of poems—rather than cultural amnesia provides our best hope for survival. Lying and covering up, not truth-telling, threaten democracy. Traditional cultures have great potential in contemporary society because of the power they attribute to the word as a force for change.

Further, the creation of new stories that take into account modern circumstances is as important as the maintenance of old ones. Traditions can be carried forward into the present by imagining, remembering, telling. Seneca clan mother Aliquippa prophesies,

> Again
> we will eat succotash, drink soup.
> Singers will stand and sing, our daughters will
> pick strawberries, wild and red, from the mead-
> ows.
> Our men will thank the deer for his flesh.
> Wolf will trot the old mountains
> and the elders lead us in prayer.
> We will have forgotten nothing.

Maurice Kenny and Aliquippa have shown us a way of taking back our own history.

Additional coverage of Kenny's life and career is contained in the following sources published by Gale Research: *Contemporary Authors*, Vol. 144; and *Native North American Literature.*

Beloved

Toni Morrison

The following entry presents criticism on Morrison's novel *Beloved* (1987). For further information on her life and works, see *CLC,* Volumes 4, 10, 22, 55, and 81.

INTRODUCTION

Awarded the Pulitzer Prize for Fiction in 1988, *Beloved* is the most celebrated and controversial of Morrison's novels. Inspired by the story of Margaret Garner, a runaway slave who attempted to kill her children rather than have them returned to slavery, Morrison's novel explores the psychological and physical violence caused by slavery, its lingering effects on successive generations of black Americans, and the dynamics of mother-child relationships. *Beloved* became a source of controversy several months after its publication. When it failed to win a 1987 National Book Award or National Book Critics Circle Award, forty-eight prominent black writers and critics signed a tribute to Morrison's career and published it in the 24 January 1988 edition of *The New York Times Book Review.*

Plot and Major Characters

Set twelve years after the end of the Civil War, *Beloved* focuses on Sethe, a former slave who escaped with her four children from a Kentucky plantation known as Sweet Home in 1855. The traumatic events of her past—which include attempted suicide and her decision to murder her eldest daughter in an attempt to save her once and for all from bondage—are narrated in discontinuous flashbacks. Having been released from prison through the aid of abolitionists, Sethe lives with her youngest daughter, Denver, in an isolated farmhouse near Cincinnati, Ohio, and believes that the ghost of her deceased daughter, "Beloved," haunts the house. The novel opens with the unannounced arrival of Paul D., a former slave from the Sweet Home plantation. His attempts to form a sexual relationship with Sethe, however, are thwarted by a mysterious woman named Beloved, whom Sethe and Denver believe to be an incarnation of Sethe's dead child. Although rumored to be a ghost, Beloved becomes Paul D.'s lover as well as a close friend to Denver. Beloved's memories of her past, however, suggest that she is not a ghost, but someone who has suffered the rigors of a transatlantic crossing aboard a slave ship and the trauma of watching her mother throw herself overboard. While Beloved, who considers Sethe her long-lost mother, initially shows spite and anger towards Sethe, she is gradually appeased by Sethe and Denver's attempts at reconciliation. The novel closes with Beloved's apparent departure, after Sethe inadvertently reenacts her "defense" of her late daughter by attacking a Quaker abolitionist, whom she mistakes for a slave trader, in order to protect Denver.

Major Themes

The central concerns of *Beloved* are the ethical dilemmas posed by slavery, the complex imperatives of individual and collective memory, the dynamics of the mother-child relationship, and the importance of community. By focusing on a violent infanticide, which is publicly denounced despite its mitigating circumstances, Morrison illuminates slavery from the anguished perspective of its victims. Memories too painful and "evil" to bear can be submerged but inevitably return in the form of "ghosts": Sethe views Beloved as the ghost of her daughter, while the distraught Beloved transfers her feelings for her late mother to Sethe. In contrast to traditional abolitionist accounts of slavery, in which the evils of slavery and the virtues of the oppressed are rendered in stark opposition, Morrison focuses on difficult ethical problems regarding relations among slaves and former slaves. Prominent among the dilemmas Morrison addresses within the mother-child context are abandonment, infanticide, and suicide—the complexity and ambiguity of which are exacerbated by the realities of slavery. Through her dramatization of Sethe and Denver's isolation from the black community, Sethe's refusal to seek expiation, and their eventual reintegration into the community, Morrison demonstrates the importance of community ties for the individual's well-being.

Critical Reception

Despite its popularity and status as one of Morrison's most accomplished novels, *Beloved* has never been universally hailed as a success. Some reviewers have excoriated the novel for what they consider its excessive sentimentality and sensationalistic depiction of the horrors of slavery, including its characterization of the slave trade as a Holocaust-like genocide. Others, while concurring that *Beloved* is at times overwritten, have lauded the novel as a profound and extraordinary act of imagination. Noting the work's mythic dimensions and political focus, these commentators have treated the novel as an exploration of family, trauma, and the repression of memory as well as an attempt to restore the historical record and give voice to the collective memory of African Americans. Indeed, critics and Morrison herself have indicated that the controversial epitaph to *Beloved*, "Sixty Million and More," is drawn from a number of studies on the African slave trade which estimate that approximately half of each ship's "cargo" perished in transit to America. Scholars have additionally debated the nature of the character Beloved, arguing whether she is actually a ghost or a real person. Numerous reviewers, assuming Beloved to be a supernatural incarnation of Sethe's daughter, have subsequently faulted *Beloved* as an unconvincing and confusing ghost story. Elizabeth E. House, however, has argued that Beloved is not a ghost, and the novel is actually "a story of two probable instances of mistaken identity. Beloved is haunted by the loss of her African parents and thus comes to believe that Sethe is her mother. Sethe longs for her dead daughter and is rather easily convinced that Beloved is the child she has lost." Such an interpretation, House contends, clears up many puzzling aspects of the novel and emphasizes Morrison's concern with familial ties.

PRINCIPAL WORKS

The Bluest Eye (novel) 1970
Sula (novel) 1973
The Black Book [editor] (nonfiction) 1974
Song of Solomon (novel) 1977
Tar Baby (novel) 1981
Dreaming Emmett (drama) 1986
Beloved (novel) 1987
Jazz (novel) 1992
Playing in the Dark: Whiteness and the Literary Imagination (essays) 1992
Rac-ing, Justice, En-gendering Power: Essays on Anita Hill, Clarence Thomas and the Construction of Social Reality (nonfiction) 1992

CRITICISM

Walter Clemons   (review date 28 September 1987)

SOURCE: "A Gravestone of Memories," in *Newsweek*, Vol. CX, No. 13, September 28, 1987, pp. 74-5.

[*Clemons is an American critic and short story writer. In the following review, he praises* Beloved *as a masterpiece of psychological and historical evocation which re-creates the "interior life" of black slaves "with a moving intensity no novelist has even approached before."*]

In 1855 a runaway slave from Kentucky named Margaret Garner was tracked by her owner to Cincinnati, where she had taken refuge with her freed mother-in-law. Cornered, she tried to kill her four children. Afterward, she was quite serene about what she had done. A newspaper account of this stark event taken from a documentary sourcebook stayed in Toni Morrison's mind over the years. Now it has become the germ of a magnificent novel.

In a lecture last year [1986], Morrison spoke about omissions in slave narratives written for abolitionist readers during the 19th century. Addressing sympathetic whites, blacks tactfully suppressed feelings of outrage that might offend their hearers. They mentioned "proceedings too terrible to relate" only in formulaic euphemism. They "forgot" many things. "Most importantly—at least for me," Morrison said, "—there was no mention of their interior life."

In *Beloved,* this interior life is re-created with a moving intensity no novelist has even approached before. Morrison has been able to imagine an existence of almost unimaginable precariousness, in which it was illegal for slaves to be taught to read or write, to love and marry with any expectation of permanence, to become parents with any hope of living with their children to maturity.

Through Morrison's bold imagination, the historical Margaret Garner has become Sethe, a stoic outcast; she lives with one daughter in the house outside Cincinnati given to her mother-in-law by a kindly abolitionist. Eighteen years have passed; it's 1873. Sethe's mother-in-law—an eloquent preacher known as Baby Suggs—has died and her two sons have run away, frightened by their mother and by the capricious ghost that shakes the house—the malicious spirit, apparently, of the baby daughter Sethe succeeded in killing before she was prevented from killing the others.

To this house comes Paul D, a former slave on the plantation in Kentucky from which Sethe escaped. Soon there's another arrival—a mysterious, blank-eyed young woman from nowhere, whom Sethe's daughter Denver at once accepts as her murdered sister, grown up and come back from the dead. This is Beloved, who takes her name from the word chiseled on the gravestone of Sethe's dead child.

To outline this story is to invite the very resistance I felt on first reading it. A specter returned to bedevil the living? A Gothic historical romance from Toni Morrison? But with magisterial confidence Morrison has employed a monstrous anecdote as entrance key to the monstrosity of slavery. The Emancipation Proclamation was issued exactly a decade before this novel begins. Though technically "freed," the book's black characters have stumbled into post-Civil War existence unable to free themselves from memories of a system in which they had no rightful ownership of a Self. Memory is so oppressive for the novel's characters that stifling it is a means of survival. The splintered, piecemeal revelation of the past is one of the technical wonders of Morrison's narrative. We gradually understand that this isn't tricky storytelling but the intricate exploration of trauma.

Morrison casts a formidable spell. The incantatory, intimate narrative voice disarms our reluctance to enter Sethe's haunted house.

—*Walter Clemons*

Under a system in which "men and women were moved around like checkers," Sethe's murderous act was a distorted exertion of her balked maternal instinct. "She ain't crazy. She love those children," says a black man who was at the scene. "She was trying to outhurt the hurter." "My children my best thing," Sethe says, her sense of her own value having been maimed. She wanted to rescue her children from the life she'd fled, and killing them to prevent their return to slavery was the expedient that occurred to her. She welcomes the arrival of the spectral Beloved as a chance to explain herself. Sethe's arrogance has made the black community of Cincinnati shun her, and Paul D, who has not heard of her bloody past during his own 18 years of wandering, deserts her when he learns of it. Her isolation binds her in an unholy relation with Beloved.

At the heart of this astounding book, prose narrative dissolves into a hypnotic, poetic conversation among Sethe, Denver and the otherworldly Beloved. The broken speech of Beloved reveals that she's something other than the ghost of Sethe's murdered baby. "You think she sure 'nough your sister?" Paul D asks Denver. Denver replies: "At times I think she was—more." In Beloved's monologue we can grasp that this something "more" is that she remembers passage on a slave ship, which Sethe's murdered baby couldn't have. Though Sethe and Denver have accepted Beloved as the reincarnation of the dead baby, grown up into a young woman with a baby's insatiable demands—and Sethe never learns otherwise—Beloved is also a ghost from the slave ships of Sethe's ancestry. Beloved rose from water in a nearby river to come to Sethe's doorstep. Sethe invited the invasion, wanting to justify herself, but the Beloved who materialized has an anterior life deeper than the ghostly role she fulfills in the Cincinnati household she visits.

Morrison casts a formidable spell. The incantatory, intimate narrative voice disarms our reluctance to enter Sethe's haunted house. We are reassured by feeling that the eerie story is reinforced by exact attention to verifiable detail about the lives of postwar Cincinnati blacks and the inferno from which they emerged. When Sethe's Cincinnati neighbors come to her rescue, and the incubus child who nearly consumed her life has vanished, the flood of daylight that ends the book is overpowering. I think we have a masterpiece on our hands here: difficult, sometimes lushly overwritten, but profoundly imagined and carried out with burning fervor.

Gail Caldwell   (essay date 6 October 1987)

SOURCE: "Author Toni Morrison Discusses Her Latest Novel *Beloved*," in *Conversations with Toni Morrison,* edited by Danille Taylor-Guthrie, University Press of Mississippi, 1994, pp. 239-45.

[*The essay excerpted below was originally published in* The Boston Globe *in October 1987 and was based on an interview with Morrison in which Caldwell questioned her about the sources for* Beloved, *the difficulties Morrison faced in writing it, and its major themes.*]

If **The Bluest Eye** and her next novel, **Sula** found eager audiences, **Song of Solomon,** published in 1977, found an exuberant one, going on to win the National Book Critics Circle Award in 1978. **Tar Baby** followed in 1981; by then, Morrison had been at the crest of a new wave of Afro-American literature for more than a decade. An editor at Random House since 1967, she resigned in 1983 to write full time; at 56, she lives in Rockland County, N.Y., with the younger of her two sons.

Morrison spent two years thinking about the story of **Beloved** and another three writing it; she says now that she was so frightened by the effort that she hit a writing impasse in 1985. She had conceived of the novel as a three-volume work; when she gave the manuscript to her editor, Bob Gottlieb (formerly of Knopf, now of the *New Yorker*), she was already convinced that she had failed.

"I had decided that I was never going to meet the deadline, and I would just have to live with it. But I gave Bob what I had, and said, 'I'm sorry, because I really and truly have only a third of a book.'

"And he read it and said, 'Whatever else you're doing, do it, but this *is* a book.' I said, 'Are you sure?' "

Morrison laughs. "I was happy that, after all these years, what I had done could be published. I was not sure for a long time. I mean, I trust Bob a lot, but I kept saying, 'What do you think?' Not meaning, 'is it any good?' but 'are you sure this is IT?' "

This was most certainly it, as Gottlieb realized immediately, for Morrison had given him **Beloved** in its entirety, save the page-and-a-half coda at the end. The novel is extraordinary, even by Morrison standards, with a lyricism equal to the sadnesses it plumbs. Set in Ohio in 1873, **Beloved** tells the story of Sethe, an ex-slave who fled the South with her children 18 years earlier. She now lives alone with her youngest daughter, Denver, but their isolation is threatened by a presence in the house: the ghost of her other girl, Beloved, who was murdered as an infant.

How that tragedy came about—and just who was responsible—is the mystery at the center of *Beloved,* which is as much about the mother-daughter bond as it is the crimes of slavery.

Morrison says she works from the ground up, conceiving of "the smaller details, the images," before the entire architecture of a novel appears. But unlike her four previous books, the idea for the plot of *Beloved* came from an actual event—gleaned from a 19th-century newspaper story she'd discovered while editing *The Black Book* (an overview of black American history) at Random House. The woman in the news story became Sethe, and Morrison began to write.

"What was on my mind," says Morrison, "was the way in which women are so vulnerable to displacing themselves, into something other than themselves. And how now, in the modern and contemporary world, women had a lot of choices and didn't have to do that anymore. But nevertheless, there's still an enormous amount of misery and self-sabotage, and we're still shooting ourselves in the foot.

"It occurred to me that I'd read these stories about black women . . . because we were at the forefront of making certain kinds of decisions, modern decisions that hadn't been made in 1873.

"The past, until you confront it, until you live through it, keeps coming back in other forms. The shapes redesign themselves in other constellations, until you get a chance to play it over again."

Morrison still views *Beloved* as the first of three works, and that, she says, has helped counteract the melancholy that usually accompanies a book's completion. The struggles she encountered along the way paid off: *Beloved* is driven by a voice so pure that it half-seems as though its narrators are gathered around the reader's kitchen table. Its shifting narration builds to a crescendo of voices at the end of the novel, particularly that of Beloved—who has come back as a young woman looking to reclaim her past.

"I couldn't get Beloved's voice," says Morrison, "I just couldn't get there. I wrote around it: She was there, but she couldn't say anything . . . I could get Denver's and Sethe's voices, but I just couldn't get that girl to say where she had been."

Paul D, the former slave from Sethe's past, has his own way of saying where he's been, a poetry of lament that seems written from the inside looking out. "I'll tell you," says Morrison about capturing his voice, "you know how actresses do? You just get in there, and see what the world looks like in there. I can even write dialogue when he's talking and I'm inside him, and then I have to come out and get in the other person. Rewriting was that constant shifting, and trying to do him justice. I don't want to shortchange anybody. It has something to do with honorably rendering another life.

"Paul D's like a lot of other black men I used to know, and listen to—my father, my uncles, and the way they used to talk."

It's not the only time Morrison's family had a hand in *Beloved*. As a child, she listened to the ghost stories her parents told; all her novels are rich with supernatural lore; from the dream imagery of *Sula* to the flying metaphors of *Song of Solomon*. When Beloved's flesh-and-blood manifestation shows up at Sethe's house one day—no lines on her palms and no history to speak of—her presence seems as ordinary as an afternoon visit from the local preacher.

"As a child, everybody knew there were ghosts," says Morrison. "You didn't put your hand under the bed when you slept at night. It's that place that you go to [in *Beloved*], right away . . . a shared human response to the world. And that's where I had to go to, with Beloved's voice, because I couldn't confuse it with my own." Morrison laughs. "It starts getting crazy, you know, trying to do that."

With its lush, Gauguin-like imagery and commonplace mysticism, *Beloved* draws from a wellspring not unlike that of the Latin American fabulists. Morrison nods at the comparison between black American folklore and magic realism, though she says she was well into *Song of Solomon* before she discovered Gabriel Garcia Marquez.

"Their stuff was so readily available to them—that mixture of Indian and Spanish. Whereas I felt the preachers, the storytelling, the folklore, the music was very accessible to me, but I felt almost alone. It wasn't only mine, but I didn't have any literary precedent for what I was trying to do with the magic.

"So I thought, boy, those guys—they've got it. Everybody understood the sources of their magic right away. Whereas mine was discredited, because it was held by discredited people. 'Folklorists!' Now it's sort of a little subject in the academy, but it did not have any currency . . . it's perceived of as illiterate.

"People give a lot of credence to the intelligence, the concentration, the imagination necessary for listening to music, but never for listening to stories. That somehow seems like a dumb thing that people who can't read do. And I know how hard it is to listen, and what's engaged when you listen."

If Morrison's early work quickly became required reading in Afro-American literature courses around the country, it was [on] lists of standard English courses, Afro-American or otherwise. Still, the embrace of "ethnic" and "women's" literature in the last 15 years—read: non-white-male—is viewed by some as a ghettoization of literature, more stifling than liberating. And while Morrison herself has received superlative-laden praise for her work, the words "black" and "female" almost always preface such claims.

"Well, I get unnerved by all of it," says Morrison. "When they say I'm a great American novelist, I say, 'Ha! They're trying to say I'm not black.' When they say I'm a wonderful woman novelist, I think, 'Aha, they think I don't belong.' So I've just insisted—insisted!—upon being called a black woman novelist. And *I* decided what that meant—in terms of this big world that has become broader and deeper through the process of reclamation, because I have claimed it. I have claimed what I know. As a black and a woman, I have had access to a range of emotions and perceptions that were unavailable to people who were neither.

"So I say, 'Yes, I'm a black woman writer.' And if I write well enough, then maybe in about five years—or 10, or 15—it'll be like, 'Do you write for the Russians, or do you write for the French?' I mean, that kind of question, you can't put to anyone other than women and blacks."

Morrison laughs. "I've always had a secret desire to write reviews of white people's books from that point of view, and make all these observations. I think that would be a scream. I'd say, 'This is a better book because that's the way white people *really are.*' I mean, what does that mean?"

The color and gender demarcations of contemporary fiction have begun to blur in the last decade, in part due to writers such as Morrison, whose contributions stand tall against any literary standard. And while she underplays her own participation in that change, she says she's witnessed its effects, particularly in the schools and universities.

"The black kids [where I lectured], when they would ask questions, they used to say—vis a vis *Song of Solomon* or *Sula*—they'd say, 'I don't know anybody like that.' Or, 'wear shoes.'"

"And I would say, 'I don't know anybody like that either.'"

"They were always disassociating themselves from the class of blacks to which they did not belong. And they weren't talking to me anyway; they were talking to their fellow [white] students. All of the time, at least one person would make sure that I understood that a wine-maker like Pilate [in *Song of Solomon*] they loved, but that was not part of *their* experience.

"They were at great pains to let me know that they were literate. That doesn't happen anymore."

"Painful as it is, there was a void before, and now there's something in it. And you know, I'm not the first black writer. So that it means that the cumulative effect of all those writers who went before—the Zoras [Neale Hurston] and the [Ralph] Ellisons—in its real sense, it means it is there now."

The difficulties Morrison encountered with *Beloved* came from the heights and depths she tried to conquer: The girl Beloved's voice at the end of the novel is wrenching testimony, not just her private suffering but of all the ravages of slavery. For Morrison, it was more than a personal triumph.

"When I had problems, I thought: If they can live it, I can write about it. I refuse to believe that that period, or that thing [slavery] is beyond art. Because the consequences of practically everything we do, art alone can stand up to. It's not the historians' job to do that—you know what I'm saying? You will get some truth out of it that is not just the province of the natural or social sciences.

"I said, then the slaveholders have won if this experience is beyond my imagination and my powers. It's like humor: You have to take the authority back; you realign where the power is. So I wanted to *take* the power. They were very inventive and imaginative with cruelty, so I have to take it back—in a way that I can tell it. And that is the satisfaction."

Clarence Major   (review date January-February 1988)

SOURCE: "In the Name of Memory," in *The American Book Review,* Vol. 9, No. 6, January-February, 1988, p. 17.

[*Major is an American poet, novelist, short story writer, critic, and educator. In the following review of* Beloved, *he identifies its dominant theme as the residual power of memory and extols Morrison's ability to "disappear" from her own writing.*]

I am not an innocent reader approaching a book by a writer I have not known before. Only long ago was that innocence possible. Long ago was the excitement of that innocence. Now, only something close to that excitement happens. But I actually bought Toni Morrison's novel, *Beloved,* with my own money and I bought it out of some vestige of that earlier excitement; I bought it in Washington, D.C., on a dry, windy afternoon in October. I was excited by the possibility of a great reading experience, like those I had as a boy discovering books such as *The Catcher in the Rye* and *The Drunken Boat Party.*

Another kind of magic—perhaps more critical and equally valuable—had taken possession of the experience. Maybe that earlier and apparently unrecoverable innocence was best unrecovered. I was not disappointed although I had not entirely left my body for the magical world of the text; had not entirely entered the world of Sethe, Baby Suggs, Denver, Paul D, and Beloved. That world was certainly magical enough and full of the lyrical power necessary for the experience. Listen to this:

> A fully dressed woman walked out of the water.
> She barely gained the bank of the stream before
> she sat down and leaned against a mulberry tree.

That is the arrival of Beloved. From this moment on she enters the lives of the people who live at 124 Bluestone Road, but she is there primarily because she *belongs* in an unbroken, passionate, blood-tied way to Sethe.

Let me explain who these characters are and what they are about and why they are where they are. Sethe, who is at the center of the action with Beloved, a ghost from the past, is the mother of Denver, a feisty young woman who is uneasy about the presence of Paul D, Sethe's live-in man. Then there is the profound, even mythic presence of old Baby Suggs herself, Sethe's mother-in-law. All of these folk are refugees from slavery or the legacy of it; escapees from the hardship of a slave plantation with an ironic name, Sweet Home. Although they are not exactly in limbo, they are like a group of survivors waiting on a rock in the middle of the ocean: not exactly without hope, but hard enough and realistic enough not to get too excited about what tomorrow might bring.

Morrison is the type of writer who would
tell me that she works hard to make the
presence of the writer disappear.

—*Clarence Major*

Yes, it is a ghost story, but not because things move
around in 124, not because strange lights invade rooms;
it is a ghost story because of the history of the human
heart, because of the inability of the human spirit to shrug
off that which might be best forgotten. Beloved, the ghost
of Sethe's dead infant, brings to 124 a living presence that
confirms all of this, a presence that is not meant to redeem
anybody—certainly not Sethe in the murder of her own
infant in no matter how noble a cause—not meant to punish anybody. Beloved comes in the name of memory—its
right to exist in the present; in the name of its unbroken
truce with the flesh and its earth-place.

This truce, as acted out between Sethe and Beloved, spins
its way down through the novel like a cyclone, possessing
every other human force in its wake. Yes, the reading experience was about as innocent and good as a reading experience can be for me these days.

And the writing itself helped to make that possible. But
Morrison is the type of writer who would tell me that she
works hard to make the presence of the writer disappear.
Even so. Even so. When one goes to a book for a great
reading experience, one does not wish to escape the page
one is looking at. I found Morrison's disappearing act to
be as skillful as Vermeer's when he is pretending he has
nothing to do with the view of a street in Delft. No matter
how successful he is in realistically submerging himself
into the vortex of representation, it is precisely his disappearing act that most reveals his incredible presence. So
it is with Toni Morrison.

Deborah Horvitz   (essay date Autumn 1989)

SOURCE: "Nameless Ghosts: Possession and Dispossession in *Beloved*," in *Studies in American Fiction*, Vol. 17,
No. 2, Autumn, 1989, pp. 157-67.

[*Horvitz is a critic and psychiatric social worker. In the
essay below, she provides a thematic analysis of* Beloved,
*noting Morrison's focus on bonding, bondage, alienation,
loss, memory, and mother-daughter relationships.*]

Toni Morrison's fifth novel, *Beloved* (1987), explores the
insidious degradation imposed upon all slaves, even when
they were owned by, in Harriet Beecher Stowe's term, "a
man of humanity." The novel is also about matrilineal ancestry and the relationships among enslaved, freed, alive,
and dead mothers and daughters. Equally it is about the
meaning of time and memory and how remembering either destroys or saves a future. Written in an anti-
minimalist, lyrical style in which biblical myths, folklore,
and literary realism overlap, the text is so grounded in his-

torical reality that it could be used to teach American history classes. Indeed, as a simultaneously accessible and yet
extremely difficult book, *Beloved* operates so complexly
that as soon as one layer of understanding is reached, another, equally as richly textured, emerges to be unravelled.
[In Judith Thurman's "A House Divided," *The New
Yorker*, November 2, 1987] Morrison has referred to her
novel as a "ghost story" and begins and ends with Beloved, whose name envelops the text.

The powerful corporeal ghost who creates matrilineal connection between Africa and America, Beloved stands for
every African woman whose story will never be told. She
is the haunting symbol of the many Beloveds—
generations of mothers and daughters—hunted down and
stolen from Africa; as such, she is, unlike mortals, invul-
nerable to barriers of time, space, and place. She moves
with the freedom of an omnipresent and omnipotent spirit
who weaves in and out of different generations within the
matrilineal chain. Yet, Morrison is cautious not to use Beloved as a symbol in a way that either traps the reader in
polemics or detaches one from the character who is at different times a caring mother and a lonely girl. Nor is Beloved so universalized that her many meanings lose specificity. She is rooted in a particular story and is the embodiment of specific members of Sethe's family. At the same
time she represents the spirit of all the women dragged
onto slave ships in Africa and also all Black women in
America trying to trace their ancestry back to the mother
on the ship attached to them. Beloved is the haunting presence who becomes the spirit of the women from "the other
side." As Sethe's mother she comes from the geographic
other side of the world, Africa; as Sethe's daughter, she
comes from the physical other side of life, death. There is
a relationship, too, between Beloved's arrival and the blos-
soming of Sethe's memory. Only after Beloved comes to
Sethe's house as a young woman does Sethe's repression
of countless painful memories begin to lift. Beloved generates a metamorphosis in Sethe that allows her to speak
what she had thought to be the unspeakable.

In *Beloved* the ghost-child who comes back to life is not
only Sethe's two-year-old daughter, whom she murdered
eighteen years ago; she is also Sethe's African mother.
This inter-generational, inter-continental, female ghost-
child teaches Sethe that memories and stories about her
matrilineal ancestry are life-giving. Moreover, Beloved
stimulates Sethe to remember her own mother because, in
fact, the murdered daughter and the slave mother are a
conflated or combined identity represented by the ghost-
child Beloved.

Mother-daughter bonding and bondage suffuses Morrison's text. Sethe's nameless mother is among the African
slaves who experienced the Middle Passage and, late in the
text, she relates that ordeal through a coded message from
the ship revealing that she too is a Beloved who, like Sethe,
has been cruelly separated from her own mother. This
cycle of mother-daughter loss, perceived abandonment,
betrayal, and recovery is inherent in and characterizes
each mother-daughter relationship in the novel. But in the
present tense of the novel—Ohio in 1873—Sethe barely remembers, from so long ago,

her own mother, who was pointed out to her by the eight-year-old child who watched over the young ones—pointed out as the one among many backs turned away from her, stooping in a watery field. Patiently Sethe waited for this particular back to gain the row's end and stand. What she saw was a cloth hat as opposed to a straw one, singularity enough in that world of cooing women each of whom was called Ma'am.

This is mainly how she remembers her mother, simply as an image, a woman in a field with a stooped back in a cloth hat.

Sethe does, however, have one other quite specific memory of this obscure mother, of what may have been their only interaction following the two weeks the nameless Ma'am was allowed to nurse her. She remembers that Ma'am

> picked me up and carried me behind the smoke-house. Back there she opened up her dress front and lifted her breast and pointed under it. Right on her rib was a circle and a cross burnt right in the skin. She said, "This is your ma'am. This," and she pointed. "I am the only one got this mark now. The rest dead. If something happens to me and you can't tell me by my face, you can know me by this mark." Scared me so. All I could think of was how important this was and how I needed to have something important to say back, but I couldn't think of anything so I just said what I thought. "Yes, Ma'am," I said. "But how will you know me? How will you know me? Mark me, too," I said. "Mark the mark on me too."

Because Sethe is not marked, she thinks she has no link with her mother. In fact, before Beloved helps Sethe's memory unfold, Sethe firmly believes that because Ma'am is physically dead, they are not emotionally tied. When her mother was hanged, Sethe did not know why. Probably Ma'am was caught trying to escape from the plantation, but the daughter born in bondage refuses to believe her mother could have run. It would mean that she left Sethe behind, emphasizing in this generation the continuous pattern of severed mother-daughter relationships. In other words, her memories of Ma'am are buried not only because their relationship was vague and their contact prohibited but also because those recollections are inextricably woven with feelings of painful abandonment. If Sethe remembers her mother, she must also remember that she believes her mother deserted her.

The powerful corporeal ghost who creates matrilineal connection between Africa and America, Beloved stands for every African woman whose story will never be told.

—Deborah Horvitz

As Sethe tells this story to Denver and Beloved, she becomes frightened: "She was remembering something [Ma'am's language] she had forgotten she knew." Murky pictures and vague words begin to creep into her mind and she knows that they come from that place inside her—the place Paul D. refers to as the locked and rusted tobacco tin—that stores, but can never lose, forgotten memories. Ma'am's language erupts into her conscious mind signaling the beginning of Sethe's slow metamorphosis. "Something privately shameful . . . had seeped into a slit in her mind right behind the . . . circled cross," and she remembers that she does or did have a link with her mother that transcends the cross in the circle. She is afraid to remember but ashamed not to. Recollections of "the language her ma'am spoke . . . which would never come back" creep into her consciousness. She remembers one-armed Nan, the slave who was in charge of Sethe and the other children on the plantation where Sethe grew up. Nan "used different words," words that expressed her mother's native African, and these words link Sethe back both to her mother and to her mother's land, the place where women gathered flowers in freedom and played in the long grass before the white men came:

> Words Sethe understood then but could neither recall nor repeat now. She believed that must be why she remembered so little before Sweet Home except singing and dancing and how crowded it was. What Nan told her she had forgotten, along with the language she told it in. But the message—that was and had been there all along. Holding the damp white sheets against her chest, she was picking meaning out of a code she no longer understood. Nighttime.

Although Sethe has forgotten the words of her mother's language, they continue to exist inside her as feelings and images that repeatedly emerge as a code that she relies on without realizing it. This code holds animated, vital memories, such as the one of her mother dancing juba, as well as the most painful fact of Sethe's life: her mother's absence.

Sethe is shocked as she continues to find meaning in a code she thought she no longer understood. She remembers that she felt the dancing feet of her dead mother as she was about to give birth to Denver. Pregnant and thinking she is going to die because her swollen feet cannot take another step, she wants to stop walking; every time she does so, the movement of her unborn child causes her such pain that she feels she is being rammed by an antelope. Although Sethe wonders why an antelope, since she cannot remember having ever seen one, it is because the image of the antelope is really an image of Ma'am dancing. Sethe's antelope kicking baby and her antelope dancing mother are one and the same:

> Oh but when they sang. And oh but when they danced and sometimes they danced the antelope. The men as well as the ma'ams, one of whom was certainly her own. They shifted shapes and became something other. Some unchained demanding other whose feet knew her pulse better than she did. Just like this one in her stomach.

Stored in childhood but only now unlocked, the link between the unborn Denver's kicks and the dead ma'am's kicks as she danced the antelope erupts in Sethe's memory. As she bears the next generation in her matrilineal line, Sethe keeps her mother's African antelope dancing alive: she links the pulses of her unchained, vigorously moving mother and her energetic, womb-kicking daughter forever.

A second and perhaps the most crucial part of this story from her past is that Sethe, as Nan tells her, is the only child her mother did not kill:

> She told Sethe that her mother and Nan were together from the sea. Both were taken up many times by the crew. "She threw them all away but you. The one from the crew she threw away on the island. The others from more whites she also threw away. Without name she threw them. You she gave the name of the black man. She put her arms around him. The others she did not put her arms around. Never. Never. Telling you. I am telling you, small girl Sethe."

Conceived with a Black man in love, rather than with a white master through rape, Sethe, named after her father, is the only child her mother allowed to survive.

Significantly, she is flooded with these memories in response to questions from her own daughter, Beloved, who wants to know everything in Sethe's memory and actually feeds and fattens on these stories. What Beloved demands is that Sethe reveal memory and story about her life before Sweet Home, memory about her African speaking, branded mother and her life right after Sweet Home when she cut Beloved's throat. In other words, because they share identities, the ghost-child's fascination lies in the "joined" union between Sethe's mother and herself. Sethe's memory is being pried wide open by Beloved's presence. She forces Sethe to listen to her own voice and to remember her own mother, her ma'am with the special mark on her body, along with her mother's native language, songs, and dances.

This cycle of mother-daughter fusion, loss, betrayal, and recovery between Sethe and her mother plays itself out again in the present relationship between Sethe and Beloved. Beloved transforms from a lonely, affectionate girl into a possessive, demanding tyrant, and her ruthlessness almost kills Sethe. There is even a connection between this ruling Beloved and the slave-driver. Because any attempt to possess another human being is reminiscent of the slave-master relationship, Denver links Sethe and the slave-drivers when she warns Beloved that Sethe, like "the men without skin" from the ship, "chews and swallows." Beloved is furious and ferocious. When she first comes to the farmhouse where Sethe and Denver live, she appears because the other side is lonely—devoid of love and memory. She yearns for Sethe and cannot take her eyes off her. "Sethe was licked, tasted, eaten by Beloved's eyes." But what starts out as a child's love and hunger for a mother from whom she has long been separated turns into a wish to own Sethe, to possess her, to merge with her and be her. Beloved gets rid of Paul D. and eventually excludes Denver from their play. Just as the disembodied baby ghost Beloved hauntingly possessed Sethe, so the flesh-and-blood adolescent Beloved tries to own and dominate her. Sethe is as haunted by the girl's presence as she was by her

absence because possession of any kind involving human beings is destructive.

These "possessive" attachments raise the important moral dilemma underlying Sethe's act; either Sethe must be held accountable for Beloved's death or the institution of slavery alone killed the child. If Morrison wants to humanize and individualize the "great lump called slaves," then perhaps she is suggesting that Sethe, like any individual, is answerable and responsible for her own actions. The namesake for Beloved's Sethe is the biblical Seth, born to replace his brother, the murdered Abel. Perhaps Morrison's Sethe, too, is a "replacement" for her brothers and sisters murdered by the system of slavery and lost to her nameless ma'am. If so, then the inevitable confrontation between Sethe, the replacement child saved by her ma'am, and Beloved, the protected child murdered by hers, represents the impossible choice available to the enslaved mother.

Certainly one reason Beloved comes back is to pass judgment on Sethe. When Sethe first realizes that Beloved is the ghost of her third child, she wants desperately for the girl to understand that she tried to kill her babies so that they would be protected from captivity forever. Sethe assumes Beloved will forgive her. She does not. For Beloved, her mother's protection became the act of possession that led to her own death, which was murder. Beloved becomes mean-spirited and exploits her mother's pain. Sethe gives Beloved story after story of her love and devotion to her. She tells her how nothing was more important than getting her milk to her, how she waved flies away from her in the grape arbor, how it pained her to see her baby bitten by a mosquito, and how she would trade her own life for Beloved's. Sethe tries to impress upon her how slavery made it impossible for her to be the mother she wanted to be.

For Sethe her children are her "best thing," yet they have all been ruined. The murdered Beloved torments Sethe, Howard and Buglar have left home, and Denver is so afraid of the world that it is only starvation that forces her off the front porch. Sethe begs the ruling Beloved not only for forgiveness for the obvious but also for the return of her "self." But Beloved does not care:

> She said when she cried there was no one. That dead men lay on top of her. That she had nothing to eat. Ghosts without skin stuck their fingers in her and said beloved in the dark and bitch in the light. Sethe never came to her, never said a word to her, never smiled and worst of all never waved goodbye or even looked her way before running away from her.

What is most striking here is that Beloved responds to Sethe's entreaties not only in the language of the murdered daughter but also in the tortured language of the "woman from the sea." Death and the Middle Passage evoke the same language. They are the same existence; both were experienced by the multiple-identified Beloved.

To appreciate fully Beloved's attack on her mother, it is important to look back to Morrison's previous pages, written without punctuation, composed of some lines written in complete sentences with spaces after them, while others are not. The writing is fluid, open, created in the first person with no names and no reference to time or place. This rhetoric communicates what may at first appear to be an unintelligible experience, a story of images which the reader must grope and finally fail to figure out. In fact, breaking the barriers of form, this key passage, much like Morrison's ghost moving beyond human barriers, communicates the death-like Middle Passage suffered by Sethe's mother. She, Sethe's mother, is the woman "from the sea."

In the remembered ghost story, a woman is crouching on a ship where there is not enough room; there is bread that she is too hungry to eat and so little water that she cannot even make tears. Prisoner on a rat infested ship where she is urinated on by the "men without skin," which is how the clothed white men look to her, she uses words almost identical to the ones Beloved shouts at Sethe: Beloved says "dead men lay on top of [me]"; the speaker "from the sea" says "the man on my face is dead." Beloved tells Sethe that "ghosts without skin stuck their fingers in [me]"; the woman from the ship says that "he puts his finger there." Beloved blames Sethe for not coming to her, not smiling and not waving goodbye before she left her; the woman on the ship says "she was going to smile at me   she was going to   a hot thing." The point is that "Beloved" exists in several places and has more than one voice. While in the pages of unpunctuated writing she is the voice of the woman on the ship, thirty pages later she uses almost the same words as Sethe's daughter, and each voice shouts to a Sethe. At the end of this section, the collective voice screams: "I am not dead   Sethe's is the face that left me   Sethe sees me see her now we can join   a hot thing." The "hot thing," referred to repeatedly by both voices, expresses the passion that permeates the text, the fantasy that it is possible to join with and possess the lost Beloved. It expresses the desperately writhing and thwarted wish to be both "self" and "other" so as to regain the lost Beloved by becoming her. This is what each means when she says "her face is my own," or "the woman is there with the face I want the face that is mine." The "hot thing" expresses the wish to join, merge, and fuse with the lost mother.

Referring to the dead slaves being dumped overboard, the voice of the woman from the sea says "the men without skin push them through with poles," and then the speaker, Sethe's mother, enraged and mournful, protests: "The woman is there with the face I want   they fall into the sea   if I had the teeth of the man who died on my face I would bite the circle around her neck   bite it away." Terrified and outraged by the iron collar placed on the slaves, she wants to "bite the circle around her neck   bite it away" because she knows the woman hates its being there. The "woman with the face I want" is never definitively identified, but at the very end of the novel, Morrison, referring to the African women whose stories are lost, writes, "they never knew . . . whose was the underwater face she needed like that." Perhaps she, "the woman with the face I want," the lost underwater, drowned face, is someone on the ship with Sethe's mother. Most likely, given that she sees her own face reflected in the "underwater face," she is her own mother, Sethe's grandmother. If so, there is another generation in the line of tortured, invisible women, all of them Beloveds, who

have been cruelly severed from their mothers and daughters. The loss of "the underwater face" represents not only the death of a woman, but the death of a mother and therefore the rupture of the mother-daughter bond, probably the strongest, most important relationship women can have. In this novel grief is not only for one deceased woman but for the empty space that she leaves inside all her daughters.

The two voices, Sethe's ma'am's and her daughter's, both of them Beloveds, merge. Yet within the fused voice, each describes her own, individual experience of horrific loss:

> I am Beloved and she is mine. [Sethe] was about to smile at me when the men without skin came and took us up into the sunlight with the dead and shoved them into the sea. Sethe went into the sea. . . . They did not push her. . . . She was getting ready to smile at me. . . . All I want to know is why did she go in the water in the place where we crouched? Why did she do that when she was just about to smile at me? I wanted to join her in the sea but I could not move.

From the "place where we crouched," the slave ship, Sethe's mother has lost someone who jumped in the water—the woman Morrison says will never be known, but surely it is Sethe's grandmother. The author creates a fluidity of identity among Sethe's mother, Sethe's grandmother, and the murdered two-year-old, so that Beloved is both an individual and a collective being. They are the primary losses to Sethe, more so, even, than her husband, Halle. Beloved is the crucial link that connects Africa and America for the enslaved women. She is Sethe's mother; she is Sethe herself; she is her daughter.

Although at different times Sethe, her mother, and her daughter all live with the agonizing feeling that they have been betrayed by their mothers, perhaps most heartbreaking is the image of mother-daughter separation evoked when Beloved insists that a "Sethe," voluntarily and without being pushed, went into the sea. The agony stems from the child's assumption that she is being deliberately abandoned by her ma'am. A little girl stands on an enormous ship not understanding why her mother jumps overboard. Beloved lost her mother when she "went into the sea instead of smiling at [her]." And Sethe's mother wants an unidentified, lost woman on the ship, probably her ma'am, to know how urgently she tries "to help her but the clouds are in the way." This Beloved, Sethe's mother, wants desperately either to save her own mother or die with her, but she loses her again "because of the noisy clouds of smoke." (Beloved also says she lost "Sethe" again "because of the noisy clouds of smoke.") There was a riot on the ship and the noisy clouds of smoke were caused by guards' gunfire, which prevented the daughter from reaching her mother. Perhaps the sick slaves were forced overboard; maybe it was a mass suicide or an attempt to escape through the water. Or the gunfire could have occurred in Africa, before the ships were boarded, when the white traders were hunting down and capturing native Blacks. What is clear is that a woman on the ship went into the sea leaving a girl-child alone, bereft; and each was to the other a Beloved. What is also clear is that the novel is structured by a series of flashbacks, which succeed in bridging the shattered generations by repeating meaningful and multi-layered images. That is, contained in the narrative strategy of the novel itself are both the wrenching, inter-generational separations and the healing process.

The American and African Beloveds join forever in the last two pages of the novel as symbols of the past—exploding, swallowing, and chewing—and fuse with these same images in the present. The sickening fear of her body exploding, dissolving, or being chewed up and spit out links each enslaved Beloved with her sister in captivity. Africa is "the place where long grass opens," the slave ship is the crouching place, and the ghost-child is the girl seen "that day on the porch." The Beloved from each place is another's matrilineal heritage and future; and each Beloved merges with her other "selves" in the shared and horrific fear of losing her body. The gap is bridged between America and Africa, the past and the present, the dead and the living, the flesh and the spirit. But they are joined in a specific shared, secret horror, perhaps the most devastating effect of the violence heaped upon them by "the men without skin." Each lives in terror that her body will disintegrate or, quite literally, explode. Earlier in the text the ghost-child loses a tooth and

> Beloved looked at the tooth and thought, This is it. Next would be her arm, her hand, a toe. Pieces of her would drop maybe one at a time, maybe all at once. Or on one of those mornings before Denver woke and after Sethe left she would fly apart. It is difficult keeping her head on her neck, her legs attached to her hips when she is by herself. Among the things she could not remember was when she first knew that she could wake up any day and find herself in pieces. She had two dreams: exploding and being swallowed. When her tooth came out—an odd fragment, last in the row—she thought it was starting.

She cannot remember when she first knew "she could wake up any day and find herself in pieces," not simply because she was only two when her mother cut her throat, but because the fear predates her birth; it comes from the Beloveds in Africa and the ship: "In the place where long grass opens, the girl who waited to be loved and cry shame erupts into her separate parts, to make it easy for the chewing laughter to swallow her all away." The voice on the ship repeatedly hears "chewing and swallowing and laughter." The point is that enslaved women, not in possession of their own bodies, survived barbaric beatings, rapes, and being "swallowed" without total decompensation by emotionally dissociating themselves from their bodies. The price they paid was, of course, an enormous one; those that survived often did so with no shred of basic integrity or dignity regarding their bodies. The imagery emphasizes, too, those African women who did not survive the Middle Passage—those who were chewed up, spit out, and swallowed by the sea—those whose bodies and stories were never recovered. Morrison, speaking of the women whose stories are lost, says they are "disremembered," meaning not only that they are forgotten, but also that they are dismembered, cut up and off, and not remembered.

The very end of the novel paradoxically appears to belie the crucial theme of the book, that it is imperative to preserve continuity through story, language, and culture between generations of Black women. The authorial voice says repeatedly "this is not a story to pass on," although it seems in this text that not to repeat is to lose stories crucial to Black heritage and American history and to the personal lives of Black women.

The paradox is the one posed by memory and history themselves when past memories hurt so much they feel as though they must be forgotten. Sethe could not pass on her mother's story for the same reason that, before Beloved came, she could not talk about the murder: "Every mention of her past life hurt. The hurt was always there—like a tender place in the corner of her mouth that the bit left." Remembering horrors of such enormous magnitude can cause a despair so profound that the memories cancel out the possibility of resolution or pleasure in the present and future. For example, the happiness that seemed possible between Sethe and Paul D. at the carnival was obliterated by the past, in the form of Beloved's arrival that very day. However, Morrison implies, even though memory of the past can prevent living in the present, to pursue a future without remembering the past has its own and even deeper despair for it denies the reality and sacrifice of those who died. Assuming individual and collective responsibility is a crucial concern of *Beloved,* and it is a responsibility to remember.

Like Sethe, Beloved herself is trapped by painful memories of the past at the end of her narrative. When white Mr. Bodwin comes to pick up Denver, Sethe becomes terrified because she associates Bodwin's hat with Schoolteacher's. She temporarily forgets where she is and who he is, and she tries to kill him. Sethe runs from Beloved into the crowd of women outside her house. The ghost-child, left "Alone Again," watches Sethe run "away from her to the pile of people out there. They make a hill. A hill of black people, falling." What Beloved sees is the "little hill of dead people" from the slave ship; she sees "those able to die . . . in a pile." She sees "rising from his place with a whip in his hand, the man without skin, looking. He is looking at her." While Sethe sees Bodwin as Schoolteacher, Beloved sees him as a slave-driver from the slave ship looking at her, suggesting again that Beloved, the daughter, is also the woman "from the sea," Sethe's mother. She runs away, naked and pregnant with stories from the past, back to the water from which she emerged, where the narrator says she will be forgotten.

The paradox of how to live in the present without cancelling out an excruciatingly painful past remains unresolved at the end of the novel. At the same time, something healing has happened. Sethe's narrative ends with her considering the possibility that she could be her own "best thing." Denver has left the front porch feeling less afraid and more sure of herself. Now that Beloved is gone there is the feeling that perhaps Sethe can find some happiness with Paul D., who "wants to put his story next to hers." As the embodiment of Sethe's memories, the ghost Beloved enabled her to remember and tell the story of her past, and in so doing shows that between women words used to make and share a story have the power to heal. Although Toni Morrison states that "it was not a story to pass on," she herself has put words to Beloved's tale. Though the ghost-child-mother-sister returns, unnamed, to the water, her story is passed on.

Karen E. Fields   (essay date 1989)

SOURCE: "To Embrace Dead Strangers: Toni Morrison's *Beloved*," in *Mother Puzzles: Daughters and Mothers in Contemporary American Literature*, edited by Mickey Pearlman, Greenwood Press, 1989, pp. 159-69.

[*In the following essay, Fields explores Morrison's emphasis on "the nature of love," focusing primarily on the personal relationships between Sethe, Beloved, Paul D., and Denver.*]

The most obvious feature of Toni Morrison's ***Beloved*** has been least noted that, whatever else, it profoundly is a meditation on the nature of love. The meditation begins as a love story about a man and a woman. In it Paul D and Sethe meet again after many years and redeem one another. Paul D redeems Sethe from her entrapment in a haunted present; and Sethe, Paul D from his fate of continual wandering. At the time of meeting both are afloat on the surface of the present, set adrift by pasts that have burned away most human connection. To both the future exists only after the fact, as time elapsed for Sethe, as distance traveled for Paul D.

Paul D's travels eventually bring him to Sethe's haunted house, which stands off to itself at the far end of a road, on the outskirts of Cincinnati. It is a house the townspeople avoid altogether or hurry past. But Paul D walks up to it and then into it, as if it has been his destination of many years; and he banishes Sethe's ghost. By so doing, he unlocks her desire and his own to envision the future and to plan. In a sense, they bring one another back to life. Like that of the man and woman in a fairy tale, whose coming together ends an enchantment, their love is activated, as it were, the instant they meet; yet it is wholly personal, existing only because it is he, because it is she. In the telling of who they both were, the story's meditation about love unfolds. By the end they seem poised to live happily together thereafter: "Me and you, we got more yesterday than anybody," Paul D tells Sethe. "We need some kind of tomorrow."

Their reunion occurs eighteen years after a lovingly planned but hideously aborted escape from a plantation in Kentucky called Sweet Home, on which embarked Paul D and his half-brother, Paul A, Six-O, Sethe (pregnant), her husband, Halle, and their three children. Paul D, Sethe, and one daughter are, to their knowledge, the only survivors. The "yesterday" Paul D refers to unfolds as concrete events and spiritual passages. Sethe has resisted being retaken with her children a month after the escape, by trying to kill her children and herself. She succeeds in killing a baby girl, who returns to haunt the house, injecting her spite into the lives of her two brothers, who leave, her grandmother, who dies, her sister, Denver, and Sethe, who make their own separate peace with it. Paul D has escaped and been retaken five times since the day they all tried to leave Sweet Home together; he has traveled America far and wide, witnessing its physical beauty and its human monstrosity, and has concluded with both a hard-edged peace.

Their spiritual passages over those years are revealed through their separate struggles with another apparition, which entered Sethe's life at about the same time as Paul D. This new apparition is a strange-looking girl of about twenty, who says her name is Beloved. She may or may not be a ghost and may or may not be the ghost of Sethe's child. Who or whatever she is, she takes up residence in the lives of Sethe, Paul D, and Denver, Sethe's bottomlessly lonely daughter. She resides with them as Need itself—need for human connection, for warmth, for identity, for stories and on ad infinitum through all the things one human can willingly give to another, and more than that. But there is also reciprocity with this ghost-or-girl. In giving to this being of unbounded demand, the three also receive. Beloved gives by taking.

In the way of ghosts, Beloved manifests herself differently to the different people who experience her. In that, of course, she is not different from an ordinary human being. To Paul D she is a terrifying seductress who compromises his loyalty to Sethe, but from whom he at the same time gets back parts of his living self long shut away. To Denver she is a dominant sister who extorts devotion, but who gives her the secret-sharing, storytelling complicity of childhood and, therewith, instruction in loving and caring for another. To Sethe she is a destroyer, who tries by turns to kill Sethe and to absorb her; but she is also by turns a daughter to care for and the daughter she killed. She is a chance to make up for and a chance to explain; she is a compensation and a retribution.

The retribution is not for the murder, however, but for the separation. Beloved will not hear that Sethe intended to kill all her children and herself so that they could go together to the other side or that Sethe's killing her had been a mother's act of protection. Beloved is not interested in plans or intentions, only in the result: that where she went she had no mother. She hurls at Sethe again and again the accusation of abandonment. In repeating this accusation, she becomes confounded with Sethe crying out herself against abandonment by her own mother and crying out for reunion.

> I am Beloved and she is mine. I am not separate from her there is no place where I stop her face is my own and I want to be there in the place where her face is and to be looking at it too a hot thing.

Morrison makes this cry reverberate up and down generations, placing in a single poetic vision a long stream of disembodied memory that encompasses Sethe's mother, perhaps also her mother's mother and Denver. It encompasses slaves, living and dead, and their captors, those who survived the raids, the middle passage, slavery itself, and those who did not. The conundrum of individuation and kinship alternates with that of individuation and reciprocity throughout Morrison's slow and ramifying meditation about love.

As a meditation about love, ***Beloved*** is sober yet optimistic, intent yet undidactic. Above all, it has mind and senses attuned to what can be learned in general from the world of a particular place and time. Morrison explores love in its interested and disinterested forms, in forms that uplift the human person and in forms that carry profound moral danger. She follows out its convolutions as pride and self-sacrifice, as possession and domination, as subjective emotion and objective experience. She considers how love could be manifest in ties between people as nearly equal as fellow slaves and as fully unequal as slave and master. Sometimes she detaches love from particular objects and relationships and lets it appear simply as itself, unshaped by rules of human feeling and connectedness. Love standing on its own is personified by the ghost-or-girl Beloved.

We habitually think of love as an inhabitant of the familiar human relations that at once construct and constrict it. It seems to lean and grow upon human relationships known to us, much as ivy leans and grows upon a familiar wall. But love can also be thought of as a part of nature that exists in and for itself, as a free-growing plant that enters the world of human beings on its own. With a wall the growing ivy reveals the wall. Without a wall, the ivy entwines upon itself, revealing a luxuriance of ramification and convolution that the wall conceals. Love considered standing for itself reveals complexity that is concealed by the simplifying elements of law, rules, conventional emotions, moral conduct, and behavior unequivocal or transparent in its import. Morrison meditates upon the nature of love by imagining its autonomous existence in the world. What appears in the personage of Beloved as disembodied demand appears in that of Paul D as embodied kindness.

> Not even trying, he had become the kind of man who could walk into a house and make the women cry. Because with him, in his presence they could. There was something blessed in his manner. Women saw him and wanted to weep. . . . Strong women and wise saw him and told him things they only told each other. . . . Young girls sidled up to him to confess.

Love expressed as disinterested kindness appears again in the encounter of Sethe and Amy Denver, two runaways:

> "You ain't got no business walking around these hills, miss." "Looka here who's talking. I got more business here'n you got. They catch you they cut your head off. Ain't nobody after me but I know somebody after you." Amy pressed her fingers into the soles of the slavewoman's feet. "Whose baby that?"

That simply, Amy pauses in her own flight, to massage Sethe's feet and ask a question. She continues for a night and a day letting one task after the next signal its immediacy and detain her: helping the wounded and very pregnant Sethe to shelter ("Thank your maker I come along so's you wouldn't have to die out there in them weeds"); finding wild medicine with which to treat Sethe's wounds ("Amy returned with two palmfuls of web, which she . . . draped on Sethe's back saying it was like stringing a tree for Christmas"); talking a blue streak and singing a little while Sethe swung between survival and death; later, making it possible for Sethe to walk on her own ("She tore two pieces from Sethe's shawl, filled them with leaves and tied

them over her feet, chattering all the while. 'How old are you, Lu?' I been bleeding for four years but I ain't having nobody's baby. 'Won't catch me sweating milk cause. . . .' 'I know,' said Sethe. 'You going to Boston' "); she stayed on when Sethe suddenly went into labor, washed and wrapped the baby, tied it to Sethe's chest, then continued on her lone way to Boston: the Good Samaritan.

This story of Amy stands for a moment on its own, as a perfect portrayal of disinterested love—wholly contained in the actions that express it, needing no request and no reward, purely contingent, transient, and impersonal. The next moment we remember that it does not stand on its own, for it is told elsewhere quite differently. In the present idealized form, it is one of Denver's unfree gifts to Beloved: "She swallowed twice to prepare for the telling, to construct out of the strings she had heard all her life a net to hold Beloved." To hold Beloved, she must satisfy Beloved's appetite for knowledge about Sethe's past. She tells it as it relates to herself. Along this way she arrives at a secret of her own. It is a recurrent nightmare made the more frightening by the resemblance of Sethe's act of murder to the kindly caring of the Good Samaritan. In the dream Sethe slowly mounts the stairs to Denver's room to cut off her head, then take it back downstairs to comb and braid the hair: "Her pretty eyes looking at me like I was a stranger. Not mean or anything, but like I was somebody she found and felt sorry for."

Because *Beloved* is set among slave owners, slaves, and ex-slaves a decade before and after the Civil War, it can appear to be about a subject and human predicament of less than universal scope. But the details about slavery and Reconstruction serve as resources with which to create real human beings, alive in real circumstances. They are not the story itself. Without specifics of place and time, we cannot tell a love story, for we cannot say who loved. *Beloved* is no more about Afro-Americans in mid-nineteenth-century America than *Romeo and Juliet* is about Renaissance Veronese. And no less. We cannot grasp the movement of either story without knowing what facts in each case shape the human capacity to love. The facts that confront Romeo and Juliet are the inverse of those that confront Sethe and Paul D. Romeo and Juliet love outside the law, in a world where individual identity is inscribed within membership in a family. In their world love can climb and grow upon—or grow away from—walls that are authoritatively upheld in social life. It is a world in which the love that joins men and women, parents and children, siblings and friends is subject to well-established orderliness. Sethe and Paul D, by contrast, were reared in a world from which order in human relations is excluded for practical reasons and where individuation is stretched to its very limit.

The essence of slavery was the creation of free-standing individuals, not families or communities. As units of a commodity to be bought, sold, or put to use, individual slaves stood apart from any authoritative claim to human connection. Any such claim compromised the owner's property in the commodity. In consequence, even gender and generation, the primordial constraints upon individuality, were broken—and, with them, the building blocks of the wall upon which love ordinarily grows. What would elsewhere have been "man" and "woman" became simply "male" and "female"; and what could have been differences of generation amounted to no more than differences of physique. Paul D and Sethe were reared in such a world of individuals. The drama of their love is not a struggle against social constraint but, on the contrary, a struggle to create constraint out of the bits and pieces available to them. Their love thus has as its prehistory the creation of order out of lawlessness. In **Beloved** slavery as a state of nature offers a vantage point from which to contemplate love afresh.

Some of Morrison's characters live life, in this respect, as they find it. "Don't love nothing" is the beginning and end of what Ella has to say about children. Sethe's husband's mother, Baby Suggs, achieves the equivalent by forgetting: "My first-born. All I can remember of her is how she loved the burned bottom of bread. Can you beat that? Eight children and that's all I remember." Sethe's own mother aborted all her children but Sethe, whom she nursed very briefly before being returned to work in the rice, forced to leave Sethe to struggle for her share from a wet nurse. Sethe remembered that her mother scarcely ever looked at her, and when she did always with a smile—not her own but a deformity, the result of being punished with an iron bit in her mouth. Sethe grieved that her mother had never even combed her hair and that she had never known a real smile. The one time she said in effect "I want to be like you," the mother slapped her but said nothing. Her mother left her by being hanged and Sethe, remembering, wished to think that her mother would not have been trying to escape without her. Throughout the story Sethe does not know and sometimes suspects the worst.

As a mother herself Sethe struggles against the logic that puts her to use without leaving any room for her to make the physical connection between female and offspring into a moral connection between mother and child. She scurries back and forth, between her work for Mrs. Garner and a grape arbor under which she has sheltered her daughter, rushing in to do her ironing, rushing out to shoo the flies from the baby's face. Later on, in freedom, she combs her daughter Denver's hair so memorably that it figures in the girl's recurrent nightmare. Again, during the escape when Sethe is dragging herself along, horribly violated and brutally whipped, she keeps herself going with the single idea of delivering her milk to the baby, who has been sent ahead.

If in such miniatures we witness the destruction and construction of generation, we witness the construction of gender in the contract Paul F, Paul D, Paul A, Halle, and Six-O make when Sethe is brought to Sweet Home. She is a beautiful girl of fourteen, the only girl on the farm, and they are men. But they are the Sweet Home men and proud of it. So although they lust as males after this solitary female, they agree to let her choose and wait the year it takes for her to choose Halle: "A year of yearning, when rape seemed the solitary gift of life. The restraint they exercised possible only because they were Sweet Home men—the ones Mr. Garner bragged about." By an act of collective will, which Morrison marks off with an act of pollution, they make a contract that lets them be men and lets Sethe be a woman who can be loved lawfully. Unlike other contracts, this one is durable only so long as the parties sustain their generosity to one another and to Sethe—and will it to be durable. That this act of generosity is powerfully connected with personal pride adds to the depth of Morrison's Paul D, "the last of the Sweet Home men."

While it provided a social residence for different kinds of love, the bond the Sweet Home men forged among themselves and then between themselves and Sethe was no more protected than the bond between the slaves and the Garners. Its fragility was exhibited when Paul F's sale away undid his status as a Sweet Home man. Sethe's status as Halle's wife could have easily been undone in many ways (although as things happened it was not). But the Sweet Home men's status as men collapsed as soon as Mr. Garner died. While he lived, however, a convolution of generosity and love of self, not unlike the men's, revealed itself in Garner's esteem for his slaves. It is not clear that, if he had had sons, he would have "raised" his slaves as he did. Perhaps by sad happenstance, he taught his slaves to read and count if they wanted, let them have hunting guns, listened to what they thought and felt, which mattered to him; and he worked with them. In the process, he was consciously making them men by his own proud creation; but by the same act he consciously made himself a man in a sense he could not be without them.

> "Beg to differ, Garner. Ain't no nigger men."
> "Not if you scared, they ain't. . . . But if you a man yourself, you'll want your niggers to be men too." "I wouldn't have no nigger men around my wife." It was the reaction Garner loved and waited for. "Neither would I," . . . and there was always a pause before the neighbor, or stranger, or peddler, or brother-in-law . . . got the meaning.

Out of the brawl or hot argument that invariably followed there came home to Lillian Garner a scratched-up but happy man's man and slave owner's slave owner, "a real Kentuckian, one strong enough and smart enough to make and call his own niggers men."

The same ramifying branches that join the Sweet Home men to each other, to Mr. Garner, and to Sethe, also join Sethe to Mrs. Garner. After choosing Halle, she wonders about a wedding:

> There should be . . . dancing, a party, a something. She and Mrs. Garner were the only women there, so she decided to ask her. . . . "Is there a wedding?"
>
> Mrs. Garner put down her cooking spoon. Laughing a little, she touched Sethe on the head, saying, "You are one sweet child." And then no more.

But she did respond. She overlooked (and Sethe knew she overlooked) the temporary theft of two pillowcases, a dresser skirt, an old sash, and some mosquito netting, the bits and pieces out of which Sethe made the dress she wore the day she and Halle became a couple. The day after, according to Sethe, "Mrs. Garner crooked her finger at me and took me upstairs to her bedroom. She opened a wooden box and took out a pair of crystal earrings. She said, 'I want you to have these, Sethe.' " The gesture was authentically maternal, in manner as much as in content, and no doubt both enjoyed it as such, until Mrs. Garner's next question revealed the loose end: "Are your ears pierced?" Still, she said and meant that Halle was nice, that she wanted them to be happy; and Sethe said and meant her thank you. But Sethe tied the earrings in her skirt and did not put them on until she had left her Kentucky home.

And so we begin to see an infinitely delicate imagining of love on its own, without the authority of the conventional ties that could make it coherent and durable. It is a makeshift. Here it is stitched to an outlying bit of the conventionally intimate mother-daughter relation; there it returns to the conventionally distant slave-mistress relation. The mother-daughter relation Sethe and Mrs. Garner stitch together is inherently unstable because it cannot be upheld beyond the voluntary complicity of the two, and because nothing sustains it but their separate desires. This lack of social authority means, among other things, that the relationship cannot demand of either party more than she wills voluntarily to give it. So while the tie between Sethe and Mrs. Garner exhibits the disinterested traits of the categorical mother-daughter relation—some things are given without expectation of reward, but simply "because it was she"—it also exhibits some of the traits of a mutually self-interested exchange—each woman for her own reasons needs part of the other. This portrayal of an undomesticated love relation, growing on itself, invites reflection on the parts of its domesticated relative that grow well away from the pruned surface.

It would be a simpler task than Morrison set herself not to explore the inner and outer limits of authentic love between slave owner and slaves. But as the creator of a man and woman capable of love despite their rearing as slaves, she reckons with the fact that no ties enjoy protection, neither those that join slaves to other slaves nor those that join slaves to owners. Therefore to disparage a priori the possible makeshifts between owners and slaves is not to leave those between slaves credible. The makeshift we see, of Sethe's becoming a daughter, and the daughterless Mrs. Garner's becoming a mother to her, is as important to Sethe as her unrealized relationship with her own mother. Indeed, the two fuse together in her mind. We learn how important Mrs. Garner was to Sethe at the moment when she embraced Beloved as her dead daughter. "Beloved, she my daughter, she mine. . . . She come back to me of her own free will and I don't have to explain a thing." But, farther on: "I'll explain to her even though I don't have to." And then the explanation moves from how Sethe braved everything to deliver milk to her baby, to how the Garners' grown nephews forcibly nursed her, to the act of murder to keep her daughter safe, to Mrs. Garner's sickness the night the sign came that it was time to run:

> I tended her like I would have tended my own mother if she needed me. If they had let her out of the rice field, because I was the only one she didn't throw away. I couldn't have done more for that woman than I could my own

ma'am . . . and I'd have stayed with her until she got well or died. And I would have stayed after that except Nan snatched me back.

She told Mrs. Garner how the grown-up nephews had taken her behind the stable and nursed her: "Last time I saw her she couldn't do anything but cry, and I couldn't do a thing for her but wipe her face when I told her what they done to me." The sick and feeble Mrs. Garner's protest to her nephews against this violation led to the brutal whipping Sethe got.

In Denver's story of Sethe's escape, Amy's selflessness during an awful night and day is matched by Sethe's own. She will endure any hardship to get milk to the baby who has been sent ahead. In Sethe's account to Paul D, this selfless striving promotes something more:

> I did it. I got us all out. . . . I had help . . . but still it was me doing it. . . . Me using my own head. But it was more than that. It was a kind of selfishness I never knew anything about before. . . . I was big, Paul, deep and wide and when I stretched out my arms all my children could get in between. I was *that* wide.

It was this exultant exultant Sethe, not the Sethe groping with the others toward the decision to escape, who had found it within herself to resist recapture, whatever the cost. The community picked up Sethe's pride and judged her for it. As Janey said, when she heard of Sethe's last tribulation: "This Sethe had lost her wits, finally, as Janey knew she would—trying to do it all alone with her nose in the air." "Like she was better," said another. "Guess she had it coming," someone else put in. When one of them whispered to Paul D about the day the patrollers arrived, and Paul questioned her, he concluded: "There could have been a way. Some other way." Having been seduced by Beloved (his "stepdaughter" to the extent she was Sethe's "daughter"), and guilty himself, he was primed for judging and so he judged. At the end of their conversation, he broke his promise to hold onto her ankles and not let her fall. He left Sethe's house, taking up nighttime residence in the basement of the Church of the Redeemer and daytime residence on its front steps, with a bottle in his hand.

On the day the patrollers arrived, Sethe had acted without hesitation and without regret, without need to explain anything to anyone or to seek forgiveness anywhere. In any case, it was not an act to be forgiven. Perhaps it was one to be gotten beyond by placing oneself into the hands of the community's capacity for mercy after its judgment. Sethe invited no one's participation either way. When she returned from jail with Denver, neighbors and former friends left her to herself, and she sought no one. She went back and forth to her drab work in a restaurant kitchen, did housework from day to day, and kept plodding as her sons left to follow the Union army, Denver retreated into deaf and dumb shock, and Baby Suggs decided to take to her bed, pine, and die. After a brief notion of moving, quickly abandoned, she accepted matter-of-factly the baby ghost's interfering presence in the house and made practical allowance for it. She accommodated Denver's solitude, loving in parallel with her when anything else was impossible. She managed her life, a full survivor of the terrible events that happened twenty-eight days after her declaration of freedom. She simply pinned her life into the present during the next eighteen years; and then everything came undone.

Beloved has the property Walter Benjamin attributed to all great stories. Its essence is not expended in one telling.

—Karen E. Fields

What really happened to Sethe and how is left to the reader's own meditation. The paradox of the story is that, with the arrival of the two apparitions that boded better things, Sethe collapsed. First was Paul D, who as the last of the Sweet Home men rejoined her with her past. He interrupted her sober practicality with laughter, a "bed life," the comfort of past acquaintance, a vision of the future, and the offer of safety in which to entertain an inward life: "Jump, if you want to, 'cause I'll catch you, girl. I'll catch you 'fore you fall. Go as far inside as you need to, I'll hold your ankles. Make sure you get back out." Beloved interrupted Sethe's sober practicality with the deadliest of temptations: "to take care of and make up for" and to explain, to seize the forbidden fruit of doing the past over again, better. The miraculous gift of having her murdered daughter back and doing the past over, therefore came at the cost of remorse, guilt, self-doubt, and unending self-justification. The attempt to do the past over, as an ordinary mother, brought her within reach of the community's judgment. She had not been before.

Beloved did not seem to her to be "the daughter," as distinct from "a daughter," until the moment when "the click" came, and Sethe began to see the scar around the young woman's neck and three fingernail marks on her head. As simply a daughter and one of a threesome with Sethe and Denver, Beloved added to their joy frolicking together on ice skates, planning the next summer's garden, sewing fancy clothes, eating fancy foods, telling stories and jokes, singing. Denver's "click" came long before Sethe's, and so her love evolved into holding onto Beloved and then into holding Beloved together before Sethe's did. When Sethe's came, she held on too, and Denver let go. Giving up her job so as never to leave Beloved alone again, giving up eating or caring for herself, Sethe gradually became weak and weary of life, as she tried, ever more ineffectually, to explain to Beloved the colossal act of a mother who had been "that wide." Watching, and remembering how Baby Suggs had let herself pass away, Denver set in motion the events that saved her mother but exorcized Beloved.

With Beloved gone, Paul D came back to the house. He found Sethe in a physical state that told her spiritual connection to the dead. She was lying in Baby Suggs's bed and decay was in the air. He thought he saw what she was

planning and asked. "Oh, I don't have no plans," she told him, "No plans at all." He said:

> "Look. . . . Denver be here in the day. I be here in the night. I'm a take care of you, you hear? Starting now. First off, you don't smell right. Stay there. Don't move. Let me heat up some water." He stops. "Is it all right, Sethe, if I heat up some water?"

And then, with Paul D's simple acts of bathing Sethe and rubbing her feet, Morrison turns the light brilliantly up around Baby Suggs's bed. Sethe "opens her eyes, knowing the danger of looking at him. . . . The peachstone skin, the crease between his ready, waiting eyes, and sees it—the thing in him, the blessedness, that has made him the kind of man who can walk in a house and make the women cry."

In keeping with the grandeur of her subject, Morrison moves us from the happy ending, in which Paul D and

---

An excerpt from *Beloved*

Sethe knew that the circle she was making around the room, him, the subject, would remain one. That she could never close in, pin it down for anybody who had to ask. If they didn't get it right off—she could never explain. Because the truth was simple, not a long-drawn-out record of flowered shifts, tree cages, selfishness, ankle ropes and wells. Simple: she was squatting in the garden and when she saw them coming and recognized schoolteacher's hat, she heard wings. Little hummingbirds stuck their needle beaks right through her headcloth into her hair and beat their wings. And if she thought anything, it was No. No. Nono. Nonono. Simple. She just flew. Collected every bit of life she had made, all the parts of her that were precious and fine and beautiful, and carried, pushed, dragged them through the veil, out, away, over there where no one could hurt them. Over there. Outside this place, where they would be safe. And the hummingbird wings beat on. Sethe paused in her circle again and looked out the window. She remembered when the yard had a fence with a gate that somebody was always latching and unlatching in the time when 124 was busy as a way station. She did not see the whiteboys who pulled it down, yanked up the posts and smashed the gate leaving 124 desolate and exposed at the very hour when everybody stopped dropping by. The shoulder weeds of Bluestone Road were all that came toward the house.

When she got back from the jail house, she was glad the fence was gone. That's where they had hitched their horses—where she saw, floating above the railing as she squatted in the garden, schoolteacher's hat. By the time she faced him, looked him dead in the eye, she had something in her arms that stopped him in his tracks. He took a backward step with each jump of the baby heart until finally there were none.

Toni Morrison, in her Beloved, *Plume, 1987.*

Sethe seem poised to begin a sunlit new story, to a twilight in which to contemplate the old one: the meaning of Beloved's appearance in the lives of three people; the permutations of happenstance and will that made Paul D and Sethe the people they were; the content of their tie to one another. And who was the girl, Beloved? The ending offers new material with which to return to the beginning. "There is loneliness that can be rocked. . . . Then there is loneliness that roams. . . . A dry and spreading thing that makes the sound of one's own feet seem to come from a far-off place." Morrison's narrator continues by insisting, "It was not a story to pass on. So they forgot her."

It also is not a story to be retold in only one way. For *Beloved* has the property Walter Benjamin attributed [in "The Storyteller," in *Illuminations,* 1969] to all great stories. Its essence is not expended in one telling. The psychological connections are not made but are left to the readers, from each according to his ability, to each according to his need. In that way, *Beloved* lays claim to a place in memory and in retelling. I have retold *Beloved* as a meditation upon the nature of love. To me, it is a story that trains this meditation by inviting us, from the very beginning, to embrace dead strangers. "Sixty million and more," Morrison tells us in her own voice—and then, in God's, "I will call them my people which were not my people; and her beloved which was not beloved." But *Beloved* is not a story to be retold in only one way. It is a story to pass on.

Susan Bowers   (essay date Spring 1990)

SOURCE: "*Beloved* and the New Apocalypse," in *The Journal of Ethnic Studies,* Vol. 18, No. 1, Spring, 1990, pp. 59-77.

[*In the following essay, Bowers analyzes* Beloved *in the context of the "long tradition of African-American apocalyptic writing."*]

Toni Morrison's *Beloved* joins a long tradition of African-American apocalyptic writing. Early African-American writers believed that "America, after periods of overwhelming darkness, would lift the veil and eternal sunshine would prevail" [Addison Gayle, *The Way of the World: The Black Novel in America,* 1975]. By the Harlem Renaissance, African-American writers had begun to doubt a messianic age, but the middle and late 1960s saw a return to apocalypticism, emphasizing Armageddon. Many of these works by such writers as John Williams and John Oliver Killens conceived "the longed-for racial battle" as "the culmination of history and the revelatory moment of justice and retribution" [A. Robert Lee, ed., *Black Fiction: New Studies in the Afro-American Novel Since 1945,* 1980]. Morrison's novel maps a new direction for the African-American apocalyptic tradition which is both more instructive and potentially more powerful than the end-of-the-world versions of the sixties. She has relocated the arena of racial battle from the streets to the African-American psyche from where the racial memories of Black people have been taken hostage.

Morrison has remarked on the dearth of any "songs or dances or tales" about those who died in the Middle Passage and on what was left out of slave narratives.

> People who did dwell on it, it probably killed them, and the people who did not dwell on it probably went forward. They tried to make a life. I think that Afro-Americans in rushing away from slavery, which was important to do—it meant rushing out of bondage into freedom—also rushed away from the slaves because it was painful to dwell there, and they may have abandoned some responsibility in so doing. ["In the Realm of Responsibility: A Conversation with Toni Morrison," *Women's Review of Books,* March 1988]

She believes that her "job as a writer in the last quarter of the 20th century, not much more than a hundred years after Emancipation, becomes how to rip that veil drawn over 'proceedings too terrible to relate.' "

The word "apocalypse" means unveiling, and this novel unveils the angry presence of the "disremembered and unaccounted for" (Morrison, *Beloved*) those who died from slavery and on the Middle Passage (at least 50% of all Africans on slave ships died between Africa and the American plantations during the 320 years of the slave trade).

Apocalypticism is a form of eschatology. The root meaning of *eschaton* is "furthermost boundary" or "ultimate edge" in time or space. Apocalypses can be read

> as investigations into the edge, the boundary, the interface between radically different realms. If the apocalypse is an unveiling (*apo* [from or away], *kalupsis* [covering] from *kalupto* [to cover], and *kalumma*[veil]), then clearly the veil is the *eschaton,* that which stands between the familiar and whatever lies beyond. In this sense the apocalypse becomes largely a matter of *seeing.* [Douglas Robinson, *American Apocalypses,* 1985]

The veil or *eschaton* in *Beloved* is forgetting. The etymological sense of "forget" is to miss or lose one's hold. The characters of *Beloved*—and by implication, contemporary African-Americans—have lost touch with those who have died from slavery and even with their own pasts. As a result they have lost part of themselves, their own interior lives. Their struggle is to lift the veil of Lethe to reveal the truth of their personal and collective histories. Morrison fuses Christian notions of apocalypse with West African beliefs to create a revised apocalyptic which principally looks backward, not forward in time, and concentrates on the psychological devastation which began with the horrors of slavery and continued when African-Americans had to let the horrors of the Middle Passage and slavery disappear into the black hole of Lethe, that vortex of forgetting. Working from the foundation of West African philosophy, at the heart of which is communion with ancestors, Morrison presents an apocalyptic demolition of the boundaries between the earthly and spiritual realms, an invasion of the world of the living by the world beyond the veil. The narrative does not drive toward its apocalyptic moment, but recounts the struggle of living through and beyond the reign of the Anti-Christ and of surviving the "mumbling of the black and angry dead" (*Beloved*).

Beloved's focus on the past may seem contrary to the forward-looking spirit of apocalypse, especially in American literature, where the apocalyptic is considered fundamental. However, African-American apocalypse must be clearly differentiated from White American apocalypse. The fact is that "American apocalypse" is founded on a premise which necessarily excludes African-American writing: that America is the New World, land of rebirth and new life, as opposed to Europe, the Old World of decadence, decay and death. When Europeans discovered America in the sixteenth century, "America was conceived as mankind's last great hope, the Western site of the millenium," and "its future destiny was firmly and prophetically linked with God's plan for the world" [Robinson, *American Apocalypses*]. As a result, most White American apocalyptic literature has been based on the optimistic expectation of historical, material change. The reverse experience, of course, is true for African-Americans. They did not leave an Old World of death and decadence for a New World of hope and rebirth, but were torn from the world of their families, communities, their own spiritual traditions and languages, to be taken to a world of suffering, death, and alienation. The good life lay not before them, but behind them; yet, every attempt was made to crush their memories of the past. Slaves were isolated from other members of their tribes to keep them from communicating in their own languages and maintaining their own traditions. In *Beloved,* only when characters can recover the past do they begin to imagine a future.

One way Morrison avoids the end-of-the-world perspective of most apocalyptic fiction is by basing her novel, like Ralph Ellison's *Invisible Man,* on West African philosophy, including the notion of cyclical time. The West African sense of time is part of an organic philosophy that views the world as living—"subject to the law of becoming, of old age and death" [Mircea Eliade, *Myth and Reality,* 1963]. For such a culture, apocalypse is repeatable and survivable. On the other hand, there can be only one apocalypse if time is conceived of as linear and irreversible as it is in the Judeo-Christian tradition. The constant circling of the narrative in *Beloved* from present to past and back again enacts the West African perspective and reinforces the importance of the past for both the individual and collective psyche.

Morrison shares with post-Holocaust Jewish artists the monumental difficulties attendant of depicting the victims of racial genocide. What Elie Weisel has stated about the Holocaust applies to the slaughter of ten times as many Africans and African-Americans as the six million Jews killed by Hitler (Morrison has said that 60 million is the smallest figure she had gotten from anyone for the number of slaves who died as a result of slavery).

> The Holocaust is not a subject like all the others. It imposes certain limits. . . . In order not to betray the dead and humiliate the living, this particular subject demands a special sensibility, a different approach, a rigor strengthened by respect and reverence and, above all, faithfulness to memory. [Elie Weisel, "Art and the Holocaust: Trivializing Memory," *New York Times,* June 11, 1989]

Betrayal would include sentimentalizing and thus trivializing the victims of slavery, rendering them merely pathetic and pitiable. Morrison does not do that. She dedicated *Beloved* to the "Sixty Million and More," and her novel conjures slaves back to life in many-dimensional characters with a full range of human emotions. They love and hate, sin and forgive, are heroic and mean, self-sacrificing and demanding. They endure incredible hardships to sustain relationships, but the inconceivable brutality and degradation which they experience fractures their communities and inflicts both physical and perhaps irreparable psychological damage on individuals.

One of the questions which *Beloved* asks is whether it is possible to transform unspeakably horrific experiences into knowledge. Is the magnitude of their horror too great to assimilate? Perhaps because the novel asks its readers, especially African-Americans, to "dwell on the horror" which those rushing away from slavery could not, it addresses what happens when the magnitude of that horror is acknowledged, even suggesting how to survive the bringing into consciousness of what has lain hidden for so long. The struggle of *Beloved*'s characters to confront the effects of the brutality and to recover their human dignity, their selves "dirtied" by White oppression—to transform their experiences into knowledge—is presented in the form of a slave narrative that can be read as a model for contemporary readers attempting to engage these brutal realities. Slave narratives emphasize personal quest as a means of "wrest[ing] the black subject out of anonymity, inferiority and brutal disdain" [Susan Willis, "Black Women Writers: Taking a Critical Perspective," *Making a Difference,* edited by Gayle Greene and Coppelia Kahn, 1985]. *Beloved* combines the personal quest theme with the collective memory of racial brutality, for although apocalyptic literature features the destiny of the individual and personal salvation, its "overall perspective is still that of the community" [D. S. Russell, *Apocalyptic: Ancient and Modern,* 1968.]

It is important to note that *Beloved* is more explicit than most early slave narratives which could not reveal fully the horror of slave experience, either because their authors dared not offend their White abolitionist audiences or because they too could not bear to dwell on the horror. *Beloved* does not subordinate the stories of slave life to abstract ideas, unlike the slave narratives which were usually "sandwiched between white abolitionist documents, suggesting that the slave has precious little control over his or her life—even to its writing" [John Sekora, "Is the Slave Narrative a Species of Autobiography?" *Studies in Autobiography,* edited by James Olney, 1988]. Moreover, Morrison's modeling of her novel on the slave narrative is one way of giving African-Americans back their voices. The slave narrative was an extremely popular form of literature until the Civil War. But after the war, the narratives were "expelled from the center of our literary history."

While an editor at Random House, Morrison worked for 18 months in the early 1970s on a project to unveil the reality of African-American life, *The Black Book,* which she called "a genuine Black history book—one that simply recollected Black life as lived" [Morrison, **"Behind the Making of *The Black Book*,"** *Black World*, February 1974]. *The Black Book* contains what became the germ of *Beloved*: the story of a slave woman in Cincinnati who killed one child and tried to kill the other three, to, in her words, "end their sufferings, [rather] than have them taken back to slavery, and murdered by piecemeal." But this "folk journey of Black America" had a far more profound impact upon Morrison than providing her with an initial spark, because it was a model of attempting to tell the truth about a part of African-American life that has been either whitewashed or forgotten, a truth so horrible that it could make a mother see death as desirable for her child.

What *The Black Book* models is an uncensored exposure of brutality through newspaper clippings and photographs of lynchings and burnings of Black people, for instance, juxtaposed with the celebration of African-American strengths and achievements and folkways. Essentially, *The Black Book* models the remembering of African-American experience.

One of the questions which *Beloved* asks is whether it is possible to transform unspeakably horrific experiences into knowledge. Is the magnitude of their horror too great to assimilate?

—*Susan Bowers*

"Rememorying" is what Morrison's characters call it, and it is the central activity in *Beloved*. Because of it the narrative moves constantly back and forth between past and present, mixing time inextricably, as memory escalates its battle against amnesia. The voice of the former slave "above all *remembering* his ordeal in bondage" can be "the single most impressive feature of a slave narrative" [Robert B. Stepto, *From Behind the Veil: A Study of Afro-American Narrative*, 1979]. The characters' rememorying in *Beloved* epitomizes the novel's purpose of conjuring up the spirits and experiences of the past and thus ultimately empowering both characters and readers. *Beloved* pairs the stories of a woman and a man, Sethe and Paul D. Sethe's name may be an allusion to Lethe, the spring of forgetfulness in Greek myth. The past that was too painful for either to remember alone can be recovered together: "Her story was bearable because it was his as well." Their stories reveal that the worst brutality they have suffered "is less a single act than the systematic denial of the reality of black lives" [Cynthia Davis, "Self, Society and Myth in Toni Morrison's Fiction," *Contemporary Literature*, 1982], the profound humiliation which both know can be worse than death:

> That anybody white could take your whole self for anything that came to mind. Not just work, kill, or maim you, but dirty you. [*Beloved*]

Remembering is part of reversing the "dirtying" process that robbed slaves of self-esteem.

The concentration on the horrors of the past and present—the misuse of power, the cruelty and injustice—is characteristic of apocalyptic writing. However, the traditional apocalyptic anticipation of the messianic age—the time of freedom and redemption—is missing among these slaves and ex-slaves for whom hope has come to seem a cruel trick. The members of Paul D's chain gang try to destroy that part of themselves as they crush stone: "They killed the flirt whom folks called Life for leading them on."

The typical format of the slave narrative is to trace the story of the individual's life in slavery, escape, and the journey to freedom. What Morrison reveals is that the process must be repeated twice: first to leave physical enslavement by whites and the second time to escape the psychological trauma created by their brutality. The physical escapes of both Sethe and Paul D create the patterns for their psychological escapes: archetypal journeys of courage, descents into almost certain death, and rebirths into beauty and freedom. Sethe gives birth with the help of a young White girl when she reaches the Ohio River and thus freedom. Paul D is helped by Cherokees, who "describe the beginning of the world and its end and tell him to follow the tree flowers to the North and freedom."

But the novel opens with characters still traumatized many years after their escapes from slavery. They are numb, almost incapable of emotion because they have suffered so deeply and seen such terror. Sethe and her daughter are literally haunted by the ghost of her murdered baby. Sethe is unable to feel; every morning she sees the dawn, but never acknowledges its color. Paul D experiences his heart as a "tobacco tin lodged in his chest," which holds the painful memories of his own past, the memories of one friend being burned to death, of others hanging from trees, his brothers being sold and taken away, of being tortured. "By the time he got to 124 nothing in this world could pry it open." Paul D's arrival at 124, Sethe's home, 18 years after the two had last seen each other, begins their long and excruciating process of thawing frozen feeling.

Contemporary research on treatment for post-traumatic stress syndrome indicates that support and caring from others can help victims to heal, but that the most crucial part of healing is the unavoidable confrontation with the original trauma and feeling the pain again. *Beloved* enacts that theory. Sethe and Paul D are able to help each other to a point, but until they have intimate contact with the original pain and the feelings it created that had to be suppressed, they cannot be purged of its paralyzing effect.

What breaks open Paul D's tin heart and allows Sethe to see and love color again (color often appears in Morrison's fiction as a sign of the ability to feel) is Beloved's return from the dead, not as a ghost but a living being. She climbs fully dressed out of the water—perhaps representing the collective unconscious of African-Americans—while, appropriately, Sethe, Paul D., and Sethe's daughter Denver are at a carnival (etymologically, "festival of flesh"). Beloved has "new skin, lineless and smooth," no expression in her eyes, three thin scratches on her head where Sethe had held her head after severing her neck, and a small neck scar. Although Sethe does not consciously recognize her daughter for some time, her bladder fills the moment she sees her face and she voids "endless" water as if giving birth. For each of the three residents of 124—Sethe, Paul D and Denver—relating to Beloved addresses her or his most profound individual anguish, whatever lies at the core of each identity. For Sethe, it is mothering; for Paul D, his ability to feel, and for Denver, her loneliness. Their individual reactions to her reflect their respective voids, and reveal their deepest selves.

Angela Davis has pointed out that slave women were not recognized as mothers having bonds with their children, but considered only "breeders" and workers. Thus, slave-owners had no scruples about selling children away from their mothers: "Their infant children could be sold away from them like calves from cows" [Davis, *Women, Race and Class,* 1981]. ***Beloved*** is characterized by mothers losing their children: Sethe's mother-in-law barely glanced at the last of her eight children "because it wasn't worth the trouble." Sethe's own mother, hanged when Sethe was a small child, had not been allowed to nurse her. But Sethe defines herself as mother in defiance of the near-impossibility of that role. Even 18 years after her escape, Paul D recognizes that Sethe's mother-love is risky. "For a used-to-be slave woman to love anything that much was dangerous, especially if it was her children she had settled on to love." It was to avoid a future in slavery for her children that led Sethe to plan escape, and to get her milk to her baby—sent ahead with the other children—that made her attempt it alone. She experiences having her milk stolen from her by the nephews of her slavemaster as the ultimate brutality, even worse than the savage beating she received just before escaping. "They handled me like I was the cow, no, the goat, back behind the stable because it was too nasty to stay in with the horses." Beloved's return enables Sethe to mother her abundantly with "lullabies, new stitches, the bottom of the cake bowl, the top of the milk."

If mothering is at the core of Sethe's identity, feeling is at the core of Paul D's. "Not even trying, he had become the kind of man who could walk into a house and make the women cry. Because with him, in his presence, they could." What had led to his own inability to feel was the systematic destruction of his manhood. Like many men, women and children, he had had a bit in his mouth, but the worst part of the experience for Paul D was feeling the superiority of a rooster (called Mister):

> Mister was allowed to be and stay what he was. . . . But wasn't no way I'd ever be Paul D again, living or dead. Schoolteacher changed me. I was something else and that something was less than a chicken sitting in the sun on a tub.

When Beloved seduces Paul D, making love with her breaks open the tobacco tin in his chest to release his red heart.

Sethe's anguish is about her mothering, and Paul D's, the ability to feel. Denver's is her loneliness. Its original cause is Beloved's murder, which alienated the community, made Denver afraid of her mother and of whatever was terrible enough to make her kill her own, and caused the haunting of 124 that made Denver's two brothers leave. She had gone deaf and withdrawn from others for a time after having been asked if she hadn't been in jail with her when her mother was charged with murder. Beloved's gift to Denver is attention. Under her gaze, "Denver's skin dissolved . . . and became soft and bright."

But Beloved is much more than Sethe's resurrected daughter. She is the embodiment of the collective pain and rage of the millions of slaves who died on the Middle Passage and suffered the tortures of slavery. Therefore, her unconscious knows the desperately crowded conditions of a ship of the Middle Passage:

> . . . there will never be a time when I am not crouching and watching others who are crouching too   I am always crouching   the man on my face is dead   his face is not mine   his mouth smells sweet but his eyes are locked

West African religion believes that after physical death, the individual spirit lives, but because it is no longer contained by its "carnal envelope," it gains in power. Spirits "may cause havoc to people if they are spirits of people who were killed in battle or unjustly," and the spirits feel punished if their names are obliterated or forgotten [John S. Mbiti, *The Prayers of African Religion,* 1975]. (Beloved has no name but the epitaph on her gravestone, a word Sethe remembered from the funeral and which she could pay to have engraved only by enduring the sexual assault of the engraver). The invasion of the world of the living by Beloved's physical presence is evidence of the terrible destruction of the natural order caused by slavery. No one had thought anything about a ghost haunting the house, because ancestral spirits were known to linger in the world. But her physical presence has the effect of Judgment Day on all those whom she encounters: Sethe, Paul D, Denver, and the community. However, because the West African sense of time is non-linear, judgment can be endured and redemption still achieved.

> . . . if the apocalypse stands as one constant pole of the black imagination, as a present possibility, the other pole is an unfashionable conviction that change is possible—that the ghosts of the past can be laid if only they are freely engaged and honestly confessed. [C.W.E Bigsby, "Judgment Day is Coming! The Apocalyptic Dream in Recent Afro-American Fiction," *Black Fiction: New Studies in the Afro-American Novel Since 1945,* edited by A. Robert Lee, 1980]

Beloved proclaims that apocalypse and change are not necessarily at opposite poles: an apocalypse—that lifting of the veil on whatever lies beyond—can stimulate change. Its catharsis can be the beginning of transformation; apocalypse can thus become a bridge to the future, passage to freedom.

This novel makes very clear that physical escape into physical freedom was only the first step for the slaves.

That fact is symbolized by *Beloved*'s equivalent of Charon, the figure in Greek mythology who ferries the souls across the Acheron to the underworld. This character is an ex-slave who, after handing over his wife to his master's son, changed his name from Joshua to Stamp Paid because "whatever his obligations were, that act paid them off." By ferrying escaped slaves across the Ohio into freedom, he "gave them their own bill of sale," except that the freedom on the Ohio side of the river is illusory, and not only for political and economic reasons. The slaves who cross the river bring with them the memories of lynchings and torture, family members sold away, degradation, and cumulative loss, so that Stamp Paid, like Charon, actually carries them physically to an underworld, to "free" territory where, in *Beloved,* souls are dead even if bodies are alive. However, Stamp Paid also attempts to carry them out of this underworld into genuine freedom. He "extended the debtlessness [that he believed he had achieved by handing over his wife] to other people by helping them pay out and off whatever they owed in misery."

Stamp Paid interprets the angry mumbling of the spirits around Sethe's home as "the jungle whitefolks planted" in Black people, a jungle which grew and spread, "In, through and after life." Among other things, Beloved is the embodiment of the White folks' jungle, the psychological effects of slavery. The three residents of 124—Sethe, Paul D, and Denver—find out that although Beloved, once no longer a ghost, did address their deepest needs, she is also malevolent. Sethe realizes that Beloved will never accept her explanation for the murder and that Sethe can never make it up to her. Sethe becomes Beloved's slave, goes without food so that Beloved can eat, and begins to die. Paul D recognizes that making love with Beloved "was more like a brainless urge to stay alive." Denver is finally deserted by Beloved when her mother recognizes her dead daughter. When Denver accuses her of strangling Sethe from a distance of several feet, Beloved denies it. "The circle of iron choked it." Her reply reflects the complexity of her character, as both the ghost of Sethe's murdered baby who can't get enough love from her mother and as also the representative of all the angry spirits—the manifestation of the murderous rage created by Whites in enslaved African-Americans. Beloved as the spirit of slavery—the circle of iron around slave necks—did try to kill Sethe; murdered indirectly by Sethe's slavemaster, Beloved is an unquiet spirit. The enormity of the wrongs wreaked upon the "60 million and more" has produced her, obsessed with revenge, desperately needy for love, but incapable of giving it. Beloved is the tangible presence of the painful past. When Sethe finally recognizes her, Sethe is "excited to giddiness by all the things she no longer had to remember." Even though sex with her filled Paul D with repulsion and shame, "he was thankful too for having been escorted to some ocean-deep place he once belonged to."

Beloved's stream of consciousness reveals that she had waited "on the bridge." She herself becomes a bridge between the "other side" and the living, the apocalyptic manifestation of the world beyond the veil. Like a bridge, Beloved enables passage to knowledge of the other side that otherwise would be impossible. We know that medieval chapels were constructed in the middle of bridges so that passengers could contemplate passage from one state of being to another. Beloved's very being forces such contemplation.

In terms of Christian apocalypse, Beloved is not the Anti-Christ; that role belongs to Sethe's slavemaster, representative of the Whites who oppressed African-Americans through slavery. But as the product of slavery, she could be the Anti-Christ's beast. She is a constant sign that this novel is dealing with another level of reality, but also a reminder of the paradoxes about which the novel circles: the killing of a child to protect her and the combined pathos and wrathfulness of the ancestral spirits. Yet, although Sethe's murder of Beloved is the center of the paradox, which occurred 18 years before the action that begins the novel, it is not depicted until nearly the mid-point of *Beloved*. Instead, the murder is anticipated so often that a dark foreboding is created, just as Sethe's mother-in-law sensed something "dark and coming" as the slavemaster and his accomplices were arriving.

The slavemaster, Schoolteacher, is definitely an Anti-Christ figure, the kind of character who usually functions in apocalyptic writing as a sign of the end. The Anti-Christ signals a return to chaos, and Schoolteacher's arrival produces chaos which permeates Sethe's life and in the lives of everyone in her family and in the entire community. Schoolteacher and the three other White men: his nephew, the slavecatcher, and the sheriff, are Morrison's four horsemen of the apocalypse. Their appearance crystallizes the terror and horror of slavery, emphasized by the fact that this episode is the only one in the novel told from the point of view of a white person. When they discover Sethe's sons bleeding at her feet, her baby's head nearly severed, and her trying to kill the other infant, Schoolteacher concedes his economic loss. He believes that Sethe would be useless as a slave to him because she has "gone wild" due to his nephew having "overbeaten" her; she resembles a hound beaten too hard and which, therefore, can never be trusted. He reflects slavery's treatment of African-Americans as animals. Sethe's reaction to seeing the four horsemen is to protect her children in the only way she has left: to remove them from the reach of evil, to try to carry them "through the veil, out, away, over there where no one could hurt them."

This prefiguring of the novel's climactic, redemptive moment is the most violent episode in the novel. Although violence is characteristic of apocalyptic literature, this violence is especially notable because it consists of the victim inflicting the violence on her own children out of utter hopelessness. Stamp Paid calls this event "the Misery" and "Sethe's response to the Fugitive Act." It demonstrates what the characters in *Beloved* recognize—that actual battle with Whites is impossible because the odds are so stacked against Blacks: "Lay down your sword. This ain't a battle; it's a rout."

Biblical scholars read the four horsemen of the apocalypse as agents of divine wrath; Morrison's four horsemen are only emblems of evil. Her revision of the classic apocalyptic image suggests that she does not share with many apocalyptic writers a belief in a moral force at work in history, the invisible presence of a god who will come again to judge sinners and rescue and reward the oppressed. Instead, *Beloved* insists that if change is possible, it will happen only when individuals are integrated with the natural world and each other. The only moral agency is human, represented in *Beloved* by Denver. Born in a boat filling with the "river of freedom," she represents the generation born outside slavery—the future.

Denver is the redemptive figure in this novel. She was only a few days old when her mother murdered Beloved, and Sethe's nipple was covered with her sister's blood when she nursed. "So Denver took her mother's milk right along with the blood of her sister." The image can be read as an allusion to Christ in Revelation "robed in the blood of martyrs" (Rev. 19:13). Like a Christ figure, Denver often functions as an intermediary between spirits and living. Even before Beloved materialized, she saw her in a white dress kneeling beside Sethe, and she was the first to recognize Beloved. Denver not only represents the future; she brings it into being. When neither Sethe nor Beloved seem to care what the next day might bring, "Denver knew it was on her. She would have to leave the yard; step off the edge of the world," and find help. Her efforts lead to everyone's salvation: the reunion of the community. It begins with gifts of food accompanied by the givers' names, but culminates in the women coming to the yard of 124 to exorcise Beloved.

Ella, the former slave woman who had led Sethe and the just-born Denver from the Ohio River, leads Sethe's rescue. She had guided them to the community of former slaves, then led the community's ostracizing of Sethe for 18 years when Sethe had seemed not to need anyone after Beloved's death. Now, it is the idea of Beloved's physical presence which enrages Ella, for she understands that Beloved represents the invasion of one world by the other, and specifically, "the idea of past errors taking possession of the present." As long as Beloved was only a ghost, even a violent ghost, Ella respected it.

> But if it took on flesh and came in her world, well, the shoe was on the other foot. She didn't mind a little communication between the two worlds, but this was an invasion.

Ella and the others recognize that Beloved's being violates the boundary between the dead and the living. They know that she is the representative of "the people of the broken necks, of fire-cooked blood" whose anger and suffering could not be contained in the other world as long as the living neither heard nor remembered them: the apocalyptic presence come to demand attention. When the community is forced to acknowledge what she represents in their own interior lives, Beloved can be exorcised. Like Beloved's murder, the exorcism takes place in the yard of 124. It shares several other characteristics with that appearance of the Anti-Christ: the arrival of a White man with a horse, a violent reaction by Sethe, and the demise of Beloved. But it is the contrasts that are most important. This time, the White man's mission is innocent; Sethe does not succeed; Beloved's demise is necessary and beneficial, the community supports Sethe instead of deserting her,

and, most important of all, the community achieves a shared revelation that ushers in a new age.

This second momentous gathering at 124 has a fated quality. For instance, at precisely the same moment that the Black women are marching toward 124, Edward Bodwin, the White abolitionist who owns 124, is coming to take Denver to his house to work as a night maid. The women are coming to purge the house of the demon beating up on Sethe, armed with whatever they believe will work: amulets, their Christian faith, anything. It has been 30 years since Bodwin saw 124, the house where he was born, a place about which "he felt something sweeter and deeper" than its commercial value. The thought of it takes him back to his childhood, a time when he had buried his precious treasures in the yard. It has been 18 years since the women were in the yard of 124, at the picnic Sethe's mother-in-law had given the day before Schoolteacher's arrival to celebrate Sethe's escape. If the house is symbolic for Bodwin, it has symbolic value also for the women approaching it. Seeing Beloved on the porch makes them see themselves as young girls picnicking in the yard 18 years earlier, the day before Beloved was killed. What they see is also a reminder of how the community shares responsibility for Beloved's death. The community of former slaves had been so jealous of the huge party which Sethe's mother-in-law had thrown that no one warned 124 of the approaching horsemen. Then the community had not gathered around Sethe when she climbed into the cart for the ride to jail because they felt that she held her head too high. However, Beloved's presence does enable the women to go back in time to being "young and happy." She also lets them recapture the paradisal time they had spent in the Clearing with Sethe's mother-in-law Baby Suggs as their spiritual leader. It is significant that by the end of the novel "rememorying" calls back positive moments instead of the painful, collective oppressive past. United in memories of joy and collective strength, the women can respond to the need to banish Beloved, the objectification of the angry and revengeful ancestral spirits, with the full power of their spiritual tradition. It is especially important that their leader Ella recognizes at last that she shares something very significant with Sethe. What Ella remembers is the "hairy white thing," fathered by her slavemaster, which she had let die. "The idea of that pup coming back to whip her too set her jaw working." And she hollers, to be joined at once by the others.

> They stopped praying and took a step back to the beginning. In the beginning there were no words. In the beginning was the sound, and they all know what that sound sounded like.

The primal sound exorcises Beloved and thus the evil of the "White folks' jungle" in their own lives as well as Sethe's family's. The moment takes them all outside of linear time into a type of apocalypse in which all is reduced to its most fundamental terms, to a purity of emotion and a brilliant clarity. In this moment the cycle has rolled around to begin again. When the women take a step back to the beginning, they touch the eschaton, the boundary, and momentarily escape from the flux of time to the place where clear vision is possible. They remind us that apocalypse is not a synonym for disaster or cataclysm; it is linked to revelation. Seeing clearly into the past, the women can take hold again of what they had lost in forgetting.

Apocalyptic literature is very like Greek tragedy in arousing emotion and creating the conditions for catharsis. Morrison's novel raises all kinds of emotion—pain, grief, remorse, anger, fear—and purges it once "intensified and given objective expression." Beloved focuses the objective expression of emotion. When the women create the powerful, timeless sound which exorcises Beloved, they purge themselves and Sethe and Denver of the emotion which had imprisoned them. It returns them all to a new beginning where, cleansed, they can create a new life.

> The apocalyptic imagination may finally be defined in terms of its philosophical preoccupation with that moment of juxtaposition and consequential transformation or transfiguration when an old world of mind discovers a believable new world of mind, which either nullifies and destroys the old system entirely or, less likely, makes it part of a larger design. [David Ketterer, *New Worlds for Old; The Apocalyptic Imagination, Science Fiction, and American Literature*, 1974]

The women's song or shout creates the moment of redemptive transfiguration in **Beloved**. Still caught in the mode of forgetting which had been their method of survival after physically escaping slavery, when the women focused on the image of Beloved standing on the front porch of 124, they were themselves dragged through the veil into a world rich with memory of their personal and collective lives and of the "unnamed, unmentioned people left behind."

> For Sethe it was as though the Clearing had come to her with all its heat and simmering leaves, where the voices of women searched for the right combination, the key, the code, the sound that broke the back of words.

The Clearing was the open place in the woods where Sethe's mother-in-law, Baby Suggs had led the community in spiritual ceremonies. Baby Suggs had begun those ceremonies by asking the children to laugh, the men to dance, but the women to cry, "For the living and the dead." Then she would direct them all to love themselves deeply.

> 'Here,' she said, 'in this here place, we flesh; flesh that weeps, laughs, flesh that dances on bare feet in grass. Love it. Love it hard. Yonder they do not love your flesh.'

But Baby Suggs gave up after the "Misery" and went to bed to die. When Sethe is taken back to the Clearing by the women's song in her yard, it is a sign of both personal and community redemption; the community at this apocalyptic moment has returned finally to loving themselves, but also to feeling compassion for those who have died. In the yard of 124 when the women found "the sound that broke the backs of words,"

> it was a wave of sound wide enough to sound deep water and knock the pods off chestnut trees. It broke over Sethe and she trembled like the baptized in its wash.

The women's song was powerful enough to break "the back of words"—words used to define African-Americans, such as "animal" and "breeding stock" and "slaves." it baptizes Sethe into a new life, into a radical spiritual transformation.

Ironically, Bodwin arrives at the peak of the women's song/shout. His appearance recalls Sethe to that moment when four White horsemen rode into her yard: and so she acts again to protect her child, but this time she runs to kill the oppressor—whom she sees as Bodwin—instead of her own child. Denver stops her. We should not read Sethe's seeing Bodwin as her enemy as a crazed mistake, but rather as evidence of a kind of clear-sightedness, Sethe having just been baptized in primal, sacred sound. Apocalyptic catharsis requires confrontation with hidden horror; it also provides a two-fold purgation by making the wronged one feel better and castigating the sinner. Although the Bodwins did help ex-slaves and worked for abolition of slavery, **Beloved** makes it clear that they are part of the problem, not the solution. They gave help to runaways "because they hated slavery worse than they hated slaves." On a shelf by their back door is the figurine of a Black child, his mouth full of money, kneeling on a pedestal with the words, " 'At Yo' Service.' " When Bodwin returns to 124, his eyes are transfixed by the sight of Beloved. After she has disappeared Beloved is described as "a naked woman with fish for hair" which may be an allusion to Medusa, the gorgon who turned men to stone. Perhaps Beloved has that effect on Bodwin. Perhaps he recognizes in her what Stamp Paid called "the white folks' jungle." Perhaps his encounter with Beloved—he doesn't even see Sethe approaching to stab him with the ice pick—is his experience of Judgment, occurring appropriately at the house where he was born, where his "treasure" lay hidden.

Apocalypse is a more diffuse experience in **Beloved** than traditionally conceived, and it is presented as something which can be survived, not as an event at the end of linear time. In **Beloved** it is an attempt to free African-Americans from guilt and past suffering. What **Beloved** suggests is that while the suffering of the "black and angry dead" is the inescapable psychological legacy of all African-Americans, they can rescue themselves from the trauma of that legacy by directly confronting it and uniting to loosen its fearsome hold. **Beloved**'s redemptive community of women epitomizes the object of salvation in biblical apocalyptic literature: "the creation of a new society."

Thus, like much African-American writing, **Beloved** does not conclude with a climactic moment. "For the black writer, incompletion is a fact of private and public life and the basis for social and cultural hope" (Bigsby). The experience of suffering and guilt can begin to be transformed into knowledge, once the trauma is purged, so that the novel leaves the powerful apocalyptic scene of the community's expurgation of Beloved to observe Sethe and Paul D rejoining their stories to each other's. Paul D, who had left upon learning of the murder, must return to Sethe's house to re-establish the intimate connection which will allow them each to find his or her own self and love it. Paul D, despite his inability to feel when he had first arrived at

Sethe's, has a deep understanding of the meaning of slavery and freedom, that under slavery "you protected yourself and loved small," but finding freedom means "to get to a place where you could love anything you chose." Linked with Sethe's mother in several ways, including the wearing of the bit, he mothers Sethe as her own mother never could, and when he does, the voice of his lynched best friend enters his mind, speaking about the woman he loved, "She is a friend of my mind. She gather me, man. The pieces I am, she gather them and give them back to me in all the right order."

Beloved is a novel about collecting fragments and welding them into beautiful new wholes, about letting go of pain and guilt, but also recovering what is lost and loving it into life. One of its most poignant images is the ribbon that Stamp Paid finds on the river bottom—"a red ribbon knotted around a curl of wet woolly hair, clinging still to its bit of scalp." Although he knows all the horrors of 1874—the lynchings, whippings, burnings of colored schools, rapes, and lynch fires—it is this discovery which finally weakens Stamp Paid's bone marrow and makes him "dwell on Baby Suggs' wish to consider what in the world was harmless."

What Morrison creates is far from harmless. She knows how painful it is to remember the horrors she presents. She has said in an interview that she expected *Beloved* to be the least read of all her books because "it is about something that the characters don't want to remember, I don't want to remember, black people don't want to remember, white people don't want to remember. I mean, it's national amnesia" [Bonnie Angelo, "The Pain of Being Black," *Time,* 22 May 1989]. However, because *Beloved* insists on remembering, the novel is able to recover and honor the symbolic spirit of the Black girl whose ribbon and piece of scalp Stamp Paid found. In so doing, it makes possible the contemplation and creation of a future in which African-Americans can respect and honor themselves and their ancestors—be beloved. As Paul D says to Sethe, "Me and you, we got more yesterday than anybody. We need some kind of tomorrow." What *Beloved* suggests is that tomorrow is made possible by the knowledge of yesterday, a knowledge that for contemporary African-Americans can be gained from imagining what it was like to walk in the flesh of their slave ancestors.

> Auschwitz lies on the other side of life and on the other side of death. There, one lives differently, one walks differently, one dreams differently. . . . Only those who lived it in their flesh and their minds can possibly transform their experience into knowledge. [Wiesel]

By giving its readers the inside view of slaves' lives—which bore uncanny resemblance to the holocaust—the novel enables its African-American readers to live the experience of slavery in their minds and to join in the healing primal sound of the women who come to Sethe's yard. By speaking the horror, Morrison assumes and helps to create the community that can hear it and transform it.

Elizabeth B. House (essay date Spring 1990)

SOURCE: "Toni Morrison's Ghost: The Beloved Who Is Not Beloved," in *Studies in American Fiction,* Vol. 18, No. 1, Spring, 1990, pp. 17-26.

[*In the following essay, House argues that the character Beloved in Morrison's novel is not literally a reincarnation of Sethe's slain infant, but an orphaned child upon whom it is convenient for Sethe to project her anguished feelings of remorse and guilt.*]

Most reviewers of Toni Morrison's novel *Beloved* have assumed that the mysterious title character is the ghostly reincarnation of Sethe's murdered baby, a flesh and blood version of the spirit Paul D. drives from the house. Judith Thurman, for example, writes in *The New Yorker* [2 November 1987] that the young stranger "calls herself by the name of the dead baby—Beloved—so there isn't much suspense, either about her identity or about her reasons for coming back." In *The New York Review of Books* [5 November 1987], Thomas R. Edwards agrees that the "lovely, historyless young woman who calls herself Beloved . . . is unquestionably the dead daughter's spirit in human form," and, concurring with these ideas, the *Ms.* reviewer, Marcia Ann Gillespie, adds that "Beloved, blindly seeking retribution, is a succubus leeching Sethe's . . . spirit" [*Ms.,* Vol. 16, No. 5, 1987]. Similarly, Stanley Crouch, in his *New Republic* review [19 October 1987], chides Morrison for creating unreal characters and then laments that "nothing is more contrived than the figure of Beloved herself, who is the reincarnated force of the malevolent ghost that was chased from the house." And, in the same vein, Carol Rumens says in the *Times Literary Supplement* [16-22 October 1987] that the baby ghost, after being driven from the house, "loses little time in effecting a more solid manifestation, as a young woman runaway." Then Rumens faults Morrison for using a spirit as a main character, for, as she says, "the travails of a ghost cannot be made to resonate in quite the same way as those of a living woman or child."

Clearly, these writers evaluate Morrison's novel believing that Beloved is unquestionably a ghost. [In a footnote, House adds: "A few other reviewers take the more moderate position of expressing puzzlement about Beloved rather than claiming that she is either ghost or human. For example, in her *New York Times* review of the novel, Margaret Atwood concludes, 'The reader is kept guessing; there's a lot more to Beloved than any one character can see, and she manages to be many things to several people.' See 'Haunted by Their Nightmares,' *The New York Times Book Review* (September 13, 1987). Similarly, in a *Newsweek* piece, Walter Clemons writes that 'Beloved . . . has an anterior life deeper than the ghostly role she fulfills in the . . . household she visits.' See 'A Gravestone of Memories,' *Newsweek* (September 28, 1987). And, Paul Gray in a *Time* review says that 'the flesh-and-blood presence of Beloved roils the novel's intense, realistic surface. This young woman may not actually be Sethe's reincarnated daughter, but no other explanation of her identity is provided.' See 'Something Terrible Happened,' *Time* (September 21, 1987)."] Such uniform acceptance of this notion is surprising, for evidence throughout the book suggests that the girl is not a supernatural being of any kind but simply a young woman who has herself suffered the horrors of slavery.

In large part, Morrison's Pulitzer Prize-winning fifth novel is about the atrocities slavery wrought both upon a mother's need to love and care for her children as well as a child's deep need for a family: Sethe murders her baby girl rather than have her taken back into slavery; Baby Suggs grieves inconsolably when her children are sold; Sethe sees her own mother, a woman who was brought from Africa on a slave ship, only a few times before the woman is killed; Denver loves her mother, Sethe, but also fears the woman because she is a murderer. These and other incidents illustrate the destruction of family ties brought by slavery, and Beloved, seen as a human being, emphasizes and illuminates these themes. [In a footnote, House continues: "Sethe's own need for a parent is expressed in a pained suspicion that her mother had been hanged for attempting to run away, an action that would have separated the woman not only from the horrors of slavery but also from her own daughter. Speaking to Beloved in a stream-of-conscious remembering, Sethe explains, 'My plan was to take us all to the other side where my own ma'am is. They stopped me from getting us there, but they didn't stop you from getting here. . . . You came right on back like a good girl, like a daughter which is what I wanted to be and would have been if my ma'am had been able to get out of the rice long enough before they hanged her and let me be one. . . . I wonder what they was doing when they was caught. Running, you think? No. Not that. Because she was my ma'am and nobody's ma'am would run off and leave her daughter, would she? Would she, now?' "]

Unraveling the mystery of the young woman's identity depends to a great extent upon first deciphering chapters four and five of Part II, a section that reveals the points of view of individual characters. Both of these chapters begin with the line "I AM BELOVED and she is mine," and in these narratives Morrison enters Beloved's consciousness. From Beloved's disjointed thoughts, her stream-of-conscious rememberings set down in these chapters, a story can be pieced together that describes how white slave traders, "men without skin," captured the girl and her mother as the older woman picked flowers in Africa. In her narrative, Beloved explains that she and her mother, along with many other Africans, were then put aboard an abysmally crowded slave ship, given little food and water, and in these inhuman conditions, many blacks died. To escape this living hell, Beloved's mother leaped into the ocean, and, thus, in the girl's eyes, her mother willingly deserted her.

In order to grasp the details of this story, chapters four and five of Part II must be read as a poem: thus, examining the text line by line is often necessary. As Beloved begins her narrative, she is recalling a time when she was a young girl, for she says "I am not big" and later remarks again "I am small." However, the memory of these experiences is so vivid that, to her, "all of it is now." One of the first traumas Beloved describes is being in the lower hold of a slave ship. The captured Africans have been crouching,

crammed in the overcrowded space for so long that the girl thinks "there will never be a time when I am not crouching and watching others who are crouching" and then she notes that "someone is thrashing but there is no room to do it in." At first the men and women on the ship are separated, but then Beloved says that "storms rock us and mix the men into the women and the women into the men   that is when I begin to be on the back of the man." This person seems to be her father or at least a father figure, for he carries the young girl on his back. Beloved says "I love him because he has a song" and, until he dies on the ship, this man sings of his African home, of the "place where a woman takes flowers away from their leaves and puts them in a round basket   before the clouds."

These lyrics bring to mind the first scene in Part II, chapter four. Beloved's tale begins with the girl watching her mother as the woman takes "flowers away from leaves   she put them in a round basket. . . . She fills the basket   she opens the grass." This opening of the grass is probably caused by the mother's falling down, for Beloved next says, "I would help her but the clouds are in the way." In the following chapter, the girl clarifies this thought when she explains, "I wanted to help her when she was picking the flowers, but the clouds of gunsmoke blinded me and I lost her." Thus, what the girl is remembering is the capture of her mother by the men without skin, the armed white slave traders. Later, Beloved sums up her story by explaining that the three crucial points in her life have been times when her mother left her: "Three times I lost her: once with the flowers because of the noisy clouds of smoke; once when she went into the sea instead of smiling at me; once under the bridge when I went in to join her and she came toward me but did not smile." Thus, the slave traders' capture of her mother is the first of three incidents that frame the rest of Beloved's memories.

Once incarcerated on the ship, Beloved notices changes in her mother. She remembers seeing the diamond earrings, "the shining in her ears," as they were picking flowers. Now on the ship, her mother "has nothing in her ears," but she does have an iron collar around her neck. The child knows that she "does not like the circle around her neck" and says "if I had the teeth of the man who died on my face I would bite the circle around her neck   bite it away   I know she does not like it." Sensing her mother's unhappiness, her longing for Africa, Beloved symbolizes the woman's emotions by ascribing to her a wish for physical items: "She wants her earrings   she wants her round basket."

As Beloved continues her tale, she explains that in the inhuman conditions of the ship, many blacks die. She says "those able to die are in a pile" and the "men without skin push them through with poles," evidently "through" the ship's portholes, for the hills of dead people "fall into the sea which is the color of the bread." The man who has carried her on his back is one of those who succumbs, and as he takes his last breath, he turns his head and then Beloved can "see the teeth he sang through." She knows that "his song is gone," so now she loves "his pretty little teeth instead." Only after the man's head drops in death is the girl able to see her mother; Beloved remembers, "when he dies on my face I can see hers   she is going to smile at me." However, the girl never receives this gesture of affection, for her mother escapes her own pain by jumping into the ocean, thus committing suicide. The scene is etched in Beloved's memory: "They push my own man through   they do not push the woman with my face through   she goes in   they do not push her   she goes in   the little hill is gone she was going to smile at me." Beloved is haunted by this second loss of her mother for, unlike the separation caused by the slavetraders' attack, this time the mother chooses to leave her. The girl agonizes as she tries to understand her mother's action and later thinks that "all I want to know is why did she go in the water in the place where we crouched? Why did she do that when she was just about to smile at me? I wanted to join her in the sea but I could not move." [In a footnote, House remarks: "In an interview with Walter Clemons, Morrison brought to his attention *Beloved*'s dedication, 'Sixty Million and more,' and explained that 'the figure is the best educated guess at the number of black Africans who never even made it into slavery—those who died either as captives in Africa or on slave ships.' Morrison notes, too, that 'one account describes the Congo as so clogged with bodies that the boat couldn't pass. . . . They packed 800 into a ship if they'd promised to deliver 400. They assumed that half would die. And half did.' And, the author wryly adds, 'A few people in my novel remember it. . . . Baby Suggs came here out of one of those ships. But mostly it's not remembered at all.' See 'A Gravestone of Memories,' *Newsweek* (September 28, 1987). Of course, Beloved is the most important person in the novel who remembers the slave ships' horrors. However, Morrison does not reveal that fact here; she merely hints at it."]

Time passes and Beloved notes that "the others are taken   I am not taken." These lines suggest that when the other slaves are removed from the ship, Beloved, whose beauty is noted by several characters, is perhaps kept by one of the ship's officers. At any rate, she is now controlled by a man who uses her sexually, for "he hurts where I sleep," thus in bed, and "he puts his finger there." In this situation, Beloved longs for her mother and explains, "I wait on the bridge because she is under it." Although at this point she may be on an inland bridge, Beloved is most likely waiting for her mother on the ship's bridge; if she is being kept by one of the vessel's officers, the girl would logically be there. But, wherever she is at this time, Beloved last saw her mother as the woman went into the sea; thus, the girl associates water with her parent and believes she can be found in this element.

Beloved's stream-of-consciousness narrative then jumps to the time, apparently several years later, when she arrives at the creek behind Sethe's house. Morrison does not specify exactly how Beloved comes to be there, but various characters give possible explanations. The most plausible theory is that offered by Stamp Paid who says, "Was a girl locked up in the house with a whiteman over by Deer Creek. Found him dead last summer and the girl gone. Maybe that's her. Folks say he had her in there since she was a pup." This possibility would explain Beloved's

"new" skin, her unlined feet and hands, for if the girl were constantly kept indoors, her skin would not be weathered or worn. Also, the scar under Beloved's chin could be explained by such an owner's ill-treatment of her. Morrison gives credence to Stamp Paid's guess by having Sethe voice a similar hypothesis and then note that her neighbor, Ella, had suffered the same fate. When Beloved first comes to live with the family, Sethe tells Denver "that she believed Beloved had been locked up by some whiteman for his own purposes, and never let out the door. That she must have escaped to a bridge or someplace and rinsed the rest out of her mind. Something like that had happened to Ella. . . ." In addition, Beloved's own words suggest that she has been confined and used sexually. The girl explains to Denver that she "knew one whiteman," and she tells Sethe that a white man "was in the house I was in. He hurt me." In a statement that reveals the source of her name, Beloved says that men call her "beloved in the dark and bitch in the light," and in response to another question about her name, she says, "in the dark my name is Beloved."

Whatever situation Beloved has come from, when she reaches the creek behind Sethe's house, she is still haunted by her mother's absence. The lonely girl sees the creek, remembers the water under the ship's bridge where she last glimpsed her mother, and concludes that her lost loved ones are beneath the creek's surface. In her soliloquy, Beloved links the scene to her mother and father figure by evoking images of the African mother's diamond earrings and the father's teeth. She says that she knows the man who carried her on his back is not floating on this water, but his "teeth are down there where the blue is . . . so is the face I want the face that is going to smile at me." And, in describing the creek she says, "in the day diamonds are in the water where she is and turtles in the night I hear chewing and swallowing and laughter it belongs to me." [In a footnote, House explains: "In *The Golden Bough: A Study in Magic and Religion* (1940), James G. Frazier notes that several American Indian groups believed that the dead souls of their relatives returned to earth in the form of water turtles. This concept fits with Morrison's use of the turtles in the scene in which Beloved decides that her lost loved ones are beneath the creek's surface."] The diamonds Beloved thinks she sees in the water are most likely reflected bits of sunlight that make the water sparkle. Similarly, the noises the girl interprets as "chewing and swallowing and laughing" are probably made by the turtles. Alone in the world, Beloved's intense need to be with those she loves undoubtedly affects her interpretation of what her senses perceive.

If Stamp Paid is right and the girl has been locked up for years, then she has not had normal experiences with people or places. She lacks both formal learning and the practical education she would have gained from a family life. These deficiencies also undoubtedly affect her perceptions, and, thus, it is not especially surprising that she does not distinguish between the water under the ship's bridge and that in the creek behind Sethe's house. To the untutored girl, all bodies of water are connected as one.

Apparently, Beloved looks into the creek water, sees her

own reflection, and concludes that the image is her mother's face. She then dives into the water, believing that in this element her mother will at last give her the smile that was cut short on the slave ship. Beloved says,

> "I see her face which is mine it is the face that was going to smile at me in the place where we crouched now she is going to her face comes through the water . . . her face is mine she is not smiling. . . . I have to have my face I go in. . . . I am in the water and she is coming there is no round basket no iron circle around her neck."

In the water, Beloved cannot "join" with the reflection, and thus she thinks her mother leaves her for a third time; distraught, she says, "my own face has left me I see me swim away. . . . I see the bottoms of my feet I am alone."

Beloved surfaces, sees Sethe's house, and by the next day she has made her way to the structure. Exhausted by her ordeal, the girl is sleeping near the house when Sethe returns from the carnival. [In a footnote, House continues: "The narrator says that all of Sethe's neighbors are eager to see the carnival, a show that advertises performances by people who have two heads, are twenty feet tall, or weigh a ton, and 'the fact that none of it was true did not extinguish their appetite a bit.' That Sethe and Denver attend this carnival immediately before meeting Beloved foreshadows their willingness, in fact their need, to believe that the mysterious girl is something other than an ordinary human. Neither the carnival world nor Beloved's status as a child returned from the dead is based on truth, but both provide much desired escapes from the pain of everyday reality."] Beloved says,

> "I come out of blue water. . . . I need to find a place to be. . . . There is a house. . . . I sit the sun closes my eyes when I open them I see the face I lost Sethe's is the face that left me. . . . I see the smile. . . . It is the face I lost she is my face smiling at me doing it at last."

Thus, when Beloved awakens and sees Sethe smiling at her, the girl mistakenly thinks that the woman is her long lost mother. In the second half of her narrative, Beloved even more clearly states her erroneous conclusions when she asserts, "Sethe is the one that picked flowers . . . in the place before the crouching. . . . She was about to smile at me when the men without skin came and took us up into the sunlight with the dead and shoved them into the sea. Sethe went into the sea. . . . They did not push her. . . ."

What finally emerges from combining Beloved's thoughts and the rest of the novel is a story of two probable instances of mistaken identity. Beloved is haunted by the loss of her African parents and thus comes to believe that Sethe is her mother. Sethe longs for her dead daughter and is rather easily convinced that Beloved is the child she has lost.

Morrison hints at this interpretation in her preface to the novel, a quotation from Romans 9:25: "I will call them my people, which were not my people; and her beloved, which was not beloved." As Margaret Atwood notes, the biblical context of these lines emphasizes Paul's message that people once "despised and outcast, have now been redefined as acceptable." However, Morrison's language, especially in the preface, is rich in meaning on many levels. In view of the ambiguity about Beloved's identity found in the rest of the novel, it seems probable that in this initial line Morrison is suggesting an answer to the riddle of who Beloved really is or, to be more exact, who she is not. The words "I will call . . . her beloved, which was not beloved" suggest that the mysterious girl is not really Sethe's murdered daughter returned from the grave; she is "called" Beloved, but she is not Sethe's child. Also, the line "I will call them my people, which were not my people" hints that Beloved mistakenly thinks Sethe and her family are her blood kin.

Seen in this light, Beloved's story illuminates several other puzzling parts of the novel. For example, after Sethe goes to the Clearing and feels that her neck is being choked, Denver accuses Beloved of causing the distress. Beloved replies, " 'I didn't choke it. The circle of iron choked it.' " Since she believes Sethe and her African mother are the same person, Beloved reasons that the iron collar her African mother was forced to wear is bothering Sethe.

Beloved's questions about Sethe's earrings are one reason the woman comes to believe that the mysterious girl is her murdered child. Before her death, Sethe's baby girl had loved to play with her mother's crystal earrings. Sethe had "jingled the earrings for the pleasure of the crawling-already? girl, who reached for them over and over again." Thus, when Beloved asks "where your diamonds? . . . Tell me your earrings," the family wonders, "How did she know?" Of course, Beloved asks this question remembering the "shining" in her African mother's earrings, the diamonds that were probably confiscated by the slave traders. However, Sethe thinks Beloved is remembering the crystal earrings with which the dead baby played.

This instance of misunderstanding is typical, for throughout the novel Sethe, Denver, and Beloved often fail to communicate clearly with each other. In fact, the narrator describes Beloved's and Denver's verbal exchanges as "sweet, crazy conversations full of half sentences, daydreams and misunderstandings more thrilling than understanding could ever be." This evaluation is correct, for as the three women talk to each other, each person's understandings of what she hears is slanted by what she expects to hear. For example, Denver, believing Beloved to be a ghost, asks the girl what the "other world" was like: " 'What's it like over there, where you were before? . . . Were you cold?' " Beloved, of course, thinks Denver is asking her about Africa and the slave ship, and so she replies, " 'Hot. Nothing to breathe down there and no room to move it.' " Denver then inquires whether Beloved saw her dead grandmother, Baby Suggs, or Jesus on the other side: " 'You see Jesus? Baby Suggs?' " and Beloved, remembering the death laden ship, replies that there were many people there, some dead, but she did not know their names. Sethe has a similar conversation with Beloved and begins "Tell me the truth. Didn't you come from the other side?" and Beloved replies "Yes. I was on the other side."

Of course, like Denver, Sethe is referring to a life after death world, while Beloved again means the other side of the ocean, Africa.

Encased in a deep and destructive need for what each thinks the other to be, Sethe and Beloved seclude themselves in Sethe's house, Number 124, and the home becomes like a prison cell for the two disturbed women. They separate themselves completely from the rest of humanity, even Denver, and they begin to consume each other's lives: Beloved continually berates Sethe for having deserted her. Sethe devotes every breath to justifying her past actions to Beloved. Their home life deteriorates to the point that the narrator says "if the whitepeople . . . had allowed Negroes into their lunatic asylum they could have found candidates in 124."

Sethe's and Beloved's obsession with the past clearly affects their perception of what happens when the singing women and Edward Bodwin approach Sethe's house. Ella and the other women are there, singing and praying, hoping to rid Sethe of the ghost they think is plaguing her. Edward Bodwin is the white man who helped Sethe when she was jailed for murdering her baby; now he has come to give Denver a ride to her new job. However, when Sethe comes out of her house and views the scene, her mind reverts to the time when another white man, her slave owner, had come into the yard.

On that fateful day Sethe had killed her child, and she had first sensed danger when she glimpsed her slave master's head gear. When she saw the hated "hat, she heard wings. Little hummingbirds stuck their needle beaks right through her headcloth into her hair and beat their wings. And if she thought anything, it was No. No. Nono. Nonono. Simple. She just flew." Years later, as Sethe stands holding Beloved's hand, she sees Bodwin approach, and her unsettled mind replays her thoughts from long ago. She recognizes "his . . . hat wide-brimmed enough to hide his face but not his purpose. . . . She hears wings. Little hummingbirds stick needle beaks right through her headcloth into her hair and beat their wings. And if she thinks anything, it is no. No no. Nonono. She flies." Apparently deciding that this time she will attack the white intruder and not her own child, Sethe rushes toward Bodwin with an ice pick. Ella strikes Sethe, and then the other women apparently fall on the distraught mother, pinning her to the ground.

As this commotion occurs, Beloved also has a sense of *déjà vu.* First, the girl stands on the porch holding Sethe's hand. Then Sethe drops the hand, runs toward the white man and group of black women, and Beloved thinks her mother has deserted her again. Remembering that her African mother's suicide came after the hill of dead black people were pushed from the slave ship, Beloved sees the horrible scene being recreated:

> But now her hand is empty. . . . Now she is running into the faces of the people out there, joining them and leaving Beloved behind. Alone. Again . . . [she is running away]. Away from her to the pile of people out there. They make a hill. A hill of black people, falling. And above them all, . . . the man without skin, looking.

Beloved connects this "hill" of falling people with the pile of dead blacks who were pushed from the ship, and, terrified, the girl apparently runs away.

In his introduction to *The House of the Seven Gables,* Nathaniel Hawthorne notes that romances, one of the literary traditions to which *Beloved* is heir, are obliged to reveal the "truth of the human heart." And, in *Beloved,* Morrison does just that. An important facet of this truth is that emotional ghosts of hurt, love, guilt, and remembrance haunt those whose links to family members have been shattered; throughout the novel, Morrison shows that family ties can be severed only at the cost of distorting people's lives. In *Beloved,* Morrison also shows that past griefs, hurts ranging from the atrocities of slavery to less hideous pains, must be remembered, but they should not control life. At the end of the novel, Paul D. tells Sethe " 'me and you, we got more yesterday than anybody. We need some kind of tomorrow.' " And, throughout *Beloved,* Morrison's theme is that remembering yesterdays, while not being consumed by them, gives people the tomorrows with which to make real lives.

Karla F. C. Holloway   (essay date Summer 1990)

SOURCE: "*Beloved:* A Spiritual," in *Callaloo,* Vol. 13, No. 3, Summer, 1990, pp. 516-25.

[*In the essay below, Holloway examines myth, historical revisionism, voice, and remembrance in* Beloved *on both thematic and structural levels.*]

> I have to cast my lot with those
> who age after age, peversely,
> with no extraordinary power,
> reconstitute the world.
>
>   —Adrienne Rich, "Natural Resources"

The literary and linguistic devices which can facilitate the revision of the historical and cultural texts of black women's experiences have perhaps their most sustained illustration in Toni Morrison's *Beloved.* Here, narrative structures have been consciously manipulated through a complicated interplay between the implicit orature of recovered and (re)membered events and the explicit structures of literature. The reclamation and revision of history function as both a thematic emphasis and textual methodology. The persistence of this revision is the significant strategic device of the narrative structures of the novel.

Myth dominates the text. Not only has Morrison's reclamation of this story from the scores of people who interviewed Margaret Garner shortly after she killed her child in 1855 constituted an act of recovery, it has accomplished a mythic revisioning as well. Morrison refused to do any further research on Margaret Garner beyond her reviewing of the magazine article that recounted the astonishment of the preachers and journalists who found her to be "very calm . . . very serene" after murdering her child [as recounted in Mervyn Rothstein's "Morrison Discusses New Novel," *The New York Times,* 26 August 1987]. The imagination that restructures the initial article Morrison read into her novel *Beloved* is the imagination of a mythmaker. The mythological dimensions of her story, those that recall her earlier texts, that rediscover the altered universe of the black diaspora, that challenge the Western valuations of time and event (place and space) are those that, in various quantities in other black women writers and in sustained quantities in Morrison's works, allow a critical theory of text to emerge. [The critic adds in a footnote: "My position is that a critical theory of black *women*'s writing emerges as the dimensions of a cultural expression within an African-American literary tradition and specifies, through an interpretation of literary style and substance and its formal modes and figurations, certain textual modes of discourse. Such a specification underscores my primary argument that black women's literature reflects its community—its cultural ways of knowing as well as its ways of framing that knowledge in language. The figures of language that testify to that cultural mooring place—the inversive, recursive, and sometimes even subversive structures that layer the black text—give it a dimension only accessed when the cultural and gendered points of its initiation are acknowledged."]

Morrison revisions a history both spoken and written, felt and submerged. It is in the coalescence of the known and unknown elements of slavery—the events, miniscule in significance to the captors but major disruptions of black folks' experience in nurturing and loving and *being*—where Morrison's reconstruction of the historical text of slavery occurs. Morrison's reformulation propels a backlog of memories headlong into a postemancipation community that has been nearly spiritually incapacitated by the trauma of slavery. For Morrison's novel, what complicates the physical and psychic anguish is the reality that slavery itself defies traditional historiography. The victim's own chronicles of these events were systematically submerged, ignored, mistrusted, or superceded by "historians" of the era. This novel positions the consequences of black invisibility in both the records of slavery and the record-keeping as a situation of primary spiritual significance. Thus, the "ghostly"/"historical" presence that intrudes itself into this novel serves to belie the reportage that passes for historical records of this era as well as to reconstruct those lives into the spiritual ways that constituted the dimensions of their living.

Because slavery effectively placed black women outside of a historical universe governed by a traditional (Western) consideration of time, the *aspect* of their being—the quality and nature of their "state" of being—becomes a more appropriate measure of their reality. In historian Joan Kelly's essays the exclusion of women throughout "historical time" is discussed in terms that clarify how the activities of civilization were determined by and exclusive to males. In defining a "feminist historiography" (a deconstruction of male-centered formulations of historical periods), Kelly focuses [in her *Women, History and Theory,* 1984] on the ways in which history is "rewritten and periodized" according to issues that affect women. In black women's writing, this deperiodization is more fully articulated because of the propensity of this literature to strategically place a detemporalized universe into the centers of their texts. Not surprisingly, black women have experienced the universe that Kelly's essays on women's history theoretically discuss.

It is perhaps the insistence of this alternative perspective in regards to black women's experiences that explains some dimension of the strident element in the critical response to *Beloved.* Stanley Crouch, who wrote ["Aunt Medea: *Beloved* by Toni Morrison"] in *The New Republic* [19 October 1987] that "[i]t seems to have been written in order to enter American slavery into the big-time martyr ratings contest," missed the point entirely. Morrison wrote *Beloved* precisely because:

> It was not a story to pass on.
>
> They forgot her like a bad dream.
> After they made up their tales, shaped
> and decorated them . . . in the end,
> they forgot her too. Remembering seemed
> unwise. . . .
>
> It was not a story to pass on. . . .
>
> This is not a story to pass on.

Like the litany of repetition that is a consistent narrative device in black women's literature, these closing phrases of the novel echo between the seeming contradiction of the initial "it was/this is not . . ." and the final words "pass on." The phrase becomes a directive. Its message reveals that this was not a story to die. Morrison revisions "Pass on," inverting it to mean go on through. . . continue . . . tell. She privileges the consequences of the sustained echo and in this way forces the sounds of these words (orature) to contradict the appearance of the visual (literate) text. Morrison has "passed on" this story in defiance of those who would diminish the experience she voices back into presence.

The final pages of the novel, where these lines appear, illustrate what I see as the interplay between structures that are implicitly orate but explicitly literate in black women's writing. In Morrison, this contrapuntal structure dominates the novel and appears as a device that mediates speech and narrative, the visual and the cognitive, and time and space. These paired elements of text and philosophy are central to my discussion in this essay.

Mediation such as the contrapuntal interplay sustains the text and rescues it from formlessness. Even when the narrative structure, for example, dissolves into the eddying recollection of Beloved's memory, the text survives and the reader, almost drowning in the sheer weight of her overwhelmingly tactile recollection, survives this immersion into text because of Morrison's comforting mediation. In a discussion with a group of Virginia Polytechnic Institute students in 1988, Morrison explained to them that one of her goals for this work was to acknowledge the reader's presence and participation in what she admitted was a difficult and painful story. Her strategy was in part an assurance of her mediative narrative presence. She spoke of writing with the sense that she was inviting the reader to "Come on in," and that she would assure safe passage. As I listened to her, I was reminded of the pie-ladies in the basement churches Son remembers in *Tar Baby,* whose "Come on in, you honey you" echoed through his adult memories. A similar guide, ancestral and essentially beneficent, also mediates the story of *Beloved*.

The signals of "telling" as a survival strategy—dialect, narrative recursion, suspension of time and place—are all in this text, especially in the compact and powerful passages where Sethe's, Denver's and Beloved's voices are prosopopeic (re)memory. Morrison introduces this section with a particularly beautiful and haunting recollection of the elements of speech and the devices of narrative that black women writers have used so effectively. Morrison's blending of voice and text privileges neither. Instead they both collapse into the other and emerge as an introspective that enfolds the dimensions of both the mind and history in a visually rich and dazzling projection of a revisioned time and space. The narrative streams that (re)member and chronicle these events are prefigured in an episode when Denver, Sethe, and Beloved are ice-skating in a place where the "sky above them was another country. Winter stars, close enough to lick, had come out before sunset." It is at this moment that Beloved sings the song that fulfills her mother's intimation that this is indeed the spirit of her dead daughter. At that time, Morrison writes, "Outside, snow solidified itself into graceful forms. The peace of winter stars seemed permanent." In this way of removing hours from their reality (Sethe tells her daughters that it's "time to sleep") and placing them into a seasonal metaphor (they stumbled over the snow, but—and Morrison uses the following recursive, repeated structure—"nobody saw them falling" at least three times), the text prepares itself, the reader, and these three women for its temporal lapse. The chapter just prior to Sethe's discursive monologue ends in this way:

> When Sethe locked the door, the women inside were free at last to be what they liked, see whatever they saw and say whatever was on their minds.

> Almost. Mixed in with the voices surrounding the house . . . were the thoughts of the women of 124, unspeakable thoughts, unspoken.

But they are spoken, for the next voice is Sethe's. And her first statement is in dialect—a sign that the text is about to embrace recursion and signify upon itself: "Beloved, she my daughter. She mine."

Sethe's version of her awareness of Beloved, and each of the three passages that follows hers are indeed "versions" of the same story with a different narrator. This is not particularly structurally ambiguous even though it is instead crowded with information that makes any attention to time or place simply inappropriate. French theorist and philosopher Cathérine Clément, in a dialogue with Hélène Cixous about the nature of their discourse in *La Jeune Née* [translated as *The Newly Born Woman,* 1986], accepts that:

> there can be two women in the same space who are *differently* engaged, speaking of almost exactly the *same things,* investing in two or three different kinds of discourse and going from one to the other and then on to the spoken exchange.

Cixous replies how she basically "distrust[s] the identification of a subject with a single discourse."

At this space in ***Beloved,*** Morrison cannot entrust this story to the single, individual discourse of any of the three women who are implicated in the myth. Instead, it is their collective telling that accomplishes the creative process of their task—to tell, (re)member and validate their own narratives and to place them, full-bodied and spoken, into the space they share. Each of their voices is distinct, examples of the "different kind of discourse" Clément refers to, even though the three women are in the same dissolved space of Beloved's ephemeral presence.

Sethe's discourse is dense—interwoven with dialect and poetry and complicated with the smells and touches and colors that are left to frame her reality.

> Think what the spring will be for us! I'll plant carrots just so she can see them, and turnips . . . white and purple with a tender tail and a hard head. Feels good when you hold it in your hand and smells like the creek when it floods . . . we'll smell them together.

Hers is a discourse vibrant and redolent—almost as if the vitality of her description would defy the dying and killing she acknowledges with her wintry declaration that, "Beloved, she my daughter."

Beloved's discourse is the Derridean trace element—the one that dislocates the other two by challenging—disrupting what semblance of narrative structure of sense there had been in Sethe's or Denver's thinking.

—*Karla F. C. Holloway*

Denver's discourse, in the same space as Sethe's, for she too uses her "unspeakable thoughts" to acknowledge Beloved, is the "different engagement" but "same thing" that Cixous and Clément discuss. Morrison highlights this "same difference" with the technique of repetition that functions as a recursion strategy—a means of accessing memory and enabling its domination of the text. Denver's first words "Beloved is my sister" take us back to Sethe's. Her discourse also recollects her first memories, and then propels her into her current dilemma. It (re)members her sister's death from a variety of perspectives—what she did (went to her secret house in the woods), what she tasted (her mother's milk along with her sister's blood), what she was told (by Grandma Baby). But it is the final repetition of her opening claim of Beloved as "my sister" that encircles her narrative discourse and encloses it within the safety of kinship acknowledged—"She's mine, Beloved. She's mine."

Beloved's discourse is the Derridean trace element—the one that dislocates the other two by challenging—disrupting what semblance of narrative structure of sense there had been in Sethe's or Denver's thinking. But her discourse also supports the narrative because her dialogue accomplishes the same kind of disruption that her presence actualized. It was she who denied them their space in a secure and memory-less present. So her discourse opens with an elliptical "I am Beloved and she is mine." That opening pronouncement is the last structure syntactically marked as a sentence. The rest evidences a fully divested text. Western time is obliterated, space is not even relevant because Beloved's presence is debatable, and the nature of her being is a nonissue because her belonging ("she is mine") has been established by her mother and sister.

> I am not dead   I am not   there is a
>   house
> there is what she whispered to me   I am
>   where
> she   told   me   the   sun   closes   my
>   eyes   when I
> open them I see the face I lost.

Emptied of the values that mark and specify dimension in a Western tradition, Morrison's narrative now belongs to itself—the text claims its text. Voice ("I am where she told me") is the only certain locus that remains. Her next chapter verifies the creation of this oracular space. It collapses all their voices into a tightened poetic chant. Finally the identity of the speaker is absolutely unclear and singularly irrelevant. Sethe's, Denver's, and Beloved's voices blend and merge as text and lose the distinction of discourse as they narrate:

> You are my face; I am you.
> Why did you leave me who am you?
> I will never leave you again
> Don't ever leave me again
> You went in the water
> I drank your blood
> I brought your milk . . .
> I waited for you
> You are mine
> You are mine
> You are mine.

When Zora Neale Hurston described dialect as the "urge to adorn"—an oral "hieroglyph"—she probably was not prefiguring the dimensions that Morrison has brought to the glyph of black language. However, Hurston certainly recognized the potential in black language to dissolve the artificial constructs of time that confine it to a tradition that belies its origin. What Morrison does with language is an act of liberation. The consequences of this freedom is that the text which seems to be literate, i.e., written, is revealed as an oracular, i.e., a spoken, event. This is a blend that Walter Ong explicitly acknowledges when he writes [in *Orality and Literacy: The Technology of the World,* 1983] that orality is "never completely eradicable; reading a text oralizes it." Morrison enriches Ong's observation. Her texts are a constant exchange between an implicit mythic voice, one that struggles against the wall of history to assert itself and an explicit narrator, one that is inextricably bound to its spoken counterpoint.

The structures within African and African-American novels consistently defy the collected eventualities of time "past, present, and future" and in consequence a consideration of *aspect* may be a more appropriate frame through which to consider the chronicle of events in this story. [In

an endnote, the critic states: "Aspect describes action in terms of its duration without a consideration of its place in time. In *Caribbean and African Languages* Morgan Dalphini's discussion explores how aspect is a better descriptor of such basic cultural concepts than those traditionally measured by a '(past/present/future) time-based yardstick.' The implications of such a measure for literature that reflects its culture in the arrangement and use of language is clearly relevant to literatures of the African diaspora."] Temporal time represents a narrow specific moment of occurrence. The relatively limited idea of time as being either in the past, the present, or the future is inadequate for a text like *Beloved,* where the pattern of events criss-crosses through these dimensions and enlarges the spaces that they suggest. This novel immediately makes it clear that a traditional (Western) valuation of time is not definitive of the experience it (re)members, instead it is an intrusion on a universe that has existed seemingly without its mediation. Weeks, months, and years become irrelevant to the spite of 124—the house that Beloved's spirit inhabits. Baby Suggs, Morrison writes, was "suspended between the nastiness of life and the meanness of the dead." This suspension was shared by more than Baby Suggs. Living itself is suspended in this story because of the simultaneous presence of the past.

In "Toward the Solstice" Adrienne Rich writes:

>   if I could know
> in what language to address
> the spirits that claim a place
> beneath these low and simple ceilings,
> tenants that neither speak nor stir
> yet dwell in mute insistence
> till I can feel utterly ghosted in this house.

When spirits "claim a place" there must be a simultaneous disruption of the spaces occupied not only by others, but by their aspect—their beings. The "tenants" in Rich's poem who "neither speak nor stir" still manage to pull her into their places until she feels "utterly ghosted." Morrison's spirit is a tug as well, and yet it is not only the dimensions of being that Beloved has claimed as her own, it is dimensionality itself—including the fourth dimension, time. Once time is implicated in Beloved's "insistence" a pattern familiar to Morrison's work asserts itself.

Sula's time "ends" on earth with her death, and yet, after she has died we hear her remark that it didn't even hurt— and her urge to tell her best friend Nel of that revelation. Her voice survived, suspended through the dimensions, or across them, as did her urge to share her knowledge, to continue to "tell." Circe, in Morrison's *Song of Solomon,* clearly defies time. How old is she? It's immaterial. What is critical is that she has lived past (and through) time to assure that the myth Milkman needed to reclaim his legacy would one day be his. She alone is able to retell the story he must hear if he is to solve the riddle that is his life. Milkman, who tells her "They think you're dead," is easily claimed by her mythic dimensions. The fruity, ginger odor of her house that smells like Pilate's and her dark embracing presence draw him into her fabric. Time is suspended long enough for him to lose his place in the dangerous present that threatens his spirituality and find his place in a nurturing past. *Tar Baby,* Morrison's sustained mythic text, begins with a water lady, a goddess reminiscent of the African water goddesses, nudging Son to an island where reclamation is the only surety. On Isles des Chevaliers, the mythology of ancestral blind horsemen dominates the present and everyone there is waiting for the past to renew itself through them. For Morrison, myth becomes a metaphorical abandonment of time because its function is to reconnect the poetry that the development in languages has shifted away from the word. The sense of a metaphor is represented as origin in myth—the two are not separable and therefore to be metaphorical is to abandon the dissonance of time. Within such a cosmology, the potential of *Beloved* is freed from the dominance of a history that would submerge this story. This liberation is perhaps the most critical issue of Morrison's novel.

If Beloved is not only Sethe's dead daughter returned, but the return of all the faces, all the drowned, but remembered, faces of mothers and their children who have lost their being because of the force of the EuroAmerican slave-history, then she has become a cultural mooring place, a moment for reclamation and for naming. Morrison's epigraph to her novel cites the Old Testament: "I will call her Beloved who was not Beloved." I will *call.* I will name her who was not named. "I need to find a place to be," Beloved's discourse insists. Her being depended on not losing her self again. "Say my name," Beloved insists to Paul D. She demands to be removed from her nothingness, to be specified, to be "called."

If history has disabled human potential, then assertion, the ghostly insistence that Rich writes of in "Toward the Solstice" must come outside of history. Beloved's existence is liminal. Between worlds, being neither "in," nor "of " a past or a present, she is a confrontation of a killing history and a disabling present. Since neither aspect allows the kind of life that a postemancipation black community would have imagined for itself because at the very least, "not a house in the county ain't packed to the rafters with some dead Negro's grief," *Beloved* becomes a text collected with the textures of living and dying rather than with a linear movements of events. Morrison has written novels marked by seasons (*The Bluest Eye*) and years (*Sula*) but this story is marked by the shifting presence of the house, number 124 on Bluestone Road, that was introduced in Book One as "spite[ful]," in Book Two as "loud," and in Book Three, as finally "quiet." This shift allows the focus of the novel to ignore the possible time frames. Neither distance nor years mattered to the white house where Beloved insisted herself back into reality. For Sethe, "the future was a matter of keeping the past at bay" and since this story (not a story to "pass on") demystifies time, allowing it to "be" where/whenever it must be, we know, even before the story assumes this "text," that there was neither future nor present in the woman who walked fully dressed out of the water.

The recursion of this text, its sublimation of time and its privileging of an alternative not only to history, but to reality, places it into the tradition of literature by black women because of its dependence on the alternative, the inversion that sustains the "place" that has re-placed reality. Certainly not all recursive texts sublimate time, but

temporal displacement is clearly a possibility of such technique. This is why Hurston's note that black folk think in glyphs rather than writing is not only an acknowledgement of another cosmology, but an acknowledgement of the necessity of evolution in the basic design of the ways we think about thought. Thomas Kuhn's discussion in *The Structure of Scientific Revolutions* considers "evolution from the community's state of knowledge at any given time" as the appropriate visual dimension of progress. It is evolution, i.e. a changing and shifting conceptualization that identifies the aspective nature of recursion, rather than temporicity as the operative narrative space of Morrison's text. In her re-visioning of the history of slavery, Morrison proposes a paradigm of that history that privileges the vision of its victims and that denies the closure of death as a way of side-stepping any of that tragedy. The houses of the counties held grief; Sethe practiced, without success, holding back the past, and Beloved held not only her own history, but those of "sixty million and more." In these ways, the vision of this novel is innervision, the cognitive reclamation of our spiritual histories.

Marilyn Judith Atlas   (essay date 1990)

SOURCE: "Toni Morrison's *Beloved* and the Reviewers," in *Midwestern Miscellany,* Vol. XVIII, 1990, pp. 45-57.

[*In the following essay, Atlas discusses the differences between various reviews of* Beloved *and suggests that the novel's subject and design pose unusual difficulties for most critics.*]

Even before the publication of *Beloved,* Toni Morrison was clearly a writer's writer. Toni Cade Bambara, author of *Gorilla, My Love* and *The Salt-Eaters,* herself an impressive crafter of fiction, wrote of Morrison's fourth novel, *Tar Baby:* "That voice of hers is so *sure.* She lures you in, locks the door and encloses you in a special, very particular universe—all in the first three pages." Outrage among black writers was so great after *Beloved* failed to win the National Book Award during the fall of 1987 that forty-eight black writers, among them, June Jordon, Toni Cade Bambara, Amiri Baraka, Maya Angelou, Paule Marshall, John Wideman and Alice Walker signed an open letter in January, published in the *New York Times Book Review* [28 January 1988], protesting that Morrison had never won that award or the Pulitzer.

Walter Goodman saw this letter as lobbying: "Literary lobbying goes on all the time: the form it takes, perhaps just a friendly telephone call or some cocktail party chit-chat, is generally more discreet than a salvo in the *Times Book Review,* but the intent is the same" ["The Lobbying for Literary Prizes," *New York Times*, 28 January 1988]. Others, such as one of its signers, novelist John Wideman, whose "Sent for You Yesterday" won a PEN/Faulkner Award for fiction, explained that the purpose of the letter was "not to mount a public relations campaign for Toni Morrison, but merely to point out that sometimes the pie doesn't get shared equally" [Kathy Hogan Trockeck, "Black Writers Protest Lack of Recognition for Morrison," *Journal*, 20 January 1988]. The letter, penned by June Jordan, whatever else it was, was also a letter of respect and admiration acknowledging the power of Morrison's writings:

> Your gifts to us have changed and made more gentle our time together. And so we write, here, hoping not to delay, not to arrive, in any way, late with this, our simple tribute to the seismic character and beauty of your writing. And furthermore, in grateful wonder at the advent of *Beloved* your most recent gift to our community, our country, our conscience, our courage flourishing as it grows, we here record our pride, our respect and our appreciation for the treasury of your findings and invention.

Toni Morrison did win the Pulitzer for *Beloved* in March of 1988. Although this was a very important literary honor, it was not her first: her third novel, *Song of Solomon,* won the National Book Critics Circle Award in 1977; her second novel, *Sula,* is excerpted in a major American literary anthology, Random House's *The American Tradition in Literature;* and her first novel, *The Bluest Eye,* is excerpted in *The Norton Anthology of Literature by Women.* She is a writer of international status: although there was no winner in 1988, she was one of three contenders for the Ritz Hemingway prize in Paris.

To review Morrison for an important publication is to take risks, the risk that you will be read by people who know her work, that you will be publicly perceived as wrong—wrong because your view is clearly political, or wrong because it is not; wrong because the importance of her issues make artistic assessment difficult, or wrong because her artistic brilliance may make her ideas, her psychological insights, seem more original, more true, than they are. One is afraid of being seduced by rhythmic prose, provocative images, and easy, warm, answers. And yet all types of reviewers take the plunge and respond to a work like *Beloved*.

In the *London Review of Books* [15 September 1988], Mary-Kay Wilmers wrote, and correctly so, ". . . while there have been many great books, there are few great book reviews." One can learn much from them, however, because they are important reflectors of politics and culture and, like books themselves, they help shape the ideas and art of a particular culture's values.

I collected approximately twenty reviews of *Beloved,* all published before the results of the Pulitzer Prize were announced in March of 1988. Winning such an important award under any conditions does not make the book reviewer's job any easier. There is even more pressure than before to see the novel as Morrison's best. But even before the Pulitzer committee honored the book, assessment was complicated by the novel's subject—the horror of slavery and its fallout—reminding both reviewer and reader not only of the existence of past atrocities, but that these atrocities can never be totally annihilated. Between Morrison's prestige, her race and her subject, *Beloved* was difficult to evaluate with even a semblance of objectivity.

Some reviewers, such as Charles Larson, writing for the [*Chicago Tribune*, 30 August 1987], and Helen Dudar for the *Wall Street Journal* [30 September 1987], seemed to have no difficulty declaring that *Beloved* was Morrison's

masterpiece. Larson found the work as original as anything that had appeared in our literature in the last twenty years and an understandable culmination for Morrison: "*Beloved* is the context out of which all of Morrison's earlier novels were written. In her darkest and most probing novel, Toni Morrison has demonstrated once again the stunning powers that place her in the first ranks of our living novelists."

But the judgments of reviewers are certainly not written in stone. In an introduction to her own book review on *Tar Baby,* Barbara Christian in *Black Feminist Criticism: Perspectives on Black Women Writers* discusses the nature of book reviews, particularly about books written by black authors:

> Book reviews are an immediate, succinct response to a writer's work, quite different, it seems to me, from essays in which one has the time and space to analyze their craft and ideas. They are necessary to the creating of a wider, more knowledgable audience for the writer's work—an important responsibility of the critic. Often, however, book reviews of works by Afro-Americans are written as if the reviewer is not aware that an Afro-American intellectual tradition exists, that certain ideas may, at the time, be under critical discussion, or as if the writers had not written anything else.

This was not usually a problem in the reviews of *Beloved*. Morrison is too famous a novelist for that to occur. The majority of reviews responded to it in context to her previous work and to an Afro-American intellectual tradition. And they assumed that their job was not to convince others to read her. Rosellen Brown when reviewing *Beloved* for *The Nation* [17 October 1987] begins her essay making some assumptions in exact opposition to Christian's concerns: "Can we not assume that most people interested in new fiction will want to read Toni Morrison's latest book, drawn to it not by rave reviews but by an understanding that she is a gifted novelist who always has something to say?" Most reviewers did seem to begin with this assumption and to focus their attention not so much on whether the novel deserved to be read, but how it fits into the world of modern American literature, how it connects the past with the future and whether or not it was one of Morrison's best novels. Many reviews were actually review essays, trying to analyze as well as describe the nature of Morrison's writing and ideas. Most would agree with Thomas R. Edward who wrote in the *New York Review of Books* [5 November 1987], "A novel like Toni Morrison's *Beloved* makes the reviewer's usual stereotypes of praise and grumbling seem shallow."

In reviewing *Beloved,* a few critics noted that in this book Morrison is turning the tradition of autobiographies and slave narratives into a complex piece of work which is both historical and mythic. Morrison attempted in this novel to recreate the era of Reconstruction, using the true story of Margaret Garner, a slave who actually killed her child in order to prevent the child's capture, but who unlike Sethe, was herself returned to slavery. Unlike nineteenth century slave narratives which avoided horrifying details so as not to discourage middle class abolitionists by

> In reviewing *Beloved,* a few critics noted that in this book Morrison is turning the tradition of autobiographies and slave narratives into a complex piece of work which is both historical and mythic.
>
> —*Marilyn Judith Atlas*

overwhelming them, Morrison mentions terrifying events in all their disgusting cruelty and horror. As a writer who understands the power of myth, Morrison skillfully created a novel in which archetypal quests and archetypal errors are presented. Without apology, Morrison weaves her characters' stories from both this world and one inhabited by the dead. Realistic and mythic techniques are intertwined and Morrison does not explain or apologize: the eponymous Beloved, the child slaughtered by her mother with a handsaw, is a restless ghost, self-reflective enough to tell part of her own story. Believing in that ghost, accepting a black folk-world where ghosts exist, is as necessary in *Beloved* as accepting human flight was in *Song of Solomon,* and believing in the plague of robins was in *Sula*.

Reviewers far from agree about Morrison's use of the supernatural in *Beloved*. Paul Gray, writing for *Time* [21 September 1987], found it problematic both in conception and language:

> The flesh-and-blood presence of Beloved roils the novel's intense, realistic surface. This young woman may not actually be Sethe's reincarnated daughter, but no other explanation of her identity is provided. Her symbolic significance is confusing; she seems to represent both Sethe's guilt and redemption. And Morrison's attempt to make the strange figure come to life strains unsuccessfully toward the rhapsodic.

Rosellen Brown of *The Nation,* however, found Morrison's methods, her unwillingness to explain the walking dead, a successful ploy allowing an intimacy with her reader that explanations would shatter: "Saints and spirits routinely walk the roads of the black South; to explain would be to acknowledge that outsiders were listening." Anita Snitow of *The Village Voice* [September 1987] also found the character of Beloved a "drag" on the narrative, and Carol Rumens of *Times Literary Supplement* [22 October 1987] found the ghost a failure: "The travails of a ghost cannot be made to resonate in quite the same way as those of a living woman or child." But Margaret Atwood, in her *New York Times* [17 September 1987] book review, found the magical world of *Beloved* successful. Atwood had no problem with the ghost: "In this book, the other world exists, and magic works, and the prose is up to it. If you can believe page one—and Ms. Morrison's verbal authority compels belief—you're hooked on the rest of the book."

The reviewers also disagreed about the quality of Morri-son's realism. While some found her style perfect, others found it cloying. As Rosellen Brown of *The Nation* noted, Morrison rarely mentioned anything once. But for Brown, this repetition across an "increasingly familiar psychological field" ends in the coherence of the whole deadly scene. For her, the novel is a successful opera: "*Beloved* brings us into the mind of the haunt as well as the haunted. That is an invitation no other American writer has offered, let alone fulfilled with such bravery and grace."

Stanley Crouch of *The New Republic* [19 October 1987] refused to be moved by the novel. He found it nothing more than another "blessed are the victims" novel, a tradition in Afro-American literature begun, he asserts, by James Baldwin, but one that is shabby, unrealistic and which should not be emulated. He found her folk material "poorly digested," her feminism "rhetoric," and her use of magic realism "labored." While he acknowledged that she has "real talent," "an ability to organize her novel in a musical structure, deftly using images as motifs," he found that she "perpetually interrupts her narrative with maudlin ideological commercials." He felt distant from the horrors of slavery as presented in the novel: "In *Beloved* Morrison only asks that her readers tally up the sins committed against the darker people and feel sorry for them, not experience the horrors of slavery as they do." In summary, Crouch found her work "melodramatic," containing too many attempts at "biblical grandeur," showing no courage to face the ambiguities of the human soul, a sentimental text. He found Morrison "American" in a cheap sense, "as American as P. T. Barnum."

Crouch's review was angry and, it seemed to me, self-protective. While other reviewers found flaws, none found the ideas and sentiments as cheap as he did. Most found the book extremely valuable. Hope Hale Davis of *The New Leader* [2 November 1987] found the drama ringing inescapably true and Judith Thurman of *The New Yorker* [2 November 1987] found the novel not only realistic, but originally so in its depiction of the differences between male and female hardship, how women's pride is damaged by the world on an even more intimate level than men's. Thurman found the risks taken by the characters to honor their own autonomy realistic and impressive and the choice they made between the claims of past grief and potential happiness, universal. In essence, Thurman focused on what she learned from the text: that the illusion of autonomy may be more debilitating in the long run and more cruel than a full consciousness of servility. For her *Beloved* is psychologically realistic. She is hooked: "But if you read *Beloved* with a vigilant eye, you should also listen to it with a vigilant ear. There's something great in it: a play of human voices, consciously exalted, perversely stressed, yet holding true. It gets you."

Beloved also "gets" Marcia Ann Gillespie, former editor of *Essence,* and reviewer for *Ms.* Gillespie noted that Morrison succeeded in this novel to give voice to pain by exploring the parameters of maternal love and human understanding. For Gillespie, the characters of this novel "soar off the page into our blood." Gillespie believes Morrison is asking important questions concerning power, love, the cost of living, control, compromise, self-acceptance, individual and cultural progress. And she, like the majority of reviewers, found Morrison "an impressive explorer of the psyche and spirit of a people" [*Ms.*, November 1988 and January 1988].

Charles Johnson, director of creative writing at the University of Washington, believes that this is her best book despite its flaws: "In novelistic terms, there isn't much of a plot, and Toni has a real problem with dramatic scenes . . . [also] the characters are not given the full, three dimensional development that we might see in other writing." He adds, however: "Nevertheless *Beloved* is the book that every black cultural nationalist writer has been trying to write for the last 20 years" [*Seattle Times*, 22 January 1988].

Why such contradictory responses? Why does Thomas R. Edwards of the *New York Review of Books* find "wisdom" and D. Keith Mano of the *National Review* [4 December 1987] find that Morrison successfully avoids melodrama by being mistress of what he calls the "theatrical retard" while Stanley Crouch thinks the novel is nothing more than New York glitz and cheap thrills Afro-American style? Perhaps the contradictions reflect the novel's emotional atmosphere—perhaps *Beloved* simply makes some reviewers extremely uncomfortable, forcing confrontations not usually required by literature. These critics do not want to reflect upon these particular human issues and they are unable to see how exploring these new details from new perspectives permanently expands the tradition of American literature, and allows valuable characters into the world, ones they can see no value in examining. Not every reviewer wants his or her consciousness transformed by these particular insights, and Morrison's prose in this novel is pushy: for me, as for Marsha Jean Darling of *Women's Review of Books* [March 1988], *Beloved* seeks to transform the consciousness of the reader through the telling of the tale. Morrison, in an interview with Darling, puts the responsibility back on the reader, an uncomfortable position for some:

> They always say that my writing is rich. It's not—what's rich, if there is any richness, is what the reader gets and brings him or herself. That's part of the way in which the tale is told. The folktales are told in such a way that whoever is listening is in it and can shape it and figure it out. It's not over just because it stops. It lingers and it's passed on. It's passed on and somebody else can even alter it later. You can even end it if you want. It has a moment beyond which it doesn't go, but the end is never like in a Western folktale where they all drop dead or live happily ever after.

Perhaps the fact that the novel did not stop for me is what initiated this study. I wanted to, but could not, go further into what Morrison set up as a possible, positive life for Sethe with Paul D. and Denver. For the novel to have integrity, I needed to believe in Sethe's ability to begin a new life and get past her relationship to Beloved and Sweet Home, something it seemed Morrison wanted me to be able to accomplish. At first, because I could not believe in the novel's positive continuation, potentially positive ending, I looked for reasons to defend my disbelief. I was a milder version of Stanley Crouch: the scene in which Sethe was suckled by the nephews annoyed and offended me because the characters were destroyed by it, and at first I preferred to think inappropriately destroyed. Why couldn't Halle or Sethe get over it? Why was this, after so many humiliations, so pivotal? I argued with myself, then a nursing mother, that the nephews couldn't even get the milk—that a nursing woman's body would shut down, but came to realize that this was Morrison's point and that shutting down itself was a privilege, one that Sethe's body was unable to provide because she was too vulnerable. Overwhelming personal humiliation was the point, being treated like a cow and having no alternative but to accept one's treatment was the point, a point I was as unwilling to face because it deeply frightened me, as Crouch was somehow unwilling to face that the holocaust is more than a sentimental symbol of hell, that being a victim is not always a choice.

A fan of Toni Morrison ever since my first reading of *Song of Solomon*—I read *The Bluest Eye* and *Sula* shortly after—my anger, my inability to suspend my disbelief, to be stuck on such a detail, surprised me. I had not felt so personally, so intimately, threatened reading her other four novels.

I had found *The Bluest Eye* elegantly symbolic, extraordinarily beautiful, unusually musical, the characters very human and the ending appropriate for the novel: while *The Bluest Eye* ended with sorrow—the marigolds would not grow, Pecola Breedlove was mad, and Cholly was dead, I trusted that Claudia would survive because she was the subject, the actor, the lover, the judge, and even while she narrated that it was "much too late" on the edge of town for anything to grow, one never sensed that this included her. Reading *The Bluest Eye,* I never questioned the details, or the depth of my response. Where the narrator and characters led, I was able to follow.

Sula also ended with partial destruction, but with enough insight so that I trusted a certain community healing. Nel was the center of this healing because she realized that Sula, the destructive and brilliant artist without the proper art object, was part of her, immortal, and that their bond was indestructable, and beyond measurable value. Nel's final cry of intimacy was a fine cry—loud and long—without top or bottom—a connecting cry from which one could continue. *Sula* saddened but satisfied me. I believed in Sula, and in the town, and in the robins, and in the art of the novel and the world, and in the future.

Song of Solomon also worked for me. Even when I disliked the characters, I believed in their existence. I had no problems with the magic realism and none with the characters' veritability. The novel, examining magic, history, community and responsibility, may have ended with the possible death of Milkman and Guitar as well as Pilate, but I felt, as the narrator seemed to want me to feel, mostly the resurrection, the possibility of a more whole, spiritual, and worthy future.

Morrison's fourth and most controversial novel, *Tar Baby,* her tropical novel, too plush, too slick, too mechanical for some, also worked for me, probably because the characters as types have a vitality which separated them from the usual flat characters, much the way Charles Dickens' characters function. When Jadine broke free from Son, I felt relief, because Son belonged to the past and I wanted Jadine, as she herself wanted, to have the future. However flawed civilization was, Jadine needed the physical earth more than myth, and at this point of her life, if one believed the details of the plot, and I did, she really could not have both Son and reality. I was glad when Son joined the horseman, partially to have him safely out of Jadine's way, partially because he was finding his way home, fulfilling what seemed like the only destiny which was his to follow, making peace with his mythical, cultural depth. I was not sure how far Jadine would get in her Parisian world, but I was not without hope. Morrison had not created her as much of a compromiser, but then she also had not forced me to accept that Jadine necessarily would do fine, just that she had been successful in the past and had learned something about herself in her encounter with Son. I trusted Jadine to pull her own weight, more than I trusted the brutalized Sethe to get out of bed and find the energy to create from her experiences a healthy family and a viable future.

My ambivalence toward *Beloved,* my anger and confusion, surprised me, so I turned to the reviewers. Of course, I knew I would have to return to the text, but I was taking an emotional break. I was comforted when Ann Snitow preferred *Sula,* but oddly, not satisfied. The reviewers could not and did not solve my problems with *Beloved:* when others found the ending problematic, it was not for the same reason that I found it so. Perhaps Stanley Crouch, ironically, turned me around. After reading him, I felt compelled to defend *Beloved.* This novel was not cheap. Morrison, I came to realize, was simply touching new vulnerabilities with a precision so poignant that I was unable to come to terms with its profound impact on me.

As Judith Thurman notes, in *Beloved* Morrison is exploring the difference between male and female hardship. A woman's pride can be damaged even more than a man's because a woman can be humiliated as a mother: a woman while able to give birth is not necessarily able to see her child through to safety, to spiritual as well as physical viability. Few, not even the generally sensitive Paul D., could comprehend the depth of this damage and the permission it gave Sethe to do outrageous, seemingly inhuman, things such as taking a handsaw to her child to keep it from knowing such humiliation. What I needed to do was acknowledge this vulnerability because I could not imagine surviving it. The ending of *Beloved* was a beginning, a second chance, named, but not dramatically portrayed, handed to the reader to create, if he or she was able.

Accepting the vulnerability, I was able to accept the possibility of a positive future for Sethe, even for a happy enough family life. After all, Sethe's surviving daughter, Denver, was working, part of the community, independent enough to continue maturing, and Paul D. wanted a life with Sethe and Denver. Although imperfect, he could make the world weep, and open the first steps toward healing. The fact that he used the traditional male excuse for sleeping with Beloved—"I couldn't help it"—did not make him much worse than the average man and his excuse was certainly more impressive. Sethe was weakened, but not alone, and if nurtured might heal, might heal herself, and her support staff, Denver, Paul D. and the remainder of the community, if imperfect, clearly was in place.

As another gesture toward peacemaking with Sethe, I looked her name up in the *New English Dictionary.* The eighteenth century Indian meaning of Seth is a "leading Hindoo merchant or banker" and its fourteenth century Scottish meaning is "atonement." And of course, Seth is the name of Adam's and Eve's son, the ancestor of Noah and hence of the existing human race: without his survival there is no human history according to the Book of Genesis. A number of Gnostic sects of the second century, according to this same source, held Seth in great veneration, believing that Christ was Seth reborn.

I had at my disposal, after this encounter with the dictionary, some new reasons why it was difficult, but linguistically essential, for me to accept Sethe's future: Sethe is the banker, the subject, the owner, like Claudia, the namer and therefore cannot die if the world is to continue; and she is atonement, the mending and fixing which also accounts for her survival, her second chance; and she is the essential parent whose legacy is the human race itself; and she is Christ, crucified but resurrected. Sethe, Morrison implies, may continue journeying and in choosing her name Morrison shows us that she must. So I, after a good deal of squirming, after studying the reviewers and their complicated responses, made a certain peace with this Pulitzer prize winning novel. My recommendation as a reviewer, as a critic, as a fan of Morrison: read it and grow.

Eusebio L. Rodrigues   (essay date Spring 1991)

SOURCE: "The Telling of *Beloved,*" in *The Journal of Narrative Technique,* Vol. 21, No. 2, Spring, 1991, pp. 153-69.

[*In the essay below, Rodrigues comments on the narrative techniques in* Beloved, *which he calls "a triumph of storytelling" and an example of "the blues mode in fiction."*]

Beloved is a triumph of storytelling. Toni Morrison fuses arts that belong to black oral folk tradition with strategies that are sophisticatedly modern in order to create the blues mode in fiction, and tell a tale thick in texture and richly complex in meaning. The reader has to be a hearer too. For the printed words leap into sound to enter a consciousness that has to suspend disbelief willingly and become that of a child again, open to magic and wonder.

"124 was spiteful": thus the narrative shock tactics begin. Here is no fairy tale opening but an entrance (124 is not a number but a house as the last sentence of the first paragraph will confirm) into a real unreal world. Toni Morrison's narrator—it is a woman's voice, deep, daring, folkwise—has full faith in her listeners (curious males have gathered around her) and in their ability to absorb multiple meanings. She plunges into *medias res* and begins her tale with the arrival of Paul D.

Paul's arrival sets the story in motion. Outraged by the

spiteful persecution of a "haunt" that resents his sudden irruption into a house it has taken possession of, Paul attacks it and drives it out. The incident has a tremendous impact—on Paul, on Sethe, who has resigned herself to a certain way of life, on Denver, who feels deprived of the only companion she ever had, and especially on the listener, who is bewildered, utterly disoriented. For he is flung into a dark fictional world without any bearings or explanations. He has to be patient and wait for light to filter in through cracks in the thick darkness. Exhalations from the dim past arise—a baby is furious at having its throat cut, a grandmother's name is Baby Suggs, a baby is born in 1855, Sethe's milk is taken—but they lack meaning and cannot, yet, be chronologically aligned or connected with the events of the present, the year 1873.

Toni Morrison begins the slow process of conjuring up a world that has receded into the past. Here is no extended Proustian act of remembering a lost world with the help of a madeleine dipped in tea. For the past, racial and personal, seared into the being of her characters, has to be exorcized by "rememory." Unspeakable, it emerges reluctantly. The major characters, Sethe and Paul, have to tear the terrible past, bit by painful bit, out of their being so that they, and Denver, can confront it and be healed. Toni Morrison's narrator will stage an extended blues performance, controlling the release of these memories, syncopating the accompanying stories of Sixo, Stamp Paid and Grandmother Suggs, making rhythms clash, turning beats into offbeats and crossbeats, introducing blue notes of loneliness and injustice and despair, generating, at the end, meanings that hit her listeners in the heart, that region below the intellect where knowledge deepens into understanding.

The structural ordering of this "aural" novel is not spatial but musical. [In an endnote, Rodrigues quotes Morrison on the "oral-aural" qualities of her fiction: "Ah well, that may mean that my efforts to make aural literature—A-U-R-A-L—work because I do hear it. It has to be read in silence and that's just one phase of the work but it also has to *sound* and if it doesn't *sound* right . . . Even though I don't speak it when I'm writing it, I have this interior piece, I guess, in my head that reads, so that the way I hear it is the way I write it and I guess that's the way I would read it aloud. The point is not to need the adverbs to say how it sounds but to have the sound of it in the sentence, and if it needs a lot of footnotes or editorial remarks or description in order to say how it sounded, then there's something wrong with it."] It consists of a title, a dedication to Sixty Million and more, an epigraph from an obscure Biblical passage, and three unequal parts. Part I, of eighteen sections, appears to be lopsidedly long, a stretch of 163 pages; Part II, with its seven sections, goes on for 70 pages; Part III, of 3 sections and only 38 pages, ends with a word that is an isolate, at once a re-dedication and a whispered prayer, Beloved.

Part I takes its time in order to establish the many modes Toni Morrison uses to create a world. Her narrator begins the tale, and immediately allows an interplay of voices to begin. Torn fragments of the past float out of Sethe and Paul, who have met again after eighteen long years. Their

voices join those of Baby Suggs, dead for eight years, and of Denver, for whom only the present matters. The voices set a world spinning, the world of slaves and slavery whose horrors can no longer be visualized today but whose sounds of pain and suffering still linger on. They issue out of the shared stories of Sethe and Paul D set in two focal regions: in Sweet Home, a farm in Kentucky, where events take place that project and compress rural slave life before 1865; and in 124 Bluestone Road on the outskirts of Cincinnati, Ohio, an urban setting that highlights the painful consequences of post Civil War freedom. The narrator transforms the interlinked stories of Sethe and Paul into a paradigm of what it meant to be a slave, especially a woman slave in America.

History, however, is not treated as mere documentary. For that readers could turn to slave narratives. Toni Morrison makes history integral to her novel. In musical terms her narrative melodies are sung against the groundbeat of historical detail. The details are thrown in casually, understated, as in the true blues idiom, to intensify the horror. Baby Suggs' eight children had six fathers. Men were put out to stud, slave women were sold suddenly, children vanished into the unknown. After the war there was chaos, black human blood cooked in a lynch fire stank, there was madness, segregation, the South was "infected by the Klan." Before the war hangings were common (Sethe saw her mother's unrecognizable corpse cut down), slaves were branded (Sethe's mother's identification mark was a cross and circle burnt into the skin under her breast), and an iron bit was thrust into the mouth for days as punishment (Paul complained not about sucking iron but about his intense need to spit). What happened before the slaves got to America was, for them, only a dim memory. At times Sethe remembers her mother dancing the antelope (there is no such animal in America) and remembers, at times, faintly, the ghostly voice of Nan, her mother's friend, speaking about a sea voyage in a language Sethe knew but has now forgotten. The memories of the other characters do not extend to the African past. The narrator will devise a way to resurrect this past.

But before this past can spring to life for the community of listeners (women, their work done, have joined the semi-circle now), the present has to be made alive and exciting. The telling therefore does not begin from a point fixed in time. Nor will the narrator use symbolism (an overused mode), or channel her stories through points of view (too thin, too limited), or through a consciousness that flows like a stream. The words will not have a Hemingway translucence but a Faulknerian density, for the language, slow moving, will be thick with history. Tenses will shift when needed to quicken pace. The oral-aural mode will use repetition to intensify the experience. Words will be repeated; phrases and images will be used over and over again to generate rhythmic meanings; fragments of a story will recur, embedded in other fragments of other stories. A born bard, the narrator, a blueswoman, will cast a spell on her audience so that fragments, phrases, words accelerate and work together to create a mythic tale.

The words repeated are simple but vibrant. Plans, repeated to warn slaves not to make any, for they have no future, anything could happen any time. Interlinked words, pieces, parts, sections, warn a slave about the lack of a unitary self. The slave is a bundle of pieces, of names, food, shelter provided by changing masters; a collection of fractured parts, outer and inner, that have been defiled. Sethe knows she could easily break into pieces. That is why Baby Suggs bathed the rescued Sethe in sections; that is why Paul D will have to wash off Sethe's defilement part by piece by section at the end, before his love (like that of Sixo's woman) can make the pieces come together. Beloved, it becomes clear, is afraid of breaking up into pieces, an indication that she is a composite of slave pieces of the past.

Smile/smiling: these word-forms, tossed out casually at first, begin to resound when associated with Beloved, who emerges from the water smiling mysteriously, fascinating Denver. They gather more resonance when Sethe connects the smile with her mother's smile, and realizes that her mother "had smiled when she did not smile," realizes further that it was the iron bit clamped on the tongue that had produced that perpetual smile. It was the same smile worn by the Saturday prostitutes who worked the slaughterhouse yard on pay day. Sethe's own smile, as she makes these connections, is one of knowledge. Paul D, during the telling of his story to Sethe, can understand why, when he was led away, iron bit in the mouth, his hatred had focused on Mister, "the smiling boss of roosters." What Paul saw on the rooster was a white smile of supreme contempt and arrogance, a looking down on one less than a chicken. In Part III the full force of the word-forms rings loud and clear. Beloved smiles dazzlingly before she explodes out of existence. What remains at the end is the scar on her handsawed throat, the "smile under the chin," the memory for Sethe of "the little shadow of a smile." Smiling, the listener realizes, is a silent statement of endurance. To smile is to know the horror of what it means to be a slave.

The narrator makes words function as musical notes. She also makes use of musical phrases together with chordal accompaniments to produce assonance, consonance, dissonance. "Wear her out": associated at first with the young Denver, who is always tired, this phrase is applied to Sethe and then modulated and amplified when linked with Baby Suggs and Stamp Paid. Stamp Paid himself feels bone tired towards the end; only then does he understand the marrow weariness that made Baby Suggs give up the struggle, and get into bed to die. "Lay it all down," she advises Sethe and Denver, echoing a line out of a spiritual. Sword and shield, lay it all down; she urges resignation, it's useless to fight, one cannot ever defend oneself. The phrase becomes a refrain, a burden (in both senses), that insists on the unbearable weight of racial suffering and injustice.

Images and metaphors of food intensify this suffering. "The stone had eaten the sun's rays": a mere trick of style, did the verb not compel listener and reader to pause, for "eaten" springs out of the consciousness of the famished Sethe. Sethe is constantly chewing and swallowing; she keeps "gnawing" at the past. The narrator uses the language of hunger lest her listeners forget essential truths, that all food was decided and provided by the masters, and that hunger was yet another burden of slave life. Sugar was never provided; that's why Denver and Beloved crave sweet things. The only food the slave mother could provide her babies was her own milk. "All I ever had," Sethe tells Paul. That's why she felt outraged when the two white boys stole her nursing milk. That is why she was ready to bite out the eyes, to gnaw the cheek of anyone who would stop her from getting to her starving baby. That's what drove her on from Kentucky to Ohio.

Milk, more than just food, was the flow of love Sethe wanted to release into her babies. Denver, sucking on a bloody nipple, took in Sethe's milk with her sister's blood. The baby sister never did get enough of Sethe's milk. That is why, when she returns as Beloved, she has a "hungry" face. Sethe, says the narrator, "was licked, tasted, eaten by Beloved's eyes." Beloved was "greedy" to hear Sethe talk, and Sethe "feeds" her with stories of the past it always hurt her to tell others, even Denver. The narrator's language becomes thick with insistent references to and images and metaphors of food and hunger, so that listener and reader become aware of many slave hungers—for food, for things sweet, for an understanding of the past, for communion, for community, and, above all, for a form of sustenance slaves were deprived of, love. It was dangerous to love, for the beloved could be torn away at any time. Beloved, as name, title and emanation, now gathers significance but the meanings do not come together yet. Nor can the hearers grasp the connections between food and religion—"the berries that tasted like church," the Biblical references to "loaves and fishes," the setting-up of the food after Baby Suggs' funeral. All connections and meanings, all notes and musical phrases, will be made to converge and resonate in Parts II and III.

Before such a convergence can occur there has to be an awareness of the magical sounds of the language through which meanings flow. Toni Morrison undermines the heaviness of print by turning word-shapes into word-sounds in order to allow her narrator to chant, to sing, to exploit sound effects. ". . . No. No. Nono. Nonono": these staccato drumbeats—single, double, triple—translate Sethe's fears of the threatening white world into ominous sounds. Word-sounds enact the rhythmic steps of a dance: "A little two-step, two-step, make-a-new-step, slide, slide and strut on down." A page presents consecutive paragraphs that have a one-word beginning, "but" with a period. The reader can see the pattern the buts make; the listener hears the repeated thuds that drive in the utter futility of slaves making plans to escape. At one point the narrator refers to Sethe's "bedding" dress made up of pieces Sethe put together—two pillow cases, a dresser scarf with a hole in it, an old sash, mosquito netting. The strange adjective is used to trigger an ironic rhyme-echo, for a slave woman could never have a "wedding" with a ceremony and a preacher, but only a coupling. Sad, but full of admiration and affection for Sethe, the narrator herself turns celebrant, the music of her language transforming the mating into a unique fertility rite in a tiny cornfield, witnessed by their friends who partake of the young corn. Fourteen-year-old Sethe's virgin surrender to

Halle, her moments of pain and joy, have as accompaniments the dance of the cornstalks, the husk, the cornsilk hair, the pulling down of the tight sheath, the ripping sound, the juice, the loose silk, the jailed-up flavor running free, the joy. Light monosyllabic sounds bring this epithalamium to a close: "How loose the silk. How fine and loose and free."

Beloved makes many aural demands for its musical patterns are many. Toni Morrison turns her narrator into a Bakhtinian ventriloquist who throws her voice into Baby Suggs. Oh my people, cries Baby Suggs, that preacher without a church, calling out to her congregation in the Clearing, repeating the words "here" and "yonder," and "flesh" and "heart" and "love," exhorting her people to love their unloved flesh, their beating hearts, so moving them that they make music for her dance. By using repetition for emphasis, participles for movement, internal rhyme and alliteration, the narrator heightens the voice and the word-patterns of Paul D (who cannot read) to translate into thudbeats the unspeakable fears and cravings of forty-six chain-linked chain-dancing men pounding away at rocks with their sledge hammers:

> They sang it out and beat it up, garbling the words so they could not be understood; tricking the words so their syllables yielded up other meanings. They sang the women they knew; the children they had been; the animals they had tamed themselves or seen others tame. They sang of bosses and masters and misses; of mules and dogs and the shamelessness of life. They sang lovingly of graveyards and sisters long gone. Of pork in the woods; meal in the pan; fish on the line; cane, rain, and rocking chairs.

Toni Morrison endows her narrator with a voice that has both range and energy, without being artificial or literary. It is a human voice, warm and friendly, not detached or distant, a voice that reaches out to touch the whole village community now gathered around her. She is, after all, their bard; she knows their language and can speak the vernacular. There is no need, therefore, for any comments, or for the language of explanations; only the need for a heightening of the black idiom in order to summon up a world buried in their racial memory.

Hence the language intensification. "Knees wide open as the grave": this startling simile erupts as Sethe remembers rutting among the headstones to get the seven letters of "Beloved" chiseled for free. A flirtation "so subtle you had to scratch for it": Sethe's verb springs out of her world; the implied image is that of hens in a farmyard. A memory of something shameful seeps "into a slit" in Sethe's mind; she is poised on the "the lip" of sleep; Beloved has "rinsed" certain memories out of her mind, explains Sethe to Denver. The language becomes intensely vibrant at times, as when Paul D suddenly realizes he was completely wrong about Sethe:

> This here Sethe was new. The ghost in her house didn't bother her for the very same reason a room-and-board witch with new shoes was welcome. This here Sethe talked about love like any other woman; talked about baby clothes like any other woman, but what she meant could cleave the bone. This here Sethe talked about safety with a handsaw. This here new Sethe didn't know where she stopped and the world began.

The verbal phrase, "cleave the bone," the repetition of "talked," of "like any other woman," the repetition of thematic words used earlier in the story, "love," "safety," "world," the insertion of "here" between "this" and "Sethe" to colloquialize the phrase, its repetition three times, and then the modulation into a four beat phrase "this here new Sethe"—all work together to produce the thick flow of Paul's realization.

Toni Morrison's ability to charge the vernacular with power and sound enables her to give a mythic form to the story of her people, the Afro-Americans. Oh my people, cries Toni Morrison, hear the voice of the bard. This bard is a Blakean *griot* in whom the ancestral experience is stored and who can see and sing the past, present, and future. She sings an ongoing story of the savage uprooting of sixty million and more, of a sea passage from Africa to America, of selves fractured and reduced to things lower than animals, of freedom imposed by others from the outside, and then the painful process of healing, of the achieving of inner freedom, and of slowly discovering themselves as human beings in a new world. It is a story of generations, of two hundred years and more compressed in time and channeled through a few individuals. The telling is a teaching, too, directed to the generations yet to come, lest they forget. History had to be transformed into myth.

Toni Morrison's ability to charge the vernacular with power and sound enables her to give a mythic form to the story of her people, the Afro-Americans.

—Eusebio L. Rodrigues

Toni Morrison has her narrator employ the technique of circling round and round the subject that Sethe, her central character, uses for telling the essentials of her story to Paul D: "Circling, circling, now she was gnawing something else instead of getting to the point." All the stories—that of Sethe and Paul D, of Baby Suggs and Stamp Paid, of Beloved and Denver, and of Sixo—have their chronologies fractured and the "pieces" made to spin together to form one story, monstrous and heroic. The fragments keep sliding into and out of each other for they cannot be separated. Their love for each other makes Sethe's story Paul's too. The stories of Baby Suggs and Stamp Paid tell of an earlier generation. The stories of Sixo and the Cherokee Indians present yet another account of suffering and injustice. Denver's story leads into the future, while Beloved's reaches to the past. Sure her people will slowly understand the story of their own past, the narrator begins with Sethe.

Sethe, in 1873, has resigned herself to her situation. Isolated from the Bluestone community, terrified of the exhalations of the past she kept buried within her damaged being, Sethe needs healing. The re-entry of Paul D and of Beloved into her life begins the slow process that leads her to understanding, love and community. Sethe is compelled to re-live two ordeals, the birth of Denver and the killing of her third child.

The story of Sethe's harrowing escape and of Denver's miraculous birth takes eight sections of Part I to be told, but the narrator does not release all its meanings. Certain clues are offered; the listener gets accustomed to a mode of telling that involves delay, repetition, and a slow but controlled release of information. Sethe casually mentions "that girl looking for velvet" to Paul D. Only later is her name, Amy, revealed (the first clue, the name, from Old French, means *beloved*). The story is relayed through dialogue, recall and narration. Sethe begins the narrative; Denver remembers parts that Sethe told her, and, as if under a spell, she "steps into the told story" to recreate it for Beloved. The narrator takes over and finishes the telling which is exciting, full of horror and pathos and beauty. She smuggles in significant truths through the words of Amy—that anything dead coming back to life hurts, that nothing can heal without pain—that she hopes some of her listeners will ponder. The unexpected aria that bursts out of the narrator towards the end, just after the birth of Denver, is a musical celebration the audience can respond to but cannot understand, yet:

> Spores of bluefern growing in the hollows along the riverbank float toward the water in silver-blue lines hard to see unless you are in or near them, lying right at the river's edge when the sunshots are low and drained. Often they are mistook for insects—but they are seeds in which the whole generation sleeps confident of a future. And for a moment it is easy to believe each one has one—will become all of what is contained in the spore: will live out its days as planned. This moment of certainty lasts no longer than that; longer, perhaps, than the spore itself.

The story of Sethe's other ordeal is told in "pieces" that are scattered through all 18 sections of Part I, and that have to be put together. The focus is on two consecutive days, four weeks after Sethe's arrival at 124. On the first day the whole community is invited to a feast, a communion, a ritual "celebration of blackberries that put Christmas to shame." The second day is one of foreboding for Baby Suggs, who smells two odors, one of disapproval, the other of a "dark and coming thing." What happens in the shed appears to be both a killing and a ritual sacrifice, the red blood spurting out of the cut throat of the baby held against the mother's chest.

The horror is not immediate, nor are the details graphic. The scene has a stabbing intensity, for it is a chill horror that takes time to penetrate and implode. The narrative tactics shift; the temperature of the language drops. The scene (section 16 of Part I) is relayed through four voices that slide one into the other to form a "white" composite. That of the slave catcher presents a hunter calculating his profit: "Unlike a snake or a bear, a dead nigger could not be skinned for profit and was not worth his own dead weight in coin." The nephew simply cannot understand

why and how a mere beating could cause such a reaction. The schoolteacher presents a doleful view of "creatures God has given you the responsibility of." The sheriff sees before him a proof that freedom should not have been imposed so soon on these poor savages. The language of all four voices is cold, aloof, detached, clinical. After all these are creatures and cannibals, aren't they, what else can one expect. Drenched in savage irony the scene becomes almost unbearable. Mercifully the narrator takes over; the ironic mode loses its edge but still continues with the sudden entry (as in a Hitchcock movie) of two white children, one bearing shoes for Baby Suggs to repair. The unmentioned color emits a tiny scream as the narrator's voice drops into silence at the end: "The hot sun dried Sethe's dress, stiff as rigor mortis."

The story of Sethe and her ordeals forms the spinning center around which the other stories of collapse spin. The outer circle is made up of the stories of the Cherokee (yet another people decimated, and uprooted from the lands they owned) and of Sixo the Indian, Paul's "brother," who laughs when his feet are roasted and sings "Seven-O!, Seven-O!" before he is shot. Then the story of Baby Suggs, seventy years old, who had proclaimed the gospel of love after she got her freedom. She realizes that she had preached a lie, and that it was all useless. White folks came into my yard, she says, using the language of understatement. She "lays down" in bed to die there. Two sentences sum up the slave life of Paul, whose heart has become a rusty tobacco tin into which he has stuffed his experiences: "It was some time before he could put Alfred, Georgia, Sixo, Halle, his brothers, Sethe, Mister, the taste of iron, the sight of butter, the smell of hickory, notebook paper, one by one, into the tobacco tin lodged in his chest. By the time he got to 124 nothing in this world could pry it open." How much is a nigger supposed to take, he asks. All he can, Stamp Paid replies, and Paul can only repeat why why why why why. The Stamp Paid story is of one who had dedicated his entire life to the rescue and service of his people. He finds himself in a state of despair in 1874, nine years after his people were set free. He had found in his boat a tiny red ribbon that smelt of skin and embodied for him all the lynchings and the burnings that his people still had to endure. "What *are* these people? You tell me, Jesus. What *are* they?" he asks.

The narrator is confident that this question to Jesus will direct her audience (some white people have drifted into the group now) to the Christian dimensions of her tale. After all, they also have been sustained and comforted by their Christian faith and by the Bible. They would pick up the Biblical references to "loaves and fishes" during the celebratory feast, to Stamp Paid's real name, Joshua (the successor to Moses), and to the origins in Genesis of Sethe's name. They would realize that Baby Suggs had lost faith in the God she once believed in; that Stamp Paid, who had relied on the Word and who had believed that "these things too will pass," abandoned his efforts to rescue the inhabitants of 124 menacingly "ringed with voices like a noose." And they would sense that additional help was needed from other sources to deal with things "older, but not stronger, than He Himself was."

Listeners (aware of African religious beliefs) and readers (familiar with books by Janheinz Jahn and Geoffrey Parrinder, and with the Indic tradition) slowly begin to realize that Beloved has sprung out of pre-Christian sources. A complex creation, Beloved is made up of "pieces" that Toni Morrison has spun into being so skillfully that it is difficult to isolate their sources. Some elements derive from the Afro-American belief, shared by the Bluestone community, that the unfulfilled dead can return to the scene of their former existence. According to Baby Suggs almost every house is "packed to its rafters with some dead Negro's grief." Other elements spring from the belief, purely African, that "the departed are spiritual forces which can influence their living descendants. In this their only purpose is to increase the life force of their decendants" [Janheinz Jahn, *Muntu*, 1961]. Toni Morrison fuses these elements with others of her own invention in order to intensify her tale and raise it to the level of myth. She makes her narrator control the pace of the telling, releasing the story slowly so that listener and reader are persuaded to accept Beloved as a "presence," allowing a number of meanings to accumulate so that, at the end, it becomes a story of haunting significance.

In the beginning the baby ghost is merely a disturbance, mysterious not to Sethe and Denver but to the listeners, exciting their interest in a good story. Only after the Thursday carnival, after Beloved returns from the other side of the grave, does the tale become more than a ghost story. Toni Morrison set herself two fictional problems. She had to delay Sethe's recognition of Beloved as her baby daughter, while allowing Denver to be aware that Beloved is her sister almost from the beginning. The second problem was to provide Beloved with a voice and a language. Toni Morrison carefully controls the release of details about Beloved. That Beloved is a nineteen-year-old (the age she would have been had she lived) who acts like a baby in the beginning is clear (though not to Sethe who is distracted by her love of Paul D): Beloved has sleepy eyes, her hands and feet are soft, her skin is flawless, she cannot hold her head up, she is incontinent. She "grows" up in the course of a few days because Sethe "feeds" her with stories of her own past. This "feeding," a form of narrative strategy, allows the novelist to evoke Sethe's past for her readers, and it allows Sethe to exorcize what she had kept buried within herself. Sethe's rememory pours out of her in response to the many questions Beloved keeps asking, using a strange, raspy voice. It takes over four weeks for Beloved's "gravelly" voice, with its African cadence, to shift unobtrusively into the rhythms of Afro-American speech.

The talks with Sethe establish the reality of Beloved as a human being. The scenes with Denver and with Paul suggest that Beloved is also a catalytic life force. The shed behind 124 becomes the locale where the racial past is reenacted. Beloved "moves" Paul D (the way slaves were moved from place to place; there was nothing they or Paul could do about it), "like a rag doll," out of Sethe's bed and into the dark shed where she forces him, much against his will, to have sex with her, and to call her by her true name, Beloved, not the one the "ghosts without skin" called her in the daylight, bitch. Paul turns into a version of Seth, the black man on the slave ship whom Sethe's mother loved and after whom Sethe was named. The dark shed becomes the ship's hold as Beloved forces Denver to re-live the experience of panic, suffocation and thick darkness (with cracks of daylight) where the self is reduced to nothing. These painful experiences will be healing (as Amy had said). Denver, who belongs to the future, lives through a racial past without whose knowledge she would not be complete. Paul's rusty tobacco tin, which "nothing *in this world* could pry open" (my italics), opens up into a red, warm heart.

Before presenting Sethe's sorrows and sufferings the narrator halts the recitative and turns into a blueswoman, making a trio of voices sing "unspeakable thoughts, unspoken." The timing of this musical interlude sung by a mother and her two daughters is exactly right: Paul D has been made to leave 124; Sethe knows that her baby has come back from the other side; and the past has been disinterred. The interlude of four sections provides a time of rest and slowdown before the final narrative outburst.

The first two sections open with the voiced thoughts of Sethe and of Denver, recapitulating, in fragments, the significant moments of their past. The third section begins in the present with "I am Beloved and she is mine." Then the I swells into a collective choric I that comes as if from a distant time and place, as though sixty million and more voices had been compressed into one. Toni Morrison could use only a few typographical devices to activate print into tempo. All punctuation is banished (except for the period that ends the opening sentence). There is quadruple spacing between sentences and there are double gaps between paragraphs. These pauses slow down the voice and make it resonate, so that a lamentation fills the air as the African beginnings of the horror are reenacted. Visual details blur and dissolve: women crouch in the jungle picking flowers in baskets, there is gunsmoke during the hunt for slaves, the men are crammed into the ship's hold, children and women, naked, crouch on the deck and on the bridge, storms at sea force men and women to be packed together, there is the sweet rotten smell of death, corpses are stacked in piles on the deck and then pushed out into the sea with poles, suicide by jumping into the sea and rapes are common. [In a footnote, Rodrigues remarks: "In the *Time* interview (May 22, 1989) Toni Morrison refers to 'travel accounts of people who were in the Congo—that's a wide river—saying, "We could not get the boat through the river, it was choked with bodies." That's like a logjam. A lot of people died. Half of them died in those ships.' In his introduction to *Adventures of an African Slaver* by Captain Theodore Canot, Malcolm Cowley mentions a strange phenomenon: that 'in Bonny River . . . the bodies of slaves washed backwards and forwards with the tide, the women floating, it is said, face downwards; the men on their backs, staring into perpetual clouds which were almost the color of their eyes.' In the slaveship's hold 'the slaves were packed as tightly as cases of whisky. . . . The slaves were laid on their sides, spoon-fashion, the bent knees of one fitting into the hamstrings of his neighbour. On some vessels they could not even lie down; they spent the voyage sitting on each other's laps.'

Beloved demonstrates this position to Denver in the shed when she 'bends over, curls up and rocks.' "]

Out of such visual horror arise cries of anguish as beloved is torn from beloved, women from their children, mothers from their daughters. The anguish is never ending, for "all of it is now it is all now." The past is still present, as those who have listened to the tale so far know. Beloved becomes the embodiment of all slave daughters; Sethe stands for generations of slave mothers. Denver experiences something worse than death, the utter lack of self in the shed; Paul trembles uncontrollably in Georgia like the man in the hold packed so tight he had no room even to tremble in order to die; Sethe experiences choking to make her know what it felt like to wear an iron circle around her neck; Beloved gazes in tears at the turtles in the stream behind 124, as if her earlier self were looking for her Seth who had leapt from the bridge of the slave ship. All experiences repeat or parallel each other. The fourth section returns the listeners to the present where the trio of voices chant a dirge in liturgical fashion as the interlude ends.

The narrator then takes up again the story of Sethe, who lavishes all her love on her baby daughter, excluding Denver and feeding the uncomprehending Beloved with explanations, telling her that she had to kill her in order to save her. Beloved grows monstrously fat devouring Sethe's love while Sethe wastes away. Denver, through whom most of Part III is channeled, does not understand what is happening but is afraid there could be another killing.

Both reader and listener have to understand why Beloved and Sethe behave in this unnatural manner. Sethe does not realize that Beloved's demands are not those of a human being, but of an impersonal life force that has got what it wanted, but cannot stop its blind, unreasonable demands for more. The narrator calls her "wild game." The Bluestone community refers to her as an "it" that will destroy Sethe, who has committed a crime. Sethe, on the other hand, believes that "what she had done was right because it came from true love."

Toni Morrison does not judge Sethe. Neither does her narrator allow her listeners to pass judgment on Sethe. The Bluestone community cannot forgive what they regard as an act of senseless murder. Even Baby Suggs was horrified on that day, and fell on her knees begging God's pardon for Sethe. Denver, who is afraid of her mother even though she loves her, has an inkling of what it was that drove Sethe on: it was a "something" in her mother that made it all right to "kill her own." The thing was "coiled" up in her, too, for Denver felt it leap within her at certain moments.

What the "thing" is is never made clear. But Sethe's story provides some clues. The process begins at edenic Sweet Home, that "cradle" of innocence, at the moment when Sethe's knowledge of evil begins, the knowledge that the white world, in the person of schoolteacher, considered her part animal. He had told his nephews to categorize Sethe by setting down her animal characteristics on the right, her human ones on the left. Overhearing these words, Sethe feels her head itch as if somebody were sticking fine needles in her scalp. During the escape, before the meeting with Amy, Sethe senses a *"something"* that came out of the earth into her and impelled her to attack: "like a snake. All jaws and hungry."

It was this "something," a blind animal force perhaps, that leapt within Sethe just before the killing. At the sight of schoolteacher's hat she heard wings: "Little hummingbirds stuck their needle beaks right through her headcloth and beat their wings." Stamp Paid, who was present, saw a dramatic change in Sethe, whose face "beaked" and whose hands worked like claws before she snatched up her children "like a hawk on the wing," and dragged them into the shed.

Stamp Paid tries to tell Paul D that love drove Sethe to "outhurt the hurter." Paul cannot understand such love. Too thick, he tells Sethe, adding that Sethe had two legs not four, implying that she was not an animal but a human being. A "forest" sprang up between them, adds the narrator who, reluctant to explain anything to listener or reader, compels them to ponder the image of the forest.

Yet another clue had been provided earlier when, asked by Paul to have his baby, Sethe thought: "Unless carefree, motherlove was a killer." Paul D had observed that, for a slave, any form of love was fraught with danger, and that human love needed freedom. One can only speculate that mother love, when not allowed free expression and growth in human society, remains a primal instinct. Fiercely possessive and predatory, it kills to protect the young from the enemy. That explains perhaps why there are so many animal references. Slaves were regarded as property, as possessions, as animals.

In this light Sethe's act of murder transforms itself from a mere killing into a ritual sacrifice of the beloved, an expression of the helpless rage and outrage of many slave mothers who either wanted to or did kill their young to deliver them from slavery. But one sin cannot cancel out another. 124 with its shed is more than a gray and white house: it becomes the arena where the resurrected past demands vengeance and threatens to overwhelm the present. A ritual atonement is needed. Denver, the future, has to step out of this dark world to seek help. She goes to the community.

With a few deft touches all through Parts I & II, the narrator has established the reality of the Bluestone community, a loosely knit group of colored folks living at the city's edge. They are a good bunch, Stamp Paid tells Paul D, a little proud and mean at times, but ready to help anyone in need. They had two meeting centers: the Church of the Holy Redeemer with Reverend Pike as preacher, and the Clearing in the woods where that unchurched preacher, Baby Suggs, holy, restored their faith in themselves and in their bodies. 124, at that time, had been a "cheerful, buzzing house," a way station and a place of refuge for runaways, where Baby Suggs provided food, comfort and help. What led to the estrangement between 124 and the community is not quite clear, but the narrator is confident that her listeners (their circle has now expanded into a vast human congregation) will understand and forgive human failings.

A few listeners might be aware of the term *hubris,* but all would know that pride and arrogance were sins that could lead to misunderstanding. Baby Suggs knew that she had been guilty of pride on the day of the celebration, knew that she had "offended them by excess." That is why, on the next day, she could smell the disapproval of the community. The ninety friends and neighbors were guilty too, of enjoying the feast of "loaves and fishes" and then displaying anger, envy and resentment towards the provider. Sethe, too, is guilty, of arrogantly isolating herself and not going to the community for help, even after the death of Baby Suggs. The setting-up after the funeral did not lead to communion. Sethe did not eat of their food, and they would not eat what she provided. It is Stamp Paid, that Soldier of Christ, who tries to help. Driven by a sense of guilt and by the memory of his friend, Baby Suggs, he tries to pass through two barriers: the circle of nightmarish voices, and the door that remains locked despite his knocking. He abandons his efforts to reach the inhabitants of 124.

Having made her listeners fully aware of the many meanings of 124, the narrator now quickens the pace of the telling. The tempo increases, the sound effects grow intense. "124 was loud," the opening of Part II, echoes the opening of Part I, "124 was spiteful," and there is a re-echo in the opening of Part III, "124 was quiet." Quiet because its inhabitants, locked in a meaningless love, were starving and would die of hunger. Denver is afraid of stepping off the porch of this prison:

> *Out there where* small things scratched and sometimes touched. *Where* words could be spoken that would close your ears shut. *Where,* if you *were* alone, feeling could overtake you and stick to you like a shadow. *Out there where there were* places in which things so bad had happened that when you *were* near them it would happen again. Like Sweet Home *where* time didn't pass and *where,* like her mother said, the bad was waiting for her as well. How would she know these places? What was more—much more—*out there were* whitepeople and how could you tell about them? (italics mine)

The listener can easily respond to the reference to Sweet Home as a place where time had stopped, to the rhyme-echoes and repetition (with variation) of "out there," "where," and "were" that enact Denver's fears and hesitations, and trigger Denver's rememory of the rats in prison and her sudden deafness.

Neither Sethe nor Denver can hear the loud voices that menace 124. Only Stamp Paid, that witness of his people's sufferings, listens and can recognize the two sets of voices: the roaring of all the slaves who were lynched and burned; and the terrified mutterings, near the porch, of whites (like the schoolteacher who had created a "jungle" in Sethe) in whom the jungle of hate and terror had entered. The pack of haunts is ready to pounce.

The listeners can tell the end is near. The narrator summons up techniques that tellers of tales use to create suspense—tantalizing pauses, breaks in the narrative, switches and cross-telling (like cross-cutting in film). It is an ominous Friday, three in the afternoon, a steaming tropical day reeking with foul odors. Three narrative movements

converge: Bluestone women, thirty of them, led by Ella, make their way to 124 to rescue Sethe from the devil child; Mr. Bodwin, who had helped in the defense of Sethe, is on his way to 124 (where he had been born), to fetch Denver, who is waiting for him on the porch; Sethe, inside 124, uses an ice pick to break some ice for the sweating Beloved.

To amplify her story the narrator now summons her co-tellers, the blueswoman and the bard. The blueswoman vocalizes the rhythms of the approaching mumbling chorus of thirty women (significantly, no man, not even Stamp Paid, is present). Some of them kneel outside the yard, as though in church, and begin a series of responses to a prayer call: "Yes, yes, yes, oh yes. Hear me. Hear me. Do it, Maker, do it. Yes." Then Ella begins to holler, an elemental cry that sweeps all the women to the very beginning, of time perhaps, even before the Christian Word. "In the beginning was the sound," the blueswoman announces.

The narrative pauses, then the narrator switches to Edward Bodwin, driving a cart to 124, haunted by time and by the recent wars and the fight over abolition that made him lose faith in what his father had told him, that human life is holy. The narrative breaks again to Sethe and Beloved standing on the porch of 124. The three movements converge and combine.

The blueswoman becomes one with the community of women out of whose being sounds explode, and rise to a crescendo of pure sound. More than a speech act, it is a *mantra*like utterance that rises from the creative female depths of their self, an act of exorcism: "Building voice upon voice until they found it, and when they did it was a wave of sound wide enough to sound deep water and knock the pods off chestnut trees. It broke over Sethe and she trembled like the baptized in its wash." The reference to water, the word "sound" used as a verb and noun, the allusion to Baby Suggs and to her powers associated with nature, "tremble," the word linked with Paul D, the double implication of "wash," all insist that this unpremeditated rite combines a pre-Christian archetypal cleansing with Christian baptism. Beloved's dazzling smile suggests that she does "understand" what has happened. But the listeners are puzzled.

It is the bard who knows what has been exorcised and begins to chant, switching from the past to the present tense because "all is now." The events of the past are once again made present. The words used earlier for what happened in 1855 (the definite green of the leaves, the staccato drumbeats of Sethe's fears) are repeated and relayed through Sethe's rememory. But this time, ice pick in hand, Sethe (after she sees Edward Bodwin's hat) attacks not her beloved but the "schoolteacher" attacker, a normal human reaction for the "thing" has been exorcised out of her. Denver and the women move in to stop her. The words used in the interlude (pile, faces, people, the man without skin) are also repeated to summon back from the remote past Beloved's ordeals on the slave ship. Then Beloved, her belly swollen with the past, vanishes. But this monstrous African past cannot be completely exorcised. It will linger on, wanting to be at least remembered.

The listeners, held spellbound by these events, experience catharsis. The tale has reached into their hearts and touched basic human emotions. It moves them, but not to action. For Toni Morrison is an artist, not a sociologist or a politician. Like Conrad, who wanted, before all, to make his readers *see,* Toni Morrison wants to make her people *listen* and, like the spirit of Baby Suggs urging Denver, know the truth about themselves and their "roots." Like Conrad, too, Toni Morrison feels compelled to "render the highest kind of justice to the visible universe" [Joseph Conrad, *The Nigger of the Narcissus*]. The institution of slavery is condemned, but all white people are not. The listeners remember Amy (a "slave" herself who, significantly, is on her pilgrim way to Boston), the Garners (Sethe looked upon Mrs. Garner as if she was her mother), the Bodwins, even the sheriff (who had looked away when Sethe nursed Denver). But Toni Morrison insists that true freedom is essential and that equality between peoples is of absolute necessity. That is why the goodness of the Garners and the Bodwins is somehow flawed: on a shelf in the Bodwin house Denver sees a black boy figurine kneeling on a pedestal that reads: "At Yo Service."

Toni Morrison's sense of justice and compassion leads her to introduce notes of hope. The many Christian references suggest such a possibility, especially the name of the community church, and the redemptive tree of suffering that Sethe carries on her back and will carry for a lifetime. Paul's love will heal Sethe, rescue her from the fate that befell Baby Suggs, and put her pieces together. In the tableau at the end Paul touches Sethe's face as he whispers his tribute to her: "You your best thing, Sethe. You are." The story of Sethe and Paul will gradually recede into the past. Denver *is* the future. She is the child of the race, "my heart," Stamp Paid tells Paul D. Lady Jones can see "everybody's child" in her face. Clever and intelligent, she will go to Oberlin. Denver is like Seven-O, which is not just a cry of warning to his woman, but a continuation of Sixo, the name of his "seed" which she bears away with her. Denver needs no tribute, for the narrator has already sung an aria to celebrate her birth; she is the seed "in which the whole generation sleeps confident of the future."

With the stories of Sethe, Paul, and Denver told, the narrator and the bard know that the telling has to come to a stop. Their listeners have been rapt into a mythic world. But humankind cannot live there for long. The account of what happened to Paul D, which balances the story of Sethe, allows the listeners to return to ordinary human reality. When Paul D and Stamp Paid talk about what happened at 124, a strange laughter, like Sixo's, erupts out of them. "To keep from cryin' I opens my mouth an' laughs," as Langston Hughes puts it. Narrator and bard have finished their tasks, but something remains to be done. The blueswoman takes over.

She begins to keen, as though at a wake, a ceremony held in order to remember, to celebrate, and then to forget. But the lament soon changes into the sound of a biblical voice from on high (sounded in the epigraph), that summons an alien people unto itself and calls them beloved. The community remembers what Sethe rememoried, the voice of the preacher at the baby's funeral telling them who they are, addressing them all as Dearly Beloved. The voice of the blueswoman now develops a powerful hum, for she expresses, as in basic blues, not her own feelings but those of all her people. It uses not the minor (though it sounds plaintive) but the major mode of the classical blues. The words are unimportant for they all have been heard before, except the twice repeated, two-word word, "disremembered," which associates memory with pieces. The blueswoman and the community know that the past can linger on but has to be laid to rest. As in a blues ending they announce, then repeat, then repeat again, mixing the past and present tenses, that it was/is "not a story to pass on." Till, finally, the blueswoman allows her voice to sink into silence after a whispered prayer, Beloved.

Barbara Schapiro (essay date Summer 1991)

SOURCE: "The Bonds of Love and the Boundaries of Self in Toni Morrison's *Beloved,*" in *Contemporary Literature,* Vol. 32, No. 2, Summer, 1991, pp. 194-210.

[*In the following essay, Schapiro discusses the psychological and emotional dimensions of slavery in* Beloved, *which she praises for its historical depth and insight.*]

Toni Morrison's ***Beloved*** penetrates, perhaps more deeply than any historical or psychological study could, the unconscious emotional and psychic consequences of slavery. The novel reveals how the condition of enslavement in the external world, particularly the denial of one's status as a human subject, has deep repercussions in the individual's internal world. These internal resonances are so profound that even if one is eventually freed from external bondage, the self will still be trapped in an inner world that prevents a genuine experience of freedom. As Sethe succinctly puts it, "Freeing yourself was one thing; claiming ownership of that freed self was another." The novel wrestles with this central problem of recognizing and claiming one's own subjectivity, and it shows how this cannot be achieved independently of the social environment.

A free, autonomous self, as Jessica Benjamin argues in *The Bonds of Love,* is still an essentially relational self and is dependent on the recognizing response of an other. ***Beloved*** powerfully dramatizes the fact that, in Benjamin's words, "In order to exist for oneself, one has to exist for an other"; in so doing, it enacts the complex interrelationship of social and intrapsychic reality. For Morrison's characters, African-Americans in a racist, slave society, there is no reliable other to recognize and affirm their existence. The mother, the child's first vital other, is made unreliable or unavailable by a slave system which either separates her from her child or so enervates and depletes her that she has no self with which to confer recognition. The consequences on the inner life of the child—the emotional hunger, the obsessive and terrifying narcissistic fantasies—constitute the underlying psychological drama of the novel.

"124 was spiteful. Full of a baby's venom." The opening lines of the novel establish its psychic source: infantile rage. A wounded, enraged baby is the central figure of the book, both literally, in the character of Beloved, and symbolically, as it struggles beneath the surface of the other major characters. Even the elderly grandmother is significantly named "Baby," and the ferocity of a baby's frustrated needs colors the novel's overt mother-child relationships as well as the love relationship between Sethe and Paul D and that between Beloved and her sister Denver. "A baby's frustrated needs" refers here not to physical needs but to psychic and emotional ones. The worst atrocity of slavery, the real horror the novel exposes, is not physical death but psychic death. The pivotal event, or crisis, of the novel is Sethe's murder of her baby daughter Beloved. The reader is allowed to feel, however, the paradoxical nature of the murder. Sethe, having run away from the sadistic slave-master Schoolteacher, is on the verge of being recaptured. Her humanity has been so violated by this man, and by her entire experience as a slave woman, that she kills her daughter to save her from a similar fate; she kills her to save her from psychic death: "if I hadn't killed her she would have died and that is something I could not bear to happen to her."

Psychic death, as the novel makes clear, involves the denial of one's being as a human subject. The infant self has an essential, primary need to be recognized and affirmed as a whole being, as an active agent of its own legitimate desires and impulses, and the fulfillment of this need is dependent on the human environment, on other selves. The premise of the object relations school of psychoanalysis, as Jessica Benjamin notes [in *The Bonds of Love: Psychoanalysis, Feminism, and the Problem of Domination*, 1988], is that "we are fundamentally social beings." According to this theory, human beings are not innately sexual or aggressive; they are innately responsive and relational. As Harry Guntrip explains, the "need of a love-relationship is the fundamental thing" in life, and "the love-hunger and anger set up by frustration of this basic need must constitute the two primary problems of personality on the emotional level" [*Schizoid Phenomena, Object Relations, and the Self,* 1969]. The experience of one's cohesiveness and reality as a self is dependent on this primary relationship, on the loving response and recognition from an other. This issue is repeatedly illustrated and explored in Morrison's novels. Sula, for instance, speaks of the two most formative experiences of her life: the first concerns her overhearing her mother state matter-of-factly that she simply doesn't "like" her (Sula), and the second involves her having thrown a child, seemingly by accident, into the river to drown. "The first experience taught her there was no other that you could count on; the second that there was no self to count on either. She had no center, no speck around which to grow" (*Sula*). These experiences are intimately related: the lack of an affirming, reliable other leads to an unconscious, murderous rage and the lack of a coherent, reliable self.

In *The Bonds of Love,* a feminist psychoanalytic study of the problem of domination in Western culture, Benjamin modifies object relations theory to form what she calls "intersubjective theory." She maintains the primacy of relationship in self-development but argues that the self grows through relationship with another *subject* rather than through relations with its object. The child has a need to see the mother, or his or her most significant other, "as an independent subject, not simply as the 'external world' or an adjunct of his ego." The intersubjective view, which Benjamin sees as complementary to intrapsychic theory, conceives of self and other "as distinct but interrelated beings" who are involved in an intricate dance of assertion and recognition. The essential need is for *mutual* recognition—"the necessity of recognizing as well as being recognized by the other." Benjamin also emphasizes the concept of attunement, a "combination of resonance and difference" in which self and other are empathically in tune while maintaining their distinct boundaries and separateness. When the boundaries break down and the necessary tension between self and other dissolves, domination takes root. The search for recognition then becomes a struggle for power and control, and assertion turns into aggression.

Beloved does not delve into the roots of white domination, but there is a suggestion of fear and inadequate selfhood underlying the problem. The white farmer Mr. Garner, while still sharing in the cultural objectification of blacks, nevertheless boasts that his "niggers is men every one of 'em." When another farmer argues that there "Ain't no nigger men," Garner replies, "Not if you scared, they ain't. . . . But if you a man yourself, you'll want your niggers to be man too." A self wants the recognition of another self; this form of mutuality is more desirable, Garner implies, than mastery of an object. Garner, however, dies—his perspective cannot prevail in a world in which domination and the denial of recognition are built into the social system.

Beloved explores the interpersonal and intrapsychic effects of growing up as a black person in such a system, one in which intersubjectivity is impossible. How can a child see self or mother as subjects when the society denies them that status? The mother is made incapable of recognizing the child, and the child cannot recognize the mother. As a young girl, Sethe had to have her mother "pointed out" to her by another child. When she becomes a mother herself, she is so deprived and depleted that she cannot satisfy the hunger for recognition, the longed for "look," that both her daughters crave. The major characters in the novel are all working out of a deep loss to the self, a profound narcissistic wound that results from a breakdown and distortion of the earliest relations between self and other. In the case of Beloved, the intense desire for recognition evolves into enraged narcissistic omnipotence and a terrifying, tyrannical domination.

The infantile rage in the novel is a form of frustrated, murderous love. The baby ghost of Beloved wreaks havoc in Sethe's home, prompting Denver to comment, "For a baby she throws a powerful spell," to which Sethe replies, "No more powerful than the way I loved her." The power of Beloved's rage is directly linked to the power of Sethe's love. The intimacy of destructive rage and love is asserted in various ways throughout the book—Sethe's love for Beloved is indeed a murderous love. The violation or murder of children by their parents is a theme that runs throughout much of Morrison's work, from Cholly raping his daughter in *The Bluest Eye* to Eva setting fire to her son in *Sula,* and in these cases too the acts are incited by feelings of love. If the infant is traumatically frustrated in its first love relationship, if it fails to receive the affirmation and recognition it craves, the intense neediness of the infant's own love becomes dangerous and threatening. The fear, as Guntrip and others have discussed, is that one's love will destroy. The baby's enraged, destructive love is also projected outward onto the parent, which suggests one perspective on the strain of destructive parental love in Morrison's novels.

Because the first physical mode of relationship to the mother is oral, the earliest emotional needs in relation to the mother are also figured in oral terms in the child's inner world. Frustration in this first oral stage of relationship leads to what object relations theorists call "love made hungry," a terrifying greediness in which the baby fears it will devour and thus destroy mother and, conversely, that mother (due to projection) will devour and destroy the self. A preponderance of oral imagery characterizes Morrison's novel. Beloved, in her fantasies, repeatedly states that Sethe "chews and swallows me," while the metaphor of Beloved chewing and swallowing Sethe is almost literal: "Beloved ate up her life, took it, swelled up with it, grew taller on it." Denver's problems of identity and self-cohesion, too, are often imaged in oral terms: leaving the house means being prepared to "be swallowed up in the world beyond the edge of the porch." When Denver temporarily loses sight of Beloved in the shed, she experiences a dissolution of self—"she does not know where her body stops, which part of her is an arm, a foot or a knee"—and feels she is being "eaten alive by the dark." Beloved, in the second part of the novel, is said to have two dreams: "exploding, and being swallowed." Everywhere in the novel, the fantasy of annihilation is figured orally; the love hunger, the boundless greed, that so determines the life of the characters also threatens to destroy them.

Sethe repeatedly asserts that the worst aspect of her rape was that the white boys "took my milk!" She feels robbed of her essence, of her most precious substance, which is her maternal milk. We learn that as a child, Sethe was deprived of her own mother's milk: "The little whitebabies got it first and I got what was left. Or none. There was no nursing milk to call my own." Sethe was not physically starved as a baby—she did receive milk from another nursing slave woman—but she was emotionally starved of a significant nurturing relationship, of which the nursing milk is symbolic. That relationship is associated with one's core being or essence; if she has no nursing milk to call her own, she feels without a self to call her own. Thus even before she was raped by the white farm boys, Sethe was ravaged as an infant, robbed of her milk/essence by the white social structure.

Beloved's first appearance in her incarnated form is marked by her excessive drinking, by her downing "cup after cup of water," while Sethe, suddenly feeling her "bladder filled to capacity," lifts her skirts and "the water she voided was endless." The dynamic suggests a mother being drained by the child's greedy, excessive need. Sethe's voiding is also associated with her own child-self in relation to her mother: "Not since she was a baby girl, being cared for by the eight-year-old girl who pointed out her

mother to her, had she had an emergency that unmanageable." One might rather expect Sethe to experience thirst upon seeing her mother, but perhaps that thirst is so extreme, so potentially violent and destructive, that the more urgent need is to void, to empty oneself completely of this unmanageable hunger and rage. Sethe must drain herself in order to avoid draining, and therefore destroying, her mother. This is the fearful fantasy so central to the book; it is precisely what Beloved almost succeeds in doing to Sethe. The nursing dynamic also characterizes Denver and Beloved's relationship: "so intent was her (Denver's) nursing" of Beloved, "she forgot to eat," and she hides Beloved's incontinence. Paul D, as I will discuss more fully later, also plays a maternal, nurturing role in relation to Sethe. When he arrives, Sethe feels "that the responsibility for her breasts, at last, was in somebody else's hands."

The primal nursing relationship is so fraught with ambivalence that frequently in the novel satiation leads to disaster. The most obvious example is the grand feast Baby Suggs prepares for ninety people—"Ninety people who ate so well, and laughed so much, it made them angry." The feast is the prelude to the abandonment of the community, the return of Schoolteacher, and Sethe's consequent murder of her baby. Melanie Klein has discussed the baby's extreme "envy" of the withholding breast, and this projected envy may underlie the anger of the neighbors at the maternal bounty of Baby Suggs—she has "given too much, offended them by excess." Similarly, the prelude to Beloved's appearance in the flesh and the ensuing disruption of Sethe's relationship with Paul D is the festive plentitude of the carnival at which Paul D plies both Sethe and Denver with candy and sweets. Paul D's abandonment of Sethe, too, is preceded by a special dinner that Sethe, feeling confident that "she had milk enough for all," prepares for him.

The rage and ambivalence surrounding the love hunger in the novel is illustrated again in the scene in which Sethe, while sitting in the Clearing associated with Baby Suggs and her sermons on love, experiences fingers touching her throat. The fingers are first soothing and comforting but then begin to choke and strangle her, and the hands are associated with those of both Baby Suggs and Beloved, of both mother and child. When Denver accuses Beloved of choking Sethe, Beloved insists that she "fixed" Sethe's neck—"I kissed her neck. I didn't choke it." The incident, of course, parallels Sethe's murder of Beloved by sawing through her neck, the oral associations once more enforced by mention of the "teeth" of the saw having chewed through the skin. After denying that she choked Sethe's neck, Beloved adds, "The circle of iron choked it," and the image recalls the collars locked around the necks of the black slaves. Her statement is thus true in that the slave system has choked off the vital circulation between mother and child so crucial to the development of the self. Some of the most vivid, disturbing passages in the novel describe the experience of having a horse's bit forced into one's mouth; the sense of deep, searing injury to one's humanity that these descriptions evoke is perhaps compounded by unconscious resonances of violation at the earliest oral roots of our human identity.

The oral imagery in the novel is also closely associated with ocular imagery, with images of eyes and seeing. Sethe is described as being "licked, tasted, eaten by Beloved's eyes"; when Sethe lies hidden in the field, anticipating the approach of one of the white boys, she "was eager for his eyes, to bite into them; . . . 'I was hungry,' she told Denver, 'just as hungry as I could be for his eyes'." For Denver, "looking" at Beloved "was food enough to last. But to be looked at in turn was beyond appetite; it was breaking through her own skin to a place where hunger hadn't been discovered." In the logic of the unconscious world, the desire to get and "drink in" with the eyes is akin to the oral wish to consume. Psychoanalyst Heinz Kohut has written about the oral-visual relationship [in *The Analysis of the Self,* 1971]. If the mother is physically and emotionally distant from the child, if she withholds her body, he says, the visual will become "hypercathectic" for the child. One can also understand the connection from Benjamin's perspective in that the real hunger in this first relationship between self and other is the hunger for recognition—the desire to be, in Denver's words, "pulled into view by the interested, uncritical eyes of the other." The gaze of the beloved other recognizes and affirms the wholeness and intrinsic value of one's being. Denver describes the quality of being looked at by Beloved: "Having her hair examined as a part of her self, not as material or a style. Having her lips, nose, chin caressed as they might be if she were a moss rose a gardener paused to admire." The look takes Denver to a "place beyond appetite," to where she is "Needing nothing. Being what there was." To be recognized by the beloved is all the nourishment one needs; it brings one into coherence, into meaningful existence. Before Beloved's arrival, Denver craved this look from Sethe: none of the losses in her life mattered, she felt, "as long as her mother did not look away."

Sethe's eyes, however, are described as "empty"; Paul D thinks of Sethe's face as "a mask with mercifully punched-out eyes. . . . Even punched out they needed to be covered, lidded, marked with some sign to warn folks of what that emptiness held." Her eyes reflect the psychic loss and denial of self she has experienced on all levels in her life. The face of Sethe's mother was also masklike, distorted into a permanent false smile from too many times with the bit. Sethe comments that she never saw her mother's own smile. Sethe's mother, deprived of her authentic selfhood, her status as a human subject, cannot provide the recognition and affirmation that her child craves. The cycle is vicious, and thus Sethe's children, Beloved and Denver, will suffer the same loss. Beloved's eyes too are remarkable for their emptiness: "deep down in those big black eyes there was no expression at all."

The craving for mutual recognition—for simultaneously "seeing" the beloved other and being "seen" by her—propels the central characters in the novel. Beloved says she has returned in order to "see" Sethe's face, and she wants "to be there in the place where her face is and to be looking at it too." When, as a child, Sethe is shown the brand burned into her mother's skin and is told that she will be able to "know" her by this mark, Sethe anxiously responds, "But how will you know me? How will you

Toni Morrison's *Beloved* penetrates, perhaps more deeply than any historical or psychological study could, the unconscious emotional and psychic consequences of slavery.

—Barbara Schapiro

know me? Mark me, too, . . . Mark the mark on me too." Love is a form of knowing and being known. Beloved repeatedly commands Paul D, "I want you to touch me on the inside part and call me my name." The hunger is to be touched, recognized, known in one's inner being or essential self. This yearning is poignantly captured in the image of two turtles mating. Denver and Beloved observe the turtles on the bank of the river: "The embracing necks—hers stretching up toward his bending down, the pat pat pat of their touching heads. No height was beyond her yearning neck, stretched like a finger toward his, risking everything outside the bowl just to touch his face. The gravity of their shields, clashing, countered and mocked the floating heads touching."

The yearning of Beloved, Sethe, and Denver to touch faces with the beloved other, to know and be known, is, like that of the turtles, obstructed and mocked by the shields or shells each has constructed. The shell, however, is a necessary defense; it attempts to preserve the self from a culture that seeks to deny it. As Joseph Wessling argues in ["Narcissism in Toni Morrison's *Sula*," *College Language Language Journal*, 1988] an article on narcissism in *Sula,* narcissistic defenses, such as "self-division" and an inability to empathize or experience human sympathy, may be "the price of survival" in an oppressive, unjust society. The shell also serves to protect the self and its boundaries from the intensity of its own frustrated desire. The hunger for recognition, as discussed, may be so overwhelming that it threatens to swallow up the other and the self, destroying all boundaries in one total annihilation.

The novel as a whole is characterized by a fluidity of boundaries, by a continuously altering narrative perspective that slides in and out of characters' minds, by a mutable, nonsequential time structure, and by an absence of the conventional lines between fantasy and reality. Such fluidity, as Nancy Chodorow [in *The Reproduction of Mothering,* 1978] and Carol Gilligan [in *In a Different Voice,* 1982] have argued, is characteristic of female, as opposed to male, modes of perception and expression. It derives from the preservation of an original identity and preoedipal bondedness between self and mother. The series of monologues by Beloved, Sethe, and Denver in Part 2 of Morrison's novel, however, suggest something more extreme and dangerous than mere fluidity of boundaries: the monologues reveal an utter breakdown of the borders between self and other, a collapse that is bound up with incorporative fantasies. Sethe's section begins, "Beloved, she my daughter. She mine." Denver's opens, "Beloved is my sister. I swallowed her blood right along with my mother's milk," and Beloved's with the line, "I am Beloved and she is mine." After that sentence, Beloved's monologue is marked by a total absence of punctuation, highlighting the fantasy of merging and oneness at the essence of her plaintive ramblings: "I am not separate from her   there is no place where I stop   her face is my own." Her words reveal the psychic loss—the denial of recognition—at the core of the fantasy:

> there is no one to want me   to say me my
> name . . . she chews and swallows me   I
> am gone   now I am her face   my own
> face has left me. . . Sethe sees me see her and
> I see the smile   her smiling face is the place
> for me   it is the face I lost   she is my
> face smiling at me   doing it at last   a
> hot thing   now we can join   a hot
> thing.

A similar merging fantasy also figures prominently in *Sula,* in the relationship between Sula and Nel. The two characters are described as so close that "they themselves had difficulty distinguishing one's thoughts from the other's"; for Nel, "talking to Sula had always been a conversation with herself"; and Sula eventually realizes that neither Nel nor anyone else "would ever be that version of herself which she sought to reach out to and touch with an ungloved hand." Each is compelled continually to seek the self through an other, and such blurring of boundaries can lead to one of the forms of domination and submission Benjamin describes: the self can surrender totally to the will and agency of the other, or the self can consume and appropriate the other as part of itself, as an object of its possession.

The repetition of the word "mine" in the monologues of Sethe, Denver, and Beloved suggests exactly this sort of possession and incorporation of the other as an object. "Mine" is the haunting word that Stamp Paid hears surrounding Sethe's house in ghostly whispers and is stressed again in a lyrical section following Beloved's unpunctuated monologue. In this section the voices of Beloved, Sethe, and Denver are joined (the identity of the speaker in each line is sometimes unclear) while at the same time each voice remains essentially isolated (the voices speak to but not *with* each other):

> Beloved
> You are my sister
> You are my daughter
> You are my face; you are me
> I have found you again; you have come back to
>   me
> You are my Beloved
> You are mine
> You are mine
> You are mine

This form of possessing and objectifying the other, however, cannot satisfy—it imprisons the self within its own devouring omnipotence, its own narcissism. True satisfaction or joy, as Benjamin explains, can only be achieved through "mutual recognition" between self and other, between two subjects or selves.

Both sides of the power dynamic, both surrender to and incorporation of the other, are apparent in the relationship between Sethe and Beloved. Toward the end of the novel, Sethe relinquishes herself completely to the will and desire of Beloved. She neglects to feed or care for herself and becomes physically drained and emotionally depleted. Sethe literally shrinks while Beloved literally expands and swells; both are caught up in a mutually destructive, frighteningly boundless narcissism. The prelude to Sethe's decline is an incident that again stresses lack of recognition at the source of this narcissistic condition. Sethe has been abandoned once again, this time by Paul D (her previous abandonments include those by her mother, her husband Halle, Baby Suggs, and her two sons), and to cheer herself, she takes Denver and Beloved ice-skating on the frozen creek. The three are unable to keep their balance, and as they fall on the ice, they shriek with both pain and laughter. The scene is redolent of childhood and of childlike helplessness. "Making a circle or a line, the three of them could not stay upright for one whole minute, but nobody saw them falling." The phrase "nobody saw them falling" becomes the dominant motif of the scene; the line is repeated four times in the two-page description. Sethe's laughter turns into uncontrollable tears, and her weeping in the context of the scene's refrain suggests a child's aching sense of loss or absence, specifically the absence of the confirming, legitimizing gaze of the other.

Once it is asserted that "nobody saw" her falling, that there is no "other" to confer the reality of her own existence on her, Sethe falls prey to a consuming narcissism. Suddenly she consciously recognizes Beloved as the incarnation of her dead child and surrenders herself totally to her. Sethe now feels that "there is no world outside" her door and that since her daughter has come back, "she can sleep like the drowned." In psychological terms, she retreats from external reality and succumbs to her destructive, narcissistic fantasies, to her murderously enraged child-self as well as her insatiable need to make reparation for her murderous love. Paul D recognizes, and fears, the narcissistic nature of Sethe's love: "This here new Sethe didn't know where the world stopped and she began . . . more important than what Sethe had done was what she claimed. It scared him."

Paul D is the one character in the novel who has the power to resist and disrupt the destructive, narcissistic mother-child dyad. Sethe recalls, "There was no room for any other thing or body until Paul D arrived and broke up the place, making room, shifting it, moving it over to someplace else, then standing in the place he had made." Sethe also tells Beloved that she would have recognized her "right off, except for Paul D." Paul D is the external "other" who triangulates the dyad, as the image of the "three shadows" of Sethe, Denver, and Paul D "holding hands" as they walk to the carnival emphasizes. The excursion to the carnival is Sethe's first venture into the community since the murder; Paul D has the capacity to lead Sethe out of her narcissistic isolation and into relationship with the external world. The claims of the angry baby Beloved, however, are still too powerful to allow for these other attachments: she makes her first appearance in the flesh immediately following the excursion.

While Paul D plays the role of the saving other in contradistinction to Beloved and the narcissistic dyad, he does not represent the typical world of the father. He is not, for instance, a token of male rationality countering the irrationality of the female world. He too is deeply affected by Beloved's irrational power—she literally "moves" him, making him physically restless and forcing him to sleep with her in the shed outside the house. His power lies precisely in his maternal, nurturing quality; he is that "other" with the power to recognize and affirm the inner or essential self. He is described as "the kind of man who could walk into a house and make the women cry. Because with him, in his presence, they could." The women see him and not only want to weep; they also want to confess their deepest secrets, to expose all the pain and rage bound up with their true selves. Sethe thinks of how he "cradled her before the cooking stove" and is deeply comforted by "the mind of him that knew her own."

Paul D has the power to satisfy the craving that fuels the novel, the craving to be "known," to have one's existence sanctioned by the empathic recognition of the other. That Morrison bestows this quality on an African-American male character is an interesting, and unusual, point. A common criticism of black women novelists is that their portrayals of black males are often flat, stereotypic, or unempathic. For Morrison, the maternal nurturing quality is a form of love that is not restricted by gender; this view expands the possibilities, and is a liberating factor, for her characters. Yet Paul D, too, is not a totally reliable other: he temporarily retreats after learning of Sethe's murder of her child. Like all of the other black characters in the novel, he must work out of a condition of psychic fragmentation—his selfhood has been severely impaired, his status as a human subject denied by the slave culture. He feels that even the old rooster Mister was allowed an essential integrity of being denied him: "Mister was allowed to be and stay what he was. But I wasn't allowed to be and stay what I was. Even if you cooked him you'd be cooking a rooster named Mister. But wasn't no way I'd ever be Paul D again, living or dead."

Only Denver does not see Paul D as the other women do; for her he does not play the same nurturing role. She sees him only as a threat, as an intruder into her intense, and deeply ambivalent, relationship with her mother. Denver is terrified of Sethe's murderous love: she has "monstrous and unmanageable dreams about Sethe" and is afraid to fall asleep while Sethe braids her hair at night. In her fantasies, "She cut my head off every night." For Denver, the idealized, saving other is her father Halle, whom she calls "Angel Man." Yet the father is significantly incapable of playing the savior role. The "other"—whether represented by mother or father—is always untrustworthy in Morrison's world, rendered thus by the social environment. As a result, the self remains trapped within its own destructive narcissism.

Sethe regards Halle as the ultimate betrayer: he witnessed her rape, she learns, but did not protest or try to protect her. His absent presence is worse than mere absence, for it confirms an essential hollowness and undependability of the other and of love. Yet Halle is not simply a "bad guy"; again, Morrison extends her compassion equally to her male characters. The reader is allowed to see Halle too as a deeply wounded child. Traumatized by the rape of Sethe and the maternal violation that it also represents, Halle literally loses his mind—his selfhood shatters. Paul D observes him later squatting by a churn, with "butter all over his face." He smeared that butter on his face, Sethe thinks, "because the milk they took is on his mind." The image of Halle here recalls Beloved and the image at the psychological base of the book: it is the picture of a lost, greedy child whose ravenous hunger/love is out of control.

Ultimately Denver is able to escape the narcissistic vacuum, and she is helped not, as she had fantasized, by Halle, but by another maternal figure in the novel, Mrs. Jones. Denver is first propelled out of the house by literal hunger, for Sethe, locked in her obsession with Beloved, has become oblivious to food and to all external or physical considerations. Denver realizes that "it was she who had to step off the edge of the world and die because if she didn't, they all would." Excluded from the Beloved-Sethe dyad, Denver is forced into the role of the outside other, and assuming that role is her salvation. She goes first to her former teacher Lady Jones, an old woman of mixed race who has long struggled with the contempt of the black community and, equally, with self-contempt. Lady Jones thus has a special "affection for the unpicked children," an empathy with those, like Denver, who have never been recognized or "picked," who have never had their existence validated or confirmed. After Denver asks her for food, Mrs. Jones compassionately croons, "Oh, baby," and that empathic recognition of the hungry baby within finally frees Denver from the trap of her infantile needs: "Denver looked up at her. She did not know it then, but it was the word 'baby,' said softly and with such kindness, that inaugurated her life in the world as a woman."

With this recognition, Denver for the first time begins to experience the contours of her own separate self. When Nelson Lord, an old school acquaintance, affectionately says, "Take care of yourself, Denver," Denver "heard it as though it were what language was made for," and she realizes that "It was a new thought, having a self to look out for and preserve." Self-recognition is inextricably tied up with self-love, and this is precisely the message of the sermons that Baby Suggs preaches to her people in the Clearing. In a white society that does not recognize or love you, she tells them, you must fight to recognize and love yourself:

> "Here," she said, "in this here place, we flesh; flesh that weeps, laughs; flesh that dances on bare feet in grass. Love it. Love it hard. Yonder they do not love your flesh. They despise it. They don't love your eyes; they'd just as soon pick em out. . . . Love your hands! Love them. Raise them up and kiss them. Touch others with them, pat them together, stroke them on your face 'cause they don't love that either. *You* got to love it, *you!*"

Baby Suggs continues to enjoin her people to love every appendage, every organ in their bodies, and especially to "love your heart." This is the crucial lesson, but it cannot be learned in isolation; self-love needs a relational foundation and a social context. Thus even Baby Suggs is unable to sustain her convictions and heed her own teachings. After Sethe's murder, Baby Suggs retreats and ceases to care about herself or others, showing interest in nothing except "colors."

Morrison's novel, however, is not hopelessly bleak or despairing. Her characters are wounded, but not all of them are ruined. Denver and Paul D, by courageously facing their inner terrors—Denver leaves the house even though she expects to be "swallowed up," and Paul D returns to Sethe and her fearful, murderous love—are able to salvage out of the wreckage a bolstering faith in both self and other. Paul D tries to pass this faith on to Sethe at the end. He assumes again a maternal, nurturing role. He holds Sethe, calls her "baby," and gently tells her not to cry. Beloved is gone and Sethe feels bereft and lost: "She was my best thing," she tells Paul D. He "leans over and takes her hand. With the other he touches her face. 'You your best thing, Sethe. You are.' His holding fingers are holding hers." While the word "thing" still suggests a sense of self as object (an objectification of self that perhaps no black person in the slave culture could ever totally escape), the scene between Sethe and Paul D at the end comes closest to that state of mutual recognition and attunement that Benjamin describes. Paul D's gently touching Sethe's face recalls the touching faces of the mating turtles; the relationship here is not one of merging or of domination but of resonating "likeness" and empathic understanding. Paul D recalls Sixo's description of his mistress, the "Thirty-Mile Woman": "She is a friend of my mind. She gather me, man. The pieces I am, she gather them and give them back to me in all the right order. It's good, you know, when you got a woman who is a friend of your mind." The beloved other has the power to give to the self its own essential wholeness. The role of the other here is neither as an object to possess nor even as a mirror for the self; as a "friend of [the] mind," the other is a subject in its own right, with an inner life that corresponds with that of the self. In such correspondence, in that mutuality of inner experience and suffering, lies the self-confirming and consoling power of the relationship.

Paul D tells Sethe in this final scene that "He wants to put his story next to hers." Throughout the novel, stories and storytelling are associated with the self and with the primary oral relationship at its root. Beloved is tireless in her demand, in "her thirst for hearing" Sethe's stories: "It became a way to feed her . . . Sethe learned the profound satisfaction Beloved got from storytelling." Denver too feeds Beloved's craving for stories about Sethe, "nursing Beloved's interest like a lover whose pleasure was to overfeed the loved." Denver's storytelling, because of the empathic identification it involves, also allows her to feel a closer bond and oneness with her mother. As she narrates the tale of Sethe's escape to Beloved, "Denver was seeing it now and feeling it—through Beloved. Feeling how it must have felt to her mother." Paul D does not want to merge or incorporate Sethe's story into his own at the end; rather, he wants to "put his story next to hers." This suggests again an essential maintenance of boundaries, a balance of two like but separate selves, an attunement.

The novel does not end, however, with the scene between

Sethe and Paul D, but with one last lyrical section on Beloved. The refrain of the last two pages is the line, repeated three times: "It was not a story to pass on." The final section arouses a deep sense of pathos for that unrecognized, ravenously needy infant-self that is Beloved:

> Everybody knew what she was called, but nobody anywhere knew her name. Disremembered and unaccounted for, she cannot be lost because no one is looking for her, and even if they were, how can they call her if they don't know her name? Although she has claim, she is not claimed. In the place where long grass opens, the girl who waited to be loved and cry shame erupts into her separate parts, to make it easy for the chewing laughter to swallow her all away.

> It was not a story to pass on.

The poignancy of Beloved's story/self is that it is *not* a story/self. She has been denied the narrative of her being, the subjectivity and continuity of inner experience that should be everyone's birthright. Beloved's desolation, her sorrow, is a more extreme version of the same sorrow that all of the black characters in the novel experience. Thus Baby Suggs, finally freed from slavery, expresses not the elation of freedom but the deep sadness of not knowing her self, of not being able to read her own story: "The sadness was at her center, the desolated center where the self that was no self made its home. Sad as it was that she did not know where her children were buried or what they looked like if alive, fact was she knew more about them than she knew about herself, having never had the map to discover what she was like." In the end, the novel is more about Beloved than Sethe. Beloved's character is both the frame and center of the book, and it is her story—or her desperate struggle to know and experience her own story—that is the pumping heart of the novel. Beloved's struggle is Sethe's struggle; it is also Denver's, Paul D's, and Baby Suggs's. It is the struggle of all black people in a racist society, Morrison suggests, to claim themselves as subjects in their own narrative.

Beloved demonstrates, finally, the interconnection of social and intrapsychic reality. The novel plays out the deep psychic reverberations of living in a culture in which domination and objectification of the self have been institutionalized. If from the earliest years on, one's fundamental need to be recognized and affirmed as a human subject is denied, that need can take on fantastic and destructive proportions in the inner world: the intense hunger, the fantasized fear of either being swallowed or exploding, can tyrannize one's life even when one is freed from the external bonds of oppression. The self cannot experience freedom without first experiencing its own agency or, in Sethe's words, "claiming ownership" of itself. The free, autonomous self, *Beloved* teaches, is an inherently social self, rooted in relationship and dependent at its core on the vital bond of mutual recognition.

FURTHER READING

Criticism

Bell, Bernard W. "*Beloved:* A Womanist Neo-Slave Narrative; or Multivocal Remembrances of Things Past." *African American Review* 26, No. 1 (Spring 1992): 7-15.

> Discusses *Beloved* as an exploration of the "double consciousness" of Black Americans.

Bender, Eileen T. "Repossessing *Uncle Tom's Cabin:* Toni Morrison's *Beloved*." In *Cultural Power/Cultural Literacy: Selected Papers from the Fourteenth Annual Florida State University Conference on Literature and Film,* edited by Bonnie Braendlin, pp. 129-42. Tallahassee: Florida State University Press, 1991.

> Argues that *Beloved* is Morrison's meditated reaction against the sentimental stereotypes of Harriet Beecher Stowe's famous novel. According to Bender, Morrison's novel represents a "new act of emancipation for a culture still enslaved by false impressions and factitious accounts."

Bjork, Patrick Bryce. "*Beloved:* The Paradox of a Past and Present Self and Place." In his *The Novels of Toni Morrison: The Search for Self and Place within the Community,* pp. 141-62. New York: Peter Lang Publishing, 1992.

> Examines the contradictions of personal identity and memory in Morrison's novel.

Chandler, Marilyn R. "*Housekeeping* and *Beloved:* When Women Come Home." In her *Dwelling in the Text: Houses in American Fiction,* pp. 291-318. Berkeley: University of California Press, 1991.

> Analyzes *Beloved* and Marilynne Robinson's *Housekeeping* "under the rubric of house and home as ideas in relation to which women in every generation and in every situation have had to 'work out their salvation' and define their identities."

Darling, Marsha Jean. "Ties That Bind." *The Women's Review of Books* V, No. 6 (March 1988): 4-5.

> Praises *Beloved* as a masterpiece of historical fiction which "challenges, seduces, cajoles and enjoins us to visualize, contemplate, to know, feel and comprehend the realities of the material world of nineteenth-century Black women and men."

Davis, Christina. "*Beloved:* A Question of Identity." *Présence Africaine* 145 (1988): 151-56.

> Extols Morrison's gift for giving expression to the subjective consciousness of Sethe, a slave whose voice "is clear, its pain full of anguish, its beauty unbearable, its truth stunning."

Demetrakopoulos, Stephanie A. "Maternal Bonds as Devourers of Women's Individuation in Toni Morrison's *Beloved*." *African American Review* 26, No. 1 (Spring 1992): 51-9.

> Argues that *Beloved* "develops the idea that maternal bonds can stunt or even obviate a woman's individuation or sense of self," and that "the conclusion of the book effects a resolution of the tension between history and nature which underlies the movement of the work as a whole."

Duvall, John N. "Authentic Ghost Stories: *Uncle Tom's Cabin, Absalom, Absalom!,* and *Beloved*." *The Faulkner Journal* IV, Nos. 1 and 2 (Fall 1988-Spring 1989): 83-97.

> Compares the ghost story elements in novels by Morrison, Harriet Beecher Stowe, and William Faulkner.

Goldman, Anne E. " 'I Made the Ink': (Literary) Production and Reproduction in *Dessa Rose* and *Beloved*." *Feminist Studies* 16, No. 2 (Summer 1990): 313-30.

> Argues that *Beloved* and Sherley Anne Williams's *Dessa Rose* "comment implicitly on the gap between mainstream critical theories and modern literary practice" by their construction of strong heroines who integrate themselves through writing, in contrast to the narrative fragmentation of postmodern fiction.

Malmgren, Carl D. "Mixed Genres and the Logic of Slavery in Toni Morrison's *Beloved*." *Critique* XXXVI, No. 2 (Winter 1995): 96-106.

> Notes *Beloved*'s incorporation of elements from various genres, including the ghost story and historical novel, and argues that "[it] is the institution of slavery that supplies the logic underwriting the novel, the thematic glue that unifies this multifaceted text."

Harris, Trudier. "Of Mother Love and Demons." *Callaloo* 11, No. 2 (Spring 1988): 387-89.

> Analyzes Morrison's treatment of the "mother love" theme in *Beloved*. Harris argues that in "exorcising" Beloved "the women favor the living over the dead, mother love over childish punishment of parents, reality over the legend of which they have become a part."

Rigney, Barbara Hill. " 'A Story to Pass On': Ghosts and the Significance of History in Toni Morrison's *Beloved*." In *Haunting the House of Fiction: Feminist Perspectives on Ghost Stories by American Women,* edited by Lynette Carpenter and Wendy K. Kolmar, pp. 229-35. Knoxville: University of Tennessee Press, 1991.

> Explains the meaning of history in *Beloved* as "the reality of slavery. The 'rememories' are a gross catalogue of atrocities, gross sexual indignities, a denial of human rights on every level."

Additional coverage of Morrison's life and career is contained in the following sources published by Gale Research: *Authors and Artists for Young Adults*, Vol. 1; *Black Literature Criticism; Black Writers*, Vol. 2; *Concise Dictionary of American Literary Biography, 1968-1988; Contemporary Authors*, Vols. 29-32, rev. ed.; *Contemporary Authors New Revision Series*, Vols. 27 and 42; *Contemporary Literary Criticism*, Vols. 4, 10, 22, 55, 81; *Dictionary of Literary Biography*, Vols. 6, 33, 143; *Dictionary of Literary Biography Yearbook, 1981; DISCovering Authors; Major 20th-Century Writers;* and *Something about the Author*, Vol. 57.

Ben Okri

1959-

Nigerian novelist, short story writer, and poet.

The following entry provides an overview of Okri's career through 1994.

INTRODUCTION

Winner of the 1991 Booker Prize for *The Famished Road* (1991), Okri is known for works that focus on life in modern-day Nigeria. His tales, often black and ominous in outlook, depict the problems which beset his homeland, particularly poverty, famine, and political corruption. Okri also examines the relationship between the natural and spiritual world in his writings, combining Western literary techniques with elements of traditional African folklore and myth.

Biographical Information

Of Urhobo descent, Okri was born in Minna, Nigeria. Although he spent his earliest years in England, where his father was studying law, Okri returned to Nigeria with his parents at age seven. He received formal schooling at Urhobo College in Warri, Nigeria, and, after returning to England, earned a B.A. in comparative literature from the University of Essex in Colchester. Working as a journalist, he began writing essays and short stories, publishing his first novel, *Flowers and Shadows* (1980), before the age of twenty-one. In addition to the Booker Prize, Okri—who has worked as a broadcaster for the BBC World Service and as poetry editor for *West Africa*—has been awarded the Commonwealth Writers Prize for Africa for *Incidents at the Shrine* (1986) and the *Paris Review* Aga Khan Prize for Fiction. Okri has spent much of his adult life in England but acknowledges that "Africa is the only place that I really want to write about. It's a gift to the writer."

Major Works

Okri's works frequently focus on the political, social, and economic conditions of contemporary Nigeria. In *Flowers and Shadows,* for example, Okri employs paradox and dualism to contrast the rich and poor areas of a typical Nigerian city. Set in the capital city of Lagos, the novel focuses on Jeffia, the spoiled child of a rich man, who realizes his family's wealth is the result of his father's corrupt business dealings. In *The Landscapes Within* (1981) the central character, Omovo, is an artist who, to the consternation and displeasure of family, friends, and government officials, paints the corruption he sees in his daily life. Detailing the growth and development of the protagonist as well as that of Nigeria, *The Landscapes Within* has been classified as a *künstlerroman*—a novel that traces the evolution of an artist—and favorably compared to other works in the genre, notably James Joyce's *A Portrait of the Artist as*

a Young Man (1916) and Ayi Kwei Armah's *The Beautyful Ones Are Not Yet Born* (1968). Frequently set in Lagos or London, the stories collected in *Incidents at the Shrine* focus on individuals trying to survive—or at least mentally escape—the violence and squalor that characterize their daily existence. Critics note that the disparate settings of England and Nigeria are unified by Okri's recurring focus on the dangers of modern civilization and on conservative government officials who idly watch the moral and physical collapse of their constituents and cities. Oppression, economic disparity, political repression, alienation, and loss are likewise central to the short story collection *Stars of the New Curfew* (1988) and the poetry volume entitled *An African Elegy* (1992), both of which have been recognized for their use of myth and surrealistic detail, and their focus on dreams, visions, and the spirit world. The story "When the Light Returns," for instance, updates the myth of Eurydice and Orpheus, recounting a young man's search for his love among the dead; in another piece from *Stars of the New Curfew* a politician drops coins out of a helicopter onto voters. In the course of the tale, which is based on actual events, people are hurt by the falling currency and the resulting mayhem only to discover that the money is worthless. As Giles Foden notes, the poems in

An African Elegy are similarly infused with anger and draw on everything from "African myth to Western sci-fi." Okri's combination of myth and Western literary traditions is also employed in *The Famished Road* and its sequel, *Songs of Enchantment* (1993). Drawing on the culture and tradition of Nigeria's Yoruba tribe, *The Famished Road* concerns a young Nigerian named Azaro, who is an *abiku*—a spirit-child torn between the natural and spiritual world. His desire to free himself from the spirit world is paralleled by his father's and people's attempt to rise above their poverty. Though considered less successful than *The Famished Road, Songs of Enchantment* stresses the problems of cultural nationalism and continues Azaro and his community's struggle against corrupt government officials.

Critical Reception

Stressing his inclusion of African myth and folklore, emphasis on spirituality and mysticism, and focus on Nigerian society and the attendant problems associated with the country's attempts to rise above its third-world status, critics have lauded Okri's writings for capturing the Nigerian worldview. Okri has additionally received praise for his use of surrealistic detail, elements of Nigerian storytelling traditions, and Western literary techniques, notably the magic realism popularized by Gabriel García Márquez. Placing Okri's works firmly within the tradition of postcolonial writing and favorably comparing them to those of such esteemed Nigerian authors as Chinua Achebe, critics cite the universal relevance of Okri's writings on political and aesthetic levels. As Okri has written: "Politics take their place beside myth and facts, each one in turn has ascendency. People can say this is a triumph for the African novel if it gives them comfort, but I say it is a triumph for the imagination, for what Baudelaire calls voluptuousness, the texture of our sensuality."

PRINCIPAL WORKS

Flowers and Shadows (novel) 1980
The Landscapes Within (novel) 1981
Incidents at the Shrine (short stories) 1986
Stars of the New Curfew (short stories)   1988
The Famished Road (novel) 1991
An African Elegy (poetry) 1992
Songs of Enchantment (novel) 1993

CRITICISM

Jane Bryce (review date 19 September 1980)

SOURCE: "Out of the Earth," in *The Times Literary Supplement,* No. 4042, September 19, 1980, p. 1047.

[*In the following favorable review, Bryce discusses the themes, characters, and setting of* Flowers and Shadows.]

Flowers and Shadows is a first novel by a young Nigerian of nineteen. A striking feature of the book is its sureness of touch, the self-confidence with which the author handles both characterization and events. Above all, the language reflects a keen ear for the cadences of speech, whether pidgin or standard English.

Some aspects of the setting are familiar from such novels as *Violence,* by another young Nigerian author, Festus Iyayi: squalor, filth and poverty reduce the inhabitants of Lagos's poorer quarters to despair, yet ultimately refine them. Okri spares us no detail of the smells, the jostling for buses, the excreta in the gutters, the clamour of the maimed, begging for coins. These details emerge as the physical correlative of the social reality of Lagos, the mental violence practised by the powerful, the dog-eat-dog struggles for political and financial survival. Poverty is a curse, and in the face of such poverty luxury is a flagrant denial of humanity. The two are skilfully juxtaposed in passages such as the description of a Lagos go-slow, in all its confusion, from the interior of a chauffeured, air-conditioned limousine.

The experience of the darker side of Lagos life seems at first sight a long way from that of the protagonist, Jeffia, a young man who has arrived "at the ante-chamber of his childhood dreams", and who is portrayed as the pampered child of a rich man. The dialogue of Innocence and Experience is, however, made explicit in Jeffia's realization that his peace of mind is founded on the ruthlessness of his father, Jonan. Perhaps because the author's attention is concentrated on this process of revelation, coincidences and violent deaths proliferate, and the description almost loses its way at the moment of impact between the two cars of Jeffia's father and his uncle.

This is no way impairs the mood of the whole, however. Many such contrasts are present in the substructure of the book. The title *Flowers and Shadows* encapsulates this dualism. Jeffia's mother, whose role in the novel is that of the creative artist, has a gentleness of spirit which is directly in conflict with her husband's violent nature. Jonan's character is tinged with darkness: the childhood of poverty from which he can escape only through power and money is hinted at in his native mannerisms, juju worship, his family's belief in witchcraft, and even his wielding of the decorative Hausa sword in murderous rage towards his brother.

The sins of the father are visited on the son. This starkly biblical message is enacted in the novel, but the flowers survive, albeit sickly and stunted. Cynthia, the young woman whose history is unknowingly interwoven with Jeffia's, stands as a reminder of hope throughout. A flower growing in tragic soil, her love transforms the final scenes of squalor so that the book ends on a note of triumphant optimism. The beautiful ones are born, though their beauty is both obscured and tempered by the shadow of society's evils. Drawing inspiration from its own culture, Okri's is a voice which speaks to those outside, and promises to be one worth listening to.

Michelene Wandor   (review date July 1986)

SOURCE: "Terrors of Civilisation," in *Books and Bookmen*, No. 369, July, 1986, p. 36.

[*Wandor is an English playwright, scriptwriter, short story writer, poet, novelist, editor, and nonfiction writer who frequently writes on feminist themes. In the review below, she presents a thematic discussion of* Incidents at the Shrine.]

A series of oppositions form the themes underlying this collection of short stories [entitled **Incidents at the Shrine**]: black/white; civilisation/superstition; survival/destruction. The war between indigenous African culture and white civilisation is laid out in the first story, **'Laughter Beneath the Bridge'**, where a group of children are left behind, abandoned after an unnamed civil war in an unnamed African country. Violence comes from all sides, and is there in the threatening presence of the ordinary and everyday, as the young boy hero finally survives, but not before having seen violence done to others.

A young boy is also the hero/observer of another story, **'A Crooked Prayer'**, in which the anguish of African family life is played out through the desire of his uncle for a child. These children embody a sort of innocent eye, but it is an innocence which is not just confined to Okri's child characters. The adult men all seem in many different ways to be caught at the meeting point of social conflicts, and some survive more intact than others.

In **'Converging City'**, a nameless down-and-out takes up residence in a house peopled by young post-punk whites—or does he? In the psyches of people for whom tribal meanings make little distinction between the material and the spiritual, it is not always easy to see what is dream and what is reality: at his strongest, Okri's prose itself blurs the line between them. In this story, the alien aggression of white undergraduate culture is reflected in the hero's obsession with decay, which affects his perspective on everything.

The book's title story brings together the conflicts of east and west, of civilisation and the tribal. In an ironic beginning, Anderson, late for work in a museum, is sacked; he becomes ill, is treated by orthodox medicine, and finally, in despair, returns to his village where the urban 'evils' are exorcised by the Image maker. Okri manages to convey fear, persecution, the comprehended and the obscure, in a prose which is direct and evocative, and able to penetrate the way the unconscious and dreams find their equivalents in cultures seen as 'primitive', where civilisation has only brutish power to offer. In the most effective stories in this short book, Okri poses himself between the fearful purifications of the primitive and the looming terrors of civilisation. It is a painful area for the imagination to tread; it is interesting to speculate on where it might go. He could, of course, continue to explore the same theme, with variations. Or his prose could entirely self-destruct in a scatology of fear, outsiderness and hate; or he may opt for one half of the divide against the other. He is a strong writer, so perhaps all options are possible. I look forward to his next fiction with interest.

John Melmoth   (review date 8 August 1986)

SOURCE: "From Ghetto to Badland," in *The Times Literary Supplement*, No. 4349, August 8, 1986, p. 863.

[*In the following highly laudatory review, Melmoth briefly describes the plots and themes of some of the short stories contained in* Incidents at the Shrine, *concluding that Okri's Lagos stories are his best.*]

Reversing the more usual course of events, Ben Okri has followed the two novels he wrote while in his teens—*Flowers and Shadows* and *The Landscapes Within*—with a collection of short stories [entitled **Incidents at the Shrine**]. Whereas the novels could be regarded as juvenilia, the stories are terse, poised, poetic. *Flowers and Shadows* was oddly reminiscent of Lawrence's *The White Peacock;* the stories owe more to Joyce and Chekhov and, less to their advantage, to Hemingway. With them Okri has found a voice and established a style of his own.

Not only is Okri working in a different medium, he is also exploring a different milieu: the ghettoes of Lagos and the badlands of London. *Flowers and Shadows* toyed uneasily with the *haute arrivisme* of manicured lawns, cocktail parties and Japanese cars. Although Omovo in *The Landscapes Within* had to work for a living, as an artist he escaped the class system. This new volume [*Incidents at the Shrine*], in contrast, immerses itself in poverty and deprivation, and the ways of dealing with it in the bars and discos of Lagos and the baleful wastes of London's high-rises. Only the first story, **"Laughter Beneath the Bridge"**, deals with a recognizably bourgeois world of public schools, and it does so only to put it at risk in the Nigerian civil war of 1967-71.

For most of Okri's protagonists life is singularly lacking in comfort and glamour, and their attempts at escape range from signing up for correspondence courses guaranteed to develop their business acumen to dabbling in the supernatural. The baroque contortions, delusions and indulgences of their mental lives contrast with their unpromising physical existences. Agodi, in **"Converging City"**, responds to one commercial disappointment by braiding his hair and beard, donning yellow and purple robes and going into business as the true prophet. **"Masquerades"** inspects the social life of a night-soil worker who compensates for the vileness of his job by creating a spotless slum penthouse, hung with his terylene suits, photographs of himself, a picture of Christ and a Benin mask. Compulsively dousing himself with lavender and jasmine is his only way of coping with the inchoate nihilism which goes with the job: "When I look at people I see nothing—what doesn't turn to shit turns to dust." Ajegunle Joe, eponymous focus of **"The Dream Vendor's August"**, the longest and most complex of the stories, combats futility with occultism, selling pamphlets on "How to Fight Witches and Wizards" and protecting himself from disaster with rings, one of which was taken from the body of Isaac Newton and one of which belonged to King Solomon.

> Okri maintains that "Africa is the only place I really want to write about. It's a gift to the writer." One hopes that, as an expatriate, he will be able to go on doing so, and as memorably.
>
> —*John Melmoth*

Okri's preoccupation with mental flights to various destinations gives his stories a heightened and surreal quality. In **"Laughter Beneath the Bridge"** three boys haunt a deserted school in a state of superheated reverie induced by fear and hormonal promptings: "I dreamed of her new-formed breasts when the lizards chased us from the dormitories, and when the noise of the fighter planes drove us to the forests." In **"The Dream Vendor's August"** Joe converses regularly with a dwarf who visits his dreams.

The two stories set in London are similarly concerned with cognitive dissonances: the narrator of **"Disparities"** is all twitching and inconsequentiality; the watcher in **"A Hidden History"** spots a lunatic beating his coat against a lamp-post. They are, however, principally remarkable for their exaggerated treatment of the unspeakable, an accumulation of nastiness that flirts with bathos. **"Disparities"** wanders into a reeking pub, peopled with the "very cream of leftovers"—trendies, deadbeats and old men coughing up phlegm while the jukebox plunges the "human cesspit into perfect, unmelodious gloom". **"A Hidden History"** presses between its pages the flora of urban decay, the "vegetable life" of corruption, "purple and green . . . beautiful to look at like the fata Morgana". The problem is that the facts of depression themselves become merely depressing if they remain without context or explanation. Okri's account of the decline and fall of London is metaphysical and somewhat unconvincing: he couches it in terms of "a monstrous negative force" which emanates from "the wild gardens of all the rotting houses".

The distinction between the Lagos stories and the London ones is revealing. Those set in Africa are the more complex and fertile, the language of the shanties has a vitality which the inevitable solecisms can only enhance: "Try us for size. A trial will convict you." Okri maintains that "Africa is the only place I really want to write about. It's a gift to the writer." One hopes that, as an expatriate, he will be able to go on doing so, and as memorably.

Suzanne Cronje   (review date 22 July 1988)

SOURCE: "Powerlessness Corrupts," in *New Statesman & Society*, Vol. 1, No. 7, July 22, 1988, pp. 43-4.

[*In the following positive review, Cronje examines Okri's focus on Nigeria in* Stars of the New Curfew.]

In the title story of Ben Okri's book, *Stars of the New Curfew*, two local politicians, both millionaires, hold a crude contest for power. This consists of distributing money to the crowd. One of them produces an air-conditioned Rolls Royce with a large refrigerator which stores and cools his banknotes: "The fridge was brought on stage and the stacks of notes were unloosened from their bindings and thrown at the crowd." This goes on for a while, until the rival chief makes his counter-bid: "The helicopter hovered over us. Then a door opened and coins were emptied over us. No one moved for a while . . . The silvery sparkles floated down through the air like tangible stars . . . The coins rained on us as if it were our punishment for being below". In the end the crowd disperses: "We were the garbage carried away on the waves of mud." The torrential rain in the town misses the houses belonging to members of a secret cult.

The nightmarish setting of this scene may disguise the fact that it actually took place, money-helicopter and all, during Nigeria's 1983 election campaign—before the military rule so angrily denounced by Okri in this book. (I noted with some amusement in the Nigerian press the other day that the real-life tycoon who presumably inspired this tale continues with his "philantropic gestures" to win people's hearts, despite the present military government's ban on politics.)

With the possible exception of **"What the Tapster Saw,"** which is more allegorical than the rest, Okri's six stories are all "true" reflections on life in Nigeria. The first goes back to the Biafran war; the rest are set in the present; all are vivid and frightening. The love story, **"When the Lights Return,"** is like a guilt-ridden dream in which the heroine, white-clad Maria, is presented with Okri's consummate skill as the archetypal mistress of moral blackmail. In the background: the Lagos ghetto of Munshin, peopled with loathsome soldiers and a dead man who rises from a rubbish heap to preach revolt.

Okri's writing is suffused with helpless anger at the alienation of Nigerian society, the corruption not only of the rulers but also of the ruled who seem to connive at their own oppression. "The strongest fear in this town", one of his characters says, "is to be defenceless, to be without a powerful godfather, and therefore at the mercy of the drums. New starts are growing every day. They grow from the same powers, the same rituals . . ." The trouble with most people is that they cannot *see* the nature of the evil surrounding them. In **"Worlds that Flourish,"** the hero, a clerk who is sacked without apparent reason, leaves his job without bitterness and tells his neighbour he feels "fine". This is "because you go around as if you don't have any eyes", the neighbour says. But even vision does not protect you in Okri's Nigeria. When the ex-clerk begins to see, he flees the city in horror, to end up in the village of the dead. There he rediscovers his neighbour who has been killed by a soldier and who now displays *three* eyes.

Stars of the New Curfew is an important comment on Nigerian society. Only time will tell whether its unremitting pessimism is fully justified, but it leaves no doubt about Okri's passion and talent.

Abioseh Michael Porter   (essay date Autumn 1988)

SOURCE: "Ben Okri's *The Landscapes Within:* A Metaphor for Personal and National Development," in *World Literature Written in English,* Vol. 28, No. 2, Autumn, 1988, pp. 203-10.

[*In the following essay, Porter analyzes how Okri uses elements of the* künstlerroman *in* The Landscapes Within *to discuss problems of contemporary Nigeria. He also briefly compares the story line of* The Landscapes Within *to other novels within this genre, notably James Joyce's* Portrait of the Artist as a Young Man *(1916) and Ayi Kwei Armah's* The Beautyful Ones Are Not Yet Born *(1968).*]

Although African writers have often treated the subject of national and cultural development in their writings, very few of these authors have focused specifically on the role or contribution of the young artist towards national development in modern African society. My aim in this essay is to demonstrate how Ben Okri, a promising young novelist from Nigeria, successfully uses the literary conventions of the *künstlerroman*—a novel portraying the early learnings and growth of a young artist—in his work *The Landscapes Within* to address some important questions dealing with national and cultural development in Nigeria. Okri's text is different from several of its other West African literary cousins—*Bildungsromane* such as *La Pauvre Christ de Bomba, Mission terminée, Kocoumbo, l'étudiant noir, Le Regard du roi, Second Class Citizen,* and *The White Man of God*—because of the way he seems to have used literary influences as varied as Achebe, Ngugi, Soyinka, and James Joyce to give a new twist both to the novel of personal (and artistic) development as genre and his treatment of the cultural aspects of development.

The Landscapes Within deals with the process of maturation of a young, bright, sensitive and lonely artist as he tries to survive the general philistinism, corruption and inhumanity that characterize big city life in Lagos. As a child, Omovo had moved with his parents from Igbo-land after the Nigeria-Biafra civil war and had progressed quite well in school until being prevented from taking the all-important school certificate examinations because of his father's failure to pay the necessary fees on time. Life becomes increasingly miserable for the young man when, not long after the death of his mother, his father re-marries and, as a result of domestic tension, Omovo's elder brothers—Okur and Umeh—are kicked out of the family fold by their father.

Although after the struggle that usually accompanies a novel dealing with personal development, Omovo is finally able to find a job and though he does have some friends (such as a painter called Dr. Okocha, Keme, the journalist, and Okoro, a veteran of the Nigerian civil war) he becomes a lonely and sad person who finds solace only in painting and in the company of his lover-cum-friend Ifeyinwa, a married neighbour. Omovo and Ifeyinwa become attracted to each other because of some similar qualities (they are both sensitive, introverted, impressionable, intelligent, and great lovers of both literature and the visual arts), and also because they both feel trapped in a morally corrupt and physically degrading environment. Ifeyinwa

has been forced into a life of misery because she was pushed into a loveless marriage after her father's suicide.

In scenes that clearly echo Ayi Kwei Armah's *The Beautyful Ones Are Not Yet Born* (on both the literal and symbolic levels), Okri shows how Omovo becomes more and more aware of the extensive malaise that pervades his society. But, unlike Armah's anonymous protagonist, who merely drifts aimlessly and helplessly in a sea of corruption, Omovo thinks that not only can he see through the wholly materialistic nature of the society, but that he can even depict the dirty quality of the corrupt society on canvas. He increasingly learns, however, that for his actions to be more meaningful he has to do more than merely express a symbolic disgust with corruption. Thus, by the end of *The Landscapes Within* Omovo, who is often depicted as passive, nearly always given to reverie, has become capable of making down-to-earth assessments of events around him and able to act accordingly. After a series of terrible, even tragic, events (for example, he is forced to resign from his job because he dares display some modicum of integrity; Ifeyinwa, while trying to escape from her brutal husband, is senselessly killed in an insane war between her village and a neighbouring village), the protagonist finally sees the need to forge a new vision of reality. Inspired by a poem written by his brother, Okur, Omovo suggests (albeit implicitly) that it is not enough for him as an artist to be merely cognizant of the filth around him; he should be ready to act. Such, in bare outline, is the plot of *The Landscapes Within*.

As I mentioned earlier, there are some hints of influences of Joyce's *Portrait of the Artist as a Young Man* on this novel: we see this not only in the choice of the young artist as hero but also in several other distinct ways. For example, one of the quotations Okri uses to preface the text is Stephen Dedalus' aspiration at the end of *A Portrait* to "go encounter for the millionth time the reality of experience and to forge in the smithy of my soul the uncreated conscience of my race." This quotation is important because, just as Stephen uses it to express the belief that for him to survive as an artist he has to free himself from the shackles of church, family, and country, so does Okri use it as a way of foreshadowing the end of *The Landscapes Within* where Omovo will suggest that for him to survive as an artist he needs to have a more realistic and less fanciful approach to things and events around him. The episodic narrative and the solitary nature of the hero also recalls Joyce's method of narration and portrayal of the hero in *A Portrait*.

All this is not to suggest that *The Landscapes Within* is a mere transplant of Joyce's text into an African environment. On the contrary, we can say that one of the hallmarks of Okri's writing is the way he uses and goes beyond a mosaic of literary sources to create his own masterpiece. One of the most literary of African novelists, Okri shows familiarity not only with Joyce but, perhaps more significantly, other African writers such as Achebe, Armah, Ngugi, Ousmane, and Soyinka. But, together with Joyce's *Portrait,* Armah's *The Beautyful Ones Are Not Yet Born* seems to be the most important literary influence on *The Landscapes Within*. It is, in fact, when we compare

Armah's description of the man with Okri's portrayal of Omovo that the latter's process of personal development becomes clear; hence a comparison allows us to see not only the apprenticeship qualities of *The Landscapes Within,* but also the hero's potential for contributing to the cultural development of his society. It is thus appropriate to summarize Armah's characterization of the man.

The man is depicted as a character who has absolute integrity and is definitely beyond reproach in a society crowded with moral degenerates. Exposed to humiliation and ridicule by his mother-in-law and quiet but pointed indictment by his wife and children, he refuses to be caught in the web of corruption that seems to embrace almost everyone in the novel. It is also manifest, however, that despite his high ideals the man is too weak to be a real hero. Though he tries to rise above the corruption (physical and moral) that evidently surrounds him, he neither seeks to understand its nature nor actually to fight against it. The scene on board the bus where the conductor, who has given the man and other passengers short change, imagines that he has been caught by the man, can be seen as a microcosmic representation of Armah's portrayal of his leading character. The conductor, fearing that he has been caught and will thus be exposed by the man "whose pair of wide-open staring eyes met his," attempts to bribe the man before he discovers that the man had actually been sleeping. Adopting a very serious and self-righteous pose, the conductor wakens the man, showers him with invective, and finally kicks him out of the bus.

The importance of this episode lies in the way it illustrates how a lack of positive action by decent people such as the man actually encourages corruption to continue. Certainly, the man is asleep for the greater part of this episode (and hence cannot do anything) but, as Eustace Palmer points out in *An Introduction to the African Novel,* the man's somnambulant behaviour in this scene is symptomatic of his overall lack of action in the entire novel. Although he is fully aware of the extent of the corruption in Ghanaian society, the man generally behaves as he unwittingly does in this scene. He literally and symbolically sleeps in the midst of moral decay. It is not surprising, therefore, that he does not show any sign of development in the course of Armah's novel.

Though Omovo resembles the man in many ways, he demonstrates by the end of *The Landscapes Within* that he has grown out of the sleepy and passive state that characterizes the man's behaviour. In other words, as in all novels dealing with personal growth and development, there is a movement from a state of passivity to one of action in Okri's novel. Like the man, Omovo demonstrates an ability to act for the greater part of the text. Even though he is very much aware of the putrefying nature of the society, he does nothing to stop the corruption and decay.

There are several ways in which Okri reveals Omovo's disgust with the corruption and decay around him and, like Armah, the Nigerian novelist takes full advantage of a central symbol—scum—to communicate his revulsion at the moral squalor in Lagos. Omovo's attention is constantly being drawn towards some scum or other and it is therefore quite in place that the scum ultimately becomes the outlet through which he thinks he can fight against or at least express his loathing for the corruption in society. Inspired by a greenish scum close to their house, Omovo initially makes a scum painting which he captions *Related Losses.* This picture is stolen, however, and he then decides to paint "a large vanishing scumscape—snot coloured." But this painting, labelled *Drift,* nearly gets him into serious trouble when he displays it at an art exhibition. He is harangued by a government official for being "a reactionary" who wants "to mock our independence . . . great progress . . . us."

It should be stressed, however, that though Omovo might seem to be taking a stand against corruption in such a scene, his action has been carefully planned or even thought out. The fact is that in spite of his own high ideals Omovo is initially too wrapped up in his own thoughts and too submissive seriously to oppose corruption at this stage. Several incidents can serve as illustrations of the protagonist's docility: in one instance Omovo is witness to a scene in which some children unnecessarily taunt and, in fact, beat up a small goat, apparently with the silent approval of some adults standing close by; he tries to stop the children but is soon cowed into silence and inactivity when one of the grown ups asks in a rather harmless manner "wetin" (what is it)? Like the man in *The Beautyful Ones,* Omovo is just too feeble to act. Thus even when Ifeyinwa's husband jealously and rashly destroys the painting Omovo had been making of Ifeyinwa, or when his portrait is illegally seized at the art exhibition, Okri's leading character does nothing but mutter a few words of protest. When he does try to act he imagines that he can use his painting to solve the world's problems:

> After his mother's death painting became a little world full of his bizarre feelings. Now it was something of a passion, a means to explore the deeper, more unconscious meanings and miasma of his life and the landscapes about him. His painting was a part of his response to life; a personal prism.

The novelist seems to be making the point, though, that Omovo is using his art as a means of escape and that he needs to show more conviction and develop a more realistic approach towards life problems if he really is to succeed in contributing to moral, cultural, social, and political changes.

But, in spite of Omovo's initial display of passivity, we notice that by the end of *The Landscapes Within* he starts showing the need for more positive action—thereby exhibiting some evidence of growth. We will look at two identical scenes from *The Beautyful Ones Are Not Yet Born* and *The Landscapes Within* respectively as illustrations of this assertion. The first focuses on the encounter in *The Beautyful Ones* between the timber merchant and the man at the man's place of work. When the merchant attempts to bribe the man for favoured space allocation (which the merchant has been doing successfully with the man's colleagues), the man, of course, refuses to accept the bribe but, as he himself admits, he does not even know the reason for his refusal to accept the money. Omovo, on the other hand, not only refuses to accept a bribe in the chemical company where he works, he decides to stand up against corruption before the end of the story. He, in fact, lets some of those who are involved in such corruption know what he thinks of them. After he is forced to resign, ostensibly for failing to appear at work for three days without sick leave (even though he has genuinely been ill), Omovo informs the cringing puppet of an office manager that he knows he is being fired because he demonstrates a rare quality in the office—moral rectitude:

> I can see right through your pretences at good office and public relations. You don't have to try further to make me frustrated. Yes, the company is accommodating, after all it is international and you are a very civilised man and very very clean—*a scum*. (emphasis added.)

It is from an episode such as this one that Omovo shows signs of beginning to comprehend that in such a society he has to do more than merely express an abhorrence for corruption on canvas; he realizes that he has to act. (One cannot imagine the man taking such a principled stand in a conscious manner.)

The protagonist also demonstrates an awareness of the need for action when he promises to read a short poem by his brother Okur (a poem which he says "holds a lot for me" to his friend Keme). Even before reading the poem Omovo mentions to Keme that his experiences have been teaching him (Omovo) something else: "It's about surviving, but it's more about becoming a life-artist." It is significant that Omovo should choose Okur's poem, which seems to stress the need for a more unromantic way of looking at the world as his final watchword. According to the persona in the poem, as a little boy, he used to roam down the beach looking for "bright pebbles" and "strange corals" but sometimes he also found other things "like half-defaced sketches on the sand / painting a way through the tormented seas." I think that Okri is implicitly suggesting that Omovo has now realized that he had previously been unable to confront some of life's problems because he had not been prepared for all its vicissitudes. Now, however, the protagonist knows that there are not only the bright spots which are represented by the "bright pebbles" and "strange corals" but also some rough terrain—symbolized in the poem by the "half-defaced sketches"—which might lead eventually to some good.

There is no doubt that Omovo's personal experiences contribute to this awareness but (in the true tradition of novels dealing with growth and development), it is also clear that there are certain other characters who are partially responsible for the young artist's growth. Dr. Okocha, the old painter, is obviously one such character. He is the one who provides the necessary motivation and encouragement for the young man to continue his painting and who also currently reminds Omovo about the need to face grim reality:

> You feel things too much. You have a truly broad vision. It is such visions that make great works. But they are no substitute for the real life. Omovo, I have known you for some time now. I like you. Try and live, try and act when you should. I don't know . . . It's always a duty to try and manifest whatever good visions we

have . . . In dreams begin responsibilities. An Indian poet said that.

It is Dr. Okocha who in the end is able to convince Omovo to face the truth, especially when nearly all seems lost to the young man. Omovo is psychologically shaken when (almost simultaneously) he learns of both his father's arrest and the death of his lover, Ifeyinwa. But, as usual, Dr. Okocha is around with a helping hand and he prods Omovo to adopt a more positive or even life-embracing approach to his calamities: "You going mad? Madness is a stupid escape, eh, it is a stupid escape. What is the matter with you?"

The journalist, Keme, is another of Omovo's friends who helps him on the road to progress. If Dr. Okocha is remarkable because of the way he lends psychological support to the protagonist, Keme deserves mention because of the manner in which he guides Omovo on the path towards moral and social responsibility. As a character who always shows concern for social justice and probity, he serves as a complement to Omovo and, indeed, as one of the moral positives in the text.

Because the didactic strain is never absent from novels in the *Bildungsroman* tradition, it seems totally in place for Okri to use certain other characters as symbols to portray and, ultimately, condemn corruption, hypocrisy, and other such vices in Lagos society. These characters include Omovo's father, their neighbour, Tuwo, Omovo's office manager, Mr. Akwu, and a host of others. Instead of offering guidance and leadership to his family, Omovo's father merely becomes a source of dissension and destruction. Also, Tuwo and Mr. Akwu are hypocrites; they practice the exact opposite of what they preach. For instance, Tuwo, while claiming to have Takpo's best interest at heart, tells Takpo that the latter's wife, Ifeyinwa, has been having an affair with Omovo—a story which not only leads to Omovo receiving a severe beating from thugs hired by Takpo but to Ifeyinwa's eventual death—when in actual fact Tuwo himself has been having an affair with Omovo's stepmother, Blackie. The same can be said of Mr. Akwu who, while engaged in the most blatant form of corruption and nepotism in the office, exhorts and harangues Omovo and others about hard and decent work for the company.

In proper apprenticeship manner, *The Landscapes Within* is replete with irony. Also, in conformity with the demands of a work dealing with national development, Okri uses several events and episodes to satirize the false values that seem not only to be the norm but actually serve as impediments to cultural development in that society. His description of the gathering at the art exhibition will serve as an example:

> . . . the whole place reverberated with ceaseless streams of murmurs, shouted conversations, steamed speeches, clinking glasses, throaty monologues, octaves of borrowed accents, screeching pretences and raging in the background, Walton's "Belshazzar's Feast." He [Omovo] felt lost amidst the dense clutter and crowding. Somewhere in the dead centre of the ceaseless collective clamour was a child scream-

ing. He pushed his way through fat women, spitting women, pretty women, tall bearded men, nondescript men, stammering men, sharp, neat university satellites; through stinging sweat smells, fresh perfumes, jaded aftershaves, mingled farts. Drinks were spilt, conversations grooved, textbook theories on the devirations of healthiness of modern African art were flung about like mind traps—and the child in the dead centre screamed even louder.

This passage, vaguely reminiscent of the opening of the writers' club exhibition in Achebe's *A Man of the People*, is not only representative of Okri's general style, it displays some of his most frequently used symbols. We are impressed, of course, by the way he uses language with economy to throw his ironic barbs at the foibles of Lagos high society—pretentious behaviour, ostentation, hypocrisy, and so forth—but what makes the description here and elsewhere even more salient is Okri's use of imagery and symbols. As on other occasions, there is the image of the scum (though not explicitly referred to as such in this scene) which is symbolic of the rotten nature of the society, and that of the individual who is entrapped by authorities or powers-that-be who just do not care—as we see in the way the child is completely ignored by adults who are indulging in the most banal of conversations. It is needless to emphasize that the child-adult relationship here is symbolic of the broad electorate-ruler relationship in the society at large. Okri also deserves praise for his suggestive use of language; taut and at the same time unpretentious, it often succeeds in conveying the right picture or image, a technique most appropriate for a novel about a painter:

> Dr. Okocha, as he was fondly called, was thickset like a wrestler. His face was strong and sweaty and his massive forehead was a deep dry brown. His small nose, snub and blunt, repeated the curves of his rather large, friendly lips. He was reminiscent of some crude bark-brown paintings of Igbo wrestlers. He had reddish-brown-white eyes that were piercing in their depths and over which were thick bushy eyebrows. His hair was thinning and had white straggling strands. A brown threadbare *agbada* covered his thickset frame and made him seem shorter than he really was.

Another virtue demonstrated in *The Landscapes Within* is a very fine handling of dialogue. In fact Okri's conscious use of a variety of languages gives this novel a particularly Lagosian flavour. The blending of pidgin (spiced at times with some Yoruba expressions) and different levels of English (including those deliberately borrowed from thrillers by James Hadley Chase) at strategically convenient positions is one method Okri uses successfully to develop his varied characters.

It is perhaps fitting to conclude this discussion of *The Landscapes Within* by looking at the novel within the context of the *künstlerroman* tradition. Had we not taken into account at least some of the conventions of this type of novel in our present study, it is probable that we would have been less sensitive to Okri's use of the genre's elements in both the shaping of his narrative and his very serious treatment of the theme of national and cultural de-

velopment. That, in turn, might have tempted one to read the text only as a quasi-political document. Genres exist to cue responses and, for reading a writer steeped in both the African and European literary traditions like Okri, it becomes even more imperative for the critic to be alert to certain generic pointers that might help give clearer meanings to the text.

Linda Grant on *The Famished Road*:

Far from being polemical, politics and magic are part of the everyday experience of [*The Famished Road* and] its characters. Okri's gift is to present a world view from inside a belief system. Here are people who have never heard of vacuums, for whom spaces are pregnant with beings which they think of as spirits. For influences one would look to Blake rather than Franz Fanon.

Linda Grant, in her "The Lonely Road from Twilight to Hard Sun," in The Observer, *27 October 1991.*

Neil Bissoondath   (review date 13 August 1989)

SOURCE: "Rage and Sadness in Nigeria," in *The New York Times Book Review,* August 13, 1989, p. 12.

[*Bissoondath is an Trinidadian-born short story writer and novelist. In the following review, he offers a highly favorable assessment of* Stars of the New Curfew, *praising the volume's universal relevance.*]

"That afternoon three soldiers came to the village. They scattered the goats and chickens. They went to the palm-frond bar and ordered a calabash of palm-wine. They drank amidst the flies."

This first paragraph of the first story—**"In the Shadow of War"**—in Ben Okri's collection *Stars of the New Curfew* beautifully illustrates the power of his writing. The language is simple, the details striking, the whole powerfully observed scene pulled together by the final sentence.

Mr. Okri, a Nigerian who lives in London, is a natural storyteller, to the point where these stories if read aloud would acquire yet another dimension, and possibly their greatest effect. With rare exceptions, he maintains this quality of narrative focus throughout.

"In the City of Red Dust," a relentless tale of exploitation and degradation, is probably the most effective story. Men make their way through their surreal and chilling lives by selling their own blood, by picking pockets, by drinking themselves into a stupor. A woman once the victim of a rape by soldiers escapes another by slitting her own throat. The governor preens, soldiers parade, jet fighters swoop overhead in a display of agile omnipotence. It is a frightening picture of urban life in Nigeria in recent times, and one full of political commentary.

The title story, **"Stars of the New Curfew,"** which tells of a virtual civil war in "the town of W.," is also hauntingly effective, evoking the fear of nothingness, fantasies of flight, the rot of politics. Here, as in other stories, Mr. Okri shrinks from nothing, offering sharp comments on a variety of issues.

On the future: "The town of W. revolves, amongst its youths, around dreams of escape. Everyone is stretched between being a nobody and going to America." On politics: "I felt up to my neck with our powerful people, our politicians, our governors, who had their cults as a way of maintaining and spreading their influence. I was tired of those who create our realities and who encircle themselves with dread." On music: "It occurred to him that when chaos is the god of an era, clamorous music is the deity's chief instrument."

These comments are built upon rage and sadness finely sieved through an admirable artistic sensibility. And they are truths, offered without romanticism or apology, that apply not just to the town of W., not just to Nigeria, but to much of what, for want of a better term, we call the third world. In *Stars of the New Curfew,* Mr. Okri, who is the author of two novels and another collection of stories that have not been published here, and a former poetry editor of *West Africa* magazine, has fashioned tales that resonate well beyond their immediate settings, striking chords of recognition in anyone with more than a nodding acquaintance with underdeveloped countries.

His talent fails him only when his imagination gets ahead of him, as in **"What the Tapster Saw,"** a tale of life after death in which the fantastical strides beyond the wondrous into the chaotic. There the details are overwhelming and, ultimately, pointless. But—interestingly enough, the only story in *Stars of the New Curfew* that is devoid of social observation—it is the sole disappointment in an otherwise striking collection.

Maria Thomas   (review date 24 September 1989)

SOURCE: "The Forest in the City," in *Los Angeles Times Book Review,* September 24, 1989, pp. 3, 13.

[*The pseudonym of the late Roberta Warrick, Thomas was best known for her fiction and nonfiction writings about Africa, where she spent numerous years working for the Peace Corps. In the following favorable review, Thomas lauds Okri's use of detail, his blending of realism and surrealism, and his focus on West African life in* Stars of the New Curfew.]

Ben Okri is Nigerian. His collection of six stories, *Stars of the New Curfew,* is made of Nigeria—heat, rain, car crashes, tyrants, millionaires, raw sewage, zinc huts, soldiers, rubbish mounds, palm wine, ghosts, music, forests. This is not an Africa of travel writers of journalist-fiction: It's an Africa of its own myths, thronged and bewitched.

In style and imagery Okri follows closely in the footsteps of Amos Tutuola, a strange and amazing writer from Nigeria who emerged in the late '50s, totally unfamiliar with Western culture, whose English was the simple and relentless language of incantation but whose imagination was wild and supercharged, a devastating formula.

Tutuola wandered in fabulous territories of mind where metamorphosis was a way of life and the land of the dead and its secrets was as immediate as the next tree or the other side of the river.

Okri is an updated Tutuola, his stories moved from the bush to the teeming slums of urban Nigeria. Here life is described as loss—loss of jobs, loss of power, loss of sleep, loss of blood—and loss is the force moving men back to and through their worst nightmares and turmoils. Readers may wonder how to translate these dense allegories but will recognize where they are if there's anything in what Jung said about common dream pools or in what Kafka told us about men living in mad worlds programmed by unknown forces, obeying unintelligible laws.

The stories proceed as journeys, sometimes from only one side of the town to the other, but always crossing dark uncharted territories. Forest impinges no matter where, a clash reminding us that imported overlays in Africa are as thin as the covering cloth on a radio-made fetish in the first pages of the book. In Okri's forests, characteristic of West African myth and fable, event and image have equal value, merge with intensity. The protagonist is witness and chronicler.

Okri's skill is in taking the reader steady on, step by step as in matters of fact, a way of grounding the most bizarre tales. We are told of men who are arrested as accomplices to their own robberies, of cars that drive in the air over rain, of earth that bites like insects, of towns where everything is upside down and backwards, of winged people who come out of trees. Typified by the palm-wine tapster of the last story, Okri's heroes are not so much personalities as they are forms of consciousness, thrown into regions where the outside world and the inner mate with unchecked energy in a waking dream. It reminds me of journeying in some far reaches of Eastern Nigeria, watching between terror and seduction as masked dancers dropped from trees like giant fruits or birds, bristling and shouting.

These stories ought to be read slowly, carefully, or the passages of Okri's heroes may seem monotonous, like an endless LSD trip or the DTs, in which the faceless men go from one ghastly vision to the next—cups that drip blood, bodies eaten by ringworm. Not so; Okri's imagination yields bounty.

In Okri's Nigeria life is described as loss—loss of jobs, loss of power, loss of sleep, loss of blood—and loss is the force moving men back to and through their worst nightmares and turmoils.

—*Maria Thomas*

In one wonderful episode, fish are absorbed into the sky and rain down, apocalypse style, on a city similar to Port Harcourt—oil corrupted and boasting two monstrous millionaires who, like overblown tyrants from Latin-

American fictions, stage a contest that in North America is known as "potlatch" and in Lagos is known as "declaring surplus"; that is, seeing who can throw around the most money in the fastest, most elaborate way. One millionaire has it chilled in a fridge. The other drops it from a helicopter. A joke of course: After crowds have fought a life-and-death battle for it, the ink washes off the bogus currencies in the rain, a perfect metaphor for all the vanities exposed here.

The humor is black, as it were, but Okri can be hilarious if you have the eye for it. In the title story, **"Stars of the New Curfew,"** the protagonist sells quack medicine which in fact causes disease, a central image of inversions that make real life as hallucinated as nightmare and nightmare as traumatized as real life. The impulse is surreal, not limited to describing Africa, but the quack-medicine career culminates in a sublimely Nigerian moment when his boss comes up with a big money maker, the drug for all things, POWER DRUG. Adventures with it begin on a packed bus. While a Rastafarian in fake dreads is declaiming for Jah and Africa, the salesman makes his pitch. Soon everyone is stoned on POWER DRUG, including the driver who crashes into a lagoon green with raw sewage as pickpockets squeeze money out of the commuters. This is Lagos, as real as it can possibly be.

In **"When the Lights Return"** a singer, Ede, crosses Lagos darkened by a power failure to retrieve his love from the land of the dead. It is the most sadly haunting of the stories, the figure of Ede's woman, Maria, always luminous and rising, appearing where she shouldn't be and in other forms, like life cycles of a butterfly. The city has been waiting for him, holding the woman's face before him as a lure, preparing its images of violence and redemption. We see an eerie bonfire as people burn away mountains of trash, a prophetess decrying vanity and the government, beggars covered with diseases, stunned silent crowds at intersections, traditional musicians playing sorrowful songs of the past, a corpse rising from ashes calling for revolt. All these things and more are catalogued with an increasing sense of archetype or shape to make you absorb the visions or be absorbed by them, in the same way you look at birds (if you look at birds) and know at a glance this one's a raptor, a hornbill, a finch, a shrike without any words having to pass over your brain.

We know well before Okri gives away the secret that we're reading about Orpheus and Eurydice and that the ending will be double edged. The hero is beaten to death by a crowd, mistaken for a thief, just as he receives word that the woman is lost.

But after the deaths, in a quiet way, "deep in the marketplace, amid all the cacophony, a woman sang in a voice of agonized sweetness" in counterpoint to clamorous music from the record shops. The lights have come on. Couples have made up their quarrels with each other. The sound of frogs croaking in the marshland is heard. All as if in preparation, perhaps for a new era, Okri seems to hope, in which chaos will no longer be the god.

Hopefulness does not grow easily in stories like these. It has to be coaxed, tacked on like the final paragraph (or even the title) of **"When the Lights Return."** Or like the Rastaman shouting "Africa! We counting on yuh!," an odd refrain to such songs of terror. But hope there is because you come from these stories with a sense of an underlying vitality that will not be destroyed.

Joe Wood (review date October 1989)

SOURCE: A review of *Stars of the New Curfew*, in *VLS*, No. 79, October, 1989, p. 8.

[*In the following review, Wood discusses Okri's use of language and thematic focus in the short story collection* Stars of the New Curfew.]

Once, when traveling in Africa, I asked a friend whether he ever confused the languages he knew. "Do you sometimes, for instance, find yourself speaking English when you're thinking Twi?" No, he said: "Languages to me are clothes, and I'm a natty dresser wherever I go."

Ben Okri sports his languages, too. Born in Nigeria, Okri lives and writes in London, the dying heart of Nigeria's erstwhile oppressor. *Stars of the New Curfew,* his second collection of short stories, measures the remains left behind by colonials—and the decay administered by their African inheritors—in a distinctly African-English idiom, a choice combination of Nigerian and European styles, politics, and myths. The elements never clash, but they don't pack a serious wallop either—though if the reader were Nigerian-English instead of Afro-American, the concert of voices might feel richer than it does.

Sleep plays a central role in *Stars:* the book's eyes, Nigeria's citizens, tour epic-style among the dreams and nightmares that roam and rule ruined Nigeria. Having risen from British colonialism, Okri's Nigeria finds itself overwhelmed by rot—in its leaders, in its streets, in the exasperation of its people. "First they shat on us," one character observes, "now we shit on ourselves." Through **"In the City of Red Dust,"** Okri follows two impoverished men, Emokhai and Marjomi, as they sell pints of their blood to pay for food, and for the beers that feed their dreams, while out in the town's plaza the local potentate erects pricey images of himself. In **"Stars of the New Curfew,"** a quack drug salesman tries to run away from the physical and psychological nightmares his medicines give him and his clientele, financing his escape with the profits of false pretenses:

> When I left the office I thought about what it meant to go back to the molues overcrowded with screaming children and traders. I had to choose. The blank or the authentic. Then, slowly, I began to tease out an understanding of my nightmares. I had to choose if I wanted to be on the block or a buyer, to be protected by power or to be naked, to laugh or to weep. There are few consolations for an honest man, and no one is really sure if this isn't the only chance a poor man has on this planet. I am ashamed to admit it, but I hate suffering. So, resigned to the lengthening curfews, to the lights blinking out in small firmaments, I chose to accept my old job. For a while I took batches of the new POWER-

DRUG and made my speeches on buses, by the roadsides, but without my former conviction.

When the new inadequacies of the drug began to manifest themselves again I changed my mind. My boss began to contemplate making medicines to cure the problems that POWER-DRUG created. Where will it end: Like most of our leaders, he creates a problem, then creates another problem to deal with the first one—on and on, endlessly fertile, always creatively spiralling to greater chaos. But it was when I discovered that my boss didn't really use the medicines he manufactured, and after I had saved up enough money, that I decided to quit and attempt to start up my own business.

Okri clearly finds little to his satisfaction in Nigeria, apart from the characters he sympathetically draws, and the hope his characters represent. Less clear are the sources of Okri's references: Readers may get impatient hacking through the unfamiliar mythic fantasies of, for instance, "When the Lights Return," in which Okri puts the Orpheus/Eurydice myth to work with Afro-twists that make Camus's "Black Orpheus" look pale, and easy, by comparison. Okri's contortions are seriously tricky, as in "What the Tapster Saw":

> And then one day, fired by memories of ancient heroes, he pursued a course in the borehole. In the strange environment he saw the multi-coloured snake twisted round a soapstone image. He saw alligators in a lake of bubbling green water. He saw an old man who had died in a sitting position while reading a bible upside-down. Everything seemed on fire, but there was no smoke. Thick slimes of oil seeped down the walls. Roseate flames burned everywhere without consuming anything. He heard a noise behind him. He turned and a creature forced a plate containing a messy substance of food into his hands. . . . While the tapster ate the snake slid over and began to tell him bad jokes. The snake told him stories of how they hang black men in quiet western towns across the great seas, and of how it was possible to strip the skin off a baby without it uttering a sound.

Most readers will sense *Stars'* mythic resonance, hear its poetic fun, and even get some of both. They will also be tempted to ask, to whom is Okri telling these stories? And whom is he trying to impress? The answer, it seems, is Nigerians on both counts. Check it out: Brother Okri's rearranging the clothes in his closet—and letting the rest of us watch.

Nadežda Obradovic   (review date Autumn 1990)

SOURCE: A review of *Flowers and Shadows,* in *World Literature Today,* Vol. 64, No. 4, Autumn, 1990, p. 687.

[In the following review, Obradovic gives a brief plot summary of Flowers and Shadows.]

"Little flowers in the shadows that's what we all are. Nobody knows what the larger shadows will do to the flowers; nobody knows what the flowers will become," says the mother to Jeffia, the protagonist of Ben Okri's novel *Flow-*

ers and Shadows. The titular leitmotiv iterates through the entire book, in variants spoken by different characters, as an omnipresent scorching sun beats down upon them all and surveys their actions.

Jeffia, an eighteen-year-old boy, suddenly starts noticing things about himself, as if the hushed, smooth life of his big home with its well-kept gardens, nicely furnished and air-conditioned rooms, servants, three cars, and other luxuries of well-to-do Nigerian society had ceased to exist. He is faced with the squalor of his surroundings, the filthy roads full of beggars and hungry people, the corrupt police, and suspicions about his father's integrity. The death of his best friend aggravates the situation even further and deepens his insight.

Parallel with his discovery of his father's various machinations and shady transactions, the latter's downfall begins: he is tricked in several deals, is culpably implicated in his partner's death, loses the company, and finally meets his death in a car accident. Life changes drastically for Jeffia and his beloved mother as a consequence, as he must give up hope of higher education in order to provide for day-to-day life. In the long run, with the help of his girlfriend (a hospital nurse), Jeffia achieves a certain mental balance and peace of mind and is able to envision calm and even happy days for his mother and himself. He learns how he, the flower, can emerge at last from his father's shadow.

Ben Okri was nineteen when he wrote *Flowers and Shadows,* and the acclaim it received was confirmed by the success of his second, *The Landscapes Within* (1981). The short-story collections *Incidents at the Shrine* (1986) and *Stars of the New Curfew* (1989) offered further proof of his gifts. Okri has served as poetry editor of *West Africa* and in 1987 received the Commonwealth Writers Prize for Africa and the Aga Khan Prize for Fiction, sponsored by the *Paris Review*.

Okri on writing about Nigeria:

[If] my characters are going to be set in Nigeria and I am going to write about them truthfully, I've got several different options. First, I've got the option of naturalism, which means I write about them from the viewpoint that only what I see is what exists. Secondly, I have got the mythic dimension, which is a very important part of our world view. It's not separable from anything else. Third, I've got all the different dimensions of our world view plus naturalism. So what seems like surrealism or fantastic writing actually is not fantastic writing, it's simply writing about the place in the tone and the spirit of the place. I'm not trying in the slightest to produce any strange effects. All I'm trying to do is write about the world from the world view of that place so that it is true to the characters.

Ben Okri, in an interview in Contemporary Authors, *Vol. 138, Gale Research, 1993.*

Giles Foden   (review date 17 April 1992)

SOURCE: "Speaking for Africa," in *The Times Literary Supplement,* No. 4646, April 17, 1992, p. 8.

[*In the following review, Foden presents a mixed assessment of* An African Elegy, *questioning the collection's relevance for non-Africans since "every poem contains an exhortation to climb out of the African miasma."*]

In an essay in the *Guardian* in August 1990, Ben Okri wrote of how the suffering of the oppressed could make them farmers of their dreams. "Their harvest could make the world more just and more beautiful. It is only the oppressed who have this sort of difficult and paradoxical responsibility." Dreams are the currency of Okri's writing, particularly in this first book of poems, *An African Elegy,* but also in his books of short stories and Booker Prize-winning novel *The Famished Road*.

Okri's dreams are made on the stuff of Africa's colossal economic and political problems, and reading the poems is to experience a constant succession of metaphors of resolution, in both senses of the word. Virtually every poem contains an exhortation to climb out of the African miasma, and virtually every poem harvests the dream of itself with an upbeat, restorative ending.

But these are not the poems of a placard-carrier, nor of an escapist. As Okri documents the slum-life of Lagos, the dusty tropical lassitude of a sleepy country town or the lonely life of the African exile in London, the (sometimes wearing) zest of his surrealistic imagery is tempered by an acute observation of physical detail. Invocations and incantations, drawing on everything from African myth to Western sci-fi, his poems present a phantasmagoric series of apocalyptic images. Though some spring from urban dereliction (Eliot's unreal city doubly unreal under the African sun), most are agricultural in spirit, intimately connected with the idea of organic putrescence and the spoilt harvest. They work as allegories for the failure of development:

> The yam-tubers bleed our sorrows.
> Crows in the field
> scream of despair.
> Machetes pollute our food
> with rust.
> The masters conduct their
> plunderings
> with quiet murders:
> The victims perform maypole dances
> around the village shrines

or:

> Who can rouse the memories
> Of dead animals
> Rotting in the fields
> And the drops of bad milk dripping
> Into the mouths
> Of ghost-ridden children?
> Harmattan grips the lights.
> The sound of thunder stirs recollections:
> Cataclysms forefelt blow over our bodies.

Authenticity shines out of these poems in the way it does from the work of some East European and Russian poets, and there is little of the sleight-of-hand and evasive irony of much British poetry. Of course, sleight-of-hand and evasive irony can be part of an authentic vision, but Okri's is an authenticity of voice, not naïve but not studied either. Sometimes the voice is unconvincing, though. For example, when he asks, "Is there a searing clarity / about the noises / rising daily / from this riverbed we call our own?" one feels like saying, well, you should know, if clarity is the right word.

Another question is, who is Okri addressing when he says "we call our own"? Nearly all the poems in *An African Elegy* are in the first person plural, and the reader usually feels he is listening to Okri speak for Africa in this mode, an option more or less closed now to a Western poetic tradition beset by worries about coherence and universality. But what of those readers (such as myself) neither from Africa nor products of its diaspora? As readers they are drawn into the poem's collective, wondering whether to universalize the subject or attribute a difference. This "we" problem caused a keen cultural disjuncture when Okri read out the unashamedly lyrical title poem at the Booker presentation:

> We are the miracle that God made
> To taste the bitter fruits of Time.
> We are precious.
> And one day our suffering
> Will turn into the wonders of the earth.

This had some squirming in their seats. It certainly made me feel uncomfortable, sitting watching the ceremony at home. And, reading it now, I still don't feel like a miracle that God made to taste etc, and the poem can only seem embarrassing.

Nicolas Tredell   (review date 25 June 1992)

SOURCE: "Uncertainties of the Poet," in *London Review of Books,* Vol. 14, No. 12, June 25, 1992, pp. 22-3.

[*In the excerpt below, Tredell argues that the poems collected in* An African Elegy *are better suited for public oration than the printed page.*]

Violence, and the resistance to it, are important themes in Ben Okri's *An African Elegy:* but his declamatory mode largely proscribes subtle registrations like those of [John] Burnside. Okri's greatest public exposure as a poet came on the 1991 Booker Prize night, when he read what is now the title poem of this collection; that public reading, indeed, prompted this volume's publication. But a poetry effective on the podium can seem doubtful on the printed page. Okri often deals with some of the most serious of public themes: above all, the sufferings and conflicts of the post-colonial world, whether 'post-colonial' is understood to apply to the formerly colonised countries or the old Imperial centres—in Okri's case, Africa and London. He makes much use of abstraction and personification, which are, as the 18th century recognised, right for public poetry: but, in a manner more like that of a certain kind of 19th-century Romanticism, that of Shelley and Swinburne, those abstractions and personifications tend to float loose from semantic and syntactic armatures. The result is a weak phantasmagoria, a vague simulacrum of England and Africa. Okri likes the sentence that runs on over short lines, sometimes no more than one word in length, but there seems little semantic or rhythmic justification for his breaking the lines where he does. He is fond of parallelism and repetition with variation, and this can produce some of his better effects—for example, the repetition of 'remember the history well' in **'On Edge of Time Future'**. But potentially powerful parallelisms falter because some of the parallel phrases are loosely filled out. This is not to charge Okri with a merely aesthetic slackness: it is a matter of a proper rhetoric for public poetry.

To criticise Okri in this way is, of course, to invoke the 'close reading' criteria implicit in the early work of [I. A.] Richards and [F. R.] Leavis, and these may seem inappropriate to a poetry that employs a different rhetorical strategy. But it is worth recalling that those criteria can be seen as, in part, a reaction against the inflation and abuse of public language in the First World War, not least in its public poetry. The insistence on linguistic precision was no mere pedantry, but sprang from a sense that loose language had potentially lethal consequences. That case was doubtless itself inflated, particularly when extended into the belief that good poetry and fiction could save us, but its more modest versions did have some truth. In the post-colonial world, a similar linguistic precision seems most important. There is now a vast range of post-colonial writing of remarkable subtlety—to take only some of the most prominent instances, there is the prose of Achebe and Selvon, and the poetry of Walcott or, closer to home, James Berry (Okri might also learn a thing or two from Grace Nichols). It may be that Okri wishes, as a poet and a novelist, to define himself against these older generations, but he is not yet a strong enough poet to spurn their lessons.

Henry Louis Gates, Jr.   (review date 28 June 1992)

SOURCE: "Between the Living and the Unborn," in *The New York Times Book Review,* June 28, 1992, pp. 3, 20.

[*Gates is an American educator, critic, editor, and nonfiction writer who frequently writes on race relations and culture in America. In the following review, he examines Okri's use of African lore and myth in* The Famished Road.]

Perhaps because of the literary authority it has earned, we can easily forget that the black African novel in English is (a few scattered anomalies aside) only some three decades old—as old, or as young, as African independence itself. This relationship isn't just a matter of parallel time lines, for many of the earliest of these novels were infused with the spirit—sometimes heady, sometimes rueful—of nation-building in a postcolonial era.

With the self-consciousness of an educated elite, the authors of such novels announced the arrival of a new burst of literary creativity. A generation of the formerly colonized would write themselves into being—but on their own terms, and as subjects rather than objects. Consider, for example, the sheer energy that Chinua Achebe's classic *Things Fall Apart*—the most widely read book in any genre by a black African—breathed into so-called Commonwealth literature when it was published in 1958, just before Nigerian independence. The relationship between nationhood and narrative voice in African literature seemed real, palpable and direct.

Despite the fact that the novel enjoyed the role of primogenitor among the genres of contemporary African literature, few authors have chosen to test the limits of the conventional "well made" realistic novel, a form inherited from Europe. Mr. Achebe's early fiction, in some respects an extended engagement with Conrad's *Heart of Darkness,* sought to rewrite the figure of the black in the English novel of Africa (as seen, for example, in the works of writers like Joyce Cary) by presenting in thick and telling detail the heretofore veiled universe of the Ibo people. In fact, it is only recently that his marvelous works have made their way out of anthropology syllabuses in American universities and onto the reading lists of the English departments. Ngugi wa Thiong'o, black Africa's other great Anglophone novelist, has used the form expansively to forge political allegories of important Kenyan historical events, such as the Mau Mau uprising, thus charting a vision of contemporary political liberation from one of Africa's most repressive regimes. (Mr. Ngugi, a native of Kenya, now teaches at Yale University, forced into exile by the Government of President Daniel arap Moi.)

Clearly, the major figures of modern African fiction in English have had other, evidently more pressing, tasks than wholesale formal experimentation. But in an era of literary innovation—and grievous political disillusionment—boundaries exist to be trespassed, conventions to be defied. So it should not be surprising that African novelists would eventually seek to combine Western literary antecedents with modes of narration informed by Africa's powerful tradition of oral and mythic narrative, much as the Nobel laureate Wole Soyinka has in the realm of drama. And such is the case with Ben Okri's third novel, *The Famished Road*.

It is the redoubtable accomplishment of this book (which won Britain's Booker Prize in 1991) to have forged a narrative that is both engagingly lyrical and intriguingly postmodern. And Mr. Okri has done so not merely, as we might expect, by adapting techniques of the magic realism associated with the great Latin American novelists (especially Gabriel García Márquez), but by returning to the themes and structures of traditional Yoruba mythology and the relatively little-known achievements of the Yoruba novel.

The Yoruba, one of the three dominant cultures in contemporary Nigeria, have a particularly lyrical and densely metaphorical tradition of oral literature. What is so curious about Mr. Okri's use of Yoruba mythology and narrative techniques is that he is not Yoruba himself, though he speaks the language fluently. Rather, he comes to this tradition largely through the plays and poems of Mr. Soyinka and the novels of D. O. Fagunwa, notably *Forest of a Thousand Daemons,* which Mr. Soyinka translated from the Yoruba. Indeed, the title of Mr. Okri's book is taken from Mr. Soyinka's poem "Death in the Dawn"—"May you never walk / when the road waits, famished." The metaphor of the road is a central image in Mr. Soyinka's tragedies, seen as a place of both death and possibility. Mr. Okri's sense of the Yoruba tradition, then, is derived from his reading of its literature and was not simply gained (as some anthropologists still fancy about "third world" authors) at his mother's knee.

Ben Okri is a member of the Urhobo people, from the delta region of Nigeria. He published his first novel, *Flowers and Shadows,* in 1980, at the age of 21. His second novel, *The Landscapes Within,* appeared two years later. A collection of short stories, *Incidents at the Shrine,* which deals with the Nigerian civil war, won the Commonwealth Prize for Africa in 1987.

Even in his second novel, Mr. Okri was less concerned with the mechanics of plot than with the consciousness of his protagonist, who is presented amid the chaos and despair of post-civil-war Nigeria. While his latest novel, *The Famished Road,* does not abandon linear narrative completely, its organization turns on the keen perceptions of its narrator, Azaro (a shortened version of Lazaro, or Lazarus), a being known as an *abiku,* one who lives in the limited realm between the worlds of the living and the unborn, with one foot in each. His struggles to escape his destiny to die in childhood and return to his *abiku* kinsmen are reflected in the episodic shape of this epic tale.

An *abiku,* Mr. Soyinka tells us in the first volume of his autobiography, is "a child which is born, dies, is born again and dies in a repetitive cycle." A traditional Yoruba proverb speaks of a "wanderer" child: "It is the same child who dies and returns again and again to plague the mother." As Mr. Soyinka puts it in his poem, "Abiku":

> Night and Abiku sucks the oil
> from lamps. Mothers! It'll be the
> Suppliant snake coiled on the doorstep
> Yours the killing cry.
>
> The ripest fruit was saddest;
> where I crept, the warmth was cloying.
> In silence of webs, Abiku moans, shaping
> Mounds from the yolk.

One can scarcely imagine a more suitable metaphor for the frustrated hopes of African independence and democracy.

The Famished Road's publication may well prove as significant for the evolution of the post-modern African novel as Chinua Achebe's *Things Fall Apart* was for the beginning of the tradition itself, or as Gabriel García Márquez's *One Hundred Years of Solitude* was for the novel in Latin America.

—*Henry Louis Gates, Jr.*

Thus drawing on a subgenre that we can think of as the fantastic, Mr. Okri sketches Africa's perilous quest to free

itself from the cyclical enslavement of colonial and post-colonial forms of oppression. In his hands, the enigmatic, mythical figure of the *abiku* sustains enormous thematic and narrative freight, as we follow the progress of a being who wishes to break his destined cycle of death and rebirth:

> I was a spirit-child rebelling against the spirits, wanting to live the earth's life and contradictions. Ade wanted to leave, to become a spirit again, free in the captivity of freedom. I wanted the liberty of limitations, to have to find or create new roads from this one which is so hungry, this road of our refusal to be. I was not necessarily the stronger one; it may be easier to live with the earth's boundaries than to be free in infinity.

In this cosmogony, all that separates the realm of existence from that of death is the will, so that even beyond the very real political and social dimensions of Mr. Okri's work, the novel is a study of the strength of being and the mythic power of death, which are also the central concerns of Wole Soyinka's works.

As Mr. Okri explores these themes, he also presents us with Azaro's misadventures, both in a luminously rendered spirit world, ever present at his elbow, and in the "real" world of his second sight:

> I was falling in love with life and the four-headed spirit had chosen the best moment to dance with me, turning and twisting me through strange spaces, making me dance my way out of the world of the living. . . . The four-headed spirit led me in a dance through the desert, holding me in an iron grip. The harder I fought the tougher the grip became, till my arms turned blue. He danced me through the desert winds, which concealed the forms of master spirits and powerful beings who borrowed the sandstorms to clothe their nakedness; through the striated sands, over the vast desert worms, through the mirage cities in which the liquid apparitions of air concealed cities throbbing in rich bazaars and marketplaces and dens of hallucinations; he danced me through the mirage cities where tall women had breasts of glass and beautiful women had the phosphorescent tails of cats, over the wells, past the oasis where obscure figures turned silver into water, through the streets of the elite quarters where people cried out for love, past the slave alleys where innumerable souls had written their names on the walls with their flesh.

Abundant scenes like this overlap with Azaro's father's fantasies of escaping desperate poverty through a return to the sport of boxing, in which he was once known as Black Tyger. Set in the years just before Nigerian independence, his epic street battle with a legendary adversary called the Green Leopard takes place against a backdrop of political conflict, as the Party of the Rich and the Party of the Poor compete for the hearts and minds and blind loyalty of the would-be citizens of a free and democratic nation.

Plot structure may not be this lengthy novel's main concern, but the fine art of storytelling certainly is. *The Famished Road* succeeds magnificently in telling a story heretofore untold in English, and it does so in a bold and brilliant new way. The book's publication may well prove as significant for the evolution of the postmodern African novel as Mr. Achebe's was for the beginning of the tradition itself, or as *One Hundred Years of Solitude* was for the novel in Latin America. Comparisons with Mr. García Márquez's magic realism will no doubt be made by Western reviewers, but Mr. Okri's magical sense of reality stems primarily from Yoruba sources. (Mr. García Márquez, incidentally, has cited a visit to Angola as pivotal to his own development of this mode.)

The novel's elusive, lyrical beauty is marred only by a tendency, at its very end, to *name* the terms of its allegory, to tell readers where we've been, as the author betrays an unwillingness to trust the uninitiated to understand his message:

> The spirit-child is an unwilling adventurer into chaos and sunlight, into the dreams of the living and the dead. Things that are not ready, not willing to be born or to become, things for which adequate preparations have not been made to sustain their momentous births, things that are not resolved, things bound up with failure and with fear of being, they all keep recurring, keep coming back, and in themselves partake of the spirit-child's condition. They keep coming and going till their time is right. History itself fully demonstrates how things of the world partake of the condition of the spirit-child. . . .
>
> It shocked him that ours too was an abiku nation, a spirit-child nation, one that keeps being reborn and after each birth come blood and betrayals, and the child of our will refuses to stay till we have made propitious sacrifice and displayed our serious intent to bear the weight of a unique destiny.

Fortunately, these lapses toward the literal fail to diminish the power of *The Famished Road* or its importance for African—indeed, for contemporary—fiction. Ben Okri, by plumbing the depths of Yoruba mythology, has created a political fable about the crisis of democracy in Africa and throughout the modern world. More than that, however, he has ushered the African novel into its own post-modern era through a compelling extension of traditional oral forms that uncover the future in the past. But while *The Famished Road* may signal a new achievement for the African novel in English, it would be a dazzling achievement for any writer in any language.

K. Anthony Appiah (review date 3-10 August 1992)

SOURCE: "'Spiritual Realism,'" in *The Nation*, New York, Vol. 255, No. 4, August 3-10, 1992, pp. 146-48.

[*An English-born educator, editor, novelist, and critic, Appiah specializes in African studies. In the following review, he discusses the plot, characters, and stylistic features of* The Famished Road, *noting, in particular, Okri's focus on the spiritual world.*]

Ben Okri's *The Famished Road* is nothing if not audacious. It is 500 pages with only the barest semblance of a plot; a postmodern *Thousand and One Nights,* with a boy Scheherazade who refuses the ordinary courtesies of the realist narrator. In three sections, eight "books" and seventy-eight chapters, through episode after episode, we follow the travails of Azaro, an *abiku,* or spirit-child—one who, according to a Nigerian tradition, is born and reborn, only to die in infancy and return to the joyful play of the spirit world.

And indeed, Azaro almost dies at the start of the life that begins in this book. As an infant he is very ill, spending "most of the time in the other world trying to reason with my spirit companions, trying to get them to leave me alone." Returning to his body one day from playing with these companions, he wakens in a coffin, weeping fiercely in the hubbub of his own funeral: His parents have given him up for dead. From then on, his mother calls him not Lazaro, as she and her husband had named him, but Azaro, wanting to avoid the echo of the tale of Lazarus.

Sometimes an *abiku* can be coaxed into staying in the flesh, however, and Azaro is one such. He decides to cease his coming and going, but instead of settling on one explanation, he tells us: "I sometimes think it was a face that made me want to stay. I wanted to make happy the bruised face of the woman who would become my mother." This bruised face is that of a working woman in the slums of an African city around the time of independence. "Mum," as the narrator calls her, adds a meager sum to her husband's equally meager earnings as a porter by trading commodities from a small tray in the market. Theirs are lives of backbreaking labor, of exploitation by the landlord, of oppression by the thugs who serve the politicians and the rich, and of diseases of body and spirit fated by the inscrutable wills of spirits and ancestors. And yet, in the midst of squalor, as the rain pours in through their roof, as the rats squabble in their closet and the little money they have is siphoned off for the barest necessities, they manage to celebrate the small triumphs of their lives and to grow in dignity.

Azaro's "Dad" discovers partway through the book a vocation in boxing. His triumphs over human and spirit adversaries leave him richer (from his bets) but always near to death. In her struggles to bring him back, Azaro's mother must sometimes follow her husband into the world of spirits in her dreams. The love of these two people for each other and for their son, in a world where all the odds are stacked against them, is beautifully—and, one might add, unsentimentally—realized.

Aside from Azaro and his "Mum" and "Dad," the central characters are few. The most fantastic is Madame Koto, proprietor of a "chop bar" where palm wine and pepper soup and a good time are available at all hours. Madame Koto is enormous. She is also a witch. As she grows in spiritual potency (from her dark dealings with the other world) and in temporal power (from her equally depraved dealings with the new political order of the Party of the Rich), her corruption is manifested in her increasing volume, in her distended foot, in her swelling belly (swollen, as we finally discover, with three *abiku* children, so that her fertility is in vain). With electricity, arranged by Madame Koto's political cronies for her alone among all in the ghetto, come the prostitutes and the political thugs; with the fetish pinned over her door come strange, many-headed invisible monsters, feeding off the energies of her corruption. Azaro returns daily from a school we never see to sit in her bar, able, with his spirit-child vision, to see the monstrous phantoms that inhabit it but are invisible to the more ordinary mortals who gather there.

And then there is the International Photographer (a typical half-jesting, half-boastful nickname from English-speaking West Africa), who gets into trouble photographing the antecedents and the consequences of a handout of free powdered milk, offered as a pre-election bribe to the people of Azaro's neighborhood by one of the new political parties. The handout causes a riot; the milk causes food poisoning; the photographs appear in the national newspapers; the International Photographer must go underground, disappearing and reappearing in the dark at Azaro's home.

Finally, looming, like these others, out of the shadowy mass of the denizens of the city and of the spirit world, there is Ade, another spirit-child, whom we meet three-quarters of the way through the book; another *abiku*, like Azaro, but one who, it seems, has decided not to stay. Ade is the character who finally speaks the allegory that the book has hinted at all along, the allegory in which, as he says, "Our country is an *abiku* country. Like the spirit-child, it keeps coming and going. One day it will decide to remain."

Okri's novel makes and breaks promises with mischievous abandon, so that though Ade's death is foreshadowed, it never quite happens. And this is only one of the ways in which he challenges us. It takes a while, for example, to get accustomed to the ease with which Azaro moves between this world and the other, traveling out of his body to the spirit world, in his dreams and in the daytime, or venturing into the forest to find many-headed spirit monsters. The narrative yokes the familiar and the miraculous in a language that is richly synaesthetic (every odor has a color, every feeling a smell) and in which the sinuous syntax repeatedly enfolds contradictions.

The result is an often densely figurative style. Once, for example, Azaro stumbles into a shrine dominated by "an ancient mother who had been turned into wood. . . . She gave off accumulated odours of libations, animal blood, kaolin, the irrepressible hopes of strangers, and a yellow impassivity." Zeugma is one of Okri's many rhetorical predilections; as here, where the giving off of odors is literal and the giving off of impassivity presumably figurative. But this coloring of emotions, the "yellow impassivity," is characteristic, too. And so is the strange list. (Two pages later we find: "the shapes of captors, the albumen of unbounded monsters, genies in murky bottles, homunculi in the nests of bats.") But it is the merging of the senses that strikes one above all: Once, a "blue wind whistled" in Madame Koto's bar, captured in these three words for the eye, the ear and the skin; once, when he returns from one of his midnight wanderings, Azaro's mother takes him home "under an arpeggio of watery stars." Until now work of this rhetorical complexity has largely been found in Africa in Francophone fiction such as Yambo

Ouologuem's *Bound to Violence* or Ahmadou Kourouma's *The Suns of Independence*. We have traveled a long distance from the spare prose of Chinua Achebe or the narrative thrust of Ngugi wa Thiong'o; we are far, too, from the naturalism of Buchi Emecheta. It will be interesting to see how this novel finds readers at home.

Since this is bravura writing, it is not surprising that sometimes in this lush excess one may feel that Okri has gone too far. And yet, we (here in the United States) are likely to forgive him, in part because, though he lives and writes in London, he has chosen to speak as an African writer (which, as someone born in Nigeria in 1959, he is surely entitled to do). This choice is part of what gains him the license *outside* Africa to invent—from the resources of Nigerian folklore and the English language and his own wide reading and ample imagination—a language and a universe of his own. The laudatory reviews this book received in Britain, where the novel won the 1991 Booker Prize, are being followed by raves here, many of which speak of "magical realism," explicitly connecting Okri with postcolonial Latin America, another place where Otherness has lowered our barriers to "disorders" of language and the imagination.

> If *The Famished Road* does not always succeed in its ambitions, they are high literary ambitions, higher than most in our day, and in the moments when they pay off, what you get is sheer magic.
>
> —*K. Anthony Appiah*

My own sense is that there is a difference between the ways in which Latin American writers draw on the supernatural and the way that Okri does: For Okri, in a curious way, the world of spirits is not metaphorical or imaginary; rather, it is more real than the world of the everyday. And so tales of that world have, like tales of our own, their own justification. What is exciting is the energy of this rendering of the reality of the spirit world (which does not, of course, require us to suppose that Okri is a "true believer") linked to, and sometimes in tension with, his exile's passion for the project of Nigerian national politics. Together the spiritual realism and the moral seriousness generate heat, light, fire. This is an energy that excuses much, but it also serves to generate what there is to excuse.

There is, for example, the matter of Okri's need, rooted in the moral seriousness, to draw attention to his messages, a fault whose effect is amplified by the author's apparent recognition that it is a failing. The matter of Azaro/Lazaro's name is typical. On the one hand, the child *is*—almost—named Lazarus. But this would be too crude an anticipation of his return from the dead; and so, on the other hand, we hear the name only once, before he becomes Azaro. Just so, Okri cannot resist decoding one level of his own allegory in the words of Ade, the spirit-child I quoted above. But he also knows that this is a crude gesture, and so it is briskly, almost furtively, done close to the end, when we have already figured it out for ourselves. (The tension between spiritual realism and moral vision shows itself here. The tale of the spirit world could surely be taken on its own terms, but is offered up as allegory in order to give it moral weight. One has the suspicion that this is, in part, a concession to readers who do not put much stock in spirits.)

And the spiritual realism, which gives the writer access to a world of almost unlimited powers, may also lead him sometimes into an irritatingly pseudomystical New Age mode. Thus, on one of his many journeys in the other world, Azaro asks the three-headed spirit that accompanies him: "Are we travelling this road to the end?"

> "Yes," the spirit said, walking as if distance meant nothing.
>
> "But you said the road has no end."
>
> "That's true," said the spirit.
>
> "How can it be true?"
>
> "From a certain point of view the universe appears to be composed of paradoxes. But everything resolves. That is the function of contradiction."
>
> "I don't understand."
>
> "When you see everything from every imaginable point of view you might begin to understand."
>
> "Can you?"
>
> "No."

It is a mark of Okri's fundamental good judgment that he undercuts such high-flown talk with other exchanges; but one has the feeling that the message is the medium a little too often. But then, this is a one-of-a-kind book, a rambling monster with the loose structure of epic, conducted, however, on the scale of a single human life. And it is, to return to my earliest point, brave in the extreme. If it does not always succeed in its ambitions, they are high literary ambitions, higher than most in our day, and in the many moments when they pay off, what you get is, well, sheer magic.

Tom Wilhelmus   **(review date Spring 1993)**

SOURCE: "Time and Distance," in *The Hudson Review*, Vol. XLVI, No. 1, Spring, 1993, pp. 247-52, 254-55.

[*In the following excerpt, Wilhelmus examines stylistic and thematic aspects of* The Famished Road.]

In *Thus Spoke Zarathustra*, the animals say to Nietzsche's philosopher-mystic:

> "Look, we know what you teach: that all things return forever, and we along with them, and that we have already been here an infinite number of times, and all things along with us."

According to Milan Kundera, this "mad myth" is Nietz-

sche's means of forcing us to contemplate the horror as well as the beauty and sublimity of life's events in a way which prevents our overlooking them because they are so fleeting. Without some such concept—that an event may return again and again to haunt us—"We would need take no more note of it than of a war between two African kingdoms in the fourteenth century, a war that altered nothing in the destiny of the world, even if a hundred thousand blacks perished in excruciating torment" (*The Unbearable Lightness of Being*). Repetition, recurrence, the myth of eternal return show the weight of history and create the awareness that life has significance and depth. In some fashion, this fact is illustrated in . . . [*The Famished Road*. It] is concerned with time, and [it] creates perspective and distance. [The novel] also deals with recurrence, without which time itself is only duration. . . .

[*The Famished Road* by Nigerian Ben Okri] won the Booker Prize in 1991. It is an unusual novel which could appeal to whatever politically correct feelings we are suffering from at the moment. For the first 250 unrelentingly paratactic pages, simple sentence followed simple sentence, scene followed simple scene, nothing connected, nothing was subordinated, and every experience seemed as important as every other. And I thought political correctness might well be the point. Moreover, the narrator jumped so freely from realistic passages depicting African village life into surrealist passages of fantasy and dream that to me they exhibited a blurred—and possibly primitive?—inability to separate fact from fiction. Yet I should have known: important works are not distinguished by how you read but how they require you to read them by their standards. And now I'm convinced that *The Famished Road* displays immense integrity in doing what it does.

Here, now, is what I think is going on. In Azaro, his child narrator, Okri has created a naive consciousness removed from prejudice and able to comment on events from a fresh and, presumably, natural point of view. Such devices are not new in literature (a similar narrator occurs in Grass's *The Tin Drum* as the dust jacket points out). And in this novel, the device allows us to experience the wonder Azaro discovers in his own childhood while observing for ourselves an all-too-familiar pattern of exploitation, industrialization, and environmental ruin that is encroaching on his family because of Africa's postcolonial history.

Similarly, Okri's use of the Yoruba myth of the *abiku* or spirit-child allows us to compare the family's present cruel circumstances to an ideal that lies beyond them. Azaro's (his name is short for "Lazarus") awareness that he is a spirit-child and only a temporary resident on the earth, who may return to his origins at any time if the real world proves too heartless, gives the novel much of its poignancy and motivation. "There was not one" among the *abiku*, says the opening, "who looked forward to being born." They disliked the "rigours of existence, the unfulfilled longings, the enshrined injustices of the world, the labyrinths of love, the ignorance of parents, the fact of dying, and the amazing indifference of the Living in the midst of simple beauties of the universe."

Much of the stylistic difficulty of the first half of the novel results from Okri's attempt to dramatize this gulf between the ideal and the real and from his desire to present Azaro's emerging consciousness alongside a community's emerging sense of modern social and political life. Ontogeny recapitulates phylogeny, and just as Azaro's attention swings from family to the road outside, from village to the surrounding forest, from reality to dream, the villagers also struggle to reconcile the present with the fetishistic past.

Such experiences are common to most emerging cultures and along with modernization a new dream, based on personal achievement, captures the village's interest. Thus, Azaro's father's improbable ambition to become first a boxer and then a politician constitutes an effort to defeat the existing political parties, at the time divided in self-interest and ignoring the needs of the poor: "He conjured an image of a country in which he was the invincible ruler and in which every citizen must be completely aware of what is going on in the world, be versed in tribal, national, continental, and international events, history, poetry, and science," and to aid him in his quest he demands Azaro must learn to read—philosophy, politics, anatomy, sciences, astrology, Chinese medicine, Greek and Roman classics, the Bible, the cabbala, the *Arabian Nights,* classical Spanish love poetry and retellings of the lives of Shaka the Zulu and Sundiata the beast. For a while this bizarre conviction brings hope to the community—and makes the second half of the book stylistically and intellectually more interesting as well. But ultimately, it seems, the myth of personal accomplishment will fail because no amount of personal knowledge or courage will completely solve all the earth's contradictions.

As it happens, however, the spirit-child myth is able to include this paradox: that it is important to rebel against the past and to know one never escapes it. At the beginning of the last chapter, the narrator explains that rebellion introduces ideas about "nations, civilizations, revolutions, art forms, experiments" that are not new though "they are perceived as new" because they come to us without the visible "marks of their recurrence," a fact which makes personal achievement both tragic and absurd. It does, however, represent a "cry into being, scorched by the strange ecstasy of the will ascending to say yes to destiny and illumination." So that when Azaro's father fails his actions seem heroic though they are ridiculous as well.

A more humanizing depiction of the contradictions among life, recurrence, knowledge, and will (outside of Nietzsche) would be hard to find. I have read that Okri derives both his image of the famished road and the spirit-child from the writings of Wole Soyinka, the Nigerian Nobel Laureate. And Soyinka himself is known for the subtle interweaving of Yoruba mythology with other African and European literary models and ideas. Moreover, Okri, though Nigerian, is not Yoruban, a fact which argues that his choice of mythology was made on aesthetic rather than racial grounds. It does not matter. His use of time and recurrence is eloquent, full of integrity, and comprehensive though it may not be entirely new.

Okri on African writers:

Some writers who write about Africa are good and say very interesting things, but what strikes me on the whole is the absence of humility, not taking the opportunity to see yourself as a stranger. I think it's saddening, because there's a great dialogue that we can all hold with one another here; we can try to enlighten our spirits a lot more, to learn. It will change. This is not a criticism, it's just a sadness.

Ben Okri, in an interview in Contemporary Authors, *Vol. 138, Gate Research, 1993.*

Judy Cooke   (review date 26 March 1993)

SOURCE: "Strong Spirits," in *New Statesman & Society,* Vol. 6, No. 245, March 26, 1993, p. 41.

[*In the following review of* Songs of Enchantment, *Cooke favorably assesses the novel's themes and characters.*]

"Sometimes we have to redream ourselves," declares the narrator of Ben Okri's new book, which in many ways continues the exploration started in **The Famished Road. Songs of Enchantment** is closer to a collection of short stories, or rather folk tales, than to the novel form. It describes a pilgrimage through danger and violent struggle into some kind of stasis—not a retreat, since Azaro's redeemed world remains as astonishing as any nightmare, but an acceptance that "to see anew is not enough. We must also create our new lives, everyday, with will and light and love."

This very personal statement, centred on the reconciliation between man, wife and child, conveys a familial warmth and provides a necessary weight of feeling. The richness of the descriptive writing—"sprawling ghommid-infested alabaster landscapes of the recently dead"—might otherwise leap away into a purely Blakean text in which everything is of equal significance.

"The world is holy", Azaro's Dad concludes, having won an epic victory against demonic possession, blindness and the anger of a corpse: the unburied carpenter who is confined at last, shut in a cave and kept there by a great black rock. Whatever interpretation is given to Okri's drama as it moves between the natural and the supernatural world, his superb storytelling comes back to the simple, puzzling themes of poverty and oppression. How can Azaro dream his own future and that of his nation?

Mum was the linchpin of Okri's Booker-winner, a sustaining presence scraping together money for rent and food, a mysterious priestess who recounts the story of how death was conquered. Dad is very much the central character here: on one level, a labouring man, exhausted and fallible; on another, the hero of the kingdom created within the timespan of the book. He is a fitting adversary for the vividly realised sorceress, snake-slayer and fantastically dressed seller of palm-wine, Madame Koto.

> **Okri's Africa is above all a place of fertility and energy where the immense forces of nature sustain the visionary, the "spirit-child", and death can be deflected by a joke or a good story.**
>
> —*Judy Cooke*

Dad's triumphant naming of the new kingdom brings the story to its climax in a linguistic *tour de force,* Okri at his lyrical, authoritative best:

> He named the night birds who were never what they seemed, the ones with the eyes of wise old men, the owl that was a benign witch: he named the plants, the secret herbs, the poisonous vegetations which themselves cured other poisons, the wild roses of the forest, the tranquil agapanthus . . . He named the gods of the ghetto: the god of poverty, distant relation of the god of rainbows, the god of fear and transferences, the god of timidity and suspicion, the god of self-imposed limitation and fatalism. . .

Many folk tales are working towards a creation myth, examining causation and identity. The youngest son saves the stranger, names the monster, brings about the new order. Okri's work is perhaps best enjoyed in this context. It returns to certain themes and images, expressed in forms that are related: the poems connected with the prose, the brief fables a spark to illuminate the dense perplexities of the longer fictions.

There are some consistent external realities, but never any close political analysis. The jungle villages of Nigeria, where most of the action takes place, are a harsh enough environment, tyrannised by the Party of the Poor as much as by the Party of the Rich. Life is brutalised by thugs, soldiers, conmen. Yet Okri's Africa is above all a place of fertility and energy where the immense forces of nature sustain the visionary, the "spirit-child", and death can be deflected by a joke or a good story. The gods of Azaro's people are there to be touched.

Michael Gorra   (review date 10 October 1993)

SOURCE: "The Spirit Who Came to Stay," in *The New York Times Book Review,* October 10, 1993, p. 24.

[*Gorra is an educator. In the following unfavorable review of* Songs of Enchantment, *he faults the novel's focus and structure.*]

I had looked forward to reading the Nigerian writer Ben Okri's novel *The Famished Road.* It had won England's Booker Prize for the best novel of 1991, people I respect had admired it, and reviewers had compared Mr. Okri to other writers I enjoyed.

So when I was asked to look at its sequel, I happily sat down with both books, ready to follow the adventures of its child narrator, Azaro, a boy who can step into the realm of the spirits, into "the mesmeric dreams of hidden gods . . . susurrant marketplaces of the unborn . . . alabaster landscapes of the recently dead." For Azaro is an *abiku,* a child who, in the cosmology of Nigeria's Yoruba people, is born only to die in infancy and then to be reborn, "often to the same parents." Such a child is "unwilling to come to terms with life." His attachment to the spirit world is too strong; it allows him "to will [his own] death," causing "much pain to mothers." But sometimes these children "grow tired of coming and going," and without fully losing their links to the land of the spirits, they decide, like Azaro, to stay alive in this one.

Well, I sat down—and almost immediately wanted to get back up, to read something else, anything else, from *Pride and Prejudice* to *The Satanic Verses.* Mr. Okri's sentences are usually short and monotonously punchy: "The air turned green. A hyena laughed in the dark. An owl called. Ritual noises surfaced among the bushes. Suddenly, everything was alive. The air crackled with resinous electricity." I'm not sure just what a "ritual noise" is. But that imprecision wouldn't have been such a problem if only there'd been some logic to Mr. Okri's narrative—and by "logic" I don't mean a European plausibility.

When Azaro spends days and chapters in the spirit world, and then finds that he's suddenly back in a "real" world in which no time has passed, I accept that he's found a way into another realm of experience; one that is, as it were, perpendicular to our own. No, by "logic" I mean a sense of purposeful form and structure.

The new novel is continuous with **The Famished Road**. The "political thugs" still terrorize the neighborhood in which Azaro lives with his parents. The sinister and otherworldly Mme. Koto still runs her palm-wine bar in league with the Party of the Rich. The great pre-election rally that was in the offing for the last half of the previous book still hasn't happened by the end of **Songs of Enchantment**. So when after 600 pages spread between the two volumes Azaro sees "the sight which was to bring terror into our lives," I almost shut the book for good. Terror hadn't been there before? But maybe Azaro needed to remind us, for these characters are so perpetually on the verge of crisis that the reader stops believing in it. Or stops believing, rather, that the crisis will ever be in any way resolved.

The idea of an *abiku* does, admittedly, imply a cyclical rather than a linear conception of human existence, as indeed do many African models of history. Yet in reading, I still want to know why one incident follows another; if the dream world of the novel's opening chapters is interchangeable with that in the middle or at the end, then what's the point of all those pages in between? But no matter how many times these characters shift into "a completely new reality," everything stays pretty much the same. And I don't think it's just my (relative) ignorance of Yoruba mythology that makes it seem that way. It's that Mr. Okri has simply asserted that his world has undergone a series of "cyclical transformations," rather than made them perceptible.

In fact, so many of this book's scenes contribute so little, and seem so loosely linked, to any overall design that I began to wonder if they might perhaps be outtakes from a single enormously long manuscript, one whose best pages became **The Famished Road**. That novel at least had passages of real power. The ease with which Azaro could step from an ordinary forest and into the bush of ghosts; his father's boxing match with the shade of a dead fighter; above all, the central myth of its title, of a great King of the Road who swallows all the sustenance of the world—these are impossible to forget. Nothing in **Songs of Enchantment** has that intensity, and its repetitiveness can only diminish what pleasure one took in its predecessor.

FURTHER READING

Criticism

Brent, Frances Padorr. Review of *The Famished Road,* by Ben Okri. *Chicago Tribune—Books* (14 June 1992): 1, 9.
   Describes the characters, imagery, and plot of *The Famished Road.*

Johnson, Charles. "Fighting the Spirits." *The Times Literary Supplement,* No. 4594 (19 April 1991): 22.
   Offers a mixed assessment of *The Famished Road.* Discussing the novel's characters, setting, and focus on history, Johnson asserts that "Okri is, if not yet a careful craftsman, a gifted poet of the African experience."

Miller, Faren. Review of *The Famished Road,* by Ben Okri. *Locus* 29, No. 2 (August 1992): 15, 17.
   Relates Okri's focus on magic and fantasy in *The Famished Road.*

Olshan, Joseph. "Fever Dreams from Nigeria's Troubled Soul." *Chicago Tribune—Books* (16 July 1989): 6.
   Thematic analysis of *Stars of the New Curfew.*

Onwordi, Sylvester Ike. "Beneath the Waves." *The Times Literary Supplement,* No. 4453 (5-11 August 1988): 857.
   Compares Okri's writing style and focus as evinced in *Stars of the New Curfew* to those of African writer Ken Saro-Wiwa.

Rubin, Merle. "Nigerian Tales Pack Power of True Art." *The Christian Science Monitor* 81, No. 185 (18 August 1989): 11.
   Offers a favorable review of *Stars of the New Curfew,* noting Okri's blending of real and surreal elements in the collection.

Thorpe, Michael. Review of *Stars of the New Curfew,* by Ben Okri. *World Literature Today* 64, No. 2 (Spring 1990): 349.
   Examines narrative style, setting, and themes of *Stars of the New Curfew,* characterizing the pieces in the collection as "quest narratives."

Turner, Jenny. "Blithe Spirits." *New Statesman & Society* 4, No. 143 (22 March 1991): 44.
   Offers a highly favorable review of *The Famished Road,* stressing Okri's prose style and focus on mysticism.

Delmore Schwartz

1913-1966

(Full name Delmore David Schwartz) American poet, short story writer, novelist, essayist, playwright, and critic.

The following entry presents criticism of Schwartz's career and works from 1981 through 1988. For further information, see *CLC,* Volumes 2, 4, 10, and 45.

INTRODUCTION

Best known for poems and stories deeply informed by his experiences as the son of Jewish immigrants, Schwartz often focused on middle-class New York immigrant families whose children are alienated both from their parents and from American culture and society. In his writings Schwartz explored such themes as the importance of self-discovery, the necessity of maintaining hope in the presence of despair, free will versus determinism, and the immanence of the subconscious. Thematically influenced by the writings of Sigmund Freud, Karl Marx, and Plato, Schwartz's work, particularly his inventive use of symbolism, also displays his admiration for the work of such Modernists as William Butler Yeats and T. S. Eliot.

Biographical Information

Schwartz was born in Brooklyn to Jewish immigrants whose troubled marriage created a turbulent environment during his childhood. Following his graduation from high school, Schwartz studied philosophy at several universities. In 1937 his short story "In Dreams Begin Responsibilities" appeared in the inaugural issue of *Partisan Review.* This work was immediately hailed as a masterpiece and is widely considered Schwartz's finest achievement. He published frequently and taught composition at a variety of universities, including Harvard and Princeton. Schwartz also served as the editor of *Partisan Review* from 1943 to 1947 and as poetry editor and film critic for the *New Republic* from 1955 to 1957. Although the quality of his fiction and poetry is generally considered to have declined after the late 1940s, Schwartz continued to earn respect for his insightful literary criticism, which he had been writing and contributing to periodicals since the mid-1930s. Plagued by insomnia, manic depression, and a growing dependence on drugs and alcohol, Schwartz died of a heart attack in 1966.

Major Works

Schwartz's poetry and short stories are characterized by the themes of separation and isolation, often featuring a Jewish-American protagonist struggling to find his place in American society. The title piece of *In Dreams Begin*

Responsibilities, and Other Stories (1938) is an account of an evening spent viewing a film about the narrator's parents. *In Dreams Begin Responsibilities* also contains some of Schwartz's most highly praised and frequently anthologized verse, including "The Heavy Bear Who Goes with Me," a tragicomic lyric concerning the conflict between mind and flesh; and "In the Naked Bed, in Plato's Cave," based on Plato's famous allegory on the limits of human perception. In *Shenandoah, or, the Naming of the Child* (1941), a surrealistic verse play, the narrator, Shenandoah Fish, revisits the past and witnesses the acquisition of his unorthodox name and his circumcision. Through such events, Schwartz examines conflicts between the Jewish heritage and modern American culture. Jewish life in the United States is also the subject of *The World Is a Wedding* (1948), a short story collection that is sometimes regarded as a novella in ten sections. "The Child Is the Meaning of This Life" displays Schwartz's interest in family relationships, the role of the artist, and feelings of alienation; "America! America!," which further examines the character of Shenandoah Fish, focuses on a writer's sense of isolation from his fellow New Yorkers, his family, and his Jewish heritage.

Critical Reception

While the story "In Dreams Begin Responsibilities" has generally been praised, Schwartz's overall critical reception has been mixed. His literary criticism has always been regarded as perceptive and reliable—informed not only by his immense knowledge of individual writers but also by his understanding of cultural traditions and trends—but the quality of his later poetry and fiction is considered to have steadily declined. Nevertheless, such posthumously released works as *Selected Essays of Delmore Schwartz* (1970) and *The Ego Is Always at the Wheel* (1986), as well as James Atlas's biography *Delmore Schwartz: The Life of an American Poet* (1977) and Saul Bellow's novel *Humboldt's Gift* (1975)—the protagonist of which was based on Schwartz—revived interest in his career and provided further evidence of his insight into the conflicts associated with Jewish-American identity. As David Lehman observed: "It is hard not to see Schwartz as an emblematic figure, capable of stirring us in his ravings no less than in his brilliant and original literary creations, meant to reproach and admonish us with the purity and grandeur of his aspirations as well as with the unbanished image of his demise."

PRINCIPAL WORKS

In Dreams Begin Responsibilities, and Other Stories (poetry and prose)   1938
Shenandoah, or, the Naming of the Child (one-act verse play)   1941
Genesis, Book One (prose and poetry)   1943
The World Is a Wedding (short stories)   1948
Vaudeville for a Princess, and Other Poems (poetry)   1950
Summer Knowledge: New and Selected Poems, 1938-1958 (poetry)   1959; also published as *Selected Poems: Summer Knowledge,* 1967
Successful Love, and Other Stories (short stories)   1961
Selected Essays of Delmore Schwartz (essays)   1970
Last and Lost Poems of Delmore Schwartz (poetry)   1979
Letters of Delmore Schwartz (letters)   1985
The Ego Is Always at the Wheel: Bagatelles (fiction)   1986
Portrait of Delmore: Journals and Notes of Delmore Schwartz, 1939-1959 (journals and correspondence)   1986

CRITICISM

Jay L. Halio   (review date Summer 1981)

SOURCE: "Fiction and the Malaise of Our Time," in *The Southern Review,* Louisiana State University, Vol. 17, No. 3, Summer, 1981, pp. 622-30.

[*In the following review, Halio favorably assesses* The World Is a Wedding.]

If literature is the light that imagination shines upon reality, then reading literature inevitably uncovers reality as various, complex, and often strange. Perhaps that is why critics used to refer to the "world" of the writer (some still do), or more grandiloquently to his "universe." Yet in opening a work of literature, of fiction, do we not still look for light that it may shine upon our own world, our own reality, the existence that we daily live? Escapist or sensationalist literature apart, does not fiction bear upon our lives, if not directly, then none the less incisively for being indirect? This is the justification for science fiction that aspires to be taken seriously, but it must also be the justification for any fiction that pretends to serious literature, which mediates between the unsifted experiences of our lives and the recurrent need to find some coherence or at least intelligibility in those experiences. Lacking that sort of literature, Alfred Kazin says ("American Writing Now," *The New Republic,* October 18, 1980), we suffer from a profound cultural malaise. Best-sellers and the literary hype that goes with them are not symptoms but, along with other examples of the "breakdown of intellectual authority," *are* the malaise.

Although the situation is bleak, it is not hopeless. . . . Delmore Schwartz's stories from the 1930s and 1940s, republished along with several others under the title **In Dreams Begin Responsibilities,** not only show what the form was capable of, but invoke a strong sense of their times and demonstrate in fiction a sensibility as powerful as that which is demonstrated in Schwartz's poetry. The longest piece, **The World Is a Wedding,** a novella in ten sections, recreates the social and cultural milieu of a group of young intellectuals who gather on Saturday nights during the Depression to talk about their experiences and their ideas. But the story accomplishes a good deal more than the evocation of what is now a lost era; hence, as Irving Howe indicates in his Foreword, the value of this story and others in the volume is hardly to satisfy nostalgia. In the opposing views of Jacob Cohen, the "conscience and noble critic" of the group, and of Laura Bell, Rudyard's sister in whose small apartment the circle meets, the story sustains a tension that remains unresolved to the end. For Laura's bitter disillusionment about herself, about her brother (to whom despite her carping she is profoundly devoted), and about the life they all lead can scarcely be reconciled with Jacob's generally more optimistic realism. He recognizes that indeed the "world is a wedding," uniting not only God and Nature, but also the variety of human types represented, for example, in the very circle of friends who gather to express their hopes and disappointments, their accomplishments and failures. Jacob's positive acceptance contrasts with Laura's bitter condemnation of an existence that is anything but cheerful. The world is a wedding, not a funeral as Laura claims, although she is allowed the last word. But to recognize this requires the thoughtful disposition of a Jacob Cohen, the wanderer of neighborhoods who, like Socrates, refuses to let materialistic attitudes and values overwhelm him, tempted as many of his friends are to do so. It is his point of view, I think, that permeates other stories in this collection, notwithstanding the strident note of despair that Schwartz often sounds, especially when, as in **"The Track Meet,"** he is recounting the experience of a particularly horrifying nightmare.

Irving Howe on Delmore Schwartz:

Of dismay and disintegration, chaos and ugliness, waste and malaise there was more than enough in the life, sometimes also the work, of Delmore Schwartz. Yet there is something else in his poems and stories, so rare in our time and so vulnerable to misuse and ridicule I hesitate to name it. What complicates and enriches Schwartz's comedy is, I think, a reaching out toward nobility, a shy aspiring spirituality, a moment or two of achieved purity of feeling.

Irving Howe in the foreword to Delmore Schwartz's In Dreams Begin Responsibilities, and Other Stories, *New Directions, 1978.*

Irving S. Saposnik   (essay date Spring 1982)

SOURCE: "Delmore Schwartz's America," in *Studies in Short Fiction,* Vol. 19, No. 2, Spring, 1982, pp. 151-55.

[*Saposnik is an American educator and critic who specializes in Jewish-American literature. In the following essay, he discusses Schwartz's treatment of Jewish-American identity in his fiction and poetry.*]

Of all his contemporaries among the New York intellectuals—those who, as Wallace Markfield puts it, used to run with the Trilling bunch—none was seemingly more bothered by his Jewish-American identity than Delmore Schwartz. While he himself would sometimes joke about his origins—"I am of Russian-Jewish distraction"— others among his friends described his neurosis and eventual paranoia as "obsession" (Dwight Macdonald) and "anguish" (William Barrett) [Dwight Macdonald in "Delmore Schwartz: 1913-1966" from *Selected Essays of Delmore Schwartz,* ed. by Donald A. Dike and David H. Zucker, 1970; William Barrett in "Delmore: A 30's Friendship and Beyond," *Commentary* 58, No. 3 (September 1974)]. However variable the symptom, the cause remained constant: in story, poem, and verse drama Schwartz's subject was ever and again the hyphenated and marginal Jewish-American self, never able to cast off the burden of its Jewishness, while never able to achieve the supposed comforts of being at home in America. Whether as distraction, obsession, or anguish; whether the persona's name was Belmont Weiss (the 1940 **"America! America!"**), Shenandoah Fish (several stories), or Hershey Green (*Genesis*), the irreconcilable duality of being a Jewish American remained central.

For Schwartz, as for his characters, it is not so much the burden of being a Jewish American, as being a Jewish-American intellectual. Whether musician, artist, or poet, the Jewish-American intellectual, that sometime child of immigrant parents who wanted nothing more than to be an American, saw himself as different, not only from his parents but also from his peers. By achieving some degree of success, or at least sustenance, in the intellectual world, he was now marked by his separation from the Jewish tradition, whose foreign manners and mannerisms he could no longer share, and yet unable to share in an American tradition that was not his by title. Such a burden often proved difficult and sometimes damaging, though the danger was more in the life than in the literature.

Whatever the difficulties of Schwartz's personal struggle, and however autobiographical his fiction, his stories, particularly those written in the forties and collected under the title *The World is a Wedding* (1948), indicate an attempted reconciliation of the several conflicting forces that haunted him throughout his life. While Schwartz's characters, like him, are haunted by their Jewishness and by their inescapable necessity to reconcile both their incongruous names and their ambiguous identities, they succeed, in part, in holding their lives together. Although their success may be only partial, and their condition, in Saul Bellow's formulation, little more than dangling, they at least point the way out of that "post-Munich sensibility" that Schwartz identified with those of his generation who passed from economic to emotional depression.

Of the several stories collected in *The World is a Wedding,* perhaps none is more indicative of Schwartz's maturing attitude towards his Jewish-American identity than **"America! America!"** While it has generally been overshadowed by Schwartz's acknowledged masterpiece **"In Dreams Begin Responsibilities,"** **"America! America!"** is perhaps only now beginning to come into its own as for some his best story (Morris Dickstein), and for others the story in which "all of Schwartz's themes come to fulfillment and his literary voice strikes its characteristic note" [Irving Howe, "Delmore Schwartz: An Appreciation," in *Celebration and Attacks,* 1979]. In addition to its literary merits, it allows for a comparative analysis unique among the stories in *The World is a Wedding* collection, for it is the only story in the collection, and indeed the only work among what might be termed the "Shenandoah Fish quartet," that exists in two separate but complementary published versions: its initial appearance in *Partisan Review* (March-April 1940) in which, among other differences, the central character is a musician named Belmont Weiss; and the more familiar version (1948), in which Belmont Weiss, the musician, becomes Shenandoah Fish, the writer, a character who appears as well in two other stories in the collection, **"New Year's Eve"** (1945) and **"A Bitter Farce"** (1946), and in the verse drama *Shenandoah* (1941).

Between the first appearance of **"America! America!"** in *Partisan Review* and its final appearance in *The World is a Wedding* collection, Schwartz revised and refined the story's language, and redrew its central character to conform to his other fictional appearances in story and poem. Shenandoah Fish becomes not only a better realized persona for his author's dual identity than Belmont Weiss, but a more accurate barometer of Schwartz's maturing fictional voice. In his repeated presence in story and poem, Shenandoah Fish becomes perhaps the quintessential Schwartz persona (he certainly appears more often than any of the others), for he personifies the essential ambiguity in Schwartz's attitude toward his origins: as a Jew he is both in exile and exotic; the Ancient Mariner with a touch of Byron. As he himself stated in a 1951 essay, **"The Vocation of the Poet in the Modern World"** [published in his *Collected Essays*]: "the Jew is at once alienated and indestructible, he is in exile from his own country and in exile even from himself, yet he survives the annihilating fury of history."

Being Jewish is thus both a blessing and a curse, though the latter is often prominent. For Schwartz, as for his characters, alienation and exile are implicit in the Jewish birthright, and that separation is most recognizable in one's given name. By focusing on the names that immigrant Jewish parents were wont to give their children in order to certify their American credentials, Schwartz developed a telling metaphor for that sense of separation that was ever to haunt both him and his characters. And yet the name is not all. While there may indeed be something fishy about Shenandoah's name, it is no more pretentious than many of the names given to Schwartz's contemporaries: Lionel (Trilling), Clifton (Fadiman), Clifford (Odets), Hilton (Kramer), Leslie (Fiedler), and Walt Whitman (Rostow). It is not the name alone, but the burden of the name, that proves significant. Dangling between given name and surname, Shenandoah is a fish out of water, attractive perhaps for his oddity, but soon left to rot.

In the early forties, when he was writing the first version of **"America! America!,"** Schwartz was still unable to distance himself sufficiently from the pains of his Jewish-American heritage. Thus while the 1940 version of **"America! America!"** outwardly resembles the later version, the essential differences are largely contained in the concurrent voices of mother and son which become strikingly complementary only in 1948. It is this dramatic quality that above all singles out the second version as superior to the first, and which links **"America! America!"** with those other successful stories and poems, such as **"In Dreams Begin Responsibilities"** and *Shenandoah* in which Schwartz uses the dramatic device of ironic distance to examine the past and present of the incomplete self.

Schwartz is able to define more sharply the dramatic quality of **"America! America!"** because it already contained two voices and two stories at the beginning: the story told by Belmont's mother of the Baumann family and their mounting disappointment as their family moves from first-generation success to second-generation failure; and the story which forms the outer narrative, a story told in commentary by Belmont as he reveals his own felt displacement. The two narrators, mother and son—for Schwartz it is always the world of his mothers with which he has to wrestle—form a double vision which is as critical to **"America! America!"** as the movie metaphor is to **"In Dreams Begin Responsibilities"**: each establishes the distance necessary to confront self history, and each confirms

the necessary sympathy with which to understand that history. Even as Belmont listens as his mother tells him the story of the Baumann's unrealized dreams, he realizes that he will remain as unrealized as they unless and until he incorporates their history into his own. Only at his mother's kitchen table, when the Depression has disrupted his own dreams, is he able to redefine himself. As he listens to his mother, and as he makes her language his own, he insures that the present becomes meaningful only by looking backward, the self becomes whole only by looking beyond itself.

A closer look at Schwartz's revisions during the eight years between the first and second versions of **"America! America!"** suggests that he made most of his changes in order to bring mother and son closer together, as well as to remove most of the son's comments from the cloying confines of subjective complaint. While the Baumann's story is hardly changed at all—it remains, as it was in the first version, a story of familial dissolution amid an increasing disillusion with America—Shenandoah and his mother reinforce their familial ties. While listening to his mother's monologue, Shenandoah reflects upon his mother's native wisdom. With increasing frequency, he begins to join in her narrative until they become as one speaker, each telling a part of the story that each must share: "Each incident cited by his mother suggested another one to Shenandoah, and he began to interrupt his mother's story and tell her what he himself remembered. She would seize whatever he mentioned and augment it with her own richness of knowledge and experience" (*The World is a Wedding*). Shared language and shared narration insure shared experience.

The 1948 **"America! America!"** reinforces a linguistic and structural balance between mother and son which seemingly reflects Schwartz's more balanced attitude toward his own Jewish-American identity. Whereas Belmont had to force himself to listen to his mother's "inexhaustible talk," Shenandoah finds his mother's monologue "pleasant," even as he acknowledges her "richness of knowledge and experience." Furthermore, the revised story more clearly emphasizes Schwartz's characteristic concern with "the mystery of the family life." By contrasting the reconciliation between Shenandoah and his mother with the Baumann family's increasing disintegration, Schwartz indicates that it is within the family that one must begin to solve the mystery of self. The Baumann children move away from their parents because, as one puts it, "the old oil" won't work anymore. In contrast, the more Shenandoah listens to his mother the more he tries to understand her and identify with her. While the 1940 **"America! America!"** ends with Belmont's grudging acceptance of his family ties—"The relationship which he now recognized did not seem a pleasant matter to him"—the 1948 story emphasizes Shenandoah's growing realization of "how closely bound he was to these people. His separation was actual enough, but there existed also an unbreakable unity. As the air was full of the radio's unseen voices, so the life he breathed in was full of these lives and the age in which they had acted and suffered" (*The World is a Wedding*).

Shenandoah accepts his hyphenated identity as naturally, and yet as mysteriously as "the radio's unseen voices." His unseen voices are the voices of generations dead, while his visible voice is his mother's which so dominates his story. Both voices speak to him, as he speaks to himself, of the necessity to understand their lives, even as they force him to admit that he can never fully share their experiences. And yet, that realization is itself a beginning, even as that beginning ends the story. As Shenandoah looks at himself in the mirror, reflection becomes self-reflection, and past and present compose one history. Seeing himself as if for the first time, he accepts his historical identity in the continuous and unceasing flow of time: "No one truly exists in the real world because no one knows all that he is to other human beings, all that they say behind his back, and all the foolishness that the future will bring him" (*The World is a Wedding*).

Schwartz's revisions of **"America! America!"** suggest that during the forties he was better able to view history as more vision than nightmare. With Shenandoah Fish now at the center of his story, he is able to bring **"America! America!"** closer to his other forties stories. The strident self-justification and even anger of the first version of **"America! America!"** and the 1941 verse play *Shenandoah* become muted in the later forties stories, and is largely absent in the revised version. While the earlier stories echo the somber mood of **"In Dreams Begin Responsibilities,"** with its wish never to have been born, the later stories move toward an acceptance of self in the flow of history. While to be born a Jewish American is perhaps not the best of all possible births, it is the beginning (and perhaps the end) of necessary self-exploration.

Among young Jewish-American intellectuals like himself, Schwartz's stories offered immediate recognition, for like many of them he too was "another son slipping into estrangement." In **"America! America!,"** Schwartz offers a world in which that estrangement, while acknowledged, must be resisted. America, as the Yiddish expression suggests, may be a thief, but we must learn to give her only what we want her to take. While success in America may be discontinuous, and while to be born a Jewish American may be more burden than blessing, parents and children must accept their place in history and then build upon it. As Schwartz observes: "The lower middle-class of the generation of Shenandoah's parents had engendered perversions of its own nature, children full of contempt for everything important to their parents" (*The World is a Wedding*). Yet that is the place to start. Listening to his mother's story, even while knowing that he can never fully put himself in her place, Shenandoah transforms her words and thoughts into new meanings, meanings which become newly meaningful to him: "Her words descended into the marine world of his mind and were transformed there, even as swimmers and deep-sea divers seen in a film moving underwater through new pressures, and compulsions, and raising heavy arms to free themselves from the dim and dusky green weight of underseas" (*The World is a Wedding*).

Metaphors of film and water suggest a deeply entangled mental and emotional underworld from which children of the second generation must emerge to make their own way. It is not an easy journey. As Schwartz suggests in **"The Ballad of the Children of the Czar"**: "The innocent are overtaken, / They are not innocent. / They are their fathers' fathers. / The past is inevitable. Yet as it is difficult so is it necessary. Shenandoah Fish's progression as a native-born alien is typical of the struggle endemic to all Jewish Americans, and his reappearance in story and poem reinforces the centrality of that struggle in Schwartz's writings. If the world is truly a wedding, as the title of the 1948 collection implies, then it must surely be a Jewish wedding, where tears are mixed with laughter, sadness with joy.

Philip Rahv on Schwartz's fiction:

It cannot be said of Schwartz that he was a born writer of fiction. He was not endowed with the capacity to create a solid fictional world seemingly self-governing in structure and possessed of an energy supple enough to establish a necessary congruity between interior and external event and circumstance. In Schwartz's narratives the best writing (and effects) is mostly achieved in lyrical moments and in passages embodying the emotional and intellectual pathos of self-recognition or self-identification.

Philip Rahv, in his Essays on Literature and Politics: 1932-1972, *Houghton Mifflin, 1978.*

Elisa New   (essay date September 1985)

SOURCE: "Reconsidering Delmore Schwartz," in *Prooftext*, Vol. 5, No. 3, September, 1985, pp. 245-62.

[*In the following essay, New examines Schwartz's fiction in the larger context of American and Jewish-American literature.*]

If Jewish-American literature is not entirely at home in Jewish literary history, this is probably because it has so thoroughly learned and integrated the homelessness endemic to American literature. Before we know it, the Jewish-American novel has, in Podhoretz's terms, "made it," its hero become American hero, its forms as much defining as defined by standards of what American literature should be. Thus, on the one hand, we see Jewish-American literature prodigiously fulfilling the requirements of that American genre spelled out by Huck Finn: "The widow Douglas she took me for her son, and allowed she would sivilize me; but it was rough living in a house all the time . . . and so when I couldn't stand it no longer, I lit out. . . ." "Lighting out," putting distance between themselves and the "sivilizing" influences of women and home, Jewish-American heroes achieve their manhood and their Americanness simultaneously, simply by leaving the house. This flight is both mark of citizenship and the Jewish hero's redemption from a greenhorn cultural childhood: by making it, the hero frees Jewish culture from its adolescence, reflecting glory on us all, serving, paradoxically, as apotheosis of Jewishness precisely for living beyond the hyphen that separates Jewish from American. Alfred Kazin's "walker in the city," crossing the bridge from Brooklyn to Manhattan; Henry's Roth's David, defying his father in a moment of epiphany; Saul Bellow's Augie, freewheeling in South America; and even Philip Roth's Portnoy, reliving the family romance from the safe remove of a psychiatrist's couch—all these heroes, adventuring in narratives bordering on the picaresque, offer paradigms of a mobile success we hasten to canonize.

The rewards for such travel flow from the other side as well. As Jewish literature has learned the American formulas of flight, it has ironically come also to originate formulas of its own, defining what American literature should do, and, as Yankee John Updike's assumption of the Jewish persona "Bech" would indicate, what an American writer should be. The rise of the Jew has come to symbolize the rise of all marginal people; Jewish success figures American success. And inasmuch as this appropriation of Jewish uniqueness has been lavishly paid for in mainstream critical acclaim, even in Nobel Prizes, the conflation of Jewish and American has come to emit a mesmerizing aura, if an aura which tends to perplex critical efforts to disentangle the two.

Delmore Schwartz is anamalous in this scheme, and tellingly so. To study Schwartz's career is to find points of access into a genre that preempts investigation; it is to encounter some of those cultural wishes and myths a canny criticism of Jewish-American literature would describe. For even as the young Schwartz precociously lived out the myth of "walker"—becoming in his mid-twenties an editor of the *Partisan Review;* writer of masterful critical prose, a few fine modernist poems and letters which are the emininently quotable documents of a young man on the verge of intellectual prominence—he left behind him as well a body of creative work that subverts the adult poise of the Jewish-American canon as completely as the latter half of the Schwartz biography subverts the early half. If what Schwartz leaves in this work is adolescent in subject, ungainly in tone and finally so uneven and undignified as to count Schwartz out of a canon that lets Philip Roth in, it is yet work that uniquely reflects on aspects of the New World experience either transcended, or perhaps more accurately, repressed by the more mobile work of other figures. As such, it is work that does not evade but solicits attention as Jewish-American, and so our critical attention.

The vision Schwartz's creative work offers is anything but appetizing. Even as the late, profligate Delmore Schwartz, that Delmore remembered in so many recent memoirs, adds a racy flourish to the myth by falling in such a way as to claim kinship with Berryman, Crane and other American versions of the New World Byronic hero, too many of Schwartz's young heroes, by ignoble contrast, linger in their mother's kitchens through middle age, eating late breakfasts and rehashing petty quarrels. Symbiotic sufferers, Schwartz's children and parents endure together, and with bad grace, what Kazin's or Bellow's heroes do not endure at all. The typical Schwartz son, stranded at home, exhibits not freewheeling manliness portending

wider cultural maturity, but a whiney adolescence indicating an intergenerational and cultural torpor perhaps summed up best in the Schwartz title, **"A Child is the Meaning of This Life."** Schwartz's work is interesting, then, not for its success, but for its failure, or at least for its doubleness. Both adult and childish, mobile and grounded, the Schwartz corpus is truncated, sad, broken; not American, but Jewish-American; riding the myth of American urban adulthood only so long before regressing to languish in the boroughs, in Brooklyn, at home.

In recent years, of course, that part of the Schwartz canon which can be read as adult and American has been slowly excavated. James Atlas' biography, *Delmore Schwartz: The Life of an American Poet,* William Barrett's *The Truants* and more recent articles by Elizabeth Hardwick, Anatole Broyard and Helen Vendler locate Schwartz in the American grain, among the ranks of other doomed American prodigies. Dwight Macdonald's "appreciation" prefacing the *Selected Essays* and Karl Shapiro's preface to William Phillips's recently published edition of Schwartz's letters pay tribute to the Schwartz whose literary adulthood was at least as memorable and impressive as his later regression. One is struck in all these documents by just how vividly Schwartz is remembered and how tenaciously, despite all later insanity, admired. One senses, in fact, that the visceral quality of these memoirs is best laid to Schwartz himself who had a gift not only for breathing his personality into the memories of his friends, but for making, in a complicated way, the intellectual, visceral.

Schwartz writes with an immediacy that goes some way to explaining the pungency of writing about him; his prose has an embodying power, an accuracy of style, that evokes almost physical pang. Writing of Yeats, for example, in an early issue of the *Partisan Review,* Schwartz notes, "the poet's initial gift for versifying has become the power to get into verbal behavior, into meter and diction, the slightest shift of emotion." In a review of Wallace Stevens' *The Man with The Blue Guitar,* Schwartz writes "the poet has been compelled to consider the nature of poetry in its travail among things as they are." Such phrases as "verbal behavior," "poetry in its travail" are characteristic of Schwartz, phrases that seem drawn from the very bloodstream of a poet's praxis, from inside; they indicate not only native understanding, but also hard study of the poetic labor behind the poems.

Schwartz's letters have the same quality. They are letters that read with the force of a poetic mind realizing, or bodying itself, in prose. Distinguished by an intellectual intimacy, a constant acknowledgement of the other partner in dialogue, the letters, like the critical prose, show what Elizabeth Hardwick, writing of that prose, describes as a "valiant and disinterested attention to important texts," and what I would like to call, following Schwartz, a sense of *responsibility*.

Arguing, for example, in a letter to Philip Horton, Hart Crane's first biographer, over Crane's acknowledged failure in "The Bridge" to write the American epic he envisioned, Schwartz is resolute in objecting to the idea that Crane's poetic failures are attributable to his personal failure; Schwartz insists that the work not be seen through the prism of the suicide. Bucking, in this view, every contemporary critic of Crane—including his own mentor Allen Tate—Schwartz fixes his eye on Crane's work, on "The Bridge" as a poetic mechanism, and attempts to explicate that mechanism in its own terms:

> I said that I did not contradict myself when I said that Crane's sensibility was for things, and yet on the other hand, that Crane's emotion was religious. No contradiction, because some people do have religious emotion, merely about things, particularly primitive animists. And yet, on the other hand, a contradiction on the part of the animists who attribute conscious attributes to wood and stone—or, as in Crane, to steel. . . . But you must be tired of my repetitious discourse by now. I'd like, by the way, to use your letters—not in quotations, but merely as explicative of your book in revising my article. I won't do so . . . if you object, but if I do not hear from you I will assume that it is all right. (December 14, 1937)

The resolve of the twenty-four-year-old Schwartz here— not diverted by prevailing opinion—takes as its only support a conscientious attention to the subtlety of Crane's poetry. Where other critics, ruffled by Crane's difficulty, write off that difficulty as the detritus of a growing instability, Schwartz advances, in a few sentences, an argument about the "disunity" of "The Bridge" that is not merely sympathetic but is, as well, acute. Even at his scrappiest, the young Schwartz maintains a sane and responsible attitude toward his task. It is this same consideration—this responsibility—that is evident in Schwartz's much reprinted letter to Ezra Pound, a letter that notes the limits of a reader's loyalty even as it circumspectly allows Pound's greatness.

> Dear Mr. Pound:
>
> I have been reading your last book, *Culture.* Here I find numerous remarks about the Semite or Jewish race, all of them damning. . . .
>
> A race cannot commit a moral act. Only an individual can be moral or immoral. No generalization from a sum of particulars is possible, which will render a moral judgment. In a court of law, the criminal is always one individual, and when he is condemned, his whole family is not, qua family, condemned. This is not to deny, however, that there are such entities as races. Furthermore, your view of individual responsibility is implicit in the poetry for which you are justly famous.
>
> But I do not doubt that this is a question which you have no desire to discuss with anyone who does not agree with you, and even less with one who will be suspected of an interested view. Without ceasing to distinguish between past activity and present irrationality, I should like you to consider this as a letter of resignation: I want to resign as one of your most studious and faithful admirers.
>
> Sincerely yours,

> Delmore Schwartz
>
> (March 5, 1939)

Other letters reveal such critical tact developing in tandem with a lyric gift in which one reads, as in the prose, a certain determination to exercise, in Milton's terms, both "the right hand and the left," to become as canny an observer of the landscape, or prospect, as of the self. Early letters reveal Schwartz training his sight on what lies outside.

> For, hurried by the winds, the lake drifts, runs, ever unwrinkling, unravelling, comes southwestward toward me. But the trees and the ground stand still. Motion against perfect rest. The gray blue influx parallel to the low brown and the tall black and the thin grass, that is fixed. . . . (October 26, 1931)

as assiduously as reports have him perusing what lay inside:

> I dream at night. I dream of reading and writing. When I dreamed of reading I saw myself greeting and shaking hands with urchinous birds who entered my room on a tree, by my room, one of those branches had extended themselves into the room. Each bird dropped from his mouth numberless squirming twisting white fish which I delighted to touch. These images followed my dream of reading Emily Dickinson. I see the book of hers that I have, opened. Then I saw what I have just written. (November 1, 1931)

Such rich passages from Schwartz's early letters, the letters of a young poet on the verge of prominence, explain why at least the letters have been collected. They are letters of the critic to be. Even as they reveal an extreme sensitivity, they lack, to borrow Elizabeth Hardwick's phrase, the "nerve-wrung" quality of the work Schwartz took to be his central task. It is precisely to this "nerve-wrung" work, however, that I should like to now turn: to work that, in its very limitations, offers insights that more established Jewish-American fiction does not. If I thus begin by speaking about these limitations, it is not to qualify but rather to ground my argument. For while it would be absurd to call Schwartz's creative work uniformly good, or unpardonably ignored, still, if much of Schwartz's work is abysmal, it is abysmal in the same way that much of Whitman is abysmal, or even indeed as much of Wordsworth is abysmal. Schwartz, like Whitman and Wordsworth, had a knack for making his worst out of his best, for making calamitous use of the gift that in other places elevates and distinguishes his writing.

A penchant for making too much of a good thing is often the trouble. Thus, for example, Schwartz's very gift for breathing life into literary precursors can turn on him: Plato and Aristotle, absurdly literalized, linger around the young Schwartz's imagined bed, counseling the poet on the most mundane matters. It is this lack of proportion, this tendency to pour it on, that we have in mind when we read in a February 1941 letter to Dwight MacDonald, "The enclosed *jeu d'esprit,* written last summer but just typed, is sent to you on the off chance that you might want to print a scene or two . . . it seems good to me, though

I have been wrong many times before." Whether he is wrong or not here, the verse play to which Schwartz refers in this letter, *Shenandoah*, is one of his productions rather too prodigiously sprinkled with lines like "So Hegel and Empedocles have taught." And in such lines Schwartz is merely clearing his throat. The work climaxes in the birth of a not so ordinary Jewish child, Shenandoah, whose proper cultural context is supplied in a tone we would just as soon take for vaudeville but fear we must take straight:

> Let us consider where the great men are
> Who will obsess this child when he can read:
> Joyce in Trieste in a Berlitz school . . .
> Eliot works in a bank and there he learns
> The profit and the loss . . . Rilke endures
> Of silence and of solitude the unheard music
> . . . The child will learn of life from these men,
> He will participate in their solitude. . . .

Shenandoah strains the reader's tolerance. One wants to believe that Schwartz is burlesquing in such lines, and yet it is this same grandiloquence—pushed beyond decency but not quite far enough for irony—that characterizes so much of Schwartz's work. The tone is too much the greenhorn's at having mastered the classics as others master the subway; the pride too much that of the recently arrived, written, as Irving Howe suggests, in the diction of the "nightschool." **Shenandoah**'s speaker is, moreover, too unconcealedly Schwartz himself. And that particular Schwartz himself, too unabashedly the culture climber, the bounder like father Harry Schwartz who achieved his dandyism, his air of "an Arab on a horse," by selling swamp land in New Jersey to immigrants. Schwartz's heavy handed citations are insufficient either to conceal or dignify biographical material that is so frankly *material* we recoil. The question is, then, why a writer of such subtle critical gifts as Schwartz possessed is not more circumspect about displaying his bill of goods; the dilemma, how, or why, should we go on reading work that savors so distinctly of showmanship and the hard sell?

The solution to this problem thus far, as I have said, has been to read only that part of the Schwartz corpus that transcends this greenhorn flashiness, to remember only those texts which prove able to "grow up" or naturalize themselves as American texts. What we lose by such reading, I would suggest, is understanding of that acquisitiveness, both intellectual and material, that is Schwartz's great topic. This topic is, in the tradition of *David Levinsky*, the acculturation of the European Jew. Schwartz's contribution to that tradition is to describe how this acculturation is mediated through objects of mass culture that bind Jewish parents and children. In their buying up of America, Harry Schwartz the real estate sharpy and Delmore Schwartz, proprietor of a literary emporium, become alienated from traditional culture as from each other. The "cut glass bowls" that ostentatiously grace the tables of the parents are recapitulated in the Plato and Empedocles of the sons. It is this, I suppose, sociological phenomenon, and Schwartz's willingness to reveal himself as its apogee, that defines the real significance of Schwartz's work in Jewish-American literature. As it is based in social criticism and cultural self-scrutiny, this other, largely decanonized, work treats areas of our experience nowhere else touched. Even in its excess this work is eminently responsible. If we remember that Schwartz's final criticism of Hart Crane, contained in a November 1939 letter, was to say that "Crane lacked the understanding of ideas and human character which would have made him sufficiently critical of his age," we will better recognize in Schwartz's most ambitious work the resolve of the "cultural critic" who would criticize his age, not stinting to allow his own place within that age.

Indeed, I would like to borrow for this discussion the term "cultural critic," a term more usually found applied to the work of members of the Frankfurt School like Walter Benjamin, Theodor Adorno and Ernst Bloch. Though never explicitly involved with these thinkers—who were, in fact, his exact contemporaries—and though not a Marxist, as most members of the Frankfurt School assuredly were, Schwartz, as one intimately connected with the aggressively social *Partisan Review*, took a view of the specificity of literature that always placed it within the wider social context. Schwartz's fiction evidences a broadening and narrowing of focus compatible with such a context, an indexing of the personal to the social and the social to the personal that claims only consideration of both will yield accurate representation of "reality."

Schwartz's earliest undergraduate letters to Julian Sawyer show an acute, even punitive, awareness of this relation of personal life to certain social forms. In an October 1931 letter to Sawyer that Schwartz whimsically titles "Exhortations of D. Schwartz," the young Schwartz, among other tasks, betakes himself to "use words as translations of reality, not a cheap band music" and "to see no moving pictures, read no cheap books, listen to no catgut music at all." Such exhortations illuminate Schwartz's sense of a tension between "reality" and the modern art forms that may "cheapen" or elevate that reality: "catgut" music is to be shunned, precision of language to be pursued. The callow didacticism of 1931 presages the Schwartz of 1951 who will, in the *Partisan Review*, sound a caustic alarm about television, "the supreme dragon . . . which may transform motion picture palaces into bare ruined choirs where late Bing Crosby sang." But more to my point here, Schwartz's attention to mass culture puts him in intellectual relationship with thinkers like Benjamin, Adorno and Bloch, whose writings of the 1930s show an identical, if of course clearly more disciplined and comprehensive, preoccupation with detecting the right relation to "reality" and with locating the place of mass culture in that "reality."

It is in this critical context that I would situate, and that I would like to discuss, Schwartz's best remembered but incompletely understood story, **"In Dreams Begin Responsibilities."**

We may understand Schwartz's accomplishment in that story as twofold. First, **"In Dreams Begin Responsibilities"** is an investigation, and finally an indictment, of the power of certain mass media. And second, the story is a dramatization of a specifically Jewish symbiosis and paralysis, a conflating of generations, that Schwartz will increasingly draw in relation to such media. If **"In Dreams Begin Responsibilities"** is a work that, as Irving Howe puts it, exposes our "presumptuous but inevitable desire to unwind the reel of our lives," beyond this metaphoric formulation, it is a work that chronicles the unreeling of Jewish-American life as that life is displaced in mass culture; or, we might say, as that life becomes *film,* a medium public, technological and finally alien to itself. Film, the paradigmatic modern medium for Schwartz, functions as a kind of agora for the transactions of Jewish parents and Jewish children, even as it records, at the same time, the pathetic and parallel self-evacuations of both. By tracing the projection of value into objects and into public mass forms, **"In Dreams Begin Responsibilities"** traces, on the same trajectory, the alienation of generation from generation.

It is this relationship of alienation to mass forms, and especially to film, that brings Schwartz as social critic into particular relationship with Walter Benjamin. Benjamin, whose father's antiques financed his own famous *flaneuring* and whose suicide on the Spanish border bears uncanny resemblance to Schwartz's death—both men dying gripped by paranoia and more importantly, perhaps, by disappointment—wrote his master essay, "Art in the Age of Mechanical Reproduction," in 1934, in the same year that Schwartz wrote **"In Dreams Begin Responsibilities."** Both works, the story and the essay, survey technological innovation as it enters traditional life, exposing that life to unfamiliar transformations. The works may be read to gloss one another: Schwartz dramatizes Benjamin; Benjamin lends theoretical sinew to Schwartz.

Let me turn, then, to Benjamin's evocation of "aura" in "Art in the Age of Mechanical Reproduction." We remember that for Benjamin, "aura" is that presence attaching to a work of art that exists for the work's being "imbedded in the fabric of tradition." This aura, which ineluctably belongs to the past, to tradition, "withers in the age of mechanical reproduction," and with its withering comes, to use Benjamin's charged term, "exile": the complex state of exclusion that is inclusion, the being outside that is more gripping than being inside. It is this state of exile, rendered as the *vicarious* by Schwartz, that informs the opening paragraphs of **"In Dreams Begin Responsibilities":**

> I think it is the year 1909. I feel as if I were in a motion picture theatre, the long arm of light crossing the darkness and spinning, my eyes fixed on the screen. This is a silent picture as if an old Biograph one, in which the actors are dressed in ridiculously old fashioned clothes, and one flash succeeds another with sudden jumps. The actors too seem to jump about and walk too fast. The shots themselves are full of dots and rays, as if it were raining when the picture was photographed. The light is bad.

> It is Sunday afternoon, June 12th, 1909, and my father is walking down the quiet streets of Brooklyn on his way to visit my mother. His clothes are newly pressed and his tie is too tight in his high collar. He jingles the coins in his pockets, thinking of the witty things he will say. I feel as if I had by now relaxed entirely in the soft darkness of the theatre; the organist peals out the obvious and approximate emotions on

which the audience rocks unknowingly. I am anonymous and I have forgotten myself. It is always so when one goes to the movies, it is, as they say, a drug.

The grip of family history, of the ritual past, is, in this remarkable opening, taken over by the grip of the film, that most disaffected of media. If the power of the film is like, as Schwartz puts it, "a drug," or as Benjamin puts it, "surgery," then the irony is how indifferent, as apparatus, is film, and how potent. As the French film critic, Jean Louis Baudry, writing of the identity that obtains between cinematic and psychological projection remarks, "The cinematographic apparatus brings about a state of total regression." Thus, even as the film, with all its "dots and rays," its mimetic banality, its brute technicality, declares its own uncrossable distance from that which it records, still it delivers its apprehender both into that distance and into a past, an experience, the distance closes. It is this regression, this powerlessness, or state of arrest, that makes the film suspect for both Schwartz and Benjamin. Film is too much like "cheap band music . . ."; it invokes not alert and critical response but "obvious approximate emotions" that hold the speaker, as us, in thrall. There is a Brechtian kind of resistance here to catharsis, to emotional engagement, worth noting. But the real complexity of **"In Dreams Begin Responsibilities"** rests not simply in its indictment of the tawdriness of the movies, but in how Schwartz twines that tawdriness around the family romance, a romance that corresponds to the literal and biographical courtship of Schwartz's own parents.

This courtship, the fait accompli which is the narrative unreeled by the film, is viewed "presumptuously," as Howe puts it, because publicly. If the story is a dream and the movie the substance of that dream, still the narrator's burden as dreamer is a guilt, or sense of lapsed responsibility, for making his parents courtship a spectacle which, as a consciously crafted story of an unconscious film, it is. The dreamer is not mere spectator, but also producer; not passive, but culpable; not a child unborn who will avert catastrophe, but an adult who airs and profits from that catastrophe, who only intensifies his guilt by ostentatiously parading it as pain. And pain which, it turns out, is but another disreputable public act.

The eye of the narrator, then, an eye both exhibitionist and voyeuristic, is the cinematic lens through which we glimpse this particular family history, a history which, as we shall see, only compounds, by doubling upon, the narrator's anguish. The courtship of the narrator's parents unfolds as if, in Benjamin's terms, to exemplify the dissolution of aura in mass culture that gives the story its regretful perspective.

The action opens in a young woman's Brooklyn living room where the narrator's mother lingers with her beau while her traditional father looks skeptically on: the form is portentously that of the tableau, the freeze frame that prepares us for the "withering of aura," or ritual, to come. And it does come, soon enough, in a stuttering of the film that shows the narrator's grandfather surveying his daughter and her suitor doubtfully: "but the film has returned to a portion just shown, and once more I see my grandfather rubbing his bearded cheek and pondering my father's character." This double-take figures the last moment of ritual potency; the vision of the old bearded man stroking his cheek, an almost tragic anegnoresis: cinematic notation codes moments of cultural loss even as it enforces that loss. Like Benjamin, often described as a writer clinging to the mast of a sinking culture, elegizing its passing in a language already ousted from that culture, Schwartz here writes the demise of a ritual past in the very twitching, sepia medium that dissolves that past.

We should pause to note again just how implicated Schwartz's narrator is, the narrator who goes on, "It is difficult to get back into the picture and lose myself, but as my mother giggles at my father's words, the darkness drowns me." To whatever degree the film is voyeuristic, what we witness, as what the narrator witnesses among spectators, is his own guilty projection. The film is as much his present malady as it is etiology of the cultural malady that brought him to make a career of the past. Nor should we forget how this career qua career is vexed with its own inevitable guilt: the narrator's film surely functions too as metaphor for that older imitation of life that is any artist's guilt and obsession. This production, then—which offers the oddest kind of escape imaginable, a claustrophic escape looping deeper than catharsis into the narrator's own psyche, own dreams—points to what Benjamin notes as the odd simultaneity of film, the paradox on which it is founded:

> . . . the technique of reproduction detaches the reproduced object from the domain of tradition. . . . And in permitting the reproduction to meet the beholder or listener in his own particular situation, it reactivates the object produced. These two processes lead to a tremendous shattering of tradition which is the obverse of the contemporary crisis and renewal of mankind. Both processes are intimately connected with the contemporary mass movements. Their most powerful agent is the film. Its social significance, particularly in its most positive form, is inconceivable without its destructive cathartic aspect, that is, the liquidation of the traditional value of cultural heritage.

There is a double process here, a process in which the past and the present of the story converge. As the narrator's alienation is wrought by a medium that destroys to create, defrauds the past in order to activate it, the vision of that past delivered by the medium, its "content," is that of an identical alienation coming over the narrator's parents. This alienation, which first sets in when tradition is disenfranchised in the fade-out of the bearded patriarch, is sealed with the young couple's fatal seduction by media whose enticements are nothing less than those of the film in embryo. Less abstractly, as the narrator submits to the film, he watches his parents submit to the merry-go-round, the photographer's booth and the crystal ball—all blandishments which deliver them into the same depression which wracks him by the end of the story. Even as the narrator watches the film, suffering as he watches, dizziness, weeping, vertigo, perspiration, his parents submit to a series of temptations, making, in effect, a greenhorn

pilgrimage into the mass monster in whose grip their son already struggles.

If I verge here on the allegorical, I should, for **"In Dreams Begin Responsibilities"** is a story plotted with allegorical urgency, a story of overdetermined symbols: the "merry go round making its eternal circuit," the photographer's booth where "my father's smile turns to a grimace and my mother's bright and false," and the "crystal ball," an image of sham and the blighted future that establishes the narrator's claim to his parents' romance. As a prospective apparatus of dreaming, the crystal ball finds its mirror image in the film; thus, naturally enough, it is with the crystal ball on the screen that the narrator breaks into the illusion of the film, shouting, entering the guilty spectacle of his creation by "making a spectacle of himself." What the narrator suffers is apprehension of a spinning history, a history torn loose from the linear progression of tradition, a history wheeling in a confusion of the revocable and the irrevocable. In perhaps his greatest poem, **"In the Naked Bed, In Plato's Cave,"** a work which, like **"In Dreams Begin Responsibilities,"** mingles projection and regression, memory and stasis, Schwartz puts it this way:

> So, so,
> O son of man, the ignorant night, the travail
> Of early morning, the mystery of beginning
> Again and again,
>   while History is unforgiven.

As history, particularly as Jewish history, **"In Dreams Begin Responsibilities"** is guilty and unforgiven. Chronicle of a Jewish world emptied of ritual content, it suffers exile, the confusion of self-evacuation. Only by its own form—tragicomic allegory, megillah scrolling forward and backward—will it secure redemption.

I believe it is amply redeemed by that form. As a pained and hyperconscious record of a culture's self-erasure, and as a work of art that formally masters some of the most obstreperous social questions bearing on Jewish acculturation, **"In Dreams Begin Responsibilities"** is a great story, perhaps the greatest ever written of the adjustments by which we enter the New World. But beyond this, **"In Dreams Begin Responsibilities"** is a story that offers a blueprint, if we would read it, for the appreciation of other Schwartz works, indeed a blueprint for the excavation of the worthiest of Schwartz's work. At this point, then, I would like to look at some of that other work as it picks up certain themes that I have suggested distinguish **"In Dreams Begin Responsibilities."**

Perhaps the most poignant, and certainly Schwartz's most focused treatment of what we might, following Benjamin, call the "reification" of aura comes in a work that I have already perhaps unwisely maligned, Schwartz's verse play, *Shenandoah*. *Shenandoah* is a play about the naming of a Jewish child. Like **"In Dreams Begin Responsibilities,"** its cast includes denizens of an immigrant generation (that generation of the "grandfathers") as well as "first generation" champions of Americanization. Negotiations between the two generations are witnessed, as in **"In Dreams Begin Responsibilities"** by the child, now adult, of that first generation. This child, who watches his parents' courtship in the earlier story with a dread that finally impels him to cry out "Stop! It's not too late," here stands on the wings, similarly helpless because "too late," as he is given his ridiculous first name. The voice of tradition issues here as well from a grandfather who chides his daughter, if sympathetically, for her ignorance of Jewish traditions of naming, for her disavowal of forms with "aura" and the history those forms preserve:

> Elsie, I do not blame you for not knowing the beliefs of your religion and your people. You are only a woman, and in this great new America, anyone might forget everything but such wonderful things as tall buildings, subways, automobiles and iceboxes.

The grandfather is right about the distractions of the New World, for Elsie, rather than reinscribe her child within tradition by subscribing to Jewish traditions of naming, subscribes rather to the society section of the local paper, and finds his name there—the paper, of course, an organ of mass culture analogous to film. Indeed it is in a filmic "bit" worthy of the dizziest of thirties dames that Elsie and Mrs. Goldmark arrive at the name "Shenandoah Fish":

> Elsie Fish: Let's get the morning paper and see what luck I have.
>
> [Mrs. Goldmark goes in the living room . . . and returns with the newspaper.]
>
> Mrs. Goldmark: Now let us see what names are mentioned today . . . Russell, Julian, Christopher, Nicholas, Glenn, Llewellyn, Murray, Franklin, Alexander: do you like any of those?
>
> Elsie Fish: I like some of them, Mrs. Goldmark, but I might as well pick one from a whole many . . .
>
> Mrs. Goldmark: . . . Marvin, Irving, Martin, James, Elmer, Oswald, Rupert, Delmore . . .
>
> Elsie Fish: Delmore! What a pretty name, Mrs. Goldmark—
>
> Mrs. Goldmark: Vernon, Allen . . . Do you know, I could read the society page for weeks at a time. If I am ever sick I will. I feel as if I had known some members of the Four Hundred, the Vanderbilts and the Astors, for years. And I know about the less important families also. I know their friends and where they go in winter and in summer. For instance, the Talbot Brewsters, who are mentioned today: every year they go to Florida in January. Mrs. Brewster has an estate in the Shenandoah Valley—
>
> Elsie Fish: Shenandoah! What a wonderful name! Shenandoah Fish!

Here is our quintessential example of aura, in this case the aura surrounding a traditionally assigned name, displaced or exiled in what Benjamin calls "star" quality. What is unique in the traditional context, the Jewish name as mark of continuation, of linear history, is supplanted by that public image which is uniqueness reified. "Shenandoah Fish," like "Delmore Schwartz," marks not achievement of an intrinsic quality guaranteed by the tradition, but pursuit of such quality through externally determined forms.

The self, in such mass ritual, is conceived as object to be filled: tradition has become prospective: the character must unreel itself, make its own history, and make that history by way of an image.

Now this matter of image brings us, inevitably, to wonder at the identity of this child-adult, this narrator in the wings, replaying his family home movies so tirelessly. How are we to respond to this persona who, upon witnessing the triumphant selection of his name by Mrs. Goldmark and Elsie, hisses melodramatically?

> Now it is done! quickly! I am undone!
> This is the crucial crime, the accident
> Which is more than an accident because
> It happens only to certain characters,
> As only Isaac Newton underwent
> The accidental apple's happy fall.

One wants to read this too as burlesque, as the inflated aside of an arch arch-victim whose over self-consciousness reflects irony on the vulgar and utterly unself-conscious Mrs. Goldmark and Elsie. And yet the spectator's obvious investment, his very brooding presence at his own *bris* is unnerving. What is Shenandoah Fish *doing* witnessing his naming with such vampirish attention? By the same token, what was the narrator of **"In Dreams Begin Responsibilities"** *doing* at the movie of his parents' courtship? Like the usher in that story, such scenes make us want to ask "What are *you* doing? . . . Why should a young man like you, with your whole life before you, get hysterical like this?" Why do Shenandoah Fish and Delmore Schwartz linger in the wings so long, brooding over family mistakes? Why don't they act like other heroes from out of Jewish-American fiction: manly, rebellious, picaresque?

What we are up against here is the distinctly uncomfortable part of Schwartz's work; that is, his refusal, or incapacity, to be, in Kazin's terms, "a walker in the city"; if not a hero, at least post-adolescent, one who leaves Brooklyn and the family to recover them if need be—like Augie, like Portnoy—in nostalgia or rancour, but to *get out of the house.* There is no nostalgia in Schwartz's writing and that is the trouble: there is no leaving home.

The film in **"In Dreams Begin Responsibilities,"** the newspaper in *Shenandoah,* the SCREENO wheel in **"SCREENO,"** the shoes in **"America! America!"** all function in Schwartz's fiction as the circumstantial evidence of a symbiosis that infantilizes Jewish parents and Jewish children alike by showing them alienated by, yet in frantic pursuit of, the same objects. The telling of a linear Jewish history that would free and redeem, the story that would lend fathers and sons individuation in a world where value is the continuous preservation of aura in tradition—this is all dissolved. What Schwartz's fiction does and does best is arrest growth; it underlines stasis by working always from a formal premise of repetition. Searching out images of the "again and again," the circular—the reel, the merry-go-round, the crystal—it delivers us into a vison we shun: that of grown men malingering in a cultural freeze-frame, Delmores and Shenandoahs and Belmonts mocking their parents' speech in speech of their own that all too unwittingly "reactivates" what they would destroy, yokes present to past:

Shenandoah's mother proceeded to explain how insurance was a genial medium for a man like Mr. Baumann. The important thing in insurance was to win one's way into the homes and into the confidences of other people. Insurance could not be sold as a grocer or druggist sells his *goods* (here Shenandoah was moved again by his mother's choice of words); you could not wait for the customer to come to you; nor could you like the book salesman go from house to house, plant your foot in the doorway and start talking quickly before the housewife shut the door in your face.

"Genial medium"—not to mention "nor could you like the book salesman go"—is the narrator's locution: the merging of child and parent in **"America! America!"** is figured in an indirect discourse—a compromised intersecting terrain—that functions as film did in **"In Dreams Begin Responsibilities."** Even to criticize one's parents is to dog their language, their steps. When later in **"America! America!"** Mr. Baumann accuses a ne'er-do-well son, another Shenandoah, of failing to make a success of himself, the son reproaches the father, in kind, for never "making a million dollars." The argument is precipitated by a pair of shoes, a mediant object that marks the empty space where ritual was. Thus parents and children, regressing together in a common projection of identity into mass objects, find their relations shipwrecked in those objects, all discourse determined by those objects.

There is, we inevitably discover, something ignoble, self-hating, and finally even un-American about all this. Schwartz is, it turns out, even harder to take than Roth, for Roth's stories contain always an escape plan; they are nascent Bellow novels, as Bellow's novels are bildungsroman of a Jewish Tom Jones or, better, Huck Finn, who flees a stultifying past to patriate himself as American adult: Corde, Bellow's picaresque Dean, is a runaway who only earns his return to Chicago, its oddly hostile and nostalgic evocation, by straying far far away. If the Jewish-American canon is the scene of that intergenerational showdown through which Jewish-American heroes define themselves as American heroes, Schwartz's stories map out danger zones of intergenerational paralysis where we languish in the throes of a cultural adolescence that will not let us stop selling ourselves as Americans, hawking our goods, both material and intellectual.

That, at least, is Schwartz's case as I see it; that is the intensity of the criticism he levels at us. And by offering himself, despite our protestations, as eternally adolescent scapegoat of a rather massive cultural denial, inviting us to identify with that usher who remonstrates "Why don't you *think* of what you are doing! You can't act like this even if other people aren't around! You will be sorry if you do not do what you should do, you can't carry on like this, it is not right, you will find that out soon enough, everything you do matters too much," Schwartz heralds his own decanonization, his own unceremonious removal from the theatre on the arm of an usher. In our identification with that usher, in our very protestations, Schwartz prophesies his own oddly infamous celebrity, his own truncated posthumous reputation.

Awaking from a dream on the morning of his twenty-first birthday, the narrator of **"In Dreams Begin Responsibilities"** apprehends a double vision of responsibility: one, the usher's version, would enforce an adult poise, a decorum; the other, Shenandoah's or Belmont's or Hershey's, would reveal the cultural adolescence of which they are exemplars. Schwartz's work falls, as I have read it here, into two halves, expressing rather neatly these two versions of responsibility. Delmore Schwartz's critical prose is that of the adult: whose dreams have yielded to reputability, whose early letters thrill with the power of the "walker in the city." The accomplished editor and stylist of the *Partisan Review*—grasping Yeats and Stevens, Crane and television with a confidence and verve born of steady and conscientious contemplation—Schwartz writes letters which, to the end, even as friends recall the desperation behind them, retain a chastity, a decorum and a poise as great as any usher would ask. It is difficult to reconcile these letters with the stories revealing a different vision of responsibility, if an equally exacting one, and it is dispiriting to match the letters or the fiction with the portrait of the legendary profligate who, as the Atlas biography informs us, called loyal friend Dwight Macdonald a "fucking Yalie," whined to Robert Lowell about his poverty, perfected anecdotes about T. S. Eliot's sex life and left scribbled on a bank statement in his last hotel room the Baudelairian message, "Into the destructive element . . . that is the way."

The problem we face in evaluating Delmore Schwartz, however, is a problem that can only energize and sharpen our cultural criticism. If Schwartz leaves us work that belies its own ambition, dissolves its own success, subverts its own adulthood, it is yet work that exposes the fragility of ambition, success, adulthood. It is work that, all of a sudden, reveals just what communal hopes an Augie March articulates and just what communal fears a Delmore Schwartz betrays. It is, on the one hand, work that arouses the distaste we feel at the return of the repressed, but, on the other, work that is nothing if not responsible, giving Jewish-American culture of an era perhaps en-

---

James Atlas on Schwartz's writing:

Having invented a diction that reproduced American speech while heightening its effects through the use of a standard blank verse line, Schwartz went on to devise a new mode of ironic detachment and pathos in his fiction. Even his criticism, especially the long essays on Dos Passos, Faulkner and Eliot, revealed a wry personal voice that made his lucid social and literary commentaries distinctive. More vividly than any writer of that period, Delmore captured its temper and intellectual style. Above all, though, he was the great chronicler of the Jewish immigration, its aspirations and anxieties; by concentrating his genius on that experience, Delmore gave life to one of the most significant dramas in American history.

James Atlas, in "Reconsidering Delmore Schwartz," in The New Republic, *1 November 1975.*

croaching on our own the kind of painful scrutiny it nowhere else receives; doing so bravely, and often at its own expense.

Schwartz offers compassionate insight into the lives of our Jewish failed sons. He offers, in the image of the cinema, a vision of the imprint of mass culture on immigrant life that is both resonant and useful as it shows us American culture going through the kinds of transformations Americans can scarcely keep up with. Much of Schwartz's work is unimpressive, immature and inflated, but Schwartz at his best, and yes, even at his worst, gives us critical tools to study those genres of adulthood that assure us we belong.

Mark Shechner (review date 1987)

SOURCE: "More on Delmore," in *Partisan Review,* Vol. 54, No. 3, 1987, pp. 497-502.

[*Shechner is an American educator and critic who specializes in Jewish-American literature. In the following essay, he reviews* Portrait of Delmore: Journals and Notes of Delmore Schwartz: 1939-1959.]

It is possible to feel overwhelmed by Delmore Schwartz in death as it was in life. Twenty years after his death on July 11, 1966, the movement to resurrect Schwartz has taken an aggressive turn. The publication of his journals is just a ripple in the tide of Schwartziana that has been swelling since 1975, when Saul Bellow's *Humboldt's Gift* brought Schwartz back into public consciousness as the kibbitzer maudit and insomniac laureate of his age. That wave includes Robert Phillips's edition of Schwartz's *Letters,* published in 1984; Schwartz's *Last and Lost Poems* (1979); the collection of "bagatelles," *The Ego is Always at the Wheel* (1986); James Atlas's *Delmore Schwartz: The Life of an American Poet* (1977); the extended portrait of Schwartz in William Barrett's *The Truants* (1982); and Bruce Bawer's essay on Schwartz's poetry in *The Middle Generation: The Lives and Poetry of Delmore Schwartz, Randall Jarrell, John Berryman, and Robert Lowell* (1986). Virtually forgotten after his death, Schwartz has now been brought back to life as a symbol of Jewish intellectual life and a small but vigorous cottage industry.

Much of this industry is the work of Schwartz's literary executor Robert Phillips, who has been toiling in the ruins of Schwartz's career in the hopes, it seems, of making a museum out of all that shattered masonry. The *Letters,* the *Last and Lost Poems* and *The Ego is Always at the Wheel* are his doing, and he cautions us in the last book that other publications are likely to be forthcoming: verse plays, unpublished novels, stories, a book-length critical study of T. S. Eliot, and the autobiographical poem that Schwartz wrestled with for years, *Genesis, Book II.* "Much of this material," Phillips has been candid to admit in the preface to *The Ego is Always at the Wheel,* "is not Schwartz at his best," and it is doubtful that any reader of the most recent gleanings will take issue with him.

Phillips has not been alone. Working in tandem to edit, decipher, and publish Schwartz's gargantuan journals has been Schwartz's exwife, Elizabeth Pollett, who had been estranged from Schwartz for nine years at the time of his death. The journals, some 2,400 pages of lava and ash, were among the papers rescued by Dwight Macdonald from a moving company, after their whereabouts came to light during a chance encounter in a bar between Macdonald's son and the proprietor of the company. Those 2,400 pages were eventually transcribed into 1,400 pages of typescript, then edited down to something like 900 pages [entitled *Portrait of Delmore: Journals and Notes of Delmore Schwartz: 1939-1959*]. Entries after 1959, which Elizabeth Pollett found virtually indecipherable, are omitted.

Schwartz began the journal of his twenty-sixth birthday, December 8, 1939, and kept at it for twenty-seven years until his death. It began as a diary of the most conventional kind: "In the evening I went to the movie. . . . Yesterday we went to see the Fergussons. . . . Jay called from Mt. Vernon." Except that literature is Schwartz's constant preoccupation, this is fairly indistinguishable from the diary of an ordinary teenager. It is self-conscious, gossipy, and bristling with resentment. Keeping track of social encounters and the social injuries he invariably provoked was Schwartz's chief preoccupation. But by 1942, the journal had become a catch-all for whatever impressions were bubbling through his mind: poems, limericks, epigrams, puns, sendups, assaults, appeals, diatribes—the effluvia of his restless imagination. When Schwartz was in one of his manic moods, the journal took on the qualities of a Joycean *monologue interieur,* and Schwartz's lifelong fascination with Joyce, whom he transcribed into his notebooks as a discipline of style, may have inspired his erratic and spontaneous method of notation. But in Schwartz's hands the Joycean manner—fleeting impressions joined by threads of association—often dispensed with the associations. Early on, the journal suggests a basic disorganization. By 1942, when Schwartz was twenty-nine and at the height of his powers, the private writing was already showing signs of decomposition, as though the tide of impressions was no longer under control. Two years later, while keeping up a brave front as a poet and man of letters, he privately admitted defeat:

> This lifelong sickness which robs me of my self, which takes away my power, which made me a poor student, the author of unfinished works, or works which deceive me very much: at last I know it is a sickness, and that I am hardly to blame, to blame myself—at least that much is understood.

The sickness was never precisely pinpointed, though insomnia was Schwartz's chief torment, and the remedies he indulged to combat it had a shattering effect on every mental faculty: his concentration, his character, his work habits. The journal is a twenty-year-long pathogram, which shows us Schwartz sliding into a limbo of alcohol, amphetamines, and barbiturates until disorder has become his only order, scatter his only unity, everywhere his sole direction.

> *July 5 [1945]* I took Benzedrine at 3:30. St. Louis 7, Giants 5. I rejected ten mss. I took a haircut. I had breakfast with E.; lunch with [Milton] Klonsky; I dined with *The New Yorker* at the Sevilla. I wrote one painful page. I glanced through

Auden's collected poems and was distressed by the titles. "Don't be Careful." Spoke to Edna [Phillips] on the phone.

Page after hopeless page, the journal proceeds in this fractured and banal fashion, the self-regard punctuated by jokes and epiphanies and, on good days, poems on the theme of his torment:

> I held a seashell to my ear and heard
> My heart roar PANDEMONIUM which was to
>   say
> Every demon from hell yells in your heart
> —Although you thought you heard the senseless
>   sea,
> You only heard yourself.

Schwartz's poetry was all misery and form, and the misery being constant, his perennial quest was for a proper form. "Form is an endless effort," he writes, "and not only that, but perhaps the secret of life." Again, "Every success I knew was from the fecundative power of form." These are standard claims, and yet in the context of these journals they seem like pleas for redemption. Cut loose from any sustaining ideas, Schwartz took form alone for his grail, one that was at times no larger than a shotglass: "All literature," he would declare nonchalantly, "is an effort at the formal character of the epigram," and he hoarded his epigrams the way a comedian hoards punch lines.

Schwartz's performance, as he turned the inner pandemonium into a theater of personality, had a hypnotic effect on others. "Mankind is stunned by the Exuberance and Beauty of certain individuals," observed Bellow in *Humboldt's Gift*. "When a Manic Depressive escapes from his Furies he's irresistible." In *New York Jew*, Alfred Kazin would remember "the headlong rush of words that seemed to engage every muscle in his face as he twisted and spat in the rage of his opinions." But Schwartz's improvisations are not so compelling in print as they were face to face. The command was in the delivery, which wedded the manic-depressive's intoxication to the *tummler*'s sense of timing, without which the exuberant lines fade into narcissism and exaggeration; they seem merely gaudy without being particularly potent, and Pollett herself steps outside the glow of her own devotion long enough to express disappointment in "the lopsidedness of the entries and the impossibilities, finally, of language to render life." This book might be thought of as the script for a great tragicomic performance in which puns and one-liners take the place of heroic verse. Schwartz was a dynamo of quips, a machine for generating *bon mots* and a few *mauvais* ones as well. "What this country needs is a good five-cent psychiatrist"; "Philip Rahv has his good qualities, but he never lets them stand in his way"; "She was the wife of the party; he was engaged in holy wedlock"; "How do you like Kipling?' 'I never drink it' "; "A horse divided against itself cannot stand"; "All gall is divided into three parts: arrogance, insensitivity, self-dramatization." Schwartz aspired, it seems, to be Milton Berle, but such a Berle as himself might yarn to be T. S. Eliot, taking the measure of modern life in iambs and singing to the mermaids with a cigar in his teeth.

Schwartz was a study in contradictions. On the one side

lay a heaviness, immanence, a nervous, exasperated life, and a sluggish physicality, "the heavy bear who goes with me."

> When I go down to sleep
>   To sleep
> I am wood I am
>   Stone I am a slow
> River, hardly flowing
> & all is warm & all is animal
> —I am stone, I am river
> I am wood—a wood but not
>   A leaf . . .

Then again, in raptures of illumination, he was the bard of air and wind, music and light.

> Music is not water, but it moves like water
> It is not fire but it soars as warm as the sun
> It is not rock, it is not fountain,
> But rock and fountain, clock and mountain
> Abide within it, bound together
> In radiance pulsing, vibrating, and reverberat-
>   ing,
> Dominating the domination of the weather.

This cadenza appears in 1959, when, gloomy and dazed, Schwartz could still snatch a grace beyond the reach of amphetamines. Playing Ariel to his own Caliban, he could outflank his depression long enough to strike the silver note. It is remarkable. The journal, otherwise sodden and world weary, suddenly melts into air. Perhaps these were no more than the normal gyrations of the manic depressive, whose capricious moods can drag him from the suburbs of heaven to the porches of hell in minutes, but one is struck all the same by their extremity: how utterly black were the black moods and how dazzling the light ones.

I wish I could report that [*Portrait of Delmore*] was a joy to read or that it returned me to Schwartz's writing with renewed appreciation. Unfortunately, it is a trial that no one will pick up casually. The scatter is appalling, and if these journals in any way can be said to capture Schwartz's furious presence, it is only by documenting in brutal detail his confusion and grief and the venom that poisoned all his social relations. The brilliant range of reference that Bellow recorded in *Humboldt's Gift*—"Yeats, Apollinaire, Lenin, Freud, Morris R. Cohen, Gertrude Stein, baseball statistics, and Hollywood gossip"—was no more than that, a range of reference and evidence of a mind that had mistaken gossip for thought and had gotten lost in the cosmopolitan wilderness somewhere between James Joyce and Walter Winchell. Schwartz's mind was an encyclopedia from which everything had been scratched but the titles, and he had an inkling of his own depthlessness: "As with an onion," he wrote, "illusion after illusion is peeled off—what remains? Nothing at all—".

What did Schwartz believe? These journals show us a man without a gospel, who by that fact alone stood apart from his fellow *Partisan Review* editors, all of whom were virtuosi of gospel. One looks in vain for a significant politics: Roosevelt appears seven times in the index, Trotsky four times, Stalin only twice, and they are only names among names. One looks for an emotional agenda, a social doctrine, a code of human relations, a burning metaphysic—anything. Even a poetic. The terrible truth was that behind the poetry was a void that Schwartz sought desperately to fill with words, as if to hide from himself the absence of meaning. Instead of meaning we find personality, instead of thought, declamation. Schwartz performed the rare feat of baring his breast while hiding his heart, electing to complain, to joke, to dramatize himself, and above all to itemize with dull perseverance every drink, every pill, every slight, every grievance, every frivolity, every frisson, and every pang, until the tabula rasa was smudged with grief and clotted with verse.

It is not too strong to say that this is an appalling book and that Schwartz is diminished by these raids on his papers. The journals are 663 pages long, the letters 384, the "bagatelles" 143. By comparison, a fine little compendium of Schwartz's best poems published in England in 1976, **What Is to Be Given?**, is but 75 pages long and is simply overwhelmed by the ephemera. **Portrait of Delmore** shows us the poet at his most dishevelled, stripped of his defenses and his dignity. Maybe what is lacking is only the ersatz dignity of literary form and verbal composure, but ersatz or real it is vital to the artist who digs deep into himself and mines the seams of his own shame for his art. At such times, one sympathizes with Kafka's plea to Max Brod to destroy all his papers after his death. We're all the richer for Brod's betrayal of his friend, but Schwartz left nothing like *The Trial* behind him when he died.

Delmore Schwartz in all his vanity and turmoil, his narcissism and pain, is growing uncommonly familiar to us these days, while the poetry is sliding out of focus. A generation of readers that knows nothing of Schwartz's great poem **"Seurat's Sunday Afternoon Along the Seine"** is now expert in his insomnia, his drinking, his rages, and his crackup. There have got to be better forms of homage than these 648 pages of undigested journal. Surely there are shorter ones.

Harry Levin on the legacy of Delmore Schwartz:

Delmore's peculiar gift was his *Angst,* his unreassuring certainty that discomfort is a basic component of our psychological condition, his accusation leveled against all who are complacent enough to feel at home in the universe he rejected.

Harry Levin, in his Memories of the Moderns, *New Directions, 1980.*

Mark Ford (essay date 31 March 1988)

SOURCE: "No One Else Can Take a Bath for You," in *London Review of Books,* Vol. 10, No. 7, March 31, 1988, pp. 20-1.

[*In the following essay, Ford offers an overview of Schwartz's literary career, focusing on his achievements and limitations as an artist.*]

It is unfortunate, really, that Schwartz has filtered into the general public's consciousness more because of the outstanding copy his life has proved for other writers than because of his own work. Saul Bellow's superb *roman à clef, Humboldt's Gift,* was modelled loosely on his relations with Schwartz in the late Forties and early Fifties, and—his first book after winning the Nobel Prize—was a colossal seller. By now, most of those who knew him best have had their say. There are essays from many of the old *Partisan* crowd, Dwight Macdonald, Irving Howe, William Barrett, Philip Rahv; a compassionate reminiscence from Harry Levin, who was much abused by Schwartz when they were neighbours in Cambridge in 1940; there are Lowell's elegies and Berryman's Dreamsongs, and even an awkward commemoration on his *The Blue Mask* album from Lou Reed, a student of Schwartz's at Syracuse in the early Sixties. And James Atlas's sensitive biography, published in 1977, provides an exhilarating mass of circumstantial evidence about Schwartz's day-to-day existence.

But the best introduction to his achievement remains his extraordinary first book. He really was onto something, though it's difficult even now to say exactly what:

> In the naked bed, in Plato's cave,
> Reflected headlights slowly slid the wall,
> Carpenters hammered under the shaded
> window,
> Wind troubled the window curtains all night
> long,
> A fleet of trucks strained uphill, grinding,
> Their freights covered, as usual.
> The ceiling lightened again, the slanting
> diagram
> Slid slowly forth.
> Hearing the milkman's chop,
> His striving up the stair, the bottle's chink,
> I rose from bed, lit a cigarette,
> And walked to the window . . .

It is perhaps the earnestness of this that is its most appealing feature, its implicit faith in poetry. It teems with echoes of Eliot, Yeats, Auden, Baudelaire, but, as in much of Eliot's own earlier work, the poem's intentness acts as a kind of crucible for each of the borrowings, making them seem like urgent data needing to be processed and understood by anyone with a serious interest in remaining alive in the modern world. Schwartz is describing his recurring insomnia, but the lines are at once rigorously impersonal and absolutely self-confident. The poem's subject is anxiety, guilt, doubt, but the poetry itself is authoritative and precise. Schwartz admired the way the early Auden could evoke atmospheres of imminent crisis with a jokey, fluent detachment, and in his excellent essay **'The Two Audens'** he pictured Auden plugging into England's 'collective unconscious . . . delivering its obsessions to the page'. These lines certainly covet that ability.

Pretty well all of Schwartz's best work is overwritten, almost violently so. His short story **'In Dreams Begin Responsibilities'**, for instance, which first made his name, heading the opening issue of the newly revived *Partisan Review* in 1937 in front of contributions from Edmund Wilson, Lionel Trilling, and even Picasso, has an intensity that seems both unique to Schwartz and bound up with its own moment of composition. There is nothing in it from which one might learn how to compose short stories, or how to achieve certain effects. Schwartz was 21 when he wrote it, and part of its charm and power certainly derives from its gaucheness, its schoolboy earnestness. Though it aims to be wise in a passionate, Dostoevskian way, it really succeeds through its awkwardness and innocence. The domestic situation which **'In Dreams Begin Responsibilities'** describes—the incompatibility of his mother and father from the very moment of their engagement—was Schwartz's major theme. Especially touching is the way the story seems to be driven by a kind of misplaced confidence in the omnipotence of art: the 'divine vibrations' Nabokov admired in it perhaps derive from the firmness of this trust. But as Schwartz went on, exploring his family's miseries over and over, in verse plays, lyrics, more stories, across the two hundred numbing pages of *Genesis: Book 1,* he never found himself quite able to discover within his life's vicissitudes the Wordsworthian coherence he so desired. As a child, he suffered a great deal from his parents' unhappy marriage, and was often treated as a pawn in their wranglings. His father was rarely at home, and had endless affairs. In addition, there were all the cultural dilemmas of first-generation Jewish immigrants to be endured. His personal history, Schwartz felt, which had complicated his character to the point of neurosis, would surely receive some sort of ultimate justification and annealment in the perfection of his art—a common thought since Edmund Wilson, but one that few successful artists can ever have taken as seriously as Schwartz did.

Passionate for absolutes, he expanded it into the full-blooded conception of the poet as Christ-like hero in the capitalist wilderness, involved in a continual act of unacknowledged self-sacrifice for the common good. He described how the modern poet 'must dedicate himself to poetry, although no one else seems likely to read what he writes; and he must be indestructible as a poet until he is destroyed as a human being'—a comment that might be funny if it weren't so sincere.

The irony was that Schwartz was quite incapable of exploiting his sufferings to artistic effect. His artistic friends have proved much better at these sufferings. His gifts were lyrical, not narrative or dramatic. None of the fictional personae he invented for himself really connects his life to his work, as happens in Lowell or Berryman. Essentially Schwartz was, like Dylan Thomas, a dazzling phrase-maker. His first lines were usually his best, and these often became the poems' titles: **'Dogs are Shakespearean, Children are strangers', 'In the Naked Bed, in Plato's Cave', 'The Beautiful American Word, Sure'**. Phrases like these, and sometimes whole poems, are exciting for no single clear reason, although probably most important is the way they seem to subdue the needs of the individual sensibility in favour of an awareness of the possibilities of language for its own sake. Disparate and vatic, they aim vaguely at some private, or perhaps universal, *angst*: but most of the poems' pleasures remain contingent on the strange convolutions of imagery and syntax in individual lines or phrases.

Given the unstable nature of his talent, Schwartz's assault

on the long poem was doomed from the start. But by the time he began *Genesis* he had read Freud—according to William Barrett, this was the central disaster of his life—and the Family Romance seemed the answer to all his problems, the obvious, indeed the only possible plot. His earlier work is, to use his own phrase for Auden, full of 'the residue of undigested meaning', but Schwartz's middle poems and stories tend more towards tedious psychologising. *Genesis* is a family history; by detailing the exploits of grandparents, uncles, cousins, aunts, Schwartz seems to have hoped to establish once and for all his identity and the sources of his genius: while the story of their emigration is interesting enough, however, the touchingly absurd poetry and Biblical prose in which it is told never ignite. Schwartz's reputation suffered for it on all fronts. His publisher James Laughlin was unenthusiastic, Auden advised him not to publish, and, when it did come out in 1943, it received, at best, tepidly polite reviews.

Schwartz never abandoned poetry. In fact, over the next twenty years he wrote reams of it, much of it still unpublished—Yale's manuscript library has twenty or so large boxes of his papers, including hundreds of pages of the typescript for *Genesis: Book II*. And much of it makes eerie reading. As his life fell apart, and the exhaustive doses of Nembutal, Seconal and alcohol with which he combated his insomnia took their toll, and as his fits of paranoia and mania became more frequent, his poetry grew eccentrically chirpy and spontaneous:

> 'I am cherry alive,' the little girl sang,
> 'Each morning I am something new . . . '

Schwartz's literary executor, Robert Philips, thinks this is one of Schwartz's permanent contributions to 20th-century American poetry, but I don't think he can be serious. There are occasional strikes, such as **'Mr. Seurat's Sunday Afternoon'**, and he never lost his gift for good titles (**'Dusk shows us what we are and hardly mean'**), but most of his later poems are too loosely put together to conceal their baffled inner emptiness. Conceived as the unchecked effusions of a naive lyricism, they too often end up sounding like bad imitations of early Roethke. Dwight Macdonald acutely spoke of Schwartz's 'invincible innocence'. In his later life he grew both violently suspicious—it was Schwartz who coined the aphorism 'Even paranoiacs have real enemies'—and litigious, and slapped trumped-up writs on all his old friends: but his poetry from these years seems to yearn ever more nostalgically for the sweet and pristine.

His critical faculties, on the other hand, never really deserted him. Schwartz wrote a great quantity of good criticism during his life, mainly essays and reviews. Books on Eliot and Fitzgerald were advertised, but never appeared. His critical prose tends towards the orotund—Eliot's criticism is the overwhelming model—but it can also be shrewd and personal. Schwartz studied the literary stockmarket like a broker, monitoring reputations as they dropped a point, gained a point, and this gives his assessments of his contemporaries—he never wrote on earlier authors—a certain relish. 'Pound is not as learned as he seems to be,' he cautions, before predicting the *Cantos'* 'immense usefulness for future writing'. His high seriousness rarely unbent, even when he became film-reviewer for *The New Republic* in the mid-Fifties. His joke-free cultural analyses of Mary Pickford and Marilyn Monroe are perceptive.

Schwartz did feel, however, that he had a lighter vein to cultivate. *The ego is always at the wheel* (another brilliant title) is a selection of bagatelles he wrote mainly in the late Forties and early Fifties; about half were previously published in magazines and Schwartz's *Vaudeville for a Princess* collection (1950), which inventively interspersed poetry and prose, while half were found among his papers. The previously unpublished essays are especially baffling. It's hard to imagine anyone, let alone Schwartz, sitting down to write these limp trifles except on commission.

He was an explosive conversationalist and a great raconteur, but his attempts in these pieces at the middlebrow columnist's garrulous humour, as perfected by Thurber, Ring Lardner (one of Schwartz's heroes) or S. J. Perelman, are quite disastrous. The required tone of wide-eyed pedantry was simply alien to him. Most of the pieces in question convey a grimmer comedy—that of the self-conscious intellectual reaching for a populist style in order to escape for a while from his obsessions. Many are facetious descriptions of literary classics, without punch or point. *Hamlet* can only be understood 'if we suppose that everyone is roaring drunk from the beginning to the end of the play.' The only thing we can know for certain about Don Giovanni is that he 'was a Lesbian, that is to say, someone who likes to sleep with girls'. The definition of Existentialism is that 'no one else can take a bath for you.'

Others are personal reminiscences in which Schwartz dramatises himself as a picaresque innocent. **'The ego is always at the wheel'** describes the cars in his life, from a 1929 Royal Coupé in 1929 to a 1936 Buick in 1949, and how the dealers rooked him on each trade-in. In another, he is hired by Ma Bell to lecture her junior executives on

The Brothers Karamazov, in the hope of reducing 'patterns of over-conformity' among the staff. Schwartz is unable to appear natural or at ease in these pieces, and it is hard to believe that each one underwent numerous revisions. Even the best, a description of adolescent gloom following a precocious immersion in Spengler's *The Decline of the West* and a violent dip in the fortunes of the Giants, has a dispiriting vagueness to it. Though the Giants buy the formidable batter Rogers Hornsby in the close season, they still miss out on the Pennant race the following year. Schwartz concludes:

> It is now years since I first became aware that the reality of the future was very likely to be very different than any present image or expectation: Yet this awareness, recognition, or knowledge are likely to be astonishing and unpredictable in many ways so essentially the same as they were so long ago that I must make an admission which may be a confession: Experience has taught me nothing.

The publication of these curiosities now can only re-affirm the drift of this self-analysis, and deepen our awareness of the extraordinary misunderstandings that accompanied Schwartz's enormous original talent.

FURTHER READING

Criticism

Wilson, Raymond. "Delmore Schwartz and Purgatory." *Partisan Review* LVII, No. 2 (Summer 1990): 363-70.

> Analyzes the similarities between Schwartz's "In Dreams Begin Responsibilities" and William Butler Yeats's *Purgatory.*

Additional coverage of Schwartz's life and career is contained in the following sources published by Gale Research: *Contemporary Authors,* Vols. 17-18, 25-28 (rev. ed., obituary); *Contemporary Authors New Revision Series,* Vol. 35; *Contemporary Authors Permanent Series,* Vol. 2; *Contemporary Literary Criticism,* Vols. 2, 4, 10, 45; *Dictionary of Literary Biography,* Vols. 28, 48; *Major 20th-Century Writers;* and *Poetry Criticism,* Vol. 8.

Robert Towne

1936(?)-

(Full name Robert Burton Towne; also wrote under the pseudonyms P. H. Vazak and Edward Wain) American screenwriter, director, and actor.

The following entry provides an overview of Towne's career through 1994.

INTRODUCTION

Towne is most famous for his Academy Award-winning screenplay for the film *Chinatown* (1974). Widely regarded as the best screenwriter in Hollywood, he is also renowned for his uncredited rewriting—or "screen doctoring"—of the scripts for such noted films as *Bonnie and Clyde* (1967) and *The Godfather* (1972). *Chinatown,* directed by Roman Polanski, epitomizes Towne's cinematic trademarks of rigidly structured and meticulously detailed plots, controversial themes, and intriguing, offbeat characters. Having gained critical acclaim for directing his own screenplays, namely *Personal Best* (1982) and *Tequila Sunrise* (1988), Towne has been compared to such prominent and influential Hollywood writers as Ben Hecht, Joseph and Herman Mankiewicz, and Charles Brackett.

Biographical Information

Born in San Pedro, California, Towne studied philosophy and literature at Pomona State College before dropping out to join the army. After military service, he took a series of acting classes where he met producer-director Roger Corman—for whom he wrote his first screenplay, *The Last Woman on Earth* (1960)—and his longtime friend and collaborator Jack Nicholson. While "doctoring" screenplays for a variety of Hollywood directors during the 1960s and early 1970s—most notably rewriting much of *Bonnie and Clyde* for director Arthur Penn and devising a crucial scene between Michael Corleone and his father, Vito, in Francis Ford Coppola's *The Godfather*—Towne also scripted episodes for the television series *The Outer Limits* and *The Man from U.N.C.L.E.* In the 1970s Towne wrote three highly acclaimed screenplays: *The Last Detail* (1973), based on the novel by Darryl Ponicsan; *Chinatown;* and *Shampoo* (1975), an Academy Award-nominated collaboration with Warren Beatty. In the 1980s Towne produced and directed two of his own scripts, *Personal Best* and *Tequila Sunrise*. However, because of budgeting difficulties and his reputation for costly, painstaking attention to detail, studios were reluctant to back Towne on future producing and directing assignments. In 1990 Jack Nicholson starred in and directed Towne's screenplay *The Two Jakes,* the long-awaited sequel to *Chinatown;* and in the 1990s Towne and Beatty worked together on the script for *Love Affair* (1994), which is based on two earlier films, *Love Affair* (1939) and *An Affair to Remember* (1957).

Major Works

While his plots and settings vary widely from script to script, nearly all of Towne's screenplays explore complex moral and social themes. His first critical success came with the script for *The Last Detail,* a story about two seasoned navy petty officers, played by Jack Nicholson and Otis Young, who are assigned to escort a young, naive seaman to the naval prison in Portsmouth, Virginia. Before completing their mission, however, the two men treat their troubled but good-hearted prisoner to a final good time. The offbeat humor and dark side of life portrayed in *The Last Detail* are explored in much greater depth in *Chinatown.* A detective story modeled after those written by Dashiell Hammett and Raymond Chandler, *Chinatown* evokes the style of the *film noir* genre of the 1940s and deals with moral and ethical questions. In telling the story of detective Jake Gittes, played by Jack Nicholson, and his search for a missing girl, the film explores the history of Los Angeles and examines the depths of moral corruption. Towne summed up the film succinctly: "I wanted to tell a story about a man who raped the land and his daughter in the name of the future." The following year, Towne and Beatty's script for *Shampoo* addressed what Joel Bellman called "the social contradictions and manic energy" of the 1960s; with director Hal Ashby they examined the libidinous life of a hairdresser named George, whose many relationships bring him in contact with the social and political leaders of Los Angeles on the eve of the 1968 presidential election. In *Personal Best* Towne explored female intimacy among young American women athletes who prepared for the 1980 Olympic games. The film details the relationship of two women, depicting their growth from competitors to friends, lovers, and, finally, to competitors again; the lesbian element of the story generated considerable controversy at the time. Like *Personal Best,* Towne both wrote and directed *Tequila Sunrise,* a story about a drug dealer, played by Mel Gibson, trying to retire from his illegal business; a narcotics detective, played by Kurt Russell, who has long been trying to arrest him; and a restaurateur, played by Michelle Pfeiffer, who comes between them. The tortuously complex plot and the script's refusal to make moral judgments prompted Mark Horowitz to describe Towne as "a moral filmmaker in the French sense of the word: he's preoccupied with choices and ideas. . . . Like [Jean] Renoir before him, Towne's lack of moral rigidity has often been misperceived as moral laxity."

Critical Reception

Critical reaction to Towne's work has generally been very favorable. Many critics contend that Towne's reworking of the original storyline in *The Last Detail*—for example, having the two shore patrol officers deliver their prisoner at the end, rather than allowing him to escape as they do in the novel—together with his superb use of salty dialogue and humor, are considerable improvements on the book. *Chinatown* is generally considered a masterpiece of narrative structure and plot development. Commentators have praised Towne's interweaving of a multilayered mystery plot with an examination and evocation of the history of southern California. Tony Slade has remarked that the depiction of Jake Gittes as an "ingenious but naive quester seeking answers to questions he can barely comprehend . . . aims toward the high reaches of tragedy." Several commentators, however, have pointed out inconsistencies in the development of Towne's characters. For example, Slade argues that Gittes's true motivation for following his case to its bitter end is never made clear and that Gittes's stated purpose of protecting his reputation is ultimately unconvincing. Similarly, some critics find implausible the final scenes of *Shampoo,* when George begins to question his undisciplined lifestyle. Some critics have also suggested that *Tequila Sunrise* and *The Two Jakes* suffer from overly complex, "out of control" plots that impair the believability of both the stories and their characters. Additionally, while many applaud Towne's determination to address issues with strong moral implications, some commentators have faulted his refusal to take a clear-cut moral stand. Nevertheless, filmmakers and critics generally agree that Towne is an extremely talented screenwriter and filmmaker and that his work represents a major contribution to the art of American film.

*PRINCIPAL WORKS

The Last Woman on Earth [as Edward Wain] (screenplay) 1960
The Tomb of Ligeia [adaptor; from the short story "Ligeia" by Edgar Allan Poe] (screenplay) 1965
Villa Rides [with Sam Peckinpah; adaptors from the book *Pancho Villa* by William Douglas Lansford] (screenplay) 1968
The Last Detail [adaptor; from the novel by Darryl Ponicsan] (screenplay) 1973
Chinatown (screenplay) 1974
Shampoo [with Warren Beatty] (screenplay) 1975
The Yakuza [with Paul Schrader] (screenplay) 1975
†*Personal Best* (screenplay) 1982
Greystoke: The Legend of Tarzan, Lord of the Apes [as P. H. Vazak, with Michael Austin; adaptors from the novel *Tarzan of the Apes* by Edgar Rice Burroughs] (screenplay) 1984
The Natural [with Phil Dusenberry; adaptors from the novel by Bernard Malamud] 1984
†*Tequila Sunrise* (screenplay) 1988
Days of Thunder [with Tom Cruise] (screenplay) 1990
The Two Jakes (screenplay) 1990
Love Affair [with Warren Beatty; adaptors from the screenplays for the films *Love Affair,* written by Delmer Daves and Donald Ogden Stewart, and *An Affair to Remember,* written by Daves and Leo McCarey] (screenplay) 1994

---

*In addition to the films listed above, for which Towne received either sole or shared screenwriting credit, he has also worked without screen credit on numerous films. The most prominent of these include *Bonnie and Clyde* (1967), for which he is credited as "special consultant"; *The Godfather* (1972); *Marathon Man* (1976); *Reds* (1981); *Swing Shift* (1984); *8 Million Ways to Die* (1985); *Fatal Attraction* (1987); and *Frantic* (1988).

†Towne also directed these films.

CRITICISM

Pauline Kael   (review date 11 February 1974)

SOURCE: "Nicholson's High," in *The New Yorker,* Vol. XLIX, No. 51, February 11, 1974, pp. 95-6.

[*Kael is one of the foremost film critics in the United States. In the following mixed review of* The Last Detail, *she argues that despite Towne's improvements on the novel by Darryl Ponicsan, the film remains calculatingly sentimental.*]

In *The Last Detail,* you can see the kid who hasn't grown up in Nicholson's grin, and that grin has the same tickle it had when he played the giddy, drunken Southern lawyer in *Easy Rider,* but now it belongs to the ravaged face of an aging sailor. The role of Buddusky, the tattooed signalman, first class, is the best full-scale part he's had; the screenwriter Robert Towne has shaped it to Nicholson's gift for extremes. After Buddusky's fourteen years in the

Navy, his mind and emotions have been devastated, and he lives on nostalgia, ingrained resentment, a lewd prole's quick anger, and booze. The role has the highs that Nicholson glories in. He plays it like a spaced-out, dissipated James Cagney; his face always has something going on in it, and you feel that you can't get too much of him—though you do. At its best, his performance is so full it suggests a sustained version of Barry Fitzgerald's small but classic portrait of a merchant seaman in *The Long Voyage Home;* it's easy to imagine Buddusky a few years hence returning to his ship after a binge as Fitzgerald did—a wizened little man with his tail between his legs. The movie is about blasted lives: Buddusky's and those of Mulhall (the black actor Otis Young), a gunner's mate, first class, and Meadows (Randy Quaid), a morose eighteen-year-old seaman who has been sentenced to eight years in a Navy prison for attempting to steal forty dollars from a polio-donation box. Buddusky and Mulhall are dispatched to take Meadows from the brig in Norfolk, Virginia, to the naval prison in Portsmouth, New Hampshire. The movie is the record of their dallying, beer-soaked journey and of their self-discoveries en route.

Nicholson gets a chance to demonstrate his enormous skill, and he keeps the picture going, but he's playing a mawkish role—a sentimentalist with a coward's heart. This time, the emotions he's expressing are, if anything, too clear. **The Last Detail,** based on Darryl Ponicsan's novel, is the newest version of a heart-wrenching genre that used to work with a huge popular audience—and possibly it will this time, too. Essentially, it's the story of doomed people who discover their humanity too late, and nothing in the movie can keep this from being a sell—not Nicholson's and Quaid's imaginative performances, and not Robert Towne's finely tuned script. It's doubtful if there's any way to extract an honest movie from a Ponicsan novel—Ponicsan also wrote the book from which *Cinderella Liberty* was derived—because Ponicsan works on us for a canned response. His material didn't play in *Cinderella Liberty* and it does here, but the same manipulative streak runs through both films, and the same obviousness. Everything in **The Last Detail** tells you how to feel at each point; that's how the downer-tearjerker has always worked. This picture sounds realistically profane and has a dark, grainy surface, and by Hollywood standards it's strong, adult material, but the mechanism is a vise for our emotions—the mechanism is schlock. The downer-tearjerker congratulates you for your sensitivity in seeing the touching hopelessness and misery that are all you've got to look at.

Meadows, the eighteen-year-old, is a petty pilferer, a bawling, uncommunicative kid, too sluggish and demoralized to be angry at the injustice of his harsh sentence. He doesn't know that he has any rights; he has never learned to fight back. As the story is set up, he's a sleeping beauty; on the drunken trip, Buddusky and Mulhall offer him comradeship, and he awakens and discovers his manhood. We perceive the possibilities in him, knowing that prison life will crush him back down to the listless, almost catatonic state he was in. And, in a parallel process, the tough, damaged Buddusky, who has felt warm and paternal while bringing the kid out, can only retreat to his guzzling

and brawling. Buddusky couldn't function except in the service; he's quick to identify with the kid, because he's an emotional wreck himself, living in the past, spinning out tired anecdotes. We're programmed to recognize that he's a man who is always spoiling for a fight so he can let out his frustrations, and we're programmed to respond to each pointedly ironic episode. When the three men go to a Village party, Buddusky comes on with a "line" and he doesn't register that he's bombing out; his peppy cock-of-the-walk act is all he's got—he has no other way to make contact. We see him through the girls' contemptuous eyes; to them he's just a crude blowhard. In contrast, the depressed kid's innocent, solemn dignity is a hit with them. The movie is about the lost possibilities in both Buddusky and Meadows, and about the acceptance of a restricted life by Mulhall. Otis Young's Mulhall has chosen the Navy because it's not a bad deal for him; we can't tell much more about the character. Otis Young has the cheekbones and facial contours of a stronger version of the young Frank Sinatra; his eyes slant upward the same way, and he's marvellous to look at, but the role isn't as flamboyant as Nicholson's or as affecting as Quaid's, and Young's restrained performance doesn't add up to as much as his face suggests. He never quite comes across; he stays as nice-guyish as a black Gregory Peck.

The direction, by Hal Ashby, is not all it might be. I loved much of Ashby's first film, *The Landlord*—a story about a rich white boy (Beau Bridges) who bought a building in a black ghetto and had an affair with a tenant (Diana Sands). It was adapted by William Gunn from Kristin Hunter's novel (both writers are black), and it had a complicated sense of why people behave as they do. It was full of characters; more and more people kept getting into the young landlord's life, and I became interested in every one of them. In several cases, I don't think those performers have been as good since; maybe the writing accounted for the quality as much as the directing did, but I missed Ashby's second film, *Harold and Maude,* and I'd been looking forward to more of his work, hoping for a film full of people whose lives can't be reduced to formulas. The material here, though, is on a single track; we go from city to city, but there's never anything to look at. Visually, the movie is relentlessly lower-depths gloomy; it doesn't allow us to think of anything but the pushy central situation. And though Nicholson does suggest some of the qualities of the characters in *The Landlord,* and Quaid transforms himself before our eyes, they play within a preordained scheme. It's all *required.* The effectiveness of the movie depends on the director's wringing pathos out of the two older men's gruff tenderness toward the kid and their desire to show him a good time before he's locked away; and though Ashby, to his credit, keeps the pathos down, there is still more mugging than necessary. Ashby's weaknesses show—not so much with the three leads as with the minor players and the staging of the large-scale sequences. That's where you can feel the director trying to get a certain emotional effect, and he gets it, all right (an effect I hate anyway), but he's also heavy and clumsy about getting it (which makes me even more aware of how I hate it). There's a fight aboard a train, and the passengers don't react adequately; there's a church scene in which followers of an Eastern religion chant together, and though it may well be authentic, the way it has been shot it doesn't feel authentic; in a Boston brothel scene Carol Kane does her Pre-Raphaelite wasted-beauty number; and so on. And I think I'd be happier without the Johnny Mandel score, with its antic use of military airs, orchestrated in an unfamiliarly thin way to add a musical layer of irony. It all works together, of course, but the overstressed style and the systematized ironies tighten one's responses. Ponicsan has talent, but he degrades his own material; he milks tragedy for pathos. Towne improves on the novel, and his ear for dialogue gives the film some distinction, but there is only one line that seems to be there for its own sweet sake—when Nicholson tells a story about a whore in Wilmington who had a glass eye—and this was the only minute I freely enjoyed.

Stanley Kauffmann   (review date 23 February 1974)

SOURCE: A review of *The Last Detail,* in *The New Republic,* Vol. 170, No. 8, February 23, 1974, pp. 22, 33-4.

[*Kauffmann, one of the most respected and well-known film critics in the United States, has reviewed movies for* The New Republic *for many years. In the following positive review of* The Last Detail, *he notes a number of Towne's improvements to the novel upon which the film is based.*]

There's a kind of film that reveals its entire shape very early, with a cleverness that makes us both interested and wary. During such a picture the main question isn't "What happens next?" It's "Are they going to muff it?" Some examples, differently successful: *The Gunfighter, The African Queen, The Informer, Lifeboat, The Lost Patrol, The Defiant Ones.* Latest example: *The Last Detail.*

The script by Robert Towne is based on, and better than, the novel by Darryl Ponicsan. Two US Navy sailors, old pros, are assigned to escort a young sailor from the Norfolk, Virginia naval base to the naval prison in Portsmouth, New Hampshire. The story deals with the three men in transit, and the moment you understand that, you see that this is going to be a symbolic film with overtones. The situation is far from new: innumerable Westerns have dealt with a marshal bringing back a prisoner to justice, the two men traveling through wilds and hostiles, facing danger together. But *The Last Detail* is better than most like it because the story is not so consciously abstracted and, chiefly, because the drama results from the struggle *not* to change, rather than building to some kind of rosy affirmation. This script ends exactly where it was headed from the beginning. Nothing is bettered. The real agon comes from the fact that, after temptations to go somewhere else, the script gets right back where it was heading—into reality, habit, fear and compliance. The result is not ironic; it's flatly truthful.

Jack Nicholson, of *Five Easy Pieces* and *Carnal Knowledge,* is the senior of the Shore Patrol duo. The other is a black actor named Otis Young, previously unknown to me. Their prisoner is Randy Quaid, a big fellow who has been seen before in small parts. Quaid plays a kleptomaniacal 18-year-old boy, insecure, apathetic, uncomplaining. He tried to steal a collection box containing $40—he didn't even get away with it. The collection was

for polio, the pet charity of the admiral's wife. Quaid got an eight-year sentence, with a possible two years off for good behavior. The two old toughies have to take this kid to the prison and turn him over to begin this sentence.

Nicholson's first plan is to hustle the kid up to Portsmouth as quickly as possible, so that he and Young can have the rest of the allotted five days on their own. But the boy's continuous presence, the grotesqueness of his sentence, his incompetence to handle his life, his inexperience of practically everything, his puppy-like regard for his guards, all of these have a foreseen but nicely handled effect. Instead of rushing, Nicholson dallies. He obviously wants to give the boy something, some fun, some pleasantness, before he gets shut away. This of course includes first sex, in a Boston brothel. Young argues with Nicholson about his sentimentality. (In other language. The dialogue is, justly, very raunchy.) They either have to let the kid escape or turn him over, and they're not going to let him escape because that would mean *their* asses; so why all this silk wrapping? Why not just get it over with, without sops to their own nobility? But Nicholson insists, and Young, who really wants to do the same thing, agrees.

"Don't let it go pulpy," we keep hoping. Except for a contrived encounter with some Greenwich Village types engaged in Nichiren Shoshu chanting and some fisticuffs with marines that are right out of Paramount service comedies of the '30s, the script hews to its line. No one short of a beast could have responded less than these escorts; no one but fictional characters would have let the boy escape as a result of that response. They deliver him to prison at the end and walk away, chatting about what they're going to do before they get back to Norfolk. (An improvement over the novel, which has a long tediously ironic coda.) Responsibility, the script implies, is always elsewhere; the lower man bucks it to the higher, and the highest bucks it back to the lowest, en masse. This last is called duty to the corps or the service or the People.

A strong undercurrent of the script is the implication, not new but still true, that the armed forces are the career for you if you want to remain a boy. Substitute cokes for beer; eliminate sex, which is only one number on a program, an incidental chance for triumph or patronization; and you have three 12-year-olds on an outing with overeating and dormitory hijinks. A uniform, particularly for the lower ranks, is armor against growing up.

Jack Nicholson, tattooed, comes back. He was figuratively away in *The King of Marvin Gardens* and *A Safe Place;* here he has a part that is exactly right for him—a rough romantic, innately furious, frequently gentle but knowingly cruel. To cavil, the only thing wrong with his taking over this picture is that his role has been built for him to take over the picture. Aside from the faint air of virtuoso occasion, he and the role are perfect for each other, and together they galvanize the film.

As his sidekick Young is less effective. He's passable, but I was always conscious of his working; he lacks that last access of confidence in the medium, confidence that the camera will reach in and *get* the performance from him. Quaid, I thought at first, was not going to be good. But physically he reminded me of so many big country boys that I used to know, with spaces between their teeth (I don't mean missing teeth) his very lack of appeal contributed so much to his pathos that my reaction soon became that of his guards. Michael Moriarty, now so fine on Broadway in *Find Your Way Home,* has a nice bit as an uppity marine lieutenant.

The director was Hal Ashby, who made *Harold and Maude* and *The Landlord.* I saw only the latter and disliked its inflated cinema rhetoric. Here his work is hard, businesslike, clean. (But he ought to have watched the fellow-passengers on train and bus; they are strangely oblivious to the trio's broilings.) The opening credits are whipped past briskly to staccato drum rolls. (Military marches occasionally underpin matters—the only attempt at irony, and superfluous, I think.) At Portsmouth Quaid is whisked upstairs into prison without even a chance to say goodbye; it's just the effect that's needed, like the abrupt clanging of a steel door. And two other moments are especially well handled. Nicholson and Young take the boy on a detour to Camden to see his mother who lives there alone. The mother isn't home—another improvement over the novel, which has a trite scene with the mother and her seedy lover. After some chuffing and blowing on the wintry porch, Nicholson tries the door. It's open. We get just a quick look at the scruffy living room. The boy doesn't even step inside. Our look at the room and the boy's reaction to it tell us all we need to know about the past life that has put him where he is.

Then, during a childishly perverse picnic in a snowy Boston park, the boy makes a last-minute unplanned attempt to escape. The guards chase him. He slips; they catch him and subdue him. Ashby holds the camera back from the struggle in a long shot. It's an excellent touch. Ashby doesn't want to maul us with immediate violence; he wants us to see the three men, former friends, struggling in the middle of open space, three physically and humanely entangled items of humanity. Instead of being shocking or gory, which it might have been, the moment is perfectly sad.

Martin Kasindorf (essay date 14 October 1974)

SOURCE: "Hot Writer," in *Newsweek,* Vol. LXXXIV, No. 16, October 14, 1974, pp. 114-114B.

[*In the following, Kasindorf discusses Towne's approach to screenwriting and his experiences working on* Chinatown.]

The Hollywood star system is back stronger than ever. Once again it's an age of the hot performer, the hot director—and now the hot screenwriter. Where for years studios were reluctant to take chances on original screenplays, preferring adaptations of "sure-fire" hit plays and books, now the bidding for original scripts is fierce. The success of originals like David S. Ward's Oscar-winning *The Sting,* William Goldman's *Butch Cassidy and the Sundance Kid* and Carole Eastman's *Five Easy Pieces* has put a big premium on originals. Willard Huyck and Gloria Katz, the husband-wife team who created *American Graffiti,* were paid $400,000 for their new story of rum-running in the '20s, *Lucky Lady,* which will star Liza Minnelli. All

this has given the screenwriter a status he hasn't had since the '30s and '40s, when people like Ben Hecht, Herman Mankiewicz and Charles Brackett were pounding typewriters and bending elbows in palm-shaded bungalows.

Right now there's no hotter screenwriter than Robert Towne, whose salty adaptation of Darryl Ponicsan's novel *The Last Detail* earned him an Oscar nomination last year, and whose brilliant *Chinatown* will be hard to beat for the best original screenplay of 1974. At 38, after unsung years of "doctoring" others' efforts as an Abe Burrows of Hollywood, Towne now gets $150,000 for adaptations and up to $300,000 for his original stories, with juicy percentages of the box office. Long handicapped by a chronic sickliness that he shrugged off as "writer's hypochondriasis" until it was diagnosed two years ago as a complex of allergies, the bearded, rumpled Towne had been considered, he wryly recalls, "a relief pitcher who could come in for an inning, not pitch the whole game."

Towne got his start by writing horror movies for producer Roger Corman whom he met in 1958 at acting classes along with Jack Nicholson, James Coburn and Sally Kellerman. After some television scripting, Towne moved into rewriting scripts. He put a final polish on *Bonnie and Clyde* and added the brilliant, crucial last scene between Marlon Brando and Al Pacino to *The Godfather* at the request of director Francis Ford Coppola, a superb screenwriter himself. But not until he was cured of his allergies did Towne begin the sustained productivity that has brought him to the top.

The first choice of Paramount production chief Robert Evans to do the screen adaptation of *The Great Gatsby,* Towne luckily turned down that job, convincing Evans in the process to commission *Chinatown.* Then, among other projects, Towne teamed with Warren Beatty to write *Shampoo,* a forthcoming comedy about a fashionable Beverly Hills hairdresser, starring Beatty, Julie Christie and Goldie Hawn. Nowadays the busy Towne hangs out with big-name buddies like Beatty and Nicholson (the star of both *The Last Detail* and *Chinatown*), and lives in an idyllic hillside cottage with his girlfriend of six years, actor John Payne's daughter, Julie.

Doing most of his writing in a tiny Los Angeles apartment, Towne likes to follow his solitary drafting with daily visits to the set to solve problems once filming starts. A classic craftsman who uses no gimmicks, Towne believes that "People want to escape into stories with strong narrative lines. A well-made screenplay has to go somewhere, not just ramble around. A good script should have air in it, to allow everybody latitude. If you don't want to totally alienate directors and actors and drive them crazy, don't tell them what they're feeling." Not surprisingly, Towne finds it easier to adapt material than create his own. "Fear and vanity don't come into the process in the same way as in original material," he notes.

Nevertheless, *Chinatown* succeeds largely because Towne, like the best novelists, chose to work close to his own roots. Raised in the San Pedro harbor district of Los Angeles, he worked on a tuna clipper and noted the paranoid fear of the fishermen that their wives were cheating on them. He began *Chinatown* with a scene playing on this theme involving his private eye, J.J. Gittes. A longtime devotee of Dashiell Hammett and Raymond Chandler, Towne fused their hard-boiled atmospherics with his own concern for the violation of the land. His archvillain, Noah Cross, played by John Huston, is an amalgam of several portentous figures from California's history of land and water scandals. "I wanted to tell a story about a man who raped the land and his own daughter in the name of the future," says Towne. "Men like Cross believe that as long as they can keep building, keep reproducing, they'll live forever."

For all their new star status, writers are still the low men in the director-dominated movie hierarchy. On *Chinatown* Towne found himself at loggerheads with director Roman Polanski, a strong creative force with ideas of his own. After wrenching debates, Polanski changed Towne's original ending, in which virtue at least partially triumphs, to a denouement of unrelieved despair. "The ending is so relentlessly cynical that it works against itself," says the still bitter Towne. During one dispute, Polanski asked Towne, in his Polish accent, "Bob, do you think I'm a schmock?" No, Towne shot back: "You're a terrific .400 hitter, which means that I think you're right less than half the time." Even before the cameras rolled, the two had stopped speaking to each other. "I would never work with Roman again, nor he with me," Towne says.

Nevertheless, Towne accepts the screenwriter's lot. "Film is totally a director's medium," he says. "And I would rather work with a strong director, because the chances are it will be a better movie. Ideally, your relationship with the director should be one of loving contentiousness."

Jack Nicholson and Faye Dunaway in Chinatown.

J.J. Gittes may live on in a sequel, sans Polanski. Meanwhile Towne is working on his most bizarre project, *Lord Greystoke,* based on Edgar Rice Burroughs's original Tarzan story. Towne is converting the ape-man from a mighty, monosyllabic mumbler to a marooned idealist. "The original myth showed that an English lord could conquer nature on the Dark Continent," says Towne. "This lord will have a communion with nature."

Charles Michener (review date 10 February 1975)

SOURCE: "Don Juan in Beverly Hills," in *Newsweek,* Vol. LXXXV, No. 6, February 10, 1975, p. 51.

[*In the following excerpt, Michener favorably reviews Towne's collaboration with Warren Beatty on* Shampoo, *suggesting that "many people will view* Shampoo *as 'Warren Beatty's film,' not just because he is listed as producer, co-author and star, but because his public persona is . . . in many ways its central subject and joke."*]

Warren Beatty, a rich, complicated man with a reputation as Hollywood's most active Don Juan, has made a rich, complicated comedy about the perils of Don Juan-ing called *Shampoo.* To imply that Beatty alone is responsible for its success is unfair to his sharp-eared co-screenwriter, Robert Towne, his sensitive director, Hal Ashby, and his brilliant co-stars, Julie Christie, Goldie Hawn, Jack Warden and Lee Grant. But many people will view *Shampoo* as "Warren Beatty's film," not just because he is listed as producer, co-author and star, but because his public persona is, as Marlon Brando's was in *Last Tango in Paris,* in many ways its central subject—and joke.

Beatty's fictional alter ego is a hairdresser named George who practices his art in that citadel of hairdressing, Beverly Hills. His subjects are women who are preparing themselves for one of America's favorite social rituals, an election-night party—in this instance, Nov. 5, 1968, the year that both mini-skirts and Richard Nixon were "in." George worries, in one of the film's funniest moments of self-meditation: "I've been cutting too much hair lately; I'm losing my concept." But his energy is mostly directed outward, since it is the core of Beatty's joke that, contrary to popular folklore, his hairdresser is a helplessly heterosexual stud, entangled not only in wet hair but in post-adolescent wet dreams—and having no trouble at making them come true.

From its opening sequence, which finds him in coitus interruptus with the most voracious of his clients (Lee Grant), it is clear that his dreams have become waking nightmares. His nominal girlfriend (Goldie Hawn), an insomniac actress who is kept awake by "gunshots in the canyons," is pressing him for a greater show of feeling ("After work," he grumbles). A former girlfriend (Julie Christie), who is being kept by the Republican fat-cat husband of Lee Grant (Jack Warden), turns up unpropitiously. George hops from body to body on his motorcycle, but by the time the bodies start colliding on election night it is also clear that we are in an updated Don Juan fable that can end only in comeuppance for the hopper.

But in the meantime, *Shampoo* has become something

much more: a satirical account of human disaster that is far more devastating than that other study of disaster in Los Angeles, *Earthquake.* "I don't take up your time, don't take up my time," goes the love song of Lee Grant. "I wish my son knew what to do . . . anything . . . as long as it's *something,*" complains Jack Warden. "Are you married?" Goldie Hawn asks a young director. "Sometimes," he answers. Before an urgent copulation in a Louis XVI bedroom, it is necessary to turn on Herb Alpert and the Tijuana Brass.

Shampoo achieves a fine comic distance by setting itself so specifically in "the past," but it doesn't—to its credit—try to get *us,* in the present, off the hook. And how could it? For as its ending implies, George the hairdresser is still alive, a bit older—and burning up energy in the midst of the energy crisis.

Which is a good description of Warren Beatty, who has been involved with *Shampoo* ever since his initial producing effort in 1967, the resoundingly successful *Bonnie and Clyde.* "Robert Towne and I independently came up with the idea of doing a modern version of *The Country Wife,* the Restoration comedy about a compulsive Don Juan," says Beatty. "It seemed like a good idea to make the character a hairdresser—to upset the conventional idea that all hairdressers are homosexual as well as the Freudian assumption that all Don Juans are latently homosexual."

Other movies and a two-year sabbatical from films to work full-time for George McGovern's Presidential candidacy intervened. But about a year ago, he and Towne holed up for eleven days and turned out a final script. "I just wanted to get the subject out of my system," says Beatty—which suggests that George is closer to Beatty himself than most of his previous characters were. "People can make what they want of it," he says. "There's a lot of me in every character I play. And I think that all of us have to close out that promiscuous phase in our lives. But, in a lot of important ways, George is simply not me."

Robert Towne with John Brady   (interview date 1981)

SOURCE: An interview in *The Craft of the Screenwriter: Interviews with Six Celebrated Screenwriters,* Simon and Schuster, 1981, pp. 366-432.

[Brady is an American nonfiction writer, interviewer, and critic. In the following excerpt, Towne discusses his screenwriting career, focusing on his scripts for Chinatown *and* Shampoo, *and describes his "script-doctoring" work on such films as* The Godfather *and* Bonnie and Clyde.*]*

[Brady]: When did you start writing for movies?

[Towne]: About 1960. It was on and off. I started with Roger Corman doing horror and science fiction films—almost the same time that Jack Nicholson started acting. Nicholson and I were in the same acting class (run by Jeff Corey), but I always thought I was going to write. It was a class that included many directors, producers—Irv Kirschner was in the class, for instance. Roger Corman was in the class. That's how I got my first job. He was producing and directing. There were a lot of actors, too— Sally Kellerman was in there, Jimmy Coburn was in

there . . . Dick Chamberlain. It was invaluable for me— for all kinds of reasons. I met a lot of people, who I thought were terrific at the time, and as it turns out most have done very well professionally. In some cases—Jack's, in particular—the acting influenced me as a writer. Watching Jack improvise really had an effect.

In what way?

His improvisations were inventive. When he was given a situation, he would not improvise on the nose. He'd talk around the problem, and good writing is the same way: It's not explicit. Take a very banal situation—a guy trying to seduce a girl. He talks about everything *but* seduction, anything from a rubber duck he had as a child to the food on the table or whatever. But you know it's all oriented toward trying to fuck this girl. It's inventive, and it teaches you something about writing.

You started writing for Corman. Can you tell me about the writing that goes into a horror movie?

It's the toughest kind. Really, it's a tough form. Roger and I were really a classic mismatch. It was very painstaking, the screenplay of *The Tomb of Ligeia.* In fact, I worked harder on the horror screenplay for him than on anything I think I have ever done. And I still like the screenplay. I think it's good.

Roger works so fast, and you seem to have a slower sense of craftsmanship. How did you adapt?

Actually, I didn't. It just meant I practically starved to death while I was writing.

Not even time for meals?

No, it just meant that Roger was not really lavish with the money he paid anybody. I think that *Ligeia* may have been made for about a hundred and fifty thousand dollars, and the amount of money on the script was negligible. So if you take a long time writing something like that, it works against you.

How do you write a horror movie, particularly when you have a short story in front of you that must be expanded into some ninety minutes of screen time?

Well, "Ligeia" was a *very* short story. I remember reading all the body of Poe's work, and I felt the best thing to do would be to take Poe's themes and expand on them. There was a strong hint of mesmerism in the story. I decided to make it overt—with all that emphasis on Ligeia's eyes and how they held the beholder. Also in Poe there is a lot of necrophilia—implied if not expressed. So I took the combination of mesmerism, which was there, and necrophilia, which was sort of there (because the first wife was always in the background), and brought them together. It provided a natural explanation for this woman. She had hypnotized the protagonist, and he was making love to this body under posthypnotic suggestion, literally being controlled by someone who was dead—which is kind of a gruesome notion, but perfectly consistent with Poe. I was trying to use a theme consistent with him, even though it wasn't in the story.

American horror stories tend to provide natural explanations for events—like "Oh, well, she was hypnotized"—whereas the English tend to go for supernatural explanations. I tried to have my cake and eat it too in *Ligeia.* There was that natural explanation of posthypnotic suggestion, along with the supernatural explanation of a possession. That was also a theme in the story—this vaguely pantheistic notion of being able to come back from the dead in a blade of grass or an animal—and there was the cat and all that.

Some people liked the movie quite a bit. I think it was a little dull. I think it would have been better if it had been done with a man who didn't look like a necrophiliac to begin with.

You disapprove of Vincent Price?

I love Vincent. He's very sweet. But, going in, you suspect that Vincent could bang cats, chickens, girls, dogs, everything. You just feel that necrophilia might be one of his Basic Things. I'd felt the role called for an almost unnaturally handsome guy who the second wife could fall in love with. There should also be a sense of taboo about the really close tie he had with his first wife—as though it were something incestuous, two halves of the same person. The intensity of the relationship is a sacrilege in itself; just *being* together is almost an unnatural act.

At the outset, Corman told me he wouldn't cast Vincent Price in the film, but when it was done he called me in L.A. from London. He told me he had cast Vincent, and added: "It's OK, we've got Marlene Dietrich's makeup man." I've never been able to figure out what difference *that* made.

I did a couple of films for Roger Corman—*Ligeia,* and another horror film I'd rather not mention. Then I did some television work—*The Outer Limits,* some *Man from U.N.C.L.E.* work, a show called *Breaking Point, The Richard Boone Show,* an anthology. I also did *The Lloyd Bridges Show,* an anthology he did after his *Sea Hunt* shows.

Can you draw any comparisons between TV and movie work?

I think that dramatic writing for television is, if anything, almost harmful to the potential screenwriter. The only good thing about it is that it allows you to, theoretically anyway, make a living writing. Censorship is one problem. It was then, anyway. There is more permissiveness in television today, but a lot of it is still the same. I once did a script for *Outer Limits* which presented an interesting problem. These guys came to me and said, "We want to do a story on how adaptable man is, how chameleonlike human beings are. We want a story in which creatures come to earth from outer space, and, in order to study them, a man gets transformed into one of them to figure out what they are." Which is a wildly improbable story. I remember saying, "Fellas, did it ever occur to you what would happen if we went on a five-man space mission to Mars, and we're walking around and suddenly a sixth man shows up that none of us knew? Don't you think we'd be a little dubious about the new guy?" It's an impossible problem. But they said, "No, go ahead and do it."

Well, in those days I would try anything. I was just trying

to work. So I came up with these creatures who were almost bear-like. I had them in these weird iron bars high up in the Rockies or the Sierras or someplace, and a forestman came across them. He was killed by them. People found his body, and they realized that his killers had taken him apart, literally, system by system. His vascular system, his muscular system . . . and so on. They had literally pulled him apart. Then they tried to put him back together, but they didn't do it quite right. People were appalled and frightened. They didn't know quite what to do with these creatures because they seemed so brilliant, yet erratic.

> The toughest scenes in a piece of material may not only have been the toughest for the writer who worked ahead of you, but may also be the most difficult scenes to solve, period. So they are the ones you have to keep redoing, whether it's you or somebody else. Tough scenes create problems.
>
> —*Robert Towne*

They got a piece of tissue from beneath the fingernails of the dead ranger and tried to program these creatures genetically to learn how they could transform a guy who goes there to find out how they can be so brilliant and so erratic. What he finds out is that they are children, and that they are literally in a playpen waiting for their mother, who has deposited them there temporarily. Which would explain why they could be precocious and bright but unpredictable.

Well, ABC Continuity read it and said, "No, we can't do this because we don't want to have anything to do with children." I said, they're not *children* children. They're these creatures from outer space. "No, can't have it." Well, that's insane. I don't know if it would happen today, but it was deeply demoralizing, and it was the only solution I could come up with for the particular problem that these guys wanted to do. The script had to be entirely rewritten. I did the rewrite in one day—eight hours—and it was terrible. I just didn't care what I wrote. It was shot (I don't know who did it—Bobby Duvall, maybe), but it was no good at all.

That sort of thing would happen time after time after time. Censorship like that is so demoralizing. Also, you had to write so explicitly. If a story had a theme, you had to *state* the theme. Scenes had to really be kind of on the nose. In every way. It got you into the habit of writing too much. Too much dialogue. Because they wanted it.

I think by and large it was not a terrific period for me, and I did not enjoy it in any way, shape or form. I should say one thing, though. I think that comedy writing on television is terrific—all those *Mary Tyler Moore* scripts, for instance, were very well written. But one of the things that is almost implicit in comedy is something that is repetitious, static—that is, you pretty much leave a character the way you find him. That's OK in *all* comedy. Repetitive or even compulsive behavior is what *makes* comedy. Archie Bunker is funny because he keeps repeating his prejudices in one form or another, and you expect these things. Jack Benny's repetitive behavior, his stinginess, was funny, and you came to appreciate him for it. Comedy in that sense lends itself better to television, where you have to have a running character the same every week, whereas in dramatic writing the very *essence* is character change. The character at the end is not the same as he was at the beginning. He's changed—psychologically, maybe even physically. He may be dead by the end of a show. Yet in a running dramatic series for television, you have to leave the characters the way that you find them—and that is basically antithetical to good writing.

Do you think you came too late to television? Do you believe in the so-called golden age of television in the 1950s?

No. I believe that there was some good stuff written in the fifties, and there were some terrific writers. But who knows? I've seen some of the stuff. Some of it was dogshit—pretentious, silly and precious. But some of it was great. There's nobody better than Paddy Chayefsky. An incredible writer. But he would have been incredible anywhere. A talent like that is as responsible for the golden age as is the so-called climate that went into creating him.

After working in TV, how did you get back into movies?

Corman again. He was doing a supposedly big-budget film at Columbia and needed a western script rewritten. He asked me to do it. I did, but there was a lot of subsequent difficulty between Roger and the studio over the movie. Roger left the picture, somebody else did it, and I took my name off it. But the script attracted attention from Warren Beatty. That's how I met Warren. At the time he and Arthur Penn were having trouble with the script for *Bonnie and Clyde*. They felt that they had reached a dead end with it, so I was asked to read it. I was brought together with Arthur, did the rewrites on the film, and that's how I got back into the movies.

Arthur Penn has called you Warren's best friend.

We're as close as two people are likely to be, I suppose.

The work on Bonnie and Clyde *sounds like it must have been especially close.*

It was. I was rewriting scenes time after time. The movie was impromptu in the sense that there was rewriting going on constantly, but once Arthur was satisfied with a scene, once the rewriting was done to everybody's satisfaction, there was no deviation whatsoever from those lines. That's the way it was shot. There was less improvising in *Bonnie and Clyde* than in any other movie I have worked on. Which speaks well for the acting and directing, I think, because the film was praised for its freewheeling sense, as though the cameras just *happened* to be there to record real life.

What were the rewrite problems on Bonnie and Clyde?

The original script, by David Newman and Robert Benton, was very talented, but it was written as a *ménage à trois* among Clyde, Bonnie and W.D. At that time the climate was not so permissive that it would be easy to do something like that, so, for several reasons (partly because of the studio), it had to be changed. Also, the script was kind of static. I mean, it was funny—Clyde and W.D., Bonnie and W.D., and so on—but ultimately it didn't go anywhere. If you're going to do a movie about shifting relationships, like Truffaut's *Jules and Jim,* it is tough to do a gangster movie at the same time.

Arthur Penn and Warren decided that they didn't want the *ménage à trois,* but instead a relationship between Bonnie and Clyde, and asked Benton and Newman to do it. But the script just didn't seem to work after that change was made. One of the problems was in making that relationship go somewhere. Arthur was very unhappy with it. That was when I was called in—things had reached an impasse. I remember the first suggestion I made. It was obvious that everybody knew the people in the picture were going to get killed, so that was never an element of mystery, but rather one of suspense. *When* was it going to happen? The other element was: Would Bonnie and Clyde resolve some element in their relationship before it happened? Which is one of the first things I think I said—that we would have to heighten the fact that the particular roads they were traveling on led to one place.

In the original script the mortician episode came *after* Bonnie went to see her family. She went and saw her mother, had a nice time, then picked these people up along the road, after stealing their car and chasing them, had hamburgers with them, then learned that Gene Wilder was a mortician—and kicked him and his girl out of the car. I suggested that they take that scene and place it *before* Bonnie sees her mother so that the impetus of having a good time, only to find out that the guy is a mortician, strikes Bonnie, who is the most sensitive and open of the group, and makes her say, "I wanna go see my Mama." It scared her. Pacing like that gives the character a little drive, makes her want to *do* something as a result of it. And then, at her mother's, instead of having a happy scene, I suggested that the scene end up with Clyde saying to Bonnie's mother, "We're gonna end up living by you," and with the mother replying, "If you're gonna live three miles from here, you're not gonna live long." In effect, Bonnie can't go home anymore. All of these avenues are being closed off, and she is being thrown back on Clyde for a ride that is going one way. Then came a scene in a hotel room where Bonnie says, "I thought we were really going someplace," with disillusionment setting in. And Clyde says, "Well, I'm your family," heightening the intensity, the meaning and the need of that relationship for her, and hopefully something will be resolved about it before they are killed. Of course, they eventually end up sleeping together.

Then one had to be careful (we all worried about it) about Clyde. Suddenly, just because he could have a normal heterosexual relationship, it could not mean that he would put down his gun and stop robbing banks, which is a script problem to deal with. Those were the initial changes. I started working with it then, always under Arthur's guidance—he would have me rewrite something ten or fifteen times, until I felt I just couldn't write at all. He used to scare me. I used to think, "Gee, I must really be terrible if he keeps having me rewrite like this. God, I'm really bad." Then they asked me to come down to Texas, where I stayed all during the picture, working even in postproduction, writing wild lines for background.

From a writing point of view, the thing that was interesting was the number of times I rewrote scenes. But when you're rewriting, very often you're doing the scenes that *don't* work. The toughest scenes in a piece of material may not only have been the toughest for the writer who worked ahead of you, but may also be the most difficult scenes to solve, period. So they are the ones you have to keep redoing, whether it's you or somebody else. Tough scenes create problems. All other things being equal, some scenes are easy for seven out of ten writers to do—the actions of characters are clear, and it's simple to get through. But other scenes are more difficult. There may be more ways in which a scene can go. Maybe a scene reaches a point where you have to carry both plot information and character information, which makes it difficult. There are all these problems, which I didn't realize at the time.

But afterward I realized that was one of the reasons why I was rewriting scenes so many times. There were other reasons, too. It was very valuable for me. I was learning an awful lot from Arthur just by doing and redoing. From Warren, too. There was constant collaborative effort. Story conferences. Arthur, Warren and myself down there in Texas.

When you come in to do rewrites on a script, do you ever work with the original writer?

I did work with Francis Ford Coppola when he called me in on *The Godfather.*

Mario Puzo shared the credit on that. Did you work with him?

No, I didn't meet Mario until afterward.

The reason I asked is that he wrote an article afterward which made it sound like that was a rather traumatic period for him.

It always is. Your first movie is terribly traumatic. But I'm sure he's gotten over it. He's survived, hands down. He's a terrific guy. But I didn't work with him.

I wondered how far the rewrite man works from the guy he's replaced. It sounds as if they want a fresh opinion, and don't want any . . .

Usually *very* far removed. Invariably. But sometimes the person who does the rewrite can write a whole new script. Literally, a whole new script. It wasn't the case in *Bonnie and Clyde* or in *The Godfather,* but in other films I've done, it's been entirely new scripts. I mean, the rewrite in that western I did was virtually a new script. Rewrites at times can be entire.

What were the rewrite problems on The Godfather?

Mainly, Francis was perplexed. In the book there wasn't any resolution between Vito Corleone and his son Mi-

chael—their relationship. He needed a scene between the two of them. Francis kept saying, "Well, I want the audience to know that they love each other." He put it that way. But you couldn't do a scene about two people loving each other. So I wrote a scene about the succession of power, and *through* that it was obvious that the two men had a great deal of affection for each other. Through Brando's anxiety about what would happen to his son, and his anxiety about giving up his power—his ambivalent feelings about, in effect, forcing his son to assume his role, and having to give up his role—that was the key to that scene.

If you want to use the "script doctor" analogy, it wasn't a major operation—just spot surgery in a highly specific area. That creates all sorts of problems by itself. I wasn't rewriting the script from beginning to end, which I've done most often. Instead, I was adding outside material and had to fit it in with what existed, make it consistent— and this meant knowing everything that had been shot, and everything that the director had in mind. An interesting problem. Usually you're rewriting right along with the director as you know where you're going. On *The Godfather* it was a case of someone saying, "This is where I think I'm going, but I don't know where to go anymore. You help me make up my mind where I want to go next." And yet I hadn't been in on any of the original process. They'd been shooting for five or six weeks before I even got there. So I had to look at the footage and say either, "This is terrific" or, "This is so bad, I can't possibly fix it." Which, of course, was the last thing in the world from the truth.

You were called in under extreme pressure, weren't you?

That was the scariest situation I've ever been in, because I knew they were going to lose Brando within twenty-four hours. It was a tense situation at that particular point because no one figured that the film was going to be the big hit that it was. I saw about an hour of assembled footage, and I thought it was brilliant. Francis was troubled. There was a lot of backstabbing on the set, and he was constantly being undermined. So I couldn't get over it: The footage was so extraordinary. I felt that I was going to make a contribution to a film that was virtually assured of being a major hit, although that was not the prevailing opinion on the set.

I worked on a few minor scenes. I remember restructuring Michael's speech for the scene where he tells how he is going to kill the cop. I just did a simple thing there. The way that Francis had originally written the speech, Michael says at the beginning he's going to kill the cop, and then he tells about the newspaper story and other things to justify it. But it was much more dramatic for him to withhold what he was going to do until the end of the speech. I just reversed it. There were a few other little things like that.

But mainly Francis was concerned about having a scene between Michael and his father. So we sat down with Marlon and Al Pacino, got their feelings, and began writing about eight o'clock that night and did a scene about the transfer of power: Uneasy lies the head that wears the crown. I don't know if you remember the scene at all, but that's the gist of it. The don is saying, "We've got to see about this," and Michael is saying, "Dad, I told you I'd take care of it, and I'm taking care of it." What seems to be a kind of absentmindedness on the part of Vito Corleone as far as protective measures are concerned is really his unwillingness to accept the position he's placed his youngest son in.

But the two men in the course of the scene really accept the dictates of fate. It's sort of a perverse *noblesse oblige:* Vito is obliged to pass the cup, and Michael is obliged to take it. He does, and through that you see that the two men love each other very much, rather than my writing a scene about love, which wouldn't have worked in that movie. It's illustrative in a way of writing in general. Most scenes are rarely about what the subject matter is.

You mentioned this earlier in relation to Jack Nicholson improvising scenes at Jeff Corey's school—improvising off the point.

Corey had an exercise in which he would take a scene from, say, *Three Men on a Horse,* which is a farce, and he would say, "OK, you're a junkie, and you're trying to sell this guy some dope." In other words, the situation that he would give would be totally contrary to the text, and it was the task of the actors, through their interpretation of the various bits of business they could come up with, to suggest the real situation through lines that had no bearing on the situation. When you see that for three years running, when you are asked for improvisations in which you are given a situation and told that you must talk about everything *but* the situation to advance the action, you soon see the power of dealing obliquely or elliptically with situations, because most people rarely confront things head-on. They're afraid to. I think that most people try to be accommodating in life, but in back of their accommodation is suppressed fear or anger or both. What happens in a dramatic situation is that it surfaces. And it shouldn't surface too easily, or it's not realistic.

How much do you take from your actors when you sit down and have to structure a scene with twenty-four-hour notice?

It depends on the actors. I took a lot from Marlon and Al. Particularly Marlon. He said, "Just once in this part I'd like *not* to be inarticulate." So I took the notion that he wanted to have this man try to express himself. I took the notion of Vito Corleone trying to talk, then, rather than having him give sage nods. Through most of the film it is the power of his silence that carries force. But in the situation I was asked to write, he actually talks. Most of the time the power of the character is conveyed through pregnant silence.

I took a lot of things from Jack Nicholson in life for the character of Gittes in *Chinatown,* too. Things that happened. I used his idiosyncrasies, but, more importantly, I tried to use his way of working. I've seen him work so much that I feel I know what he does well. In fact, I don't even think about it. I just do it. I saw Jack work and improvise two or three times a week for maybe five straight years. It's hard *not* to think about Jack even when I'm not writing for him. His work literally affected the way that I work, totally independent of doing a movie with Jack. He and other people in that class.

In the case of working with Warren on *Shampoo,* obviously there's an effect there. I definitely take him into account when I am writing scenes for him, because I feel that I know what he does well. I feel that Warren always has to be tougher than he thinks. He presents a peculiar problem as an actor because he is a man who is deeply embarrassed by acting. Unlike Jack. Warren is a very talented man, but he's so embarrassed by his acting that you have to constantly force him, one way or another, to use himself, whereas Jack doesn't have that reluctance. He doesn't mind using himself. Warren has the instincts of a character actor. He'd rather hobble around on one foot in *Bonnie and Clyde,* or wear a gold tooth in *McCabe and Mrs. Miller.* He's a little bit like another great actor who is embarrassed about using his own instrument—and that's Albert Finney. In *Murder on the Orient Express,* for instance, he plays Hercule Poirot and manages to cover himself up completely as a character actor. Both men have the instincts of character actors, and that's not really good for movies, because after a time if an actor is playing a "leading man" he has to be willing to use aspects of his own personality for a role. It won't look real if he doesn't. Film is just too sensitive. When you are dealing with someone like that, if you know him well, you are obliged as a writer to try to push situations where an actor must use aspects of himself, and you remind him of it in the way in which you write scenes. Or when you write scenes together, as Warren and I did in *Shampoo,* you've got to say, "Look, you've got to be tough with yourself here, and not be afraid of yourself."

Now I am talking about two cases in which I enjoy close personal relationships with actors whom I respect professionally. In many ways I'm as close to Jack and Warren as I am to anybody. When you work with people you don't know so well, the problems are much more complex. Then you've got to go through a lot of diplomatic crises. When you say you don't approve of something (whether it's with an actor, a director or whatever), then they assume that what you are saying is you don't approve of their talent or of them—the way they part their hair, whatever. That's very time-consuming and exhausting, and there is not that kind of time on a movie when it's being shot—which is one reason why, whenever possible, you should do movies with people whom you are intimate with at one level or another. You can cut through that shit. The disadvantage, of course, is that over a period of years you can get sloppy, I suppose. John Ford finally just got tired, got very old. But for years he was working with people he knew. All really good directors do it. Fellini does it. Bergman.

He has a repertory company, I think.

Sure. And there's a reason for it; it's just too hard otherwise, too hard to keep working with strangers. It's like starting a marriage over and over and over again.

I'm very interested in how you write with somebody else. On **Shampoo,** *you and Beatty shared writing credits. Does it come down to two men sitting in a room, or is it a back-and-forth type of arrangement?*

In the case of **Shampoo,** it goes so far back I can't tell you. I had done an early draft—about two hundred and twenty pages—of the thing that I was interested in having Warren do around the time of *Bonnie and Clyde.* It was very amorphous, though. Warren looked at it and said, "You really seem lost, though the writing is interesting." I still have that draft, as a matter of fact. We sat and we talked for about a month about a new shape it might take. Warren went to Europe for a couple of months while I rewrote the script. When he came back we had a big argument over the script because there were *two* strong female parts. He had wanted one part for Julie Christie, and a very secondary part for another female. As it happens, there were two major parts in the final script—for Julie and Goldie Hawn—but at this time it was very dicey, and Warren was very unhappy, and we didn't speak for about six months. I thought that was the end of that particular arrangement. He had given me option money, but I felt the script would never be made, and there was some mutual confusion as to who had the rights to it. So it was left in limbo for three years. I went on to do other things—*The Last Detail, Chinatown,* and so forth. I did *The Yakuza* during this period, too.

Finally, Warren sat down and took the script and did a draft with some new material, including a couple of party sequences. He was trying to restructure it in a more interesting way, particularly after a lapse of three years. One particular sequence in the old script which involved dope was bad. He did a draft that really just didn't work. It wasn't much related to what I had done. Then he did another in which he rearranged a lot of the original material. We talked, and I took that draft and in a seven-day period in December 1973 we sat down in the Beverly Wilshire Hotel with Hal Ashby, whom Warren had hired as director, and the real collaboration took place.

We thrashed out and rewrote entirely the rewrite of the draft I had done in 1970—if that makes any sense. It's a very convoluted history. Hal, Warren and I would sit in a room and thrash out the sequence of events in the picture. We had very little time to do this because they were going to try to shoot it in six weeks. In order to get Warren, Julie, Goldie, Lee Grant and Jack Warden together meant you had to be ready to *go* during these six weeks, or you'd end up costing yourself a lot of money. Warren had committed himself financially to people prior to finalizing the deal with the studio, which meant that he was personally on the hook for a *lot* of money. So there was enormous pressure to get it done immediately. We went through the draft then, and in many ways it ended up, at least in spirit, very close to the earliest version—that is, with two women, and with the guy more attached emotionally to the less naive of the two. The work on that final draft, though, was the most intensive I've been through in a long time. We'd start about nine in the morning and work until about eleven at night, then sleep and start again.

We would talk through the scenes, and I would go into another room and do the writing of the scenes themselves. Some writers can collaborate and write on the spot. I can't. Maybe comedy writers work that way: You say this line, and I'll say that line. But I prefer to talk through the scenes, reworking their structure, arguing back and forth

about the party sequences, trying to make them an organic part of the whole script, and making relationships between characters come to a head during the parties, and not just having a party for a party's sake. It was completely rewritten in about seven days. Then I went to Japan to do the finishing touches on *The Yakuza,* then came back to do the rewriting on *Shampoo* as it was being shot.

In *Shampoo* the rewriting during shooting was less extensive than it has been in many other cases. It's a film that I like about as much as I like anything I've written in a while. Maybe other people don't, but I feel very positive about it. I was given an ongoing voice in the process of the making of the film. I was on the set every day, rewriting every day. At one point I even asked to have a scene reshot because I saw that there had been a crucial mistake. I rewrote the scene, and it was reshot.

Which scene?

It's between Warren and Goldie—the climactic scene in their relationship. She has caught him with her best girl friend. She faces him and says, "There were others, too, weren't there?" And he says, "What do you want to know for?" "Well, there were, and I want to know," she says. Finally, he blows up, and tells her to grow up, everybody fucks everybody else, and he goes into this whole speech about why he went to beauty school.

I took a couple of my dogs for a walk, and it occurred to me that as the scene was shot, he advanced on her; but as it was written, she advanced on *him.* In order for the scene to work at all, he had to be the passive agent and have it forced out of him. Anger or fear, as I've said, can't come out of a person too easily. It has to be *forced* out of him to be realistic, to make him more of a person. I realized, too, that the speech itself wasn't working. It was didactic when it should have been personal. He should have said it's *me,* not that's what *people* do. The speech was changed. He sits down (so she's towering over him), and he fumbles, but he gets it out—and it's a speech that we worked out with Warren. The part that's most important to me occurs when he says, "Well, look, I don't know what I'm apologizing for. I go into an elevator or walk down the street and see a pretty girl, and that's it: It makes my day. I can't help it. I feel like I'm gonna live forever. Maybe it means I don't love them, and maybe it means I don't love you, but nobody's gonna tell me I don't *like* them very much."

What I was getting at with the last half of that speech— the notion of seeing pretty girls and feeling like he was going to live forever—was someone as far away as possible from compulsive Don Juanism, or latent homosexuality, or someone who is trying to prove his masculinity. None of these things interested me, nor did I believe in them in the case of this guy. Instead, I perceived him as sort of a crude Pygmalion—he makes women pretty, then falls in love with them, moment to moment. They're pretty, they're nice to touch, they smell great, they look great, they feel great—which is what he says in the speech. They are a life force for him in the classic Don Juan sense. The man just has more *life* in him. He is a rebel in the sense that he doesn't want to deny himself. The man sort of goes through a breakdown. He really is getting old in the course of the two days in the film. It's never quoted in the film, but that line from William Butler Yeats's "Sailing to Byzantium"—That is no country for old men—is never far from the back of my mind when I think of this film and of Southern California. And never far from the front of my mind.

Julie Christie has gone with George, the hairdresser, and at one point wanted to marry him. But he's always running around, having a hell of a good time, and she says, "You know why I always used to be so angry with you?" And he says, "Because I wouldn't settle down." And she says, "No, because you were always so happy about everything." And he says, "I was?" Because in the two days of the film he's kind of frenetic and occasionally very funny. But he's not happy. It's *that* element which it was necessary to deal with and carry through in the speech to Goldie, from a guy who really had a greater, more genuine appetite for certain kinds of enjoyment—particularly because the film is filled with people who *settle* for things. They settle for things because they *feel* they should, or because they are *told* they should, or because they're afraid not to. But the hairdresser is a guy who is dumber than the rest of them, in a way. He doesn't even *know* enough to settle for things, and he's lived his life in a certain sybaritic way. But there's nothing corrupt or crude about the guy at all. He's very sweet.

You've been called an Abe Burrows of Hollywood because of the years you spent doctoring the scripts of others. What's your attitude toward that kind of reputation? Is it an exalted role, like that of a star relief pitcher? Or is it a minor role, like someone who plays only when the star pulls up with an injury?

I don't know if a relief pitcher is an exalted role, but I think it's more like that than the other. It's misleading, though, to talk about script doctoring or polishing as though it were a specialized art. *All* scripts are rewritten, whether they be yours or somebody else's. The only question is whether it is rewritten well or badly. But everything is and should be rewritten. Movies are not done under laboratory conditions. They are done over a period of time, under the gun of a budget—maybe a film will cost a hundred thousand dollars a day—and there are all sorts of problems: weather problems, people problems, lots of surprises. People may not know each other, and there may not be enough time to rehearse. You can lose locations. You can lose light. You can lose your fucking mind. So there are tremendous numbers of variables.

Also, when you are looking at something, and then it is blown up thirty-two times, just *that* can surprise you. You don't know what you've got. You see it on the set, and then you see it on the screen, and you say, "Hey, that's good!" or, "That's bad!" For example, at an early point in *Bonnie and Clyde,* everybody was worried about establishing their relationship in a particular scene. I must have written seven or eight little scenes. Then, one day, we were looking at dailies when they came in, and there they were in the same frame on the screen, and Warren was saying, "I'm Clyde Barrow, and we rob banks." It was obvious.

> **Some people may think there's something pejorative about the term "script doctor." But on the whole it's better to have a reputation for fixing things up than for messing them up. I have enjoyed the role, and conceivably would and will do it again.**
>
> **—Robert Towne**

Their relationship *was* established. It would be stupid to write any other scenes. You are always miscalculating in a movie, partially because of the disparity between what you see on the set and what you see on the screen. No matter how skilled you are in anticipating what the image is going to look like finally, you can still be fooled. So you have to rewrite, and be rewritten—not because the original is necessarily badly *written,* but because, ultimately, if it doesn't *work* for a film, it's bad.

Some people may think there's something pejorative about the term "script doctor." But on the whole it's better to have a reputation for fixing things up than for messing them up. I have enjoyed the role, and conceivably would and will do it again. If for no other reason than you force yourself into somebody else's world and you learn things at every level that you don't if you are doing original material. It's a way of revitalizing yourself. You learn things from other people. In rewriting someone or in adapting a work, you can come to feel it's your very own, too. Or you can feel that you are in the service of somebody else's material that you love very much, and you *want* to work. We all have rescue fantasies. . . .

Is good writing enough? Or does a screenwriter also have to be good at story conference strategies for dealing with producers, directors, and the like?

Well, it helps. But the best answer to that problem is to work with your friends, because no matter how much moxie you've got, if you're with a guy who is fundamentally not congenial to your point of view, or if he's worried about what somebody else is going to think, it just doesn't matter. So if you can sidestep such things, it's best to work with people you know and trust—and who know you and trust you—and to work from that vantage point. There are going to be disagreements, for sure. But there is also mutual respect, and work that is bound to be satisfying insofar as everyone on a movie *can* be satisfied with the outcome.

I assume that you had some enemies on **Chinatown.** *The early drafts of that script are completely different from the shooting script, especially at the end.*

Yeah, there was some conflict there between Roman Polanski and me. We went over everything, and he said he didn't like the ending. In the original, I had Evelyn Mulwray going to jail and her daughter escaping to Mexico. Roman wanted Evelyn to die at the end. "You're kidding," I said. "Well, think of something else," he said.

And I did. I came up with an alternative ending about four or five days before shooting. I brought it over to him, and he said, "Well, it's too late. We're going to shoot in a week and I can't change anything. I just can't do it." That was the last we spoke during the picture. It was very quiet, subdued, although we'd had several fights in which I'd blown up and yelled at him, and he at me. But I must also say that except for Arthur, Roman taught me more about screenwriting than anybody I've ever worked with, both in spite of and because of our conflicts. Roman is great at the elucidation of the narrative—to go from point A to B to C. In that sense, he is excellent.

The shooting script of **Chinatown** *is such a reversal of everything the first, second and third drafts build toward. Can you recall the compromise version that you came up with?*

I never wanted Evelyn killed. I can't recall the specifics of the original scene because I've lost it—but in it she did kill her father in Chinatown.

I remember that the second draft was very clumsy, and I was forced to embark on a third draft. One of the things about the first and second drafts is that Gittes is told by Evelyn, when she feels backed up to the wall, that she is seeing somebody else, that she's seeing a married man and that's her reason for not wanting to go to the police. It was a little lame in the third draft, a little vague in the shooting script, but in the earlier drafts it was very clear. Gittes says, "OK, I'm going to the police unless you tell me what is going on." And she gives the most plausible reason to her mind that he would accept, because it involved a certain amount of culpability on her part: She's a married woman, and she's making it with somebody else. Because he thinks that she's being honest with him, and because he's been kind of a sucker, he decides to go along with her. Then he becomes slowly jealous of this mythical character. So when he goes to see who she's seeing—when he follows her—he thinks he's going to find her lover. Which I felt would have been much more interesting.

The postcoital love scene, in which Evelyn adores Gittes (in the shooting script), was improvised on the set. In the original scene, Evelyn was so upset after having sex that she was ignoring him completely. And he was misconstruing it as her being concerned about her other lover, whereas, as she'd indicated earlier, her reaction to sex was very neurotic. But, frankly, I don't think Roman Polanski could be interested in a woman who is involved with somebody else, or, in this case, a hero who would *worry* that his lover was fucking somebody else. And it was Roman's identification with the hero that was making the film work. It has to be unqualified involvement with him. As with the love scene. The woman has to approve wholeheartedly of the man's performance in bed.

Roman needs that kind of approbation from both women, men and everybody on the set. He's the little king. That's a case where that kind of attitude warped the mystery, the tension at a point in the film. Also, it prevented the film from dealing with what I thought was the most important missing thing of all—namely, that Gittes was getting progressively, insanely crazy about this woman. He was jealous, and really falling in love with her. Although she came

to like him very much, her other problems were so overwhelming that she couldn't . . . she came to admire and like him and really find him enormously attractive. But he was falling in love with her.

That kind of passion I felt was very important for the film, in order for his betrayal of her to have any significance. He had to really love her.

At any rate, the script had to be turned into a shooting script. I was struggling through the first and second drafts simply trying to figure out the story for myself. The second draft was so complex that a shooting script based upon it would have run close to three hours. I would have had to do a radical rewrite in order to simplify it.

There's incredible texture to it.

In the film I missed that kind of progressive jealousy by Gittes—his thinking that she was involved with someone else. And the ending, as shot, is very harsh.

Didn't you want to direct **Chinatown** *yourself?*

Initially I did. That's why I wrote a detective script. I figured that no matter how badly it was directed, if I wrote a story that people wanted to know the outcome of, it would carry. That was one of the reasons for the genre. There were others that I discovered as I went along with it.

I hope you do the novel. There's so much puzzlement in the film of **Chinatown**. *I came away wondering, "What does this or that line mean? Why does Gittes repeat 'as little as possible' at the end?" The reference to Evelyn's flawed eye. There's so much going on in the film that is cerebral, that is just not visual enough—it's like a tease. I think the novel would answer many questions the film poses.*

The novel would be very different, all right. What do you mean about the eye reference—are you referring to Evelyn's getting shot in the eye in the end?

Yes, but earlier Gittes notices some flaw in her eye. It's a point of discussion. Then, at the end, she is shot in the eye.

That shot in the eye at the end *does* make you think of that earlier line, which is unfortunate. The flaw in her iris was intended for another purpose. You may remember an early speech in the script, and Gittes says, "Who does she think she is? She's no better than anybody else in this town." She was sort of a perfect, upper-class lady. So Gittes comes up against this woman who is infuriatingly correct, and everything about her is an insult to this lower-class guy who monograms everything and is made to feel like a crude, dumb asshole. And finally: He sees a flaw in the iris. It's emblematic at that moment of her vulnerability. If you've ever seen such eyes, you know they are very pretty. To me it was also emblematic of the fact that she is psychologically flawed. The fact that she was shot in the eye later is a coincidental echo.

All the more reason for doing the novel.

Either I will do it, or it won't be done. It's a highly personal thing. In fact, most of the locations that Roman chose for the film were ones that I directed him to. I remembered them from my childhood.

What sort of childhood did you have?

I grew up in California, around San Pedro. I grew up amidst fishermen, Mexicans, chief petty officers in the merchant marine with three-day growths of beard who would come up and *wheeeeze* on you. Sailors and guys with raspy voices. It was kind of a fun neighborhood, actually. Rather polyglot: Slavs, Italians, a total melting pot. I was the only Jew on the block, I think. It was terrific. I've never regretted it. I even worked as a fisherman for a while on a boat, and when I was in college I wrote maybe half a dozen short stories that were largely descriptions of my life on that boat. Even today, I don't think they're bad. Every writer has to use the world he lives in as source material, I think, though it shouldn't impose restrictions or limitations on what you write. You have to be able to get into the worlds, the fantasies of people outside yourself as well.

Besides writing out of experience, how much research goes into a script like **Chinatown?**

I did a lot of research—mostly reading to get a feeling for the ambience of the time, the way people spoke, what their inhibitions were. For example, today it's perfectly proper to talk about all sorts of intimate sexual things, but people are rather chary of talking about how much money they make—whereas in the 1930s I think the reverse would have been true. People wouldn't have minded talking about how much money, but *boy,* would they not have talked about sex. To get attitudinal differences like that, you have to read, and I suppose that's research. You have to find out what people would say or would not say in a social situation. And the basic premise of the scandal was researched, too. I read about the Owens Valley, and became interested in it. But I didn't base a single character in **Chinatown** on any person I read about in the Owens Valley episode. My characters fulfilled roles that in some cases were analogous to roles in the original scandal but were wholly made up. Mulwray was perhaps somewhat like Mulholland of the Owens Valley deal, but in **Chinatown** Mulwray was depicted as a very decent guy, whereas I think that Mulholland was a corrupt man who allowed himself to be used by Chandler and everybody else. He was ambitious. The Mulwray of the film was intended to be a tough but decent man who was trying to avoid a scandal that would have ruined the public ownership of his department, which he had fought for, while at the same time trying to keep the thing from taking place which eventually took place.

And yet you have a William Mulholland statement as a prefatory quote to the first and second drafts of your script.

Which I would use in the novel. Sure: "There it is, take it." That's what the attitude had always been out here about everything. L.A. has never been viewed as a city, but as a place where hustlers come. It's like a mine, and everyone's trying to hit the main vein and get it out, then leave the fucking place. It's never viewed as a city. Never has been. It's a place where you just Get Yours, then get out. It doesn't matter what happens to the land, the air or any of its natural beauty. That's the attitude. So I felt that the Mulholland quote was apropos not only of Mulholland,

but of everyone who was here to make a fast buck, to make it big and fast.

I liked the Seabiscuit material in the early drafts. That shows research, too, I suppose.

Right. That was an interesting thing. Big argument over it. Remember the early draft of the barbershop scene?

Yes.

Remember when he gets mad? Somebody says "Boy, did Seabiscuit fold in the stretch the other day," and Gittes gets furious. He threatens to get in a fight over it. And later, when he goes to see Noah Cross, Cross offers him, by way of payment, a horse. The point (and I would have smoothed it out in the final draft if I'd continued to use it) was that I wanted to show a venal, corrupt man in Gittes—well, pettily venal and crude, rather than corrupt, really—crass, crude, self-serving, social-climbing—who admired the character of this tiny horse named Seabiscuit. At one point in an early draft he is asked why he thinks so much of the animal. I don't know how much you know about Seabiscuit, but it was a horse that came back from a complete breakdown, and *won* the following year. The animal didn't look like it could win anything, but really was one of the classiest horses that ever lived. A small horse with tremendous character. And Gittes' admiration of that character was meant to be an early tip-off that the guy was susceptible to class in one form or another. Of course, he would be susceptible to class in a woman, too. Seabiscuit was meant to be the transfer. But Roman said, "That's folklore," although he ended up using the Seabiscuit thing in the paper. What he insisted on using in the barbershop scene as a means of getting Gittes mad was a story in the newspaper and some guy calling him a headline seeker. Gittes is then called upon to justify his work—which he had to do with Evelyn anyway, when he went to her house after being threatened with a suit. I disliked the self-serving moment there in the barbershop. I wanted to suggest at that point that the guy had the capacity to admire something, just for the sake of its beauty or its character. In one way or another, it was thoroughbred. Which is a tip-off that he could be in real trouble with a woman he admired. I missed that. I felt it was a mistake to get rid of it. It made that moment kind of petty and dumb, whereas if the Seabiscuit idea had been developed, I think it would have been more insightful to the guy.

It's an angle on Gittes that is simply not fleshed out in the film at all.

That would have done it, really. Everything I was doing was driving toward Gittes falling in love with Evelyn. Everything that Roman was doing was blunting that.

An influence that I see in the early writing is Dashiell Hammett. In the first draft, Gittes at one point says, "In my case, being respectable would be bad for business." Hammett's Sam Spade in The Maltese Falcon *says, "Don't be too sure I'm as crooked as I'm supposed to be. That kind of reputation makes it easier to deal with the enemy."*

I remember the line very well from *The Maltese Falcon.* It may be an unconscious echo there.

Are there any parallels between Sam Spade and Brigid in Falcon *and Jake Gittes and Evelyn in* **Chinatown?**

The relationship in **Chinatown** is meant to be the opposite. In *Falcon,* Brigid is the villain. The woman is usually a femme fatale, and I was trying to suggest that that was the way I was going, but go against that convention and make her the only decent person in the story, which is what Evelyn is meant to be. She is acting from a pure, basic motive—mother love. That's generally conceded to be the most unselfish motive there is, and that was the basis for all her actions in the film. I was trying to make Evelyn the opposite of what someone like Brigid was.

Every writer has to use the world he lives in as source material, I think, though it shouldn't impose restrictions or limitations on what you write. You have to be able to get into the worlds, the fantasies of people outside yourself as well.

—Robert Towne

Hammett's toughness of character was the main value in his work, I would say, at least for me. If you reread all of Hammett and Raymond Chandler, though, I don't think you can touch Chandler. Hammett ages badly in some of his short stories. Chandler doesn't. Both Hammett and Chandler, though, were so much better than anybody else. Chandler's prose about the city of Los Angeles at that time is really inspiring. I'm old enough to remember what the city was like then, and reading Chandler filled me with such a sense of loss that it was probably the main reason why I did the script. Just reading Chandler kept me going.

Your background readings, then, were used more often to acquire a mood for your own writing than to acquire outside material, it would seem.

No question. That's what it was really all about.

Who else did you read?

John Fante, who wrote one of the best books about L.A. ever—called *Ask the Dusk.* A terrible title, but a terrific book. I had read Nathanael West before. A very telling writer, but I'm not one of the unqualified admirers of *The Day of the Locust.* I don't think it's that good a book. West was brilliant, but *Locust* was not a great book in the manner that *Miss Lonelyhearts* was.

How did you decide on the names in the film?

I picked my names on the basis of sounds. I thought Mulwray had a romantic sound, redolent of some heroines of the past. It had a ring to it. Hollis Mulwray sounded good for the husband. Julian was the original name for Noah Cross, but there was a Julian Cross living, so it had to be changed. For which I'm sorry, because Julian Cross is now actually dead. If I do the novel, I'll return his name to Julian. Gittes' name was chosen because I wanted an

antiromantic name for him—a name that sounded like a hustler. Jack Nicholson and I have a friend called Harry Gittes, and I've always loved his name. Just pronouncing the name is vaguely insulting: Gittes. Jake is a good name from the time period, and it is also the name I have always called Nicholson. Jack's full name is actually John J. —so I took that, too, and it became J. J. Gittes, which seemed like a reasonable name, a real name. I tend to name characters that way, on the basis of their sound.

How did you decide on the dirty joke that Gittes is telling when Evelyn comes into the room?

I was talking to a fellow who lived out here in L.A. in the thirties, when there was much antipathy toward the Chinese and when that joke had its origins out here. I asked him to tell me everything he could remember—what people called people, what they did when they went out, how they fucked, did they use rubbers, and so on. I went crazy with details like that. I talked to guys in their fifties and their sixties who were resilient, sharp. There was one writer in particular, and he told me this joke.

I thought, that's the perfect kind of joke for that time, because it was a time when people's prejudices were much more out front, and I wanted to make use of that throughout the movie. "Do you accept anyone of the Jewish persuasion?" Gittes asks at the old folks' home. "Sorry, we don't," he is told. Jake: "Well, that's good; neither does Dad."

I wanted to be consistent with that. I had some Mexican stuff that I wanted to use, too. People then were more ashamed of their origins. Prejudices were more open. They all wanted to be Americans, and were vaguely ashamed of being anything else. Society was more stratified at *every* level. People had principles. There were certain things they would do, and certain things they would not do. Fucking. Not fucking. Marriage. Adultery. Abortion. All these things were really major issues. Behavior was much more codified, and people were much more certain of the limits on their behavior—which is what Gittes learned. Gittes thinks he understands people's limitations, and then he comes up against a monster, Noah Cross, who will do *everything.* There is *nothing* he won't do. Man *has* no limits. That was the point of that confrontation scene, which Gittes didn't understand: Cross tells him that some people have *no* limitations. At a given place and a given time, people are capable of anything. Gittes' cynicism, by comparison, is petty, naive, and almost sweet.

When and why did you decide to call it **Chinatown?**

The origin of that was the vice cop who sold me one of my dogs and who used to work in Chinatown. "Down there," he said, "we never do anything, because the tongs are still working. We don't know all the dialects, and they say don't do anything, because you could make a mistake. You don't know who's a crook and who isn't a crook. You don't know who you're helping and who you're hurting. So in Chinatown they say just don't do a goddamn thing." Which I found an intriguing notion, and when I started working on the script I tried to elaborate on that idea—turning it into a metaphor. Chinatown is the place where Gittes fucked up, and Evelyn is a *person* where he fucked up. That was the idea. But ultimately, I think China-town—where if you're smart you do nothing—suggests the futility of good intentions.

Did you have trouble getting the name through?

Oh, yeah. That was why the last scene was set in China-town. These guys sat around like Harry Cohn saying, "How can you call a movie *Chinatown* when there's no Chinatown in it?" Roman led the way. One highly sensi-tive man whom I *love* went so far in this discussion—and things had gotten so out of hand—that he actually said, "Well, maybe if Gittes liked Chinese *food*." At which point I blew up. It was one of those story conferences with the best of men, I'm afraid, saying these crazy things.

How did the idea for slitting Gittes' nose come about?

I didn't want to use a lot of overt violence in the film, be-cause I felt that the only real way you could be scared for your hero is emotionally—that is, if he got hung up on somebody you were afraid he shouldn't have gotten hung up on. Or if he committed some act that destroyed him as a character, because your identification with him as a de-tective is probably the greatest instant identification an au-dience can have with any hero. You follow the guy, the mystery, and try to unravel it the way you follow yourself around in a dream. You know you're not going to die—in the dream, anyway. So the only fear you can threaten the viewer with is something suggestive of a deeper horror. So I just sat back and asked, "What is the most horrible thing I can think of that would really scare you?" And I just came up with that. I thought of slitting his ears and every-thing else, but he's a nosy guy, and a knife up his nose just seemed to work.

I would think it takes a special actor to agree to a role re-quiring that he go around in half the film with a piece of gauze over his face.

That's Jack. A grand guy.

Which is easier, adapting the material of others or creating your own?

I think that almost always it's easier to adapt. Your writ-ing inhibitions are lower. In a sense, you might even be writing a little bit better when you're adapting somebody else's material because vanity, fear and all the things that inhibit you as a writer don't come into play. You tend to be a little looser, taking shots from different parts of the court that you wouldn't normally attempt—and making them—just because you are looser. Sometimes with your own material you get constipated, vain and stupid. For that reason it's somewhat easier to adapt. But not always.

Jack Kroll   (review date 8 February 1982)

SOURCE: "Chariots of Desire," in *Newsweek*, Vol. XCIX, No. 6, February 8, 1982, p. 60.

[*In the following review, Kroll favorably discusses* Personal Best, *contending that it not only "takes the world of track and field as a microcosm for the ecstacies and pains of self-striving," but also explores lesbianism as "a paradigm of authentic human intimacy."*]

Robert Towne's splendid film *Personal Best* opens at the 1976 Olympic track tryouts at Eugene, Ore. In the first shot you're looking at a screen filled with blurred, sun-gold images. Then, slowly, the profiled face of Mariel Hemingway drops into the frame in sharp focus, two beads of sweat glistening at the tip of her nose and chin as she crouches at the start of the 100-meter hurdles. It's an image of beauty and concentration, which is what this original, compelling and no doubt controversial film is all about—the beauty of human beings focusing all their en-ergy on excellence. Just as the recent *Chariots of Fire* did, Robert Towne's *Personal Best* takes the world of track and field as a microcosm for the ecstasies and pains of self-striving. And it dares, with great delicacy and insight, to show a loving sexual relationship between two young women, not as a statement about homosexuality but as a paradigm of authentic human intimacy.

Chris Cahill (Hemingway), a young track athlete, and Tory Skinner (Patrice Donnelly), a more advanced ath-lete, meet at the 1976 trials. Their sexual desire flows from the concern each feels for the other in a world where phys-ical pain and psychic anxiety are the ingredients of self-development. One of the best things in this picture is its feeling for the wisdom of the body. The love scenes be-tween Hemingway and Donnelly have the dignity of true sensuality. Hemingway and Donnelly are friends, lovers and competitors, and Towne traces their shifting relation-ship through the four years they work to make the 1980 Olympic team—the team that never got to Moscow.

You don't have to be a sports nut to enjoy the excitement and the kinetic drive of this story. The relationship be-tween Hemingway and Donnelly is a casualty of relentless competitive intensity, fueled by the women's win-at-any-price coach, played with a kind of poignant *machismo* by Scott Glenn. Hemingway winds up with a man, a swim-mer named Denny (Kenny Moore), and it's this hetero-sexual pair who play the film's central scene. Watching Hemingway work out in the weight-training room, Moore has a revelation as he sees a power that both enhances her femininity and becomes an inspiration to him.

The beautifully controlled humor of this scene reflects the wit, lyricism and dramatic sense shown by screenwriter Robert Towne in his first directorial venture. Towne gets an appealing humanity from all his players, not only the colt-like Hemingway but the many women athletes in the film and Kenny Moore, a former Olympic marathoner who is now a writer for *Sports Illustrated*. Most astonish-ing is the performance of Patrice Donnelly. A former Olympic hurdler, she not only has a ravishing physical grace but in her first acting role plays with unerring emo-tional truth and sensitivity.

Technically, Towne and his brilliant cinematographer Mi-chael Chapman (*Taxi Driver, Raging Bull*) achieve many stunning scenes: the long-legged Hemingway in super-slow motion seeming to soar forever over one hurdle; a montage of the women's shot put, in which all the compet-itors merge in an explosive burst of balletic power; the final 800-meter run that's the most excitingly filmed race since Leni Riefenstahl's controversial epic film of the 1936

"Nazi" Olympics in Berlin. This is an original movie, full of feeling, fire and thought.

Robert Towne made his reputation as the phantom script doctor, the man producers called in to do uncredited revisions on other writers' screenplays. His masterpiece in this respect was his rewrite of *Bonnie and Clyde,* which led to similar work on *The Godfather* and finally to his original screenplays for **Chinatown** (for which he won an Oscar) and **Shampoo.**

Personal Best is a personal project for him, a labor of love. "I have an absolutely blatant prejudice for women athletes," he says, "for their bodies, the way they move, their temperament. Just watching them check their sweat socks knocks me out."

For the leads in **Personal Best** he needed a rare combination of acting and athletic ability. When he found out that Mariel Hemingway (who played Woody Allen's teen-age lover in *Manhattan*) was a cross-country skier and trampoline expert, he persuaded her to go through the exhausting, yearlong workouts to prepare for the film. After trying out actresses like Sigourney Weaver for the other lead, he decided on Donnelly against the advice of Hollywood professionals who warned him that she was a great athlete who'd never be able to act.

Doing the love scenes with two straight, shy young women wasn't easy. "I'm going to try some things that will shame you and anger you," he told them. During rehearsal of a scene in which the two girls arm-wrestle one another, Towne yanked a towel away, leaving Donnelly to play the scene naked. Such methods did arouse anger. Towne would tell her, "You're used to having pain in workouts but if I give you psychic pain you rebel. It's the same thing—pain is your teacher in athletics and in art. You get roses for winning but the real tribute is to offer you not a rose but a thorn."

Towne is a lean, intense, bearded 47-year-old who has conquered chronic illness by physical conditioning. He expects some people to be upset by the sexual odyssey of his two heroines. "To me the story is about innocence, purity, growing up," he says. "My idea is that they're children, like my daughter, discovering who they are with their bodies. They learn to come to terms with someone else without violating their need to excel." Towne recalls an article the great Jesse Owens wrote, urging President Carter to modify the Olympics boycott to allow athletes to compete as "free individuals." "Owens said that the Olympics leads not to Moscow or Los Angeles or even to Athens. It leads to the best within ourselves."

Laurie Stone (review date 16 March 1982)

SOURCE: "*Personal Best:* What's New in Towne," in *The Village Voice,* Vol. XXVII, No. 11, March 16, 1982, pp. 52-3.

[*In the following review, Stone discusses Towne's treatment of women's sports and lesbian sex in* Personal Best, *contending that "the themes are entwined in a startlingly innovative way."*]

Nervous sweat drips off Mariel Hemingway's face as she sets up for a sprint in **Personal Best,** and real life bursts through decades of movie convention. We've seen sport as background to romance in the charming caprice, *Pat and Mike.* We've seen the athlete as manipulated beauty: Susan Anton in *Golden Girl.* But we've never before seen the beauty as jock *foremost;* and, amazingly, the woman's commitment isn't presented as some dazzling exception or aberrant piece of sublimation. Writer-director Robert Towne doesn't explain it at all. It's simply a given.

Women's sports are treated with an altogether new seriousness in **Personal Best,** and so is lesbian sex. The themes are entwined in a startlingly innovative way, but most reviewers, even those who liked the movie, have failed to identify its novelty and daring. **Personal Best** is striking resonant chords and pinching sensitive nerves among feminists and gay activists too. Some love it. Others think it's exploitive and distorting. Herewith, an attempt to sort out the controversy and distinguish what works in the film from what doesn't.

Personal Best is about Olympic contenders Chris Cahill (played by Hemingway) and Tory Skinner (Patrice Donnelly). They meet at a track event, become lovers, and then teammates at the University of California. When we first see Chris, she's an emotional wreck, unable to perform under her father's goading. When we first see Tory, a seasoned competitor, she's lifting her male coach in the air after a victory. Tory attracts Chris because she displays the self-confidence the younger woman lacks and desires, and Tory recognizes in Chris the great physical potential she has always longed for. Tory encourages Chris as no one ever has, and she blossoms into a champion. After three years of living with Tory and working out with her, however, Chris hungers to test experience on her own. The women break up and Chris eventually takes a male lover, but sport remains the center of both women's lives.

I found Michael Chapman's cinematography intoxicating, with its close-up and slow-motion adoration of female anatomy and racially integrated sport ritual, and I was surprised to learn that others thought it leering and reductive. I first heard the charge from a magazine editor. "But what about all those crotch shots?" she asked, with obvious distaste. She was referring to a sequence of high jumps. At the peak of the event, the pelvis, of course, is thrust upward, and that astonishing arch is what the camera recorded.

For a fuller elaboration of her chagrin I recommend Robert Hatch's denunciation in the February 27 *Nation.* "What gravels me about the film is its persistent treatment of its large cast of women as sex objects in situations that are unrelated to sex. We wander into their steam room, where they are relaxing in languorous nudity," Hatch fumes and then adds: "This is cheesecake; it demeans women, and the lubricious chuckles in the audiences suggest that it does so successfully."

Hatch has completely misread the film's images. His category "not related to sex" seems vast to me, and Towne's naturalistic depiction of sport life and its innate eroticism is thus lost to him. Does Hatch imagine that women in steam rooms sit at attention in dress-for-success ensembles? Towne's depiction of women athletes is an unqualified triumph. He sees sport with a voluptuary's eye—a far sight from the ascetic, running-for-God/running-for-the-Jews sensibility which steered *Chariots of Fire.* He makes Chris's and Tory's physical attachment—and that between men and women, and men and men, who train together—seem a natural concomitant of the pared-down jock world of group saunas, massages, gallops on the beach, and salty embraces. The lines dividing sex and sport are easily blurred, for both genders: there's a playfulness to the sex and a sexiness to the carousing. These are people who can think of fucking as building lower body muscle.

Personal Best is a celebration of the life lived entirely in and of the body. Tory and Chris are both raw material and the artists who mold it. They know sensation—the agony of ripped tendons; the exhilaration of achieving new feats—as nonathletes never can. And they are wonderfully unsqueamish about physical functions. In a funny, revolutionary scene, Chris gets behind her male lover and holds his penis while he urinates, exclaiming: "I've always wanted to pee standing up."

But the indignant response to the film (it's in a lot of other reviews too) belies more than ignorance about sports. It's a muddled, knee-jerk puritanism, also known as antiporn feminism, a line far more focused on how women are damaged than how they are pleasured. To claim that Towne sees his characters merely as sex objects is preposterous, since his camera is almost always revealing the nitty-gritty of women's training. Towne makes women's sexiness a function of their power: he shows that women are alluring when they're strong, graceful, accomplished, and rippling with muscle. What a long, salubrious way Mariel Hemingway is from the poignantly helpless flesh of Marilyn Monroe, or an anorectic wisp like Audrey Hepburn, earlier exemplars of female sexiness.

This month's *Playboy* photo layout on *Personal Best* unwittingly documents the difference between empathetic images of female sexiness and the other kind. First there are four pages of stills from the movie: the camera has observed women in their lives, engaged in either athletic activity or sex with one another. Then boom! On the next double page is a classic, posed *Playboy* shot of Hemingway nude except for pearls, doing a spilt with her head bent forward. She's photographed from behind, so the camera targets her ass, legs, and back in a darkened room.

It's a disturbing picture, partly because the photographer flaunts his advantages over his model—you're on display; I have put you there—and partly because the photographer's advantage is precisely what makes the shot sexy to its intended audience. The *Playboy* viewer needs to see configurations which declare, unequivocally, that the woman is displaying herself for no reason other than to arouse the viewer and that never, for one moment, has she forgotten she exists only to be seen by potentially excitable men. The less the *Playboy* viewer sees a woman's strength and accomplishment, the less he is reminded that she can be distracted from her role as turn-on for him.

Personal Best is a male fantasy too—only Towne gets off on female vigor and self-will. He really tries to get feminism right (unlike poor George Cukor who, in his recent debacle, *Rich and Famous,* depicted liberation as a woman's right to get humiliated by increasingly younger men). Towne is careful to show how good women are to one another and how successful they've become at telling pushy men to fuck off. He dramatizes both the gratitude and the impatience the women feel for their coach, a man who wants them to win, but *his* way. And Towne subtly reveals how sport and lesbianism—two choices which make women marginal in society—reinforce his characters' independence. Eventually, their inner lives match the radicalism of their outer situations and both are able to feel fine without male approval.

Towne's treatment of lesbianism—despite the problems it raises, and there are some—is completely new in films. *Personal Best* is a gratifying, clarifying departure from lesbian-punishing movies like *The Children's Hour, The Killing of Sister George, The Fox,* and *Windows.* A friend who recently saw *Personal Best* at the Greenwich Theater, with an audience consisting largely of lesbian couples, said that spontaneous applause and cheering broke out after the initial lovemaking scene.

It is gloriously sensual, if too brief. Tory and Chris drink beer, smoke dope, get silly, and whip off their clothes, ex-

Mariel Hemingway in Personal Best.

ulting in their nerves and cells. The camera traces their long thighs and flat stomachs like an amorous tongue. It's intent but unsmutty, partly because Towne doesn't view their sex as neurotic. He rescues lesbianism from a number of other bum raps as well, including the belief—advanced by some lesbians and gay men—that lesbians disdain lustiness in favor of affectionate cuddling (while gay men supposedly do the opposite). The movie cuts against the stereotype that lesbians accept each other as a consolation prize, because they can't attract men; Tory and Chris are known as "the two best-looking women in San Luis Obispo" and choose each other freely. There's no butch/femme division: both women combine tomboyish swaggering with womanly tenderness. And most remarkable—a first among movies with lesbian characters—their sexuality isn't made the Problem around which everyone else's emotions quiver and congeal.

Towne's good will notwithstanding, a number of gay men and women have come down hard on *Personal Best.* Recently interviewed in the *Times,* Vito Russo said that Towne trivialized lesbian sex, and therefore all homosexuality by having Chris go from Tory to a man. It made the women's affair seem adolescent, Russo argued. A lesbian friend, who came back railing against this movie I'd suggested she see, thought the lesbian sex insultingly tame, nothing like genuine eroticism which, she said, Towne didn't come close to portraying.

I don't think these charges make a case for Towne as a homophobe. Tory is clear about what she wants. Chris isn't. She *is* young, an experimenter who wants to taste the full sexual menu. If anything, it was bold of Towne to make a movie which didn't lock characters into an either/or rigid sexual identity. Tory has had male lovers—she describes one at the beginning of the movie. She may have a man again, and it's certainly possible that Chris could fall in love with another woman. Chris is uncertain about how her male lover will feel about her affair (he accepts it), but she never disavows this aspect of her sexuality.

Towne doesn't make lesbianism like beginner sex. When Chris makes love to a man, she's just as coltish as she was with Tory. In fact, her lesbian affair is presented as more intense than her heterosexual one. There's no hot-and-heavy eroticism *anywhere* in this film. It's about people obsessed with sport, not sex.

The trouble with *Personal Best* is that Towne doesn't know how to dramatize his characters' conflicts, and, as a result, the film portrays athletes more astutely than it does a lesbian relationship. The women's break-up is awkward and unimaginative. Chris isn't exactly a fount of introspective eloquence, and with her grazing-animal, Renoir face and squeaky drawl of a voice, Hemingway is terrific as a jock required to look dumber than she is. Still, the women's emotions deserve a more intelligent treatment than the few fuzzy hurt-feeling episodes Towne provides. By not permitting us to understand or probe his characters, Towne distances us from them irretrievably.

He makes another crucial error by abandoning Tory. Until the split-up, *Personal Best* is about two women, but afterwards, Tory is glimpsed in snippets and only in rela-

tion to Chris. It's unfair to the character, and it severely unbalances the film. We need to see Tory in her own life— miserable, or with friends, or with another lover—because Towne has made us care about her. Tory and Chris are thrown together once more at the Olympic finals, and Chris gets a chance to return the support which Tory first gave to her, but the ending is slapdash, and Chris's relationships with both Tory and her coach are left frustratingly unresolved. After the astonishing and lengthy first section—well worth seeing—the story goes nowhere, like the athletes who cannot get to Moscow.

The abandonment of Tory as a character is the one uncontestable antilesbian charge that can be leveled at the movie. I did get the feeling that Towne wanted to see Hemingway in bed with a man—not to legitimatize her, however, but because that's what he likes. Towne clearly doesn't get off on the spectacle of affirmed, second-round lesbianism, or he would have shown Tory with another woman. It's not believable that this beautiful, adventurous character would just mope and pine indefinitely.

In a similar vein, Towne and Hemingway have been telling reporters that *Personal Best* is not about lesbianism, which is rather like saying that *Moby Dick* is about men at sea, nature, and change, but not about whale-hunting. Having made the most enlightened movie about lesbians to date, is Towne now afraid the theme will hurt the movie commercially, and if so, why doesn't he come right out and say so? The producers of *Making Love* made a big, newsy deal out of their risk in doing a movie on gay men. What's up?

By advertising the financial chanciness of male gay sex and not mentioning that lesbians are risky too, everyone seems to be agreeing that homophobia is essentially about male/male sex—that sex with penises is the kind that's truly threatening. Lesbians aren't a turnoff to straights of either gender, the rationale goes, because what women do together isn't serious.

But this doesn't quite square with Towne's denial of the content of his film, or with the fact that Towne's film company was harassed with bomb threats and guns while on location in Oregon, or with the fact that lesbianism is a far more closeted subject in society than male gay sex. Gay men are a reality in popular culture, even if only as a Phil Donahue "issue." There are male gay characters on sitcoms, and comedians satirize the cruising life, while lesbians rarely show up on the tube and are never joked about. *Gay* means *gay man* on TV, and to most Americans, therefore, the questions of who lesbians are and what they do in bed are still mysterious and fraught. Why else the morbid gravity when the subject comes up?

Maybe the relative openness with which male homosexuality is now discussed is partly a cover for, and distraction from, the possibility that lesbian sex evokes even deeper terrors. Perhaps Towne denies his subject because he's realized that nowhere, save the laid-back world of *Personal Best,* are people relaxed about female sexuality. Maybe most people feel that sex without penises isn't safe and sweet but scary and subversive. It's certainly not good for the family. It's certainly not good for men. That's dangerous enough for me.

Michael Sragow (essay date January-February 1989)

SOURCE: "Darkness at the Edge of Towne," in *American Film,* Vol. XIV, No. 4, January-February, 1989, pp. 40-61.

[*In the following excerpt, Sragow surveys Towne's career, focusing on* Chinatown, Tequila Sunrise, *and his reputation in Hollywood.*]

> ". . . Nobody wants me to quit. 'Don't quit, don't get caught, stay on top long enough for us to knock you off.' That's the motto around here. Nobody wants me to quit. The cops wanna bust me, the Colombians want my connections, my wife wants my money, her lawyer agrees and mine likes getting paid to argue with them. Nobody wants me to quit—hey, I haven't even mentioned my customers. You know they don't want me to quit."

That speech belongs to the drug-dealer protagonist of writer-director Robert Towne's new movie, *Tequila Sunrise,* but it may echo the sentiments of Towne himself, a prodigiously gifted filmmaker who's never been able to shake his reputation as simply the best screenwriter in Hollywood.

Tequila Sunrise producer Thom Mount is not alone in considering Towne's directorial debut, *Personal Best,* among "the best first movies ever made." But in the nearly seven years between that film's release and *Sunrise,* Towne's only other writing-directing project, *The Two Jakes,* tripped at the starting block. Pundits and industry gossips seemed to be pressuring Towne back into what they saw to be his proper place—as a great writer, period.

In some ways, who could blame them? A short list of the most memorable movie moments of the last 15 years would have to include a bunch of speeches, confrontations and revelations written by Robert Towne, such as the crisis in *The Last Detail* (1973) when the cantankerous Navy signalman harasses a redneck bartender until the latter threatens to call the shore patrol. The signalman slaps his service revolver on the bar and proclaims, "I AM THE MOTHER-FUCKING SHORE PATROL!" Or the time in *Chinatown* (1974) when an alternately slick and seedy '30s private eye, taking on a case that ripples through the power circles of Los Angeles, gets his nose slit by a verminy punk. "It looks like half the city is trying to cover it all up, which is fine with me. But Mrs. Mulwray—I goddamn near lost my nose! And I like it. I like breathing through it. And I still think you're hiding something."

Or maybe the magnetically shaggy oration of the charming Beverly Hills hairdresser in *Shampoo* (1975) when he explains why he's such an unregenerate womanizer:

> "I go into that shop and they're so great-looking you know. And I, I'm doing their hair, and they feel great, and they smell great. Or I could be out on the street, you know, and I could just stop at a stoplight, or go into an elevator, or I . . .

there's a beautiful girl. I, I, I don't know . . . I mean, that's it. I, it makes my day. Makes me feel like I'm gonna live forever. And, as far as I'm concerned, with what I'd like to have done at this point in my life, I know I should have accomplished more. But I've got no regrets. . . . Maybe that means I don't love 'em. Maybe it means I don't love you. I don't know. Nobody's going to tell me I don't like 'em very much."

These speeches, casual and simple in their language yet vivid and revelatory in their dramatic impact, are so intimately keyed to the performances that they bring to mind the actors and—amazingly for movies—their edgy, vernacular characters: Jack Nicholson as Billy "Badass" Buddusky in *The Last Detail,* Nicholson again as J. J. Gittes in *Chinatown* and Warren Beatty as George in *Shampoo.*

What's more, the outbursts arrive at just the right instant to clinch the stories and the characters. You immediately comprehend Buddusky's volatile dissatisfaction with life, Gittes' drawling slyness and romantic curiosity, and George's fundamentally innocent sensuality. Just listening to the lines brings back the movies in their entirety.

Creating scripts like these, which are full of existential showdowns, diversely expressive speeches, and characters that bring out the vitality in stars such as Nicholson and Beatty, helped make Robert Towne the first superstar screenwriter of the current Hollywood era.

Towne, now 54, was no Wunderkind when he hit it big. Raised in San Pedro, California, he worked as a tuna fisherman, studied literature and philosophy at Pomona College in Claremont, and reportedly did a stint in military intelligence before landing in Jeff Corey's Hollywood acting class in 1958, where he met Nicholson and quickie movie king Roger Corman.

Madison Avenue-man-turned-producer Harry Gittes, the friend of Nicholson and Towne whose last name became immortalized in *Chinatown,* refers to Towne as

> "the best example of an actor-turned-writer in the business. If you're an actor first, you know what's tough to play, how much exposition you need to get a point across. I ended up coproducing *Drive, He Said* [Nicholson's 1972 directorial debut]. Towne was in it as an actor. He was in a scene that was extremely tough to articulate—two characters just speaking totally between the lines. The Towne character knew that the other character was having an affair with his wife. The way that Towne helped rewrite that scene, the point came across light rather than heavy-handedly. It's a lesson I'll never forget."

By the mid-'70s, Towne had parlayed his string of hits, as well as the reputation as a script doctor that he acquired on *Bonnie and Clyde* (1967) and *The Godfather* (1972), into the chance to become a writer-director. For years, Towne labored on the script he felt was the best thing he'd ever done—*Greystoke,* a version of *Tarzan of the Apes* that concentrated on the trials and tribulations of an ape raising a baby boy. Towne says that long before *Gorillas in the Mist, The Adventures of Dian Fossey,* he hoped to portray a hero "for whom the life of an ape was no less important than the life of a human being."

Still, the prospect of directing the scenes between boy and apes was daunting. So for his producing-directing debut, he chose a "smaller" script, *Personal Best* (1982), a story of female pentathletes, played by Mariel Hemingway and real-life track star Patrice Donnelly, who fall in love with each other while competing to qualify in the 1980 Olympics. Though not a commercial success, it was an audacious piece of work. A speech given by Scott Glenn, as Hemingway's coach, ranks with Towne's funniest and grittiest: "I could've coached football, I wouldn't have had to put up with this insulting shit from you. Do you actually think Chuck Noll has to worry that Franco Harris is going to cry if Terry Bradshaw won't talk to him?"

But Towne also demonstrated that he could extend his gifts for narrative structure and speech rhythms into the visual and tactile elements of movies. By concentrating his eye and ear on the athletes, he was able to recapture the unself-conscious grace that characterizes his memories of growing up in an unspoiled Southern California, and *Personal Best* became an ecstatic coming-of-age film, an indelible expression of the joy of movement.

The move into directing ultimately resulted in the stalling of his career, the loss of two dream projects and the disruption of old friendships. Where he once had been known as the consummate script doctor and Hollywood professional, he now found himself caught in a swirl of innuendo that raised questions about whether he was suited temperamentally to be a writer-director.

It all started when, as producer and writer-director of *Personal Best,* Towne clashed repeatedly with executive producer David Geffen during the completion and release of the movie. Geffen had rescued the project by taking over the financing from Warner Bros. when the 1980 Screen Actors Guild strike threatened to scuttle the movie. But a contract dispute between Towne and Geffen shut down production between December 1980 and June 1981.

In the course of what he later called a "coerced agreement" with Geffen and Warner Bros. in order to finish *Personal Best,* Towne signed away his rights to *Greystoke.* His Tarzan was made in vastly different form by Hugh Hudson, director of *Chariots of Fire,* a considerably more pompous movie about Olympic athletics. The daunting new title told the story: *Greystoke: The Legend of Tarzan, Lord of the Apes.*

Meanwhile, Towne endured years of gossip centering on Geffen's countercharges that the director had taken "a picture budgeted at $7 million and made it incompetently for $16 million." (Towne rebutted that the original budget was $11.7 million, renegotiated to $12.7 million and that it rose to $15 million partly because of the interest paid during the six-month contract dispute.)

In 1985, after some odd writing jobs, Towne was once again a writer-director, all set to launch *The Two Jakes,* the highly anticipated sequel to *Chinatown.* Jack Nicholson had gotten back into leading-man shape to repeat the role of Gittes, and, in the boldest, weirdest stroke, Robert Evans co-starred as the second Jake, a mysterious real estate operator named Jake Berman. According to the one full report ever published on the film (by David Thomson in *Vanity Fair*), that oddball move may have killed the production. Whatever the ultimate reason, when Evans couldn't cut it as Berman, things fell apart, and the production was halted almost before it began. Towne once again became the center of scrutiny, which this time questioned his leadership ability.

Over the years, Towne kept busy with writing chores—rewriting an unproduced fantasy named *Mermaid* for Beatty and Ray Stark (*Splash* beat this prestige team to the punch), and doing script surgery on Hal Ashby's *8 Million Ways to Die* and Roman Polanski's *Frantic.* Still, since *Personal Best,* the only times his name appeared on-screen were as the executive producer for his friend Curtis Hanson's *The Bedroom Window,* and as an actor (and uncredited creative consultant) in writer-director James Toback's comedy *The Pick-up Artist.*

But, as Toback says, "Robert Towne is a Hollywood outsider with the compulsiveness, determination and slyness to crack into the center whenever the need arises." And with the help of independent producer Thom Mount, Towne has cracked back in with *Tequila Sunrise,* an "under $20 million" romantic comedy-drama starring Mel Gibson as a former cocaine dealer who now sells ecologically sound leaky-pipe irrigation systems, Kurt Russell as his best high-school buddy, who happens to be a star narcotics cop, and Michelle Pfeiffer as the chic Manhattan Beach restaurant owner who gets caught between them.

Towne asked Mount to produce *Tequila Sunrise,* a project he had been trying to make for a number of years, while they both were working on *Frantic. Frantic* star Harrison Ford, who was originally penciled in for the Mel Gibson role, had second thoughts about playing an ex-dealer. Mount downplays the difficulties he had selling the project to Warner Bros., where he worked out a negative pick-up deal for the film's distribution. (As part of the "coerced" 1981 agreement, Warners had the right to a first look at *Tequila Sunrise.*)

"Let's just say everyone looked very carefully at the balance between the drug dealer's current life and his past life," says Mount. "And, as a director, Robert has one of the most important weapons anyone could have to sell a project—a concrete vision of what he wants."

To Curtis Hanson, the clouds hanging over recent Towne productions have wrongfully obscured Towne's creative steadiness and industry clout. Shortly after *The Two Jakes* fell apart, Towne called Hanson and asked what he was doing. Hanson replied that he got *The Bedroom Window* back from Paramount in turnaround and was trying to set it up with himself directing. "And Robert just went crazy. Over the course of a holiday weekend, he got the go-ahead at Fox." Eventually, with Towne's help, Hanson ended up making the movie at the De Laurentiis Entertainment Group.

"Think about the gossip surrounding Robert," says Hanson.

"You know, when he was a writer, people used to say, 'Yeah, he's good, but he's too slow,' and now that he's a director, people say, 'Yeah, but does he have the temperament?' This is a very small town. A lot of guys who have bad experiences making movies don't work any more. Yet Robert commands great respect at Orion. He commands great respect at Paramount. And now, after the nightmare of the release of *Personal Best* and the further nightmare of *Greystoke,* he's back at Warner Bros. with *Tequila Sunrise.* They wouldn't be in bed with him if they didn't think he could perform!"

Mount says he wasn't disappointed on *Tequila Sunrise:* "Robert took 'the long view' on every scene and every shot; the flip side of that was intense work on issues of performance. There was a lot of night shooting (40 nights out of a total of 68 days), a lot of high-powered actors. And 10 days into production, he had to fire the cinematographer, Jost Vacano (*Das Boot*), a terrific guy who just wasn't in sync with his ideas. Robert handled it."

I found Towne at the Evergreen Studios, where he was overseeing the film's music scoring. He was paunchier than the last time I saw him, right after *Personal Best* when he was in the middle of a physical fitness obsession. But otherwise he seemed steadier now. The gaze of his eyes—his dominant feature—was more direct. There has always been something dolphinlike and slippery about his imposing physical presence. Instinctive in all his convictions, spontaneous in their expression, he sends out thought waves not only when he's speaking in his surprisingly soft voice, but also when he's punctuating his talk with silence.

"One of the reasons the first cinematographer and I had difficulties," Towne explained during a break,

> "is that he wanted it to look grainy and gritty, because it was a drug world and everything else. And to me, it's like being in the olive oil business. I mean, what makes *The Godfather* real is all the glamour in it, which is what most of us would see in our daily lives. You'd see Sam Giancana sitting in a beautiful restaurant, very gentlemanly, and quiet, retired.
>
> "So if you're trying to tell a movie about cops and robbers, you withhold the underbelly of it as long as you can. You show what most of us see, and it's not that different from our lives, when we're living well. And then, gradually, the audience starts getting scared, because they realize there's this underbelly, and they haven't seen it yet, and something is going to sneak up on them and bite them on the ass if they're not careful."

As the movie evolved, Towne turned parts of it into a celebration of West Coast light:

> "There was a piece of graffiti I once saw that I tried to put in the movie and couldn't find a place for—'There's no life east of Sepulveda.' And this movie is about life west of Sepulveda, as I knew it. San Pedro, Redondo, Hermosa made up a magical place for me. It was unlike L.A., it was unlike anywhere I'd ever been. I was

setting the movie in the place of my magical memories, even though the movie is contemporary.

> "Conrad Hall [the cinematographer who replaced Vacano] has the same understanding of Southern California that I have, and that Richard Sylbert [the production designer] has. I always start out saying, 'I'm just going to show how this place has turned to shit.' And then I can't stop myself. My eye keeps going to the things that were beautiful, the things that I remembered as a kid—like people having trailers in the backyard, and bougainvillea in the backyard, and crab grass and those funny little redwood fences."

At the heart of *Tequila Sunrise* is the triangular tale of an honest master criminal who tries to be loyal to all his friends, including a Latin drug dealer; a good cop who's emotionally dishonest but redeemable; and the slick yet feeling woman who's caught between them. As a minor character comments, their interplay poses the question, "Who says friendship lasts forever? We'd all like it to, maybe, but maybe it wears out like everything else, like tires."

Over the years, many names had been dropped as possible players in *Tequila Sunrise,* including Warren Beatty and L.A. Lakers coach Pat Riley. After Harrison Ford dropped out, Towne saw *Lethal Weapon* and sent Gibson the script. "I just got stupidly lucky; no one could have been a better choice than Mel," he says. Towne was banking on Gibson bringing to the part the unhinged, reckless quality that it needed in its final act.

Towne thought of Michelle Pfeiffer after seeing Alan Alda's *Sweet Liberty.*

> "She gave a very witty performance, one in which she displayed an ability to have a surface persona and then break into a whole other character. And somebody who owns and runs a restaurant has to have those two speeds, this surface persona as the hostess, dealing with people regardless of what's going on, gracious even in the face of crises, which has its own kind of comedy. And then there's also intrigue in, 'What's that woman like when she's not being so fucking gracious that she drives you nuts?' Her sangfroid and her beauty become a challenge and a kind of rebuke. . . ."

Kurt Russell was the actor most firmly set in Towne's mind:

> "Hanging out with him and Goldie [Hawn, Russell's live-in mate], I saw something in Kurt that was so right for the character—the irrepressibly mischievous nature of the man. It's an expression of the life force that allows you to take a character who has certain complexities that would normally be unacceptable or unappealing—enough to vitiate the drama—and with Kurt, he makes the movie a horse race."

Towne explained that each character is an amalgamation of several people.

> "For example, in Kurt you will see a physical re-

semblance to Pat Riley that's unmistakable. Pat never comes unglued on the sidelines, never undoes his ties, and nobody can read into his behavior one way or the other. That's good for a glamorous cop who's trying to get a job done; it's useful with cops and criminals alike.

> "What I wanted to create was a character who is politically very adroit, which is the reason for his success in his professional life and for his undoing in his personal life. He's charming and mischievous and basically decent, but he's also manipulative and damn near gets a lot of people seriously hurt."

From the beginning, Towne's Hollywood identity has been tied in with that of his friends Nicholson and Beatty. Towne has often given credit to Nicholson for teaching him the art of indirection—of playing the action of a scene against the ostensible subject, so that (as he once told John Brady) "a guy trying to seduce a girl . . . talks about everything *but* seduction, anything from a rubber duck he had as a child to the food on the table or whatever."

But after Towne toiled on cheap movies and television (including *The Outer Limits* and *Breaking Point*), it was Beatty who brought him into big time when, impressed by an unproduced western Towne had rewritten, Beatty asked the unknown writer to work on *Bonnie and Clyde*. Though Towne didn't get any screenwriting credit, the movie made him legendary as a script doctor, a reputation that was cinched when he provided Francis Coppola with a crucial scene in *The Godfather*—the one in which Don Vito tries to pass his wisdom along to his son Michael. And it was with Beatty that Towne wrote the critical and commercial hit, *Shampoo.*

"In my life," Towne says,

> "I have known, at a little distance, what were putatively my closest friends for 20 years. I read about them in the paper, I see them in the movies, I get glimpses of them from the gossip columns, and yet they're my close friends. And I think we get lulled into a false sense of seeming that we know each other better than we do, because we read about each other in the newspapers and elsewhere."

"Movies are insulating experiences," says Towne, "and unless you have those experiences with your intimate friends, you inevitably lose contact with them but think you haven't." *Tequila Sunrise* took shape when Towne began to explore

> "that feeling, and what it does to you, and the increasing willingness, in movies and in all kinds of business, to be able to use anything that's personal in the name of your business is OK. People use the name of art and the name of business the way they're given to saying, 'I swear on my child's life.' That feeling seemed transferable to a cop who could do anything in the name of his business because he's got justification—drug dealers being what they are and the world being what it is.

> "When the characters get crazy over certain issues, none of them are venal. . . . They're al-

ways a matter of personal honor. The drug dealer has a very strict belief that there's a right and wrong way to behave. And, unlike most drug lords, the only thing that upsets the Latin so-called villain is that he feels an old friend may have behaved in a way contrary to the way friends are supposed to behave. They all operate out of an elemental code of honor. If your girl lies to you, that's it."

In its witty, sophisticated and surprisingly soft-spoken way, *Tequila Sunrise* protests the opportunistic morality that has held sway in this country's public life for 30 years. Although the movie focuses on the ethical corners present-day cops cut in order to nab drug dealers, Towne feels that the drama has its roots in the '50s.

> "When Eisenhower admitted that we flew a spy plane over Russia, it was a big shock in this century. It was a bad thing to do. It wasn't fair. We were engaging in an underhanded activity.

> "In the old westerns, before drawing your gun, the other guy had to draw his gun and fire. Take that and World War II, and you have a rather elevated way of viewing how you were supposed to deal with your adversary. The U-2 came along and just didn't square with that. It affected me, my thinking, strongly. We were doing that to them. From that moment on, the end justified the means.

> "And that thinking is transferable in this country to any scourge, whether it's communism or drugs or whatever it is. You know, everything's fair. You've got to do whatever you can to get rid of the problem. It's another version of what you have to do to ferret out witches. And if you're like me, you never end up knowing how valid the problem is because you're so pissed off."

The most daring part of *Tequila Sunrise* is that the drug dealer is more of a traditional hero than the cop is. McKussick (the Mel Gibson character) still does drug-related favors for family and friends. But he's trying to go straight and devote himself solely to his legitimate business—his leaky pipes that irrigate fields without wasting water or endangering the ecology.

How upset were the folks at Warner Bros. at this sympathetic portrait of a drug dealer? "Oh, well, man, I tell you, I like and respect Bob Daly [Warner Bros.' chairman of the board and CEO], but at first he was terrified," says Towne.

> "He couldn't believe it. Couldn't the guy be in the numbers racket? Couldn't he be anything else? Couldn't he just sell marijuana? But if a man is trying to escape his past and it's difficult, he's got to have a difficult past to escape from, and you've really got to identify with the problem. I mean, if the underlying dynamic of your story is that a gunfighter is desperate to hang up his guns, you've got to have some sense of what it was like to be a gunman, sort of unsavory. You can't have a gambler or a numbers runner ashamed and desperate to stop—the difficulties

of trying to escape that kind of past are just not the same."

Towne can be indirect and disarmingly frank at the same time—like some of his best characters—even when he's discussing the current anti-drug crusade:

> "I mean, if I were Rip van Winkle and went to sleep in 1968 and woke up in 1988, and they told me that drugs were bad and that sex could kill me, I'd say, 'I'm going back to sleep, man.'

> "Of course I don't think drugs are good for people in general, they're just not. But I think the current preoccupation with drugs is more damaging than anything else. The real lie is, you CAN'T say no. You can't say no to the kid making thousands and thousands of dollars in the ghetto. You can't go around saying no—that's the lesson of William Blake, he knew that 250 years ago. He's the one who knew you can't have a 'Thou Shalt Not' writ over the door—people will just lose themselves in gin, because life is miserable. You can't just say no, you have to provide an alternative. You have to find something you want to do. Drugs is a way of saying that you haven't found anything you want to do."

Does he speak from personal experience?

> "Hey, I'm just the wrong person to ask. In my life, until I was 28 years old, I smoked three packs of cigarettes a day, until one day I decided, 'That makes me sick.' Up to eight, nine years ago, I smoked Cuban cigars. I've still got a thousand Cuban cigars in London in a beautiful humidor that James Fox has for me. I don't smoke them anymore because they make me sick. Certain things just tend to give *me* up, whether I want to give them up or not. But I do know that Bob Daly's position on drugs isn't so far from mine, and he's on Nancy Reagan's 'Just Say No' committee."

The last six years have been a tumultuous time for a man who believes in simple codes. He's gone through divorce, remarriage and a custody fight for his young daughter, and the fracas over ***The Two Jakes*** strained his long-standing friendships with Nicholson and Evans. But Towne, who feels that the ***Jakes*** script is now "as solid and disciplined" as ***Chinatown,*** says he's happy that the film seems to be headed for production with Nicholson directing as well as starring, and will be glad to offer his help. (Although nothing has been officially announced, Nicholson's friends regard it as a done deal.)

Towne and his second wife, Luisa, are devoted to each other. Over her protests, he calls her "the keeper of the flame"—the person who keeps reminding him of his dreams whenever the pressures of production threaten to bury them.

Curtis Hanson, once described by Towne as "one of three close friends who one way or another have helped me through scripts and through my life over the years," has known Towne well for over two decades. Hanson admits that he and Towne have had their ups and downs—severe ones. And he agrees with Towne that things got more

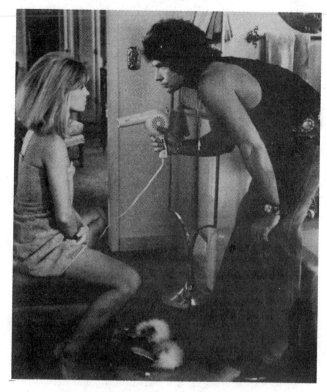

Warren Beatty and Julie Christie in Shampoo.

complicated for the writer when he became a director, "around the time of ***Personal Best,*** when he got into the center of the hurricane." Still, says Hanson, "Robert is an emotional guy and a complicated guy.

"My feeling," Hanson continues,

> "is that Robert likes being in the middle and working with the actors and the cameraman and doing all the things that go with carrying your vision out. At the same time, I think Robert would also be happy to work with a director on a given project and see the picture go off and kind of godfather it—if he felt it was going to be made right. Of course, the question is, would he ever feel the projects would be made right?"

One project that Towne feels is sure to be made right is Hanson's next film, *The Brotherhood of the Grape,* in development at Orion. Based on John Fante's roisterous 1977 novel of California-Italian family life, Towne and Francis Ford Coppola were to team up on the movie, but instead will serve as co-executive producers.

Towne has fought hard when trying to preserve the form and meaning of his own scripts, never more notoriously than when he clashed with ***Chinatown*** director Roman Polanski over the bleak ending and cynical slant that Towne felt Polanski had imposed on the material. (Towne gets his revenge in his script to the sequel, ***The Two Jakes.*** By the end, the sleazy private eye J. J. Gittes turns into a romantic hero.)

"If he's really convinced of the rightness of something," says James Toback, "and he's given a couple of shots to explain why it's the way to go, he starts to get quite frustrated if you don't see it the same way." This willingness to take a stand over artistic issues, along with his stubborn attention to details, have helped to give Towne a reputation for integrity, and, in recent years, for "difficulty." But Toback admires Towne for his intellectual tenacity, which he calls "a very un-Hollywood trait. There, the attitude is, 'You don't like my script? I don't like it either, here's my other one.'"

Towne's sense of craftsmanship would seem to link him to Hollywood's glory days. "If we were back in the '30s and '40s, it might be that Robert would have become like Nunnally Johnson, more of a writer-producer," says Hanson. "But today, directors get all the praise and a lot of the power."

But Towne says that Hollywood tradition

> "isn't important to me at all, personally. I think that I have always felt that people respond best to structure, especially if you're going to make an unorthodox point. I mean, to show how the farmers were blown out of the Owens Valley, I'm not going to do a Frank Norris novel like *The Octopus* or Mary Austin's *The Land of Little Rain*. Nobody would go to see it—nobody would let me make it.

> "So I figure I do a detective movie and do it about a real crime, which is fucking up land and water rather than stealing a jewel-encrusted falcon. *The Maltese Falcon* is one of my favorite stories. It's about greed and something else, and so's *Chinatown*. But *Chinatown* is about greed and its consequences, not just in the present, but to the future. The land is raped as surely as the daughter, and these things have far-reaching consequences.

> "I mean, the important thing is, how much better can you write? How much better can you lead? Why are you doing it?"

Towne says, echoing the words he wrote years ago in *Chinatown*. "For the future."

Mark Horowitz (essay date November-December 1990)

SOURCE: "Fault Lines," in *Film Comment*, Vol. 26, No. 6, November-December, 1990, pp. 52-5, 57-8.

[*In the following essay, Horowitz analyzes Towne's career through* The Two Jakes *and reassesses the significance of* Chinatown *as "the lens through which all of his other films are judged."*]

Sixteen years have gone by since we first met *Chinatown*'s Jake Gittes, the Los Angeles private eye who specialized in divorce cases, though he preferred the more delicate term "matrimonial work." By whatever name, Gittes' métier was still the sleazy but lucrative snooping on adulterers that his closest professional rival, Philip Marlowe, fastidiously eschewed. It has also been sixteen years since we met the doomed and beautiful Evelyn Mulwray, she of the anxious hunted look and the nervous habit of lighting up

a cigarette when she already had one going. Mrs. Mulwray and her family had terrible secrets, and Gittes, regrettably, learned them all. The year was 1937.

Robert Towne's screenwriting career divides easily into two parts: 1) *Chinatown* and 2) Not-*Chinatown*. The second category includes an impressive list of credits, among them *The Last Detail* (1973), from the novel by Darryl Ponicsan; *Shampoo* (1975), co-written with Warren Beatty; *Greystoke* (the original version by Towne, not the final film version written, according to the credits, by Michael Austin and P.H. Vazak, Towne's sheep dog, now deceased); *Personal Best* (1982) and *Tequila Sunrise* (1988), both of which Towne also directed; *Days of Thunder*, this summer's Tom Cruise retread; and *The Two Jakes*, this year's long-awaited continuation of the Jake Gittes saga.

But of all that Towne has written, *Chinatown* remains the keystone. Critics still treat it as his definitive statement. It is the lens through which all his other films are judged, and, if they are found wanting, it provides a convenient rhetorical club to beat them with. In view of how often this has happened over the years, it's possible to conclude that writing *Chinatown* was the worst mistake Robert Towne ever made.

Chinatown's artistic ambitions were as grand as they were apocalyptic. It promised to lay bare the sinister roots of modern capitalist society by proposing a countermyth to the traditional American story of benevolent founding fathers. Evelyn Mulwray's father, the all-powerful Noah Cross, begat modern Los Angeles by bending man as well as nature to his will.

Named for the founding father in another popular origin myth, Cross was the paragon of unrestrained capitalism, monstrous and heroic, destructive and creative. No meat was unfit for his insatiable appetite. He was the secret id of modernity, the Oedipal nightmare turned on its head: Dad kills son and rapes daughter. He was unstoppable.

When the movie hit theaters in July 1974, unbridled pessimism was the currency of the day. Political disillusion was epidemic. OPEC had the West by the short hairs. Watergate was at high tide. Less than a month into the film's successful run, President Nixon resigned from office. The formal burial of the sincere Sixties came nine months later when Saigon, without American support, fell to the North Vietnamese Army and was renamed Ho Chi Minh City. The country was in foul spirits. *Chinatown*, set in the deepest, darkest Great Depression, captured the mood of 1974 to perfection.

But as grim a portrait of American society as *Chinatown* was, the film still wasn't dark enough to match the true depths of the contemporary mood. *Chinatown* was a modest hit and won Towne an Academy Award for best screenplay, but the Oscar for best picture that year went to its rival in radical despair, *Godfather II*, an even darker and more tragic vision of corruption in high places. *Chinatown* still had a hero, albeit an impotent one; *Godfather II* had none.

Towne never intended to create a classic of despair. Granted, he took Raymond Chandler's detective genre and enriched it with a more fully articulated social critique, giving the pessimism inherent in all detective fiction a stronger foundation. But Towne also preserved intact Chandler's romantic notion that, despite the odds, there were occasional candles against the darkness. Marlowe and Gittes were both cynical private eyes, but they were also closet knights-in-shining-armor who occasionally made a difference.

Towne wrote *Chinatown* but it was directed by Roman Polanski, a man whose philosophical views had been uniquely shaped by his tragic encounters with both Adolf Hitler and Charles Manson. He lost family members to both. Towne's and Polanski's artistic agendas diverged at times, and Polanski, as director, had his way at the crucial moments.

At the end of the film Evelyn Mulwray confronts her father over custody of their daughter, the product of their incestuous union. "She's mine, too," he moans pitifully. Apparently, in Towne's original draft Evelyn shoots her father and goes to jail, but, with Gittes' help, the daughter escapes to Mexico. There was a partial victory; hope was kept alive, even if only a glimmer.

Polanski took Towne's romantic pessimism and twisted the knife until it metamorphosed into his own brand of East European nihilism. In the final Polanski version, Evelyn dies and Noah Cross gets his hands on the girl. The forces of darkness are unbeatable. No one makes a difference and Gittes' meddling probably made matters worse. At the end of the tunnel Polanski saw only . . . more tunnel.

Since 1974, the libraries of few aspiring screenwriters have been complete without a tenth-generation Xerox of the script for *Chinatown.* The true connoisseur possesses several different drafts. Towne's script is held up in film schools and how-to-write-a-screenplay books as a masterpiece of construction, noted for its layered plot in which one revelation after another unwinds with absolute precision, no scene ever lasting longer than it has to.

Thanks to Polanski, Towne not only acquired a reputation for unqualified pessimism despite the fact that he intended something far more equivocal—he was also given too much credit for *Chinatown*'s tight, clockwork plot structure.

Towne was tagged as an avatar of crystalline screenplay structure when nothing could have been further from the truth. Admirers confuse his craftsmanlike respect for the formal demands of a particular genre—the detective film—with an overall commitment to rigid story structure in every case.

Such discriminating attention to craft has always stood Towne in good stead with producers who happily pay him unimaginable sums to take a look at their ailing properties. (His uncredited interventions as script doctor are known to include *Bonnie and Clyde, The Godfather, Reds, Swing Shift, Eight Million Ways to Die, Frantic,* and *Fatal Attraction.* Some of these were major page-one rewrites and some were brief hit-and-run consultations. A complete list of credits will probably never be known.) But in his original screenplays Towne prefers a loose approach to storytelling. *Chinatown* was the only exception, and Towne readily gave Polanski credit for a large part of the film's narrative precision.

Towne revels in the kinds of conventions previously at home in the well-made plays of Feydeau or Sardou, not the least of which is his nearly fetishistic use of symbolic objects as foci for the shifting meanings that surround his characters.

—Mark Horowitz

Chinatown's canonization wreaked havoc with critical perceptions of Towne's career. To borrow a perverse line from *The Producers, Chinatown* was just "too good." It created a vivid but false impression. Towne is most famous for a film whose content is darkly pessimistic and whose form is crystalline and succinct. These qualities are uncharacteristic of everything else he's written, and this anomaly has been interpreted as clear evidence of a decline in artistic quality since 1974.

Chinatown, so the argument goes, is perfect, while the rest of Towne's scripts are all over the place, like big sloppy shaggy dogs (like P.H. Vazak, in fact!): *Personal Best* feels improvised and unstructured, the plot of *Tequila Sunrise* is incomprehensible and its climax is sentimental, *Shampoo* is too light and ambivalent, and *The Last Detail* pulls its final punch, compromising the novel's dark conclusion by having Badass Buddusky (Jack Nicholson) deliver his prisoner to the brig, then go back about his business, whereas in the novel he feels so guilty he goes AWOL and destroys himself. The novel ends with the doleful finality of *Chinatown,* while Towne's adaptation substitutes a wishy-washy conclusion.

Oh what a falling-off there's been. In every instance, *Chinatown*'s moral certitude (life is shit) has given way to moral vagueness (life is kind of complicated). Or so it appears.

What if you turn the painting around and try looking at it another way? What if the sins of an artist unable to find his way back to his one single moment of perfection are actually the hallmarks of his true style? What if *Chinatown,* far from being quintessential Towne in theme, style, and structure, is really his most atypical and misleading work?

> "The greatest filmmaker that I know of, the one who moves me the most, is Jean Renoir. If I ever were to do a course on screenwriting, I would deal a lot with Renoir . . . [who] got more of life into his art than anybody I've seen before or since." [Robert Towne, in a interview with John Brady]

Many of Towne's alleged weaknesses are also those of his

avowed master, Jean Renoir, whose artistic universe is as far from Polanski's *Chinatown* as Frank Capra is from the Coen brothers. Renoir's is a world where villainy and heroism are never clear cut, where each character has his reasons, where scenes end only after every last ambiguous bit of meaning, buried intent, and misunderstood motive has been teased out, where the moral terrain is constantly shifting and where actors and camera alike appear to be freely improvising rather than fatalistically following their well-worn path to oblivion.

Towne's affinity for Renoir may not be the master key that unlocks all his films, but it's a useful corrective to the tunnel vision engendered by *Chinatown.* For starters, Towne finds justification in Renoir for ignoring many of the innovations of modernist cinema. Towne is a classicist—at least in form—not an innovator. He does not subvert or "appropriate" old forms in the postmodern fashion; he embraces the conventions of whatever genre he happens to be working in—whether detective story, romantic melodrama, even Restoration comedy (*Shampoo* was inspired by Wycherly's *The Country Wife*).

He shares this deference to existing forms with Renoir, who also moved freely from costume drama to war film to Hollywood melodrama to Technicolor musical, always leaving the conventions of the form as he found them. His interests, like Towne's, lay elsewhere: in the moral relationships of the characters.

It is a conundrum of 20th century modernism, familiar to literary critics, that stylistic radicalism is no guide to anyone's politics. (Eliot and Pound come to mind.) For all their dynamic innovativeness, Scorsese, Schrader, DePalma, Cronenberg, and Lynch are, to a man, rigid moralists. They subscribe to the profoundly conservative line that man is born bad and only society restrains him, though just barely. The cosmological specifics may vary according to their religious backgrounds, but corruption always lies just beneath the surface, sin is everywhere, and redemption is possible only through violence, death, or, less frequently, love. It is one of the many ironies of postmodernity that our hottest cinematic rebels are the true heirs to the moral intransigence of old Hollywood's Production Code. Flesh betrays spirit, and transgression must bring punishment.

Towne prefers ambiguous, morally compromised characters because they're real. His attitude is that no individual can walk through life along a perfectly straight line. He must live and work in the real world.

—*Mark Horowitz*

In stark contrast to so many of his peers, Towne is moral without being moralistic. He is a moral filmmaker in the French sense of the word: he's preoccupied with choices and ideas. In an earlier day, we might simply have called him a liberal humanist. The same goes for Renoir (despite a brief flirtation with Communism in the Thirties). Their style of psychological realism is rooted in the brilliant bourgeois culture of the 19th century European novel.

Like Renoir before him, Towne's lack of moral rigidity has often been misperceived as moral laxity. Moral absolutists of the right have attacked Towne for glorifying drug use in *Tequila Sunrise* because the drug dealer (Mel Gibson) is not a villain and, what's worse, in the end he gets the girl. Moral commissars on the left denounced the same film for its allegedly shameless revival of old-fashioned, hero-worshiping Hollywood decadence, not to mention its cop-out of a happy ending.

But Towne prefers ambiguous, morally compromised characters because they're real. His attitude is that no individual can walk through life along a perfectly straight line. He must live and work in the real world.

Money is usually a problem; so is job stability. Towne has the common man's contempt for those who enjoy enough material luxury to never have to compromise their high-priced values. *Shampoo*'s George the hairdresser (Warren Beatty) caters to the rich, but he himself is not; he desperately needs others' capital if he is to open his own shop. Mac, the drug dealer in *Tequila Sunrise,* used to be rich, but his decision to go straight has caused financial problems that are driving him to the wall.

Another dose of reality is that Towne's characters aren't all geniuses, either. George, Mac, Buddusky, and Jake Gittes are all explicitly portrayed as intellectual underachievers. They cannot easily discern the truth of their situations, or see clearly what's right and wrong. They have the desire to be faithful and good, but they make mistakes, they misread events, and they always, always are forced into unpleasant compromises.

Those characters who have the greatest luxury of all, the luxury of moral certainty, like the track coach in *Personal Best,* are never the heroes of a Towne story. The coach (Scott Glenn) knows he's right, and his certainty is very seductive, at first, to his two young protégés (Mariel Hemingway and Patrice Donnelly). He "knows" that any athlete who wants to make it to the Olympics has to be selfish, singleminded, and completely alone. But the two young women develop an intimate friendship, at first erotic, then platonic. Their innocence turns to experience and challenges the ideological authority of the coach. *Personal Best* is about testing the limits of the self, on and off the track. It's a sexy, physically intimate film about the life of the mind.

In *The Last Detail,* Buddusky escorts a young sailor to prison. The poor dumb kid (Randy Quaid) is being put away for years—for stealing just a few dollars. Buddusky gives the kid a happy last few days, but he still follows his orders and takes him to the brig in the end. In Towne's version of Darryl Ponicsan's novel, Buddusky hates himself for doing it but he accepts it as part of his job and lives with it. Towne's ending is compromised, unresolved, unheroic, but true to life. In a corrupt and compromising world where everyone eventually gets their hands dirty, the important question is: how dirty.

"Most people just do their job," Towne said à propos *The Last Detail,* "whether it's shove Jews in ovens or take a kid who's stolen forty bucks and rob him of eight years of his life. You're nice about it. You're polite . . . I'm just doing my job. . . . The ending of that screenplay is more consonant with my sensibility than the ending of *Chinatown.*" Not surprisingly, Ponicsan is said to have hated it.

Towne not only wrote *Personal Best* and *Tequila Sunrise,* he directed them as well. And directing style is another area where *Chinatown* can be misleading when it comes to analyzing Towne's other work.

In his first two directorial efforts, Towne has shown more affinity for the sympathetic and accommodating directing style of Hal Ashby (with whom Towne made three films) than for Polanski, whose sharply controlled technique gave *Chinatown* its edge. Towne, Ashby, and, at a much higher level of development, Renoir share a flexible method that allows greater room for the contributions of the actors. Their styles are slightly rough around the edges, with a looser, more spontaneous feel. Towne has even gone so far as to use nonprofessional actors in *Personal Best,* not for their malleability (as Bresson does), but for their unpredictability, perhaps taking his cue from Renoir's *Toni.* (Jack Nicholson, who years ago directed his acting-class colleague Towne in *Drive, He Said,* also leans toward a more improvisatory style. All the more reason we should have expected that *The Two Jakes,* directed by Nicholson, would be a disappointment to hardcore purists awaiting a literal reprise of the Polanski *Chinatown.*)

Towne's penchant for informality has been harmful in one respect. His plots have grown increasingly complex, even to the point of incomprehensibility, and he is reluctant to pare them back. This is especially true of the last two, *Tequila Sunrise* and *The Two Jakes.* Towne might agree with Raymond Chandler—another writer whose plots have gotten out of control at times—who once wrote: "With me a plot . . . is an organic thing. It grows and often it overgrows. So that my problem invariably ends up as a desperate attempt to justify a lot of material that, for me at least, has come alive and insists on staying alive."

I am reluctant to defend either of them on this point, though Oscar Wilde might take their case: "Incomprehensibility is a gift," Wilde said. "Not everyone has it."

If plot construction is not among Towne's evident strengths, character certainly is—even though film is a difficult medium for a psychological realist. Unlike the novel, film permits no direct view into a character's mind. The filmmaker's tools are acting, dialogue, visual style, and whatever tricks of the trade can be found amidst the artifice of 19th century drama, the unsung source of many a classic Hollywood dramatic mode.

Towne revels in the kinds of conventions previously at home in the well-made plays of Feydeau or Sardou, not the least of which is his nearly fetishistic use of symbolic objects as foci for the shifting meanings that surround his characters. Cigarette lighters, watches, missing eyeglasses,

even scars recur within and between films, each time imparted with a new and different symbolic meaning by the character who touches them. We often come to truly know Towne's people through their bric-a-brac.

Take the common envelope. In *Chinatown* Evelyn Mulwray mails a check to Jake. She's trying to buy him off. He tries to return the envelope—and the check—but not before noticing her engraved initials, which reveal her relationship to Noah Cross. Not much; but the same envelope reappears in *Tequila Sunrise* with a vengeance. (At least, I prefer to believe it's the same one.)

Tequila Sunrise is about two high-school buddies—one who grew up to be a cop, the other a dealer—and the woman they both love. Mac (Mel Gibson) is suspected of still dealing drugs. Envelopes of cash are a drug dealer's stock-in-trade. So when Mac gives an envelope to his cousin to deliver to Jo Ann (Michelle Pfeiffer), everyone eyes it suspiciously. Is it evidence that Jo Ann is involved with Mac in some sort of drug-dealing scheme? Is it a love letter? In fact, he's just asking her restaurant to cater a party for him.

The envelope reappears, in duplicate now, when Mac hands one to Jo Ann as payment for the party and then hands another to his ex-wife as his monthly alimony installment. This time they really are filled with cash, but he has accidentally mixed the two up and given too much money to Jo Ann and too little to his ex-wife. The envelopes move from hand to hand in an elaborately choreographed dance of meaning and misunderstanding. Jo Ann assumes he's trying to buy her affection. Mac "explains" everything, but the symbolic envelopes are closer to the awkward truth.

Or how about cigarettes and lighters? In *Chinatown* Evelyn Mulwray lights a cigarette everytime she tells a lie—it's as reliable as Pinocchio's nose. In *Tequila Sunrise,* Mac the dealer and Nick the cop both nervously flick matching Zippo lighters bearing the initials, in raised brass letters, of the high school they attended together. The lighters are constant visual reminders of the bond of experience and affection that ties the two unlikely friends together.

And if not lighters, then ordinary matches. In the film's finest scene—one of Towne's all-time best—Nick the cop (Kurt Russell) gives a long, confessional speech in front of Jo Ann. He's saying he loves her and will no longer be the suspicious cop with her. It is a moment of absolute sincerity and it wins her heart.

Then the phone rings. Jo Ann goes to the other end of the bar to answer it. Nick's police instincts get the better of him. He has to know who she's talking to. He thinks it may be Mac. He decides to eavesdrop. Let the screenplay finish it:

> He reaches for a cigarette, doesn't seem to be able to find a match. He moves down the bar ostensibly to pick up a pack by the cash register which is close to Jo Ann and her conversation. She turns questioningly when she senses he's at her back. He holds up the pack of matches by way of reply. She nods, "oh"—then stops. She

looks down the bar—two packs of matches are crammed under the ashtray in front of Nick's bar stool. . . .

Betrayed by a book of matches. With that eloquent gesture, more truthful than his long confession, Nick drives the woman he loves into the arms of his rival. Nick will always be a cop. That's his strength and his fatal flaw.

Like *Personal Best* before it, *Tequila Sunrise* is a portrait of a tense and competitive friendship. Towne has shown an increasing interest in how friendships and love affairs survive in the real world. Where the public and the private overlap, professional demands impinge on personal and romantic ones. (He may have drawn inspiration from his own highly publicized friendships with Jack Nicholson and Warren Beatty, with each of whom he has collaborated on numerous film projects.)

The public and private realms do not peacefully coexist; the choices between the two are often impossible, but choices have to be made. "Given the choice between betraying my country or my friends," E.M. Forster provocatively wrote, "I hope I will have the courage to betray my country." Towne can be infuriating in the same way.

Lately Towne has taken to doubling the number of protagonists as a way of upping the moral ante. The moral dilemmas of individuals has given way to the moral distractions of pairs and couples. The trend continues with his most recent film. Where there was only one Jake sixteen years ago, today there are two.

In *The Two Jakes* we meet Gittes eleven years after the events of *Chinatown.* He's added a few pounds and lost some hair, but is prosperous and content. The Great Depression is over, World War II (in which he served with distinction) has come and gone, and the postwar boom is in full swing. His company, Gittes Investigations, has its own building now, and the proprietor has his own parking space. All that remains of the unpleasant past are a few scars: one on his nose, others hidden deeper.

The script for *The Two Jakes* (which circulated in samizdat form for several years) again concerns a character trying to do good but making a mess of it. This time there are two knights-errant, both named Jake—and two fetishistic cigarette lighters as well.

It is also the next chapter in Towne's history of the social and economic development of Southern California. The harsh social realism precariously coexists with the romantic recollection of the Southern California of his youth.

In *Chinatown* the historic focus of desire was water; in *The Two Jakes* the smart money is on real estate and oil. The original tenants of the San Fernando Valley land appropriated by Noah Cross in the first film are long gone; postwar tract houses are going up where walnut groves once stood. The second Jake of the title is a Jewish real estate developer who at first seems like the bad guy but (shades of Marcel Dalio in *Grand Illusion* and *Rules of the Game*) turns out to be, well, more complicated. Is he another cynical megalomaniac who'll stop at nothing to further his own interests and mint more money? Or is he a different kind of

dreamer, and Gittes' doppelgänger in more than name only?

The Two Jakes is a continuation of the *Chinatown* story, but on a deeper level it is also a rebuttal. Part of the new script's subtext seems to be how Towne himself, in the form of Jake Gittes, must atone for his mistake in the previous film—namely, letting Polanski give a dark, nihilistic twist to the original ending by killing Evelyn Mulwray. Towne and Jake failed to save Evelyn in *Chinatown.* The failure still haunts them both. In *The Two Jakes* they want to protect the memory of her daughter, Katherine, as a way of atoning for Evelyn's death.

Katherine was always a perfectly balanced Towne symbol: the tainted product of a horrible incestuous rape—but also a symbol of innocence and hope for the future. Would Robert Towne, the third Jake, manage to protect her this time? (Part of him must have been confident. After all, four years after the release of *Chinatown,* his wife gave birth to a daughter. They named her Katherine.)

As he did with Polanski, Towne had some differences of opinion with director Nicholson, and he apparently absented himself from L.A. during the latter part of the shooting. Nicholson reportedly reworked the ending to suit his own artistic instincts—and, no doubt, to simplify the very long and convoluted script.

But finally . . . so what? The compromises of filmmaking are a perfect mirror to the compromises in life, and they do not always lead to inevitable failure. Towne once called *Chinatown* the first part of a projected trilogy, so there's always hope for another shot—though prospects are dim: after all, the second film took sixteen years to reach the screen, and was soon playing to empty houses. Still, anything is possible. Like the old revolutionary, Robert Towne is a pessimist of the intellect, but an optimist of the will.

David Ansen (review date 24 October 1994)

SOURCE: "An Old Affair Revisited," *Newsweek,* Vol. CXXIV, No. 17, October 24, 1994, p. 76.

[*In the following mixed review of Towne's* Love Affair, *Ansen asks: "Why do another remake of the sentimental classics* Love Affair *and* An Affair to Remember . . . *if you're not prepared to wallow in four-hankie heaven?"*]

Like every movie Warren Beatty has produced, *Love Affair* is made with skill, the participation of topnotch talents and considerable taste. There are times, however, when good taste can get in your way. Why do another remake of the sentimental classics *Love Affair* and *An Affair to Remember* (both directed by Leo McCarey, in 1939 and 1957) if you're not prepared to wallow in four-hankie heaven? Beatty, who stars and co-wrote the script with Robert Towne (Glenn Gordon Caron directs), follows the originals' plot line with great fidelity, with a sprinkling of contemporary details to drag it into the '90s. He's a former pro quarterback and notorious womanizer engaged to a TV talk-show host (Kate Capshaw). On a flight to Australia he meets the woman of his dreams—piano teacher Terry McKay (Annette Bening), herself engaged to marry a wealthy financier (Pierce Brosnan). The plane crash-lands on a Pacific island; the two embark on a ship for Tahiti, fall in love and vow to meet in three months atop the Empire State Building. If you don't know what happens next, you didn't see *Sleepless in Seattle*.

Aside from the autobiographical echoes—famous philanderer discovers monogamy late in the day—Beatty offers no fresh take. The movie, bathed in soft focus, is as reticent about sex as the Cary Grant/Deborah Kerr version, and half as romantic. The only fun is in the lively first third: Beatty and Bening are at their best in push-pull seduction mode, when they can be a bit naughty. But once the couple clinch their bond—just when the story gets really shameless—the life drains out of the movie. *Love Affair* takes such pains to dodge vulgarity it forgets to put anything in its place.

FURTHER READING

Criticism

Alpert, Hollis. "Jack, The Private Eye." *Saturday Review/World* 1, No. 23 (27 July 1974): 46.

> Positive review of *Chinatown* that concludes the film "is clever, cunning, tricky, and superbly acted."

Cocks, Jay. "Lost Angelenos." *Time* 104, No. 1 (1 July 1974): 42.

> Contends that *Chinatown* successfully recreates "the ambience of Los Angeles before the [Second World] war," but argues that the story's protagonist, J. J. Gittes, though "a kind of genial guide through all the thickets of plot," is not a fully developed character.

———. "Blow Dry." *Time* 105, No. 8 (24 February 1975): 4-5.

> Praises *Shampoo* as a "fast bedroom farce" that realistically depicts Southern California living in the late 1960s. Cocks, however, faults Towne for the "grossly sentimental" ending of the film, which he feels is inconsistent with the protagonist's character and the direction of the plot.

Ellsworth, Elizabeth. "Illicit Pleasures: Feminist Spectators and *Personal Best*." *Wide Angle* 8, No. 2 (1986): 45-56.

> Surveys critical reactions to *Personal Best*, focusing on Towne's treatment of lesbianism and other feminist issues.

Hatch, Robert. Review of *Personal Best*, by Robert Towne. *The Nation* 234, No. 8 (27 February 1982): 251-52.

> Contends that *Personal Best* treats women as sex objects and takes "crass advantage" of Mariel Hemingway's "comeliness."

Kael, Pauline. "The Man Who Understands Women." In her *Taking It All In*, pp. 302-07. New York: Holt, Rinehart and Winston, 1984.

> Enthusiastic 1982 review of *Personal Best*, complimenting Towne's natural dialogue, character development, and cinematography. Kael asserts that Towne wants to show "that the beauty that excites him is the same as 'character,' and that a woman [athlete] who moves beautifully is beautiful through and through, right to her soul."

Moore, Kenny. "You Oughta Be in Pictures." *Sports Illustrated* 56, No. 4 (1 February 1982): 50-4, 56, 58-62.

> Behind-the-scenes account of the making of *Personal Best*. Moore, an athlete and writer, played the character Denny in the film.

Young, Vernon. "Film Chronicle: *Personal Best*, Three Levels." *The Hudson Review* XXXV, No. 3 (Autumn 1982): 447-52.

> Negatively reviews *Personal Best*, contending that the film lacks beauty and tenderness, and focuses on "vindictive competition, macho assumptions, and gutter language."

Zimmerman, Paul D. "Tars and Bars." *Newsweek* LXXXIII, No. 6 (11 February 1974): 85-6.

> Mixed review of *The Last Detail*. Zimmerman contends that "Towne's sharp dialogue and inventive episodes, and [Hal] Ashby's spirited direction can go just so far in transforming an essentially depressing dead-end situation into a satisfying comedy."

Additional coverage of Towne's life and career is contained in the following sources published by Gale Research: *Contemporary Authors,* Vol. 108; and *Dictionary of Literary Biography,* Vol. 44.

Marguerite Yourcenar

1903-1987

(Born Marguerite Antoinette Jeanne Marie Ghislaine Cleenewerck de Crayencour) Belgian-born French and American novelist, short story writer, essayist, critic, poet, dramatist, and translator.

The following entry provides an overview of Yourcenar's career. For further information on her life and works, see *CLC,* Volumes 19, 38, and 50.

INTRODUCTION

Esteemed for her magisterial literary style and classical erudition, Yourcenar was the first woman elected to the Académie Française, the highly prestigious French cultural institution established in the 1600s by Cardinal Richelieu for the perfection and preservation of the French language. Her primary artistic preoccupations included the mythology, history, and verse of ancient Greece and Rome; the nature of love and its relationship to sexuality; and the possibility of morality in the absence of myth and religion. Although she was conservative in aesthetic temperament, defying the modernist trends of the century and eschewing the social conventions of Parisian literary life, Yourcenar was a lifelong champion of civil rights, equality for women, and environmental and antinuclear causes.

Biographical Information

Yourcenar was born into two very old, wealthy, and influential families from Belgium and France. Her mother, a native of Brussels, died ten days after giving birth. Consequently, Yourcenar was raised and educated by her father, Michel de Crayencour, a Frenchman, in Mont-Noir, Lille, and Paris. As her teacher, mentor, and sole intellectual companion, Yourcenar's father encouraged her to study the classics, to begin writing poetry, and to read French, Latin, Greek, and English literature. She wrote her first poems when she was fourteen and her first volume, *Le jardin des chimères,* was privately published in 1921; she later dismissed this work as possessing only "the virtue of childish simplicity." For this book, she and her father anagrammatized "Crayencour" to devise the pen name Yourcenar, which she adopted as her legal name in 1947. For most of the 1920s she and her father traveled through Europe enjoying a life devoted to literary, aesthetic, and intellectual pursuits. In 1929, after her father's death and the loss of much of her inherited fortune in the stock market crash of that year, Yourcenar published her first novel, *Alexis* (*Alexis*); this was her first work to be accepted by a commercial publisher and was her only major work that her father read. In the 1930s, she published prolifically in a variety of genres, including a critical volume on the Greek poet Pindar simply entitled *Pindare* (1932); a unique book of prose, poetry, and aphorisms examining various aspects of love, *Feux* (1938; *Fires*); two collections

of short fiction, *La mort conduit l'attelage* (1934) and *Nouvelles orientales* (1938; *Oriental Tales*); and a book-length essay on dreams, *Les songes et les sorts* (1938). She also translated Virginia Woolf's 1931 novel *The Waves* into French in 1937 and two years later published her second major novel, *Le coup de grâce* (1939; *Coup de Grâce*). Able to support herself with her writing in these years, she traveled widely in Italy, Germany, and Greece; in 1937 she briefly visited the United States, where she lectured at several colleges and studied the life of the Roman emperor Hadrian (A.D. 76-138) at Yale University. Travel restrictions imposed throughout Europe during World War II forced Yourcenar back to the United States, where she worked briefly as a journalist and commercial translator before becoming a part-time instructor at Sarah Lawrence College in 1942. Her literary output was slight until 1948, when trunks containing her collected notes on Hadrian arrived from France. Inspired by these notes, Yourcenar began composing what many critics consider her greatest work, *Mémoires d'Hadrien* (1951; *Memoirs of Hadrian*). While she continued to travel extensively over the next twenty years, she and Grace Frick, her close companion and English translator, established their permanent home on Mount Desert Island, Maine, in 1950. Yourcenar's life from this time on was consumed by travel and literary projects, many of the latter involving the revision or completion of work from previous decades; notable in this regard is the 1968 novel *L'oeuvre au noir* (*The Abyss*), which is widely considered her second masterpiece. During the 1960s and 1970s she received many international literary awards and numerous honorary degrees from colleges and universities in the United States. In 1980 she became the first woman elected to the Académie Française in the three-century history of the institution whose members include writers, politicians, scholars, and scientists; in her address to the Académie she acknowledged the importance and influence of such illustrious French women writers as Germaine de Staël, George Sand, and Colette, saying that she was "accompanied by an invisible troupe of women who perhaps should have received this honor long before, so that I am tempted to stand aside to let their shadows pass." Yourcenar remained an active traveler and writer for the rest of her life, nearly completing the final volume, *Quoi? L'éternite* (1990), of her autobiographical trilogy known as *Le labyrinthe du monde* before her death at the age of 84.

Major Works

Although Yourcenar produced important works in a variety of genres, her reputation rests primarily on her novels. Her first attempt in the genre, *Alexis,* is structured as a *récit,* a classical form of the French short story designed to recount, ostensibly as an aid to the examination of conscience, a significant deed or event in a concise, rapid narrative. The novel proceeds as a letter written by the title character, a talented musician finally avowing his homosexuality, to his wife, Monique, as an apologia for deserting her and their new baby, and to express his regret at having lived misleadingly with her for so long. Anticipating *Memoirs of Hadrian* with its epistolary form, the novel also inaugurates many of Yourcenar's signature themes, namely the artist's struggle to maintain and express his sensibilities in a hostile environment; male homosexuality; love and pleasure; and the emergence of self-identity and its relation to guilt. *Coup de Grâce,* which also uses the first-person *récit* form, examines the lives of three characters caught in romantic and political turmoil. Set in the late 1930s during the civil wars touched off by the Russian Revolution in the Baltic states of Estonia, Latvia, and Lithuania, the novel is "remembered" by Eric von Lhommond, an aristocratic adventurer and romantic mercenary whose purely class-based, nonideological objections to Communism provide his pretext for participating in Europe's military conflicts. He recounts his relationships with Conrad, a young man whom he loved, and Conrad's idealistic sister Sophie, who fell in love with Eric but was rejected and finally executed by him. *Coup de Grâce* further develops Yourcenar's notion of love as fate and examines the abuse of power in its physical, emotional, and political forms. Critics note that the novel also presents, in the character of Eric, the prototype for Yourcenar's hallmark larger-than-life protagonist, clearly prefiguring the Hadrian of *Memoirs of Hadrian* and Zeno of *The Abyss.* As Ann M. Begley has pointed out, Yourcenar's fascination with Hadrian began when she read Gustave Flau-

bert's description of the emperor's era: "Just when the gods had ceased to be and the Christ had not yet come, there was a unique moment in history, between Cicero and Marcus Aurelius, when man stood alone." *Memoirs of Hadrian* is an epistolary novel consisting of the aging emperor Hadrian's letter to his seventeen-year-old adoptive grandson and heir, Marcus Aurelius, the purpose of which is to pass on the lessons learned in an eventful, varied life. With her stated intention of conveying the psychology of the age, Yourcenar largely avoids plot and melodrama, focusing instead on anecdotal depictions of Hadrian's career and his meditations on politics, war, art, religion, destiny, and love between and among the sexes. Yourcenar depicts Hadrian as the quintessential warrior-poet, an agnostic who has succeeded in forging a personal moral code with the support of neither ancient myth nor Christian faith. Like Hadrian, Zeno in *The Abyss* is a faithless man, but one whose personal understanding is achieved through lifelong study and service to the sick. Set during the sixteenth century, the novel details the divergent paths taken by Henri-Maximilian Ligre, scion of a wealthy and powerful family who seeks adventure and fame as a soldier, and his bastard cousin Zeno, a studious, metaphysically-oriented man who despises his cousin's life and devotes himself to the investigation of philosophy, alchemy, medicine, and mysticism. Portrayed in a Faustian light, Zeno's quest for an authentic life and truth is seen as heresy by the leaders of his age. *The Abyss* is a further examination of Yourcenar's interests in the implications of fate, emergent self-identity, and the relation of magic and philosophy.

Critical Reception

Before the publication of *Memoirs of Hadrian,* Yourcenar's works received little attention outside a relatively small group of intellectual readers. *Le jardin des chimères,* for example, was ignored by most reviewers, but attracted the enthusiastic attention of Nobel laureate Rabindranath Tagore, who invited Yourcenar to live in India. In general, critics have praised Yourcenar's classical writing style, the breadth of her interests, and the depth of her understanding. Others, however, have faulted what they consider her obsession with the past, the auxiliary role female characters play in her fiction, and her reluctance to discuss the personal experiences that influenced her work; this last charge is frequently raised by readers of her autobiographical trilogy *Le labyrinthe du monde,* which investigates and re-creates the lives of her forebears but does not focus on the events of her own life. Furthermore, at least one critic, Elaine Marks, has discerned anti-Semitic sentiments in *Coup de Grâce*—Marks's opinions, however, do not appear to be widely shared. Yourcenar's novels, particularly *Memoirs of Hadrian* and *The Abyss,* are widely hailed as masterpieces; scholar Anthony Levi has called them "high points in the development of the French historical novel." Begley has also noted that Yourcenar's scholarship in *Hadrian* is so scrupulous, and her portrait of the emperor's mind and times so accurate, that the novel is "read by historians, and . . . is cited in historical bibliographies dealing with Hadrian."

PRINCIPAL WORKS

Le jardin des chimères (poetry) 1921

Les dieux ne sont pas morts (poetry) 1922

Alexis; ou, Le traité du vain combat [*Alexis*; translated and revised edition, 1984] (novel) 1929

La nouvelle Eurydice (novel) 1931

Pindare (criticism) 1932

*Denier du rêve [*A Coin in Nine Hands*; translated and revised edition, 1982] (novel) 1934

La mort conduit l'attelage (novellas) 1934

Feux [*Fires*] (poetry and prose) 1938

Nouvelles orientales [*Oriental Tales*; translated and revised edition, 1985] (short stories) 1938

Les songes et les sorts (essay) 1938

†Le coup de grâce [*Coup de Grâce*] (novel) 1939

Mémoires d'Hadrien [*Memoirs of Hadrian*] (novel) 1951

‡Electre; ou, La chute des mosques (drama) 1954

Les charités d'Alcippe et autres poèmes [*The Alms of Alcippe*] (poetry) 1956

Sous bénéfice d'inventaire [*The Dark Brain of Piranesi, and Other Essays*] (essays) 1962

‡Le mystère d'Alceste, suivi de Qui n'a pas son minotaure? (dramas) 1963

§L'oeuvre au noir [*The Abyss*] (novel) 1968

Théâtre. 2 vols. [*Plays*; partial translation, 1984] (dramas) 1971

Souvenirs pieux [*Dear Departed*] (autobiography) 1974

Archives du nord (autobiography) 1977

La couronne et la lyre: Poèmes traduits du grec (translations and criticism) 1979

Mishima; ou, La vision du vide [*Mishima: A Vision of the Void*] (criticism) 1980

Les yeux ouverts; entretiens avec Matthieu Galey [*With Open Eyes: Conversations with Matthieu Galey*] (interviews) 1980

Anna, soror . . . (novella) 1981

§Comme l'eau qui coule [*Two Lives and a Dream*] (novellas) 1982

Le temps, ce grand sculpteur [*That Mighty Sculptor, Time*] (essays) 1983

La voix des choses (photographs and translations) 1987

En pèlerin et en étranger (essays) 1990

|| *Quoi? L'éternite* (autobiography) 1990

**Conte bleu (short stories) 1993

---

*Yourcenar later reworked *Denier du rêve* into the play *Rendre à César* (published in the first volume of *Théâtre*).

†This novel served as the basis for the 1978 film directed by Volker Schlöndorff and written by Genevieve Dorman, Margarethe von Trotta, and Jutta Bruckner.

‡*Electre; ou, la chute des mosques* was translated as *Electra* in *Plays. Qui n'a pas son minotaure?* was translated as *To Each His Minotaur* in *Plays*.

§*L'oeuvre au noir* is based on the novella *D'après Dürer*, one of three in *La mort conduit l'attelage* (the other two are *D'après Greco* and *D'après Rembrandt*). Two of the three novellas in *Comme l'eau qui coule*—*Un homme obscur* and *Une belle matinée*—are based on *D'après Rembrandt* from *La mort*.

|| Collectively these works are known as *Le labyrinthe du monde*.

**This work contains "Conte bleu," "Le premier soir," and "Maléfice."

CRITICISM

Marguerite Yourcenar with Matthieu Galey (interview date 1980)

SOURCE: An interview in *With Open Eyes* by Marguerite Yourcenar, translated by Arthur Goldhammer, Beacon Press, 1984, 271 p.

[*In the following excerpt from a series of interviews conducted over many years and first published in France as* Les yeux ouverts: Entretiens avec Matthieu Galey *in 1980, Yourcenar discusses a number of topics, including her literary influences, some of her major works, and her thoughts on politics and feminism.*]

[Yourcenar]: In the course of preparing to write **Quoi? l'Eternité,** the third volume of **Labyrinthe du monde,** I had occasion recently to list some of the books I read as a child and adolescent. Two periods are sharply differentiated: the childhood influences have nothing in common with those that follow. In the end there were so many influences, they must have cancelled one another out.

To begin with, there were the fairy tales, of which I was very fond. Like any other child I attempted to act them out, for instance by walking around with a magic wand, touching it to some object, and commanding it to turn to gold. The objects may not have changed much, but it was a wonderful game.

Then there was the reading I did out loud with my father of books that he liked, such as *Le trésor des humbles*. . . . I was eleven when he read me the historical novels of Merezhkovski, which were then in vogue; that mysterious man, though somewhat effete and something of a high-society figure, just may have exerted some influence on the direction I was to take. These readings took place in our Paris apartment. I didn't understand them very well, but the books left me with the sense of a crowd that all Russian novels give, whether by Merezhkovski or Tolstoy.

I also read Shakespeare. I read all my classics in cheap editions that I purchased myself. . . : Racine, La Bruyère, and the rest. I remember an impression I had just after I began reading, or, rather, when I had just learned how to read and reading was still an entirely new experience for me. I must have been six-and-a-half, seven at most. It was a day when we were moving, and my father had left me alone in his bedroom while he busied himself with sealing our trunks. He had handed me a book that happened to be lying on the table: it was a novel by a woman who is completely forgotten today, whose name I happened to run across on a plaque affixed to the house she had occupied in Montpellier when I was staying in that beautiful city some years ago. Born of a good Languedocian family, Protestant I think, her name was Renée Montlaur and she wrote novels based on the Gospels and the Bible. Books of that sort were never among my favorites, but I remember that this one was set in Egypt at around the time of Christ. I barely knew where Egypt was, and I've forgotten the plot, but my eyes happened to fall on a passage in which several of the characters board a boat on the Nile at sunset. That is the impression I remember: the glint of sunlight on the Nile, when I was six or seven. And that impression stayed with me, though it took quite a while before it became an episode in Hadrian's travels through Egypt. It stuck in my memory. I'm sure it would have astonished the author of the pious novel from which I borrowed it.

[*Galey*]: *What other French novels did you read?*

In early adolescence virtually none. It was not until later, when I was almost fifteen, that I began to read everything. I read Barrès, of course. He was the man of the hour. The patriotic side of his work didn't interest me. *Les déracinés* (*The Uprooted*) struck me then as forced and artificial, and that opinion still holds. But the Barrès of *La colline inspirée* (*The Inspired Hillside*) was overwhelming, again because it combined the invisible world with another world, that of the peasant's everyday reality. I still think that it is a great book. Obviously there are slack passages, places where Barrès merely tosses off a bit of Barrès, but there are other places where he achieves the level of truly great art: the Lorraine landscapes, so wonderfully described, and especially the solitude and old age of Leopold, the magician and practitioner of occult arts, and his devotion unto death to Vintras, half fanatic and half charlatan, despite the fact that Vintras is the cause of all his woes.

Did Barrès's style have any influence on your own?

It's hard to say. Certainly not at the time of my first "major experiments," when I was twenty, and not when I was writing *Alexis* either. But after that, maybe a little. Overall I have had two or three periods in which I wrote in different styles, which I can pinpoint fairly accurately. The first includes my early sketches, my *Pindare,* written by an adolescent who knew practically nothing, the first "Hadrian," the first "Zeno," the two other short stories in *La mort conduit l'attelage,* first drafted when I was twenty and subsequently rewritten in a style that was, though still immature, something approaching the "free" style I finally settled on. I hope that these stories, which I wrote or, rather, rewrote in this free style from beginning to end, will soon be published. It pleases me to think that one's style improves throughout life, as one sheds the scale of imitation, simplifies, finds one's path, while the underpinnings remain, shored up or, rather, strengthened by experience.

Then came my first published attempts to write in the genre known in French as the *récit,* very reserved, moderate, limited in scope: this was the period of *Alexis.* The development of my own personal style came to a halt until I was almost twenty-five, as I attempted to get in step with contemporary literature, especially the *récit* form as it was being used by Gide and Schlumberger; I wanted to confine myself to a more literary, more restrained form of art, which was in fact an excellent sort of discipline.

This was followed by a reaction against *Alexis.* In the next period I wrote *Fires* and the original *Coin in Nine Hands,* in an ornate style that may have been influenced by Barrès but that was certainly also influenced by many others, Suarès for example and all the baroque painters and poets of Italy. And after that I think I more or less found my own voice, beginning with *Hadrian.*

Did your father have literary enthusiasms that he passed on to you?

He was very fond of reading and had his favorite authors, but enthusiasms, no, I think not. He loved Shakespeare and Ibsen, for instance. We read Ibsen together when I was sixteen or seventeen: he wanted to teach me to read out loud, and he conceived a sort of musical notation to mark the places where one should pause and where the voice should rise and fall. Ibsen taught me a great deal about man's total independence, as in *An Enemy of the People,* where the hero is the only person who sees that the town is polluted. The great nineteenth-century writers were often rebels, subversives, opponents of their age and their society, of all mediocrity. Ibsen, Nietzsche, and Tolstoy were like that, and I might add that it was with my father that I read all three.

On the other hand, my father didn't read much Balzac. Though it may appear arrogant to say so, I would even go so far as to suggest that it was I who forced him to read a part of nineteenth-century French literature. For example, I was the one who said, "Let's read *La Chartreuse de Parme.*"

We read together a great deal, out loud. We passed the book back and forth. I would read, and when I became tired my father would spell me. He read very well, far better than I: he put much more of himself into the characters.

When did you discover Proust?

Shortly after his (i.e., Proust's) death. I must have been twenty-four or twenty-five. But my father didn't go along with me there. It was his age that refused: he hated the thought of reading the latest books. For him Proust was the incomprehensible. He preferred the Russians, of whom we were enormously fond. And Selma Lagerlöf, about whom I was later to write an essay and whom I still regard as a writer of genius.

And Dostoevsky?

I read him later on and admired him so much that I was virtually dumbstruck. How shall I put it? At times he took my breath away, so great did he seem. But he didn't exert much of an influence on me. His Christianity was—or at any rate seemed to me—poles apart from what mattered to me, though I was moved by the starets, Zosima. Yet I've never gone back to reread much Dostoevsky, and that's the real index of influence.

We read some French writers too, such as Saint-Simon. My father particularly liked the seventeenth-century writers. I read almost all of Saint-Simon with him. He introduced me to whole crowds of humanity, and I thought of him as the great observer of what happens and what passes by. As for style, his is so great that, unless one is a writer, one doesn't notice that he has one. His diction is admirable, but I sometimes wonder if it's because of the moment of history in which we now find ourselves that I find it particularly impressive.

And what about poets?

Poets? The seventeenth-century poets, of course, and the Renaissance poets, and Hugo. I've always liked Hugo a great deal, despite the vagaries of fashion. I recognize that at times he can be heavily rhetorical, but there are also tremendous, dazzling moments. All the other poets, Rimbaud and Apollinaire, I discovered later in life. As I wrote in the preface to **Alexis,** I think that young writers are quite often not particularly involved with their own age, unless they happen to belong body and soul to a "school" with its finger in the wind, which tries to anticipate or at least latch on to every change in outlook. Generally speaking, the young writer takes his nourishment from the work of preceding generations. You see this very strikingly when you study the work of the Romantics. They hark back not to their immediate predecessors but invariably to artists somewhat further back in time.

If you're looking for influences, you'd probably do better to look to the philosophers. It would be impossible to overestimate Nietzsche's influence, for example.

—*Marguerite Yourcenar*

Who were your predecessors?

Oh, perhaps Yeats, Swinburne, and D'Annunzio. D'Annunzio was widely read at the time. Mainly the poems, many of them quite beautiful, which I read in Italian. I was capable of distinguishing between his novels, which are very dated, and those of his poems that have stood up well, provided, of course, that one is willing to overlook the rhetorical passages and baroque ornamentation which are as embarrassing in D'Annunzio as they are in Barrès.

Who else? Péguy? I never got very far with Péguy. I didn't like his aggressive brand of Christianity any more than I did Claudel's. Neither one really mattered to me. Baudelaire? Yes, but I didn't sample him until rather late, as a connoisseur—I read him with the eye of the professional, appraising the extraordinary perfection of the Baudelairean line. It was too late for naïve enthusiasm, so to speak.

My enthusiasm was reserved mainly for the seventeenth-century and Renaissance poets: Racine, to a lesser extent La Fontaine (it was not until much later that I came to appreciate the rhythmic beauty of La Fontaine's verse),

and the English poets, especially the Metaphysicals, whom I read, of course, in the original.

If you're looking for influences, you'd probably do better to look to the philosophers. It would be impossible to overestimate Nietzsche's influence, for example: the Nietzsche not of *Zarathustra* but of *Joyful Wisdom* and *Human, All Too Human,* the Nietzsche who had a certain way of looking at things, from close up and at the same time from afar, a man lucid and acute as a writer yet light of touch.

What about someone like Schopenhauer? Was he important to you?

Yes, but his influence soon became confused with that of Buddhism, because basically Schopenhauer represents the earliest attempt to develop the philosophy of Buddhism in a European climate. Still, I am moved whenever I think of Mann's Thomas Buddenbrook, discouraged after a long life lived according to the conventions of his time, discovering in Schopenhauer not only the meaning of despair but also, perhaps, the utmost peace.

. . . . .

You seem to take a greater interest in literature than in writers.

I have always been happy to know the writers I have met, such as Cocteau, Martin du Gard, Schlumberger, and others who are still living, because knowing a writer personally allows you to make certain judgments that you couldn't make otherwise, judgments of the person rather than the work. But at bottom it's all rather illusory: such judgments add nothing as far as the work is concerned. The problem, the mystery of the work remains. Besides, I've never felt any particular desire to know writers as distinct from other people I've had the opportunity to meet.

For one thing, I always felt that I would bore other writers to death. Even today, I'm not absolutely delighted to open my door every time a young writer appears on the doorstep: many have nothing to say. And then, so little goes on between two people in a half hour's conversation. Why not spend the time rereading the books of a writer you admire? The writer's solitude is profound indeed. Each writer is unique, with his own problems and his own technique, painstakingly acquired. And every writer has a life of his own. There isn't much to be gained from talking about literary subjects with writers you happen to know (or don't know, for that matter).

Broadly speaking, you're quite hostile to literary schools and coteries. I'm thinking, for example, of Gide and his friends, who read their works to one another.

I must confess that I don't understand that sort of thing. Which is not to say I'm shocked—everyone has to find a style that suits. But really, Gide's little circle gathering to read their works out loud—imagine! Think of the embarrassment, the shame, the artificiality that such meetings could engender! Gide had no reason to be astonished that Madame Gide chose that day for her dental appointment: how right she was! That manner of working I don't understand at all.

But aren't literary movements rather like the lyceum, like the Greek philosophers with their disciples? Haven't you ever been tempted to seek out someone's intellectual heritage?

I've never sought out a person whom I looked upon as a master, the way some people looked upon Gide as a master. I'll grant you that I may have gained a considerable amount from knowing certain writers, even writers whose work I don't appreciate. For example, Jaloux's work as a novelist meant nothing to me, but as a critic and simply as a person to talk to he was important, but no more, in a way, than the carpenter who lived next door. My purpose in saying this is not to disparage Jaloux. On the contrary. What is important is a lasting relationship with any person. The accent here is on *lasting:* I'm talking about people one sees every day, or with whom intensity of exchange makes up for periods when contact is lost. Literary groups and movements never contribute anything but wind, and plenty of it! Wind full of dross and dust.

I must confess that I don't understand literary schools and coteries. Consider Gide's little circle gathering to read their works out loud—imagine! Think of the embarrassment, the shame, the artificiality! Gide had no reason to be astonished that Madame Gide chose that day for her dental appointment!

—*Marguerite Yourcenar*

***Fires** stands out in this period as an unusual book.*

Yes, it was unusual from the standpoint of technique, because it's a personal monologue that is—how shall I put it?—somehow externalized, disembodied. It's not me so much as myth again, the grand vistas of human existence. Of course I'm also present, but what you have in addition is access to various possibilities, to a number of imposing images of human life.

Nearly all of the stories in the book depict characters from Greek and occasionally Christian history (there is one story about Mary Magdalene, but with the same Near Eastern setting as the others). I was traveling frequently in the Near East at this time, and the setting of all the stories is based on what I saw.

To take one example, **"Léna ou le secret"** is about a woman who is part of a conspiracy and who allows herself to be tortured rather than betray her coconspirators. The real tragedy, though, is that, in my presentation of the situation, she doesn't really know the group's secrets: for reasons of security she has not been told everything. Yet she won't admit, even under torture, that she doesn't know everything and isn't a full-fledged member of the group. Plutarch, it seems, took a different view of the matter: he saw the woman as the lover of one of the conspirators, fully cognizant of the plans of Harmodius and Aristogiton. But in my story, Léna, like nearly all my female characters, is both humbler and more humiliated, yet at the same time a woman in love.

Even though the story actually took place almost a century before Pericles, I present it as though it might have taken place at around the time of writing, in the Greece of 1936. When you think about Greece and the Near East, whether in the past or in the present, you see that partisan struggles of the sort described in the story have been going on continually, or nearly so. Needless to say, at the time of writing Spain was also much on my mind.

This is possibly the only book of yours in which the word "I" occasionally occurs.

No, there are brief passages in which I use "I," speaking in my own name, in my prefaces and notebooks, as for example in the notes accompanying **Hadrian.** I did use "I" on occasion in **Fires,** but in much the same way as a musician tunes his instrument before a concert. I wanted to go beyond the narrow framework of the tale and to attempt to show what lay behind it, a joyful, durable passion. Passion in many guises: love *tout court* as in *Phèdre;* love of the absolute, as in the *Phaedo;* love of God, as in the story of Mary Magdalene; or love of justice, as in *Antigone.*

The book contains almost no adjectives.

That may be fortunate, because adjectives generally play such tricks on you! When we reread the writers we admire, it's usually their adjectives that bother us. Still, adjectives are surely necessary.

The tone of the book is dry.

No, it's altogether ardent, it's truly **Fires.** I suppose you regard fire as a dry element. Champagne is also "dry." And as far as I know, precious gems don't exude moisture either.

Why, in discussing this book, did you say, "I hope it will never be read"?

Because people will probably mistake its nature or fail to enter into the emotions that still overwhelm me whenever I reread it. To some extent every writer has to balance the desire to be read against the desire not to be read. The same thing is also true of many poets. Otherwise they wouldn't fill their poems with so many obstacles to discourage potential readers. I put a few such obstacles into **Fires**—the situation lent itself to doing so. Writers have always liked to toy with enigmas. But the lines of force in **Fires** are quite visible. They're all related to passion, but passion tugs in many directions. Including, of course, the direction of transcendence.

What do you mean by passion? How do you distinguish it from love?

Most people see no difference, viewing passion simply as love pitched one degree higher. But it would be more accurate to say that the two emotions are close to being opposites. In passion there is a desire to satisfy oneself, to slake one's thirst, in some cases coupled with a desire to control, to dominate another person. By contrast, in love there is abnegation. When I wrote *Fires* I combined the two, sometimes describing love-as-abnegation, sometimes love-as-passion. Ultimately, though, passion has more to do with aggression than with abnegation. Etymologically speaking, it should be the other way around. Passion comes from a word meaning "to suffer," a passive condition, as when we speak of the "Passion" of Jesus Christ, the flagellation and crucifixion. Love, on the other hand, is an active condition.

Time also plays a part. Passions are briefer.

I suppose so, though one does find instances in history and in life of great loves that have endured, and from my point of view it is difficult to distinguish between a great love and a great passion. There are women who've managed to sustain love for difficult men for more than forty years, like Mrs. Carlyle.

Was her love reciprocated?

Reciprocity may not be very important: Laura wasn't especially preoccupied with Petrarch. His was a case of love-as-fervor, in which Laura somehow figured as an image of God. The same remark applies to Beatrice. When it comes to reciprocity in love, there is always a question of how much reciprocity, and reciprocity in what respects. Did Hugo, for example, love Juliette as much as Juliette loved Hugo? Certainly not. For two or three years, perhaps, they enjoyed what they thought of as mutual love, following which she became the great man's humble servant.

The impression one gets is that she was never uppermost in his mind except for a very brief period. Many other women must have found themselves in similar circumstances. With men, love-as-abnegation is less common, because men have always felt that there were other things in life and in the world than love.

In that case, how do you account for the fact that all literature, including your own work, revolves around this problem?

Not *all* my work, surely—far from it—and not all literature. Love plays only a minor role in *The Abyss.* In *Hadrian* many readers focus on the story of Antinous, which is of course a love affair, but in fact it only takes up one-fifth of the book, admittedly the most moving part. It's very important, I grant you, since it must have been very important, too, in Hadrian's life. But in no way is it typical of the book as a whole. It is possible to imagine writing Hadrian's memoirs without dealing at all with the subject of love, in which case they would describe a life incomplete to be sure but still great.

But the book would then lack its crucial radiance. And if Hadrian's story could be told without mentioning love, why does the happenstance of the emperor's meeting this Bithynian shepherd change everything?

To begin with, Antinous was probably not a shepherd (nor was he, in all probability, a slave, as we have been told). Antinous as I have tried to describe him was closer to a "middle-class" Bithynian adolescent of his day. As for the change that comes over Hadrian and what you call the episode's "radiance," I would say that both have to do with

the fact that the encounter with Antinous is the only point at which Hadrian renounces his lucid self-mastery, the only point, apart from certain occult experiences, at which he feels that life transcends him. Love is a disorder in the same sense in which Thomas Mann maintained that genius is a disorder. Or, to put it another way, love is dangerous. Of course it's also a kind of happiness—fundamentally, happiness is also dangerous. Hadrian collapses when Antinous dies but later regains control of himself, after a hard struggle, by dint of what he calls "Augustan discipline." But some traits of his character very likely die forever, along with Antinous.

Even before Antinous dies, however, Hadrian had begun, I fear, to blunder quite frightfully on the subject of love. He mistakes the amount of happiness and security that he is able to bring to his young friend. He behaves quite badly toward the end of the relationship, mired as he is in a routine of business mixed with facile pleasures that makes him a rather odious and rather ordinary character. Then comes the death of his friend, when he comes close to losing his grip entirely, after which he gradually proceeds toward the *patientia* of his final years. I have always viewed Hadrian's story as having a sort of pyramidal shape (though few of my readers have noticed this): the slow ascent to self-possession and power; the years of equipoise followed by the brief period of intoxication, which is also the peak of his ascent; and then the collapse, the rapid descent, followed by a new beginning in the final years, when his feet are once again firmly planted on the ground; after the earlier years of exotic experience, lavish building, and suffering, Hadrian finally comes to accept Roman customs and religion.

But the death of Antinous is not the only cause of collapse in Hadrian. Hadrian gives the impression of being a man who tended to push his strength to the limit and beyond. He came quite close to collapse during the period of uncertainty surrounding the imperial succession prior to the death of Trajan and was saved only thanks to Plotina. As an old man, even after his misfortune, he needs to muster all his self-control to surmount the despair that seizes him during the war in Palestine. Then, however, it is his body that collapses as heart disease takes hold. Frightfully ill, he suffers bouts of despair that bring him within an inch of suicide. His collapse on the ship's deck after the death of Antinous was not Hadrian's only experience with an affliction affecting both body and soul.

You often assimilate love to disease.

The ancients did it before me, for the very reason that I mentioned earlier, namely, that love involves danger. I do not subscribe to the notion, common to so much of French literature, that "love" is the center of life, the center of human existence—not continuously at any rate. It may be life's nadir, rather, or its summit. Love brings good and ill alike, but it is not necessarily what matters most, or, if it is, it is something more than love, something that words lack the power to express.

. . . . .

The time, or rather the atmosphere of the period, must have been of some importance when you wrote **Coup de Grâce** *in 1938. You must have sensed the imminence of war.*

One would have had to have been deaf and blind not to have seen the war coming in 1938. And remember that I knew Germany fairly well and Austria even better, and that I had personally witnessed the growing anxiety in the Near East. But whenever I returned to France from either Greece or central Europe, I saw people sitting in the cafés who gave no sign of suspecting that anything was amiss.

In those days I had a very strong feeling of imminent danger, heightened by the war in Spain and by what I knew of the underside of Italian fascism. The scenes of torture in **"Léna ou le secret"** and *Fires,* along with Antigone's suicide, also in *Fires,* seemed almost to anticipate what history was to enact.

France seemed relatively safe. In part this had to do with life's being so agreeable there, certainly much more noticeably so than elsewhere. No one seemed to anticipate what lay ahead. But a trip on the Orient Express in those days was enough to reveal the hatred that festered in every country along the line, a clear sign that terrible things lay in store. My purpose in writing wasn't to describe the current situation, however.

With *Coup de Grâce* I made the discovery that it was better to work toward a certain perspective in time and space, as I tried to do by evoking the Baltic Wars of 1919-21 (which of course I had not lived through). This was already history, and I was therefore forced to deal with a specific social setting at a specific point in time, far enough in the past so that the resolution of at least some of the issues of that period could already be discerned—which for me may be the essence of what history is about.

Incidentally, the story was a true one, told to me by a friend and subsequently by the brother of the person involved, who is called Eric in the novel. The story appealed to me because it concerned a love affair involving three young people left isolated in a country devastated by war. I sensed in this situation a tragic beauty, together with a unity of place, time, and danger, as the French classic canon so wonderfully puts it. The place was Livonia, or rather Kurland, and the time that of the German putsches of 1919-21, directed against the Communist government. As for danger, there was the drama, the human drama, of three isolated young people set against the larger drama of war, poverty, and conflicting ideologies.

Eric, the main character, the voice in the monologue, looks on as the world into which he was born crumbles around him: Germany collapses in the wake of its defeat in World War I, the Baltic world collapses into chaos, and even the French world of his ancestors falls apart— because his German father was killed on the French front. Finally, the world of ideology, the foundation on which he might have built his life, collapses under him. His only bulwark against the general ruin is the castle in which he is living with his friend, Conrad, and Conrad's sister, Sophie. With the stage thus set, all that remained was to involve these three characters in the action.

I'm still quite interested in the character Sophie, who is a very generous woman, generous even to the man she loves—not as common a thing as one might think. The story ends in the book as it ended in life, in the kind of tragic incident that is inevitable in the ferocity of guerrilla warfare. But love, loyalty to a way of life, and the close bonds that unite three human beings of similar type— these are the things that count, far more than the political background.

What sort of welcome did **Coup de Grâce** *receive, given that its main character, a German, is portrayed with a certain amount of sympathy?*

Many readers liked it a great deal. A critic once told me that Eric was, for some people, the young Werther of his generation. What he had in mind was probably the character's emotional makeup, which resembles Werther's to the extent that "romanticism" is possible in this day and age. Politics is not important to Eric. He is an adventurer, as well as a champion of lost causes. At the very beginning of the book he dismisses all ideologies.

I'm sure I won't be telling you anything you don't already know if I remind you that a person who describes him or herself as apolitical generally stands politically on the right.

Let me think a moment about that statement, which strikes me as too cut and dried to accept on its face. . . . What your proposition proves is simply that, for the time being, left-wing ideology is dominant over right-wing ideology, or at any rate is attempting to assert its dominance. Any minority appears apolitical to the surrounding majority. Mussolini, for example, surely looked upon any writer who did not subscribe to his imperial policy as an "apolitical" person with anarchist tendencies.

In this respect, people described as "left wing" are all too often as naïve as the early Christians, who believed that their answers had to be right and who dreamed, as true believers invariably do, that Eden was at hand—even though Eden always turns out in the end to be inaccessible, because man is imperfect and because any halfway attempt to establish perfection invariably brings violence and error in its wake.

I am not arguing that such eschatological fantasies are wrong because they are left wing; I am saying that they are wrong because, inevitably, they are distorted and turned into hollow formulas. I am utterly convinced that there is no form of government that cannot be perfect, provided that both ruler and ruled are also perfect. An ideal communist would be divine. But an enlightened monarch of the sort Voltaire desired would be equally divine. Where are they, though? A monarchy with a sublime king would be able to find sublime, perfect advisers! Show me such men. That's the error of the monarchists, if there are any monarchists left. They don't see that their king would soon call upon someone like Mr. Giscard d'Estaing or Mr. Mitterrand to serve as prime minister and that the post office would still be staffed by the same people as today, or by others just like them. And as far as I'm concerned, the capitalist technocrat who claims that by using the methods of a sorcerer's apprentice he can bring happiness to human kind is in the same boat. The old political labels have outlived their usefulness, or ought to have.

But in the period just after the Popular Front, when many writers, like Gide, Malraux, Bernanos, and even Mauriac, suddenly became "committed," what was your attitude?

One of indifference. I was spending so little time in France then that it seemed more remote to me than Spain or Greece. Of course, you're right, at that time people like Malraux were pouring forth torrents of eloquence, but I detected a certain rhetoric in that eloquence. To my mind, Malraux was never very sure of what he was doing until he discovered de Gaulle. Underneath it all, I always felt, was *Les conquérants,* Malraux's same old poetic anarchism.

I greatly admire Malraux in certain respects, but he never impressed me as being a convinced man. He was a great actor. In the end it all had a rather hollow ring, as one senses in *Antimémoires.* It's impossible to tell truth and falsehood apart in that book, and Malraux doesn't even seem to care since he can no longer tell the difference himself. In *Les chênes qu'on abat* (based on Malraux's conversations with de Gaulle—Trans.), it's impossible to say who's asking the questions and who's giving the answers. It's all Malraux, always and everywhere, and in many places he is indeed superb. Both his commitment to the left and his later commitment to General de Gaulle seemed a magma of words, that formed and reformed like clouds in the setting sun.

. . . . .

[*What are your thoughts on feminism?*]

I am opposed to particularism, whether it is based on nationality, religion, or species. So don't count on me to support sexual particularism either. I believe that a good woman is worth just as much as a good man, and that an intelligent woman is worth just as much as an intelligent man. That is a simple truth. If the issue is one of fighting to insure that women with qualifications equal to men receive the same pay, then I am involved in the struggle. If it is to defend a woman's right to use contraceptives, then I am an active supporter of several organizations that do just that. Even if the issue is abortion, if the man or the woman involved was for some reason unable to take appropriate steps in time, or ignorant of what those steps might be, then I am for abortion, and I am a member of a number of groups that aid women in trouble, though I should add that abortion, in my view, is always a very serious matter. However, in a world that is already overpopulated and in which poverty and ignorance are the lot of the majority, I believe that it is preferable to end a life at its inception rather than allow it to develop in shameful conditions. When it comes to education or schooling, I am of course in favor of equality between the sexes; that is self-evident. As for political rights, not only the right to vote but the right to participate in government, I am strongly in favor of equal rights for women, though I doubt that women, or men either, will be able to do much to improve the current detestable political situation unless there is a profound change in both sexes as well as in the methods of political action.

I have, on the other hand, strong objections to feminism as it now presents itself. It is usually aggressive, and aggression rarely succeeds in bringing about lasting change. Furthermore—and this will doubtless strike you as paradoxical—feminism is conformist with respect to the existing order, in that what women seem to want is the freedom and well-being of the bureaucrat who goes to work each morning briefcase in hand, or of the worker who each day punches in and out of his plant. The ideal that women wish to imitate, apparently, is that of bureaucratic, technocratic homo sapiens, and they fail to see the frustrations and dangers implicit in that ideal because, like men, they think (in this respect at any rate) in terms of immediate profit and individual "success." What is important for women, I think, is to take an as-active-as-possible role in useful causes of every description and to win respect by their competence. A century ago the English authorities showed themselves to be harsh and grudging toward Florence Nightingale and her work at the Scutari hospital, but they couldn't do without her. Every gain that women achieve in the areas of civil rights, urbanism, environmentalism, and in protecting the right of animals, children, and minorities, every victory over war and over the monstrous exploitation of science by the forces of greed and violence, is a triumph for women if not for feminism, and in any case feminism reaps the benefit. I even believe that women may be better equipped to play this role than men, because women are in day-to-day contact with the realities of life, of which many men remain comparatively ignorant.

I also find it distressing that women seem willing to play a double game. There are magazines, for example, that follow fashion (there are fashions in opinion just as there are in clothing) by publishing supposedly incendiary feminist articles, while at the same time serving up for the benefit of female readers idly flipping pages at the hairdresser's the same old photographs of pretty young girls, or rather, young girls who would be pretty if they weren't all too plainly the embodiment of some advertiser's ideal. Today's bizarre commercial psychology forces models to sulk and pout in ways that are supposedly seductive, exciting, and sensual, at times using seminude females in layouts bordering on the pornographic.

That feminists tolerate these woman-objects astonishes me. I'm also astonished that they still flock in droves to buy the latest fashions, as if fashion and elegance were the same thing, and that millions of them acquiesce, quite unwittingly to be sure, in the torture of the hundreds of animals martyred every year in tests of cosmetic products, to say nothing of the thousands of animals that suffer in traps or are clubbed to death on ice floes so that these same women can grace themselves with bloody furs. Whether those furs are bought with money earned by the women themselves in their "careers" or given as gifts by husbands or lovers has no bearing on the issue. In the United States one frequently sees advertisements that show a pretty girl smoking a cigarette with a slightly defiant air, and this image presumably induces readers of the magazine to go out and buy cigarettes, despite the warning in almost invisible fine print at the bottom of the page that smoking may cause cancer and endanger health. I think that on the day women succeed in outlawing this kind of advertising, their cause will have taken a major step forward.

Last but not least, women who use the word "men" and men who use the word "women," generally to complain about supposed flaws in the opposite sex, inspire tremendous boredom in me, as people generally do when they mumble platitudes. There are specifically "feminine" virtues that feminists pretend to disdain, though that hardly means that the virtues in question were ever shared by all women: gentleness, kindness, subtlety, delicacy—virtues so important that a man who did not at least possess a modicum of them would be a brute and not a man. There are also so-called masculine virtues, though, again, this hardly means that all men possess them: courage, endurance, physical strength, self-control—and any woman who didn't share at least some of these qualities would be a slight or spineless creature indeed. It would be lovely if these complementary virtues could be combined for the good of all concerned. But to eliminate the social and psychological differences that do exist between the sexes, however fluid and variable they may be, strikes me as a deplorable thing, on a par with all the other forces that have lately been driving mankind in the direction of dull uniformity.

What would I have gained from being a man, other than the privilege of taking a somewhat more direct part in a number of wars?

—*Marguerite Yourcenar*

Didn't you ever suffer from being a woman?

Not in the slightest, and I never wanted to be a man, nor would I have wanted to be a woman had I been born a man. Besides, what would I have gained from being a man, other than the privilege of taking a somewhat more direct part in a number of wars? To be sure, it is just this sort of advancement that the future seems to hold in store for women too.

In the Mediterranean countries, where you lived for many years, didn't you ever feel that you were "creating a scandal"?

Never, except perhaps once when I went swimming in the nude below the ruins of Selinunte and no doubt shocked several *contadini* who happened to pass by. But in the Mediterranean countries, you must remember, I was a foreigner, and people tolerated in foreigners what they would not tolerate in their own women.

I don't mean to imply, though, that Mediterranean women are as mistreated as they are often said to be. Quite often I saw Greek men in the villages berated by their wives because they had tarried too long in some café, drinking a *metrio* or *poligliki* with three glasses of water. I have the impression, moreover, that today's militant feminists are extrapolating from current ideas and conditions when they discuss the very low status of French

women in the past. Mme Du Deffand certainly never dreamed of entering the Académie française. But she invited members of the Académie to her salon and very likely entertained them on her own terms. It is hard to think of women like Marguerite d'Angoulême, Marguerite de Navarre, and Mme Roland as having been mistreated. [In a footnote, the translator identifies these women as: "Marguerite d'Angoulême, 1492-1549, sister of King Francis I of France, poet, and patron of the arts"; "Marguerite de Navarre, known as Queen Margot, 1553-1615, daughter of King Henry II of France and wife of King Henry III of Navarre (later Henry IV of France, who repudiated their marriage); writer, poet, and patron of the arts"; and "Madame Manon Philipon Roland, 1754-1793, held a celebrated Parisian salon before being guillotined during the Reign of Terror; memoirist."] In *Souvenirs pieux* and *Archives du Nord* I portrayed three nineteenth-century women, tyrannical wives and mothers, and two of them I showed in an odious light, while the third was more attractive, a woman who even at a ripe old age still resembled a fine frigate in full sail. But it is impossible to be sure that even Reine Bieswal de Briarde always exerted a beneficial influence, since she forced her son, my grandfather, to make a rather unhappy marriage for the sake of money.

What do you think about rape?

That it is a crime, one of the most repugnant of all crimes. If I believed in the death penalty, I confess that rape is one crime to which I would be tempted to apply it. A rape can ruin a woman's life and psyche forever. In most rape cases only psychiatry can find extenuating circumstances. Occasionally, though, rapes are motivated by female sexual provocation, whether conscious or not.

That is the kind of argument put forward by the most "macho" of men.

I've never heard anything of the sort except from the lips of women: mothers, sisters, or relatives of the victim forced to conclude, against their will, that the woman was imprudent. A woman who goes hitchhiking wearing fancy clothes and make-up and half-naked besides is quite naïve if she doesn't expect the worst. Last year, a twenty-seven-year-old tourist went hitchhiking through the national park here, on roads that she must have known would be quite deserted, and got herself raped and murdered by some imbecile brute; there is no way around the fact that such want of prudence comes dangerously close to stupidity, or else involves a good deal of provocation. That of course in no way diminishes the extraordinary sadness of such a horrible end.

Sad, yes, but also revolting. A man wouldn't have run the same risk.

But he would have run others: the danger of war, of working in a mine, of doing dangerous jobs hitherto rarely open to women (I'm thinking just now of two quarry workers from this island who were buried alive in a rock slide). And above all the danger of having been brought up so vilely, so wretchedly, amidst such frustration and hatred and unsatisfied envy as to become the kind of man *capable* of wanting to commit a rape. Rape is the crime of a society that has been unable to resolve not so much the problem of the sexes as the problem of sexuality. Children must be taught very early in life a truth known to primitive civilizations, that coitus is a sacred act and that sexual satisfaction depends in large part on mutual tenderness and good will. (Incidentally, the rapist involved in the incident I mentioned earlier was a recidivist; it emerged that a warrant had been issued for his arrest on a charge of having bludgeoned his brother in a fit of rage.) Sensual pleasure cannot be had through violence or money or even insane love. Mutual understanding is indispensable.

But such comprehension requires equality between the sexes.

Equality doesn't mean identity.

In your books, however, you've always hidden behind men in giving your view of the world.

Hidden? The word offends me. In any event it isn't true of *Fires,* in which it is a woman who speaks almost the whole time. Nor is it true of *A Coin in Nine Hands,* in which male and female characters balance one another. Nor is it true of some of the "oriental tales" such as **"Le lait de la mort"** or **"La veuve Aphrodissia."** In *Memoirs of Hadrian* the object was to present a final vision of the ancient world as seen by one of its last great figures, and this had to be a person who had enjoyed supreme power, known war, traveled widely, and concerned himself as a high official with economic and political reform. History offered no woman who filled the bill; yet hidden away discreetly in the shadows Hadrian does have his female [paramour]. The woman I have in mind is not one of his young mistresses but Plotina, his counselor and friend, a woman with whom he was associated in "amorous friendship," to quote verbatim from one of the ancient chronicles. In *Coup de Grâce* it is Eric who has the advantage of lucidity, if only because he is the narrator, but it is Sophie who, as he says, "takes the lead," with such generosity and spirit as to dumbfound even Eric. They too are [paramours]; they understand each other to the bitter end, despite all their differences, and even in the moment of death. There are also women and young men in the life of Zeno, a character infinitely more intellectual than he is sensual, but who accepts what little life has to offer him of sensual gratification only to renounce it in the end. But he too has his discreet [paramour], the Lady of Froso, the only women who might have been his companion and shared his medical work; and Zeno can't be sure that they didn't have a son together. But it would have been impossible to convey the whole broad panorama of the sixteenth century through the Lady of Froso in her Swedish manor, just as it would have been impossible to convey the ancient world through Plotina.

If women's lives are as limited as you claim, . . .

[In a footnoted comment added to the manuscript sometime after the interview, Yourcenar stated: "I must take the liberty of interrupting my interviewer to protest. . . . A traditional woman's existence was not necessarily limited in every sense: Phaedra and Andromache (and even— why not?—Felicité in *Un coeur simple*) essay the infinite."] . . .

how do you account for the fact that there are novelists who are interested exclusively in women?

Precisely because they are women, perhaps, and interested only in themselves. If men were the same way, we would not have Virgil's Dido or Mme Bovary or Mme de Langeais or Anna Karenina. Still, when Tolstoy and Flaubert want to describe the great currents of the nineteenth century, they are forced to choose male characters: Prince André and Pierre Bezukhov for the Napoleonic period, or, to capture the social and political life of nineteenth-century France, either that rather tarnished mirror, Frédéric Moreau, or that more somber mirror, Vautrin.

Still, there have been exceptional women in history who might have inspired you.

They did inspire me in some of my essays and, as we've just been discussing, as deuteragonists in some of my books. The life of a woman of action like Florence Nightingale might have tempted me; Strachey has told her story and very well too, whatever people may say. Antigone and Mary Magdalene are sublime characters, however good or bad the poems I've written about them may be. Yet there is, in some very great men, a tendency toward complete impersonality, of which Hadrian speaks to us: "A man who reads, reflects, or plans belongs to his species rather than his sex; in his best moments he rises even above the humans." Such impersonality is much more rare, at least up to now, in even the most eminent of women.

You are a counterexample.

Even if that is true, one swallow does not a summer make.

Judith L. Johnston   (essay date Fall 1982)

SOURCE: "Marguerite Yourcenar's Sexual Politics in Fiction, 1939," in *Faith of a (Woman) Writer,* edited by Alice Kessler-Harris and William McBrien, Greenwood Press, 1988, pp. 221-28.

[*Johnston is an American critic and educator who has written extensively on twentieth-century history and literature. In the following essay, which was originally presented at a conference on twentieth-century women writers held at Hofstra University in the fall of 1982, she analyzes the sexual and political relationships of the three main characters in* Coup de Grâce, *arguing that they reflect "the European state of mind" on the brink of World War II.*]

Marguerite Yourcenar, the first woman elected to the Académie Française, is a French novelist and dramatist, born in Brussels in 1903, who resides on Mount Desert Island in Maine. She published her first play in 1921; her most famous novel in the United States is *Memoirs of Hadrian;* she translated Virginia Woolf's *The Waves* in 1937; and, since her election to the "immortals," she is beginning to receive the international critical attention her large body of work deserves. Her career as a twentieth-century writer spans more than half the century.

When I consider her place in literary history, I am amazed that she has received so little attention as a writer responding to the sexual and political crises of the twentieth century. Defining "political" broadly, to include all relations of power, I find that Yourcenar's political analysis of sexuality and modern culture shapes both her characters and her narratives. Here, I would like to explore sexual politics in her 1939 novel, *Coup de Grâce,* which is a confessional narrative set between the two world wars.

Although her preface to the 1981 translation denies any political value in this human document, the mutual bonding of authoritarian and submissive personalities portrayed in the love triangle of Erick, Sophie, and Conrad certainly derives from a political critique of her culture. In the same preface, she implicitly acknowledges the contemporary historical relevance of her 1939 novel, by alluding to Racine's *Bajazet* as "a tragedy of events close to his own time but occurring in what was then the closed world of the Ottoman Empire." Yourcenar's own novel is a tragedy of events relevant to the impending second European war, but occurring two decades earlier, in 1919-20. Although she has refused to accept the concepts of "feminine discourse" or "feminine writing," her narrative nevertheless reveals that language reflects the gender-linked relations of power. The sexual identity of her narrator, Erick, shapes his "récit." *Coup de Grâce* calls for a radical revisioning of culturally based gender stereotypes and requires the reader to envision alternatives to passivity when faced with the threat of violence.

Although Yourcenar denies that political confrontation was her subject, *Coup de Grâce* offers a political critique of modern culture.

—*Judith L. Johnston*

Yourcenar has stated that she began writing *Coup de Grâce* in 1938, in response to the September Munich conference, at which Daladier and Chamberlain, the French and British prime ministers, hoping by their submission to gain peace in their time, yielded to Hitler's demand to "repatriate" Germanic peoples dwelling in the Sudetenland of Czechoslovakia. The conference raised questions about nationality, cultural history, and the proper response to the threat of force; *Coup de Grâce* demands consideration of these same three issues. The novel was published in May of 1939, after the failure of the Munich compromise was evident, but before the German invasion of Poland.

Yourcenar's historical fiction interprets the origin of the Nazi movement in the post-World War I *Freikorps* fighting in the Baltic against Bolshevik revolutionaries. The Baltic cross, or Swastika, those soldiers of fortune brought back to Germany symbolizes the continuity between the Baltic terror of 1919 and the threat of 1939. Like the broken string of pearls Erick carried with him as a memento of Sophie, the Baltic cross is a sign of past actions predicting and defining future character. *Coup de Grâce* is a con-

temporary historical parable, in which the events of 1919 forecast the events of 1939.

In 1939, reviewers failed to connect contemporary politics with the narrative of Yourcenar's historical novel. Edmond Jaloux, reviewing the novel in August 1939, in *Les Nouvelles Littéraires,* defined it as "une histoire vraie," and Jean Charpentier, in the September 1, 1939 issue of *Mercure de France,* noted "la vérité historique," but neither noted that Yourcenar's psychological tragedy might be relevant to France's moral dilemma of choosing submission or resistance to violent force. Her novel portrays individuals facing that dilemma, and the implications for her national culture in 1939 should have been sobering.

The narrator and principal character is Erick von Lhomond, a German soldier of fortune. In a brief preface, a third-person narrator introduces Erick in his late thirties, as he is returning wounded from fighting for Franco in Spain, specifically in the battle of Saragossa, which dates this part of the narrative in 1937. In a train station, Erick solicits unenthusiastic listeners for his Baltic war story; ominously, a nearly blind beggar also solicits the travelers, offering a tour of Pisa's famous Leaning Tower. As in *Madame Bovary,* the blind man's presence portends death, here the death of a culture. The narrative shifts into Erick's own voice as he tells his story, which he admits is a "text full of holes."

Erick narrates a complicated tale of terrorist war and unrequited love. An impoverished aristocrat, born too late to have fought in World War I, Erick had allied himself with the Russian aristocracy displaced by the revolution. Erick describes his participation in the Baltic civil wars and in a love triangle with a brother and a sister, Conrad and Sophie, the Count and Countess de Reval. His story encompasses the ruin of their Edenic estate, and the deaths of both Sophie and Conrad in the war.

Erick's prejudices, his cult of force, and his self-deluding revision of history resemble those of other unreliable, biased characters of twentieth-century confessional fiction. Erick and his egocentric historical narrative most closely resemble Ernst von Salomon, the popular German fascist writer, and his autobiographical novel about his participation in the Baltic civil wars, *The Outlaws (Die Geächteten,* 1930). *Coup de Grâce* also invites comparison with André Gide's *The Immoralist* (1902), Louis-Ferdinand Céline's *Journey to the End of the Night* (1932), and Gunter Grass's *The Tin Drum* (1962), all novels in which narrators who are paradoxically both attractive and repulsive reflect the author's critical image of his own culture. Although Yourcenar, a French woman, chose a voice that was both German and male, her portrayal of Erick does not suggest that fascism was the symptom of a national neurosis, nor that it was peculiar to German culture; instead, Yourcenar's novel analyzes the authoritarian personality by presenting Erick's confession as a case history. His brutal first-person narrative provokes the reader's active, energetic, analytical response. This interplay between reader and narrator generates an alternative to the passive acceptance of authoritarian violence.

In Yourcenar's historical parable, Sophie may represent

Russia, Conrad England and France, and Erick Germany; however, Sophie, Conrad, and Erick transcend national stereotypes. Their mixed national heritage signals their role as representative Europeans of the generation that became young adults in 1919. All three were orphaned by World War I. Erick is a "Prussian with French and Baltic blood," and Conrad and Sophie are "Balt with some Russian ancestry." Separate national stereotypes dissolve in Erick's and Sophie's partial comprehension of each other, a comprehension both limited and empowered by their complex sexual relationship. Both Erick and Sophie are the age of their century; Conrad is a few years younger. Erick is not simply a proto-Fascist, but, as Carlos Baker vividly suggested [in *The New York Times Book Review*, 21 July 1957], "a veritable Judas-goat of a stricken continent, a bad European leading his conferees toward the *coup de grâce*." I agree, and wish to extend Baker's insight.

Erick is the European without roots after World War I, seeking identity in violent action. His lust for adventure is not satisfied in the Baltic civil war; throughout the 1920s and 1930s, he seeks out violent confrontations. He participates in the political agitations in central Europe which lead to Hitler's rise, and he takes part as well in the Japanese attack on Manchuria 1931-32, the Chaco war in Paraguay 1932-35, and the Spanish Civil War with Franco 1936-37. His active engagement in repressive military violence contradicts his claim to be apolitical. Although Erick asserts that fighting the Bolsheviks in 1919 was for him a "matter of caste" and not an ideological commitment, his hostility toward "Jewish money-lenders everywhere" suggests a psychological complex that, in the 1930s, was being exploited for ideological ends. As he reconstructs his past, he envisions himself as a modern Napoleon, a great leader doomed to defeat at Waterloo.

Conrad is a "disciple" of this authoritarian leader, an "aide-de-camp" to "Bonaparte." He adopts his master's views, and he relinquishes his independent opinions when ridiculed. In the context of the 1930s, Conrad represents all those individual Europeans, in France and England as well as in Germany or Italy, who docilely welcomed a strong national leader.

Conrad's "susceptibility and softness" also suggests France's and England's compliance with Germany's demand at Munich. Facing the threat of violence, they became impotent. Had Conrad survived into the 1920s, Erick contemptuously imagines he might have become "a poet cut to the pattern of T. S. Eliot or Jean Cocteau."

Speaking in 1937, Erick pictures Conrad as resembling Rembrandt's portrait of a Polish cavalier, a youth on a pale horse, his anxious face turned toward the viewer, and the comparison seems the sign of a coming apocalypse. Yourcenar perhaps foresaw the tragedy of a second European war, but her narrator Erick exploits the apocalyptic image to prepare his listeners for his account of Conrad's slow, painful death. Erick considered "putting him out of his agony," but could not deliver the *coup de grâce* to his friend. Wounded in the stomach, the Count de Reval spent his last hours in agony, but Erick idealizes and then immortalizes his body: "first he was like a wounded officer of the time of Charles the Twelfth, then like a medieval knight lying upon a tomb, and finally like any dying man." Erick's nostalgia for "the time of Charles the Twelfth" colors his history, in which Conrad's death, prefaced by an evocation of the lost Polish cavalier, represents the downfall of European aristocracy.

Conrad's sister, though born an aristocrat, did not seek to preserve the domination of her class. Sophie, whose name recalls Dostoyevsky's Sophia in *Crime and Punishment*, believes in Marxism as Sophia believes in Christianity. Sophie represents the engaged European intellectual, but her ideological commitment is linked to her experience as a woman. Amid the death and terror of civil war, Sophie had been raped by a soldier. The rape ends her privileged and protected life, but for several months longer, she remains bound to her aristocratic past through Conrad and his friend Erick, with whom she had fallen in love. Her political sympathy for the Reds, which Erick acknowledges as "the one thing she had of her own," remains steady, even against Erick's ridicule and criticism. Except in her political convictions, Sophie yields to Erick's mastery, and he manipulates "Sophie's subservience." Her submissiveness ends only after she discovers the nature of his close relationship with her brother. Then, she denounces Erick in obscenities, and responds to his calling her a streetwalker by spitting in his face. Abandoning her position as Countess de Reval and joining the workers' revolution, she acts on her convictions. Her rebellion against Erick's sadistic domination combines political and sexual liberation.

Yourcenar's portrayal of Sophie is a complex rendering of the possible responses to the threat of violence. Her irregular affair with an authoritarian figure seems to parallel Russia's changing relationship to Germany between 1917 and 1938. Sophie's early submissiveness to Erick represents Bolshevik Russia's 1917 armistice with Germany, and her later defiance suggests Russia's 1938 resistance to Hitler's demand for the partition of Czechoslovakia.

Sophie and Erick meet once more, after Conrad's death, but she refuses to submit to his mercy. She defies Erick's authority to the end. By requesting that Erick, not one of his subordinates, be her executioner, Sophie assumes the dominant role. Erick executes her as a revolutionary, and when his first shot fails to kill her, he delivers the *coup de grâce*.

At the end of her novel, Yourcenar chooses not to close the narrative frame, inflicting without mediation Erick's final self-justifying assertion: "One is always trapped, somehow, in dealings with women." The reader rejects his appropriation of the universal "one" and reinterprets the story just concluded.

Erick, in his self-deluding, falsely heroic narrative, seeks to intimidate his listeners into accepting his interpretation of events. He anticipates his audience's objections by admitting, "this summary that I am dishing up to you is made in retrospect, like History itself," thus claiming the authority of History for his summary. Earlier, he had asserted, "I feel too strongly that each of our actions is an absolute, a thing complete, necessary and inevitable, although unforeseen a moment before and past history the moment after," but his principle seems manufactured in retrospect to explain his executing Sophie. If Erick cannot foresee how he will act, if his violence has meaning only in retrospect, then he cannot be held responsible for killing Sophie, any more than he holds himself responsible for drunkenly taking a prostitute. The reader, however, is not trapped in Erick's persona.

Yourcenar, by forcing us to endure Erick's domineering voice, compels our active response. Her portrayal of his authoritarian personality, embodied in the form as well as the content of his confessional narrative, is so clearly defined that we recoil from it, appalled. The interplay between Erick's history and our response, guided by Sophie's acts and few words, explores the bond between domineering and submissive personalities. The tension is defined sexually, as well as politically, in terms of authority and power.

Erick's confession reveals his penchant for violence whenever his desires have been frustrated. Though he proudly rejects cruelty, his assertion unconsciously slips from killing to making love: "I preferred to deal out death without embellishment. . . . In the matter of love, too, I hold for perfection unadorned." His sadism is revealed as he imagines Sophie as flesh yielding equally to his knife or his lips: "the ravishing sweetness of a fruit that is ripe for the cutting, or consuming." His assertion that "Love had made her a glove in my hands" reminds us of the peculiarly cruel torture of the Letts, which Erick had earlier described to deny its attraction for him: the "Chinese Hand" involved slapping the victim "with the skin of his own hand stripped from him while he was alive." The image of a slap becomes actual when Erick slaps Sophie so forcefully that he breaks her string of pearls.

In Erick, Yourcenar offers a savage caricature that is repulsive; and yet, Erick's personality is fascinating. He is as much a victim of his cult of force as is Sophie. Erick cannot imagine himself except as a victim, "a crushed finger," or as a powerful leader, like Napoleon. He can envision Conrad as his disciple or brother, and therefore not threatening, but Sophie, in his fantasy, must be either an asexual saint or an eager whore.

He candidly admits: "Between Sophie and me an intimacy swiftly sprang up like that between victim and executioner. The cruelty was not of my making . . . but it is not so certain that the whole situation was not to my liking." Erick's comparison of their intimacy to "that between victim and executioner" predicts his final act, and his admission that he liked the situation is a truth that slips out, like others in his confession, as if by accident. The psychological source of his cruelty toward Sophie is his repulsion from female sexuality. He shudders just as he is about to kiss her, and at that moment recalls being terrified by a starfish thrust into his little hand by his mother. Since his fear and loathing of female genitalia are linked to his resentment of his mother's authority, his hostility toward Sophie finds expression in images of authoritative, destructive, passionate heroines.

Significantly, Erick compares Sophie to "a heroine in Ibsen utterly fed up with life." He envisions her savagely poking a fire, so she embodies for him the volatile, threatening, and self-destructive Hedda Gabler. Though Sophie cannot burn Erick's confessional narrative, he nevertheless associates her with fire. Sophie, dancing, twirls "like a flame." Asserting his mastery over her element, he notes, "Fire may be trusted, provided one knows that its law is to burn, or to die." Because her desire threatens him, he tries to stand aloof, allowing her fire to consume herself alone. Like Dido and Aeneas, Sophie and Erick take shelter together during a rainstorm, but Sophie's well-lit fire dries their clothes without kindling Erick's desire or turning him aside from his aimless career as a soldier of fortune. On their journey home from this interlude, he put his "arm round her, like a lover, to force her down beside me in a ditch," to shelter her from bullets, but he physically reasserts his mastery. The passionate Dido threw herself on a funeral pyre, but Sophie escapes.

Conrad also escapes, but only through his death. Linking his youthful docility to an inevitable decline, Erick imagines with dread an older Conrad, prey to an "insidious dissolution, like the loathsome decay of iris; those sombre flowers, though nobly shaped like a lance, die miserably in their own sticky secretion, in marked contrast to the slow, heroic dying of the rose." This extraordinary passage, with its phallic iris and its genital rose, suggests the sexual roles Erick unconsciously assigns to himself and to Conrad.

Erick describes Conrad as "pale and elated as Orestes in the opening of Racine's play," and he lovingly notes "a small scar on his lip, like a dark violet." This allusion to the opening scene of *Andromache,* where the dialogue between Orestes and his comrade Pylades establishes them as a couple, hints at Erick's love for Conrad; however, the allusion also recalls the violence and the entrapment of Andromache's tragic passion.

The connection between sexuality, violence, and entrapment appears in a powerful image, which Erick once consciously employs as he defines the relationship between individual actions and history: "They say that fate excels in tightening the cord round the victim's neck, but to my knowledge her special skill is to break all ties." Erick might wish all ties with his past were broken, but his narrative reveals only tightening cords. The image recurs without his explicit commentary in the pearl necklace he breaks from around Sophie's neck as he slaps her. Despite his disingenuous claim that the necklace was worthless, he carried it with him for years. The image also recurs in the torture suffered by one of Sophie's lovers: Franz von Aland, captured by the enemy, had a cord tied round his neck, and then set on fire; his body was found "with a charred wound round the neck." Two explications of this image, one political and one sexual, are connected.

German diplomats and intellectuals justified both their aggression in the First World War and their 1938 demand for the Sudetenland by depicting the German nation surrounded by hostile rivals, seeking only to break free of the encirclement. The humiliation of German defeat in 1918 fueled support for the nationalistic claims on territory in 1938-39, as a buffer against the Communist Slavs in Russia. Fear of encirclement and the humiliation of defeat combine in Erick's actions at Gourna, where his leadership in the retreat is one of the blots on his military career.

In Yourcenar's psychological portrait of Erick, we see the child feeling trapped by the mother who gave birth. The son rebels against her authority and seeks to break free of the woman's body. The trap is linked to marriage in Erick's ambiguous admission, on his return from the Gourna retreat, "perhaps I was avoiding stepping back immediately into the trap where I now consented to be caught," which alludes to his earlier assertion, "I was prepared to pledge myself to her immediately upon my return." His frantic desire to escape from encirclement by the Bolsheviks at Gourna corresponds to his fear of entrapment by Sophie. By sending Volkmar back to Sophie's estate, Erick insures that she will learn of his homosexual relationship with Conrad. Such knowledge ends Sophie's desire for Erick and releases him from the trap. The connection between the political and the sexual may be seen in Erick's final assertion: "One is always trapped, somehow, in dealings with women." The trap, *piège,* is a noose, a circle used to catch the victim's head.

Yourcenar's timely and sensitive evaluation of the historical and psychological roots of fascism deserves critical appreciation. She has admitted that in writing this historical novel she immersed herself in documents about the Germans fighting in the Baltic in 1919-1920, and, though she denies that the political confrontation was her subject, *Coup de Grâce* offers a political critique of modern culture. By defining her three characters in the context of their sexual identities and political history, she requires the reader's personal, intimate, judgment to make appropriate connections with contemporary events.

Yourcenar has stated, "In our epoch, more than in preceding epochs, politics plays a major role in our lives, whether we wish it and sense it or not. Consequently, even if we evoke a completely private adventure no more than five or ten years old, we encounter certain deeds which are already 'historical,' in the most official sense of the term, and of which we must take account." Erick's apparently open confession of his private adventure requires the reader's collaborative, close study to determine the historical significance of his affair in 1919. Looking back, the reader must evaluate Erick's authoritarian domination by force, as well as Conrad's subservience and Sophie's defiance. In her portrait of these three complex personalities, Yourcenar held a mirror up to the European state of mind in 1939.

Sven Birkerts (essay date 1984)

SOURCE: "Marguerite Yourcenar," in *An Artificial Wilderness: Essays on 20th-Century Literature,* William Morrow and Company, Inc., 1987, pp. 157-61.

[*Birkerts is an American critic and educator who has won numerous awards and grants for his essays on literature. In the following essay, which was originally published in 1984, he addresses the theme of male homosexuality in* Alexis *and* Memoirs of Hadrian.]

In her **"Reflections on the Composition of *Memoirs of Hadrian,*"** Marguerite Yourcenar has described in some detail the halting yet seemingly fated progress of that book. Originally begun between 1924 and 1930, abandoned, resumed, it was abandoned again before the war, for the last time—or so the author thought then. In 1948, however, when Yourcenar was living in America, an old trunk full of papers and letters was returned to her. She tells how she seated herself in front of a fire and undertook the sad reconnaissance of her past. Letters were read and consigned to the flames, long-forgotten faces were recalled. Then: "I came upon four or five typewritten sheets, the paper of which had turned yellow. The salutation told me nothing. 'My dear Mark . . .' *Mark . . .* What friend or love, what distant relative was this? It was several minutes before I remembered that *Mark* stood here for *Marcus Aurelius,* and that I had in hand a fragment of the lost manuscript. From that moment there was no question but that this book must be taken up again, whatever the cost."

The long gestation bore magnificent results: the narrative, at once intimate and austere, reconstitutes with its burnished images the empire of second-century Rome. Largely on the strength of *Hadrian,* Yourcenar was elected to the Académie Française in 1981. She was the first woman ever thus honored.

During the period of the original drafting of Hadrian's letter to Marcus Aurelius, Yourcenar also completed the short novel *Alexis* (published in 1929), which appeared in English for the first time in 1984. *Alexis* is, like *Hadrian,* an epistolary self-accounting. But whereas *Hadrian* hoards the memories of a turbulent life against the onset of death, *Alexis* is little more than a congeries of hints and evasions. What Oscar Wilde called "the love that dare not speak its name" tries to come across in a low whisper.

Alexis, a successful young pianist, is writing to Monique, his aristocratic young wife, to explain his desertion. He has decided, after some agonizing (which is either genuine or pro forma—part of the trouble is that we're not sure), that he must be free to indulge his sexual preference. But this is Europe at the turn of the century, and with his refined sensibility, Alexis cannot come right out with the news. No, he constructs a lacework of hints and withholdings and coy reprimands to himself: nothing must injure the delicacy of feeling that is between them. It is of freedom that Alexis speaks, but his idiom is that of entrapment: "But, you see, I am hesitating; every word I write takes me a little further from what I wanted to express at the very outset. . . ." One thinks recurrently of Prufrock.

The apologia begins with some muted evocations of childhood. Alexis was a solitary dreamer; he grew up in a once-fine manor in Bohemia, surrounded by the ghosts of energetic ancestors and by the tranquil affections of his mother and sisters. We are to imagine the subtle ways in which a disposition is shaped, though from time to time Alexis supplies a speculative nudge. Recalling his sister's girlhood friends, for example, he writes: "Nothing would appear to have prevented me from loving one of these girls, and perhaps you yourself find it strange that I did not. . . . One does not lose one's heart to what one respects, nor perhaps even to what one loves; above all, one does not lose one's heart to what resembles oneself—and it was not women I was most different from." To this he adds, bringing himself to the threshold of confession: "Monique, do you understand me?"

In time, of course, Alexis has to come to the point—a good letter, like any other prose, needs to develop in some direction. So, after endless tergiversation, he avers that there was an original incident, an initiation. Not that he is especially graphic: it happened somewhere along a road, by a hedge, with someone, somehow. He gives no name, face, or sensation. And yet we are to believe that this furtive, shameful event set him on his track. Not right away, naturally. Before he can accept himself, Alexis must suffer the lacerating cycle: penitence, denial, sudden abandoned indulgence, reaffirmed penitence. He comes to see that his marriage represents the supreme denial, and that the letter of confession is the record of his victory.

All of this could make for a fascinating narrative. The opposition of passion and the taboo has always been a source of the most irresistible tension in fiction. But this tension can neither gather nor release itself in the realm of abstraction. "I shall not describe the hallucinatory quest for pleasure," writes Alexis, "the potential mortifications, and the bitterness of a moral humiliation much worse than the sin itself. . . ." It's exactly what he *should* have done. Portrayed with such detachment Alexis's escapades do not have the force of passion that, from his perspective, is their principal justification.

Yourcenar wrote *Alexis* when she was twenty-four. She states in the recently written preface that she has resisted the temptation to revise or modernize the book; though she obviously recognizes the radically changed social perception of the homosexual, she contends that the difficulties facing the individual are much the same. Doubtless she is right, but my guess is that few homosexuals will find confirmation or self-recognition in the maunderings of this young man. Their value is mainly historical—they tell us something about the status of the unspoken, or unspeakable, in a certain milieu at a certain time.

How very different is the gravid fullness of *Hadrian* (1955) or the warts-and-all portraiture of *The Abyss* (1976). In those novels, too, Yourcenar represents love between men—Hadrian's devotion to the young Antinous is especially moving; but in both the rendering is so robust and unconstrained that it scarcely seems we are reading about a reality long proscribed. One could argue, obviously, that both novels are historical and treat of periods less distorted by sexual repression (Rome in the early empire, Flanders in the sixteenth century). At some point, however, the psychobiographer will get restive and demand his say.

Male love, not lesbianism, is a central subject in Yourcenar's novels. And yet Yourcenar has never made any secret of her own sexual preference. Clearly she has found in male homosexual love a useful figure, one that affords certain emblematic similarities and at the same time allows her to keep artistic distance. If this is so, then it is not unreasonable to speculate that the lapse of time between *Alexis* and *Hadrian*—more than two decades—coincided with a great personal liberation, that *Alexis* was the projection of a crisis that had been overcome by the time *Hadrian* was written. Or, to put it another way, that there was a tension about sexual identity that *had* to be overcome in order that *Hadrian* could take the form it does. Yourcenar's essay on that novel has a great deal to say about the difficulty of achieving historical empathy. Nothing is said about the matter of sexual empathy, which is hardly irrelevant.

Yourcenar's imaginative transformations raise some interesting, if unanswerable, questions. Why, for instance, does she not write about lesbian love? Or, if we accept that she has a need to distance and refigure the personal, then we have to ask whether there is, in fact, a ready interchangeability between lesbian and male homosexual love. Are the emotional and situational registers so parallel that one can stand in for the other, or is this possible only through some obscure private conversion?

Provocative though they may be, these are topics better left in the biographer's care. For us it is enough that Yourcenar in her best work is one of the great anatomists of the human psyche. The sexual disposition of Hadrian, or the philosopher Zeno in *The Abyss,* is less important, ultimately, than the highly kindled flux of inner life she depicts, that hovering between passion and detachment that, to a greater or lesser extent, characterizes us all.

Inseparable from this is her superb craftsmanship. Yourcenar is one of the last exponents of what used to be known, at least in France, as the "classical" prose style. Such a style aspires to lucidity and balance, a certain cool stateliness. In Yourcenar's hands it achieves a supple sensuousness as well, for she will freely modulate from the abstract to the concrete wherever appropriate. Here is Hadrian discoursing on love:

> That mysterious play which extends from love of a body to love of an entire person has seemed to me noble enough to consecrate to it one part of my life. Words for it are deceiving, since the word for pleasure covers contradictory realities comprising notions of warmth, sweetness, and intimacy of bodies, but also feelings of violence and agony, and the sound of a cry. The short and obscene sentence of Poseidonius about the rubbing together of two small pieces of flesh, which I have seen you copy in your exercise books with the application of a good schoolboy, does no more to define the phenomenon of love than the cord touched by a finger accounts for the infinite miracle of sounds. Such a dictum is less an insult to pleasure than to the flesh itself, that amazing instrument of muscles, blood and skin, that red-tinged cloud whose lightning is the soul.

With the passing of the classical style we have lost this kind of music. It may not be suited to the transmission of the modern sense of discord, but it embodies an element of human continuity that literature cannot easily do without.

Marguerite Yourcenar with Shusha Guppy (interview date 11 April 1987)

SOURCE: An interview in *The Paris Review,* Vol. 30, No. 106, Spring, 1988, pp. 229-49.

[*Guppy is an Iranian-born writer and critic who has served as the London editor of* The Paris Review. *In the following interview, which was conducted in April 1987, Yourcenar discusses her life, career, and literary influences.*]

I had an appointment with Marguerite Yourcenar on Saturday, November 14, 1987 at her hotel in Amsterdam. I was told that she had not arrived, that several people had been looking for her, including her driver, and that no one knew where she was. Further telephone calls to her home in Maine and to her publishers in Paris revealed that she had had a slight stroke and was recovering, and that there was no cause for concern. She did not recover, and died on December 18th. She was eighty-four.

I had first interviewed her on April 11th in London and later sent her the typescript for corrections. It had come back with a good deal of amendment, carefully written on the text and on separate sheets of paper. I was grateful that she had taken so much trouble over it, but she was still not quite satisfied and wanted to see me again, go through it with me and make sure that everything was exactly as she intended. I was happily anticipating our meeting in Amsterdam, but it was not to be. The following introduction was written after our meeting in London. I have left it in the present tense.

. . . . .

Marguerite Yourcenar has the ardent imagination and clear, intense blue eyes of her Flemish ancestors. The rich, many-colored subtlety of her great novels—**Memoirs of Hadrian, The Abyss, Alexis, Coup de Grâce,** and others—is reminiscent of their intricate tapestries, while her sublime mystical appreciation of Nature and its beauty evokes the golden age of landscape painting in the Low Countries. For years she has been considered one of France's most distinguished and original writers; yet it was not until 1981, when she was the first woman ever to "join the Immortals" and be elected to the French Academy in the four hundred years of its existence, that she was discovered by the general public.

Marguerite Yourcenar was born in 1903 into a patrician Franco-Belgian family. (Yourcenar is an anagram of her real name *à particule,* de Crayencour.) Her mother died of puerperal fever shortly after her birth, and she was brought up by her father, a great reader and traveler, who taught her Latin and Greek and read the French classics with her. They lived in various European countries and she learned English and Italian as well.

She published two volumes of poetry in her teens, "which are frankly *oeuvres de jeunesse* and never to be republished." Her two novellas, *Alexis* and *Coup de Grâce,* appeared in 1929 and 1939 respectively, during which time she lived mostly in Greece, and won her critical acclaim. In 1938 she met Grace Frick in Paris, who later "admirably translated" three of her major books. When the war came in 1939 and she could not return to Greece, she was offered hospitality in the USA by Grace Frick, "since she had not the means of living in Paris." To support herself, she took a teaching job at Sarah Lawrence College. She also began to write her masterpiece, **Memoirs of Hadrian,** which was published in 1954.

In 1950 Yourcenar and Frick bought a house in Mount Desert Island, off the coast of Maine, where they lived between long journeys abroad. Grace Frick died in 1979 after a long illness, but Marguerite Yourcenar still lives there, though she continues to travel extensively.

Her latest book, **Two Lives and a Dream,** was published recently in England, and she is now working on **Le Labyrinthe du Monde,** completing the autobiographical triptych which began with **Souvenirs Pieux** and **Archives du Nord.** She has just written a long essay on Borges—a lecture given recently at Harvard.

Marguerite Yourcenar's intellectual vigor and curiosity are still prodigious, despite age and an open-heart operation two years ago. She has just translated James Baldwin's *The Amen Corner* and Yukio Mishima's *Five Modern No Plays* into French, from the original English and Japanese, helped for the latter by her friend J.M. Shisagi, Mishima's executor. She was in London briefly for the publication of **Two Lives and a Dream,** and this interview took place at her hotel in Chelsea. She was elegantly dressed in black and white and spoke an exquisite French, with a markedly patrician accent, in a deep, mellifluous tone.

. . . . .

[*Guppy*]: *You have just spent the day in Richmond; was it just to walk in the beautiful park there or for some other reason?*

[Yourcenar]: Well, it had to do with the book I am writing at the moment, which is a book built entirely of memories, and in the present chapter I evoke the fourteen months I spent in England when I was twelve and we lived in Richmond. But where exactly I can't recall. I saw dozens of little houses in as many streets, all looking alike, with tiny gardens, but I couldn't tell which one was ours. It was during the first and second years of World War I, which unlike the Second World War did not drop from the sky in England—there were no bomb alerts or blitzes. I used to go for long walks in Richmond Park on fine days and to museums in London when it rained. I saw the Elgin Marbles at the British Museum and went to the Victoria and Albert frequently. I used to drop my sweet wrappings in a porcelain dragon there—I bet they're still there!

What is your new book to be called?

The French title is **Quoi? L'Eternité,** which is from a poem of Rimbaud's: "*Quoi? L'Eternité, elle est retrouvée.*" The book is the third volume of my memoirs. The other two are being translated into English at the moment. There are certain words one can't translate literally, and one has to change them. For example the first volume is called **Souvenirs Pieux** in French, and I have translated it as **Dear Departed,** which conveys the same nuance of irony. The second volume is called **Archives du Nord,** but "the North" in another language evokes a different image: in England the North refers to Manchester, or even Scotland; in Holland it is the Fresian Isles, which has nothing to do with the North of France. So I have changed it completely, and taken the first line of a Bob Dylan song—"Blowin' in the Wind." I quote the song inside as an epigraph: "How many roads must a man walk down / Before you can call him a man?" It is very beautiful, don't you think? At least it defines well my father's life, and many lives. But to come to the present volume, I don't think *"Quoi? L'Eternité"* would work in English, and we will have to find another title. Among the Elizabethan poets there must be quantities of quotations about eternity, so I think I might find something there.

Let's go back to the beginning. You were very close to your father. He encouraged you to write and he published your first poems. It was a limited edition and I believe is now unobtainable. What do you think of them in retrospect?

My father had them published at his own expense—a sort of compliment from him. He shouldn't have done—they were not much good. I was only sixteen. I liked writing, but I had no literary ambitions. I had all these characters and stories in me, but I had hardly any knowledge of history and none of life to do anything with them. I could say that all my books were conceived by the time I was twenty, although they were not to be written for another thirty or forty years. But perhaps this is true of most writers—the emotional storage is done very early on.

This relates to what you once said, that "Books are not life, only its ashes." Do you still believe that?

Yes, but books are also a way of learning to feel more acutely. Writing is a way of going to the depth of Being.

From your father's death in 1929 to 1939 you only published two novellas, Alexis *and* Coup de Grâce, *which you said were based on people you knew. Who were they?*

My father loved an extraordinary woman, exceedingly free in her private life yet of an almost heroic morality. She chose to remain with her husband though her real attraction was for a man who was *Alexis.* As for *Coup de Grâce,* I can now tell you that Sophie is very close to me at twenty, and Eric, the young man ardently attached to her own brother whom she falls in love with, was someone I knew, but political problems separated us. Of course one never knows how close fictional characters are to real people. At the beginning of my memoirs I say, *"L'être que j'appelle moi"*—the person I call myself—which means that I don't know who I am. Does one ever?

Next came Memoirs of Hadrian *which was immediately hailed as a masterpiece and became a bestseller all over the world. Why did you choose the historical novel as a genre?*

I have never written a historical novel in my life. I dislike most historical novels. I wrote a monologue about Hadrian's life, as it could have been seen by himself. I can point out that this *treatise-monologue* was a common literary genre of the period and that others besides Hadrian had done it. Hadrian is a very intelligent man, enriched by all the traditions of his time, while Zenon, the protagonist of *The Abyss (L'Oeuvre au Noir)* is also very intelligent and in advance of his time—indeed of all other epochs too—and is defeated at the end. Nathanaël, the hero of the third panel, *Two Lives and a Dream,* is by contrast a simple, nearly uneducated man who dies at twenty-eight of tuberculosis. He is a sailor at first who becomes shipwrecked off the coast of Maine in America, marries a girl who dies of

T.B., travels back to England and Holland, marries a second time a woman who turns out to be a thief and a prostitute, and is finally taken up by a wealthy Dutch family. For the first time he comes into contact with culture—listens to music, looks at paintings, lives in luxury. But he keeps a clear head and sharp eyes, because he knows that while he is listening to music in the hospital, opposite his house men and women are suffering and dying of disease. Eventually he is sent away to an island in the North and dies in peace, surrounded by wild animals and nature. The question is: how far can one go without accepting any culture? The answer is, for Nathanaël, very far, through lucidity of mind and humility of heart.

You met Grace Frick, who later translated Hadrian, *in 1938. Did you move to the States straight away?*

At first only for a few months. I was living in Greece then, in Athens. I came to Paris for a visit and the War broke out. I could not go back to Greece and had no money to live in Paris. Grace, with infinite kindness, asked me to come to America for a while. I thought it would be for six months, but there I still am!

What made you choose Mount Desert Island?

We had a friend who was a Professor of Theology at Yale. In 1940 he took a house in Maine while he was on sabbatical, and asked his friends to come and stay. Grace and I went to visit him, and thought that it would be nice to have a house in this still (then) peaceful island. Grace went all over the villages on horseback and became known as "the lady who is looking for a house"! There were luxury houses, sort of chalets for millionaires, or village houses with no facilities, and nothing in between. We finally bought a simple house and modernized it, putting in central heating and a few other amenities. Did you know that Mount Desert was discovered by the French sailor and explorer Champlain? His ship developed some trouble and he had to stay there for a while to have it repaired. He named it Mount Desert, but alas it is now anything but deserted, and in summer boatloads of tourists pour in from everywhere.

One striking aspect of your work is that nearly all your protagonists have been male homosexuals: Alexis, Eric, Hadrian, Zenon, Mishima. Why is it that you have never created a woman who would be an example of female sexual deviance?

I do not like the word homosexual, which I think is dangerous—for it enhances prejudice—and absurd. Say "gay" if you must. Anyway, homosexuality, as you call it, is not the same phenomenon in a man as in a woman. Love for women in a woman is different from love for men in a man. I know a number of "gay" men, but relatively few openly "gay" women. But let us go back to a passage in *Hadrian* where he says that a man who *thinks,* who is engaged upon a philosophical problem or devising a theorem, is neither a man nor a woman, nor even human. He is something else. It is very rare that one could say that about a woman. It does happen, but very seldom; for example the woman whom my father loved was very sensuous and also in terms of her times an "intellectual," but the greatest element of her life was love, especially love for her husband. Even without reaching the high level of someone like Hadrian, one is in the same mental space, and it is unimportant whether one is a man or a woman. Can I say also that love between women interests me less, because I have never met with a great example of it.

But there are writers, like Gertrude Stein and Colette, who have tried to illuminate female homosexuality.

I do not happen to like Colette and Gertrude Stein. The latter is completely foreign to me; Colette, in matters of eroticism, often falls to the level of a Parisian concierge. You look for an example of a woman who is in love with another woman, but *how* is she in love? Is it an ardent passion of a few months? Or a bond of friendship over a long period? Or something in between? When you are in love you're in love—the sex of the beloved does not matter very much. What matters is the feelings, emotions, relationships between people.

Nonetheless, having portrayed Hadrian so eloquently, could you have done something similar on, say, Sappho? And you have been very discreet about your own life, with Grace Frick for example.

We must set Sappho aside, since we know next to nothing about her. As for my own life: there are times when one must reveal certain things, because otherwise things could not be said with verisimilitude. For example, as I said, Sophie's story in **Coup de Grâce** is based on a true incident. But I was always, as they say, "more intellectually oriented" than Sophie. And I was not raped by a Lithuanian sergeant, nor lodged in a ruined castle! As for my relationship with Grace Frick, I met her when we were both women of a certain age, and it went through different stages: first passionate friendship, then the usual story of two people living and travelling together for the sake of convenience and because they have common literary interests. During the last ten years of her life she was very ill. For the last eight years she couldn't travel and that's why I stayed in Maine during those winters. I tried to help her til the end, but she was no longer the center of my existence, and perhaps had never been. The same is true reciprocally, of course. But what is love? This species of ardor, of warmth, that propels one inexorably towards another being? Why give so much importance to the genito-urinary system of people? It does not define a whole being, and it is not even erotically true. What matters, as I said, concerns emotions, relationships. But *whom* you fall in love with depends largely on chance.

Do you think the emphasis on the physical, sexual aspect of love is due partly to psychoanalysis? Perhaps this is what Anna Akhmatova meant when she said "Freud ruined literature."

Freud turns sexuality into a sort of metaphor, and a metaphor not quite worked out. It seems that he was a great innovator, being the first to speak of sexuality with frankness. But that does not make his theories acceptable. But he did not ruin literature—it was not in his power to do so, since literature is a very great thing. And then no one thinks of Freud in terms of his time and circumstances. He came from a poor, orthodox Jewish family, living in a little provincial town. Naturally, as a young professor,

he was struck by examples of pleasure in Vienna. As a result he saw the world from this double perspective.

It is not so much his pioneering work as a doctor one questions now, but his philosophic-psychological extrapolations.

Quite so. He makes a number of extravagant extrapolations, starting from very limited, restricted and small premises. Hence its attraction for the modern world. But he was the first man to speak about sexuality with sincerity and frankness, when it was still taboo. So everyone was fascinated. But we can now say to him: Thank you for your pioneering effort, but to us it is not a new venture, nor a total discovery. As a great psychologist I prefer Jung. He was sometimes strange, but there was genius in his madness. He was more a poet and had a larger perception of human nature. In his memoirs (*Memories, Dreams and Reflections*) you are often confronted with the mystery of life itself. For example, his mother hatred, so strong that a table breaks itself in two when they are together! A stunning para-psychological episode or a beautiful symbol?

Is it because beyond a certain level the male-female dichotomy is irrelevant to you that you have not been interested in feminism? What has been your relationship to the feminist movement of the last few decades?

It does not interest me. I have a horror of such movements, because I think that an intelligent woman is worth an intelligent man—if you can find any—and that a stupid woman is every bit as boring as her male counterpart. Human wickedness is almost equally distributed between the two sexes.

Is that why you did not wish to be published by Virago Press in England?

I did not want to be published by them—what a *name!* —because they publish *only* women. It reminds one of ladies' compartments in nineteenth-century trains, or of a ghetto, or simply of those basements of restaurants where one is confronted by a door marked *Women* and another marked *Men*. But of course there are social differences, and geographical ones. The Muslim woman is somewhat more restricted. But even there, I have just spent the winter in Morocco, and when I saw women walking arm in arm, going to the *Hammam* (public baths)—a place which is not all like the Turkish baths one imagines through Ingres's pictures, and where any minute one risks one's neck, so slippery it is—well, those women often seem happier than their Parisian or New Yorker sisters. They get a lot out of their friendships. There was a Mughol princess called Jahanara, the daughter of Sultan Jahan, an admirable poet. I have found too little information concerning her, but she was initiated to Sufism by her brother, the admirable Prince Dara, assassinated in his thirties by his brother, the fanatic Aurangzarb. So you see even Muslim women could achieve eminence despite their circumstances, if they had it in them.

Because Sufism liberates them from the rigid confines of Orthodox Islam. There is another Sufi poetess, Rabe'a. She wrote most of her surviving poems with her blood when they opened her veins in a warm bath until she bled to death. At least that's the story. It was a common punishment for heretics then, and Sufis were, on and off, considered heretical.

Jahanara was not murdered, but the Sufi Master who had initiated her and her brother Dara was finally put to death.

Going back to your work, your book **Fires** *is a series of monologues written from the point of view of women . . .*

The impersonal narrator, who writes the small linking sentences, is also evidently a woman, but her reflections on love are genderless. There are three monologues which concern men—Achilles, Petroclus, and Phedros—and with them we are in the world of *Alexis.* On the other hand Phedre, Antigone, Clytemnestra, Sappho, Lena, are women, ranging from supreme greatness (Antigone) to vulgarity (Clytemnestra).

You mentioned once that what you wished to do through your work was to revive le sense du sacré. *It is a common complaint that today we have lost the sense of the sacred— even those who have greatly contributed to this state of affairs complain about it! Will you expand on it a bit more, in relation to your work?*

The sacred is the very essence of life. To be aware of the sacred even as I am holding this glass is therefore essential. I mean this glass has a form, which is very beautiful, and which evokes the great mystery of void and plenitude that has haunted the Chinese for centuries. Inside, the glass can serve as a receptacle, for ambrosia or poison. What matters to the Taoists is the Void. And glass was invented by someone we don't know. As I say in **The Abyss,** when Zenon is lying down in his monk's cell, "the dead are far away and we can't reach them, nor even the living." Who made this table? If we tried to find our how every object around us came into being we would spend our lives doing it. Everything is too far away in the past, or mysteriously too close.

To what do you attribute this loss of the sacred? Is it due, as some maintain, to the development of capitalism and its corollary, consumerism?

Certainly consumerism has a lot to answer for. One lives in a commercialized society against which one *must* struggle. But it is not easy. As soon as one is dealing with the media one becomes their victim. But have we really lost the sense of the sacred? I wonder! Because unfortunately in the past the sacred was intricately mixed with superstition, and people came to consider superstitious even that which was not. For example, peasants believed that it was better to sow the grain at full moon. But they were quite right: that is the moment when the sap rises, drawn by gravitation. What is frightening is the loss of the sacred in human, particularly sexual relationships, because then no true union is possible.

Perhaps this feeling for the sacred is the reason why you are particularly interested in ecology and conservation?

It is most important. The Dutch have kindly elected me to their Academy, the Erasmus Institute for the Arts and Letters. Unlike its French counterpart it includes a substantial prize, half of which one has to donate to a charity. I gave mine to the World Wildlife Organization. They pro-

tested at first, saying that the Institute was for the promotion of the Arts and Letters, not lions and birds! But I said that I would have to refuse the prize unless I could make my gift, and they accepted. How sincere are the Green and Ecology parties, and how much of it is political posturing, I simply do not know. But something has to be done before it is too late. It is almost too late already, with the acid rain destroying Europe's forests and the defoliation of the tropical forests in South America.

Talking about the Academy, you were the first woman in four hundred years to be elected to the French Academy. How did it happen? I ask this because traditionally one must make an application and go canvassing with other members. One reads heart-wrenching letters from past candidates, notably Baudelaire, begging the members to vote for them.

Poor Baudelaire! He had greatly suffered from the condemnation of some of his poems, *Les Fleurs du Mal,* and membership in the Academy for him could have been revenge. In my case Jean d'Ormesson wrote asking me if I would object to being nominated, without any visit or other effort on my part. I said no, finding it discourteous to refuse. I was wrong. There are a few serious and interesting Academicians; there are also, and always have been, more mediocre choices. Furthermore, the Academy, like the *Figaro,* where most Academicians do write, represents now a more or less strongly rightist group. I am myself neither rightist nor leftist. I did refuse to wear the Academy's uniform—my long black velvet skirt and cape were designed by St. Laurent. And of course I refused the customary gift of the sword. But I received a Hadrian coin from voluntary contributors.

Since your election to the Academy you have become much better known to the general public and lionized by the literary world. Do you mix with the Parisian literary society?

I do not know what being lionized means, and I dislike all literary worlds, because they represent false values. A few great works and a few great books are important. They are aside and apart from any "world" or "society."

I would like to go back again to the early days and talk about your influences. You have been compared to Gide by many people. Was he an influence? For example, they say that Nathanaël, the hero of your **Two Lives and a Dream,** *is named after the one in Gide's* Les Nourritures Terrestres. *Is that true?*

I don't like Gide very much. I find him dry and sometimes superficial. I chose Nathanaël because it is a Puritan name, and he is a young Dutch sailor from a Puritan family. Other members of the family are called Lazarus or Eli for the same reason. They are Biblical names and have no connection with Gide's book. We are very far from the state of happy inebriation presented by Gide in the *Nourritures,* and which is no longer possible in our time, in the face of so much madness and chaos.

But **Alexis** *has the form of a Gidian* récit. . .

A *récit* in the form of a letter is an old literary French form. I have said that the gratitude young writers felt for Gide was, to a large extent, because of his use of classical prose forms. But why choose any one in particular? There are hundreds of great books in different languages by which we all are or should be influenced.

Of course, but there are always certain affinities with various writers. Who are they in your case? Baudelaire, Racine, the Romantics?

Baudelaire certainly; and some of the Romantics. The French Middle Ages much more, and certain poets of the seventeenth century, such as Ménard, *"La Belle Vieille,"* and many, many other poets, French and non-French. Racine up to a point, but he is such a unique case that no one can be compared to him.

Except for Britanicus all his protagonists were women: Phedre, Berenice, Nathalie, Roxane, etc. . .

Proust had this idea that Racine's Phedre could be identified with a man as well as a woman. But Racine's Phedre is much more French than Greek: you will see it at once if you compare her to the Greek Phedre. Her passionate jealousy is a typical theme of French literature, just as it is in Proust. That is why even in Phedre Racine *had* to find her a rival, Aricie, who is an insignificant character, like a bridal from a popular dress shop. In other words, love as possession, *against* someone. And that is prodigiously French. Spanish jealousy is quite different: it is real hatred, the despair of someone who has been deprived of his/her food. As for the Anglo-Saxon love, well, there is nothing more beautiful than Shakespeare's sonnets, while German love has produced some wonderful poetry too.

I have this theory that the French do not understand Baudelaire and never have. They speak of his rhetoric, yet he is the least rhetorical of poets. He writes like an Oriental poet—dare I say like a Persian poet?

Baudelaire is a sublime poet. But the French don't even understand Hugo, who is also a sublime poet. I have—as Malraux also did—taken titles from Hugo's verses: *Le Cerveau Noir de Piranèse,* and others. Whenever I am passing by Place Vendôme in Paris I recall Hugo's poem in which he is thinking of Napoleon, wondering if he should prefer *"la courbe d'Hannibal et l'angle d'Alexandre au carré de César."* A whole strategy contained in one line of Alexandrine! Of course there are times when Hugo is bad and rhetorical—even great poets have their off days—but nonetheless he is prodigious.

Is this what Gide meant when he said: "Victor Hugo, hélas"?

To have said *"hélas"* is proof of a certain smallness in Gide.

He also rejected Proust's manuscript of Swann's Way, *saying, "Here is the story of a little boy who can't go to sleep"!*

We were talking about jealousy: maybe Gide was jealous of Proust; or perhaps he honestly could not like the long and subjective beginning of the *Temps Perdu.* He was not, as we are, cognizant of Proust's whole work.

So who was a decisive influence on you in youth?

As I said in the preface to *Alexis,* at the time it was Rilke. But this business of influence is a tricky one. One reads thousands of books, of poets, modern and ancient, as one meets thousands of people. What remains of it all is hard to tell.

You mentioned modern poets. Which ones for example?

There is a Swedish poet whom I have never succeeded in introducing to my French friends: Gunnard Ekelof. He has written three little books called *Divans,* I suppose influenced by Persian poetry. And, of course, Borges, and some of Lorca's poems, and Pessoa, Apollinaire.

Talking about, Borges, what about other South American writers, the whole school of Magical Realism?

I don't like them—they are like factory products.

What about the literature of your adopted country, the United States?

I'm afraid I haven't read much. I have read a lot of things unconnected with Western literature. At the moment I am reading a huge book by a Moroccan Sufi poet, books on ecology, sagas from Iceland, and so on.

But surely you must have read writers like Henry James, Faulkner, Hemingway, Edith Wharton?

Some. There are great moments in Hemingway, for example "The Battler" or, even better, "The Killers," which is a masterpiece of the American short story. It is a tale of revenge in the underworld, and it is excellent. Edith Wharton's short stories seem to me much better than her novels. *Ethan Frome,* for example, is the story of a peasant of New England. In it the protagonist, a woman of the world, puts herself in his place and describes the life of these people in winter, when all the roads are frozen, isolated. It is short and very beautiful. Faulkner brings with him the true horror of the South, the illiteracy and racism of poor whites. As for Henry James, the best definition is the one by Somerset Maugham, when he said that Henry James was an alpinist, equipped to conquer the Himalayas, and walked up Beaker Street! Henry James was crushed by his stifling milieu—his sister, his mother, even his brother who was a genius but of a more philosophical and professorial kind. James never told his own truth.

You have just translated The Amen Corner, *and I know that you admire James Baldwin and are a friend of his. What do you think of his work now?*

Baldwin has written some admirable pages, but he does not have the courage to go to the end of his conclusions. He should have hit much harder. His life has been hard. He was one of nine children in Harlem, poor, a preacher at fifteen, a runaway at eighteen, working as a laborer, first in the Army during the War and later in the street, earning barely enough to survive. Somehow he gets to Paris where he manages to get himself incarcerated for the crime of having no fixed address and no profession. He has a drink problem now, but many American writers have had problems with drinking; perhaps it is due to the puritanism which has reigned over the American soul for so long. But at the same time, when the Americans are generous, cordial, intelligent, they are somehow more so than the Europeans. I know at least five or six Americans like that.

You are also interested in Japanese literature and your book on Mishima is considered one of the best essays on him. When did you get involved with Japan?

My interest in Japanese literature goes back to when I was about eighteen, and first discovered it through certain books. I read Mishima in French when he first appeared and found some of his work very beautiful. Later I saw that a great deal of absurdities were written about him and decided to write my book in order to present a more genuine Mishima. Now they have even made a detestable film of his life. Mrs. Mishima went to Hollywood and tried to stop it, but in vain. Four years ago I started learning Japanese, and after a while with the help of a Japanese friend translated Mishima's *Five Modern No Plays* into French. They are beautiful.

Traveling extensively as you do, how do you manage to write? Where do you find so much energy, and what is your work routine?

I write everywhere. I could write here, as I am talking to you. When in Maine or elsewhere, when I am traveling, I write wherever I am or whenever I can. Writing doesn't require too much energy—it is a relaxation, and a joy.

Looking back on your life, do you feel that you have had a "good" life, as the expression goes?

I don't know what a good life is. But how can one not be sad looking at the world around us at present? But there are also moments when I feel—to use a military expression my father liked—that "it is all counted as leave" (*Tout ça compte dans le congé!*). Happiness sometimes exists.

You are also interested in Sufism, and are planning an essay on Jahanara. What attracts you to it? I am particularly interested because I come from that tradition.

It is a philosophy which deals with the Divine as the essence of perfection, which is the Friend, and which the Buddhists seek within themselves, knowing that it comes from themselves, that liberation is from within. But I can't say that I am a Buddhist or a Sufi, or a socialist. I don't belong to any doctrine in particular. But there are spiritual affinities.

It seems crass to ask of someone as remarkably youthful and energetic as you are whether you ever think of death?

I think about it all the time. There are moments when I am tempted to believe that there is at least a part of the personality that survives, and others when I don't think so at all. I am tempted to see things as Honda does, in Mishima's last book, the one he finished the day he died. Honda, the principal character, realizes that he has been lucky enough to have loved four people, but that they were all the same person in different forms, in, if you like, successive reincarnations. The fifth time he has made a mistake and the error has cost him dearly. He realizes that the essence of these people is somewhere in the universe and that some day, perhaps in ten thousand years or more, he will find them again, in other forms, without even recognizing them. Of course, reincarnation here is only a word, one of the many possible words to stress a *certain* continuity. Certainly all the physical evidence points to our total annihilation, but if one also considers all the metaphysical *données,* one is tempted to say that it is not as simple as that.

Konrad Czynski   **(review date September 1987)**

SOURCE: A review of *Oriental Tales,* in *Comparative Literature Studies,* Vol. 24, No. 3, September, 1987, pp. 302-07.

[*In the following review, Czynski lauds Yourcenar's writing style and discusses* Oriental Tales *in relation to the development of the short story genre. Czynski also comments on some of the inadequacies he sees in Alberto Manguel's translation of the collection.*]

To journey is to appropriate the world; distances hitherto descried as limitless barriers are resolved into horizons of the mind, unified therein. The journeyer may voyage in space and time: Marco Polo's *Description of the World* (c. 1300), Kipling's *From Sea to Sea* (1899), Kazantzakis' *Voyage to Japan and China* (1938). The journeyer may set forth within the realm of the literary imagination: James Hilton's *Lost Horizon* (1933), Peter Shaffer's *The Royal Hunt of the Sun* (1964), Endō Shūsaku's *Samurai* (1980; English trans., 1982). Marguerite Yourcenar's collection of ten **Oriental Tales** (**Nouvelles orientales,** 1938) is a transposition at once of both modes of journeying, exemplifying as well a unique meeting of East and West.

During the 1920s and '30s, when Marguerite Yourcenar voyaged to Greece visiting the countries bordering the Adriatic and the eastern Mediterranean, her ever-exploring mind transposed what she saw and heard into the domain of prose fiction. She pursued thus her eastward journey along the paths of folk-tale, legend, and literature, her gaze seeking out the distant horizons of India, China, and Japan. Hence, the adjective "Oriental" in the title is justified, all the more so since in French "the Orient" encompasses eastern Europe (Polish is considered a *langue orientale,* an "eastern tongue"), Russia, the Near East, and all the countries and seas extending as far as the Land of the Rising Sun.

Marguerite Yourcenar, a resident of Mount Desert Island, Maine, is known to English-speaking readers as the authoress of **Memoirs of Hadrian,** splendidly translated almost three decades ago by Grace Frick in collaboration with Ms. Yourcenar, and as the first woman writer to be elected to the Académie Française (1980). She herself has translated into French "Negro Spirituals," with commentaries, under the title **Deep torrent, Dark river** (1964). Her long-standing interest in Japan is especially manifest in a 125-page essay (recently translated into English) on the novelist Mishima Yukio entitled **Mishima, or the Vision of Emptiness** (1980).

The reproduction of a detail from a painting by Tao-chi (China, 1641-1710)—*Returning Home* (Metropolitan Museum of Art, New York)—as the central image of the dust-jacket design, executed by Cynthia Krupat, is to be commended as an appropriate choice. The publisher's blurb thereon is, however, a simplification that misrepresents the nature of this recital of tales. Specifically, it is an error to state that Marguerite Yourcenar's stories "follow no established tradition."

First of all, the volume had its precedent, as Ms. Yourcenar avows in **Les Yeux ouverts,** in Gobineau's six *Nouvelles asiatiques,* published in 1876. As in the case of Gobineau's *nouvelles,* the majority of Ms. Yourcenar's short stories originally appeared in periodicals, hers during the years 1928-1937. Whereas Gobineau's romantic and exotic *Tales of Asia* are longer than the **Nouvelles orientales,** both collections do illustrate the genre termed *nouvelle.* In essence, this designates a short piece of narrative prose, occasionally enclosed within a prologue and an epilogue, the primary focus of which is a brief sequence of events undertaken, or undergone, by the principal figure or figures, rather than, as in the novel, character-development in a psychological or *Bildungsroman* sense. Indeed, the central character is more or less static, sketched monochromatically, and in some measure allegorical, while the events, situations, or episodes of conflict to which the narrative framework is restricted culminate in a comic, or tragic, climax that surprises even as it is seen to be the inevitable outcome of the circumstances. The inexorable unfolding of the plot-logic of Somerset Maugham's short stories is exemplary in this regard; John Barth's volume of novellas *Chimera* (1973) is a contemporary illustration of the genre's survival.

Secondly, Marguerite Yourcenar did indeed deliberately compose within the traditions of the *nouvelle* (short story) and the *conte* (tale), for both terms appear in her Postscript as applicable to one or another of the ten stories. The first edition of this work appeared in 1938 in the Gallimard series "La Renaissance de la Nouvelle," such designation likewise underscoring the literary lineage. Since then, the collection, augmented with a tenth story in 1978, underwent two stylistic revisions, published in 1963 and 1979. Both editions contain slightly different Postscripts offering authorial insights into the origins and themes of these culturally diverse prose-fantasias and retellings of folk and classical literature and myth. The ten stories are individually so multifariously rich and so gracefully wrought, novels-in-miniature one is tempted to say, that the delights of rereading—surprise renewed, wisdom gleaned, reflections provoked—are most devoutly, and long-lastingly, to be savoured.

"How Wang-Fo was saved" (or "spared"; the hyphen is unnecessary between the surname and the given-name), the opening piece in the recital, is a retelling of a Taoist morality-tale concerning an aged painter, Master Wang "the Buddha-aspirant" ("Fo" signifies "the Buddha"). It illustrates a certain magical dimension intrinsic to the metaphysical continuum bridging a work of art and imitated reality. It may well have been inspired by a passage in Arthur Waley's book on Chinese painting *Introduction to the Study of Chinese Painting* (1923) wherein Waley alludes to the T'ang dynasty painter Wu Tao-tzu (*fl.* early eighth century): "The Taoists have annexed [Wu] as one of their divinities and tell us that he disappeared into one of his own pictures." In like manner, master of the brush Wang Fo comes to be spared the evil designs of imperial wrath through both his art and the (post-mortem!) devo-

tion of his faithful disciple Ling. The realm of the fantastic is thus one with the domain of the real.

The second piece introduces the reader to a Serbian folk-hero, Marko Kraljević, whose patriotic and death-defying exploits in the face of Turkish brutality reveal a singular and admirable weakness, itself a moral strength leading to more than military victory. A conquest of a different order ensues: *omnia vincit amor,* as Vergil has said. The ninth piece, composed in 1978, tells of Marko's fateful encounter with a formidable Old Man, he who has always vanquished Life with the relentless grip of his invisible hands.

The third is based on a mediaeval Balkan folk-ballad, as naively touching as any work of hagiography evoking the miraculous powers of motherhood.

The fourth depicts the twilight hours of Genji the Shining Prince's long day's journey into night. This account of the death of the Shining Prince was inspired, as Ms. Yourcenar informs us in **Les Yeux ouverts,** by her reading of Arthur Waley's majestic translation in several volumes of the greatest Japanese novel, *The Tale of Genji,* written in the early eleventh century by Lady Murasaki Shikibu. (It has been devotedly and masterfully translated anew by Edward Seidensticker.) The impending darkness of Genji's eternal rest is metaphorically anticipated by both his physical blindness and that of his heart, blind to the devotion of the noblewoman whose love was never truly acknowledged. In this prose-fantasia Marguerite Yourcenar has succeeded, as indeed she so intended, in portraying with poignantly drawn strokes of poetry Prince Genji's late years and last days in a manner worthy of Japan's preeminent novelist, who was, we should reiterate, an authoress. Herein Genji's death, passed over in silence by Murasaki Shikibu, incarnates a pathos surpassed only by the tragedy that darkened Ling's wedded life, told in the opening tale.

The fifth takes the reader to twentieth-century Greece where the Nereids, beauteous nymph-daughters of the sea in the pre-Homeric age, bestow upon an innocent youth the calamitous delights of courtship unsought, the euphoria of mythic misfortune. The sixth transports us to fourth-century Greece at the time of Athanasius, bishop of Alexandria, whose disciple Therapion encounters the compassionate Blessed Virgin while he is engaged in the zealous pursuit, indeed persecution, of a different species of nymph, denied by him their rightful place in the divine economy. In this fantasia the authoress suggests the origin of the name of a chapel found in the Athens countryside. The seventh piece returns us to Greece of the 1920s and '30s, calling to mind the village world of Zorba the Greek. It is the retelling of a folk-anecdote which unfolds, in dramatically poised, heart-laden steps, the grim tale of primitive passions incarnate in a peasant widow whose very name, Aphrodissia, betrays her nature, if not her fate.

The eighth, set in India, retells a Hindu myth concerning the Fierce Goddess, Kali, demonic consort of Śiva, she who symbolizes the inherent discords of human nature, its broken harmonies, the spirit ever in conflict with what Tennessee Williams called, in *Night of the Iguana,* "the earth's obscene, corrupting love."

The tenth and closing piece concerns a Dutch portrait

painter, Cornelius Berg, an embittered contemporary of Rembrandt's who comes to wish that God had never created mankind. For man the city-dweller and Nature-queller has defiled Creation's primordial beauties. The tulips cultivated by Berg's old friend symbolize an artificial paradise, insofar as they cannot obliterate awareness of all manner of ugliness and squalor brought by men into the world, robbing it thus of its blessed, pristine harmony. The recital thus opens and closes with reflections on man's possible redemption attained through a self-effacing Art. Indeed, this little book embodies such an endeavor as it proclaims that very hope.

The present translation was carried out by Alberto Manguel, apparently in collaboration with Ms. Yourcenar. Unfortunately, the original texts, having had to wait almost half a century to receive their English garb, were not, in contrast to the collaborative fruit *Memoirs of Hadrian,* as well outfitted as they deserved to be. Far greater justice could have been rendered to the *poetic* virtues of the French. The choice of English rendering is often not equal to the literary level of the original; moreover, a few clauses have been unjustifiably omitted, as well as a word or phrase here and there. Furthermore, a spontaneous dimension of storytelling is lost when *car* ("for") is, in all but one or two occurrences, turned into the expository "because." In several instances the word chosen is inaccurate. *Chevreuil* is given once as "she-goat" (ludicrously incongruous in the context), and in the second occurrence as the plural "wild deer"; in both cases it signifies the miniature and delicate "roe-deer." In the language of the King James Version, Creation is characterized as God's "handiwork," not "His handicraft" as in the translation (the French is *oeuvre*). In the short story about Wang Fo, the *Tu* addressed to the Emperor should be rendered "Thou" and "Thee," thereby maintaining the distinction between the honorific second-person singular and the informal *tu* ("you") uttered to the humble painter, the latter *tu* conveying the nuance of "lowly subject."

In the tale of Prince Genji linguistic matters are more complicated. The name Murasaki, shared by the authoress and a quasi-autobiographical character, and correctly rendered in the French as *Violette,* was exotically transformed into "Wisteria." This is unjustified, despite the common attribute of color: *fuji* is the flower (forming only part of Murasaki Shikibu's clan name, Fujiwara, "Fields-of-Wisteria"), *murasaki* its purple and blue-lilac hues. "Lady-of-the-Convulvulus-Pavilion" is rather stilted. The flower in question is the morning glory (*asago* in Japanese: lit. "Face of the dawn"; *volubilis* in French). Hence, "Lady-of-the-Morning-glory-Pavilion" is preferable. Chujo, a court-rank used as an appellation, should have a macron over the "u" indicating a prolonged vowel: thus, Chūjo. "Lady-Cricket-in-the-Garden" should more evocatively be "Lady-of-the-Cicada-Arbour." This late-summer insect (*semi* in Japanese, *cigale* in French) is a perennial subject of Japanese poetry, as in the haikai verse of Bashō (1644-94) wherein the short-lived insect's chirping cry, innocent of imminent death in the unrestrained vigor of its voice, bespeaks an intimation of mortality, symbolizing thus the pathos known only to humankind.

By way of conclusion, then, these are not stories told just for the telling. If we seek to discern a *leitmotif* in this sequence of old tales poured into new wine bottles, we shall find variations of Vergil's *sunt lacrimae rerum.* In **"How Wang-Fo was saved"** the Emperor, denouncing the old master's art as a deception, exclaims (in my translation): "The world is nought but a jumble of indistinct brush-strokes cast pell-mell by an artist void of reason, and ceaselessly washed away by the purifying flow of our tears." There are, as each story testifies, tears of joy and of sorrow for what befalls us: hearts will ever be moved by the vicissitudes to which we are prey, the ills and blessings of mortality to which we are, saints and sinners, heir. Marguerite Yourcenar is a journeyer who, having appropriated the world, has transcended space and time in her noble and masterly evocations of this, our so benighted heritage.

Joanne Schmidt   (review date Fall 1988)

SOURCE: "Marguerite Yourcenar: 1903-1987," in *Belles Lettres: A Review of Books by Women,* Vol. 4, No. 1, Fall, 1988, p. 8.

[*Schmidt is an American critic and educator. In the following review of* With Open Eyes, A Coin in Nine Hands, *and* Two Lives and a Dream, *she lauds Yourcenar's work.*]

The date March 6, 1980, was memorable for French women writers. On that day, Marguerite Yourcenar became the first and so far only woman ever elected to the prestigious 345-year-old body of French writers, the French Academy. However, as she recounts in *With Open Eyes,* the informative series of conversations she had with French literary critic Matthieu Galey, she herself was publicly indifferent to membership in the academy of "Immortals."

For two contradictory reasons, Yourcenar remains an enigma to many feminists. First, she was not interested in striking a victory for women by becoming a member of the Academy, and second, she was, above all other contemporary French women writers, extremely acceptable to the French male literary establishment. At the core of any attempt by a feminist to understand Yourcenar's acceptability to that establishment, both in France and abroad, is the essential fact found in her biography that the only parent she ever knew was her father, since her mother died only days after her birth in 1903 in Brussels.

In *With Open Eyes,* Yourcenar sums up the father/daughter relationship in two succinct yet revealing statements: "We helped each other" and "We thought of each other as equals." Her father, Michel Crayencourt (*Yourcenar* is an anagram of her family name, which her father helped her invent), was a French aristocrat who welcomed his daughter into the world of male privilege. Early in her childhood, her ambition was to write something important and make an impression on people through her pen. Because of her father, she grew to believe that being female would never be a tremendous obstacle. She also shared the feeling with him that she was destined for something great. "I had a strange certainty that I *was* somebody."

Yourcenar was twenty-four years old when her father died. Their bond had been loving, respectful, and meaningful. He was the one who told her many stories about her mother, a highly intelligent Belgian aristocrat who read avidly, loved the classics, and, in the 1890s despite her family's disapproval, arranged to learn Greek and Latin with tutors. One can easily see how the seeds of Yourcenar's life were present in her mother's life and why loss and separation would be recurring themes in her works.

The void of never having known her mother was filled by her companion Grace Frick, an American academic whom Yourcenar met while in her early twenties. After her father's death, she found solace in their friendship and the deep bond they shared. Frick invited Marguerite to move to New York City in 1939 during an obviously troubled time in Europe, helped find their future home in 1949 on Mount Desert Island off the coast of Maine, and translated her monumental novel *The Memoirs of Hadrian* into English. In total, Frick and Yourcenar spent almost forty years together.

Besides the many details of Yourcenar's personal life, *With Open Eyes* reveals her political opinions and her views on love, racism, and feminism. She was suspicious of labels and never called herself a feminist, viewing feminism as "particularism" or a type of "racism in reverse," which is not difficult to understand from the point of view of a European who witnessed fascism firsthand. Yet she told each woman to reject the "artificial image" that society "reflects back to her" and encouraged women to be full human beings who are also women (*"un être humain femme"*). Furthermore, she was always in the vanguard of many issues important to feminists: the fight against nuclear power and weapons, pollution, and cruelty to animals, and the belief in ecology. She frequently sent telegrams to public officials and government agencies to support these causes: her way to be engaged in direct activism. To her, all living things were part of a greater whole, a view that was also present in her novels. Although Yourcenar never embraced feminism, she exemplified part of the diversity of female responses and experiences under patriarchal rule.

Attentive readers of Yourcenar find that she has added immensely to women's writing about being caught in a double bind. She also started her literary career addressing taboo topics such as homosexuality ("a word I find annoying"), bisexuality, and incest. She demonstrated great courage in these themes. Through development of them by her and by her protagonists of both sexes, she successfully analyzed and exposed the social structure or deconstructed the patriarchy, in current feminist terminology. She chose bisexuality and sexual "inversion" (a seventeenth-century French literary device still used in Yourcenar's time, in which females are endowed with some "male" qualities and males are endowed with some "female" qualities) as means to a solution for dealing with the reality of the human condition for both men and women in a patriarchal society. The implicit subtext in her novels sets out to solve the sexual problem, which for her was an admitted inability "to see why anyone would want to make a distinction between homosexual love and love in general." For the rest of her life, she swam against the tide in her pursuit of bisexuality as a topic of interest because she saw men as they were and did not assume that their masculinity was total and exclusive. She made the same supposition concerning femininity.

A Coin in Nine Hands was written in the 1930s while Yourcenar was living in Italy. This carefully constructed novel set in fascist Italy examines the world of male power gone mad. The presence of the dictator Mussolini looms above the lives of the characters like Big Brother in *1984*. Yourcenar connected the major characters through the device of a coin passed from one to the next. This novel, begun in 1934, was revised and rewritten in 1958-59 because the author felt that the first version was too stylized and not reflective of the real and tangible misery of the period.

The antifascist hero in this novel, Carlo Stevo, never appears directly. Marcella, the proletarian heroine and one of Stevo's followers, holds political views diametrically opposed to those of her husband, Dr. Alessandro Sarte, a doctor for fascists. The couple have been estranged from the beginning of the novel. Her husband delivers the news of Stevo's death, and at first she does not believe him but later finds out it is true. Marcella then reveals her plan to kill Mussolini. She even tells him that she will use his gun, for which she exchanges some coins as a token payment. Alessandro does not believe her plan and thinks she is crazy. At this point, coins begin to forebode doom by being linked to the coins found in Judas Iscariot's pocket.

" 'How alone I am,' she thought." Yourcenar purposely pointed out the extreme isolation of women in acts of courage such as the one Marcella commits: Marcella saw her target, then "fired and missed." She will be killed by the mob. Only the character Mother Dida validates her act: "She must have had courage to do a thing like that." The novel ends with images of darkness and all characters sleeping.

Unlike authors of the past, Yourcenar left ample explanations of her work. In *A Coin in Nine Hands,* she furnished her readers with an afterword, in which she explained why she revised this novel after being distanced from it over time. She was proud of the book because "it was one of the first French novels (maybe the very first) to confront the hollow reality behind the bloated facade of Fascism."

Two Lives and a Dream (1987) is a collection of three novellas. Nathaniel, the protagonist in *An Obscure Man,* is a highly sympathetic character with strong similarities to Voltaire's Candide and to Félicité in Flaubert's *A Simple Heart.* The novella, set in Amsterdam, opens with a flashback before Nathaniel's death. He wanders through life in an "ebb and flow" as a gentle, loyal, and sensitive man with some education in English and Latin. A picaro type of character, he flees to the New World after thinking he has killed a man in self-defense.

Sexual inversion and role reversal are used throughout. Nathaniel is thought "effeminate" because he cannot kill an animal without being ill. In the same way, Foy, one of the female characters, is characterized as working "like a man."

For Nathaniel, every living organism is connected. He becomes ill and is exiled on an island, where he faces death alone, surrounded by the sounds and wonders of nature. He has lived in harmony with nature, and he seeks his favorite place on the island to die. Some time before death, he reflects on his sense of self and identity. In summing up his character, Yourcenar notes, "nor did he particularly consider himself male in contrast with the gentle order of women."

The second novella, *A Lovely Morning,* is also set in Amsterdam. Lazarus, Nathaniel's twelve-year-old son from a disintegrated marriage, is the protagonist. Like his father, he is sensitive and kind. He knows about his mother's death but not his father's, and he lives in his grandmother's house, where a visitor teaches him to read, and, eventually, to act parts in plays. Lazarus is content to play different roles, both male and female, and is convincing in the latter. His life is filled with infinite possibilities through acting. The novella ends on a positive note with one of Lazarus's theatrical performances.

Anna, Soror, the most intriguing of the three novellas, focuses on Yourcenar's most taboo topic: incest. The setting is Naples in 1575. As in *The Memoirs of Hadrian,* Yourcenar used a French neoclassical practice of distancing herself from her own period in order to gain perspective on her characters.

The aristocrat Don Alvaro and his beautiful wife, Valentina, have two children, Anna and Miguel, who are mirror images. "One could have been mistaken for the other." Valentina contracts malaria, and as her illness worsens, an attraction builds between her children. At her deathbed, Anna and Miguel reveal their true feelings claiming, "We love each other." And Valentina replies, "I know."

Eventually they consummate their love, keeping it a secret. But Miguel dies in a naval battle, and Anna tries to deny to herself that incest ever occurred. Yet Miguel's memory lives on in her mind. Years later, on her own deathbed, she utters, *"Mi amado"* ("My lover"). But the nuns in the convent where she dies assume the predictable. "They thought she was speaking to God. Perhaps she was."

Throughout her career as a writer, Marguerite Yourcenar championed one taboo topic after another in her oeuvre. Among her many accomplishments were eight novels, four books of essays, three books of autobiography, four volumes of plays, four books of poetry and prose poems, and six translations, the most notable being Virginia Woolf's *The Waves.* Yourcenar was thus a poet, novelist, playwright, essayist, critic, translator, activist, ecologist, and citizen of the world. She was remarkable because she never ceased working. Before her death at age eighty-four in a Maine hospital, she was in the process of finishing the last volume of her autobiography, entitled *Quoi? l'Éternité,* or *What? Eternity.* That word, *eternity,* is her final message. Her opus will assure her place in literature as a true "Immortal."

David Cowart   (essay date 1989)

SOURCE: "The Way It Was," in *History and the Contemporary Novel,* Southern Illinois University Press, 1989, pp. 31-75.

[*Cowart is an American critic and educator who has written extensively on modern literature. In the following excerpt, he provides a detailed discussion of the main themes in* Memoirs of Hadrian, *analyzing in particular Yourcenar's re-creation of the classical world and ancient "Rome's mental life."*]

The reader who would know the feel of Roman life in the second century finds in Yourcenar's *Memoirs of Hadrian* an extraordinary feat of literary, spiritual, and mental archeology. Yourcenar makes the past live through her literary skill and through the exercise of an imagination disciplined by scrupulous scholarship. By focusing the novel on one man's lifelong pursuit of order, liberty, self-knowledge, and the good life, she makes his story a cultural history of politics, society, and thought in ancient Rome. She brings to life a Roman emperor almost two thousand years dead, and with him the myths, the science, the mores, the philosophy, the very consciousness of an age long past. She overcomes the disparities between ancient and modern cultural attitudes. She shows her reader the way it was.

Memoirs of Hadrian stands up well in comparison with other modern and contemporary novels set in the Roman world, including Graves's *I, Claudius* and *Claudius the God,* Broch's *The Death of Virgil,* Robert DeMaria's *Clodia,* John Williams's *Augustus,* Hersey's *The Conspiracy,* Wilder's *The Ides of March,* and Vidal's *Julian.* Yourcenar matches Williams for psychological precision, and she matches Graves for erudition. Indeed, her erudition is less eccentric, and one suspects a comment on Graves when her Hadrian hints that Suetonius—Graves's chief source for the *Claudius* novels—may have distorted the history he was charged with recording. Though less technically innovative than Broch, Yourcenar achieves substantially more control, precision, and economy. In her prose, finally, and in her direct sensuous apprehension of a bygone reality, she outclasses all these other writers.

Though Vidal, Williams, and Hersey all follow Yourcenar in the epistolary structure of their novels, none manages the acuteness of her psychological portrait. By casting her novel in the form of an autobiographical letter from the Emperor Hadrian to Marcus Aurelius, his adoptive grandson and a future caesar himself, she enables the reader to experience the mental life of the refined and hellenized ruler who did much to consolidate Rome's fabled status as "eternal city." Early in his letter Hadrian promises Marcus Aurelius "a recital stripped of preconceived ideas and of mere abstract principles; it is drawn wholly from the experience of one man, who is myself. I am trusting to this examination of facts to give me some definition of myself, and to judge myself, perhaps, or at the very least to know myself better before I die." Hadrian's personal goal mirrors the goal of both history and art: knowledge of the human reality. Yourcenar, through Hadrian, intimates a relationship between self-knowledge and knowledge of the past. One of the things that makes *Memoirs of Hadrian* a good historical novel is the interweaving in it of psychology and history, personal self-knowledge and cultural self-knowledge, the manifest psychological and spiritual rewards of the one enriched and made yet more meaningful by the other.

In *Memoirs of Hadrian,* Yourcenar brings to life a Roman emperor almost two thousand years dead, and with him the myths, the science, the mores, the philosophy, the very consciousness of an age long past.

—*David Cowart*

Hadrian offers an instructive contrast to that other aged monarch, King Lear. Lear "hath ever but slenderly known himself," as one of his vicious daughters remarks, and Shakespeare's drama demonstrates, among other things, the ramifications of such culpable and dangerous nescience. Lear's ignorance on this point reflects what seems a generalized ignorance among the characters of the play with regard to the past, or at least the civilized past, of the kingdom they inhabit. Thus no one—not even the sensible Kent—thinks to advance the argument of history against Lear's proposed division of a kingdom. Lacking both personal and collective self-knowledge, Lear and his realm easily revert or regress to a savage state—from which "history" must begin all over again.

Unlike Lear, Hadrian maintains contact with a cultural and personal past. He is a man of historical sensibility, like his imperial predecessor Claudius. But in contrast to Claudius, who could do little more than study history, Hadrian actually directs it. As Yourcenar conceives of him, he is that rarity, the thinker who can also lead.

He can also write. The emperor's prose discovers an accomplished man of letters, a modest poet, a discriminating lover of literature. He produces a shapely narrative, with well-turned paragraphs and sentences that hover at the distant periphery of epigram. Every expression combines what Chaucer calls "solas" and "sentence."

But Hadrian's stylistic virtues generate difficulties. In conferring upon her narrator these literary gifts, which complicate his task of self-examination, Yourcenar complicates her own task of historical re-creation, which depends greatly on the emperor's credibility. Hadrian aspires to candor in his narrative yet cannot help the tendency of his polished prose to gainsay all that might make him seem less than exemplary. One becomes suspicious of such an artful narrator. One notices, for example, his remarkable ability to reveal his virtues without seeming proud and his flaws without seeming vicious. At times, after all, Hadrian cloaks actions that might seem vicious or unbalanced in language so measured and reasonable as to forestall opprobrium, and only by acts of rigorous discrimination

does the reader perceive a disparity between the thing reported—the endless and extravagant memorials to Antinous, say—and the elegant terms of the reporting. Throughout the narrative, in fact, Hadrian affects a tone implying passions long since banked.

The point is not that Hadrian means to deceive. One can recollect and report a violent action or a violent grief in tranquility, but sometimes one can belie an emotion's original violence by the artful language in which one describes it. The problem—it is really Yourcenar's—concerns narrative technique: how to circumscribe the tendency of a rhetorically sophisticated narrator to compromise psychological and historical accuracy. Yourcenar, the translator into French of Henry James and Virginia Woolf, handles this technical challenge with great resourcefulness. She creates in Hadrian a narrator just unreliable enough to remain human. She reports in her **"Reflections on the Composition of *Memoirs of Hadrian*"** that as her fictional emperor took on autonomous life—as the characters of a good writer properly do—she retained the necessary detachment. "At certain moments, though very seldom, it has occurred to me that the emperor was lying. In such cases I had to let him lie, like the rest of us." Thus the reader encounters Antinous, for example, "through the emperor's memories, that is to say, in passionately meticulous detail, not devoid of a few errors." Even when the emperor does not lie consciously, the ideal of psychological accuracy dictates that he make mistakes or color certain events with his own mild prejudice.

Yourcenar's refusal to make the emperor a paragon, a Roman King Arthur, argues a judicious and discriminating approach to recapturing the way it was. Though she perceives Hadrian as "a very great man," she seeks to give her readers a real person whose essential honesty and wisdom do not preclude occasional mistakes, poor judgment, and moral lapses. Her emperor, however admirable, remains a human being, subject to the distortions of character that inevitably accompany power. Thus he admits to striking Antinous; he exiles Favorinus for his sharp tongue and Juvenal for mocking a favorite actor; Suetonius he forces into retirement, and Apollodorus he has executed as part of the Servianus faction. Most shocking of all, perhaps, he drives a stylus into the eye of a contentious scribe in a fit of pique. Some readers find this last detail simply incredible—an odd lapse on the part of both author and character. Jean Blot, a French critic, complains that "this act remains impossible, unrealistic, gratuitous. The gentleman of the *Memoirs* is constitutionally incapable of this kind of brutality." But the inclusion of this incident is of crucial importance to balancing the insidious effects of the narrator's elegant prose. It forces the reader, in a moment of empathic mortification, to recognize other objectionable acts in their true light, acts for which allowances have perhaps too willingly been made. Between the shock value of this incident and the surprising number of dubious acts it causes to come suddenly into focus, Hadrian—and behind him Yourcenar—corrects for the tendency of good writing to neutralize confessional revelations.

Hadrian's candor regarding the number and the occasional severity of his lapses, then, has the effect of compensating for his artful presentation of them. His admissions ultimately witness to his essential honesty and integrity, for he could easily have passed over these embarrassing actions. His forthrightness in such matters makes one believe him when he disclaims the villainies imputed to him by his enemies—when, for example, he says that he did not poison his wife Sabina, that he does not prepare his own food out of fear, or that he did not order the deaths of "three intriguing scoundrels and a brute" who threatened his position after the death of Trajan. Both his real and imputed lapses, on the other hand, weigh less in the scale than his gestures of kindness and mature restraint— pardoning the slave's attempt on his life, for example, or declining the Senate's gestures of empty fawning ("the long series of honorary appellations which is draped like a fringed shawl round the necks of certain emperors"). Hadrian's civilized distaste for bloodletting, whether in the coliseum or in Parthia, would compensate for much more villainy than that with which the emperor manages to charge himself. One forgives any number of minor sins in a man who sanely turns his back on meaningless and counterproductive wars of conquest.

The emperor prefers to invest his energies in consolidating the peace and conserving the heritage of the past. As he remarks on his restoration of the tomb of Epaminondas, Hadrian feels the need "to commemorate . . . a time when everything, viewed at a distance, seems to have been noble, and simple, too, whether tenderness, glory, or death." He has ordered tombs, monuments, shrines, temples, and public buildings refurbished or rebuilt throughout the empire, and this work symbolizes the more abstract and awesome task of refurbishing Rome itself—its institutions, its power, its security, its ideals, its splendor, even its Hellenic pedigree. All of these had suffered under Tiberius, Caligula, Nero, and the rest of the mad or inverted or merely incompetent rulers between Augustus and Nerva.

"I have done much rebuilding. To reconstruct is to collaborate with time gone by, penetrating or modifying its spirit, and carrying it toward a longer future. Thus beneath the stones we find the secret of the springs." These remarks describe historical fiction no less than conservationism, for the author of an historical novel—this one, for example—also engages in an act of reconstruction, of collaboration with time gone by. Yourcenar seeks to uncover the vital origins of her own moribund culture. She, too, seeks the secret of the springs.

In addition to his other acts of cultural conservation, Hadrian builds libraries and orders books copied and recopied, for "each man fortunate enough to benefit to some degree from this legacy of culture seemed to me responsible for protecting it and holding it in trust for the human race." Yourcenar, herself an accomplished classical scholar, a beneficiary of Hadrian's sense of cultural responsibility, does her part to preserve and pass on the special vitality of the ancient world, to effect in some small measure the reinvigoration of a culture whose classical antecedents seem to lie in ruins. But to disinter the values of antiquity, she must first disinter a whole set of perceptions common to that world but now alien. She accomplishes this end primarily through an act of psychological reconstruction. Focusing on one man's psychological reality, she re-creates the mind of Hadrian and thereby re-creates Hadrian's time as well. The reader looks into that mind as into a mirror angled to catch the light of a remote age.

Occasionally, however, the mirror reflects the age of the reader. . . . [A] historical novel will commonly function in one primary and one secondary mode; in this one the primary attention to the way it was does not preclude secondary reflections in a distant mirror. Thus Hadrian, with various degrees of conscious prevision, can from time to time address posterity and even show a later century its own face. He imagines at one point "a hypothetical empire governed from the West, an Atlantic world," and he sounds even more prescient when he describes the puritan work ethic and the materialistic and antlike societies of the future: "I can well imagine forms of servitude worse than our own, because more insidious, whether they transform men into stupid, complacent machines, who believe themselves free just when they are most subjugated, or whether to the exclusion of leisure and pleasures essential to man they develop a passion for work as violent as the passion for war among barbarous races. To such bondage for the human mind and imagination I prefer even our avowed slavery."

These touches alone represent mere glances toward the twentieth century, rather than an actual mirroring of the present in the past. The real mirroring is more a matter of atmosphere, for in her depiction of the autumnal civilization of Hadrian's Rome, the author invites the reader to recognize a later civilization, also past its prime. In her **"Reflections on the Composition of *Memoirs of Hadrian,"*** Yourcenar explains that the novel, after a number of false starts beginning as early as the 1920s, really began to come together in her mind late in 1948, when "everything that the world . . . had gone through" seemed to illuminate her reading of ancient source materials on Hadrian, to cast "upon that imperial existence certain other lights and shades." She felt a special affinity with the long-dead emperor and his age, because "the fact of having lived in a world which is toppling" gave her a real appreciation of an age and a civilization that had to suffer a like dissolution of old values, old certainties, old sources of strength. "Both Plutarch and Marcus Aurelius knew full well that gods, and civilizations, pass and die. We are not the first to look upon an inexorable future."

But these features merely enhance the creation of an author whose primary energies serve the end of a faithful capturing of the past in its own unique character. Yourcenar realizes the difficulties of getting at historical truth, but she does not assume that it must therefore remain forever out of reach. In her **"Reflections"** on the novel she emphasizes the necessity of scrupulous research animated by an imagination capable of filling gaps with authority: "Learn everything, read everything, inquire into everything," she declares. Fill "hundreds of card notes," call before the mind's eye both people and actions, and recognize that divergent texts do not call each other into question but rather represent "different facets, or two successive stages, of the same reality, a reality convincingly human just because it is complex." She aspires to "constant participation, as intensely aware as possible, in *that which has been,*" and she refuses "to suggest, as is too often done, that historical truth is never to be attained, in any of its aspects. With this kind of truth, as with all others, the problem is the same: one errs *more* or *less.*" She recognizes that Hadrian himself seeks the truth, no less than the writer who aspires to present him accurately. True to her Roman orientation, she even invokes Pontius Pilate, whom the Western world has been conditioned to think singularly blind on the subject, as a wise man in matters of truth: "He who seeks passionately for truth, or at least for accuracy, is frequently the one best able to perceive, like Pilate, that truth is not absolute or pure."

Notwithstanding her respect for the usual kinds of historical research, Yourcenar places special emphasis on a kind of linking up with the mind of the past, and she reflects that "some five and twenty aged men, their withered hands interlinked to form a chain, would be enough to establish an unbroken contact between Hadrian and ourselves." She suggests with this figure the essential identity of history and personal memory. She elaborates by pointing out the "historical" aspects of a writer like Proust:

> Those who put the historical novel in a category apart are forgetting that what every novelist does is only to interpret, by means of the techniques which his period affords, a certain number of past events; his memories, whether consciously or unconsciously recalled, whether personal or impersonal, are all woven of the same stuff as History itself. . . . In our day, when introspection tends to dominate literary forms, the historical novel, or what may for convenience's sake be called by that name, must take the plunge into time recaptured, and must fully establish itself within some inner world.

To know the past, this author implies, one must enter a representative mind of the past, live in that "inner world." But the attainment of such historical empathy remains problematic because of the extrinsic mental baggage accumulated over the centuries. The most cumbersome of this baggage is the set of religious and cultural assumptions intervening—and strengthened, down through the ages—between ancient Rome and today. When the Supreme Pontiff, the Vicar of Christ, supplanted the Pontifex Maximus (an event actually imagined by Hadrian), an enormous change in values took place. Julian, the fourth-century Byzantine emperor who tried, too late, to halt the Christian transformation, allegedly died murmuring "*Vicisti Galilæe,*" and only the occasional Gibbon, who associated the rise of Christianity with the decline and fall of Rome, or Swinburne, who translated Julian's last words in the famous line "Thou hast conquered, O pale Galilean," has registered the toll of Christian hegemony, given adequate expression to what the world lost by the new dispensation's displacement of the old.

Even the waning of Christianity in the modern world has done little to restore an older set of attitudes or perceptions in matters spiritual. Consequently, Yourcenar must take strong measures to bring home the radically different worldview of Hadrian and his age. She allows the emperor

to express opinions about Jews and Christians—mere common sense to the cultivated Romans of his day—that run shockingly counter to the received views of a later age. Hadrian, nonetheless, speaks as a religious man—but a religious man in the Roman tradition of thoroughgoing religious tolerance. He has little sympathy with all forms of fanaticism and intolerance. Receiving an apologia from one "Quadratus, a bishop of the Christians," Hadrian reads it thoughtfully and concedes the value of the solace that Christianity affords to simple and poor folk.

> But I was aware, too, of certain dangers. Such glorification of virtues befitting children and slaves was made at the expense of more virile and intellectual qualities; under the narrow, vapid innocence I could detect the fierce intransigence of the sectarian in presence of forms of life and of thought which are not his own, the insolent pride which makes him value himself above other men, and his voluntarily circumscribed vision.

The Christians at least render unto Caesar the things that are Caesar's. The Jews, on the other hand, cultivate a really monumental intransigence. Their resistance to the rebuilding of Jerusalem leads to blood-shed on a scale that appalls and sickens the "pacifically inclined" Hadrian. The costs of the savage conflict in Palestine, as the emperor recounts them, make grim reading: "In those four years of war fifty fortresses and more than nine hundred villages and towns had been sacked and destroyed; the enemy had lost nearly six hundred thousand men; battles, endemic fevers, and epidemics had taken nearly ninety thousand of ours." Hadrian reasons that only fanatics, "sectarians so obsessed by their god that they have neglected the human," could resist the *Pax Romana* so long and at such cost.

Hadrian overstates the fanaticism of the Jewish rebels. As Yourcenar remarked to Patrick de Rosbo, "He is incapable of admitting . . . that these people do not desire the benefits of Greco-Roman civilization." He also fails to consider how zealously he and his countrymen might resist another Carthaginian invasion of Italy. But in expressing his contempt for religious absolutism, Hadrian does not, as at least one critic has hinted, become the mouthpiece for an anachronistic and monstrous anti-Semitism. To impute anti-Semitism in the modern sense to either this character or his creator implies an odd expectation that the author will impose on historical material an inappropriate modern perspective. Yourcenar, writing only a few years after the opening of the death camps and the first modern Palestinian war (1948), takes certain risks here to establish the profound difference between the way ancient Romans thought about religion and the way those influenced by the Judeo-Christian heritage think about it.

One should note, however, that Yourcenar ironically undercuts her narrator when he speaks of "leaning against the trunk of a leafless fig tree" to observe the Roman assault on Bethar, the last Jewish stronghold. The oblique reference to an earlier Jew's least sensible gesture, the cursing of the fig tree, would seem to have something to do with the senselessness of the present bloodshed. But Hadrian probably remains unaware that he has touched on a famous incident in the New Testament, an incident traditionally held to symbolize the fate of the old Judaic dispensation at the coming of a new order. According to biblical interpreters, the fig tree cursed by Christ represents the tree of Judah, inherently unripe for miracle. In Yourcenar's context, the tree no longer vital enough for the new dispensation is ironically associated with Romans and Jews alike. Both face superannuation by crescive Christianity.

The toll of the Jewish war also figures in the novel's central myth—a myth so familiar to Hadrian and his correspondent as to require little direct reference. In writing of his life as a progression from early vigor and happiness to declining health and vitality, Hadrian recapitulates the Ages of Man, and the presence of this myth in his narrative, resonant with but distanced from its Judeo-Christian and psychoanalytic congeners, provides further evidence of Yourcenar's having immersed herself in psychological givens that differ from those of her own age. Yourcenar's subtle exploitation of the myth contributes to the accuracy of her historical reconstruction, so that the reader experiences not only the events of the past but also its half-conscious mythic thinking. This mythic thinking shapes Hadrian's narrative. From his accession to power and his relationship with Antinous to the dissolution of love and peace, Hadrian follows the archetypal pattern of slow wasting established in the cosmology of Hesiod and Ovid. According to the myth, the world began in an age of Gold, then declined successively to ages of Silver, Bronze, and Iron, with attendant changes in tutelary deities. Saturn ruled in the Golden Age, Jupiter in the Silver, and lesser gods thereafter. The terrestrial environment and its human inhabitants also changed. During the Golden Age, humanity lived peacefully in a kind of perennial spring, but subsequently the climate became harsher, the human beings more warlike and knavish.

Hadrian's recollections of the years with Antinous elicit the few direct references to this myth. "When I think back on these years," he declares in the chapter entitled "Saeculum Aureum," "I seem to return to the Age of Gold." Subsequently he describes this period as "truly an Olympian height in my life. All was there, the golden fringe of cloud, the eagles, and the cupbearer of immortality." The eagles belong iconographically to Rome, over which he reigns, and to Olympian Zeus, or Jupiter, with whom he identifies, and he recognizes his cupbearer, his Ganymede, in Antinous. But according to Hesiod, such voluptuousness—Hadrian even notes the anagrammatic relationship of *Roma* and *Amor*—belongs to the Age of Silver, not the Age of Gold. Hadrian, identifying with Jupiter, is actually at one remove from the Golden Age. Ironically, the emperor fails to see that the process of decline has already begun, that his real Golden Age had slipped by during his successful defense of the Dacian frontier, his rise to power, his wise treaties, his early, judicious rule. Then was he Saturnlike, enjoying "the virgin gold of respect," untouched as yet by the passing years because Saturn, qua Kronos, is master of time.

After Saturn and Jupiter comes Mars, and with him the Age of Bronze. In this age, says Ovid, "men were of a fiercer character, more ready to turn to cruel warfare" (*Metamorphoses,* I). Hadrian enters his Age of Bronze in the Jewish war, which seems in the narrative to follow hard upon the death of Antinous. The emperor understands that this war, with its multiple cruelties and endless bloodshed, represents a terrible decline from what has gone before in his life and in his reign, and he begins to glimpse an elemental process at work, eroding civilization itself. In a bleak moment he catalogues the cultural slippage: "I was beginning to find it natural, if not just, that we should perish. Our literature is nearing exhaustion, our arts are falling asleep; Pancrates is not Homer, nor is Arrian a Xenophon; when I have tried to immortalize Antinous in stone no Praxiteles has come to hand. Our sciences have been at a standstill from the times of Aristotle and Archimedes; our technical development is inadequate to the strain of a long war; even our pleasure-lovers grow weary of delight."

As Hadrian himself grows weary of delight, he enters the Age of Iron and even identifies with Pluto, its grim deity. Ovid says of the Iron Age: "friend was not safe from friend, nor father-in-law from son-in-law, and even between brothers affection was rare. Husbands waited eagerly for the death of their wives, and wives for that of their husbands." Thus at the end of his narrative Hadrian speaks with greatest frankness about the hostility between himself and his wife Sabina, and almost casually he orders the execution of his brother-in-law and grandnephew, Servianus and Fuscus. He even recapitulates his identification with the various deities associated with the Ages of Man: "men . . . no longer compare me, as they once did, to serene and radiant Zeus, but to Mars Gradivus, god of long campaigns and austere discipline. . . . Of late this pale, drawn visage, these fixed eyes and this tall body held straight by force of will, suggest to them Pluto, god of shades."

More painful to Hadrian than his personal griefs are the signs by which he recognizes Rome's fate, recognizes that "catastrophe and ruin will come." The Romans restore order on one frontier after another, but gradually the defenses crumble: "I could see the return of barbaric codes, of implacable gods, of unquestioned despotism of savage chieftains, a world broken up into enemy states and eternally prey to insecurity. . . . Our epoch, the faults and limitations of which I knew better than anyone else, would perhaps be considered one day, by contrast, as one of the golden ages of man." Thus the myth at the heart of ***Memoirs of Hadrian*** operates on several levels: one sees it in Hadrian's life, in the decline of the Roman Empire, and, most chillingly, in the decline over the centuries from Golden antiquity to the present Age of Iron. Part of the power of this myth, like the myth of Eden and its loss, lies in its ability to capture and reflect a sense of the progressive decay that time visits on individual human beings and on nations. It even anticipates the entropic decline posited by modern physicists.

Considerations of this kind prey on the mind of the emperor at the end of his reign because he has devoted his life to the promotion and consolidation of order. Hadrian's pursuit of this ideal constitutes the most important thematic thread in the novel; the prominence of the theme reveals how fully Yourcenar understands the man and the age that she sets out to present with fidelity. She recognizes, for example, that Hadrian's love of order springs from his regard for Greek culture no less than from the Roman values he must, as Caesar, preserve and protect. As Jacques Vier has remarked [in his *"L'Empereur Hadrien vu par* Marguerite Yourcenar," in the April 1979 issue of *Etudes Littèraires*], Hadrian embodies "the perfect accord of the Greek genius and the Latin genius." Thus he delights in contributing to the dissemination of the Greek heritage, and he labors to accelerate the grafting of the older culture onto its successors. He dreams, early in his career, "of Hellenizing the Barbarians and Atticizing Rome, thus imposing upon the world by degrees the only culture which has once for all separated itself from the monstrous, the shapeless, and the inert, the only one to have invented a definition of method, a system of politics, and a theory of beauty."

Yet despite his own Hellenism, Hadrian remains a true Roman, for his vision of order goes beyond anything the Greeks ever achieved or even imagined. Alexander, after all, subjugated but did not stabilize, and *The Republic,* that most comprehensive Greek statement on the subject of political order, seems conceived exclusively on the scale of the city-state. Only a Roman could dream of *tellus stabilita,* and Hadrian, true to his heritage, wants an abiding imperial peace: "I could see myself as seconding the deity in his effort to give form and order to a world." This passion of Hadrian's extends to his most mundane imperial duties—he fosters a solid and capable civil service bureaucracy to ensure that poor rule will not undermine stability—and even to his casual observations: "Pompey, in endeavoring to bring order to this uncertain world of Asia, sometimes seemed to me to have worked more effectively for Rome than Caesar himself." But readers probably find most attractive Hadrian's refusal, in the name of greater security and order, to pursue wars of imperial expansion. "I dreamed of an army trained to maintain order on frontiers less extended, if necessary, but secure. Every new increase in the vast imperial organism seemed to me an unsound growth, like a cancer or dropsical edema which would eventually cause our death." Hadrian's Wall, the most famous relic of this enlightened attitude, survives to this day in England, an "emblem of my renunciation of the policy of conquest."

One must work to create and maintain order because it does not flourish in the natural state. Hadrian, a contemporary of the astronomer Ptolemy, seems to distinguish between sublunary and cosmic spheres. He hints at the distinction in the opening pages, where he mentions his interest in the possible meaning contained in "the random twitter of birds, or . . . the distant mechanism of the stars." Here the translation, presumably with the approval of Yourcenar, clarifies a point left ambiguous in the original French. *Babillage,* "babbling" or "chatter," becomes *"random* twitter," the adjective implying the disorder of the sublunary sphere. Thus in the English translation Hadrian differentiates stars and birdsong: the one is mechanical, remotely orderly, and accessible to the astronomer; the other is "random" or orderless, yielding at best problematic messages to haruspices. Sublunary life, in other words, progressing from organic to inorganic and back to organic, amounts only to a crude approximation of order, and from moment to moment life tends to wallow in disorder. Only in moments like the one in which he lies out under the Syrian stars all one night can Hadrian affirm that "disorder is absorbed in order." Elsewhere he speaks of "the order of the universe" as of something divine, a referent for all human aspirations to harmony.

But wherever one achieves order on earth, it must dissolve sooner or later into chaos. "One has always to begin over again," says Hadrian. "Nature prefers to start again from the very clay, from chaos itself, and this horrible waste is what we term natural order." Nevertheless, Hadrian remains as impressed by the human capacity to rebuild as by the tendency toward dissolution. "Catastrophe and ruin will come; disorder will triumph, but order will too, from time to time. Peace will again establish itself between two periods of war." Whatever the fate of the actual political entity he has served, the emperor reflects, the *idea* of Rome will survive, a beacon in the realm of the attainable ideal. "Rome would be perpetuating herself in the least of the towns where magistrates strive to demand just weight from the merchants, to clean and light the streets, to combat disorder, slackness, superstition and injustice, and to give broader and fairer interpretation to the laws. She would endure to the end of the last city built by man."

> **Yourcenar depicts, in the representative and empathic mind of Hadrian, Rome's mental life, and she achieves psychological mimesis of a very high order.**
>
> *—David Cowart*

For Hadrian, the ideal of order subsumes a number of other philosophically related goals, goals definable only through a sustained inquiry into the good life. This inquiry, another part of the Greek legacy to Roman civilization, leads the emperor to reflect on the relative value of pleasure versus duty, freedom versus discipline, and the life of the senses versus the life of the mind. With remarkable lucidity he analyzes everything from his own sexuality to his official function and the sacrifices it entails. As Hadrian explores the political and ethical philosophy of the age, he completes, as it were, an inventory of his own mind, and Yourcenar, the presence behind this voice out of the remote past, completes her picture of a bygone intellectual reality.

Philosophically, Hadrian represents a curious mixture of stoic and hedonist, and here again, in the coexistence of a tropism for pleasure and a tropism for duty, one sees the rich flowing together of Greek and Roman traditions. The emperor's hedonism finds its definitive expression in a kind of polymorphous sexuality. Homosexual in the great passion of his life, he moves on the periphery of Roman tolerance, apologist for a relationship the Greeks, in an earlier age, would have viewed as natural. Yet he actually describes himself as bisexual, intimating that only the shallowness of women in second-century Rome has precluded their becoming his lovers more often. The one exceptional woman he has known, Plotina, is unavailable to him as a lover (or so Yourcenar interprets a relationship that Hadrian's enemies viewed as sexual). Nevertheless, he does encounter in her a genteel variety of hedonism, for she "leaned toward Epicurean philosophy, that narrow but clean bed whereon I have sometimes rested my thoughts." If Hadrian inclines toward embracing pleasure more frankly, he does so on reflection and on principle. In his most direct apologia for his life, the emperor rebukes the "so-called wise, who denounce the danger of habit and excess in sensuous delight, instead of fearing its absence or its loss." He replies, too, to the puritans of every age who see early pleasures requited in later sorrows: "My own felicity is in no way responsible for those of my imprudences which shattered it later on; in so far as I have acted in harmony with it I have been wise. I think still that someone wiser than I might well have remained happy till his death." He compares himself, finally, to Alcibiades, "that great artist in pleasure."

If Hadrian tends to speak of his hedonism more often and more directly than of his stoicism, one should remember that he addresses Marcus Aurelius, famous even as a youth for his sobriety and indifference to pleasure. Hadrian offers this earnest young man an eloquent paean to an alternative philosophy. But the attentive reader discovers indications of philosophical balance on the emperor's part. Part of the evidence presents itself in the composition of the imperial circle, for Hadrian keeps about him not only beautiful youths like Antinous, Celer, and Diotimus but also [as Yourcenar notes in her **"Bibliographical Note"** in *Memoirs of Hadrian*] a "circle of Platonist or Stoic philosophers" led by Chabrias. He gives further proof of philosophical duality in his arrangements for the succession. He chooses first Lucius Ceionius, a hedonist, then Antoninus Pius and Marcus Aurelius, a brace of stoics. In fact, he obliges Antoninus to adopt Lucius's son along with Marcus Aurelius, as if to insure the continued presence of a hedonist counterweight in the succession.

The courtliness and civilized discourse of the emperor notwithstanding, one may still resist or despise some of the practices and attitudes for which he apologizes. But all resistance vanishes, at least among readers who value freedom, when Hadrian addresses himself to political questions. Yourcenar makes her narrator the spokesman for a philosophy that anticipates the reasoning of the eighteenth-century architects of political liberty in France, England, and America. Thus one hears echoes of "Life, Liberty, and the Pursuit of Happiness" and *Liberté, Egalité, Fraternité"* when Hadrian introduces his own ringing triad of political desiderata. This triad, however, undergoes a revealing modification in the course of the narrative. Hadrian speaks first of *"Humanitas, Libertas, Felicitas,"* but at the end, having surrendered his own personal happiness and no longer buoyed by pleasant recollections, he speaks of *"humanity, liberty, and justice."* The substitution of *iustitia* for *felicitas* hints at a revision dictated by

sobering experience, a transition from the hedonism of youth to the stoicism of age. Humanity and liberty, on the other hand, he embraces with lifelong consistency, though fully aware of the faults of the one and the dangers of the other.

Hadrian's regard for liberty begins with his own sense of freedom and its value—a sense he calls the "one thing" that makes him "superior to most men":

> [Others] fail to recognize their due liberty, and likewise their true servitude. They curse their fetters, but seem sometimes to find them matter for pride. Yet they pass their days in vain license, and do not know how to fashion for themselves the lightest yoke. For my part I have sought liberty more than power, and power only because it can lead to freedom. What interested me was not a philosophy of the free man (all who try that have proved tiresome), but a technique: I hoped to discover the hinge where our will meets and moves with destiny, and where discipline strengthens, instead of restraining, our nature.

Observations like these reveal a man who knows how "to command, and what is perhaps in the end slightly less futile, to serve." They express, according to Michel Aubrion [in "Marguerite Yourcenar *ou la mesure de l'homme"* in the January 1970 issue of *La Revue Générale*], "the whole doctrine of classicism" and provide "the key to the character and to the novel, the key, too, to the entire *oeuvre* of Marguerite Yourcenar, to her philosophy and to her aesthetic."

In *Memoirs of Hadrian,* then, the reader experiences the way it was in the Roman Empire of the second century. Yourcenar depicts Rome's pleasures, political intrigues, and wars. Most of all she depicts, in the representative and empathic mind of her narrator, Rome's mental life, and she achieves psychological mimesis of a very high order. In the act of reconstruction, according to Hadrian, one collaborates with time gone by to uncover the secret of the springs. Yourcenar reconstructs a rich classical world to uncover a spring, a source of ideas and values, that flows around many obstacles into all subsequent Western culture. In **"Reflections on the Composition of *Memoirs of Hadrian,"*** she describes setting out to "do, from within, the same work of reconstruction which the nineteenth-century archaeologists have done from without," and surely Clio smiles on the result, a book in which history and fiction blend with pathos and grace.

John Taylor   (review date 2-8 February 1990)

SOURCE: "First Person Third," in *The Times Literary Supplement,* No. 4531, February 2-8, 1990, p. 108.

[*In the following review of the final volume of Yourcenar's autobiography,* Quoi? L'éternité, *and the essay collection* En pèlerin et étranger, *Taylor criticizes Yourcenar for the pretentious tone of the former—which he finds lacking in autobiographical detail—and for the uneven quality of the essays collected in the latter.*]

When Marguerite Yourcenar died on December 17, 1987, she had almost finished *Quoi? L'Eternité,* the final volume of her autobiographical trilogy. The book had been impatiently awaited, for in the first two volumes the autobiographer, as a "character", especially as an adult character, is remarkably absent. *Souvenirs pieux* (1974) deals mainly with the maternal side of the author's family, and *Archives du Nord* (1977) concerns itself with paternal ancestors and the life of her father, Michel de Crayencour. Yourcenar had revealed that in the third volume she would evoke her own life, from her birth in 1903 until the outbreak of the First World War or perhaps even the declaration of the Second; she would write until, as she put it melodramatically, "the pen fell from [her] hands". She never intended, however, to write about the nearly fifty years—roughly two-thirds of her lifetime—during which she lived in the United States and wrote all her major works.

Quoi? L'Eternité disappoints in many ways. First, Yourcenar barely keeps her promise about examining her own life. Though she provides glimpses of herself as a child, the book once again focuses on her father. (According to Yvon Bernier, who edited the volume, Yourcenar intended to write approximately fifty more pages; presumably she would have described her father's death, then her travels in Austria, Italy and Greece just before the Second World War.) The interest of Yourcenar's family, as this third volume reveals, has its limits; and it is a strange autobiography indeed which, after three volumes, tells us almost nothing about the author's adult life.

Yourcenar would also, presumably, have completed the already engaging portrait of Jeanne de Reval. A close friend of Yourcenar's mother, Fernande de Reval (the name is fictitious), was a maternal figure to Marguerite and a mistress to Michel Crayencour during a part of the author's childhood. (Fernande died a few days after Marguerite's birth, as readers of a compelling passage of *Souvenirs pieux* will remember.) Though the best pages of *Quoi? L'Eternité* depict Michel and Jeanne's tormented relationship, the many other passages about Michel add little to the fine portrait already drawn in the preceding volumes.

Suspense and drama appear only in the final chapter, in which Egon, Jeanne's husband and a composer of avantgarde music, returns to his native Latvia and is caught up in the Russian Revolution. Yourcenar always portrays such intellectuals brilliantly, setting them squarely amid the political and philosophical upheavals of their times.

The fundamental disappointment of *Quoi? L'Eternité,* however, comes not from our speculations as to what Yourcenar might have written, had she lived longer; and not from our frustrated curiosity about her personal feelings or private life. Instead, it lies in the gap between the admirable philosophy underlying her innovative project and the pretentious tone that so often vitiates it. Behind the claims of self-effacement (presented with Buddhist overtones) is a moralizing, condescending narrator who uses an authorial "je" to judge others, otherwise referring to herself as "elle" or "l'enfant" or "l'enfant du Mont Noir", terms reminiscent of Goethe's overbearing "der Knabe" in *Dichtung und Wahrheit*. Her portraits of others are perceptive, but often lack tenderness or pity (except for

those of Jeanne and her father). Her rare self-portraits lack irony, and sometimes their earnestness rings false, as when Yourcenar declares: "Il y avait en moi, venu de je ne sais où, un besoin inné, non seulement de m'instruire, mais de m'améliorer, un souci passionné d'être chaque jour un peu meilleure qu'hier." Time and again she reminds her reader that she has conscientiously employed family archives—or memories of conversations with her father and other relatives—to "reconstruct" events which took place years, decades, even centuries before her birth; or while she was too young to understand what was happening or being said. At best, extraneous explanations temporarily interrupt the narrative; at worst, academic fastidiousness spoils entire passages. Elsewhere she proclaims her political opinions with the artlessness of a mere militant for ecological causes.

En pèlerin et en étranger, her posthumous collection of essays, articles and occasional pieces, is equally disappointing. The scope of Yourcenar's interests, however, as in her earlier (and superior) collections, *Sous bénéfice d'inventaire* (1978) and *Le Temps, ce grand sculpteur* (1983), is impressively displayed. Twenty-six miscellaneous texts range from a somewhat pedestrian article on Oscar Wilde, written in 1929 and (as with many other articles here) "touched up" at a much later date, to a magisterial lecture on Borges given at Harvard in 1987. There is a gentle remembrance of Virginia Woolf, whom the author met while working on her translation of *The Waves*. There are also several *inédits;* particularly enlightening is an unpublished text on that French painter whom the non-French find so difficult to admire: Poussin. Some passages in the **"Carnets de notes 1942-1948"** are memorable, such as one concluding with the wish that "ce voyage dans le temps aboutisse à l'extrême bord de l'éternel". Conceived as an exercise in the apprehension of time, her best historical fiction does seem to bring eternity within our grasp. Such, no doubt, was also her intention in *Quoi? L'Eternité* (its title taken from Rimbaud: "Elle est retrouvée! / Quoi? l'éternité. / C'est la mer mêlée / Au soleil . . . ".) Yet most of the articles in this collection, while soundly researched and carefully written, represent honest journalistic work rather than original contributions. Running through some of them is the self-congratulatory tone of the *écrivain académique* Yourcenar sometimes could be, instead of the thoroughly convincing stylist of the historical novels—of *Mémoires d'Hadrien,* of *L'Oeuvre au noir* and *Anna, soror.* As in *Quoi? L'Eternité,* these occasional pieces come alive only when the author is truly absent, when Marguerite Yourcenar forgets that she is Marguerite Yourcenar.

Elaine Marks   (essay date Spring 1990)

SOURCE: " 'Getting Away with Murd(h)er': Author's Preface and Narrator's Text, Reading Marguerite Yourcenar's *Coup de Grâce* 'After Auschwitz,' " in *The Journal of Narrative Technique,* Vol. 20, No. 2, Spring, 1990, pp. 210-20.

[*Marks is an American educator and critic who has written extensively on French literature, focusing mainly on the works of Colette and Simone de Beauvoir. In the following essay, she analyzes the relationship between the novel* Coup de Grâce, *written in 1938, and the preface Yourcenar added to it in 1962. Marks argues that the novel harbors anti-Semitic sentiments and that the preface was designed to make the reader believe they do not reflect Yourcenar's actual feelings.*]

Since the early summer of 1987 the focus of my research has shifted. It began, as one might imagine, with a book, Bram Dijkstra's *Idols of Perversity: Fantasies of Feminine Evil in Fin de Siècle Culture,* and the intersection of this book with two essays that I was writing. One of the essays was on the Anglo-American lesbian poet Renée Vivien, who wrote in French in the early years of the twentieth century, the other on Jean Larnac's study of French women writers from Marie de France to Colette. *Idols of Perversity* and my essays dealt with the effects of late-nineteenth-century antisemitic, nationalist, racist and sexist discourses on the question of "littérature féminine" and the ways in which these discourses, and the theories and ideology that nourish them, continue today. But it is the phrase "the early summer of 1987" that is the key to explaining the shift. That was the summer of the trial of Klaus Barbie in Lyon, and the summer of the first two issues of the journal *Annales d'Histoire révisionniste,* whose articles affirmed what a few French, North American and Swiss historians have been claiming since the late 1970s, namely that the systematic destruction of European Jews in the Nazi death camps had not taken place. It occurred to me that much of French writing "after Auschwitz" (and this simple two-word phrase has, since its initial coinage by Adorno in 1955, its own fascinating development) was obsessed with the death camps, with the complicity of the Vichy régime in the extermination of 78,000 Jews deported from France, although this had not as yet, except in the most obvious cases, been adequately analyzed. It now seems to me important not only to locate and identify sexist and antisemitic discourses in French literature and culture, but also to uncover and to contextualize the presence of this obsession, which recalls the obsession with the guillotine in nineteenth-century French texts. Thus I am involved in reading again, but from a different perspective, a certain number of narrative texts with which I have long been familiar. And "after Auschwitz" does not apply exclusively to cultural production since the end of World War II. It applies as well to texts written at any moment in the long history of French writing, texts that are today being read in the knowledge of "Auschwitz" by readers whose interpretive universe has been permanently changed by "Auschwitz" as event and as metaphor.

The reading I would like to propose involves a short novel, *Coup de Grâce,* published in 1939, and a preface to this novel, published twenty-three years later in 1962. Both *Coup de Grâce* and its preface were written by Marguerite Yourcenar, the pseudonymous anagram of Marguerite de Crayencour, the first woman to be elected to the French Academy since its creation three hundred forty-five years ago. Not all of the questions that prompted my investigation receive primary attention in this essay, but I include them because they have directed my thinking: Why did Marguerite Yourcenar find it imperative to write the 1962

> **It may seem strange that in 1938, when Nazi Germany was already actively persecuting Jews and antisemitic tracts were being published regularly in Germany and in France, Marguerite Yourcenar should have chosen to write a story in which antisemitism is allowable because it is professed by European aristocrats.**
>
> **—Elaine Marks**

preface and to insist on its being read as part of *Coup de Grâce?* How does the author, in the preface, blatantly manipulate the reader? What are the connections between antisemitism, racism, classism, and sexism in the preface? What kind of political agenda does the preface propose and refuse? How are these connections maintained and reinforced in the narrative? How do they work together through the selection and ordering of events, metaphors, and metonymies, as well as the narrator's first person discourse, to destroy the female protagonist by shooting her twice, the first time in the face? How can psychoanalytic and deconstructionist concepts such as the "repression of the feminine" help us to read together the silence surrounding the male narrator's homosexuality and the narrator's aversion for the mother figure and for Jews? What shall we do with the author's intentions and with her affirmations about nobles and nobility, about the "natural" antisemitism of her Baltic-Prussian-French aristocratic protagonist, and her generalizations about the behavior of women in love? How does the preface affect our reading of the narrative it now precedes? What are the connections between the "I" in the preface and the "I" in the narrative; between the ideology that permeates both preface and *récit?* More seriously, do the so-called "realistic" conventions of narrative inevitably reproduce stereotypes and clichés as has been claimed by leading contemporary literary and cultural theorists? What are the political and social consequences of rejecting these conventions? And finally, how might we read this first person narrative, written by a woman and narrated by an aristocratic male homosexual "after Auschwitz"? My reading will explore three levels of interpretation with which we are familiar in literary studies: the intentions of the writer-author; the ideology, or the non-conscious presuppositions that inform the text; and the unconscious of the text which we will look for in the signifiers of *Coup de Grâce,* primarily in the title. These signifiers, more than the overt references to Eric von Lhomond's antisemitism, will lead us linguistically and textually to some of the connections between sexism, antisemitism, and nationalism with which I began my inquiry.

In the introduction to his book *Legacies of Antisemitism,* Jeffrey Mehlman writes: "These pages, then, are exploratory rather than accusatory." I am aware that when dealing with questions of such a delicate and powerful nature it is almost impossible to maintain a non-judgmental tone. Although I would rather accuse the text of reproducing an antisemitic ideology than the author of being antisemitic, it is impossible, as my analysis will show, not to implicate the author and not to hold her responsible. May I remind the readers in the most general way of what was happening in Europe in 1938, the fifth year of Hitler's Third Reich, and the year Marguerite Yourcenar wrote her novel? And may I insist more precisely on books that were published in France between 1937 and 1939 in which antisemitism held the center of the page, both reflecting and reinforcing its importance in France? Two of the most significant books published during this period include Céline's violent polemic against the Jewish peril, *Bagatelles pour un massacre,* 1937, and Sartre's *récit,* "L'Enfance d'un chef," 1939, which locates antisemitism within a prefascist, nationalist, aesthetic sensibility.

In the Pléiade edition of her collected prose fiction, which she edited herself, Marguerite Yourcenar insists that the preface to *Coup de Grâce* must accompany and precede the narrative. The eight page preface, in the American edition published by Farrar, Straus and Giroux, and translated by Marguerite Yourcenar's companion, "compagne de vie" since 1937, Grace Frick, is a curious document. It is as if the author had wanted to present as unquestionable truths the following points: that this short novel must be read as a human and not a political document; that the protagonist is neither a sadist nor an antisemite; that this narrative belongs within the double tradition of seventeenth-century French tragedy and the Russian and French first person *récit.* Corneille is mentioned and his insistence on the importance of the unity of peril, as is Racine and his preface to *Bajazet;* Tolstoy's *Kreutzer Sonata* is mentioned as well as Gide's *L'Immoraliste.* Marguerite Yourcenar does not make the connection, however, between the protagonists in these two *récits* who kill their wives, and Eric von Lhomond who shoots Sophie de Reval. The preface justifies and defends *Coup de Grâce* in terms of the "authenticity" of the documentation (Racine does the same in the opening sentences of the preface to *Bajazet*), and because it places the narrative within the most prestigious literary traditions. Readers are called upon to read with care and to rectify the inevitable deformation in a first person narrative. Readers are invited to be sympathetic towards the "moral nobility" of the three protagonists. Readers are also expected to consent to generalizations in the author's preface about the behavior of women in love and the behavior of men involved in "chivalric dreams of comradeship."

In my efforts to locate as many as possible of the reviews that followed the publication of *Coup de Grâce* in France, Great Britain and the United States I have not found more than one or two reviews that accuse the writer of antisemitism. [In an endnote, Marks adds: "The English translation omits at least one reference to Jews that exists in the French version, suggesting that the author and the translator were conscious of possible reader reactions in the United States. . . ."] Nevertheless, it is clearly as a response to such a charge that the preface was written. And the charge is answered, by the author, in terms of fidelity to reality and the conventions of verisimilitude. Antisemitism, she maintains in the preface, is a natural phenomenon; it is endemic to certain geographical areas and certain social groups. This is why Eric von Lhomond's narrative contains so many of the stereotypes and clichés that have developed since the Middle Ages to depict Jews: they are usurers, jewellers, furriers; omnivorous readers; obese and ugly; revolutionary and pusillanimous.

Eric von Lhomond, according to Marguerite Yourcenar's logic in the preface, is in no way responsible for his antisemitic references and allusions any more than he is responsible for the murder of Sophie de Reval. He is not presented as following orders, but rather as reproducing the language inherited from his ethnic and class positions. These forms are, in her scheme, both internalized and irrelevant. They are no more than local color, divorced from the central dramas of *Coup de Grâce,* which are the difficulty of narrating the past and the tragic implications of a particular amorous triangular configuration. Clearly the author is annoyed that her 1939 narrative has been misinterpreted by some readers who have made connections—unintended by the author—between the protagonist's attitudes towards his narrative, towards the past, towards women and towards Jews. She seems to suggest in the preface that what was intended as marginal description should never have become a center of critical attention.

Marguerite Yourcenar's uneasiness is revealed throughout the preface by omissions and silences about the killing of women by their husbands and lovers; by her refusal, or inability, to understand antisemitism as anything other than a class or cultural prejudice; by her resistance to making certain obvious connections between the pieces of her own narrative.

The preface to *Coup de Grâce* is followed by a brief, two and a half page, third person narrative that sets the stage for the first person *récit.* These pages give the reader abundant information: a wounded aristocratic mercenary has been fighting most recently for Franco; because of "birth and inclination," he has fought during the past fifteen years for right-wing causes in which he did not believe in Central Europe, China, South America, and Latvia; he now tells his story, in the words of the text his "interminable confession," to two comrades while waiting for a train to Germany at the station buffet in Pisa. If the mercenary's "fractured and bandaged foot" suggests Oedipus and his complex, the presence of the Leaning Tower and of "an old beggar of a coachman blind in one eye" further suggests confusions of sexual identity that reinforce the confusions of national identity and contribute to the reader's sense of a tottering phallocentric Europe. The third person narrator sustains these ambiguities by refusing to qualify Eric as belonging either to the group of "men of feeling" or to the group of "criminals." Eric von Lhomond is presented as a victim of circumstance, subject to determinants he cannot control. He will later present himself in similar fashion.

Eric von Lhomond's first person narrative, like the first person author's preface, is an ordering and a justification of events that took place fifteen years earlier, during the civil war that followed the Russian Revolution of 1917. In this section of the essay, I will focus on the representation of women and of the feminine with particular emphasis on the figure of the mother and the death (murder) of the main female character, Sophie de Reval. Four passages are central to my reading. The first is the presentation of Eric von Lhomond's mother, sandwiched between the description of the death of his father at Verdun, fighting for the Germans and killed, ironically, by an "African soldier fighting for France" and the description of his beloved friend Conrad, "a fixed point, a center a heart." "As for my mother, she was half lost in dreams; she passed her time reading Buddhist scripture, or the poems of Rabindranath Tagore." The second passage is the presentation of Sophie de Reval, Conrad's sister, which follows a four page description of Eric's adolescent paradise, a golden age spent in the company of Conrad de Reval: "As for the young girl, she did not count; she was careless about her attire, and did nothing but devour books lent to her by a young Jewish student at Riga; she had no use for boys."

Both the narrator's mother and Sophie are associated with books and their evil effects. The mother is "lost in dreams" and in another, foreign culture: Conrad's sister is initially coupled with "a young Jewish student," an equally foreign and dangerous influence. The verb "devour" will accompany Sophie throughout the text as an indication of the danger that the "feminine" poses for Eric.

The third passage describes a screen memory that overwhelms Eric von Lhomond during a nocturnal bombardment when Sophie, who, he tells us, is desperately in love with him, falls into his arms and he kisses her:

> Most amazing of all, I accepted this gesture which she had taken nearly ten weeks to bring herself to. Now that she is dead, and that I have ceased to believe in miracles, I am glad that I kissed her lips one time at least, and her wild hair. If she were to remain like a vast country subdued by me but never possessed, I was to remember, in any case, the exact taste of her mouth that night, and the warmth of her living flesh. And if ever I could have loved Sophie utterly and simply with body and soul it was surely at that moment when we both were innocent as beings just resurrected. She was fairly throbbing against me, and no previous feminine encounter, whether with a chance pick-up, or with an avowed prostitute, had prepared me for that sudden, terrifying sweetness. Her body so yielding, yet rigid with delight, weighed in my arms almost as mysteriously as earth itself would have done had I entered some few hours before into death. I hardly know at what moment ecstasy changed into horror, releasing in me the memory of that starfish [*étoile de mer* in French] that Mother once forced into my hand on the beach at Scheveningen, almost provoking convulsions in me, to the consternation of the bathers. I wrenched myself from Sophie with a violence that must have seemed cruel to a body robbed of defence by felicity itself. She re-opened her eyes (they had closed) and read in my aspect something harder to bear, doubtless, than hatred or terror, for she recoiled, covering her face with her upraised arm, like a child who is slapped, and that was the last time I ever saw her actually cry.

I would like to insist on the bringing together, through the starfish, of Sophie and the narrator's mother, on the contamination of the one by the other, and on the way in which Eric's discourse blames the mother for his reactions of revulsion: "that starfish [*étoile de mer*] that Mother once forced into my hand." Without belaboring the obvious castration anxiety, and the fear of being devoured as well as penetrated by the maternal figure, I would like to note that the *étoile de mer* is connected through the text to a group of menacing marine animals whose effect is to terrify and repulse Eric von Lhomond: the octopus-like white gloved hands of a prostitute in Riga; the medusa-like head of Sophie when she has curlers in her hair. More importantly still this scene is connected to a later scene in the novel when Eric, in search of Sophie, visits the home of Mother Loew, the Jewish dressmaker and midwife, in the small Jewish community in Lilienkron. Eric describes Mother Loew as an "old creature fairly drowned in her own fat," her "revolting obsequiousness blended . . . with truly Biblical hospitality." Eric tells us that the "old Jewess" is killed by soldiers a few weeks later, thereby placing her in the series of mutilated and tortured victims beginning with a description of the "Chinese Hand" (a special form of torture for white gloved officers) and ending with the shooting of Sophie.

The fourth passage constitutes the two final paragraphs of *Coup de Grâce.* Sophie has joined a group of Bolshevik militants both out of political conviction and because she had been told that her brother Conrad and Eric were lovers. When the group to which she belongs is captured, Sophie refuses to ask for mercy and will be shot along with the others. She asks to be shot by Eric:

> One step more brought me so close to Sophie that I could almost have kissed her bared throat or laid a hand on her shoulder, now visibly shuddering, but by this time she was partly turned from me. She was breathing only slightly too fast; I clung to the thought that I had wanted to put an end to Conrad, and that this was the same thing. I fired, turning my head away like a frightened child setting off a torpedo on Christmas Eve. The first shot did no more than tear open the face, so that I shall never know (and it haunts me still) what expression Sophie would have had in death. On the second shot everything was over.
>
> At first I thought that in asking me to perform this duty she had intended to give me a final proof of her love, the most conclusive proof of all. But I understood afterwards that she only wished to take revenge, leaving me prey to remorse. She was right in that: I do feel remorse at times. One is always trapped, somehow, in dealings with women.

The words "remorse"—etymologically: to bite again— and "trapped" relate this final passage to the screen memory of the starfish [*étoile de mer*] at the beach at Scheveningen and Sophie to the narrator's mother and to Mother Loew. Or, we might say the same thing in another way: to kill Sophie is also to kill the mothers. Sophie, as a spectacle, is disappointing in much the same way as the phallic mother disappoints. With her face half blown away there is nothing to see and to know (*à voir/savoir* in French). And Eric, a victim of his mother's gesture in the earlier passage is, here again, a victim, "trapped" in Sophie's desire that he be her executioner.

Eric in his narrative and Marguerite Yourcenar in her preface almost succeed in attempting to close off to the reader paths of resistance to their discourse. They almost succeed in convincing us that to judge acts accomplished in a fiction is impossible, that time, memory and the complexities of language contribute to the formation of a linguistic barrier that stands between the readers and the possibility of condemnation or praise. The non-conscious presupposition that structures *Coup de Grâce* is that the readers can never know what really happened in the confusions of a civil war, "the Baltic imbroglio," and between Eric, Sophie and Conrad. Eric von Lhomond appears as a precursor of the revisionist historians who claim that the *Shoah*—the destruction of European Jewry—never took place, that no one can ever know what really happened in the concentration camps. Two articles that appeared in February, 1989, in *The New York Times,* one in the book review section, the other on the editorial page, reiterate my point. In a review of Charles S. Meier's *The Unmasterable Past: History, Holocaust and German National Identity,* Richard J. Evans writes:

> His [Mr. Meier's] concluding comments on the relation of the debate to the emergence of postmodernist historiography—in which more attention is paid to what people (including Hitler) thought and felt than to what they actually did—should be pondered by everyone who is thinking of jumping onto this particular contemporary intellectual bandwagon. (February 12, 1989)

And John G. McGarrahan, in an editorial whose title coincides with my own "Getting Away with Murder," writes about three cases in which "the brutal killing of a young girl by a sane, strong and rational man was found to be a not very serious crime. . . . The theme of these defenses is that it's the killer's state of mind that should determine his guilt or innocence, not his actions" (February 12, 1989).

By defending Eric von Lhomond in her 1962 preface, Marguerite Yourcenar is obliged to insist on her initial intentions and thereby to diminish the power of her narrative, the power of ideology, and the power of the reader. Her persistent denials accentuate Eric's denials and aggravate his responsibility for the killing of Sophie. Denials of the extermination of European Jews have included, among other specious arguments, one that insists on Hitler's intentions not to annihilate Jews, another that focuses on the impossibility of establishing that an event took place when there is no one who witnessed the event, and still another that attributes the fiction of the *Shoah* to Zionist propaganda. These denials continue to be made in the face of considerable and varied evidence. What allows me to connect Marguerite Yourcenar and Eric von Lhomond with the revisionist historians, in spite of the obvious differences between historical events and a fictional text, is the vehemence of the denials of judeophobia and the massive silencing of Jewish suffering.

There is, however, a dimension of the text beyond the author's intentions and the writer's non-conscious presuppositions. The unconscious of the text may help the readers to work against the weight of the authorial presence and against her implicit claims. If Marguerite Yourcenar and Eric von Lhomond both insist that they are outside ideology, the text of *Coup de Grâce* reveals that they are not. And here I am obliged to move between the French and the English versions.

The title, unchanged in translation except for the initial masculine article *Le* in the French, is a French expression, also used in English, to denote a finishing blow often performed as a deliverance to a dying person or animal. Usually a *coup de grâce* is seen as a noble gesture. Within this text, however, the signifiers *coup* and *grâce* directly relate to the body of the old Jewess, Mother Loew, whose face is described, in French as "le visage de la vieille créature noyée dans la graisse . . ." (an old creature fairly drowned in her own fat . . .). *Graisse* (fat or grease) is the noun corresponding to the adjectives *gras,* masculine, and *grasse,* feminine, for fatty or greasy. And *cou* (neck) in French is a homophone for *coup* (blow). *Cou de grasse* (neck of fat woman), through the connection with Mother Loew, becomes the repulsive, excessive flesh of women, mothers, and Jews that Eric annihilates. *Le Coup de Grâce* of the French title can, in consequence, also be read as a sadistic, sexist, and antisemitic act involving both matricide and genocide. [In an endnote, Marks adds: "I would not eliminate the possibility of reading the title as *Cou de Grâce,* 'The Neck of Grace,' Marguerite Yourcenar's companion and translator, Grace Frick. I would also like to acknowledge a suggestion made by my colleague Professor Martine Debaisieux who, having read the paper, made a connection between the sounds of the title and *Coude de Grâce* (Elbow of Grace). This connection is particularly interesting because the funny bone in French is sometimes referred to as *le petit juif* (the little Jew)."] In her prefatory attempts to get Eric von Lhomond off the hook, and in Eric von Lhomond's self-justifying discourse, the author, writer and narrator may all be read as almost "getting away with murd(h)er."

Having worked through the author's intentions, the non-conscious presuppositions, and the unconscious of the text, I would like to return to my introductory remarks and to draw some firm conclusions and some tentative observations. It would seem inevitable that between the author's stated intentions, and a reader's analysis of non-conscious presuppositions and of the unconscious of the text, there will be serious contradictions. Indeed, this reaffirms those truisms of contemporary criticism that insist on the "blindness and the insight" involved in all acts of reading, including the ones I have just performed. It would also seem inevitable that the conventions of realism as applied to the writing of fiction, in which I include Marguerite Yourcenar's claim about the "authenticity" of her *récit,* will result in the reproduction of a certain number of stereotypes. It is particularly difficult to avoid stereotyping and caricature in the representation of Jews. The signs of Jewishness with which most readers are familiar partake of the grotesque and the ugly. Without these signs Jews would not necessarily be recognizable. A possible solution, then, is to avoid the conventions of realism and to work against the dominant ideology by refusing representation. Another firm conclusion is that, in French literature at least, the juxtaposition of aristocrat and Jew is bound to lead to the opposition aristocrat and Jew, which may well be the basis for the more common opposition between being French and being Jewish so fundamental to the question of French identity. In this respect it might be suggested that Marguerite Yourcenar's *récit* depends on the binary opposition Aryan and Semite which structures so much of the antisemitic and racist discourse in France from the middle of the nineteenth century until today. Still another firm conclusion concerns the connections between antisemitism and sexism, between ideology and the representation of Jews and women both in fiction and in discourse. Within French culture, for example, the figures of "La France" and "Le Juif" provide an intriguing clue to the complex functioning of this odd couple. Because "Le Juif" is frequently portrayed as obese, with a bulbous nose and blubber lips, sexually perverse, effeminate and cowardly, radically other, there are resemblances between "le Juif" and the feminine. And because "La France" is frequently portrayed as tall, erect, brandishing a flag, leading the troops, there are, despite her often exposed breasts, resemblances between "La France" and the masculine.

More tentative observations concern the repression of the feminine in Eric von Lhomond, both his difficulty as narrator and the difficulty of the author as narrator, to acknowledge his homosexual inclinations. Eric's infatuation with Sophie's brother, Conrad, his fixation on his adolescence with Conrad as the golden age, the utopian moment that can never return, confirm an ideological position that views the present as decadent and the future as empty. It is as if this repression of the feminine within Eric were responsible both for his attitude toward the Jewish Loew family and for the shooting of Sophie. I would not venture, at this moment, even a tentative conclusion about the possible significance of this repression in the body of Marguerite Yourcenar's texts.

To conclude, my last tentative observation touches on what I referred to earlier in the essay as an obsession with the extermination camps, their explicit repression and the ways in which they are present, implicitly, through their absence. These remarks do not bear on the narrative of *Coup de Grâce,* which was published in 1939, but they do concern the preface of 1962. I would suggest that the author-narrator's refusal to acknowledge the presence of antisemitism in her text, thereby reaffirming through her resistance the antisemitic discourse in the preface, may be linked to the knowledge and the repression of the knowledge of "Auschwitz." It may seem as strange to other readers as it does to me, that in 1938, when Nazi Germany was already actively persecuting Jews and antisemitic tracts were being published regularly in Germany and in France, Marguerite Yourcenar should have chosen to write a story in which antisemitism is allowable because it is professed by European aristocrats. And that in 1962, when so much was known about what had happened to European Jews under National Socialism, the preface would castigate the "naïve reader" who "might make a sadist of Eric" and "would mistake for a professional anti-

Semite this aristocrat whose habitual irony towards Jews is a matter of caste . . ." I submit that denying the importance of antisemitic discourse and its effects, and denying "Auschwitz," are inextricably related. I submit, too, that the relationship between author-narrator and narrator-character, between Marguerite Yourcenar and Eric von Lhomond, is closer than contemporary narratological theory would have us believe.

Harold Beaver   (review date 1 March 1992)

SOURCE: "Remembering a World She Never Knew," in *The New York Times Book Review,* March 1, 1992, p. 13.

[*In the following review of* Dear Departed, *Beaver praises Yourcenar's imaginative evocation of her mother's and father's families, describing the book as "a key to the genetic sources from which [her] consciousness derived."*]

Marguerite Yourcenar never wrote an autobiography. What she had completed by the time of her death in 1987 at the age of 84 was a *Tristram Shandy*-like saga that opens on the day of her birth and then moves resolutely backward to embrace both her father's and her mother's families in three memorial volumes: *Souvenirs Pieux, Archives du Nord* and *Quoi? L'Eternité. Dear Departed* is a smooth English translation of *Souvenirs Pieux* (1974), devoted to her Belgian ancestry on her mother's side.

Instead of a self-portrait tracing the growth of her own consciousness, then, Yourcenar has supplied a key to the genetic sources from which that consciousness derived, while simultaneously allowing that consciousness (in all its adult wisdom) full play as the imaginative mediator of her text. An intimacy, intermittently acknowledged, therefore emerges, though she is at pains to hold it at arm's length. "Mildly curious" (*"avec curiosité"*), she admits to having set about collating the bric-a-brac of memoirs, letters, engravings, diaries, photographs, "to see what the completed puzzle will reveal." But she noted on an early draft of this translation (whose English title she chose): "It is *very important* that the reader *not* get the impression that the author is greatly or personally interested about her origins, since the whole quest is more sociological and historical than personal."

This can be taken with a pinch of salt. The quest clearly took on its own momentum. Born of a cross-border marriage between the Belgian and French nobility, Yourcenar was the child of a region stretching from Lille to Liège that defies modern borders simply as Flanders. But neglecting that ancient culture of Roman Catholic pieties and satanic mills, Yourcenar opted firmly for the aristocratic patrimony of her French father, Michel de Crayencour (whose name, approximately anagrammatized, she was to make world-famous with the publication of her *Memoirs of Hadrian*). For she was doubly exiled, by the loss of her mother at birth and by her loss of Belgium at around the age of 6. At the age of 12 she also had to flee France for England with her father to escape the German invasion, and she never permanently settled in Flanders again after 1918. When at last she returned for a visit in 1929, her whole Flemish past had become "merely a legend" to her. She paid a second, sustained visit to seek out her family and family estates in 1959. By that time she had further exiled herself to America, to an island off Maine.

This insistence on the impersonal, far from imparting a marmoreal coldness to the project, infuses her book with an unexpected warmth. These memories are only ironically "pious memories" in the French sense of mourning cards, inscribed with prayers, to be inserted between the pages of a missal. For here the secret sharer is her father, who alone guided her youthful years and from whom she gleaned the anecdotes and details that sustain her narrative. The warmth derives precisely from her need to fill out the magical structure of her father's memory by recovering traces of her mother's past. That task drew on all the accumulated craft of her years as a novelist. A sense of bourgeois life in the small castles of southern Belgium, at a time of rapid industrialization, is superbly conveyed. The long opening section, on the exact circumstances of her birth in Brussels in 1903, is a tour de force—detail by detail, motive for motive—of reconstruction. **Dear Departed** is not so very different, in essence, from **Memoirs of Hadrian.**

Anyone who has ever tried to sort out boxes of family effects will be astounded at what Yourcenar has achieved. For she reoccupies the past, as it were, nourishing it with her own substance to bring it alive once again. "Let us try to conjure up that house as it must have been between 1856 and 1873," she writes, and the whole Catholic household, from its newspapers to its crucifixes, is conjured up. The art is Proustian (to name one of her own literary heroes) in the intensity of this imaginative quest for a world she never knew, whose "true gods" are brilliantly summed up:

> Plutus, prince of strongboxes; the god Terminus, lord of the cadastre, who takes care of boundaries; the rigid Priapus, secret god of brides, legitimately erect in the exercise of his functions; the good Lucina, who reigns over birthing chambers; and finally, pushed as far away as possible but ever-present at family funerals and devolutions of inheritance, Libitina, goddess of burials, who concludes the procession.

The joint potency of Lucina and Libitina is certainly a haunting presence here. As her 31-year-old mother had died of puerperal fever days after her birth, so her grandmother had died a year after her mother's birth ("perhaps caused by yet another, fatal pregnancy"), and her great-grandmother had died in labor in her 21st year. Yourcenar herself remained unmarried.

Like a ghost revisiting the scenes of all those tragic childbirths, she evokes the Victorian bedroom:

> The bedroom in the 19th century is the Cave of Mysteries. At night, the wax of the candles and the oil of the lamps illuminate it with their flames, which waver and flicker like life itself and which are no more successful in reaching the shadowy recesses of the room than are the glimmers of our mind in elucidating all that is unknown and unexplained. Windowpanes hung with tulle and draped with velvet allow the light of day to enter only sparingly, and the breezes and scents of evening not at all. . . . Human

> fragments—baby teeth set into finger rings, bits of hair in lockets—pass the night in dresser-top trays. . . . The well-tucked-in bed has known the blood of deflowerings and births and the sweat of death agonies, for the fashion of going on honeymoon trips is of recent vintage and that of entering a hospital or clinic to be born or to die has yet to take hold. It is not surprising that the heavily charged atmosphere of this room should be favorable to ghosts.

There are *longueurs* in this family chronicle of provincial life, but the imaginative set pieces (her grandmother Mathilde slipping out of bed to attend Mass at the village church, or her "uncle" Octave paying a deathbed visit to an old relative) constantly enliven it. The weakest link is possibly the third section, devoted to Octave Pirmez (a minor but influential Belgian essayist) and his revolutionary brother Fernand (nicknamed Rémo). No doubt Yourcenar was thrilled to discover and re-create a literary ancestry in a family resolutely opposed to any hint of artistic, religious or political subversion. Here too is sounded a theme familiar from the rest of her *oeuvre:* that of a mysterious, veiled sexuality. For Octave was clearly what we would today call a "closet homosexual," whose youthful repressed longing for Walloon boys as they fished half-naked filled him (in his own words) with "the same emotions that the Parthenon frieze would later inspire."

This urge to turn a Belgian estate into a version of Virgilian pastoral is subtly revealed; Yourcenar's portrait of the rural eccentric as mother's boy and aristocratic Orpheus, wandering at dusk into the woods with his Guarneri violin, strikes one as authentic precisely because Pirmez so lacked the passionate or intellectual verve of exotic characters like the extravagant creator of Fonthill Abbey and author of "Vathek," William Beckford, or the even more extravagant creator of Gothic fantasies, King Ludwig II of Bavaria. The English countryside too abounded with such gloomy Victorian bachelors, high on Theocritus and the ideal of two minds uniting "in a kind of virile marriage." It needed all Yourcenar's skill to bring off a sketch of someone whose outer demeanor—and writing—verge on quite such pompous dullness.

The theme of a homosexual liaison again briefly emerges in the final section, at a boarding school run by nuns in Brussels, this time between Yourcenar's mother and a young Dutch baroness in the 1880's. It amounted to no more than a startling decline of her mother's grades and her eventual removal home. Yet for all its fine scenes from a corner of Europe more renowned for its coal mines and war graves, this first volume of her ancestral trilogy will leave Yourcenar's readers restive because she never deals with her own homosexual life. But her life, spanning the Atlantic from the Académie Française (whose first female immortal she became) to Mount Desert Island in Maine, must have seemed all too perspicuous to her. Her art flourished best in the imaginative penetration of secret places. In this final quest for an absent mother, and a largely destroyed or ruined motherland, that art was triumphantly vindicated.

Joan E. Howard (essay date 1992)

SOURCE: "Rise and Fall of an Emperor: *Mémoires d'Hadrien,*" in her *From Violence to Vision: Sacrifice in the Works of Marguerite Yourcenar,* Southern Illinois University Press, 1992, pp. 184-219.

[*Howard is an American critic and educator who has done extensive research into Yourcenar's life and works. In the following essay, she examines the narrative structure of* Memoirs of Hadrian *and the life of its narrator and main character.*]

Mémoires d'Hadrien was the work that, in 1951, catapulted Marguerite Yourcenar to international literary prominence. Begun and abandoned several times over the course of the preceding decades, this fictionalized autobiography of one of the last enlightened Roman emperors takes the form of a letter to Marcus Aurelius, Hadrian's eventual successor. The book was the fruit, by the author's own admission, of a certain postwar optimism regarding the future of mankind. In the speech that Yourcenar delivered upon the occasion of her induction to the Académie française in 1981 [published in *En pèlerin et en étranger*], she recalls her outlook during those years:

> Ces années furent celles où, cherchant dans le passé un modèle resté imitable, j'imaginais comme encore possible l'existence d'un homme capable de 'stabiliser la terre', donc d'une intelligence humaine portée à son plus haut point de lucidité et d'efficacité.

> Those were the years when, searching in the past for a model that remained imitable, I imagined as still possible the existence of a man capable of "stabilizing the earth," thus of a human intelligence extended to its highest point of lucidity and efficacy.

In discussing the genesis of *Mémoires d'Hadrien* with Matthieu Galey in *Les yeux ouverts,* Yourcenar is more explicit regarding the unfortunate inaccuracy of that optimism. The hope of a long-lived Pax Americana or Pax Europeana to which the establishment of the United Nations gave rise was not realized. Nor were any political geniuses forthcoming. "Il ne s'est présenté que de brillants seconds. Mais, à l'époque, j'avais la naïveté de croire que c'était encore possible"/"Only brilliant second-raters made their appearance. At the time, however, I was still naive enough to believe in the possibility of such a thing."

Given the markedly negative portrait painted by Yourcenar in *Le coup de grâce* of another man of arms and the degradation unto dictatorship of the 1930s Rome we have just left, one can hardly fail to be perplexed that Yourcenar should look to the hierarchical model of imperial authority in search of renewal for a war-battered world. Who could more closely resemble a Hitler or a Mussolini than an ancient Roman despot? The eminent French author and critic Michel Tournier has addressed this issue in his "Gustave et Marguerite." According to Tournier, the question raised by *Mémoires d'Hadrien* is whether or not it is possible to be a "good tyrant." Yourcenar's entire book, he asserts, provides an emphatically affirmative response to this question. "Il serait donc faux que le pouvoir rende fou, et que le pouvoir absolu rende absolument fou, comme semblent le prouver cent exemples historiques de Néron à Hitler en passant par Robespierre et Napoléon"/"Thus it would appear to be false that power drives one crazy, and that absolute power drives one absolutely crazy, as a hundred historical examples from Nero to Hitler by way of Robespierre and Napoleon would seem to prove." As Tournier goes on to say, Yourcenar's book recreates the twenty-one years of "imperial wisdom" that Hadrian's reign, beginning in the year A.D. 117 and ending with his death in 138, bestowed upon the citizens of the Roman Empire:

> Cette sagesse se signale par l'intégration sans la moindre discordance de la sphère privée à la chose publique. Alors que les fous sanglants, que nous avons cités, menaient une politique sans contact avec leur vie d'homme ou perturbées par leurs passions personnelles, Hadrien se présente à nous comme un cosmos harmonieux où ses chasses, ses expéditions et ses amours occupent chacune leur juste place.

> This wisdom distinguishes itself by integrating the private sphere with the state without the slightest discordance. Whereas the blood-soaked madmen, whom we have cited, carried out political policies bearing no relation to their life as men or perturbed by their personal passions, Hadrian presents himself to us as a harmonious cosmos in which his hunting parties, his expeditions and his loves each occupy their rightful place.

As this passage so accurately notes, the factor that distinguishes Hadrian from his destructive peers and presumptive political legatees is his capacity to integrate the personal and the private with the functions of his public office, to keep an ever-watchful eye on the human consequences of his imperial decisions. It is also this integrative facility that differentiates Hadrian from the protofascist narrator of Yourcenar's *Le coup de grâce.*

Madeleine Boussuges situates Hadrian with regard to the empire he governed: "Le siècle d'or des Antonins, où s'inscrit le règne de l'Empereur Hadrien, correspond à la fois à l'apogée de l'empire romain et au début de son déclin"/"The golden century of the Antonines, of which the reign of the emperor Hadrian was a part, corresponds at once to the apogee of the Roman Empire and to the beginning of its decline." The rise to a zenith and subsequent fall also characterize the structure of Yourcenar's account of Hadrian's life. During the first half of the text, the emperor climbs to dizzying heights of personal and professional success. Though seemingly irrepressible, his ascent is transformed nonetheless into decline with the sacrificial death of his beloved young companion Antinous. With this novel that inaugurates the period of her most renowned works, nearly two decades after her Athenian victims began wending their way toward Crete, sacrifice finds itself still at the center of the material—be it that of myth, that of daily life, or that of history—to which Marguerite Yourcenar devotes her creative attention.

It is a sixty-year-old Hadrian, already long afflicted by the ailing heart that will kill him two years later, who addresses the story of his life to the young man who will one day take his place. The narrator thus possesses a store of experience and wisdom that the Hadrian he narrates did not necessarily possess. Nowhere is this more evident than in the pages of reflection that open the emperor's letter to his adopted imperial grandson. Addressing topics as varied as Hadrian's health, his erstwhile hunting expeditions, and the virtues of a sound sleep, these meditations brim with benevolent sagacity. They paint a picture of a man whose acute intelligence is matched by his humaneness and form a kind of philosophical backdrop against which the story of Hadrian's life will be projected. Two themes emerge as paramount from these pages of reflection. They testify to traits of character that will play a crucial role throughout the book: Hadrian's will to maintain contact with the rudiments of life and his uncanny capacity to open himself to and partake of the Other, be that Other friend or foe.

Hadrian's nearly constant volition, much like that of Hercules in *Le mystère d'Alceste,* to keep in close touch with the elemental sources of life is first alluded to in a passage pertaining to the differences between Roman and Greek cuisine. The former is described as excessively rich and refined, whereas the latter is simple and better suited to the body's assimilative capacities. "J'ai goûté," affirms Hadrian,

> dans tel bouge d'Egine ou de Phalère, à des nourritures si fraîches qu'elles demeuraient divinement propres, en dépit des doigts sales du garçon de taverne, si modiques, mais si suffisantes, qu'elles semblaient contenir sous la forme la plus résumée possible quelque essence d'immortalité.

> In the merest hole of a place in Aegina or Phaleron I have tasted food so fresh that it remained divinely clean despite the dirty fingers of the tavern waiter; its quantity, though modest, was nevertheless so satisfying that it seemed to contain in the most reduced form possible some essence of immortality.

As is frequently the case, Hadrian's thoughts, having moved from the complicated gastronomy of Roman imperial banquets to the unadorned sufficiency of simple Greek taverns, turn subsequently to an even more primitive form of sustenance recalled from his past, that of the hunt. In this passage we learn that if the simple courses served by Greek waiters somehow suggest immortality, there is something sacramental in the sharing of the flesh of the hunt:

> La viande cuite au soir des chasses avait elle aussi cette qualité presque sacramentelle, nous ramenait plus loin, aux origines sauvages des races. Le vin nous initie aux mystères volcaniques du sol, aux richesses minérales cachées: une coupe de Samos bue à midi, en plein soleil, ou au contraire absorbée par un soir d'hiver dans un état de fatigue qui permet de sentir immédiatement au creux du diaphragme son écoulement chaud, sa sure et brûlante dispersion le long de nos artères, est une sensation presque sacrée, parfois trop forte pour une tête humaine; je ne la retrouve plus si pure sortant des celliers numérotés de Rome, et le pédantisme des grands connaisseurs de crus m'impatiente. Plus pieusement encore, l'eau bue dans la paume ou à même la source fait couler en nous le sel le plus secret de la terre et la pluie du ciel.

> Likewise meat cooked at night after a hunt had that same almost sacramental quality, taking us far back to the primitive origins of the races of men. Wine initiates us into the volcanic mysteries of the soil, and its hidden mineral riches; a cup of Samos drunk at noon in the heat of the sun or, on the contrary, absorbed of a winter evening when fatigue makes the warm current be felt at once in the hollow of the diaphragm and the sure and burning dispersion spreads along our arteries, such a drink provides a sensation which is almost sacred, and is sometimes too strong for the human head. No feeling so pure comes from the vintage-numbered cellars of Rome; the pedantry of great connoisseurs of wine wearies me. Water drunk more reverently still, from the hands or from the spring itself, diffuses within us the most secret salt of earth and the rain of heaven.

Like no Roman repast concocted by chefs of renown, wild game connects man to a primeval past. A cup of wine links the emperor to riches coursing through the earth like blood through veins. Simpler still, and thus more sacred, fresh water ties man to both heaven and earth. Hadrian's tendency to move from the complex to the simple, from the phenomenon at hand to its origins, displays again that same will to make contact with the real that fills his musings. Later Hadrian describes this volition as the "attention constante que j'avais toujours donnée aux moindres détails de mes actes"/"constant attention [I had always paid to] the smallest details of my acts." This unmediated connection to his world is one of the cornerstones of Hadrian's ascension to imperial eminence.

Standing beside this connectedness is Hadrian's ability to open himself to the Other. The second half of his opening reflections meditates on the question of the self and the Other, on the relations of alterity. This topic is broached first in a discussion of the seamless rapport that in earlier, more active, times had linked the emperor to his horse, Borysthenes. Though his own days as an equestrian are behind him, a vivid memory of the perfect harmony that had reigned between him and his horse continues to inform Hadrian's ability to participate viscerally in the pleasure "du cavalier et celui de la bête"/"both of horse and of rider" as he watches his aide Celer exercise the imperial mount. He still partakes in a similar way of the joys of swimming and running, though they too are forbidden him now. As the following passage suggests, there have even been times when Hadrian has tried to extend his empathic capacities beyond the realm of the human:

> J'ai cru, et dans mes bons moments je crois encore, qu'il serait possible de partager de la sorte l'existence de tous, et cette sympathie serait l'une des espèces les moins révocables de l'immortalité. Il y eut des moments où cette compréhension s'efforça de dépasser l'humain, alla du nageur à la vague.

> I have supposed, and in my better moments

think so still, that it would be possible in this manner to participate in the existence of everyone; such sympathy would be one of the least revocable kinds of immortality. There have been moments when that comprehension tried to go beyond human experience, passing from the swimmer to the wave.

Just as Hadrian's ingestion of seared flesh, simple wines, and fresh water creates a sacred tie between him and the natural world, so too does his faculty for sympathetic engagement make it possible for him to participate meaningfully in modes of being beyond the boundaries of his own, seemingly limited, self.

Nowhere is this more evident than in the heightened state of sensual and spiritual receptivity to the Other which is love. Unlike Erick von Lhomond [the warrior character in *Le coup de grâce*] who closed out the Other in fear, the aging Hadrian insists on the necessity of abdicating one's masterful hold on oneself in complete surrender to the object of love:

> De tous nos jeux, [l'amour] est le seul qui risque de bouleverser l'âme, le seul aussi où le joueur s'abandonne nécessairement au délire du corps. Il n'est pas indispensable que le buveur abdique sa raison, mais l'amant qui garde la sienne n'obéit pas jusqu'au bout à son dieu. L'abstinence ou l'excès n'engagent partout ailleurs que l'homme seul: sauf dans le cas de Diogène, dont les limitations et le caractère de raisonnable pis-aller se marquent d'eux-mêmes, toute démarche sensuelle nous place en présence de l'Autre, nous implique dans les exigences et les servitudes du choix.

> Of all our games, love's play is the only one which threatens to unsettle the soul, and is also the only one in which the player has to abandon himself to the body's ecstasy. To put reason aside is not indispensable for a drinker, but the lover who leaves reason in control does not follow his god to the end. In every act save that of love, abstinence and excess alike involve but one person; any step in the direction of sensuality, however, places us in the presence of the Other, and involves us in the demands and servitudes to which our choice binds us (except in the case of Diogenes, where both the limitations and the merits of reasonable expedient are self-evident).

In much more graphic expression of the self-abandonment that amorous relations entail, Hadrian refers to himself some two pages later as "cloué au corps aimé comme un crucifié à sa croix"/"[n]ailed to the beloved body like a slave to a cross."

When his thoughts progress from love to sleep, the guiding thread remains the issue of the self and its relation to otherness. In a passage that seems to allude to the notions about love just evoked, Hadrian comments on the subject of sleep that: "Là, comme ailleurs, le plaisir et l'art consistent à s'abandonner consciemment à cette bienheureuse inconscience, à accepter d'être subtilement plus faible, plus lourd, plus léger, et plus confus que soi"/"There, as elsewhere, the pleasure and the art consist in conscious surrender to that blissful unconsciousness, and in accept-

ing to be slightly less strong, less light, less heavy and less definite than our waking selves." Providing as it does the daily experience of a radical relinquishment of self, sleep also suggests to Hadrian the possibility not just of surrendering to but of being the Other. He recalls that the profound slumbers following the exhaustion of the hunt were abrupt and total departures from the confines of his normal mode of being:

> Si totale était l'éclipse, que j'aurais pu chaque fois me retrouver autre, et je m'étonnais, ou parfois m'attristais, du strict agencement qui me ramenait de si loin dans cet étroit canton d'humanité qu'est moi-même. Qu'étaient ces particularités auxquelles nous tenons le plus, puisqu'elles comptaient si peu pour le libre dormeur, et que, pour une seconde, avant de rentrer à regret dans la peau d'Hadrien, je parvenais à savourer à peu près consciemment cet homme vide, cette existence sans passé?

> So total was the eclipse that each time I could have found myself to be someone else, and I was perplexed and often saddened by the strict law which brought me back from so far away to re-enter this narrow confine of humanity which is myself. What are those particularities upon which we lay so much store, since they count so little for us when we are liberated in sleep, and since for one second before returning, regretfully, into the body of Hadrian I was about to savor almost consciously that new existence without content and without a past? . . .

[The] narrator of *Le coup de grâce* [engages] in a desperate attempt to build barriers of difference between himself and the frightening encroachment of the Other. *Mémoires d'Hadrien,* on the contrary, begins with an effort to break down those barriers. It undermines thus the differences upon which the notion of hierarchy, so crucial to the masculinist mindset of an Erick von Lhomond, depends. Perhaps this is all the more remarkable inasmuch as they are also, of course, the differences upon which reposes the imperial foundation of Hadrian's power: "Endormis, Caïus Caligula et le juste Aristide se valent; je dépose mes vains et importants privilèges; je ne me distingue plus du noir janiteur qui dort en travers de mon seuil"/"Asleep, Caius Caligula and Aristides the Just are alike; my important but empty privileges are forgotten, and nothing distinguishes me from the black porter who lies guard at my door." Whereas the narrator of *Le coup de grâce* seeks continually to emphasize differences in his attempt to define himself against a fearsome Otherness, Hadrian actively engages with difference in an effort to integrate himself with alterity of all kinds. The opening reflections of this fictional memoir place Hadrian in a network that connects the animals, the plants, the peoples of his realm, and the heavens, thus forging a sharp distinction between the narrating Hadrian and that other first person narrator. . . . Erick von Lhomond. At the same time, these pages lay the philosophical foundation for the pyramidal structure of this novel.

Born in the Roman city of Italica, in Spain, the young Hadrian was a cousin of Trajan, successor to Nerva as emperor of Rome. Though Hadrian's own accession to this position was by no means a foregone conclusion, his rise to power was steady and swift. A succession of administrative and military appointments during Trajan's reign, each more demanding than the one before, both developed and demonstrated the qualities that would eventually secure for Hadrian the title of emperor. Despite his reputation for military prowess, it became clear even before his reign began that Hadrian would refuse to continue his predecessor's politics of conquest. He describes his first consulate as a secret, unceasing struggle "en faveur de la paix"/"on behalf of peace." The most important thing, at that time, "c'est que quelqu'un s'opposât à la politique de conquêtes, en envisageât les conséquences et la fin, et se préparât, si possible, à en réparer les erreurs"/"was that someone should be in opposition to the policy of conquest, envisaging its consequences and the final aim, and should prepare himself, if possible, to repair its errors."

Having already been chosen to administer the civil affairs of the empire during Trajan's last campaign against the Parthians, Hadrian succeeded to the throne upon his cousin's death. His reign began with the first fulfillment of that pledge to peace that he had secretly made before his advent and that would continue to guide his development as emperor:

> Les négociations reprirent, ouvertement désormais; je fis répandre partout que Trajan lui-même m'en avait chargé avant de mourir. Je raturai d'un trait les conquêtes dangereuses: non seulement la Mésopotamie, où nous n'aurions pas pu nous maintenir, mais l'Arménie trop excentrique et trop lointaine, que je ne gardai qu'au rang d'Etat vassal. . . . Je tâchai de faire passer dans les pourparlers cette ardeur que d'autres réservent pour le champ de bataille; je forçai la paix.

> Negotiations were resumed, this time openly; I let it be generally understood that Trajan himself had told me to do so before he died. With one stroke of the pen I erased all conquests which might have proved dangerous: not only Mesopotamia, where we could not have maintained ourselves, but Armenia, which was too far away and too removed from our sphere, and which I retained only as a vassal state. . . . I tried to put into these diplomatic conversations the same ardor that others reserve for the field of battle; I forced a peace.

As trade flourishes along routes made safe by peace, the pulse of a world that has suffered the convulsions of grave illness begins to beat again its healthy rhythm. Traveling merchants exchange not only goods with their customers but also "un certain nombre de pensées, de mots, de coutumes bien à nous, qui peu à peu s'empareraient du globe plus sûrement que les légions en marche"/"a certain number of thoughts, words, and customs genuinely our own, which little by little would take possession of the globe more securely than can advancing legions."

Having made peace with his Parthian adversary, King Osroës, Hadrian then turns his attention to settling the differences between those "eternal incompatibles," the

Greeks and the Jews. A week spent in the boiling heat of an Egyptian tribunal yields a subtly wrought compromise:

> Il m'importait assez peu que l'accord obtenu fût extérieur, imposé du dehors, probablement temporaire: je savais que le bien comme le mal est affaire de routine, que le temporaire se prolonge, que l'extérieur s'infiltre au-dedans, et que le masque, à la longue, devient visage. Puisque la haine, la sottise, le délire ont des effets durables, je ne voyais pas pourquoi la lucidité, la justice, la bienveillance n'auraient pas les leurs. L'ordre aux frontières n'était rien si je ne persuadais pas ce fripier juif et ce charcutier grec de vivre tranquillement côte à côte.

> It mattered little to me that the accord obtained was external, imposed from without and perhaps temporary; I knew that good like bad becomes a routine, that the temporary tends to endure, that what is external permeates to the inside, and that the mask, given time, comes to be the face itself. Since hatred, stupidity, and delirium have lasting effects, I saw no reason why good will, clarity of mind and just practice would not have their effects, too. Order on the frontiers was nothing if I could not persuade a Jewish peddler and a Greek grocer to live peaceably side by side.

It is with just such scrupulous attention to concrete, simple facts of everyday existence that Hadrian approaches every problem he seeks to resolve during the early years of his rule. His repeated successes are proof that his confidence in his methods is well-placed. Hadrian emphasizes the importance of maintaining contact with the elemental forces of life in the meditative pages that open this novel. This example illustrates that same kind of attention to the real in Hadrian's execution of his imperial duties.

Similarly vital to his efforts to pacify and stabilize the empire is Hadrian's ability to open himself to the Other. When, three years after the conclusion of his peace treaty with King Osroës, border incidents in the Orient threaten to erupt into full-scale war, Hadrian travels once again to the Parthian territory. He is determined to reach a negotiated, not a military, settlement that will satisfy both sides and that will last. After making the good-faith gesture of returning the Parthian king's daughter, taken hostage years before, Hadrian proceeds to hammer out with Osroës terms which both sides will be able to abide. The crux of his method is to put himself in Osroës' shoes:

> Mes curieuses disciplines mentales m'aidaient à capter cette pensée fuyante: assis en face de l'empereur parthe, j'apprenais à prévoir, et bientôt à orienter ses réponses; j'entrais dans son jeu; je m'imaginais devenu Osroès marchandant Hadrien.

> My peculiar mental disciplines helped me to grasp this elusive intelligence: seated facing the Parthian emperor, I learned to anticipate, and soon to direct, his replies; I entered into his game; last, I imagined myself as Osroës bargaining with Hadrian.

When Hadrian narrates these events to his adopted imperial grandson, the agreement concluded between him and his Parthian counterpart had held for fifteen years. All signs suggest that a permanent peace had been won.

It is by virtue of these skills that Hadrian's efforts during the first years of his reign meet almost invariably with success. His accomplishments are legion. He improves the plight of Roman slaves by establishing laws that protect them from common abuses. He enhances the condition of women, granting them legal rights that heretofore have been denied them. He institutes reforms in the realms of economic organization and agriculture. A unionist before the letter, Hadrian counts among his most satisfying days as emperor the one on which he persuades a group of seamen to join together in a kind of corporation. On the island of Britain he puts up a wall, proclaiming to the world that he has renounced the policy of conquest so aggressively pursued by his predecessor. In his beloved Greece, Hadrian sets about repairing the damages done by the invasions of Sulla, proceeding to double the size of Athens. As is always the case in these years of reparation and construction, Hadrian's gaze is constantly trained on the future.

Though I have contrasted the opening meditative pages of **Mémoires d'Hadrien** with those that follow, the chronological account of Hadrian's ascent to the pinnacle of his achievement is by no means bereft of reflection. Interspersed among the pages of Hadrian's narration are lyrical passages attesting to the depth and beauty of his vision. Under Hadrian's tutelage, Rome will be even more than a flourishing capital city. Rome will come to represent forever those ideals of justice and peace that Hadrian vows to extend to the farthest reaches of the empire:

> Elle échapperait à son corps de pierre; elle se composerait du mot d'Etat, du mot de citoyenneté, du mot de république, une plus sûre immortalité. Dans les pays encore incultes, sur les bords du Rhin, du Danube, ou de la mer des Bataves, chaque village défendu par une palissade de pieux me rappelait la hutte de roseaux, le tas de fumier où nos jumeaux romains dormaient gorgés de lait de louve: ces métropoles futures reproduiraient Rome. Aux corps physiques des nations et des races, aux accidents de la géographie et de l'histoire, aux exigences disparates des dieux ou des ancêtres, nous aurions à jamais superposé, mais sans rien détruire, l'unité d'une conduite humaine, l'empirisme d'une expérience sage. Rome se perpétuerait dans la moindre petite ville où des magistrats s'efforcent de vérifier les poids des marchands, de nettoyer et d'éclairer leurs rues, de s'opposer au désordre, à l'incurie, à la peur, à l'injustice, de réinterpréter raisonnablement les lois. Elle ne périrait qu'avec la dernière cité des hommes.

> She would no longer be bound by her body of stone, but would compose for herself from the words *State, citizenry,* and *republic* a surer immortality. In the countries as yet untouched by our culture, on the banks of the Rhine and the Danube, or the shores of the Batavian Sea, each village enclosed within its wooden palisade brought to mind the reed hut and dunghill where our Roman twins had slept content, fed by the milk of the wolf; these cities-to-be would

follow the pattern of Rome. Over separate nations and races, with their accidents of geography and history and the disparate demands of their ancestors or their gods, we should have superposed for ever a unity of human conduct and the empiricism of sober experience, but should have done so without destruction of what had preceded us. Rome would be perpetuating herself in the least of the towns where magistrates strive to demand just weight from the merchants, to clean and light the streets, to combat disorder, slackness, superstition and injustice, and to give broader and fairer interpretation to the laws. She would endure to the end of the last city built by man.

As this and other passages demonstrate, in every project undertaken, Hadrian knows he is renewing the traditions of the past so that they will stand the test of time to come: "J'ai beaucoup reconstruit: c'est collaborer avec le temps sous son aspect de passé, en saisir ou en modifier l'esprit, lui servir de relais vers un plus long avenir; c'est retrouver sous les pierres le secret des sources"/"I have done much rebuilding. To reconstruct is to collaborate with time gone by, penetrating or modifying its spirit, and carrying it toward a longer future. Thus beneath the stones we find the secret of the springs." Like the hands-on contact with the real that is a key to Hadrian's diplomatic successes, it is here, once again, an intimate contact with the elemental that provides the foundation upon which the future foreseen is erected.

All indications suggest that Hadrian's successes will be as limitless as they are spectacular. Hadrian compares himself, so many and varied are his triumphs, to a "joueur qui gagne à tout coup"/"player who wins at every throw." It is during this period of his ascending fortunes that the emperor meets up with young Antinous. Their love will be the crowning glory of an already glorious existence.

From the very beginning, Hadrian's liaison with Antinous is shown to partake of that same adhesion to the real that plays such a crucial role in the emperor's realization of his imperial goals. Hadrian meets the Bithynian Antinous for the first time, significantly, "au bord d'une source consacrée à Pan"/"beside a spring consecrated to Pan." Perhaps it is the spring's consecration to this Greek god of forests, flocks, and shepherds that prompts Hadrian to compare Antinous, upon first catching sight of him, to "un berger au fond des bois, vaguement sensible à quelque obscur cri d'oiseau"/"some shepherd, deep in the woods, vaguely aware of a strange bird's cry." In any event, our first view of the youth, seated on the edge of the basin into which flows an underground spring, cannot but recall the early passage in which Hadrian speaks so reverently of the water that "diffuses within us the most secret salt of earth and the rain of heaven," thus heralding that privileged and sensual relation to the primordial that Antinous will incarnate in the pages to follow.

Encountered under the sign of that life-giving element, water, Antinous will also be associated time and again with the earth, with plants, or with wild animals.

> Sa présence était extraordinairement silencieuse:
> il m'a suivi comme un animal ou comme un

génie familier. Il avait d'un jeune chien les capacités infinies d'enjouement et d'indolence, la sauvagerie, la confiance. Ce beau lévrier avide de caresses et d'ordres se coucha sur ma vie.

His presence was extraordinarily silent: he followed me like some animal, or a familiar spirit. He had the infinite capacity of a young dog for play and for swift repose, and the same fierceness and trust. This graceful hound, avid both for caresses and commands, took his post at my feet.

Later on, as clouds of doom begin to gather on the horizon, Antinous' connection to the animal world, as well as to the earth and to the emperor, comes once again to the fore. It is the eve of Hadrian's dedication of the Olympieion in Athens. He enters a temple with Antinous where a sacrificial python awaits his fate:

[A]u pied de l'échafaudage, le grand python que j'avais fait chercher aux Indes pour le consacrer dans ce sanctuaire grec reposait déjà dans sa corbeille de filigrane, bête divine, emblème rampant de l'esprit de la Terre, associé de tout temps au jeune homme nu qui symbolise le Génie de l'empereur. Antinoüs, entrant de plus en plus dans ce rôle, servit lui-même au monstre sa ration de mésanges aux ailes rognées.

[A]t the foot of the scaffolding lay the great python brought from India at my order to be consecrated in this Greek sanctuary. Already reposing in its filigree basket, the divine snake, emblem of Earth on which it crawls, has long been associated with the nude youth who symbolizes the emperor's Genius. Antinous, entering more and more into that role, himself fed the monster its ration of wing-clipped wrens.

Of all the passages in which Antinous signifies the intimate contact with primary forces that stands Hadrian in such good stead over the course of his first years as emperor, none is more explicit than this one from the next-to-last segment of the *"Saeculum aureum"* section. As Hadrian sails with Antinous upon the Nile, he reaches over to caress his young favorite:

Ma main glissait sur sa nuque, sous ses cheveux. Dans les moments les plus vains ou les plus ternes, j'avais ainsi le sentiment de rester en contact avec les grands objets naturels, l'épaisseur des forêts, l'échine musclée des panthères, la pulsation régulière des sources.

My hand passed over his neck, under his heavy hair; thus even in the dullest or most futile moments I kept some feeling of contact with the great objects of nature, the thick growth of the forests, the muscular back of the panther, the regular pulsation of springs.

It is as if Antinous becomes the primary means whereby Hadrian keeps touch with those primordial forces that figure so importantly in the reflections with which his memoirs begin and that are so central to Hadrian's efforts to pacify, rebuild, and amplify the freedoms of the Roman empire he inherited.

Scrupulous attention to the smallest details of his reign played a role in Hadrian's spectacular imperial success. It is to his capacity for engaging in a similarly passionate physical attention to his partner that Hadrian also attributes his felicity as a lover:

Tout bonheur est un chef-d'oeuvre: la moindre erreur le fausse, la moindre hésitation l'altère, la moindre lourdeur le dépare, la moindre sottise l'abêtit. Le mien n'est responsable en rien de celles de mes imprudences qui plus tard l'ont brisé: tant que j'ai agi dans son sens, j'ai été sage. Je crois encore qu'il eût été possible à un homme plus sage que moi d'être heureux jusqu'à sa mort.

Every bliss achieved is a masterpiece, the slightest error turns it awry, and it alters with one touch of doubt; any heaviness detracts from its charm, the least stupidity renders it dull. My own felicity is in no way responsible for those of my imprudences which shattered it later on; in so far as I have acted in harmony with it I have been wise. I think still that someone wiser than I might well have remained happy till his death.

The importance of this kind of "passionate attention" to all aspects of existence has been stressed in Yourcenar's works time and time again. In **"Borges ou le voyant,"** for example, which appears in the posthumous *En pèlerin et en étranger,* Yourcenar states that "Les Hindous ont raison de faire de l'Ekagrata, l'attention, l'une des plus hautes qualités mentales"/"The Hindus are right to make *Ekagrata,* or attention, one of the highest mental qualities." She addresses this issue as well, with specific reference to the emperor Hadrian, in her interviews with Matthieu Galey [in *Les yeux ouverts*]:

Ce qu'on vous recommande toujours, et ce qui est extraordinairement difficile à acquérir, c'est ce que les sages hindous appelaient l'*attention,* une attention qui élimine les trois quarts, les neuf dixièmes de ce que l'on croit penser, tandis qu'en réalité on ne pense pas; . . . C'est extrêmement difficile à réaliser: il y a toute espèce d'astuces, différentes manières d'arriver à cet état, que j'ai fait d'ailleurs décrire à Hadrien lui-même apprenant à vivre. . . .

Generally speaking, one must try against considerable difficulty to achieve what Hindu sages describe as a state of "attentiveness," in which you get rid of three-quarters or nine-tenths of what you seem to think but really don't. . . . It's extremely difficult to do. There are all sorts of tricks, a whole variety of ways, for arriving at this state of attentiveness, some of which I have Hadrian describe. . . .

In turning to the question of the sacrificial death that ravages Hadrian's world, forming the pivot of this novel's structural pyramid, we must ask to what extent it is a coincidence that that death takes place at a time when the emperor's attention, both to Antinous and to the smallest details of his acts, is at its lowest ebb.

Antinous' death puts an end to that "Age of Gold" chronicled in the fourth section of *Mémoires d'Hadrien,* entitled *"Saeculum aureum."* It does not occur without warning. Indeed a series of progressively more ominous incidents prepares the reader, if not the narrated emperor, for the impending catastrophe. Many of these involve acts, either personal or ritual, that are themselves sacrificial in nature.

The first concerns Hadrian's imperial reader, the Stoic philosopher Euphrates. Having suffered for years from a debilitating ailment, Euphrates one day requests permission from Hadrian to put an end to his misery by suicide. "Ce problème du suicide, qui m'a obsédé depuis, me semblait alors de solution facile. Euphratès eut l'autorisation qu'il réclamait"/"The problem of suicide which has obsessed me since seemed then of easy solution. Euphrates received the authorization which he sought." It was Antinous whom the emperor dispatched to bear this news to the Stoic philosopher, who killed himself the following day. The incident was a sobering one for Hadrian's favorite, who could not seem to shake it from his thoughts: "Nous reparlâmes plusieurs fois de cet incident: l'enfant en demeura assombri durant quelques jours. Ce bel être sensuel regardait la mort avec horreur; je ne m'apercevais pas qu'il y pensait déjà beaucoup"/"We talked over the incident several times; the boy remained somber for some days thereafter. This ardent young creature held death in horror; I had not observed that he already gave it much thought."

Two pages thereafter is recounted the first of several sacrificial rites to which Antinous will be witness. Hadrian recalls this event, which takes place in Phrygia, as one that formed "l'image la plus complète et la plus lucide"/"the clearest and most complete idea" of his happiness with the Bithynian youth who had come to occupy such an important place in his affections. As is frequently the case regarding the scenes of his commerce with Antinous that Hadrian recounts in these memoirs, this recollection is set in surroundings untouched by the reach of civilization, so appropriate to the just-barely-tame creature he cherishes. Hadrian had ordered a statue placed on the abandoned tomb of Alcibiades to commemorate this Greek hero who had died on this spot several centuries before. He had also made arrangements for the sacrifice of a young bull to be consumed later during the evening's festivities. The relation between Antinous and this night spent paying homage to Alcibiades is signaled early on by Hadrian's reference to its illustration of their happiness. But this is not the only link. It is surely not hard to imagine a connection between the much-traveled Alcibiades and Hadrian himself—all the more so given the former's reputation for intelligence and statesmanship. Nor is another possibility to be dismissed outright. In light of what is to come, this brief passage on a figure of the past who, in addition to his finer qualities, was also noted for his debauchery and prodigality can be read as foreshadowing an aspect of Hadrian's character that has yet to come to the fore. In any event, there can be little doubt that the site on which this first ritual sacrifice takes place is a meaningful one. Phrygia is located "sur les confins où la Grèce et l'Asie se mélangent"/"on the borderlands where Greece melts into Asia." Antinous is a Greek with Asian blood: "Antinoüs était Grec. . . . Mais l'Asie avait produit sur ce sang un epu âcre l'effet de la goutte de miel qui trouble et parfume un vin pur"/"Antinous was Greek. . . . But Asia had produced its effect upon that rude blood, like the drop of honey which clouds and perfumes a pure wine." This first in a series of ritual sacrifices is clearly linked in an intimate way to the evolving destiny of the young man from Bithynia.

I have already evoked the next sacrifice recounted by Hadrian: that of an Indian python offered up as part of the Olympieion festivities in Athens. It is upon this occasion that Hadrian remarks that his young favorite seems to be entering more and more deeply into the role of the emperor's Genius, or attendant spirit. According to the ancients, one's Genius bore the burden of presiding, for good or for ill, over one's destiny. With the perspective of hindsight, Hadrian's text hints that the prayer made by his lover within the walls of that sanctuary already contained at least the seed of the plan that he would later carry out: "Je savais que cette prière, faite pour moi, ne s'adressait qu'à moi seul, mais je n'étais pas assez dieu pour en deviner le sens, ni pour savoir si elle serait un jour ou l'autre exaucée"/"I knew that this prayer, made for me, was addressed to no one but myself, though I was not god enough to grasp its sense, nor to know if it would some day be answered." Shadows begin here to gather, and Hadrian expresses relief upon emerging from the darkness of the temple into the brightly lit Athenian streets.

From this point forward, the sacrifices leading up to that of Antinous take on a more violent character, one following fast upon the other in a kind of bloody spiral. Hadrian describes this period as one in which "la danse devient vertige, où le chant s'achève en cri"/"the dance leaves us reeling and song ends in outcry." He who had years before taken part in the savage initiation rituals connected with certain Asian mystery sects consents to attend, despite having forbidden such practices, the orgies of Cybele. They are gruesome rites of human mutilation. Hadrian's account of the event highlights the morbid fascination that the ceremony holds for the young Antinous:

> j'ai vu l'affreux tourbillonnement des danses ensanglantées; fasciné comme un chevreau mis en présence d'un reptile, mon jeune compagnon contemplait avec terreur ces hommes qui choisissaient de faire aux exigences de l'âge et du sexe une réponse aussi définitive que celle de la mort, et peut-être plus atroce.

> I witnessed the hideous whirling of bleeding dancers; fascinated as a kid in presence of a snake, my young companion watched with terror these men who were electing to answer the demands of age and of sex with a response as final as that of death itself, and perhaps more dreadful.

Though the "demands of age" might well seem a topic far removed from the thoughts of a still adolescent Antinous, the previous paragraph informs us that this youth, described now as brooding and melancholic, is anxiously concerned that he will shortly turn nineteen.

No sooner do the blood-spattered dancers to the orgiastic glory of Cybele come to rest than another sanguinary ritual begins. As befits the ever more rapidly spinning gyre of sacrifices into whose vortex Antinous will soon leap, this time Hadrian's companion will himself take part in the rite. Harking back to that first ritual offering of a young bull, so pointedly related to Antinous, the taurobolium takes place in a sacred cave. Its dark shadows recall those of the temple in which the boy from Bithynia voiced his prayer for the emperor's welfare, adopting the role of his Genius.

It is the emperor's Syrian host in the city of Palmyra who suggests that Antinous be initiated into the cult of Mithra, as Hadrian himself had done some years before. A rigorous religion, widespread during the second century, Mithraism exacted above all other values an unflinching loyalty among its adepts. There is no wonder, then, that Antinous embraces this chance to join the cult with such fervor. Though the emperor's youthful attraction to such passionate fraternal values and feverish ceremonies is a thing of the past, he agrees to serve as sponsor for his ardent young friend.

> Mais quand je vis émerger de la fosse ce corps strié de rouge, cette chevelure feutrée par une boue gluante, ce visage éclaboussé de taches qu'on ne pouvait laver, et qu'il fallait laisser s'effacer d'elles-mêmes, le dégoût me prit à la gorge, et l'horreur de ces cultes souterrains et louches.

> But when I saw his body, streaked with red, emerging from the ditch, his hair matted with sticky mud and his face spattered with stains which could not be washed away but had to be left to wear off themselves, I felt only disgust and abhorrence for all such subterranean and sinister cults.

Shortly thereafter, Hadrian issues an order forbidding his troops, which are stationed nearby, to enter the underground chamber of Mithra.

An equally disturbing and equally premonitory sacrifice takes place shortly after the bloody taurobolium of Palmyra. Its setting is the summit of Mount Casius, near Antioch, where Hadrian had often held such ceremonies during his tenure as governor of Syria. As he had done once before in order to witness the much-reputed beauty of dawn from the mountaintop, Hadrian climbs Mount Casius at night with a small group of friends. This time, however, as never before, the emperor experiences a shortness of breath that causes him to stop for a moment and lean on his young lover's shoulder. This unprecedented lapse in Hadrian's vigor is taken as a sign by Antinous that the propitiatory sacrifice that he has perhaps already planned is, in fact, more urgent than he thought.

When the imperial party has nearly reached the summit of the mountain, a thunderstorm breaks out. Both priest and sacrificial victim are struck by lightning a moment before the ceremony can begin. They die instantly. This extraordinary event is immediately seen as propitious. Witnesses proclaim that:

> L'homme et le faon sacrifiés par cette épée divine s'unissaient à l'éternité de mon Génie: ces vies substituées prolongeaient la mienne. Antinoüs agrippé à mon bras tremblait, non de terreur, comme je le crus alors, mais sous le coup d'une pensée que je compris plus tard.

> The man and fawn thus sacrificed by this divine sword were uniting with the eternity of my Genius; that these lives, by substitution, were prolonging mine. Antinous gripping fast to my arm was trembling, not from terror, as I then supposed, but under the impact of a thought which I was to understand only later on.

We have already seen how frequently the text associates Antinous with various animals. It is surely no coincidence that, only six pages prior to Hadrian's account of the sacrificial thunderbolt, the youth is called precisely a "jeune faon"/"young fawn." Nor can it be denied that the young man who understands himself to embody the emperor's Genius sees this incident as a significant one. Looking back on this part of his past, Hadrian views it as a decisive factor in what was so soon to take place: "L'éclair du mont Cassius lui montrait une issue: la mort pouvait devenir une dernière forme de service, un dernier don, et le seul qui restât"/"The lightning of Mount Casius had revealed to him a way out: death could become a last form of service, a final gift, and the only one which seemed left for him to give." And give it he soon would.

Having traveled first to Jerusalem, then to Alexandria, Hadrian consents to a trip to Canopus where a magician of local repute resides. Both Antinous and Lucius Ceionius, who much earlier in Hadrian's reign had been the emperor's lover for a time, accompany him. Night has fallen over Egypt, as it soon will descend upon Hadrian's life.

The predictions of the sorceress are ominous. Problems of every sort will soon beset the emperor upon whom fate has smiled for so long. Everything can be set straight, however, with a magical sacrifice that the Egyptian prophetess will be only too willing to perform. The victim of choice is an "animal familier" or "pet animal"—designations, of course, recalling similar textual references to Antinous—belonging, if possible, to the emperor. Antinous proposes a much cherished falcon that Hadrian had given him after receiving it himself from the king of Osroëne.

Several aspects of the falcon's death will presently find themselves repeated in that of young Antinous. As was seen to be the case with priest and fawn atop Mount Casius, the bird's years of earthly life will serve to extend that of Hadrian; its soul will unite with the emperor's Genius. After his death, this invisible spirit may appear before Hadrian and continue to serve him. Above all, it is important that

> la victime ne se débattît pas et que la mort parût volontaire. Enduite rituellement de miel et d'essence de rose, la bête inerte fut déposée au fond d'une cuve remplie d'eau du Nil; la créature noyée s'assimilait à l'Osiris emporté par le courant du fleuve.

> the victim should not struggle, and that the death should appear voluntary. Rubbed over with ritual honey and attar of roses, the animal, now inert, was placed in the bottom of a tub filled with Nile water; in drowning thus it was to be assimilated to Osiris borne along on the river's current.

With the seemingly interminable service completed, the

sorceress inters the casketed bird "au bord du canal, dans un cimetière abandonné"/"at the edge of the canal, in an abandoned cemetery." A few days later, Hadrian will find his lover face down in the mud of a similar site at the edge of the same river in whose water his falcon before him had drowned.

The indelible tragedy of Antinous's death is conveyed, before the fact of its narration, in the opening words of the antepenultimate segment of *"Saeculum aureum"* section. In its agonized length and precision, Hadrian's remembrance of the date that his companion chose to die conveys, perhaps more vividly than any other passage, the grief that would be his from that day forth: "Le premier jour du mois d'Athyr, la deuxième année de la deux cent vingt-sixième Olympiade . . ."/"The first of the month of Athyr, the second year of the two hundred and twenty-sixth Olympiad . . ." It is the anniversary of the death of the same god, Osiris, to which Antinous's falcon had so recently been sacrificed.

The night before his death, Antinous joins Hadrian for dinner aboard Lucius's boat. He wears a robe recalling the description, from an earlier period in Hadrian's reign, of *"Tellus stabilita,* le Génie de la Terre pacifiée"/"*Tellus Stabilita,* the Genius of the Pacified Earth," represented "sous l'aspect d'un jeune homme couché qui tient des fruits et des fleurs"/"in the guise of a reclining youth who holds fruits and flowers." In a subtle reminder, on the eve of his drowning, of his role as the emperor's Genius, Antinous appears clad in a "longue robe syrienne, mince comme une pelure de fruit, toute semée de fleurs et de Chimères"/"long Syrian robe, sheer as the skin of a fruit and strewn over with flowers and chimeras." In this poetic way, we are alerted once again that Antinous is now the symbol of both a personal and an imperial ideal.

When the fatal day arrives, a ritual wailing has gone on for three days in lamentation for the drowned Osiris. Antinous' disappearance brings Hadrian and Chabrias to a chapel the old tutor once visited with the Bithynian youth. "Sur une table à offrandes, les cendres d'un sacrifice étaient encore tièdes. Chabrias y plongea les doigts, et en retira presque intacte une boucle de cheveux coupés"/"On an offering table lay ashes still warm from a sacrifice; turning them with his fingers, Chabrias drew forth a lock of hair, almost intact." In a basin near a bend in the Nile lies the body of Hadrian's young companion. Antinous, it seems, has sacrificed himself to ensure the good fortune of the man he had loved and the emperor he had worshipped. The consequences of his act, however, are thoroughly contrary to his intentions. With Antinous' death a series of events begins, both public and private, that cause Hadrian to sink, as the years wear on, to an existential nadir.

Antinous' death provides the lamentable climax to a long series of sacrifices that cannot have failed to have their effect on this impressionable youth. He was inclined, moreover, to a certain heroic romanticization of his liaison with Hadrian, as is suggested, for example, by the similarity he saw between them and the legendary Achilles and Patroclus. As we have found to be the case regarding other self-sacrifices, however, there remains a certain equivocality regarding the nature of Antinous' death to which Hadrian

refers in the following passage. It affords him a horrible joy to view Antinous' death as a sacrifice made in his honor:

> Mais j'étais seul à mesurer combien d'âcreté fermente au fond de la douceur, quelle part de désespoir se cache dans l'abnégation, quelle haine se mélange à l'amour. Un être insulté me jetait à la face cette preuve de dévouement; un enfant inquiet de tout perdre avait trouvé ce moyen de m'attacher à jamais à lui. S'il avait espéré me protéger par ce sacrifice, il avait dû se croire bien peu aimé pour ne pas sentir que le pire des maux serait de l'avoir perdu.

> But I was the only one to measure how much bitter fermentation there is at the bottom of all sweetness, or what degree of despair is hidden under abnegation, what hatred is mingled with love. A being deeply wounded had thrown this proof of devotion at my very face; a boy fearful of losing all had found this means of binding me to him forever. Had he hoped to protect me by such a sacrifice he must have deemed himself unloved indeed not to have realized that the worst of ills would be to lose him.

What are the sources and the nature of this bitterness, this hatred, this despair? How had Antinous been so deeply wounded? Why would the beloved youth fear losing all? We must answer these questions, for Antinous' death is not merely the result of a romanticized notion of sacrifice, nor even of the desire to serve the man he loved, however fervently sincere that desire may have been. *Mémoires d'Hadrien,* after all, recounts Hadrian's life. And there is a sense in which Antinous' fatal gesture can be viewed as the physical enactment of another sacrificial event that had already taken place within Hadrian himself.

The two constitutive elements of Hadrian's personal happiness and political success, keeping in touch with the real and staying open to the Other, were both factors in the intimacy that developed between Hadrian and the youth from Bithynia. In fact, in his role as the emperor's Genius, Antinous comes to serve as the textual symbol of these qualities. But with the dizzying success of his every endeavor, Hadrian begins to betray the principles upon which those successes were erected.

"Peu à peu, la lumière changea"/"Little by little the light changed." The passage of time transforms the child whom Hadrian encountered on the edge of a spring into a young prince. A process of distancing begins that, however slightly at first, attenuates the intimacy of yore:

> Durant les chasses organisées dans les domaines de Lucius, en Toscane, j'avais pris plaisir à mêler ce visage parfait aux figures lourdes et soucieuses des grands dignitaires, aux profils aigus des Orientaux, aux mufles épais des veneurs barbares, à obliger le bien-aimé au rôle difficile de l'ami.

> At the hunts organized in Tuscany, in Lucius' domains, it had pleased me to place this perfect visage in among the heavy and care-laden faces of high officials, or alongside the sharp Oriental profiles and the broad, hairy faces of barbarian

huntsmen, thus obliging the beloved to maintain also the difficult role of friend.

In the past, even the humblest and most anonymous of Hadrian's subjects could be assured of the emperor's passionate attention to their plight. At the height of his happiness with Antinous, however, and lost in his own fantasies,

> il m'arriva d'oublier la personne humaine, l'enfant qui s'efforçait vainement d'apprendre le latin, priait l'ingénieur Décrianus de lui donner des leçons de mathématiques, puis y renonçait, et qui, au moindre reproche, s'en allait bouder à l'avant du navire en regardant la mer.

> I sometimes forgot the purely human, the boy who vainly strove to learn Latin, who begged the engineer Decrianus for lessons in mathematics, then quickly gave up, and who at the slightest reproach used to take himself off to the prow of the ship to gaze broodingly at the sea.

Though the narrating Hadrian continues to protest that he loved his young companion more, rather than less, as time went by, it is increasingly clear that the figure narrated wished to disentangle himself from a commitment that weighed on him more and more heavily. Hadrian started taking other lovers; he frequented brothels. One night in Smyrna, he forced "l'objet aimé à subir la présence d'une courtisane"/"the beloved one to endure the presence of a courtesan." Antinous, whose notion of love included that of exclusivity, was nauseated by this experience.

Several pages earlier, Hadrian describes a trip to Sardinia where he and Antinous take refuge in a peasant's hut during a storm. It is a remembrance of the joy of their early years together. As his young lover helps their host prepare dinner, he reflects on his bliss: "je me crus Zeus visitant Philémon en compagnie d'Hermès. Ce jeune homme aux jambes repliées sur un lit était ce même Hermès dénouant ses sandales; Bacchus cueillait cette grappe, ou goûtait pour moi cette coupe de vin rose; ces doigts durcis par la corde de l'arc étaient ceux d'Eros"/"I felt like Zeus visiting Philemon in company with Hermes. The youth half reclining on a couch, knees upraised, was that same Hermes untying his sandals; it was Bacchus who gathered grapes or tasted for me the cup of red wine; the fingers hardened by the bowstring were those of Eros." The euphoric nature of this vision contrasts sharply with Hadrian's reaction when Antinous, some time later, engages in a similar mythification of their liaison. The emperor had journeyed to Troas. He stopped for a moment to pay his respects at Hector's tomb; Antinous, meanwhile, visited that of Patroclus. "Je ne sus pas reconnaître dans le jeune faon qui m'accompagnait l'émule du camarade d'Achille: je tournai en dérision ces fidélités passionnées qui fleurissent surtout dans les livres; le bel être insulté rougit jusqu'au sang"/"I failed to recognize in the devoted young fawn who accompanied me an emulator of Achilles' friend: when I derided those passionate loyalties which abound chiefly in books the handsome boy was insulted, and flushed crimson."

It was not only at the level of his intimate affairs that the emperor's relations with his world had changed. Hadrian's phenomenal imperial success had multiplied what he

once calls his "chances de vertige"/"sense of vertiginous heights"—heights, one might add, from which one risks falling. Not long before Antinous' death, Hadrian and his entourage made a stop in Jerusalem, where the emperor intended to construct a new city on the ruins of the old. To be called Aelia Capitolina, it would be a modern metropolis of the Roman design that had served so well in other locations. But Jerusalem is not a location like any other. The Jews are outraged by Hadrian's plans to violate their sacred ruins; the first workers to raise a pickax are assaulted by an angry crowd. With a disregard for the local population that Hadrian has never shown before, he presses on with his project. Passionate personal attention to every single detail, in the past, has assured the success of Hadrian's endeavors. Before the walls of Jerusalem, however, he not only fails but refuses to see that he has lit a fire of hatred that will not soon be extinguished: "Je refusai de voir, sur ces tas de débris, la croissance rapide de la haine"/"I refused to see in those heaps of rubble the rapid growth of hatred." Three years after Antinous' death, Hadrian will find himself waging war against those he had so heedlessly and thoroughly offended.

He will provoke a similar, though less virulent, animosity from his subjects in Alexandria upon arriving there. In a passage of remarkable hostility, Hadrian criticizes the useless proliferation of Christian sects in that city, referring to two rival leaders as charlatans. As for the dregs of Egyptian society, they amuse themselves by cudgeling foreigners. Those of higher station find their pleasure in religious conversions.

> Mais l'or est leur seule idole: je n'ai vu nulle part solliciteurs plus éhontés. Des inscriptions pompeuses s'étalèrent un peu partout pour commémorer mes bienfaits, mais mon refus d'exonérer la population d'une taxe, qu'elle était fort à même de payer, m'aliéna bientôt cette tourbe.

> But gold is their only idol: nowhere have I seen more shameless importuning. Grandiose inscriptions were displayed all about to commemorate my benefactions, but my refusal to exempt the inhabitants from a tax which they were quite able to pay soon alienated that rabble from me.

The antipathy that pervades this account could be a sign of increasing arrogance on the part of the narrated Hadrian or else the mark of an impatient narrator rationalizing the mistakes of his past; perhaps both. But in any event, this passage points once again to Hadrian's failure, indeed refusal, to engage with a discontented populace in a meaningful way. Both Lucius and Antinous are subjected to the insults of a scornful people.

These incidents make only too clear that the alienation from his former self upon arriving at the summit of his powers affects Hadrian's actions as emperor in the same unfortunate way that it influences his behavior as a lover. The decline that follows the loss of Antinous will manifest itself similarly in both the personal and the professional spheres.

The section of *Mémoires d'Hadrien* that follows Antinous' death bears the heading "*Disciplina augusta.*" As this title suggests, from now on it is to a rigorous discipline that Hadrian will make himself adhere. But, while self-discipline may be better than distraction, it is no substitute for that lucid and supple adhesion to the real that underlay the triumphs of a now bygone era. Nor can it restore the joy that once had been his.

Those people and places he had formerly loved are suddenly seen as despicable. Returning to Antioch, where he had governed toward the end of Trajan's reign, he calls the populace stupid, mocking, and frivolous. His plans for reform in Asia are not being properly realized; everyone's concern is for personal gain. No one, in short, can do anything right.

The intellectual pursuits that had previously given him pleasure have also gone sour:

> Les trois quarts de nos exercices intellectuels ne sont plus que broderies sur le vide; je me demandais si cette vacuité croissante était due à un abaissement de l'intelligence ou à un déclin du caractère; quoi qu'il en fût, la médiocrité de l'esprit s'accompagnait presque partout d'une étonnante bassesse d'âme.

> Three quarters of our intellectual performances are no more than decorations upon a void; I wondered if that increasing vacuity was due to the lowering of intelligence or to moral decline; whatever the cause, mediocrity of mind was matched almost everywhere by shocking selfishness and dishonesty.

Philosophers themselves fare no better. Once respected companions, they now are pedants who revel in malicious remarks. When Hadrian adds what he believes to be the too-long-neglected works of Hesiod and Ennius to the school curriculum, "ces esprits routiniers me prêtèrent aussitôt l'envie de détrôner Homère, et le limpide Virgile que pourtant je citais sans cesse. Il n'y avait rien à faire avec ces gens-là"/"those routine minds promptly attributed to me the desire to dethrone Homer, and the gentle Virgil as well (whom nevertheless I was always quoting). There was nothing to be done with people of that sort."

Hadrian once had been calm and even-tempered. Now he is impatient and easily angered. He indulges as well in a period of morbid suspicion. Someone, he fears, is planning to poison him. In an effort to foreclose an attack upon his life, he stoops to reading personal letters addressed to his friends. They are not amused.

These character changes may seem to be harmless enough, but such is not the case. Depicting the depths to which Hadrian sinks, and explicitly linked to the loss of his favorite, this incident concerns an imperial secretary, perverse and stubbornly set in his outmoded ways: "Ce sot m'irrita un jour plus qu'à l'ordinaire; je levai la main pour frapper; par malheur, je tenais un style, qui éborgna l'oeil droit. Je n'oublierai jamais ce hurlement de douleur, ce bras maladroitement plié pour parer le coup, cette face convulsée d'où jaillissait le sang"/"This fool irritated me one day more than usual; I raised my hand to slap him; unhappily, I was holding a style, which blinded his right eye. I shall never forget that howl of pain, that arm awkwardly bent to ward off the blow, that convulsed visage from which the blood spurted." When Hadrian asks him to fix a compen-

sation for the harm he has been done, the only thing he wants is another right eye. The passage concludes, revealingly, thus: "Je n'avais pas voulu éborgner ce misérable. Mais je n'avais pas voulu non plus qu'un enfant qui m'aimait mourût à vingt ans"/"I had not wished to injure the wretch. But I had not desired, either, that a boy who loved me should die in his twentieth year."

Many incidents reveal the negative changes in Hadrian's outlook and person after Antinous' death. The structural symmetry of Hadrian's rise and fall shows through most clearly, however, in those contrapuntal scenes that, echoing the period of Hadrian's ascension, punctuate that of his decline. The first of these concerns the founding of a city in honor of the emperor's companion.

During his early years as ruler, Hadrian had taken great joy in the building or rebuilding of imperial cities. We have already observed the lyrical manner in which he describes constructing city after city where Roman culture will flourish. Much more than mere structures of stone, every new metropolis provides the terrain upon which the values of *Humanitas, Felicitas, Libertas* can take root and thrive. Here is a typical passage from *"Tellus stabilita,"* in which Hadrian addresses the value of those "ruches de l'abeille humaine"/"human beehives" that he did his best to multiply:

> Dans un monde encore plus qu'à demi dominé par les bois, le désert, la plaine en friche, c'est un beau spectacle qu'une rue dallée, un temple à n'importe quel dieu, des bains et des latrines publiques, la boutique où le barbier discute avec ses clients les nouvelles de Rome, une échoppe de pâtissier, de marchand de sandales, peut-être de libraire, une enseigne de médecin, un théâtre où l'on joue de temps en temps une pièce de Térence.

> In a world still largely made up of woods, desert, and uncultivated plain, a city is indeed a fine sight, with its paved streets, its temple to some god or other, its public baths and toilets, a shop where the barber discusses with his clients the news from Rome, its pastry shop, shoestore, and perhaps a bookshop, its doctor's sign, and a theatre, where from time to time a comedy of Terence is played.

When the time comes to build Antinoöpolis, however, Hadrian's hymn to the life of the city becomes a bitter dirge:

> La mort est hideuse, mais la vie aussi. Tout grimaçait. La fondation d'Antinoé n'était qu'un jeu dérisoire: une ville de plus, un abri offert aux fraudes des marchands, aux exactions des fonctionnaires, aux prostitutions, au désordre, aux lâches qui pleurent leurs morts avant de les oublier.

> Death is hideous, but life is too. Everything seemed awry. The founding of Antinoöpolis was a ludicrous endeavor, after all, just one more city to shelter fraudulent trading, official extortion, prostitution, disorder, and those cowards who weep for a while over their dead before forgetting them.

Grief, of course, is no small factor in the so marked transformation of this man. It alone does not explain, however, the long, steep slope down which Hadrian continues to hurtle.

At the beginning of *"Disciplina augusta,"* Hadrian returns to Athens, his spiritual home. Here he embarks on another endeavor that reveals the growing contrast between his present and his former selves: the rereading of history. There had once been a time when Hadrian discerned eternal order beneath the surface chaos of human events. He evokes it in connection with his initiation to the Eleusian mysteries. The Eleusis ritual, according to an earlier Hadrian, explained "chacun de nos gestes en termes de mécanique éternelle"/"each of our motions in terms of celestial mechanism." Because of these ritual practices, "J'avais entendu les dissonances se résoudre en accord; j'avais pour un instant pris appui sur une autre sphère, contemplé de loin, mais aussi de tout près, cette procession humaine et divine où j'avais ma place, ce monde où la douleur existe encore, mais non l'erreur"/"I had heard the discords resolving into harmonies; for one moment I had stood on another sphere and contemplated from afar, but also from close by, that procession which is both human and divine, wherein I, too, had my place, this our world where suffering existed still, but error was no more." In his passionate study of astronomy as well, Hadrian looked for and found laws governing the movement of the stars. Though the constellations may appear to wander aimlessly across the heavens, scientists can, in fact, predict their cycles. He sees equally orderly forces presiding over human affairs.

These are not the conclusions that emerge from Hadrian's return to the authors of history after Antinous' death: "leur oeuvre, commentée par ma propre expérience, m'emplit d'idées sombres; l'énergie et la bonne volonté de chaque homme d'Etat semblaient peu de chose en présence de ce déroulement à la fois fortuit et fatal, de ce torrent d'occurrences trop confuses pour être prévues, dirigées, ou jugées"/"their works, judged in the light of my own experience, filled me with somber thoughts; the energy and good intentions of each statesman seemed of slight avail before this flood so fortuitous and so fatal, this torrent of happenings too confused to be foreseen or directed, or even appraised." Where hidden order once had reigned, now there was naught but a fatal flood of anarchy.

And fatal indeed the flood would prove to be—most disastrously so in the campaign of Palestine. The people of Jerusalem were already opposed, as we have seen, to the reconstruction of their city. Certain insults to their faith, though inadvertent, were enough to ignite a rebellion. Revolt then turned into full-scale war. So the emperor who had devoted his life to bringing peace to his realm spent his last active years on the Judaean front.

It is a protracted, guerrilla-type war, which Hadrian's troops are ill-equipped to fight. To make matters worse, living conditions are such that disease claims almost as many soldiers' lives as does the fighting. Though the Romans eventually overcome the fierce resistance of the Jewish partisans, Hadrian counts this war among his failures: "Je ne le nie pas: cette guerre de Judée était un de mes échecs. Les crimes de Simon et la folie d'Akiba n'étaient pas mon oeuvre, mais je me reprochais d'avoir été aveugle à Jérusalem, distrait à Alexandrie, impatient à Rome"/"There is no denying it; that war in Judaea was one of my defeats. The crimes of Simon and the madness of Akiba were not of my making, but I reproached myself for having been blind in Jerusalem, heedless in Alexandria, impatient in Rome." He also notes that it was almost as if the war-torn times that had preceded his reign were beginning all over again.

This is not the only way that the Judaean campaign serves to recall that era of ascent to happiness and glory that ended on the banks of the Nile. The war provides as well the backdrop for a nocturnal meditation, symphonic in its thematic complexity, which is the last and in many ways the bleakest of those contrapuntal passages undergirding the structure of this novel.

In both *"Tellus stabilita,"* which precedes the account of his "Age of Gold," and *"Disciplina augusta,"* which comes after, the narrative dwells for several vivid pages on the late-night reflections of a solitary Hadrian. The first scene takes place in the Syrian desert after the emperor's successful peace negotiations with king Osroës. We have already noted his fervent passion for the stars. Upon this particular occasion, he decides to offer "aux constellations le sacrifice d'une nuit tout entière"/"sacrifice to the constellations of an entire night." Hadrian calls these dark hours of crystalline lucidity "le plus beau de mes voyages"/"the most glorious of all my voyages." It was during that same time of his life that he began to feel himself a kind of god, divine and eternal. Both the passage describing his night beneath the stars and *"Tellus stabilita"* come to an end with an emphatic affirmation of his part in eternity: "la nuit syrienne représente ma part consciente d'immortalité"/"the Syrian night remains as my conscious experience of immortality."

Things are turned around, however, in *"Disciplina augusta."* Whereas the emperor's nocturnal voyage in the Syrian desert had taken place under the sign of a recently established peace, its companion scene is set amidst the death and desolation of the Palestine campaign. Unable to sleep, Hadrian leaves his tent for a breath of fresh air. His senses are accosted instead by the stench of dysentery that emanates from the camp hospital. No night of lucidity this, with not a star in sight. The emperor who once had known himself to be a god now declares such notions null and void: "On me suppose depuis quelques années d'étranges clairvoyances, de sublimes secrets. On se trompe, et je ne sais rien"/"For some years now people have credited me with strange insight, and with knowledge of divine secrets. But they are mistaken; I have no such power." The statesman who had once believed that good could triumph over evil and do so in a manner that would last now renounces that faith:

> Nos faibles efforts pour améliorer la condition humaine ne seraient que distraitement continués par nos successeurs; la graine d'erreur et de ruine contenue dans le bien même croîtrait monstrueusement au contraire au cours des siècles. Le monde las de nous se chercherait d'autres maîtres; ce qui nous avait paru sage paraîtrait insipide, abominable ce qui nous avait paru beau.

Comme l'initié mithriaque, la race humaine a peut-être besoin du bain de sang et du passage périodique dans la fosse funèbre.

Our feeble efforts to ameliorate man's lot would be but vaguely continued by our successors; the seeds of error and ruin contained even in what is good would, on the contrary, increase to monstrous proportions in the course of centuries. A world wearied of us would seek other masters; what had seemed to us wise would be pointless for them, what we had found beautiful they would abominate. Like the initiate to Mithraism the human race has need, perhaps, of a periodical bloodbath and descent into the grave.

The man who once had taken the "most glorious of voyages" beneath a star-studded Syrian sky is now "irrité contre moi-même d'avoir consacré à de creuses méditations sur l'avenir une nuit que j'aurais pu employer à préparer la journée du lendemain, ou à dormir"/"provoked with myself for having devoted to hollow meditations upon the future a night which I could have employed to prepare the work of the next day, or to sleep."

It is no doubt clear by now that Hadrian's affairs, both imperial and personal, are in precipitous decline. Yet they have not reached their nadir. This they will do as a result, at least in part, of his physical health, which, over the course of the events just related, has progressively deteriorated.

We have already observed Hadrian's shortness of breath upon climbing Mount Casius for the last time. This incident was a harbinger of things to come. Just before visiting the sorceress from Canopus he experienced a brief fainting spell. At the encampment in Judaea he becomes seriously ill. A persistent nosebleed saps his strength, and, shortly thereafter, Hadrian suffers the first attack of what his doctor diagnoses as an hydropic heart. As time goes by, his sickness gets worse. The last years of Hadrian's life are spent in almost total confinement.

It is in this state of infirmity that the emperor hits bottom. He decides to put an end to his life. As fear of murder had obsessed him in a healthier time, now suicide obsesses him. Afraid he lacks the strength to stab himself to death, Hadrian implores his young doctor Iollas to provide him with a mortal toxin. Though he indignantly refuses at first, Iollas finally promises to seek out the requested dose of poison. "Je l'attendis vainement jusqu'au soir. Tard dans la nuit, j'appris avec horreur qu'on venait de le trouver mort dans son laboratoire, une fiole de verre entre les mains. Ce coeur pur de tout compromis avait trouvé ce moyen de rester fidèle à son serment sans rien me refuser"/"I awaited him in vain until evening. Late in the night I learned with horror that he had just been found dead in his laboratory, with a glass phial in his hands. That heart clean of all compromise had found this means of abiding by his oath while denying me nothing." Having fallen so far, Hadrian finally sees that his life is not his own to dispose of. He agrees to submit to the painful exigencies of his fate:

> Je ne refuse plus cette agonie faite pour moi, cette fin lentement élaborée au fond de mes ar-

tères, héritée peut-être d'un ancêtre, née de mon tempérament, préparée peu à peu par chacun de mes actes au cours de ma vie. L'heure de l'impatience est passée; au point où j'en suis, le désespoir serait d'aussi mauvais goût que l'espérance. J'ai renoncé à brusquer ma mort.

> I no longer refuse the death agony prepared for me, this ending slowly elaborated within my arteries and inherited perhaps from some ancestor, or born of my temperament, formed little by little from each of my actions throughout my life. The time of impatience has passed; at the point where I now am, despair would be in as bad taste as hope itself. I have ceased to hurry my death.

The next and final chapter of *Mémoires d'Hadrien* recounts nothing less than a renascence. It begins and continues, as had his long-ago paeon to the virtues of Rome in a brisk present tense that looks toward the future: "Tout reste à faire"/"There is still much to be done." No fewer than thirteen imperial projects are listed in rapid-fire succession. These are not the only signs of renewal. Having rejected the idea of his divinity during the period of decline, Hadrian now embraces it again: "Comme au temps de mon bonheur, ils me croient dieu; ils continuent à me donner ce titre au moment même où ils offrent au ciel des sacrifices pour le rétablissement de la Santé Auguste. Je t'ai déjà dit pour quelles raisons cette croyance si bienfaisante ne me paraît pas insensée"/"As in the days of my felicity, people believe me to be a god; they continue to give me that appellation even though they are offering sacrifices to the heavens for the restoration of the Imperial Health. I have already told you the reasons for which such a belief, salutary for them, seems to me not absurd." Such prodigious powers do his subjects attribute to their emperor-god that Hadrian finds himself curing the sick by virtue of their faith in him.

Though he is nearing the end of his life, Hadrian returns to that passionate attention to his acts that had informed his past successes. It is not by chance that the latter are recalled in this last chapter of *Mémoires d'Hadrien,* nor that the passage that does so highlights Hadrian's unmediated contact with his work, recalling as well his openness to alterity. These are the emperor's comments on the verses of an Alexandrian Jew who, once an adversary, is now a friend:

> [J]'ai accueilli sans sarcasmes cette description du prince aux cheveux gris qu'on vit aller et venir sur toutes les routes de la terre, s'enfonçant parmi les trésors des mines, réveillant les forces génératrices du sol, établissant partout la prospérité et la paix, de l'initié qui a relevé les lieux saints de toutes les races, du connaisseur en arts magiques, du voyant qui plaça un enfant au ciel.

> [W]ithout irony I welcomed that description of an elderly prince who is seen going back and forth over all the roads of the earth, descending to the treasures of the mines, reawakening the generative forces of the soil, and everywhere establishing peace and prosperity; the initiate who has restored the shrines of all races, the connois-

seur in magic arts, the seer who raised a youth
to the heavens.

Having lost his moorings for several long years, Hadrian
succeeds at the end of his reign at reconstructing himself
as, in times past, he had succeeded at rebuilding Roman
cities. The footsteps of wisdom in which he follows are
those of his own former self. They cut a path of fervent
attachment to every aspect of the real, a path that Hadrian
will walk, as in his finest moments, until his final breath
is drawn. "Tâchons,"/"Let us try, if we can," he ends
his lengthy letter, "d'entrer dans la mort les yeux
ouverts . . ."/"to enter into death with open eyes. . .".

Ann M. Begley   (review date Winter 1993)

SOURCE: "Death and the Maiden," in *The American
Scholar,* Vol. 62, No. 1, Winter, 1993, pp. 141-42,
144-45.

[*In the following review of* Dear Departed, *Begley provides
an introduction to Yourcenar's major themes and worldview.*]

Marguerite Yourcenar's genius was such that she had at
her command an extraordinary range of literary genres.
Yet her oeuvre often tends to resist classification. Poetry
informs all of her work, without exception. Two of her
novels were awarded prizes for excellence in expository
prose, and—with considerable justification—she elected
to include a volume of prose poems in the collection of her
fiction. It is not surprising, then, to find that *Le labyrinthe
du monde,* which the author has called a memoir and some
have labeled an autobiography, is, in reality, a three-
volume chronicle of her family lineage, replete with polemical commentaries, and in which the writer scarcely
appears on stage at all.

In *Dear Departed,* the first volume of the trilogy to be
translated into English, the reader is taken back to four-
teenth-century Belgium and then led swiftly forward
through generations of the bourgeois aristocracy—
privileged, land-owning families, pausing now and again
to view and ponder those of Yourcenar's forebears who arrest her attention. The writer lingers longest, as one might
suspect, on the courtship and brief marriage of her parents, "already fissured by tiny cracks," in an era when
marriage was looked upon as a commercial transaction
and women "took care not to know too much about conception and parturition and would not have thought they
could name the organs involved. Everything that touched
on the center of the body was the province of husbands,
midwives and physicians."

"It is very important," Yourcenar advised Maria Louise
Ascher, whose fine translation this is, "that the reader not
get the impression that the author is greatly or personally
interested about her origins, since the whole quest is more
sociological and historical than personal." She nevertheless dwells, on the very first page, on "the hopeless tangle
of incidents and circumstances which to a greater or lesser
extent shape us all," and in particular on "the being I refer
to as me," "that girl-child, already fixed by the space-time
coordinates of the Christian era and twentieth-century
Europe." One is tempted to conclude that, just as a num-

ber of her fictive characters examined past events, ostensibly for other reasons but in reality in order to come to a
better understanding of who and what they were, so, too,
might Yourcenar's quest have been a dual one. Contrary
to the expectations of some and the wishes of many, the
book does not reveal the author's own story. However, the
"I," which was so carefully eliminated from much of her
writings, is either present or hovering in the wings. In any
case, as the protagonist of her first novel, Alexis, remarks,
"It is always of oneself that one speaks."

Very little is actually recalled. Rather it is through exhaustive research and impeccable scholarship that Yourcenar,
née Marguerite de Crayencour, evokes a portrait of her
maternal ancestors and the era in which they lived. For
this reason her "memoir" has been compared to *Memoirs
of Hadrian,* the book that first brought her the interest and
respect of American readers. Scrupulous about the authenticity of details, the novelist spent years reading what
the emperor had read and written, traveling where he had
traveled, touching objects he had touched. Her scholarship is so highly valued that she has had the distinction
of being included in the bibliographies of historical works.
To attain what she terms "inner reality," she transported
herself in thought into the body and soul of Hadrian to
permit him to express himself, as much as it is possible,
without an authorial intermediary.

In doing so, to be sure, Yourcenar goes further than the
orthodox historian is willing to tread. Always seeking the
truth, she nevertheless is not opposed to letting her imagination lend her assistance. She describes a method she employed to participate in the events of the past, to permit
those long departed to speak for themselves. Adapting the
Spiritual Exercises of Saint Ignatius of Loyola as well as
those of certain Hindu ascetics, she placed herself on the
scene of events as a silent observer, emptying her mind of
everything but the drama unfolding before her eyes, attaining the contemplative state of recollection in order to
convey what she saw and heard in the manner of a medium.

In *Dear Departed,* she does not achieve the same result.
Precisely because of the continual authorial intrusion, the
reader is sharply aware that the I-narrator/commentator
is speculating much of the time about the feelings and motivations of the constantly changing large cast of characters passing through the mind of the writer, whereas with
Hadrian she lived in a kind of symbiotic relationship so
intense and for so long that it approached, in her words,
"controlled delirium."

As in all of Yourcenar's work, however, what absorbs the
reader of this volume is her examination of the metaphysical questions that have always fascinated the "thinking
reeds"—to use Pascal's metaphor—that we are: the universal fear of death and desire for immortality, the unity
and indestructibility of all in matter, the tension between
divine immanence and transcendence, the strangeness yet
banality of life, the splendor and mystery of love, the unfathomable link between time and eternity.

Yourcenar's mother, Fernande de Cartier de Marchienne,
left French Flanders with her husband, Michel de Crayen-

cour, where they resided on his family estate, to undergo the ordeal of giving birth to her first and only child in familiar and familial surroundings. Thus it was, in 1903, that the first woman ever to have been elected to the French Academy "happened," as she liked to put it, to be born in Brussels. Ten days after giving birth, Fernande died of puerperal fever and peritonitis. And it is this drama that is first presented to the reader.

Yourcenar (the surname is a near anagram of Crayencour) was preoccupied with death, which she defined as "the supreme form of life." In an interview with a journalist, she expressed her desire to die slowly, completely conscious of the "passage," so as not to miss the "ultimate experience." It was in this spirit, she notes, that Hadrian and Zeno, the protagonist of her novel *The Abyss,* die—"with their eyes open." To ensure a dignified encounter with this "friend," she espoused living in constant intimacy with the thought of the inevitable.

In her study of Yukio Mishima, she quotes from a Japanese treatise: "Imagine your death every morning, and you will no longer be afraid to die." There are two kinds of people, she remarks, those who drive the thought of their death out of their minds so as to live more comfortably, and those who feel it wiser and less stressful to live while watching out for death, anticipating its sure arrival. "What some label a morbid mania," she continues, "is for others a heroic discipline." Returning to this theme in *Dear Departed,* Yourcenar observes: "Our love lives are public; our death seems to be conjured out of sight." In this work, as in a number of others, she expresses her admiration for those who elect to die.

The title of the French edition, *Souvenirs pieux* (1974), translated roughly as "devotional remembrances," refers to the small cards with prayers and sometimes pious pictures, distributed by the family of the deceased for the implied purpose of requesting the prayers of the recipients for the "dear departed." (The author also chose the title of the English edition.) In both French and English, the word *pieux* (pious) carries ironic overtones of conspicuous religiosity, hypocrisy, even lack of charity. The *souvenirs pieux* of near and distant relatives, reproduced throughout the book, function as a unifying element, adding cohesiveness to the text. They are at the same time a symbol of death and continuous creation.

Although, in *With Open Eyes,* Yourcenar expresses satisfaction in the rituals, imagery, and liturgy of her Catholic origins, her aversion to what she viewed as the superficial, mechanical, tepid, sometimes superstitious religious observance of her forebears—of whom only a few "make an effort to discover the meaning of Christ's tragic sacrifice"—is clearly evident in *Dear Departed.* Their real gods, she says, are "Plutus, prince of strongboxes; the god Terminus, lord of the cadastre, who takes care of boundaries; the rigid Priapus, secret god of brides, legitimately erect in the exercise of his functions; the good Lucina, who reigns over birthing chambers; and finally, pushed as far away as possible but ever-present at family funerals and devolutions of inheritance, Libitina, goddess of burials, who concludes the procession."

Just prior to her death, Fernande instructed her husband not to let anyone prevent "the little one" from becoming a nun if that should be her wish. The daughter, seventy-one years later, observes that, late in life and in her own fashion, she has embraced religion, but that her mother's "desire has been realized in a way she doubtless would have neither approved nor understood."

While she never renounced Christ, she preferred, she has said, the beauty and mystery of Eastern thought, espousing the concept of divine immanence over transcendence. She subscribed to a "mysticism of matter," a kind of world soul present in every particle of nature, in a continual process of birth, death, and rebirth. The narrator of her powerful short story **"Anna, soror"** comments: "The book of creation has two interpretations, both valid: no one knows whether everything lives only to die, or dies only to be reborn." Her eulogy to her predecessor in the French Academy is essentially a hymn to nature, in which she quotes the medieval mystic Meister Eckhart: "The stone is God, but it doesn't know that it is, and it is the lack of this knowledge that defines its nature as stone."

Setting in relief the blurred boundary she saw between beginning and end, merging present, past, and future, the author chose as an epigraph to *Dear Departed* the Zen koan: "What did your face look like before your father and mother met?" Where time and eternity are juxtaposed in Western thought, Yourcenar perceived a cyclical unity. In *That Mighty Sculptor, Time,* she declares: "There is neither past nor future, only a series of presents, a road, perpetually destroyed and rebuilt, on which we all move forward." *Dear Departed* ends with Fernande, presumably pregnant, reclining on a chaise longue; the writer remarks: "My face begins to take shape on the screen of time." The voyage before life, she has written, of which we know nothing, is as important as the afterlife, of which we are equally ignorant.

After the death of his wife, Michel returned to France with his infant daughter where they lived in a Europe that was still a lovely park where the privileged could stroll about as they pleased, the author notes, and where identification papers were most useful when one was calling for letters at the general delivery window. The child was educated at home by governesses and tutors. When World War I erupted, with the threat of a German invasion, they took refuge in England. After the war, the family seat having been destroyed by the Germans, father and daughter moved to the south of France. After the death of Michel, whose lineage is similarly traced in the second volume of the trilogy, *Archives du nord* (1977), at the end of which the infant Marguerite is not quite six weeks old, Yourcenar traveled extensively throughout Europe, giving serious consideration to settling in Greece. The last volume, *Quoi? L'Eternite* (1988), recounts, to a large extent, Michel's liaison with a friend who had considerable influence in the molding of the author's overview of life.

In 1939, with Europe once more in turmoil, Yourcenar accepted an invitation from Grace Frick to visit the United States. She decided to remain. With Frick, who became her lifelong companion and translator of a number of her books, she bought a house in Northeast Harbor on Mount

Desert Island off the coast of Maine. This was to be her home for the rest of her life, though she continued to be a world traveler and returned many times to France.

In 1947, she became a naturalized American (taking Yourcenar as her legal name), forfeiting her French nationality. Thirty-two years later, at the suggestion of certain French notables, in order to facilitate her election to the Academie française, she petitioned to be reinstated as a French citizen. So it was that, in 1987, she died with dual citizenship. Ironically, in her heart, she was probably neither French nor American. She seemed to prefer Greek culture and liked to think of herself as kin to the universe. In **With Open Eyes,** she remarks: "I have several homelands, so that in one sense I belong perhaps to none." **Dear Departed** is at the same time a quest for roots, an examination of certain metaphysical questions, and a sustained critique of the significant cultural, political, and sociological factors of a society that, in part, spawned the author.

FURTHER READING

Criticism

Brown, John L. Review of *En pèlerin et en étranger,* by Marguerite Yourcenar. *World Literature Today* 65, No. 1 (Winter 1991): 78-9.
    Brief, generally positive review of the collection of previously published essays.

————. Review of *Le labyrinthe du monde: Souvenirs pieux, Archives du nord, Quoi? L'éternité,* by Marguerite Yourcenar. *World Literature Today* 66, No. 1 (Winter 1992): 89.
    Brief, positive overview of Yourcenar's three-volume autobiography.

Epstein, Joseph. "Read Marguerite Yourcenar!" *Commentary* 74, No. 2 (August 1982): 60-5.
    Appreciative introduction to Yourcenar's life and major works. Epstein begins by harshly critiquing George Steiner's 1981 *New Yorker* article in which he negatively assessed Yourcenar's importance and questioned the appropriateness of her induction into the Académie Française.

Farrell, Frederick C., Jr., and Farrell, Edith R. *Marguerite Yourcenar in Counterpoint.* Lanham, MD: University Press of America, 1983, 118 p.
    Contains essays on some of Yourcenar's early works—including *Alexis, Denier du rêve,* and *Feux*—as well as essays that consider such issues as the role of women in her works, the relation of her essays to her fiction, and her penchant for revising and rewriting her work.

Gorman, Kay. "Fact and Fiction in Marguerite Yourcenar's *Le labyrinthe du monde.*" *Essays in French Literature,* No. 23 (November 1986): 60-70.
    Examines Yourcenar's literary technique in the first two volumes of her autobiography, *Souvenirs pieux* and *Archives du nord.* The essay contains many untranslated quotations from the original French.

————. "Marguerite Yourcenar's Encounter with a Feminist Critic." *Journal of the Australasian Universities Language and Literature Association* 73 (May 1990): 59-73.
    Disputes the major points made by Georgia H. Shurr in her *Marguerite Yourcenar: A Reader's Guide,* arguing that "Shurr consistently confuses author, narrator and fictional characters" in her search for autobiographical clues in Yourcenar's works. "Unlike most modern critics," Gorman adds, "Shurr seems to think that there is a 'true' reading of a text, and that autobiographical detail gives some privileged access to it."

Langhorne, Elizabeth. "Bridging East and West." *The Virginia Quarterly* 63, No. 3 (Summer 1987): 521-28.
    Examines and positively reviews *Mishima, or the Vision of the Void* and *Two Lives and Dream.*

Rutledge, Harry C. "Marguerite Yourcenar: The Classicism of *Feux* and *Memoires d'Hadrien.*" *Classical and Modern Literature* 4, No. 2 (Winter 1984): 87-99.
    Argues that both *Feux* and *Memoires d'Hadrien* are "significant contributions to the present-day vitality of the classical tradition." The essay contains many untranslated quotations from the original French.

Sarnecki, Judith Holland. Review of *Conte bleu,* by Marguerite Yourcenar. *The French Review* 68, No. 4 (March 1995): 756-57.
    Laudatory review of *Conte bleu* praising the volume's cohesiveness and focus on gender stereotypes. Sarnecki states: "Fans of Yourcenar's elegant prose will delight in finding new texts to savor, while newcomers to her work will discover many of the themes developed at greater length in [her] masterpieces."

Shurr, Georgia H. *Marguerite Yourcenar: A Reader's Guide.* Lanham, MD: University Press of America, 1987, 150 p.
    Feminist study of Yourcenar's major works.

Steiner, George. "Ladies' Day." *The New Yorker* LVII, No. 26 (17 August 1981): 104-06.
    Negative review of *Fires* and generally unfavorable assessment of Yourcenar's career.

Straus, Dorothea. "Petite Plaisance." *Partisan Review* LVI, No. 3 (Summer 1989): 370-73.
    Reminiscence of meeting Yourcenar at her home while she worked on her critical study of Yukio Mishima.

Taylor, John. "Waiting for Hadrian." *The Georgia Review* XLII, No. 1 (Spring 1988): 147-51.
    Appreciation and personal reminiscence of Yourcenar's life and work.

Weightman, John. "Twilight in Flanders." *The New York Review of Books* XXXIX, Nos. 1-2 (16 January 1992): 30-3.
    Detailed review of *Dear Departed,* which, though he finds it an interesting and entertaining depiction of "the twilight of a social class," he deems ultimately disappointing in its lack of information and insight into its author.

Wineapple, Brenda. "Digging Up the Family Plot." *The Women's Review of Books* IX, No. 6 (March 1992): 12-13.
    Positive review and analysis of *Dear Departed.*

Interviews

Cismaru, Alfred. "Marguerite Yourcenar: The Final Interview." *Michigan Quarterly Review* XXXI, No. 1 (Winter 1992): 96-103.

Yourcenar discusses her reputation and her thoughts on literature and aging. The interview was conducted a few months before she died, and at the time she was recovering from open-heart surgery.

Additional coverage of Yourcenar's life and career is contained in the following sources published by Gale Research: *Contemporary Authors,* Vols. 69-72; *Contemporary Authors New Revision Series,* Vol. 23; *Contemporary Literary Criticism,* Vols. 19, 38, 50; *Dictionary of Literary Biography,* Vol. 72; *Dictionary of Literary Biography Yearbook 1988;* and *Major 20th-Century Writers.*

☐ Contemporary Literary Criticism

Indexes

Literary Criticism Series
Cumulative Author Index
Cumulative Topic Index
Cumulative Nationality Index
Title Index, Volume 87

How to Use This Index

The main references

Calvino, Italo
    1923-1985.....CLC 5, 8, 11, 22, 33, 39,
                            73; SSC 3

---

list all author entries in the following Gale Literary Criticism series:

BLC = *Black Literature Criticism*
CLC = *Contemporary Literary Criticism*
CLR = *Children's Literature Review*
CMLC = *Classical and Medieval Literature Criticism*
DA = *DISCovering Authors*
DC = *Drama Criticism*
HLC = *Hispanic Literature Criticism*
LC = *Literature Criticism from 1400 to 1800*
NCLC = *Nineteenth-Century Literature Criticism*
PC = *Poetry Criticism*
SSC = *Short Story Criticism*
TCLC = *Twentieth-Century Literary Criticism*
WLC = *World Literature Criticism, 1500 to the Present*

The cross-references

See also CANR 23; CA 85-88;
  obituary CA 116

---

list all author entries in the following Gale biographical and literary sources:

AAYA = *Authors & Artists for Young Adults*
AITN = *Authors in the News*
BEST = *Bestsellers*
BW = *Black Writers*
CA = *Contemporary Authors*
CAAS = *Contemporary Authors Autobiography Series*
CABS = *Contemporary Authors Bibliographical Series*
CANR = *Contemporary Authors New Revision Series*
CAP = *Contemporary Authors Permanent Series*
CDALB = *Concise Dictionary of American Literary Biography*
CDBLB = *Concise Dictionary of British Literary Biography*
DLB = *Dictionary of Literary Biography*
DLBD = *Dictionary of Literary Biography Documentary Series*
DLBY = *Dictionary of Literary Biography Yearbook*
HW = *Hispanic Writers*
JRDA = *Junior DISCovering Authors*
MAICYA = *Major Authors and Illustrators for Children and Young Adults*
MTCW = *Major 20th-Century Writers*
NNAL = *Native North American Literature*
SAAS = *Something about the Author Autobiography Series*
SATA = *Something about the Author*
YABC = *Yesterday's Authors of Books for Children*

Literary Criticism Series
Cumulative Author Index

Anthony, Peter
See Shaffer, Anthony (Joshua); Shaffer, Peter (Levin)

Anthony, Piers 1934- . . . . **CLC 35**
See also AAYA 11; CA 21-24R; CANR 28; DLB 8; MTCW

Antoine, Marc
See Proust, (Valentin-Louis-George-Eugene-) Marcel

Antoninus, Brother
See Everson, William (Oliver)

Antonioni, Michelangelo 1912- . . . . . **CLC 20**
See also CA 73-76; CANR 45

Antschel, Paul 1920-1970
See Celan, Paul
See also CA 85-88; CANR 33; MTCW

Anwar, Chairil 1922-1949 . . . . **TCLC 22**
See also CA 121

Apollinaire, Guillaume . . **TCLC 3, 8, 51; PC 7**
See also Kostrowitzki, Wilhelm Apollinaris de

Appelfeld, Aharon 1932- . . . . **CLC 23, 47**
See also CA 112; 133

Apple, Max (Isaac) 1941- . . . . **CLC 9, 33**
See also CA 81-84; CANR 19; DLB 130

Appleman, Philip (Dean) 1926- . . . . . **CLC 51**
See also CA 13-16R; CAAS 18; CANR 6, 29

Appleton, Lawrence
See Lovecraft, H(oward) P(hillips)

Apteryx
See Eliot, T(homas) S(tearns)

Apuleius, (Lucius Madaurensis)
125(?)-175(?) . . . . **CMLC 1**

Aquin, Hubert 1929-1977 . . . . **CLC 15**
See also CA 105; DLB 53

Aragon, Louis 1897-1982 . . . . **CLC 3, 22**
See also CA 69-72; 108; CANR 28; DLB 72; MTCW

Arany, Janos 1817-1882 . . . . **NCLC 34**

Arbuthnot, John 1667-1735 . . . . **LC 1**
See also DLB 101

Archer, Herbert Winslow
See Mencken, H(enry) L(ouis)

Archer, Jeffrey (Howard) 1940- . . . . **CLC 28**
See also BEST 89:3; CA 77-80; CANR 22

Archer, Jules 1915- . . . . **CLC 12**
See also CA 9-12R; CANR 6; SAAS 5; SATA 4

Archer, Lee
See Ellison, Harlan (Jay)

Arden, John 1930- . . . . **CLC 6, 13, 15**
See also CA 13-16R; CAAS 4; CANR 31; DLB 13; MTCW

Arenas, Reinaldo
1943-1990 . . . . **CLC 41; HLC**
See also CA 124; 128; 133; DLB 145; HW

Arendt, Hannah 1906-1975 . . . . **CLC 66**
See also CA 17-20R; 61-64; CANR 26; MTCW

Aretino, Pietro 1492-1556 . . . . **LC 12**

Arghezi, Tudor . . . . **CLC 80**
See also Theodorescu, Ion N.

Arguedas, Jose Maria
1911-1969 . . . . **CLC 10, 18**
See also CA 89-92; DLB 113; HW

Argueta, Manlio 1936- . . . . **CLC 31**
See also CA 131; DLB 145; HW

Ariosto, Ludovico 1474-1533 . . . . **LC 6**

Aristides
See Epstein, Joseph

Aristophanes
450B.C.-385B.C. . . . . **CMLC 4; DA; DC 2**

Arlt, Roberto (Godofredo Christophersen)
1900-1942 . . . . **TCLC 29; HLC**
See also CA 123; 131; HW

Armah, Ayi Kwei 1939- . . . . **CLC 5, 33; BLC**
See also BW 1; CA 61-64; CANR 21; DLB 117; MTCW

Armatrading, Joan 1950- . . . . **CLC 17**
See also CA 114

Arnette, Robert
See Silverberg, Robert

Arnim, Achim von (Ludwig Joachim von Arnim) 1781-1831 . . . . **NCLC 5**
See also DLB 90

Arnim, Bettina von 1785-1859 . . . . **NCLC 38**
See also DLB 90

Arnold, Matthew
1822-1888 . . . . . **NCLC 6, 29; DA; PC 5; WLC**
See also CDBLB 1832-1890; DLB 32, 57

Arnold, Thomas 1795-1842 . . . . . . **NCLC 18**
See also DLB 55

Arnow, Harriette (Louisa) Simpson
1908-1986 . . . . **CLC 2, 7, 18**
See also CA 9-12R; 118; CANR 14; DLB 6; MTCW; SATA 42; SATA-Obit 47

Arp, Hans
See Arp, Jean

Arp, Jean 1887-1966 . . . . **CLC 5**
See also CA 81-84; 25-28R; CANR 42

Arrabal
See Arrabal, Fernando

Arrabal, Fernando 1932- . . . **CLC 2, 9, 18, 58**
See also CA 9-12R; CANR 15

Arrick, Fran . . . . **CLC 30**

Artaud, Antonin 1896-1948 . . . . . **TCLC 3, 36**
See also CA 104

Arthur, Ruth M(abel) 1905-1979 . . . . **CLC 12**
See also CA 9-12R; 85-88; CANR 4; SATA 7, 26

Artsybashev, Mikhail (Petrovich)
1878-1927 . . . . **TCLC 31**

Arundel, Honor (Morfydd)
1919-1973 . . . . **CLC 17**
See also CA 21-22; 41-44R; CAP 2; CLR 35; SATA 4; SATA-Obit 24

Asch, Sholem 1880-1957 . . . . **TCLC 3**
See also CA 105

Ash, Shalom
See Asch, Sholem

Ashbery, John (Lawrence)
1927- . . . . . . **CLC 2, 3, 4, 6, 9, 13, 15, 25, 41, 77**
See also CA 5-8R; CANR 9, 37; DLB 5; DLBY 81; MTCW

Ashdown, Clifford
See Freeman, R(ichard) Austin

Ashe, Gordon
See Creasey, John

Ashton-Warner, Sylvia (Constance)
1908-1984 . . . . **CLC 19**
See also CA 69-72; 112; CANR 29; MTCW

Asimov, Isaac
1920-1992 . . . . . . **CLC 1, 3, 9, 19, 26, 76**
See also AAYA 13; BEST 90:2; CA 1-4R; 137; CANR 2, 19, 36; CLR 12; DLB 8; DLBY 92; JRDA; MAICYA; MTCW; SATA 1, 26, 74

Astley, Thea (Beatrice May)
1925- . . . . **CLC 41**
See also CA 65-68; CANR 11, 43

Aston, James
See White, T(erence) H(anbury)

Asturias, Miguel Angel
1899-1974 . . . . **CLC 3, 8, 13; HLC**
See also CA 25-28; 49-52; CANR 32; CAP 2; DLB 113; HW; MTCW

Atares, Carlos Saura
See Saura (Atares), Carlos

Atheling, William
See Pound, Ezra (Weston Loomis)

Atheling, William, Jr.
See Blish, James (Benjamin)

Atherton, Gertrude (Franklin Horn)
1857-1948 . . . . **TCLC 2**
See also CA 104; DLB 9, 78

Atherton, Lucius
See Masters, Edgar Lee

Atkins, Jack
See Harris, Mark

Atticus
See Fleming, Ian (Lancaster)

Atwood, Margaret (Eleanor)
1939- . . . . . **CLC 2, 3, 4, 8, 13, 15, 25, 44, 84; DA; PC 8; SSC 2; WLC**
See also AAYA 12; BEST 89:2; CA 49-52; CANR 3, 24, 33; DLB 53; MTCW; SATA 50

Aubigny, Pierre d'
See Mencken, H(enry) L(ouis)

Aubin, Penelope 1685-1731(?) . . . . **LC 9**
See also DLB 39

Auchincloss, Louis (Stanton)
1917- . . . . **CLC 4, 6, 9, 18, 45**
See also CA 1-4R; CANR 6, 29; DLB 2; DLBY 80; MTCW

Auden, W(ystan) H(ugh)
1907-1973 . . . . . . **CLC 1, 2, 3, 4, 6, 9, 11, 14, 43; DA; PC 1; WLC**
See also CA 9-12R; 45-48; CANR 5; CDBLB 1914-1945; DLB 10, 20; MTCW

Audiberti, Jacques 1900-1965 . . . . . . **CLC 38**
See also CA 25-28R

Audubon, John James
1785-1851 . . . . **NCLC 47**

Auel, Jean M(arie) 1936- . . . . **CLC 31**
See also AAYA 7; BEST 90:4; CA 103; CANR 21

Auerbach, Erich 1892-1957 . . . . **TCLC 43**
See also CA 118

Augier, Emile   1820-1889 . . . . NCLC 31

August, John
    See De Voto, Bernard (Augustine)

Augustine, St.   354-430 . . . . CMLC 6

Aurelius
    See Bourne, Randolph S(illiman)

Austen, Jane
    1775-1817 . . . .   NCLC 1, 13, 19, 33; DA;
                                                WLC
    See also CDBLB 1789-1832; DLB 116

Auster, Paul   1947- . . . . CLC 47
    See also CA 69-72; CANR 23

Austin, Frank
    See Faust, Frederick (Schiller)

Austin, Mary (Hunter)
    1868-1934 . . . . TCLC 25
    See also CA 109; DLB 9, 78

Autran Dourado, Waldomiro
    See Dourado, (Waldomiro Freitas) Autran

Averroes   1126-1198 . . . . CMLC 7
    See also DLB 115

Avison, Margaret   1918- . . . . CLC 2, 4
    See also CA 17-20R; DLB 53; MTCW

Axton, David
    See Koontz, Dean R(ay)

Ayckbourn, Alan
    1939- . . . . CLC 5, 8, 18, 33, 74
    See also CA 21-24R; CANR 31; DLB 13;
        MTCW

Aydy, Catherine
    See Tennant, Emma (Christina)

Ayme, Marcel (Andre)   1902-1967 . . . CLC 11
    See also CA 89-92; CLR 25; DLB 72

Ayrton, Michael   1921-1975 . . . . CLC 7
    See also CA 5-8R; 61-64; CANR 9, 21

Azorin . . . . CLC 11
    See also Martinez Ruiz, Jose

Azuela, Mariano
    1873-1952 . . . . TCLC 3; HLC
    See also CA 104; 131; HW; MTCW

Baastad, Babbis Friis
    See Friis-Baastad, Babbis Ellinor

Bab
    See Gilbert, W(illiam) S(chwenck)

Babbis, Eleanor
    See Friis-Baastad, Babbis Ellinor

Babel, Isaak (Emmanuilovich)
    1894-1941(?) . . . . . . TCLC 2, 13; SSC 16
    See also CA 104

Babits, Mihaly   1883-1941 . . . . TCLC 14
    See also CA 114

Babur   1483-1530 . . . . LC 18

Bacchelli, Riccardo   1891-1985 . . . . . CLC 19
    See also CA 29-32R; 117

Bach, Richard (David)   1936- . . . . CLC 14
    See also AITN 1; BEST 89:2; CA 9-12R;
        CANR 18; MTCW; SATA 13

Bachman, Richard
    See King, Stephen (Edwin)

Bachmann, Ingeborg   1926-1973 . . . . . CLC 69
    See also CA 93-96; 45-48; DLB 85

Bacon, Francis   1561-1626 . . . . LC 18
    See also CDBLB Before 1660

Bacon, Roger   1214(?)-1292 . . . . . . CMLC 14
    See also DLB 115

Bacovia, George . . . . TCLC 24
    See also Vasiliu, Gheorghe

Badanes, Jerome   1937- . . . . CLC 59

Bagehot, Walter   1826-1877 . . . . . NCLC 10
    See also DLB 55

Bagnold, Enid   1889-1981 . . . . CLC 25
    See also CA 5-8R; 103; CANR 5, 40;
        DLB 13; MAICYA; SATA 1, 25

Bagrjana, Elisaveta
    See Belcheva, Elisaveta

Bagryana, Elisaveta
    See Belcheva, Elisaveta
    See also DLB 147

Bailey, Paul   1937- . . . . CLC 45
    See also CA 21-24R; CANR 16; DLB 14

Baillie, Joanna   1762-1851 . . . . NCLC 2
    See also DLB 93

Bainbridge, Beryl (Margaret)
    1933- . . . . CLC 4, 5, 8, 10, 14, 18, 22, 62
    See also CA 21-24R; CANR 24; DLB 14;
        MTCW

Baker, Elliott   1922- . . . . CLC 8
    See also CA 45-48; CANR 2

Baker, Nicholson   1957- . . . . CLC 61
    See also CA 135

Baker, Ray Stannard   1870-1946 . . . TCLC 47
    See also CA 118

Baker, Russell (Wayne)   1925- . . . . . . CLC 31
    See also BEST 89:4; CA 57-60; CANR 11,
        41; MTCW

Bakhtin, M.
    See Bakhtin, Mikhail Mikhailovich

Bakhtin, M. M.
    See Bakhtin, Mikhail Mikhailovich

Bakhtin, Mikhail
    See Bakhtin, Mikhail Mikhailovich

Bakhtin, Mikhail Mikhailovich
    1895-1975 . . . . CLC 83
    See also CA 128; 113

Bakshi, Ralph   1938(?)- . . . . CLC 26
    See also CA 112; 138

Bakunin, Mikhail (Alexandrovich)
    1814-1876 . . . . NCLC 25

Baldwin, James (Arthur)
    1924-1987 . . . . . . CLC 1, 2, 3, 4, 5, 8, 13,
                    15, 17, 42, 50, 67; BLC; DA; DC 1;
                                        SSC 10; WLC
    See also AAYA 4; BW 1; CA 1-4R; 124;
        CABS 1; CANR 3, 24;
        CDALB 1941-1968; DLB 2, 7, 33;
        DLBY 87; MTCW; SATA 9;
        SATA-Obit 54

Ballard, J(ames) G(raham)
    1930- . . . . CLC 3, 6, 14, 36; SSC 1
    See also AAYA 3; CA 5-8R; CANR 15, 39;
        DLB 14; MTCW

Balmont, Konstantin (Dmitriyevich)
    1867-1943 . . . . TCLC 11
    See also CA 109

Balzac, Honore de
    1799-1850 . . . . NCLC 5, 35; DA; SSC 5;
                                                WLC
    See also DLB 119

Bambara, Toni Cade
    1939- . . . . CLC 19; BLC; DA
    See also AAYA 5; BW 2; CA 29-32R;
        CANR 24; DLB 38; MTCW

Bamdad, A.
    See Shamlu, Ahmad

Banat, D. R.
    See Bradbury, Ray (Douglas)

Bancroft, Laura
    See Baum, L(yman) Frank

Banim, John   1798-1842 . . . . NCLC 13
    See also DLB 116

Banim, Michael   1796-1874 . . . . . . NCLC 13

Banks, Iain
    See Banks, Iain M(enzies)

Banks, Iain M(enzies)   1954- . . . . CLC 34
    See also CA 123; 128

Banks, Lynne Reid . . . . CLC 23
    See also Reid Banks, Lynne
    See also AAYA 6

Banks, Russell   1940- . . . . CLC 37, 72
    See also CA 65-68; CAAS 15; CANR 19;
        DLB 130

Banville, John   1945- . . . . CLC 46
    See also CA 117; 128; DLB 14

Banville, Theodore (Faullain) de
    1832-1891 . . . . NCLC 9

Baraka, Amiri
    1934- . . . . CLC 1, 2, 3, 5, 10, 14, 33;
                                        BLC; DA; PC 4
    See also Jones, LeRoi
    See also BW 2; CA 21-24R; CABS 3;
        CANR 27, 38; CDALB 1941-1968;
        DLB 5, 7, 16, 38; DLBD 8; MTCW

Barbellion, W. N. P. . . . . TCLC 24
    See also Cummings, Bruce F(rederick)

Barbera, Jack (Vincent)   1945- . . . . . . CLC 44
    See also CA 110; CANR 45

Barbey d'Aurevilly, Jules Amedee
    1808-1889 . . . . NCLC 1; SSC 17
    See also DLB 119

Barbusse, Henri   1873-1935 . . . . TCLC 5
    See also CA 105; DLB 65

Barclay, Bill
    See Moorcock, Michael (John)

Barclay, William Ewert
    See Moorcock, Michael (John)

Barea, Arturo   1897-1957 . . . . TCLC 14
    See also CA 111

Barfoot, Joan   1946- . . . . CLC 18
    See also CA 105

Baring, Maurice   1874-1945 . . . . TCLC 8
    See also CA 105; DLB 34

Barker, Clive   1952- . . . . CLC 52
    See also AAYA 10; BEST 90:3; CA 121;
        129; MTCW

Barker, George Granville
    1913-1991 . . . . CLC 8, 48
    See also CA 9-12R; 135; CANR 7, 38;
        DLB 20; MTCW

Barker, Harley Granville
    See Granville-Barker, Harley
    See also DLB 10

Barker, Howard 1946-.......... **CLC 37**
See also CA 102; DLB 13

Barker, Pat 1943-.............. **CLC 32**
See also CA 117; 122

Barlow, Joel 1754-1812 .... **NCLC 23**
See also DLB 37

Barnard, Mary (Ethel) 1909-....... **CLC 48**
See also CA 21-22; CAP 2

Barnes, Djuna
1892-1982 ... **CLC 3, 4, 8, 11, 29; SSC 3**
See also CA 9-12R; 107; CANR 16; DLB 4,
9, 45; MTCW

Barnes, Julian 1946-.............. **CLC 42**
See also CA 102; CANR 19; DLBY 93

Barnes, Peter 1931- .... **CLC 5, 56**
See also CA 65-68; CAAS 12; CANR 33,
34; DLB 13; MTCW

Baroja (y Nessi), Pio
1872-1956 .... **TCLC 8; HLC**
See also CA 104

Baron, David
See Pinter, Harold

Baron Corvo
See Rolfe, Frederick (William Serafino
Austin Lewis Mary)

Barondess, Sue K(aufman)
1926-1977 .... **CLC 8**
See also Kaufman, Sue
See also CA 1-4R; 69-72; CANR 1

Baron de Teive
See Pessoa, Fernando (Antonio Nogueira)

Barres, Maurice 1862-1923 .... **TCLC 47**
See also DLB 123

Barreto, Afonso Henrique de Lima
See Lima Barreto, Afonso Henrique de

Barrett, (Roger) Syd 1946- .... **CLC 35**

Barrett, William (Christopher)
1913-1992 .... **CLC 27**
See also CA 13-16R; 139; CANR 11

Barrie, J(ames) M(atthew)
1860-1937 .... **TCLC 2**
See also CA 104; 136; CDBLB 1890-1914;
CLR 16; DLB 10, 141; MAICYA;
YABC 1

Barrington, Michael
See Moorcock, Michael (John)

Barrol, Grady
See Bograd, Larry

Barry, Mike
See Malzberg, Barry N(athaniel)

Barry, Philip 1896-1949.......... **TCLC 11**
See also CA 109; DLB 7

Bart, Andre Schwarz
See Schwarz-Bart, Andre

Barth, John (Simmons)
1930- ...... **CLC 1, 2, 3, 5, 7, 9, 10, 14,**
27, 51; SSC 10
See also AITN 1, 2; CA 1-4R; CABS 1;
CANR 5, 23; DLB 2; MTCW

Barthelme, Donald
1931-1989 ...... **CLC 1, 2, 3, 5, 6, 8, 13,**
23, 46, 59; SSC 2
See also CA 21-24R; 129; CANR 20;
DLB 2; DLBY 80, 89; MTCW; SATA 7;
SATA-Obit 62

Barthelme, Frederick 1943-........ **CLC 36**
See also CA 114; 122; DLBY 85

Barthes, Roland (Gerard)
1915-1980 .... **CLC 24, 83**
See also CA 130; 97-100; MTCW

Barzun, Jacques (Martin) 1907-.... **CLC 51**
See also CA 61-64; CANR 22

Bashevis, Isaac
See Singer, Isaac Bashevis

Bashkirtseff, Marie 1859-1884 ... **NCLC 27**

Basho
See Matsuo Basho

Bass, Kingsley B., Jr.
See Bullins, Ed

Bass, Rick 1958-................. **CLC 79**
See also CA 126

Bassani, Giorgio 1916-............ **CLC 9**
See also CA 65-68; CANR 33; DLB 128;
MTCW

Bastos, Augusto (Antonio) Roa
See Roa Bastos, Augusto (Antonio)

Bataille, Georges 1897-1962 .... **CLC 29**
See also CA 101; 89-92

Bates, H(erbert) E(rnest)
1905-1974 .... **CLC 46; SSC 10**
See also CA 93-96; 45-48; CANR 34;
MTCW

Bauchart
See Camus, Albert

Baudelaire, Charles
1821-1867 ..... **NCLC 6, 29; DA; PC 1;**
SSC 18; WLC

Baudrillard, Jean 1929-........... **CLC 60**

Baum, L(yman) Frank 1856-1919 ... **TCLC 7**
See also CA 108; 133; CLR 15; DLB 22;
JRDA; MAICYA; MTCW; SATA 18

Baum, Louis F.
See Baum, L(yman) Frank

Baumbach, Jonathan 1933- ...... **CLC 6, 23**
See also CA 13-16R; CAAS 5; CANR 12;
DLBY 80; MTCW

Bausch, Richard (Carl) 1945- ...... **CLC 51**
See also CA 101; CAAS 14; CANR 43;
DLB 130

Baxter, Charles 1947-.......... **CLC 45, 78**
See also CA 57-60; CANR 40; DLB 130

Baxter, George Owen
See Faust, Frederick (Schiller)

Baxter, James K(eir) 1926-1972 .... **CLC 14**
See also CA 77-80

Baxter, John
See Hunt, E(verette) Howard, (Jr.)

Bayer, Sylvia
See Glassco, John

Baynton, Barbara 1857-1929 ...... **TCLC 57**

Beagle, Peter S(oyer) 1939-........ **CLC 7**
See also CA 9-12R; CANR 4; DLBY 80;
SATA 60

Bean, Normal
See Burroughs, Edgar Rice

Beard, Charles A(ustin)
1874-1948 .... **TCLC 15**
See also CA 115; DLB 17; SATA 18

Beardsley, Aubrey 1872-1898 ..... **NCLC 6**

Beattie, Ann
1947-.... **CLC 8, 13, 18, 40, 63; SSC 11**
See also BEST 90:2; CA 81-84; DLBY 82;
MTCW

Beattie, James 1735-1803 .... **NCLC 25**
See also DLB 109

Beauchamp, Kathleen Mansfield 1888-1923
See Mansfield, Katherine
See also CA 104; 134; DA

Beaumarchais, Pierre-Augustin Caron de
1732-1799 .... **DC 4**

**Beauvoir, Simone (Lucie Ernestine Marie
Bertrand) de**
1908-1986 .... **CLC 1, 2, 4, 8, 14, 31, 44,**
50, 71; DA; WLC
See also CA 9-12R; 118; CANR 28;
DLB 72; DLBY 86; MTCW

Becker, Jurek 1937-.......... **CLC 7, 19**
See also CA 85-88; DLB 75

Becker, Walter 1950-............. **CLC 26**

Beckett, Samuel (Barclay)
1906-1989 ...... **CLC 1, 2, 3, 4, 6, 9, 10,**
11, 14, 18, 29, 57, 59, 83; DA; SSC 16;
WLC
See also CA 5-8R; 130; CANR 33;
CDBLB 1945-1960; DLB 13, 15;
DLBY 90; MTCW

Beckford, William 1760-1844 .... **NCLC 16**
See also DLB 39

Beckman, Gunnel 1910-........... **CLC 26**
See also CA 33-36R; CANR 15; CLR 25;
MAICYA; SAAS 9; SATA 6

Becque, Henri 1837-1899........ **NCLC 3**

Beddoes, Thomas Lovell
1803-1849 .... **NCLC 3**
See also DLB 96

Bedford, Donald F.
See Fearing, Kenneth (Flexner)

Beecher, Catharine Esther
1800-1878 .... **NCLC 30**
See also DLB 1

Beecher, John 1904-1980......... **CLC 6**
See also AITN 1; CA 5-8R; 105; CANR 8

Beer, Johann 1655-1700............ **LC 5**

Beer, Patricia 1924-.............. **CLC 58**
See also CA 61-64; CANR 13, 46; DLB 40

Beerbohm, Henry Maximilian
1872-1956 .... **TCLC 1, 24**
See also CA 104; DLB 34, 100

Beerbohm, Max
See Beerbohm, Henry Maximilian

Begiebing, Robert J(ohn) 1946-..... **CLC 70**
See also CA 122; CANR 40

Behan, Brendan
1923-1964 .... **CLC 1, 8, 11, 15, 79**
See also CA 73-76; CANR 33;
CDBLB 1945-1960; DLB 13; MTCW

Behn, Aphra
1640(?)-1689 .... **LC 1; DA; DC 4; WLC**
See also DLB 39, 80, 131

Behrman, S(amuel) N(athaniel)
1893-1973 .... **CLC 40**
See also CA 13-16; 45-48; CAP 1; DLB 7,
44

Bertrand, Aloysius   1807-1841 . . . .   **NCLC 31**

Bertran de Born   c. 1140-1215 . . . . .   **CMLC 5**

Besant, Annie (Wood)   1847-1933 . . .   **TCLC 9**
   See also CA 105

Bessie, Alvah   1904-1985 . . . .   **CLC 23**
   See also CA 5-8R; 116; CANR 2; DLB 26

Bethlen, T. D.
   See Silverberg, Robert

Beti, Mongo . . . .   **CLC 27; BLC**
   See also Biyidi, Alexandre

Betjeman, John
      1906-1984 . . . .   **CLC 2, 6, 10, 34, 43**
   See also CA 9-12R; 112; CANR 33;
      CDBLB 1945-1960; DLB 20; DLBY 84;
      MTCW

Bettelheim, Bruno   1903-1990 . . . . . .   **CLC 79**
   See also CA 81-84; 131; CANR 23; MTCW

Betti, Ugo   1892-1953 . . . .   **TCLC 5**
   See also CA 104

Betts, Doris (Waugh)   1932- . . . .   **CLC 3, 6, 28**
   See also CA 13-16R; CANR 9; DLBY 82

Bevan, Alistair
   See Roberts, Keith (John Kingston)

Bialik, Chaim Nachman
      1873-1934 . . . .   **TCLC 25**

Bickerstaff, Isaac
   See Swift, Jonathan

Bidart, Frank   1939- . . . .   **CLC 33**
   See also CA 140

Bienek, Horst   1930- . . . .   **CLC 7, 11**
   See also CA 73-76; DLB 75

Bierce, Ambrose (Gwinett)
      1842-1914(?) . . . .   **TCLC 1, 7, 44; DA;
                                                       SSC 9; WLC**
   See also CA 104; 139; CDALB 1865-1917;
      DLB 11, 12, 23, 71, 74

Billings, Josh
   See Shaw, Henry Wheeler

Billington, (Lady) Rachel (Mary)
      1942- . . . .   **CLC 43**
   See also AITN 2; CA 33-36R; CANR 44

Binyon, T(imothy) J(ohn)   1936- . . . .   **CLC 34**
   See also CA 111; CANR 28

Bioy Casares, Adolfo
      1914- . . . . . .   **CLC 4, 8, 13; HLC; SSC 17**
   See also CA 29-32R; CANR 19, 43;
      DLB 113; HW; MTCW

Bird, Cordwainer
   See Ellison, Harlan (Jay)

Bird, Robert Montgomery
      1806-1854 . . . .   **NCLC 1**

Birney, (Alfred) Earle
      1904- . . . .   **CLC 1, 4, 6, 11**
   See also CA 1-4R; CANR 5, 20; DLB 88;
      MTCW

Bishop, Elizabeth
      1911-1979 . . . . . .   **CLC 1, 4, 9, 13, 15, 32;
                                                       DA; PC 3**
   See also CA 5-8R; 89-92; CABS 2;
      CANR 26; CDALB 1968-1988; DLB 5;
      MTCW; SATA-Obit 24

Bishop, John   1935- . . . .   **CLC 10**
   See also CA 105

Bissett, Bill   1939- . . . .   **CLC 18**
   See also CA 69-72; CAAS 19; CANR 15;
      DLB 53; MTCW

Bitov, Andrei (Georgievich)   1937- . . .   **CLC 57**
   See also CA 142

Biyidi, Alexandre   1932-
   See Beti, Mongo
   See also BW 1; CA 114; 124; MTCW

Bjarme, Brynjolf
   See Ibsen, Henrik (Johan)

Bjornson, Bjornstjerne (Martinius)
      1832-1910 . . . .   **TCLC 7, 37**
   See also CA 104

Black, Robert
   See Holdstock, Robert P.

Blackburn, Paul   1926-1971 . . . . . .   **CLC 9, 43**
   See also CA 81-84; 33-36R; CANR 34;
      DLB 16; DLBY 81

Black Elk   1863-1950 . . . .   **TCLC 33**
   See also CA 144; NNAL

Black Hobart
   See Sanders, (James) Ed(ward)

Blacklin, Malcolm
   See Chambers, Aidan

Blackmore, R(ichard) D(oddridge)
      1825-1900 . . . .   **TCLC 27**
   See also CA 120; DLB 18

Blackmur, R(ichard) P(almer)
      1904-1965 . . . .   **CLC 2, 24**
   See also CA 11-12; 25-28R; CAP 1; DLB 63

Black Tarantula, The
   See Acker, Kathy

Blackwood, Algernon (Henry)
      1869-1951 . . . .   **TCLC 5**
   See also CA 105

Blackwood, Caroline   1931- . . . .   **CLC 6, 9**
   See also CA 85-88; CANR 32; DLB 14;
      MTCW

Blade, Alexander
   See Hamilton, Edmond; Silverberg, Robert

Blaga, Lucian   1895-1961 . . . .   **CLC 75**

Blair, Eric (Arthur)   1903-1950
   See Orwell, George
   See also CA 104; 132; DA; MTCW;
      SATA 29

Blais, Marie-Claire
      1939- . . . .   **CLC 2, 4, 6, 13, 22**
   See also CA 21-24R; CAAS 4; CANR 38;
      DLB 53; MTCW

Blaise, Clark   1940- . . . .   **CLC 29**
   See also AITN 2; CA 53-56; CAAS 3;
      CANR 5; DLB 53

Blake, Nicholas
   See Day Lewis, C(ecil)
   See also DLB 77

Blake, William
      1757-1827 . . . . .   **NCLC 13, 37; DA; WLC**
   See also CDBLB 1789-1832; DLB 93;
      MAICYA; SATA 30

Blasco Ibanez, Vicente
      1867-1928 . . . .   **TCLC 12**
   See also CA 110; 131; HW; MTCW

Blatty, William Peter   1928- . . . .   **CLC 2**
   See also CA 5-8R; CANR 9

Bleeck, Oliver
   See Thomas, Ross (Elmore)

Blessing, Lee   1949- . . . .   **CLC 54**

Blish, James (Benjamin)
      1921-1975 . . . .   **CLC 14**
   See also CA 1-4R; 57-60; CANR 3; DLB 8;
      MTCW; SATA 66

Bliss, Reginald
   See Wells, H(erbert) G(eorge)

Blixen, Karen (Christentze Dinesen)
      1885-1962
   See Dinesen, Isak
   See also CA 25-28; CANR 22; CAP 2;
      MTCW; SATA 44

Bloch, Robert (Albert)   1917-1994 . . .   **CLC 33**
   See also CA 5-8R; 146; CAAS 20; CANR 5;
      DLB 44; SATA 12

Blok, Alexander (Alexandrovich)
      1880-1921 . . . .   **TCLC 5**
   See also CA 104

Blom, Jan
   See Breytenbach, Breyten

Bloom, Harold   1930- . . . .   **CLC 24**
   See also CA 13-16R; CANR 39; DLB 67

Bloomfield, Aurelius
   See Bourne, Randolph S(illiman)

Blount, Roy (Alton), Jr.   1941- . . . . .   **CLC 38**
   See also CA 53-56; CANR 10, 28; MTCW

Bloy, Leon   1846-1917 . . . .   **TCLC 22**
   See also CA 121; DLB 123

Blume, Judy (Sussman)   1938- . . .   **CLC 12, 30**
   See also AAYA 3; CA 29-32R; CANR 13,
      37; CLR 2, 15; DLB 52; JRDA;
      MAICYA; MTCW; SATA 2, 31, 79

Blunden, Edmund (Charles)
      1896-1974 . . . .   **CLC 2, 56**
   See also CA 17-18; 45-48; CAP 2; DLB 20,
      100; MTCW

Bly, Robert (Elwood)
      1926- . . . .   **CLC 1, 2, 5, 10, 15, 38**
   See also CA 5-8R; CANR 41; DLB 5;
      MTCW

Boas, Franz   1858-1942 . . . .   **TCLC 56**
   See also CA 115

Bobette
   See Simenon, Georges (Jacques Christian)

Boccaccio, Giovanni
      1313-1375 . . . .   **CMLC 13; SSC 10**

Bochco, Steven   1943- . . . .   **CLC 35**
   See also AAYA 11; CA 124; 138

Bodenheim, Maxwell   1892-1954 . . .   **TCLC 44**
   See also CA 110; DLB 9, 45

Bodker, Cecil   1927- . . . .   **CLC 21**
   See also CA 73-76; CANR 13, 44; CLR 23;
      MAICYA; SATA 14

Boell, Heinrich (Theodor)
      1917-1985 . . . .   **CLC 2, 3, 6, 9, 11, 15, 27,
                                                 32, 72; DA; WLC**
   See also CA 21-24R; 116; CANR 24;
      DLB 69; DLBY 85; MTCW

Boerne, Alfred
   See Doeblin, Alfred

Bogan, Louise   1897-1970 . . . . .   **CLC 4, 39, 46**
   See also CA 73-76; 25-28R; CANR 33;
      DLB 45; MTCW

Cable, George Washington
1844-1925 . . . . TCLC 4; SSC 4
See also CA 104; DLB 12, 74

Cabral de Melo Neto, Joao 1920-. . . CLC 76

Cabrera Infante, G(uillermo)
1929- . . . . CLC 5, 25, 45; HLC
See also CA 85-88; CANR 29; DLB 113;
HW; MTCW

Cade, Toni
See Bambara, Toni Cade

Cadmus and Harmonia
See Buchan, John

Caedmon fl. 658-680. . . . . CMLC 7
See also DLB 146

Caeiro, Alberto
See Pessoa, Fernando (Antonio Nogueira)

Cage, John (Milton, Jr.) 1912- . . . . . CLC 41
See also CA 13-16R; CANR 9

Cain, G.
See Cabrera Infante, G(uillermo)

Cain, Guillermo
See Cabrera Infante, G(uillermo)

Cain, James M(allahan)
1892-1977 . . . . CLC 3, 11, 28
See also AITN 1; CA 17-20R; 73-76;
CANR 8, 34; MTCW

Caine, Mark
See Raphael, Frederic (Michael)

Calasso, Roberto 1941- . . . . CLC 81
See also CA 143

Calderon de la Barca, Pedro
1600-1681 . . . . LC 23; DC 3

Caldwell, Erskine (Preston)
1903-1987 . . . . CLC 1, 8, 14, 50, 60
See also AITN 1; CA 1-4R; 121; CAAS 1;
CANR 2, 33; DLB 9, 86; MTCW

Caldwell, (Janet Miriam) Taylor (Holland)
1900-1985 . . . . CLC 2, 28, 39
See also CA 5-8R; 116; CANR 5

Calhoun, John Caldwell
1782-1850 . . . . NCLC 15
See also DLB 3

Calisher, Hortense
1911- . . . . CLC 2, 4, 8, 38; SSC 15
See also CA 1-4R; CANR 1, 22; DLB 2;
MTCW

Callaghan, Morley Edward
1903-1990 . . . . CLC 3, 14, 41, 65
See also CA 9-12R; 132; CANR 33;
DLB 68; MTCW

Calvino, Italo
1923-1985 . . . . . CLC 5, 8, 11, 22, 33, 39,
73; SSC 3
See also CA 85-88; 116; CANR 23; MTCW

Cameron, Carey 1952- . . . . CLC 59
See also CA 135

Cameron, Peter 1959- . . . . CLC 44
See also CA 125

Campana, Dino 1885-1932. . . . . . . TCLC 20
See also CA 117; DLB 114

Campbell, John W(ood, Jr.)
1910-1971 . . . . CLC 32
See also CA 21-22; 29-32R; CANR 34;
CAP 2; DLB 8; MTCW

Campbell, Joseph 1904-1987 . . . . . . CLC 69
See also AAYA 3; BEST 89:2; CA 1-4R;
124; CANR 3, 28; MTCW

Campbell, Maria 1940-. . . . . CLC 85
See also CA 102; NNAL

Campbell, (John) Ramsey 1946- . . . . CLC 42
See also CA 57-60; CANR 7

Campbell, (Ignatius) Roy (Dunnachie)
1901-1957 . . . . TCLC 5
See also CA 104; DLB 20

Campbell, Thomas 1777-1844 . . . . NCLC 19
See also DLB 93; 144

Campbell, Wilfred. . . . . TCLC 9
See also Campbell, William

Campbell, William 1858(?)-1918
See Campbell, Wilfred
See also CA 106; DLB 92

Campos, Alvaro de
See Pessoa, Fernando (Antonio Nogueira)

Camus, Albert
1913-1960 . . . . CLC 1, 2, 4, 9, 11, 14, 32,
63, 69; DA; DC 2; SSC 9; WLC
See also CA 89-92; DLB 72; MTCW

Canby, Vincent 1924-. . . . . CLC 13
See also CA 81-84

Cancale
See Desnos, Robert

Canetti, Elias
1905-1994 . . . . . . CLC 3, 14, 25, 75, 86
See also CA 21-24R; 146; CANR 23;
DLB 85, 124; MTCW

Canin, Ethan 1960-. . . . . CLC 55
See also CA 131; 135

Cannon, Curt
See Hunter, Evan

Cape, Judith
See Page, P(atricia) K(athleen)

Capek, Karel
1890-1938 . . . . . TCLC 6, 37; DA; DC 1;
WLC
See also CA 104; 140

Capote, Truman
1924-1984 . . . . . . CLC 1, 3, 8, 13, 19, 34,
38, 58; DA; SSC 2; WLC
See also CA 5-8R; 113; CANR 18;
CDALB 1941-1968; DLB 2; DLBY 80,
84; MTCW

Capra, Frank 1897-1991. . . . . CLC 16
See also CA 61-64; 135

Caputo, Philip 1941-. . . . . CLC 32
See also CA 73-76; CANR 40

Card, Orson Scott 1951- . . . . CLC 44, 47, 50
See also AAYA 11; CA 102; CANR 27, 47;
MTCW

Cardenal (Martinez), Ernesto
1925- . . . . CLC 31; HLC
See also CA 49-52; CANR 2, 32; HW;
MTCW

Carducci, Giosue 1835-1907. . . . . . . TCLC 32

Carew, Thomas 1595(?)-1640. . . . . . . LC 13
See also DLB 126

Carey, Ernestine Gilbreth 1908-. . . . CLC 17
See also CA 5-8R; SATA 2

Carey, Peter 1943-. . . . . CLC 40, 55
See also CA 123; 127; MTCW

Carleton, William 1794-1869. . . . . . NCLC 3

Carlisle, Henry (Coffin) 1926-. . . . . . CLC 33
See also CA 13-16R; CANR 15

Carlsen, Chris
See Holdstock, Robert P.

Carlson, Ron(ald F.) 1947-. . . . . CLC 54
See also CA 105; CANR 27

Carlyle, Thomas 1795-1881 . . NCLC 22; DA
See also CDBLB 1789-1832; DLB 55; 144

Carman, (William) Bliss
1861-1929 . . . . TCLC 7
See also CA 104; DLB 92

Carnegie, Dale 1888-1955 . . . . TCLC 53

Carossa, Hans 1878-1956. . . . . TCLC 48
See also DLB 66

Carpenter, Don(ald Richard)
1931-. . . . . CLC 41
See also CA 45-48; CANR 1

Carpentier (y Valmont), Alejo
1904-1980 . . . . CLC 8, 11, 38; HLC
See also CA 65-68; 97-100; CANR 11;
DLB 113; HW

Carr, Caleb 1955(?)-. . . . . CLC 86

Carr, Emily 1871-1945. . . . . TCLC 32
See also DLB 68

Carr, John Dickson 1906-1977 . . . . . . CLC 3
See also CA 49-52; 69-72; CANR 3, 33;
MTCW

Carr, Philippa
See Hibbert, Eleanor Alice Burford

Carr, Virginia Spencer 1929-. . . . . . . CLC 34
See also CA 61-64; DLB 111

Carrier, Roch 1937-. . . . . CLC 13, 78
See also CA 130; DLB 53

Carroll, James P. 1943(?)-. . . . . CLC 38
See also CA 81-84

Carroll, Jim 1951- . . . . CLC 35
See also CA 45-48; CANR 42

Carroll, Lewis . . . . NCLC 2; WLC
See also Dodgson, Charles Lutwidge
See also CDBLB 1832-1890; CLR 2, 18;
DLB 18; JRDA

Carroll, Paul Vincent 1900-1968. . . . CLC 10
See also CA 9-12R; 25-28R; DLB 10

Carruth, Hayden
1921-. . . . CLC 4, 7, 10, 18, 84; PC 10
See also CA 9-12R; CANR 4, 38; DLB 5;
MTCW; SATA 47

Carson, Rachel Louise 1907-1964. . . CLC 71
See also CA 77-80; CANR 35; MTCW;
SATA 23

Carter, Angela (Olive)
1940-1992 . . . . . . CLC 5, 41, 76; SSC 13
See also CA 53-56; 136; CANR 12, 36;
DLB 14; MTCW; SATA 66;
SATA-Obit 70

Carter, Nick
See Smith, Martin Cruz

Carver, Raymond
1938-1988 . . . CLC 22, 36, 53, 55; SSC 8
See also CA 33-36R; 126; CANR 17, 34;
DLB 130; DLBY 84, 88; MTCW

Cary, (Arthur) Joyce (Lunel)
1888-1957 .... TCLC 1, 29
See also CA 104; CDBLB 1914-1945;
DLB 15, 100

Casanova de Seingalt, Giovanni Jacopo
1725-1798 .... LC 13

Casares, Adolfo Bioy
See Bioy Casares, Adolfo

Casely-Hayford, J(oseph) E(phraim)
1866-1930 .... TCLC 24; BLC
See also BW 2; CA 123

Casey, John (Dudley) 1939-........ CLC 59
See also BEST 90:2; CA 69-72; CANR 23

Casey, Michael 1947-.............. CLC 2
See also CA 65-68; DLB 5

Casey, Patrick
See Thurman, Wallace (Henry)

Casey, Warren (Peter) 1935-1988 ... CLC 12
See also CA 101; 127

Casona, Alejandro................. CLC 49
See also Alvarez, Alejandro Rodriguez

Cassavetes, John 1929-1989........ CLC 20
See also CA 85-88; 127

Cassill, R(onald) V(erlin) 1919-... CLC 4, 23
See also CA 9-12R; CAAS 1; CANR 7, 45;
DLB 6

Cassity, (Allen) Turner 1929- .... CLC 6, 42
See also CA 17-20R; CAAS 8; CANR 11;
DLB 105

Castaneda, Carlos 1931(?)-........ CLC 12
See also CA 25-28R; CANR 32; HW;
MTCW

Castedo, Elena 1937-............. CLC 65
See also CA 132

Castedo-Ellerman, Elena
See Castedo, Elena

Castellanos, Rosario
1925-1974 .... CLC 66; HLC
See also CA 131; 53-56; DLB 113; HW

Castelvetro, Lodovico 1505-1571..... LC 12

Castiglione, Baldassare 1478-1529 ... LC 12

Castle, Robert
See Hamilton, Edmond

Castro, Guillen de 1569-1631....... LC 19

Castro, Rosalia de 1837-1885 ..... NCLC 3

Cather, Willa
See Cather, Willa Sibert

Cather, Willa Sibert
1873-1947 .... TCLC 1, 11, 31; DA;
SSC 2; WLC
See also CA 104; 128; CDALB 1865-1917;
DLB 9, 54, 78; DLBD 1; MTCW;
SATA 30

Catton, (Charles) Bruce
1899-1978 .... CLC 35
See also AITN 1; CA 5-8R; 81-84;
CANR 7; DLB 17; SATA 2;
SATA-Obit 24

Cauldwell, Frank
See King, Francis (Henry)

Caunitz, William J. 1933-......... CLC 34
See also BEST 89:3; CA 125; 130

Causley, Charles (Stanley) 1917-..... CLC 7
See also CA 9-12R; CANR 5, 35; CLR 30;
DLB 27; MTCW; SATA 3, 66

Caute, David 1936-.............. CLC 29
See also CA 1-4R; CAAS 4; CANR 1, 33;
DLB 14

Cavafy, C(onstantine) P(eter)...... TCLC 2, 7
See also Kavafis, Konstantinos Petrou

Cavallo, Evelyn
See Spark, Muriel (Sarah)

Cavanna, Betty .... CLC 12
See also Harrison, Elizabeth Cavanna
See also JRDA; MAICYA; SAAS 4;
SATA 1, 30

Caxton, William 1421(?)-1491(?)..... LC 17

Cayrol, Jean 1911-............... CLC 11
See also CA 89-92; DLB 83

Cela, Camilo Jose
1916- .... CLC 4, 13, 59; HLC
See also BEST 90:2; CA 21-24R; CAAS 10;
CANR 21, 32; DLBY 89; HW; MTCW

Celan, Paul ...... CLC 10, 19, 53, 82; PC 10
See also Antschel, Paul
See also DLB 69

Celine, Louis-Ferdinand
.... CLC 1, 3, 4, 7, 9, 15, 47
See also Destouches, Louis-Ferdinand
See also DLB 72

Cellini, Benvenuto 1500-1571 .... LC 7

Cendrars, Blaise
See Sauser-Hall, Frederic

Cernuda (y Bidon), Luis
1902-1963 .... CLC 54
See also CA 131; 89-92; DLB 134; HW

Cervantes (Saavedra), Miguel de
1547-1616 ...... LC 6, 23; DA; SSC 12;
WLC

Cesaire, Aime (Fernand)
1913- .... CLC 19, 32; BLC
See also BW 2; CA 65-68; CANR 24, 43;
MTCW

Chabon, Michael 1965(?)- .... CLC 55
See also CA 139

Chabrol, Claude 1930-............ CLC 16
See also CA 110

Challans, Mary 1905-1983
See Renault, Mary
See also CA 81-84; 111; SATA 23;
SATA-Obit 36

Challis, George
See Faust, Frederick (Schiller)

Chambers, Aidan 1934- .... CLC 35
See also CA 25-28R; CANR 12, 31; JRDA;
MAICYA; SAAS 12; SATA 1, 69

Chambers, James 1948-
See Cliff, Jimmy
See also CA 124

Chambers, Jessie
See Lawrence, D(avid) H(erbert Richards)

Chambers, Robert W. 1865-1933... TCLC 41

Chandler, Raymond (Thornton)
1888-1959 .... TCLC 1, 7
See also CA 104; 129; CDALB 1929-1941;
DLBD 6; MTCW

Chang, Jung 1952- .... CLC 71
See also CA 142

Channing, William Ellery
1780-1842 .... NCLC 17
See also DLB 1, 59

Chaplin, Charles Spencer
1889-1977 .... CLC 16
See also Chaplin, Charlie
See also CA 81-84; 73-76

Chaplin, Charlie
See Chaplin, Charles Spencer
See also DLB 44

Chapman, George 1559(?)-1634...... LC 22
See also DLB 62, 121

Chapman, Graham 1941-1989 ...... CLC 21
See also Monty Python
See also CA 116; 129; CANR 35

Chapman, John Jay 1862-1933 ..... TCLC 7
See also CA 104

Chapman, Walker
See Silverberg, Robert

Chappell, Fred (Davis) 1936-.... CLC 40, 78
See also CA 5-8R; CAAS 4; CANR 8, 33;
DLB 6, 105

Char, Rene(-Emile)
1907-1988 .... CLC 9, 11, 14, 55
See also CA 13-16R; 124; CANR 32;
MTCW

Charby, Jay
See Ellison, Harlan (Jay)

Chardin, Pierre Teilhard de
See Teilhard de Chardin, (Marie Joseph)
Pierre

Charles I 1600-1649 .... LC 13

Charyn, Jerome 1937- .... CLC 5, 8, 18
See also CA 5-8R; CAAS 1; CANR 7;
DLBY 83; MTCW

Chase, Mary (Coyle) 1907-1981 ...... DC 1
See also CA 77-80; 105; SATA 17;
SATA-Obit 29

Chase, Mary Ellen 1887-1973 .... CLC 2
See also CA 13-16; 41-44R; CAP 1;
SATA 10

Chase, Nicholas
See Hyde, Anthony

Chateaubriand, Francois Rene de
1768-1848 .... NCLC 3
See also DLB 119

Chatterje, Sarat Chandra 1876-1936(?)
See Chatterji, Saratchandra
See also CA 109

Chatterji, Bankim Chandra
1838-1894 .... NCLC 19

Chatterji, Saratchandra .... TCLC 13
See also Chatterje, Sarat Chandra

Chatterton, Thomas 1752-1770 .... LC 3
See also DLB 109

Chatwin, (Charles) Bruce
1940-1989 .... CLC 28, 57, 59
See also AAYA 4; BEST 90:1; CA 85-88;
127

Chaucer, Daniel
See Ford, Ford Madox

Chaucer, Geoffrey
1340(?)-1400 .... LC 17; DA
See also CDBLB Before 1660; DLB 146

Chaviaras, Strates 1935-
See Haviaras, Stratis
See also CA 105

Chayefsky, Paddy .... CLC 23
See also Chayefsky, Sidney
See also DLB 7, 44; DLBY 81

Chayefsky, Sidney 1923-1981
See Chayefsky, Paddy
See also CA 9-12R; 104; CANR 18

Chedid, Andree 1920- .... CLC 47
See also CA 145

Cheever, John
1912-1982 ...... CLC 3, 7, 8, 11, 15, 25,
                        64; DA; SSC 1; WLC
See also CA 5-8R; 106; CABS 1; CANR 5,
27; CDALB 1941-1968; DLB 2, 102;
DLBY 80, 82; MTCW

Cheever, Susan 1943- .... CLC 18, 48
See also CA 103; CANR 27; DLBY 82

Chekhonte, Antosha
See Chekhov, Anton (Pavlovich)

Chekhov, Anton (Pavlovich)
1860-1904 ..... TCLC 3, 10, 31, 55; DA;
                              SSC 2; WLC
See also CA 104; 124

Chernyshevsky, Nikolay Gavrilovich
1828-1889 .... NCLC 1

Cherry, Carolyn Janice 1942-
See Cherryh, C. J.
See also CA 65-68; CANR 10

Cherryh, C. J. .... CLC 35
See Cherry, Carolyn Janice
See also DLBY 80

Chesnutt, Charles W(addell)
1858-1932 .... TCLC 5, 39; BLC; SSC 7
See also BW 1; CA 106; 125; DLB 12, 50,
78; MTCW

Chester, Alfred 1929(?)-1971 ...... CLC 49
See also CA 33-36R; DLB 130

Chesterton, G(ilbert) K(eith)
1874-1936 .... TCLC 1, 6; SSC 1
See also CA 104; 132; CDBLB 1914-1945;
DLB 10, 19, 34, 70, 98; MTCW;
SATA 27

Chiang Pin-chin 1904-1986
See Ding Ling
See also CA 118

Ch'ien Chung-shu 1910- .... CLC 22
See also CA 130; MTCW

Child, L. Maria
See Child, Lydia Maria

Child, Lydia Maria 1802-1880 .... NCLC 6
See also DLB 1, 74; SATA 67

Child, Mrs.
See Child, Lydia Maria

Child, Philip 1898-1978 .... CLC 19, 68
See also CA 13-14; CAP 1; SATA 47

Childress, Alice
1920-1994 .. CLC 12, 15, 86; BLC; DC 4
See also AAYA 8; BW 2; CA 45-48; 146;
CANR 3, 27; CLR 14; DLB 7, 38; JRDA;
MAICYA; MTCW; SATA 7, 48, 81

Chislett, (Margaret) Anne 1943- .... CLC 34

Chitty, Thomas Willes 1926- .... CLC 11
See also Hinde, Thomas
See also CA 5-8R

Chomette, Rene Lucien 1898-1981
See Clair, Rene
See also CA 103

Chopin, Kate .... TCLC 5, 14; DA; SSC 8
See also Chopin, Katherine
See also CDALB 1865-1917; DLB 12, 78

Chopin, Katherine 1851-1904
See Chopin, Kate
See also CA 104; 122

Chretien de Troyes
c. 12th cent. - .... CMLC 10

Christie
See Ichikawa, Kon

Christie, Agatha (Mary Clarissa)
1890-1976 ...... CLC 1, 6, 8, 12, 39, 48
See also AAYA 9; AITN 1, 2; CA 17-20R;
61-64; CANR 10, 37; CDBLB 1914-1945;
DLB 13, 77; MTCW; SATA 36

Christie, (Ann) Philippa
See Pearce, Philippa
See also CA 5-8R; CANR 4

Christine de Pizan 1365(?)-1431(?) .... LC 9

Chubb, Elmer
See Masters, Edgar Lee

Chulkov, Mikhail Dmitrievich
1743-1792 .... LC 2

Churchill, Caryl 1938- ... CLC 31, 55; DC 5
See also CA 102; CANR 22, 46; DLB 13;
MTCW

Churchill, Charles 1731-1764 .... LC 3
See also DLB 109

Chute, Carolyn 1947- .... CLC 39
See also CA 123

Ciardi, John (Anthony)
1916-1986 .... CLC 10, 40, 44
See also CA 5-8R; 118; CAAS 2; CANR 5,
33; CLR 19; DLB 5; DLBY 86;
MAICYA; MTCW; SATA 1, 65;
SATA-Obit 46

Cicero, Marcus Tullius
106B.C.-43B.C. .... CMLC 3

Cimino, Michael 1943- .... CLC 16
See also CA 105

Cioran, E(mil) M. 1911- .... CLC 64
See also CA 25-28R

Cisneros, Sandra 1954- ...... CLC 69; HLC
See also AAYA 9; CA 131; DLB 122; HW

Clair, Rene .... CLC 20
See also Chomette, Rene Lucien

Clampitt, Amy 1920-1994 .... CLC 32
See also CA 110; 146; CANR 29; DLB 105

Clancy, Thomas L., Jr. 1947-
See Clancy, Tom
See also CA 125; 131; MTCW

Clancy, Tom .... CLC 45
See also Clancy, Thomas L., Jr.
See also AAYA 9; BEST 89:1, 90:1

Clare, John 1793-1864 .... NCLC 9
See also DLB 55, 96

Clarin
See Alas (y Urena), Leopoldo (Enrique
Garcia)

Clark, Al C.
See Goines, Donald

Clark, (Robert) Brian 1932- .... CLC 29
See also CA 41-44R

Clark, Curt
See Westlake, Donald E(dwin)

Clark, Eleanor 1913- .... CLC 5, 19
See also CA 9-12R; CANR 41; DLB 6

Clark, J. P.
See Clark, John Pepper
See also DLB 117

Clark, John Pepper
1935- .... CLC 38; BLC; DC 5
See also Clark, J. P.
See also BW 1; CA 65-68; CANR 16

Clark, M. R.
See Clark, Mavis Thorpe

Clark, Mavis Thorpe 1909- .... CLC 12
See also CA 57-60; CANR 8, 37; CLR 30;
MAICYA; SAAS 5; SATA 8, 74

Clark, Walter Van Tilburg
1909-1971 .... CLC 28
See also CA 9-12R; 33-36R; DLB 9;
SATA 8

Clarke, Arthur C(harles)
1917- ...... CLC 1, 4, 13, 18, 35; SSC 3
See also AAYA 4; CA 1-4R; CANR 2, 28;
JRDA; MAICYA; MTCW; SATA 13, 70

Clarke, Austin 1896-1974 .... CLC 6, 9
See also CA 29-32; 49-52; CAP 2; DLB 10,
20

Clarke, Austin C(hesterfield)
1934- .... CLC 8, 53; BLC
See also BW 1; CA 25-28R; CAAS 16;
CANR 14, 32; DLB 53, 125

Clarke, Gillian 1937- .... CLC 61
See also CA 106; DLB 40

Clarke, Marcus (Andrew Hislop)
1846-1881 .... NCLC 19

Clarke, Shirley 1925- .... CLC 16

Clash, The
See Headon, (Nicky) Topper; Jones, Mick;
Simonon, Paul; Strummer, Joe

Claudel, Paul (Louis Charles Marie)
1868-1955 .... TCLC 2, 10
See also CA 104

Clavell, James (duMaresq)
1925-1994 .... CLC 6, 25, 87
See also CA 25-28R; 146; CANR 26;
MTCW

Cleaver, (Leroy) Eldridge
1935- .... CLC 30; BLC
See also BW 1; CA 21-24R; CANR 16

Cleese, John (Marwood) 1939- ..... CLC 21
See also Monty Python
See also CA 112; 116; CANR 35; MTCW

Cleishbotham, Jebediah
See Scott, Walter

Cleland, John 1710-1789 .... LC 2
See also DLB 39

Clemens, Samuel Langhorne 1835-1910
   See Twain, Mark
   See also CA 104; 135; CDALB 1865-1917;
      DA; DLB 11, 12, 23, 64, 74; JRDA;
      MAICYA; YABC 2

Cleophil
   See Congreve, William

Clerihew, E.
   See Bentley, E(dmund) C(lerihew)

Clerk, N. W.
   See Lewis, C(live) S(taples)

Cliff, Jimmy . . . . **CLC 21**
   See also Chambers, James

Clifton, (Thelma) Lucille
   1936- . . . . **CLC 19, 66; BLC**
   See also BW 2; CA 49-52; CANR 2, 24, 42;
      CLR 5; DLB 5, 41; MAICYA; MTCW;
      SATA 20, 69

Clinton, Dirk
   See Silverberg, Robert

Clough, Arthur Hugh 1819-1861 . . **NCLC 27**
   See also DLB 32

Clutha, Janet Paterson Frame 1924-
   See Frame, Janet
   See also CA 1-4R; CANR 2, 36; MTCW

Clyne, Terence
   See Blatty, William Peter

Cobalt, Martin
   See Mayne, William (James Carter)

Coburn, D(onald) L(ee) 1938- . . . . . . **CLC 10**
   See also CA 89-92

Cocteau, Jean (Maurice Eugene Clement)
   1889-1963 . . . . **CLC 1, 8, 15, 16, 43; DA;**
                                                     WLC
   See also CA 25-28; CANR 40; CAP 2;
      DLB 65; MTCW

Codrescu, Andrei 1946- . . . . **CLC 46**
   See also CA 33-36R; CAAS 19; CANR 13,
      34

Coe, Max
   See Bourne, Randolph S(illiman)

Coe, Tucker
   See Westlake, Donald E(dwin)

Coetzee, J(ohn) M(ichael)
   1940- . . . . **CLC 23, 33, 66**
   See also CA 77-80; CANR 41; MTCW

Coffey, Brian
   See Koontz, Dean R(ay)

Cohen, Arthur A(llen)
   1928-1986 . . . . **CLC 7, 31**
   See also CA 1-4R; 120; CANR 1, 17, 42;
      DLB 28

Cohen, Leonard (Norman)
   1934- . . . . **CLC 3, 38**
   See also CA 21-24R; CANR 14; DLB 53;
      MTCW

Cohen, Matt 1942- . . . . **CLC 19**
   See also CA 61-64; CAAS 18; CANR 40;
      DLB 53

Cohen-Solal, Annie 19(?)- . . . . **CLC 50**

Colegate, Isabel 1931- . . . . **CLC 36**
   See also CA 17-20R; CANR 8, 22; DLB 14;
      MTCW

Coleman, Emmett
   See Reed, Ishmael

Coleridge, Samuel Taylor
   1772-1834 . . **NCLC 9; DA; PC 11; WLC**
   See also CDBLB 1789-1832; DLB 93, 107

Coleridge, Sara 1802-1852 . . . . . . **NCLC 31**

Coles, Don 1928- . . . . **CLC 46**
   See also CA 115; CANR 38

Colette, (Sidonie-Gabrielle)
   1873-1954 . . . . . . **TCLC 1, 5, 16; SSC 10**
   See also CA 104; 131; DLB 65; MTCW

Collett, (Jacobine) Camilla (Wergeland)
   1813-1895 . . . . **NCLC 22**

Collier, Christopher 1930- . . . . **CLC 30**
   See also AAYA 13; CA 33-36R; CANR 13,
      33; JRDA; MAICYA; SATA 16, 70

Collier, James L(incoln) 1928- . . . . . **CLC 30**
   See also AAYA 13; CA 9-12R; CANR 4,
      33; CLR 3; JRDA; MAICYA; SATA 8,
      70

Collier, Jeremy 1650-1726 . . . . **LC 6**

Collins, Hunt
   See Hunter, Evan

Collins, Linda 1931- . . . . **CLC 44**
   See also CA 125

Collins, (William) Wilkie
   1824-1889 . . . . **NCLC 1, 18**
   See also CDBLB 1832-1890; DLB 18, 70

Collins, William 1721-1759 . . . . **LC 4**
   See also DLB 109

Colman, George
   See Glassco, John

Colt, Winchester Remington
   See Hubbard, L(afayette) Ron(ald)

Colter, Cyrus 1910- . . . . **CLC 58**
   See also BW 1; CA 65-68; CANR 10;
      DLB 33

Colton, James
   See Hansen, Joseph

Colum, Padraic 1881-1972 . . . . **CLC 28**
   See also CA 73-76; 33-36R; CANR 35;
      CLR 36; MAICYA; MTCW; SATA 15

Colvin, James
   See Moorcock, Michael (John)

Colwin, Laurie (E.)
   1944-1992 . . . . **CLC 5, 13, 23, 84**
   See also CA 89-92; 139; CANR 20, 46;
      DLBY 80; MTCW

Comfort, Alex(ander) 1920- . . . . **CLC 7**
   See also CA 1-4R; CANR 1, 45

Comfort, Montgomery
   See Campbell, (John) Ramsey

Compton-Burnett, I(vy)
   1884(?)-1969 . . . . . . **CLC 1, 3, 10, 15, 34**
   See also CA 1-4R; 25-28R; CANR 4;
      DLB 36; MTCW

Comstock, Anthony 1844-1915 . . . . **TCLC 13**
   See also CA 110

Conan Doyle, Arthur
   See Doyle, Arthur Conan

Conde, Maryse 1937- . . . . **CLC 52**
   See also Boucolon, Maryse
   See also BW 2

Condillac, Etienne Bonnot de
   1714-1780 . . . . **LC 26**

Condon, Richard (Thomas)
   1915- . . . . **CLC 4, 6, 8, 10, 45**
   See also BEST 90:3; CA 1-4R; CAAS 1;
      CANR 2, 23; MTCW

Congreve, William
   1670-1729 . . . **LC 5, 21; DA; DC 2; WLC**
   See also CDBLB 1660-1789; DLB 39, 84

Connell, Evan S(helby), Jr.
   1924- . . . . **CLC 4, 6, 45**
   See also AAYA 7; CA 1-4R; CAAS 2;
      CANR 2, 39; DLB 2; DLBY 81; MTCW

Connelly, Marc(us Cook)
   1890-1980 . . . . **CLC 7**
   See also CA 85-88; 102; CANR 30; DLB 7;
      DLBY 80; SATA-Obit 25

Connor, Ralph . . . . **TCLC 31**
   See also Gordon, Charles William
   See also DLB 92

Conrad, Joseph
   1857-1924 . . . . **TCLC 1, 6, 13, 25, 43, 57;**
                                       DA; SSC 9; WLC
   See also CA 104; 131; CDBLB 1890-1914;
      DLB 10, 34, 98; MTCW; SATA 27

Conrad, Robert Arnold
   See Hart, Moss

Conroy, Pat 1945- . . . . **CLC 30, 74**
   See also AAYA 8; AITN 1; CA 85-88;
      CANR 24; DLB 6; MTCW

Constant (de Rebecque), (Henri) Benjamin
   1767-1830 . . . . **NCLC 6**
   See also DLB 119

Conybeare, Charles Augustus
   See Eliot, T(homas) S(tearns)

Cook, Michael 1933- . . . . **CLC 58**
   See also CA 93-96; DLB 53

Cook, Robin 1940- . . . . **CLC 14**
   See also BEST 90:2; CA 108; 111;
      CANR 41

Cook, Roy
   See Silverberg, Robert

Cooke, Elizabeth 1948- . . . . **CLC 55**
   See also CA 129

Cooke, John Esten 1830-1886 . . . . . **NCLC 5**
   See also DLB 3

Cooke, John Estes
   See Baum, L(yman) Frank

Cooke, M. E.
   See Creasey, John

Cooke, Margaret
   See Creasey, John

Cooney, Ray . . . . **CLC 62**

Cooper, Douglas 1960- . . . . **CLC 86**

Cooper, Henry St. John
   See Creasey, John

Cooper, J. California . . . . **CLC 56**
   See also AAYA 12; BW 1; CA 125

Cooper, James Fenimore
   1789-1851 . . . . **NCLC 1, 27**
   See also CDALB 1640-1865; DLB 3;
      SATA 19

Coover, Robert (Lowell)
   1932- . . **CLC 3, 7, 15, 32, 46, 87; SSC 15**
   See also CA 45-48; CANR 3, 37; DLB 2;
      DLBY 81; MTCW

Copeland, Stewart (Armstrong)
  1952- . . . . CLC 26

Coppard, A(lfred) E(dgar)
  1878-1957 . . . . TCLC 5
  See also CA 114; YABC 1

Coppee, Francois 1842-1908 . . . . . . TCLC 25

Coppola, Francis Ford 1939- . . . . CLC 16
  See also CA 77-80; CANR 40; DLB 44

Corbiere, Tristan 1845-1875 . . . . . NCLC 43

Corcoran, Barbara 1911- . . . . CLC 17
  See also AAYA 14; CA 21-24R; CAAS 2;
  CANR 11, 28; DLB 52; JRDA; SATA 3,
  77

Cordelier, Maurice
  See Giraudoux, (Hippolyte) Jean

Corelli, Marie 1855-1924 . . . . TCLC 51
  See also Mackay, Mary
  See also DLB 34

Corman, Cid. . . . . CLC 9
  See also Corman, Sidney
  See also CAAS 2; DLB 5

Corman, Sidney 1924-
  See Corman, Cid
  See also CA 85-88; CANR 44

Cormier, Robert (Edmund)
  1925- . . . . CLC 12, 30; DA
  See also AAYA 3; CA 1-4R; CANR 5, 23;
  CDALB 1968-1988; CLR 12; DLB 52;
  JRDA; MAICYA; MTCW; SATA 10, 45

Corn, Alfred (DeWitt III) 1943- . . . . CLC 33
  See also CA 104; CANR 44; DLB 120;
  DLBY 80

Corneille, Pierre 1606-1684 . . . . LC 28

Cornwell, David (John Moore)
  1931- . . . . CLC 9, 15
  See also le Carre, John
  See also CA 5-8R; CANR 13, 33; MTCW

Corso, (Nunzio) Gregory 1930- . . . CLC 1, 11
  See also CA 5-8R; CANR 41; DLB 5, 16;
  MTCW

Cortazar, Julio
  1914-1984 . . . . . . CLC 2, 3, 5, 10, 13, 15,
                              33, 34; HLC; SSC 7
  See also CA 21-24R; CANR 12, 32;
  DLB 113; HW; MTCW

Corwin, Cecil
  See Kornbluth, C(yril) M.

Cosic, Dobrica 1921- . . . . CLC 14
  See also CA 122; 138

Costain, Thomas B(ertram)
  1885-1965 . . . . CLC 30
  See also CA 5-8R; 25-28R; DLB 9

Costantini, Humberto
  1924(?)-1987 . . . . CLC 49
  See also CA 131; 122; HW

Costello, Elvis 1955- . . . . CLC 21

Cotter, Joseph Seamon Sr.
  1861-1949 . . . . TCLC 28; BLC
  See also BW 1; CA 124; DLB 50

Couch, Arthur Thomas Quiller
  See Quiller-Couch, Arthur Thomas

Coulton, James
  See Hansen, Joseph

Couperus, Louis (Marie Anne)
  1863-1923 . . . . TCLC 15
  See also CA 115

Coupland, Douglas 1961- . . . . CLC 85
  See also CA 142

Court, Wesli
  See Turco, Lewis (Putnam)

Courtenay, Bryce 1933- . . . . CLC 59
  See also CA 138

Courtney, Robert
  See Ellison, Harlan (Jay)

Cousteau, Jacques-Yves 1910- . . . . . . CLC 30
  See also CA 65-68; CANR 15; MTCW;
  SATA 38

Coward, Noel (Peirce)
  1899-1973 . . . . CLC 1, 9, 29, 51
  See also AITN 1; CA 17-18; 41-44R;
  CANR 35; CAP 2; CDBLB 1914-1945;
  DLB 10; MTCW

Cowley, Malcolm 1898-1989 . . . . CLC 39
  See also CA 5-8R; 128; CANR 3; DLB 4,
  48; DLBY 81, 89; MTCW

Cowper, William 1731-1800 . . . . NCLC 8
  See also DLB 104, 109

Cox, William Trevor 1928- . . . CLC 9, 14, 71
  See also Trevor, William
  See also CA 9-12R; CANR 4, 37; DLB 14;
  MTCW

Coyne, P. J.
  See Masters, Hilary

Cozzens, James Gould
  1903-1978 . . . . CLC 1, 4, 11
  See also CA 9-12R; 81-84; CANR 19;
  CDALB 1941-1968; DLB 9; DLBD 2;
  DLBY 84; MTCW

Crabbe, George 1754-1832 . . . . NCLC 26
  See also DLB 93

Craig, A. A.
  See Anderson, Poul (William)

Craik, Dinah Maria (Mulock)
  1826-1887 . . . . NCLC 38
  See also DLB 35; MAICYA; SATA 34

Cram, Ralph Adams 1863-1942 . . . . TCLC 45

Crane, (Harold) Hart
  1899-1932 . . . . TCLC 2, 5; DA; PC 3;
                                              WLC
  See also CA 104; 127; CDALB 1917-1929;
  DLB 4, 48; MTCW

Crane, R(onald) S(almon)
  1886-1967 . . . . CLC 27
  See also CA 85-88; DLB 63

Crane, Stephen (Townley)
  1871-1900 . . . . TCLC 11, 17, 32; DA;
                                      SSC 7; WLC
  See also CA 109; 140; CDALB 1865-1917;
  DLB 12, 54, 78; YABC 2

Crase, Douglas 1944- . . . . CLC 58
  See also CA 106

Crashaw, Richard 1612(?)-1649 . . . . . . LC 24
  See also DLB 126

Craven, Margaret 1901-1980 . . . . . . CLC 17
  See also CA 103

Crawford, F(rancis) Marion
  1854-1909 . . . . TCLC 10
  See also CA 107; DLB 71

Crawford, Isabella Valancy
  1850-1887 . . . . NCLC 12
  See also DLB 92

Crayon, Geoffrey
  See Irving, Washington

Creasey, John 1908-1973 . . . . CLC 11
  See also CA 5-8R; 41-44R; CANR 8;
  DLB 77; MTCW

Crebillon, Claude Prosper Jolyot de (fils)
  1707-1777 . . . . LC 28

Credo
  See Creasey, John

Creeley, Robert (White)
  1926- . . . . . CLC 1, 2, 4, 8, 11, 15, 36, 78
  See also CA 1-4R; CAAS 10; CANR 23, 43;
  DLB 5, 16; MTCW

Crews, Harry (Eugene)
  1935- . . . . CLC 6, 23, 49
  See also AITN 1; CA 25-28R; CANR 20;
  DLB 6, 143; MTCW

Crichton, (John) Michael
  1942- . . . . CLC 2, 6, 54
  See also AAYA 10; AITN 2; CA 25-28R;
  CANR 13, 40; DLBY 81; JRDA;
  MTCW; SATA 9

Crispin, Edmund . . . . CLC 22
  See also Montgomery, (Robert) Bruce
  See also DLB 87

Cristofer, Michael 1945(?)- . . . . CLC 28
  See also CA 110; DLB 7

Croce, Benedetto 1866-1952 . . . . . . TCLC 37
  See also CA 120

Crockett, David 1786-1836 . . . . NCLC 8
  See also DLB 3, 11

Crockett, Davy
  See Crockett, David

Crofts, Freeman Wills
  1879-1957 . . . . TCLC 55
  See also CA 115; DLB 77

Croker, John Wilson 1780-1857 . . NCLC 10
  See also DLB 110

Crommelynck, Fernand 1885-1970 . . CLC 75
  See also CA 89-92

Cronin, A(rchibald) J(oseph)
  1896-1981 . . . . CLC 32
  See also CA 1-4R; 102; CANR 5; SATA 47;
  SATA-Obit 25

Cross, Amanda
  See Heilbrun, Carolyn G(old)

Crothers, Rachel 1878(?)-1958 . . . . . TCLC 19
  See also CA 113; DLB 7

Croves, Hal
  See Traven, B.

Crowfield, Christopher
  See Stowe, Harriet (Elizabeth) Beecher

Crowley, Aleister. . . . . TCLC 7
  See also Crowley, Edward Alexander

Crowley, Edward Alexander 1875-1947
  See Crowley, Aleister
  See also CA 104

Crowley, John 1942- . . . . CLC 57
  See also CA 61-64; CANR 43; DLBY 82;
  SATA 65

Day Lewis, C(ecil)
1904-1972 .... **CLC 1, 6, 10; PC 11**
See also Blake, Nicholas
See also CA 13-16; 33-36R; CANR 34;
CAP 1; DLB 15, 20; MTCW

Dazai, Osamu .... **TCLC 11**
See also Tsushima, Shuji

de Andrade, Carlos Drummond
See Drummond de Andrade, Carlos

Deane, Norman
See Creasey, John

de Beauvoir, Simone (Lucie Ernestine Marie
Bertrand)
See Beauvoir, Simone (Lucie Ernestine
Marie Bertrand) de

de Brissac, Malcolm
See Dickinson, Peter (Malcolm)

de Chardin, Pierre Teilhard
See Teilhard de Chardin, (Marie Joseph)
Pierre

Dee, John 1527-1608 .... **LC 20**

Deer, Sandra 1940-............... **CLC 45**

De Ferrari, Gabriella .... **CLC 65**

Defoe, Daniel
1660(?)-1731 .... **LC 1; DA; WLC**
See also CDBLB 1660-1789; DLB 39, 95,
101; JRDA; MAICYA; SATA 22

de Gourmont, Remy
See Gourmont, Remy de

de Hartog, Jan 1914-............. **CLC 19**
See also CA 1-4R; CANR 1

de Hostos, E. M.
See Hostos (y Bonilla), Eugenio Maria de

de Hostos, Eugenio M.
See Hostos (y Bonilla), Eugenio Maria de

Deighton, Len .... **CLC 4, 7, 22, 46**
See also Deighton, Leonard Cyril
See also AAYA 6; BEST 89:2;
CDBLB 1960 to Present; DLB 87

Deighton, Leonard Cyril 1929-
See Deighton, Len
See also CA 9-12R; CANR 19, 33; MTCW

Dekker, Thomas 1572(?)-1632....... **LC 22**
See also CDBLB Before 1660; DLB 62

de la Mare, Walter (John)
1873-1956 .. **TCLC 4, 53; SSC 14; WLC**
See also CDBLB 1914-1945; CLR 23;
DLB 19; SATA 16

Delaney, Franey
See O'Hara, John (Henry)

Delaney, Shelagh 1939-........... **CLC 29**
See also CA 17-20R; CANR 30;
CDBLB 1960 to Present; DLB 13;
MTCW

Delany, Mary (Granville Pendarves)
1700-1788 .... **LC 12**

Delany, Samuel R(ay, Jr.)
1942- .... **CLC 8, 14, 38; BLC**
See also BW 2; CA 81-84; CANR 27, 43;
DLB 8, 33; MTCW

De La Ramee, (Marie) Louise 1839-1908
See Ouida
See also SATA 20

de la Roche, Mazo 1879-1961 ...... **CLC 14**
See also CA 85-88; CANR 30; DLB 68;
SATA 64

Delbanco, Nicholas (Franklin)
1942- .... **CLC 6, 13**
See also CA 17-20R; CAAS 2; CANR 29;
DLB 6

del Castillo, Michel 1933-......... **CLC 38**
See also CA 109

Deledda, Grazia (Cosima)
1875(?)-1936 .... **TCLC 23**
See also CA 123

Delibes, Miguel .... **CLC 8, 18**
See also Delibes Setien, Miguel

Delibes Setien, Miguel 1920-
See Delibes, Miguel
See also CA 45-48; CANR 1, 32; HW;
MTCW

DeLillo, Don
1936- ..... **CLC 8, 10, 13, 27, 39, 54, 76**
See also BEST 89:1; CA 81-84; CANR 21;
DLB 6; MTCW

de Lisser, H. G.
See De Lisser, Herbert George
See also DLB 117

De Lisser, Herbert George
1878-1944 .... **TCLC 12**
See also de Lisser, H. G.
See also BW 2; CA 109

Deloria, Vine (Victor), Jr. 1933-.... **CLC 21**
See also CA 53-56; CANR 5, 20; MTCW;
NNAL; SATA 21

Del Vecchio, John M(ichael)
1947- .... **CLC 29**
See also CA 110; DLBD 9

de Man, Paul (Adolph Michel)
1919-1983 .... **CLC 55**
See also CA 128; 111; DLB 67; MTCW

De Marinis, Rick 1934-.......... **CLC 54**
See also CA 57-60; CANR 9, 25

Demby, William 1922-...... **CLC 53; BLC**
See also BW 1; CA 81-84; DLB 33

Demijohn, Thom
See Disch, Thomas M(ichael)

de Montherlant, Henry (Milon)
See Montherlant, Henry (Milon) de

Demosthenes 384B.C.-322B.C. ... **CMLC 13**

de Natale, Francine
See Malzberg, Barry N(athaniel)

Denby, Edwin (Orr) 1903-1983..... **CLC 48**
See also CA 138; 110

Denis, Julio
See Cortazar, Julio

Denmark, Harrison
See Zelazny, Roger (Joseph)

Dennis, John 1658-1734........... **LC 11**
See also DLB 101

Dennis, Nigel (Forbes) 1912-1989.... **CLC 8**
See also CA 25-28R; 129; DLB 13, 15;
MTCW

De Palma, Brian (Russell) 1940-.... **CLC 20**
See also CA 109

De Quincey, Thomas 1785-1859 ... **NCLC 4**
See also CDBLB 1789-1832; DLB 110; 144

Deren, Eleanora 1908(?)-1961
See Deren, Maya
See also CA 111

Deren, Maya .... **CLC 16**
See also Deren, Eleanora

Derleth, August (William)
1909-1971 .... **CLC 31**
See also CA 1-4R; 29-32R; CANR 4;
DLB 9; SATA 5

Der Nister 1884-1950........... **TCLC 56**

de Routisie, Albert
See Aragon, Louis

Derrida, Jacques 1930-........ **CLC 24, 87**
See also CA 124; 127

Derry Down Derry
See Lear, Edward

Dersonnes, Jacques
See Simenon, Georges (Jacques Christian)

Desai, Anita 1937-............ **CLC 19, 37**
See also CA 81-84; CANR 33; MTCW;
SATA 63

de Saint-Luc, Jean
See Glassco, John

de Saint Roman, Arnaud
See Aragon, Louis

Descartes, Rene 1596-1650 .... **LC 20**

De Sica, Vittorio 1901(?)-1974 ..... **CLC 20**
See also CA 117

Desnos, Robert 1900-1945 .... **TCLC 22**
See also CA 121

Destouches, Louis-Ferdinand
1894-1961 .... **CLC 9, 15**
See also Celine, Louis-Ferdinand
See also CA 85-88; CANR 28; MTCW

Deutsch, Babette 1895-1982 .... **CLC 18**
See also CA 1-4R; 108; CANR 4; DLB 45;
SATA 1; SATA-Obit 33

Devenant, William 1606-1649 .... **LC 13**

Devkota, Laxmiprasad
1909-1959 .... **TCLC 23**
See also CA 123

De Voto, Bernard (Augustine)
1897-1955 .... **TCLC 29**
See also CA 113; DLB 9

De Vries, Peter
1910-1993 .... **CLC 1, 2, 3, 7, 10, 28, 46**
See also CA 17-20R; 142; CANR 41;
DLB 6; DLBY 82; MTCW

Dexter, Martin
See Faust, Frederick (Schiller)

Dexter, Pete 1943-............ **CLC 34, 55**
See also BEST 89:2; CA 127; 131; MTCW

Diamano, Silmang
See Senghor, Leopold Sedar

Diamond, Neil 1941- .... **CLC 30**
See also CA 108

di Bassetto, Corno
See Shaw, George Bernard

Dick, Philip K(indred)
1928-1982 .... **CLC 10, 30, 72**
See also CA 49-52; 106; CANR 2, 16;
DLB 8; MTCW

Dickens, Charles (John Huffam)
1812-1870 . . . . . . **NCLC 3, 8, 18, 26, 37;**
DA; SSC 17; WLC
See also CDBLB 1832-1890; DLB 21, 55,
70; JRDA; MAICYA; SATA 15

Dickey, James (Lafayette)
1923- . . . . **CLC 1, 2, 4, 7, 10, 15, 47**
See also AITN 1, 2; CA 9-12R; CABS 2;
CANR 10; CDALB 1968-1988; DLB 5;
DLBD 7; DLBY 82, 93; MTCW

Dickey, William 1928-1994 . . . . . . **CLC 3, 28**
See also CA 9-12R; 145; CANR 24; DLB 5

Dickinson, Charles 1951- . . . . **CLC 49**
See also CA 128

Dickinson, Emily (Elizabeth)
1830-1886 . . **NCLC 21; DA; PC 1; WLC**
See also CDALB 1865-1917; DLB 1;
SATA 29

Dickinson, Peter (Malcolm)
1927- . . . . **CLC 12, 35**
See also AAYA 9; CA 41-44R; CANR 31;
CLR 29; DLB 87; JRDA; MAICYA;
SATA 5, 62

Dickson, Carr
See Carr, John Dickson

Dickson, Carter
See Carr, John Dickson

Diderot, Denis 1713-1784 . . . . **LC 26**

Didion, Joan 1934- . . . . . **CLC 1, 3, 8, 14, 32**
See also AITN 1; CA 5-8R; CANR 14;
CDALB 1968-1988; DLB 2; DLBY 81,
86; MTCW

Dietrich, Robert
See Hunt, E(verette) Howard, (Jr.)

Dillard, Annie 1945- . . . . **CLC 9, 60**
See also AAYA 6; CA 49-52; CANR 3, 43;
DLBY 80; MTCW; SATA 10

Dillard, R(ichard) H(enry) W(ilde)
1937- . . . . **CLC 5**
See also CA 21-24R; CAAS 7; CANR 10;
DLB 5

Dillon, Eilis 1920- . . . . **CLC 17**
See also CA 9-12R; CAAS 3; CANR 4, 38;
CLR 26; MAICYA; SATA 2, 74

Dimont, Penelope
See Mortimer, Penelope (Ruth)

Dinesen, Isak. . . . . **CLC 10, 29; SSC 7**
See also Blixen, Karen (Christentze
Dinesen)

Ding Ling. **CLC 68**
See also Chiang Pin-chin

Disch, Thomas M(ichael) 1940- . . . **CLC 7, 36**
See also CA 21-24R; CAAS 4; CANR 17,
36; CLR 18; DLB 8; MAICYA; MTCW;
SAAS 15; SATA 54

Disch, Tom
See Disch, Thomas M(ichael)

d'Isly, Georges
See Simenon, Georges (Jacques Christian)

Disraeli, Benjamin 1804-1881 . . **NCLC 2, 39**
See also DLB 21, 55

Ditcum, Steve
See Crumb, R(obert)

Dixon, Paige
See Corcoran, Barbara

Dixon, Stephen 1936- . . . . . **CLC 52; SSC 16**
See also CA 89-92; CANR 17, 40; DLB 130

Dobell, Sydney Thompson
1824-1874 . . . . **NCLC 43**
See also DLB 32

Doblin, Alfred . . . . **TCLC 13**
See also Doeblin, Alfred

Dobrolyubov, Nikolai Alexandrovich
1836-1861 . . . . **NCLC 5**

Dobyns, Stephen 1941- . . . . **CLC 37**
See also CA 45-48; CANR 2, 18

Doctorow, E(dgar) L(aurence)
1931- . . . . . **CLC 6, 11, 15, 18, 37, 44, 65**
See also AITN 2; BEST 89:3; CA 45-48;
CANR 2, 33; CDALB 1968-1988; DLB 2,
28; DLBY 80; MTCW

Dodgson, Charles Lutwidge 1832-1898
See Carroll, Lewis
See also CLR 2; DA; MAICYA; YABC 2

Dodson, Owen (Vincent)
1914-1983 . . . . **CLC 79; BLC**
See also BW 1; CA 65-68; 110; CANR 24;
DLB 76

Doeblin, Alfred 1878-1957. . . . . . . **TCLC 13**
See also Doblin, Alfred
See also CA 110; 141; DLB 66

Doerr, Harriet 1910- . . . . **CLC 34**
See also CA 117; 122; CANR 47

Domecq, H(onorio) Bustos
See Bioy Casares, Adolfo; Borges, Jorge
Luis

Domini, Rey
See Lorde, Audre (Geraldine)

Dominique
See Proust, (Valentin-Louis-George-Eugene-)
Marcel

Don, A
See Stephen, Leslie

Donaldson, Stephen R. 1947- . . . . . . **CLC 46**
See also CA 89-92; CANR 13

Donleavy, J(ames) P(atrick)
1926- . . . . **CLC 1, 4, 6, 10, 45**
See also AITN 2; CA 9-12R; CANR 24;
DLB 6; MTCW

Donne, John
1572-1631 . . . . **LC 10, 24; DA; PC 1**
See also CDBLB Before 1660; DLB 121

Donnell, David 1939(?)- . . . . **CLC 34**

Donoghue, P. S.
See Hunt, E(verette) Howard, (Jr.)

Donoso (Yanez), Jose
1924- . . . . **CLC 4, 8, 11, 32; HLC**
See also CA 81-84; CANR 32; DLB 113;
HW; MTCW

Donovan, John 1928-1992 . . . . **CLC 35**
See also CA 97-100; 137; CLR 3;
MAICYA; SATA 72; SATA-Brief 29

Don Roberto
See Cunninghame Graham, R(obert)
B(ontine)

Doolittle, Hilda
1886-1961 . . . . . **CLC 3, 8, 14, 31, 34, 73;**
DA; PC 5; WLC
See also H. D.
See also CA 97-100; CANR 35; DLB 4, 45;
MTCW

Dorfman, Ariel 1942- . . . . **CLC 48, 77; HLC**
See also CA 124; 130; HW

Dorn, Edward (Merton) 1929- . . . **CLC 10, 18**
See also CA 93-96; CANR 42; DLB 5

Dorsan, Luc
See Simenon, Georges (Jacques Christian)

Dorsange, Jean
See Simenon, Georges (Jacques Christian)

Dos Passos, John (Roderigo)
1896-1970 . . . . . . **CLC 1, 4, 8, 11, 15, 25,**
34, 82; DA; WLC
See also CA 1-4R; 29-32R; CANR 3;
CDALB 1929-1941; DLB 4, 9; DLBD 1;
MTCW

Dossage, Jean
See Simenon, Georges (Jacques Christian)

Dostoevsky, Fedor Mikhailovich
1821-1881 . . . . . . **NCLC 2, 7, 21, 33, 43;**
DA; SSC 2; WLC

Doughty, Charles M(ontagu)
1843-1926 . . . . **TCLC 27**
See also CA 115; DLB 19, 57

Douglas, Ellen. . . . . **CLC 73**
See also Haxton, Josephine Ayres;
Williamson, Ellen Douglas

Douglas, Gavin 1475(?)-1522. . . . . . . **LC 20**

Douglas, Keith 1920-1944 . . . . **TCLC 40**
See also DLB 27

Douglas, Leonard
See Bradbury, Ray (Douglas)

Douglas, Michael
See Crichton, (John) Michael

Douglass, Frederick
1817(?)-1895 . . . . **NCLC 7; BLC; DA;**
WLC
See also CDALB 1640-1865; DLB 1, 43, 50,
79; SATA 29

Dourado, (Waldomiro Freitas) Autran
1926- . . . . **CLC 23, 60**
See also CA 25-28R; CANR 34

Dourado, Waldomiro Autran
See Dourado, (Waldomiro Freitas) Autran

Dove, Rita (Frances)
1952- . . . . **CLC 50, 81; PC 6**
See also BW 2; CA 109; CAAS 19;
CANR 27, 42; DLB 120

Dowell, Coleman 1925-1985. . . . . . . **CLC 60**
See also CA 25-28R; 117; CANR 10;
DLB 130

Dowson, Ernest Christopher
1867-1900 . . . . **TCLC 4**
See also CA 105; DLB 19, 135

Doyle, A. Conan
See Doyle, Arthur Conan

Doyle, Arthur Conan
1859-1930 ...... **TCLC 7; DA; SSC 12;**
WLC

See also AAYA 14; CA 104; 122;
CDBLB 1890-1914; DLB 18, 70; MTCW;
SATA 24

Doyle, Conan
See Doyle, Arthur Conan

Doyle, John
See Graves, Robert (von Ranke)

Doyle, Roddy 1958(?)- .... **CLC 81**
See also AAYA 14; CA 143

Doyle, Sir A. Conan
See Doyle, Arthur Conan

Doyle, Sir Arthur Conan
See Doyle, Arthur Conan

Dr. A
See Asimov, Isaac; Silverstein, Alvin

Drabble, Margaret
1939- .... **CLC 2, 3, 5, 8, 10, 22, 53**
See also CA 13-16R; CANR 18, 35;
CDBLB 1960 to Present; DLB 14;
MTCW; SATA 48

Drapier, M. B.
See Swift, Jonathan

Drayham, James
See Mencken, H(enry) L(ouis)

Drayton, Michael 1563-1631 .... **LC 8**

Dreadstone, Carl
See Campbell, (John) Ramsey

Dreiser, Theodore (Herman Albert)
1871-1945 ...... **TCLC 10, 18, 35; DA;**
WLC

See also CA 106; 132; CDALB 1865-1917;
DLB 9, 12, 102, 137; DLBD 1; MTCW

Drexler, Rosalyn 1926- .... **CLC 2, 6**
See also CA 81-84

Dreyer, Carl Theodor 1889-1968 .... **CLC 16**
See also CA 116

Drieu la Rochelle, Pierre(-Eugene)
1893-1945 .... **TCLC 21**
See also CA 117; DLB 72

Drinkwater, John 1882-1937 ...... **TCLC 57**
See also CA 109; DLB 10, 19

Drop Shot
See Cable, George Washington

Droste-Hulshoff, Annette Freiin von
1797-1848 .... **NCLC 3**
See also DLB 133

Drummond, Walter
See Silverberg, Robert

Drummond, William Henry
1854-1907 .... **TCLC 25**
See also DLB 92

Drummond de Andrade, Carlos
1902-1987 .... **CLC 18**
See also Andrade, Carlos Drummond de
See also CA 132; 123

Drury, Allen (Stuart) 1918- .... **CLC 37**
See also CA 57-60; CANR 18

Dryden, John
1631-1700 ... **LC 3, 21; DA; DC 3; WLC**
See also CDBLB 1660-1789; DLB 80, 101,
131

Duberman, Martin 1930- .... **CLC 8**
See also CA 1-4R; CANR 2

Dubie, Norman (Evans) 1945- ...... **CLC 36**
See also CA 69-72; CANR 12; DLB 120

Du Bois, W(illiam) E(dward) B(urghardt)
1868-1963 ...... **CLC 1, 2, 13, 64; BLC;**
DA; WLC

See also BW 1; CA 85-88; CANR 34;
CDALB 1865-1917; DLB 47, 50, 91;
MTCW; SATA 42

Dubus, Andre 1936- ... **CLC 13, 36; SSC 15**
See also CA 21-24R; CANR 17; DLB 130

Duca Minimo
See D'Annunzio, Gabriele

Ducharme, Rejean 1941- .... **CLC 74**
See also DLB 60

Duclos, Charles Pinot 1704-1772 ..... **LC 1**

Dudek, Louis 1918- .... **CLC 11, 19**
See also CA 45-48; CAAS 14; CANR 1;
DLB 88

Duerrenmatt, Friedrich
1921-1990 ...... **CLC 1, 4, 8, 11, 15, 43**
See also CA 17-20R; CANR 33; DLB 69,
124; MTCW

Duffy, Bruce (?)- .... **CLC 50**

Duffy, Maureen 1933- .... **CLC 37**
See also CA 25-28R; CANR 33; DLB 14;
MTCW

Dugan, Alan 1923- .... **CLC 2, 6**
See also CA 81-84; DLB 5

du Gard, Roger Martin
See Martin du Gard, Roger

Duhamel, Georges 1884-1966 .... **CLC 8**
See also CA 81-84; 25-28R; CANR 35;
DLB 65; MTCW

Dujardin, Edouard (Emile Louis)
1861-1949 .... **TCLC 13**
See also CA 109; DLB 123

Dumas, Alexandre (Davy de la Pailleterie)
1802-1870 .... **NCLC 11; DA; WLC**
See also DLB 119; SATA 18

Dumas, Alexandre
1824-1895 .... **NCLC 9; DC 1**

Dumas, Claudine
See Malzberg, Barry N(athaniel)

Dumas, Henry L. 1934-1968 ..... **CLC 6, 62**
See also BW 1; CA 85-88; DLB 41

du Maurier, Daphne
1907-1989 ...... **CLC 6, 11, 59; SSC 18**
See also CA 5-8R; 128; CANR 6; MTCW;
SATA 27; SATA-Obit 60

Dunbar, Paul Laurence
1872-1906 ...... **TCLC 2, 12; BLC; DA;**
PC 5; SSC 8; WLC

See also BW 1; CA 104; 124;
CDALB 1865-1917; DLB 50, 54, 78;
SATA 34

Dunbar, William 1460(?)-1530(?) .... **LC 20**
See also DLB 132, 146

Duncan, Lois 1934- .... **CLC 26**
See also AAYA 4; CA 1-4R; CANR 2, 23,
36; CLR 29; JRDA; MAICYA; SAAS 2;
SATA 1, 36, 75

Duncan, Robert (Edward)
1919-1988 .... **CLC 1, 2, 4, 7, 15, 41, 55;**
PC 2

See also CA 9-12R; 124; CANR 28; DLB 5,
16; MTCW

Dunlap, William 1766-1839 ...... **NCLC 2**
See also DLB 30, 37, 59

Dunn, Douglas (Eaglesham)
1942- .... **CLC 6, 40**
See also CA 45-48; CANR 2, 33; DLB 40;
MTCW

Dunn, Katherine (Karen) 1945- ..... **CLC 71**
See also CA 33-36R

Dunn, Stephen 1939- .... **CLC 36**
See also CA 33-36R; CANR 12; DLB 105

Dunne, Finley Peter 1867-1936 .... **TCLC 28**
See also CA 108; DLB 11, 23

Dunne, John Gregory 1932- .... **CLC 28**
See also CA 25-28R; CANR 14; DLBY 80

Dunsany, Edward John Moreton Drax
Plunkett 1878-1957
See Dunsany, Lord
See also CA 104; DLB 10

Dunsany, Lord .... **TCLC 2**
See also Dunsany, Edward John Moreton
Drax Plunkett
See also DLB 77

du Perry, Jean
See Simenon, Georges (Jacques Christian)

Durang, Christopher (Ferdinand)
1949- .... **CLC 27, 38**
See also CA 105

Duras, Marguerite
1914- ...... **CLC 3, 6, 11, 20, 34, 40, 68**
See also CA 25-28R; DLB 83; MTCW

Durban, (Rosa) Pam 1947- .... **CLC 39**
See also CA 123

Durcan, Paul 1944- .... **CLC 43, 70**
See also CA 134

Durkheim, Emile 1858-1917 ...... **TCLC 55**

Durrell, Lawrence (George)
1912-1990 .... **CLC 1, 4, 6, 8, 13, 27, 41**
See also CA 9-12R; 132; CANR 40;
CDBLB 1945-1960; DLB 15, 27;
DLBY 90; MTCW

Durrenmatt, Friedrich
See Duerrenmatt, Friedrich

Dutt, Toru 1856-1877 .... **NCLC 29**

Dwight, Timothy 1752-1817 ...... **NCLC 13**
See also DLB 37

Dworkin, Andrea 1946- .... **CLC 43**
See also CA 77-80; CANR 16, 39; MTCW

Dwyer, Deanna
See Koontz, Dean R(ay)

Dwyer, K. R.
See Koontz, Dean R(ay)

Dylan, Bob 1941- ...... **CLC 3, 4, 6, 12, 77**
See also CA 41-44R; DLB 16

Eagleton, Terence (Francis) 1943-
See Eagleton, Terry
See also CA 57-60; CANR 7, 23; MTCW

Eagleton, Terry .... **CLC 63**
See also Eagleton, Terence (Francis)

Early, Jack
  See Scoppettone, Sandra

East, Michael
  See West, Morris L(anglo)

Eastaway, Edward
  See Thomas, (Philip) Edward

Eastlake, William (Derry) 1917-..... **CLC 8**
  See also CA 5-8R; CAAS 1; CANR 5;
    DLB 6

Eastman, Charles A(lexander)
  1858-1939 .... **TCLC 55**
  See also NNAL; YABC 1

Eberhart, Richard (Ghormley)
  1904-............... **CLC 3, 11, 19, 56**
  See also CA 1-4R; CANR 2;
    CDALB 1941-1968; DLB 48; MTCW

Eberstadt, Fernanda 1960-........ **CLC 39**
  See also CA 136

Echegaray (y Eizaguirre), Jose (Maria Waldo)
  1832-1916 .... **TCLC 4**
  See also CA 104; CANR 32; HW; MTCW

Echeverria, (Jose) Esteban (Antonino)
  1805-1851 .... **NCLC 18**

Echo
  See Proust, (Valentin-Louis-George-Eugene-)
    Marcel

Eckert, Allan W. 1931-.......... **CLC 17**
  See also CA 13-16R; CANR 14, 45;
    SATA 29; SATA-Brief 27

Eckhart, Meister 1260(?)-1328(?) .. **CMLC 9**
  See also DLB 115

Eckmar, F. R.
  See de Hartog, Jan

Eco, Umberto 1932-.......... **CLC 28, 60**
  See also BEST 90:1; CA 77-80; CANR 12,
    33; MTCW

Eddison, E(ric) R(ucker)
  1882-1945 .... **TCLC 15**
  See also CA 109

Edel, (Joseph) Leon 1907-...... **CLC 29, 34**
  See also CA 1-4R; CANR 1, 22; DLB 103

Eden, Emily 1797-1869 .... **NCLC 10**

Edgar, David 1948-.............. **CLC 42**
  See also CA 57-60; CANR 12; DLB 13;
    MTCW

Edgerton, Clyde (Carlyle) 1944-.... **CLC 39**
  See also CA 118; 134

Edgeworth, Maria 1767-1849...... **NCLC 1**
  See also DLB 116; SATA 21

Edmonds, Paul
  See Kuttner, Henry

Edmonds, Walter D(umaux) 1903-.. **CLC 35**
  See also CA 5-8R; CANR 2; DLB 9;
    MAICYA; SAAS 4; SATA 1, 27

Edmondson, Wallace
  See Ellison, Harlan (Jay)

Edson, Russell.................... **CLC 13**
  See also CA 33-36R

Edwards, Bronwen Elizabeth
  See Rose, Wendy

Edwards, G(erald) B(asil)
  1899-1976 .... **CLC 25**
  See also CA 110

Edwards, Gus 1939-............. **CLC 43**
  See also CA 108

Edwards, Jonathan 1703-1758.... **LC 7; DA**
  See also DLB 24

Efron, Marina Ivanovna Tsvetaeva
  See Tsvetaeva (Efron), Marina (Ivanovna)

Ehle, John (Marsden, Jr.) 1925-.... **CLC 27**
  See also CA 9-12R

Ehrenbourg, Ilya (Grigoryevich)
  See Ehrenburg, Ilya (Grigoryevich)

Ehrenburg, Ilya (Grigoryevich)
  1891-1967 .... **CLC 18, 34, 62**
  See also CA 102; 25-28R

Ehrenburg, Ilyo (Grigoryevich)
  See Ehrenburg, Ilya (Grigoryevich)

Eich, Guenter 1907-1972 .... **CLC 15**
  See also CA 111; 93-96; DLB 69, 124

Eichendorff, Joseph Freiherr von
  1788-1857 .... **NCLC 8**
  See also DLB 90

Eigner, Larry...................... **CLC 9**
  See also Eigner, Laurence (Joel)
  See also DLB 5

Eigner, Laurence (Joel) 1927-
  See Eigner, Larry
  See also CA 9-12R; CANR 6

Eiseley, Loren Corey 1907-1977..... **CLC 7**
  See also AAYA 5; CA 1-4R; 73-76;
    CANR 6

Eisenstadt, Jill 1963-............. **CLC 50**
  See also CA 140

Eisenstein, Sergei (Mikhailovich)
  1898-1948 .... **TCLC 57**
  See also CA 114

Eisner, Simon
  See Kornbluth, C(yril) M.

Ekeloef, (Bengt) Gunnar
  1907-1968 .... **CLC 27**
  See also CA 123; 25-28R

Ekelof, (Bengt) Gunnar
  See Ekeloef, (Bengt) Gunnar

Ekwensi, C. O. D.
  See Ekwensi, Cyprian (Odiatu Duaka)

Ekwensi, Cyprian (Odiatu Duaka)
  1921-................... **CLC 4; BLC**
  See also BW 2; CA 29-32R; CANR 18, 42;
    DLB 117; MTCW; SATA 66

Elaine........................ **TCLC 18**
  See also Leverson, Ada

El Crummo
  See Crumb, R(obert)

Elia
  See Lamb, Charles

Eliade, Mircea 1907-1986 .... **CLC 19**
  See also CA 65-68; 119; CANR 30; MTCW

Eliot, A. D.
  See Jewett, (Theodora) Sarah Orne

Eliot, Alice
  See Jewett, (Theodora) Sarah Orne

Eliot, Dan
  See Silverberg, Robert

Eliot, George
  1819-1880 .... **NCLC 4, 13, 23, 41; DA;
    WLC**
  See also CDBLB 1832-1890; DLB 21, 35, 55

Eliot, John 1604-1690 .... **LC 5**
  See also DLB 24

Eliot, T(homas) S(tearns)
  1888-1965 ..... **CLC 1, 2, 3, 6, 9, 10, 13,
    15, 24, 34, 41, 55, 57; DA; PC 5; WLC 2**
  See also CA 5-8R; 25-28R; CANR 41;
    CDALB 1929-1941; DLB 7, 10, 45, 63;
    DLBY 88; MTCW

Elizabeth 1866-1941............. **TCLC 41**

Elkin, Stanley L(awrence)
  1930- ... **CLC 4, 6, 9, 14, 27, 51; SSC 12**
  See also CA 9-12R; CANR 8, 46; DLB 2,
    28; DLBY 80; MTCW

Elledge, Scott.................... **CLC 34**

Elliott, Don
  See Silverberg, Robert

Elliott, George P(aul) 1918-1980..... **CLC 2**
  See also CA 1-4R; 97-100; CANR 2

Elliott, Janice 1931-.............. **CLC 47**
  See also CA 13-16R; CANR 8, 29; DLB 14

Elliott, Sumner Locke 1917-1991 ... **CLC 38**
  See also CA 5-8R; 134; CANR 2, 21

Elliott, William
  See Bradbury, Ray (Douglas)

Ellis, A. E........................ **CLC 7**

Ellis, Alice Thomas............... **CLC 40**
  See also Haycraft, Anna

Ellis, Bret Easton 1964-........ **CLC 39, 71**
  See also AAYA 2; CA 118; 123

Ellis, (Henry) Havelock
  1859-1939 .... **TCLC 14**
  See also CA 109

Ellis, Landon
  See Ellison, Harlan (Jay)

Ellis, Trey 1962-................. **CLC 55**

Ellison, Harlan (Jay)
  1934- .... **CLC 1, 13, 42; SSC 14**
  See also CA 5-8R; CANR 5, 46; DLB 8;
    MTCW

Ellison, Ralph (Waldo)
  1914-1994 .... **CLC 1, 3, 11, 54, 86;
    BLC; DA; WLC**
  See also BW 1; CA 9-12R; 145; CANR 24;
    CDALB 1941-1968; DLB 2, 76; MTCW

Ellmann, Lucy (Elizabeth) 1956-.... **CLC 61**
  See also CA 128

Ellmann, Richard (David)
  1918-1987 .... **CLC 50**
  See also BEST 89:2; CA 1-4R; 122;
    CANR 2, 28; DLB 103; DLBY 87;
    MTCW

Elman, Richard 1934-............. **CLC 19**
  See also CA 17-20R; CAAS 3; CANR 47

Elron
  See Hubbard, L(afayette) Ron(ald)

Eluard, Paul................. **TCLC 7, 41**
  See also Grindel, Eugene

Elyot, Sir Thomas 1490(?)-1546 ..... **LC 11**

Elytis, Odysseus 1911-...... **CLC 15, 49**
  See also CA 102; MTCW

Emecheta, (Florence Onye) Buchi
1944- . . . . CLC 14, 48; BLC
See also BW 2; CA 81-84; CANR 27;
DLB 117; MTCW; SATA 66

Emerson, Ralph Waldo
1803-1882 . . . . . . NCLC 1, 38; DA; WLC
See also CDALB 1640-1865; DLB 1, 59, 73

Eminescu, Mihail 1850-1889 . . . . . NCLC 33

Empson, William
1906-1984 . . . . CLC 3, 8, 19, 33, 34
See also CA 17-20R; 112; CANR 31;
DLB 20; MTCW

Enchi Fumiko (Ueda) 1905-1986 . . . . CLC 31
See also CA 129; 121

Ende, Michael (Andreas Helmuth)
1929- . . . . CLC 31
See also CA 118; 124; CANR 36; CLR 14;
DLB 75; MAICYA; SATA 61;
SATA-Brief 42

Endo, Shusaku 1923- . . . . . CLC 7, 14, 19, 54
See also CA 29-32R; CANR 21; MTCW

Engel, Marian 1933-1985 . . . . CLC 36
See also CA 25-28R; CANR 12; DLB 53

Engelhardt, Frederick
See Hubbard, L(afayette) Ron(ald)

Enright, D(ennis) J(oseph)
1920- . . . . CLC 4, 8, 31
See also CA 1-4R; CANR 1, 42; DLB 27;
SATA 25

Enzensberger, Hans Magnus
1929- . . . . CLC 43
See also CA 116; 119

Ephron, Nora 1941- . . . . CLC 17, 31
See also AITN 2; CA 65-68; CANR 12, 39

Epsilon
See Betjeman, John

Epstein, Daniel Mark 1948- . . . . CLC 7
See also CA 49-52; CANR 2

Epstein, Jacob 1956- . . . . CLC 19
See also CA 114

Epstein, Joseph 1937- . . . . CLC 39
See also CA 112; 119

Epstein, Leslie 1938- . . . . CLC 27
See also CA 73-76; CAAS 12; CANR 23

Equiano, Olaudah
1745(?)-1797 . . . . LC 16; BLC
See also DLB 37, 50

Erasmus, Desiderius 1469(?)-1536 . . . . LC 16

Erdman, Paul E(mil) 1932- . . . . CLC 25
See also AITN 1; CA 61-64; CANR 13, 43

Erdrich, Louise 1954- . . . . CLC 39, 54
See also AAYA 10; BEST 89:1; CA 114;
CANR 41; MTCW; NNAL

Erenburg, Ilya (Grigoryevich)
See Ehrenburg, Ilya (Grigoryevich)

Erickson, Stephen Michael 1950-
See Erickson, Steve
See also CA 129

Erickson, Steve . . . . CLC 64
See also Erickson, Stephen Michael

Ericson, Walter
See Fast, Howard (Melvin)

Eriksson, Buntel
See Bergman, (Ernst) Ingmar

Eschenbach, Wolfram von
See Wolfram von Eschenbach

Eseki, Bruno
See Mphahlele, Ezekiel

Esenin, Sergei (Alexandrovich)
1895-1925 . . . . TCLC 4
See also CA 104

Eshleman, Clayton 1935- . . . . CLC 7
See also CA 33-36R; CAAS 6; DLB 5

Espriella, Don Manuel Alvarez
See Southey, Robert

Espriu, Salvador 1913-1985 . . . . CLC 9
See also CA 115; DLB 134

Espronceda, Jose de 1808-1842 . . . NCLC 39

Esse, James
See Stephens, James

Esterbrook, Tom
See Hubbard, L(afayette) Ron(ald)

Estleman, Loren D. 1952- . . . . CLC 48
See also CA 85-88; CANR 27; MTCW

Eugenides, Jeffrey 1960(?)- . . . . CLC 81
See also CA 144

Euripides c. 485B.C.-406B.C. . . . . DC 4
See also DA

Evan, Evin
See Faust, Frederick (Schiller)

Evans, Evan
See Faust, Frederick (Schiller)

Evans, Marian
See Eliot, George

Evans, Mary Ann
See Eliot, George

Evarts, Esther
See Benson, Sally

Everett, Percival L. 1956- . . . . CLC 57
See also BW 2; CA 129

Everson, R(onald) G(ilmour)
1903- . . . . CLC 27
See also CA 17-20R; DLB 88

Everson, William (Oliver)
1912-1994 . . . . CLC 1, 5, 14
See also CA 9-12R; 145; CANR 20; DLB 5,
16; MTCW

Evtushenko, Evgenii Aleksandrovich
See Yevtushenko, Yevgeny (Alexandrovich)

Ewart, Gavin (Buchanan)
1916- . . . . CLC 13, 46
See also CA 89-92; CANR 17, 46; DLB 40;
MTCW

Ewers, Hanns Heinz 1871-1943 . . . TCLC 12
See also CA 109

Ewing, Frederick R.
See Sturgeon, Theodore (Hamilton)

Exley, Frederick (Earl)
1929-1992 . . . . CLC 6, 11
See also AITN 2; CA 81-84; 138; DLB 143;
DLBY 81

Eynhardt, Guillermo
See Quiroga, Horacio (Sylvestre)

Ezekiel, Nissim 1924- . . . . CLC 61
See also CA 61-64

Ezekiel, Tish O'Dowd 1943- . . . . CLC 34
See also CA 129

Fadeyev, A.
See Bulgya, Alexander Alexandrovich

Fadeyev, Alexander . . . . TCLC 53
See also Bulgya, Alexander Alexandrovich

Fagen, Donald 1948- . . . . CLC 26

Fainzilberg, Ilya Arnoldovich 1897-1937
See Ilf, Ilya
See also CA 120

Fair, Ronald L. 1932- . . . . CLC 18
See also BW 1; CA 69-72; CANR 25;
DLB 33

Fairbairns, Zoe (Ann) 1948- . . . . CLC 32
See also CA 103; CANR 21

Falco, Gian
See Papini, Giovanni

Falconer, James
See Kirkup, James

Falconer, Kenneth
See Kornbluth, C(yril) M.

Falkland, Samuel
See Heijermans, Herman

Fallaci, Oriana 1930- . . . . CLC 11
See also CA 77-80; CANR 15; MTCW

Faludy, George 1913- . . . . CLC 42
See also CA 21-24R

Faludy, Gyoergy
See Faludy, George

Fanon, Frantz 1925-1961 . . . . . CLC 74; BLC
See also BW 1; CA 116; 89-92

Fanshawe, Ann 1625-1680 . . . . LC 11

Fante, John (Thomas) 1911-1983 . . . CLC 60
See also CA 69-72; 109; CANR 23;
DLB 130; DLBY 83

Farah, Nuruddin 1945- . . . . CLC 53; BLC
See also BW 2; CA 106; DLB 125

Fargue, Leon-Paul 1876(?)-1947 . . . TCLC 11
See also CA 109

Farigoule, Louis
See Romains, Jules

Farina, Richard 1936(?)-1966 . . . . CLC 9
See also CA 81-84; 25-28R

Farley, Walter (Lorimer)
1915-1989 . . . . CLC 17
See also CA 17-20R; CANR 8, 29; DLB 22;
JRDA; MAICYA; SATA 2, 43

Farmer, Philip Jose 1918- . . . . CLC 1, 19
See also CA 1-4R; CANR 4, 35; DLB 8;
MTCW

Farquhar, George 1677-1707 . . . . LC 21
See also DLB 84

Farrell, J(ames) G(ordon)
1935-1979 . . . . CLC 6
See also CA 73-76; 89-92; CANR 36;
DLB 14; MTCW

Farrell, James T(homas)
1904-1979 . . . . CLC 1, 4, 8, 11, 66
See also CA 5-8R; 89-92; CANR 9; DLB 4,
9, 86; DLBD 2; MTCW

Farren, Richard J.
See Betjeman, John

Farren, Richard M.
See Betjeman, John

Folke, Will
See Bloch, Robert (Albert)

Follett, Ken(neth Martin) 1949- .... **CLC 18**
See also AAYA 6; BEST 89:4; CA 81-84;
CANR 13, 33; DLB 87; DLBY 81;
MTCW

Fontane, Theodor 1819-1898..... **NCLC 26**
See also DLB 129

Foote, Horton 1916-............. **CLC 51**
See also CA 73-76; CANR 34; DLB 26

Foote, Shelby 1916- .... **CLC 75**
See also CA 5-8R; CANR 3, 45; DLB 2, 17

Forbes, Esther 1891-1967......... **CLC 12**
See also CA 13-14; 25-28R; CAP 1;
CLR 27; DLB 22; JRDA; MAICYA;
SATA 2

Forche, Carolyn (Louise)
1950- .... **CLC 25, 83, 86; PC 10**
See also CA 109; 117; DLB 5

Ford, Elbur
See Hibbert, Eleanor Alice Burford

Ford, Ford Madox
1873-1939 .... **TCLC 1, 15, 39, 57**
See also CA 104; 132; CDBLB 1914-1945;
DLB 34, 98; MTCW

Ford, John 1895-1973............. **CLC 16**
See also CA 45-48

Ford, Richard 1944-.............. **CLC 46**
See also CA 69-72; CANR 11, 47

Ford, Webster
See Masters, Edgar Lee

Foreman, Richard 1937-.......... **CLC 50**
See also CA 65-68; CANR 32

Forester, C(ecil) S(cott)
1899-1966 .... **CLC 35**
See also CA 73-76; 25-28R; SATA 13

Forez
See Mauriac, Francois (Charles)

Forman, James Douglas 1932-...... **CLC 21**
See also CA 9-12R; CANR 4, 19, 42;
JRDA; MAICYA; SATA 8, 70

Fornes, Maria Irene 1930-...... **CLC 39, 61**
See also CA 25-28R; CANR 28; DLB 7;
HW; MTCW

Forrest, Leon 1937-.............. **CLC 4**
See also BW 2; CA 89-92; CAAS 7;
CANR 25; DLB 33

Forster, E(dward) M(organ)
1879-1970 ..... **CLC 1, 2, 3, 4, 9, 10, 13,
15, 22, 45, 77; DA; WLC**
See also AAYA 2; CA 13-14; 25-28R;
CANR 45; CAP 1; CDBLB 1914-1945;
DLB 34, 98; DLBD 10; MTCW;
SATA 57

Forster, John 1812-1876 .... **NCLC 11**
See also DLB 144

Forsyth, Frederick 1938-...... **CLC 2, 5, 36**
See also BEST 89:4; CA 85-88; CANR 38;
DLB 87; MTCW

Forten, Charlotte L. .... **TCLC 16; BLC**
See also Grimke, Charlotte L(ottie) Forten
See also DLB 50

Foscolo, Ugo 1778-1827......... **NCLC 8**

Fosse, Bob .... **CLC 20**
See also Fosse, Robert Louis

Fosse, Robert Louis 1927-1987
See Fosse, Bob
See also CA 110; 123

Foster, Stephen Collins
1826-1864 .... **NCLC 26**

Foucault, Michel
1926-1984 .... **CLC 31, 34, 69**
See also CA 105; 113; CANR 34; MTCW

Fouque, Friedrich (Heinrich Karl) de la Motte
1777-1843 .... **NCLC 2**
See also DLB 90

Fournier, Henri Alban 1886-1914
See Alain-Fournier
See also CA 104

Fournier, Pierre 1916-........... **CLC 11**
See also Gascar, Pierre
See also CA 89-92; CANR 16, 40

Fowles, John
1926- ...... **CLC 1, 2, 3, 4, 6, 9, 10, 15,
33, 87**
See also CA 5-8R; CANR 25; CDBLB 1960
to Present; DLB 14, 139; MTCW;
SATA 22

Fox, Paula 1923-................ **CLC 2, 8**
See also AAYA 3; CA 73-76; CANR 20,
36; CLR 1; DLB 52; JRDA; MAICYA;
MTCW; SATA 17, 60

Fox, William Price (Jr.) 1926- ..... **CLC 22**
See also CA 17-20R; CAAS 19; CANR 11;
DLB 2; DLBY 81

Foxe, John 1516(?)-1587 .... **LC 14**

Frame, Janet .... **CLC 2, 3, 6, 22, 66**
See also Clutha, Janet Paterson Frame

France, Anatole................... **TCLC 9**
See also Thibault, Jacques Anatole Francois
See also DLB 123

Francis, Claude 19(?)- .... **CLC 50**

Francis, Dick 1920- .... **CLC 2, 22, 42**
See also AAYA 5; BEST 89:3; CA 5-8R;
CANR 9, 42; CDBLB 1960 to Present;
DLB 87; MTCW

Francis, Robert (Churchill)
1901-1987 .... **CLC 15**
See also CA 1-4R; 123; CANR 1

Frank, Anne(lies Marie)
1929-1945 .... **TCLC 17; DA; WLC**
See also AAYA 12; CA 113; 133; MTCW;
SATA-Brief 42

Frank, Elizabeth 1945-............ **CLC 39**
See also CA 121; 126

Franklin, Benjamin
See Hasek, Jaroslav (Matej Frantisek)

Franklin, Benjamin 1706-1790... **LC 25; DA**
See also CDALB 1640-1865; DLB 24, 43,
73

Franklin, (Stella Maraia Sarah) Miles
1879-1954 .... **TCLC 7**
See also CA 104

Fraser, (Lady) Antonia (Pakenham)
1932- .... **CLC 32**
See also CA 85-88; CANR 44; MTCW;
SATA-Brief 32

Fraser, George MacDonald 1925-.... **CLC 7**
See also CA 45-48; CANR 2

Fraser, Sylvia 1935-............. **CLC 64**
See also CA 45-48; CANR 1, 16

Frayn, Michael 1933-...... **CLC 3, 7, 31, 47**
See also CA 5-8R; CANR 30; DLB 13, 14;
MTCW

Fraze, Candida (Merrill) 1945-..... **CLC 50**
See also CA 126

Frazer, J(ames) G(eorge)
1854-1941 .... **TCLC 32**
See also CA 118

Frazer, Robert Caine
See Creasey, John

Frazer, Sir James George
See Frazer, J(ames) G(eorge)

Frazier, Ian 1951-................ **CLC 46**
See also CA 130

Frederic, Harold 1856-1898...... **NCLC 10**
See also DLB 12, 23

Frederick, John
See Faust, Frederick (Schiller)

Frederick the Great 1712-1786 ...... **LC 14**

Fredro, Aleksander 1793-1876..... **NCLC 8**

Freeling, Nicolas 1927- .... **CLC 38**
See also CA 49-52; CAAS 12; CANR 1, 17;
DLB 87

Freeman, Douglas Southall
1886-1953 .... **TCLC 11**
See also CA 109; DLB 17

Freeman, Judith 1946-............ **CLC 55**

Freeman, Mary Eleanor Wilkins
1852-1930 .... **TCLC 9; SSC 1**
See also CA 106; DLB 12, 78

Freeman, R(ichard) Austin
1862-1943 .... **TCLC 21**
See also CA 113; DLB 70

French, Albert 1943- .... **CLC 86**

French, Marilyn 1929-...... **CLC 10, 18, 60**
See also CA 69-72; CANR 3, 31; MTCW

French, Paul
See Asimov, Isaac

Freneau, Philip Morin 1752-1832.. **NCLC 1**
See also DLB 37, 43

Freud, Sigmund 1856-1939 .... **TCLC 52**
See also CA 115; 133; MTCW

Friedan, Betty (Naomi) 1921-...... **CLC 74**
See also CA 65-68; CANR 18, 45; MTCW

Friedman, B(ernard) H(arper)
1926- .... **CLC 7**
See also CA 1-4R; CANR 3

Friedman, Bruce Jay 1930- .... **CLC 3, 5, 56**
See also CA 9-12R; CANR 25; DLB 2, 28

Friel, Brian 1929-........... **CLC 5, 42, 59**
See also CA 21-24R; CANR 33; DLB 13;
MTCW

Friis-Baastad, Babbis Ellinor
1921-1970 .... **CLC 12**
See also CA 17-20R; 134; SATA 7

Frisch, Max (Rudolf)
1911-1991 ..... **CLC 3, 9, 14, 18, 32, 44**
See also CA 85-88; 134; CANR 32;
DLB 69, 124; MTCW

Gates, Henry Louis, Jr. 1950-...... **CLC 65**
See also BW 2; CA 109; CANR 25; DLB 67

Gautier, Theophile 1811-1872 ..... **NCLC 1**
See also DLB 119

Gawsworth, John
See Bates, H(erbert) E(rnest)

Gaye, Marvin (Penze) 1939-1984 ... **CLC 26**
See also CA 112

Gebler, Carlo (Ernest) 1954-....... **CLC 39**
See also CA 119; 133

Gee, Maggie (Mary) 1948-........ **CLC 57**
See also CA 130

Gee, Maurice (Gough) 1931-...... **CLC 29**
See also CA 97-100; SATA 46

Gelbart, Larry (Simon) 1923-... **CLC 21, 61**
See also CA 73-76; CANR 45

Gelber, Jack 1932-........**CLC 1, 6, 14, 79**
See also CA 1-4R; CANR 2; DLB 7

Gellhorn, Martha (Ellis) 1908-.. **CLC 14, 60**
See also CA 77-80; CANR 44; DLBY 82

Genet, Jean
1910-1986 ... **CLC 1, 2, 5, 10, 14, 44, 46**
See also CA 13-16R; CANR 18; DLB 72;
DLBY 86; MTCW

Gent, Peter 1942-................. **CLC 29**
See also AITN 1; CA 89-92; DLBY 82

Gentlewoman in New England, A
See Bradstreet, Anne

Gentlewoman in Those Parts, A
See Bradstreet, Anne

George, Jean Craighead 1919-...... **CLC 35**
See also AAYA 8; CA 5-8R; CANR 25;
CLR 1; DLB 52; JRDA; MAICYA;
SATA 2, 68

George, Stefan (Anton)
1868-1933 .... **TCLC 2, 14**
See also CA 104

Georges, Georges Martin
See Simenon, Georges (Jacques Christian)

Gerhardi, William Alexander
See Gerhardie, William Alexander

Gerhardie, William Alexander
1895-1977 .... **CLC 5**
See also CA 25-28R; 73-76; CANR 18;
DLB 36

Gerstler, Amy 1956-............. **CLC 70**

Gertler, T. .... **CLC 34**
See also CA 116; 121

Ghalib 1797-1869 .... **NCLC 39**

Ghelderode, Michel de
1898-1962 .... **CLC 6, 11**
See also CA 85-88; CANR 40

Ghiselin, Brewster 1903-.......... **CLC 23**
See also CA 13-16R; CAAS 10; CANR 13

Ghose, Zulfikar 1935-............ **CLC 42**
See also CA 65-68

Ghosh, Amitav 1956-............. **CLC 44**

Giacosa, Giuseppe 1847-1906 ...... **TCLC 7**
See also CA 104

Gibb, Lee
See Waterhouse, Keith (Spencer)

Gibbon, Lewis Grassic .... **TCLC 4**
See also Mitchell, James Leslie

Gibbons, Kaye 1960- .... **CLC 50**

Gibran, Kahlil
1883-1931 .... **TCLC 1, 9; PC 9**
See also CA 104

Gibson, William 1914-....... **CLC 23; DA**
See also CA 9-12R; CANR 9, 42; DLB 7;
SATA 66

Gibson, William (Ford) 1948-... **CLC 39, 63**
See also AAYA 12; CA 126; 133

Gide, Andre (Paul Guillaume)
1869-1951 .... **TCLC 5, 12, 36; DA;**
SSC 13; WLC
See also CA 104; 124; DLB 65; MTCW

Gifford, Barry (Colby) 1946-....... **CLC 34**
See also CA 65-68; CANR 9, 30, 40

Gilbert, W(illiam) S(chwenck)
1836-1911 .... **TCLC 3**
See also CA 104; SATA 36

Gilbreth, Frank B., Jr. 1911-....... **CLC 17**
See also CA 9-12R; SATA 2

Gilchrist, Ellen 1935-.. **CLC 34, 48; SSC 14**
See also CA 113; 116; CANR 41; DLB 130;
MTCW

Giles, Molly 1942-............... **CLC 39**
See also CA 126

Gill, Patrick
See Creasey, John

Gilliam, Terry (Vance) 1940-....... **CLC 21**
See also Monty Python
See also CA 108; 113; CANR 35

Gillian, Jerry
See Gilliam, Terry (Vance)

Gilliatt, Penelope (Ann Douglass)
1932-1993 .... **CLC 2, 10, 13, 53**
See also AITN 2; CA 13-16R; 141; DLB 14

Gilman, Charlotte (Anna) Perkins (Stetson)
1860-1935 .... **TCLC 9, 37; SSC 13**
See also CA 106

Gilmour, David 1949-............. **CLC 35**
See also CA 138

Gilpin, William 1724-1804...... **NCLC 30**

Gilray, J. D.
See Mencken, H(enry) L(ouis)

Gilroy, Frank D(aniel) 1925-........ **CLC 2**
See also CA 81-84; CANR 32; DLB 7

Ginsberg, Allen
1926- ...... **CLC 1, 2, 3, 4, 6, 13, 36, 69;**
DA; PC 4; WLC 3
See also AITN 1; CA 1-4R; CANR 2, 41;
CDALB 1941-1968; DLB 5, 16; MTCW

Ginzburg, Natalia
1916-1991 .... **CLC 5, 11, 54, 70**
See also CA 85-88; 135; CANR 33; MTCW

Giono, Jean 1895-1970............ **CLC 4, 11**
See also CA 45-48; 29-32R; CANR 2, 35;
DLB 72; MTCW

Giovanni, Nikki
1943- ...... **CLC 2, 4, 19, 64; BLC; DA**
See also AITN 1; BW 2; CA 29-32R;
CAAS 6; CANR 18, 41; CLR 6; DLB 5,
41; MAICYA; MTCW; SATA 24

Giovene, Andrea 1904-............ **CLC 7**
See also CA 85-88

Gippius, Zinaida (Nikolayevna) 1869-1945
See Hippius, Zinaida
See also CA 106

Giraudoux, (Hippolyte) Jean
1882-1944 .... **TCLC 2, 7**
See also CA 104; DLB 65

Gironella, Jose Maria 1917-....... **CLC 11**
See also CA 101

Gissing, George (Robert)
1857-1903 .... **TCLC 3, 24, 47**
See also CA 105; DLB 18, 135

Giurlani, Aldo
See Palazzeschi, Aldo

Gladkov, Fyodor (Vasilyevich)
1883-1958 .... **TCLC 27**

Glanville, Brian (Lester) 1931-...... **CLC 6**
See also CA 5-8R; CAAS 9; CANR 3;
DLB 15, 139; SATA 42

Glasgow, Ellen (Anderson Gholson)
1873(?)-1945 .... **TCLC 2, 7**
See also CA 104; DLB 9, 12

Glaspell, Susan (Keating)
1882(?)-1948 .... **TCLC 55**
See also CA 110; DLB 7, 9, 78; YABC 2

Glassco, John 1909-1981 .... **CLC 9**
See also CA 13-16R; 102; CANR 15;
DLB 68

Glasscock, Amnesia
See Steinbeck, John (Ernst)

Glasser, Ronald J. 1940(?)-........ **CLC 37**

Glassman, Joyce
See Johnson, Joyce

Glendinning, Victoria 1937-........ **CLC 50**
See also CA 120; 127

Glissant, Edouard 1928-........ **CLC 10, 68**

Gloag, Julian 1930- .... **CLC 40**
See also AITN 1; CA 65-68; CANR 10

Glowacki, Aleksander
See Prus, Boleslaw

Glueck, Louise (Elisabeth)
1943-............**CLC 7, 22, 44, 81**
See also CA 33-36R; CANR 40; DLB 5

Gobineau, Joseph Arthur (Comte) de
1816-1882 .... **NCLC 17**
See also DLB 123

Godard, Jean-Luc 1930-.......... **CLC 20**
See also CA 93-96

Godden, (Margaret) Rumer 1907-... **CLC 53**
See also AAYA 6; CA 5-8R; CANR 4, 27,
36; CLR 20; MAICYA; SAAS 12;
SATA 3, 36

Godoy Alcayaga, Lucila 1889-1957
See Mistral, Gabriela
See also BW 2; CA 104; 131; HW; MTCW

Godwin, Gail (Kathleen)
1937-............. **CLC 5, 8, 22, 31, 69**
See also CA 29-32R; CANR 15, 43; DLB 6;
MTCW

Godwin, William 1756-1836...... **NCLC 14**
See also CDBLB 1789-1832; DLB 39, 104,
142

Goethe, Johann Wolfgang von
1749-1832 . . . . NCLC 4, 22, 34; DA;
PC 5; WLC 3
See also DLB 94

Gogarty, Oliver St. John
1878-1957 . . . . TCLC 15
See also CA 109; DLB 15, 19

Gogol, Nikolai (Vasilyevich)
1809-1852 . . . . NCLC 5, 15, 31; DA;
DC 1; SSC 4; WLC
Goines, Donald
1937(?)-1974 . . . . CLC 80; BLC
See also AITN 1; BW 1; CA 124; 114;
DLB 33

Gold, Herbert   1924- . . . . . . CLC 4, 7, 14, 42
See also CA 9-12R; CANR 17, 45; DLB 2;
DLBY 81

Goldbarth, Albert   1948- . . . . CLC 5, 38
See also CA 53-56; CANR 6, 40; DLB 120

Goldberg, Anatol   1910-1982 . . . . CLC 34
See also CA 131; 117

Goldemberg, Isaac   1945- . . . . CLC 52
See also CA 69-72; CAAS 12; CANR 11,
32; HW

Golding, William (Gerald)
1911-1993 . . . . CLC 1, 2, 3, 8, 10, 17, 27,
58, 81; DA; WLC
See also AAYA 5; CA 5-8R; 141;
CANR 13, 33; CDBLB 1945-1960;
DLB 15, 100; MTCW

Goldman, Emma   1869-1940 . . . . . . TCLC 13
See also CA 110

Goldman, Francisco   1955- . . . . CLC 76

Goldman, William (W.)   1931- . . . . CLC 1, 48
See also CA 9-12R; CANR 29; DLB 44

Goldmann, Lucien   1913-1970 . . . . . . CLC 24
See also CA 25-28; CAP 2

Goldoni, Carlo   1707-1793 . . . . LC 4

Goldsberry, Steven   1949- . . . . CLC 34
See also CA 131

Goldsmith, Oliver
1728-1774 . . . . LC 2; DA; WLC
See also CDBLB 1660-1789; DLB 39, 89,
104, 109, 142; SATA 26

Goldsmith, Peter
See Priestley, J(ohn) B(oynton)

Gombrowicz, Witold
1904-1969 . . . . CLC 4, 7, 11, 49
See also CA 19-20; 25-28R; CAP 2

Gomez de la Serna, Ramon
1888-1963 . . . . CLC 9
See also CA 116; HW

Goncharov, Ivan Alexandrovich
1812-1891 . . . . NCLC 1

Goncourt, Edmond (Louis Antoine Huot) de
1822-1896 . . . . NCLC 7
See also DLB 123

Goncourt, Jules (Alfred Huot) de
1830-1870 . . . . NCLC 7
See also DLB 123

Gontier, Fernande   19(?)- . . . . CLC 50

Goodman, Paul   1911-1972 . . . . CLC 1, 2, 4, 7
See also CA 19-20; 37-40R; CANR 34;
CAP 2; DLB 130; MTCW

Gordimer, Nadine
1923- . . . . CLC 3, 5, 7, 10, 18, 33, 51, 70;
DA; SSC 17
See also CA 5-8R; CANR 3, 28; MTCW

Gordon, Adam Lindsay
1833-1870 . . . . NCLC 21

Gordon, Caroline
1895-1981 . . . CLC 6, 13, 29, 83; SSC 15
See also CA 11-12; 103; CANR 36; CAP 1;
DLB 4, 9, 102; DLBY 81; MTCW

Gordon, Charles William   1860-1937
See Connor, Ralph
See also CA 109

Gordon, Mary (Catherine)
1949- . . . . CLC 13, 22
See also CA 102; CANR 44; DLB 6;
DLBY 81; MTCW

Gordon, Sol   1923- . . . . CLC 26
See also CA 53-56; CANR 4; SATA 11

Gordone, Charles   1925- . . . . CLC 1, 4
See also BW 1; CA 93-96; DLB 7; MTCW

Gorenko, Anna Andreevna
See Akhmatova, Anna

Gorky, Maxim . . . . TCLC 8; WLC
See also Peshkov, Alexei Maximovich

Goryan, Sirak
See Saroyan, William

Gosse, Edmund (William)
1849-1928 . . . . TCLC 28
See also CA 117; DLB 57, 144

Gotlieb, Phyllis Fay (Bloom)
1926- . . . . CLC 18
See also CA 13-16R; CANR 7; DLB 88

Gottesman, S. D.
See Kornbluth, C(yril) M.; Pohl, Frederik

Gottfried von Strassburg
fl. c. 1210- . . . . CMLC 10
See also DLB 138

Gould, Lois . . . . CLC 4, 10
See also CA 77-80; CANR 29; MTCW

Gourmont, Remy de   1858-1915 . . . . TCLC 17
See also CA 109

Govier, Katherine   1948- . . . . CLC 51
See also CA 101; CANR 18, 40

Goyen, (Charles) William
1915-1983 . . . . CLC 5, 8, 14, 40
See also AITN 2; CA 5-8R; 110; CANR 6;
DLB 2; DLBY 83

Goytisolo, Juan
1931- . . . . CLC 5, 10, 23; HLC
See also CA 85-88; CANR 32; HW; MTCW

Gozzano, Guido   1883-1916 . . . . PC 10
See also DLB 114

Gozzi, (Conte) Carlo   1720-1806 . . NCLC 23

Grabbe, Christian Dietrich
1801-1836 . . . . NCLC 2
See also DLB 133

Grace, Patricia   1937- . . . . CLC 56

Gracian y Morales, Baltasar
1601-1658 . . . . LC 15

Gracq, Julien . . . . CLC 11, 48
See also Poirier, Louis
See also DLB 83

Grade, Chaim   1910-1982 . . . . CLC 10
See also CA 93-96; 107

Graduate of Oxford, A
See Ruskin, John

Graham, John
See Phillips, David Graham

Graham, Jorie   1951- . . . . CLC 48
See also CA 111; DLB 120

Graham, R(obert) B(ontine) Cunninghame
See Cunninghame Graham, R(obert)
B(ontine)
See also DLB 98, 135

Graham, Robert
See Haldeman, Joe (William)

Graham, Tom
See Lewis, (Harry) Sinclair

Graham, W(illiam) S(ydney)
1918-1986 . . . . CLC 29
See also CA 73-76; 118; DLB 20

Graham, Winston (Mawdsley)
1910- . . . . CLC 23
See also CA 49-52; CANR 2, 22, 45;
DLB 77

Grant, Skeeter
See Spiegelman, Art

Granville-Barker, Harley
1877-1946 . . . . TCLC 2
See also Barker, Harley Granville
See also CA 104

Grass, Guenter (Wilhelm)
1927- . . . . . CLC 1, 2, 4, 6, 11, 15, 22, 32,
49; DA; WLC
See also CA 13-16R; CANR 20; DLB 75,
124; MTCW

Gratton, Thomas
See Hulme, T(homas) E(rnest)

Grau, Shirley Ann
1929- . . . . CLC 4, 9; SSC 15
See also CA 89-92; CANR 22; DLB 2;
MTCW

Gravel, Fern
See Hall, James Norman

Graver, Elizabeth   1964- . . . . CLC 70
See also CA 135

Graves, Richard Perceval   1945- . . . . CLC 44
See also CA 65-68; CANR 9, 26

Graves, Robert (von Ranke)
1895-1985 . . . . . . CLC 1, 2, 6, 11, 39, 44,
45; PC 6
See also CA 5-8R; 117; CANR 5, 36;
CDBLB 1914-1945; DLB 20, 100;
DLBY 85; MTCW; SATA 45

Gray, Alasdair (James)   1934- . . . . . . CLC 41
See also CA 126; CANR 47; MTCW

Gray, Amlin   1946- . . . . CLC 29
See also CA 138

Gray, Francine du Plessix   1930- . . . . CLC 22
See also BEST 90:3; CA 61-64; CAAS 2;
CANR 11, 33; MTCW

Gray, John (Henry)   1866-1934 . . . . TCLC 19
See also CA 119

Gray, Simon (James Holliday)
1936- . . . . CLC 9, 14, 36
See also AITN 1; CA 21-24R; CAAS 3;
CANR 32; DLB 13; MTCW

Howard, Elizabeth Jane 1923- ... **CLC 7, 29**
See also CA 5-8R; CANR 8

Howard, Maureen 1930- ..... **CLC 5, 14, 46**
See also CA 53-56; CANR 31; DLBY 83;
MTCW

Howard, Richard 1929- ...... **CLC 7, 10, 47**
See also AITN 1; CA 85-88; CANR 25;
DLB 5

Howard, Robert Ervin 1906-1936... **TCLC 8**
See also CA 105

Howard, Warren F.
See Pohl, Frederik

Howe, Fanny 1940- .... **CLC 47**
See also CA 117; SATA 52

Howe, Irving 1920-1993........... **CLC 85**
See also CA 9-12R; 141; CANR 21;
DLB 67; MTCW

Howe, Julia Ward 1819-1910 ..... **TCLC 21**
See also CA 117; DLB 1

Howe, Susan 1937-............... **CLC 72**
See also DLB 120

Howe, Tina 1937-................ **CLC 48**
See also CA 109

Howell, James 1594(?)-1666 .... **LC 13**

Howells, W. D.
See Howells, William Dean

Howells, William D.
See Howells, William Dean

Howells, William Dean
1837-1920 .... **TCLC 7, 17, 41**
See also CA 104; 134; CDALB 1865-1917;
DLB 12, 64, 74, 79

Howes, Barbara 1914-............. **CLC 15**
See also CA 9-12R; CAAS 3; SATA 5

Hrabal, Bohumil 1914-......... **CLC 13, 67**
See also CA 106; CAAS 12

Hsun, Lu .... **TCLC 3**
See also Shu-Jen, Chou

Hubbard, L(afayette) Ron(ald)
1911-1986 .... **CLC 43**
See also CA 77-80; 118; CANR 22

Huch, Ricarda (Octavia)
1864-1947 .... **TCLC 13**
See also CA 111; DLB 66

Huddle, David 1942- .... **CLC 49**
See also CA 57-60; CAAS 20; DLB 130

Hudson, Jeffrey
See Crichton, (John) Michael

Hudson, W(illiam) H(enry)
1841-1922 .... **TCLC 29**
See also CA 115; DLB 98; SATA 35

Hueffer, Ford Madox
See Ford, Ford Madox

Hughart, Barry 1934-............. **CLC 39**
See also CA 137

Hughes, Colin
See Creasey, John

Hughes, David (John) 1930- ...... **CLC 48**
See also CA 116; 129; DLB 14

Hughes, (James) Langston
1902-1967 ..... **CLC 1, 5, 10, 15, 35, 44;
BLC; DA; DC 3; PC 1; SSC 6; WLC**
See also AAYA 12; BW 1; CA 1-4R;
25-28R; CANR 1, 34; CDALB 1929-1941;
CLR 17; DLB 4, 7, 48, 51, 86; JRDA;
MAICYA; MTCW; SATA 4, 33

Hughes, Richard (Arthur Warren)
1900-1976 .... **CLC 1, 11**
See also CA 5-8R; 65-68; CANR 4;
DLB 15; MTCW; SATA 8;
SATA-Obit 25

Hughes, Ted
1930- .... **CLC 2, 4, 9, 14, 37; PC 7**
See also CA 1-4R; CANR 1, 33; CLR 3;
DLB 40; MAICYA; MTCW; SATA 27,
49

Hugo, Richard F(ranklin)
1923-1982 .... **CLC 6, 18, 32**
See also CA 49-52; 108; CANR 3; DLB 5

Hugo, Victor (Marie)
1802-1885 .. **NCLC 3, 10, 21; DA; WLC**
See also DLB 119; SATA 47

Huidobro, Vicente
See Huidobro Fernandez, Vicente Garcia

Huidobro Fernandez, Vicente Garcia
1893-1948 .... **TCLC 31**
See also CA 131; HW

Hulme, Keri 1947-............... **CLC 39**
See also CA 125

Hulme, T(homas) E(rnest)
1883-1917 .... **TCLC 21**
See also CA 117; DLB 19

Hume, David 1711-1776............. **LC 7**
See also DLB 104

Humphrey, William 1924-........ **CLC 45**
See also CA 77-80; DLB 6

Humphreys, Emyr Owen 1919-..... **CLC 47**
See also CA 5-8R; CANR 3, 24; DLB 15

Humphreys, Josephine 1945-.... **CLC 34, 57**
See also CA 121; 127

Hungerford, Pixie
See Brinsmead, H(esba) F(ay)

Hunt, E(verette) Howard, (Jr.)
1918- .... **CLC 3**
See also AITN 1; CA 45-48; CANR 2, 47

Hunt, Kyle
See Creasey, John

Hunt, (James Henry) Leigh
1784-1859 .... **NCLC 1**

Hunt, Marsha 1946-............. **CLC 70**
See also BW 2; CA 143

Hunt, Violet 1866-1942 .... **TCLC 53**

Hunter, E. Waldo
See Sturgeon, Theodore (Hamilton)

Hunter, Evan 1926- .... **CLC 11, 31**
See also CA 5-8R; CANR 5, 38; DLBY 82;
MTCW; SATA 25

Hunter, Kristin (Eggleston) 1931-... **CLC 35**
See also AITN 1; BW 1; CA 13-16R;
CANR 13; CLR 3; DLB 33; MAICYA;
SAAS 10; SATA 12

Hunter, Mollie 1922-............. **CLC 21**
See also McIlwraith, Maureen Mollie
Hunter
See also AAYA 13; CANR 37; CLR 25;
JRDA; MAICYA; SAAS 7; SATA 54

Hunter, Robert (?)-1734............. **LC 7**

Hurston, Zora Neale
1903-1960 .... **CLC 7, 30, 61; BLC; DA;
SSC 4**
See also BW 1; CA 85-88; DLB 51, 86;
MTCW

Huston, John (Marcellus)
1906-1987 .... **CLC 20**
See also CA 73-76; 123; CANR 34; DLB 26

Hustvedt, Siri 1955-............. **CLC 76**
See also CA 137

Hutten, Ulrich von 1488-1523....... **LC 16**

Huxley, Aldous (Leonard)
1894-1963 ..... **CLC 1, 3, 4, 5, 8, 11, 18,
35, 79; DA; WLC**
See also AAYA 11; CA 85-88; CANR 44;
CDBLB 1914-1945; DLB 36, 100;
MTCW; SATA 63

Huysmans, Charles Marie Georges
1848-1907
See Huysmans, Joris-Karl
See also CA 104

Huysmans, Joris-Karl............. **TCLC 7**
See also Huysmans, Charles Marie Georges
See also DLB 123

Hwang, David Henry
1957- .... **CLC 55; DC 4**
See also CA 127; 132

Hyde, Anthony 1946-............. **CLC 42**
See also CA 136

Hyde, Margaret O(ldroyd) 1917- ... **CLC 21**
See also CA 1-4R; CANR 1, 36; CLR 23;
JRDA; MAICYA; SAAS 8; SATA 1, 42,
76

Hynes, James 1956(?)-............ **CLC 65**

Ian, Janis 1951- .... **CLC 21**
See also CA 105

Ibanez, Vicente Blasco
See Blasco Ibanez, Vicente

Ibarguengoitia, Jorge 1928-1983.... **CLC 37**
See also CA 124; 113; HW

Ibsen, Henrik (Johan)
1828-1906 .... **TCLC 2, 8, 16, 37, 52;
DA; DC 2; WLC**
See also CA 104; 141

Ibuse Masuji 1898-1993........... **CLC 22**
See also CA 127; 141

Ichikawa, Kon 1915-............. **CLC 20**
See also CA 121

Idle, Eric 1943-................. **CLC 21**
See also Monty Python
See also CA 116; CANR 35

Ignatow, David 1914-...... **CLC 4, 7, 14, 40**
See also CA 9-12R; CAAS 3; CANR 31;
DLB 5

Ihimaera, Witi 1944- .... **CLC 46**
See also CA 77-80

Ilf, Ilya........................ **TCLC 21**
See also Fainzilberg, Ilya Arnoldovich

Immermann, Karl (Lebrecht)
   1796-1840 .... **NCLC 4**
   See also DLB 133

Inclan, Ramon (Maria) del Valle
   See Valle-Inclan, Ramon (Maria) del

Infante, G(uillermo) Cabrera
   See Cabrera Infante, G(uillermo)

Ingalls, Rachel (Holmes) 1940- ..... **CLC 42**
   See also CA 123; 127

Ingamells, Rex 1913-1955 .... **TCLC 35**

Inge, William Motter
   1913-1973 .... **CLC 1, 8, 19**
   See also CA 9-12R; CDALB 1941-1968;
   DLB 7; MTCW

Ingelow, Jean 1820-1897 .... **NCLC 39**
   See also DLB 35; SATA 33

Ingram, Willis J.
   See Harris, Mark

Innaurato, Albert (F.) 1948(?)- .. **CLC 21, 60**
   See also CA 115; 122

Innes, Michael
   See Stewart, J(ohn) I(nnes) M(ackintosh)

Ionesco, Eugene
   1909-1994 .... **CLC 1, 4, 6, 9, 11, 15, 41,
                                86; DA; WLC**
   See also CA 9-12R; 144; MTCW; SATA 7;
   SATA-Obit 79

Iqbal, Muhammad 1873-1938 ..... **TCLC 28**

Ireland, Patrick
   See O'Doherty, Brian

Iron, Ralph
   See Schreiner, Olive (Emilie Albertina)

Irving, John (Winslow)
   1942- .... **CLC 13, 23, 38**
   See also AAYA 8; BEST 89:3; CA 25-28R;
   CANR 28; DLB 6; DLBY 82; MTCW

Irving, Washington
   1783-1859 .... **NCLC 2, 19; DA; SSC 2;
                                WLC**
   See also CDALB 1640-1865; DLB 3, 11, 30,
   59, 73, 74; YABC 2

Irwin, P. K.
   See Page, P(atricia) K(athleen)

Isaacs, Susan 1943- .... **CLC 32**
   See also BEST 89:1; CA 89-92; CANR 20,
   41; MTCW

Isherwood, Christopher (William Bradshaw)
   1904-1986 .... **CLC 1, 9, 11, 14, 44**
   See also CA 13-16R; 117; CANR 35;
   DLB 15; DLBY 86; MTCW

Ishiguro, Kazuo 1954- ...... **CLC 27, 56, 59**
   See also BEST 90:2; CA 120; MTCW

Ishikawa Takuboku
   1886(?)-1912 .... **TCLC 15; PC 10**
   See also CA 113

Iskander, Fazil 1929- .... **CLC 47**
   See also CA 102

Ivan IV 1530-1584 .... **LC 17**

Ivanov, Vyacheslav Ivanovich
   1866-1949 .... **TCLC 33**
   See also CA 122

Ivask, Ivar Vidrik 1927-1992 .... **CLC 14**
   See also CA 37-40R; 139; CANR 24

Jackson, Daniel
   See Wingrove, David (John)

Jackson, Jesse 1908-1983 .... **CLC 12**
   See also BW 1; CA 25-28R; 109; CANR 27;
   CLR 28; MAICYA; SATA 2, 29;
   SATA-Obit 48

Jackson, Laura (Riding) 1901-1991
   See Riding, Laura
   See also CA 65-68; 135; CANR 28; DLB 48

Jackson, Sam
   See Trumbo, Dalton

Jackson, Sara
   See Wingrove, David (John)

Jackson, Shirley
   1919-1965 .... **CLC 11, 60, 87; DA;
                                SSC 9; WLC**
   See also AAYA 9; CA 1-4R; 25-28R;
   CANR 4; CDALB 1941-1968; DLB 6;
   SATA 2

Jacob, (Cyprien-)Max 1876-1944 ... **TCLC 6**
   See also CA 104

Jacobs, Jim 1942- .... **CLC 12**
   See also CA 97-100

Jacobs, W(illiam) W(ymark)
   1863-1943 .... **TCLC 22**
   See also CA 121; DLB 135

Jacobsen, Jens Peter 1847-1885 .. **NCLC 34**

Jacobsen, Josephine 1908- .... **CLC 48**
   See also CA 33-36R; CAAS 18; CANR 23

Jacobson, Dan 1929- .... **CLC 4, 14**
   See also CA 1-4R; CANR 2, 25; DLB 14;
   MTCW

Jacqueline
   See Carpentier (y Valmont), Alejo

Jagger, Mick 1944- .... **CLC 17**

Jakes, John (William) 1932- .... **CLC 29**
   See also BEST 89:4; CA 57-60; CANR 10,
   43; DLBY 83; MTCW; SATA 62

James, Andrew
   See Kirkup, James

James, C(yril) L(ionel) R(obert)
   1901-1989 .... **CLC 33**
   See also BW 2; CA 117; 125; 128; DLB 125;
   MTCW

James, Daniel (Lewis) 1911-1988
   See Santiago, Danny
   See also CA 125

James, Dynely
   See Mayne, William (James Carter)

James, Henry
   1843-1916 ...... **TCLC 2, 11, 24, 40, 47;
                                DA; SSC 8; WLC**
   See also CA 104; 132; CDALB 1865-1917;
   DLB 12, 71, 74; MTCW

James, M. R.
   See James, Montague (Rhodes)

James, Montague (Rhodes)
   1862-1936 .... **TCLC 6; SSC 16**
   See also CA 104

James, P. D. .... **CLC 18, 46**
   See also White, Phyllis Dorothy James
   See also BEST 90:2; CDBLB 1960 to
   Present; DLB 87

James, Philip
   See Moorcock, Michael (John)

James, William 1842-1910..... **TCLC 15, 32**
   See also CA 109

James I 1394-1437 .... **LC 20**

Jameson, Anna 1794-1860 .... **NCLC 43**
   See also DLB 99

Jami, Nur al-Din 'Abd al-Rahman
   1414-1492 .... **LC 9**

Jandl, Ernst 1925- .... **CLC 34**

Janowitz, Tama 1957- .... **CLC 43**
   See also CA 106

Jarrell, Randall
   1914-1965 .... **CLC 1, 2, 6, 9, 13, 49**
   See also CA 5-8R; 25-28R; CABS 2;
   CANR 6, 34; CDALB 1941-1968; CLR 6;
   DLB 48, 52; MAICYA; MTCW; SATA 7

Jarry, Alfred 1873-1907....... **TCLC 2, 14**
   See also CA 104

Jarvis, E. K.
   See Bloch, Robert (Albert); Ellison, Harlan
   (Jay); Silverberg, Robert

Jeake, Samuel, Jr.
   See Aiken, Conrad (Potter)

Jean Paul 1763-1825 .... **NCLC 7**

Jefferies, (John) Richard
   1848-1887 .... **NCLC 47**
   See also DLB 98, 141; SATA 16

Jeffers, (John) Robinson
   1887-1962 .... **CLC 2, 3, 11, 15, 54; DA;
                                WLC**
   See also CA 85-88; CANR 35;
   CDALB 1917-1929; DLB 45; MTCW

Jefferson, Janet
   See Mencken, H(enry) L(ouis)

Jefferson, Thomas 1743-1826 .... **NCLC 11**
   See also CDALB 1640-1865; DLB 31

Jeffrey, Francis 1773-1850....... **NCLC 33**
   See also DLB 107

Jelakowitch, Ivan
   See Heijermans, Herman

Jellicoe, (Patricia) Ann 1927- ...... **CLC 27**
   See also CA 85-88; DLB 13

Jen, Gish .... **CLC 70**
   See also Jen, Lillian

Jen, Lillian 1956(?)-
   See Jen, Gish
   See also CA 135

Jenkins, (John) Robin 1912- .... **CLC 52**
   See also CA 1-4R; CANR 1; DLB 14

Jennings, Elizabeth (Joan)
   1926- .... **CLC 5, 14**
   See also CA 61-64; CAAS 5; CANR 8, 39;
   DLB 27; MTCW; SATA 66

Jennings, Waylon 1937- .... **CLC 21**

Jensen, Johannes V. 1873-1950.... **TCLC 41**

Jensen, Laura (Linnea) 1948- ...... **CLC 37**
   See also CA 103

Jerome, Jerome K(lapka)
   1859-1927 .... **TCLC 23**
   See also CA 119; DLB 10, 34, 135

Jerrold, Douglas William
   1803-1857 .... **NCLC 2**

Kaiser, Georg 1878-1945 . . . . **TCLC 9**
See also CA 106; DLB 124

Kaletski, Alexander 1946- . . . . **CLC 39**
See also CA 118; 143

Kalidasa fl. c. 400- . . . . **CMLC 9**

Kallman, Chester (Simon)
1921-1975 . . . . **CLC 2**
See also CA 45-48; 53-56; CANR 3

Kaminsky, Melvin 1926-
See Brooks, Mel
See also CA 65-68; CANR 16

Kaminsky, Stuart M(elvin) 1934- . . . **CLC 59**
See also CA 73-76; CANR 29

Kane, Paul
See Simon, Paul

Kane, Wilson
See Bloch, Robert (Albert)

Kanin, Garson 1912- . . . . **CLC 22**
See also AITN 1; CA 5-8R; CANR 7;
DLB 7

Kaniuk, Yoram 1930- . . . . **CLC 19**
See also CA 134

Kant, Immanuel 1724-1804 . . . . . . **NCLC 27**
See also DLB 94

Kantor, MacKinlay 1904-1977 . . . . . . **CLC 7**
See also CA 61-64; 73-76; DLB 9, 102

Kaplan, David Michael 1946- . . . . . . **CLC 50**

Kaplan, James 1951- . . . . **CLC 59**
See also CA 135

Karageorge, Michael
See Anderson, Poul (William)

Karamzin, Nikolai Mikhailovich
1766-1826 . . . . **NCLC 3**

Karapanou, Margarita 1946- . . . . **CLC 13**
See also CA 101

Karinthy, Frigyes 1887-1938 . . . . . . **TCLC 47**

Karl, Frederick R(obert) 1927- . . . . . **CLC 34**
See also CA 5-8R; CANR 3, 44

Kastel, Warren
See Silverberg, Robert

Kataev, Evgeny Petrovich 1903-1942
See Petrov, Evgeny
See also CA 120

Kataphusin
See Ruskin, John

Katz, Steve 1935- . . . . **CLC 47**
See also CA 25-28R; CAAS 14; CANR 12;
DLBY 83

Kauffman, Janet 1945- . . . . **CLC 42**
See also CA 117; CANR 43; DLBY 86

Kaufman, Bob (Garnell)
1925-1986 . . . . **CLC 49**
See also BW 1; CA 41-44R; 118; CANR 22;
DLB 16, 41

Kaufman, George S. 1889-1961 . . . . . **CLC 38**
See also CA 108; 93-96; DLB 7

Kaufman, Sue . . . . **CLC 3, 8**
See also Barondess, Sue K(aufman)

Kavafis, Konstantinos Petrou 1863-1933
See Cavafy, C(onstantine) P(eter)
See also CA 104

Kavan, Anna 1901-1968 . . . . . . **CLC 5, 13, 82**
See also CA 5-8R; CANR 6; MTCW

Kavanagh, Dan
See Barnes, Julian

Kavanagh, Patrick (Joseph)
1904-1967 . . . . **CLC 22**
See also CA 123; 25-28R; DLB 15, 20;
MTCW

Kawabata, Yasunari
1899-1972 . . . . . **CLC 2, 5, 9, 18; SSC 17**
See also CA 93-96; 33-36R

Kaye, M(ary) M(argaret) 1909- . . . . . **CLC 28**
See also CA 89-92; CANR 24; MTCW;
SATA 62

Kaye, Mollie
See Kaye, M(ary) M(argaret)

Kaye-Smith, Sheila 1887-1956 . . . . . **TCLC 20**
See also CA 118; DLB 36

Kaymor, Patrice Maguilene
See Senghor, Leopold Sedar

Kazan, Elia 1909- . . . . **CLC 6, 16, 63**
See also CA 21-24R; CANR 32

Kazantzakis, Nikos
1883(?)-1957 . . . . **TCLC 2, 5, 33**
See also CA 105; 132; MTCW

Kazin, Alfred 1915- . . . . **CLC 34, 38**
See also CA 1-4R; CAAS 7; CANR 1, 45;
DLB 67

Keane, Mary Nesta (Skrine) 1904-
See Keane, Molly
See also CA 108; 114

Keane, Molly . . . . **CLC 31**
See also Keane, Mary Nesta (Skrine)

Keates, Jonathan 19(?)- . . . . **CLC 34**

Keaton, Buster 1895-1966 . . . . **CLC 20**

Keats, John
1795-1821 . . . **NCLC 8; DA; PC 1; WLC**
See also CDBLB 1789-1832; DLB 96, 110

Keene, Donald 1922- . . . . **CLC 34**
See also CA 1-4R; CANR 5

Keillor, Garrison . . . . **CLC 40**
See also Keillor, Gary (Edward)
See also AAYA 2; BEST 89:3; DLBY 87;
SATA 58

Keillor, Gary (Edward) 1942-
See Keillor, Garrison
See also CA 111; 117; CANR 36; MTCW

Keith, Michael
See Hubbard, L(afayette) Ron(ald)

Keller, Gottfried 1819-1890 . . . . **NCLC 2**
See also DLB 129

Kellerman, Jonathan 1949- . . . . **CLC 44**
See also BEST 90:1; CA 106; CANR 29

Kelley, William Melvin 1937- . . . . . . **CLC 22**
See also BW 1; CA 77-80; CANR 27;
DLB 33

Kellogg, Marjorie 1922- . . . . **CLC 2**
See also CA 81-84

Kellow, Kathleen
See Hibbert, Eleanor Alice Burford

Kelly, M(ilton) T(erry) 1947- . . . . . . **CLC 55**
See also CA 97-100; CANR 19, 43

Kelman, James 1946- . . . . **CLC 58, 86**

Kemal, Yashar 1923- . . . . **CLC 14, 29**
See also CA 89-92; CANR 44

Kemble, Fanny 1809-1893 . . . . **NCLC 18**
See also DLB 32

Kemelman, Harry 1908- . . . . **CLC 2**
See also AITN 1; CA 9-12R; CANR 6;
DLB 28

Kempe, Margery 1373(?)-1440(?) . . . . . **LC 6**
See also DLB 146

Kempis, Thomas a 1380-1471 . . . . **LC 11**

Kendall, Henry 1839-1882 . . . . **NCLC 12**

Keneally, Thomas (Michael)
1935- . . . . . . **CLC 5, 8, 10, 14, 19, 27, 43**
See also CA 85-88; CANR 10; MTCW

Kennedy, Adrienne (Lita)
1931- . . . . **CLC 66; BLC; DC 5**
See also BW 2; CA 103; CAAS 20; CABS 3;
CANR 26; DLB 38

Kennedy, John Pendleton
1795-1870 . . . . **NCLC 2**
See also DLB 3

Kennedy, Joseph Charles 1929-
See Kennedy, X. J.
See also CA 1-4R; CANR 4, 30, 40;
SATA 14

Kennedy, William 1928- . . . **CLC 6, 28, 34, 53**
See also AAYA 1; CA 85-88; CANR 14,
31; DLB 143; DLBY 85; MTCW;
SATA 57

Kennedy, X. J. . . . . **CLC 8, 42**
See also Kennedy, Joseph Charles
See also CAAS 9; CLR 27; DLB 5

Kenny, Maurice (Francis) 1929- . . . . . **CLC 87**
See also CA 144; NNAL

Kent, Kelvin
See Kuttner, Henry

Kenton, Maxwell
See Southern, Terry

Kenyon, Robert O.
See Kuttner, Henry

Kerouac, Jack . . . . . **CLC 1, 2, 3, 5, 14, 29, 61**
See also Kerouac, Jean-Louis Lebris de
See also CDALB 1941-1968; DLB 2, 16;
DLBD 3

Kerouac, Jean-Louis Lebris de 1922-1969
See Kerouac, Jack
See also AITN 1; CA 5-8R; 25-28R;
CANR 26; DA; MTCW; WLC

Kerr, Jean 1923- . . . . **CLC 22**
See also CA 5-8R; CANR 7

Kerr, M. E. . . . . **CLC 12, 35**
See also Meaker, Marijane (Agnes)
See also AAYA 2; CLR 29; SAAS 1

Kerr, Robert . . . . **CLC 55**

Kerrigan, (Thomas) Anthony
1918- . . . . **CLC 4, 6**
See also CA 49-52; CAAS 11; CANR 4

Kerry, Lois
See Duncan, Lois

Kesey, Ken (Elton)
1935- . . . . . . **CLC 1, 3, 6, 11, 46, 64; DA;**
　　　　　　　　　　　　　　　　　　　　　　WLC
See also CA 1-4R; CANR 22, 38;
CDALB 1968-1988; DLB 2, 16; MTCW;
SATA 66

Kesselring, Joseph (Otto)
1902-1967 . . . . **CLC 45**

Kopit, Arthur (Lee) 1937- .... **CLC 1, 18, 33**
See also AITN 1; CA 81-84; CABS 3;
DLB 7; MTCW

Kops, Bernard 1926-.............. **CLC 4**
See also CA 5-8R; DLB 13

Kornbluth, C(yril) M. 1923-1958.... **TCLC 8**
See also CA 105; DLB 8

Korolenko, V. G.
See Korolenko, Vladimir Galaktionovich

Korolenko, Vladimir
See Korolenko, Vladimir Galaktionovich

Korolenko, Vladimir G.
See Korolenko, Vladimir Galaktionovich

Korolenko, Vladimir Galaktionovich
1853-1921 .... **TCLC 22**
See also CA 121

Kosinski, Jerzy (Nikodem)
1933-1991 .... **CLC 1, 2, 3, 6, 10, 15, 53,**
70
See also CA 17-20R; 134; CANR 9, 46;
DLB 2; DLBY 82; MTCW

Kostelanetz, Richard (Cory) 1940- .. **CLC 28**
See also CA 13-16R; CAAS 8; CANR 38

Kostrowitzki, Wilhelm Apollinaris de
1880-1918
See Apollinaire, Guillaume
See also CA 104

Kotlowitz, Robert 1924-.......... **CLC 4**
See also CA 33-36R; CANR 36

Kotzebue, August (Friedrich Ferdinand) von
1761-1819 .... **NCLC 25**
See also DLB 94

Kotzwinkle, William 1938- ... **CLC 5, 14, 35**
See also CA 45-48; CANR 3, 44; CLR 6;
MAICYA; SATA 24, 70

Kozol, Jonathan 1936-........... **CLC 17**
See also CA 61-64; CANR 16, 45

Kozoll, Michael 1940(?)- .... **CLC 35**

Kramer, Kathryn 19(?)- .... **CLC 34**

Kramer, Larry 1935- .... **CLC 42**
See also CA 124; 126

Krasicki, Ignacy 1735-1801....... **NCLC 8**

Krasinski, Zygmunt 1812-1859 .... **NCLC 4**

Kraus, Karl 1874-1936........... **TCLC 5**
See also CA 104; DLB 118

Kreve (Mickevicius), Vincas
1882-1954 .... **TCLC 27**

Kristeva, Julia 1941- .... **CLC 77**

Kristofferson, Kris 1936-.......... **CLC 26**
See also CA 104

Krizanc, John 1956-.............. **CLC 57**

Krleza, Miroslav 1893-1981........ **CLC 8**
See also CA 97-100; 105; DLB 147

Kroetsch, Robert 1927- ...... **CLC 5, 23, 57**
See also CA 17-20R; CANR 8, 38; DLB 53;
MTCW

Kroetz, Franz
See Kroetz, Franz Xaver

Kroetz, Franz Xaver 1946- .... **CLC 41**
See also CA 130

Kroker, Arthur 1945-............. **CLC 77**

Kropotkin, Peter (Aleksieevich)
1842-1921 .... **TCLC 36**
See also CA 119

Krotkov, Yuri 1917-.............. **CLC 19**
See also CA 102

Krumb
See Crumb, R(obert)

Krumgold, Joseph (Quincy)
1908-1980 .... **CLC 12**
See also CA 9-12R; 101; CANR 7;
MAICYA; SATA 1, 48; SATA-Obit 23

Krumwitz
See Crumb, R(obert)

Krutch, Joseph Wood 1893-1970.... **CLC 24**
See also CA 1-4R; 25-28R; CANR 4;
DLB 63

Krutzch, Gus
See Eliot, T(homas) S(tearns)

Krylov, Ivan Andreevich
1768(?)-1844 .... **NCLC 1**

Kubin, Alfred 1877-1959 .... **TCLC 23**
See also CA 112; DLB 81

Kubrick, Stanley 1928-............ **CLC 16**
See also CA 81-84; CANR 33; DLB 26

Kumin, Maxine (Winokur)
1925- .... **CLC 5, 13, 28**
See also AITN 2; CA 1-4R; CAAS 8;
CANR 1, 21; DLB 5; MTCW; SATA 12

Kundera, Milan
1929- .... **CLC 4, 9, 19, 32, 68**
See also AAYA 2; CA 85-88; CANR 19;
MTCW

Kunene, Mazisi (Raymond) 1930-... **CLC 85**
See also BW 1; CA 125; DLB 117

Kunitz, Stanley (Jasspon)
1905- .... **CLC 6, 11, 14**
See also CA 41-44R; CANR 26; DLB 48;
MTCW

Kunze, Reiner 1933-............. **CLC 10**
See also CA 93-96; DLB 75

Kuprin, Aleksandr Ivanovich
1870-1938 .... **TCLC 5**
See also CA 104

Kureishi, Hanif 1954(?)-.......... **CLC 64**
See also CA 139

Kurosawa, Akira 1910-............ **CLC 16**
See also AAYA 11; CA 101; CANR 46

Kushner, Tony 1957(?)- .... **CLC 81**
See also CA 144

Kuttner, Henry 1915-1958........ **TCLC 10**
See also CA 107; DLB 8

Kuzma, Greg 1944-................ **CLC 7**
See also CA 33-36R

Kuzmin, Mikhail 1872(?)-1936 .... **TCLC 40**

Kyd, Thomas 1558-1594...... **LC 22; DC 3**
See also DLB 62

Kyprianos, Iossif
See Samarakis, Antonis

La Bruyere, Jean de 1645-1696...... **LC 17**

Lacan, Jacques (Marie Emile)
1901-1981 .... **CLC 75**
See also CA 121; 104

**Laclos, Pierre Ambroise Francois Choderlos
de** 1741-1803 .... **NCLC 4**

Lacolere, Francois
See Aragon, Louis

La Colere, Francois
See Aragon, Louis

La Deshabilleuse
See Simenon, Georges (Jacques Christian)

Lady Gregory
See Gregory, Isabella Augusta (Persse)

Lady of Quality, A
See Bagnold, Enid

**La Fayette, Marie (Madelaine Pioche de la
Vergne Comtes** 1634-1693...... **LC 2**

Lafayette, Rene
See Hubbard, L(afayette) Ron(ald)

Laforgue, Jules 1860-1887........ **NCLC 5**

Lagerkvist, Paer (Fabian)
1891-1974 .... **CLC 7, 10, 13, 54**
See also Lagerkvist, Par
See also CA 85-88; 49-52; MTCW

Lagerkvist, Par
See Lagerkvist, Paer (Fabian)
See also SSC 12

Lagerloef, Selma (Ottiliana Lovisa)
1858-1940 .... **TCLC 4, 36**
See also Lagerlof, Selma (Ottiliana Lovisa)
See also CA 108; SATA 15

Lagerlof, Selma (Ottiliana Lovisa)
See Lagerloef, Selma (Ottiliana Lovisa)
See also CLR 7; SATA 15

La Guma, (Justin) Alex(ander)
1925-1985 .... **CLC 19**
See also BW 1; CA 49-52; 118; CANR 25;
DLB 117; MTCW

Laidlaw, A. K.
See Grieve, C(hristopher) M(urray)

Lainez, Manuel Mujica
See Mujica Lainez, Manuel
See also HW

Lamartine, Alphonse (Marie Louis Prat) de
1790-1869 .... **NCLC 11**

Lamb, Charles
1775-1834........ **NCLC 10; DA; WLC**
See also CDBLB 1789-1832; DLB 93, 107;
SATA 17

Lamb, Lady Caroline 1785-1828.. **NCLC 38**
See also DLB 116

Lamming, George (William)
1927- .... **CLC 2, 4, 66; BLC**
See also BW 2; CA 85-88; CANR 26;
DLB 125; MTCW

L'Amour, Louis (Dearborn)
1908-1988 .... **CLC 25, 55**
See also AITN 2; BEST 89:2; CA 1-4R;
125; CANR 3, 25, 40; DLBY 80; MTCW

Lampedusa, Giuseppe (Tomasi) di ... **TCLC 13**
See also Tomasi di Lampedusa, Giuseppe

Lampman, Archibald 1861-1899 .. **NCLC 25**
See also DLB 92

Lancaster, Bruce 1896-1963........ **CLC 36**
See also CA 9-10; CAP 1; SATA 9

Landau, Mark Alexandrovich
See Aldanov, Mark (Alexandrovich)

Landau-Aldanov, Mark Alexandrovich
See Aldanov, Mark (Alexandrovich)

Lee, Lawrence 1941-1990......... **CLC 34**
See also CA 131; CANR 43

Lee, Manfred B(ennington)
1905-1971 .... **CLC 11**
See also Queen, Ellery
See also CA 1-4R; 29-32R; CANR 2;
DLB 137

Lee, Stan 1922-.................. **CLC 17**
See also AAYA 5; CA 108; 111

Lee, Tanith 1947-............... **CLC 46**
See also CA 37-40R; SATA 8

Lee, Vernon..................... **TCLC 5**
See also Paget, Violet
See also DLB 57

Lee, William
See Burroughs, William S(eward)

Lee, Willy
See Burroughs, William S(eward)

Lee-Hamilton, Eugene (Jacob)
1845-1907 .... **TCLC 22**
See also CA 117

Leet, Judith 1935- .... **CLC 11**

Le Fanu, Joseph Sheridan
1814-1873 .... **NCLC 9; SSC 14**
See also DLB 21, 70

Leffland, Ella 1931- .... **CLC 19**
See also CA 29-32R; CANR 35; DLBY 84;
SATA 65

Leger, Alexis
See Leger, (Marie-Rene Auguste) Alexis
Saint-Leger

Leger, (Marie-Rene Auguste) Alexis
Saint-Leger 1887-1975....... **CLC 11**
See also Perse, St.-John
See also CA 13-16R; 61-64; CANR 43;
MTCW

Leger, Saintleger
See Leger, (Marie-Rene Auguste) Alexis
Saint-Leger

Le Guin, Ursula K(roeber)
1929- .... **CLC 8, 13, 22, 45, 71; SSC 12**
See also AAYA 9; AITN 1; CA 21-24R;
CANR 9, 32; CDALB 1968-1988; CLR 3,
28; DLB 8, 52; JRDA; MAICYA;
MTCW; SATA 4, 52

Lehmann, Rosamond (Nina)
1901-1990 .... **CLC 5**
See also CA 77-80; 131; CANR 8; DLB 15

Leiber, Fritz (Reuter, Jr.)
1910-1992 .... **CLC 25**
See also CA 45-48; 139; CANR 2, 40;
DLB 8; MTCW; SATA 45;
SATA-Obit 73

Leimbach, Martha 1963-
See Leimbach, Marti
See also CA 130

Leimbach, Marti .... **CLC 65**
See also Leimbach, Martha

Leino, Eino .... **TCLC 24**
See also Loennbohm, Armas Eino Leopold

Leiris, Michel (Julien) 1901-1990... **CLC 61**
See also CA 119; 128; 132

Leithauser, Brad 1953-........... **CLC 27**
See also CA 107; CANR 27; DLB 120

Lelchuk, Alan 1938-.............. **CLC 5**
See also CA 45-48; CAAS 20; CANR 1

Lem, Stanislaw 1921-........ **CLC 8, 15, 40**
See also CA 105; CAAS 1; CANR 32;
MTCW

Lemann, Nancy 1956-............. **CLC 39**
See also CA 118; 136

Lemonnier, (Antoine Louis) Camille
1844-1913 .... **TCLC 22**
See also CA 121

Lenau, Nikolaus 1802-1850...... **NCLC 16**

L'Engle, Madeleine (Camp Franklin)
1918- .... **CLC 12**
See also AAYA 1; AITN 2; CA 1-4R;
CANR 3, 21, 39; CLR 1, 14; DLB 52;
JRDA; MAICYA; MTCW; SAAS 15;
SATA 1, 27, 75

Lengyel, Jozsef 1896-1975.......... **CLC 7**
See also CA 85-88; 57-60

Lennon, John (Ono)
1940-1980 .... **CLC 12, 35**
See also CA 102

Lennox, Charlotte Ramsay
1729(?)-1804 .... **NCLC 23**
See also DLB 39

Lentricchia, Frank (Jr.) 1940-..... **CLC 34**
See also CA 25-28R; CANR 19

Lenz, Siegfried 1926-............ **CLC 27**
See also CA 89-92; DLB 75

Leonard, Elmore (John, Jr.)
1925- .... **CLC 28, 34, 71**
See also AITN 1; BEST 89:1, 90:4;
CA 81-84; CANR 12, 28; MTCW

Leonard, Hugh.................... **CLC 19**
See also Byrne, John Keyes
See also DLB 13

Leopardi, (Conte) Giacomo
1798-1837 .... **NCLC 22**

Le Reveler
See Artaud, Antonin

Lerman, Eleanor 1952-............. **CLC 9**
See also CA 85-88

Lerman, Rhoda 1936-............. **CLC 56**
See also CA 49-52

Lermontov, Mikhail Yuryevich
1814-1841 .... **NCLC 47**

Leroux, Gaston 1868-1927....... **TCLC 25**
See also CA 108; 136; SATA 65

Lesage, Alain-Rene 1668-1747...... **LC 28**

Leskov, Nikolai (Semyonovich)
1831-1895 .... **NCLC 25**

Lessing, Doris (May)
1919- ..... **CLC 1, 2, 3, 6, 10, 15, 22, 40;
DA; SSC 6**
See also CA 9-12R; CAAS 14; CANR 33;
CDBLB 1960 to Present; DLB 15, 139;
DLBY 85; MTCW

Lessing, Gotthold Ephraim
1729-1781 .... **LC 8**
See also DLB 97

Lester, Richard 1932-............ **CLC 20**

Lever, Charles (James)
1806-1872 .... **NCLC 23**
See also DLB 21

Leverson, Ada 1865(?)-1936(?) .... **TCLC 18**
See also Elaine
See also CA 117

Levertov, Denise
1923- ...... **CLC 1, 2, 3, 5, 8, 15, 28, 66;
PC 11**
See also CA 1-4R; CAAS 19; CANR 3, 29;
DLB 5; MTCW

Levi, Jonathan.................... **CLC 76**

Levi, Peter (Chad Tigar) 1931-..... **CLC 41**
See also CA 5-8R; CANR 34; DLB 40

Levi, Primo
1919-1987 .... **CLC 37, 50; SSC 12**
See also CA 13-16R; 122; CANR 12, 33;
MTCW

Levin, Ira 1929- .... **CLC 3, 6**
See also CA 21-24R; CANR 17, 44;
MTCW; SATA 66

Levin, Meyer 1905-1981 .... **CLC 7**
See also AITN 1; CA 9-12R; 104;
CANR 15; DLB 9, 28; DLBY 81;
SATA 21; SATA-Obit 27

Levine, Norman 1924-............ **CLC 54**
See also CA 73-76; CANR 14; DLB 88

Levine, Philip 1928-... **CLC 2, 4, 5, 9, 14, 33**
See also CA 9-12R; CANR 9, 37; DLB 5

Levinson, Deirdre 1931-.......... **CLC 49**
See also CA 73-76

Levi-Strauss, Claude 1908-........ **CLC 38**
See also CA 1-4R; CANR 6, 32; MTCW

Levitin, Sonia (Wolff) 1934- .... **CLC 17**
See also AAYA 13; CA 29-32R; CANR 14,
32; JRDA; MAICYA; SAAS 2; SATA 4,
68

Levon, O. U.
See Kesey, Ken (Elton)

Lewes, George Henry
1817-1878 .... **NCLC 25**
See also DLB 55, 144

Lewis, Alun 1915-1944........... **TCLC 3**
See also CA 104; DLB 20

Lewis, C. Day
See Day Lewis, C(ecil)

Lewis, C(live) S(taples)
1898-1963 ..... **CLC 1, 3, 6, 14, 27; DA;
WLC**
See also AAYA 3; CA 81-84; CANR 33;
CDBLB 1945-1960; CLR 3, 27; DLB 15,
100; JRDA; MAICYA; MTCW;
SATA 13

Lewis, Janet 1899-............... **CLC 41**
See also Winters, Janet Lewis
See also CA 9-12R; CANR 29; CAP 1;
DLBY 87

Lewis, Matthew Gregory
1775-1818 .... **NCLC 11**
See also DLB 39

Lewis, (Harry) Sinclair
1885-1951 ..... **TCLC 4, 13, 23, 39; DA;
WLC**
See also CA 104; 133; CDALB 1917-1929;
DLB 9, 102; DLBD 1; MTCW

Lewis, (Percy) Wyndham
1884(?)-1957 .... **TCLC 2, 9**
See also CA 104; DLB 15

Loti, Pierre . . . . TCLC 11
    See also Viaud, (Louis Marie) Julien
    See also DLB 123

Louie, David Wong   1954- . . . . CLC 70
    See also CA 139

Louis, Father M.
    See Merton, Thomas

Lovecraft, H(oward) P(hillips)
    1890-1937 . . . . TCLC 4, 22; SSC 3
    See also AAYA 14; CA 104; 133; MTCW

Lovelace, Earl   1935- . . . . CLC 51
    See also BW 2; CA 77-80; CANR 41;
    DLB 125; MTCW

Lovelace, Richard   1618-1657 . . . . LC 24
    See also DLB 131

Lowell, Amy   1874-1925 . . . . TCLC 1, 8
    See also CA 104; DLB 54, 140

Lowell, James Russell   1819-1891 . . NCLC 2
    See also CDALB 1640-1865; DLB 1, 11, 64,
    79

Lowell, Robert (Traill Spence, Jr.)
    1917-1977 . . . CLC 1, 2, 3, 4, 5, 8, 9, 11,
        15, 37; DA; PC 3; WLC
    See also CA 9-12R; 73-76; CABS 2;
    CANR 26; DLB 5; MTCW

Lowndes, Marie Adelaide (Belloc)
    1868-1947 . . . . TCLC 12
    See also CA 107; DLB 70

Lowry, (Clarence) Malcolm
    1909-1957 . . . . TCLC 6, 40
    See also CA 105; 131; CDBLB 1945-1960;
    DLB 15; MTCW

Lowry, Mina Gertrude   1882-1966
    See Loy, Mina
    See also CA 113

Loxsmith, John
    See Brunner, John (Kilian Houston)

Loy, Mina . . . . CLC 28
    See also Lowry, Mina Gertrude
    See also DLB 4, 54

Loyson-Bridet
    See Schwob, (Mayer Andre) Marcel

Lucas, Craig   1951- . . . . CLC 64
    See also CA 137

Lucas, George   1944- . . . . CLC 16
    See also AAYA 1; CA 77-80; CANR 30;
    SATA 56

Lucas, Hans
    See Godard, Jean-Luc

Lucas, Victoria
    See Plath, Sylvia

Ludlam, Charles   1943-1987 . . . . . CLC 46, 50
    See also CA 85-88; 122

Ludlum, Robert   1927- . . . . CLC 22, 43
    See also AAYA 10; BEST 89:1, 90:3;
    CA 33-36R; CANR 25, 41; DLBY 82;
    MTCW

Ludwig, Ken . . . . CLC 60

Ludwig, Otto   1813-1865 . . . . NCLC 4
    See also DLB 129

Lugones, Leopoldo   1874-1938 . . . . TCLC 15
    See also CA 116; 131; HW

Lu Hsun   1881-1936 . . . . TCLC 3

Lukacs, George . . . . CLC 24
    See also Lukacs, Gyorgy (Szegeny von)

Lukacs, Gyorgy (Szegeny von)   1885-1971
    See Lukacs, George
    See also CA 101; 29-32R

Luke, Peter (Ambrose Cyprian)
    1919- . . . . CLC 38
    See also CA 81-84; DLB 13

Lunar, Dennis
    See Mungo, Raymond

Lurie, Alison   1926- . . . . CLC 4, 5, 18, 39
    See also CA 1-4R; CANR 2, 17; DLB 2;
    MTCW; SATA 46

Lustig, Arnost   1926- . . . . CLC 56
    See also AAYA 3; CA 69-72; CANR 47;
    SATA 56

Luther, Martin   1483-1546 . . . . LC 9

Luzi, Mario   1914- . . . . CLC 13
    See also CA 61-64; CANR 9; DLB 128

Lynch, B. Suarez
    See Bioy Casares, Adolfo; Borges, Jorge
    Luis

Lynch, David (K.)   1946- . . . . CLC 66
    See also CA 124; 129

Lynch, James
    See Andreyev, Leonid (Nikolaevich)

Lynch Davis, B.
    See Bioy Casares, Adolfo; Borges, Jorge
    Luis

Lyndsay, Sir David   1490-1555 . . . . . . LC 20

Lynn, Kenneth S(chuyler)   1923- . . . . CLC 50
    See also CA 1-4R; CANR 3, 27

Lynx
    See West, Rebecca

Lyons, Marcus
    See Blish, James (Benjamin)

Lyre, Pinchbeck
    See Sassoon, Siegfried (Lorraine)

Lytle, Andrew (Nelson)   1902- . . . . . . CLC 22
    See also CA 9-12R; DLB 6

Lyttelton, George   1709-1773 . . . . LC 10

Maas, Peter   1929- . . . . CLC 29
    See also CA 93-96

Macaulay, Rose   1881-1958 . . . . . TCLC 7, 44
    See also CA 104; DLB 36

Macaulay, Thomas Babington
    1800-1859 . . . . NCLC 42
    See also CDBLB 1832-1890; DLB 32, 55

MacBeth, George (Mann)
    1932-1992 . . . . CLC 2, 5, 9
    See also CA 25-28R; 136; DLB 40; MTCW;
    SATA 4; SATA-Obit 70

MacCaig, Norman (Alexander)
    1910- . . . . CLC 36
    See also CA 9-12R; CANR 3, 34; DLB 27

MacCarthy, (Sir Charles Otto) Desmond
    1877-1952 . . . . TCLC 36

MacDiarmid, Hugh
    . . . . CLC 2, 4, 11, 19, 63; PC 9
    See also Grieve, C(hristopher) M(urray)
    See also CDBLB 1945-1960; DLB 20

MacDonald, Anson
    See Heinlein, Robert A(nson)

Macdonald, Cynthia   1928- . . . . . . CLC 13, 19
    See also CA 49-52; CANR 4, 44; DLB 105

MacDonald, George   1824-1905 . . . . . TCLC 9
    See also CA 106; 137; DLB 18; MAICYA;
    SATA 33

Macdonald, John
    See Millar, Kenneth

MacDonald, John D(ann)
    1916-1986 . . . . CLC 3, 27, 44
    See also CA 1-4R; 121; CANR 1, 19;
    DLB 8; DLBY 86; MTCW

Macdonald, John Ross
    See Millar, Kenneth

Macdonald, Ross . . . . . CLC 1, 2, 3, 14, 34, 41
    See also Millar, Kenneth
    See also DLBD 6

MacDougal, John
    See Blish, James (Benjamin)

MacEwen, Gwendolyn (Margaret)
    1941-1987 . . . . CLC 13, 55
    See also CA 9-12R; 124; CANR 7, 22;
    DLB 53; SATA 50; SATA-Obit 55

Macha, Karel Hynek   1810-1846 . . NCLC 46

Machado (y Ruiz), Antonio
    1875-1939 . . . . TCLC 3
    See also CA 104; DLB 108

Machado de Assis, Joaquim Maria
    1839-1908 . . . . TCLC 10; BLC
    See also CA 107

Machen, Arthur . . . . TCLC 4
    See also Jones, Arthur Llewellyn
    See also DLB 36

Machiavelli, Niccolo   1469-1527 . . LC 8; DA

MacInnes, Colin   1914-1976 . . . . . . CLC 4, 23
    See also CA 69-72; 65-68; CANR 21;
    DLB 14; MTCW

MacInnes, Helen (Clark)
    1907-1985 . . . . CLC 27, 39
    See also CA 1-4R; 117; CANR 1, 28;
    DLB 87; MTCW; SATA 22;
    SATA-Obit 44

Mackay, Mary   1855-1924
    See Corelli, Marie
    See also CA 118

Mackenzie, Compton (Edward Montague)
    1883-1972 . . . . CLC 18
    See also CA 21-22; 37-40R; CAP 2;
    DLB 34, 100

Mackenzie, Henry   1745-1831 . . . . NCLC 41
    See also DLB 39

Mackintosh, Elizabeth   1896(?)-1952
    See Tey, Josephine
    See also CA 110

MacLaren, James
    See Grieve, C(hristopher) M(urray)

Mac Laverty, Bernard   1942- . . . . CLC 31
    See also CA 116; 118; CANR 43

MacLean, Alistair (Stuart)
    1922-1987 . . . . CLC 3, 13, 50, 63
    See also CA 57-60; 121; CANR 28; MTCW;
    SATA 23; SATA-Obit 50

Maclean, Norman (Fitzroy)
    1902-1990 . . . . CLC 78; SSC 13
    See also CA 102; 132

MacLeish, Archibald
1892-1982 . . . . CLC 3, 8, 14, 68
See also CA 9-12R; 106; CANR 33; DLB 4,
7, 45; DLBY 82; MTCW

MacLennan, (John) Hugh
1907-1990 . . . . CLC 2, 14
See also CA 5-8R; 142; CANR 33; DLB 68;
MTCW

MacLeod, Alistair   1936- . . . . CLC 56
See also CA 123; DLB 60

MacNeice, (Frederick) Louis
1907-1963 . . . . CLC 1, 4, 10, 53
See also CA 85-88; DLB 10, 20; MTCW

MacNeill, Dand
See Fraser, George MacDonald

Macpherson, (Jean) Jay   1931- . . . . . . CLC 14
See also CA 5-8R; DLB 53

MacShane, Frank   1927- . . . . CLC 39
See also CA 9-12R; CANR 3, 33; DLB 111

Macumber, Mari
See Sandoz, Mari(e Susette)

Madach, Imre   1823-1864 . . . . NCLC 19

Madden, (Jerry) David   1933- . . . . CLC 5, 15
See also CA 1-4R; CAAS 3; CANR 4, 45;
DLB 6; MTCW

Maddern, Al(an)
See Ellison, Harlan (Jay)

Madhubuti, Haki R.
1942- . . . . CLC 6, 73; BLC; PC 5
See also Lee, Don L.
See also BW 2; CA 73-76; CANR 24;
DLB 5, 41; DLBD 8

Maepenn, Hugh
See Kuttner, Henry

Maepenn, K. H.
See Kuttner, Henry

Maeterlinck, Maurice   1862-1949 . . . TCLC 3
See also CA 104; 136; SATA 66

Maginn, William   1794-1842 . . . . . . NCLC 8
See also DLB 110

Mahapatra, Jayanta   1928- . . . . CLC 33
See also CA 73-76; CAAS 9; CANR 15, 33

Mahfouz, Naguib (Abdel Aziz Al-Sabilgi)
1911(?)-
See Mahfuz, Najib
See also BEST 89:2; CA 128; MTCW

Mahfuz, Najib . . . . CLC 52, 55
See also Mahfouz, Naguib (Abdel Aziz
Al-Sabilgi)
See also DLBY 88

Mahon, Derek   1941- . . . . CLC 27
See also CA 113; 128; DLB 40

Mailer, Norman
1923- . . . . . . CLC 1, 2, 3, 4, 5, 8, 11, 14,
28, 39, 74; DA
See also AITN 2; CA 9-12R; CABS 1;
CANR 28; CDALB 1968-1988; DLB 2,
16, 28; DLBD 3; DLBY 80, 83; MTCW

Maillet, Antonine   1929- . . . . CLC 54
See also CA 115; 120; CANR 46; DLB 60

Mais, Roger   1905-1955 . . . . TCLC 8
See also BW 1; CA 105; 124; DLB 125;
MTCW

Maistre, Joseph de   1753-1821 . . . . NCLC 37

Maitland, Sara (Louise)   1950- . . . . . . CLC 49
See also CA 69-72; CANR 13

Major, Clarence
1936- . . . . CLC 3, 19, 48; BLC
See also BW 2; CA 21-24R; CAAS 6;
CANR 13, 25; DLB 33

Major, Kevin (Gerald)   1949- . . . . CLC 26
See also CA 97-100; CANR 21, 38;
CLR 11; DLB 60; JRDA; MAICYA;
SATA 32

Maki, James
See Ozu, Yasujiro

Malabaila, Damiano
See Levi, Primo

Malamud, Bernard
1914-1986 . . . . . . CLC 1, 2, 3, 5, 8, 9, 11,
18, 27, 44, 78, 85; DA; SSC 15; WLC
See also CA 5-8R; 118; CABS 1; CANR 28;
CDALB 1941-1968; DLB 2, 28;
DLBY 80, 86; MTCW

Malaparte, Curzio   1898-1957 . . . . . TCLC 52

Malcolm, Dan
See Silverberg, Robert

Malcolm X . . . . CLC 82; BLC
See also Little, Malcolm

Malherbe, Francois de   1555-1628 . . . . . LC 5

Mallarme, Stephane
1842-1898 . . . . NCLC 4, 41; PC 4

Mallet-Joris, Francoise   1930- . . . . . . CLC 11
See also CA 65-68; CANR 17; DLB 83

Malley, Ern
See McAuley, James Phillip

Mallowan, Agatha Christie
See Christie, Agatha (Mary Clarissa)

Maloff, Saul   1922- . . . . CLC 5
See also CA 33-36R

Malone, Louis
See MacNeice, (Frederick) Louis

Malone, Michael (Christopher)
1942- . . . . CLC 43
See also CA 77-80; CANR 14, 32

Malory, (Sir) Thomas
1410(?)-1471(?) . . . . LC 11; DA
See also CDBLB Before 1660; DLB 146;
SATA 33, 59

Malouf, (George Joseph) David
1934- . . . . CLC 28, 86
See also CA 124

Malraux, (Georges-)Andre
1901-1976 . . . . CLC 1, 4, 9, 13, 15, 57
See also CA 21-22; 69-72; CANR 34;
CAP 2; DLB 72; MTCW

Malzberg, Barry N(athaniel)   1939- . . . CLC 7
See also CA 61-64; CAAS 4; CANR 16;
DLB 8

Mamet, David (Alan)
1947- . . . . CLC 9, 15, 34, 46; DC 4
See also AAYA 3; CA 81-84; CABS 3;
CANR 15, 41; DLB 7; MTCW

Mamoulian, Rouben (Zachary)
1897-1987 . . . . CLC 16
See also CA 25-28R; 124

Mandelstam, Osip (Emilievich)
1891(?)-1938(?) . . . . TCLC 2, 6
See also CA 104

Mander, (Mary) Jane   1877-1949 . . . TCLC 31

Mandiargues, Andre Pieyre de . . . . . . CLC 41
See also Pieyre de Mandiargues, Andre
See also DLB 83

Mandrake, Ethel Belle
See Thurman, Wallace (Henry)

Mangan, James Clarence
1803-1849 . . . . NCLC 27

Maniere, J.-E.
See Giraudoux, (Hippolyte) Jean

Manley, (Mary) Delariviere
1672(?)-1724 . . . . LC 1
See also DLB 39, 80

Mann, Abel
See Creasey, John

Mann, (Luiz) Heinrich   1871-1950 . . . TCLC 9
See also CA 106; DLB 66

Mann, (Paul) Thomas
1875-1955 . . . . TCLC 2, 8, 14, 21, 35, 44;
DA; SSC 5; WLC
See also CA 104; 128; DLB 66; MTCW

Manning, David
See Faust, Frederick (Schiller)

Manning, Frederic   1887(?)-1935 . . . TCLC 25
See also CA 124

Manning, Olivia   1915-1980 . . . . . . CLC 5, 19
See also CA 5-8R; 101; CANR 29; MTCW

Mano, D. Keith   1942- . . . . CLC 2, 10
See also CA 25-28R; CAAS 6; CANR 26;
DLB 6

Mansfield, Katherine
. . . . TCLC 2, 8, 39; SSC 9; WLC
See also Beauchamp, Kathleen Mansfield

Manso, Peter   1940- . . . . CLC 39
See also CA 29-32R; CANR 44

Mantecon, Juan Jimenez
See Jimenez (Mantecon), Juan Ramon

Manton, Peter
See Creasey, John

Man Without a Spleen, A
See Chekhov, Anton (Pavlovich)

Manzoni, Alessandro   1785-1873 . . NCLC 29

Mapu, Abraham (ben Jekutiel)
1808-1867 . . . . NCLC 18

Mara, Sally
See Queneau, Raymond

Marat, Jean Paul   1743-1793 . . . . LC 10

Marcel, Gabriel Honore
1889-1973 . . . . CLC 15
See also CA 102; 45-48; MTCW

Marchbanks, Samuel
See Davies, (William) Robertson

Marchi, Giacomo
See Bassani, Giorgio

Margulies, Donald . . . . CLC 76

Marie de France   c. 12th cent. - . . . . CMLC 8

Marie de l'Incarnation   1599-1672 . . . . LC 10

Mariner, Scott
See Pohl, Frederik

Marinetti, Filippo Tommaso
1876-1944 . . . . TCLC 10
See also CA 107; DLB 114

Marivaux, Pierre Carlet de Chamblain de
1688-1763 .... **LC 4**

Markandaya, Kamala .... **CLC 8, 38**
See also Taylor, Kamala (Purnaiya)

Markfield, Wallace 1926- .... **CLC 8**
See also CA 69-72; CAAS 3; DLB 2, 28

Markham, Edwin 1852-1940 ...... **TCLC 47**
See also DLB 54

Markham, Robert
See Amis, Kingsley (William)

Marks, J
See Highwater, Jamake (Mamake)

Marks-Highwater, J
See Highwater, Jamake (Mamake)

Markson, David M(errill) 1927- .... **CLC 67**
See also CA 49-52; CANR 1

Marley, Bob. .... **CLC 17**
See also Marley, Robert Nesta

Marley, Robert Nesta 1945-1981
See Marley, Bob
See also CA 107; 103

Marlowe, Christopher
1564-1593 ..... **LC 22; DA; DC 1; WLC**
See also CDBLB Before 1660; DLB 62

Marmontel, Jean-Francois
1723-1799 .... **LC 2**

Marquand, John P(hillips)
1893-1960 .... **CLC 2, 10**
See also CA 85-88; DLB 9, 102

Marquez, Gabriel (Jose) Garcia
See Garcia Marquez, Gabriel (Jose)

Marquis, Don(ald Robert Perry)
1878-1937 .... **TCLC 7**
See also CA 104; DLB 11, 25

Marric, J. J.
See Creasey, John

Marrow, Bernard
See Moore, Brian

Marryat, Frederick 1792-1848 .... **NCLC 3**
See also DLB 21

Marsden, James
See Creasey, John

Marsh, (Edith) Ngaio
1899-1982 .... **CLC 7, 53**
See also CA 9-12R; CANR 6; DLB 77;
MTCW

Marshall, Garry 1934- .... **CLC 17**
See also AAYA 3; CA 111; SATA 60

Marshall, Paule
1929- .... **CLC 27, 72; BLC; SSC 3**
See also BW 2; CA 77-80; CANR 25;
DLB 33; MTCW

Marsten, Richard
See Hunter, Evan

Martha, Henry
See Harris, Mark

Martial c. 40-c. 104 .... **PC 10**

Martin, Ken
See Hubbard, L(afayette) Ron(ald)

Martin, Richard
See Creasey, John

Martin, Steve 1945- .... **CLC 30**
See also CA 97-100; CANR 30; MTCW

Martin, Violet Florence
1862-1915 .... **TCLC 51**

Martin, Webber
See Silverberg, Robert

Martindale, Patrick Victor
See White, Patrick (Victor Martindale)

Martin du Gard, Roger
1881-1958 .... **TCLC 24**
See also CA 118; DLB 65

Martineau, Harriet 1802-1876.... **NCLC 26**
See also DLB 21, 55; YABC 2

Martines, Julia
See O'Faolain, Julia

Martinez, Jacinto Benavente y
See Benavente (y Martinez), Jacinto

Martinez Ruiz, Jose 1873-1967
See Azorin; Ruiz, Jose Martinez
See also CA 93-96; HW

Martinez Sierra, Gregorio
1881-1947 .... **TCLC 6**
See also CA 115

Martinez Sierra, Maria (de la O'LeJarraga)
1874-1974 .... **TCLC 6**
See also CA 115

Martinsen, Martin
See Follett, Ken(neth Martin)

Martinson, Harry (Edmund)
1904-1978 .... **CLC 14**
See also CA 77-80; CANR 34

Marut, Ret
See Traven, B.

Marut, Robert
See Traven, B.

Marvell, Andrew
1621-1678 ..... **LC 4; DA; PC 10; WLC**
See also CDBLB 1660-1789; DLB 131

Marx, Karl (Heinrich)
1818-1883 .... **NCLC 17**
See also DLB 129

Masaoka Shiki. .... **TCLC 18**
See also Masaoka Tsunenori

Masaoka Tsunenori 1867-1902
See Masaoka Shiki
See also CA 117

Masefield, John (Edward)
1878-1967 .... **CLC 11, 47**
See also CA 19-20; 25-28R; CANR 33;
CAP 2; CDBLB 1890-1914; DLB 10, 19;
MTCW; SATA 19

Maso, Carole 19(?)- .... **CLC 44**

Mason, Bobbie Ann
1940- .... **CLC 28, 43, 82; SSC 4**
See also AAYA 5; CA 53-56; CANR 11,
31; DLBY 87; MTCW

Mason, Ernst
See Pohl, Frederik

Mason, Lee W.
See Malzberg, Barry N(athaniel)

Mason, Nick 1945- .... **CLC 35**

Mason, Tally
See Derleth, August (William)

Mass, William
See Gibson, William

Masters, Edgar Lee
1868-1950 ...... **TCLC 2, 25; DA; PC 1**
See also CA 104; 133; CDALB 1865-1917;
DLB 54; MTCW

Masters, Hilary 1928- .... **CLC 48**
See also CA 25-28R; CANR 13, 47

Mastrosimone, William 19(?)- ...... **CLC 36**

Mathe, Albert
See Camus, Albert

Matheson, Richard Burton 1926- ... **CLC 37**
See also CA 97-100; DLB 8, 44

Mathews, Harry 1930- .... **CLC 6, 52**
See also CA 21-24R; CAAS 6; CANR 18,
40

Mathews, John Joseph 1894-1979... **CLC 84**
See also CA 19-20; 142; CANR 45; CAP 2;
NNAL

Mathias, Roland (Glyn) 1915- ...... **CLC 45**
See also CA 97-100; CANR 19, 41; DLB 27

Matsuo Basho 1644-1694 .... **PC 3**

Mattheson, Rodney
See Creasey, John

Matthews, Greg 1949- .... **CLC 45**
See also CA 135

Matthews, William 1942- .... **CLC 40**
See also CA 29-32R; CAAS 18; CANR 12;
DLB 5

Matthias, John (Edward) 1941- ...... **CLC 9**
See also CA 33-36R

Matthiessen, Peter
1927- .... **CLC 5, 7, 11, 32, 64**
See also AAYA 6; BEST 90:4; CA 9-12R;
CANR 21; DLB 6; MTCW; SATA 27

Maturin, Charles Robert
1780(?)-1824 .... **NCLC 6**

Matute (Ausejo), Ana Maria
1925- .... **CLC 11**
See also CA 89-92; MTCW

Maugham, W. S.
See Maugham, W(illiam) Somerset

Maugham, W(illiam) Somerset
1874-1965 ...... **CLC 1, 11, 15, 67; DA;
SSC 8; WLC**
See also CA 5-8R; 25-28R; CANR 40;
CDBLB 1914-1945; DLB 10, 36, 77, 100;
MTCW; SATA 54

Maugham, William Somerset
See Maugham, W(illiam) Somerset

Maupassant, (Henri Rene Albert) Guy de
1850-1893 .... **NCLC 1, 42; DA; SSC 1;
WLC**
See also DLB 123

Maurhut, Richard
See Traven, B.

Mauriac, Claude 1914- .... **CLC 9**
See also CA 89-92; DLB 83

Mauriac, Francois (Charles)
1885-1970 .... **CLC 4, 9, 56**
See also CA 25-28; CAP 2; DLB 65;
MTCW

Mavor, Osborne Henry 1888-1951
See Bridie, James
See also CA 104

Melanter
See Blackmore, R(ichard) D(oddridge)

Melikow, Loris
See Hofmannsthal, Hugo von

Melmoth, Sebastian
See Wilde, Oscar (Fingal O'Flahertie Wills)

Meltzer, Milton 1915- . . . . **CLC 26**
See also AAYA 8; CA 13-16R; CANR 38;
CLR 13; DLB 61; JRDA; MAICYA;
SAAS 1; SATA 1, 50, 80

Melville, Herman
1819-1891 . . . . **NCLC 3, 12, 29, 45; DA;
SSC 1, 17; WLC**
See also CDALB 1640-1865; DLB 3, 74;
SATA 59

Menander
c. 342B.C.-c. 292B.C. . . . . **CMLC 9; DC 3**

Mencken, H(enry) L(ouis)
1880-1956 . . . . **TCLC 13**
See also CA 105; 125; CDALB 1917-1929;
DLB 11, 29, 63, 137; MTCW

Mercer, David 1928-1980. . . . . **CLC 5**
See also CA 9-12R; 102; CANR 23;
DLB 13; MTCW

Merchant, Paul
See Ellison, Harlan (Jay)

Meredith, George 1828-1909 . . . **TCLC 17, 43**
See also CA 117; CDBLB 1832-1890;
DLB 18, 35, 57

Meredith, William (Morris)
1919- . . . . **CLC 4, 13, 22, 55**
See also CA 9-12R; CAAS 14; CANR 6, 40;
DLB 5

Merezhkovsky, Dmitry Sergeyevich
1865-1941 . . . . **TCLC 29**

Merimee, Prosper
1803-1870 . . . . **NCLC 6; SSC 7**
See also DLB 119

Merkin, Daphne 1954- . . . . **CLC 44**
See also CA 123

Merlin, Arthur
See Blish, James (Benjamin)

Merrill, James (Ingram)
1926- . . . . **CLC 2, 3, 6, 8, 13, 18, 34**
See also CA 13-16R; CANR 10; DLB 5;
DLBY 85; MTCW

Merriman, Alex
See Silverberg, Robert

Merritt, E. B.
See Waddington, Miriam

Merton, Thomas
1915-1968 . . **CLC 1, 3, 11, 34, 83; PC 10**
See also CA 5-8R; 25-28R; CANR 22;
DLB 48; DLBY 81; MTCW

Merwin, W(illiam) S(tanley)
1927- . . . . . . **CLC 1, 2, 3, 5, 8, 13, 18, 45**
See also CA 13-16R; CANR 15; DLB 5;
MTCW

Metcalf, John 1938- . . . . **CLC 37**
See also CA 113; DLB 60

Metcalf, Suzanne
See Baum, L(yman) Frank

Mew, Charlotte (Mary)
1870-1928 . . . . **TCLC 8**
See also CA 105; DLB 19, 135

Mewshaw, Michael 1943- . . . . **CLC 9**
See also CA 53-56; CANR 7, 47; DLBY 80

Meyer, June
See Jordan, June

Meyer, Lynn
See Slavitt, David R(ytman)

Meyer-Meyrink, Gustav 1868-1932
See Meyrink, Gustav
See also CA 117

Meyers, Jeffrey 1939- . . . . **CLC 39**
See also CA 73-76; DLB 111

Meynell, Alice (Christina Gertrude Thompson)
1847-1922 . . . . **TCLC 6**
See also CA 104; DLB 19, 98

Meyrink, Gustav . . . . **TCLC 21**
See also Meyer-Meyrink, Gustav
See also DLB 81

Michaels, Leonard
1933- . . . . **CLC 6, 25; SSC 16**
See also CA 61-64; CANR 21; DLB 130;
MTCW

Michaux, Henri 1899-1984 . . . . . . **CLC 8, 19**
See also CA 85-88; 114

Michelangelo 1475-1564. . . . . **LC 12**

Michelet, Jules 1798-1874 . . . . . . **NCLC 31**

Michener, James A(lbert)
1907(?)- . . . . **CLC 1, 5, 11, 29, 60**
See also AITN 1; BEST 90:1; CA 5-8R;
CANR 21, 45; DLB 6; MTCW

Mickiewicz, Adam 1798-1855 . . . . . **NCLC 3**

Middleton, Christopher 1926- . . . . . . **CLC 13**
See also CA 13-16R; CANR 29; DLB 40

Middleton, Richard (Barham)
1882-1911 . . . . **TCLC 56**

Middleton, Stanley 1919- . . . . **CLC 7, 38**
See also CA 25-28R; CANR 21, 46;
DLB 14

Middleton, Thomas 1580-1627. . . . . . . **DC 5**
See also DLB 58

Migueis, Jose Rodrigues 1901- . . . . . **CLC 10**

Mikszath, Kalman 1847-1910 . . . . . **TCLC 31**

Miles, Josephine
1911-1985 . . . . **CLC 1, 2, 14, 34, 39**
See also CA 1-4R; 116; CANR 2; DLB 48

Militant
See Sandburg, Carl (August)

Mill, John Stuart 1806-1873 . . . . . **NCLC 11**
See also CDBLB 1832-1890; DLB 55

Millar, Kenneth 1915-1983 . . . . **CLC 14**
See also Macdonald, Ross
See also CA 9-12R; 110; CANR 16; DLB 2;
DLBD 6; DLBY 83; MTCW

Millay, E. Vincent
See Millay, Edna St. Vincent

Millay, Edna St. Vincent
1892-1950 . . . . . . **TCLC 4, 49; DA; PC 6**
See also CA 104; 130; CDALB 1917-1929;
DLB 45; MTCW

Miller, Arthur
1915- . . . . **CLC 1, 2, 6, 10, 15, 26, 47, 78;
DA; DC 1; WLC**
See also AITN 1; CA 1-4R; CABS 3;
CANR 2, 30; CDALB 1941-1968; DLB 7;
MTCW

Miller, Henry (Valentine)
1891-1980 . . . . **CLC 1, 2, 4, 9, 14, 43, 84;
DA; WLC**
See also CA 9-12R; 97-100; CANR 33;
CDALB 1929-1941; DLB 4, 9; DLBY 80;
MTCW

Miller, Jason 1939(?)- . . . . **CLC 2**
See also AITN 1; CA 73-76; DLB 7

Miller, Sue 1943- . . . . **CLC 44**
See also BEST 90:3; CA 139; DLB 143

Miller, Walter M(ichael, Jr.)
1923- . . . . **CLC 4, 30**
See also CA 85-88; DLB 8

Millett, Kate 1934- . . . . **CLC 67**
See also AITN 1; CA 73-76; CANR 32;
MTCW

Millhauser, Steven 1943- . . . . . . **CLC 21, 54**
See also CA 110; 111; DLB 2

Millin, Sarah Gertrude 1889-1968 . . **CLC 49**
See also CA 102; 93-96

Milne, A(lan) A(lexander)
1882-1956 . . . . **TCLC 6**
See also CA 104; 133; CLR 1, 26; DLB 10,
77, 100; MAICYA; MTCW; YABC 1

Milner, Ron(ald) 1938- . . . . **CLC 56; BLC**
See also AITN 1; BW 1; CA 73-76;
CANR 24; DLB 38; MTCW

Milosz, Czeslaw
1911- . . . **CLC 5, 11, 22, 31, 56, 82; PC 8**
See also CA 81-84; CANR 23; MTCW

Milton, John 1608-1674. . . **LC 9; DA; WLC**
See also CDBLB 1660-1789; DLB 131

Min, Anchee 1957- . . . . **CLC 86**

Minehaha, Cornelius
See Wedekind, (Benjamin) Frank(lin)

Miner, Valerie 1947- . . . . **CLC 40**
See also CA 97-100

Minimo, Duca
See D'Annunzio, Gabriele

Minot, Susan 1956- . . . . **CLC 44**
See also CA 134

Minus, Ed 1938- . . . . **CLC 39**

Miranda, Javier
See Bioy Casares, Adolfo

Mirbeau, Octave 1848-1917 . . . . **TCLC 55**
See also DLB 123

Miro (Ferrer), Gabriel (Francisco Victor)
1879-1930 . . . . **TCLC 5**
See also CA 104

Mishima, Yukio
. . . . . . **CLC 2, 4, 6, 9, 27; DC 1; SSC 4**
See also Hiraoka, Kimitake

Mistral, Frederic 1830-1914 . . . . . . **TCLC 51**
See also CA 122

Mistral, Gabriela. . . . . **TCLC 2; HLC**
See also Godoy Alcayaga, Lucila

Mistry, Rohinton 1952- . . . . **CLC 71**
See also CA 141

Mitchell, Clyde
See Ellison, Harlan (Jay); Silverberg, Robert

Mitchell, James Leslie 1901-1935
See Gibbon, Lewis Grassic
See also CA 104; DLB 15

Morris, Wright 1910-... **CLC 1, 3, 7, 18, 37**
See also CA 9-12R; CANR 21; DLB 2;
DLBY 81; MTCW

Morrison, Chloe Anthony Wofford
See Morrison, Toni

Morrison, James Douglas 1943-1971
See Morrison, Jim
See also CA 73-76; CANR 40

Morrison, Jim .... **CLC 17**
See also Morrison, James Douglas

Morrison, Toni
1931- .... **CLC 4, 10, 22, 55, 81, 87;
BLC; DA**
See also AAYA 1; BW 2; CA 29-32R;
CANR 27, 42; CDALB 1968-1988;
DLB 6, 33, 143; DLBY 81; MTCW;
SATA 57

Morrison, Van 1945- .... **CLC 21**
See also CA 116

Mortimer, John (Clifford)
1923- .... **CLC 28, 43**
See also CA 13-16R; CANR 21;
CDBLB 1960 to Present; DLB 13;
MTCW

Mortimer, Penelope (Ruth) 1918-... **CLC 5**
See also CA 57-60; CANR 45

Morton, Anthony
See Creasey, John

Mosher, Howard Frank 1943-...... **CLC 62**
See also CA 139

Mosley, Nicholas 1923-........ **CLC 43, 70**
See also CA 69-72; CANR 41; DLB 14

Moss, Howard
1922-1987 .... **CLC 7, 14, 45, 50**
See also CA 1-4R; 123; CANR 1, 44;
DLB 5

Mossgiel, Rab
See Burns, Robert

Motion, Andrew 1952-........... **CLC 47**
See also DLB 40

Motley, Willard (Francis)
1909-1965 .... **CLC 18**
See also BW 1; CA 117; 106; DLB 76, 143

Motoori, Norinaga 1730-1801.... **NCLC 45**

Mott, Michael (Charles Alston)
1930- .... **CLC 15, 34**
See also CA 5-8R; CAAS 7; CANR 7, 29

Mowat, Farley (McGill) 1921- ..... **CLC 26**
See also AAYA 1; CA 1-4R; CANR 4, 24,
42; CLR 20; DLB 68; JRDA; MAICYA;
MTCW; SATA 3, 55

Moyers, Bill 1934-.............. **CLC 74**
See also AITN 2; CA 61-64; CANR 31

Mphahlele, Es'kia
See Mphahlele, Ezekiel
See also DLB 125

Mphahlele, Ezekiel 1919-..... **CLC 25; BLC**
See also Mphahlele, Es'kia
See also BW 2; CA 81-84; CANR 26

Mqhayi, S(amuel) E(dward) K(rune Loliwe)
1875-1945 .... **TCLC 25; BLC**

Mr. Martin
See Burroughs, William S(eward)

Mrozek, Slawomir 1930-........ **CLC 3, 13**
See also CA 13-16R; CAAS 10; CANR 29;
MTCW

Mrs. Belloc-Lowndes
See Lowndes, Marie Adelaide (Belloc)

Mtwa, Percy (?)-................ **CLC 47**

Mueller, Lisel 1924-........... **CLC 13, 51**
See also CA 93-96; DLB 105

Muir, Edwin 1887-1959 .... **TCLC 2**
See also CA 104; DLB 20, 100

Muir, John 1838-1914 .... **TCLC 28**

Mujica Lainez, Manuel
1910-1984 .... **CLC 31**
See also Lainez, Manuel Mujica
See also CA 81-84; 112; CANR 32; HW

Mukherjee, Bharati 1940-........ **CLC 53**
See also BEST 89:2; CA 107; CANR 45;
DLB 60; MTCW

Muldoon, Paul 1951-.......... **CLC 32, 72**
See also CA 113; 129; DLB 40

Mulisch, Harry 1927-............. **CLC 42**
See also CA 9-12R; CANR 6, 26

Mull, Martin 1943-.............. **CLC 17**
See also CA 105

Mulock, Dinah Maria
See Craik, Dinah Maria (Mulock)

Munford, Robert 1737(?)-1783 .... **LC 5**
See also DLB 31

Mungo, Raymond 1946-........... **CLC 72**
See also CA 49-52; CANR 2

Munro, Alice
1931- .... **CLC 6, 10, 19, 50; SSC 3**
See also AITN 2; CA 33-36R; CANR 33;
DLB 53; MTCW; SATA 29

Munro, H(ector) H(ugh) 1870-1916
See Saki
See also CA 104; 130; CDBLB 1890-1914;
DA; DLB 34; MTCW; WLC

Murasaki, Lady.................. **CMLC 1**

Murdoch, (Jean) Iris
1919- ...... **CLC 1, 2, 3, 4, 6, 8, 11, 15,
22, 31, 51**
See also CA 13-16R; CANR 8, 43;
CDBLB 1960 to Present; DLB 14;
MTCW

Murnau, Friedrich Wilhelm
See Plumpe, Friedrich Wilhelm

Murphy, Richard 1927-........... **CLC 41**
See also CA 29-32R; DLB 40

Murphy, Sylvia 1937-............. **CLC 34**
See also CA 121

Murphy, Thomas (Bernard) 1935-... **CLC 51**
See also CA 101

Murray, Albert L. 1916- .... **CLC 73**
See also BW 2; CA 49-52; CANR 26;
DLB 38

Murray, Les(lie) A(llan) 1938- ..... **CLC 40**
See also CA 21-24R; CANR 11, 27

Murry, J. Middleton
See Murry, John Middleton

Murry, John Middleton
1889-1957 .... **TCLC 16**
See also CA 118

Musgrave, Susan 1951- .... **CLC 13, 54**
See also CA 69-72; CANR 45

Musil, Robert (Edler von)
1880-1942 .... **TCLC 12; SSC 18**
See also CA 109; DLB 81, 124

Musset, (Louis Charles) Alfred de
1810-1857 .... **NCLC 7**

My Brother's Brother
See Chekhov, Anton (Pavlovich)

Myers, Walter Dean 1937- ... **CLC 35; BLC**
See also AAYA 4; BW 2; CA 33-36R;
CANR 20, 42; CLR 4, 16, 35; DLB 33;
JRDA; MAICYA; SAAS 2; SATA 27, 41,
71

Myers, Walter M.
See Myers, Walter Dean

Myles, Symon
See Follett, Ken(neth Martin)

Nabokov, Vladimir (Vladimirovich)
1899-1977 ..... **CLC 1, 2, 3, 6, 8, 11, 15,
23, 44, 46, 64; DA; SSC 11; WLC**
See also CA 5-8R; 69-72; CANR 20;
CDALB 1941-1968; DLB 2; DLBD 3;
DLBY 80, 91; MTCW

Nagai Kafu.................... **TCLC 51**
See also Nagai Sokichi

Nagai Sokichi 1879-1959
See Nagai Kafu
See also CA 117

Nagy, Laszlo 1925-1978............ **CLC 7**
See also CA 129; 112

Naipaul, Shiva(dhar Srinivasa)
1945-1985 .... **CLC 32, 39**
See also CA 110; 112; 116; CANR 33;
DLBY 85; MTCW

Naipaul, V(idiadhar) S(urajprasad)
1932-.......... **CLC 4, 7, 9, 13, 18, 37**
See also CA 1-4R; CANR 1, 33;
CDBLB 1960 to Present; DLB 125;
DLBY 85; MTCW

Nakos, Lilika 1899(?)-............ **CLC 29**

Narayan, R(asipuram) K(rishnaswami)
1906-.............. **CLC 7, 28, 47**
See also CA 81-84; CANR 33; MTCW;
SATA 62

Nash, (Fredric) Ogden 1902-1971 .. **CLC 23**
See also CA 13-14; 29-32R; CANR 34;
CAP 1; DLB 11; MAICYA; MTCW;
SATA 2, 46

Nathan, Daniel
See Dannay, Frederic

Nathan, George Jean 1882-1958... **TCLC 18**
See also Hatteras, Owen
See also CA 114; DLB 137

Natsume, Kinnosuke 1867-1916
See Natsume, Soseki
See also CA 104

Natsume, Soseki .... **TCLC 2, 10**
See also Natsume, Kinnosuke

Natti, (Mary) Lee 1919-
See Kingman, Lee
See also CA 5-8R; CANR 2

Ossoli, Sarah Margaret (Fuller marchesa d')
1810-1850
See Fuller, Margaret
See also SATA 25

Ostrovsky, Alexander
1823-1886 . . . . NCLC 30

Otero, Blas de 1916-1979. . . . . CLC 11
See also CA 89-92; DLB 134

Otto, Whitney 1955- . . . . CLC 70
See also CA 140

Ouida . . . . TCLC 43
See also De La Ramee, (Marie) Louise
See also DLB 18

Ousmane, Sembene 1923- . . . . CLC 66; BLC
See also BW 1; CA 117; 125; MTCW

Ovid 43B.C.-18(?) . . . . CMLC 7; PC 2

Owen, Hugh
See Faust, Frederick (Schiller)

Owen, Wilfred (Edward Salter)
1893-1918 . . . . . . TCLC 5, 27; DA; WLC
See also CA 104; 141; CDBLB 1914-1945;
DLB 20

Owens, Rochelle 1936- . . . . CLC 8
See also CA 17-20R; CAAS 2; CANR 39

Oz, Amos 1939- . . . CLC 5, 8, 11, 27, 33, 54
See also CA 53-56; CANR 27, 47; MTCW

Ozick, Cynthia
1928- . . . . CLC 3, 7, 28, 62; SSC 15
See also BEST 90:1; CA 17-20R; CANR 23;
DLB 28; DLBY 82; MTCW

Ozu, Yasujiro 1903-1963 . . . . CLC 16
See also CA 112

Pacheco, C.
See Pessoa, Fernando (Antonio Nogueira)

Pa Chin . . . . CLC 18
See also Li Fei-kan

Pack, Robert 1929- . . . . CLC 13
See also CA 1-4R; CANR 3, 44; DLB 5

Padgett, Lewis
See Kuttner, Henry

Padilla (Lorenzo), Heberto 1932- . . . CLC 38
See also AITN 1; CA 123; 131; HW

Page, Jimmy 1944- . . . . CLC 12

Page, Louise 1955- . . . . CLC 40
See also CA 140

Page, P(atricia) K(athleen)
1916- . . . . CLC 7, 18
See also CA 53-56; CANR 4, 22; DLB 68;
MTCW

Paget, Violet 1856-1935
See Lee, Vernon
See also CA 104

Paget-Lowe, Henry
See Lovecraft, H(oward) P(hillips)

Paglia, Camille (Anna) 1947- . . . . CLC 68
See also CA 140

Paige, Richard
See Koontz, Dean R(ay)

Pakenham, Antonia
See Fraser, (Lady) Antonia (Pakenham)

Palamas, Kostes 1859-1943 . . . . TCLC 5
See also CA 105

Palazzeschi, Aldo 1885-1974 . . . . . . CLC 11
See also CA 89-92; 53-56; DLB 114

Paley, Grace 1922- . . . . CLC 4, 6, 37; SSC 8
See also CA 25-28R; CANR 13, 46;
DLB 28; MTCW

Palin, Michael (Edward) 1943- . . . . . CLC 21
See also Monty Python
See also CA 107; CANR 35; SATA 67

Palliser, Charles 1947- . . . . CLC 65
See also CA 136

Palma, Ricardo 1833-1919 . . . . TCLC 29

Pancake, Breece Dexter 1952-1979
See Pancake, Breece D'J
See also CA 123; 109

Pancake, Breece D'J . . . . CLC 29
See also Pancake, Breece Dexter
See also DLB 130

Panko, Rudy
See Gogol, Nikolai (Vasilyevich)

Papadiamantis, Alexandros
1851-1911 . . . . TCLC 29

Papadiamantopoulos, Johannes 1856-1910
See Moreas, Jean
See also CA 117

Papini, Giovanni 1881-1956 . . . . . . TCLC 22
See also CA 121

Paracelsus 1493-1541 . . . . LC 14

Parasol, Peter
See Stevens, Wallace

Parfenie, Maria
See Codrescu, Andrei

Parini, Jay (Lee) 1948- . . . . CLC 54
See also CA 97-100; CAAS 16; CANR 32

Park, Jordan
See Kornbluth, C(yril) M.; Pohl, Frederik

Parker, Bert
See Ellison, Harlan (Jay)

Parker, Dorothy (Rothschild)
1893-1967 . . . . CLC 15, 68; SSC 2
See also CA 19-20; 25-28R; CAP 2;
DLB 11, 45, 86; MTCW

Parker, Robert B(rown) 1932- . . . . . . CLC 27
See also BEST 89:4; CA 49-52; CANR 1,
26; MTCW

Parkin, Frank 1940- . . . . CLC 43

Parkman, Francis, Jr.
1823-1893 . . . . NCLC 12
See also DLB 1, 30

Parks, Gordon (Alexander Buchanan)
1912- . . . . CLC 1, 16; BLC
See also AITN 2; BW 2; CA 41-44R;
CANR 26; DLB 33; SATA 8

Parnell, Thomas 1679-1718 . . . . LC 3
See also DLB 94

Parra, Nicanor 1914- . . . . CLC 2; HLC
See also CA 85-88; CANR 32; HW; MTCW

Parrish, Mary Frances
See Fisher, M(ary) F(rances) K(ennedy)

Parson
See Coleridge, Samuel Taylor

Parson Lot
See Kingsley, Charles

Partridge, Anthony
See Oppenheim, E(dward) Phillips

Pascoli, Giovanni 1855-1912 . . . . . TCLC 45

Pasolini, Pier Paolo
1922-1975 . . . . CLC 20, 37
See also CA 93-96; 61-64; DLB 128;
MTCW

Pasquini
See Silone, Ignazio

Pastan, Linda (Olenik) 1932- . . . . . . CLC 27
See also CA 61-64; CANR 18, 40; DLB 5

Pasternak, Boris (Leonidovich)
1890-1960 . . . . . . CLC 7, 10, 18, 63; DA;
PC 6; WLC
See also CA 127; 116; MTCW

Patchen, Kenneth 1911-1972 . . . CLC 1, 2, 18
See also CA 1-4R; 33-36R; CANR 3, 35;
DLB 16, 48; MTCW

Pater, Walter (Horatio)
1839-1894 . . . . NCLC 7
See also CDBLB 1832-1890; DLB 57

Paterson, A(ndrew) B(arton)
1864-1941 . . . . TCLC 32

Paterson, Katherine (Womeldorf)
1932- . . . . CLC 12, 30
See also AAYA 1; CA 21-24R; CANR 28;
CLR 7; DLB 52; JRDA; MAICYA;
MTCW; SATA 13, 53

Patmore, Coventry Kersey Dighton
1823-1896 . . . . NCLC 9
See also DLB 35, 98

Paton, Alan (Stewart)
1903-1988 . . . . . . CLC 4, 10, 25, 55; DA;
WLC
See also CA 13-16; 125; CANR 22; CAP 1;
MTCW; SATA 11; SATA-Obit 56

Paton Walsh, Gillian 1937-
See Walsh, Jill Paton
See also CANR 38; JRDA; MAICYA;
SAAS 3; SATA 4, 72

Paulding, James Kirke 1778-1860 . . NCLC 2
See also DLB 3, 59, 74

Paulin, Thomas Neilson 1949-
See Paulin, Tom
See also CA 123; 128

Paulin, Tom . . . . CLC 37
See also Paulin, Thomas Neilson
See also DLB 40

Paustovsky, Konstantin (Georgievich)
1892-1968 . . . . CLC 40
See also CA 93-96; 25-28R

Pavese, Cesare 1908-1950 . . . . TCLC 3
See also CA 104; DLB 128

Pavic, Milorad 1929- . . . . CLC 60
See also CA 136

Payne, Alan
See Jakes, John (William)

Paz, Gil
See Lugones, Leopoldo

Paz, Octavio
1914- . . . . CLC 3, 4, 6, 10, 19, 51, 65;
DA; HLC; PC 1; WLC
See also CA 73-76; CANR 32; DLBY 90;
HW; MTCW

Peacock, Molly 1947-............. CLC 60
See also CA 103; DLB 120

Peacock, Thomas Love
1785-1866 .... NCLC 22
See also DLB 96, 116

Peake, Mervyn 1911-1968....... CLC 7, 54
See also CA 5-8R; 25-28R; CANR 3;
DLB 15; MTCW; SATA 23

Pearce, Philippa .... CLC 21
See also Christie, (Ann) Philippa
See also CLR 9; MAICYA; SATA 1, 67

Pearl, Eric
See Elman, Richard

Pearson, T(homas) R(eid) 1956- .... CLC 39
See also CA 120; 130

Peck, Dale 1968(?)- .... CLC 81

Peck, John 1941- .... CLC 3
See also CA 49-52; CANR 3

Peck, Richard (Wayne) 1934- ...... CLC 21
See also AAYA 1; CA 85-88; CANR 19,
38; CLR 15; JRDA; MAICYA; SAAS 2;
SATA 18, 55

Peck, Robert Newton 1928-.... CLC 17; DA
See also AAYA 3; CA 81-84; CANR 31;
JRDA; MAICYA; SAAS 1; SATA 21, 62

Peckinpah, (David) Sam(uel)
1925-1984 .... CLC 20
See also CA 109; 114

Pedersen, Knut 1859-1952
See Hamsun, Knut
See also CA 104; 119; MTCW

Peeslake, Gaffer
See Durrell, Lawrence (George)

Peguy, Charles Pierre
1873-1914 .... TCLC 10
See also CA 107

Pena, Ramon del Valle y
See Valle-Inclan, Ramon (Maria) del

Pendennis, Arthur Esquir
See Thackeray, William Makepeace

Penn, William 1644-1718.......... LC 25
See also DLB 24

Pepys, Samuel
1633-1703 .... LC 11; DA; WLC
See also CDBLB 1660-1789; DLB 101

Percy, Walker
1916-1990 .... CLC 2, 3, 6, 8, 14, 18, 47,
65
See also CA 1-4R; 131; CANR 1, 23;
DLB 2; DLBY 80, 90; MTCW

Perec, Georges 1936-1982........ CLC 56
See also CA 141; DLB 83

Pereda (y Sanchez de Porrua), Jose Maria de
1833-1906 .... TCLC 16
See also CA 117

Pereda y Porrua, Jose Maria de
See Pereda (y Sanchez de Porrua), Jose
Maria de

Peregoy, George Weems
See Mencken, H(enry) L(ouis)

Perelman, S(idney) J(oseph)
1904-1979 ... CLC 3, 5, 9, 15, 23, 44, 49
See also AITN 1, 2; CA 73-76; 89-92;
CANR 18; DLB 11, 44; MTCW

Peret, Benjamin 1899-1959 .... TCLC 20
See also CA 117

Peretz, Isaac Loeb 1851(?)-1915... TCLC 16
See also CA 109

Peretz, Yitzkhok Leibush
See Peretz, Isaac Loeb

Perez Galdos, Benito 1843-1920 ... TCLC 27
See also CA 125; HW

Perrault, Charles 1628-1703 .... LC 2
See also MAICYA; SATA 25

Perry, Brighton
See Sherwood, Robert E(mmet)

Perse, St.-John .... CLC 4, 11, 46
See also Leger, (Marie-Rene Auguste) Alexis
Saint-Leger

Peseenz, Tulio F.
See Lopez y Fuentes, Gregorio

Pesetsky, Bette 1932-............ CLC 28
See also CA 133; DLB 130

Peshkov, Alexei Maximovich 1868-1936
See Gorky, Maxim
See also CA 105; 141; DA

Pessoa, Fernando (Antonio Nogueira)
1888-1935 .... TCLC 27; HLC
See also CA 125

Peterkin, Julia Mood 1880-1961.... CLC 31
See also CA 102; DLB 9

Peters, Joan K. 1945-............ CLC 39

Peters, Robert L(ouis) 1924-........ CLC 7
See also CA 13-16R; CAAS 8; DLB 105

Petofi, Sandor 1823-1849........ NCLC 21

Petrakis, Harry Mark 1923-........ CLC 3
See also CA 9-12R; CANR 4, 30

Petrarch 1304-1374................ PC 8

Petrov, Evgeny .... TCLC 21
See also Kataev, Evgeny Petrovich

Petry, Ann (Lane) 1908- ...... CLC 1, 7, 18
See also BW 1; CA 5-8R; CAAS 6;
CANR 4, 46; CLR 12; DLB 76; JRDA;
MAICYA; MTCW; SATA 5

Petursson, Halligrimur 1614-1674 .... LC 8

Philipson, Morris H. 1926-........ CLC 53
See also CA 1-4R; CANR 4

Phillips, David Graham
1867-1911 .... TCLC 44
See also CA 108; DLB 9, 12

Phillips, Jack
See Sandburg, Carl (August)

Phillips, Jayne Anne
1952-................ CLC 15, 33; SSC 16
See also CA 101; CANR 24; DLBY 80;
MTCW

Phillips, Richard
See Dick, Philip K(indred)

Phillips, Robert (Schaeffer) 1938-... CLC 28
See also CA 17-20R; CAAS 13; CANR 8;
DLB 105

Phillips, Ward
See Lovecraft, H(oward) P(hillips)

Piccolo, Lucio 1901-1969......... CLC 13
See also CA 97-100; DLB 114

Pickthall, Marjorie L(owry) C(hristie)
1883-1922 .... TCLC 21
See also CA 107; DLB 92

Pico della Mirandola, Giovanni
1463-1494 .... LC 15

Piercy, Marge
1936-......... CLC 3, 6, 14, 18, 27, 62
See also CA 21-24R; CAAS 1; CANR 13,
43; DLB 120; MTCW

Piers, Robert
See Anthony, Piers

Pieyre de Mandiargues, Andre 1909-1991
See Mandiargues, Andre Pieyre de
See also CA 103; 136; CANR 22

Pilnyak, Boris .... TCLC 23
See also Vogau, Boris Andreyevich

Pincherle, Alberto 1907-1990 ... CLC 11, 18
See also Moravia, Alberto
See also CA 25-28R; 132; CANR 33;
MTCW

Pinckney, Darryl 1953-........... CLC 76
See also BW 2; CA 143

Pindar 518B.C.-446B.C......... CMLC 12

Pineda, Cecile 1942-.............. CLC 39
See also CA 118

Pinero, Arthur Wing 1855-1934 ... TCLC 32
See also CA 110; DLB 10

Pinero, Miguel (Antonio Gomez)
1946-1988 .... CLC 4, 55
See also CA 61-64; 125; CANR 29; HW

Pinget, Robert 1919- .... CLC 7, 13, 37
See also CA 85-88; DLB 83

Pink Floyd
See Barrett, (Roger) Syd; Gilmour, David;
Mason, Nick; Waters, Roger; Wright,
Rick

Pinkney, Edward 1802-1828 ..... NCLC 31

Pinkwater, Daniel Manus 1941- .... CLC 35
See also Pinkwater, Manus
See also AAYA 1; CA 29-32R; CANR 12,
38; CLR 4; JRDA; MAICYA; SAAS 3;
SATA 46, 76

Pinkwater, Manus
See Pinkwater, Daniel Manus
See also SATA 8

Pinsky, Robert 1940-........ CLC 9, 19, 38
See also CA 29-32R; CAAS 4; DLBY 82

Pinta, Harold
See Pinter, Harold

Pinter, Harold
1930-..... CLC 1, 3, 6, 9, 11, 15, 27, 58,
73; DA; WLC
See also CA 5-8R; CANR 33; CDBLB 1960
to Present; DLB 13; MTCW

Pirandello, Luigi
1867-1936 ..... TCLC 4, 29; DA; DC 5;
WLC
See also CA 104

Pirsig, Robert M(aynard)
1928-.................. CLC 4, 6, 73
See also CA 53-56; CANR 42; MTCW;
SATA 39

Pisarev, Dmitry Ivanovich
1840-1868 .... NCLC 25

Pix, Mary (Griffith)   1666-1709 . . . . LC 8
    See also DLB 80

Pixerecourt, Guilbert de
    1773-1844 . . . . NCLC 39

Plaidy, Jean
    See Hibbert, Eleanor Alice Burford

Planche, James Robinson
    1796-1880 . . . . NCLC 42

Plant, Robert   1948- . . . . CLC 12

Plante, David (Robert)
    1940- . . . . CLC 7, 23, 38
    See also CA 37-40R; CANR 12, 36;
    DLBY 83; MTCW

Plath, Sylvia
    1932-1963 . . . . . CLC 1, 2, 3, 5, 9, 11, 14,
        17, 50, 51, 62; DA; PC 1; WLC
    See also AAYA 13; CA 19-20; CANR 34;
    CAP 2; CDALB 1941-1968; DLB 5, 6;
    MTCW

Plato   428(?)B.C.-348(?)B.C. . . . CMLC 8; DA

Platonov, Andrei . . . . TCLC 14
    See also Klimentov, Andrei Platonovich

Platt, Kin   1911- . . . . CLC 26
    See also AAYA 11; CA 17-20R; CANR 11;
    JRDA; SAAS 17; SATA 21

Plick et Plock
    See Simenon, Georges (Jacques Christian)

Plimpton, George (Ames)   1927- . . . . . CLC 36
    See also AITN 1; CA 21-24R; CANR 32;
    MTCW; SATA 10

Plomer, William Charles Franklin
    1903-1973 . . . . CLC 4, 8
    See also CA 21-22; CANR 34; CAP 2;
    DLB 20; MTCW; SATA 24

Plowman, Piers
    See Kavanagh, Patrick (Joseph)

Plum, J.
    See Wodehouse, P(elham) G(renville)

Plumly, Stanley (Ross)   1939- . . . . . . CLC 33
    See also CA 108; 110; DLB 5

Plumpe, Friedrich Wilhelm
    1888-1931 . . . . TCLC 53
    See also CA 112

Poe, Edgar Allan
    1809-1849 . . . . . NCLC 1, 16; DA; PC 1;
                        SSC 1; WLC
    See also AAYA 14; CDALB 1640-1865;
    DLB 3, 59, 73, 74; SATA 23

Poet of Titchfield Street, The
    See Pound, Ezra (Weston Loomis)

Pohl, Frederik   1919- . . . . CLC 18
    See also CA 61-64; CAAS 1; CANR 11, 37;
    DLB 8; MTCW; SATA 24

Poirier, Louis   1910-
    See Gracq, Julien
    See also CA 122; 126

Poitier, Sidney   1927- . . . . CLC 26
    See also BW 1; CA 117

Polanski, Roman   1933- . . . . CLC 16
    See also CA 77-80

Poliakoff, Stephen   1952- . . . . CLC 38
    See also CA 106; DLB 13

Police, The
    See Copeland, Stewart (Armstrong);
    Summers, Andrew James; Sumner,
    Gordon Matthew

Pollitt, Katha   1949- . . . . CLC 28
    See also CA 120; 122; MTCW

Pollock, (Mary) Sharon   1936- . . . . . . CLC 50
    See also CA 141; DLB 60

Pomerance, Bernard   1940- . . . . CLC 13
    See also CA 101

Ponge, Francis (Jean Gaston Alfred)
    1899-1988 . . . . CLC 6, 18
    See also CA 85-88; 126; CANR 40

Pontoppidan, Henrik   1857-1943 . . . TCLC 29

Poole, Josephine . . . . CLC 17
    See Helyar, Jane Penelope Josephine
    See also SAAS 2; SATA 5

Popa, Vasko   1922- . . . . CLC 19
    See also CA 112

Pope, Alexander
    1688-1744 . . . . LC 3; DA; WLC
    See also CDBLB 1660-1789; DLB 95, 101

Porter, Connie (Rose)   1959(?)- . . . . . CLC 70
    See also BW 2; CA 142; SATA 81

Porter, Gene(va Grace) Stratton
    1863(?)-1924 . . . . TCLC 21
    See also CA 112

Porter, Katherine Anne
    1890-1980 . . . . . . CLC 1, 3, 7, 10, 13, 15,
                        27; DA; SSC 4
    See also AITN 2; CA 1-4R; 101; CANR 1;
    DLB 4, 9, 102; DLBD 12; DLBY 80;
    MTCW; SATA 39; SATA-Obit 23

Porter, Peter (Neville Frederick)
    1929- . . . . CLC 5, 13, 33
    See also CA 85-88; DLB 40

Porter, William Sydney   1862-1910
    See Henry, O.
    See also CA 104; 131; CDALB 1865-1917;
    DA; DLB 12, 78, 79; MTCW; YABC 2

Portillo (y Pacheco), Jose Lopez
    See Lopez Portillo (y Pacheco), Jose

Post, Melville Davisson
    1869-1930 . . . . TCLC 39
    See also CA 110

Potok, Chaim   1929- . . . . CLC 2, 7, 14, 26
    See also AITN 1, 2; CA 17-20R; CANR 19,
    35; DLB 28; MTCW; SATA 33

Potter, Beatrice
    See Webb, (Martha) Beatrice (Potter)
    See also MAICYA

Potter, Dennis (Christopher George)
    1935-1994 . . . . CLC 58, 86
    See also CA 107; 145; CANR 33; MTCW

Pound, Ezra (Weston Loomis)
    1885-1972 . . . . . CLC 1, 2, 3, 4, 5, 7, 10,
        13, 18, 34, 48, 50; DA; PC 4; WLC
    See also CA 5-8R; 37-40R; CANR 40;
    CDALB 1917-1929; DLB 4, 45, 63;
    MTCW

Povod, Reinaldo   1959-1994 . . . . CLC 44
    See also CA 136; 146

Powell, Anthony (Dymoke)
    1905- . . . . CLC 1, 3, 7, 9, 10, 31
    See also CA 1-4R; CANR 1, 32;
    CDBLB 1945-1960; DLB 15; MTCW

Powell, Dawn   1897-1965 . . . . CLC 66
    See also CA 5-8R

Powell, Padgett   1952- . . . . CLC 34
    See also CA 126

Powers, J(ames) F(arl)
    1917- . . . . CLC 1, 4, 8, 57; SSC 4
    See also CA 1-4R; CANR 2; DLB 130;
    MTCW

Powers, John J(ames)   1945-
    See Powers, John R.
    See also CA 69-72

Powers, John R. . . . . CLC 66
    See also Powers, John J(ames)

Pownall, David   1938- . . . . CLC 10
    See also CA 89-92; CAAS 18; DLB 14

Powys, John Cowper
    1872-1963 . . . . CLC 7, 9, 15, 46
    See also CA 85-88; DLB 15; MTCW

Powys, T(heodore) F(rancis)
    1875-1953 . . . . TCLC 9
    See also CA 106; DLB 36

Prager, Emily   1952- . . . . CLC 56

Pratt, E(dwin) J(ohn)
    1883(?)-1964 . . . . CLC 19
    See also CA 141; 93-96; DLB 92

Premchand . . . . TCLC 21
    See also Srivastava, Dhanpat Rai

Preussler, Otfried   1923- . . . . CLC 17
    See also CA 77-80; SATA 24

Prevert, Jacques (Henri Marie)
    1900-1977 . . . . CLC 15
    See also CA 77-80; 69-72; CANR 29;
    MTCW; SATA-Obit 30

Prevost, Abbe (Antoine Francois)
    1697-1763 . . . . LC 1

Price, (Edward) Reynolds
    1933- . . . . CLC 3, 6, 13, 43, 50, 63
    See also CA 1-4R; CANR 1, 37; DLB 2

Price, Richard   1949- . . . . CLC 6, 12
    See also CA 49-52; CANR 3; DLBY 81

Prichard, Katharine Susannah
    1883-1969 . . . . CLC 46
    See also CA 11-12; CANR 33; CAP 1;
    MTCW; SATA 66

Priestley, J(ohn) B(oynton)
    1894-1984 . . . . CLC 2, 5, 9, 34
    See also CA 9-12R; 113; CANR 33;
    CDBLB 1914-1945; DLB 10, 34, 77, 100,
    139; DLBY 84; MTCW

Prince   1958(?)- . . . . CLC 35

Prince, F(rank) T(empleton)   1912- . . CLC 22
    See also CA 101; CANR 43; DLB 20

Prince Kropotkin
    See Kropotkin, Peter (Aleksieevich)

Prior, Matthew   1664-1721 . . . . LC 4
    See also DLB 95

Pritchard, William H(arrison)
    1932- . . . . CLC 34
    See also CA 65-68; CANR 23; DLB 111

Pritchett, V(ictor) S(awdon)
1900- . . . . CLC **5, 13, 15, 41; SSC 14**
See also CA 61-64; CANR 31; DLB 15,
139; MTCW

Private 19022
See Manning, Frederic

Probst, Mark 1925- . . . . CLC **59**
See also CA 130

Prokosch, Frederic 1908-1989. . . . CLC **4, 48**
See also CA 73-76; 128; DLB 48

Prophet, The
See Dreiser, Theodore (Herman Albert)

Prose, Francine 1947- . . . . CLC **45**
See also CA 109; 112; CANR 46

Proudhon
See Cunha, Euclides (Rodrigues Pimenta) da

Proulx, E. Annie 1935- . . . . CLC **81**

Proust, (Valentin-Louis-George-Eugene-)
Marcel
1871-1922 . . . TCLC **7, 13, 33; DA; WLC**
See also CA 104; 120; DLB 65; MTCW

Prowler, Harley
See Masters, Edgar Lee

Prus, Boleslaw 1845-1912 . . . . TCLC **48**

Pryor, Richard (Franklin Lenox Thomas)
1940- . . . . CLC **26**
See also CA 122

Przybyszewski, Stanislaw
1868-1927 . . . . TCLC **36**
See also DLB 66

Pteleon
See Grieve, C(hristopher) M(urray)

Puckett, Lute
See Masters, Edgar Lee

Puig, Manuel
1932-1990 . . . CLC **3, 5, 10, 28, 65; HLC**
See also CA 45-48; CANR 2, 32; DLB 113;
HW; MTCW

Purdy, Al(fred Wellington)
1918- . . . . CLC **3, 6, 14, 50**
See also CA 81-84; CAAS 17; CANR 42;
DLB 88

Purdy, James (Amos)
1923- . . . . CLC **2, 4, 10, 28, 52**
See also CA 33-36R; CAAS 1; CANR 19;
DLB 2; MTCW

Pure, Simon
See Swinnerton, Frank Arthur

Pushkin, Alexander (Sergeyevich)
1799-1837 . . . . NCLC **3, 27; DA; PC 10;
WLC**
See also SATA 61

P'u Sung-ling 1640-1715 . . . . LC **3**

Putnam, Arthur Lee
See Alger, Horatio, Jr.

Puzo, Mario 1920- . . . . CLC **1, 2, 6, 36**
See also CA 65-68; CANR 4, 42; DLB 6;
MTCW

Pym, Barbara (Mary Crampton)
1913-1980 . . . . CLC **13, 19, 37**
See also CA 13-14; 97-100; CANR 13, 34;
CAP 1; DLB 14; DLBY 87; MTCW

Pynchon, Thomas (Ruggles, Jr.)
1937- . . . . . CLC **2, 3, 6, 9, 11, 18, 33, 62,
72; DA; SSC 14; WLC**
See also BEST 90:2; CA 17-20R; CANR 22,
46; DLB 2; MTCW

Qian Zhongshu
See Ch'ien Chung-shu

Qroll
See Dagerman, Stig (Halvard)

Quarrington, Paul (Lewis) 1953- . . . . CLC **65**
See also CA 129

Quasimodo, Salvatore 1901-1968 . . . CLC **10**
See also CA 13-16; 25-28R; CAP 1;
DLB 114; MTCW

Queen, Ellery. . . . . CLC **3, 11**
See also Dannay, Frederic; Davidson,
Avram; Lee, Manfred B(ennington);
Sturgeon, Theodore (Hamilton); Vance,
John Holbrook

Queen, Ellery, Jr.
See Dannay, Frederic; Lee, Manfred
B(ennington)

Queneau, Raymond
1903-1976 . . . . CLC **2, 5, 10, 42**
See also CA 77-80; 69-72; CANR 32;
DLB 72; MTCW

Quevedo, Francisco de 1580-1645. . . . LC **23**

Quiller-Couch, Arthur Thomas
1863-1944 . . . . TCLC **53**
See also CA 118; DLB 135

Quin, Ann (Marie) 1936-1973 . . . . . . CLC **6**
See also CA 9-12R; 45-48; DLB 14

Quinn, Martin
See Smith, Martin Cruz

Quinn, Simon
See Smith, Martin Cruz

Quiroga, Horacio (Sylvestre)
1878-1937 . . . . TCLC **20; HLC**
See also CA 117; 131; HW; MTCW

Quoirez, Francoise 1935- . . . . CLC **9**
See also Sagan, Francoise
See also CA 49-52; CANR 6, 39; MTCW

Raabe, Wilhelm 1831-1910 . . . . TCLC **45**
See also DLB 129

Rabe, David (William) 1940- . . . CLC **4, 8, 33**
See also CA 85-88; CABS 3; DLB 7

Rabelais, Francois
1483-1553 . . . . LC **5; DA; WLC**

Rabinovitch, Sholem 1859-1916
See Aleichem, Sholom
See also CA 104

Racine, Jean 1639-1699 . . . . LC **28**

Radcliffe, Ann (Ward) 1764-1823 . . NCLC **6**
See also DLB 39

Radiguet, Raymond 1903-1923 . . . . TCLC **29**
See also DLB 65

Radnoti, Miklos 1909-1944 . . . . TCLC **16**
See also CA 118

Rado, James 1939- . . . . CLC **17**
See also CA 105

Radvanyi, Netty 1900-1983
See Seghers, Anna
See also CA 85-88; 110

Rae, Ben
See Griffiths, Trevor

Raeburn, John (Hay) 1941- . . . . CLC **34**
See also CA 57-60

Ragni, Gerome 1942-1991 . . . . CLC **17**
See also CA 105; 134

Rahv, Philip 1908-1973 . . . . CLC **24**
See also Greenberg, Ivan
See also DLB 137

Raine, Craig 1944- . . . . CLC **32**
See also CA 108; CANR 29; DLB 40

Raine, Kathleen (Jessie) 1908- . . . CLC **7, 45**
See also CA 85-88; CANR 46; DLB 20;
MTCW

Rainis, Janis 1865-1929 . . . . TCLC **29**

Rakosi, Carl. CLC **47**
See also Rawley, Callman
See also CAAS 5

Raleigh, Richard
See Lovecraft, H(oward) P(hillips)

Rallentando, H. P.
See Sayers, Dorothy L(eigh)

Ramal, Walter
See de la Mare, Walter (John)

Ramon, Juan
See Jimenez (Mantecon), Juan Ramon

Ramos, Graciliano 1892-1953 . . . . . TCLC **32**

Rampersad, Arnold 1941- . . . . CLC **44**
See also BW 2; CA 127; 133; DLB 111

Rampling, Anne
See Rice, Anne

Ramuz, Charles-Ferdinand
1878-1947 . . . . TCLC **33**

Rand, Ayn
1905-1982 . . . . . . CLC **3, 30, 44, 79; DA;
WLC**
See also AAYA 10; CA 13-16R; 105;
CANR 27; MTCW

Randall, Dudley (Felker)
1914- . . . . CLC **1; BLC**
See also BW 1; CA 25-28R; CANR 23;
DLB 41

Randall, Robert
See Silverberg, Robert

Ranger, Ken
See Creasey, John

Ransom, John Crowe
1888-1974 . . . . CLC **2, 4, 5, 11, 24**
See also CA 5-8R; 49-52; CANR 6, 34;
DLB 45, 63; MTCW

Rao, Raja 1909- . . . . CLC **25, 56**
See also CA 73-76; MTCW

Raphael, Frederic (Michael)
1931- . . . . CLC **2, 14**
See also CA 1-4R; CANR 1; DLB 14

Ratcliffe, James P.
See Mencken, H(enry) L(ouis)

Rathbone, Julian 1935- . . . . CLC **41**
See also CA 101; CANR 34

Rattigan, Terence (Mervyn)
1911-1977 . . . . CLC **7**
See also CA 85-88; 73-76;
CDBLB 1945-1960; DLB 13; MTCW

Riefenstahl, Berta Helene Amalia   1902-
   See Riefenstahl, Leni
   See also CA 108

Riefenstahl, Leni . . . . CLC 16
   See also Riefenstahl, Berta Helene Amalia

Riffe, Ernest
   See Bergman, (Ernst) Ingmar

Riggs, (Rolla) Lynn   1899-1954 . . . . TCLC 56
   See also CA 144; NNAL

Riley, James Whitcomb
   1849-1916 . . . . TCLC 51
   See also CA 118; 137; MAICYA; SATA 17

Riley, Tex
   See Creasey, John

Rilke, Rainer Maria
   1875-1926 . . . . TCLC 1, 6, 19; PC 2
   See also CA 104; 132; DLB 81; MTCW

Rimbaud, (Jean Nicolas) Arthur
   1854-1891 . . . . . NCLC 4, 35; DA; PC 3;
                                                      WLC

Rinehart, Mary Roberts
   1876-1958 . . . . TCLC 52
   See also CA 108

Ringmaster, The
   See Mencken, H(enry) L(ouis)

Ringwood, Gwen(dolyn Margaret) Pharis
   1910-1984 . . . . CLC 48
   See also CA 112; DLB 88

Rio, Michel   19(?)- . . . . CLC 43

Ritsos, Giannes
   See Ritsos, Yannis

Ritsos, Yannis   1909-1990 . . . . . CLC 6, 13, 31
   See also CA 77-80; 133; CANR 39; MTCW

Ritter, Erika   1948(?)- . . . . CLC 52

Rivera, Jose Eustasio   1889-1928 . . . TCLC 35
   See also HW

Rivers, Conrad Kent   1933-1968 . . . . . . CLC 1
   See also BW 1; CA 85-88; DLB 41

Rivers, Elfrida
   See Bradley, Marion Zimmer

Riverside, John
   See Heinlein, Robert A(nson)

Rizal, Jose   1861-1896 . . . . NCLC 27

Roa Bastos, Augusto (Antonio)
   1917- . . . . CLC 45; HLC
   See also CA 131; DLB 113; HW

Robbe-Grillet, Alain
   1922- . . . . . . CLC 1, 2, 4, 6, 8, 10, 14, 43
   See also CA 9-12R; CANR 33; DLB 83;
      MTCW

Robbins, Harold   1916- . . . . CLC 5
   See also CA 73-76; CANR 26; MTCW

Robbins, Thomas Eugene   1936-
   See Robbins, Tom
   See also CA 81-84; CANR 29; MTCW

Robbins, Tom . . . . CLC 9, 32, 64
   See also Robbins, Thomas Eugene
   See also BEST 90:3; DLBY 80

Robbins, Trina   1938- . . . . CLC 21
   See also CA 128

Roberts, Charles G(eorge) D(ouglas)
   1860-1943 . . . . TCLC 8
   See also CA 105; CLR 33; DLB 92;
      SATA 29

Roberts, Kate   1891-1985 . . . . CLC 15
   See also CA 107; 116

Roberts, Keith (John Kingston)
   1935- . . . . CLC 14
   See also CA 25-28R; CANR 46

Roberts, Kenneth (Lewis)
   1885-1957 . . . . TCLC 23
   See also CA 109; DLB 9

Roberts, Michele (B.)   1949- . . . . CLC 48
   See also CA 115

Robertson, Ellis
   See Ellison, Harlan (Jay); Silverberg, Robert

Robertson, Thomas William
   1829-1871 . . . . NCLC 35

Robinson, Edwin Arlington
   1869-1935 . . . . TCLC 5; DA; PC 1
   See also CA 104; 133; CDALB 1865-1917;
      DLB 54; MTCW

Robinson, Henry Crabb
   1775-1867 . . . . NCLC 15
   See also DLB 107

Robinson, Jill   1936- . . . . CLC 10
   See also CA 102

Robinson, Kim Stanley   1952- . . . . . . CLC 34
   See also CA 126

Robinson, Lloyd
   See Silverberg, Robert

Robinson, Marilynne   1944- . . . . CLC 25
   See also CA 116

Robinson, Smokey . . . . CLC 21
   See also Robinson, William, Jr.

Robinson, William, Jr.   1940-
   See Robinson, Smokey
   See also CA 116

Robison, Mary   1949- . . . . CLC 42
   See also CA 113; 116; DLB 130

Rod, Edouard   1857-1910 . . . . TCLC 52

Roddenberry, Eugene Wesley   1921-1991
   See Roddenberry, Gene
   See also CA 110; 135; CANR 37; SATA 45;
      SATA-Obit 69

Roddenberry, Gene . . . . CLC 17
   See also Roddenberry, Eugene Wesley
   See also AAYA 5; SATA-Obit 69

Rodgers, Mary   1931- . . . . CLC 12
   See also CA 49-52; CANR 8; CLR 20;
      JRDA; MAICYA; SATA 8

Rodgers, W(illiam) R(obert)
   1909-1969 . . . . CLC 7
   See also CA 85-88; DLB 20

Rodman, Eric
   See Silverberg, Robert

Rodman, Howard   1920(?)-1985 . . . . . CLC 65
   See also CA 118

Rodman, Maia
   See Wojciechowska, Maia (Teresa)

Rodriguez, Claudio   1934- . . . . CLC 10
   See also DLB 134

Roelvaag, O(le) E(dvart)
   1876-1931 . . . . TCLC 17
   See also CA 117; DLB 9

Roethke, Theodore (Huebner)
   1908-1963 . . . . . . CLC 1, 3, 8, 11, 19, 46
   See also CA 81-84; CABS 2;
      CDALB 1941-1968; DLB 5; MTCW

Rogers, Thomas Hunton   1927- . . . . . CLC 57
   See also CA 89-92

Rogers, Will(iam Penn Adair)
   1879-1935 . . . . TCLC 8
   See also CA 105; 144; DLB 11; NNAL

Rogin, Gilbert   1929- . . . . CLC 18
   See also CA 65-68; CANR 15

Rohan, Koda . . . . TCLC 22
   See also Koda Shigeyuki

Rohmer, Eric . . . . CLC 16
   See also Scherer, Jean-Marie Maurice

Rohmer, Sax . . . . TCLC 28
   See also Ward, Arthur Henry Sarsfield
   See also DLB 70

Roiphe, Anne (Richardson)
   1935- . . . . CLC 3, 9
   See also CA 89-92; CANR 45; DLBY 80

Rojas, Fernando de   1465-1541 . . . . . . LC 23

Rolfe, Frederick (William Serafino Austin
   Lewis Mary)   1860-1913 . . . . . . TCLC 12
   See also CA 107; DLB 34

Rolland, Romain   1866-1944 . . . . . . TCLC 23
   See also CA 118; DLB 65

Rolvaag, O(le) E(dvart)
   See Roelvaag, O(le) E(dvart)

Romain Arnaud, Saint
   See Aragon, Louis

Romains, Jules   1885-1972 . . . . CLC 7
   See also CA 85-88; CANR 34; DLB 65;
      MTCW

Romero, Jose Ruben   1890-1952 . . . TCLC 14
   See also CA 114; 131; HW

Ronsard, Pierre de
   1524-1585 . . . . LC 6; PC 11

Rooke, Leon   1934- . . . . CLC 25, 34
   See also CA 25-28R; CANR 23

Roper, William   1498-1578 . . . . LC 10

Roquelaure, A. N.
   See Rice, Anne

Rosa, Joao Guimaraes   1908-1967 . . . CLC 23
   See also CA 89-92; DLB 113

Rose, Wendy   1948- . . . . CLC 85
   See also CA 53-56; CANR 5; NNAL;
      SATA 12

Rosen, Richard (Dean)   1949- . . . . . . CLC 39
   See also CA 77-80

Rosenberg, Isaac   1890-1918 . . . . . . TCLC 12
   See also CA 107; DLB 20

Rosenblatt, Joe . . . . CLC 15
   See also Rosenblatt, Joseph

Rosenblatt, Joseph   1933-
   See Rosenblatt, Joe
   See also CA 89-92

Rosenfeld, Samuel   1896-1963
   See Tzara, Tristan
   See also CA 89-92

Rosenthal, M(acha) L(ouis)   1917- . . . CLC 28
   See also CA 1-4R; CAAS 6; CANR 4;
      DLB 5; SATA 59

Salamanca, J(ack) R(ichard)
1922- . . . . **CLC 4, 15**
See also CA 25-28R

Sale, J. Kirkpatrick
See Sale, Kirkpatrick

Sale, Kirkpatrick 1937- . . . . **CLC 68**
See also CA 13-16R; CANR 10

Salinas (y Serrano), Pedro
1891(?)-1951 . . . . **TCLC 17**
See also CA 117; DLB 134

Salinger, J(erome) D(avid)
1919- . . . . . . **CLC 1, 3, 8, 12, 55, 56; DA;**
SSC 2; WLC
See also AAYA 2; CA 5-8R; CANR 39;
CDALB 1941-1968; CLR 18; DLB 2, 102;
MAICYA; MTCW; SATA 67

Salisbury, John
See Caute, David

Salter, James 1925- . . . . **CLC 7, 52, 59**
See also CA 73-76; DLB 130

Saltus, Edgar (Everton)
1855-1921 . . . . **TCLC 8**
See also CA 105

Saltykov, Mikhail Evgrafovich
1826-1889 . . . . **NCLC 16**

Samarakis, Antonis 1919- . . . . **CLC 5**
See also CA 25-28R; CAAS 16; CANR 36

Sanchez, Florencio 1875-1910 . . . . . **TCLC 37**
See also HW

Sanchez, Luis Rafael 1936- . . . . **CLC 23**
See also CA 128; DLB 145; HW

Sanchez, Sonia 1934- . . . **CLC 5; BLC; PC 9**
See also BW 2; CA 33-36R; CANR 24;
CLR 18; DLB 41; DLBD 8; MAICYA;
MTCW; SATA 22

Sand, George
1804-1876 . . . . . . **NCLC 2, 42; DA; WLC**
See also DLB 119

Sandburg, Carl (August)
1878-1967 . . . . **CLC 1, 4, 10, 15, 35; DA;**
PC 2; WLC
See also CA 5-8R; 25-28R; CANR 35;
CDALB 1865-1917; DLB 17, 54;
MAICYA; MTCW; SATA 8

Sandburg, Charles
See Sandburg, Carl (August)

Sandburg, Charles A.
See Sandburg, Carl (August)

Sanders, (James) Ed(ward) 1939- . . . **CLC 53**
See also CA 13-16R; CANR 13, 44;
DLB 16

Sanders, Lawrence 1920- . . . . **CLC 41**
See also BEST 89:4; CA 81-84; CANR 33;
MTCW

Sanders, Noah
See Blount, Roy (Alton), Jr.

Sanders, Winston P.
See Anderson, Poul (William)

Sandoz, Mari(e Susette)
1896-1966 . . . . **CLC 28**
See also CA 1-4R; 25-28R; CANR 17;
DLB 9; MTCW; SATA 5

Saner, Reg(inald Anthony) 1931- . . . . **CLC 9**
See also CA 65-68

Sannazaro, Jacopo 1456(?)-1530 . . . . . . **LC 8**

Sansom, William 1912-1976 . . . . . . **CLC 2, 6**
See also CA 5-8R; 65-68; CANR 42;
DLB 139; MTCW

Santayana, George 1863-1952 . . . . . **TCLC 40**
See also CA 115; DLB 54, 71

Santiago, Danny . . . . **CLC 33**
See also James, Daniel (Lewis); James,
Daniel (Lewis)
See also DLB 122

Santmyer, Helen Hoover
1895-1986 . . . . **CLC 33**
See also CA 1-4R; 118; CANR 15, 33;
DLBY 84; MTCW

Santos, Bienvenido N(uqui) 1911- . . . **CLC 22**
See also CA 101; CANR 19, 46

Sapper . . . . **TCLC 44**
See also McNeile, Herman Cyril

Sappho fl. 6th cent. B.C.- . . . . **CMLC 3; PC 5**

Sarduy, Severo 1937-1993 . . . . **CLC 6**
See also CA 89-92; 142; DLB 113; HW

Sargeson, Frank 1903-1982 . . . . **CLC 31**
See also CA 25-28R; 106; CANR 38

Sarmiento, Felix Ruben Garcia
See Dario, Ruben

Saroyan, William
1908-1981 . . . . . **CLC 1, 8, 10, 29, 34, 56;**
DA; WLC
See also CA 5-8R; 103; CANR 30; DLB 7,
9, 86; DLBY 81; MTCW; SATA 23;
SATA-Obit 24

Sarraute, Nathalie
1900- . . . . **CLC 1, 2, 4, 8, 10, 31, 80**
See also CA 9-12R; CANR 23; DLB 83;
MTCW

Sarton, (Eleanor) May
1912- . . . . **CLC 4, 14, 49**
See also CA 1-4R; CANR 1, 34; DLB 48;
DLBY 81; MTCW; SATA 36

Sartre, Jean-Paul
1905-1980 . . . . **CLC 1, 4, 7, 9, 13, 18, 24,**
44, 50, 52; DA; DC 3; WLC
See also CA 9-12R; 97-100; CANR 21;
DLB 72; MTCW

Sassoon, Siegfried (Lorraine)
1886-1967 . . . . **CLC 36**
See also CA 104; 25-28R; CANR 36;
DLB 20; MTCW

Satterfield, Charles
See Pohl, Frederik

Saul, John (W. III) 1942- . . . . **CLC 46**
See also AAYA 10; BEST 90:4; CA 81-84;
CANR 16, 40

Saunders, Caleb
See Heinlein, Robert A(nson)

Saura (Atares), Carlos 1932- . . . . **CLC 20**
See also CA 114; 131; HW

Sauser-Hall, Frederic 1887-1961 . . . . **CLC 18**
See also CA 102; 93-96; CANR 36; MTCW

Saussure, Ferdinand de
1857-1913 . . . . **TCLC 49**

Savage, Catharine
See Brosman, Catharine Savage

Savage, Thomas 1915- . . . . **CLC 40**
See also CA 126; 132; CAAS 15

Savan, Glenn 19(?)- . . . . **CLC 50**

Sayers, Dorothy L(eigh)
1893-1957 . . . . **TCLC 2, 15**
See also CA 104; 119; CDBLB 1914-1945;
DLB 10, 36, 77, 100; MTCW

Sayers, Valerie 1952- . . . . **CLC 50**
See also CA 134

Sayles, John (Thomas)
1950- . . . . **CLC 7, 10, 14**
See also CA 57-60; CANR 41; DLB 44

Scammell, Michael . . . . **CLC 34**

Scannell, Vernon 1922- . . . . **CLC 49**
See also CA 5-8R; CANR 8, 24; DLB 27;
SATA 59

Scarlett, Susan
See Streatfeild, (Mary) Noel

Schaeffer, Susan Fromberg
1941- . . . . **CLC 6, 11, 22**
See also CA 49-52; CANR 18; DLB 28;
MTCW; SATA 22

Schary, Jill
See Robinson, Jill

Schell, Jonathan 1943- . . . . **CLC 35**
See also CA 73-76; CANR 12

Schelling, Friedrich Wilhelm Joseph von
1775-1854 . . . . **NCLC 30**
See also DLB 90

Schendel, Arthur van 1874-1946 . . . **TCLC 56**

Scherer, Jean-Marie Maurice 1920-
See Rohmer, Eric
See also CA 110

Schevill, James (Erwin) 1920- . . . . **CLC 7**
See also CA 5-8R; CAAS 12

Schiller, Friedrich 1759-1805 . . . . **NCLC 39**
See also DLB 94

Schisgal, Murray (Joseph) 1926- . . . . . **CLC 6**
See also CA 21-24R

Schlee, Ann 1934- . . . . **CLC 35**
See also CA 101; CANR 29; SATA 36, 44

Schlegel, August Wilhelm von
1767-1845 . . . . **NCLC 15**
See also DLB 94

Schlegel, Friedrich 1772-1829 . . . . **NCLC 45**
See also DLB 90

Schlegel, Johann Elias (von)
1719(?)-1749 . . . . **LC 5**

Schlesinger, Arthur M(eier), Jr.
1917- . . . . **CLC 84**
See also AITN 1; CA 1-4R; CANR 1, 28;
DLB 17; MTCW; SATA 61

Schmidt, Arno (Otto) 1914-1979 . . . . **CLC 56**
See also CA 128; 109; DLB 69

Schmitz, Aron Hector 1861-1928
See Svevo, Italo
See also CA 104; 122; MTCW

Schnackenberg, Gjertrud 1953- . . . . . **CLC 40**
See also CA 116; DLB 120

Schneider, Leonard Alfred 1925-1966
See Bruce, Lenny
See also CA 89-92

Schnitzler, Arthur
1862-1931 . . . . **TCLC 4; SSC 15**
See also CA 104; DLB 81, 118

Schor, Sandra (M.) 1932(?)-1990 . . . **CLC 65**
See also CA 132

Shaffer, Peter (Levin)
1926-. . . . . **CLC 5, 14, 18, 37, 60**
See also CA 25-28R; CANR 25, 47;
CDBLB 1960 to Present; DLB 13;
MTCW

Shakey, Bernard
See Young, Neil

Shalamov, Varlam (Tikhonovich)
1907(?)-1982 . . . . **CLC 18**
See also CA 129; 105

Shamlu, Ahmad 1925- . . . . **CLC 10**

Shammas, Anton 1951-. . . . . **CLC 55**

Shange, Ntozake
1948- . . . . **CLC 8, 25, 38, 74; BLC; DC 3**
See also AAYA 9; BW 2; CA 85-88;
CABS 3; CANR 27; DLB 38; MTCW

Shanley, John Patrick 1950-. . . . . . . **CLC 75**
See also CA 128; 133

Shapcott, Thomas William 1935- . . . **CLC 38**
See also CA 69-72

Shapiro, Jane. . . . . **CLC 76**

Shapiro, Karl (Jay) 1913- . . **CLC 4, 8, 15, 53**
See also CA 1-4R; CAAS 6; CANR 1, 36;
DLB 48; MTCW

Sharp, William 1855-1905 . . . . **TCLC 39**

Sharpe, Thomas Ridley 1928-
See Sharpe, Tom
See also CA 114; 122

Sharpe, Tom. **CLC 36**
See also Sharpe, Thomas Ridley
See also DLB 14

Shaw, Bernard. . . . . **TCLC 45**
See also Shaw, George Bernard
See also BW 1

Shaw, G. Bernard
See Shaw, George Bernard

Shaw, George Bernard
1856-1950 . . . . **TCLC 3, 9, 21; DA; WLC**
See also Shaw, Bernard
See also CA 104; 128; CDBLB 1914-1945;
DLB 10, 57; MTCW

Shaw, Henry Wheeler
1818-1885 . . . . **NCLC 15**
See also DLB 11

Shaw, Irwin 1913-1984. . . . . . . **CLC 7, 23, 34**
See also AITN 1; CA 13-16R; 112;
CANR 21; CDALB 1941-1968; DLB 6,
102; DLBY 84; MTCW

Shaw, Robert 1927-1978 . . . . **CLC 5**
See also AITN 1; CA 1-4R; 81-84;
CANR 4; DLB 13, 14

Shaw, T. E.
See Lawrence, T(homas) E(dward)

Shawn, Wallace 1943- . . . . **CLC 41**
See also CA 112

Shea, Lisa 1953-. . . . . **CLC 86**

Sheed, Wilfrid (John Joseph)
1930- . . . . **CLC 2, 4, 10, 53**
See also CA 65-68; CANR 30; DLB 6;
MTCW

Sheldon, Alice Hastings Bradley
1915(?)-1987
See Tiptree, James, Jr.
See also CA 108; 122; CANR 34; MTCW

Sheldon, John
See Bloch, Robert (Albert)

Shelley, Mary Wollstonecraft (Godwin)
1797-1851 . . . . **NCLC 14; DA; WLC**
See also CDBLB 1789-1832; DLB 110, 116;
SATA 29

Shelley, Percy Bysshe
1792-1822 . . . . **NCLC 18; DA; WLC**
See also CDBLB 1789-1832; DLB 96, 110

Shepard, Jim 1956-. . . . . **CLC 36**
See also CA 137

Shepard, Lucius 1947- . . . . **CLC 34**
See also CA 128; 141

Shepard, Sam
1943- . . . . **CLC 4, 6, 17, 34, 41, 44; DC 5**
See also AAYA 1; CA 69-72; CABS 3;
CANR 22; DLB 7; MTCW

Shepherd, Michael
See Ludlum, Robert

Sherburne, Zoa (Morin) 1912-. . . . . . **CLC 30**
See also AAYA 13; CA 1-4R; CANR 3, 37;
MAICYA; SAAS 18; SATA 3

Sheridan, Frances 1724-1766. . . . . **LC 7**
See also DLB 39, 84

Sheridan, Richard Brinsley
1751-1816 . . . **NCLC 5; DA; DC 1; WLC**
See also CDBLB 1660-1789; DLB 89

Sherman, Jonathan Marc. . . . . **CLC 55**

Sherman, Martin 1941(?)-. . . . . **CLC 19**
See also CA 116; 123

Sherwin, Judith Johnson 1936-. . . **CLC 7, 15**
See also CA 25-28R; CANR 34

Sherwood, Frances 1940-. . . . . **CLC 81**

Sherwood, Robert E(mmet)
1896-1955 . . . . **TCLC 3**
See also CA 104; DLB 7, 26

Shestov, Lev 1866-1938. . . . . **TCLC 56**

Shiel, M(atthew) P(hipps)
1865-1947 . . . . **TCLC 8**
See also CA 106

Shiga, Naoya 1883-1971. . . . . **CLC 33**
See also CA 101; 33-36R

Shilts, Randy 1951-1994 . . . . **CLC 85**
See also CA 115; 127; 144; CANR 45

Shimazaki Haruki 1872-1943
See Shimazaki Toson
See also CA 105; 134

Shimazaki Toson. . . . . **TCLC 5**
See also Shimazaki Haruki

Sholokhov, Mikhail (Aleksandrovich)
1905-1984 . . . . **CLC 7, 15**
See also CA 101; 112; MTCW;
SATA-Obit 36

Shone, Patric
See Hanley, James

Shreve, Susan Richards 1939-. . . . . . **CLC 23**
See also CA 49-52; CAAS 5; CANR 5, 38;
MAICYA; SATA 46; SATA-Brief 41

Shue, Larry 1946-1985. . . . . **CLC 52**
See also CA 145; 117

Shu-Jen, Chou 1881-1936
See Hsun, Lu
See also CA 104

Shulman, Alix Kates 1932- . . . . . . **CLC 2, 10**
See also CA 29-32R; CANR 43; SATA 7

Shuster, Joe 1914- . . . . **CLC 21**

Shute, Nevil. . . . . **CLC 30**
See also Norway, Nevil Shute

Shuttle, Penelope (Diane) 1947- . . . . . **CLC 7**
See also CA 93-96; CANR 39; DLB 14, 40

Sidney, Mary 1561-1621 . . . . **LC 19**

Sidney, Sir Philip 1554-1586. . . . **LC 19; DA**
See also CDBLB Before 1660

Siegel, Jerome 1914- . . . . **CLC 21**
See also CA 116

Siegel, Jerry
See Siegel, Jerome

Sienkiewicz, Henryk (Adam Alexander Pius)
1846-1916 . . . . **TCLC 3**
See also CA 104; 134

Sierra, Gregorio Martinez
See Martinez Sierra, Gregorio

Sierra, Maria (de la O'LeJarraga) Martinez
See Martinez Sierra, Maria (de la
O'LeJarraga)

Sigal, Clancy 1926-. . . . . **CLC 7**
See also CA 1-4R

Sigourney, Lydia Howard (Huntley)
1791-1865 . . . . **NCLC 21**
See also DLB 1, 42, 73

Siguenza y Gongora, Carlos de
1645-1700 . . . . **LC 8**

Sigurjonsson, Johann 1880-1919. . . **TCLC 27**

Sikelianos, Angelos 1884-1951 . . . . **TCLC 39**

Silkin, Jon 1930- . . . . **CLC 2, 6, 43**
See also CA 5-8R; CAAS 5; DLB 27

Silko, Leslie (Marmon)
1948- . . . . **CLC 23, 74; DA**
See also AAYA 14; CA 115; 122;
CANR 45; DLB 143; NNAL

Sillanpaa, Frans Eemil 1888-1964. . . **CLC 19**
See also CA 129; 93-96; MTCW

Sillitoe, Alan
1928-. . . . . **CLC 1, 3, 6, 10, 19, 57**
See also AITN 1; CA 9-12R; CAAS 2;
CANR 8, 26; CDBLB 1960 to Present;
DLB 14, 139; MTCW; SATA 61

Silone, Ignazio 1900-1978 . . . . **CLC 4**
See also CA 25-28; 81-84; CANR 34;
CAP 2; MTCW

Silver, Joan Micklin 1935- . . . . **CLC 20**
See also CA 114; 121

Silver, Nicholas
See Faust, Frederick (Schiller)

Silverberg, Robert 1935- . . . . **CLC 7**
See also CA 1-4R; CAAS 3; CANR 1, 20,
36; DLB 8; MAICYA; MTCW; SATA 13

Silverstein, Alvin 1933- . . . . **CLC 17**
See also CA 49-52; CANR 2; CLR 25;
JRDA; MAICYA; SATA 8, 69

Silverstein, Virginia B(arbara Opshelor)
1937-. . . . . **CLC 17**
See also CA 49-52; CANR 2; CLR 25;
JRDA; MAICYA; SATA 8, 69

Sim, Georges
See Simenon, Georges (Jacques Christian)

Simak, Clifford D(onald)
1904-1988 . . . . CLC **1, 55**
See also CA 1-4R; 125; CANR 1, 35;
DLB 8; MTCW; SATA-Obit 56

Simenon, Georges (Jacques Christian)
1903-1989 . . . . CLC **1, 2, 3, 8, 18, 47**
See also CA 85-88; 129; CANR 35;
DLB 72; DLBY 89; MTCW

Simic, Charles 1938-. . . CLC **6, 9, 22, 49, 68**
See also CA 29-32R; CAAS 4; CANR 12,
33; DLB 105

Simmons, Charles (Paul) 1924-. . . . . CLC **57**
See also CA 89-92

Simmons, Dan 1948-. . . . . CLC **44**
See also CA 138

Simmons, James (Stewart Alexander)
1933- . . . . CLC **43**
See also CA 105; DLB 40

Simms, William Gilmore
1806-1870 . . . . NCLC **3**
See also DLB 3, 30, 59, 73

Simon, Carly 1945-. . . . . CLC **26**
See also CA 105

Simon, Claude 1913-. . . . . . . CLC **4, 9, 15, 39**
See also CA 89-92; CANR 33; DLB 83;
MTCW

Simon, (Marvin) Neil
1927- . . . . CLC **6, 11, 31, 39, 70**
See also AITN 1; CA 21-24R; CANR 26;
DLB 7; MTCW

Simon, Paul 1942(?)- . . . . CLC **17**
See also CA 116

Simonon, Paul 1956(?)- . . . . CLC **30**

Simpson, Harriette
See Arnow, Harriette (Louisa) Simpson

Simpson, Louis (Aston Marantz)
1923- . . . . CLC **4, 7, 9, 32**
See also CA 1-4R; CAAS 4; CANR 1;
DLB 5; MTCW

Simpson, Mona (Elizabeth) 1957-. . . CLC **44**
See also CA 122; 135

Simpson, N(orman) F(rederick)
1919- . . . . CLC **29**
See also CA 13-16R; DLB 13

Sinclair, Andrew (Annandale)
1935- . . . . CLC **2, 14**
See also CA 9-12R; CAAS 5; CANR 14, 38;
DLB 14; MTCW

Sinclair, Emil
See Hesse, Hermann

Sinclair, Iain 1943-. . . . . CLC **76**
See also CA 132

Sinclair, Iain MacGregor
See Sinclair, Iain

Sinclair, Mary Amelia St. Clair 1865(?)-1946
See Sinclair, May
See also CA 104

Sinclair, May. . . . . TCLC **3, 11**
See also Sinclair, Mary Amelia St. Clair
See also DLB 36, 135

Sinclair, Upton (Beall)
1878-1968 . . . . . . CLC **1, 11, 15, 63; DA;
WLC**
See also CA 5-8R; 25-28R; CANR 7;
CDALB 1929-1941; DLB 9; MTCW;
SATA 9

Singer, Isaac
See Singer, Isaac Bashevis

Singer, Isaac Bashevis
1904-1991 . . . . CLC **1, 3, 6, 9, 11, 15, 23,
38, 69; DA; SSC 3; WLC**
See also AITN 1, 2; CA 1-4R; 134;
CANR 1, 39; CDALB 1941-1968; CLR 1;
DLB 6, 28, 52; DLBY 91; JRDA;
MAICYA; MTCW; SATA 3, 27;
SATA-Obit 68

Singer, Israel Joshua 1893-1944 . . . TCLC **33**

Singh, Khushwant 1915-. . . . . CLC **11**
See also CA 9-12R; CAAS 9; CANR 6

Sinjohn, John
See Galsworthy, John

Sinyavsky, Andrei (Donatevich)
1925- . . . . CLC **8**
See also CA 85-88

Sirin, V.
See Nabokov, Vladimir (Vladimirovich)

Sissman, L(ouis) E(dward)
1928-1976 . . . . CLC **9, 18**
See also CA 21-24R; 65-68; CANR 13;
DLB 5

Sisson, C(harles) H(ubert) 1914-. . . . . CLC **8**
See also CA 1-4R; CAAS 3; CANR 3;
DLB 27

Sitwell, Dame Edith
1887-1964 . . . . CLC **2, 9, 67; PC 3**
See also CA 9-12R; CANR 35;
CDBLB 1945-1960; DLB 20; MTCW

Sjoewall, Maj 1935-. . . . . CLC **7**
See also CA 65-68

Sjowall, Maj
See Sjoewall, Maj

Skelton, Robin 1925-. . . . . CLC **13**
See also AITN 2; CA 5-8R; CAAS 5;
CANR 28; DLB 27, 53

Skolimowski, Jerzy 1938-. . . . . CLC **20**
See also CA 128

Skram, Amalie (Bertha)
1847-1905 . . . . TCLC **25**

Skvorecky, Josef (Vaclav)
1924- . . . . CLC **15, 39, 69**
See also CA 61-64; CAAS 1; CANR 10, 34;
MTCW

Slade, Bernard. . . . . CLC **11, 46**
See also Newbound, Bernard Slade
See also CAAS 9; DLB 53

Slaughter, Carolyn 1946-. . . . . CLC **56**
See also CA 85-88

Slaughter, Frank G(ill) 1908- . . . . . . CLC **29**
See also AITN 2; CA 5-8R; CANR 5

Slavitt, David R(ytman) 1935-. . . . CLC **5, 14**
See also CA 21-24R; CAAS 3; CANR 41;
DLB 5, 6

Slesinger, Tess 1905-1945 . . . . TCLC **10**
See also CA 107; DLB 102

Slessor, Kenneth 1901-1971. . . . . . . CLC **14**
See also CA 102; 89-92

Slowacki, Juliusz 1809-1849 . . . . . NCLC **15**

Smart, Christopher 1722-1771. . . . . . . LC **3**
See also DLB 109

Smart, Elizabeth 1913-1986. . . . . . . CLC **54**
See also CA 81-84; 118; DLB 88

Smiley, Jane (Graves) 1949- . . . . CLC **53, 76**
See also CA 104; CANR 30

Smith, A(rthur) J(ames) M(arshall)
1902-1980 . . . . CLC **15**
See also CA 1-4R; 102; CANR 4; DLB 88

Smith, Anna Deavere 1950-. . . . . . . CLC **86**
See also CA 133

Smith, Betty (Wehner) 1896-1972. . . CLC **19**
See also CA 5-8R; 33-36R; DLBY 82;
SATA 6

Smith, Charlotte (Turner)
1749-1806 . . . . NCLC **23**
See also DLB 39, 109

Smith, Clark Ashton 1893-1961 . . . . CLC **43**
See also CA 143

Smith, Dave. . . . . CLC **22, 42**
See also Smith, David (Jeddie)
See also CAAS 7; DLB 5

Smith, David (Jeddie) 1942-
See Smith, Dave
See also CA 49-52; CANR 1

Smith, Florence Margaret 1902-1971
See Smith, Stevie
See also CA 17-18; 29-32R; CANR 35;
CAP 2; MTCW

Smith, Iain Crichton 1928- . . . . CLC **64**
See also CA 21-24R; DLB 40, 139

Smith, John 1580(?)-1631 . . . . LC **9**

Smith, Johnston
See Crane, Stephen (Townley)

Smith, Lee 1944-. . . . . CLC **25, 73**
See also CA 114; 119; CANR 46; DLB 143;
DLBY 83

Smith, Martin
See Smith, Martin Cruz

Smith, Martin Cruz 1942-. . . . . CLC **25**
See also BEST 89:4; CA 85-88; CANR 6,
23, 43; NNAL

Smith, Mary-Ann Tirone 1944-. . . . . CLC **39**
See also CA 118; 136

Smith, Patti 1946- . . . . CLC **12**
See also CA 93-96

Smith, Pauline (Urmson)
1882-1959 . . . . TCLC **25**

Smith, Rosamond
See Oates, Joyce Carol

Smith, Sheila Kaye
See Kaye-Smith, Sheila

Smith, Stevie . . . . CLC **3, 8, 25, 44**
See also Smith, Florence Margaret
See also DLB 20

Smith, Wilbur (Addison) 1933-. . . . . CLC **33**
See also CA 13-16R; CANR 7, 46; MTCW

Smith, William Jay 1918- . . . . CLC **6**
See also CA 5-8R; CANR 44; DLB 5;
MAICYA; SATA 2, 68

Smith, Woodrow Wilson
See Kuttner, Henry

Smolenskin, Peretz 1842-1885 .... **NCLC 30**

Smollett, Tobias (George) 1721-1771 .. **LC 2**
See also CDBLB 1660-1789; DLB 39, 104

Snodgrass, W(illiam) D(e Witt)
1926- .... **CLC 2, 6, 10, 18, 68**
See also CA 1-4R; CANR 6, 36; DLB 5;
MTCW

Snow, C(harles) P(ercy)
1905-1980 ...... **CLC 1, 4, 6, 9, 13, 19**
See also CA 5-8R; 101; CANR 28;
CDBLB 1945-1960; DLB 15, 77; MTCW

Snow, Frances Compton
See Adams, Henry (Brooks)

Snyder, Gary (Sherman)
1930- .... **CLC 1, 2, 5, 9, 32**
See also CA 17-20R; CANR 30; DLB 5, 16

Snyder, Zilpha Keatley 1927- ...... **CLC 17**
See also CA 9-12R; CANR 38; CLR 31;
JRDA; MAICYA; SAAS 2; SATA 1, 28,
75

Soares, Bernardo
See Pessoa, Fernando (Antonio Nogueira)

Sobh, A.
See Shamlu, Ahmad

Sobol, Joshua .... **CLC 60**

Soderberg, Hjalmar 1869-1941 .... **TCLC 39**

Sodergran, Edith (Irene)
See Soedergran, Edith (Irene)

Soedergran, Edith (Irene)
1892-1923 .... **TCLC 31**

Softly, Edgar
See Lovecraft, H(oward) P(hillips)

Softly, Edward
See Lovecraft, H(oward) P(hillips)

Sokolov, Raymond 1941- .... **CLC 7**
See also CA 85-88

Solo, Jay
See Ellison, Harlan (Jay)

Sologub, Fyodor .... **TCLC 9**
See also Teternikov, Fyodor Kuzmich

Solomons, Ikey Esquir
See Thackeray, William Makepeace

Solomos, Dionysios 1798-1857 ... **NCLC 15**

Solwoska, Mara
See French, Marilyn

Solzhenitsyn, Aleksandr I(sayevich)
1918- ...... **CLC 1, 2, 4, 7, 9, 10, 18, 26,
34, 78; DA; WLC**
See also AITN 1; CA 69-72; CANR 40;
MTCW

Somers, Jane
See Lessing, Doris (May)

Somerville, Edith 1858-1949 ...... **TCLC 51**
See also DLB 135

Somerville & Ross
See Martin, Violet Florence; Somerville,
Edith

Sommer, Scott 1951- .... **CLC 25**
See also CA 106

Sondheim, Stephen (Joshua)
1930- .... **CLC 30, 39**
See also AAYA 11; CA 103; CANR 47

Sontag, Susan 1933-... **CLC 1, 2, 10, 13, 31**
See also CA 17-20R; CANR 25; DLB 2, 67;
MTCW

Sophocles
496(?)B.C.-406(?)B.C..... **CMLC 2; DA;
DC 1**

Sorel, Julia
See Drexler, Rosalyn

Sorrentino, Gilbert
1929- .... **CLC 3, 7, 14, 22, 40**
See also CA 77-80; CANR 14, 33; DLB 5;
DLBY 80

Soto, Gary 1952-........ **CLC 32, 80; HLC**
See also AAYA 10; CA 119; 125; DLB 82;
HW; JRDA; SATA 80

Soupault, Philippe 1897-1990 ...... **CLC 68**
See also CA 116; 131

Souster, (Holmes) Raymond
1921- .... **CLC 5, 14**
See also CA 13-16R; CAAS 14; CANR 13,
29; DLB 88; SATA 63

Southern, Terry 1926- .... **CLC 7**
See also CA 1-4R; CANR 1; DLB 2

Southey, Robert 1774-1843 .... **NCLC 8**
See also DLB 93, 107, 142; SATA 54

Southworth, Emma Dorothy Eliza Nevitte
1819-1899 .... **NCLC 26**

Souza, Ernest
See Scott, Evelyn

Soyinka, Wole
1934- .... **CLC 3, 5, 14, 36, 44; BLC;
DA; DC 2; WLC**
See also BW 2; CA 13-16R; CANR 27, 39;
DLB 125; MTCW

Spackman, W(illiam) M(ode)
1905-1990 .... **CLC 46**
See also CA 81-84; 132

Spacks, Barry 1931-............. **CLC 14**
See also CA 29-32R; CANR 33; DLB 105

Spanidou, Irini 1946- .... **CLC 44**

Spark, Muriel (Sarah)
1918-........ **CLC 2, 3, 5, 8, 13, 18, 40;
SSC 10**
See also CA 5-8R; CANR 12, 36;
CDBLB 1945-1960; DLB 15, 139; MTCW

Spaulding, Douglas
See Bradbury, Ray (Douglas)

Spaulding, Leonard
See Bradbury, Ray (Douglas)

Spence, J. A. D.
See Eliot, T(homas) S(tearns)

Spencer, Elizabeth 1921-.......... **CLC 22**
See also CA 13-16R; CANR 32; DLB 6;
MTCW; SATA 14

Spencer, Leonard G.
See Silverberg, Robert

Spencer, Scott 1945-............. **CLC 30**
See also CA 113; DLBY 86

Spender, Stephen (Harold)
1909- .... **CLC 1, 2, 5, 10, 41**
See also CA 9-12R; CANR 31;
CDBLB 1945-1960; DLB 20; MTCW

Spengler, Oswald (Arnold Gottfried)
1880-1936 .... **TCLC 25**
See also CA 118

Spenser, Edmund
1552(?)-1599 .... **LC 5; DA; PC 8; WLC**
See also CDBLB Before 1660

Spicer, Jack 1925-1965 ...... **CLC 8, 18, 72**
See also CA 85-88; DLB 5, 16

Spiegelman, Art 1948- .... **CLC 76**
See also AAYA 10; CA 125; CANR 41

Spielberg, Peter 1929- .... **CLC 6**
See also CA 5-8R; CANR 4; DLBY 81

Spielberg, Steven 1947- .... **CLC 20**
See also AAYA 8; CA 77-80; CANR 32;
SATA 32

Spillane, Frank Morrison 1918-
See Spillane, Mickey
See also CA 25-28R; CANR 28; MTCW;
SATA 66

Spillane, Mickey .... **CLC 3, 13**
See also Spillane, Frank Morrison

Spinoza, Benedictus de 1632-1677 .... **LC 9**

Spinrad, Norman (Richard) 1940-... **CLC 46**
See also CA 37-40R; CAAS 19; CANR 20;
DLB 8

Spitteler, Carl (Friedrich Georg)
1845-1924 .... **TCLC 12**
See also CA 109; DLB 129

Spivack, Kathleen (Romola Drucker)
1938- .... **CLC 6**
See also CA 49-52

Spoto, Donald 1941-.............. **CLC 39**
See also CA 65-68; CANR 11

Springsteen, Bruce (F.) 1949- ...... **CLC 17**
See also CA 111

Spurling, Hilary 1940-............. **CLC 34**
See also CA 104; CANR 25

Spyker, John Howland
See Elman, Richard

Squires, (James) Radcliffe
1917-1993 .... **CLC 51**
See also CA 1-4R; 140; CANR 6, 21

Srivastava, Dhanpat Rai 1880(?)-1936
See Premchand
See also CA 118

Stacy, Donald
See Pohl, Frederik

Stael, Germaine de
See Stael-Holstein, Anne Louise Germaine
Necker Baronn
See also DLB 119

**Stael-Holstein, Anne Louise Germaine Necker
Baronn** 1766-1817 .... **NCLC 3**
See also Stael, Germaine de

Stafford, Jean 1915-1979 ... **CLC 4, 7, 19, 68**
See also CA 1-4R; 85-88; CANR 3; DLB 2;
MTCW; SATA-Obit 22

Stafford, William (Edgar)
1914-1993 .... **CLC 4, 7, 29**
See also CA 5-8R; 142; CAAS 3; CANR 5,
22; DLB 5

Staines, Trevor
See Brunner, John (Kilian Houston)

Stairs, Gordon
See Austin, Mary (Hunter)

Stannard, Martin 1947- . . . . CLC 44
See also CA 142

Stanton, Maura 1946- . . . . CLC 9
See also CA 89-92; CANR 15; DLB 120

Stanton, Schuyler
See Baum, L(yman) Frank

Stapledon, (William) Olaf
1886-1950 . . . . TCLC 22
See also CA 111; DLB 15

Starbuck, George (Edwin) 1931- . . . . CLC 53
See also CA 21-24R; CANR 23

Stark, Richard
See Westlake, Donald E(dwin)

Staunton, Schuyler
See Baum, L(yman) Frank

Stead, Christina (Ellen)
1902-1983 . . . . CLC 2, 5, 8, 32, 80
See also CA 13-16R; 109; CANR 33, 40;
MTCW

Stead, William Thomas
1849-1912 . . . . TCLC 48

Steele, Richard 1672-1729 . . . . LC 18
See also CDBLB 1660-1789; DLB 84, 101

Steele, Timothy (Reid) 1948- . . . . CLC 45
See also CA 93-96; CANR 16; DLB 120

Steffens, (Joseph) Lincoln
1866-1936 . . . . TCLC 20
See also CA 117

Stegner, Wallace (Earle)
1909-1993 . . . . CLC 9, 49, 81
See also AITN 1; BEST 90:3; CA 1-4R;
141; CAAS 9; CANR 1, 21, 46; DLB 9;
DLBY 93; MTCW

Stein, Gertrude
1874-1946 . . . . . . TCLC 1, 6, 28, 48; DA;
WLC
See also CA 104; 132; CDALB 1917-1929;
DLB 4, 54, 86; MTCW

Steinbeck, John (Ernst)
1902-1968 . . . . . . CLC 1, 5, 9, 13, 21, 34,
45, 75; DA; SSC 11; WLC
See also AAYA 12; CA 1-4R; 25-28R;
CANR 1, 35; CDALB 1929-1941; DLB 7,
9; DLBD 2; MTCW; SATA 9

Steinem, Gloria 1934- . . . . CLC 63
See also CA 53-56; CANR 28; MTCW

Steiner, George 1929- . . . . CLC 24
See also CA 73-76; CANR 31; DLB 67;
MTCW; SATA 62

Steiner, K. Leslie
See Delany, Samuel R(ay, Jr.)

Steiner, Rudolf 1861-1925 . . . . TCLC 13
See also CA 107

Stendhal
1783-1842 . . . . . NCLC 23, 46; DA; WLC
See also DLB 119

Stephen, Leslie 1832-1904 . . . . TCLC 23
See also CA 123; DLB 57, 144

Stephen, Sir Leslie
See Stephen, Leslie

Stephen, Virginia
See Woolf, (Adeline) Virginia

Stephens, James 1882(?)-1950 . . . . . TCLC 4
See also CA 104; DLB 19

Stephens, Reed
See Donaldson, Stephen R.

Steptoe, Lydia
See Barnes, Djuna

Sterchi, Beat 1949- . . . . CLC 65

Sterling, Brett
See Bradbury, Ray (Douglas); Hamilton,
Edmond

Sterling, Bruce 1954- . . . . CLC 72
See also CA 119; CANR 44

Sterling, George 1869-1926 . . . . TCLC 20
See also CA 117; DLB 54

Stern, Gerald 1925- . . . . CLC 40
See also CA 81-84; CANR 28; DLB 105

Stern, Richard (Gustave) 1928- . . . CLC 4, 39
See also CA 1-4R; CANR 1, 25; DLBY 87

Sternberg, Josef von 1894-1969 . . . . . CLC 20
See also CA 81-84

Sterne, Laurence
1713-1768 . . . . LC 2; DA; WLC
See also CDBLB 1660-1789; DLB 39

Sternheim, (William Adolf) Carl
1878-1942 . . . . TCLC 8
See also CA 105; DLB 56, 118

Stevens, Mark 1951- . . . . CLC 34
See also CA 122

Stevens, Wallace
1879-1955 . . . . TCLC 3, 12, 45; DA;
PC 6; WLC
See also CA 104; 124; CDALB 1929-1941;
DLB 54; MTCW

Stevenson, Anne (Katharine)
1933- . . . . CLC 7, 33
See also CA 17-20R; CAAS 9; CANR 9, 33;
DLB 40; MTCW

Stevenson, Robert Louis (Balfour)
1850-1894 . . . . NCLC 5, 14; DA;
SSC 11; WLC
See also CDBLB 1890-1914; CLR 10, 11;
DLB 18, 57, 141; JRDA; MAICYA;
YABC 2

Stewart, J(ohn) I(nnes) M(ackintosh)
1906- . . . . CLC 7, 14, 32
See also CA 85-88; CAAS 3; CANR 47;
MTCW

Stewart, Mary (Florence Elinor)
1916- . . . . CLC 7, 35
See also CA 1-4R; CANR 1; SATA 12

Stewart, Mary Rainbow
See Stewart, Mary (Florence Elinor)

Stifle, June
See Campbell, Maria

Stifter, Adalbert 1805-1868 . . . . . . NCLC 41
See also DLB 133

Still, James 1906- . . . . CLC 49
See also CA 65-68; CAAS 17; CANR 10,
26; DLB 9; SATA 29

Sting
See Sumner, Gordon Matthew

Stirling, Arthur
See Sinclair, Upton (Beall)

Stitt, Milan 1941- . . . . CLC 29
See also CA 69-72

Stockton, Francis Richard 1834-1902
See Stockton, Frank R.
See also CA 108; 137; MAICYA; SATA 44

Stockton, Frank R. . . . . TCLC 47
See also Stockton, Francis Richard
See also DLB 42, 74; SATA-Brief 32

Stoddard, Charles
See Kuttner, Henry

Stoker, Abraham 1847-1912
See Stoker, Bram
See also CA 105; DA; SATA 29

Stoker, Bram . . . . TCLC 8; WLC
See also Stoker, Abraham
See also CDBLB 1890-1914; DLB 36, 70

Stolz, Mary (Slattery) 1920- . . . . CLC 12
See also AAYA 8; AITN 1; CA 5-8R;
CANR 13, 41; JRDA; MAICYA;
SAAS 3; SATA 10, 71

Stone, Irving 1903-1989 . . . . CLC 7
See also AITN 1; CA 1-4R; 129; CAAS 3;
CANR 1, 23; MTCW; SATA 3;
SATA-Obit 64

Stone, Oliver 1946- . . . . CLC 73
See also CA 110

Stone, Robert (Anthony)
1937- . . . . CLC 5, 23, 42
See also CA 85-88; CANR 23; MTCW

Stone, Zachary
See Follett, Ken(neth Martin)

Stoppard, Tom
1937- . . . . . . CLC 1, 3, 4, 5, 8, 15, 29, 34,
63; DA; WLC
See also CA 81-84; CANR 39;
CDBLB 1960 to Present; DLB 13;
DLBY 85; MTCW

Storey, David (Malcolm)
1933- . . . . CLC 2, 4, 5, 8
See also CA 81-84; CANR 36; DLB 13, 14;
MTCW

Storm, Hyemeyohsts 1935- . . . . CLC 3
See also CA 81-84; CANR 45; NNAL

Storm, (Hans) Theodor (Woldsen)
1817-1888 . . . . NCLC 1

Storni, Alfonsina
1892-1938 . . . . TCLC 5; HLC
See also CA 104; 131; HW

Stout, Rex (Todhunter) 1886-1975 . . . CLC 3
See also AITN 2; CA 61-64

Stow, (Julian) Randolph 1935- . . CLC 23, 48
See also CA 13-16R; CANR 33; MTCW

Stowe, Harriet (Elizabeth) Beecher
1811-1896 . . . . NCLC 3; DA; WLC
See also CDALB 1865-1917; DLB 1, 12, 42,
74; JRDA; MAICYA; YABC 1

Strachey, (Giles) Lytton
1880-1932 . . . . TCLC 12
See also CA 110; DLBD 10

Strand, Mark 1934- . . . . . . CLC 6, 18, 41, 71
See also CA 21-24R; CANR 40; DLB 5;
SATA 41

Straub, Peter (Francis) 1943- . . . . . . CLC 28
See also BEST 89:1; CA 85-88; CANR 28;
DLBY 84; MTCW

Strauss, Botho 1944- .... **CLC 22**
See also DLB 124

Streatfeild, (Mary) Noel
1895(?)-1986 .... **CLC 21**
See also CA 81-84; 120; CANR 31;
CLR 17; MAICYA; SATA 20;
SATA-Obit 48

Stribling, T(homas) S(igismund)
1881-1965 .... **CLC 23**
See also CA 107; DLB 9

Strindberg, (Johan) August
1849-1912 ...... **TCLC 1, 8, 21, 47; DA;
WLC**
See also CA 104; 135

Stringer, Arthur 1874-1950 .... **TCLC 37**
See also DLB 92

Stringer, David
See Roberts, Keith (John Kingston)

Strugatskii, Arkadii (Natanovich)
1925-1991 .... **CLC 27**
See also CA 106; 135

Strugatskii, Boris (Natanovich)
1933- .... **CLC 27**
See also CA 106

Strummer, Joe 1953(?)- .... **CLC 30**

Stuart, Don A.
See Campbell, John W(ood, Jr.)

Stuart, Ian
See MacLean, Alistair (Stuart)

Stuart, Jesse (Hilton)
1906-1984 .... **CLC 1, 8, 11, 14, 34**
See also CA 5-8R; 112; CANR 31; DLB 9,
48, 102; DLBY 84; SATA 2;
SATA-Obit 36

Sturgeon, Theodore (Hamilton)
1918-1985 .... **CLC 22, 39**
See also Queen, Ellery
See also CA 81-84; 116; CANR 32; DLB 8;
DLBY 85; MTCW

Sturges, Preston 1898-1959 ...... **TCLC 48**
See also CA 114; DLB 26

Styron, William
1925- .... **CLC 1, 3, 5, 11, 15, 60**
See also BEST 90:4; CA 5-8R; CANR 6, 33;
CDALB 1968-1988; DLB 2, 143;
DLBY 80; MTCW

Suarez Lynch, B.
See Bioy Casares, Adolfo; Borges, Jorge
Luis

Su Chien 1884-1918
See Su Man-shu
See also CA 123

Suckow, Ruth 1892-1960
See also CA 113; DLB 9, 102; SSC 18

Sudermann, Hermann 1857-1928 .. **TCLC 15**
See also CA 107; DLB 118

Sue, Eugene 1804-1857 .... **NCLC 1**
See also DLB 119

Sueskind, Patrick 1949- .... **CLC 44**
See also Suskind, Patrick

Sukenick, Ronald 1932- ..... **CLC 3, 4, 6, 48**
See also CA 25-28R; CAAS 8; CANR 32;
DLBY 81

Suknaski, Andrew 1942- .... **CLC 19**
See also CA 101; DLB 53

Sullivan, Vernon
See Vian, Boris

Sully Prudhomme 1839-1907 ...... **TCLC 31**

Su Man-shu .... **TCLC 24**
See also Su Chien

Summerforest, Ivy B.
See Kirkup, James

Summers, Andrew James 1942- ..... **CLC 26**

Summers, Andy
See Summers, Andrew James

Summers, Hollis (Spurgeon, Jr.)
1916- .... **CLC 10**
See also CA 5-8R; CANR 3; DLB 6

Summers, (Alphonsus Joseph-Mary Augustus)
Montague 1880-1948 .... **TCLC 16**
See also CA 118

Sumner, Gordon Matthew 1951- .... **CLC 26**

Surtees, Robert Smith
1803-1864 .... **NCLC 14**
See also DLB 21

Susann, Jacqueline 1921-1974 ...... **CLC 3**
See also AITN 1; CA 65-68; 53-56; MTCW

Suskind, Patrick
See Sueskind, Patrick
See also CA 145

Sutcliff, Rosemary 1920-1992 ...... **CLC 26**
See also AAYA 10; CA 5-8R; 139;
CANR 37; CLR 1; JRDA; MAICYA;
SATA 6, 44, 78; SATA-Obit 73

Sutro, Alfred 1863-1933 .... **TCLC 6**
See also CA 105; DLB 10

Sutton, Henry
See Slavitt, David R(ytman)

Svevo, Italo .... **TCLC 2, 35**
See also Schmitz, Aron Hector

Swados, Elizabeth 1951- .... **CLC 12**
See also CA 97-100

Swados, Harvey 1920-1972 .... **CLC 5**
See also CA 5-8R; 37-40R; CANR 6;
DLB 2

Swan, Gladys 1934- .... **CLC 69**
See also CA 101; CANR 17, 39

Swarthout, Glendon (Fred)
1918-1992 .... **CLC 35**
See also CA 1-4R; 139; CANR 1, 47;
SATA 26

Sweet, Sarah C.
See Jewett, (Theodora) Sarah Orne

Swenson, May
1919-1989 .... **CLC 4, 14, 61; DA**
See also CA 5-8R; 130; CANR 36; DLB 5;
MTCW; SATA 15

Swift, Augustus
See Lovecraft, H(oward) P(hillips)

Swift, Graham (Colin) 1949- .... **CLC 41**
See also CA 117; 122; CANR 46

Swift, Jonathan
1667-1745 ...... **LC 1; DA; PC 9; WLC**
See also CDBLB 1660-1789; DLB 39, 95,
101; SATA 19

Swinburne, Algernon Charles
1837-1909 ...... **TCLC 8, 36; DA; WLC**
See also CA 105; 140; CDBLB 1832-1890;
DLB 35, 57

Swinfen, Ann .... **CLC 34**

Swinnerton, Frank Arthur
1884-1982 .... **CLC 31**
See also CA 108; DLB 34

Swithen, John
See King, Stephen (Edwin)

Sylvia
See Ashton-Warner, Sylvia (Constance)

Symmes, Robert Edward
See Duncan, Robert (Edward)

Symonds, John Addington
1840-1893 .... **NCLC 34**
See also DLB 57, 144

Symons, Arthur 1865-1945 .... **TCLC 11**
See also CA 107; DLB 19, 57

Symons, Julian (Gustave)
1912- .... **CLC 2, 14, 32**
See also CA 49-52; CAAS 3; CANR 3, 33;
DLB 87; DLBY 92; MTCW

Synge, (Edmund) J(ohn) M(illington)
1871-1909 .... **TCLC 6, 37; DC 2**
See also CA 104; 141; CDBLB 1890-1914;
DLB 10, 19

Syruc, J.
See Milosz, Czeslaw

Szirtes, George 1948- .... **CLC 46**
See also CA 109; CANR 27

Tabori, George 1914- .... **CLC 19**
See also CA 49-52; CANR 4

Tagore, Rabindranath
1861-1941 .... **TCLC 3, 53; PC 8**
See also CA 104; 120; MTCW

Taine, Hippolyte Adolphe
1828-1893 .... **NCLC 15**

Talese, Gay 1932- .... **CLC 37**
See also AITN 1; CA 1-4R; CANR 9;
MTCW

Tallent, Elizabeth (Ann) 1954- ..... **CLC 45**
See also CA 117; DLB 130

Tally, Ted 1952- .... **CLC 42**
See also CA 120; 124

Tamayo y Baus, Manuel
1829-1898 .... **NCLC 1**

Tammsaare, A(nton) H(ansen)
1878-1940 .... **TCLC 27**

Tan, Amy 1952- .... **CLC 59**
See also AAYA 9; BEST 89:3; CA 136;
SATA 75

Tandem, Felix
See Spitteler, Carl (Friedrich Georg)

Tanizaki, Jun'ichiro
1886-1965 .... **CLC 8, 14, 28**
See also CA 93-96; 25-28R

Tanner, William
See Amis, Kingsley (William)

Tao Lao
See Storni, Alfonsina

Tarassoff, Lev
See Troyat, Henri

Tarbell, Ida M(inerva)
1857-1944 .... **TCLC 40**
See also CA 122; DLB 47

Tarkington, (Newton) Booth
        1869-1946 .... **TCLC 9**
        See also CA 110; 143; DLB 9, 102;
        SATA 17

Tarkovsky, Andrei (Arsenyevich)
        1932-1986 .... **CLC 75**
        See also CA 127

Tartt, Donna   1964(?)- .... **CLC 76**
        See also CA 142

Tasso, Torquato   1544-1595 .... **LC 5**

Tate, (John Orley) Allen
        1899-1979 .... **CLC 2, 4, 6, 9, 11, 14, 24**
        See also CA 5-8R; 85-88; CANR 32;
        DLB 4, 45, 63; MTCW

Tate, Ellalice
        See Hibbert, Eleanor Alice Burford

Tate, James (Vincent)   1943- ... **CLC 2, 6, 25**
        See also CA 21-24R; CANR 29; DLB 5

Tavel, Ronald   1940- .... **CLC 6**
        See also CA 21-24R; CANR 33

Taylor, C(ecil) P(hilip)   1929-1981... **CLC 27**
        See also CA 25-28R; 105; CANR 47

Taylor, Edward   1642(?)-1729.... **LC 11; DA**
        See also DLB 24

Taylor, Eleanor Ross   1920- .... **CLC 5**
        See also CA 81-84

Taylor, Elizabeth   1912-1975 ... **CLC 2, 4, 29**
        See also CA 13-16R; CANR 9; DLB 139;
        MTCW; SATA 13

Taylor, Henry (Splawn)   1942- ...... **CLC 44**
        See also CA 33-36R; CAAS 7; CANR 31;
        DLB 5

Taylor, Kamala (Purnaiya)   1924-
        See Markandaya, Kamala
        See also CA 77-80

Taylor, Mildred D. .... **CLC 21**
        See also AAYA 10; BW 1; CA 85-88;
        CANR 25; CLR 9; DLB 52; JRDA;
        MAICYA; SAAS 5; SATA 15, 70

Taylor, Peter (Hillsman)
        1917- ...... **CLC 1, 4, 18, 37, 44, 50, 71;
                                                  SSC 10**
        See also CA 13-16R; CANR 9; DLBY 81;
        MTCW

Taylor, Robert Lewis   1912- .... **CLC 14**
        See also CA 1-4R; CANR 3; SATA 10

Tchekhov, Anton
        See Chekhov, Anton (Pavlovich)

Teasdale, Sara   1884-1933......... **TCLC 4**
        See also CA 104; DLB 45; SATA 32

Tegner, Esaias   1782-1846........ **NCLC 2**

Teilhard de Chardin, (Marie Joseph) Pierre
        1881-1955 .... **TCLC 9**
        See also CA 105

Temple, Ann
        See Mortimer, Penelope (Ruth)

Tennant, Emma (Christina)
        1937- .... **CLC 13, 52**
        See also CA 65-68; CAAS 9; CANR 10, 38;
        DLB 14

Tenneshaw, S. M.
        See Silverberg, Robert

Tennyson, Alfred
        1809-1892 .. **NCLC 30; DA; PC 6; WLC**
        See also CDBLB 1832-1890; DLB 32

Teran, Lisa St. Aubin de .... **CLC 36**
        See also St. Aubin de Teran, Lisa

Terence   195(?)B.C.-159B.C...... **CMLC 14**

Teresa de Jesus, St.   1515-1582 ...... **LC 18**

Terkel, Louis   1912-
        See Terkel, Studs
        See also CA 57-60; CANR 18, 45; MTCW

Terkel, Studs .... **CLC 38**
        See also Terkel, Louis
        See also AITN 1

Terry, C. V.
        See Slaughter, Frank G(ill)

Terry, Megan   1932- .... **CLC 19**
        See also CA 77-80; CABS 3; CANR 43;
        DLB 7

Tertz, Abram
        See Sinyavsky, Andrei (Donatevich)

Tesich, Steve   1943(?)-.......... **CLC 40, 69**
        See also CA 105; DLBY 83

Teternikov, Fyodor Kuzmich   1863-1927
        See Sologub, Fyodor
        See also CA 104

Tevis, Walter   1928-1984 .... **CLC 42**
        See also CA 113

Tey, Josephine.................... **TCLC 14**
        See also Mackintosh, Elizabeth
        See also DLB 77

Thackeray, William Makepeace
        1811-1863 .... **NCLC 5, 14, 22, 43; DA;
                                                         WLC**
        See also CDBLB 1832-1890; DLB 21, 55;
        SATA 23

Thakura, Ravindranatha
        See Tagore, Rabindranath

Tharoor, Shashi   1956- .... **CLC 70**
        See also CA 141

Thelwell, Michael Miles   1939- ..... **CLC 22**
        See also BW 2; CA 101

Theobald, Lewis, Jr.
        See Lovecraft, H(oward) P(hillips)

Theodorescu, Ion N.   1880-1967
        See Arghezi, Tudor
        See also CA 116

Theriault, Yves   1915-1983 .... **CLC 79**
        See also CA 102; DLB 88

Theroux, Alexander (Louis)
        1939- .... **CLC 2, 25**
        See also CA 85-88; CANR 20

Theroux, Paul (Edward)
        1941- .... **CLC 5, 8, 11, 15, 28, 46**
        See also BEST 89:4; CA 33-36R; CANR 20,
        45; DLB 2; MTCW; SATA 44

Thesen, Sharon   1946-............. **CLC 56**

Thevenin, Denis
        See Duhamel, Georges

Thibault, Jacques Anatole Francois
        1844-1924
        See France, Anatole
        See also CA 106; 127; MTCW

Thiele, Colin (Milton)   1920- .... **CLC 17**
        See also CA 29-32R; CANR 12, 28;
        CLR 27; MAICYA; SAAS 2; SATA 14,
        72

Thomas, Audrey (Callahan)
        1935- .... **CLC 7, 13, 37**
        See also AITN 2; CA 21-24R; CAAS 19;
        CANR 36; DLB 60; MTCW

Thomas, D(onald) M(ichael)
        1935- .... **CLC 13, 22, 31**
        See also CA 61-64; CAAS 11; CANR 17,
        45; CDBLB 1960 to Present; DLB 40;
        MTCW

Thomas, Dylan (Marlais)
        1914-1953 ... **TCLC 1, 8, 45; DA; PC 2;
                                                  SSC 3; WLC**
        See also CA 104; 120; CDBLB 1945-1960;
        DLB 13, 20, 139; MTCW; SATA 60

Thomas, (Philip) Edward
        1878-1917 .... **TCLC 10**
        See also CA 106; DLB 19

Thomas, Joyce Carol   1938- .... **CLC 35**
        See also AAYA 12; BW 2; CA 113; 116;
        CLR 19; DLB 33; JRDA; MAICYA;
        MTCW; SAAS 7; SATA 40, 78

Thomas, Lewis   1913-1993 .... **CLC 35**
        See also CA 85-88; 143; CANR 38; MTCW

Thomas, Paul
        See Mann, (Paul) Thomas

Thomas, Piri   1928-............... **CLC 17**
        See also CA 73-76; HW

Thomas, R(onald) S(tuart)
        1913- .... **CLC 6, 13, 48**
        See also CA 89-92; CAAS 4; CANR 30;
        CDBLB 1960 to Present; DLB 27;
        MTCW

Thomas, Ross (Elmore)   1926- ...... **CLC 39**
        See also CA 33-36R; CANR 22

Thompson, Francis Clegg
        See Mencken, H(enry) L(ouis)

Thompson, Francis Joseph
        1859-1907 .... **TCLC 4**
        See also CA 104; CDBLB 1890-1914;
        DLB 19

Thompson, Hunter S(tockton)
        1939- .... **CLC 9, 17, 40**
        See also BEST 89:1; CA 17-20R; CANR 23,
        46; MTCW

Thompson, James Myers
        See Thompson, Jim (Myers)

Thompson, Jim (Myers)
        1906-1977(?) .... **CLC 69**
        See also CA 140

Thompson, Judith .... **CLC 39**

Thomson, James   1700-1748 .... **LC 16**

Thomson, James   1834-1882 ...... **NCLC 18**

Thoreau, Henry David
        1817-1862 ...... **NCLC 7, 21; DA; WLC**
        See also CDALB 1640-1865; DLB 1

Thornton, Hall
        See Silverberg, Robert

Thurber, James (Grover)
1894-1961 ... **CLC 5, 11, 25; DA; SSC 1**
See also CA 73-76; CANR 17, 39;
CDALB 1929-1941; DLB 4, 11, 22, 102;
MAICYA; MTCW; SATA 13

Thurman, Wallace (Henry)
1902-1934 .... **TCLC 6; BLC**
See also BW 1; CA 104; 124; DLB 51

Ticheburn, Cheviot
See Ainsworth, William Harrison

Tieck, (Johann) Ludwig
1773-1853 .... **NCLC 5, 46**
See also DLB 90

Tiger, Derry
See Ellison, Harlan (Jay)

Tilghman, Christopher   1948(?)-..... **CLC 65**

Tillinghast, Richard (Williford)
1940- .... **CLC 29**
See also CA 29-32R; CANR 26

Timrod, Henry   1828-1867 .... **NCLC 25**
See also DLB 3

Tindall, Gillian   1938-............. **CLC 7**
See also CA 21-24R; CANR 11

Tiptree, James, Jr. .... **CLC 48, 50**
See also Sheldon, Alice Hastings Bradley
See also DLB 8

Titmarsh, Michael Angelo
See Thackeray, William Makepeace

Tocqueville, Alexis (Charles Henri Maurice
Clerel Comte)   1805-1859..... **NCLC 7**

Tolkien, J(ohn) R(onald) R(euel)
1892-1973 .... **CLC 1, 2, 3, 8, 12, 38;
DA; WLC**
See also AAYA 10; AITN 1; CA 17-18;
45-48; CANR 36; CAP 2;
CDBLB 1914-1945; DLB 15; JRDA;
MAICYA; MTCW; SATA 2, 32;
SATA-Obit 24

Toller, Ernst   1893-1939......... **TCLC 10**
See also CA 107; DLB 124

Tolson, M. B.
See Tolson, Melvin B(eaunorus)

Tolson, Melvin B(eaunorus)
1898(?)-1966 .... **CLC 36; BLC**
See also BW 1; CA 124; 89-92; DLB 48, 76

Tolstoi, Aleksei Nikolaevich
See Tolstoy, Alexey Nikolaevich

Tolstoy, Alexey Nikolaevich
1882-1945 .... **TCLC 18**
See also CA 107

Tolstoy, Count Leo
See Tolstoy, Leo (Nikolaevich)

Tolstoy, Leo (Nikolaevich)
1828-1910 ...... **TCLC 4, 11, 17, 28, 44;
DA; SSC 9; WLC**
See also CA 104; 123; SATA 26

Tomasi di Lampedusa, Giuseppe   1896-1957
See Lampedusa, Giuseppe (Tomasi) di
See also CA 111

Tomlin, Lily................... **CLC 17**
See also Tomlin, Mary Jean

Tomlin, Mary Jean   1939(?)-
See Tomlin, Lily
See also CA 117

Tomlinson, (Alfred) Charles
1927- .... **CLC 2, 4, 6, 13, 45**
See also CA 5-8R; CANR 33; DLB 40

Tonson, Jacob
See Bennett, (Enoch) Arnold

Toole, John Kennedy
1937-1969 .... **CLC 19, 64**
See also CA 104; DLBY 81

Toomer, Jean
1894-1967 ...... **CLC 1, 4, 13, 22; BLC;
PC 7; SSC 1**
See also BW 1; CA 85-88;
CDALB 1917-1929; DLB 45, 51; MTCW

Torley, Luke
See Blish, James (Benjamin)

Tornimparte, Alessandra
See Ginzburg, Natalia

Torre, Raoul della
See Mencken, H(enry) L(ouis)

Torrey, E(dwin) Fuller   1937-....... **CLC 34**
See also CA 119

Torsvan, Ben Traven
See Traven, B.

Torsvan, Benno Traven
See Traven, B.

Torsvan, Berick Traven
See Traven, B.

Torsvan, Berwick Traven
See Traven, B.

Torsvan, Bruno Traven
See Traven, B.

Torsvan, Traven
See Traven, B.

Tournier, Michel (Edouard)
1924- .... **CLC 6, 23, 36**
See also CA 49-52; CANR 3, 36; DLB 83;
MTCW; SATA 23

Tournimparte, Alessandra
See Ginzburg, Natalia

Towers, Ivar
See Kornbluth, C(yril) M.

Towne, Robert (Burton)   1936(?)-.... **CLC 87**
See also CA 108; DLB 44

Townsend, Sue   1946- .... **CLC 61**
See also CA 119; 127; MTCW; SATA 55;
SATA-Brief 48

Townshend, Peter (Dennis Blandford)
1945- .... **CLC 17, 42**
See also CA 107

Tozzi, Federigo   1883-1920....... **TCLC 31**

Traill, Catharine Parr
1802-1899 .... **NCLC 31**
See also DLB 99

Trakl, Georg   1887-1914........... **TCLC 5**
See also CA 104

Transtroemer, Tomas (Goesta)
1931- .... **CLC 52, 65**
See also CA 117; 129; CAAS 17

Transtromer, Tomas Gosta
See Transtroemer, Tomas (Goesta)

Traven, B.   (?)-1969............. **CLC 8, 11**
See also CA 19-20; 25-28R; CAP 2; DLB 9,
56; MTCW

Treitel, Jonathan   1959- .... **CLC 70**

Tremain, Rose   1943-.............. **CLC 42**
See also CA 97-100; CANR 44; DLB 14

Tremblay, Michel   1942-.......... **CLC 29**
See also CA 116; 128; DLB 60; MTCW

Trevanian...................... **CLC 29**
See also Whitaker, Rod(ney)

Trevor, Glen
See Hilton, James

Trevor, William
1928- .... **CLC 7, 9, 14, 25, 71**
See also Cox, William Trevor
See also DLB 14, 139

Trifonov, Yuri (Valentinovich)
1925-1981 .... **CLC 45**
See also CA 126; 103; MTCW

Trilling, Lionel   1905-1975.... **CLC 9, 11, 24**
See also CA 9-12R; 61-64; CANR 10;
DLB 28, 63; MTCW

Trimball, W. H.
See Mencken, H(enry) L(ouis)

Tristan
See Gomez de la Serna, Ramon

Tristram
See Housman, A(lfred) E(dward)

Trogdon, William (Lewis)   1939-
See Heat-Moon, William Least
See also CA 115; 119; CANR 47

Trollope, Anthony
1815-1882 ...... **NCLC 6, 33; DA; WLC**
See also CDBLB 1832-1890; DLB 21, 57;
SATA 22

Trollope, Frances   1779-1863 ..... **NCLC 30**
See also DLB 21

Trotsky, Leon   1879-1940........ **TCLC 22**
See also CA 118

Trotter (Cockburn), Catharine
1679-1749 .... **LC 8**
See also DLB 84

Trout, Kilgore
See Farmer, Philip Jose

Trow, George W. S.   1943-........ **CLC 52**
See also CA 126

Troyat, Henri   1911-.............. **CLC 23**
See also CA 45-48; CANR 2, 33; MTCW

Trudeau, G(arretson) B(eekman)   1948-
See Trudeau, Garry B.
See also CA 81-84; CANR 31; SATA 35

Trudeau, Garry B.................. **CLC 12**
See also Trudeau, G(arretson) B(eekman)
See also AAYA 10; AITN 2

Truffaut, Francois   1932-1984...... **CLC 20**
See also CA 81-84; 113; CANR 34

Trumbo, Dalton   1905-1976 .... **CLC 19**
See also CA 21-24R; 69-72; CANR 10;
DLB 26

Trumbull, John   1750-1831....... **NCLC 30**
See also DLB 31

Trundlett, Helen B.
See Eliot, T(homas) S(tearns)

Tryon, Thomas   1926-1991 .... **CLC 3, 11**
See also AITN 1; CA 29-32R; 135;
CANR 32; MTCW

Tryon, Tom
See Tryon, Thomas

Ts'ao Hsueh-ch'in 1715(?)-1763 . . . . . . **LC 1**

Tsushima, Shuji 1909-1948
  See Dazai, Osamu
  See also CA 107

Tsvetaeva (Efron), Marina (Ivanovna)
  1892-1941 . . . . **TCLC 7, 35**
  See also CA 104; 128; MTCW

Tuck, Lily 1938- . . . . **CLC 70**
  See also CA 139

Tu Fu 712-770 . . . . **PC 9**

Tunis, John R(oberts) 1889-1975 . . . **CLC 12**
  See also CA 61-64; DLB 22; JRDA;
  MAICYA; SATA 37; SATA-Brief 30

Tuohy, Frank . . . . **CLC 37**
  See also Tuohy, John Francis
  See also DLB 14, 139

Tuohy, John Francis 1925-
  See Tuohy, Frank
  See also CA 5-8R; CANR 3, 47

Turco, Lewis (Putnam) 1934- . . . **CLC 11, 63**
  See also CA 13-16R; CANR 24; DLBY 84

Turgenev, Ivan
  1818-1883 . . . . . . **NCLC 21; DA; SSC 7;**
                         WLC

Turgot, Anne-Robert-Jacques
  1727-1781 . . . . **LC 26**

Turner, Frederick 1943- . . . . **CLC 48**
  See also CA 73-76; CAAS 10; CANR 12,
  30; DLB 40

Tutu, Desmond M(pilo)
  1931- . . . . **CLC 80; BLC**
  See also BW 1; CA 125

Tutuola, Amos 1920- . . . **CLC 5, 14, 29; BLC**
  See also BW 2; CA 9-12R; CANR 27;
  DLB 125; MTCW

Twain, Mark
  . . . **TCLC 6, 12, 19, 36, 48; SSC 6; WLC**
  See also Clemens, Samuel Langhorne
  See also DLB 11, 12, 23, 64, 74

Tyler, Anne
  1941- . . . . **CLC 7, 11, 18, 28, 44, 59**
  See also BEST 89:1; CA 9-12R; CANR 11,
  33; DLB 6, 143; DLBY 82; MTCW;
  SATA 7

Tyler, Royall 1757-1826 . . . . **NCLC 3**
  See also DLB 37

Tynan, Katharine 1861-1931 . . . . **TCLC 3**
  See also CA 104

Tyutchev, Fyodor 1803-1873 . . . . . **NCLC 34**

Tzara, Tristan . . . . **CLC 47**
  See also Rosenfeld, Samuel

Uhry, Alfred 1936- . . . . **CLC 55**
  See also CA 127; 133

Ulf, Haerved
  See Strindberg, (Johan) August

Ulf, Harved
  See Strindberg, (Johan) August

Ulibarri, Sabine R(eyes) 1919- . . . . . **CLC 83**
  See also CA 131; DLB 82; HW

Unamuno (y Jugo), Miguel de
  1864-1936 . . . . **TCLC 2, 9; HLC; SSC 11**
  See also CA 104; 131; DLB 108; HW;
  MTCW

Undercliffe, Errol
  See Campbell, (John) Ramsey

Underwood, Miles
  See Glassco, John

Undset, Sigrid
  1882-1949 . . . . **TCLC 3; DA; WLC**
  See also CA 104; 129; MTCW

Ungaretti, Giuseppe
  1888-1970 . . . . **CLC 7, 11, 15**
  See also CA 19-20; 25-28R; CAP 2;
  DLB 114

Unger, Douglas 1952- . . . . **CLC 34**
  See also CA 130

Unsworth, Barry (Forster) 1930- . . . . **CLC 76**
  See also CA 25-28R; CANR 30

Updike, John (Hoyer)
  1932- . . . . . **CLC 1, 2, 3, 5, 7, 9, 13, 15,**
         23, 34, 43, 70; DA; SSC 13; WLC
  See also CA 1-4R; CABS 1; CANR 4, 33;
  CDALB 1968-1988; DLB 2, 5, 143;
  DLBD 3; DLBY 80, 82; MTCW

Upshaw, Margaret Mitchell
  See Mitchell, Margaret (Munnerlyn)

Upton, Mark
  See Sanders, Lawrence

Urdang, Constance (Henriette)
  1922- . . . . **CLC 47**
  See also CA 21-24R; CANR 9, 24

Uriel, Henry
  See Faust, Frederick (Schiller)

Uris, Leon (Marcus) 1924- . . . . **CLC 7, 32**
  See also AITN 1, 2; BEST 89:2; CA 1-4R;
  CANR 1, 40; MTCW; SATA 49

Urmuz
  See Codrescu, Andrei

Ustinov, Peter (Alexander) 1921- . . . . **CLC 1**
  See also AITN 1; CA 13-16R; CANR 25;
  DLB 13

Vaculik, Ludvik 1926- . . . . **CLC 7**
  See also CA 53-56

Valdez, Luis (Miguel)
  1940- . . . . **CLC 84; HLC**
  See also CA 101; CANR 32; DLB 122; HW

Valenzuela, Luisa 1938- . . . **CLC 31; SSC 14**
  See also CA 101; CANR 32; DLB 113; HW

Valera y Alcala-Galiano, Juan
  1824-1905 . . . . **TCLC 10**
  See also CA 106

Valery, (Ambroise) Paul (Toussaint Jules)
  1871-1945 . . . . **TCLC 4, 15; PC 9**
  See also CA 104; 122; MTCW

Valle-Inclan, Ramon (Maria) del
  1866-1936 . . . . **TCLC 5; HLC**
  See also CA 106; DLB 134

Vallejo, Antonio Buero
  See Buero Vallejo, Antonio

Vallejo, Cesar (Abraham)
  1892-1938 . . . . **TCLC 3, 56; HLC**
  See also CA 105; HW

Valle Y Pena, Ramon del
  See Valle-Inclan, Ramon (Maria) del

Van Ash, Cay 1918- . . . . **CLC 34**

Vanbrugh, Sir John 1664-1726 . . . . . . **LC 21**
  See also DLB 80

Van Campen, Karl
  See Campbell, John W(ood, Jr.)

Vance, Gerald
  See Silverberg, Robert

Vance, Jack . . . . **CLC 35**
  See also Vance, John Holbrook
  See also DLB 8

Vance, John Holbrook 1916-
  See Queen, Ellery; Vance, Jack
  See also CA 29-32R; CANR 17; MTCW

Van Den Bogarde, Derek Jules Gaspard Ulric
  Niven 1921-
  See Bogarde, Dirk
  See also CA 77-80

Vandenburgh, Jane . . . . **CLC 59**

Vanderhaeghe, Guy 1951- . . . . **CLC 41**
  See also CA 113

van der Post, Laurens (Jan) 1906- . . . **CLC 5**
  See also CA 5-8R; CANR 35

van de Wetering, Janwillem 1931- . . **CLC 47**
  See also CA 49-52; CANR 4

Van Dine, S. S. . . . . **TCLC 23**
  See also Wright, Willard Huntington

Van Doren, Carl (Clinton)
  1885-1950 . . . . **TCLC 18**
  See also CA 111

Van Doren, Mark 1894-1972 . . . . . **CLC 6, 10**
  See also CA 1-4R; 37-40R; CANR 3;
  DLB 45; MTCW

Van Druten, John (William)
  1901-1957 . . . . **TCLC 2**
  See also CA 104; DLB 10

Van Duyn, Mona (Jane)
  1921- . . . . **CLC 3, 7, 63**
  See also CA 9-12R; CANR 7, 38; DLB 5

Van Dyne, Edith
  See Baum, L(yman) Frank

van Itallie, Jean-Claude 1936- . . . . **CLC 3**
  See also CA 45-48; CAAS 2; CANR 1;
  DLB 7

van Ostaijen, Paul 1896-1928 . . . . . **TCLC 33**

Van Peebles, Melvin 1932- . . . . . . **CLC 2, 20**
  See also BW 2; CA 85-88; CANR 27

Vansittart, Peter 1920- . . . . **CLC 42**
  See also CA 1-4R; CANR 3

Van Vechten, Carl 1880-1964 . . . . . . **CLC 33**
  See also CA 89-92; DLB 4, 9, 51

Van Vogt, A(lfred) E(lton) 1912- . . . . . **CLC 1**
  See also CA 21-24R; CANR 28; DLB 8;
  SATA 14

Varda, Agnes 1928- . . . . **CLC 16**
  See also CA 116; 122

Vargas Llosa, (Jorge) Mario (Pedro)
  1936- . . . . **CLC 3, 6, 9, 10, 15, 31, 42, 85;**
                         DA; HLC
  See also CA 73-76; CANR 18, 32, 42;
  DLB 145; HW; MTCW

Vasiliu, Gheorghe 1881-1957
  See Bacovia, George
  See also CA 123

Vassa, Gustavus
  See Equiano, Olaudah

Vassilikos, Vassilis 1933- . . . . **CLC 4, 8**
  See also CA 81-84

Vaughan, Henry 1621-1695......... **LC 27**
See also DLB 131

Vaughn, Stephanie................ **CLC 62**

Vazov, Ivan (Minchov)
1850-1921 .... **TCLC 25**
See also CA 121; DLB 147

Veblen, Thorstein (Bunde)
1857-1929 .... **TCLC 31**
See also CA 115

Vega, Lope de 1562-1635.......... **LC 23**

Venison, Alfred
See Pound, Ezra (Weston Loomis)

Verdi, Marie de
See Mencken, H(enry) L(ouis)

Verdu, Matilde
See Cela, Camilo Jose

Verga, Giovanni (Carmelo)
1840-1922 .... **TCLC 3**
See also CA 104; 123

Vergil 70B.C.-19B.C. .... **CMLC 9; DA**

Verhaeren, Emile (Adolphe Gustave)
1855-1916 .... **TCLC 12**
See also CA 109

Verlaine, Paul (Marie)
1844-1896 .... **NCLC 2; PC 2**

Verne, Jules (Gabriel)
1828-1905 .... **TCLC 6, 52**
See also CA 110; 131; DLB 123; JRDA;
MAICYA; SATA 21

Very, Jones 1813-1880.......... **NCLC 9**
See also DLB 1

Vesaas, Tarjei 1897-1970......... **CLC 48**
See also CA 29-32R

Vialis, Gaston
See Simenon, Georges (Jacques Christian)

Vian, Boris 1920-1959 .... **TCLC 9**
See also CA 106; DLB 72

Viaud, (Louis Marie) Julien 1850-1923
See Loti, Pierre
See also CA 107

Vicar, Henry
See Felsen, Henry Gregor

Vicker, Angus
See Felsen, Henry Gregor

Vidal, Gore
1925- ..... **CLC 2, 4, 6, 8, 10, 22, 33, 72**
See also AITN 1; BEST 90:2; CA 5-8R;
CANR 13, 45; DLB 6; MTCW

Viereck, Peter (Robert Edwin)
1916- .... **CLC 4**
See also CA 1-4R; CANR 1, 47; DLB 5

Vigny, Alfred (Victor) de
1797-1863 .... **NCLC 7**
See also DLB 119

Vilakazi, Benedict Wallet
1906-1947 .... **TCLC 37**

Villiers de l'Isle Adam, Jean Marie Mathias
Philippe Auguste Comte
1838-1889 .... **NCLC 3; SSC 14**
See also DLB 123

Vinci, Leonardo da 1452-1519....... **LC 12**

Vine, Barbara .... **CLC 50**
See also Rendell, Ruth (Barbara)
See also BEST 90:4

Vinge, Joan D(ennison) 1948-...... **CLC 30**
See also CA 93-96; SATA 36

Violis, G.
See Simenon, Georges (Jacques Christian)

Visconti, Luchino 1906-1976...... **CLC 16**
See also CA 81-84; 65-68; CANR 39

Vittorini, Elio 1908-1966..... **CLC 6, 9, 14**
See also CA 133; 25-28R

Vizinczey, Stephen 1933-......... **CLC 40**
See also CA 128

Vliet, R(ussell) G(ordon)
1929-1984 .... **CLC 22**
See also CA 37-40R; 112; CANR 18

Vogau, Boris Andreyevich 1894-1937(?)
See Pilnyak, Boris
See also CA 123

Vogel, Paula A(nne) 1951-........ **CLC 76**
See also CA 108

Voight, Ellen Bryant 1943-........ **CLC 54**
See also CA 69-72; CANR 11, 29; DLB 120

Voigt, Cynthia 1942-............ **CLC 30**
See also AAYA 3; CA 106; CANR 18, 37,
40; CLR 13; JRDA; MAICYA;
SATA 48, 79; SATA-Brief 33

Voinovich, Vladimir (Nikolaevich)
1932-................... **CLC 10, 49**
See also CA 81-84; CAAS 12; CANR 33;
MTCW

Voloshinov, V. N.
See Bakhtin, Mikhail Mikhailovich

Voltaire
1694-1778 ... **LC 14; DA; SSC 12; WLC**

von Daeniken, Erich 1935- .... **CLC 30**
See also AITN 1; CA 37-40R; CANR 17,
44

von Daniken, Erich
See von Daeniken, Erich

von Heidenstam, (Carl Gustaf) Verner
See Heidenstam, (Carl Gustaf) Verner von

von Heyse, Paul (Johann Ludwig)
See Heyse, Paul (Johann Ludwig von)

von Hofmannsthal, Hugo
See Hofmannsthal, Hugo von

von Horvath, Odon
See Horvath, Oedoen von

von Horvath, Oedoen
See Horvath, Oedoen von

von Liliencron, (Friedrich Adolf Axel) Detlev
See Liliencron, (Friedrich Adolf Axel)
Detlev von

Vonnegut, Kurt, Jr.
1922- ...... **CLC 1, 2, 3, 4, 5, 8, 12, 22,
40, 60; DA; SSC 8; WLC**
See also AAYA 6; AITN 1; BEST 90:4;
CA 1-4R; CANR 1, 25;
CDALB 1968-1988; DLB 2, 8; DLBD 3;
DLBY 80; MTCW

Von Rachen, Kurt
See Hubbard, L(afayette) Ron(ald)

von Rezzori (d'Arezzo), Gregor
See Rezzori (d'Arezzo), Gregor von

von Sternberg, Josef
See Sternberg, Josef von

Vorster, Gordon 1924-............ **CLC 34**
See also CA 133

Vosce, Trudie
See Ozick, Cynthia

Voznesensky, Andrei (Andreievich)
1933-................. **CLC 1, 15, 57**
See also CA 89-92; CANR 37; MTCW

Waddington, Miriam 1917-........ **CLC 28**
See also CA 21-24R; CANR 12, 30;
DLB 68

Wagman, Fredrica 1937-........... **CLC 7**
See also CA 97-100

Wagner, Richard 1813-1883...... **NCLC 9**
See also DLB 129

Wagner-Martin, Linda 1936-....... **CLC 50**

Wagoner, David (Russell)
1926-................... **CLC 3, 5, 15**
See also CA 1-4R; CAAS 3; CANR 2;
DLB 5; SATA 14

Wah, Fred(erick James) 1939-...... **CLC 44**
See also CA 107; 141; DLB 60

Wahloo, Per 1926-1975 .... **CLC 7**
See also CA 61-64

Wahloo, Peter
See Wahloo, Per

Wain, John (Barrington)
1925-1994 .... **CLC 2, 11, 15, 46**
See also CA 5-8R; 145; CAAS 4; CANR 23;
CDBLB 1960 to Present; DLB 15, 27,
139; MTCW

Wajda, Andrzej 1926-............. **CLC 16**
See also CA 102

Wakefield, Dan 1932-............. **CLC 7**
See also CA 21-24R; CAAS 7

Wakoski, Diane
1937-....... **CLC 2, 4, 7, 9, 11, 40**
See also CA 13-16R; CAAS 1; CANR 9;
DLB 5

Wakoski-Sherbell, Diane
See Wakoski, Diane

Walcott, Derek (Alton)
1930- .... **CLC 2, 4, 9, 14, 25, 42, 67, 76;
BLC**
See also BW 2; CA 89-92; CANR 26, 47;
DLB 117; DLBY 81; MTCW

Waldman, Anne 1945-............. **CLC 7**
See also CA 37-40R; CAAS 17; CANR 34;
DLB 16

Waldo, E. Hunter
See Sturgeon, Theodore (Hamilton)

Waldo, Edward Hamilton
See Sturgeon, Theodore (Hamilton)

Walker, Alice (Malsenior)
1944-....... **CLC 5, 6, 9, 19, 27, 46, 58;
BLC; DA; SSC 5**
See also AAYA 3; BEST 89:4; BW 2;
CA 37-40R; CANR 9, 27;
CDALB 1968-1988; DLB 6, 33, 143;
MTCW; SATA 31

Walker, David Harry 1911-1992.... **CLC 14**
See also CA 1-4R; 137; CANR 1; SATA 8;
SATA-Obit 71

Walker, Edward Joseph 1934-
See Walker, Ted
See also CA 21-24R; CANR 12, 28

Walker, George F. 1947- . . . . **CLC 44, 61**
See also CA 103; CANR 21, 43; DLB 60

Walker, Joseph A. 1935- . . . . **CLC 19**
See also BW 1; CA 89-92; CANR 26;
DLB 38

Walker, Margaret (Abigail)
1915- . . . . **CLC 1, 6; BLC**
See also BW 2; CA 73-76; CANR 26;
DLB 76; MTCW

Walker, Ted. . . . . **CLC 13**
See also Walker, Edward Joseph
See also DLB 40

Wallace, David Foster 1962- . . . . **CLC 50**
See also CA 132

Wallace, Dexter
See Masters, Edgar Lee

Wallace, (Richard Horatio) Edgar
1875-1932 . . . . **TCLC 57**
See also CA 115; DLB 70

Wallace, Irving 1916-1990 . . . . . . **CLC 7, 13**
See also AITN 1; CA 1-4R; 132; CAAS 1;
CANR 1, 27; MTCW

Wallant, Edward Lewis
1926-1962 . . . . **CLC 5, 10**
See also CA 1-4R; CANR 22; DLB 2, 28,
143; MTCW

Walpole, Horace 1717-1797. . . . . **LC 2**
See also DLB 39, 104

Walpole, Hugh (Seymour)
1884-1941 . . . . **TCLC 5**
See also CA 104; DLB 34

Walser, Martin 1927- . . . . **CLC 27**
See also CA 57-60; CANR 8, 46; DLB 75,
124

Walser, Robert 1878-1956 . . . . **TCLC 18**
See also CA 118; DLB 66

Walsh, Jill Paton. . . . . **CLC 35**
See also Paton Walsh, Gillian
See also AAYA 11; CLR 2; SAAS 3

Walter, Villiam Christian
See Andersen, Hans Christian

Wambaugh, Joseph (Aloysius, Jr.)
1937- . . . . **CLC 3, 18**
See also AITN 1; BEST 89:3; CA 33-36R;
CANR 42; DLB 6; DLBY 83; MTCW

Ward, Arthur Henry Sarsfield 1883-1959
See Rohmer, Sax
See also CA 108

Ward, Douglas Turner 1930- . . . . **CLC 19**
See also BW 1; CA 81-84; CANR 27;
DLB 7, 38

Ward, Mary Augusta
See Ward, Mrs. Humphry

Ward, Mrs. Humphry
1851-1920 . . . . **TCLC 55**
See also DLB 18

Ward, Peter
See Faust, Frederick (Schiller)

Warhol, Andy 1928(?)-1987 . . . . **CLC 20**
See also AAYA 12; BEST 89:4; CA 89-92;
121; CANR 34

Warner, Francis (Robert le Plastrier)
1937- . . . . **CLC 14**
See also CA 53-56; CANR 11

Warner, Marina 1946- . . . . **CLC 59**
See also CA 65-68; CANR 21

Warner, Rex (Ernest) 1905-1986. . . . **CLC 45**
See also CA 89-92; 119; DLB 15

Warner, Susan (Bogert)
1819-1885 . . . . **NCLC 31**
See also DLB 3, 42

Warner, Sylvia (Constance) Ashton
See Ashton-Warner, Sylvia (Constance)

Warner, Sylvia Townsend
1893-1978 . . . . **CLC 7, 19**
See also CA 61-64; 77-80; CANR 16;
DLB 34, 139; MTCW

Warren, Mercy Otis 1728-1814. . . **NCLC 13**
See also DLB 31

Warren, Robert Penn
1905-1989 . . . . **CLC 1, 4, 6, 8, 10, 13, 18,
39, 53, 59; DA; SSC 4; WLC**
See also AITN 1; CA 13-16R;
CANR 10, 47; CDALB 1968-1988;
DLB 2, 48; DLBY 80, 89; MTCW;
SATA 46; SATA-Obit 63

Warshofsky, Isaac
See Singer, Isaac Bashevis

Warton, Thomas 1728-1790. . . . . **LC 15**
See also DLB 104, 109

Waruk, Kona
See Harris, (Theodore) Wilson

Warung, Price 1855-1911. . . . . **TCLC 45**

Warwick, Jarvis
See Garner, Hugh

Washington, Alex
See Harris, Mark

Washington, Booker T(aliaferro)
1856-1915 . . . . **TCLC 10; BLC**
See also BW 1; CA 114; 125; SATA 28

Washington, George 1732-1799. . . . . **LC 25**
See also DLB 31

Wassermann, (Karl) Jakob
1873-1934 . . . . **TCLC 6**
See also CA 104; DLB 66

Wasserstein, Wendy
1950- . . . . **CLC 32, 59; DC 4**
See also CA 121; 129; CABS 3

Waterhouse, Keith (Spencer)
1929- . . . . **CLC 47**
See also CA 5-8R; CANR 38; DLB 13, 15;
MTCW

Waters, Roger 1944- . . . . **CLC 35**

Watkins, Frances Ellen
See Harper, Frances Ellen Watkins

Watkins, Gerrold
See Malzberg, Barry N(athaniel)

Watkins, Paul 1964- . . . . **CLC 55**
See also CA 132

Watkins, Vernon Phillips
1906-1967 . . . . **CLC 43**
See also CA 9-10; 25-28R; CAP 1; DLB 20

Watson, Irving S.
See Mencken, H(enry) L(ouis)

Watson, John H.
See Farmer, Philip Jose

Watson, Richard F.
See Silverberg, Robert

Waugh, Auberon (Alexander) 1939- . . **CLC 7**
See also CA 45-48; CANR 6, 22; DLB 14

Waugh, Evelyn (Arthur St. John)
1903-1966 . . . . . . **CLC 1, 3, 8, 13, 19, 27,
44; DA; WLC**
See also CA 85-88; 25-28R; CANR 22;
CDBLB 1914-1945; DLB 15; MTCW

Waugh, Harriet 1944- . . . . **CLC 6**
See also CA 85-88; CANR 22

Ways, C. R.
See Blount, Roy (Alton), Jr.

Waystaff, Simon
See Swift, Jonathan

Webb, (Martha) Beatrice (Potter)
1858-1943 . . . . **TCLC 22**
See also Potter, Beatrice
See also CA 117

Webb, Charles (Richard) 1939- . . . . . . **CLC 7**
See also CA 25-28R

Webb, James H(enry), Jr. 1946- . . . . **CLC 22**
See also CA 81-84

Webb, Mary (Gladys Meredith)
1881-1927 . . . . **TCLC 24**
See also CA 123; DLB 34

Webb, Mrs. Sidney
See Webb, (Martha) Beatrice (Potter)

Webb, Phyllis 1927- . . . . **CLC 18**
See also CA 104; CANR 23; DLB 53

Webb, Sidney (James)
1859-1947 . . . . **TCLC 22**
See also CA 117

Webber, Andrew Lloyd. . . . . **CLC 21**
See also Lloyd Webber, Andrew

Weber, Lenora Mattingly
1895-1971 . . . . **CLC 12**
See also CA 19-20; 29-32R; CAP 1;
SATA 2; SATA-Obit 26

Webster, John 1579(?)-1634(?) . . . . **DC 2**
See also CDBLB Before 1660; DA; DLB 58;
WLC

Webster, Noah 1758-1843 . . . . **NCLC 30**

Wedekind, (Benjamin) Frank(lin)
1864-1918 . . . . **TCLC 7**
See also CA 104; DLB 118

Weidman, Jerome 1913- . . . . **CLC 7**
See also AITN 2; CA 1-4R; CANR 1;
DLB 28

Weil, Simone (Adolphine)
1909-1943 . . . . **TCLC 23**
See also CA 117

Weinstein, Nathan
See West, Nathanael

Weinstein, Nathan von Wallenstein
See West, Nathanael

Weir, Peter (Lindsay) 1944- . . . . **CLC 20**
See also CA 113; 123

Weiss, Peter (Ulrich)
1916-1982 . . . . **CLC 3, 15, 51**
See also CA 45-48; 106; CANR 3; DLB 69,
124

Weiss, Theodore (Russell)
1916- . . . . **CLC 3, 8, 14**
See also CA 9-12R; CAAS 2; CANR 46;
DLB 5

Welch, (Maurice) Denton
  1915-1948 .... **TCLC 22**
  See also CA 121

Welch, James 1940- .... **CLC 6, 14, 52**
  See also CA 85-88; CANR 42; NNAL

Weldon, Fay
  1933- .... **CLC 6, 9, 11, 19, 36, 59**
  See also CA 21-24R; CANR 16, 46;
  CDBLB 1960 to Present; DLB 14;
  MTCW

Wellek, Rene 1903- .... **CLC 28**
  See also CA 5-8R; CAAS 7; CANR 8;
  DLB 63

Weller, Michael 1942- .... **CLC 10, 53**
  See also CA 85-88

Weller, Paul 1958- .... **CLC 26**

Wellershoff, Dieter 1925-.......... **CLC 46**
  See also CA 89-92; CANR 16, 37

Welles, (George) Orson
  1915-1985 .... **CLC 20, 80**
  See also CA 93-96; 117

Wellman, Mac 1945- .... **CLC 65**

Wellman, Manly Wade 1903-1986 .. **CLC 49**
  See also CA 1-4R; 118; CANR 6, 16, 44;
  SATA 6; SATA-Obit 47

Wells, Carolyn 1869(?)-1942 ...... **TCLC 35**
  See also CA 113; DLB 11

Wells, H(erbert) G(eorge)
  1866-1946 .... **TCLC 6, 12, 19; DA;**
                              SSC 6; WLC
  See also CA 110; 121; CDBLB 1914-1945;
  DLB 34, 70; MTCW; SATA 20

Wells, Rosemary 1943-............ **CLC 12**
  See also AAYA 13; CA 85-88; CLR 16;
  MAICYA; SAAS 1; SATA 18, 69

Welty, Eudora
  1909- ...... **CLC 1, 2, 5, 14, 22, 33; DA;**
                                SSC 1; WLC
  See also CA 9-12R; CABS 1; CANR 32;
  CDALB 1941-1968; DLB 2, 102, 143;
  DLBD 12; DLBY 87; MTCW

Wen I-to 1899-1946 .... **TCLC 28**

Wentworth, Robert
  See Hamilton, Edmond

Werfel, Franz (V.) 1890-1945 ...... **TCLC 8**
  See also CA 104; DLB 81, 124

Wergeland, Henrik Arnold
  1808-1845 .... **NCLC 5**

Wersba, Barbara 1932-............ **CLC 30**
  See also AAYA 2; CA 29-32R; CANR 16,
  38; CLR 3; DLB 52; JRDA; MAICYA;
  SAAS 2; SATA 1, 58

Wertmueller, Lina 1928- .... **CLC 16**
  See also CA 97-100; CANR 39

Wescott, Glenway 1901-1987....... **CLC 13**
  See also CA 13-16R; 121; CANR 23;
  DLB 4, 9, 102

Wesker, Arnold 1932- .... **CLC 3, 5, 42**
  See also CA 1-4R; CAAS 7; CANR 1, 33;
  CDBLB 1960 to Present; DLB 13;
  MTCW

Wesley, Richard (Errol) 1945-....... **CLC 7**
  See also BW 1; CA 57-60; CANR 27;
  DLB 38

Wessel, Johan Herman 1742-1785 .... **LC 7**

West, Anthony (Panther)
  1914-1987 .... **CLC 50**
  See also CA 45-48; 124; CANR 3, 19;
  DLB 15

West, C. P.
  See Wodehouse, P(elham) G(renville)

West, (Mary) Jessamyn
  1902-1984 .... **CLC 7, 17**
  See also CA 9-12R; 112; CANR 27; DLB 6;
  DLBY 84; MTCW; SATA-Obit 37

West, Morris L(anglo) 1916-..... **CLC 6, 33**
  See also CA 5-8R; CANR 24; MTCW

West, Nathanael
  1903-1940 ...... **TCLC 1, 14, 44; SSC 16**
  See also CA 104; 125; CDALB 1929-1941;
  DLB 4, 9, 28; MTCW

West, Owen
  See Koontz, Dean R(ay)

West, Paul 1930- .... **CLC 7, 14**
  See also CA 13-16R; CAAS 7; CANR 22;
  DLB 14

West, Rebecca 1892-1983 .. **CLC 7, 9, 31, 50**
  See also CA 5-8R; 109; CANR 19; DLB 36;
  DLBY 83; MTCW

Westall, Robert (Atkinson)
  1929-1993 .... **CLC 17**
  See also AAYA 12; CA 69-72; 141;
  CANR 18; CLR 13; JRDA; MAICYA;
  SAAS 2; SATA 23, 69; SATA-Obit 75

Westlake, Donald E(dwin)
  1933-..................... **CLC 7, 33**
  See also CA 17-20R; CAAS 13; CANR 16,
  44

Westmacott, Mary
  See Christie, Agatha (Mary Clarissa)

Weston, Allen
  See Norton, Andre

Wetcheek, J. L.
  See Feuchtwanger, Lion

Wetering, Janwillem van de
  See van de Wetering, Janwillem

Wetherell, Elizabeth
  See Warner, Susan (Bogert)

Whalen, Philip 1923-........... **CLC 6, 29**
  See also CA 9-12R; CANR 5, 39; DLB 16

Wharton, Edith (Newbold Jones)
  1862-1937 ...... **TCLC 3, 9, 27, 53; DA;**
                              SSC 6; WLC
  See also CA 104; 132; CDALB 1865-1917;
  DLB 4, 9, 12, 78; MTCW

Wharton, James
  See Mencken, H(enry) L(ouis)

Wharton, William (a pseudonym)
  .... **CLC 18, 37**
  See also CA 93-96; DLBY 80

Wheatley (Peters), Phillis
  1754(?)-1784 .... **LC 3; BLC; DA; PC 3;**
                                    WLC
  See also CDALB 1640-1865; DLB 31, 50

Wheelock, John Hall 1886-1978 .... **CLC 14**
  See also CA 13-16R; 77-80; CANR 14;
  DLB 45

White, E(lwyn) B(rooks)
  1899-1985 .... **CLC 10, 34, 39**
  See also AITN 2; CA 13-16R; 116;
  CANR 16, 37; CLR 1, 21; DLB 11, 22;
  MAICYA; MTCW; SATA 2, 29;
  SATA-Obit 44

White, Edmund (Valentine III)
  1940- .... **CLC 27**
  See also AAYA 7; CA 45-48; CANR 3, 19,
  36; MTCW

White, Patrick (Victor Martindale)
  1912-1990 .. **CLC 3, 4, 5, 7, 9, 18, 65, 69**
  See also CA 81-84; 132; CANR 43; MTCW

White, Phyllis Dorothy James 1920-
  See James, P. D.
  See also CA 21-24R; CANR 17, 43; MTCW

White, T(erence) H(anbury)
  1906-1964 .... **CLC 30**
  See also CA 73-76; CANR 37; JRDA;
  MAICYA; SATA 12

White, Terence de Vere
  1912-1994 .... **CLC 49**
  See also CA 49-52; 145; CANR 3

White, Walter F(rancis)
  1893-1955 .... **TCLC 15**
  See also White, Walter
  See also BW 1; CA 115; 124; DLB 51

White, William Hale 1831-1913
  See Rutherford, Mark
  See also CA 121

Whitehead, E(dward) A(nthony)
  1933-...................... **CLC 5**
  See also CA 65-68

Whitemore, Hugh (John) 1936-..... **CLC 37**
  See also CA 132

Whitman, Sarah Helen (Power)
  1803-1878 .... **NCLC 19**
  See also DLB 1

Whitman, Walt(er)
  1819-1892 ..... **NCLC 4, 31; DA; PC 3;**
                                    WLC
  See also CDALB 1640-1865; DLB 3, 64;
  SATA 20

Whitney, Phyllis A(yame) 1903-.... **CLC 42**
  See also AITN 2; BEST 90:3; CA 1-4R;
  CANR 3, 25, 38; JRDA; MAICYA;
  SATA 1, 30

Whittemore, (Edward) Reed (Jr.)
  1919-...................... **CLC 4**
  See also CA 9-12R; CAAS 8; CANR 4;
  DLB 5

Whittier, John Greenleaf
  1807-1892 .... **NCLC 8**
  See also CDALB 1640-1865; DLB 1

Whittlebot, Hernia
  See Coward, Noel (Peirce)

Wicker, Thomas Grey 1926-
  See Wicker, Tom
  See also CA 65-68; CANR 21, 46

Wicker, Tom .... **CLC 7**
  See also Wicker, Thomas Grey

Wideman, John Edgar
  1941-......... **CLC 5, 34, 36, 67; BLC**
  See also BW 2; CA 85-88; CANR 14, 42;
  DLB 33, 143

Wiebe, Rudy (Henry) 1934-... **CLC 6, 11, 14**
See also CA 37-40R; CANR 42; DLB 60

Wieland, Christoph Martin
1733-1813 .... **NCLC 17**
See also DLB 97

Wiene, Robert 1881-1938........ **TCLC 56**

Wieners, John 1934-.............. **CLC 7**
See also CA 13-16R; DLB 16

Wiesel, Elie(zer)
1928- .... **CLC 3, 5, 11, 37; DA**
See also AAYA 7; AITN 1; CA 5-8R;
CAAS 4; CANR 8, 40; DLB 83;
DLBY 87; MTCW; SATA 56

Wiggins, Marianne 1947-......... **CLC 57**
See also BEST 89:3; CA 130

Wight, James Alfred 1916-
See Herriot, James
See also CA 77-80; SATA 55;
SATA-Brief 44

Wilbur, Richard (Purdy)
1921- .... **CLC 3, 6, 9, 14, 53; DA**
See also CA 1-4R; CABS 2; CANR 2, 29;
DLB 5; MTCW; SATA 9

Wild, Peter 1940-................ **CLC 14**
See also CA 37-40R; DLB 5

Wilde, Oscar (Fingal O'Flahertie Wills)
1854(?)-1900 .... **TCLC 1, 8, 23, 41; DA;**
SSC 11; WLC
See also CA 104; 119; CDBLB 1890-1914;
DLB 10, 19, 34, 57, 141; SATA 24

Wilder, Billy .... **CLC 20**
See also Wilder, Samuel
See also DLB 26

Wilder, Samuel 1906-
See Wilder, Billy
See also CA 89-92

Wilder, Thornton (Niven)
1897-1975 ...... **CLC 1, 5, 6, 10, 15, 35,**
82; DA; DC 1; WLC
See also AITN 2; CA 13-16R; 61-64;
CANR 40; DLB 4, 7, 9; MTCW

Wilding, Michael 1942-.......... **CLC 73**
See also CA 104; CANR 24

Wiley, Richard 1944-............. **CLC 44**
See also CA 121; 129

Wilhelm, Kate .... **CLC 7**
See also Wilhelm, Katie Gertrude
See also CAAS 5; DLB 8

Wilhelm, Katie Gertrude 1928-
See Wilhelm, Kate
See also CA 37-40R; CANR 17, 36; MTCW

Wilkins, Mary
See Freeman, Mary Eleanor Wilkins

Willard, Nancy 1936-........... **CLC 7, 37**
See also CA 89-92; CANR 10, 39; CLR 5;
DLB 5, 52; MAICYA; MTCW;
SATA 37, 71; SATA-Brief 30

Williams, C(harles) K(enneth)
1936- .... **CLC 33, 56**
See also CA 37-40R; DLB 5

Williams, Charles
See Collier, James L(incoln)

Williams, Charles (Walter Stansby)
1886-1945 .... **TCLC 1, 11**
See also CA 104; DLB 100

Williams, (George) Emlyn
1905-1987 .... **CLC 15**
See also CA 104; 123; CANR 36; DLB 10,
77; MTCW

Williams, Hugo 1942-............ **CLC 42**
See also CA 17-20R; CANR 45; DLB 40

Williams, J. Walker
See Wodehouse, P(elham) G(renville)

Williams, John A(lfred)
1925- .... **CLC 5, 13; BLC**
See also BW 2; CA 53-56; CAAS 3;
CANR 6, 26; DLB 2, 33

Williams, Jonathan (Chamberlain)
1929- .... **CLC 13**
See also CA 9-12R; CAAS 12; CANR 8;
DLB 5

Williams, Joy 1944-.............. **CLC 31**
See also CA 41-44R; CANR 22

Williams, Norman 1952- .... **CLC 39**
See also CA 118

Williams, Tennessee
1911-1983 ..... **CLC 1, 2, 5, 7, 8, 11, 15,**
19, 30, 39, 45, 71; DA; DC 4; WLC
See also AITN 1, 2; CA 5-8R; 108;
CABS 3; CANR 31; CDALB 1941-1968;
DLB 7; DLBD 4; DLBY 83; MTCW

Williams, Thomas (Alonzo)
1926-1990 .... **CLC 14**
See also CA 1-4R; 132; CANR 2

Williams, William C.
See Williams, William Carlos

Williams, William Carlos
1883-1963 .... **CLC 1, 2, 5, 9, 13, 22, 42,**
67; DA; PC 7
See also CA 89-92; CANR 34;
CDALB 1917-1929; DLB 4, 16, 54, 86;
MTCW

Williamson, David (Keith) 1942-.... **CLC 56**
See also CA 103; CANR 41

Williamson, Ellen Douglas 1905-1984
See Douglas, Ellen
See also CA 17-20R; 114; CANR 39

Williamson, Jack................. **CLC 29**
See also Williamson, John Stewart
See also CAAS 8; DLB 8

Williamson, John Stewart 1908-
See Williamson, Jack
See also CA 17-20R; CANR 23

Willie, Frederick
See Lovecraft, H(oward) P(hillips)

Willingham, Calder (Baynard, Jr.)
1922- .... **CLC 5, 51**
See also CA 5-8R; CANR 3; DLB 2, 44;
MTCW

Willis, Charles
See Clarke, Arthur C(harles)

Willy
See Colette, (Sidonie-Gabrielle)

Willy, Colette
See Colette, (Sidonie-Gabrielle)

Wilson, A(ndrew) N(orman) 1950- .. **CLC 33**
See also CA 112; 122; DLB 14

Wilson, Angus (Frank Johnstone)
1913-1991 .... **CLC 2, 3, 5, 25, 34**
See also CA 5-8R; 134; CANR 21; DLB 15,
139; MTCW

Wilson, August
1945- .. **CLC 39, 50, 63; BLC; DA; DC 2**
See also BW 2; CA 115; 122; CANR 42;
MTCW

Wilson, Brian 1942-.............. **CLC 12**

Wilson, Colin 1931- .... **CLC 3, 14**
See also CA 1-4R; CAAS 5; CANR 1, 22,
33; DLB 14; MTCW

Wilson, Dirk
See Pohl, Frederik

Wilson, Edmund
1895-1972 .... **CLC 1, 2, 3, 8, 24**
See also CA 1-4R; 37-40R; CANR 1, 46;
DLB 63; MTCW

Wilson, Ethel Davis (Bryant)
1888(?)-1980 .... **CLC 13**
See also CA 102; DLB 68; MTCW

Wilson, John 1785-1854......... **NCLC 5**

Wilson, John (Anthony) Burgess 1917-1993
See Burgess, Anthony
See also CA 1-4R; 143; CANR 2, 46;
MTCW

Wilson, Lanford 1937-........ **CLC 7, 14, 36**
See also CA 17-20R; CABS 3; CANR 45;
DLB 7

Wilson, Robert M. 1944-......... **CLC 7, 9**
See also CA 49-52; CANR 2, 41; MTCW

Wilson, Robert McLiam 1964- ..... **CLC 59**
See also CA 132

Wilson, Sloan 1920-.............. **CLC 32**
See also CA 1-4R; CANR 1, 44

Wilson, Snoo 1948-.............. **CLC 33**
See also CA 69-72

Wilson, William S(mith) 1932- ..... **CLC 49**
See also CA 81-84

Winchilsea, Anne (Kingsmill) Finch Counte
1661-1720 .... **LC 3**

Windham, Basil
See Wodehouse, P(elham) G(renville)

Wingrove, David (John) 1954-...... **CLC 68**
See also CA 133

Winters, Janet Lewis .... **CLC 41**
See also Lewis, Janet
See also DLBY 87

Winters, (Arthur) Yvor
1900-1968 .... **CLC 4, 8, 32**
See also CA 11-12; 25-28R; CAP 1;
DLB 48; MTCW

Winterson, Jeanette 1959-........ **CLC 64**
See also CA 136

Wiseman, Frederick 1930-........ **CLC 20**

Wister, Owen 1860-1938 .... **TCLC 21**
See also CA 108; DLB 9, 78; SATA 62

Witkacy
See Witkiewicz, Stanislaw Ignacy

Witkiewicz, Stanislaw Ignacy
1885-1939 .... **TCLC 8**
See also CA 105

Wittig, Monique 1935(?)-......... **CLC 22**
See also CA 116; 135; DLB 83

Wittlin, Jozef 1896-1976 .... **CLC 25**
See also CA 49-52; 65-68; CANR 3

Wodehouse, P(elham) G(renville)
1881-1975 ... **CLC 1, 2, 5, 10, 22; SSC 2**
See also AITN 2; CA 45-48; 57-60;
CANR 3, 33; CDBLB 1914-1945;
DLB 34; MTCW; SATA 22

Woiwode, L.
See Woiwode, Larry (Alfred)

Woiwode, Larry (Alfred) 1941-... **CLC 6, 10**
See also CA 73-76; CANR 16; DLB 6

Wojciechowska, Maia (Teresa)
1927- .... **CLC 26**
See also AAYA 8; CA 9-12R; CANR 4, 41;
CLR 1; JRDA; MAICYA; SAAS 1;
SATA 1, 28

Wolf, Christa 1929- .... **CLC 14, 29, 58**
See also CA 85-88; CANR 45; DLB 75;
MTCW

Wolfe, Gene (Rodman) 1931-....... **CLC 25**
See also CA 57-60; CAAS 9; CANR 6, 32;
DLB 8

Wolfe, George C. 1954- .... **CLC 49**

Wolfe, Thomas (Clayton)
1900-1938 ... **TCLC 4, 13, 29; DA; WLC**
See also CA 104; 132; CDALB 1929-1941;
DLB 9, 102; DLBD 2; DLBY 85; MTCW

Wolfe, Thomas Kennerly, Jr. 1931-
See Wolfe, Tom
See also CA 13-16R; CANR 9, 33; MTCW

Wolfe, Tom .... **CLC 1, 2, 9, 15, 35, 51**
See also Wolfe, Thomas Kennerly, Jr.
See also AAYA 8; AITN 2; BEST 89:1

Wolff, Geoffrey (Ansell) 1937- ..... **CLC 41**
See also CA 29-32R; CANR 29, 43

Wolff, Sonia
See Levitin, Sonia (Wolff)

Wolff, Tobias (Jonathan Ansell)
1945- .... **CLC 39, 64**
See also BEST 90:2; CA 114; 117; DLB 130

Wolfram von Eschenbach
c. 1170-c. 1220 .... **CMLC 5**
See also DLB 138

Wolitzer, Hilma 1930-............ **CLC 17**
See also CA 65-68; CANR 18, 40; SATA 31

Wollstonecraft, Mary 1759-1797...... **LC 5**
See also CDBLB 1789-1832; DLB 39, 104

Wonder, Stevie .... **CLC 12**
See also Morris, Steveland Judkins

Wong, Jade Snow 1922-.......... **CLC 17**
See also CA 109

Woodcott, Keith
See Brunner, John (Kilian Houston)

Woodruff, Robert W.
See Mencken, H(enry) L(ouis)

Woolf, (Adeline) Virginia
1882-1941 ...... **TCLC 1, 5, 20, 43, 56;**
DA; SSC 7; WLC
See also CA 104; 130; CDBLB 1914-1945;
DLB 36, 100; DLBD 10; MTCW

Woollcott, Alexander (Humphreys)
1887-1943 .... **TCLC 5**
See also CA 105; DLB 29

Woolrich, Cornell 1903-1968....... **CLC 77**
See also Hopley-Woolrich, Cornell George

Wordsworth, Dorothy
1771-1855 .... **NCLC 25**
See also DLB 107

Wordsworth, William
1770-1850 .... **NCLC 12, 38; DA; PC 4;**
WLC
See also CDBLB 1789-1832; DLB 93, 107

Wouk, Herman 1915-......... **CLC 1, 9, 38**
See also CA 5-8R; CANR 6, 33; DLBY 82;
MTCW

Wright, Charles (Penzel, Jr.)
1935- .... **CLC 6, 13, 28**
See also CA 29-32R; CAAS 7; CANR 23,
36; DLBY 82; MTCW

Wright, Charles Stevenson
1932- .... **CLC 49; BLC 3**
See also BW 1; CA 9-12R; CANR 26;
DLB 33

Wright, Jack R.
See Harris, Mark

Wright, James (Arlington)
1927-1980 .... **CLC 3, 5, 10, 28**
See also AITN 2; CA 49-52; 97-100;
CANR 4, 34; DLB 5; MTCW

Wright, Judith (Arandell)
1915- .... **CLC 11, 53**
See also CA 13-16R; CANR 31; MTCW;
SATA 14

Wright, L(auerali) R. 1939-........ **CLC 44**
See also CA 138

Wright, Richard (Nathaniel)
1908-1960 .... **CLC 1, 3, 4, 9, 14, 21, 48,**
74; BLC; DA; SSC 2; WLC
See also AAYA 5; BW 1; CA 108;
CDALB 1929-1941; DLB 76, 102;
DLBD 2; MTCW

Wright, Richard B(ruce) 1937- ...... **CLC 6**
See also CA 85-88; DLB 53

Wright, Rick 1945-............... **CLC 35**

Wright, Rowland
See Wells, Carolyn

Wright, Stephen Caldwell 1946- .... **CLC 33**
See also BW 2

Wright, Willard Huntington 1888-1939
See Van Dine, S. S.
See also CA 115

Wright, William 1930-............ **CLC 44**
See also CA 53-56; CANR 7, 23

Wu Ch'eng-en 1500(?)-1582(?)........ **LC 7**

Wu Ching-tzu 1701-1754 .... **LC 2**

Wurlitzer, Rudolph 1938(?)- ... **CLC 2, 4, 15**
See also CA 85-88

Wycherley, William 1641-1715 .... **LC 8, 21**
See also CDBLB 1660-1789; DLB 80

Wylie, Elinor (Morton Hoyt)
1885-1928 .... **TCLC 8**
See also CA 105; DLB 9, 45

Wylie, Philip (Gordon) 1902-1971... **CLC 43**
See also CA 21-22; 33-36R; CAP 2; DLB 9

Wyndham, John .... **CLC 19**
See also Harris, John (Wyndham Parkes
Lucas) Beynon

Wyss, Johann David Von
1743-1818 .... **NCLC 10**
See also JRDA; MAICYA; SATA 29;
SATA-Brief 27

Yakumo Koizumi
See Hearn, (Patricio) Lafcadio (Tessima
Carlos)

Yanez, Jose Donoso
See Donoso (Yanez), Jose

Yanovsky, Basile S.
See Yanovsky, V(assily) S(emenovich)

Yanovsky, V(assily) S(emenovich)
1906-1989 .... **CLC 2, 18**
See also CA 97-100; 129

Yates, Richard 1926-1992 ..... **CLC 7, 8, 23**
See also CA 5-8R; 139; CANR 10, 43;
DLB 2; DLBY 81, 92

Yeats, W. B.
See Yeats, William Butler

Yeats, William Butler
1865-1939 ..... **TCLC 1, 11, 18, 31; DA;**
WLC
See also CA 104; 127; CANR 45;
CDBLB 1890-1914; DLB 10, 19, 98;
MTCW

Yehoshua, A(braham) B.
1936- .... **CLC 13, 31**
See also CA 33-36R; CANR 43

Yep, Laurence Michael 1948- ...... **CLC 35**
See also AAYA 5; CA 49-52; CANR 1, 46;
CLR 3, 17; DLB 52; JRDA; MAICYA;
SATA 7, 69

Yerby, Frank G(arvin)
1916-1991 .... **CLC 1, 7, 22; BLC**
See also BW 1; CA 9-12R; 136; CANR 16;
DLB 76; MTCW

Yesenin, Sergei Alexandrovich
See Esenin, Sergei (Alexandrovich)

Yevtushenko, Yevgeny (Alexandrovich)
1933- .... **CLC 1, 3, 13, 26, 51**
See also CA 81-84; CANR 33; MTCW

Yezierska, Anzia 1885(?)-1970 ..... **CLC 46**
See also CA 126; 89-92; DLB 28; MTCW

Yglesias, Helen 1915-............ **CLC 7, 22**
See also CA 37-40R; CAAS 20; CANR 15;
MTCW

Yokomitsu Riichi 1898-1947 ...... **TCLC 47**

Yonge, Charlotte (Mary)
1823-1901 .... **TCLC 48**
See also CA 109; DLB 18; SATA 17

York, Jeremy
See Creasey, John

York, Simon
See Heinlein, Robert A(nson)

Yorke, Henry Vincent 1905-1974 ... **CLC 13**
See also Green, Henry
See also CA 85-88; 49-52

Yosano Akiko 1878-1942.......... **PC 11**

Yoshimoto, Banana .... **CLC 84**
See also Yoshimoto, Mahoko

Yoshimoto, Mahoko 1964-
See Yoshimoto, Banana
See also CA 144

Young, Al(bert James)
    1939- . . . . CLC 19; BLC
    See also BW 2; CA 29-32R; CANR 26;
    DLB 33

Young, Andrew (John) 1885-1971. . . . CLC 5
    See also CA 5-8R; CANR 7, 29

Young, Collier
    See Bloch, Robert (Albert)

Young, Edward 1683-1765. . . . . LC 3
    See also DLB 95

Young, Marguerite 1909-. . . . . CLC 82
    See also CA 13-16; CAP 1

Young, Neil 1945-. . . . . CLC 17
    See also CA 110

Yourcenar, Marguerite
    1903-1987 . . . . CLC 19, 38, 50, 87
    See also CA 69-72; CANR 23; DLB 72;
    DLBY 88; MTCW

Yurick, Sol 1925-. . . . . CLC 6
    See also CA 13-16R; CANR 25

Zabolotskii, Nikolai Alekseevich
    1903-1958 . . . . TCLC 52
    See also CA 116

Zamiatin, Yevgenii
    See Zamyatin, Evgeny Ivanovich

Zamyatin, Evgeny Ivanovich
    1884-1937 . . . . TCLC 8, 37
    See also CA 105

Zangwill, Israel 1864-1926. . . . . . . TCLC 16
    See also CA 109; DLB 10, 135

Zappa, Francis Vincent, Jr. 1940-1993
    See Zappa, Frank
    See also CA 108; 143

Zappa, Frank. . . . . CLC 17
    See also Zappa, Francis Vincent, Jr.

Zaturenska, Marya 1902-1982. . . . CLC 6, 11
    See also CA 13-16R; 105; CANR 22

Zelazny, Roger (Joseph) 1937- . . . . . CLC 21
    See also AAYA 7; CA 21-24R; CANR 26;
    DLB 8; MTCW; SATA 57;
    SATA-Brief 39

Zhdanov, Andrei A(lexandrovich)
    1896-1948 . . . . TCLC 18
    See also CA 117

Zhukovsky, Vasily 1783-1852. . . . NCLC 35

Ziegenhagen, Eric. . . . . CLC 55

Zimmer, Jill Schary
    See Robinson, Jill

Zimmerman, Robert
    See Dylan, Bob

Zindel, Paul 1936- . . . CLC 6, 26; DA; DC 5
    See also AAYA 2; CA 73-76; CANR 31;
    CLR 3; DLB 7, 52; JRDA; MAICYA;
    MTCW; SATA 16, 58

Zinov'Ev, A. A.
    See Zinoviev, Alexander (Aleksandrovich)

Zinoviev, Alexander (Aleksandrovich)
    1922- . . . . CLC 19
    See also CA 116; 133; CAAS 10

Zoilus
    See Lovecraft, H(oward) P(hillips)

Zola, Emile (Edouard Charles Antoine)
    1840-1902 . . . . . TCLC 1, 6, 21, 41; DA;
                                                        WLC
    See also CA 104; 138; DLB 123

Zoline, Pamela 1941-. . . . . CLC 62

Zorrilla y Moral, Jose 1817-1893. . NCLC 6

Zoshchenko, Mikhail (Mikhailovich)
    1895-1958 . . . . TCLC 15; SSC 15
    See also CA 115

Zuckmayer, Carl 1896-1977. . . . . . . CLC 18
    See also CA 69-72; DLB 56, 124

Zuk, Georges
    See Skelton, Robin

Zukofsky, Louis
    1904-1978 . . . . . . CLC 1, 2, 4, 7, 11, 18;
                                                        PC 11
    See also CA 9-12R; 77-80; CANR 39;
    DLB 5; MTCW

Zweig, Paul 1935-1984. . . . . CLC 34, 42
    See also CA 85-88; 113

Zweig, Stefan 1881-1942 . . . . TCLC 17
    See also CA 112; DLB 81, 118

Literary Criticism Series
Cumulative Topic Index

This index lists all topic entries in Gale's *Classical and Medieval Literature Criticism, Contemporary Literary Criticism, Literature Criticism from 1400 to 1800, Nineteenth-Century Literature Criticism,* and *Twentieth-Century Literary Criticism.*

Topic Index

　　　　　　　　　　　　　　　　　　　　　　　　LITERARY CRITICISM SERIES

CLC Cumulative Nationality Index

Nationality Index

Nationality Index

Nationality Index

Nationality Index

Nationality Index

CLC-87 Title Index

Title Index